Putnam's

Contemporary

Dictionaries

French-English

Anglais-Français

Dictionaries published by Berkley Books

PUTNAM'S CONTEMPORARY FRENCH DICTIONARY
PUTNAM'S CONTEMPORARY GERMAN DICTIONARY
PUTNAM'S CONTEMPORARY ITALIAN DICTIONARY
PUTNAM'S CONTEMPORARY SPANISH DICTIONARY
THE NEW ROGET'S THESAURUS

PUTNAM'S CONTEMPORARY FRENCH DICTIONARY
FRENCH ENGLISH
ENGLISH FRENCH

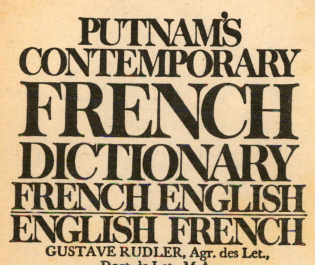

**GUSTAVE RUDLER, Agr. des Let.,
Doct. ès Let., M.A.**

Formerly Professor of French Literature,
University of Oxford

NORMAN C. ANDERSON, L-ès-L., M.A.

Formerly Senior Lecturer in French,
University of Glasgow

Revised by:

**ANTHONY C. BRENCH, M.A.
CHRISTOPHER D. BETTINSON, B.A.
W. MARY BILLINGTON, M.A.
FRANCOISE SALGUES, L-ès L.**

Lecturers in French, University of Glasgow

**CHARLES BERLITZ
MARY SOLAK**

Special Editors to the American Edition

BERKLEY BOOKS, NEW YORK

This Berkley book contains the complete
text of the original hardcover edition.
It has been completely reset in a type face
designed for easy reading, and was printed
from new film.

PUTNAM'S CONTEMPORARY
FRENCH DICTIONARY

A Berkley Book / published by arrangement with
G. P. Putnam's Sons

PRINTING HISTORY
G. P. Putnam's Sons edition published 1972
Berkley Medallion edition / January 1977
Twelfth printing / December 1980

ISBN: 0-425-04361-4

A BERKLEY BOOK ® TM 757,375
Berkley Books are published by Berkley Publishing Corporation,
200 Madison Avenue, New York, New York 10016.
PRINTED IN THE UNITED STATES OF AMERICA

Contents

Table des Matières

Introduction

In order to economize space we have not given the feminine form of those French adjectives which regularly form their feminine by adding *e* to the masculine form, e.g., *crue, grivoise, guindée*, will be found under the masculine form only, *cru, grivois, guindé*. The feminine form has been indicated in the case of all other adjectives, e.g., *audacieux, -euse, bon, bonne, décisif, -ive; moyen, -enne, premier, -ière, rêveur, -euse*. We have also on occasion omitted the adverb (often formed by adding *-ment* to the feminine singular of the adjective) and the verbal nouns in *-ment* and *-age*, where the presence of the adjective and the verb should enable the reader to recognize a family of words from one main entry.

In the case of adjectives of nationality, the French translation has been written beginning with a small letter. When used as a noun, however, such words begin with a capital letter.

Abbreviations used in the Dictionary

ABRÉVIATIONS		ABBREVIATIONS
adjectif	a	adjective
adverbe	ad	adverb
adjectif et nom	an	adjective and noun
architecture	archit	architecture
automobile	aut	automobile
aviation	av	aviation
botanique	bot	botany
chimie	chem	chemistry
conjonction	cj	conjunction
colonial	col	colonial
commerce	com	commerce
comparatif	comp	comparative
cuisine	cook	cooking
datif	dat	dative
article défini	def art	definite article
disjonctif	disj	disjunctive
ecclésiastique	eccl	ecclesiastical
électricité	el	electricity
exclamation	excl	exclamation
féminin	f	feminine
familier	fam	familiar
figuré	fig	figuratively
finances	fin	finance
gouvernement	govt	government
article indéfini	indef art	indefinite article
interrogatif	inter	interrogative
invariable	inv	invariable
juridique	jur	juridical
masculin	m	masculine
médecine	med	medicine

militaire	mil	military
mines	min	mining
musique	mus	music
nom	n	noun
nautique, marine	naut	nautical
nom féminin	nf	noun feminine
nom masculin	nm	noun masculine
numéral	num	numeral
	o.s.	oneself
péjoratif	pej	pejorative
personne	pers	person
pluriel	pl	plural
pronom	pn	pronoun
politique	pol	politics
participe passé	pp	past participle
préposition	prep	preposition
passé	pt	past tense
quelque chose	qch	
quelqu'un	qn	
relatif	rel	relative
chemins de fer	rl	railroad
singulier	s	singular
écossais	Scot	Scottish
argot, populaire	sl	slang
	s.o.	someone
	sth	something
superlatif	sup	superlative
technique	tec	technical
télévision	TV	television
généralement	usu	usually
verbe	v	verb
verbe intransitif	vi	verb intransitive
verbe impersonnel	v imp	verb impersonal
verbe intransitif, réfléchi	vir	verb intransitive, reflexive
verbe réfléchi	vr	verb reflexive
verbe transitif	vt	verb transitive
verbe transitif, intransitif	vti	verb transitive, intransitive
verbe transitif, intransitif, réfléchi	vtir	verb transitive, intransitive, reflexive
verbe transitif, réfléchi	vtr	verb transitive, reflexive
vulgaire	vul	vulgar

English and French Numerals

CARDINAL NUMBERS—NOMBRES CARDINAUX

1	one—un, une	11	eleven—onze
2	two—deux	12	twelve—douze
3	three—trois	13	thirteen—treize
4	four—quatre	14	fourteen—quatorze
5	five—cinq	15	fifteen—quinze
6	six—six	16	sixteen—seize
7	seven—sept	17	seventeen—dix-sept
8	eight—huit	18	eighteen—dix-huit
9	nine—neuf	19	nineteen—dix-neuf
10	ten—dix	20	twenty—vingt

21 twenty-one—vingt et un	90 ninety—quatre-vingt-dix
22 twenty-two—vingt-deux	91 ninety-one—quatre-vingt-onze
30 thirty—trente	
40 forty—quarante	100 a hundred—cent
50 fifty—cinquante	101 one hundred and one—cent un
60 sixty—soixante	
70 seventy—soixante-dix	300 three hundred—trois cents
71 seventy-one—soixante-et-onze	
72 seventy-two—soixante-douze	301 three hundred and one—trois cent un
80 eighty—quatre-vingts	1000 a thousand—mille
81 eighty-one—quatre-vingt-un	5000 five thousand—cinq mille
	1,000,000 a million—un million

ORDINAL NUMBERS—NOMBRES ORDINAUX

First—premier, -ère	Fiftieth—cinquantième
Second—deuxième; second, -e	Sixtieth—soixantième
	Seventieth—soixante-dixième
Third—troisième	Seventy-first—soixante-et-onzième
Fourth—quatrième	
Fifth—cinquième	Seventy-second—soixante-douzième
Sixth—sixième	
Seventh—septième	Eightieth—quatre-vingtième
Eighth—huitième	Eighty-first—quatre-vingt-unième
Ninth—neuvième	
Tenth—dixième	Ninetieth—quatre-vingt-dixième
Eleventh—onzième	
Twelfth—douzième	Ninety-first—quatre-vingt-onzième
Thirteenth—treizième	
Fourteenth—quatorzième	Hundredth—centième
Fifteenth—quinzième	Hundred-and-first—cent-unième
Sixteenth—seizième	
Seventeenth—dix-septième	Two hundredth—deux-centième
Eighteenth—dix-huitième	
Nineteenth—dix-neuvième	Two hundred-and-first—deux-cent-unième
Twentieth—vingtième	
Twenty-first—vingt-et-unième	Thousandth—millième
	Thousand-and-first—mille-et-unième
Twenty-second—vingt-deuxième	
	Thousand-and-second—mille-deuxième
Thirtieth—trentième	
Fortieth—quarantième	Millionth—millionième

Pronunciation

A simple and accurate transcription of pronunciation is given by the phonetic system of the International Phonetic Association. Although it is not as widely used in the United States as it is in other countries, we thought that its use in this dictionary would help readers to feel at ease with the spoken language. The phonetic transcription of English words is that of Received Pronunciation. It does not mention regional variations. The same convention has been applied to the transcription of French words, Standard French being roughly the pronunciation of educated people from the north of France. The readers will find below a comparative presentation of phonetic symbols (IPA) both French and English.

Length of vowels is noted thus: short—no symbol

long—[ː] after the vowel

In English, stress is shown by the symbol ['] before the stressed syllable and also secondary stress by the symbol [.].

Pour la transcription phonétique nous avons employé le système de l'Association internationale de phonétique, système qui, nous semble-t-il, permettra aux lecteurs de ce dictionnaire de se sentir à l'aise avec la langue parlée. La transcription des mots anglais est celle de la prononciation reçue, et ne tient pas compte des variations régionales. Pour le français, la même convention a été suivie. La prononciation donnée ne tient également pas compte des différences locales.

Les lecteurs trouveront en bas une présentation comparative de symboles phonétiques pour les deux langues.

La longueur des voyelles est indiquée de la façon suivante:

courte—pas de symbole

longue—[ː] après la voyelle

En anglais l'accentuation d'une voyelle est donnée par le symbole ['] placé devant le syllabe accentué, et l'accentuation secondaire par le symbole [.].

CONSONNES CONSONANTS

p	poupée	p	puppy	(in French [p, t, k] are not aspirated)
t	tente	t	tent	(en français [p, t, k] ne sont pas aspirés)
k	coq	k	cork	
b	bombe	b	bomb	

d	dinde	d	daddy	
g	gringalet	g	gag	
f	ferme	f	farm	
v	vite	v	very	
s	souci	s	so	
z	cousin	z	cousin	
		θ	thorn	
		ð	that	
ʃ	chose	ʃ	sheep	
		tʃ	church	
ʒ	juge	ʒ	pleasure	
		dʒ	judge	
w	oui	w	wall	
y	huit			
j	hier	j	yet	
		h	hat	
		x	loch (*Scots*)	
r	rentrer	r	rat	(English r is pronounced with the tip of the tongue against the front of the palate, French r with the back of the tongue against the back of the palate, not unlike, though, softer, than the Scots [x] of loch) (le r anglais se prononce avec le bout de la langue contre le palais)

m	maman	m	mummy	
n	non	n	no	
ɲ	campagne			
		ŋ	singing	
l	lait	l	little	(in English the pronunciation of the two [l] of little is not the same. There is no such difference in French [l] as in lot) (en anglais la prononciation des deux [l] de little n'est pas semblable)

VOYELLES VOWELS

i	ici	i	heel	(these equivalents are obviously only approximate because French vowels and English vowels are produced differently) (ces équivalents ne sont pas absolument semblables, les voyelles françaises et anglaises se prononcent différemment)
		i	hit	
e	est, été	ɛ	said	
ɛ	mère	ɛə	there	
a	patte	æ	bat	
ɑ	pâte	ɑː	car	
ɔ	donne	ɔ	lot	
o	côte	ɔː	all	
u	cou	u	put	
uː	cour	uː	shoe	
		ʌ	but	
œː	beurre	əː	bird	
ə	le	ə	rodent	
ø	feu	(mouth set as for [əː] of bird, lips rounded as for [uː] of shoe		
y	rue	(mouth set as for [iː], lips rounded as for [u])		

nasales (nasals); these French vowels are produced by pronouncing the corresponding oral vowel through the nose
ɑ̃ sang ɛ̃ vin œ̃ lundi ɔ̃ long

diphthongs (diphthongs)
iə beer ei date ai life au fowl ɔi boil ou low uə poor

French – English

A

à [ɑ] *prep* to, at, in, on, according to, by, of, with *etc.*

abaissement [abɛsmɑ̃] *nm* lowering, falling, degradation, derogation, humiliation.

abaisser [abɛse] *vt* to lower, bring down; *vr* to fall away, stoop, droop, demean oneself.

abandon [abɑ̃dɔ̃] *nm* surrender, relinquishing, withdrawal, desertion, neglect, abandon; à l'— neglected, at random.

abandonné [abɑ̃dɔne] *a* forsaken, forlorn, stray, desolate, derelict, shameless.

abandonnement [abɑ̃dɔnmɑ̃] *nm* surrender, desertion, abandon, degradation, profligacy.

abandonner [abɑ̃dɔne] *vt* to surrender, give up, relinquish, make over (to à), desert; *vr* to give oneself up (to), indulge (in).

abasourdir [abazurdiːr] *vt* to astound, take aback, bewilder, stun.

abat-jour [abaʒuːr] *nm* lampshade, awning.

abats [aba] *nm pl* offal.

abattage [abataːʒ] *nm* felling, slaughtering.

abattement [abatmɑ̃] *nm* dejection, prostration.

abattoir [abatwaːr] *nm* slaughterhouse, shambles.

abattre [abatr] *vt* to knock down, overthrow, bring (pull, blow) down, fell, slaughter, depress, lower, lay; *vr* to fall (swoop) down, crash, abate, become downhearted.

abattu [abaty] *a* depressed, despondent, downcast.

abbaye [abe(j)i] *nf* abbey.

abbé [abe] *nm* abbot, priest.

abbesse [abɛs] *nf* abbess.

abcès [apsɛ] *nm* abscess, gathering, fester.

abdiquer [abdike] *vt* to abdicate, (*post*) resign.

abeille [abɛːj] *nf* bee.

aberration [abɛr(r)asjɔ̃] *nf* aberration, derangement, (*mental*) lapse.

abhorrer [abɔr(r)e] *vt* to abhor, detest, loathe.

abîme [abiːm] *nm* abyss, chasm, deep.

abîmer [abime] *vt* to injure, damage, spoil; *vr* to be swallowed up, be sunk, get damaged.

abject [abʒɛkt] *a* despicable, vile.

abjurer [abʒyre] *vt* to abjure, recant.

ablation [ablasjɔ̃] *nf* ablation, removal, excision.

ablution [ablysjɔ̃] *nf* ablution.

abnégation [abnegasjɔ̃] *nf* sacrifice, selflessness.

aboiement [abwamɑ̃] *nm* bark(ing), baying.

abois [abwɑ] *nm pl* aux — at bay, hard pressed.

abolir [abɔliːr] *vt* to abolish.

abolition [abɔlisjɔ̃] *nf* abolition.

abominable [abɔminabl] *a* abominable, loathsome, wretched.

abomination [abɔminasjɔ̃] *nf* abomination; avoir en — to detest.

abondamment [abɔ̃damɑ̃] *ad* abundantly.

abondance [abɔ̃dɑ̃ːs] *nf* abundance, plenty; en — galore.

abondant [abɔ̃dɑ̃] *a* abundant, plentiful, copious.

abonder [abɔ̃de] *vi* to abound, be plentiful.

abonnement [abɔnmɑ̃] *nm* subscription, installment; carte d'— season-ticket.

abonné [abɔne] *n* subscriber, season-ticket holder.

s'abonner [sabɔne] *vr* to subscribe (to à), take a season-ticket.

abord [abɔːr] *nm* access, approach, landing; d'— first, to begin with; de prime —, au premier — at first sight; dès l'— from the start.

abordable [abɔrdabl] *a* approachable, accessible.

abordage [abɔrdaːʒ] *nm* landing, boarding, collision.

aborder [abɔrde] *vi* to land; *vt* to approach, accost, board, tackle, collide.

aboutir [abutiːr] *vi* to lead (to à), end (in), result (in), succeed, come off.

aboyer [abwaje] *vi* to bark, bay.

abrasif [abrazif] *a* abrasive.

abrégé [abreʒe] *nm* abridgment, epitome.

abréger [abreʒe] *vt* to shorten, abbreviate, abridge; *vr* to grow shorter.

abreuver [abrœve] *vt* to water, soak; *vr* to drink, quench one's thirst.

abreuvoir [abrœvwaːr] *nm* watering-place, drinking-trough.

abréviation [abrevjasjɔ̃] *nf* abbreviation, contraction.

abri [abri] *nm* shelter, cover; à l'— sheltered, immune.

abricot [abriko] *nm* apricot.

abricotier [abrikɔtje] nm apricottree.

abriter [abrite] vt to shelter, protect, house, shade; vr to take shelter.

abroger [abrɔʒe] vt to abrogate, repeal; vr to lapse.

abrupt [abrypt] a abrupt, sheer.

abruti [abryti] a besotted, sodden, stupefied, dazed; nm sot, idiot.

abrutir [abrytiːr] vt to stupefy, besot.

abrutissant [abrytisɑ̃] a stupefying, degrading, killing.

absence [apsɑ̃s] nf non-appearance.

absent [apsɑ̃] a not at home, vacant.

s'absenter [sapsɑ̃te] vr to absent oneself, stay away.

absinthe [apsɛ̃ːt] nf absinthe, wormwood.

absolu [apsɔly] a absolute, utter, unqualified.

absolument [apsɔlymɑ̃] ad absolutely, utterly; — ! quite so, just so!

absolution [apsɔlysjɔ̃] nf absolution.

absorber [apsɔrbe] vt to absorb, engross; vr to become absorbed (in), pore (over dans).

absoudre [apsudr] vt to absolve, condone, exonerate.

s'abstenir [sapstəniːr] vr to abstain, eschew, refrain.

abstinence [apstinɑ̃ːs] nf abstinence.

abstinent [apstinɑ̃] a abstinent; n teetotaller.

abstraction [apstraksjɔ̃] nf abstraction; — faite de apart from, disregarding, setting aside

abstraire [apstreːr] vt to abstract.

abstrait [apstre] a nm abstract, absent-minded.

abstrus [apstry] a abstruse.

absurde [apsyrd] a ludicrous; nm absurd.

absurdité [apsyrdite] nf absurdity, nonsense.

abus [aby] nm abuse, misuse, error; — de confiance breach of faith.

abuser [abyze] vi to misuse, take advantage of; vt to delude; vr to delude oneself.

abusif, -ive [abysif, iːv] a contrary to usage, wrong, excessive.

acabit [akabi] nm (of people) nature, stamp.

académicien [akademisjɛ̃] nm academician, member of the French Academy.

académie [akademi] nf academy, school, regional education unit, learned society, riding-school.

académique [akademik] a academic (al), choice, distinguished.

acajou [akaʒu] nm mahogany.

acariâtre [akarjaːtr] a shrewish, bad-tempered, cantankerous.

accablant [akablɑ̃] a overwhelming, crushing, oppressive.

accablé [akable] a overwhelmed, overcome, prostrate.

accablement [akabləmɑ̃] nm dejec-

tion, despondency, prostration.

accabler [akable] vt to overwhelm, overload, weigh down, snow under.

accalmie [akalmi] nf lull, respite.

accaparement [akaparmɑ̃] nm cornering, securing, monopoly.

accaparer [akapare] vt to corner, monopolize, hoard.

accéder [aksede] vi to accede, agree, have access.

accélération [akselerasjɔ̃] nf acceleration.

accélérateur [akseleratœːr] nm accelerator.

accélérer [akselere] vtr to accelerate, quicken.

accent [aksɑ̃] nm accent, emphasis, stress; pl strains.

accentuation [aksɑ̃tyasjɔ̃] nf accentuation.

accentuer [aksɑ̃tɥe] vt to accentuate, stress, emphasize, intensify; vr to become more marked.

acceptable [akseptabl] a reasonable.

acceptation [akseptasjɔ̃] nf acceptance.

accepter [aksepte] vt to accept.

acception [aksepsjɔ̃] nf acceptation, meaning.

accès [akse] nm access, approach, attack, fit, bout.

accessible [aksesibl] a available, open (to à).

accession [aksesjɔ̃] nf accession.

accessoire [akseswaːr] a adjunct, accessory, incidental; nm accessory; pl theatrical properties.

accident [aksidɑ̃] nm accident, mishap; (of ground) fold; par — accidentally, casually.

accidenté [aksidɑ̃te] a uneven, eventful; n victim (of accident).

accidentel, -elle [aksidɑ̃tɛl] a accidental.

acclamation [aklamasjɔ̃] nf acclamation; pl cheers.

acclamer [aklame] vt to acclaim, cheer.

acclimatation [aklimatasjɔ̃] nf acclimatization.

acclimater [aklimate] vt to acclimatize.

s'accointer [sakwɛ̃te] vr to take up (with avec).

accolade [akɔlad] nf embrace, accolade, bracket.

accoler [akɔle] vt to couple, bracket.

accommodant [akɔmɔdɑ̃] a accommodating, easy-going.

accommodation [akɔmɔdasjɔ̃] nf adaptation.

accommodement [akɔmɔdmɑ̃] nm compromise.

accommoder [akɔmɔde] vt to suit, adapt, settle, prepare, cook; vr to settle down, make the best (of), adapt oneself (to de), come to an agreement (with avec).

accompagnateur, -trice [akɔ̃paɲatœːr, tris] n accompanist.

accompagnement [akɔ̃paɲmɑ̃] *nm* accompaniment.

accompagner [akɔ̃paɲe] *vt* to accompany, escort.

accompli [akɔ̃pli] *a* accomplished, finished, perfect.

accomplir [akɔ̃pliːr] *vt* to accomplish, achieve, fulfill, complete; *vr* to be fulfilled.

accomplissement [akɔ̃plismɑ̃] *nm* accomplishment, fulfillment, completion.

accord [akɔːr] *nm* agreement, harmony, tune, chord; d'— agreed, (all) right; être d'— to concur, be at one (with avec), be in tune.

accorder [akɔrde] *vt* to reconcile, square, grant, award, concede, extend, tune, key; *vr* to agree, accord, harmonize.

accordeur [akɔrdœːr] *nm* tuner.

accort [akɔːr] *a* trim, pleasing.

accoster [akɔste] *vt* to accost, come alongside.

accoter [akɔte] *vt* to shore up; *vr* to lean (against contre).

accouchement [akuʃmɑ̃] *nm* confinement, labor, delivery.

accoucher [akuʃe] *vi* to be confined, give birth (to de).

s'accouder [sakude] *vr* to lean on one's elbow.

accoupler [akuple] *vt* to couple, mate, connect.

accourcir [akursiːr] *vt* to shorten.

accourir [akuriːr] *vi* to hasten, come running, rush.

accoutrement [akutrəmɑ̃] *nm* rig (-out), kit.

accoutrer [akutre] *vt* to rig out; *vr* to get oneself up.

accoutumé [akutyme] *a* accustomed, used, customary.

accoutumer [akutyme] *vt* to accustom; *vr* to get used (to à).

accréditer [akredite] *vt* to accredit.

accroc [akro] *nm* hitch, rip, infraction.

accrochage [akrɔʃaːʒ] *nm* grazing, hanging up, picking up, altercation, set-to, (*aut*) accident.

accroche-cœur [akrɔʃkœːr] *nm* kiss-curl.

accrocher [akrɔʃe] *vt* to hook, catch, collide with, hang up, pick up, tune in; *vr* to cling, hang on, get caught, clinch, have a set-to.

accroire [akrwaːr] *vt* en faire — à qn to delude s.o.

accroissement [akrwasmɑ̃] *nm* growth, increase.

accroître [akrwaːtr] *vt* to increase, enlarge, enhance.

s'accroupir [sakrupiːr] *vr* to squat, crouch (down), cower.

accueil [akœːj] *nm* welcome, reception.

accueillir [akœjiːr] *vt* to welcome, greet, receive.

acculer [akyle] *vt* to drive back, corner.

accumulateur, -trice [akymylatœːrtris] *n* hoarder; *nm* accumulator, storage battery.

accumulation [akymylasjɔ̃] *nf* accumulation.

accumuler [akymyle] *vt* to accumulate, amass, heap up.

accusateur, -trice [akyzatœːr, tris] *a* accusatory, incriminating; *n* accuser, indicter, plaintiff.

accusation [akyzasjɔ̃] *nf* charge, indictment; mettre en — to impeach, arraign.

accusé [akyze] *a* prominent; *n* accused; *nm* acknowledgment.

accuser [akyze] *vt* to accuse, indict, tax (with de), accentuate; — réception de to acknowledge receipt of.

acerbe [aserb] *a* bitter, harsh, sharp, sour.

acerbité [aserbite] *nf* bitterness, harshness, sharpness.

acéré [asere] *a* sharp-pointed, cutting.

acharné [aʃarne] *a* eager, keen, desperate, inveterate, fierce, relentless, strenuous.

acharnement [aʃarnəmɑ̃] *nm* eagerness, keenness, desperation, relentlessness.

s'acharner [saʃarne] *vr* to be dead set (against à), persist (in), be bent (on).

achat [aʃa] *nm* purchase; faire des — e to go shopping.

acheminer [aʃmine] *vt* to direct, dispatch, convey; *vr* to make one's way, proceed.

acheter [aʃte] *vt* to buy, purchase, bribe.

acheteur, -euse [aʃtœːr, øːz] *n* buyer, purchaser.

achevé [aʃve] *a* accomplished, perfect, thorough.

achèvement [aʃevmɑ̃] *nm* completion.

achever [aʃve] *vt* to complete, end, finish off; *vr* to draw to a close, end, culminate.

achoppement [aʃɔpmɑ̃] *nm* obstacle; pierre d'— stumbling-block.

acide [asid] *a* acid, tart; *nm* acid.

acidité [asidite] *nf* acidity.

acier [asje] *nm* steel.

aciérie [asjeri] *nf* steelworks.

acompte [akɔ̃t] *nm* installment.

acoquiner [akɔkine] *vr* to be thick with.

à-côté [akote] *nm* aside; *pl* side-issues, extras.

à-coup [aku] *nm* jerk, sudden stop, snatch; par —e by fits and starts, in spasms.

acoustique [akustik] *nf* acoustics.

acquérir [akeriːr] *vt* to acquire, get.

acquiescer [akjese] *vt* to acquiesce, assent.

acquis [aki] *a* acquired, established, vested; mal — ill-got(ten); — d'avance foregone; *nm* attainments, acquired knowledge.

acquisition [akizisjɔ̃] nf acquisition.
acquit [aki] nm acquittance, receipt; pour — received, paid (with thanks); par — de conscience for conscience' sake.
acquittement [akitmɑ̃] nm discharge, acquittal.
acquitter [akite] vt to discharge, acquit, clear, fulfil, receipt; vr to acquit o.s.; — de carry out, discharge.
âcre [ɑːkr] a acrid, pungent.
âcreté [ɑkrəte] nf acridity, pungency.
acrimonie [akrimɔni] nf acrimony.
acrimonieux, -euse [akrimɔnjø, jøːz] a acrimonious.
acrobate [akrɔbat] n acrobat.
acrobatie [akrɔbasi] nf acrobatics.
acte [akt] nm act, deed, record; — de naissance, de décès, de mariage birth, death, marriage certificate.
acteur, -trice [aktœːr, tris] n actor, actress.
actif, -ive [aktif, iːv] a active, busy, brisk, live, industrious; nm credit, assets.
action [aksjɔ̃] nf action, effect, shares, lawsuit.
actionnaire [aksjɔnɛːr] n shareholder.
actionner [aksjɔne] vt to sue, set in motion, drive.
activer [aktive] vt to push on, stir up, whip up.
activité [aktivite] nf activity, industry.
actuaire [aktɥɛːr -tyɛːr] nm actuary.
actualité [aktɥalite -tya-] nf reality, topical question; pl current events, newsreel.
actuel, -elle [aktɥɛl -tyɛl] a real, current, topical, of the present.
actuellement [aktɥɛlmɑ̃ -tyɛl] ad at present.
acuité [akɥite] nf keenness, sharpness.
adage [adaːʒ] nm adage.
adaptable [adaptabl] a adaptable.
adaptation [adaptasjɔ̃] nf adaptation.
adapter [adapte] vt to adapt, adjust, accommodate.
addition [adisjɔ̃] nf addition, appendage, bill.
additionner [ad(d)isjɔne] vt to add (up).
adepte [adɛpt] a adept.
adhérence [aderɑ̃ːs] nf adhesion.
adhérent [aderɑ̃] a adherent, adhesive; n adherent, member, follower.
adhérer [adere] vi to adhere, stick, hold, join.
adhésif, -ive [adezif, iːv] a nm adhesive.
adhésion [adezjɔ̃] nf adhesion.
adieu [adjø] ad good-bye; nm farewell, leave-taking; faire ses —x à to say farewell to, take leave of.

adjacent [adʒasɑ̃] a adjacent.
adjectif, -ive [adʒektif, iːv] a adjectival; nm adjective.
adjoindre [adʒwɛ̃ːdr] vt to unite, associate, add; vr to join in (with à).
adjoint [adʒwɛ̃] an assistant; — au maire deputy mayor, alderman.
adjudant [adʒydɑ̃] nm company sergeant-major, adjutant, warrant-officer.
adjudication [adʒydikasjɔ̃] nf adjudication; mettre en — to invite bids for, put up for sale by auction.
adjuger [adʒyʒe] vt to adjudge, award, knock down; vr to appropriate.
adjurer [adʒyre] vt to adjure, beseech, conjure.
admettre [admɛtr] vt to admit, assume, allow, concede, pass.
administrateur, -trice [administratœːr, tris] n administrator, director, trustee.
administration [administrasjɔ̃] nf administration, government, civil service, trusteeship.
administrer [administre] vt to administer, govern, manage, dispense.
admirable [admirabl] a admirable, wonderful.
admirateur, -trice [admiratœːr, tris] n admirer, fan.
admiratif, -ive [admiratif, iːv] a admiring.
admiration [admirasjɔ̃] nf admiration, wonderment.
admirer [admire] vt to admire, wonder at, marvel at.
admissible [admisibl] a admissible, eligible, qualified for oral examination.
admission [admisjɔ̃] nf admission.
admonestation [admɔnɛstasjɔ̃] nf reprimand.
admonester [admɔnɛste] vt to admonish.
adolescence [adɔlɛsɑ̃ːs] nf adolescence, youth.
adolescent [adɔlɛsɑ̃] n adolescent, youth, girl.
s'adonner [sadɔne] vr to give oneself up (to à), take (to).
adopter [adɔpte] vt to adopt.
adoptif, -ive [adɔptif, iːv] a adopted, adoptive.
adoption [adɔpsjɔ̃] nf adoption.
adorable [adɔrabl] a adorable, charming, lovely.
adorateur, -trice [adɔratœːr, tris] n adorer, worshipper; a adoring.
adorer [adɔre] vt to adore, worship.
adosser [adɔse] vt to place back to back, lean back (against à); vr to lean one's back (against à).
adoucir [adusiːr] vt to soften, subdue, alleviate, mitigate, mollify; vr to grow softer, milder.
adoucissement [adusismɑ̃] nm soft-

ening, toning down, alleviation, mitigation.

adresse [adrɛs] *nf* address, destination, skill, deftness, sleight, adroitness, craftiness.

adresser [adrese] *vt* to address, direct; *vr* to address, apply, ask.

adroit [adrwa] *a* skillful, deft, clever, handy, shrewd.

adulation [adylasjɔ̃] *nf* adulation.

adulte [adylt] *an* adult, grown-up, full-grown.

adultère [adyltɛːr] *a* adulterous; *n* adulterer, adulteress; *nm* adultery.

advenir [advəniːr] *v imp* to happen, occur, come to pass, become of; **advienne que pourra** come what may.

adverbe [adverb] *nm* adverb.

adversaire [adversɛːr] *nm* adversary, opponent.

adverse [advers] *a* adverse.

adversité [adversite] *nf* adversity, misfortune.

aération [aerasjɔ̃] *nf* aeration, airing, ventilation.

aérer [aere] *vt* to air, aerate, ventilate.

aérien, -ienne [aerjɛ̃, jɛn] *a* airy, aerial, ethereal; **raid —** long-distance flight, air-raid; **forces —es** air-force.

aéro-club [aeroklyb, -klœb] *nm* flying-club.

aérodrome [aerodroːm] *nm* airdrome.

aérodynamique [aerodinamik] *a* stream-lined.

aéronaute [aeronoːt] *nm* aeronaut.

aéronautique [aeronotik] *a* aeronautical; *nf* aeronautics.

aéroport [aeropoːr] *nm* airport.

aéroporté [aeroporte] *a* airborne.

aérostat [aerɔsta] *nm* airship, balloon.

aérostatique [aerostatik] *a* **barrage — balloon barrage**; *nf* aerostatics.

affabilité [afabilite] *nf* affability, graciousness.

affable [afaːbl] *a* affable.

affadir [afadiːr] *vt* to make insipid; *vr* to become insipid.

affaiblir [afebliːr] *vt* to weaken, enfeeble, impair, lower, water down; *vr* to become weaker, flag, abate.

affaiblissement [afeblismɑ̃] *nm* weakening, enfeeblement, impairment.

affaire [afɛːr] *nf* affair, thing, matter, concern, case; *pl* business, dealings, belongings; **— de cœur** love affair; **son — est faite** it's all up with him; **la belle —!** is that all!; **avoir — à, avec** to deal with; **le Ministère des — étrangères** Foreign Office.

affairé [afere] *a* busy.

affaissement [afɛsmɑ̃] *nm* subsidence, collapse.

s'affaisser [safɛse] *vr* to subside, collapse.

affamé [afame] *a* hungry, starving, famished.

affectation [afektasjɔ̃] *nf* affectation, primness, assignment, *(mil)* posting.

affecté [afɛkte] *a* affected, conceited, prim, *(mil)* posted.

affecter [afɛkte] *vt* to affect, assign (to à), post (to).

affection [afɛksjɔ̃] *nf* affection, liking, trouble.

affectionner [afɛksjɔne] *vt* to have a liking for.

affectueux, -euse [afɛktɥø, øːz] *a* affectionate, fond.

affermir [afɛrmiːr] *vt* to strengthen; *vr* to grow stronger, harden.

afféterie [afetri] *nf* affectation, primness, gewgaws.

affichage [afiʃaːʒ] *nm* bill-posting.

affiche [afiʃ] *nf* bill, poster, placard; **panneau à —s** billboard; **tenir l'—** *(of a play)* to run.

afficher [afiʃe] *vt* to stick up, post up, make a display of; **défense d'—** no bills; *vr* to show off.

afficheur [afiʃœːr] *nm* bill-poster.

affilée [afile] *nf* **d'—** at a stretch.

affiler [afile] *vt* to sharpen, grind, whet, strop.

affiliation [afiljasjɔ̃] *nf* affiliation, branch.

affilier [afilje] *vt* to affiliate.

affinité [afinite] *nf* affinity, connection.

affirmatif, -ive [afirmatif, iːv] *a* affirmative.

affirmation [afirmasjɔ̃] *nf* affirmation, assertion.

affirmative [afirmatiːv] *nf* affirmative.

affirmer [afirme] *vt* to affirm, assert, aver, avouch.

affleurer [aflœre] *vt* to make flush; *vi* to be level.

affliction [afliksjɔ̃] *nf* affliction, grief.

affligé [afliʒe] *a* afflicted, aggrieved, sorrowful.

affligeant [afliʒɑ̃] *a* distressing, sad, grievous.

affliger [afliʒe] *vt* to afflict, distress; *vr* to grieve.

affluence [aflyɑ̃ːs] *nf* flow, influx, affluence, concourse, crowd; **heures d'—** rush hours.

affluent [aflyɑ̃] *nm* tributary.

affluer [aflye] *vi* to flow, flock, abound, throng.

affolé [afole] *a* crazy, distracted, panicky.

affolement [afolmɑ̃] *nm* distraction, panic.

affoler [afole] *vt* to distract, drive crazy; *vr* to become panicky, become infatuated (with de).

affranchi [afrɑ̃ʃi] *a* freed, stamped, unscrupulous; **colis —** prepaid parcel; n emancipated man, woman.

affranchir [afrɑ̃ʃiːr] vt to set free, emancipate, stamp, enfranchise; vr to become free, shake off (de).

affranchissement [afrɑ̃ʃismɑ̃] nm freeing, setting free, stamping, postage.

affréter [afrete] vt to charter, freight.

affreux, -euse [afrø, øːz] a horrible, awful, dreadful.

affront [afrɔ̃] nm affront, insult, disgrace, public shame.

affronter [afrɔ̃te] vt to affront, face.

affût [afy] nm hiding-place, gun-carriage; à l'— on the watch.

affûter [afyte] vt to sharpen, whet.

afin [afɛ̃] ad — de in order to; cj — que so that.

africain [afrikɛ̃] an African.

Afrique [afrik] nf Africa.

agaçant [agasɑ̃] a annoying, irritating, grating.

agacer [agase] vt to annoy, irritate, set teeth on edge.

âge [ɑːʒ] nm age, period; d'un certain — elderly; prendre de l'— to be getting on in years; quel — avez-vous? how old are you?

âgé [ɑʒe] a old, aged.

agence [aʒɑ̃ːs] nf agency, office.

agencer [aʒɑ̃se] vt to arrange, fit together, set.

agenda [aʒɛ̃da] nm agenda, diary.

agenouillé [aʒnuje] a kneeling.

s'agenouiller [saʒnuje] vr to kneel (down).

agent [aʒɑ̃] nm agent; — de police policeman; — de change stockbroker; — voyer road surveyor.

agglomération [aglɔmerasjɔ̃] nf agglomeration, built-up area.

aggloméré [aglɔmere] nm conglomerate, compressed fuel, coal-dust, briquette.

agglomérer [aglɔmere] vt to agglomerate, cluster, bind.

aggraver [agrave] vt to aggravate, worsen, increase.

agile [aʒil] a agile, nimble.

agilité [aʒilite] nf agility, nimbleness.

agioteur [aʒjotœːr] nm speculator, stockbroker.

agir [aʒiːr] vi to act; v imp s'— to be in question, concern; il s'agit de it is a question of; de quoi s'agit-il? what is the matter?

agissements [aʒismɑ̃] nm pl dealings, doings.

agitateur, -trice [aʒitatœːr, tris] n agitator.

agitation [aʒitasjɔ̃] nf agitation, restlessness, bustle; faire de l'— to agitate.

agité [aʒite] a agitated, restless, excited, agog, rough.

agiter [aʒite] vt to agitate, stir up, wave, flap, dangle; vr to become agitated, bustle, fidget, toss.

agneau [aɲo] nm lamb.

agonie [agɔni] nf death agony; à l'— dying.

agonisant [agɔnizɑ̃] a dying; n dying person.

agoniser [agɔnize] vi to be dying.

agouti [aguti] nm agouti.

agrafe [agraf] nf hook, clasp, clip, fastener; —e et portes hooks and eyes.

agrafer [agrafe] vt to fasten, clip.

agrandir [agrɑ̃diːr] vt to enlarge, magnify; vr to grow larger, become more powerful.

agrandissement [agrɑ̃dismɑ̃] nm aggrandizement, enlargement.

agréable [agreabl] a pleasant, congenial, acceptable.

agréer [agree] vt to accept; veuillez— l'expression de mes sentiments distingués yours faithfully, yours truly.

agrégation [agregasjɔ̃] nf aggregation, aggregate, State competitive examination for recruitment of secondary school teachers.

agrégé [agreʒe] an teacher who has passed the aggregation.

s'agréger [sagreʒe] vr to aggregate, join together.

agrément [agremɑ̃] nm pleasure, charm, approbation.

agrès [agrɛ] nm pl rigging, tackle.

agresseur [agresœːr] nm aggressor.

agressif, -ive [agresif, iːv] a aggressive.

agression [agresjɔ̃] nf aggression, assault.

agreste [agrɛst] a rustic, rural, uncouth.

agricole [agrikɔl] a agricultural.

agriculteur [agrikyltœːr] nm farmer.

agriculture [agrikyltyːr] nf agriculture.

agripper [agripe] vt to clutch, grip; vr to cling, come to grips (with à).

aguerri [ageri] a seasoned.

aguerrir [ageriːr] vt to harden, train, season.

aguets [agɛ] nm pl être aux — to lie in wait, be on the look-out, on the lurk.

aguicher [agiʃe] vt to allure, inflame.

ahuri [ayri] a bewildered, dumbfounded, dazed.

ahurir [ayriːr] vt to bewilder, flabbergast, daze.

ahurissement [ayrismɑ̃] nm bewilderment.

aide [e(ː)d] nf aid, help, assistance; à l'— i help!, venir en — à to help, benefit; n assistant, helper, mate.

aide-mémoire [ɛdmemwaːr] nm memorandum.

aider [ede] vt to aid, help, assist, avail.

aïeul [ajœl] n ancestor, ancestress, grandfather, grandmother.

aigle [ɛgl] nm eagle, lectern.

aiglefin [ɛgləfɛ̃] nm haddock.

aiglon [ɛglɔ̃] nm eaglet.
aigre [ɛːgr] a sour, tart, bitter, crabbed, shrill, sharp.
aigre-doux, -douce [ɛgrədu, dus] a bittersweet.
aigrefin [ɛgrəfɛ̃] nm sharper, swindler, haddock.
aigrette [ɛgrɛt] nf aigrette, tuft, plume.
aigreur [ɛgrœːr] nf sourness, tartness, embitterment, crabbedness; pl heartburn.
aigrir [ɛgriːr] vt to sour, turn sour, embitter.
aigu, -uë [egy] a pointed, sharp, shrill, high-pitched.
aiguière [egjɛːr] nf ewer.
aiguille [egɥij] nf needle, hand, pointer, spire, cock, switch; pl points.
aiguiller [egɥije] vt to switch, shunt, divert.
aiguilleur [egɥijœːr] nm switchman.
aiguillon [egɥijɔ̃] nm goad, spur, prickle, sting.
aiguillonner [egɥijɔne] vt to goad, spur on, stimulate.
aiguisé [egɥize] a sharp.
aiguiser [egɥize] vt to sharpen, point, stimulate; pierre à — hone, whetstone.
ail [aːj] nm garlic.
aile [ɛl] nf wing, fender, aisle.
ailé [ɛle] a winged.
aileron [ɛlrɔ̃] nm pinion, fin, aileron, wing-flap.
ailette [ɛlɛt] nf fin, blade.
ailier [ɛlje] nm wing-player, winger.
ailleurs [ajœːr] ad elsewhere; d'— moreover, besides; par — in other respects, from another source.
aimable [ɛmabl] a amiable, pleasant, bland, kind.
aimablement [ɛmabləmɑ̃] ad amiably, agreeably.
aimant [ɛmɑ̃] a affectionate; nm magnet, lodestone.
aimanter [ɛmɑ̃te] vt to magnetize.
aimer [ɛme] vt to love, like, be fond of, care for, enjoy.
aine [ɛn] nf groin.
aîné [ɛne] a elder, eldest, senior.
ainsi [ɛ̃si] ad thus, so; et — de suite and so on; — soit-il amen, so be it; pour — dire so to speak; — que as, like, as well as.
air [ɛːr] nm air, wind, appearance, look, tune, melody; avoir l'— to look, seem; en plein — in the open air; qui tient l'— airworthy.
airain [ɛrɛ̃] nm bronze, brass.
aire [ɛːr] nf threshing-floor, area, surface, eyrie, point of the compass.
aisance [ɛzɑ̃ːs] nf ease, comfort, affluence.
aise [ɛːz] nf ease, comfort; à l'— comfortable, well-off; à votre — just as you like; mal à l'— uncomfortable, uneasy; bien — very glad.

aisé [ɛze] a easy, well-to-do.
aisément [ɛzemɑ̃] ad easily.
aisselle [ɛsɛl] nf armpit.
ajonc [aʒɔ̃] nm furze, gorse.
ajournement [aʒurnəmɑ̃] nm postponement.
ajourner [aʒurne] vt to postpone; vr to adjourn.
ajouter [aʒute] vt to add, supplement.
ajustage [aʒystaːʒ] nm adjustment, fitting.
ajustement [aʒystəmɑ̃] nm adjusting, settlement, fit.
ajuster [aʒyste] vt to adjust, fit, settle.
ajusteur [aʒystœːr] nm fitter.
alacrité [alakrite] nf alacrity.
alanguir [alɑ̃giːr] vt to enfeeble; vr to grow languid.
alanguissement [alɑ̃gismɑ̃] nm languor.
alarmant [alarmɑ̃] a alarming.
alarme [alarm] nf alarm.
alarmer [alarme] vt to alarm; vr to take fright.
alarmiste [alarmist] a alarmist, panicky; n scaremonger.
album [albɔm] nm album.
alchimie [alʃimi] nf alchemy.
alchimiste [alʃimist] nm alchemist.
alcool [alkɔl] nm alcohol, spirit(s); — à brûler methylated spirit.
alcoolique [alkɔlik] a alcoholic.
alcoolisme [alkɔlism] nm alcoholism.
alcôve [alkoːv] nf alcove, recess.
aléatoire [aleatwaːr] a risky, chancy.
alène [alɛn] nf awl.
alentour [alɑ̃tuːr] ad around; nm pl surroundings.
alerte [alɛrt] a alert, quick; nf alarm, alert, air-raid warning; fin d'— all clear.
alerter [alɛrte] vt to give the alarm to, warn.
alésage [alezaːʒ] nm (tec) boring, bore.
alèse [alɛːz] nf draw-sheet, rubber sheet.
algèbre [alʒɛbr] nf algebra.
Algérie [alʒeri] nf Algeria.
algérien, -ienne [alʒerjɛ̃, jɛn] an Algerian.
algue [alg] nf alga, seaweed.
alibi [alibi] nm alibi.
aliénation [aljenasjɔ̃] nf alienation, estrangement.
aliéné [aljene] a insane; n lunatic.
aliéner [aljene] vt to alienate, estrange.
aliéniste [aljenist] nm mental specialist.
alignement [aliɲmɑ̃] nm alignment, line, row, putting in lines.
aligner [aliɲe] vt to align, line up, draw up; vr to fall into line.
aliment [alimɑ̃] nm aliment, food.
alimentation [alimɑ̃tasjɔ̃] nf alimentation, feeding, nourishment.

alimenter [alimɑ̃te] vt to feed, nourish.

alinéa [alinea] nm paragraph, break.

s'aliter [salite] vr to take to one's bed.

allaiter [alɛte] vt to suckle.

allant [alɑ̃] nm dash, go.

allécher [al(l)eʃe] vt to entice, allure.

allée [ale] nf avenue, drive, path, lane, passage.

allégation [al(l)egasjɔ̃] nf allegation.

alléger [al(l)eʒe] vt to lighten, alleviate.

allégorie [allegɔri] nf allegory.

allègre [alɛːgr] a lively.

alléguer [al(l)ege] vt to allege, urge, plead.

Allemagne [almaɲ] nf Germany.

allemand [almɑ̃] a German.

aller [ale] vi to go, suit, fit; — chercher to fetch; comment allez-vous? how do you do?; allez-y! fire away!; cela va de soi that is a matter of course; y — de qch. to be at stake; allons donc! come along! nonsense!; vr s'en — to go away, clear off, depart; nm one-way ticket, one-way; billet d'— et retour round trip; au pis — if the worst comes to the worst.

alliage [aljaːʒ] nm alloy.

alliance [aljɑ̃ːs] nf alliance. blending, wedding ring.

allier [alje] vt to ally.

allocation [allɔkasjɔ̃] nf allocation, allowance, grant.

allonger [alɔ̃ʒe] vt to lengthen, stretch out, strike, eke out; vr to lengthen, stretch.

allumage [alymaːʒ] nm lighting, putting on, ignition.

allumer [alyme] vt to light, put on, set alight, arouse.

allumette [alymɛt] nf match.

allure [alyːr] nf carriage, gait, walk, speed, turn, style.

aloi [alwa] nm quality, standard; de bon — genuine.

alors [alɔːr] ad then, at that time, so, in that case.

alouette [alwɛt] nf lark.

alpinisme [alpinism] nm mountaineering.

altercation [alterkasjɔ̃] nf altercation, dispute.

altérer [altere] vt to change, spoil, impair, falsify, make thirsty; vr to change, be spoiled, become thirsty.

alternatif, -ive [alternatif, iːv] a alternative, alternate, alternating.

alterner [alterne] vt to alternate, to take turns.

altier [altje] a haughty, lofty.

amabilité [amabilite] nf amiability, civility.

amadouer [amadwe] vt to wheedle, coax, win over.

amaigrir [amɛgriːr] vt to make thin, reduce.

amande [amɑ̃ːd] nf almond.

amant [amɑ̃] n lover.

amarre [amaːr] nf hawser; pl moorings.

amarrer [amare] vtr to moor, tie up.

amas [ama] nm pile, heap.

amasser [amase] vt to amass, pile up; vr to mass.

amateur, -trice [amatœːr, tris] n amateur, lover.

ambages [ɑ̃baːʒ] nf pl sans — bluntly, plainly.

ambassade [ɑ̃basad] nf embassy.

ambiance [ɑ̃bjɑ̃ːs] nf surroundings, atmosphere.

ambigu, -uë [ɑ̃bigy] a ambiguous.

ambition [ɑ̃bisjɔ̃] nf ambition.

ambre [ɑ̃ːbr] nm amber.

ambulant [ɑ̃bylɑ̃] a traveling, itinerant, strolling.

âme [aːm] nf soul, spirit, core, heart, life; (of gun) bore.

améliorer [ameljɔre] vtr to improve, mend.

aménager [amenaʒe] vt to fit up (out), lay out.

amende [amɑ̃ːd] nf fine.

amender [amɑ̃de] vtr to improve.

amener [amne] vt to lead, bring, induce.

amer, -ère [ameːr] a bitter.

américain [amerikɛ̃] a an American.

Amérique [amerik] nf America.

amertume [amɛrtym] nf bitterness.

ameublement [amœblǝmɑ̃] nm furnishing, furniture.

ameuter [amøte] vt to rouse; vr to mutiny.

ami [ami] n friend, boy-, girl-friend.

amical [amikal] a friendly.

amidon [amidɔ̃] nm starch.

amincir [amɛ̃siːr] vt to make thinner, thin down; vr to grow thinner.

amiral [amiral] nm admiral.

amirauté [amirote] nf admiralty.

amitié [amitje] nf friendship, favor; pl kind regards.

amoindrir [amwɛ̃driːr] vtr to lessen, decrease.

amollir [amɔliːr] vt to soften; vr to grow weak.

amonceler [amɔ̃sle] vtr to pile up; vr to gather.

amont [amɔ̃] nm upper reaches; en — upstream.

amorce [amɔrs] nf bait, beginning, detonator.

amortir [amɔrtiːr] vt to deaden, allay, muffle, slacken, pay off, sink, redeem.

amortissement [amɔrtismɑ̃] nm deadening, redemption; fonds d'— sinking-fund.

amortisseur [amɔrtisœːr] nm shock-absorber.

amour [amuːr] nm (pl usually f) love; pour l'— de for love of, for the sake of.

s'amouracher [samuraʃe] vr to fall head over heels in love (with de).

amourette [amurɛt] *nf* passing love affair.

amoureux, -euse [amurø, øːz] *a* loving, amorous; être — de to be in love with, enamored of; *n* lover.

amour-propre [amurprɔpr] *nm* self-esteem, -respect, vanity, egotism.

amovible [amɔvibl] *a* removable, detachable.

amphibie [ɑ̃fibi] *a* amphibious; *nm* amphibian.

ample [ɑ̃ːpl] *a* ample, roomy; **plus** — further, fuller.

ampleur [ɑ̃plœːr] *nf* fullness, copiousness, magnitude.

amplificateur, -trice [ɑ̃plifikatœːr, tris] *a* amplifying; *nm* amplifier.

amplification [ɑ̃plifikasjɔ̃] *nf* amplification.

amplifier [ɑ̃plifje] *vt* to amplify.

ampoule [ɑ̃pul] *nf* blister, phial, (electric light) bulb.

ampoulé [ɑ̃pule] *a* bombastic, high-flown, stilted.

amputation [ɑ̃pytasjɔ̃] *nf* amputation.

amputer [ɑ̃pyte] *vt* to amputate, reduce.

amusant [amyzɑ̃] *a* amusing, entertaining.

amusement [amyzmɑ̃] *nm* amusement, entertainment, fun.

amuser [amyze] *vt* to amuse, entertain, interest; *vr* to enjoy oneself, take pleasure (in à), have fun.

amusette [amyzɛt] *nf* toy.

amygdale [ami(g)dal] *nf* tonsil.

amygdalite [ami(g)dalit] *nf* tonsillitis.

an [ɑ̃] *nm* year; **le jour de l'**— New Year's Day.

analogie [analɔʒi] *nf* analogy.

analogue [analɔg] *a* analogous, kindred.

analyse [analiːz] *nf* analysis, abstract.

analyser [analize] *vt* to analyze, parse.

analyste [analist] *nm* analyst.

analytique [analitik] *a* analytical.

ananas [ananɑ(ːs)] *nm* pineapple.

anarchie [anarʃi] *nf* anarchy.

anarchiste [anarʃist] *an* anarchist.

anathème [anatɛm] *nm* anathema, curse.

anatomie [anatɔmi] *nf* anatomy.

anatomiste [anatɔmist] *nm* anatomist.

ancestral [ɑ̃sɛstral] *a* ancestral.

ancêtre [ɑ̃sɛːtr] *n* ancestor, ancestress, forefather.

anchois [ɑ̃ʃwa] *nm* anchovy.

ancien, -ienne [ɑ̃sjɛ̃, jɛn] *a* ancient, old, long-standing, former, past, senior; — **combattant** ex-serviceman.

anciennement [ɑ̃sjɛnmɑ̃] *ad* formerly.

ancienneté [ɑ̃sjɛnte] *nf* antiquity, seniority.

ancre [ɑ̃ːkr] *nf* anchor; **lever l'**— to weigh anchor.

andouille [ɑ̃duːj] *nf* (chitterling) sausage, duffer, fool.

âne [ɑːn] *nm* ass, donkey, fool; **en dos d'**— hog-backed.

anéantir [aneɑ̃tiːr] *vt* to destroy, wipe out; *vr* to come to nothing.

anéantissement [aneɑ̃tismɑ̃] *nm* destruction, annihilation.

anecdote [anekdɔt] *nf* anecdote.

anémie [anemi] *nf* anemia.

anémique [anemik] *a* anemic.

anesthésie [anɛstezi] *nf* anesthesia.

anesthésier [anɛstezje] *vt* to anesthetize.

anesthésique [anɛstezik] *a* *nm* anesthetic.

anesthésiste [anɛstezist] *nm* anesthetist.

ange [ɑ̃ːʒ] *nm* angel.

angélique [ɑ̃ʒelik] *a* angelic.

angélus [ɑ̃ʒelyːs] *nm* angelus.

angine [ɑ̃ʒin] *nf* sore throat, quinsy, tonsilitis; — **de poitrine** angina (pectoris).

anglais [ɑ̃glɛ] *a* *nm* English; *n* Englishman, -woman.

angle [ɑ̃ːgl] *nm* angle.

Angleterre [ɑ̃glɛtɛːr] *nf* England.

anglican [ɑ̃glikɑ̃] *an* Anglican.

angoissant [ɑ̃gwasɑ̃] *a* distressing.

angoisse [ɑ̃gwas] *nf* anguish, anxiety, distress.

anguille [ɑ̃giːj] *nf* eel; — **sous roche** something in the wind, something brewing; — **de mer** conger-eel.

angulaire [ɑ̃gylɛːr] *a* angular; **pierre** — corner-stone.

anguleux [ɑ̃gylø] *a* angular, gaunt.

animal [animal] *a* *nm* animal.

animateur, -trice [animatœːr, tris] *n* animator, moving spirit, organizer.

animation [animasjɔ̃] *nf* animation.

animé [anime] *a* animated, lively, spirited, heated.

animer [anime] *vt* to animate, enliven, vivify, brighten, actuate; *vr* to become animated, brighten up.

animosité [animɔzite] *nf* animosity.

anis [ani] *nm* aniseed.

annales [annal] *nf pl* annals.

anneau [ano] *nm* ring, link, ringlet, quoit.

année [ane] *nf* year, vintage; **bonne** — ! a Happy New Year!

annexe [an(n)ɛks] *nm* annex.

annexer [an(n)ɛkse] *vt* to annex.

annexion [an(n)ɛksjɔ̃] *nf* annexation.

annihiler [an(n)iile] *vt* to annihilate.

anniversaire [anivɛrsɛːr] *a* anniversary; *nm* anniversary, birthday.

annonce [anɔ̃ːs] *nf* announcement, advertisement.

annoncer [anɔ̃se] *vt* to announce, herald, usher in, advertise, betoken, denote.

annonciation [anɔ̃sjasjɔ̃] *nf* Annunciation, Lady Day.

annotation [an(n)ɔtasjɔ̃] nf annotation.

annoter [an(n)ɔte] vt to annotate, note.

annuaire [an(n)ɥɛːr] nm annual, telephone directory.

annuel [an(n)ɥɛl] a annual.

annuité [an(n)ɥite] nf annuity.

annulaire [an(n)ylɛːr] a annular; nm third finger.

annulation [an(n)ylasjɔ̃] nf annulment, nullification, revocation, cancellation.

annuler [an(n)yle] vt to annul.

anoblir [anɔbliːr] vt to ennoble.

anoblissement [anɔblismɑ̃] nm ennoblement.

anodin [anɔdɛ̃] a anodyne, harmless; nm palliative.

anomalie [anɔmali] nf anomaly.

ânonner [anɔne] vt to mumble, stammer through.

anonymat [anɔnima] nm anonymity.

anonyme [anɔnim] a anonymous; société — limited company; nm anonymity.

anormal [anɔrmal] a abnormal, anomalous.

anse [ɑ̃ːs] nf handle, cove.

antagonisme [ɑ̃tagɔnism] nm antagonism.

antécédent [ɑ̃tesedɑ̃] a nm antecedent.

antenne [ɑ̃tɛn] nf antenna, feeler, aerial.

antérieur [ɑ̃terjœːr] a anterior, former, prior.

antériorité [ɑ̃terjɔrite] nf anteriority.

anthrax [ɑ̃traks] nm carbuncle.

anthropophage [ɑ̃trɔpɔfaːʒ] a nm cannibalistic, cannibal.

antiaérien, -ienne [ɑ̃tiaerjɛ̃, jɛn] a anti-aircraft.

antibiotique [ɑ̃tibiɔtik] nm antibiotic.

antichambre [ɑ̃tiʃɑ̃ːbr] nf anteroom, hall, waiting-room.

antichar [ɑ̃tiʃar] a anti-tank.

anticipation [ɑ̃tisipasjɔ̃] nf anticipation.

anticiper [ɑ̃tisipe] vt to anticipate, forestall; vi to anticipate, encroach (upon sur).

anticorps [ɑ̃tikɔr] nm antibody.

antidater [ɑ̃tidate] vt to antedate.

antidérapant [ɑ̃tiderapɑ̃] a non-skid.

antidote [ɑ̃tidɔt] nm antidote.

antipathie [ɑ̃tipati] nf antipathy, repugnance.

antipathique [ɑ̃tipatik] a antipathetic, uncongenial.

antipodes [ɑ̃tipɔd] nm pl antipodes.

antiquaille [ɑ̃tikaːj] nf lumber, junk.

antiquaire [ɑ̃tikɛːr] nm antiquarian.

antique [ɑ̃tik] a antique, ancient, old-fashioned.

antiquité [ɑ̃tikite] nf antiquity.

antiseptique [ɑ̃tiseptik] a nm antiseptic.

antithèse [ɑ̃titɛːz] nf antithesis.

antithétique [ɑ̃titetik] a antithetical.

antre [ɑ̃ːtr] nm den, lair, sinus.

anxiété [ɑ̃ksjete] nf anxiety, solicitude.

anxieux, -euse [ɑ̃ksjø, øːz] a anxious, solicitous.

aorte [aɔrt] nf aorta.

août [u] nm August.

apache [apaʃ] nm hooligan.

apaiser [apeze] vt to appease, alleviate, mollify, mitigate; vr to calm down.

aparté [aparte] nm aside, stage whisper.

apathie [apati] nf apathy, listlessness.

apathique [apatik] a apathetic, listless.

apercevoir [apersəvwaːr] vt to perceive, catch sight of; vr to notice, realize.

aperçu [apersy] nm glimpse, sidelight, outline, summary.

apéritif [aperitif] nm appetizer.

aphone [afɔn] a voiceless.

aphteux, -euse [aftø, øz] a aphthous; la fièvre aphteuse foot-and-mouth disease.

apiculteur [apikyltœːr] nm bee-keeper.

apitoyer [apitwaje] vt to move to pity; vr to commiserate (with sur).

aplanir [aplaniːr] vt to smooth (away), plane, level.

aplanissement [aplanismɑ̃] nm smoothing, leveling.

aplatir [aplatiːr] vt to flatten, iron out; vr to grovel, collapse, fall flat.

aplatissement [aplatismɑ̃] nm flattening.

aplomb [aplɔ̃] nm perpendicularity, level, self-possession, nerve; d'— upright, firm on one's feet, four-square.

apogée [apɔʒe] nm apogee, acme, zenith, peak.

apologie [apɔlɔʒi] nf vindication, justification.

apologiste [apɔlɔʒist] nm apologist.

apoplectique [apɔplɛktik] a apoplectic.

apoplexie [apɔplɛksi] nf apoplexy.

apostat [apɔsta] nm apostate.

apostolat [apɔstɔla] nm apostleship.

apostolique [apɔstɔlik] a apostolic.

apothicaire [apɔtikɛːr] nm apothecary.

apôtre [apoːtr] nm apostle.

apparaître [aparɛːtr] vi to appear, become apparent.

apparat [apara] nm pomp, show, state.

appareil [aparɛːj] nm apparatus, mechanism, plant, set, airplane; — photographique camera.

appareillage [apareja:ʒ] nm fitting

up, getting under way, equipment.

appareiller [apareje] vt to fit out; vi get under way.

apparemment [aparamã] ad apparently, evidently, seemingly.

apparence [aparãːs] nf appearance, look, show, guise.

apparent [aparã] a apparent, seeming, obvious.

apparenté [aparãte] a related.

apparier [aparje] vt to match, pair, mate.

apparition [aparisjɔ̃] nf appearance, apparition.

appartement [apartəmã] nm flat, apartment, suite, rooms.

appartenir [apartəniːr] vi to belong; v imp to appertain (to à), rest (with à).

appas [apɑ] nm pl charms.

appât [apɑ] nm bait, lure.

appâter [apate] vt to lure, bait.

appauvrir [apovriːr] vt to impoverish; vr to become poor(er).

appeau [apo] nm bird-call, decoy.

appel [apɛl] nm appeal, call, cry, call-up, roll-call, muster; aller, renvoyer en — to appeal; — d'incendie fire-alarm.

appeler [aple] vt to call (for, in, to, up); en — à to appeal to; faire — to send for; vr to be called, named.

appendice [ap(p)ɛdis] nm appendix.

appendicite [ap(p)ɛdisit] nf appendicitis.

appentis [apãti] nm outhouse, lean-to shed.

appesantir [apəzãtiːr] vt to make heavy, dull; vr to become heavy, dwell (upon sur).

appétissant [apetisã] a appetizing.

appétit [apeti] nm appetite; de bon — hearty appetite.

applaudir [aplodiːr] vt to applaud.

applaudissements [aplodismã] nm pl applause.

applicable [aplikabl] a applicable.

application [aplikasjɔ̃] nf application, enforcement, diligence, concentration.

applique [aplik] nf bracket.

appliqué [aplike] a diligent, assiduous, applied.

appliquer [aplike] vt to apply, carry out; vr to apply oneself (to à).

appoint [apwɛ̃] nm balance, odd money, contribution; faire l'— to tender exact amount, ' no change given '.

appointements [apwɛtmã] nm pl salary.

appontement [apɔ̃tmã] nm landing-stage, pier.

apport [apɔːr] nm contribution, share.

apporter [apɔrte] vt to bring (in, forward, forth).

apposer [apoze] vt to affix.

apposition [apozisjɔ̃] nf apposition, affixing.

appréciation [apresjasjɔ̃] nf appreciation, estimate, valuation.

apprécier [apresje] vt to appreciate, estimate, value.

appréhender [apreãde] vt to apprehend.

appréhension [apreãsjɔ̃] nf apprehension.

apprendre [aprãːdr] vt to learn, teach, inform, tell.

apprenti [aprãti] n apprentice.

apprentissage [aprãtisaːʒ] nm apprenticeship.

apprêté [aprete] a affected.

apprêter [aprɛte] vt to prepare, dress; vr to get ready.

apprivoiser [aprivwaze] vt to tame, domesticate.

approbateur, -trice [aprɔbatœːr, tris] a approving; n approver.

approbatif, -ive [aprɔbatif, iːv] a approving.

approbation [aprɔbasjɔ̃] nf approbation, approval, sanction.

approche [aprɔʃ] nf approach.

approcher [aprɔʃe] vt to approach, draw near; vi to approach, draw near, border (on); vr to come near.

approfondi [aprɔfɔ̃di] a deep, thorough, exhaustive.

approfondir [aprɔfɔ̃diːr] vt to deepen, go deeply into, fathom.

approfondissement [aprɔfɔ̃dismã] nm deepening, investigation.

approprié [aprɔprie] a appropriate, suitable, proper.

approprier [aprɔprie] vt to appropriate, adapt.

approuver [apruve] vt to approve of, favor, consent to.

approvisionnement [aprɔvizjɔnmã] nm provisioning, victualing, supply, stores, provisions.

approvisionner [aprɔvizjɔne] vt to stock, supply; vr to lay in supplies, get supplies.

approximatif, -ive [aprɔksimatif, iːv] a approximate, rough.

approximation [aprɔksimasjɔ̃] nf approximation.

appui [apɥi] nm support, prop, stress, rest; point d'— strong point, defended locality.

appuyer [apɥije] vt to support, prop, favor, further; vi — sur dwell on, stress, emphasize, press; vr to lean, rest (on, against sur, contre), depend, rely (on).

âpre [ɑːpr] a rough, harsh, bitter, stern, grim, keen.

après [aprɛ] prep after; d'— according to, from; ad afterward; cj — que after.

après-demain [apredmɛ̃] ad the day after tomorrow.

après-guerre [apregɛːr] nm postwar period.

après-midi [apremidi] nm or f afternoon.

âpreté [ɑprəte] nf roughness, harshness, bitterness, sternness, keenness, greed.

à-propos [aprɔpo] *nm* aptness, opportuneness.

apte [apt] *a* apt, qualified.

aptitude [aptityd] *nf* aptitude, proficiency.

apurement [apyrmɑ̃] *nm* — de comptes audit(ing).

apurer [apyre] *vt* to audit.

aquarelle [akwarɛl] *nf* water-color.

aqueduc [ak(ə)dyk] *nm* aqueduct.

aqueux, -euse [akø, ø:z] *a* aqueous, watery.

aquilin [akilɛ̃] *a* aquiline.

arabe [arab] *a* Arab, Arabian, Arabic; *n* Arab, Arabic.

arable [arabl] *a* arable.

arachide [araʃid] *nf* peanut.

araignée [arɛɲe] *nf* spider; — dans le plafond bee in the bonnet.

arbitrage [arbitra:ʒ] *nm* arbitration, umpiring, refereeing.

arbitraire [arbitrɛːr] *a* arbitrary, high-handed.

arbitre [arbi:tr] *nm* arbitrator, umpire, referee; libre — free will.

arbitrer [arbitre] *vt* to arbitrate, umpire, referee.

arborer [arbɔre] *vt* to hoist, raise, sport.

arbre [arbr] *nm* tree, shaft.

arbrisseau [arbriso] *nm* shrub.

arbuste [arbyst] *nm* bush.

arc [ark] *nm* bow, arch, arc; tir à l'— archery.

arcade [arkad] *nf* arcade.

arc-boutant [ar(k)butɑ̃] *nm* flying-buttress, stay.

arceau [arso] *nm* arch, hoop.

arc-en-ciel [arkɑ̃sjɛl] *nm* rainbow.

archaïsme [arkaism] *nm* archaism.

archange [arkɑ̃:ʒ] *nm* archangel.

arche [arʃ] *nf* ark, arch, span.

archéologie [arkeɔlɔʒi] *nf* archaeology.

archéologue [arkeɔlɔg] *nm* archaeologist.

archer [arʃe] *nm* archer.

archet [arʃe] *nm* bow.

archevêché [arʃəvɛʃe] *nm* archbishopric, archbishop's palace.

archevêque [arʃəvɛːk] *nm* archbishop.

archicomble [arʃikɔbl] *a* packed.

archipel [arʃipɛl] *nm* archipelago.

architecte [arʃitɛkt] *nm* architect.

architecture [arʃitɛkty:r] *nf* architecture.

archives [arʃiːv] *nf* *pl* archives, records, Record Office.

arctique [arktik] *a* arctic.

ardemment [ardamɑ̃] *ad* ardently, eagerly.

ardent [ardɑ̃] *a* ardent, glowing, keen, eager, live.

ardeur [ardœːr] *nf* ardor, heat, glow, eagerness, zeal, enthusiasm, spirit.

ardoise [ardwaːz] *nf* slate.

ardu [ardy] *a* arduous, tough.

arène [arɛn] *nf* arena.

arête [arɛt] *nf* fishbone, ridge, edge.

argent [arʒɑ̃] *nm* silver, money; — comptant ready money, cash down.

argenté [arʒɑ̃te] *a* silver, silver-plated.

argenterie [arʒɑ̃tri] *nf* silver-plate.

argentin [arʒɑ̃tɛ̃] *a* silvery, silvertoned.

argile [arʒil] *nf* clay.

argot [argo] *nm* slang.

argument [argymɑ̃] *nm* argument, plea, summary.

argumentation [argymɑ̃tasjɔ̃] *nf* argumentation.

argumenter [argymɑ̃te] *vi* to argue.

argutie [argysi] *nf* quibble.

aride [arid] *a* arid, dry, barren.

aridité [aridite] *nf* aridity.

aristocrate [aristɔkrat] *n* aristocrat.

aristocratie [aristɔkrasi] *nf* aristocracy.

arithmétique [aritmetik] *a* arithmetical; *nf* arithmetic.

armateur [armatœːr] *nm* shipwright, shipowner.

armature [armaty:r] *nf* framework, mainstay, reinforcement, armature.

arme [arm] *nf* arm, weapon, branch of the army; maître d'—s fencing master; prise d'—s parade.

armée [arme] *nf* army, host; — de métier professional army; — de l'air Air Force; aux —s on active service.

armement [arməmɑ̃] *nm* arming, fitting out, loading, equipment, crew; *pl* armaments.

armer [arme] *vt* to arm, strengthen, fit out, equip, load, commission, man.

armistice [armistis] *nm* armistice.

armoire [armwaːr] *nf* wardrobe, cupboard, press, closet.

armoiries [armwari] *nf* *pl* coat of arms, crest.

armure [army:r] *nf* armor.

armurerie [armyr(ə)ri] *nf* armory, arms factory.

armurier [armyrje] *nm* armorer, gunsmith.

arôme [aroːm] *nm* aroma.

arpenter [arpɑ̃te] *vt* to measure, survey, pace.

arqué [arke] *a* arched, curved, bow.

arquer [arke] *vt* to arch, bend.

arrache-pied [araʃpje] *ad* d'— steadily.

arracher [araʃe] *vt* to tear away (off, out, up), pull away (out, up), snatch.

arraisonner [arɛzɔne] *vt* to hail, stop and examine a ship.

arrangement [arɑ̃ʒmɑ̃] *nm* arrangement, order.

arranger [arɑ̃ʒe] *vt* to arrange, compose, settle; *vr* to manage, come to terms.

arrérages [arera:ʒ] nm pl arrears.
arrestation [arɛstasjɔ̃] nf arrest, detention.
arrêt [arɛ] nm stop(ping), stoppage, detention, arrest, seizure, decree, judgment; — facultatif ' stop here if required '; mandat d'— warrant; maison d'— jail.
arrêté [arete] a fixed; nm decision, decree, bylaw.
arrêter [arete] vt to stop, stem, check, clog, detain, arrest, decide; vi to halt, stop, draw up; vr to dwell (on sur), stop.
arrière [arjɛ:r] a back, rear; ad backward; en — behind, in arrears, back; en — de behind; faire marche — to reverse; nm rear, back part, full back; à l'— in the rear, at the back, behind, astern.
arrière-boutique [arjɛrbutik] nf shopyard.
arrière-bras [arjɛrbra] nm upper arm.
arrière-cour [arjɛrku:r] nf backyard.
arrière-garde [arjɛrgard] nf rearguard.
arrière-goût [arjɛrgu] nm aftertaste, smack.
arrière-grand-père, -grand'mère [arjɛrgrɑ̃pɛ:r, grɑ̃mɛ:r] n greatgrandfather, -grandmother.
arrière-pensée [arjɛrpɑ̃se] nf ulterior motive, mental reservation.
arrière-plan [arjɛrplɑ̃] nm background.
arrière-saison [arjɛrsɛzɔ̃] nf late autumn, fall.
arrière-train [arjɛrtrɛ̃] nm hindquarters, hind-carriage.
arriéré [arjere] a in arrears, backward, old-fashioned.
arrimer [arime] vt to stow, trim.
arrivage [ariva:ʒ] nm arrival, consignment.
arrivée [arive] nf arrival, coming, winning-post.
arriver [arive] vi to arrive, reach, get, succeed, happen, occur, come about.
arriviste [arivist] n careerist, gogetter.
arrogance [arɔgɑ̃:s] nf arrogance, bumptiousness.
arrogant [arɔgɑ̃] a arrogant, bumptious, assuming.
s'arroger [sarɔʒe] vr to arrogate, assume as a right.
arrondir [arɔ̃di:r] vt to round (off), make round.
arrondissement [arɔ̃dismɑ̃] nm rounding (off), subdivision of a French department, municipal ward.
arrosage [aroza:ʒ] nm watering, spraying.
arroser [aroze] vt to water, spray, sprinkle, baste.

arrosoir [arozwa:r] nm wateringcan, -cart, sprinkler.
arsenal [arsənal] nm arsenal, naval dockyard.
arsenic [arsənik] nm arsenic.
art [a:r] nm art, skill.
artère [artɛ:r] nf artery, thoroughfare.
artériel, -elle [arterjɛl] a arterial.
artichaut [artiʃo] nm globe artichoke.
article [artikl] nm article, implement, paper; pl wares; — de Paris fancy goods; à l'— de la mort at the point of death.
articulation [artikylasjɔ̃] nf articulation, joint.
articuler [artikyle] vt to articulate.
artifice [artifis] nm artifice, art, expedient, scheming; feu d'— fireworks.
artificiel, -elle [artifisjɛl] a artificial, imitation.
artillerie [artijri] nf artillery.
artimon [artimɔ̃] nm mât d'— mizzen-mast.
artisan [artizɑ̃] nm artisan, workman, maker.
artisanat [artizana] nm working classes.
artiste [artist] a artistic; n artist, performer.
artistique [artistik] a artistic.
aryen, -yenne [arjɛ̃, jɛn] an Aryan.
as [ɑ:s] nm ace, crack, swell.
asbeste [azbɛst] nm asbestos.
ascendance [as(s)ɑ̃dɑ̃:s] nf ancestry.
ascendant [as(s)ɑ̃dɑ̃] a ascending, climbing; nm ascendancy; pl ancestry.
ascenseur [asɑ̃sœ:r] nm elevator.
ascension [asɑ̃sjɔ̃] nf ascent, ascension.
ascète [asɛt] n ascetic.
ascétique [asetik] a ascetic(al).
ascétisme [asetism] nm asceticism.
asepsie [asɛpsi] nf asepsis.
aseptique [asɛptik] a aseptic.
asiatique [azjatik] a Asiatic, Oriental.
Asie [azi] nf Asia.
asile [azil] nm shelter, refuge, sanctuary, home, almshouse; — des pauvres workhouse; — d'aliénés lunatic asylum.
aspect [aspɛ] nm aspect, appearance, look, sight.
asperge [aspɛrʒ] nf asparagus.
asperger [aspɛrʒe] vt to sprinkle, splash, spray.
aspérité [asperite] nf asperity, roughness, harshness.
asphalte [asfalt] nm asphalt, bitumen, pitch.
asphyxiant [asfiksjɑ̃] a asphyxiating, poison.
asphyxie [asfiksi] nf asphyxia.
asphyxier [asfiksje] vt to asphyxiate.
aspirant [aspirɑ̃] a sucking; n candidate, aspirant; nm midshipman.
aspirateur, -trice [aspiratœ:r, tris]

a aspiratory; *nm* aspirator, vacuum cleaner.

aspiration [aspirasjɔ̃] *nf* aspiration, longing (for à), inhaling, suction, gasp.

aspirer [aspire] *vt* to aspire, long (for à), hanker (after à), inhale, suck up, aspirate.

aspirine [aspirin] *nf* aspirin.

assaillant [as(s)ajã] *nm* assailant.

assaillir [as(s)ajiːr] *vt* to assail.

assainir [aseniːr] *vt* to make healthier, cleanse.

assaisonnement [asezɔnmã] *nm* seasoning, flavoring, dressing, relish, sauce.

assaisonner [asezɔne] *vt* to season, flavor, dress.

assassin [asasɛ̃] *n* assassin, murderer.

assassinat [asasina] *nm* assassination, murder.

assassiner [asasine] *vt* to assassinate, murder.

assaut [aso] *nm* assault, onslaught, attack, bout; **emporter d'—** to storm; **troupes d'—** shock troops.

assécher [aseʃe] *vt* to drain, dry; *vir* to dry up.

assemblage [asãblaːʒ] *nm* collating, gathering, assembly, joining up.

assemblée [asãble] *nf* assembly, meeting, gathering, convocation; **Assemblée Nationale** Lower Chamber of French Parliament.

assembler [asãble] *vt* to assemble, gather, connect; *vr* to meet, assemble, flock.

assener [asɔne] *vt* to deliver, deal, land (a blow).

assentiment [asãtimã] *nm* assent.

asseoir [aswaːr] *vt* to set, lay, found; *vr* to sit down.

assermenter [asɛrmãte] *vt* to swear in.

asservir [asɛrviːr] *vt* to enslave.

asservissement [asɛrvismã] *nm* enslavement.

assesseur [asɛsœːr] *nm* assessor.

assez [ase] *ad* enough, rather, fairly.

assidu [asidy] *a* assiduous, sedulous, constant, regular.

assiduité [asidчite] *nf* assiduity, application, regularity.

assiégeant [asjeʒã] *a* besieging; *nm* besieger.

assiéger [asjeʒe] *vt* to besiege, beleaguer.

assiette [asjɛt] *nf* position, situation, set, foundation, plate; **n'être pas dans son —** to be out of sorts.

assignation [asiɲasjɔ̃] *nf* assignment, writ, subpoena.

assigner [asiɲe] *vt* to assign, allot, allocate, summon, serve a writ on.

assimiler [as(s)imile] *vt* to assimilate, digest.

assimilation [as(s)imilasjɔ̃] *nf* assimilation.

assis [asi] *a* seated, sitting, established, situated.

assise [asiːz] *nf* foundation, base, seating, course; *pl* assizes, sittings, sessions.

assistance [asistãːs] *nf* assistance, relief, presence, audience.

assistant [asistã] *n* assistant, onlooker; **—e sociale** welfare worker; *pl* audience, those present.

assister [asiste] *vt* to assist, help; *vi* to be present, witness, attend.

association [asɔsjasjɔ̃] *nf* association, society, partnership.

associé [asɔsje] *n* partner, associate.

associer [asɔsje] *vt* to associate, band, club, connect; *vr* to participate (in à), enter into a partnership (with à).

assoiffé [aswafe] *a* thirsty.

assombrir [asɔ̃briːr] *vt* to darken, dim, cast a gloom over; *vr* to become dark, cloud (over), become sad.

assommant [asɔmã] *a* overwhelming, tiresome, deadly dull, humdrum, boring.

assommer [asɔme] *vt* to knock senseless, bludgeon, tire out, wear out, bore.

assommeur [asɔmœːr] *nm* slaughterer.

assommoir [asɔmwaːr] *nm* pole-ax, bludgeon, low tavern.

assomption [asɔ̃psjɔ̃] *nf* assumption.

assortiment [asɔrtimã] *nm* matching, sorting, assortment, set.

assortir [asɔrtiːr] *vt* to match, sort, assort, stock.

assoupi [asupi] *a* dozing.

assoupir [asupiːr] *vt* to send to sleep, allay; *vr* to doze (off), die away.

assoupissement [asupismã] *nm* drowsiness, allaying.

assourdir [asurdiːr] *vt* to deafen, stun, muffle, subdue, mute; *vr* to die away.

assourdissant [asurdisã] *a* deafening, stunning.

assouvir [asuviːr] *vt* to satisfy, slake, wreak; *vr* to become sated.

assujetti [asyʒeti] *a* subject (to), tied (to).

assujettir [asyʒetiːr] *vt* to subdue, govern.

assujettissant [asyʒetisã] *a* tying.

assumer [asyme] *vt* to assume.

assurance [asyrãːs] *nf* assurance, confidence, insurance.

assurément [asyremã] *ad* certainly.

assuré [asyre] *a* sure, confident, certain, safe, steady; *n* policyholder.

assurer [asyre] *vt* to assure, ensure, make secure, insure; *vr* to make sure.

assureur [asyrœːr] *nm* underwriter.

astérisque [asterisk] *nm* asterisk.

asthmatique [asmatik] *a* asthmatic, wheezy.

asthme [asm] *nm* asthma.

asticot [astiko] nm maggot.
astiquer [astike] vt to polish.
astral [astral] a astral.
astre [astr] nm star.
astreindre [astrɛ̃:dr] vt to compel; vr to keep (to à).
astrologie [astrɔlɔʒi] nf astrology.
astrologue [astrɔlɔg] nm astrologer.
astronaute [astronot] nm astronaut.
astronef [astronɛf] nm space-ship.
astronome [astronɔm] nm astronomer.
astronomie [astronɔmi] nf astronomy.
astuce [astys] nf wile, astuteness, guile, gimmick.
astucieux, -euse [astysjø, ø:z] a wily, astute.
atelier [atəlje] nm workshop, studio.
atermoyer [atɛrmwaje] vti to put off, delay.
athée [ate] a atheistic, godless; n atheist.
athéisme [ateism] nm atheism.
athlète [atlɛt] nm athlete.
athlétique [atletik] a athletic.
athlétisme [atletism] nm athleticism, athletics.
atmosphère [atmɔsfɛ:r] nf atmosphere, environment.
atmosphérique [atmɔsferik] a atmospheric.
atome [atom] nm atom.
atomique [atomik] a atomic.
atomiser [atomize] vt to atomize, spray.
atomiseur [atomizœ:r] nm atomizer, spray.
atours [atu:r] nm pl finery, attire.
atout [atu] nm trump.
âtre [a:tr] nm hearth.
atroce [atrɔs] a atrocious, outrageous, heinous, terrible, excruciating, woeful.
atrocité [atrɔsite] nf atrocity.
'attabler [satable] vr to sit down to table.
attachant [ataʃɑ̃] a interesting, attractive, winning.
attache [ataʃ] nf tie, fastening, connection, brace, leash, fastener, paper-clip, joint; port d'— home port.
attaché [ataʃe] nm attaché.
attachement [ataʃmɑ̃] nm attachment, adherence, fondness.
attacher [ataʃe] vt to attach, fasten, tie (up), connect, lash, strap, brace; vr to cling, stick, become attached, apply oneself.
attaquable [atakabl] a assailable.
attaque [atak] nf attack, thrust, fit, stroke, seizure.
attaquer [atake] vt to attack, assault, tackle, attempt, (cards) lead; vr to attack, grapple (with à).
'attarder [satarde] vr to linger, tarry.
atteindre [atɛ̃:dr] vt to reach, attain, hit, affect.
atteint [atɛ̃] a affected, attacked, hit.

atteinte [atɛ̃:t] nf reach, blow, attack; porter — à to hurt, damage.
attelage [atla:ʒ] nm harnessing, team, yoke, coupling.
atteler [atle] vt to harness, yoke, couple, team; vr to buckle to.
attelle [atɛl] nf splint.
attenant [atnɑ̃] a adjacent, adjoining.
attendant [atɑ̃dɑ̃] ad en — meanwhile, pending; cj en — que until.
attendre [atɑ̃:dr] vt to await, wait for, expect, look for; vr to expect.
attendri [atɑ̃dri] a fond, compassionate.
attendrir [atɑ̃dri:r] vt to soften, move, touch; vr to become tender, be moved.
attendrissant [atɑ̃drisɑ̃] a touching, affecting.
attendrissement [atɑ̃drismɑ̃] nm tender emotion, pity.
attendu [atɑ̃dy] prep considering, owing to, on account of; — que seeing that, whereas.
attentat [atɑ̃ta] nm attempt, outrage, murder attempt.
attente [atɑ̃:t] nf wait, expectation, hope; salle d'— waiting-room; être dans l'— de to be awaiting.
attenter [atɑ̃te] vt make an attempt (on, against à).
attentif, -ive [atɑ̃tif, i:v] a attentive, careful, heedful, considerate.
attention [atɑ̃sjɔ̃] nf attention, care, regard, mindfulness; —! look out! faire — à to pay attention to, heed.
attentionné [atɑ̃sjɔne] a thoughtful.
atténuant [atenɥɑ̃] a extenuating.
atténuation [atenɥasjɔ̃] nf extenuation, qualification, understatement.
atténuer [atenɥe] vt to attenuate, extenuate, mitigate, qualify, understate, subdue, dim; vr to lessen, diminish.
atterrer [atere] v to overwhelm, fell, stun.
atterrir [ateri:r] vi to ground, alight, land; vt to run ashore, beach.
atterrissage [aterisa:ʒ] nm grounding, landing.
attestation [atɛstasjɔ̃] nf attestation, voucher.
attester [atɛste] vt to attest, testify, vouch.
attiédir [atjedi:r] vt to make tepid, lukewarm.
attifer [atife] vtr to dress up.
attirail [atira:j] nm outfit, tackle, gear, show.
attirance [atirɑ̃:s] nf attraction, lure.
attirant [atirɑ̃] a attractive, engaging.
attirer [atire] vt to attract, draw, entice, inveigle.
attiser [atize] vt to stir (up), poke (up).
attitude [atityd] nf attitude.

attouchement [atuʃmɑ̃] nm touch (ing), contact.

attraction [atraksjɔ̃] nf attraction, attractiveness; pl variety show.

attrait [atrɛ] nm attraction, allurement, enticement, charm.

attrape [atrap] nf trap, snare, trick, catch.

attrape-mouches [atrapmuʃ] nm fly-paper.

attrape-nigaud [atrapnigo] nm booby-trap.

attraper [atrape] vt to catch, trick, get, seize, scold.

attrayant [atrɛjɑ̃] a attractive.

attribuer [atribɥe] vt to attribute, ascribe, assign, put down (to à); vr to assume.

attribut [atriby] nm attribute.

attribution [atribysjɔ̃] nf attribution, allocation, award, conferment; pl powers, functions.

attristé [atriste] a saddened, sorrowful.

attrister [atriste] vt to sadden; vr to grow sad.

attrition [atrisjɔ̃] nf attrition.

attroupement [atrupmɑ̃] nm mob.

attrouper [atrupe] vt to gather, collect; vr to flock, form into a mob, crowd.

au [o] = à + le.

aubaine [obɛn] nf windfall, godsend.

aube [o:b] nf early dawn, paddle, blade.

subépine [obepin] nf hawthorn, may.

auberge [obɛrʒ] nf inn; — de la jeunesse youth hostel.

aubergine [oberʒin] nf egg-plant, aubergine.

aubergiste [oberʒist] n innkeeper.

aucun [okœ̃] pn anyone, no one, nobody; pl some people; a any, not any.

aucunement [okynmɑ̃] ad not at all, in no way.

audace [odas] nf audacity, boldness, daring, hardihood.

audacieux, -euse [odasjø, ø:z] a audacious, bold, daring, dashing, impudent.

au-delà [od(ə)la] ad beyond; nm the after-life.

au-dessous [odsu] ad underneath, below; prep — de below, under.

au-dessus [odsy] ad above, over (head); prep — de above, over, beyond.

au-devant [odvɑ̃] ad aller — de to go to meet.

audience [odjɑ̃:s] nf audience, hearing; lever l'— to close the session, sitting.

auditeur, -trice [oditœ:r, tris] n listener.

audition [odisjɔ̃] nf audition, hearing.

auditoire [oditwa:r] nm audience.

auge [o:ʒ] nf trough.

augmentation [ɔgmɑ̃tasjɔ̃] nf increase, rise.

augmenter [ɔgmɑ̃te] vt to augment, increase, add, raise; vr to increase, rise.

augure [ɔgy:r] nm augury, omen; de mauvais — unpropitious, inauspicious.

augurer [ɔgyre] vt to augur, promise.

auguste [ɔgyst] a august, majestic.

aujourd'hui [oʒurdɥi] ad today; d'— en huit a week from today.

aumône [omo:n] nf alms, charity.

aumônier [omonje] nm almoner, chaplain.

aune [o:n] nf alder.

auparavant [oparavɑ̃] ad before, first.

auprès [oprɛ] ad hard by, close at hand; prep — de close (to, by), near, beside, at, with, in comparison with.

auquel [okɛl] = à + lequel.

auréole [ɔreɔl] nf halo.

auriculaire [ɔrikylɛ:r] nm little finger.

aurore [ɔrɔ:r] nf dawn.

ausculter [ɔskylte] vt to sound.

auspice [ɔspis] nm auspice, omen.

aussi [osi] ad as, so, also, too; cj therefore, so.

aussitôt [osito] ad at once, immediately; cj — que as soon as; — dit, — fait no sooner said than done.

austère [ɔstɛ:r] a austere, severe, stern.

austérité [ɔsterite] nf austerity, severity, sternness.

Australie [ɔstrali] nf Australia.

australien, -ienne [ɔstraljɛ̃, jɛn] an Australian.

autant [otɑ̃] ad as much, so much, as many, so many; — que as much as, as many as, as far as; d'— que, d'— plus que more especially as, all the more . . . as.

autel [otɛl] nm altar.

auteur [otœ:r] nm author, writer, promoter, originator, perpetrator; femme — authoress; droits d'— royalties.

authenticité [otɑ̃tisite] nf authenticity.

authentique [otɑ̃tik] a authentic, genuine.

auto [oto] nf motor car, car, auto.

auto b graphie [otɔbjɔgrafi] nf autobiography.

autobus [otɔby:s] nm omnibus, bus.

autocar [otɔka:r] nm motor coach, excursion bus.

autochtone [otɔkto:n, -tɔn] a native, indigenous.

autocrate [otɔkrat] n autocrat; a autocratic.

autocratie [otɔkrasi] nf autocracy.

autocratique [otɔkratik] a autocratic.

autodémarreur [otɔdemarœːr] nm self-starter.

autodétermination [otɔdeterminasjɔ̃] nf (govt) self-determination.

autodidacte [otɔdidakt] a self-taught, -educated; nm autodidact.

autodrome [otɔdrɔm droːm] nm motor-racing track, speedway.

autographe [otɔgraf] nm autograph.

autographier [otɔgrafje] vt to autograph.

automate [otɔmat] nm automaton, robot.

automatique [otɔmatik] a automatic, automaton-like.

automnal [otɔmnal] a autumnal.

automne [otɔn] nm autumn, fall; a d'—autumnal.

automobile [otɔmɔbil] a automotive; nf automobile, motor car; salon de l'— automobile show.

automobilisme [otɔmɔbilism] nm motoring.

automobiliste [otɔmɔbilist] n motorist.

automoteur [otɔmɔtœːr] a self-propelling.

autonome [otɔnɔm] a autonomous, self-governing.

autonomie [otɔnɔmi] nf autonomy, home-rule.

autopsie [otɔpsi] nf autopsy, post-mortem examination.

autorail [otɔraːj] nm rail-car.

autorisation [otɔrizasjɔ̃, ɔt-] nf authorization, permit, license.

autorisé [otɔrize, ɔt-] a authorized, authoritative.

autoriser [otɔrize, ɔt-] vt to authorize, empower, sanction, license.

autoritaire [otɔritɛːr, ɔt-] a authoritative, domineering.

autorité [otɔrite, ɔt-] nf authority, warrant; faire — to be an authority; qui fait — authoritative.

autoroute [otɔrut] nf highway.

auto-stop [otɔstɔp] nm hitch-hiking.

autour [otuːr] ad around, about; prep — de around.

autre [oːtr] a pn other; a further, different; d'un moment à l'— any moment; de temps à — now and again; nous —s Français we French; l'un et l'— both; les uns . . . les —s some . . . others; — chose something else; quelqu'un d'— someone else; j'en ai vu bien d'—s that's nothing;— part elsewhere.

autrefois [otrəfwa] ad formerly, in the past.

autrement [otrəmɑ̃] ad otherwise, else, in a different way.

Autriche [otriʃ] nf Austria.

autrichien, -ienne [otriʃjɛ̃, ʃɛn] an Austrian.

autruche [otryʃ] nf ostrich.

autrui [otrɥi] pn indef others, other people.

aux [o] = à + les.

auxiliare [ɔksiljeːr, o-] a auxiliary, sub-; nm auxiliary.

auxquels [okel] = à + lesquels.

aval [aval] nm lower part of river; ad en — downstream; prep en — de below.

avalanche [avalɑ̃ːʃ] nf avalanche.

avaler [avale] vt to swallow, drink up, gulp down, stomach; — une insulte to pocket an insult, affront.

avance [avɑ̃ːs] nf advance, start, lead, drive, dash; loan; à l', d', par — beforehand, in advance; être en — to be fast, before time, ahead.

avancé [avɑ̃se] a advanced, forward, onward, well on, high; vous voilà bien — much good that has done you.

avancement [avɑ̃smɑ̃] nm advancing, putting forward, furtherance, rise, promotion, advancement.

avancer [avɑ̃se] vt to advance, put (forward, on), carry on, promote; vi to move forward, advance, get on, be fast, be ahead of time; vr to advance, make one's way, progress, jut out.

avant [avɑ̃] prep before; — peu presently; ad before, far (into), deep, further (in, back); en — before, forward, in front, ahead, onward; cj — que before; a fore-; nm bow, forward, front.

avantage [avɑ̃taːʒ] nm advantage; tirer — de to turn to account.

avantager [avɑ̃taʒe] vt to favor, improve.

avantageux, -euse [avɑ̃taʒø, øːz] a advantageous, beneficial, favorable, becoming, self-satisfied.

avant-bras [avɑ̃bra] nm forearm.

avant-corps [avɑ̃kɔːr] nm fore-part.

avant-cour [avɑ̃kuːr] nf forecourt.

avant-coureur [avɑ̃kurœːr] a precursory; nm forerunner.

avant-dernier, -ière [avɑ̃dɛrnje, jɛːr] a next to the last.

avant-garde [avɑ̃gard] nf van (guard), advanced guard, avant-garde.

avant-goût [avɑ̃gu] nm foretaste, earnest.

avant-guerre [avɑ̃gɛːr] nm pre-war period.

avant-hier [avɑ̃tjeːr] ad day before yesterday.

avant-plan [avɑ̃plɑ̃] nm foreground.

avant-port [avɑ̃pɔːr] nm outer harbor.

avant-poste [avɑ̃pɔst] nm outpost.

avant-première [avɑ̃prəmjeːr] nf dress rehearsal.

avant-propos [avɑ̃prɔpo] nm preface.

avare [avaːr] a miserly, tight-fisted, chary; nm miser.

avarice [avaris] nf avarice, miserliness, closeness.

avaricieux, -euse [avarisjø, jøːz] a avaricious, mean.

avarie [avari] nf damage.

avarier [avarje] *vt* to damage; *vr* to deteriorate.

avatar [avata:r] *nm* avatar; *pl* ups and downs.

avec [avɛk] *prep* with; — ça! nonsense; et — ça Monsieur? do you require anything else? d'— from; *ad* with it, with them.

avenant [avnɑ̃] *a* comely, prepossessing, buxom; à l'— in keeping, to match.

avènement [avɛnmɑ̃] *nm* advent, accession.

avenir [avnɪ:r] *nm* future; à l'— henceforth, hereafter.

aventure [avɑ̃ty:r] *nf* adventure, luck, love-affair; à l'— at random, aimlessly; d'— by chance; dire, tirer la bonne — to tell fortunes.

aventurer [avɑ̃tyre] *vtr* to venture, risk.

aventureux, -euse [avɑ̃tyrø, ø:z] *a* adventurous, venturesome, reckless, risky.

aventurier, -ière [avɑ̃tyrje, jɛ:r] *n* adventurer, adventuress.

avenu [avny] *a* non — cancelled, void.

avenue [avny] *nf* avenue, drive, walk.

avéré [avere] *a* established, proved, authenticated.

averse [avɛrs] *nf* shower of rain, downpour.

aversion [avɛrsjɔ̃] *nf* aversion, dislike, repulsion.

averti [avɛrti] *a* experienced, well-informed, knowing.

avertir [avɛrtɪ:r] *vt* to warn, caution, give notice (of).

avertissement [avɛrtismɑ̃] *nm* warning, notice, caution; sans — préalable at a moment's notice.

avertisseur [avɛrtisœ:r] *nm* alarm, warning, automobile horn.

aveu [avø] *nm* confession, avowal, admission, consent.

aveugle [avœgl] *a* blind, sightless; à l'— blindly, wildly; *nm* blind person.

aveuglement [avœgləmɑ̃] *nm* blindness.

aveuglément [avœglemɑ̃] *ad* blindly.

aveugler [avœgle] *vt* to blind, dazzle, hoodwink.

aveuglette [avœglɛt] *ad* à l'— blind(ly).

aviateur, -trice [avjatœr, tris] *n* aviator, flyer.

aviation [avjasjɔ̃] *nf* aviation, air force.

avide [avid] *a* avid, greedy, grasping, eager (for de).

avidité [avidite] *nf* avidity, greed, eagerness.

avilir [avilɪ:r] *vt* to debase, depreciate; *vr* to lower oneself, stoop, lose value.

avilissement [avilismɑ̃] *nm* abasement, degradation, depreciation.

avion [avjɔ̃] *nm* airplane, aircraft — de bombardment bomber; — de chasse, de combat fighter; — de ligne airliner; — en remorque glider; — à réaction jet plane; par — by airmail.

aviron [avirɔ̃] *nm* oar, rowing.

avis [avi] *(sl)* opinion, advice, judgment, notice, warning; à mon — to my mind; changer d'— to change one's mind.

avisé [avize] *a* far-seeing, wary, canny, shrewd, advised.

aviser [avize] *vt* to warn, perceive; *vi* to see about (à); *vr* to take it into one's head.

avocat [avɔka] *nm* lawyer, counsel, advocate.

avoine [avwan] *nf* oats; folle — wild oats.

avoir [avwa:r] *vt* to have, possess, get, obtain; — vingt ans to be twenty years old; qu'avez-vous? what is the matter with you? en — à, contre qn. to bear s.o. a grudge; y — v *imp* to be; qu'est-ce qu'il y a? what's up, what's the matter?; il y a sept ans seven years ago; *nm* property, possessions, balance in hand; doit et — debit and credit.

avoisinant [avwazinɑ̃] *a* neighboring.

avoisiner [avwazine] *vt* to be near, border on.

avorter [avɔrte] *vi* to abort, miscarry.

avortement [avɔrtmɑ̃] *nm* abortion, miscarriage.

avorton [avɔrtɔ̃] *nm* undersized, stunted creature, aborted infant.

avoué [avwe] *a* professed; *nm* solicitor, attorney.

avouer [avwe] *vt* to avow, confess, acknowledge.

avril [avril] *nm* April; un poisson d'— an April fool.

axe [aks] *nm* axis, spindle.

axiome [aksjo:m] *nm* axiom.

azimut [azimyt] *nm* azimuth, bearing, *(sl)* direction.

azote [azɔt] *nm* nitrogen.

azotique [azɔtik] *a* nitric.

azur [azy:r] *nm* azure, blue.

azyme [azim] *a* unleavened; *nm* unleavened bread.

B

baba [baba] *nm* sponge-cake; *a* dumbfounded.

babeurre [babœ:r] *nm* buttermilk.

babil [babi(l)] *nm* prattling, twittering.

babillard [babija:r] *a* talkative, babbling; *n* chatterbox.

babiller [babije] *vi* to chatter, babble, prattle.

babines [babin] *nf pl* chops, drooping lips.

babiole [babjɔl] *nf* bauble, curio, trinket, frippery.

bâbord [babɔːr] *nm* port (side).

babouin [babwɛ̃] *nm* baboon.

bac [bak] *nm* ferryboat, tub.

bâche [baːʃ] *nf* tarpaulin, awning, cistern; — **de campement** groundsheet.

bachelier, -ière [baʃəlje, jɛːr] *n* pre-university student.

bâcher [baʃe] *vt* to cover with a tarpaulin.

bachot [baʃo] *nm* baccalaureate, punt.

bacille [basil] *nm* bacillus, germ.

bâcler [bakle] *vt* to bolt, bar, block, scamp, dash off.

bactériologie [bakterjɔlɔʒi] *nf* bacteriology.

badaud [bado] *a* idle; *n* stroller, idler.

badauder [badode] *vi* to saunter, idle about.

badigeon [badiʒɔ̃] *nm* distemper, whitewash brush.

badigeonner [badiʒɔne] *vt* to distemper, color-wash, paint.

badin [badɛ̃] *a* playful, jocular, waggish; *n* joker, wag.

badinage [badinaːʒ] *nm* bantering, joking.

badine [badin] *nf* switch, cane.

badiner [badine] *vt* to tease, banter; *vi* to joke, trifle, banter.

bafoué [bafwe] *a* scorned, discomfited.

bafouer [bafwe] *vt* to scoff, jeer at, sneer at.

bafouiller [bafuje] *vti* to stammer, splutter, gabble.

bâfrer [bɑfre] *vt* to gobble, guzzle; *vi* to gormandize; *vr* to stuff.

bagage [bagaːʒ] *nm* baggage; *pl* luggage; **plier** — to pack up, clear out.

bagarre [bagaːr] *nf* brawl, disturbance, affray, scrap.

bagatelle [bagatɛl] *nf* trifle.

bagnard [baɲaːr] *n* convict.

bagne [baɲ] *nm* prison.

bagnole [baɲɔl] *nf* worn-out car, car.

bagout [bagu] *nm* avoir du — to have the gift of gab.

bague [bag] *nf* ring, cigar-band.

baguenauder [bagnode] *vi* to waste time, trifle.

baguette [bagɛt] *nf* wand, rod, stick, pointer, beading, long loaf.

bahut [bay] *nm* (*fam*) cupboard, trunk, chest; school.

bai [bɛ] *a* (*color*) bay.

baie [bɛ] *nf* bay, bight, berry, bay-window.

baignade [bɛɲad] *nf* bathe, bathing-place.

baigner [bɛɲe] *vt* to bathe, bath, wash; *vi* to soak, steep; *vr* to take a bath, bathe, welter.

baigneur, -euse [bɛɲœːr, øːz] *n* bather, bathing attendant.

baignoire [bɛɲwaːr] *nf* bath, (*theatre*) pit-box.

bail [baːj] *nm* lease.

bâillement [bɑjmɑ̃] *nm* yawn(ing), gaping.

bâiller [bɑje] *vi* to yawn, gape, be ajar.

bailleur [bɑjœːr] *nm* lessor; — **de fonds** money-lender, sleeping-partner.

bâillon [bɑjɔ̃] *nm* gag.

bâillonner [bɑjɔne] *vt* to gag, muzzle.

bain [bɛ̃] *nm* bath, bathe, dip; —**s de mer** sea-bathing.; —(**s**) **de soleil** sunbath(ing).

bain-marie [bɛ̃mari] *nm* double boiler, water-bottle.

baïonnette [bajɔnɛt] *nf* bayonet.

baiser [beze] *vt* to kiss; *nm* kiss.

baisse [bɛs] *nf* fall, drop, ebb, abatement.

baisser [bese] *vt* to lower, let down, turn down; *vi* to fall, go down, sink, droop, slump; *vr* to stoop.

baissier [besje] *nm* (*Stock Exchange*) bear.

bajoue [baʒu] *nf* cheek, chap, chop.

bal [bal] *nm* ball, dance.

balade [balad] *nf* amble, drive, stroll.

balader [balade] *vir* to go for a stroll, a drive.

baladeuse [baladøːz] *nf* handcart, trailer, inspection-lamp.

baladin [baladɛ̃] *nm* buffoon.

balafre [balafr] *nf* gash, cut, scar.

balafrer [balafre] *vt* to gash, scar, slash.

balai [balɛ] *nm* brush, broom.

balance [balɑ̃ːs] *nf* balance, scale(s), suspense; **faire la** — to strike a balance.

balancer [balɑ̃se] *vt* to balance, swing, rock; *vi* to swing, dangle, waver, hesitate; *vr* to sway, swing, rock.

balancier [balɑ̃sje] *nm* pendulum, balance-wheel, beam, balancing-pole.

balançoire [balɑ̃swaːr] *nf* swing, seesaw.

balayage [balɛjaːʒ] *nm* sweeping, (*radar*) scanning.

balayer [balɛje] *vt* to sweep (out, away, up), scour, throw out.

balayeur, -euse [balɛjœːr, øːz] *nmf* sweeper, cleaner, scavenger; *nf* carpet-sweeper.

balayures [balɛjyːr] *nf pl* sweepings.

balbutier [balbysje] *vti* to stammer, stutter, falter.

balcon [balkɔ̃] *nm* balcony, dress-circle.

baldaquin [baldakɛ̃] *nm* canopy.

baleine [balɛn] *nf* whale, whalebone, rib.

baleinière [balɛnjɛːr] *nf* whaleboat.

balise [baliːz] *nf* beacon, seamark, groundlight, radiosignal.

balistique [balistik] *a* ballistic; *nf* ballistics.

baliverne [balivɛrn] *nf* idle story; *pl* balderdash, rubbish.

ballade [balad] *nf* ballad.

ballant [balã] *a* dangling.

ballast [balast] *nm* ballast, bottom.

balle [bal] *nf* ball, bullet, franc, bale, pack, chaff, husk; **avoir la — belle** to have the ball at one's feet; **c'est un enfant de la —** he has been brought up in the trade.

ballet [balɛ] *nm* ballet (dancing).

ballon [balõ] *nm* balloon, football; **lancer un — d'essai** to fly a kite.

balloner [balɔne] *vir* to swell, balloon out, distend, bulge.

ballot [balo] *nm* bundle, bale, kitbag.

ballotage [balɔta:ʒ] *nm* shaking, tossing, second ballot.

balloter [balɔte] *vt* to shake, toss about, buffet; *vi* to toss, shake, rattle, swing.

balnéaire [balnee:r] *a* **station —** seaside resort.

balourd [balu:r] *a* uncouth, clumsy, awkward; *n* awkward person, yokel, dullard.

balourdise [balurdi:z] *nf* clumsiness, stupid mistake.

baluchon [balyʃõ] *nm* bundle, kit.

balustrade [balystrad] *nf* balustrade, rail.

balustre [balystr] *nm* baluster; *pl* banisters.

bambin [bãbɛ̃] *n* little child, urchin, baby.

bamboche [bãbɔʃ] *nf* puppet, undersized person, carousal, spree.

bambou [bãbu] *nm* bamboo.

ban [bã] *nm* ban, proclamation, round of cheers, banishment; *pl* banns; **mettre au —** to banish, ostracize.

banal [banal] *a* commonplace, hackneyed, trite, casual.

banalité [banalite] *nf* triteness, commonplace remark.

banane [banan] *nf* banana.

bananier [bananje] *nm* banana-tree.

banc [bã] *nm* bench, form, seat, bed, pew, layer, shoal; **— des accusés** dock; **— de sable** sandbank.

bancal [bãkal] *a* bow-legged, rickety.

banco [bãko] *nm* swish, baked mud, (*for building*) clay.

bandage [bãda:ʒ] *nm* bandaging, bandage, binder, truss, binding.

bande [bã:d] *nf* band, group, gang, flock, shoal, stripe, belt, shaft, wrapper, cushion, reel, film; **donner de la —** (*of ship*) to list.

bandeau [bãdo] *nm* headband, bandeau, bandage.

bander [bãde] *vt* to bind up, bandage, stretch, bend; *vr* to band together; **— les yeux à** to blindfold.

banderole [bãdrɔl] *nf* streamer, shoulder-belt, sling.

bandit [bãdi] *nm* bandit, gangster, rascal.

bandoulière [bãdulje:r] *nf* bandolier, shoulder-belt.

banlieue [bãljø] *nf* suburb.

banne [ban] *nf* hamper, awning, coal-cart.

banneau [bano] *nm* fruit-basket, hamper.

bannière [banje:r] *nf* banner.

banni [bani] *a* outlawed, exiled; *n* outlaw, exile.

bannir [bani:r] *vt* to outlaw, banish.

bannissement [banismã] *nm* exile, banishment.

banque [bã:k] *nf* bank, banking.

banqueroute [bãkrut] *nf* bankruptcy; **faire —** to go bankrupt.

banquet [bãkɛ] *nm* banquet, feast.

banquette [bãkɛt] *nf* seat, bench.

banquier, -ière [bãkje, je:r] *a* banking; *n* banker.

banquise [bãki:z] *nf* ice-field, -pack, -flow.

baptême [batɛ:m] *nm* baptism, christening; **a de —** baptismal, maiden.

baptiser [batize] *vt* to baptize, christen.

baquet [bakɛ] *nm* tub, bucket.

bar [ba:r] *nm* bar, pub; bass.

baragouiner [baragwine] *vti* to jabber, gibber.

baraque [barak] *nf* hut, booth, stall.

baraquement [barakmã] *nm* hut, lodging in huts; *pl* hutments.

baratte [barat] *nf* churn.

baratter [barate] *vt* to churn.

barbare [barba:r] *a* barbarous, cruel, barbaric; *n* barbarian.

barbarie [barbari] *nf* barbarity, barbarousness, barbarism.

barbe [barb] *nf* beard, whiskers; **se faire la —** to shave; **rire dans sa —** to laugh up one's sleeve.

barbelé [barbəle] *a* barbed.

barbiche [barbiʃ] *nf* goatee beard.

barboter [barbɔte] *vt* to splash up and down; *vi* to paddle, flounder, splash about.

barbouillage [barbuja:ʒ] *nm* smearing, scrawl, daubing, scribble, scribbling.

barbouiller [barbuje] *vt* to smear, smudge, dirty.

barbu [barby] *a* bearded.

barbue [barby] *nf* brill.

bard [ba:r] *nm* hand truck.

barde [bard] *nf* pack-saddle, slice of bacon.

barder [barde] *vt* to carry on a hand-barrow, bard; *vi* to rage; **ça va —** there will be ructions.

barème [barɛ:m] *nm* ready-reckoner, scale.

baril [bari] *nm* barrel, cask.

barillet [barijɛ] *nm* keg, drum, cylinder.

bariolé [barjɔle] *a* multicolored, motley, gaudy.

baromètre [barɔmɛtr] nm weather glass, barometer.

baroque [barɔk] a odd, quaint; nm baroque style.

barque [bark] nf boat, fishing-smack.

barrage [bara:ʒ] nm road-block, barrier, dam, weir, (sport) replay.

barre [ba:r] nf iron bar, wooden batten, rod, tiller, helm, stroke, (law courts) bar, rail, rung, surf, undertow; — des témoins witness-box; homme de — coxswain, helmsman.

barreau [baro] nm (law courts) bar, rail, rung; pl (prison) bars.

barrer [bare] vt to bar, block, dam, obstruct, cross out, steer; — un chèque to cancel a check; rue barrée no thoroughfare.

barrette [barɛt] nf biretta, barette.

barreur [barœ:r] nm helmsman, coxswain.

barricade [barikad] nf barricade.

barricader [barikade] vt to barricade.

barrière [barjɛ:r] nf gate, toll-gate, bar, rail.

barrique [barik] nf large barrel, cask, hogshead.

baryton [baritɔ̃] nm baritone.

bas, -se [ba, ba:s] a low, base, deep, mean, lower; ad low, quietly; nm lower part, end, bottom, stocking; pl hose; en — downstairs, below; en — de at the foot of; à — down (with); mettre — to lay down, bring forth.

basalte [bazalt] nm basalt.

basaner [bazane] vt to tan; vr to become tanned.

bas-bout [babu] nm bottom, lower end.

bas-côté [bakote] nm aisle, lay-by.

bascule [baskyl] nf seesaw, platform scale, rocker; chaise à — rocking-chair; wagon à — tipcart.

basculer [baskyle] vt to rock, swing; vti to dip, tip.

base [ba:z] nf foundation, basis, foot, root; de — basic; sans — unfounded.

baser [baze] vt to base, found; vr to be founded.

bas-fond [bafɔ̃] nm low ground, swamp, shoal, deep pool; pl riffraff, dregs.

basilique [bazilik] nf basilica.

basque [bask] nf tail.

basse [ba:s] nf bass.

basse-cour [basku:r] nf farmyard.

bassesse [bases] nf lowness, vileness, baseness.

basse-fosse [basfo:s] nf dungeon.

bassin [basɛ̃] nm basin, pond, ornamental lake, dock; — houiller coalfield.

bassine [basin] nf pan.

bât [ba] nm pack-saddle; cheval de — pack-horse.

bataille [bata:j] nf battle, contest.

batailleur, -euse [batajœ:r, ø:z] a pugnacious, cantankerous, quarrelsome.

bataillon [batajɔ̃] nm battalion.

bâtard [bata:r] an bastard, mongrel.

bateau [bato] nm boat, vessel; — -école training ship; — -feu light ship; — pétrolier tanker.

bateleur, -euse [batlœ:r, ø:z] n juggler, mountebank.

batelier, -ière [batəlje, jɛ:r] n boatman, -woman, ferryman, -woman, bargee.

bâter [bate] vt to put a pack-saddle on.

bath [bat] a (fam) great, swell.

batifoler [batifole] vi to frolic, lark.

bâtiment [batimɑ̃] nm building (trade), edifice, ship.

bâtir [bati:r] vt to build, erect.

bâtisse [batis] nf ramshackle building, masonry.

batiste [batist] nf cambric.

bâton [batɔ̃] nm stick, staff, baton, pole, truncheon; à — rompus desultory, by fits and starts.

bâtonner [batɔne] vt to beat, whip, cane.

battage [bata:ʒ] nm beating, threshing, churning, boosting.

battant [batɑ̃] a beating, driving, pelting, banging; porte — e swing-door; nm bell-clapper, table, counter top.

batte [bat] nf beetle, mallet.

battement [batmɑ̃] nm beating, stamping, flapping, banging, fluttering, tapping, throbbing, margin (of time), interval.

batterie [batri] nf beat of drums, roll of drums, artillery battery; set; — de cuisine set of kitchen utensils.

batteur, -euse [batœ:r, ø:z] nf threshing machine, egg whisk; nm beater, thresher.

battre [batr] vt to beat, thrash, thresh, batter, defeat, churn, whisk, (flag) fly, shuffle; vi to beat, throb, belt, flap, bang; — la campagne to scour the countryside, to be delirious; — des mains to clap one's hands; vr to fight.

battu [baty] a beaten, wrought; avoir les yeux — s to have circles under one's eyes.

battue [baty] nf beat, round-up.

baudet [bodɛ] nm donkey.

baudrier [bodrije] nm shoulder-belt, cross-belt.

bauge [bo:ʒ] nf lair, hole, squirrel's nest, pigsty.

baume [bo:m] nm balm, balsam.

bauxite [boksit] nf bauxite.

bavard [bava:r] a talkative, garrulous; n chatterbox, gossip.

bavardage [bavarda:ʒ] nm chattering, gossip.

bavarder [bavarde] vi to gossip, chatter.

bave [baːv] nf froth, foam, slaver, slime.

baver [bave] vi to slaver, dribble, foam, run.

bavette [bavɛt] nf bib.

baveur, -euse [bavœːr, øːz] a slavering, driveling; nm slobberer.

baveux, -euse [bavø, øːz] a slobbery, juicy.

bavure [bavyːr] nf burr, blot, smudge.

bayer [baje] vi — aux corneilles to gape at the moon.

bazar [bazaːr] nm bazaar, cheap stores; tout le — the whole caboodle.

béant [beɑ̃] a gaping, yawning.

béat [bea] a smug, complacent.

béatitude [beatityd] nf bliss, complacency.

beau, belle [bo, bɛl] a lovely, beautiful, fair, fine, handsome, noble; il en a fait de belles he has been up to some nice things; bel et bien well and truly, fairly; bel et bon all very well; l'échapper belle to have a narrow escape; il avait beau faire in spite of all he did.

beaucoup [boku] ad (very) much, a lot, a good deal, (very) many, lots.

beau-fils [bofis] nm son-in-law, stepson.

beau-frère [bofrɛːr] nm brother-in-law, stepbrother.

beau-père [bopɛːr] nm father-in-law, stepfather.

beaupré [bopre] nm bowsprit.

beauté [bote] nf beauty, loveliness, handsomeness, belle, beautiful woman; salon de — beauty parlor; soins de — beauty treatment; se faire une — to do oneself up; finir en — to finish in grand style.

beaux-arts [bozaːr] nm pl fine arts.

bébé [bebe] nm baby.

bébête [bebɛːt] a silly.

bec [bɛk] nm beak, bill, spout, mouthpiece, nose, nozzle; — de gaz gas burner, jet, lamp-post; — de plume pen-nib; coup de — peck; fin — gourmet; prise de — row, altercation; clouer le — à qn. to shut someone up.

bécane [bekan] nf bike.

bécasse [bekas] nf woodcock.

bécassine [bekasin] nf snipe.

bec-de-cane [bɛkdəkan] nm lever, (of door) handle, pliers.

bec-de-lièvre [bɛkdəljɛːvr] nm harelip.

bêche [bɛʃ] nf spade.

bêcher [beʃe] vt to dig, run down.

bécot [beko] nm kiss, peck.

becquée [beke] nf beakful; donner la — à to feed.

becqueter [bekte] vt to peck at, pick up, kiss.

bedaine [bədɛn] nf paunch.

bedeau [bədo] nm verger.

bedon [bədɔ̃] nm paunch.

bedonner [bədɔne] vi to get stout.

bée [be] af gaping; regarder qn bouche — to gape at someone.

beffroi [befrwa] nm belfry.

bégaiement [begɛmɑ̃] nm stammering, stuttering.

bégayer [begɛje] vt to stammer out, through; vi to stutter, splutter, stammer.

bègue [bɛg] a stammering; n stammérer.

bégueule [begœl] a priggish, prudish; nf prude.

béguin [begɛ̃] nm hood, bonnet; avoir le — pour qn. to fall for s.o.

beige [bɛːʒ] nm beige.

beignet [bɛɲɛ] nm fritter.

béjaune [beʒoːn] nm nestling, freshman, greenhorn.

bêler [bele] vi to bleat.

bel-esprit [bɛlɛspri] nm wit.

belette [bəlɛt] nf weasel.

belge [bɛlʒ] a Belgian.

Belgique [bɛlʒik] nf Belgium.

bélier [belje] nm ram, battering-ram.

bellâtre [bɛlɑːtr] a foppish; nm fop.

belle [bɛl] nf beauty; jouer la — to play the deciding game.

belle-fille [bɛlfiːj] nf daughter-in-law, stepdaughter.

belle-mère [bɛlmɛːr] nf mother-in-law, stepmother.

belles-lettres [bɛllɛtr] nf humanities.

belle-sœur [bɛlsœːr] nf sister-in-law, stepsister.

belligérance [bɛliʒerɑ̃ːs] nf belligerence.

belligérant [bɛliʒerɑ̃] a belligerent.

belliqueux, -euse [bɛlikø, øːz] a bellicose, warlike.

belvédère [bɛlvedeːr] nm viewpoint, summer-house.

bémol [bemɔl] nm (music) flat.

bénédicité [benedisite] nm grace, blessing.

bénédictin [benediktɛ̃] an Benedictine.

bénédiction [benediksjɔ̃] nf blessing.

bénéfice [benefis] nm profit, benefit (eccl) living; pl profits, drawings.

bénéficiaire [benefisjɛːr] an beneficiary.

bénéficier [benefisje] vi to benefit, (make a) profit.

benêt [bənɛ] a stupid, silly; nm ninny, simpleton.

bénévole [benevɔl] a benevolent, gentle, voluntary.

bénin, -igne [benɛ̃, iɲ] a benign, mild, kindly.

bénir [beniːr] vt to bless, consecrate.

bénit [beni] a blessed, holy, consecrated; eau —e holy water.

bénitier [benitje] nm holy-water font.

benne [bɛn] nf hamper, basket, hutch, bucket; camion à — bascculante dump truck.

benzine [bɛzin] nf benzine.

benzol [bɛzɔl] nm benzol.

béquille [beki:j] nf crutch, prop, stand.

bercail [berka:j] nm sheep fold.

berceau [berso] nm cradle, cot, arbor.

bercer [berse] vt to rock, lull, beguile, soothe; vr to rock, sway.

berceuse [bersø:z] nf cradle, lullaby.

bergamote [bergamɔt] nf bergamot.

berge [berʒ] nf bank, parapet.

berger [berʒe] nm shepherd.

bergère [berʒɛːr] nf shepherdess, easy-chair, shepherd.

bergerie [berʒəri] nf sheepfold, pen.

bergeronnette [berʒərɔnɛt] nf wagtail.

berline [berlin] nf berline, limousine, truck.

berlingot [berlɛ̃go] nm caramel, toffee.

berlue [berly] nf avoir la — to have a wrong view of things.

berne [bɛrn] nf en — at half-mast.

berner [berne] vt to toss in a blanket, take in, deceive.

bernique [bɛrnik] int nothing doing.

besicles [bezikl] nf spectacles, goggles.

besogne [bəzɔɲ] nf work, job, task, bit of work.

besogneux, -euse [bəzoɲø, øːz] a needy, poor.

besoin [bəzwɛ̃] nm need, want, necessity, poverty, urge, craving, addiction; au — if need be, in a pinch; avoir — de to need, require.

bestial [bɛstjal] a brutish, beastly.

bestialité [bɛstjalite] nf bestiality, beastliness.

bestiaux [bɛstjo] nm pl livestock, cattle.

bestiole [bɛstjɔl] nf little beast, insect.

bêta [beta] nm nincompoop, wiseacre, nitwit.

bétail [beta:j] nm livestock, cattle.

bête [bɛːt] nf animal, beast, blockhead, fool; faire la — to act the fool; — à bon Dieu ladybird, harmless creature; — noire pet aversion; chercher la petite — to quibble, be overcritical.

bêtise [beti:z] nf stupidity, foolishness, silly thing.

béton [betɔ̃] nm concrete; — armé reinforced concrete, ferro-concrete.

bétonner [betɔne] vt to concrete.

bétonnière [betɔnjɛːr] nf concrete mixer.

bette [bɛt] nf beet.

betterave [bɛtraːv] nf beetroot, mangel; — sucrière sugar-beet.

beuglement [bøgləmɑ̃] nm bellowing, lowing.

beugler [bøgle] vt to bellow, bawl out; vi to bellow, low.

beurre [bœːr] nm butter; cuit au — noir cooked in brown butter; œil au — noir black eye.

beurrer [bœre] vt to butter.

bévue [bevy] nf blunder.

biais [bjɛ] a sloping, slanting, oblique, askew; nm slant, slope, bias, expedient; de — sideways; en — on the slant.

bibelot [biblo] nm trinket, curio, knick-knack.

biberon [bibrɔ̃] nm feeding-bottle, feeder, tippler.

bible [bibl] nf Bible.

bibliographe [bibliɔgraf] nm bibliographer.

bibliographie [bibliɔgrafi] nf bibliography.

bibliomane [bibliɔman] nm book collector.

bibliophile [bibliɔfil] nm booklover.

bibliothécaire [bibliɔteke:r] nm librarian.

bibliothèque [bibliɔtɛk] nf library, bookcase.

biblique [biblik] a biblical.

bicarbonate [bikarbɔnat] nm bicarbonate.

biche [biʃ] nf hind, doe, darling.

bichon [biʃɔ̃] n lapdog, darling.

bicoque [bikɔk] nf jerry-built house, shanty.

bicyclette [bisiklɛt] nf bicycle; aller à — à to cycle to; faire de la — to cycle.

bidet [bidɛ] nm nag, bidet, trestle.

bidon [bidɔ̃] nm can, tin, drum, water-bottle; du — rubbishy; bidonville — shanty town.

bief [bjɛf] nm mill-race, -course, -lade, (of river) reach.

bielle [bjɛl] nf rod, crank-arm.

bien [bjɛ̃] ad well, good, right, proper, really, very, quite, indeed, much, many; nm property, wealth, blessing; pl belongings, chattels, assets; elle est — she is nicelooking; être — avec to be on good terms with; — que cj although.

bien-aimé [bjɛ̃neme] an beloved.

bien-être [bjɛ̃nɛ:tr] nm comfort, well-being, welfare.

bienfaisance [bjɛ̃fəzɑ̃:s] nf beneficence, generosity, charity; œuvre de — charitable society, work.

bienfaisant [bjɛ̃fəzɑ̃] a charitable, kind, beneficial.

bienfait [bjɛ̃fɛ] nm benefit, favor, boon, kindness.

bienfaiteur, -trice [bjɛ̃fɛtœːr, tris] n benefactor, -tress.

bien-fondé [bjɛ̃fɔ̃de] nm merits, justice, soundness.

bien-fonds [bjɛ̃fɔ̃] nm real estate.

bienheureux, -euse [bjɛ̃nœrø, øːz] a happy, blessed.

biennal [bjɛnnal] a biennial.

bienséance [bjɛ̃seɑ̃:s] nf decorum, propriety.

bienséant [bjɛ̃seɑ̃] a decorous, seemly, proper.

bientôt [bjɛ̃to] ad soon, before long; à — good-bye.

bienveillance [bjɛ̃vɛjɑ̃:s] nf benevolence, goodwill, kindness.
bienveillant [bjɛ̃vɛjɑ̃] a benevolent, kindly.
bienvenu [bjɛ̃vny] an welcome.
bienvenue [bjɛ̃vny] nf welcome.
bière [bjɛ:r] nf beer, ale; bier, coffin.
biffer [bife] vt to delete.
biffin [bifɛ̃] nm ragman, junkman, foot-soldier, footslogger.
bifteck [biftɛk] nm beefsteak.
bifurcation [bifyrkasjɔ̃] nf fork, branch line.
bifurquer [bifyrke] vi to fork, branch off.
bigame [bigam] a bigamous; n bigamist.
bigamie [bigami] nf bigamy.
bigarré [bigare] a variegated, mottled, motley.
bigorneau [bigɔrne] nm periwinkle, whelk.
bigot [bigo] a sanctimonious, over-devout; n bigot.
bigoudi [bigudi] nm hair-curler.
bijou [biʒu] nm jewel.
bijouterie [biʒutri] nf jewelry, jeweler's shop, jeweler's trade.
bijoutier, -ière [biʒutje, jɛːr] n jeweler.
bilan [bilɑ̃] nm balance-sheet, schedule; **dresser le —** to strike a balance.
bile [bil] nf spleen, anger; **se faire de la —** to worry, fret.
bilieux, -euse [biljø, øːz] a bilious, liverish.
billard [bijar] nm billiards, billiard-table, billiard room; **— japonais** bagatelle table.
bille [bij] nf billiard ball, marble, log; (rl) sleeper; rolling pin; **roulement à —** ball-bearing.
billet [bijɛ] nm (bank-)note, letter, ticket, bill, permit; **— simple** one-way ticket; **— d'aller et retour** return ticket; **— à ordre** promissory note.
billot [bijo] nm (of wood) block.
bimensuel, -elle [bimɑ̃sɥɛl] a fortnightly, every two weeks.
bimestriel [bimɛstriɛl] a every other month, bimonthly.
binaire [binɛːr] a binary.
bine [bin] nf hoe.
biner [bine] vt to hoe.
binette [binɛt] nf hoe.
binocle [binɔkl] nm eye-glasses, pince-nez.
binoculaire [binɔkylɛːr] a two-eyed, binocular.
biographe [biɔgraf] nm biographer.
biographie [biɔgrafi] nf biography.
biographique [biɔgrafik] a biographical.
biologie [biɔlɔʒi] nf biology.
biplan [biplɑ̃] nm biplane.
birman [birmɑ̃] an Burmese.
Birmanie [birmani] nf Burma.

bis [bis, bi] a grayish-brown; ad twice, encore, repeat; **pain —** whole-wheat bread.
bisannuel, -elle [bizanɥɛl] a biennial.
bisbille [bisbiːj] nf bickering, squabble.
biscornu [biskɔrny] a distorted, misshapen, irregular, weird, inconsistent.
biscotte [biskɔt] nf rusk.
biscuit [biskɥi] nm biscuit, plain cake.
bise [biːz] nf north wind, cold blast; kiss.
biseau [bizo] nm bevel, chamfer.
biseauter [bizote] vt to bevel, chamfer.
bison [bizɔ̃] nm bison.
bisque [bisk] nf shellfish soup; ill humor; **donner une —** to give odds.
bissecter [bisɛkte] vt to bisect.
bisser [bise] vt to encore.
bissextile [bisɛkstil] a **année —** leap year.
bistouri [bisturi] nm lancet.
bistré [bistre] a darkened, swarthy, browned.
bistro(t) [bistro] nm café, pub, tavern.
bitte [bit] nf bollard.
bitume [bitym] nm bitumen, asphalt, pitch.
bivouaquer [bivwake] vi to bivouac.
bizarre [bizaːr] a odd, peculiar, queer, weird, strange.
blackbouler [blakbule] vt to blackball, reject.
blafard [blafaːr] a wan, pale, livid, pallid.
blague [blag] nf tobacco-pouch; joke, banter; **sans —** you don't say! really!
blaguer [blage] vt to chaff, pull someone's leg; vi to joke.
blagueur, -euse [blagœːr] a scoffing, ironical; n cynical scoffer, cynic.
blaireau [blɛro] nm badger, shaving-brush.
blâmable [blɑmabl] a blameworthy.
blâme [blɑːm] nm blame, reproof.
blâmer [blame] vt to blame, reprove, rebuke.
blanc, -che [blɑ̃, blɑ̃ːʃ] a white, pale, pure, clean, blank; nm white, blank; **nuit blanche** sleepless night.
blanc-bec [blɑ̃bɛk] nm tyro, greenhorn, raw youth.
blanchâtre [blɑ̃ʃɑːtr] a whitish.
blanche [blɑ̃ːʃ] nf minim, white ball.
blancheur [blɑ̃ʃœːr] nf whiteness, purity, paleness.
blanchir [blɑ̃ʃiːr] vt to whiten, bleach, wash, whitewash; vi to turn white, pale.
blanchissage [blɑ̃ʃisaːʒ] nm laundering, whitewashing, sugar refining.
blanchisserie [blɑ̃ʃisri] nf laundry, wash-house.

blanchisseur, -euse [blãʃisœːr, øːz] n laundryman, laundress, bleacher, washer-woman.

blanc-seing [blãsɛ̃] nm (signature to a) blank document; **donner —** à to give a free hand to.

blandices [blãdis] nf pl blandishment.

blanquette [blãkɛt] nf veal stew.

blaser [blaze] vt to blunt, satiate, cloy; vr to become blasé, tired (of de).

blason [blazɔ̃] nm coat of arms, escutcheon, heraldry.

blasphémateur, -trice [blasfematœːr, tris] a blasphemous; n blasphemer.

blasphématoire [blasfematwaːr] a blasphemous.

blasphème [blasfɛːm] nm blasphemy, curse.

blasphémer [blasfeme] vti to blaspheme, curse.

blatte [blat] nf cockroach.

blé [ble] nm wheat; **— noir** buckwheat; **— d'Inde** maize, corn.

bled [blɛd] nm (pej) wilds, countryside.

blême [blɛːm] a pale, wan.

blêmir [blemiːr] vi to turn pale, blanch, grow dim.

blessé [blɛse] a wounded, hurt; n wounded man, casualty.

blesser [blɛse] vt to wound, hurt, offend, injure; vr to be wounded, be hurt, hurt oneself.

blessure [blɛsyːr] nf wound, injury, hurt, sore.

blet, -te [blɛ, blɛt] a over-ripe, soft.

bleu [blø] a blue; nm recruit, rookie, greenhorn, bruise; pl dungarees; **avoir des —s** to be black and blue; **n'y voir que du —** to be all at sea.

bleuâtre [bløɑːtr] a bluish.

bleuir [bløiːr] vt to make blue; vi to turn blue.

blindé [blɛ̃de] a armor-plated, timbered; nm pl **les —s** the armor.

blinder [blɛ̃de] vt to armor plate, line with timber.

bloc [blɔk] nm block, mass, lump, pad, coalition, clink, prison; **en —** all together, in one piece; **à —** thoroughly.

blocage [blɔkaːʒ] nm blocking up, clamping, seizing.

bloc-notes [blɔknɔt] nm writing, scribbling pad, scratch pad.

blocus [blɔkyːs] nm blockade; **braver le —** to run the blockade.

blond [blɔ̃] a fair-haired, light, blond.

blondir [blɔ̃diːr] vt to dye blond, bleach; v to turn yellow.

bloquer [blɔke] vt to block up, obstruct, blockade, jam, dam; vr to stick, jam.

se blottir [sǝblɔtiːr] vr to crouch, cower, huddle, nestle, snuggle.

blouse [bluːz] nf smock, blouse.

blouson [bluzɔ̃] nm battle-dress jacket, skiing jacket; **—s noirs** n pl young ruffians.

bluet [blyɛ] nm cornflower, bluebottle.

bluffer [blœfe] vti to bluff.

bobard [bɔbaːr] nm tall tale, fib.

bobèche [bɔbɛʃ] nf socket, sconce.

bobine [bɔbin] nf bobbin, reel, spool, coil, dial.

bocage [bɔkaːʒ] nm copse.

bocal [bɔkal] nm jar, bottle.

bock [bɔk] nm glass of beer, beer-glass.

bœuf [bœf] nm ox, bullock, beef; **— de conserve** corned beef; **— à la mode** stewed beef.

bohème [bɔɛːm] a unconventional, Bohemian; n Bohemian; nf Bohemia, art-world.

bohémien, -ienne [bɔemjɛ̃, jɛn] an gipsy, Bohemian.

boire [bwaːr] vt to drink (in, up), imbibe, absorb, soak in, up; nm drink(ing); **— un coup en vitesse** to have a quick one.

bois [bwa] nm wood, forest, timber; pl antlers, woodwind instruments.

boisage [bwazaːʒ] nm timbering, scaffold(ing), woodwork, afforestation.

boisé [bwaze] a wooded, woody, wainscoted.

boiser [bwaze] vt to timber, put under timber, wainscot.

boiserie [bwazri] nf woodwork, wainscoting, joinery.

boisseau [bwaso] nm bushel, drain, flue-tile.

boisselier [bwasǝlje] nm cooper.

boisson [bwasɔ̃] nf drink, beverage; **pris de —** under the influence.

boîte [bwaːt] nf box, case, tin, casket, jail; **— aux lettres** mailbox; **— à ordures** garbage can; **— à thé** tea-caddy; **— de nuit** night-club; **— de vitesses** gear-box.

boiter [bwate] vi to limp, hobble, be lame.

boiteux, -euse [bwatø, øːz] a lame, shaky, lop-sided.

boîtier [bwatje] nm case.

bol [bɔl] nm bowl, basin.

bolchevisme [bɔlʃevism] nm Bolshevism.

bolchevique [bɔlʃevik] an bolshevik.

bolide [bɔlid] nm meteor, fast car.

bombance [bɔ̃bãːs] nf feast(ing); **faire —** to carouse, have a blow-out.

bombardement [bɔ̃bardǝmã] nm bombardment, bombing, shelling; **— en piqué** dive-bombing.

bombarder [bɔ̃barde] vt to bombard, bomb, shell.

bombardier [bɔ̃bardje] nm bombardier, bomb-aimer, bomber plane.

bombe [bɔ̃b] nf bomb, spree; **— à retardement** time-bomb; **faire la — to go on a binge.**

bombé [bɔ̃be] *a* bulging, convex, cambered.

bomber [bɔ̃be] *vt* to stick out, arch, bend, camber; *vi* bulge, belly.

bon, -ne [bɔ̃, bɔn] *a* good, nice, right, correct, sound, righteous, kind, fitting, profitable; *nm* voucher, warrant, bond, draft, bill; **pour de — for good,** in earnest; **bon! right!;** **— à rien** good-for-nothing.

bonasse [bɔnas] *a* simple, silly.

bonbon [bɔ̃bɔ̃] *nm* candy, sweet-(meat), drop; *pl* confections.

bonbonne [bɔ̃bɔn] *nf* carboy.

bonbonnière [bɔ̃bɔnjɛːr] *nf* candy box, well-furnished little house.

bond [bɔ̃] *nm* jump, leap, spring, bounce; **faire faux —** to break.

bonde [bɔ̃d] *nf* bung, plug, bung-hole.

bondé [bɔ̃de] *a* packed, crowded, crammed.

bondir [bɔ̃diːr] *vi* to jump, leap, spring, bound, bounce, skip about.

bonheur [bɔnœːr] *nm* happiness, bliss, welfare, success; **par —** fortunately; **au petit —** indiscriminately, haphazardly.

bonhomie [bɔnɔmi] *nf* good nature, humor.

bonhomme [bɔnɔm] *a* good-natured; *nm* (good-natured) man, figure.

boni [bɔni] *nm* surplus, premium, bonus.

bonification [bɔnifikasjɔ̃] *nf* bonus, rebate, improvement.

bonifier [bɔnifje] *vti* to improve.

boniment [bɔnimɑ̃] *nm* patter, moonshine.

bonjour [bɔ̃ʒuːr] *nm* good-day, -morning, -afternoon.

bonne [bɔn] *nf* maid, servant; **— d'enfants** nursemaid.

bonnet [bɔnɛ] *nm* cap, bonnet; **gros — bigwig;** **avoir la tête près du — to be hot tempered;** **opiner du — to agree,** have no opinion of one's own.

bonneterie [bɔntri] *nf* hosiery, knitted ware.

bonneteur [bɔntœːr] *nm* cardsharper, confidence man.

bonnetier, -ière [bɔntje, jɛːr] *nm* hosier.

bon(n)iche [bɔniʃ] *nf* maidservant, slavey.

bon-papa [bɔ̃papa] *nm* grandpa, grand-dad.

bonsoir [bɔ̃swaːr] *nm* good-evening, -night.

bonté [bɔ̃te] *nf* kindness, goodness, good nature.

bonze [bɔ̃ːz] *nm* bonze, Buddhist priest, **vieux —** old fossil.

bord [bɔːr] *nm* edge, brink, brim, rim, bank, verge, side, flap, tack; **livre de —** log book; **à — de** aboard; **à pleins —s** brim-full.

bordage [bɔrdaːʒ] *nm* border(ing), curb, edging, planking.

bordeaux [bɔrdo] *nm* Bordeaux wine; **— rouge** claret.

bordée [bɔrde] *nf* broadside, watch, tack, volley; **tirer des —s** to tack; **être en —** to be on a spree.

bordel [bɔrdɛl] *nm* brothel.

border [bɔrde] *vt* to border, edge, run along, fringe, braid, plank; **— qn. dans son lit** to tuck s.o. in.

bordereau [bɔrdəro] *nm* statement, account, memorandum, docket, file.

bordure [bɔrdyːr] *nf* edge, fringe, binding, curb, rim.

borgne [bɔrɲ] *a* one-eyed, blind in one eye, shady.

borne [bɔrn] *nf* limit, boundary mark, guard-stone, terminal; **— kilométrique** milestone; **cela passe les —s** that is going too far.

borné [bɔrne] *a* limited, narrow, restricted.

borner [bɔrne] *vt* to bound, limit, restrict, stake, mark out the limits of; *vr* to confine, restrict oneself.

bosquet [bɔskɛ] *nm* thicket, grove, arbor.

bosse [bɔs] *nf* hump, lump, bump, dent, bruise; **rouler sa —** to knock about.

bosseler [bɔsle] *vt* to emboss, dent, bash.

bosselure [bɔslyːr] *nf* dent, bruise.

bossoir [bɔswaːr] *nm* davit, cathead, (of ship) bow.

bossu [bɔsy] *a* hunch-backed, humped; *n* hunchback.

bot [bo] *a* **pied —** club-foot, club-footed person.

botanique [bɔtanik] *a* botanical; *nf* botany.

botaniste [bɔtanist] *n* botanist.

botte [bɔt] *nf* boot, field-boot, bunch, truss, bundle, lunge, thrust, slip; **—s retroussées** top boots; **—s à l'écuyère** riding-boots.

botteler [bɔtle] *vt* to truss, bundle, bunch, tie up.

botter [bɔte] *vt* to put boots on, kick.

bottier [bɔtje] *nm* bootmaker.

bottin [bɔtɛ̃] *nm* directory.

bottine [bɔtin] *nf* ankle-boot.

bouc [buk] *nm* he-, billy-goat; **— émissaire,** scapegoat.

boucan [bukɑ̃] *nm* din, shindy, row, smoked meat.

boucaner [bukane] *vt* (meat) to cure, to stink.

boucanier [bukanje] *nm* buccaneer, pirate.

bouche [buʃ] *nf* mouth, muzzle, slot, opening; **— d'eau** hydrant; **garder qch. pour la bonne —** to keep something as a titbit; **fine — gourmet;** **être porté sur la —** to think of nothing but one's belly; **faire la petite —** to pick at one's food, be difficult.

bouché [buʃe] *a* plugged, stopped up, dense.

bouchée [buʃe] *nf* mouthful, bite, morsel; — à la reine vol-au-vent of chicken; mettre les —s doubles to gobble one's food, put a spurt on.

boucher [buʃe] *nm* butcher; *vt* to plug, stop (up), cork, bung, obstruct.

boucherie [buʃri] *nf* butcher's shop, -trade; slaughter, shambles.

bouchon [buʃɔ̃] *nm* cork, stopper, plug, fishing float.

boucle [bukl] *nf* buckle, loop, bow, ringlet, curl; — d'oreille earring.

bouclé [bukle] *a* curly.

boucler [bukle] *vt* to buckle on, knot, fasten, settle, clinch, curl, lock up; *vi* to buckle, be curly.

bouclier [bukli(j)e] *nm* shield, buckler.

bouder [bude] *vt* to be in the sulks with; *vi* to sulk.

bouderie [budri] *nf* sulkiness.

boudeur, -euse [budœːr, øːz] *a* sulky; *nf* double settee.

boudin [budɛ̃] *nm* black-pudding, inner tube, twist, roll, flange, beading.

boudoir [budwaːr] *nm* boudoir.

boue [bu] *nf* mud, dirt, deposit.

bouée [bwe, bue] *nf* buoy; — de sauvetage lifebuoy.

boueux, -euse [buø, øːz] *a* muddy, miry, dirty; *nm* scavenger, garbage man.

bouffant [bufã] *a* puffed, baggy.

bouffe [buf] *a* opéra — comic opera.

bouffée [bufe] *nf* whiff, puff, waft, gust, breath; tirer des —s de sa pipe to puff at one's pipe.

bouffer [bufe] *vt* to puff out, gobble; *vi* to balloon out, bag, swell.

bouffi [bufi] *a* puffed up, puffy, bloated, swollen, turgid.

bouffir [bufiːr] *vt* to bloat, inflate; *vi* to become swollen, puffed up.

bouffon, -onne [bufɔ̃, ɔn] *a* farcical; *nm* clown, jester.

bouge [buːʒ] *nm* hovel, slum, den, pigsty, (of ship) bilge.

bougeoir [buʒwaːr] *nm* candlestick.

bougeotte [buʒɔt] *nf* avoir la — to be fidgety.

bouger [buʒe] *vt* to move; *vi* to budge, stir.

bougie [buʒi] *nf* candle, taper, spark plug.

bougon, -onne [bugɔ̃, ɔn] *a* testy, grumpy; *n* grumbler.

bougonner [bugɔne] *vi* to grumble, grouse.

bougran [bugrã] *nm* buckram.

bouillabaisse [bujabes] *nf* fish-soup.

bouillant [bujã] *a* boiling, ebullient, impetuous.

bouillie [buji] *nf* gruel, pap.

bouilloire [bujwaːr] *nf* kettle.

bouillon [bujɔ̃] *nm* bubble, soup, stock, beeftea, cheap restaurant, unsold copies.

bouillonnement [bujɔnmã] *nm* boiling, seething.

bouillonner [bujɔne] *vt* to gather material into puffs; *vi* to boil up, seethe, bubble.

bouillotte [bujɔt] *nf* hot-water bottle.

boulanger, -ère [bulãʒe, ɛr] *n* baker, baker's wife; *vti* to bake.

boulangerie [bulãʒri] *nf* bread-baking, baker's shop.

boule [bul] *nf* bowl, ball, globe, bulb, lump, head, face; joueur de —s bowler; jeu de —s bowls, bowling-green.

bouleau [bulo] *nm* birch-tree.

bouledogue [buldɔg] *nm* bulldog.

boulet [bule] *nm* cannonball, fet-lock-joint.

boulette [bulɛt] *nf* pellet, meatball.

boulevard [bulvaːr] *nm* avenue, boulevard.

boulevardier, -ière [bulvardje, ɛr] *a* of the boulevards; *nm* man-about-town.

bouleversement [bulversəmã] *nm* upheaval, overthrow, disturbance, confusion.

bouleverser [bulverse] *vt* to upset, overturn, perturb, bowl over, astound, stagger.

boulon [bulɔ̃] *nm* bolt, pin.

boulot, -otte [bulo, ɔt] *a* chubby, plump, dumpy; *nm* work, food.

boulotter [bulɔte] *vt* to eat; *vi* to jog along, on.

bouquet [bukɛ] *nm* bunch, posy, bouquet, nosegay, clump, cluster, aroma, crowning-piece, highlight; c'est le — that crowns it; pour le — . . . last but not least. . .

bouquetier [buktje] *nm* flower vase.

bouquetière [buktjɛːr] *nf* flower-girl.

bouquin [bukɛ̃] *nm* old book, book, buck-rabbit, hare.

bouquiner [bukine] *vi* to collect old books, read.

bouquiniste [bukinist] *nm* second-hand bookseller.

bourbe [burb] *nf* mud, mire.

bourbeux, -euse [burbø, øːz] *a* muddy, miry.

bourbier [burbje] *nm* bog, mire.

bourde [burd] *nf* bloomer, fib.

bourdon [burdɔ̃] *nm* drone, great bell, bumble-bee.

bourdonnement [burdɔnmã] *nm* buzzing, humming, drumming, whirr.

bourdonner [burdɔne] *vt* to hum; *vi* to buzz, hum, drone, whirr.

bourg [buːr] *nm* market town.

bourgeois [burʒwa] *a* middle-class, plain, common; *n* citizen, townsman, commoner.

bourgeoisie [burʒwazi] *nf* middle class; la haute (petite) — the upper (lower) middle class.

bourgeon [burʒɔ̃] *nm* bud, pimple.

bourgeonner [burʒɔne] *vi* to bud, break out in pimples.

bourgeron [burʒərɔ̃] nm workman's overall.

Bourgogne [burgɔɲ] nf Burgundy; m Burgundy wine.

bourguignon [burgiɲɔ̃] a nmf Burgundian, of Burgundy.

bourlinguer [burlɛ̃ge] vi to labor, make heavy weather, knock about.

bourrade [burad] nf blow, thrust, thump, rough word.

bourrage [buraːʒ] nm stuffing, padding, cramming; — de crâne bunkum, eyewash, dope.

bourrasque [burask] nf squall.

bourre [buːr] nf flock, floss, wad, waste.

bourreau [buro] nm hangman, executioner, tormentor.

bourrée [bure] nf bundle of firewood, faggot.

bourreler [burle] vt to torment, rack, goad.

bourrelet [burlɛ] nm pad, cushion, fold, roll, rim, bead.

bourrelier [burəlje] nm saddler.

bourrer [bure] vt to pad, stuff, pack, cram, fill, thrash, trounce; — le crâne à qn. to fill someone's head with stuff and nonsense.

bourriche [buriʃ] nf basket, hamper.

bourrique [burik] nf she-ass, donkey, duffer.

bourru [bury] a churlish, surly, rude, gruff.

bourse [burs] nf purse, pouch, bag, grant, bursary, scholarship, stock exchange; jouer à la — to speculate.

boursier, -ière [bursje, jeːr] n scholar, paymaster, speculator.

boursouflé [bursufle] a swollen, bloated, turgid.

boursouflement [bursufləmɑ̃] nm swelling, blistering.

boursoufler [bursufle] vt to swell, blister, bloat; vi to swell, blister.

boursouflure [bursuflyːr] nf swelling, blister, turgidity.

bousculade [buskylad] nf scuffle, scurry, hustle, rush.

bousculer [buskyle] vt to jostle, hustle, upset.

bouse [buːz] nf dung.

bousiller [buzije] vt to bungle, botch, crash (plane).

boussole [busɔl] nf compass.

boustifaille [bustifaːj] nf grub, food.

bout [bu] nm end, extremity, tip, bit, tag, scrap; bas (haut) bout foot (head); à — de forces exhausted, worn out, spent; au — de at the end of, after; jusqu'au — right to the end, to the bitter end, through; de — en — through and through; venir à — de to overcome, manage, cope with; à — portant point-blank.

boutade [butad] nf whim, outburst, sally, quip.

boute-en-train [butɑ̃trɛ̃] nm bright and cheery companion, life and soul.

boutefeu [butfø] nm firebrand.

bouteille [butɛːj] nf bottle.

bouteroue [butru] nf curbstone, fender.

boutique [butik] nf shop, caboodle.

boutiquier, -ière [butikje, jeːr] n shopkeeper.

bouton [butɔ̃] nm button, bud, pimple, handle, knot; — de col stud; — de manchettes cuff-link; — d'or buttercup; tourner le — to switch on, off.

boutonner [butɔne] vt to button up; vi to bud.

boutonneux, -euse [butɔnø, øːz] a pimply.

boutonnière [butɔnjeːr] nf buttonhole, rosette.

bouture [butyːr] nf cutting.

bouvier [buvje] nm cowherd, drover.

bouvreuil [buvrœːj] nm bullfinch.

bovin [bɔvɛ̃] a bovine.

box [bɔks] nm loose box, lock-up garage, cubicle, dock.

boxe [bɔks] nf boxing.

boxer [bɔkse] vt to box with; vi to box, spar.

boxeur [bɔksœːr] nm boxer.

boy [bɔj] nmf steward.

boyau [bwajo] nm bowel, gut, inner tube, hosepipe, communication trench.

boycotter [bɔjkɔte] vt to boycott.

bracelet [braslɛ] nm bracelet, bangle, armband.

braconnage [brakɔnaːʒ] nm poaching.

braconner [brakɔne] vti to poach.

braconnier, -ière [brakɔnje, jeːr] a poaching; nm poacher.

braguette [bragɛt] nf (of trousers) fly.

braillard [brajaːr] a noisy, bawling, rowdy; n brawler.

brailler [braje] vti to bawl out, shout.

braire [breːr] vi to bray.

braise [breːz] nf embers.

braiser [breze] vt to braise.

bramer [brame] vi (of stag) to bell.

brancard [brɑ̃kaːr] nm shaft, stretcher.

brancardier [brɑ̃kardje] nm stretcher-bearer.

branche [brɑ̃ʃ] nf branch, bough, prong, leg, (of family) line.

branchement [brɑ̃ʃmɑ̃] nm branching, forking, junction, lead.

brancher [brɑ̃ʃe] vt to connect, branch, plug in; on m'a mal branché I was given the wrong number.

brandir [brɑ̃diːr] vt to brandish, flourish, wave.

brandon [brɑ̃dɔ̃] nm firebrand.

branlant [brɑ̃lɑ̃] a shaky, loose, ramshackle.

branle [brɑ̃ːl] nm swing, impetus, oscillation, motion; mettre qch. en — to set something going.

branle-bas [brɑ̃ləba] nm stir, bustle,

commotion; **faire le —** to clear decks for action.

branler [brɑ̃le] *vt* to swing, wag, shake; *vi* to shake, rock, be loose

braquage [braka:ʒ] *nm* levelling, aiming, pointing; **angle de —** lock (of car).

braquer [brake] *vt* to aim, level, point, fix, direct.

bras [bra, brɑ] *nm* arm, limb, **bracket; — droit** right-hand man, *pl* workmen, hands, **henchmen; — dessus — dessous** arm in arm; **— de mer** arm of the sea, (*Scot*) sea loch; **en — de chemise** in one's shirt sleeves; **à — le corps** round the waist; **— de rivière** backwater; **manquer de —** to be shorthanded.

brasero [brazero] *nm* brazier.

brasier [brazje] *nm* fire, inferno, furnace.

brasiller [brazije] *vt* to grill, broil; *vi* to sizzle.

brassard [brasa:r] *nm* armlet, armband.

brasse [brɑːs] *nf* arm-span, fathom, stroke; **nager à la —** to swim the breast stroke.

brassée [brase] *nf* armful.

brasser [brase] *vt* to mix, stir, brew, brace; **— de grosses affaires** to do big business.

brasserie [brasri] *nf* brewery, alehouse, restaurant.

brasseur, -euse [brasœːr, øːz] *n* brewer, puddler, mixer; **— d'affaires** big businessman.

brassière [brasjɛːr] *nf* baby's vest; *pl* slings, leading strings; **— de sauvetage** life-jacket.

bravache [bravaʃ] *a* blustering, swaggering; *nm* braggadocio, bully.

bravade [bravad] *nf* bluster.

brave [braːv] *a* brave, gallant, decent, worthy, good.

braver [brave] *vt* to brave, dare, defy, face, run (blockade).

bravoure [bravuːr] *nf* bravery, valor.

brebis [brəbi] *nf* ewe, sheep; **— galeuse** black sheep.

brèche [brɛʃ] *nf* breach, hole, gap; **battre en —** to breach.

bréchet [breʃɛ] *nm* breastbone.

bredouille [brəduːj] *a inv* empty-handed.

bredouiller [brəduje] *vt* to stammer out, mumble; *vi* to stutter, splutter, gabble.

bref, brève [brɛf, brɛːv] *a* brief, short, curt; *ad* curtly, in short.

breloque [brələk] *nf* trinket, charm.

Brésil [brezil] *nm* Brazil.

brésilien, -ienne [breziljɛ̃, jɛn] *a* Brazilian.

Bretagne [brətaɲ] *nf* Brittany.

bretelle [brətɛl] *nf* strap, sling; *pl* braces.

breton, -onne [brətɔ̃, ɔn] *an* Breton.

bretteur [brɛtœːr] *nm* duelist, swashbuckler.

breuvage [brœvaːʒ] *nm* drink, beverage, draught.

brevet [brəvɛ] *nm* patent, certificate.

breveté [brəvte] *a* certificated, by special appointment; *n* patentee.

breveter [brəvte] *vt* to grant a patent to, patent.

bréviaire [brevjɛːr] *nm* breviary.

brévité [brevite] *nf* shortness.

bribe [brib] *nf* scrap, fragment.

bric-à-brac [brikabrak] *nm* curios, bits and pieces.

bricole [brikɔl] *nf* strap, breast harness, ricochet; *pl* trifles, odd jobs.

bricoler [brikɔle] *vt* to arrange; *vi* to do odd jobs, potter about.

bricoleur [brikɔlœːr] *nm* handyman, jobber, jack of all trades.

bride [brid] *nf* bridle, string, flange, strap; **à — abattue** full tilt, at full speed; **lâcher la — à** to give free rein to, full scope to.

brider [bride] *vt* to bridle, curb, restrain, truss, flange, fasten.

bridge [bridʒ] *nm* (*game*) bridge.

bridgeur, -euse [bridʒœːr, øːz] *n* bridge player.

brièvement [brievmɑ̃] *ad* briefly, curtly, succinctly.

brièveté [brievte] *nf* brevity, shortness, conciseness.

brigade [brigad] *nf* brigade, squad, shift, gang.

brigadier [brigadje] *nm* corporal, bombardier, sergeant (*police*).

brigand [brigɑ̃] *nm* robber, brigand, highwayman.

brigandage [brigɑ̃daːʒ] *nm* brigandage, highway robbery.

brigue [brig] *nf* canvassing, intrigue, plot.

briguer [brige] *vt* to canvass for, solicit.

brillament [brijamɑ̃] *ad* brilliantly.

brillant [brijɑ̃] *a* brilliant, shining, glossy; *nm* brilliancy, gloss(iness), shine, polish.

briller [brije] *vi* to shine, sparkle, glitter.

brimade [brimad] *nf* rough joke.

brimbaler [brɛ̃bale] *vt* to lug about; *vi* to swing, wobble.

brimborion [brɛ̃bɔrjɔ̃] *nm* bauble, trifle.

brimer [brime] *vt* to haze, persecute.

brin [brɛ̃] *nm* blade, sprig, stalk, shoot, strand, bit, crumb, jot, touch, shred, chit.

brindille [brɛ̃diːj] *nf* twig, tiny branch.

bringue [brɛ̃ːg] *nf* bit, piece; **faire la —** to go on a spree.

brio [bri(j)o] *nm* vigor, dash, gusto, brilliance.

brioche [briɔʃ] *nf* bun.

brique [brik] *nf* brick.

briquet [brikɛ] *nm* flint, tinderbox, cigarette lighter.

brisant [brizɑ̃] *a* shattering; *nm* breaker, reef.

brise [bri:z] *nf* breeze.

brise-bise [brizbi:z] *nm* weather stripping, short window curtain.

brisées [brize] *nf pl* tracks; **aller sur les — de qn.** to compete with someone; **suivre les — de qn.** to follow in someone's footsteps.

brise-lames [brizlam] *nm* breakwater, mole.

briser [brize] *vt* to break (up, down, off), shatter, smash; *vr* to break.

brisure [brizy:r] *nf* break, flaw, crack.

britannique [britanik] *an* British; *n* Briton.

broc [bro] *nm* jug, pitcher.

brocanter [brɔkɑ̃te] *vt* to sell, barter; *vi* to deal in second-hand goods.

brocanteur, -euse [brɔkɑ̃tœ:r, ø:z] *n* second-hand dealer.

brocard [brɔka:r] *nm* taunt, lampoon.

brocart [brɔka:r] *nm* brocade.

broche [brɔʃ] *nf* spit, skewer, peg, brooch, spindle, pin, spigot.

brocher [brɔʃe] *vt* to stitch, sew, brocade; **livre broché** paper-bound book.

brochet [brɔʃɛ] *nm* pike.

brochette [brɔʃɛt] *nf* skewer, stick; **élevé à la — fed by hand, brought up with tender care.

brochure [brɔʃy:r] *nf* booklet, pamphlet.

brodequin [brɔdkɛ̃] *nm* sock, ankle-boot; *pl* marching boots.

broder [brɔde] *vt* to embroider, embellish, amplify.

broderie [brɔdri] *nf* (piece of) embroidery, embellishment.

bromure [brɔmy:r] *nm* bromide.

broncher [brɔ̃ʃe] *vi* to stumble, falter, flinch, shy.

bronches [brɔ̃ʃ] *nf pl* bronchial tubes.

bronchite [brɔ̃ʃit] *nf* bronchitis.

bronze [brɔ̃:z] *nm* bronze (statue).

bronzer [brɔ̃ze] *vt* to bronze, brown, tan.

brosse [brɔs] *nf* brush; **cheveux en — crewcut.

brosser [brɔse] *vt* to brush, thrash.

brouet [bruɛ] *nm* gruel, skilly.

brouette [bruɛt] *nf* wheelbarrow.

brouhaha [bruaa] *nm* uproar, din, clatter, hubbub.

brouillage [bruja:ʒ] *nm* interference, jamming, mixing.

brouillard [bruja:r] *nm* fog, mist, daybook; **il fait du — it is foggy.

brouille [bru:j] *nf* quarrel, dispute, wrangle, broil; **être en — avec qn.** to have fallen out with s.o.

brouiller [bruje] *vt* to confuse, mix (up), fuddle, scramble, perplex, jam; *vr* to get confused, mixed, blurred, quarrel, fall out.

brouillon, -onne [brujɔ̃, ɔn] *a* muddleheaded; *nm* rough copy, draft.

broussailles [brusa:j] *nf pl* undergrowth, brushwood, scrub.

broussailleux, -euse [brusajø, ø:z] *a* bushy, shaggy.

brousse [brus] *nf* bush, scrub, wilds.

brouter [brute] *vt* to graze, crop, browse.

broyer [brwaje] *vt* to crush, grind, pound; **— du noir** to have the blues.

bru [bry] *nf* daughter-in-law.

brugnon [bryɲɔ̃] *nm* nectarine.

bruine [brɥin] *nf* drizzle.

bruiner [brɥine] *vi* to drizzle, spit.

bruire [brɥi:r] *vi* to rustle, murmur, hum.

bruissement [brɥismɑ̃] *nm* rustling, whisper, humming.

bruit [brɥi] *nm* noise, clatter, din, rumor, sound, fuss, ado.

brûlant [brylɑ̃] *a* burning, blazing, scorching, fervent.

brûlé [bryle] *a* burnt, scorched; **odeur de — smell of burning.

brûle-gueule [brylgœl] *nm* clay pipe, nose warmer.

brûle-pourpoint [brylpurpwɛ̃] *ad* **à — point-blank.

brûler [bryle] *vt* to burn (up, down, out, away), singe, nip, scorch; *vi* to burn, be on fire, be aflame, singe, scorch, be eager (to); **— une gare** to run through a station without stopping; **— les feux** to jump the lights; **— la cervelle à qn.** to blow s.o.'s brains out.

brûleur, -euse [brylœ:r, ø:z] *n* burner, distiller; *nm* gas jet, Bunsen burner.

brûlot [brylo] *nm* fireship.

brûlure [bryly:r] *nf* burn, scald, blight; *pl* heartburn.

brume [brym] *nf* fog, mist, haze.

brumeux, -euse [brymø, ø:z] *a* foggy, misty, hazy.

brun [brœ̃] *a* brown, dark, dusky; *nm* brown; *n* dark person.

brunâtre [brynɑ:tr] *a* brownish.

brunir [bryni:r] *vt* to brown, darken, tan, burnish; *vi* to become dark, tan.

brusque [brysk] *a* abrupt, hasty, sudden.

brusquer [bryske] *vt* to hurry, rush, be sharp with.

brusquerie [brysk(ə)ri] *nf* bluntness, abruptness, bluffness, roughness.

brut [bryt] *a* rough, crude, unrefined, raw, unpolished, uncut, gross, extra dry.

brutal [brytal] *a* coarse, callous, rough, blunt.

brutaliser [brytalize] *vt* to bully, ill-treat.

brutalité [brytalite] *nf* (act of) brutality, brutishness, callousness.

brute [bryt] *nf* beast, bully.
bruyant [bryjɑ̃] *a* noisy, boisterous, loud, blatant.
bruyère [bryjɛ:r] *nf* heather, heath (land), briar; **coq de —** grouse.
buanderie [buɑ̃dri] *nf* wash-house.
bucarde [bykard] *nf* cockle.
bûche [by(:)ʃ] *nf* log, fall, spill, duffer.
bûcher [byʃe] *vt* to work at, cram; *vi* to work, roughhew; *nm* woodshed, woodpile, pyre, stake.
bûcheron [byʃr5] *nm* woodcutter, woodman, lumberjack.
bûcheur, -euse [byʃœ:r, ø:z] *n* hard worker, plodder.
bucolique [bykɔlik] *a* bucolic, pastoral.
budget [bydʒɛ] *nm* estimates; **boucler le —** to balance the budget.
budgétaire [bydʒete:r] *a* fiscal, financial.
buée [bye] *nf* vapor, steam.
buffet [byfɛ] *nm* sideboard, refreshment room.
buffle [byfl] *nm* buffalo, hide.
buffleterie [byflətri] *nf* leather equipment.
buis [bɥi] *nm* boxwood.
buisson [bɥis5] *nm* bush, thicket, brake.
buissonnier, -ière [bɥisɔnje, jɛːr] *a* which lives in the woods; **faire l'école buissonnière** to play truant.
bulgare [bylga:r] *an* Bulgarian.
Bulgarie [bylgari] *nf* Bulgaria.
bulbe [bylb] *nm* bulb.
bulle [byl] *nf* bubble, (eccl) bull.
bulletin [byltɛ̃] *nm* report, ticket; **— de vote** voting paper; **— de bagages** baggage check.
buraliste [byralist] *n* clerk, collector of taxes, tobacconist.
bure [by:r] *nf* frieze, homespun.
bureau [byro] *nm* desk, office, board, committee, orderly room; **— de placement** Labor Exchange, registry; **— de poste** post office; **— de tabac** tobacconist's shop.
bureaucrate [byrokrat] *nm* bureaucrat.
bureaucratie [byrokrasi] *nf* bureaucracy, officialdom, red tape.
burette [byrɛt] *nf* burette, oilcan, flagon.
burin [byrɛ̃] *nm* graving tool, etcher's pen.
buriner [byrine] *vt* to engrave.
burlesque [byrlɛsk] *a* comical.
buse [by:z] *nf* buzzard, tube, nozzle.
busqué [byske] *a* aquiline, hooked.
buste [byst] *nm* bust; **en — half-length.**
but [by(t)] *nm* aim, goal, purpose, object(ive), target, mark; **sans —** aimless(ly); **marquer un — to** score a goal; **de — en blanc** point blank.
buté [byte] *a* obstinate, set.
butée [byte] *nf* buttress, stop.

buter [byte] *vi* to knock, stumble, strike, abut; *vr* to knock, prop oneself up.
butin [bytɛ̃] *nm* booty, loot, spoils, plunder.
butoir [bytwa:r] *nm* buffer, check.
butor [byto:r] *nm* bittern, lout, bully.
butte [byt] *nf* hillock, mound, butte; **être en —** à to be exposed to.
buvable [byvabl] *a* drinkable.
buvard [byva:r] *a* **papier —** blotting paper; *nm* blotter, blotting pad.
buvette [byvɛt] *nf* refreshment bar, stand; soda fountain.
buveur, -euse [byvœːr, ø:z] *n* drinker, toper.

C

c' see **ce**
ça [sa] see **cela**.
çà [sa] *ad* here, hither; **— et là** here and there; **ah —!** now then!
caban [kabɑ̃] *nm* pea-jacket, pilot-coat.
cabane [kaban] *nf* hut, shanty, hutch.
cabanon [kaban5] *nm* padded cell, small hut.
cabaret [kabarɛ] *nm* tavern, public house, restaurant.
cabaretier, -ière [kabartje, jɛːr] *n* publican, tavern-keeper.
cabas [kaba] *nm* shopping basket, satchel, tool-bag.
cabestan [kabɛstɑ̃] *nm* capstan, windlass, winch.
cabillaud [kabijo] *nm* cod.
cabine [kabin] *nf* cabin, saloon, box, telephone booth, hut.
cabinet [kabinɛ] *nm* closet, small room, office, consulting room, cabinet, government, collection; *pl* toilet, lavatory; **— de travail** study; **— de toilette** dressing room.
câble [kɑ:bl] *nm* cable, rope, line, wire.
câbler [kɑble] *vt* to cable.
caboche [kabɔʃ] *nf* pate, head.
cabosse [kabɔs] *nm* pod.
cabot [kabo] *nm* mongrel.
cabotage [kabɔtaːʒ] *nm* coasting-trade.
caboteur [kabɔtœːr] *nm* coaster.
cabotin [kabɔtɛ̃] *n* ham actor.
cabrer [kabre] *vt* (*plane*) to elevate; *vr* to rear, buck, jib (at).
cabriole [kabriɔl] *nf* leap, caper, somersault.
cabriolet [kabriɔlɛ] *nm* gig, cabriolet, coupé.
cacahuète [kakawɛt] *nf* peanut.
cacao [kakao] *nm* cacao, cocoa.
cacaotière [kakaotjɛːr] *nf* cocoa plantation.
cacaoyer [kakaɔje] *nm* cocoa-tree.
cacatoès [kakatɔɛːs] *nm* cockatoo.
cache [kaʃ] *nf* hiding-place.

cache-cache [kaʃkaʃ] nm hide-and-seek.

cache-col [kaʃkɔl] nm man's scarf.

cachemire [kaʃmiːr] nm cashmere.

cache-nez [kaʃne] nm muffler.

cacher [kaʃe] vt to hide, conceal, keep secret; vr to lie in hiding, hide (from à).

cachet [kaʃɛ] nm seal, mark, stamp, fee, cachet.

cacheter [kaʃte] vt to seal (up).

cachette [kaʃɛt] nf hiding-place; **en — on the quiet.**

cachot [kaʃo] nm dungeon.

cachotterie [kaʃɔtri] nf mystery.

cachottier, -ière [kaʃɔtje, jeːr] a secretive, reticent.

cadastre [kadastr] nm cadastral survey.

cadavéreux, -euse [kadaverø, øːz] a cadaverous.

cadavre [kadaːvr] nm corpse, dead body, carcass.

cadeau [kado] nm present, gift.

cadenas [kadna] nm padlock, clasp.

cadenasser [kadnase] vt to padlock, clasp.

cadence [kadãːs] nf cadence, rhythm, time, tune.

cadencé [kadãse] a measured, rhythmical.

cadet, -ette [kadɛ, ɛt] a younger, junior; n youngest; nm caddie.

cadran [kadrã] nm d'il, face.

cadre [kaːdr] nm frame(work), limits, bounds, outline, plan, cadre, list, strength, management staff.

cadrer [kadre] vi to agree, square, tally, fit in.

caduc, -uque [kadyk] a declining, decrepit, weak, lapsed, null and void.

cafard [kafaːr] a sanctimonious; nm cockroach, telltale; **avoir le — to have the blues.**

cafarder [kafarde] vi to tell tales, sneak.

café [kafe] nm coffee, café; — **nature** black coffee; — **crème** white coffee; — **complet** coffee with milk, roll and butter.

caféier(e) [kafeje] n coffee plant, plantation.

cafetier, -ière [kaftje, jeːr] n owner of a café.

cafetière [kaftjeːr] nf coffee-pot.

cafouiller [kafuje] vi to splutter, (car) misfire.

cage [kaːʒ] nf cage, coop, casing, well, shaft, stairway.

cagneux, -euse [kaɲø, øːz] a knock-kneed, crooked.

cagnotte [kaɲɔt] nf pool, kitty.

cagot [kago] a hypocritical; n hypocrite.

cagoule [kagul] nf cowl, hood.

cahier [kaje] nm exercise book, copy-book.

cahin-caha [kaɛ̃kaa] ad middling, so-so, limping.

cahot [kao] nm jolt, bump.

cahoter [kaɔte] vti to jolt, bump, shake, toss about.

cahoteux, -euse [kaɔtø, øːz] a bumpy, rough.

caille [kaːj] nf quail.

caillebotte [kajbɔt] nf curds.

cailler [kaje] vtir to clot, curdle; **lait caillé** curds.

caillot [kajo] nm clot.

caillou [kaju] nm pebble.

caillouter [kajute] vt to metal, pave with pebbles.

caillouteux, -euse [kajutø, øːz] a stony, pebbly.

caïman [kaimã] nm crocodile.

caisse [kɛs] nf case, chest, casing, tub, body, cashbox, till, pay-desk, counting-house, fund, bank, drum; **tenir la — to be in charge of the money; — d'épargne savings bank.**

caissier, ière [kɛsje, jeːr] n cashier.

caisson [kɛsɔ̃] nm box, trunk, ammunition wagon, locker, caisson.

cajoler [kaʒɔle] vt to cajole, coax.

cajolerie [kaʒɔlri] nf cajolery, coaxing.

calamité [kalamite] nf calamity.

calamiteux, -euse [kalamitø, øːz] a calamitous, broken-down, seedy.

calao [kalao] nm hornbill.

calcaire [kalkeːr] a calcareous, chalky; nm limestone.

calcul [kalkyl] nm calculation, reckoning, arithmetic, calculus, (in bladder) stone.

calculé [kalkyle] a calculated, studied, deliberate.

calculer [kalkyle] vt to calculate, reckon.

cale [kal] nf hold, slipway, stocks, wedge, chock, prop; — **sèche** dry dock; — **de radoub** graving dock; **mettre sur — to lay down.**

calé [kale] a wedged, jammed, good (at en).

calebasse [kalbaːs] nf calabash, gourd.

caleçon [kalsɔ̃] nm drawers, pants.

calembour [kalãbuːr] nm pun.

calendrier [kalãdri(j)e] nm calendar.

calepin [kalpɛ̃] nm notebook.

caler [kale] vt to wedge, chock (up), prop up, adjust, stall; vi to stall, draw water, funk.

calfat [kalfa] nm caulker.

calfater [kalfate] vt to caulk.

calfeutrer [kalføtre] vt to stop (up), block (up), make draft-proof; vr to shut oneself up, make oneself cosy, comfortable.

calibre [kalibr] nm caliber, bore, gauge, pattern.

calice [kalis] nm calyx, chalice, cup.

calicot [kaliko] nm calico, draper's shop assistant.

califourchon [kalifurʃɔ̃] ad **à — astride.**

câlin [kalɛ̃] a caressing, winning, wheedling.

câliner [kɑline] *vt* to caress, fondle, pet, wheedle.

câlinerie [kɑlinri] *nf* caress(ing), petting, wheedling.

calleux, -euse [kalø, øːz] *a* horny, callous.

calligraphie [kalligrafi] *nf* penmanship, handwriting.

callosité [kallozite] *nf* callosity.

calme [kalm] *a* calm, still, quiet, composed, collected; *nm* calm(ness), stillness.

calmer [kalme] *vt* to calm, quiet, soothe; *vr* to calm down, abate.

calomniateur, -trice [kalɔmnjatœːr, tris] *n* slanderer.

calomnie [kalɔmni] *nf* calumny, slander, libel.

calomnier [kalɔmnje] *vt* to slander.

calomnieux, -euse [kalɔmnjø, øːz] *a* slanderous.

calorie [kalɔri] *nf* calory.

calorifère [kalɔrifɛːr] *nm* central-heating apparatus, hot-air stove.

calorifuge [kalɔrifyːʒ] *a* heat-insulating, heat-proof.

calorique [kalɔrik] *a* caloric, heat.

calot [kalo] *nm* forage cap, rough slate, stone.

calotte [kalɔt] *nf* skull cap, box on the ears.

calotter [kalɔte] *vt* to cuff.

calque [kalk] *nm* tracing, traced copy.

calquer [kalke] *vt* to trace.

calvitie [kalvisi] *nf* baldness.

camarade [kamarad] *n* comrade, chum, friend, mate.

camaraderie [kamaradri] *nf* comradeship, fellowship.

camard [kamaːr] *a* flat-, snub-, pug-nosed.

Cambodge [kɑmbɔdʒ] *nm* Cambodia.

cambouis [kɑbwi] *nm* dirty oil, grease.

cambré [kɑbre] *a* cambered, arched, curved, bent.

cambrer [kɑbre] *vt* to arch, bend, camber, curve; *vr* to brace oneself.

cambriolage [kɑbriɔlaːʒ] *nm* burglary.

cambrioler [kɑbriɔle] *vt* to burgle, break into.

cambrioleur, -euse [kɑbriɔlœːr, øːz] *n* burglar.

cambrure [kɑbryːr] *nf* camber, curve, arch, instep.

cambuse [kɑbyːz] *nf* steward's room, glory hole, hovel.

came [kam] *nf* cam.

camée [kame] *nm* cameo.

caméléon [kamele5] *nm* chameleon.

camélia [kamelja] *nm* camellia.

camelot [kamlo] *nm* street hawker, newsvender.

camelote [kamlɔt] *nf* rubbish, trash, shoddy goods.

caméra [kamɛra] *nf* movie camera.

camion [kamjɔ̃] *nm* wagon, dray, truck.

camionnage [kamjɔnaːʒ] *nm* cartage, haulage.

camionnette [kamjɔnɛt] *nf* light truck, van.

camionneur [kamjɔnœːr] *nm* carrier.

camisole [kamizɔl] *nf* woman's vest, dressing-jacket; **— de force** strait-jacket.

camouflage [kamuflaːʒ] *n* camouflage.

camoufler [kamufle] *vt* to disguise, fake, camouflage.

camouflet [kamuflɛ] *nm* insult, snub.

camp [kɑ̃] *nm* camp, side.

campagnard [kɑ̃paɲaːr] *a* country, rustic; *n* countryman, -woman.

campagne [kɑ̃paɲ] *nf* country(side), field, campaign; **partie de —** picnic.

campé [kɑ̃pe] *a* **bien —** well set-up, strapping.

campement [kɑ̃pmɑ̃] *nm* encampment, camping.

camper [kɑ̃pe] *vi* to (en)camp; *vt* to put under canvas, place, put, stick; **— là** to leave in the lurch; *vr* to pitch one's camp, plant oneself.

camphre [kɑ̃fr] *nm* camphor.

camphrer [kɑ̃fre] *vt* to camphorate.

camus [kamy] *a* snub-, flat-, pug-nosed.

canaille [kanaːj] *nf* rabble, mob, blackguard, rascal.

canal [kanal] *nm* canal, channel, pipe, duct.

canalisation [kanalizasjɔ̃] *nf* canalization, draining, piping, pipes, wiring, mains.

canaliser [kanalize] *vt* to canalize, pipe, lay down pipes in, wire.

canapé [kanape] *nm* sofa; canapé.

canard [kanaːr] *nm* duck, drake, false report, hoax, lump of sugar dipped in coffee.

canari [kanari] *nm* canary, earthen-ware pot.

cancan [kɑ̃kɑ̃] *nm* cancan dance, scandal.

cancanier, -ière [kɑ̃kanje, jɛːr] *a* addicted to tittle-tattle; *n* scandal-monger.

cancer [kɑ̃sɛːr] *nm* cancer.

cancéreux, -euse [kɑ̃serø, øːz] *a* cancerous.

cancrelat [kɑ̃krəla] *nm* cockroach.

candélabre [kɑ̃delaːbr] *nm* candelabrum, branched lamp-post.

candeur [kɑ̃dœːr] *nf* ingenuousness, artlessness.

candidat [kɑ̃dida] *nm* candidate.

candide [kɑ̃did] *a* ingenuous, artless, guileless.

cane [kan] *nf* duck.

caneton [kantɔ̃] *nm* duckling.

canette [kanɛt] *nf* beer-bottle, spool.

canevas [kanva] *nm* canvas, outline, sketch.

caniche [kaniʃ] *n* poodle.

canicule [kanikyl] *nf* dog-days.

canif [kanif] *nm* penknife.

caniveau [kanivo] *nm* gutter, conduit.

canne [kan] *nf* cane, walking-stick, fishing-rod; — **à sucre** sugar cane.

cannelle [kanɛl] *nf* cinnamon, spigot, tap.

cannelure [kanlyːr] *nf* groove, fluting.

canner [kane] *vt* to cane-bottom.

cannibale [kanibal] *nm* cannibal, man-eater.

cannibalisme [kanibalism] *nm* cannibalism.

canon [kanɔ̃] *nm* cannon, gun, barrel, pipe, tube, canon.

cañon [kaɲɔ̃] *nm* canyon.

canonique [kanɔnik] *a* canonical.

canoniser [kanɔnize] *vt* to canonize.

canonnade [kanɔnad] *nf* cannonade.

canonnier [kanɔnje] *nm* gunner.

canonnière [kanɔnjeːr] *nf* gunboat.

canot [kano] *nm* boat, dinghy, cutter.

canotage [kanɔtaːʒ] *nm* boating, rowing.

canoter [kanɔte] *vi* to go rowing, boating.

canotier [kanɔtje] *nm* rower, oarsman, boatman, straw hat, boater.

cantatrice [kɑ̃tatris] *nf* singer, vocalist.

cantine [kɑ̃tin] *nf* canteen.

cantinier, -ière *n* canteen-keeper.

cantique [kɑ̃tik] *nm* canticle, hymn.

canton [kɑ̃tɔ̃] *nm* canton, district.

cantonade [kɑ̃tɔnad] *nf* **à la —** in the wings, ' off '.

cantonal [kɑ̃tɔnal] *a* cantonal, district.

cantonner [kɑ̃tɔne] *vt* to divide into cantons, quarter, billet, confine, limit.

cantonnement [kɑ̃tɔnmɑ̃] *nm* cantonment, quarters, billet.

cantonnier [kɑ̃tɔnje] *nm* roadman, road-mender.

canulant [kanylɑ̃] *a* boring.

canule [kanyl] *nf* nozzle.

caoutchouc [kautʃu] *nm* (india) rubber, waterproof coat; *pl* galoshes, overshoes, rubbers.

caoutchouter [kautʃute] *vt* to rubberize, treat with rubber.

cap [kap] *nm* cape, headland.

capable [kapabl] *a* capable, fit, able.

capacité [kapasite] *nf* capacity, ability, capability.

cape [kap] *nf* cape, cloak; **rire sous — ** to laugh up one's sleeve.

capillaire [kapilleːr] *a* capillary.

capitaine [kapitɛn] *nm* captain, master, head; — **de vaisseau** captain; — **de frégate** commander; — **de corvette** lieutenant-commander; — **de port** harbor-master.

capital [kapital] *a* capital, chief, principal; *nm* capital, assets, principal.

capitale [kapital] *nf* capital, chief town.

capitaliser [kapitalize] *vt* to capitalize.

capitalisme [kapitalism] *nm* capitalism.

capitaliste [kapitalist] *n* capitalist.

capiteux, -euse [kapitø, øːz] *a* heady, strong.

capitonner [kapitɔne] *vt* to upholster, quilt.

capituler [kapityle] *vi* to capitulate.

caporal [kapɔral] *nm* corporal, (ordinary quality) tobacco.

capot [kapo] *nm* cover, hood, bonnet, cowl.

capotage [kapɔtaːʒ] *nm* capsizing, overturning.

capote [kapɔt] *nf* greatcoat, bonnet, hood, cowl, contraceptive.

capoter [kapɔte] *vt* to capsize, overturn.

câpre [kɑːpr] *nm* caper.

caprice [kapris] *nm* caprice, whim, impulse.

capricieux, -euse [kaprisjø, jøːz] *a* capricious, wayward.

capsule [kapsyl] *nf* capsule, seal, firing-cap.

captage [kaptaːʒ] *nm* catching, collecting.

captation [kaptasjɔ̃] *nf* catching, tapping, picking up.

capter [kapte] *vt* to catch, collect, obtain, pick up.

captieux, -euse [kapsjø, øːz] *a* captious, specious.

captif, -ive [kaptif, iːv] *an* captive.

captiver [kaptive] *vt* to captivate, charm.

captivité [kaptivite] *nf* captivity.

capture [kaptyːr] *nf* capture, seizure, booty.

capturer [kaptyre] *vt* to capture, catch, collect.

capuchon [kapyʃɔ̃] *nm* hood, cowl, cap.

capucine [kapysin] *nf* nasturtium.

caque [kak] *nf* keg, herring barrel.

caquet [kake] *nm* cackle, chattering.

caqueter [kakte] *vi* to cackle, chatter.

car [kaːr] *cj* for, because; *nm* motor coach.

carabin [karabɛ̃] *nm* medical student.

carabine [karabin] *nf* carbine, rifle.

carabiné [karabine] *a* stiff, violent, strong.

carabinier [karabinje] *nm* rifleman.

caractère [karakteːr] *nm* character, temper, personality, characteristic, nature.

caractériser [karakterize] *vt* to characterize; *vr* to assume the character (of *par*), be distinguished (by *par*).

caractéristique [karakteristik] *a* characteristic, typical; *nf* trait, feature.

carafe [karaf] nf decanter, carafe.

caravane [karavan] nf desert caravan, trailer.

carbone [karbɔn] nm carbon.

carbonisé [karbɔnize] a carbonized, charred, burnt to death.

carburant [karbyrɑ̃] nm motor fuel.

carburateur [karbyratœːr] nm carburetor.

carbure [karbyːr] nf carbide.

carcasse [karkas] nf carcass, frame.

cardiaque [kardjak] a cardiac; **crise** — heart attack.

cardinal [kardinal] anm cardinal.

carême [karɛm] nm Lent.

carence [karɑ̃ːs] nf insolvency, default, deficiency.

carène [karɛn] nf hull, bottom.

caresse [karɛs] nf caress.

caresser [karese] vt to caress, stroke, fondle, cherish.

cargaison [kargɛzɔ̃] nf cargo.

cargo [kargo] nm cargo boat, tramp steamer.

caricature [karikatyːr] nf caricature.

carie [kari] nf caries, decay.

carié [karje] a decayed.

carillon [karijɔ̃] nm chime, peal of bells.

carillonner [karijɔne] vi to chime, ring a peal of bells.

carillonneur [karijɔnœːr] nm bellringer.

carlingue [karlɛ̃ːg] nf fuselage, cockpit.

carnage [karnaːʒ] nm slaughter, bloodshed.

carnassier, -ière [karnasje, jɛːr] a carnivorous.

carnassière [karnasjeːr] nf gamebag.

carnaval [karnaval] nm carnival.

carnet [karnɛ] nm notebook; — de banque pass-book; — de chèques checkbook; — de bal dance program.

carnier [karnje] nm game-bag.

carnivore [karnivɔːr] a carnivorous.

carotte [karɔt] nf carrot; (of tobacco) plug; fraud, trick, catch.

carpe [karp] nf carp.

carpette [karpɛt] nf rug.

carquois [karkwa] nm quiver.

carré [kare] a square (-shouldered), straightforward; nm square, lodgings.

carreau [karo] nm tile, floor, small square, window-pane, diamonds.

carrefour [karfuːr] nm crossroads, square.

carrelage [karlaːʒ] nm tiling, tileflooring.

carreler [karle] vt to pave, lay with tiles.

carrelet [karlɛ] nm plaice.

carrément [karemɑ̃] ad squarely, firmly, bluntly.

carrer [kare] vt to square; vr to swagger, settle oneself.

carrier [karje] nm quarryman.

carrière [karjɛːr] nf career, quarry; donner libre — à to give free play, scope, vent to.

carriole [karjɔl] nf light cart.

carrossable [karɔsabl] a route — carriageway.

carrosse [karɔs] nm coach.

carrosserie [karɔsri] nf coachbuilding, body(work).

carrousel [karuzɛl] nm tournament, merry-go-round.

carrure [karyːr] nf build, stature.

cartable [kartabl] nm satchel, portfolio.

carte [kart] nf map, chart, card, bill, list, menu; — blanche free hand, carte blanche.

cartel [kartɛl] nm trust, combine, coalition.

carter [karteːr] nm gearcase, sump, spool-box.

cartographe [kartɔgraf] nm mapmaker, cartographer.

cartographie [kartɔgrafi] nf mapmaking.

cartomancie [kartɔmɑ̃si] nf fortunetelling by cards.

cartomancien, -ienne [kartɔmɑ̃sjɛ̃, jɛn] n fortune-teller by cards.

carton [kartɔ̃] nm cardboard box, carton, cartoon.

cartonné [kartɔne] a (books) bound in boards.

cartouche [kartuʃ] nf cartridge.

cartouchière [kartuʃjɛːr] nf cartridge-pouch.

cas [ka] nm case, matter, affair, instance, circumstance; le — échéant should the occasion arise; au, dans le — où in the event of; en tout — in any case; faire (grand) — de to value highly.

casanier, -ière [kazanje, jɛːr] a stay-at-home, sedentary.

cascade [kaskad] nf waterfall, cascade.

case [kaːz] nf hut, cabin, pigeonhole, compartment, space, division, square.

casemate [kazmat] nf casemate.

caser [kaze] vt to put away, stow, file, find a place for, settle; vr to settle down.

caserne [kazɛrn] nf barracks.

casier [kazje] nm set of pigeonholes, rack, cabinet; — judiciaire police record.

casque [kask] nm helmet.

casquette [kaskɛt] nf cap.

cassant [kasɑ̃] a brittle, crisp, short, blunt, abrupt.

cassation [kasasjɔ̃] nf cassation, quashing, reduction to the ranks.

casse [kaːs] nf breakage, ructions, damage.

casse-cou [kasku] nm dare-devil, death-trap.

casse-croûte [kaskrut] nm snack, quick lunch.

casse-noisettes [kɑsnwazɛt] nm nut-crackers.

casser [kɑse] vt to break, crack, cashier, degrade, annul, quash; vr to break, give way, snap; se — la tête to puzzle, rack one's brains.

casserole [kɑsrɔl] nf saucepan, stewpan, casserole.

casse-tête [kɑstɛt] nm club, loaded stick, teaser, din.

cassette [kɑsɛt] nf casket, money-box.

cassis [kɑsi(s)] nm blackcurrant (liqueur); open gutter across road.

cassonade [kɑsɔnad] nf brown sugar.

cassure [kɑsyːr] nf break, fracture, crack.

castor [kɑstɔːr] nm beaver.

casuel [kɑzɥɛl] nm perquisites, casual profits, fees.

cataclysme [kataklism] nm cataclysm.

catacombes [katakɔːb] nf pl catacombs.

catalepsie [katalɛpsi] nf catalepsy.

catalogue [katalɔg] nm catalogue.

cataloguer [kataloge] vt to catalogue, list.

catalyseur [katalizœːr] nm catalyst.

cataplasme [kataplasm] nm poultice; — sinapisé mustard poultice.

cataracte [katarakt] nf cataract.

catarrhe [kataːr] nm catarrh.

catastrophe [katastrɔf] nf catastrophe, disaster.

catch [katʃ] nm all-in wrestling.

catéchiser [kateʃize] vt to catechize, lecture, reason with, try to persuade.

catéchisme [kateʃism] nm catechism.

catégorie [kategɔri] nf category.

catégorique [kategɔrik] a categorical, positive.

cathédrale [katedral] nf cathedral.

catholicisme [katɔlisism] nm Catholicism.

catholique [katɔlik] a catholic, orthodox; universal; an Roman Catholic; ce n'est pas — that is fishy.

catimini [katimini] ad en — on the sly, stealthily.

cauchemar [koʃmaːr, ko-] nm nightmare.

cauri [kɔri] nm cowrie shell.

cause [koːz] nf cause, grounds, suit, action, brief; et pour — for a very good reason, very properly; pour — de for reasons of; à — de on account of, owing to, through; — célèbre famous case, trial; mettre en — to implicate, bring into question; en connaissance de — with full knowledge of the case.

causer [koze] vt to cause; vi to talk, converse, chat.

causerie [kozri] nf talk, chat.

causeur, -euse [kozœːr, øːz] a talkative, chatty; n talker.

caustique [kostik] a caustic, burning, cutting, biting.

cauteleux, -euse [kotlø, øːz] a cunning, sly, wary.

cautériser [koterize] vt to cauterize.

caution [kosjɔ̃] nf security, surety, bail, guarantee; sujet à — unconfirmed.

cautionnement [kosjɔnmɑ̃] nm surety, deposit, security, guarantee.

cavalerie [kavalri] nf cavalry.

cavalier, -ière [kavalje, jɛːr] a offhand, free and easy, jaunty, riding; n horseman, horsewoman, rider; nm trooper, escort, cavalier, partner, knight.

cave [kaːv] a hollow, sunken, deep-set; nf cellar, stake.

caveau [kavo] nm vault.

caverne [kavɛrn] nf cave, cavern, den, cavity.

caverneux, -euse [kavɛrnø, øːz] a cavernous, hollow, sepulchral.

caviarder [kavjarde] vt to suppress, block-out.

cavité [kavite] nf cavity, hollow, pit.

ce [s(ə)] pn it, he, she; — qui, — que what, which; sur — thereupon; pour — qui est de as regards; ce, cet, cette, ces this, that, such; pl these, those, such; — soir this evening, tonight; cette nuit last night.

ceci [səsi] pn this.

cécité [sesite] nf blindness.

céder [sede] vt to give up, surrender, assign; vi to yield, give way, sag; le — à qn. to be inferior to s.o.

cèdre [sɛːdr] nm cedar.

ceindre [sɛ̃ːdr] vt. to gird (on), encircle, encompass.

ceinture [sɛ̃tyːr] nf girdle, belt, sash, waist, circle.

ceinturon [sɛ̃tyrɔ̃] nm waistbelt, sword-belt.

cela [səla, sla] pn that, it, so; comme ci, comme ça so so; c'est ça that's right, that's it.

célèbre [selɛbr] a famous.

célébrer [selebre] vt to celebrate, observe, hold, solemnize, sing the praises of.

célébrité [selebrite] nf celebrity.

céleri [selri] nm celery.

célérité [selerite] nf celerity, speed, swiftness.

céleste [selɛst] a celestial, heavenly.

célibat [seliba] nm celibacy.

célibataire [selibatɛːr] a celibate, unmarried, single; n bachelor, spinster.

celle see celui.

cellulaire [selylɛːr] a cellular; voiture — police van.

cellule [selyl] nf cell.

celluloïd [selylɔid] nm celluloid.

cellulose [selyloːz] nf cellulose.

celte [sɛlt] n Celt.

celtique [sɛltik] a Celtic.

celui, celle, ceux, celles [səlɥi] pn he,

she, the one, those; ——ci the latter, this one; ——là the former, that one.
cendre [sɑ̃:dr] *nf* ash(es), cinders, embers.
cendré [sɑ̃dre] *a* ashy, ash-gray.
cendrier [sɑ̃drie] *nm* ashbin, -pan, -pit, -tray.
cène [sɛn] *nf* the Last Supper.
censé [sɑ̃se] *a* supposed.
censeur [sɑ̃sœ:r] *nm* censor, critic, disciplinary head of French school.
censure [sɑ̃sy:r] *nf* censorship, blame.
censurer [sɑ̃syre] *vt* to censor, criticize.
cent [sɑ̃] *a* one hundred; *nm* a hundred; **faire les — pas** to walk up and down.
centaine [sɑ̃tɛn] *nf* (about) a hundred.
centenaire [sɑ̃tnɛ:r] *an* centenarian; *nm* centenary.
centième [sɑ̃tjem] *anm* hundredth.
centigrade [sɑ̃tigrad] *a* centigrade.
centigramme [sɑ̃tigram] *nm* centigram.
centilitre [sɑ̃tilitr] *nm* centiliter.
centime [sɑ̃tim] *nm* centime.
centimètre [sɑ̃timɛtr] *nm* centimeter, tape-measure.
central [sɑ̃tral] *a* central, middle; *nm* telephone exchange.
centrale [sɑ̃tral] *nf* power-house, electricity works.
centraliser [sɑ̃tralize] *vt* to centralize.
centre [sɑ̃:tr] *nm* center, middle.
centrifuge [sɑ̃trify:ʒ] *a* centrifugal.
centuple [sɑ̃typl] *a* centuple, hundredfold.
cep [sɛ(p)] *nm* vine-plant.
cependant [s(ə)pɑ̃dɑ̃] *ad* meanwhile, meantime; *cj* still, yet, nevertheless.
cerceau [sɛrso] *nm* hoop.
cercle [sɛrkl] *nm* circle, set, club, hoop, ring, dial.
cercler [sɛrkle] *vt* to encircle, ring, hoop.
cercueil [sɛrkœ:j] *nm* coffin.
céréale [sereal] *anf* cereal.
cérébral [serebral] *a* cerebral, of the brain.
cérémonie [seremɔni] *nf* ceremony; **tenue de —** full dress; **sans —** informally.
cérémonieux, -euse [seremɔnjø, ø:z] ceremonious, formal.
cerf [sɛ:r, sɛrf] *nm* stag.
cerfeuil [sɛrfœ:j] *nm* chervil.
cerf-volant [sɛrvolɑ̃] *nm* kite.
cerise [s(ə)ri:z] *nf* cherry.
cerisier [s(ə)rizje] *nm* cherry-tree.
cerné [sɛrne] *a* **les yeux —s** with rings under the eyes.
cerner [sɛrne] *vt* to encircle, surround, hem in.
certain [sɛrtɛ̃] *a* certain, sure, fixed, stated; *pn pl* some, certain.
certainement [sɛrtɛnmɑ̃] *ad* certainly, by all means.
certes [sɛrt] *ad* yes indeed, most certainly, to be sure.

certificat [sɛrtifika] *nm* certificate, script.
certifier [sɛrtifje] *vt* to attest, authenticate.
certitude [sɛrtityd] *nf* certainty.
cerveau [sɛrvo] *nm* brain, mind; **— brûlé** hot-head.
cervelas [sɛrvəla] *nm* saveloy.
cervelle [sɛrvɛl] *nf* brain(s), mind; **se creuser la —** to rack one's brains.
ces see **ce**.
cessation [sesasjɔ̃] *nf* cessation, suspension.
cesse [sɛs] *nf* cease, ceasing.
cesser [sese] *vit* to cease, leave off, stop.
cet see **ce**.
cette see **ce**.
ceux see **celui**.
chacal [ʃakal] *nm* jackal.
chacun [ʃakœ̃] *pn* each, each one, every one, everybody, everyone.
chagrin [ʃagrɛ̃] *a* sad, glum, peevish, fretful; *nm* grief, annoyance, worry.
chagriner [ʃagrine] *vt* to grieve, afflict, vex, annoy.
chahut [ʃay] *nm* noise, uproar, rowdyism.
chahuter [ʃayte] *vi* to kick up a row, boo; *vt* to banter.
chahuteur, -euse [ʃaytœ:r, ø:z] *an* rowdy.
chaîne [ʃɛn] *nf* chain, cable, range, warp; *pl* bonds, fetters; **travail à la —** assembly-line production.
chaînon [ʃɛnɔ̃] *nm* link.
chair [ʃɛ:r] *nf* flesh, meat, pulp; **en — et en os** in the flesh; **— de poule** gooseflesh, creeps; **— à canon** cannon fodder.
chaire [ʃɛ:r] *nf* pulpit, desk, rostrum, chair, professorship.
chaise [ʃɛ:z] *nf* chair, seat.
chaise-longue [ʃɛzlɔ̃:g] *nf* couch.
chaland [ʃalɑ̃] *nm* customer, lighter, barge.
châle [ʃɑ:l] *nm* shawl, wrap.
chalet [ʃalɛ, ʃa-] *nm* chalet.
chaleur [ʃalœ:r] *nf* warmth, heat, ardor, zeal; **craint la —** keep in a cool place.
chaleureux, -euse [ʃalœrø, ø:z] *a* warm, cordial.
chaloupe [ʃalup] *nf* launch.
chalumeau [ʃalymo] *nm* straw, pipe, blowpipe.
chalutier [ʃalytje] *nm* drifter, trawler.
se chamailler [səʃamaje] *vr* to quarrel, squabble, row.
chambarder [ʃɑ̃barde] *vt* to smash up, upset, sack.
chambellan [ʃɑ̃belɑ̃] *nm* chamberlain.
chambranle [ʃɑ̃brɑ̃:l] *nm* frame, mantelpiece.
chambre [ʃɑ̃:br] *nf* (bed)room, chamber, House (parliament); **— à air** inner tube; **— d'ami** spare room.

chambrée [ʃɑ̃bre] nf roomful, barrack room.

chambrer [ʃɑ̃bre] vt to lock up in a room; (wine) take the chill off.

chameau [ʃamo] nm camel, scoundrel, beast, swine.

chamois [ʃamwa] nm chamois.

champ [ʃɑ̃] nm field, ground, course, range, scope; **à tout bout de —** at every turn.

champagne [ʃɑ̃paɲ] nm champagne; **fine —** liqueur brandy.

champêtre [ʃɑ̃pɛːtr] a rustic, rural.

champignon [ʃɑ̃piɲɔ̃] nm mushroom.

champion, -ionne [ʃɑ̃pjɔ̃, jɔn] n champion.

championnat [ʃɑ̃pjɔna] nm championship.

chance [ʃɑ̃s] nf chance, luck.

chancelant [ʃɑ̃slɑ̃] a staggering, shaky, delicate.

chanceler [ʃɑ̃sle] vi to stagger, totter.

chancelier [ʃɑ̃səlje] nm chancellor.

chancellerie [ʃɑ̃sɛlri] nf chancellery, secretaryship.

chanceux, -euse [ʃɑ̃sø, øːz] a hazardous, lucky.

chancre [ʃɑ̃ːkr] nm canker, ulcer.

chandail [ʃɑ̃daːj] nm sweater, pullover.

Chandeleur [ʃɑ̃dlœːr] nf Candlemas.

chandelier [ʃɑ̃dəlje] nm candlestick.

chandelle [ʃɑ̃dɛl] nf candle, prop, shore; **voir trente-six —s** to see stars; **économies de bouts de —** cheese-paring.

change [ʃɑ̃ːʒ] nm exchange; **lettre de —** bill of exchange.

changeable [ʃɑ̃ʒabl] a changeable, exchangeable.

changeant [ʃɑ̃ʒɑ̃] a changing, changeable, fickle.

changement [ʃɑ̃ʒmɑ̃] nm change, alteration, variation, variety; **— de vitesse** gear, change of gear; **— de voie** points.

changer [ʃɑ̃ʒe] vt to change, exchange, alter; vi to change; vr to alter, change one's clothes.

changeur [ʃɑ̃ʒœːr] nm moneychanger.

chanoine [ʃanwan] nm canon.

chanson [ʃɑ̃sɔ̃] nf song; **—s!** nonsense.

chansonnier, -ière [ʃɑ̃sɔnje, jɛːr] n songwriter; nm songbook.

chant [ʃɑ̃] nm song, singing, crow(ing), chant, canto.

chantage [ʃɑ̃taːʒ] nm blackmail.

chantant [ʃɑ̃tɑ̃] a singing, musical, sing-song.

chanter [ʃɑ̃te] vt to sing, crow, chirp, suit; **faire —** to blackmail.

chanteur, -euse [ʃɑ̃tœːr, øːz] n singer, vocalist; **maître —** mastersinger, blackmailer.

chantier [ʃɑ̃tje] nm stand, ship(building) yard, dockyard; **sur le —** in hand.

chantonner [ʃɑ̃tɔne] vt to hum.

chanvre [ʃɑ̃ːvr] nm hemp.

chaos [kao] nm chaos.

chaotique [kaotik] a chaotic.

chape [ʃap] nf cope, coping.

chapeau [ʃapo] nm hat, cover, cap, cowl, heading; **donner un coup de —** à to raise one's hat to; **— melon** bowler; **— haut-de-forme, à, de haute forme** top hat.

chapelet [ʃaplɛ] nm rosary, string.

chapelier [ʃaplje] nm hatter.

chapelle [ʃapɛl] nf chapel, coterie, clique.

chapelure [ʃaplyːr] nf breadcrumbs.

chaperon [ʃaprɔ̃] nm hood, chaperon.

chapitre [ʃapitr] nm chapter, heading, item, point; **avoir voix au —** to have a say in the matter.

chapitrer [ʃapitre] vt to lecture, reprimand.

chaque [ʃak] a each, every.

char [ʃaːr] nm chariot, car, wagon; **— d'assaut** tank.

charbon [ʃarbɔ̃] nm coal, carbon; **— de bois** charcoal.

charbonnage [ʃarbɔnaːʒ] nm pl collieries, coal-mining; (naut) bunkering.

charbonner [ʃarbɔne] vt to carbonize, blacken with charcoal.

charbonnier, -ière [ʃarbɔnje, jɛːr] nm collier, charcoal-burner, coal merchant, coalman.

charcuterie [ʃarkytri] nf porkbutcher's shop, pork-butcher's meat, pork.

charcutier, -ière [ʃarkytje, jɛːr] n pork-butcher.

chardon [ʃardɔ̃] nm thistle.

chardonneret [ʃardɔnrɛ] nm goldfinch.

charge [ʃarʒ] nf load, burden, charge, onus, care, trust, expense, office, duty, exaggeration, skit, indictment; **à la — de** chargeable to, dependent on, assigned to; **en — (el)** live; **à — de** on condition that, provided that; **témoin à —** witness for the prosecution.

chargé [ʃarʒe] a loaded, live, furred, coated, full, busy, overcast; **lettre —e** registered letter; nm **— de cours** lecturer, reader.

chargement [ʃarʒmɑ̃] nm lading, loading (up), charging, registration, freight.

charger [ʃarʒe] vt to load, charge, fill, instruct, caricature, exaggerate, saddle; vr to undertake, shoulder.

chariot [ʃarjo] nm wagon, go-cart, truck, trolley.

charité [ʃarite] nf charity, alms.

charme [ʃarm] nm charm, spell.

charmer [ʃarme] vt to charm, bewitch, delight, please.

charnel, -elle [ʃarnɛl] a carnal, sensual.

charnier [ʃarnje] nm charnel-house, ossuary.

charnière [ʃarnjɛːr] nf hinge.
charnu [ʃarny] a fleshy, plump.
charognard [ʃarɔɲar] nm vulture.
charogne [ʃarɔɲ] nf carrion, decaying carcass.
charpente [ʃarpɑ̃t] nf frame(work).
charpenter [ʃarpɑ̃te] vt to frame, build, construct.
charpenterie [ʃarpɑ̃tri] nf carpentry, carpenter's shop.
charpentier [ʃarpɑ̃tje] nm carpenter.
charpie [ʃarpi] nf lint; en — in shreds.
charretier [ʃartje] nm carter, carrier.
charrette [ʃaret] nf cart; — à bras barrow; — anglaise trap, dogcart.
charrier [ʃarje] vt to cart, carry.
charron [ʃarɔ̃] nm cartwright, wheelwright.
charrue [ʃary] nf plow.
charte [ʃart] nf charter.
chartreux [ʃartrø] nm Carthusian monk.
chasse [ʃas] nf chase, hunting, shooting, shoot; — à courre riding to hounds; — à l'affût stalking; — d'eau flush.
châsse [ʃaːs] nf reliquary, shrine, frame.
chasser [ʃase] vt to chase, hunt, shoot, drive (away, out), dismiss, expel; vi to hunt, go hunting, shooting, drive.
chasseur, -euse [ʃasœːr, øːz] n huntsman, sportsman, shooter; nm pageboy, messenger, rifleman, fighter-plane; — de fauves big-game hunter.
chassieux, -euse [ʃasjø, øːz] a blear-eyed.
chassis [ʃasi] nm frame, sash, chassis, under carriage.
chaste [ʃast] a chaste, pure.
chasteté [ʃastəte] nf chastity, purity.
chat, -atte [ʃa, -at] n cat; — de gouttières stray cat.
châtaigne [ʃatɛɲ] nf chestnut.
châtaignier [ʃatɛɲe] nm chestnut tree.
châtain [ʃatɛ̃] a chestnut-brown, auburn.
château [ʃato] nm castle, country-residence, manor, palace; —x en Espagne castles in the air; — d'eau water tower.
châteaubriand [ʃatobriɑ̃] nm grilled steak.
chat-huant [ʃaɥɑ̃] nm tawny, brown owl.
châtier [ʃatje] vt to punish, chastise, (style) polish.
châtiment [ʃatimɑ̃] nm punishment, chastisement.
chatoiement [ʃatwamɑ̃] nm shimmer, sheen.
chaton [ʃatɔ̃] nm kitten, catkin, stone in its setting.
chatouiller [ʃatuje] vt to tickle.
chatouilleux, -euse [ʃatujø, øːz] a ticklish, touchy, sensitive, delicate.

chatoyer [ʃatwaje] vi to shimmer, sparkle.
châtrer [ʃatre] vt to castrate, geld.
chatterton [ʃatɛrtɔ̃] nm insulating tape.
chaud [ʃo] a warm, hot; pleurer à —es larmes to weep bitterly; il fait — it is warm; tenir au — to keep in a warm place; avoir — to be warm.
chaudière [ʃodjɛːr] nf boiler.
chaudron [ʃodrɔ̃] nm caldron.
chaudronnerie [ʃodrɔnri] nf coppersmith's work; boiler-making, boiler-works.
chaudronnier [ʃodrɔnje] nm coppersmith, brazier, boiler-smith, boiler-maker.
chauffage [ʃofaːʒ] nm heating, firing, stoking; — central central heating.
chauffard [ʃofaːr] nm roadhog.
chauffe [ʃoːf] nf heating, stoking, firing.
chauffer [ʃofe] vt to warm, heat, stoke up, fire up, nurse, cram; vi to get hot, warm (up), get up steam.
chauffeur, -euse [ʃofœːr, øːz] n stoker, fireman, driver.
chaume [ʃoːm] nm thatch, stubble (-field).
chaumière [ʃomjɛːr] nf (thatched) cottage.
chaussée [ʃose] nf causeway, roadway, carriageway.
chausse-pied [ʃospje] nm shoehorn.
chausser [ʃose] vt to put on (shoes, stockings), make footwear for, supply with footwear; vr to put on one's shoes, stockings.
chausse-trape [ʃostrap] nf trap, ruse.
chaussette [ʃoset] nf sock.
chausson [ʃosɔ̃] nm slipper, dancing sandal, gymnasium shoe, bootee, bed-sock, footlet; — aux pommes apple turnover.
chaussure [ʃosyːr] nf footwear, boot, shoe.
chauve [ʃoːv] a bald.
chauve-souris [ʃovsuri] nf bat.
chauvin [ʃovɛ̃] a(n) chauvinist(ic).
chaux [ʃo] nf lime; — vive quicklime; blanchir à la — to whitewash.
chavirer [ʃavire] vi to capsize; vt to upset, tip (up).
chéchia [ʃeʃja] nf fez.
chef [ʃef] nm head, chief, leader, principal, foreman, master, authority, right; — de cuisine head cook, chef; — d'orchestre conductor; — de train guard.
chef-d'œuvre [ʃedœːvr] nm masterpiece.
chef-lieu [ʃefljø] nm county seat.
chelem [ʃlɛm] nm (cards) slam.
chemin [ʃmɛ̃] nm way, road, track, path, headway; — de fer railroad; — des écoliers roundabout road; — faisant on the way; se mettre en — to set out; — de traverse

crossroad; **ne pas y aller par quatre —s** to go straight to the point.
chemineau [ʃmino] *nm* tramp.
cheminée [ʃmine] *nf* fireplace, mantelpiece, chimney, funnel.
cheminer [ʃmine] *vi* to tramp, proceed, walk, trudge.
chemise [ʃmiz] *nf* shirt, chemise, jacket, folder, casing, dust jacket; **— de nuit** nightshirt (man), nightdress, nightgown (woman); **en bras de —** in one's shirt sleeves.
chenal [ʃ(ə)nal] *nm* channel.
chenapan [ʃnapã] *nm* rogue, rascal.
chêne [ʃɛn] *nm* oak (tree).
chenet [ʃ(ə)nɛ] *nm* fire-dog, andiron.
chenil [ʃ(ə)ni] *nm* kennel.
chenille [ʃ(ə)niːj] *nf* caterpillar, chenille, caterpillar tracks.
cheptel [ʃɔtɛl, ʃɛptɛl] *nm* livestock.
chèque [ʃɛk] *nm* check.
chéquier [ʃekje] *nm* checkbook.
cher, -ère [ʃɛːr] *a* dear, beloved, expensive, costly, precious; *ad* dearly, at a high price; **cela ne vaut pas —** it is not worth much.
chercher [ʃɛrʃe] *vt* to look (for, up), seek, search for, endeavor, try (to); **envoyer —** to send for.
chère [ʃɛːr] *nf* countenance, food.
chéri [ʃeri] *a* dear, beloved; *n* darling.
chérir [ʃeriːr] *vt* to love dearly, cherish.
cherté [ʃerte] *nf* dearness, high price.
chérubin [ʃerybɛ̃] *nm* cherub.
chétif, -ive [ʃetif, iːv] *a* puny, weak, sickly, poor.
cheval [ʃəval, ʃfal] *nm* horse, horsepower; **à bascule** rocking-horse; **— de bois** wooden horse; *pl* merry-go-round, roundabout; **— de trait** draft horse; **à —** on horseback; **être à — sur** to be astride, straddle, be a stickler for; **remède de —** drastic remedy.
chevaleresque [ʃ(ə)valrɛsk, ʃfal-] *a* chivalrous, knightly.
chevalerie [ʃ(ə)valri, ʃfal-] *nf* chivalry, knighthood.
chevalet [ʃ(ə)valɛ, ʃfalɛ] *nm* support, trestle, stand, easel, clothes-horse.
chevalier [ʃ(ə)valje, ʃfal-] *nm* knight; **— d'industrie** swindler, adventurer.
chevalière [ʃ(ə)valjɛːr, ʃfal-] *nf* signet-, seal-ring.
chevalin [ʃəvalɛ̃, ʃfalɛ̃] *a* equine; **boucherie —e** horse-meat butcher's shop.
cheval-vapeur [ʃəvalvapœːr] *nm* horsepower.
chevaucher [ʃ(ə)voʃe] *vti* to ride; *vt* to span, overlap.
chevelu [ʃəvly] *a* hairy.
chevelure [ʃəvlyːr] *nf* (head) of hair, locks.
chevet [ʃ(ə)vɛ] *nm* headboard, bedside, bolster.
cheveu [ʃ(ə)vø] *nm* hair; **couper un — en quatre** to split hairs; **argu-**

ment tiré par les **—x** a far-fetched argument.
cheville [ʃ(ə)viːj] *nf* pin, peg, bolt, expletive, padding, ankle; **— ouvrière** king-pin.
chèvre [ʃɛːvr] *nf* goat.
chevreau [ʃavro] *nm* kid.
chèvrefeuille [ʃɛvrəfœːj] *nm* honeysuckle.
chevreuil [ʃəvrœːj] *nm* roe-deer, roebuck.
chevron [ʃəvrɔ̃] *nm* rafter, chevron, stripe.
chevrotant [ʃəvrɔtã] *a* quavering.
chez [ʃe] *prep* at, in the house of, care of, with, among, in; **— lui** at his home; **— mon frère** at my brother's.
chic [ʃik] *a* stylish, smart, posh, swell, decent.
chicane [ʃikan] *nf* quibbling, wrangling, pettifoggery.
chicaner [ʃikane] *vt* to wrangle with; *vi* to quibble, haggle over, cavil (at **sur**).
chiche [ʃiʃ] *a* scanty, poor, stingy, sparing of; *excl* go on!, I dare you!; **pois —** chick pea.
chichis [ʃiʃi] *nm pl* affected manners, airs.
chicorée [ʃikɔre] *nf* chicory; **— (frisée)** endive.
chien, chienne [ʃjɛ̃, ʃjɛn] *n* dog, bitch; *nm* (*of gun*) hammer; **faire le — couchant** to cringe, toady; **un temps de —** filthy weather; **entre — et loup** at dusk, in the gloaming; **— loup** Alsatian dog, police dog.
chiffon [ʃifɔ̃] *nm* rag, duster, piece of lace, ribbon, material, scrap, chiffon; **parler —** to talk dress.
chiffonner [ʃifɔne] *vt* to crumple, rumple, annoy.
chiffonnier, -ière [ʃifɔnje, jɛːr] *n* ragman, rag-picker; *nm* small chest of drawers.
chiffre [ʃifr] *nm* figure, number, cipher, account, monogram; **— d'affaires** turnover.
chiffrer [ʃifre] *vt* to number, work out, cipher, mark; *vi* to calculate, reckon.
chignole [ʃiɲɔl] *nf* (hand-)drill.
chimère [ʃimɛːr] *nf* chimera, illusion.
chimérique [ʃimerik] *a* fanciful unpractical.
chimie [ʃimi] *nf* chemistry.
chimique [ʃimik] *a* chemical.
chimiste [ʃimist] *nm* chemist (scientist).
Chine [ʃin] *nf* China.
chinois [ʃinwa] *an* Chinese.
chinoiserie [ʃinwazri] *nf* Chinese curio; *pl* red tape, irksome complications.
chiper [ʃipe] *vt* to pinch, pilfer, sneak, scrounge, bag.
chipie [ʃipi] *nf* shrew, ill-natured woman.

chique [ʃik] *nf* quid (tobacco), roundworm.

chiqué [ʃike] *nm* sham, pretense, make-believe.

chiquenaude [ʃiknoːd] *nf* fillip, flick (of fingers).

chiquer [ʃike] *vt* to chew tobacco.

chiromancie [kiromãsi] *nf* palmistry.

chiromancien, -ienne [kiromãsjɛ̃, jɛn] *n* palmist.

chirurgical [ʃiryrʒikal] *a* surgical.

chirurgie [ʃiryrʒi] *nf* surgery; — **esthétique du visage** face-lifting.

chirurgien, -ienne [ʃiryrʒjɛ̃, jɛn] *n* surgeon.

chloroforme [klɔrɔfɔrm] *nm* chloroform.

choc [ʃɔk] *nm* shock, clash, impact, knock.

chocolat [ʃɔkɔla] *nm* chocolate.

chœur [kœːr] *nm* chorus, choir, chancel.

choisi [ʃwazi] *a* choice, select, picked.

choisir [ʃwaziːr] *vt* to choose, select, pick.

choix [ʃwa] *nm* choice, choosing, selection, pick; **de —** choice, best, first-class; **au —** all at the same price.

choléra [kɔlera] *nm* cholera.

chômage [ʃomaːʒ] *nm* unemployment, idleness, closing down.

chômer [ʃome] *vi* to stop work, close, shut down, be idle, be unemployed.

chômeur [ʃomœːr] *nm* unemployed person.

chope [ʃɔp] *nf* tankard.

chopine [ʃɔpin] *nf* pint mug.

choquer [ʃɔke] *vt* to shock, offend, strike, bump, clink; *vr* to come into collision, be shocked.

chose [ʃoːz] *nf* thing, case, matter; **bien des —s de ma part à** remember me to; **monsieur —** Mr. Thingummy, Mr. What's-his-name; **être tout —** to feel queer, look queer.

chou [ʃu] *nm* cabbage, rosette, cream-cake; **— de Bruxelles** Brussels sprouts; **feuille de —** rag (newspaper); **mon —** my darling, pet.

choucas [ʃuka] *nm* jackdaw.

choucroute [ʃukrut] *nf* sauerkraut.

chouette [ʃwɛt] *nf* owl; *a* great, posh, swell.

chou-fleur [ʃuflœːr] *nm* cauliflower.

choyer [ʃwaje] *vt* to pet, pamper, cherish.

chrétien, -ienne [kretjɛ̃, jɛn] *an* Christian.

chrétienté [kretjɛ̃te] *nf* Christendom.

Christ [krist] *nm* **le —** Christ.

christianisme [kristjanism] *nm* Christianity.

chromatique [krɔmatik] *a* chromatic.

chrome [kroːm] *nm* chromium, chrome.

chromo [krɔmo] *nm* color-print.

chronique [krɔnik] *a* chronic; *nf* chronicle, news, notes, reports.

chroniqueur [krɔnikœːr] *nm* chronicler, reporter.

chronologie [krɔnɔlɔʒi] *nf* chronology.

chronologique [krɔnɔlɔʒik] *a* chronological.

chronomètre [krɔnɔmɛtr] *nm* chronometer.

chronométrer [krɔnɔmetre] *vt* to time.

chronométreur [krɔnɔmetrœːr] *nm* time-keeper.

chrysalide [krizalid] *nf* chrysalis.

chrysanthème [krizɑ̃tɛ(ː)m] *nm* chrysanthemum.

chuchotement [ʃyʃɔtmɑ̃] *nm* whispering.

chuchoter [ʃyʃɔte] *vti* to whisper.

chuchoterie [ʃyʃɔtri] *nf* whispered conversation.

chut [ʃyt, ʃt] *excl* hush!

chute [ʃyt] *nf* fall, drop, downfall, collapse, chute; **la — des reins** small of the back.

Chypre [ʃipr] *nm* Cyprus.

ci [si] *ad* **par-ci, par-là** here and there; **de-ci de-là** on all sides; *dem pn neuter* **comme ci, comme ça** so-so.

ci-après [siaprɛ] *ad* hereafter, farther on, below.

cible [sibl] *nf* target.

ciboire [sibwaːr] *nm* ciborium, pyx.

ciboulette [sibulɛt] *nf* chives.

cicatrice [sikatris] *nf* scar.

ci-contre [sikɔ̃tr] *ad* opposite, annexed, on the other side, per contra.

ci-dessous [sidsu] *ad* undermentioned, below.

ci-dessus [sidsy] *ad* above (mentioned).

ci-devant [sidvɑ̃] *ad* previously, formerly, late.

cidre [si(ː)dr] *nm* cider.

ciel [sjɛl] *pl* **cieux** [sjø] *nm* sky, heaven, air, climate, canopy.

cierge [sjɛrʒ] *nm* wax candle, taper.

cigale [sigal] *nf* cicada.

cigare [sigaːr] *nm* cigar.

cigarette [sigarɛt] *nf* cigarette.

ci-gît [siʒi] here lies.

cigogne [sigɔɲ] *nf* stork.

ci-inclus [siɛ̃kly] *a* herewith, enclosed.

ci-joint [siʒwɛ̃] *a* herewith, attached, subjoined.

cil [sil] *nm* eyelash.

cime [sim] *nf* summit, top.

ciment [simɑ̃] *nm* cement; **— armé** reinforced concrete.

cimenter [simɑ̃te] *vt* to cement, consolidate.

cimetière [simtjɛːr] *nm* cemetery, graveyard.

cinéaste [sineast] *nm* film technician, producer.

cinéma [sinɛma] nm cinema, movie theater.

cinématographier [sinɛmatɔgrafje] vt to cinematograph, film.

cinématographique [sinɛmatɔgrafik] a cinematographic, film.

cinéprojecteur [sineprɔʒɛktœːr] nm movie projector.

cinglant [sɛ̃glɑ̃] a biting, cutting, scathing.

cingler [sɛ̃gle] vt to lash, cut with a lash, whip, sting; vi to sail, scud along.

cinq [sɛ̃(ː)k] num a five; moins — a near thing.

cinquantaine [sɛ̃kɑ̃tɛn] nf (about) fifty.

cinquante [sɛ̃kɑ̃ːt] num a fifty.

cinquantenaire [sɛ̃kɑ̃tnɛːr] nm fiftieth anniversary, jubilee; n a man, woman of fifty.

cinquantième [sɛ̃kɑ̃tjɛm] num an fiftieth.

cintre [sɛ̃ːtr] nm curve, bend, arch.

cintrer [sɛ̃tre] vt to curve, arch, take in at the waist.

cirage [siraːʒ] nm polishing, wax (ing), polish.

circoncire [sirkɔ̃sir] vt to circumcise.

circonférence [sirkɔ̃ferɑ̃ːs] nf circumference, perimeter, girth.

circonflexe [sirkɔ̃flɛks] a circumflex.

circonscription [sirkɔ̃skripsjɔ̃] nf circumscription, division, constituency.

circonscrire [sirkɔ̃skriːr] vt to circumscribe, encircle, limit.

circonspect [sirkɔ̃spɛ, -spɛk, -spɛkt] a circumspect, cautious.

circonspection [sirkɔ̃spɛksjɔ̃] n circumspection, prudence, caution.

circonstance [sirkɔ̃stɑ̃ːs] n circumstance, occasion, event.

circuit [sirkɥi] nm circuit, round; établir le — to switch on; couper le — to switch off, cut out.

circulaire [sirkylɛːr] anf circular.

circulation [sirkylasjɔ̃] nf circulation, traffic; — interdite no thoroughfare.

circuler [sirkyle] vi to circulate, move (on, about).

cire [siːr] nf wax.

ciré [sire] a waxed, polished; toile —e oilcloth; nm oilskins.

cirer [sire] vt to wax, polish.

cireur, -euse [sirœːr, øːz] n polisher, bootblack.

cirque [sirk] nm circus.

cisaille(s) [sizaːj] nf shears, clippers.

ciseau [sizo] nm chisel; pl scissors, shears.

ciseler [sizle] vt to chisel, carve, chase, cut.

citadelle [sitadɛl] nf citadel, stronghold.

citadin [sitadɛ̃] nm townsman.

citation [sitasjɔ̃] nf quotation, summons, (in dispatches) mention.

cité [site] nf town, (old) city,

housing scheme, students' hostel(s).

citer [site] vt to quote, cite, summon, mention.

citerne [sitɛrn] nf cistern, tank.

citoyen, -enne [sitwajɛ̃, jɛn] n citizen.

citron [sitrɔ̃] nm lemon, lime; a inv lemon-colored; — pressé lemonade.

citronnade [sitrɔnad] nf lemonade, lime-juice cordial.

citronnier [sitrɔnje] nm lemon tree, lime-tree.

citrouille [sitruːj] nf pumpkin.

civil [sivil] a civil, civic, lay, civilian, polite; en — in mufti, in plain clothes.

civilisation [sivilisasjɔ̃] nf civilization, culture.

civiliser [sivilize] vt to civilize.

civilité [sivilite] nf civility, courtesy; pl regards.

clabauder [klabode] vi to babble, chatter; — contre to run down.

claie [klɛ] nf wattle, hurdle, screen, fence.

clair [klɛːr] a clear, obvious, plain, bright, light, pale; ad clearly, plainly; nm light, clearing; tirer au — to clear up.

claire-voie [klɛrvwa] nf lattice, openwork, grating.

clairière [klɛrjɛːr] nf clearing, glade.

clairon [klɛrɔ̃] nm bugle, bugler.

clairsemé [klɛrsəme] a scattered, thin.

clairvoyance [klɛrvwajɑ̃ːs] nf perspicacity.

clairvoyant [klɛrvwajɑ̃] a perspicacious, shrewd; n clairvoyant.

clameur [klamœːr] nf outcry, clamor, howl.

clandestin [klɑ̃dɛstɛ̃] a clandestine, secret, surreptitious, underground.

clapier [klapje] nm rabbit-hutch.

claque [klak] nf smack, slap, hired applauders; nm opera hat.

claqué [klake] a dog-tired.

claquer [klake] vi to clap, bang, clatter, slap, snap, die; vt to smack.

claquettes [klakɛt] nf pl tap-dance.

clarifier [klarifje] vt to clarify.

clarinette [klarinɛt] nf clarinet.

clarté [klarte] nf clearness, brightness, light, perspicacity.

classe [klɑːs] nf class, order, form, standard, classroom, contingent, school.

classement [klɑsmɑ̃] nm classification, grading, filing.

classer [klɑse] vt to class, classify, sort out, grade, file.

classeur [klɑsœːr] nm file, filing-cabinet, sorter.

classification [klasifikasjɔ̃] nf classification.

classifier [klasifje] vt to classify.

classique [klasik] a classic, classical, standard; nm pl classics, classicists.

clavicule [klavikyl] nf collarbone.

clavier [klavje] *nm* keyboard.

clé, clef [kle] *nf* key, clue, clef;
— **anglaise** monkey wrench; — **de
voûte** keystone; **sous** — under lock
and key.

clémence [klemɑ̃:s] *nf* clemency,
mercy, mildness.

clément [klemɑ̃] *a* clement, merciful,
lenient, mild.

clerc [kle:r] *nm* clerk, cleric, scholar,
learned man.

clergé [klɛrʒe] *nm* clergy.

clérical [klerikal] *a* clerical.

cliché [klife] *nm* stereotype, block,
negative, hackneyed expression, tag.

client [kliɑ̃] *n* client, customer,
patient.

clientèle [kliɑ̃tɛl] *nf* clientele,
practice, custom, customers, public,
connection.

clignement [kliɲmɑ̃] *nm* blink(ing),
wink(ing).

cligner [kliɲe] *vti* to blink, wink,
flicker the eyelids.

clignoter [kliɲɔte] *vi* to blink,
twinkle, twitch, flicker.

climat [klima, -ma] *nm* climate.

climatique [klimatik] *a* climatic.

climatisé [klimatize] *a* air-con-
ditioned.

clin d'œil [klɛ̃dœ:j] *nm* wink,
twinkling of an eye.

clinique [klinik] *a* clinical; *nf*
nursing home, clinic.

clinquant [klɛ̃kɑ̃] *nm* foil, tinsel,
tawdriness.

clique [klik] *nf* gang, set, clique,
bugle-band.

cliqueter [klikte] *vi* to rattle, click,
clink, (*of car*) knock.

cliquetis [klikti] *nm* rattling, click,
clink(ing), jingle.

cloaque [klɔak] *nf* cesspool.

clochard [klɔʃa:r] *nm* tramp; hobo.

cloche [klɔʃ] *nf* bell, blister.

cloche-pied [klɔʃpje] *ad* **à** — on one
foot.

clocher [klɔʃe] *nm* belfry, steeple;
vi to limp, go wrong.

cloison [klwazɔ̃] *nf* partition, bulkhead.

cloître [klwa:tr] *nm* cloister(s),
monastery, convent.

clopin-clopant [klɔpɛ̃klɔpɑ̃] *ad*
hobbling about, limping along.

cloque [klɔk] *nf* lump, blister.

clos [klo] *a* closed, shut up; **maison
—e** brothel; *nm* enclosure.

clôture [kloty:r] *nf* enclosure, fence,
closing, closure, end.

clou [klu] *nm* nail, staple, (*pedestrian
crossing*) stud, boil, star turn.

clouer [klue] *vt* to nail (up, down),
pin, tie to, root to.

clouté [klute] *a* studded; **passage —**
pedestrian crossing.

coaguler [koagyle] *vt* to coagulate,
congeal, curdle.

coasser [koase] *vi* to croak.

coassement [koasmɑ̃] *nm* croaking.

cobaye [kɔba:j] *nm* guinea-pig.

cobra [kɔbra] *nm* cobra.

cocaïne [kɔkain] *nf* cocaine.

cocaïnomane [kɔkainɔman] *n* cocaïne addict.

cocarde [kɔkard] *nf* cockade, rosette.

cocasse [kɔkas] *a* comical.

coccinelle [kɔksinɛl] *nf* ladybird.

coche [kɔʃ] *nf* notch, nick; *nm*
stage-coach.

cocher [kɔʃe] *nm* coachman, cabman, driver.

cochon, -onne [kɔʃɔ̃, ɔn] *a* beastly,
obscene, swinish; *nm* pig; —
d'Inde guinea-pig.

cochonnerie [kɔʃɔnri] *nf* beastliness,
rubbish, trash, obscenity, dirty
trick.

coco [kɔko] *nm* **noix de —** coconut.

cocoteraie [kɔkɔtrɛ] *nf* coconut
plantation.

cocotier [kɔkɔtje] *nm* coconut tree.

cocotte [kɔkɔt] *nf* darling, pet,
woman of easy virtue. stew-pan.

code [kɔd] *nm* code, law, statute-
book; **mettre en —** to dim, dip
motor lights.

codicille [kɔdisil] *nm* codicil.

coefficient [koefisjɑ̃] *nm* coefficient.

coercition [koɛrsisjɔ̃] *nf* coercion.

cœur [kœ:r] *nm* heart, soul, mind,
courage, core, depth, height, hearts;
avoir mal au — to feel sick; **avoir
le — gros** to be sad at heart; **de
bon — heartily**, ungrudgingly; **de
mauvais — reluctantly.

coffre [kɔfr] *nm* box, chest, bin,
trunk.

coffre-fort [kɔfrfɔ:r] *nm* safe.

cognac [kɔɲak] *nm* brandy.

cognée [kɔɲe] *nf* ax, hatchet.

cogner [kɔɲe] *vt* to drive in, hit;
vti to knock, hit, bump.

cohérent [kɔerɑ̃] *a* coherent.

cohésion [kɔezjɔ̃] *nf* cohesion

cohue [kɔy] *nf* crowd, mob, crush.

coiffe [kwaf] *nf* head-dress, cap,
lining.

coiffer [kwafe] *vt* to cap, cover, put
on hat, dress the hair; *vr* to put on
one's hat, do one's hair, take a fancy
(to de); **du combien coiffez-vous?**
what is your size in hats?

coiffeur, -euse [kwafœ:r, ø:z] *n*
hairdresser; *nf* dressing-table.

coiffure [kwafy:r] *nf* head-dress, style
of hairdressing.

coin [kwɛ̃] *nm* corner, spot, plot,
patch, wedge, hallmark.

coincer [kwɛ̃se] *vt* to wedge (up);
vr to jam, stick.

coïncidence [kɔɛ̃sidɑ̃:s] *nf* coincidence.

coïncider [kɔɛ̃side] *vi* to coincide.

coing [kwɛ̃] *nm* quince.

col [kɔl] *nm* collar, neck, mountain
pass; **faux — detachable collar,
(*beer*) froth.

coléoptère [kɔleɔptɛ:r] *nm* beetle.

colère [kɔlɛːr] *a* angry, irascible; *nf* anger, rage, temper.

colérique [kɔlerik] *a* quick-tempered, choleric, fiery.

colifichet [kɔlifiʃɛ] *nm* trinket, knick-knack.

colimaçon [kɔlimasɔ̃] *nm* snail; **en — spiral.**

colin-maillard [kɔlɛ̃majaːr] *nm* blindman's buff.

colique [kɔlik] *a* colic; *nf* colic, gripes.

colis [kɔli] *nm* parcel, package, packet, piece of luggage; **par — postal** by parcel post.

collaborateur, -trice [kɔlabɔratœːr, tris] *n* collaborator, contributor.

collaboration [kɔlabɔrasjɔ̃] *nf* collaboration.

collaborer [kɔlabɔre] *vi* to collaborate, contribute (to à).

collant [kɔlɑ̃] *a* sticky, clinging, close-fitting; *nm* tights.

collatéral [kɔlateral] *a* collateral, side.

collation [kɔl(l)asjɔ̃] *nf* collation, conferment, snack.

collationner [kɔl(l)asjɔne] *vt* to collate, read over, repeat; *vi* to have a snack.

colle [kɔl] *nf* paste, glue, size, oral test, poser.

collecte [kɔlɛkt] *nf* collection, collect.

collecteur, -trice [kɔlɛktœːr, tris] *n* collector.

collectif, -ive [kɔlɛktif, iːv] *a* collective, joint.

collection [kɔlɛksiɔ̃] *nf* collecting, collection, file.

collectionner [kɔlɛksjɔne] *vt* to collect.

collectionneur, -euse [kɔlɛksjɔnœːr, øːz] *n* collector.

collectivité [kɔlɛktivite] *nf* collectivity.

collège [kɔlɛːʒ] *nm* college, secondary school, electoral body.

collégien, ienne [kɔleʒjɛ̃, jɛn] *n* schoolboy, -girl.

collègue [kɔlɛg] *n* colleague.

coller [kɔle] *vt* to paste, stick, glue, fail, stump; *vi* to adhere, fail, stump; *vi* to adhere, cling, stick (to); *vr* to stick, cling close (to).

collet [kɔlɛ] *nm* collar, scruff of the neck, snare; **— monté** strait-laced, prim.

colleter [kɔlte] *vt* to collar, grapple with.

collier [kɔlje] *nm* necklace, necklet, collar, band; **un coup de — tug,** great effort.

colline [kɔlin] *nf* hill.

collision [kɔllizjɔ̃] *nf* collision, clash.

colloque [kɔlɔk] *nf* colloquy, conversation.

colombe [kɔlɔ̃ːb] *nf* dove.

colombier [kɔlɔ̃bje] *nm* dovecote, pigeon-house.

colon [kɔlɔ̃] *nm* colonist, settler.

colonel [kɔlɔnɛl] *nm* colonel.

colonial [kɔlɔnjal] *a nm* colonial.

colonie [kɔlɔni] *nf* colony, settlement; **— de vacances** holiday camp.

colonisation [kɔlɔnizasjɔ̃] *nf* colonization.

coloniser [kɔlɔnize] *vt* to colonize, settle.

colonne [kɔlɔn] *nf* column, pillar; **— vertébrale** spine.

colorer [kɔlɔre] *vt* to color, stain, tint; *vr* to take on a color, grow ruddy.

coloris [kɔlɔri] *nm* color(ing), hue.

colossal [kɔlɔsal] *a* colossal, huge, gigantic.

colporter [kɔlpɔrte] *vt* to hawk, peddle.

colporteur, -euse [kɔlpɔrtœːr, øːz] *n* peddler.

combat [kɔ̃ba] *nm* combat, fight, battle, action, conflict, struggle, match.

combatif, -ive [kɔ̃batif, iːv] *a* combative, pugnacious.

combattant [kɔ̃batɑ̃] *nm* combatant, fighting-man; **anciens —s** ex-servicemen.

combattre [kɔ̃batr] *vt* to combat, fight, battle with; *vi* to strive, struggle, fight.

combien [kɔ̃bjɛ̃] *ad* how much, how many, how far; **le — sommes-nous?** what day of the month is this?

combinaison [kɔ̃binɛzɔ̃] *nf* arrangement, combine, plan, underslip, overalls, flying suit.

combine [kɔ̃bin] *nf* scheme, racket.

combiner [kɔ̃bine] *vt* to combine, arrange, contrive.

comble [kɔ̃ːbl] *nm* heap, summit, top, acme, roof(ing); **pour — de malheur** as a crowning misfortune; **ça, c'est le —** that's the limit; *a* heaped up, crowded; **faire salle —** to play to a full house.

combler [kɔ̃ble] *vt* to fill (up, in), make good, crowd, fill to overflowing, gratify.

combustible [kɔ̃bystibl] *a* combustible; *nm* fuel.

combustion [kɔ̃bystjɔ̃] *nf* combustion.

comédie [kɔmedi] *nf* comedy, play, drama; **jouer la —** to act a part.

comédien, -ienne [kɔmedjɛ̃, jɛn] *n* actor, actress.

comestible [kɔmɛstibl] *a* edible, eatable; *nm pl* food, provisions.

comète [kɔmɛt] *nf* comet.

comique [kɔmik] *a* comic, funny; *nm* comedy, comedian, humorist, joke.

comité [kɔmite] *nm* committee, board.

commandant [kɔmɑ̃dɑ̃] *nm* commanding officer, major (army), squadron leader.

commande [kɔmɑ̃ːd] *nf* order,

control, lever, driving-gear; **de —** essential, forced, feigned; **sur —** made to order, bespoke.

commandement [kɔmɑ̃dmɑ̃] nm command, order, commandment.

commander [kɔmɑ̃de] vt to order, govern, be in command of, compel, control.

commanditaire [kɔmɑ̃dite:r] nm **(associé)** — silent partner (in business).

comme [kɔm] ad as, like, such as, in the way of, how; **c'est tout —** it amounts to the same thing; cj as, since.

commémorer [kɔmmemɔre] vt to commemorate.

commençant [kɔmɑ̃sɑ̃] nm beginner, learner; a budding, beginning, early.

commencement [kɔmɑ̃smɑ̃] nm beginning.

commencer [kɔmɑ̃se] vti to commence, begin, start.

comment [kɔmɑ̃] ad how? what? excl why! what!

commentaire [kɔmɑ̃tɛ:r] nm commentary, comment.

commentateur, -trice [kɔmɑ̃tatœ:r, tris] n commentator.

commenter [kɔmɑ̃te] vti to comment (on), annotate.

commérage [kɔmɛra:ʒ] nm gossip, tittle-tattle.

commerçant [kɔmɛrsɑ̃] nm merchant, tradesman; a commercial, mercantile.

commerce [kɔmɛrs] nm commerce, trade, business, intercourse, dealings.

commercial [kɔmɛrsjal] a commercial, trading.

commettre [kɔmɛtr] vt to commit, perpetrate, entrust.

commis [kɔmi] nm clerk, book-keeper, shop-assistant; **— voyageur** traveling salesman.

commissaire [kɔmisɛ:r] nm commissioner, steward, purser, police superintendent, commissar.

commissaire-priseur [kɔmisɛrprizœ:r] nm auctioneer.

commissariat [kɔmisarja] nm commissionership, police station.

commission [kɔmisjɔ̃] nf commission, message, errand, board, committee.

commissionnaire [kɔmisjɔnɛ:r] nm (commission) agent, porter, messenger.

commode [kɔmɔd] a convenient, handy, commodious, easy-going; nf chest of drawers.

commodité [kɔmɔdite] nf convenience, comfort, commodiousness.

commotion [kɔm(m)osjɔ̃] nf commotion, shock, upheaval, concussion.

commun [kɔmœ̃] a common, usual, ordinary, vulgar; **d'un — accord**

with one accord; **peu —** out-of-the-way, uncommon; nm common run, generality, common fund; pl offices, outhouses.

communauté [kɔmynote] nf community, commonwealth, society, religious order.

commune [kɔmyn] nf commune, parish.

communément [kɔmynemɑ̃] ad commonly.

communicatif, -ive [kɔmynikatif, i:v] a communicative, talkative, infectious.

communication [kɔmynikasjɔ̃] nf communication, connection, telephone call, message.

communion [kɔmynjɔ̃] nf communion.

communiqué [kɔmynike] nm communiqué, official statement, bulletin.

communiquer [kɔmynike] vt to communicate, transmit, convey, connect; vr to be communicated.

communisant [kɔmynizɑ̃] n fellow-traveler.

communisme [kɔmynism] nm communism.

communiste [kɔmynist] n communist.

commutateur [kɔmytatœ:r] nm commutator, switch.

compagne [kɔ̃paɲ] nf companion, partner, wife.

compagnie [kɔ̃paɲi] nf company, party, firm; **de bonne, de mauvaise —** well-, ill-bred.

compagnon [kɔ̃paɲɔ̃] nm companion, fellow, mate.

comparable [kɔ̃parabl] a comparable.

comparaison [kɔ̃parɛzɔ̃] nf comparison, simile.

comparatif, -ive [kɔ̃paratif, i:v] a nm comparative.

comparé [kɔ̃pare] a comparative.

comparer [kɔ̃pare] vt to compare.

compartiment [kɔ̃partimɑ̃] nm compartment.

compas [kɔ̃pɑ] nm compass(es), scale, standard.

compassé [kɔ̃pɑse] a stiff, formal, set, prim.

compassion [kɔ̃pasjɔ̃] nf compassion, pity.

compatible [kɔ̃patibl] a compatible.

compatir [kɔ̃pati:r] vi to sympathize (with à), feel (for).

compatissant [kɔ̃patisɑ̃] a compassionate.

compatriote [kɔ̃patriɔt] nm compatriot.

compensation [kɔ̃pɑ̃sasjɔ̃] nf compensation, offset, balancing, adjustment.

compensé [kɔ̃pɑ̃se] a **semelles —es** wedge heels.

compenser [kɔ̃pɑ̃se] vt to compensate, make good, set off, balance, adjust.

compétence [kɔ̃petɑ̃:s] nf jurisdic-

tion; competence, proficiency, skill.
complaisance [kɔ̃plezɑ̃:s] *nf* complaisance, obligingness, kindness, complacency, accommodation.
complaisant [kɔ̃plezɑ̃] *a* complaisant, obliging, kind, complacent.
complémentaire [kɔ̃plemɑ̃te:r] *a* complementary, fuller.
complet, -ète [kɔ̃ple, ɛt] *a* complete, total, entire, full; *nm* suit of clothes; au — complete, at full strength.
compléter [kɔ̃plete] *vt* to complete, finish off.
complexe [kɔ̃pleks] *a* complex, complicated, compound; *nm* complex.
complexion [kɔ̃pleksjɔ̃] *nf* constitution, temperament.
complexité [kɔ̃pleksite] *nf* complexity.
complication [kɔ̃plikasjɔ̃] *nf* complication, intricacy.
complice [kɔ̃plis] *a nm* accessory, accomplice.
complicité [kɔ̃plisite] *nf* complicity, aiding and abetting.
compliment [kɔ̃plimɑ̃] *nm* compliment; *pl* greetings, regards, congratulations.
complimenter [kɔ̃plimɑ̃te] *vt* to compliment, congratulate.
compliqué [kɔ̃plike] *a* complicated, intricate, difficult.
complot [kɔ̃plo] *nm* plot.
comploter [kɔ̃plɔte] *vt* to plot, scheme.
componction [kɔ̃pɔ̃ksjɔ̃] *nf* compunction.
comporter [kɔ̃pɔrte] *vt* to admit of, require, comprise, involve; *vr* to behave.
composé [kɔ̃poze] *a* composed, impassive, composite; *a nm* compound.
composer [kɔ̃poze] *vt* to compose, form, make up, set, arrange; *vi* to come to terms; *vr* to consist.
compositeur, -trice [kɔ̃pozitœr, tris] *n* composer, compositor.
composition [kɔ̃pozisjɔ̃] *nf* composing, composition, making-up, setting, essay, test, arrangement.
compote [kɔ̃pɔt] *nf* compote, stewed fruit.
compréhensible [kɔ̃preɑ̃sibl] *a* comprehensible.
compréhensif, -ive [kɔ̃preɑ̃sif, i:v] *a* comprehensive, inclusive, understanding.
compréhension [kɔ̃preɑ̃sjɔ̃] *nf* understanding.
comprendre [kɔ̃prɑ̃:dr] *vt* to include, comprise, understand, comprehend.
compression [kɔ̃presjɔ̃] *nf* compression, crushing, repression.
comprimé [kɔ̃prime] *nm* tablet.
comprimer [kɔ̃prime] *vt* to compress, repress, restrain.
compris [kɔ̃pri] *a* y — including; non — exclusive of.

compromettre [kɔ̃prɔmetr] *vt* to compromise, implicate, endanger.
compromis [kɔ̃prɔmi] *nm* compromise.
comptabilité [kɔ̃tabilite] *nf* bookkeeping, accountancy, accounting dept.
comptable [kɔ̃tabl] *a* accounting, book-keeping, accountable, responsible; *nm* accountant, book-keeper; expert — chartered accountant.
comptant [kɔ̃tɑ̃] *a* argent — ready money; *ad* (in) cash; au — cash down.
compte [kɔ̃:t] *nm* account, reckoning, calculation, count; à bon — cheap; tout — fait all things considered; versement à — payment on account; pour mon — for my part; — rendu report, review; se rendre — to realize.
compter [kɔ̃te] *vt* to count, reckon, charge, expect; *vi* rely, reckon, depend, count.
compteur [kɔ̃tœ:r] *nm* (taxi)meter, counting-machine.
comptoir [kɔ̃twa:r] *nm* counter; — d'escompte, discount bank.
compulser [kɔ̃pylse] *vt* to go through, examine.
comte [kɔ̃:t] *nm* count.
comté [kɔ̃te] *nm* county.
comtesse [kɔ̃tes] *nf* countess.
concéder [kɔ̃sede] *vt* to concede, grant, allow.
concentrer [kɔ̃sɑ̃tre] *vt* to concentrate, focus, repress; *vr* to concentrate, center (in, on, around).
concentrique [kɔ̃sɑ̃trik] *a* concentric.
conception [kɔ̃sepsjɔ̃] *nf* conception.
concerner [kɔ̃serne] *vt* to concern, affect.
concert [kɔ̃sɛ:r] *nm* concert, agreement.
concerter [kɔ̃serte] *vt* to concert, plan; *vr* to act in concert.
concession [kɔ̃sesjɔ̃] *nf* concession, grant, compound.
concessionnaire [kɔ̃sesjɔne:r] *nm* concessionary, grantee, licenseholder.
concevable [kɔ̃s(ə)vabl] *a* conceivable.
concevoir [kɔ̃səvwa:r] *vt* to conceive, imagine, understand, word.
concierge [kɔ̃sjɛrʒ] *n* hall porter, doorkeeper, caretaker.
concilier [kɔ̃silje] *vt* to conciliate, reconcile, win over.
concis [kɔ̃si] *a* concise, terse, brief, crisp.
concision [kɔ̃sizjɔ̃] *nf* concision, terseness.
concluant [kɔ̃klyɑ̃] *a* conclusive, decisive.
conclure [kɔ̃kly:r] *vt* to conclude, end, clinch, infer.

conclusion [kɔ̃klyzjɔ̃] nf conclusion, end, settlement, inference, decision.

concombre [kɔ̃kɔ̃:br] nm cucumber.

concorde [kɔ̃kɔrd] nf concord.

concourir [kɔ̃kuri:r] vi to coincide, combine, compete.

concours [kɔ̃ku:r] nm concourse, concurrence, coincidence, cooperation, assistance, competition, contest, show.

concret, -ète [kɔ̃krɛ, -ɛt] a nm concrete.

concurrence [kɔ̃kyrɑ̃:s] nf concurrence, competition.

concurrent [kɔ̃kyrɑ̃] a competitive, rival; nm competitor, rival, candidate.

condamnable [kɔ̃danabl] a blameworthy.

condamnation [kɔ̃danasjɔ̃] nf condemnation, judgment, sentence, censure.

condamné [kɔ̃dane] n convict, condemned person.

condamner [kɔ̃dane] vt to condemn, sentence, convict, censure, block up.

condensateur [kɔ̃dɑ̃satœ:r] nm condenser.

condensation [kɔ̃dɑ̃sasjɔ̃] nf condensation.

condenser [kɔ̃dɑ̃se] vt to condense.

condenseur [kɔ̃dɑ̃sœ:r] nm condenser.

condescendance [kɔ̃desɑ̃dɑ̃:s] nf condescension.

condescendre [kɔ̃desɑ̃:dr] vt to condescend.

condition [kɔ̃disjɔ̃] nf condition, state, position, rank; pl conditions, circumstances, terms; à — on approval; à — que on condition that; être en — to be in domestic service.

conditionnel, -elle [kɔ̃disjɔnɛl, ɛl] a nm conditional.

conditionner [kɔ̃disjɔne] vt to condition.

condoléance [kɔ̃dɔleɑ̃:s] nf condolence; pl sympathy.

conducteur, -trice [kɔ̃dyktœ:r, tris] a conducting, guiding; n leader, guide, driver; nm conductor, main.

conduire [kɔ̃dɥi:r] vt to conduct, lead, guide, conduce (to), drive, convey, manage; vr to behave, conduct oneself.

conduit [kɔ̃dɥi] nm passage, pipe, conduit, duct.

conduite [kɔ̃dɥit] nf behavior, driving, pipe, management, conducting, leading.

cône [ko:n] nm cone.

confection [kɔ̃fɛksjɔ̃] nf confection, putting together, manufacture, making up, ready-made clothes.

confectionner [kɔ̃fɛksjɔne] vt to make up, manufacture.

confectionneur, -euse [kɔ̃fɛksjɔnœ:r, øːz] n ready-made outfitter, clothier.

confédération [kɔ̃federasjɔ̃] nf federation, confederacy.

confédérer [kɔ̃federe] vtr to confederate, unite.

conférence [kɔ̃ferɑ̃:s] nf conference, lecture.

conférencier, -ière [kɔ̃ferɑ̃sje, jɛːr] n lecturer.

conférer [kɔ̃fere] vt to confer, award, bestow, compare; vi to confer (with avec).

confesser [kɔ̃fese] vt to confess, own; vr to confess.

confesseur [kɔ̃fesœ:r] nm confessor.

confession [kɔ̃fesjɔ̃] nf confession, religion, denomination.

confessional [kɔ̃fesjɔnal] nm confessional(-box).

confiance [kɔ̃fjɑ̃:s] nf confidence, trust, reliance; de — on trust, reliable.

confiant [kɔ̃fjɑ̃] a confiding, (self-) confident, assured.

confidence [kɔ̃fidɑ̃:s] nf confidence, secret; en — in confidence, confidentially.

confidentiel, -elle [kɔ̃fidɑ̃sjɛl, ɛl] a confidential.

confier [kɔ̃fje] vt to confide, disclose, entrust, commit; vr to rely (on à), take into one's confidence.

confiner [kɔ̃fine] vt to confine, shut up; vi to be contiguous, border upon.

confins [kɔ̃fɛ̃] nm pl confines, borders.

confirmatif, -ive [kɔ̃firmatif, i:v] a confirmative, corroborative.

confirmation [kɔ̃firmasjɔ̃] nf confirmation, corroboration.

confirmer [kɔ̃firme] vt to confirm, corroborate.

confiscation [kɔ̃fiskasjɔ̃] nf confiscation.

confiserie [kɔ̃fizri] nf confectionery, confectioner's shop.

confiseur, -euse [kɔ̃fizœ:r, øːz] n confectioner.

confisquer [kɔ̃fiske] vt to confiscate.

confit [kɔ̃fi] a preserved, steeped in; un air — sanctimonious air; nm pl confections, comfits, sweets.

confiture [kɔ̃fity:r] nf preserves, jam; — d'orange marmalade.

conflagration [kɔ̃flagrasjɔ̃] nf conflagration, blaze, fire.

conflit [kɔ̃fli] nm conflict, clash, strife; être en — to conflict, clash.

confluent [kɔ̃flyɑ̃] nm confluence, junction, meeting.

confondre [kɔ̃fɔ̃:dr] vt to confound, mingle, blend, mistake, disconcert, put to confusion; vr to blend, intermingle, be identical; se — en excuses to apologize profusely.

confondu [kɔ̃fɔ̃dy] a overwhelmed, disconcerted.

conforme [kɔ̃fɔrm] a conformable, according (to à), in keeping (with à).

conformément [kɔ̃fɔrmemɑ̃] ad

according (to à), in keeping (with à).

conformer [kɔ̃fɔrme] *vt* to form, conform; *vr* to conform (to), comply (with à).

conformité [kɔ̃fɔrmite] *nf* conformity, agreement.

confort [kɔ̃fɔːr] *nm* comfort.

confortable [kɔ̃fɔrtabl] *a* comfortable.

confrère [kɔ̃frɛːr] *nm* colleague, fellow-member, brother.

confrérie [kɔ̃freri] *nf* brotherhood, confraternity.

confrontation [kɔ̃frɔ̃tasjɔ̃] *nf* confrontation, comparison.

confronter [kɔ̃frɔ̃te] *vt* to confront, compare.

confus [kɔ̃fy] *a* confused, jumbled, indistinct, embarrassed, abashed, ashamed.

confusion [kɔ̃fyzjɔ̃] *nf* confusion, welter, mistake, embarrassment.

congé [kɔ̃ʒe] *nm* leave, holiday, furlough, dismissal, discharge, notice to quit.

congédier [kɔ̃ʒedje] *vt* to dismiss, discharge.

congélation [kɔ̃ʒelasjɔ̃] *nf* congelation, freezing.

congeler [kɔ̃ʒle] *vtr* to congeal, freeze (up).

congénital [kɔ̃ʒenital] *a* congenital.

congestion [kɔ̃ʒɛstjɔ̃] *nf* congestion; — cérébrale stroke; — pulmonaire pneumonia.

congestionné [kɔ̃ʒɛstjɔne] *a* congested, apoplectic, red in the face.

congestionner [kɔ̃ʒɛstjɔne] *vt* to congest; *vr* to become congested.

congrégation [kɔ̃gregasjɔ̃] *nf* congregation.

congrès [kɔ̃grɛ] *nm* congress.

conique [kɔnik] *a* conic(al), cone-shaped, tapering.

conjecture [kɔ̃ʒɛktyːr] *nf* conjecture, surmise, guess.

conjecturer [kɔ̃ʒɛktyre] *vt* to conjecture, surmise.

conjoint [kɔ̃ʒwɛ̃] *a* conjoined, united, married; *nm pl* husband and wife.

conjonction [kɔ̃ʒɔ̃ksjɔ̃] *nf* union, conjunction.

conjoncture [kɔ̃ʒɔ̃ktyːr] *nf* conjuncture.

conjugaison [kɔ̃ʒygɛzɔ̃] *nf* conjugation.

conjugal [kɔ̃ʒygal] *a* conjugal, married, wedded.

conjugué [kɔ̃ʒyge] *a* conjugated, interconnected, coupled, twin.

conjuration [kɔ̃ʒyrasjɔ̃] *nf* plot, conspiracy; incantation.

conjuré [kɔ̃ʒyre] *nm* conspirator.

connaissance [kɔnɛsɑ̃ːs] *nf* knowledge, understanding, acquaintance, consciousness, senses; **en pays de —** on familiar ground, among familiar faces; **sans —** unconscious, insensible.

connaisseur, -euse [kɔnɛsœːr, øːz] *n* expert, connoisseur, judge.

connaître [kɔnɛːtr] *vt* to know, be acquainted with, take cognizance of, distinguish, have a thorough knowledge of; *vr* to be a good judge (of en), know all (about en).

connexe [kɔn(n)ɛks] *a* connected, allied, like.

connexion [kɔn(n)ɛksjɔ̃] *nf* connection, connector.

connivence [kɔnivɑ̃ːs] *nf* connivance, collusion.

conquérant [kɔ̃kerɑ̃] *a* conquering, *n* conqueror.

conquérir [kɔ̃keriːr] *vt* to conquer.

conquête [kɔ̃kɛːt] *nf* conquest.

consacré [kɔ̃sakre] *a* consecrated, hallowed, established, time-honoured, accepted, stock.

consacrer [kɔ̃sakre] *vt* to devote, ordain, consecrate.

conscience [kɔ̃sjɑ̃ːs] *nf* conscience, consciousness.

consciencieux, -euse [kɔ̃sjɑ̃sjø, jøːz] *a* conscientious.

conscient [kɔ̃sjɑ̃] *a* conscious, aware, sentient.

conscription [kɔ̃skripsjɔ̃] *nf* conscription, draft.

conscrit [kɔ̃skri] *nm* conscript, draftee.

consécration [kɔ̃sekrasjɔ̃] *nf* consecration, dedication.

consécutif, -ive [kɔ̃sekytif, iːv] *a* consecutive.

conseil [kɔ̃sɛːj] *nm* advice, decision, council, counsel, board, court; — **des ministres** cabinet; — **de guerre** council of war, court martial.

conseiller, -ère [kɔ̃sɛje, ɛːr] *n* adviser, councilor, judge.

conseiller [kɔ̃sɛje] *vt* to advise, counsel.

consentement [kɔ̃sɑ̃tmɑ̃] *nm* consent, assent.

consentir [kɔ̃sɑ̃tiːr] *vi* to consent, agree.

conséquemment [kɔ̃sekamɑ̃] *a* consequently.

conséquence [kɔ̃sekɑ̃ːs] *nf* consequence, outcome, sequel, inference, importance.

conséquent [kɔ̃sekɑ̃] *a* consistent, following, important; **par —** accordingly.

conservateur, -trice [kɔ̃sɛrvatœːr, tris] *a* preserving, conservative; keeper, guardian, curator, conservative.

conservation [kɔ̃sɛrvasjɔ̃] *nf* preservation, keeping, care.

conservatoire [kɔ̃sɛrvatwaːr] *nm* school, academy (of music).

conserve [kɔ̃sɛrv] *nf* preserve, canned food; *pl* dark glasses; — **au vinaigre** pickles; **de —** together.

conserver [kɔ̃sɛrve] *vt* to preserve, keep.

considérable [kɔ̃siderabl] *a* con

siderable, large, eminent, important.
considération [kɔ̃siderasjɔ̃] nf consideration, regard, respect.
considérer [kɔ̃sidere] vt to consider, contemplate, regard, respect, esteem.
consigne [kɔ̃siɲ] nf order(s), duty, countersign, detention, cloakroom, checkroom.
consigner [kɔ̃siɲe] vt to deposit, consign, confine to barracks, keep in, put out of bounds, hold up.
consistance [kɔ̃sistɑ̃:s] nf consistence, consistency, firmness, standing.
consistant [kɔ̃sistɑ̃]- a firm, set, solid.
consister [kɔ̃siste] vi to consist, be composed (of en).
consolateur, -trice [kɔ̃sɔlatœr, tris] a consoling; n consoler, comforter.
consolation [kɔ̃sɔlasjɔ̃] nf consolation, comfort.
console [kɔ̃sɔl] nf bracket, console (table).
consoler [kɔ̃sɔle] vt to console, solace, comfort, cheer.
consolider [kɔ̃sɔlide] vt to consolidate, fund (debt).
consommateur, -trice [kɔ̃sɔmatœːr, tris] n consumer, customer.
consommation [kɔ̃sɔmasjɔ̃] nf consummation, consumption, drink.
consommé [kɔ̃sɔme] a consummate; nm stock, clear soup.
consommer [kɔ̃sɔme] vt to consummate, consume.
consomption [kɔ̃sɔ̃psjɔ̃] nf consuming, consumption.
consonne [kɔ̃sɔn] nf consonant.
conspirateur, -trice [kɔ̃spiratœːr, tris] n conspirer, conspirator, plotter.
conspiration [kɔ̃spirasjɔ̃] nf conspiracy, plot.
conspirer [kɔ̃spire] vti to conspire, plot.
conspuer [kɔ̃spɥe] vt to decry, boo, hoot.
constamment [kɔ̃stamɑ̃] ad constantly.
constance [kɔ̃stɑ̃:s] nf constancy, steadfastness, perseverance, stability.
constant [kɔ̃stɑ̃] a constant, steadfast, firm.
constatation [kɔ̃statasjɔ̃] nf ascertainment, verification, record, statement.
constater [kɔ̃state] vt to establish, ascertain, state, record.
constellation [kɔ̃stɛllasjɔ̃] nf constellation, galaxy.
consternation [kɔ̃stɛrnasjɔ̃] nf consternation, dismay.
consterner [kɔ̃stɛrne] vt to dismay, stagger.
constipation [kɔ̃stipasjɔ̃] nf constipation.
constipé [kɔ̃stipe] a constipated, costive.

constituer [kɔ̃stitɥe] vt to constitute, form, set up, incorporate, settle (on); se — prisonnier to give oneself up.
constitution [kɔ̃stitysjɔ̃] nf constitution, composition, settlement.
constitutionnel, -elle [kɔ̃stitysjɔnel, ɛl] a constitutional.
constructeur [kɔ̃stryktœːr] nm constructor, builder, maker.
construction [kɔ̃stryksjɔ̃] nf construction, making, building, structure.
construire [kɔ̃strɥiːr] vt to construct, build, make.
consul [kɔ̃syl] nm consul.
consulaire [kɔ̃sylɛːr] a consular.
consulat [kɔ̃syla] nm consulate.
consultant [kɔ̃syltɑ̃] a consulting; nm consultant.
consultation [kɔ̃syltasjɔ̃] nf consultation, opinion, advice; cabinet de — consulting-room, doctor's office.
consulter [kɔ̃sylte] vt to consult.
consumer [kɔ̃syme] vt to consume, destroy, wear away, use up; vr to waste away, burn away.
contact [kɔ̃takt] nm contact, touch, connection, switch.
contagieux, -euse [kɔ̃taʒjø, jøːz] a contagious, infectious, catching.
contagion [kɔ̃taʒjɔ̃] nf contagion, contagiousness.
contamination [kɔ̃taminasjɔ̃] n contamination, infection.
contaminer [kɔ̃tamine] vt to contaminate, infect.
conte [kɔ̃ːt] nm story, tale, yarn, short story; — bleu fairy tale; — à dormir debout cock-and-bull story.
contemplation [kɔ̃tɑ̃plasjɔ̃] nf contemplation, meditation, gazing.
contempler [kɔ̃tɑ̃ple] vt to contemplate, meditate upon, gaze at, upon.
contemporain [kɔ̃tɑ̃pɔrɛ̃] n contemporary; a contemporaneous.
contenance [kɔ̃tnɑ̃:s] nf capacity, content, countenance, bearing.
contenir [kɔ̃tniːr] vt to contain, hold, restrain; vr to contain oneself, keep one's temper.
content [kɔ̃tɑ̃] a content, satisfied, pleased, glad; nm manger tout son— to eat one's fill.
contentement [kɔ̃tɑ̃tmɑ̃] nm satisfaction.
contenter [kɔ̃tɑ̃te] vt to content, satisfy, gratify; vr to be satisfied (with de).
contenu [kɔ̃tny] a restrained, reserved; nm contents.
conter [kɔ̃te] vt to tell.
contestable [kɔ̃tɛstabl] a questionable, debatable.
contestation [kɔ̃tɛstasjɔ̃] nf contestation, dispute.
conteste [kɔ̃tɛst] nf sans — unquestionably.
contester [kɔ̃tɛste] vt to contest, dispute, challenge.

conteur, -euse [kɔ̃tœːr, øːz] n narrator, story-teller.

contexte [kɔ̃tɛkst] nm context.

contigu, -uë [kɔ̃tigy] a contiguous, adjoining.

continent [kɔ̃tinɑ̃] a continent, chaste; nm continent, mainland.

contingent [kɔ̃tɛ̃ʒɑ̃] a contingent; nm contingent, quota, share.

continu [kɔ̃tiny] a continuous, sustained.

continuation [kɔ̃tinɥasjɔ̃] nf continuation.

continuel, -elle [kɔ̃tinɥɛl, el] a continual.

continuer [kɔ̃tinɥe] vt to continue, proceed with, go on with; vi to carry on, continue, go on.

continuité [kɔ̃tinɥite] nf continuity.

contour [kɔ̃tuːr] nm outline, contour.

contournement [kɔ̃turnəmɑ̃] nm route de — by-pass.

contourner [kɔ̃turne] vt to shape, get round, by-pass, twist, distort.

contracter [kɔ̃trakte] vt to contract, incur, draw together; vr to shrink, contract.

contraction [kɔ̃traksjɔ̃] nf contraction, shrinking.

contradiction [kɔ̃tradiksjɔ̃] nf contradiction, discrepancy, inconsistency.

contradictoire [kɔ̃tradiktwaːr] a contradictory.

contraindre [kɔ̃trɛ̃ːdr] vt to constrain, compel, force, restrain.

contraint [kɔ̃trɛ̃] a constrained, cramped, forced.

contrainte [kɔ̃trɛ̃ːt] nf constraint, compulsion, restraint.

contraire [kɔ̃trɛːr] a contrary, opposite, opposed, adverse, bad; jusqu'à avis — until further notice; nm contrary, opposite.

contrarier [kɔ̃trarje] vt to thwart, oppose, annoy, vex, provoke, interfere with.

contrariété [kɔ̃trarjete] nf contrariety, annoyance, nuisance.

contraste [kɔ̃trast] nm contrast.

contraster [kɔ̃traste] vti to contrast.

contrat [kɔ̃tra] nm contract, agreement, deed, policy.

contravention [kɔ̃travɑ̃sjɔ̃] nf contravention, breach, infringement, offense; dresser une — à to take the name and address of, prosecute.

contre [kɔ̃ːtr] prep against, contrary to, for, to, versus; ad against, hard by; le pour et le — pros and cons.

contre-amiral [kɔ̃tramiral] nm rear-admiral.

contre-attaque [kɔ̃tratak] nf counter-attack.

contre-avion(s) [kɔ̃travjɔ̃] a anti-aircraft.

contre-avis [kɔ̃travi] nm contrary opinion.

contre-balancer [kɔ̃trəbalɑ̃se] vt to counterbalance, offset.

contrebande [kɔ̃trəbɑ̃ːd] nf contraband, smuggling.

contrebandier [kɔ̃trəbɑ̃dje] nm smuggler.

contrecarrer [kɔ̃trəkare] vt to thwart, cross.

contrecœur [kɔ̃trəkœːr] ad à — reluctantly.

contre-coup [kɔ̃trəku] nm rebound, recoil, reaction, repercussion.

contredire [kɔ̃trədiːr] vt to contradict, gainsay; vr to contradict oneself, be inconsistent.

contredit [kɔ̃trədi] ad sans — unquestionably.

contrée [kɔ̃tre] nf region, district, country.

contre-espionnage [kɔ̃trɛspjɔnaːʒ] nm counter-espionage.

contrefaçon [kɔ̃trəfasɔ̃] nf counterfeit, forgery.

contrefaire [kɔ̃trəfɛːr] vt to imitate, feign, forge.

contrefait [kɔ̃trəfɛ] a disguised, feigned, sham, counterfeit, forged.

contrefort [kɔ̃trəfɔːr] nm buttress, spur.

contre-jour [kɔ̃trəʒuːr] nm unfavorable light; à — against the light, in one's own light.

contremaître, -tresse [kɔ̃trəmɛːtr, tres] n foreman, -woman, overseer.

contremander [kɔ̃trəmɑ̃de] vt to countermand, cancel, call off.

contre-ordre [kɔ̃trɔrdr] nm counter-order, countermand; sauf — unless we hear to the contrary.

contre-partie [kɔ̃trəparti] nf opposite view, other side, counterpart, contra.

contre-pied [kɔ̃trəpje] nm opposite, contrary view.

contrepoids [kɔ̃trəpwa] nm counterweight, counterbalance, counterpoise.

contre-poil [kɔ̃trəpwal] ad à — the wrong way.

contrer [kɔ̃tre] vt to counter; vi to double.

contre-sens [kɔ̃trəsɑ̃ːs] nm misconstruction, mistranslation, wrong way; à — in the wrong direction.

contresigner [kɔ̃trəsiɲe] vt to countersign.

contretemps [kɔ̃trətɑ̃] nm mishap, hitch, inconvenience; à — inopportunely.

contre-torpilleur [kɔ̃trətɔrpijœːr] nm destroyer.

contrevent [kɔ̃trəvɑ̃] nm outside shutter.

contre-voie [kɔ̃trəvwa] ad à — in the wrong direction, on the wrong side.

contribuable [kɔ̃tribɥabl] a tax-paying; nm taxpayer.

contribuer [kɔ̃tribɥe] vi to contribute.

contribution [kɔ̃tribysjɔ̃] nf contribution, share, tax, rate.

contrit [kɔ̃tri] *a* contrite, penitent.

contrition [kɔ̃trisjɔ̃] *nf* contrition, penitence.

contrôle [kɔ̃troːl] *nm* checking, inspection, roll, roster, hallmark, ticket office.

contrôler [kɔ̃trole] *vt* inspect, control, verify.

contrôleur, -euse [kɔ̃trolœːr, øːz] *n* inspector, inspectress, assessor, controller, ticket-collector, time-keeper.

controuvé [kɔ̃truve] *a* fabricated, invented.

controverse [kɔ̃trɔvɛrs] *nf* controversy, dispute.

contumace [kɔ̃tymas] *nf* contumacy.

contusion [kɔ̃tyzjɔ̃] *nf* bruise.

contusionner [kɔ̃tyzjɔne] *vt* to contuse, bruise.

conurbation [kɔnyrbasjɔ̃] *nf* conurbation.

convaincre [kɔ̃vɛ̃ːkr] *vt* to convince, convict.

convalescence [kɔ̃valɛssɑ̃ːs] *nf* convalescence.

convalescent [kɔ̃valɛssɑ̃] *an* convalescent.

convenable [kɔ̃vnabl] *a* suitable, proper, fit(ting), decent, decorous, well-behaved.

convenance [kɔ̃vnɑ̃ːs] *nf* agreement, suitability, convenience, propriety, decorum; *pl* convention.

convenir [kɔ̃vniːr] *vi* to suit, fit, agree, own, admit, be advisable, befitting.

convention [kɔ̃vɑ̃sjɔ̃] *nf* covenant, agreement, convention.

conventionnel, -elle [kɔ̃vɑ̃sjɔnɛl, ɛl] *a* conventional.

convenu [kɔ̃vny] *a* agreed, stipulated, settled.

conversation [kɔ̃vɛrsasjɔ̃] *nf* conversation, talk.

converser [kɔ̃vɛrse] *vi* to converse, talk.

conversion [kɔ̃vɛrsjɔ̃] *nf* conversion, change.

converti [kɔ̃vɛrti] *n* convert.

convertir [kɔ̃vɛrtiːr] *vt* to convert, change, win over; *vr* to become converted, turn.

convertisseur [kɔ̃vɛrtisœːr] *nm* converter, transformer.

convexe [kɔ̃vɛks] *a* convex.

conviction [kɔ̃viksjɔ̃] *nf* conviction.

convier [kɔ̃vje] *vt* to invite, urge.

convive [kɔ̃viːv] *n* table-companion, guest.

convocation [kɔ̃vɔkasjɔ̃] *nf* convocation, summons, convening, calling-up.

convoi [kɔ̃vwa] *nm* convoy, column, procession.

convoiter [kɔ̃vwate] *vt* to covet, desire.

convoitise [kɔ̃vwatiːz] *nf* covetousness, desire, lust.

convoquer [kɔ̃vɔke] *vt* to convoke, summon, convene, call up.

convulsif, -ive [kɔ̃vylsif, iːv] *a* convulsive.

convulsion [kɔ̃vylsjɔ̃] *nf* convulsion, upheaval.

coopérative [kɔɔperatiːv] *nf* cooperative stores.

coopérer [kɔɔpere] *vi* to cooperate.

coordination [kɔɔrdinasjɔ̃] *nf* coordination.

coordonner [kɔɔrdɔne] *vt* to coordinate, arrange.

copain [kɔpɛ̃] *nm* chum, pal.

copeau [kɔpo] *nm* shaving, chip.

copie [kɔpi] *nf* copy, (examination-) paper, reproduction, imitation.

copier [kɔpje] *vt* to copy, reproduce, imitate.

copieux, -euse [kɔpjø, jøːz] *a* copious, full, hearty.

copiste [kɔpist] *nm* transcriber, imitator.

coq [kɔk] *nm* cock, weathercock, ship's cook; poids — bantam weight; vivre comme un — en pâte to live in clover.

coq-à-l'âne [kɔkalɑːn] *nm* cock-and-bull story.

coque [kɔk] *nf* shell, husk, hull, bottom, loop; œuf à la — boiled egg.

coquelicot [kɔkliko] *nm* poppy.

coqueluche [kɔklyʃ] *nf* whooping-cough; darling.

coquerico [kɔkriko] *nm* cock-a-doodle-doo.

coquet, -ette [kɔkɛ, ɛt] *a* coquettish, smart, stylish, trim, interested in dress.

coquetier [kɔktje] *nm* egg-cup, egg merchant.

coquette [kɔkɛt] *nf* flirt.

coquetterie [kɔkɛtri] *nf* coquetry, affectation, love of finery, smartness.

coquillage [kɔkijaːʒ] *nm* shellfish, shell.

coquille [kɔkiːj] *nf* shell, case; misprint, printer's error.

coquin, -e [kɔkɛ̃, in] *nm* rogue, rascal, scamp; *nf* hussy, minx.

cor [kɔːr] *nm* horn, (of stag) tine, corn; réclamer à — et à cri to clamor for.

corail [kɔraːj] *nm* coral.

coran [kɔrɑ̃] *nm* Koran.

corbeau [kɔrbo] *nm* crow, raven; corbel, bracket.

corbeille [kɔrbɛːj] *nf* basket, round flowerbed; — de noces bridegroom's wedding present(s) to bride.

corbillard [kɔrbijaːr] *nm* hearse.

cordage [kɔrdaːʒ] *nm* rope, cordage.

corde [kɔrd] *nf* rope, cord, line, string, wire, thread.

cordeau [kɔrdo] *nm* tracing-line, string, fuse.

cordelière [kɔrdəljɛr] *nf* girdle, cord.

corder [kɔrde] *vt* to twist, cord, rope, string.

cordial [kɔrdjal] *a* hearty, cordial; *nm* cordial.

cordialité [kɔrdjalite] *nf* cordiality, heartiness.
cordon [kɔrdɔ̃] *nm* cordon, row, cord, ribbon, rope, string.
cordonnerie [kɔrdɔnri] *nf* shoemaking, boot and shoe trade, shoemaker's shop.
cordonnier [kɔrdɔnje] *nm* shoemaker, bootmaker.
coriace [kɔrjas] *a* tough, leathery; hard, grasping.
corne [kɔrn] *nf* (*animal*) horn; coup de — butt, gore; — du sabot horse's hoof; — d'un livre (*book*) dog-ear; — à souliers shoehorn; — de brume foghorn.
cornée [kɔrne] *nf* cornea.
corneille [kɔrnɛːj] *nf* crow, rook.
cornemuse [kɔrnəmyːz] *nf* bagpipes.
corner [kɔrne] *vt* to trumpet, din, dog-ear, turn down; *vi* to sound the horn, ring.
cornet [kɔrne] *nm* horn, trumpet, cornet; — à dés dice-box.
corniche [kɔrniʃ] *nf* cornice, ledge.
cornichon [kɔrniʃɔ̃] *nm* gherkin, simpleton.
cornu [kɔrny] *a* horned.
cornue [kɔrny] *nf* retort.
corollaire [kɔrɔlɛːr] *nm* corollary.
corporation [kɔrpɔrasjɔ̃] *nf* corporation, guild.
corporel, -elle [kɔrpɔrɛl, ɛl] *a* corporeal, corporal, bodily.
corps [kɔːr] *nm* body, substance, corpse, corps, frame, main part; — à — hand to hand, clinch; prendre — to take shape; perdu — et biens lost with all hands; à — perdu recklessly.
corpulence [kɔrpylɑ̃ːs] *nf* stoutness, corpulence.
corpulent [kɔrpylɑ̃] *a* stout, corpulent, fat.
corpuscule [kɔrpyskyl] *nm* corpuscle.
correct [kɔr(r)ɛkt] *a* correct, proper, accurate, polite, well-behaved.
correcteur, -trice [kɔr(r)ɛktœːr, tris] *n* corrector, proof-reader.
correction [kɔr(r)ɛksjɔ̃] *nf* correcting, proof-reading, correctness, accuracy, propriety, punishment.
correctionnel, -elle [kɔr(r)ɛksjɔnɛl, ɛl] *a* tribunal de police —le police court; délit — minor offense.
correspondance [kɔrɛspɔ̃dɑ̃ːs] *nf* correspondence, letters, communication, connection, intercourse.
correspondant [kɔrɛspɔ̃dɑ̃] *a* corresponding, connecting; *nm* correspondent, friend acting for parent.
correspondre [kɔrɛspɔ̃ːdr] *vi* to correspond, tally, agree, comunicate.
corridor [kɔridɔːr] *nm* corridor, passage.
corrigé [kɔriʒe] *nm* fair copy, correct version.

corriger [kɔriʒe] *vt* to correct, rectify, (*proofs*) read, cure, chastize.
corroboration [kɔrɔbɔrasjɔ̃] *nf* corroboration, confirmation.
corroborer [kɔrɔbɔre] *vt* to corroborate.
corroder [kɔrɔde] *vt* to corrode, eat away.
corrompre [kɔr(r)ɔ̃ːpr] *vt* to corrupt, spoil, bribe, taint.
corrompu [kɔr(r)ɔ̃py] *a* corrupt, depraved, tainted.
corrosif, -ive [kɔrrozif, iːv] *a nm* corrosive.
corrosion [kɔrrozjɔ̃] *nf* corrosion.
corroyer [kɔrwaje] *vt* to curry, weld, trim, puddle.
corrupteur, -trice [kɔr(r)yptœːr, tris] *a* corrupt(ing); *n* corrupter.
corruptible [kɔr(r)yptibl] *a* corruptible, bribable.
corruption [kɔr(r)ypsjɔ̃] *nf* corruption, bribery, bribing.
corsage [kɔrsaːʒ] *nm* bodice, blouse.
Corse [kɔrs] *nf* Corsica.
corse [kɔrs] *an* Corsican.
corsé [kɔrse] *a* full-bodied, strong, broad, meaty.
corser [kɔrse] *vt* to give body to, fortify, intensify; *vr* to get serious, thicken.
corset [kɔrse] *nm* corset; — de sauvetage life-jacket.
corsetier, -ière [kɔrsətje, jɛːr] *n* corset-maker.
cortège [kɔrtɛːʒ] *nm* procession, train, retinue.
corvée [kɔrve] *nf* fatigue duty, task, (piece of) drudgery.
cosmétique [kɔsmetik] *a nm* cosmetic.
cosmopolite [kɔsmɔpolit] *an* cosmopolitan.
cosse [kɔs] *nf* pod, husk.
cossu [kɔsy] *a* wealthy.
costaud [kɔsto] *a nm* strong, burly, brawny (man).
costume [kɔstym] *nm* costume, dress, suit.
costumé [kɔstyme] *a* bal — fancy-dress ball.
cote [kɔt] *nf* share, proportion, assessment, mark, number, classification, quotation, list of prices, odds.
côte [koːt] *nf* rib, hill, slope, coast, shore; — à — side by side.
côté [kote] *nm* side, way, direction, aspect, broadside, beam-ends; à — near, to one side; à — de beside by the side of, next to; de — on one side, sideways, aside, by; de mon — for my part.
coteau [kɔto] *nm* hill, hillside, slope.
côtelé [kotle] *a* ribbed, corded, corduroy (velvet).
côtelette [kotlɛt] *nf* cutlet, chop.
coter [kɔte] *vt* to assess, quote, classify, number, award marks to back.

coterie [kɔtri] nf set, clique, circle.

côtier, -ière [kotje, jɛːr] a coast, coastal, inshore; nm coaster.

cotisation [kɔtizasjɔ̃] nf share, contribution, subscription, fee.

se cotiser [səkɔtize] vr to club together, get up a subscription.

coton [kɔtɔ̃] nm cotton; filer un mauvais — to be in a poor way, go to the dogs.

cotonnerie [kɔtɔnri] nf cotton plantation.

cotonnier [kɔtɔnje] nm cotton plant.

côtoyer [kotwaje] vt to keep close to, hug, run along, skirt.

cou [ku] nm neck.

couardise [kwardiːz] nf cowardice, cowardliness.

couchage [kuʃaːʒ] nm bedding, bedclothes; sac de — sleeping-bag.

couchant [kuʃɑ̃] a setting; nm west, setting sun; chien — setter.

couche [kuʃ] nf bed, couch, layer, stratum, coat(ing), baby's diaper; pl confinement.

couché [kuʃe] a lying, recumbent, in bed.

coucher [kuʃe] vt to put to bed, lay down, set down; — en joue to aim (at); vi to sleep, spend the night; vr to go to bed, lie down, set, go down; nm night's lodging, setting.

couchette [kuʃɛt] nf crib, cot, berth, bunk, sleeper.

coucou [kuku] nm cuckoo.

coude [kud] nm elbow, bend, crank; jouer des —s to elbow one's way.

coudée [kude] nf pl elbow room, scope.

cou-de-pied [kudpje] nm instep.

coudoyer [kudwaje] vt to elbow, jostle, rub shoulders with.

coudre [kudr] vt to sew (up), stitch (on).

coudrier [kudrje] nm hazel tree.

couenne [kwan] nf thick skin, rind, membrane.

coulage [kulaːʒ] nm pouring, casting, running, sinking.

coulant [kulɑ̃] a running, flowing, easy, accommodating; nœud — slip-knot, noose.

coulé [kule] a cast, sunk, done for; nm slide, slur.

coulée [kule] nf running, flow, streak, casting.

couler [kule] vt to run, pour, cast, sink, slip, slur; vi to flow, run, leak, sink, slip, slur; vr to slip, glide, slide; se la — douce to take it easy, sit back.

couleur [kulœːr] nf color, complexion, coloring, paint, suit, flag.

couleuvre [kulœːvr] nf grass snake; avaler une — to pocket an insult.

coulisse [kulis] nf groove, slot, slide, unofficial stock-market; pl wings, slips; à — sliding; en — sidelong.

couloir [kulwaːr] nm corridor,

passage, lobby, channel, gully, lane.

coup [ku] nm blow, stroke, knock, hit, attempt, deed, attack, poke, stab, shot, blast, gust, move, ring, peal, influence, threat; manquer son — to miss the mark; — de froid cold snap, chill; boire à petits —s to sip; — d'envoi kick-off; tout d'un — all at once; du — now at last, this time; sur le — on the spot; tout à — suddenly.

coupable [kupabl] a guilty, culpable, sinful; n culprit.

coupe [kup] nf cup, glass, bowl, cut(ting), section, stroke.

coupé [kupe] a cut (up), sliced, broken, jerky, diluted; nm brougham, coupé.

coupe-coupe [kupkup] nm cutlass, long knife.

coupe-jarret [kupʒarɛ] nm cutthroat, ruffian.

coupe-papier [kuppapje] nm paperknife.

couper [kupe] vt to cut (out, up, down, off, in), intersect, cross, turn off, switch off, interrupt, stump, dilute; vr to cut oneself, cut, intersect, contradict oneself.

couperet [kuprɛ] nm chopper, cleaver, knife, blade (of guillotine).

couperosé [kuproze] a blotchy.

couple [kupl] nm couple, pair; nf two, brace, yoke, couple.

coupler [kuple] vt to couple, connect, join up.

couplet [kuplɛ] nm verse.

coupole [kupɔl] nf cupola, dome.

coupon [kupɔ̃] nm coupon, warrant, ticket, cut(ting), remnant, (short) length.

coupure [kupyːr] nf cut, gash, cutting, note.

cour [kuːr] nf court, courtship, courtyard, square, playground; faire la — à to make love to.

courage [kuraːʒ] nm courage, fortitude, spirit, heart.

courageux, -euse [kuraʒø, øːz] a brave, courageous.

couramment [kuramɑ̃] ad fluently, easily, generally.

courant [kurɑ̃] a running, current, present, standard, rife; nm current, stream, course; — d'air draft.

courbature [kurbatyr] nf stiffness, tiredness, ache.

courbaturé [kurbatyre] a aching, stiff.

courbe [kurb] nf curve, bend, sweep.

courber [kurbe] vtir to curve, bend; vr to stoop.

coureur, -euse [kurœːr, øːz] n runner, racer, sprinter, gadabout, adventurer, rake; — de dots fortune-hunter.

courge [kurʒ] nf pumpkin.

courgette [kurʒɛt] nf courgette, small marrow.

courir [kuriːr] vi to run, race, go,

be current, circulate; *vt* run (after), pursue, roam, gad about, haunt, frequent; **le bruit court** it is rumored; **par le temps qui court** nowadays, as things are.

courlis [kurli] *nm* curlew.

couronne [kurɔn] *nf* crown, coronet, wreath, corona, ring, rim.

couronnement [kurɔnmã] *nm* crowning, coronation, coping.

couronner [kurɔne] *vt* to crown, cap, reward, award a prize to, cope.

courrier [kurje] *nm* courier, messenger, mail, letters, post, newspaper paragraph.

courroie [kurwa] *nf* strap, transmission, belt, band.

courroux [kuru] *nm* anger, wrath.

cours [ku:r] *nm* course, flow, run, path, circulation, currency, quotation, price, course of lectures; *pl* classes; **en —** in progress, on hand, present, current.

course [kurs] *nf* run, race, excursion, outing, errand, course, path, flight.

court [ku:r] *a* short, brief, limited; *ad* short; **à — de** short of; **tout —** simply, merely; *nm* tennis court.

courtage [kurta:ʒ] *nm* broking, brokerage.

courtaud [kurto] *a* thickset, dumpy.

court-circuit [kursirkɥi] *nm* short-circuit.

courtier [kurtje] *nm* broker.

courtisan [kurtizã] *nm* courtier.

courtisane [kurtizan] *nf* courtesan prostitute.

courtiser [kurtize] *vt* to court, curry favor with.

courtois [kurtwa] *a* courteous, polite, courtly.

courtoisie [kurtwazi] *nf* courtesy, courteousness.

couru [kury] *a* run after, sought after, popular.

cousin [kuzɛ̃] *n* cousin; *nm* gnat, midge; **— germain** first cousin; **— à la mode de Bretagne** distant relation.

coussin [kusɛ̃] *nm* cushion.

coussinet [kusinɛ] *nm* pads, small cushion, bearing; **—s à billes** ball-bearings.

cousu [kuzy] *a* sewn, stitched; **— d'or** rolling in money.

coût [ku] *nm* cost; **— de la vie** cost of living.

couteau [kuto] *nm* knife, blade; **à —x tirés** at daggers drawn.

coutelas [kutla] *nm* cutlass, large knife.

coutelier [kutəlje] *nm* cutler.

coutellerie [kutɛlri] *nf* cutlery, cutler's shop or trade.

coûter [kute] *vi* to cost, pain, cause an effort; **coûte que coûte** at all costs.

coûteux, -euse [kutø, ø:z] *a* costly, expensive.

coutil [kuti] *nm* drill, twill, ticking.

coutume [kutym] *nf* custom, habit; **de —** usual.

couture [kuty:r] *nf* needlework, seam, scar; **battre à plate(s) —(s)** to trounce.

couturier, -ière [kutyrje, jɛ:r] *n* dressmaker.

couvée [kuve] *nf* brood, hatch, clutch.

couvent [kuvã] *nm* convent, monastery.

couver [kuve] *vt* to sit (on eggs), hatch (out), brood (over); *vi* to smolder, brew, hatch; **— des yeux** to look fondly or longingly at.

couvercle [kuvɛrkl] *nm* lid, cover, cap.

couvert [kuvɛ:r] *a* covered, clad, wearing one's hat, shady, wooded, overcast, covert, overgrown; *nm* cover(ing), shelter, place, knife and fork and spoon, cover charge.

couverture [kuvɛrty:r] *nf* cover(ing), rug, blanket, cloth, bedspread, wrapper, roofing.

couvre-feu [kuvrfø] *nm* curfew, lights out.

couvre-lit [kuvrli] *nm* bedspread.

couvre-pied [kuvrpje] *nm* quilt.

couvreur [kuvrœr] *nm* roofer, slater, tiler.

couvrir [kuvri:r] *vt* to cover (with, up), clothe, conceal, roof, drown (sound); *vr* to clothe oneself, put on one's hat, become overcast.

crabe [kra:b] *nm* crab.

crachat [kraʃa] *nm* spittle, spit.

craché [kraʃe] *a* **tout —** the dead spit of, to a tee.

cracher [kraʃe] *vt* to spit (out), splutter; *vi* to spit.

crachoir [kraʃwa:r] *nm* spittoon.

craie [krɛ] *nf* chalk.

craindre [krɛ̃:dr] *vt* to fear, dread, be afraid of; **il n'y a rien à —** there's no need to worry, nothing to worry about.

crainte [krɛ̃:t] *nf* fear, dread.

craintif, -ive [krɛ̃tif, i:v] *a* timid, afraid, fearful.

cramoisi [kramwazi] *a* crimson.

crampe [krã:p] *nf* cramp.

crampon [krãpɔ̃] *nm* clamp, fastener, crampon, stud, limpet, pest.

cramponner [krãpɔne] *vt* to cramp clamp together, fasten, pester, stick to; *vr* to hold on, hang on (to **à**).

cran [krã] *nm* safety catch, notch, hole, pluck, spirit.

crâne [krɑ:n] *nm* skull; *a* plucky, jaunty, swaggering.

crâner [krɑne] *vi* to swagger, assume a jaunty air, brazen it out.

crâneur [krɑnœr] *n* braggart, swaggerer.

crapaud [krapo] *nm* toad.

crapule [krapyl] *nf* debauchery, blackguard.

crapuleux, -euse [krapylø, ø:z] *a* debauched, dissolute, lewd, filthy.

craquelure [kraklyːr] nf crack.

craquer [krake] vi to crack, crackle, crunch, creak.

crasse [kras] af gross; nf dirt, squalor, dross, slag, meanness, dirty trick.

crasseux, -euse [krasø, øːz] a dirty, grimy, squalid.

cratère [krateːr] nm crater.

cravache [kravaʃ] nf riding-whip, horsewhip.

cravate [kravat] nf (neck)tie.

crayeux, -euse [krejø, øːz] a chalky.

crayon [krɛjɔ̃] nm pencil, pencil-drawing, crayon.

crayonner [krɛjɔne] vt to pencil, sketch, jot down.

créance [kreɑ̃ːs] nf credence, belief, credit, trust, debt, claim; lettre(s) de — letter of credit, credentials.

créancier, -ière [kreɑ̃sje, jɛːr] n creditor.

créateur, -trice [kreatœːr, tris] a creative; n creator, maker, inventor, founder.

création [kreasjɔ̃] nf creation, creating, founding.

créature [kreatyːr] nf creature, person.

crèche [krɛʃ] nf crib, manger, day-nursery.

crédence [kredɑ̃ːs] nf sideboard.

crédibilité [kredibilite] nf credibility.

crédit [kredi] nm credit, loan, bank, repute, influence.

créditeur, -trice [kreditœːr, tris] a credit; n creditor.

credo [kredo] nm creed.

crédule [kredyl] a credulous.

crédulité [kredylite] nf credulity, credulousness.

créer [kree] vt to create, make, found, build up.

crémaillère [kremajɛːr] nf pot hook; pendre la — to give a house-warming.

crématoire [krematwaːr] a four — crematorium.

crème [krɛm] nf cream, custard.

crémerie [kremri] nf creamery, dairy, milk-shop, small restaurant.

crémeux, -euse [kremø, øːz] a creamy.

crémier, -ière [kremje, jɛːr] n dairyman, dairywoman.

crémière [kremjɛːr] nf cream-jug.

créneau [kreno] nm loophole; pl battlements.

crénelé [krɛnle] a crenellated, loop-holed, notched, toothed.

créosote [kreozot] nf creosote.

crêpe [krɛːp] nf pancake; nm crape, crêpe.

crêper [krɛpe] vt to crimp, crisp, frizz, backcomb.

crépi [krepi] nm rough-cast.

crépir [krepiːr] vt to rough-cast, grain.

crépiter [krepite] vi to crackle, sputter, patter.

crépu [krepy] a crimped, crisp, frizzy, fuzzy.

crépuscule [krepyskyl] nm dusk, twilight, gloaming.

cresson [krɑsɔ̃] nm cress.

crête [krɛːt] nf comb, crest, ridge.

crétin [kretɛ̃] nm cretin, idiot, half-wit.

cretonne [krətɔn] nf cretonne.

creuser [krøze] vt to hollow (out), excavate, dig (out), go deeply into.

creuset [krøzɛ] nm crucible, melting-pot.

creux, -euse [krø, øːz] a hollow, sunk(en), empty, slack, futile; nm hollow, hole, pit, cavity.

crevaison [krəvɛzɔ̃] nf puncture, bursting, death.

crevant [krəvɑ̃] a funny, killing, exhausting.

crevasse [krəvas] nf crevice, crevasse, crack, split.

crève-cœur [krɛvkœːr] nm heart-break, disappointment.

crever [krəve] vi to burst, split, die; vt to puncture, burst, put out.

crevette [krəvɛt] nf shrimp, prawn.

cri [kri] nm cry, shout, call, squeal; le dernier — the latest fashion, the last word.

criailler [kriaje] vi to shout, bawl, whine, squeal.

criant [kriɑ̃] a crying, flagrant, glaring.

criard [kriaːr] a crying, squealing, shrill, garish.

crible [kribl] nm sieve, riddle, screen.

cribler [krible] vt to sift, riddle, screen.

cric [krik] nm jack.

cricri [krikri] nm chirping, cricket.

criée [krie] nf auction.

crier [krie] vti to cry, shout; vi scream, squeak.

crime [krim] nm crime.

criminel, -elle [kriminɛl] an criminal.

crin [krɛ̃] nm horsehair.

crinière [krinjɛːr] nf mane.

crique [krik] nf creek, cove.

crise [kriːz] nf crisis, problem, shortage, slump, attack.

crispation [krispasjɔ̃] nf twitching, clenching, wincing, shriveling up.

crisper [krispe] vt to clench, contract, contort, screw up; vr to contract, shrivel up.

crisser [krise] vi to grate.

cristal [kristal] nm crystal.

cristallin [kristalɛ̃] a crystalline, crystal-clear.

cristalliser [kristalize] vti to crystallize.

critère [kritɛːr] nm criterion.

critiquable [kritikabl] a open to criticism.

critique [kritik] a critical, crucial, ticklish, decisive; nf criticism, censure; nm critic.

critiquer [kritike] vt to criticize, censure.

croasser [krɔase] vi to caw, croak.

croc [kro] nm hook, fang, tusk.

croc-en-jambe [krɔkãʒã:b] nm **faire donner un — à qn** to trip.

croche [krɔʃ] nf quaver.

crochet [krɔʃe] nm hook, crochet, skeleton key, swerve, sudden turn; pl square brackets.

crochu [krɔʃy] a hooked, crooked.

crocodile [krɔkɔdil] nm crocodile.

croire [krwa:r] vt to believe, think; vi believe (in à, en).

croisade [krwazad] nf crusade.

croisé [krwaze] a crossed, cross, double-breasted; nm crusader.

croisée [krwaze] nf crossing, cross-roads, casement window.

croisement [krwazmã] nm crossing, meeting, intersection, interbreeding.

croiser [krwaze] vt to cross, fold, pass, meet; vi to fold over, cruise; vt to intersect, cross, meet and pass.

croiseur [krwaze:r] nm cruiser.

croisière [krwazje:r] nf cruise.

croissance [krwasã:s] nf growth.

croissant [krwasã] nm crescent, crescent roll.

croître [krwa:tr] vi to grow, increase, rise, wax, lengthen

croix [krwa] nf cross.

croque-mitaine [krɔkmiten] nm bogy(man).

croquer [krɔke] vt to crunch, munch, sketch.

croquis [krɔki] nm sketch.

crosse [krɔs] nf crook, crosier, stick, club, butt.

crotte [krɔt] nf mud, dirt, dung, chocolate sweet.

crotté [krɔte] a dirty, muddy, bespattered.

crottin [krɔtɛ̃] nm dung, droppings.

croulant [krulã] a crumbling, tottering.

croulement [krulmã] nm collapse, crumbling, falling in.

crouler [krule] vi to collapse, totter, crumble.

croupe [krup] nf croup, crupper, rump.

croupion [krupjɔ̃] nm rump, parson's nose.

croupir [krupi:r] vi to wallow, stagnate.

croustillant [krustijã] a crisp, crusty, spicy, smutty.

croûte [krut] nf crust, rind, scab, daub; **casser la —** to have a snack.

croûton [krutɔ̃] nm crust, crusty end, crouton.

croyable [krwajabl] a credible, believable, trustworthy.

croyance [krwajã:s] nf belief.

croyant [krwajã] a believing; n believer; pl the faithful.

cru [kry] a raw, crude, broad, coarse, blunt, garish; nm vintage, growth, vineyard, invention; **vin du**

— local wine; les meilleurs —s the best vineyards; **un bon —** a good vintage.

cruauté [kryote] nf cruelty.

cruche [kryʃ] nf pitcher, jug, blockhead, dolt.

crucifier [krysifje] vt to crucify.

crucifix [krysifi] nm crucifix.

crucifixion [krysifiksjɔ̃] nf crucifixion.

crudité [krydite] nf crudity, rawness, coarseness; pl raw fruit or vegetables.

crue [kry] nf rising, flood spate.

cruel, -elle [kryɛl] a cruel.

crûment [krymã] ad crudely, bluntly, roughly.

crustacés [krystase] nm pl crustaceans.

crypte [kript] nf crypt.

cube [kyb] a cubic; nm cube.

cubique [kybik] a cubic(al), cube.

cubisme [kybism] nm cubism.

cueillaison [kœjɛzɔ̃] nf gathering, picking, gathering season.

cueillette [kœjɛt] nf gathering, picking, crop.

cueillir [kœji:r] vt to gather, pick, pluck.

cuiller, -ère [kyje:r, kɥije:r] nf spoon.

cuillerée [kyjre, kɥijre] nf spoonful.

cuir [kyi:r] nm leather, hide, skin, strop; **— chevelu** scalp.

cuirasse [kɥiras] nf breastplate, armor.

cuirassé [kɥirase] a armor-plated, armored; nm ironclad, battleship.

cuire [kɥi:r] vt to cook, roast, bake, fire, burn; vi to cook, stew, burn, smart.

cuisant [kɥizã] a burning, smarting, biting, bitter.

cuisine [kɥizin] nf kitchen, cooking, cookery, food.

cuisiner [kɥizine] vt to cook; **— les comptes** manipulate the books, pull strings, (a suspect) interrogate.

cuisinier, -ière [kɥizinje, je:r] n cook.

cuisinière [kɥizinje:r] nf stove, cooker.

cuisse [kɥis] nf thigh, leg.

cuisson [kɥisɔ̃] nf cooking, baking, firing, burning, smarting.

cuistre [kɥistr] nm pedant, ill-mannered man.

cuit [kɥi] a cooked, baked, drunk; **— à point** done to a turn; **trop —** overdone; **pas assez —** underdone.

cuite [kɥit] nf baking, firing, burning, batch; **prendre une —** to get tight (drunk).

cuivre [kɥi:vr] nm copper, copperplate; **— jaune** brass; **les —s** the brass(es).

cuivré [kɥivre] a coppered, copper-colored, bronzed, metallic, brassy.

cul [ky] nm (fam) bottom, behind, rump, tail, stern.

culasse [kylas] nf breech.

culbute [kylbyt] *n* somersault, tumble, fall.

culbuter [kylbyte] *vi* to turn a somersault, tumble; *vt* to knock over, dump, trip.

cul-de-sac [kydsak] *nm* blind alley, dead end.

culinaire [kylinɛːr] *a* culinary.

culminant [kylminɑ̃] *a* culminating, highest.

culot [kylo] *nm* bottom, base, dottle, cheek, sauce.

culotte [kylɔt] *nf* breeches knickerbockers, shorts.

culotter [kylɔte] *vt* to breech, color, season.

culpabilité [kylpabilite] *nf* culpability, guilt.

culte [kylt] *nm* worship, cult.

cultivateur [kyltivatœːr] *nm* farmer, cultivator, grower.

cultivé [kyltive] *a* cultivated, cultured.

cultiver [kyltive] *vt* to farm, till, cultivate.

culture [kyltyːr] *nf* cultivation, farming, culture; *pl* fields, land under cultivation.

cumul [kymyl] *nm* plurality of offices.

cumuler [kymyle] *vt* to occupy several posts.

cupide [kypid] *a* covetous, greedy, grasping.

cupidité [kypidite] *nf* covetousness, greed.

Cupidon [kypidɔ̃] *nm* Cupid.

curatif, -ive [kyratif, iːv] *a* curative.

cure [kyːr] *nf* care, heed, presbytery, vicarage, rectory, cure.

curé [kyre] *nm* parish priest.

cure-dents [kyrdɑ̃] *nm* toothpick.

curer [kyre] *vt* to pick, clean (out), cleanse, clear.

curieux, -euse [kyrjø, øːz] *a* interested, curious, odd, quaint.

curiosité [kyrjɔzite] *nf* interestedness, inquisitiveness, curiosity, oddness, peculiarity, curio; *pl* sights.

curviligne [kyrvilin] *a* curvilinear, rounded.

cuticule [kytikyl] *nf* cuticle.

cuve [kyːv] *nf* vat, tun, tank.

cuver [kyve] *vti* to ferment; — **son vin** to sleep off one's drink.

cuvette [kyvɛt] *nf* wash-basin, dish, pan, basin.

cyanure [sjanyːr] *nm* cyanide.

cycle [sikl] *nm* cycle.

cyclisme [siklism] *nm* cycling.

cyclone [siklon] *nm* cyclone.

cygne [sin] *nm* swan.

cylindre [silɛ̃ːdr] *nm* cylinder, drum, roller.

cylindrer [silɛ̃dre] *vt* to roll, calender, mangle.

cylindrique [silɛ̃drik] *a* cylindrical.

cymbale [sɛ̃bal] *nf* cymbal.

cynique [sinik] *a* cynic(al), brazen, barefaced; *nm* cynic.

cynisme [sinism] *nm* cynicism, effrontery.

cynocéphale [sinɔsefal] *nm* baboon.

cyprès [siprɛ] *nm* cypress-tree.

cytise [sitiːz] *nm* laburnum.

D

daba [daba] *nf* hoe.

dactylo(graphe) [daktilɔgraf] *n* typist.

dactylographier [daktilɔgrafje] *vt* to type.

dada [dada] *nm* hobby (-horse).

dadais [dadɛ] *nm* ninny.

dague [dag] *nf* dagger.

daigner [deɲe] *vi* to condescend, deign.

daim [dɛ̃] *nm* deer, buck.

dais [dɛ] *nm* canopy, dais.

dallage [dalaːʒ] *nm* paving, tiled floor.

dalle [dal] *nf* flagstone, slice, slab.

daller [dale] *vt* to pave, tile.

daltonisme [daltɔnism] *nm* colorblindness.

damas [damɑ(ː)s] *nm* damask, damson.

dame [dam] *nf* lady, queen, king (checkers), beetle; *pl* checkers.

damer [dame] *vt* to crown a piece (at checkers).

damier [damje] *nm* checkerboard.

damner [dane] *vt* to damn, condemn.

dancing [dɑ̃sɛ̃g] *nm* dance hall.

dandiner [dɑ̃dine] *vt* to dandle, dance; *vr* to waddle.

Danemark [danmark] *nm* Denmark.

danger [dɑ̃ʒe] *nm* danger, peril, jeopardy, risk.

dangereux, -euse [dɑ̃ʒrø, øːz] *a* dangerous, perilous, risky.

danois [danwa, waːz] *a nm* Danish; *n* Dane.

dans [dɑ̃] *prep* in, into, within, out of, from.

danse [dɑ̃ːs] *nf* dance, dancing.

danser [dɑ̃se] *vti* to dance; *vi* to prance, bob.

danseur, -euse [dɑ̃sœːr, øːz] *n* dancer, partner.

dard [daːr] *nm* dart, javelin, harpoon, sting, tongue.

darder [darde] *vt* to dart, hurl, shoot out.

darse [dars] *nf* floating dock.

date [dat] *nf* date.

dater [date] *vti* to date; à — **de** as from.

datte [dat] *nf* date.

dattier [datje] *nm* date palm.

dauphin [dofɛ̃] *nm* dolphin, dauphin.

davantage [davɑ̃taːʒ] *ad* more, any more, any further.

de [də] *prep* from, of, by, with, in.

dé [de] *nm* thimble, dice, die, tee.

débâcle [debaːkl] *nf* collapse, breakup, downfall, rout.

déballer [debale] *vt* to unpack.

débandade [debɑ̃dad] nf rout, stampede; **à la —** in disorder, helter-skelter.

débander [debɑ̃de] vt to loosen, relax, unbend.

débarbouiller [debarbuje] vt to clean, wash; vr wash one's face.

débarcadère [debarkadɛːr] nm landing-stage, wharf.

débarder [debarde] vt to unload, discharge.

débardeur [debardœːr] nm stevedore, docker.

débarquement [debarkəmɑ̃] nm disembarking, landing, unloading, detraining.

débarquer [debarke] vti to land, disembark, detrain; vt to unload, set down.

débarras [debarɑ] nm storeroom; **bon —!** good riddance!

débarrasser [debarase] vt to rid, free, relieve; vr to get rid (of **de**).

débarrer [debare] vt to unbar.

débat [deba] nm debate, argument, discussion.

débattre [debatr] vt to discuss, debate; vr to struggle.

débauche [deboːʃ] nf debauchery, dissipation.

débaucher [deboʃe] vt to corrupt, lead astray; vr go to the bad.

débile [debil] a feeble, weak, sickly.

débilité [debilite] nf feebleness, debility.

débit [debi] nm sale, shop, flow, delivery, debit.

débiter [debite] vt to sell, retail, deliver, spin, debit.

débiteur, -trice [debitœːr, tris] n debtor.

déblai [deblɛ] nm clearing, excavation; **voie en —** railway cutting.

déblatérer [deblatere] vi to rail (against **contre**).

déblayage [deblɛjaʒ] nm clearance, clearing.

déblayer [deblɛje] vt to clear away.

déboire [debwaːr] nm nasty aftertaste, disappointment.

déboisement [debwazmɑ̃] nm deforestation.

déboîter [debwate] vt to dislocate, disjoint, disconnect.

débonder [debɔ̃de] vt to unbung.

débonnaire [debɔnɛːr] a good-natured, easy-tempered.

débordement [debɔrdəmɑ̃] nm overflowing, depravation, dissoluteness.

déborder [debɔrde] vti to overflow, boil over, brim over; vt to overlap, extend beyond, to outflank.

débouché [debuʃe] nm outlet, opening, market.

déboucher [debuʃe] vt to uncork, open, clear; vi to emerge, debouch.

déboucler [debukle] vt to unbuckle; vr (hair) to lose its curl.

déboulonner [debulɔne] vt to unbolt, unrivet.

débourber [deburbe] vt to clean out, sluice, dredge.

débours [debuːr] nm pl out of pocket expenses.

débourser [deburse] vt to spend, disburse.

debout [dəbu] ad erect, upright, standing, on end, up.

déboutonner [debutɔne] vt to unbutton.

débraillé [debraje] a untidy, disheveled, improper.

débrayer [debrɛje] vt to disconnect, throw out of gear, declutch.

débrider [debride] vt to unbridle; **sans —** without a stop.

débris [debri] nm pl fragments, bits, remains, ruins.

débrouillard [debrujaːr] a ingenious, resourceful, smart.

débrouiller [debruje] vt to unravel, disentangle; vr to find a way out, not to be stuck.

débrousser [debruse] vt to clear forest, bush.

débusquer [debyske] vt to dislodge, ferret out.

début [deby] nm beginning, start, first appearance.

débutant [debytɑ̃] n beginner.

débuter [debyte] vi to lead, begin, come out.

deçà [dəsa] ad on this side.

décacheter [dekaʃte] vt to unseal, break open.

décadence [dekadɑ̃ːs] nf decay, decline, downfall.

décaler [dekale] vt to remove wedge from, alter.

décamper [dekɑ̃pe] vi to decamp, scuttle off.

décapiter [dekapite] vt to behead.

décati [dekati] a worn out, senile.

décatir [dekatiːr] vt to sponge, steam, finish.

décéder [desede] vt to die, decease.

déceler [desle] vt to reveal, disclose, divulge.

décembre [desɑ̃ːbr] nm December.

décence [desɑ̃ːs] nf decency, propriety, decorum.

décent [desɑ̃] a decent, proper, modest.

décentraliser [desɑ̃tralize] vt to decentralize.

déception [desɛpsjɔ̃] nf deception, disappointment.

décerner [desɛrne] vt to confer, award, decree.

décès [desɛ] nm decease.

décevant [des(ə)vɑ̃] a deceptive, disappointing.

décevoir [desəvwaːr] vt to disappoint, deceive, dash.

déchaîner [deʃɛne] vt to unchain, let loose, unfetter; vr to break loose, break (out).

décharge [deʃarʒ] nf unloading, volley, discharge, acquittal, rebate; **témoin à —** witness for defense.

déchargement [deʃarʒəmɑ̃] nm unloading, discharging.

décharger [deʃarʒe] vt to dump, exonerate, unload, discharge, let off; vr to go off, run down, get rid (of de).

décharné [deʃarne] a gaunt, emaciated, skinny.

déchausser [deʃose] vt to take off s.o.'s shoes; vr take off one's shoes.

déchéance [deʃeɑ̃:s] nf fall, downfall, forfeiture.

déchet [deʃɛ] nm loss, decrease; pl refuse, scraps, failures.

déchiffrer [deʃifre] vt to decipher, decode, read.

déchiqueté [deʃikte] a torn, slashed, jagged.

déchirant [deʃirɑ̃] a heart-rending, ear-splitting, excruciating, harrowing.

déchirer [deʃire] vtr to tear, rend.

déchirure [deʃiry:r] nf tear, slit, rent.

déchoir [deʃwa:r] vi to fall.

décidément [desidemɑ̃] ad decidedly, resolutely.

décider [deside] vt to decide, settle, induce; vtr to make up one's mind, decide.

décimale [desimal] nf decimal.

décimer [desime] vt to decimate.

décisif, -ive [desizif, i:v] a decisive, crucial, conclusive.

décision [desizjɔ̃] nf decision, resolution.

déclamation [deklamasjɔ̃] nf declamation, oratory, elocution.

déclamatoire [deklamatwa:r] a declamatory.

déclamer [deklame] vti to declaim, spout.

déclarable [deklarabl] a liable to customs' duty.

déclaration [deklarasjɔ̃] nf announcement, declaration; — assermentée affidavit.

déclarer [deklare] vt to declare, state; vr declare oneself, break out, avow one's love, own up.

déclassé [deklase] a degraded, ostracized; n outcast, pariah.

déclasser [deklase] vt to transfer from one class to another, degrade.

déclencher [deklɑ̃ʃe] vt to loosen, release, launch.

déclic [deklik] nm latch, trigger, click, snap.

déclin [deklɛ̃] nm decline, close, end, deterioration.

déclinaison [deklinɛzɔ̃] nf declension, variation.

décliner [dekline] vt to decline, refuse; vi to decline, deteriorate, decay, fall; — son nom to give one's name.

déclivité [deklivite] nf declivity, slope, incline.

décocher [dekɔʃe] vt to shoot, discharge, let fly, fire.

décoiffer [dekwafe] vt to remove s.o.'s hat, undo s.o.'s hair; vr take one's hat off.

décollage [dekɔla:ʒ] nm unsticking, removal of gum, take-off (plane); piste de — runway.

décoller [dekɔle] vt to unstick, loosen, remove gum from; vi to take off; vr to come unstuck, work loose.

décolleté [dekɔlte] a low-necked.

décolorant [dekɔlɔrɑ̃] anm bleaching (agent).

décolorer [dekɔlɔre] vt to discolor, take color out of.

décombres [dekɔ̃:br] nm pl rubbish, debris.

décommander [dekɔmɑ̃de] vt to cancel, countermand, call off.

décomposer [dekɔ̃poze] vt to decompose, alter, distort; vr to decompose, become distorted.

décompte [dekɔ̃:t] nm discount, deduction.

déconcerter [dekɔ̃sɛrte] vt to confound, take aback.

déconfiture [dekɔ̃fity:r] nf defeat, discomfiture.

déconseiller [dekɔ̃sɛje] vt to dissuade, advise against.

déconsidération [dekɔ̃siderasjɔ̃] nf discredit, disrepute.

déconsidéré [dekɔ̃sidere] a disreputable.

déconsidérer [dekɔ̃sidere] vt to bring into disrepute.

décontenancer [dekɔ̃tnɑ̃se] vt to abash.

déconvenue [dekɔ̃vny] nf mishap, misfortune.

décor [dekɔr] nm decoration, scenery, set(ting).

décorateur, -trice [dekɔratœ:r, tris] n decorator, scene-painter.

décoration [dekɔrasjɔ̃] nf decoration, scene-painting.

décorer [dekɔre] vt to decorate.

décortiquer [dekɔrtike] vt to remove bark from, shell, peel, husk.

découcher [dekuʃe] vi to sleep out.

découdre [dekudr] vt to unstitch, unpick; vr to come unstitched.

découler [dekule] vi to flow, run down, fall.

découpage [dekupa:ʒ] nm cutting out, fretwork.

découper [dekupe] vt to cut out, cut up, carve; vr to stand out.

découplé [dekuple] a bien — wellbuilt.

découpure [dekupy:r] nf cutting out, cutting.

découragé [dekuraʒe] a downhearted, despondent.

décourageant [dekuraʒɑ̃] a disheartening.

découragement [dekuraʒmɑ̃] nm despondency, discouragement.

décousu [dekuzy] a disconnected, incoherent, rambling; nm incoherency.

découvert [dekuvɛːr] *a* uncovered, open, exposed; **à —** openly.

découverte [dekuvɛrt] *nf* discovery.

découvrir [dekuvriːr] *vt* to uncover, discover, reveal, detect, expose; *vr* to doff one's hat, be discovered.

décrasser [dekrase] *vt* to scour, clean.

décrépitude [dekrepityd] *nf* decay, senility.

décret [dekrɛ] *nm* decree.

décréter [dekrete] *vt* to decree, enact.

décrier [dekrie] *vt* to decry, run down, disparage.

décrire [dekriːr] *vt* to describe.

décrocher [dekrɔʃe] *vt* to unhook, take down, undo.

décroissance [dekrwasɑ̃ːs] *nf* decrease, decline.

décroître [dekrwaːtr] *vi* to decrease, grow shorter.

décrotter [dekrɔte] *vt* to clean, brush, scrape.

décrottoir [dekrɔtwaːr] *nm* scraper.

déçu [desy] *a* disappointed.

dédaigner [dedɛɲe] *vt* to disdain, scorn.

dédaigneux, -euse [dedɛɲø, øːz] *a* disdainful, supercilious.

dédain [dedɛ̃] *nm* disdain.

dédale [dedal] *nm* maze.

dedans [dədɑ̃] *ad* inside, within, in it; *nm* interior, inside.

dédicace [dedikas] *nf* dedication.

dédier [dedje] *vt* to dedicate, inscribe.

se dédire [sədediːr] *vr* to retract, take back one's words.

dédommagement [dedɔmaʒmɑ̃] *nm* compensation, damages, amends.

dédommager [dedɔmaʒe] *vt* to compensate, make amends to; *vr* to make up one's loss.

déduction [dedyksjɔ̃] *nf* deduction, inference.

déduire [deduiːr] *vt* to deduce, deduct.

déesse [deɛs] *nf* goddess.

défaillance [defajɑ̃ːs] *nf* weakness, lapse, falling-off, swoon; **tomber en —** to faint.

défaillant [defajɑ̃] *a* failing, sinking; *n* defaulter.

défaillir [defajiːr] *vi* to grow weak, fail, faint.

défaire [defɛːr] *vt* to undo, untie, defeat; *vr* to come undone, rid oneself, get rid (of).

défait [defɛ] *a* haggard, drawn, worn, undone.

défaite [defɛt] *nf* defeat.

défaitiste [defetist] *an* defeatist.

défalquer [defalke] *vt* to deduct, write off.

défaut [defo] *nm* defect, fault, lack, blemish, flaw; **à — de** for lack of; **prendre qn en —** to catch someone out.

défaveur [defavœːr] *nf* disgrace, disfavor.

défavorable [defavɔrabl] *a* unfavorable, disadvantageous.

défection [defɛksjɔ̃] *nf* disloyalty, defection.

défectueux, -euse [defɛktyø, øːz] *a* faulty, defective.

défendable [defɑ̃dabl] *a* defensible.

défendeur, -eresse [defɑ̃dœːr, ərɛs] *n* defendant.

défendre [defɑ̃ːdr] *vt* to defend, uphold, protect, forbid.

défense [defɑ̃ːs] *nf* defense, support, interdiction; *pl* tusks; **—de fumer** no smoking; **— passive** anti-aircraft defense, civil defense.

défenseur [defɑ̃sœːr] *nm* defender, protector, upholder, counsel for defense.

défensif, -ive [defɑ̃sif, iːv] *a* defensive.

défensive [defɑ̃siːv] *nf* defensive.

déférence [deferɑ̃ːs] *nf* respect, deference, compliance.

déférer [defere] *vt* to refer, hand over, administer; *vi* to assent, defer, comply.

déferler [defɛrle] *vt* to unfurl; *vi* to break.

déferrer [defɛre] *vt* to unshoe, remove the iron from; *vr* to cast a shoe.

défi [defi] *nm* defiance, challenge.

défiance [defjɑ̃ːs] *nf* distrust, suspicion, diffidence.

défiant [defjɑ̃] *a* distrustful, suspicious, wary.

déficeler [defisle] *vt* to untie.

déficit [defisit] *nm* deficit.

déficitaire [defisitɛːr] *a* deficient, unbalanced.

défier [defje] *vt* to defy, dare, challenge, beggar; *vr* to distrust.

défigurer [defigyre] *vt* to disfigure, distort, deface.

défilade [defilad] *nf* filing past.

défilé [defile] *nm* pass, defile, parade, march past.

défiler [defile] *vi* to march past, parade, flash past.

définir [definiːr] *vt* to determine, define.

définitif, -ive [definitif, iːv] *a* final, definitive.

définition [definisjɔ̃] *nf* definition.

déflation [deflasjɔ̃] *nf* deflation.

déflorer [deflɔre] *vt* to take the bloom off, take the novelty off, deflower.

défoncer [defɔ̃se] *vt* to break in, burst in, knock the bottom out of.

déformer [deforme] *vt* to disfigure, distort, put out of shape; *vr* to lose its shape.

défraîchi [defreʃi] *a* faded, soiled.

défrayer [defreje] *vt* to defray, pay s.o.'s expenses.

défricher [defriʃe] *vt* to clear, prepare, break.

défroncer [defrɔ̃se] *vt* to unplait, smooth.

défroque [defrɔk] *nf pl* cast-off clothing, wardrobe.

défroquer [defrɔke] *vt* to unfrock.

défunt [defœ̃] *a* deceased, dead, defunct.

dégagé [degaʒe] *a* free, easy, off-hand, airy.

dégagement [degaʒmɑ̃] *nm* disengagement, release, slackening, redemption.

dégager [degaʒe] *vt* to disengage, release, to redeem.

dégainer [degene] *vt* to unsheathe, draw.

dégarnir [degarniːr] *vt* to strip, deplete, dismantle; *vr* to be stripped, grow bare, empty.

dégâts [dega] *nm pl* damage, havoc.

dégauchir [degoʃiːr] *vt* to smooth, straighten, take the rough edges off.

dégel [deʒɛl] *nm* thaw.

dégeler [deʒle] *vti* to melt, thaw.

dégénération [deʒenerasjɔ̃] *nf* degeneration, degeneracy.

dégénérer [deʒenere] *vi* to degenerate.

dégingandé [deʒɛ̃gɑ̃de] *a* ungainly, gawky.

dégivreur [deʒivrœr] *nm* de-icer.

dégoiser [degwaze] *vt* to say hurriedly, race through; *vi* to chatter.

dégonfler [degɔ̃fle] *vt* to deflate, reduce, debunk, explode; *vr* to go flat, subside, climb down.

dégorger [degɔrʒe] *vt* to disgorge, clear; *vi* to flow out, overflow.

dégouliner [deguline] *vi* to drip, trickle.

dégourdi [degurdi] *a* smart, knowing, wide-awake.

dégourdir [degurdiːr] *vt* to revive, restore circulation to; *vr* to loosen one's muscles, stretch one's limbs.

dégoût [degu] *nm* disgust, aversion, distaste, annoyance.

dégoûtant [degutɑ̃] *a* disgusting, sickening.

dégoûté [degute] *a* disgusted, sick, fastidious, fed up.

dégoûter [degute] *vt* to disgust, sicken.

dégoutter [degute] *vi* to trickle, drip, drop.

dégradation [degradasjɔ̃] *nf* abasement, degeneracy, reduction in the ranks, shading off.

dégrader [degrade] *vt* to degrade, reduce to ranks, shade off, graduate.

dégrafer [degrafe] *vt* to unclasp, unhook, undo.

dégraisser [degrɛse] *vt* to scour, clean.

degré [dəgre] *nm* degree, stage, grade, step.

dégringolade [degrɛ̃gɔlad] *nf* fall, tumble, collapse, slump, bathos.

dégringoler [degrɛ̃gɔle] *vti* to rush, tumble down.

dégriser [degrize] *vt* to sober, bring s.o. to his senses; *vr* to come back to earth.

dégrossir [degrosiːr] *vt* to rough plane, rough hew, take the rough edges off.

déguenillé [degnije] *a* ragged, tattered.

déguisement [degizmɑ̃] *nm* disguise, fancy dress.

déguiser [degize] *vt* to disguise; *vr* to dress in fancy costume, disguise oneself.

déguster [degyste] *vt* to taste, sample, sip.

dehors [dəɔːr] *ad* out(side); *nm* exterior, outside.

déjà [deʒa] *ad* already, before, by this time, as it is.

déjeuner [deʒœne] *vi* to breakfast, have lunch; *nm* lunch; **petit —** breakfast.

déjouer [deʒwe] *vt* to baffle, outwit, foil, thwart.

délabrement [delabrəmɑ̃] *nm* dilapidation, disrepair, ruin, decay.

délabrer [delabre] *vt* to pull to pieces, wreck; *vr* to fall into ruins, disrepair.

délacer [delase] *vt* to unlace; *vr* to come unlaced.

délai [delɛ] *nm* delay, notice, extension.

délaissement [delɛsmɑ̃] *nm* desertion, neglect, relinquishment.

délaisser [delɛse] *vt* to desert, forsake, relinquish.

délassement [delasmɑ̃] *nm* pastime, relaxation.

délasser [delase] *vt* to refresh; *vr* to take some relaxation.

délateur, -trice [delatœːr, tris] *n* informer.

délayer [deleje] *vt* to dilute, water down, spin out.

délégation [delegasjɔ̃] *nf* delegation, assignment.

déléguer [delege] *vt* to depute, assign, delegate.

délester [delɛste] *vt* to unballast, relieve.

délibération [deliberasjɔ̃] *nf* deliberation, discussion, thought, resolution.

délibéré [delibere] *a* deliberate, purposeful.

délibérer [delibere] *vt* to discuss, think over; *vi* to deliberate, ponder.

délicat [delika] *a* delicate, dainty, fastidious, ticklish.

délicatesse [delikatɛs] *nf* delicacy, frailty, daintiness.

délice [delis] *nm (usu pl f)* delight, pleasure.

délicieux, -euse [delisjø, øːz] *a* delightful, delicious.

délié [delje] *a* slender, slim, shrewd.

délier [delje] *vt* to untie, unbind; *vr* to come loose.

délimiter [delimite] *vt* to mark the limits of, define.

délinquant [delɛ̃kɑ̃] n offender, delinquent.

délirant [delirɑ̃] a raving, frenzied, delirious.

délire [deli:r] nm frenzy, delirium.

délirer [delire] vi to rave, be delirious.

délit [deli] nm offense, misdemeanor.

délivrance [delivrɑ̃:s] nf deliverance.

délivrer [delivre] vt free, release; vr to rid oneself (of de).

déloger [delɔʒe] vt to dislodge, eject; vi to remove.

déloyal [delwajal] a unfaithful, false, unfair, unequal.

déloyauté [delwajote] nf unfaithfulness, treachery, dishonesty. disloyalty.

déluge [dely:ʒ] nm flood, deluge, downpour.

déluré [delyre] a wide-awake, cute, sly.

demain [dəmɛ̃] ad tomorrow; — en huit a week from tomorrow.

démailler [demaje] vr to run (stocking).

demande [d(ə)mɑ̃:d] nf request, question, inquiry, application, indent.

demander [d(ə)mɑ̃de] vt to ask, ask for, apply for, request, sue; vr to wonder.

demandeur, -eresse [d(ə)mɑ̃dœ:r, ɔrɛs] n claimant, petitioner.

démanger [demɑ̃ʒe] vi to itch.

démanteler [demɑ̃tle] vt to dismantle.

démarcation [demarkasjɔ̃] nf demarcation.

démarche [demarʃ] nf walk, bearing, step, approach.

démarrage [demara:ʒ] nm unmooring, start-off.

démarrer [demare] vt to unmoor; vi to leave moorings, start off.

démarreur [demarœ:r] nm selfstarter.

démasquer [demaske] vt to unmask, expose; vr to show one's true colors.

démêlé [demele] nm quarrel, tussle.

démêler [demele] vt to unravel, disentangle.

démembrer [demɑ̃bre] vt to dismember, partition.

déménagement [demenaʒmɑ̃] nm removal.

déménager [demenaʒe] vi to remove.

démence [demɑ̃:s] nf madness, insanity.

démener [demne] vr to struggle, make violent efforts.

démenti [demɑ̃ti] nm contradiction, denial, lie.

démentir [demɑ̃ti:r] vt to contradict, belie; vr to go back on one's word.

démesuré [demzyre] a huge, immoderate.

démettre [demɛtr] vt to dislocate; vr to resign.

demeurant [dəmœrɑ̃] ad eu — after all, moreover.

demeure [dəmœ:r] nf abode dwelling.

demeurer [dəmœre] vi to dwell, live remain. stay

demi [dəmi] a ad half: nm half. half-back.

demi-finale [dəmifinal] nf semifinal.

demi-pensionnaire [dəmipɑ̃sjɔnɛ:r] n day-boarder.

demi-place [dəmiplas] nf half-fare, half-price.

demi-saison [dəmisɛzɔ̃] nf betweenseason.

démission [demisjɔ̃] nf resignation.

démissionner [demisjɔne] vi to resign.

demi-tour [dəmitu:r] nm faire — to turn back.

démobilisation [demɔbilizasjɔ̃] nf demobilization.

démobiliser [demɔbilize] vt to demobilize.

démocrate [demɔkrat] a democratic; n democrat.

démocratie [demɔkrasi] nf democracy.

démocratique [demɔkratik] a democratic.

démodé [demɔde] a old-fashioned, out-of-date.

démographie [demɔgrafi] nf demography.

demoiselle [dəmwazɛl] nf young lady, maiden, spinster; dragonfly, beetle; — d'honneur bridesmaid; — de compagnie lady companion.

démolir [demɔli:r] vt to pull down, demolish.

démon [demɔ̃] nm demon, fiend, devil, imp.

démonstration [demɔ̃strasjɔ̃] nf demonstration, proof.

démonté [demɔ̃te] a dismounted, stormy, flustered.

démonter [demɔ̃te] vt to unseat, take to pieces.

démontrer [demɔ̃tre] vt to demonstrate, prove.

démoralisateur, -trice [demɔralizatœ:r, tris] a demoralizing.

démoraliser [demɔralize] vt to demoralize, dishearten; vr to lose heart, be demoralized.

démordre [demɔrdr] vi to let go, give up; en — to climb down.

démuni [demyni] a short (of), without, out (of de).

dénaturé [denatyre] a unnatural, perverted.

dénaturer [denatyre] vt to falsify, pervert.

dénégation [denegasjɔ̃] nf denial.

dénicher [deniʃe] vt to remove from the nest, find, unearth; vi to forsake the nest.

dénigrement [denigrəmɑ̃] nm disparagement.

dénigrer [denigre] *vt* to run down, disparage.

dénombrement [denɔ̃brəmɑ̃] *nm* enumeration, numbering, census.

dénommer [denɔme] *vt* to name.

dénoncer [denɔ̃se] *vt* to denounce, declare, inform against, squeal on.

dénonciateur, -trice [denɔ̃sjatœːr, tris] *a* tell-tale; *n* informer.

dénonciation [denɔ̃sjasjɔ̃] *nf* denunciation.

dénoter [denɔte] *vt* to denote, betoken.

dénouement [denumɑ̃] *nm* issue, end(ing), outcome.

dénouer [denwe] *vt* to untie, undo, unravel; *vr* to come loose, be unraveled.

denrée [dɑ̃re] *nf* commodity, food-stuff.

dense [dɑ̃ːs] *a* dense, thick.

densité [dɑ̃site] *nf* density, denseness.

dent [dɑ̃] *nf* tooth, prong, cog; **avoir une — contre** qn to bear s.o. a grudge; **à belles —s** with relish.

dentaire [dɑ̃tɛːr] *a* dental.

denté [dɑ̃te] *a* cogged.

denteler [dɑ̃tle] *vt* to indent, notch, serrate.

dentelle [dɑ̃tɛl] *nf* lace.

dentellerie [dɑ̃tɛlri] *nf* lace manufacture.

dentelure [dɑ̃tlyːr] *nf* indentation, serration.

dentier [dɑ̃tje] *nm* denture, set of false teeth.

dentifrice [dɑ̃tifris] *nm* toothpaste, -powder; **pâte —** toothpaste.

dentiste [dɑ̃tist] *nm* dentist.

dentition [dɑ̃tisjɔ̃] *nf* dentition, teething.

denture [dɑ̃tyːr] *nf* (set of) teeth (natural).

dénudation [denydasjɔ̃] *nf* laying bare, stripping.

dénudé [denyde] *a* bare, bleak.

dénuder [denyde] *vt* to lay bare, denude.

dénué [denɥe] *a* devoid (of **de**).

dénuement [denymɑ̃] *nm* destitution, distress, want.

dénuer [denɥe] *vt* to strip, divest; *vr* to part (with).

dépannage [depanaːʒ] *nm* running or emergency repairs; **équipe de —** wrecking crew.

dépanner [depane] *vt* to repair, help out.

dépaqueter [depakte] *vt* to unpack.

dépareillé [depareje] *a* odd, unmatched.

déparer [depare] *vt* to mar, spoil, disfigure.

départ [depaːr] *nm* departure, start (ing), difference.

départager [departaʒe] *vt* to decide between; **— les suffrages** to give the deciding vote.

département [departəmɑ̃] *nm* department, administrative subdivision.

départir [departiːr] *vt* to share out, divide, dispense; *vr* to depart (from **de**), part (with **de**).

dépasser [depase] *vt* to pass, surpass, exceed.

dépaysé [depe(j)ize] *a* out of one's element, strange.

dépayser [depe(j)ize] *vt* to bewilder, disconcert.

dépecer [depəse] *vt* to cut up, carve.

dépêche [depɛ(ː)ʃ] *nf* dispatch, telegram, wire.

dépêcher [depeʃe] *vt* to dispatch; *vr* to hurry, hasten.

dépeigner [depeɲe] *vt* to disarrange, ruffle s.o.'s hair.

dépeindre [depɛ̃ːdr] *vt* to depict, describe.

dépendance [depɑ̃dɑ̃ːs] *nf* dependence, appurtenance; *pl* outbuildings.

dépendant [depɑ̃dɑ̃] *a* dependent.

dépendre [depɑ̃ːdr] *vt* to take down; *vi* to depend, be answerable, hinge.

dépens [depɑ̃] *nm pl* cost, expense.

dépense [depɑ̃ːs] *nf* expenditure, outlay, expense, consumption, pantry.

dépenser [depɑ̃se] *vt* to spend, expend, consume, use up; *vr* to expend one's energies.

dépensier, -ière [depɑ̃sje, jɛːr] *a* extravagant.

dépérir [deperiːr] *vi* to pine away, decline, wilt.

dépérissement [deperismɑ̃] *nm* decline, decay.

dépêtrer [depɛtre] *vt* to extricate; *vr* to extricate oneself.

dépeupler [depœple] *vt* to depopulate, thin, empty.

dépiécer [depjese] *vt* to cut up, carve.

dépiècement [depjesmɑ̃] *nm* carving, dismemberment.

dépister [depiste] *vt* to run to earth, throw off the scent.

dépit [depi] *nm* spite, annoyance, vexation; **en — de** in spite of.

dépiter [depite] *vt* to annoy, spite.

déplacé [deplase] *a* out of place, incongruous, misplaced, uncalled for.

déplacement [deplasmɑ̃] *nm* displacing, moving, transfer; *pl* movements, journey.

déplacer [deplase] *vt* to displace, move, shift, transfer; *vr* to remove, move about, travel, shift.

déplaire [deplɛːr] *vt* to displease, offend; **ne vous en déplaise** with all due respect.

déplaisant [deplɛzɑ̃] *a* disagreeable, unpleasant.

déplaisir [deplɛziːr] *nm* displeasure, vexation, sorrow.

déplanter [deplɑ̃te] *vt* to lift (plant), transplant.

déplantoir [deplɑ̃twaːr] *nm* trowel.

déplier [deplie] *vtr* to unfold, open.
déplisser [deplise] *vt* to take out of its folds.
déploiement [deplwamɑ̃] *nm* unfolding, display, deployment.
déplorable [deplɔrabl] *a* lamentable.
déplorer [deplɔre] *vt* to deplore, bewail, mourn.
déployer [deplwaje] *vt* to unfold, spread out, display, deploy; *vr* to spread, deploy.
déplumer [deplyme] *vt* to pluck; *vr* to molt.
dépolir [depɔliːr] *vt* to take gloss off, frost (glass).
dépopulation [depɔpylasjɔ̃] *nf* depopulation.
déportements [depɔrtəmɑ̃] *nm pl* misconduct, excesses.
déporter [depɔrte] *vt* to deport.
déposant [depozɑ̃] *n* witness, depositor.
déposer [depoze] *vt* to lay down, deposit, lodge, drop; *vi* to testify, attest.
dépositaire [depozitɛːr] *n* trustee, sole agent.
déposition [depozisjɔ̃] *nf* testimony, evidence, attestation.
déposséder [deposede] *vt* to dispossess, strip.
dépossession [deposesjɔ̃] *nf* dispossessing.
dépôt [depo] *nm* deposit(ing), store, depot, warehouse, dump, coating.
dépouille [depuːj] *nf* skin, (earthly) remains, spoils, relics.
dépouiller [depuje] *vt* to skin, strip, plunder, rob; *vr* to cast its skin, rid oneself, shed; — **son courrier** to go through one's mail.
dépourvu [depurvy] *a* devoid, bereft; **pris au** — caught unawares.
dépravation [depravasjɔ̃] *nf* depravity.
dépraver [deprave] *vt* to deprave.
dépréciation [depresjasjɔ̃] *nf* depreciation, wear and tear, disparagement.
déprécier [depresje] *vt* to underrate, depreciate, disparage, cheapen.
déprédation [depredasjɔ̃] *nf* depredation, embezzlement.
dépression [depresjɔ̃] *nf* depression, fall, hollow, gloom, dejection.
déprimer [deprime] *vt* to depress; *vr* to become depressed.
depuis [dəpɥi] *prep* since, for, from; *ad* afterward, since then.
députation [depytasjɔ̃] *nf* deputation, deputing, membership in Parliament; **se présenter à la** — to stand for Parliament.
député [depyte] *n* deputy, Member of Parliament; **chambre des** —**s** parliament house.
députer [depyte] *vt* to depute, appoint as deputy.
déraciner [derasine] *vt* to uproot, root out, extirpate.

dérailler [deraje] *vi* to be derailed, run off rails; *vt* **faire** — to derail.
déraison [derɛzɔ̃] *nf* unreasonableness, folly.
déraisonnable [derɛzɔnabl] *a* unreasonable.
déraisonner [derɛzɔne] *vi* to talk nonsense.
dérangement [derɑ̃ʒmɑ̃] *nm* disarrangement, disorder, derangement.
déranger [derɑ̃ʒe] *vt* to disarrange, disturb, upset, derange; *vr* to move, inconvenience oneself, trouble.
dérapage [derapaːʒ] *nm* dragging anchor, skid.
déraper [derape] *vi* to drag its anchor, to skid.
dératé [derate] *a* spleened; **courir comme un** — to run like a hare.
derechef [dərəʃɛf] *ad* once again.
déréglé [deregle] *a* out of order, dissolute, inordinate.
dérèglement [dereglǝmɑ̃] *nm* disorder, irregularity, profligacy.
dérégler [deregle] *vt* to upset, disarrange, put out of order, unsettle; *vr* to get out of order, go wrong.
dérider [deride] *vt* to smoothe, remove wrinkles from, brighten up; *vr* to unbend.
dérision [derizjɔ̃] *nf* mockery, derision.
dérisoire [derizwaːr] *a* absurd, derisive, ridiculous.
dérivation [derivasjɔ̃] *nf* derivation, diversion, deflection, drift.
dérive [deriːv] *nf* drift, leeway; **à la** — adrift.
dériver [derive] *vt* to divert; *vi* to drift, be derived.
dernier, -ière [dɛrnje, jɛːr] *a* last, latter, latest, hindmost, utmost, extreme.
dernièrement [dɛrnjɛrmɑ̃] *ad* recently, lately.
dérobé [derɔbe] *a* secret; **à la** —**e** secretly, stealthily.
dérober [derɔbe] *vt* to steal, hide; *vr* to escape, hide, avoid, give way.
dérogatoire [derɔgatwaːr] *a* derogatory.
déroger [derɔʒe] *vi* to derogate, depart (from à), lose dignity.
dérouiller [deruje] *vt* to remove rust from, polish, brush up.
dérouler [derule] *vt* to unroll, uncoil, unfold; *vr* to unfold, stretch, spread, happen.
déroute [derut] *nf* rout, flight, downfall.
dérouter [derute] *vt* to lead astray, baffle, put off.
derrière [dɛrjɛːr] *prep* behind, beyond; *ad* behind, astern, at the back, in the rear; *nm* back, rear, bottom.
des [de, dɛ] = **de** + **les**.
dès [dɛ] *prep* since, from; — **lors** from then; — **que** as soon as.

désabuser [dezabyze] *vt* to disillusion, undeceive.

désaccord [dezakɔːr] *nm* disagreement, variance, clash.

désaccoutumer [dezakutyme] *vt* to break (s.o.) of a habit; *vr* to get out of the habit.

désaffecter [dezafɛkte] *vt* to put to another use, convert.

désaffection [dezafɛksjɔ̃] *nf* disaffection.

désagréable [dezagreabl] *a* unpleasant, offensive.

désagrégation [dezagregasjɔ̃] *nf* disintegration, breaking-up.

désagrément [dezagremɑ̃] *nm* source of irritation, vexatious incident.

désaltérer [dezaltere] *vt* to quench s.o.'s thirst; *vr* to quench one's thirst.

désappointer [dezapwɛ̃te] *vt* to disappoint.

désapprendre [dezaprɑ̃:dr] *vt* to unlearn.

désapprobateur, -trice [dezaprɔbatœːr, tris] *a* disapproving.

désapprobation [dezaprɔbasjɔ̃] *nf* disapprobation, disapproval.

désapprouver [dezapruve] *vt* to disapprove, frown upon.

désarçonner [dezarsɔne] *vt* to unseat, unsaddle.

désarmement [dezarmamɑ̃] *nm* disarming, disarmament, laying up.

désarmer [dezarme] *vt* to disarm, dismantle, lay up; *vi* to disarm, be disbanded.

désarroi [dezarwa] *nm* confusion, disorder.

désassocier [dezasɔsje] *vt* to dissociate; *vr* to dissociate o.s. (from de).

désassorti [dezasɔrti] *a* made up of odd bits.

désastre [dezastr] *nm* disaster, calamity, catastrophe.

désastreux, -euse [dezastrø, øːz] *a* disastrous.

désavantage [dezavɑ̃taːʒ] *nm* handicap.

désavantager [dezavɑ̃taʒe] *vt* to mar, handicap, put at a disadvantage.

désavantageux, -euse [dezavɑ̃taʒø, øːz] *a* detrimental, disadvantageous.

désaveu [dezavø] *nm* denial, disavowal.

désavouer [dezavwe] *vt* to repudiate, disown, disclaim.

desceller [desele] *vt* to unseal, open, loosen.

descendant [desɑ̃dɑ̃] *a* descending, downward; *n* descendant, offspring.

descendre [desɑ̃:dr] *vt* to go down, carry down, bring down; *vi* to descend, go down, alight, dismount; — **en panne** to come down with engine trouble; — **à un hôtel** to put up at a hotel.

descente [desɑ̃:t] *nf* descent, declivity, swoop, raid; — **de lit** rug.

descriptible [dɛskriptibl] *a* describable.

descriptif, -ive [dɛskriptif, iːv] *a* descriptive.

description [dɛskripsjɔ̃] *nf* description.

désemballer [dezɑ̃bale] *vt* to unpack.

désemparé [dezɑ̃pare] *a* helpless, crippled, in distress.

désemparer [dezɑ̃pare] *vt* to disable, disjoint; **sans —** without stopping.

désencombrer [dezɑ̃kɔ̃bre] *vt* to clear, free.

désenfler [dezɑ̃fle] *vt* to reduce the swelling of; *vi* to become less swollen, go down.

désengager [dezɑ̃gaʒe] *vt* to release, free, take out of pawn.

désengrener [dezɑ̃grəne] *vt* to put out of gear, disengage.

désenivrer [dezɑ̃nivre] *vt* to sober; *vr* to come to one's senses.

désenterrer [dezɑ̃tere] *vt* to disinter, dig up.

déséquilibrer [dezekilibre] *vt* to throw off balance, unbalance.

désert [dezeːr] *a* lonely, empty, deserted, bleak; *nm* desert, wilderness

déserter [dezerte] *vt* to desert, abandon; *vi* to desert.

déserteur [dezertœː] *nm* deserter.

désertion [dezersjɔ̃] *nf* desertion, running away.

désespérance [dezɛsperɑ̃:s] *nf* despair.

désespérant [dezɛsperɑ̃] *a* hopeless, heartbreaking.

désespéré [dezɛspere] *a* desperate, hopeless.

désespérer [dezɛspere] *vt* to drive to despair; *vi* to despair; *vr* to be in despair.

désespoir [dezɛspwaːr] *nm* despair, despondency.

déshabillé [dezabije] *nm* negligée.

déshabiller [dezabije] *vtr* to undress.

déshabituer [dezabitɥe] *vt* to break s.o. of the habit; *vr* to get out of the habit.

déshériter [dezerite] *vt* to disinherit.

déshonnête [dezɔnɛːt] *a* immodest, improper, indecent.

déshonnêteté [dezɔnɛtəte] *nf* impropriety.

déshonneur [dezɔnœːr] *nm* dishonor, disgrace.

déshonorer [dezɔnɔre] *vt* to dishonor, disgrace.

déshydrater [dezidrate] *vt* dehydrate.

désignation [dezinasjɔ̃] *nf* designation, appointment, choice, description.

désigner [dezine] *vt* to appoint, designate, show, fix, detail, post, draft.

désillusion [dezillyzjɔ̃] *nf* disillusion.

désillusionner [dezillyzjɔne] vt to disillusion.

désinfectant [dezɛ̃fɛktɑ̃] nm disinfectant.

désinfection [dezɛ̃fɛksjɔ̃] nf disinfection, decontamination.

désinfecter [dezɛ̃fɛkte] vt to disinfect, decontaminate.

désintégrer [dezɛ̃tegre] vt to disintegrate, split.

désintéressé [dezɛ̃terɛse] a disinterested, unselfish, selfless.

désintéressement [dezɛ̃terɛsmɑ̃] nm disinterestedness, unselfishness.

désintéresser [dezɛ̃terɛse] vr to lose interest, take no interest (de in).

désinvolte [dezɛ̃vɔlt] a free, offhand, flippant.

désinvolture [dezɛ̃vɔltyːr] nf unselfconsciousness, ease, airy manner, flippancy; avec — airily, flippantly.

désir [deziːr] nm desire, wish, longing.

désirable [dezirabl] a desirable.

désirer [dezire] vt to desire, want, long for.

désireux, -euse [dezirø, øːz] a desirous, anxious.

désobéir [dezɔbeiːr] vti to disobey.

désobéissance [dezɔbeisɑ̃s] nf disobedience.

désobligeance [dezɔbliʒɑ̃s] nf ungraciousness, disagreeableness.

désobliger [dezɔbliʒe] vt to disoblige, offend.

désobstruer [dezɔpstrye] vt to clear, free.

désœuvré [dezœvre] a idle, at loose ends.

désœuvrement [dezœvrəmɑ̃] nm idleness; par — for want of something to do.

désolant [dezɔlɑ̃] a distressing, grievous.

désolation [dezɔlasjɔ̃] nf desolation, grief.

désolé [dezɔle] a desolate, dreary, grieved; je suis — I am very sorry.

désoler [dezɔle] vt to ravage, grieve, distress.

désopilant [dezɔpilɑ̃] a screamingly funny.

désordonné [dezɔrdɔne] a disordered, untidy, dissolute.

désordre [dezɔrdr] nm confusion, disorder, untidiness, disturbance.

désorganisation [dezɔrganizasjɔ̃] nf disorganization, disarrangement.

désorganiser [dezɔrganize] vt to disorganize.

désorienter [dezɔrjɑ̃te] vt to put s.o. off his bearings, bewilder; vr to lose one's bearings, get lost.

désormais [dezɔrmɛ] ad henceforward, from now on.

désosser [dezose] vt to bone.

despote [despɔt] nm despot.

despotisme [despɔtism] nm despotism.

dessaisir [deseziːr] vt to dispossess;

se — de to give up, relinquish.

dessaler [desale] vt to remove salt from, teach s.o. a thing or two.

se dessécher [sədeseʃe] vr to dry, wither; vt parch.

dessein [desɛ̃] nm plan, design, purpose, intention; à — intentionally.

desseller [desɛle] vt to unsaddle.

desserrer [desɛre] vt to loosen, slacken, release; vr to come loose, slacken, relax.

dessert [desɛːr] nm dessert.

desservant [desɛrvɑ̃] nm officiating priest.

desservir [desɛrviːr] vt to clear (away), serve, connect.

dessin [desɛ̃] nm drawing, sketch, cartoon, design.

dessinateur, -trice [desinatœːr, tris] n designer, draftsman, black and white artist.

dessiner [desine] vt to draw, design, plan, outline; vr to stand out, be outlined.

dessouler [desule] vt to sober; vi to become sober.

dessous [dəsu] ad below, underneath, under it, them; regarder qn en — to look furtively at s.o.; avoir le — to get the worst of it; nm bottom, underside; pl seamy side.

dessus [dəsy] ad above, over, on it, them, above it, them; nm top, upper side, advantage; avoir le — to have the best of it; — d'assiette doily; — de lit bedspread; — du panier the pick of the crop.

destin [destɛ̃] nm destiny, fate.

destinataire [destinatɛːr] n addressee, payee.

destination [destinasjɔ̃] nf destination; à — de bound for.

destinée [destine] nf fate, destiny, fortune.

destiner [destine] vt to destine, intend, mean; vr to aim, intend to be; être destiné à to be fated to.

destituer [destitye] vt to dismiss, remove.

destitution [destitysjɔ̃] nf dismissal.

destructeur, -trice [destryktœːr, tris] a destructive; n destroyer.

destructif, -ive [destryktif, iːv] a destructive.

destruction [destryksjɔ̃] nf destruction.

désuet, -uète [desɥɛ, ɛt] a obsolete, out-of-date.

désuétude [desɥetyd] nf disuse, abeyance.

désunion [dezynjɔ̃] nf disunion, separation, breach.

désunir [dezyniːr] vtr to disunite.

détaché [detaʃe] a loose, detached, unconcerned.

détachement [detaʃmɑ̃] nm detaching, detachment, indifference, contingent, draft.

détacher [detaʃe] *vt* to detach, unfasten, untie, disaffect, detail, draft, remove stains from; *vr* to come loose, come off, stand out.

détail [detaːj] *nm* detail, retail; **vente au — retail** selling.

détailler [detaje] *vt* to retail, detail, divide up, look over, appraise.

détaler [detale] *vi* to clear out, scamper off, bolt.

détartrer [detartre] *vt* to scale, fur.

détection [detɛksjɔ̃] *nf* detection.

détective [detɛktiːv] *nm* detective.

déteindre [detɛ̃ːdr] *vt* to take the color out of; *vir* to fade, run; *vi* to influence.

dételer [detle] *vt* to unyoke, unharness.

détendre [detɑ̃ːdr] *vtr* to slacken, loosen, relax.

détenir [detniːr] *vt* to hold, detain, withhold.

détente [detɑ̃ːt] *nf* slackening, relaxation, trigger.

détenteur, -trice [detɑ̃tœːr, tris] *n* holder.

détention [detɑ̃sjɔ̃] *nf* detention.

détérioration [deterjɔrasjɔ̃] *nf* damage, wear and tear.

détériorer [deterjɔre] *vt* to damage, spoil; *vr* to deteriorate.

détermination [detɛrminasjɔ̃] *nf* determination.

déterminé [detɛrmine] *a* determined, definite.

déterminer [detɛrmine] *vt* to determine, fix, bring about, decide; *vr* to make up one's mind.

déterrer [detɛre] *vt* to dig up, unearth, find out.

détestable [detɛstabl] *a* wretched, hateful.

détester [detɛste] *vt* to hate, loathe, dislike.

détonateur [detɔnatœːr] *nm* detonator, fog-signal.

détonation [detɔnasjɔ̃] *nf* detonation, report.

détoner [detɔne] *vi* to detonate, bang.

détonner [detɔne] *vi* to be out of tune, jar.

détour [detuːr] *nm* turning, winding, curve, bend, roundabout way.

détourné [deturne] *a* circuitous, devious.

détournement [deturnəmɑ̃] *nm* diversion, embezzlement, abduction.

détourner [deturne] *vt* to divert, avert, ward off, abduct, alienate, embezzle; *vr* to turn aside.

détracteur, -trice [detraktœːr, tris] *n* detractor.

détraquement [detrakmɑ̃] *nm* breakdown.

détraquer [detrake] *vt* to put out of order; *vr* to break down.

détrempe [detrɑ̃ːp] *nf* distemper, wash.

détremper [detrɑ̃pe] *vt* to soak, soften.

détresse [detrɛs] *nf* distress, misery,

détriment [detrimɑ̃] *nm* detriment, prejudice, loss.

détritus [detrityːs] *nm* detritus, refuse.

détroit [detrwa] *nm* strait(s), channel, pass.

détromper [detrɔ̃pe] *vt* put right, enlighten, *vr* **détrompez-vous!** get that out of your head!

détrôner [detrone] *vt* to dethrone.

détrousser [detruse] *vt* to let down, rob.

détruire [detrɥiːr] *vt* to destroy, overthrow, demolish.

dette [dɛt] *nf* debt, indebtedness, duty.

deuil [dœːj] *nm* mourning, grief, bereavement.

deux [dø] *a* two, second; *nm* two, deuce.

deuxième [døzjɛm] *an* second.

dévaler [devale] *vti* to rush down; *vi* to slope, descend, rush down.

dévaliser [devalize] *vt* to rob, rifle, plunder.

dévaluer [devalɥe] *vt* to devaluate.

devancer [d(ə)vɑ̃se] *vt* to go before, precede, forestall.

devancier, -ière [d(ə)vɑ̃sje, jɛːr] *n* predecessor.

devant [d(ə)vɑ̃] *prep* before, in front of, in face of; *ad* ahead, in front; *nm* front; **prendre les —s sur** to steal a march on.

devanture [d(ə)vɑ̃tyːr] *nf* front, shop window.

dévastateur, -trice [devastatœːr, tris] *a* damaging, devastating; *n* ravager.

dévastation [devastasjɔ̃] *nf* devastation, havoc.

dévaster [devaste] *vt* to lay waste, devastate, gut.

déveine [devɛn] *nf* bad luck.

développement [devlɔpmɑ̃] *nm* development, growth, expansion.

développer [devlɔpe] *vt* to develop, expand, enlarge (upon); *vr* to develop, expand.

devenir [dəvniːr] *vi* to become, get, grow; **qu'est-il devenu?** what has become of him?

dévergondage [devɛrgɔ̃daːʒ] *nm* shamelessness.

dévergondé [devɛrgɔ̃de] *a* shameless, profligate.

déverrouiller [devɛruje] *vt* to unbolt.

dévers [devɛr] *a* leaning, warped, out of plumb; *nm* slope, warp, banking.

déversement [devɛrs(ə)mɑ̃] *nm* overflow, tipping.

déverser [devɛrse] *vt* to slant, incline, pour, dump; *vi* to lean, get out of true line.

dévêtir [devɛtiːr] *vt* to strip, undress, take off; *vr* to undress, divest oneself.

déviation [devjasjɔ̃] *nf* deviation,

deflexion, departure, (road) detour.
dévider [devide] vt to unwind, reel, pay out.
dévidoir [devidwa:r] nm reel, drum, winder.
dévier [devje] vt to turn aside, deflect; vi to swerve, deviate.
deviner [dəvine] vt to guess, foretell, make out.
devinette [dəvinɛt] nf conundrum, riddle.
devis [dəvi] nm estimate.
dévisager [devisaʒe] vt to stare at.
devise [dəvi:z] nf device, slogan, currency, bill.
dévisser [devise] vt to unscrew.
dévoiler [devwale] vt to unveil, disclose, reveal.
devoir [dəvwa:r] vt to owe, be indebted, have to, to be obliged to, must, ought, should; nm duty, task, exercise.
dévolu [devɔly] a devolving, devolved; nm jeter son — sur to choose.
dévorer [devɔre] vt to devour, eat up, consume.
dévot [devo] an devout, religious (person).
dévotion [devosjɔ̃] nf piety, devotion.
dévoué [devwe] a devoted, sincere, loyal.
dévouement [devumɑ̃] nm devotion, devotedness, self-sacrifice.
dévouer [devwe] vt to devote, dedicate; vr to devote oneself, sacrifice oneself.
dévoyer [devwaje] vtr to lead astray, go off the rails.
dextérité [dɛksterite] nf dexterity, skill.
diabète [djabɛt] nm diabetes.
diabétique [djabetik] an diabetic.
diable [dja:bl] nm devil; allez au —! go to hell!
diablerie [djablǝri] nf deviltry, witchcraft, mischievousness, turbulence.
diablotin [djablɔtɛ̃] nm imp, cracker.
diabolique [djabɔlik] a diabolical, fiendish.
diaconesse [djakɔnɛs] nf deaconess.
diacre [djakr] nm deacon.
diadème [djadɛm] nm diadem.
diagnostic [djagnɔstik] nm diagnosis.
diagnostiquer [djagnɔstike] vt to diagnose.
diagonal [djagɔnal] a diagonal.
dialecte [djalɛkt] nm dialect.
dialogue [djalɔg] nm dialogue.
diamant [djamɑ̃] nm diamond.
diamètre [djamɛtr] nm diameter.
diane [djan] nf reveille.
diantre [djɑ̃:tr] excl well!
diapason [djapazɔ̃] nm tuning fork, diapason, range.
diaphane [djafan] a diaphanous, transparent.
diaphragme [djafragm] nm diaphragm, sound-box.

diapré [djapre] a mottled, speckled, variegated.
dictateur [diktatœ:r] nm dictator.
dictature [diktaty:r] nf dictatorship.
dictée [dikte] nf dictation.
dicter [dikte] vt to dictate.
diction [diksjɔ̃] nf diction, elocution.
dictionnaire [diksjɔnɛ:r] nm dictionary.
dicton [diktɔ̃] nm saying, proverb, maxim.
dièse [djɛ:z] nm (mus) sharp.
diète [djɛt] nf diet, regimen.
dieu [djø] nm god; excl goodness!
diffamation [diffamasjɔ̃] nf slander, libel.
diffamatoire [diffamatwa:r] a slanderous, defamatory, libelous.
diffamer [diffame] vt to defame, slander.
différence [diferɑ̃:s] nf difference, distinction, discrepancy, gap.
différend [diferɑ̃] nm difference, dispute.
différent [diferɑ̃] a different, unlike, various.
différentiel, -ielle [diferɑ̃sjɛl] a nm differential.
différer [difere] vt to put off, postpone; vi to differ, put off.
difficile [difisil] a difficult, hard, hard to please.
difficilement [difisilmɑ̃] ad with difficulty.
difficulté [difikylte] nf difficulty; faire des —s to be fussy, raise difficulties.
difforme [difɔrm] a deformed, shapeless.
difformité [difɔrmite] nf deformity.
diffus [dify] a diffuse, wordy, diffused.
diffuser [difyze] vt to diffuse.
diffusion [difyzjɔ̃] nf spreading, broadcasting.
digérer [diʒere] vt to digest, assimilate.
digestible [diʒɛstibl] a digestible.
digestif, -ive [diʒɛstif] a digestive.
digestion [diʒɛstjɔ̃] nf digestion, assimilation.
digital, -ale, -aux [diʒital, al, o] a empreinte — fingerprint; nf foxglove, digitalis.
digne [diɲ] a worthy, stately, dignified, deserving.
dignitaire [diɲitɛ:r] nm dignitary.
dignité [diɲite] nf dignity, nobility, greatness.
digression [digresjɔ̃] nf digression.
digue [dig] nf dike, sea-wall, embankment, dam.
dilapider [dilapide] vt to waste, squander, embezzle.
dilater [dilate] vtr to dilate, expand, distend.
dilemme [dilɛm] nm dilemma.
diligence [diliʒɑ̃:s] nf application, industry, haste; stage-coach.
diligent [diliʒɑ̃] a busy.

diluer [dilɥe] *vt* to dilute, water down.

dimanche [dimɑ̃:ʃ] *nm* Sunday.

dimension [dimɑ̃sjɔ̃] *nf* size; *pl* measurements.

diminuer [diminɥe] *vt* to diminish, lessen, reduce; *vi* to decrease, abate.

diminution [diminysjɔ̃] *nf* decrease, reduction.

dinde [dɛ̃:d] *nf* turkey-hen.

dindon [dɛ̃dɔ̃] *nm* turkey-cock.

dîner [dine] *vi* to dine; *nm* dinner (party).

dîneur, -euse [dinœ:r, ø:z] *n* diner.

diocèse [djɔsɛ:z] *nm* diocese.

dioula [diula] *nm* itinerant peddler.

diphtérie [difteri] *nf* diphtheria.

diplomate [diplɔmat] *nm* diplomat (ist).

diplomatie [diplɔmasi] *nf* diplomacy, diplomatic service.

diplomatique [diplɔmatik] *a* diplomatic.

diplôme [diplo:m] *nm* diploma, certificate.

diplômé [diplome] *a* certificated.

dire [di:r] *vt* to say, tell, speak; *nm* statement, words; **dites donc!** look here!; **ce vin ne me dit rien** I don't care for this wine; **et — que and to think that; que dites-vous de cela?** what do you think of that?

direct [dirɛkt] *a* direct, straight, pointed, flat.

directeur, -trice [dirɛktœ:r, tris] *a* guiding, controlling; *n* chief, leader, manager, manageress, headmaster, headmistress, superintendent.

direction [dirɛksjɔ̃] *nf* direction, management, guidance, leadership, steering.

directives [dirɛkti:v] *nf pl* guidelines.

dirigeant [diriʒɑ̃] *a* directing, guiding, governing.

dirigeable [diriʒabl] *nm* airship.

diriger [diriʒe] *vt* to direct, manage, conduct, guide, steer, point; *vr* to make one's way, proceed.

discernement [disɛrnəmɑ̃] *nm* discernment, discrimination.

discerner [disɛrne] *vt* to discern, descry, distinguish.

disciple [disipl] *nm* disciple, follower.

discipline [disiplin] *nf* discipline, order.

discipliner [disipline] *vt* to discipline.

discontinuer [diskɔ̃tinɥe] *vt* to discontinue, leave off, break off.

disconvenance [diskɔ̃vnɑ̃:s] *nf* disparity, unsuitableness.

disconvenir [diskɔ̃vni:r] *vi* to be unsuitable, deny.

discordance [diskɔrdɑ̃:s] *nf* disagreement, clash.

discordant [diskɔrdɑ̃] *a* harsh, grating, clashing.

discorde [diskɔrd] *nf* strife, lack of unity.

discourir [diskuri:r] *vi* to talk volubly, hold forth, discourse.

discours [disku:r] *nm* discourse, speech, talk.

discourtois [diskurtwa] *a* impolite, discourteous.

discrédit [diskredi] *nm* disrepute.

discréditer [diskredite] *vt* to discredit, disparage, bring into disrepute.

discret, -ète [diskrɛ, ɛt] *a* discreet, unobtrusive.

discrétion [diskresjɔ̃] *nf* restraint.

discriminer [diskrimine] *vt* to discriminate.

disculper [diskylpe] *vt* to exonerate, clear.

discussion [diskysjɔ̃] *nf* argument, debate.

discutable [diskytabl] *a* debatable, disputable.

discuter [diskyte] *vt* to discuss, talk over, question.

disette [dizet] *nf* want, scarcity, dearth.

diseur, -euse [dizœ:r, ø:z] *n* — **de bonne aventure** fortune-teller.

disgrâce [disgrɑ:s] *nf* disfavor, misfortune.

disgracieux, -euse [disgrasjø, ø:z] *a* ungraceful, awkward, ungracious.

disjoindre [disʒwɛ̃:dr] *vt* to sever, disjoin.

dislocation [dislɔkasjɔ̃] *nf* dislocation, dismemberment.

disloquer [dislɔke] *vt* to dislocate, dismember; *vr* to fall apart, break up.

disparaître [disparɛ:tr] *vi* to disappear, vanish.

disparate [disparat] *a* unlike, illassorted.

disparition [disparisjɔ̃] *nf* disappearance.

dispendieux, -euse [dispɑ̃djø, ø:z] *a* expensive.

dispensaire [dispɑ̃sɛ:r] *nm* dispensary, out-patients' department.

dispensation [dispɑ̃sasjɔ̃] *nf* dispensing.

dispense [dispɑ̃:s] *nf* dispensation, exemption.

dispenser [dispɑ̃se] *vt* to dispense, distribute, excuse, exempt; *vr* to get exempted (from de), get out (of de).

disperser [dispɛrse] *vtr* to scatter, disperse.

dispersion [dispɛrsjɔ̃] *nf* scattering, dispersal.

disponibilité [dispɔnibilite] *nf* availability; *pl* available funds; **être en — to be on half-pay.

disponible [dispɔnibl] *a* available.

dispos [dispo] *a* fit, bright, well.

disposé [dispoze] *a* disposed, agreeable, ready; **être bien (mal) — to be in a good (bad) temper.

disposer [dispoze] *vt* to arrange, array, set out, incline; *vr* to get ready; **— de** to have at one's disposal.

dispositif [dispozitif] nm apparatus, gadget.

disposition [dispozisjɔ̃] nf disposition, disposal, arrangement, tendency; pl natural gift, provisions.

disproportion [disproporsjɔ̃] nf lack of proportion.

disproportionné [disproporsjɔne] a disproportionate, out of proportion.

disputailler [dispytaje] vi to cavil, bicker.

dispute [dispyt] nf dispute, squabble.

disputer [dispyte] vt to discuss, argue about, dispute, challenge; vi to quarrel; vr to argue, wrangle, contend for.

disqualifier [diskalifje] vt to disqualify.

disque [disk] nm discus, disc, phonograph record.

dissemblable [di(s)sãblabl] a unlike, dissimilar.

dissemblance [dis(s)ãblã:s] nf unlikeness, dissimilarity.

disséminer [dis(s)emine] vt to scatter, spread.

dissension [dis(s)ãsjɔ̃] nf dissension, discord.

dissentiment [dis(s)ãtimã] nm dissent, disagreement.

disséquer [dis(s)eke] vt to dissect.

dissertation [disertasjɔ̃] nf essay, composition.

disserter [diserte] vi to dissert, expatiate.

dissident [dis(s)idã] a dissentient, dissident.

dissimulateur, -trice [dis(s)imylatœ:r, tris] n dissembler; a deceitful.

dissimulation [dis(s)imylasjɔ̃] nf deceit, dissimulation, hiding.

dissimuler [dis(s)imyle] vt to dissimulate, conceal, disguise; vr to hide.

dissipation [disipasjɔ̃] nf dissipation, dispersion, wasting, dissolute conduct, inattentiveness.

dissipé [disipe] a dissipated, giddy, inattentive.

dissiper [disipe] vt to dissipate, dispel, waste, divert; vr to disappear, be dispelled, clear, become dissolute.

dissolu [dis(s)ɔly] a profligate, abandoned, dissolute.

dissolution [dis(s)ɔlysjɔ̃] nf disintegration, dissolving, breaking-up, solution.

dissoudre [dis(s)udr] vtr to dissolve, break up.

dissuader [dis(s)yade] vt to dissuade, talk out of.

distance [distã:s] nf distance, range.

distancer [distãse] vt to outdistance, outstrip.

distant [distã] a distant, aloof.

distillateur [distilatœ:r] nm distiller.

distillation [distilasjɔ̃] nf distillation, distilling.

distiller [distile] vt to distil, drop.

distillerie [distilri] nf distillery.

distinct [distɛ̃(:kt)] a distinct, clear, audible.

distinctif. -ive [distɛ̃ktif, i:v] a distinctive.

distinction [distɛ̃ksjɔ̃] nf distinction, honor, distinguished air.

distingué [distɛ̃ge] a eminent, distinguished.

distinguer [distɛ̃ge] vt to distinguish, discriminate, characterize, perceive, bring to notice; vr to distinguish oneself, be distinguishable.

distraction [distraksjɔ̃] nf separation, distraction, absent-mindedness, entertainment.

distraire [distre:r] vt to separate, distract, take one's mind off, amuse, entertain; vr to amuse oneself.

distrait [distre] a absent-minded, listless.

distribuer [distribɥe] vt to distribute, apportion, share out, hand out, deliver; — les rôles to cast a play.

distributeur, -trice [distribytœ:r, tris] n dispenser, distributor; — automatique slot-machine.

distribution [distribysjɔ̃] nf distribution, issue, allotting, delivery; — des prix prize-giving; — des rôles cast(ing).

dit [di] a called, named; autrement — alias, in other words.

divagation [divagasjɔ̃] nf deviation, wandering.

divaguer [divage] vi to deviate, wander, rave.

divan [divã] nm couch.

divergence [diverʒã:s] nf divergence, spread.

diverger [diverʒe] vi to diverge.

divers [dive:r] a various, sundry, divers, different, diverse; nm pl sundries.

diversion [diversjɔ̃] nf diversion, change.

diversité [diversite] nf variety, diversity.

divertir [diverti:r] vt to entertain, divert; vr to amuse oneself.

divertissement [divertismã] nm recreation, entertainment, diversion.

dividende [dividã:d] nm dividend.

divin [divɛ̃] a divine, sacred, heavenly, sublime.

divinateur, -trice [divinatœ:r, tris] n soothsayer.

divinité [divinite] nf divinity, deity.

diviser [divize] vt to divide; vr to divide, break up.

diviseur [divizœ:r] nm divisor.

divisible [divizibl] a divisible.

division [divizjɔ̃] nf division, section, dissension.

divorce [divɔrs] nm divorce.

divorcer [divɔrse] vti to divorce.

divulgation [divylgasjɔ̃] nf disclosure.

divulguer [divylge] vt to divulge, disclose, reveal.

dix [dis] a nm ten, tenth.

dixième [dizjɛm] a nm tenth.

dizaine [dizɛn] nf (about) ten.

docile [dɔsil] a complaint, manageable.

docilité [dɔsilite] nf docility.

dock [dɔk] dock(s), warehouse.

docte [dɔkt] a learned.

docteur [dɔktœːr] nm doctor.

doctoral [dɔktɔral] a doctoral, pompous.

doctorat [dɔktɔra] nm doctorate.

doctrine [dɔktrin] nf doctrine, belief, teaching.

document [dɔkymɑ̃] nm document.

documentaire [dɔkymɑ̃tɛːr] a documentary.

documentation [dɔkymɑ̃tasjɔ̃] nf gathering of facts.

documenter [dɔkymɑ̃te] vt to document, give information to; vr to collect material, information.

dodeliner [dɔdline] vti to dandle, nod, shake.

dodo [dɔdo] nm sleep; faire — to go to sleep, to go bye-bye.

dodu [dɔdy] a plump.

dogme [dɔgm] nm dogma.

dogue [dɔg] nm mastiff.

doigt [dwa] nm finger; — de pied toe.

doigté [dwate] nm tact, (mus) fingering.

doigtier [dwatje] nm finger-stall.

doit [dwa] nm debit.

doléances [dɔleɑ̃ːs] nf pl grievances, sorrows.

dolent [dɔlɑ̃] a doleful.

domaine [dɔmɛn] nm domain, estate, province, field.

dôme [doːm] nm dome.

domesticité [dɔmɛstisite] nf domesticity, staff of servants.

domestique [dɔmɛstik] a domestic; n servant.

domicile [dɔmisil] nm abode, residence.

domicilié [dɔmisilje] a residing, resident.

domicilier [dɔmisilje] vr to settle, take up residence.

dominance [dɔminɑ̃ːs] nf dominion, predominance.

dominant [dɔminɑ̃] a ruling, (pre)dominant.

dominateur, -trice [dɔminatœːr, tris] a domineering.

domination [dɔminasjɔ̃] nf rule, sway.

dominer [dɔmine] vt to dominate, rule, master, control, overlook; vi to rule.

domino [dɔmino] nm hood, domino.

dommage [dɔmaːʒ] nm harm, injury, pity; pl damage, destruction; dommages et intérêts damages (in law).

dompter [dɔ̃te] vt to tame, break in, master.

dompteur, -euse [dɔ̃tœːr, øːz] n tamer, trainer.

don [dɔ̃] nm donation, giving, gift, present, talent.

donateur, -trice [dɔnatœːr, tris] n donor, giver.

donc [dɔːk] cj so, therefore, then; ad well, just, ever.

donjon [dɔ̃ʒɔ̃] nm (of castle) keep.

donne [dɔn] nf (card games) deal.

donnée [dɔne] nf fundamental idea; pl data.

donner [dɔne] vt to give, furnish, yield, ascribe, deal; vi to look out (sur on to); — dans to have a taste for, fall into; s'en — à cœur joie to have a high old time; c'est donné it's dirt cheap.

dont [dɔ̃] pr of (by, from, with, about) whom or which, whose.

doré [dɔre] a gilt, golden.

dorénavant [dɔrenavɑ̃] ad henceforth.

dorer [dɔre] vt to gild, brown.

dorloter [dɔrlɔte] vt to cuddle, pet, coddle, pamper.

dormant [dɔrmɑ̃] a dormant, sleeping, stagnant.

dormeur, -euse [dɔrmœːr, øːz] n sleeper, sleepy-head.

dormir [dɔrmiːr] vi to sleep, be asleep, be stagnant, lie dormant.

dortoir [dɔrtwaːr] nm dormitory.

dorure [dɔryːr] nf gilt, gilding.

dos [do] nm back, bridge.

dose [doːz] nf dose, amount.

doser [doze] vt to dose, decide the amount of.

dossier [dɔsje] nm (of chair) back; record, documents, brief.

dot [dɔt] nf dowry.

doter [dɔte] vt to give a dowry to, endow.

douaire [dwɛːr] nm marriage settlement, dower.

douane [dwan] nf customs, custom-house, duty; en — in bond.

douanier, -ère [dwanje, jɛːr] a customs; n customs-officer.

double [dubl] a double, twofold; nm double, duplicate.

doubler [duble] vt to double, fold in two, line, overtake, quicken; — une classe to repeat a class; — un rôle to understudy a part; — le cap to get out of a scrape.

doublure [dublyːr] nf lining, understudy.

doucement [dusmɑ̃] ad gently, quietly, smoothly.

doucereux, -euse [dusrø, øːz] a sweetish, cloying, glib, sugary.

douceur [dusœːr] nf sweetness, smoothness, gentleness, softness, mildness; pl comforts, sweets.

douche [duʃ] nf shower-bath, douche.

doué [dwe] a gifted, endowed.

douer [dwe] vt to endow.

douille [duːj] nf case, casing, socket, sleeve.

douillet, -ette [dujɛ, ɛt] a soft, cosy, delicate, tender.

douleur [dulœːr] nf suffering, pain, grief, sorrow.

douloureux, -euse [dulurø, øːz] a painful, aching, sad, sorrowful, grievous.

doute [dut] nm doubt, misgiving, scruple; **mettre en —** to call in question; **sans —** probably.

douter [dute] vi to doubt, suspect; vt to suspect, surmise; **je m'en doutais bien** I thought as much.

douteux, -euse [dutø, øːz] a doubtful, questionable.

douve [duːv] nf ditch, moat.

doux, douce [du, dus] a sweet, gentle, smooth, soft, mild, pleasant; **eau douce** fresh water.

douzaine [duzɛn] nf dozen.

douze [duːz] nm twelve, twelfth.

doyen, -enne [dwajɛ̃, ɛn] n dean, doyen, senior.

dragage [dragaːʒ] nm dredging, dragging, mine-sweeping.

dragée [draʒe] nf sugared almond, comfit.

dragon [dragɔ̃] nm dragon, dragoon.

draguer [drage] vt to dredge, drag, sweep.

dragueur [dragœːr] nm dredger; **— de mines** mine-sweeper.

drainer [drɛne] vt to drain.

dramatique [dramatik] a dramatic; **auteur —** playwright.

dramatiser [dramatize] vt to dramatize.

dramaturge [dramatyrʒ] nm dramatist.

drame [dram] nm drama, play, sensational event.

drap [dra] nm cloth; **— de lit** bed-sheet; **être dans de beaux —s** to be in a mess.

drapeau [drapo] nm flag, colors.

draper [drape] vt to drape, hang.

draperie [drapri] nf cloth-trade, drapery.

drapier, -ière [drapje, jɛːr] n draper, clothier.

dresser [drɛse] vt to raise, set up, draw up, make out, train, break in; vr to rise, sit up, straighten up; **— les oreilles** to cock one's ears; **faire — les cheveux à qn** to make s.o.'s hair stand on end.

dresseur, -euse [drɛsœːr, øːz] n trainer, trimmer, adjuster.

dressoir [drɛswaːr] nm dresser, side-board.

drogue [drɔg] nf drug.

droguer [drɔge] vt to give medicine to, drug, dope.

droguiste [drɔgist] nm druggist.

droit [drwa] a straight, direct, upright, right(hand), honest; ad straight (on); nm right, due, fee, law; **veston —** single-breasted jacket; **— d'auteur** copyright; **—s acquis** vested interests; **à bon —**

with good reason; — d'aînesse birthright.

droite [drwat] nf right (-hand, side).

droitier, -ière [drwatje, jɛːr] a right-handed.

droiture [drwatyːr] nf integrity, uprightness.

drôle [droːl] a funny, odd, queer; n rogue, rascal.

dromadaire [drɔmadɛːr] nm dromedary.

dru [dry] a thick, dense, strong; ad thickly, heavily.

du [dy] = **de** + **le**.

duc [dyk] nm duke.

duché [dyʃe] nm duchy, dukedom.

duchesse [dyʃɛs] nf duchess.

duelliste [dɥɛlist] nm duelist.

dûment [dymɑ̃] ad duly, in due form.

dune [dyn] nf dune, sand-hill.

dunette [dynɛt] nf (deck) poop.

duo [dyo] nm duet.

dupe [dyp] nf dupe, catspaw.

duper [dype] vt to dupe, trick, take in.

duperie [dypri] nf trickery, sell, a piece of double-dealing.

duplicité [dyplisite] nf duplicity, falseness, deceit, double-dealing.

dur [dyːr] a hard, harsh, difficult, tough, inured; ad hard; **avoir l'oreille —e** to be hard of hearing; **avoir la tête —e** to be slow-witted; **œufs —s** hard-boiled eggs; **c'est un — à cuire** he is a tough nut.

durabilité [dyrabilite] nf durability, lasting quality.

durable [dyrabl] a hard-wearing, lasting, enduring.

durant [dyrɑ̃] prep during, for.

durcir [dyrsiːr] vt to harden, make hard; vi to grow hard.

durcissement [dyrsismɑ̃] nm hardening.

durée [dyre] nf duration, continuance, wear, life.

durement [dyrmɑ̃] ad hard(ly), roughly, harshly.

durer [dyre] vi to last, endure, wear well.

dureté [dyrte] nf hardness, harshness, callousness.

durillon [dyrijɔ̃] nm callosity.

duvet [dyvɛ] nm down, fluff.

duveté [dyvte] a downy, fluffy.

dynamique [dinamik] a dynamic; nf dynamics.

dynamite [dinamit] nf dynamite.

dynastie [dinasti] nf dynasty.

dysenterie [disɑ̃tri] nf dysentery.

dyspepsie [dispɛpsi] nf dyspepsia.

dyssymétrie [dis(s)imetri] nf asymmetry.

E

eau [o] nf water; **— oxygénée** hydrogen peroxide; **—x mortes** neap tides; **vives — x** spring tides; **faire — to** leak, bilge; **faire venir l'— à la bouche** to make one's mouth water; **laver à grande —** to swill.

eau-de-vie [odvi] *nf* brandy, spirits.

eau-forte [ofɔrt] *nf* aqua fortis, etching.

ébahir [ebai:r] *v'* to amaze, dumbfound; *vr* to be dumbfounded, abashed.

ébahissement [ebaismã] *nm* amazement, wonder.

ébats [eba] *nm pl* frolic, sport, gambols, revels.

s'ébattre [sebatr] *vr* to frolic, gambol, frisk about.

s'ébaubir [sebobi:r] *vr* to be astounded, flabbergasted.

ébauche [ebo:ʃ] *nf* sketch, outline.

ébaucher [eboʃe] *vt* to sketch, rough draw, outline.

ébène [ebɛn] *nf* ebony.

ébéniste [ebenist] *nm* cabinet-maker.

ébénisterie [ebenistri] *nf* cabinet-making.

éberlué [eberlɥe] *a* dumbfounded.

éblouir [eblui:r] *vt* to dazzle.

éblouissement [ebluismã] *nm* dazzling, dazzle, dizziness.

ébonite [ebɔnit] *nf* vulcanite.

éborgner [ebɔrɲe] *vt* to put s.o.'s eye out.

ébouillanter [ebujãte] *vt* to scald.

éboulement [ebulmã] *nm* falling-in, landslide.

s'ébouler [sebule] *vr* to fall in, cave in, slip.

éboulis [ebuli] *nm* mass of fallen rock and earth.

ébouriffer [eburife] *vt* to dishevel, ruffle, take aback.

ébrancher [ebrãʃe] *vt* to lop the branches off.

ébranlement [ebrãlmã] *nm* shaking, tottering, shock, commotion.

ébranler [ebrãle] *vt* to shake, loosen, set in motion; *vr* to totter, start, move off.

ébrécher [ebreʃe] *vt* to notch, chip, make inroads into.

ébriété [ebriete] *nf* intoxication.

s'ébrouer [sebrue] *vr* to snort; (*birds*) take a dust bath.

ébruiter [ebrɥite] *vt* to noise abroad, spread, make known; *vr* to be noised abroad, spread.

ébullition [ebylisjɔ̃] *nf* boiling, fever, ferment.

écaille [eka:j] *nf* scale, shell, flake, chip.

écailler [ekaje] *vt* to scale, open; *vr* to peel, flake off.

écailleux, -euse [ekajø, ø:z] *a* scaly, flaky.

écale [ekal] *nf* shell, pod.

écaler [ekale] *vt* to shell, husk.

écarlate [ekarlat] *a* scarlet.

écarquiller [ekarkije] *vtr* to open wide, spread wide apart.

écart [eka:r] *nm* step aside, swerve,

deflection, straying, divergence, difference, error, variation, discarding; **à l'—** aside; **faire un —** to shy, step aside; **faire le grand —** to do the splits.

écarté [ekarte] *a* lonely, remote, out-of-the-way.

écarteler [ekartəle] *vt* to quarter; **être écartelé** to be torn between.

écartement [ekartəmã] *nm* separation, spacing, gap, gauge.

écarter [ekarte] *vt* to separate, space, spread, pull aside, fend off, brush aside, discard; *vr* to diverge, stray, step aside.

ecclésiastique [eklezjastik] *a* ecclesiastical, clerical; *nm* clergyman.

écervelé [esɛrvəle] *a* hare-brained, giddy, rash.

échafaud [eʃafo] *nm* scaffold.

échafaudage [eʃafoda:ʒ] *nm* scaffolding.

échafauder [eʃafode] *vt* to construct, build up.

échalas [eʃala] *nm* vine-pole, hop-pole, spindle-shanks.

échalis [eʃali] *nm* stile.

échancrer [eʃãkre] *vt* to cut out, scallop, indent.

échancrure [eʃãkry:r] *nf* cut-out piece, opening.

échange [eʃã:ʒ] *nm* exchange, barter.

échangeable [eʃãʒabl] *a* exchangeable.

échanger [eʃãʒe] *vt* to exchange, barter, bandy.

échantillon [eʃãtijɔ̃] *nm* sample, pattern.

échappatoire [eʃapatwa:r] *nf* loophole, way out.

échappement [eʃapmã] *nm* escape, leakage, exhaust-pipe.

échapper [eʃape] *vi* to escape; *vr* to run away, escape, leak; **il l'a échappé belle** he had a narrow escape; **— à qn** to elude s.o.

échappée [eʃape] *nf* vista; turning space; (*racing*) spurt; (*cattle*) straying.

écharde [eʃard] *nf* splinter.

écharpe [eʃarp] *nf* scarf, sash, sling.

échasse [eʃa:s] *nf* stilt.

échauder [eʃode] *vt* to scald.

échauffant [eʃofã] *a* heating, exciting.

échauffement [eʃofmã] *nm* heating, over-heating, over-excitement.

échauffer [eʃofe] *vt* to overheat, heat, warm; *vt* to get overheated, warm up.

échauffourée [eʃofure] *nf* scuffle, skirmish.

échéance [eʃeã:s] *nf* date, expiration, falling due.

échec [eʃɛk] *nm* check, set-back, failure; *pl* chess, chessmen; **échec et mat** checkmate.

échelle [eʃɛl] *nf* ladder, scale; **après lui il faut tirer l'—** he always goes one better than anyone else; **faire la courte — à** to give a leg up to; **— de sauvetage** fire-escape.

échelon [eʃlɔ̃] nm rung, step, degree, echelon.

échelonner [eʃlɔne] vt to space out, stagger.

écheveau [eʃvo] nm skein, hank.

échevelé [eʃəvle] a disheveled, wild, frenzied.

échine [eʃin] nf spine.

échiner [eʃine] vt to work to death; vr to slave, wear o.s. out.

échiquier [eʃikje] nm chessboard, exchequer.

écho [eko] nm echo.

échoir [eʃwaːr] vi to fall (due), expire, devolve.

échoppe [eʃɔp] nf stall, booth.

échouage [eʃwaːʒ] nm stranding, grounding.

échouer [eʃwe] vt to beach; vi to run aground, ground, fail, miscarry.

éclabousser [eklabuse] vt to splash, spatter.

éclaboussure [eklabusyːr] nf splash, spatter.

éclair [eklɛːr] nm lightning, flash; eclair.

éclairage [eklɛraːʒ] nm lighting (up); **— par projecteurs** floodlighting.

éclaircie [eklɛrsi] nf break, bright interval, clearing.

éclaircir [eklɛrsiːr] vt to clarify, clear up, solve, enlighten, thin out; vr to clear, grow thin, be cleared up.

éclaircissement [eklɛrsismɑ̃] nm clearing-up, enlightenment, elucidation.

éclairer [eklɛre] vt to light, brighten, enlighten, reconnoiter; vr to light up, brighten up, clear.

éclaireur, -euse [eklɛrœːr, øːz] n scout, Boy Scout, Girl Scout.

éclat [ekla] nm splinter, chip, flash, brilliancy, glamor, burst; **rire aux —s** to laugh uproariously.

éclatant [eklatɑ̃] a bursting, loud, brilliant, resounding, flagrant.

éclater [eklate] vt to burst, split; vi to burst, explode, break out; **— en colère** to fly into a rage; **— de rire** to burst out laughing.

éclectique [eklɛktik] a eclectic, catholic.

éclipse [eklips] nf eclipse.

éclipser [eklipse] vt to eclipse, put in the shade, surpass; vr to vanish.

éclisse [eklis] nf splint; fish-plate.

éclopé [eklɔpe] a lame, limping; nm cripple, lame person.

éclore [eklɔːr] vi to hatch (out), open out, burst.

éclosion [eklozjɔ̃] nf hatching, blossoming, opening out.

écluse [eklyːz] nf lock, sluice-gate.

écœurant [ekœrɑ̃] a sickening, fulsome.

écœurement [ekœrmɑ̃] nm disgust, loathing.

écœurer [ekœre] vt to sicken, disgust.

école [ekɔl] nf school; **— polytechnique militaire** academy; **— normale** teachers college.

écolier, -ière [ekɔlje, jɛːr] n schoolboy, -girl.

éconduire [ekɔ̃dɥiːr] vt to show out, put out.

économe [ekɔnɔm] a economical, thrifty; nm steward, housekeeper, bursar.

économie [ekɔnɔmi] nf economy, thrift; pl savings; **faire des —s** to save, retrench.

économique [ekɔnɔmik] a economic (al).

économiser [ekɔnɔmize] vt to economize, save.

économiste [ekɔnɔmist] nm economist.

écope [ekɔp] nf scoop, ladle, bailer.

écoper [ekɔpe] vt to bail out; vi to catch it.

écorce [ekɔrs] nf bark, peel, rind, crust.

écorcer [ekɔrse] vt to bark, peel, husk.

écorcher [ekɔrʃe] vt to skin, flay, graze, scratch.

écorchure [ekɔrʃyːr] nf abrasion, scratch.

écorner [ekɔrne] vt to take the horns off, break the corners of, dog-ear, make inroads in.

écornifler [ekɔrnifle] vt to scrounge, cadge.

Écosse [ekɔs] nf Scotland.

écossais [ekɔsɛ] a Scottish, Scotch, Scots; **étoffe —e** tartan; n Scot, Scotsman, Scotswoman.

écosser [ekɔse] vt to shell, pod, husk.

écot [eko] nm share, quota.

écoulement [ekulmɑ̃] nm flow, discharge, waste-pipe, sale.

écouler [ekule] vt to sell, dispose of; vr to flow, run out, to pass, elapse.

écourter [ekurte] vt to shorten, curtail, cut short.

écoute [ekut] nf listening post, listening-in; **être aux —s** to be on the look-out; **faire, rester à l'—** to listen in.

écouter [ekute] vt to listen to; vi to listen; **— à la porte** to eavesdrop.

écouteur, -euse [ekutœːr, øːz] n listener; nm earphone, receiver.

écoutille [ekutiːj] nf hatchway.

écran [ekrɑ̃] nm screen.

écrasement [ekrazmɑ̃] nm crushing, crashing, defeat.

écraser [ekraze] vt to crush, run over, overburden, dwarf; vr to collapse, crash.

écrémer [ekreme] vt to skim, cream.

écrevisse [ekrəvis] nf crayfish.

s'écrier [sekrie] vr to exclaim, cry out.

écrin [ekrɛ̃] nm case, casket.

écrire [ekriːr] vt to write, note down, spell; **machine à —** typewriter.

écrit [ekri] *a* written; *nm* writing, paper with writing on it.

écriteau [ekrito] *nm* placard, notice.

écritoire [ekritwa:r] *nf* inkwell.

écriture [ekrity:r] *nf* handwriting; *pl* accounts, Scripture.

écrivain [ekrivɛ̃] *nm* writer, author.

écrou [ekru] *nm* screw-nut.

écrouer [ekrue] *vt* to send to prison, lock up.

écroulement [ekrulmɑ̃] *nm* collapse, falling in, crash.

s'écrouler [sekrule] *vr* to collapse, crumble, tumble down.

écru [ekry] *a* unbleached, raw, natural-colored.

écu [eky] *nm* shield, escutcheon, crown.

écueil [ekœːj] *nm* reef, stumbling block.

écuelle [ekyɛl] *nf* bowl, basin.

éculer [ekyle] *vt* to wear away the heels of (shoes).

écume [ekym] *nf* foam, froth, scum; — de mer meerschaum.

écumer [ekyme] *vt* to skim; *vi* to foam, froth; — les mers to scour the seas.

écumeux, -euse [ekymø, øːz] *a* foamy, frothy, scummy.

écumoire [ekymwaːr] *nf* skimming ladle.

écurer [ekyre] *vt* to scour.

écureuil [ekyrœːj] *nm* squirrel.

écurie [ekyri] *nf* stable.

écusson [ekysɔ̃] *nm* escutcheon, coat-of-arms, shield.

écuyer, -ère [ekɥije, ɛːr] *n* rider, horseman, -woman; *nm* equerry, squire; bottes à l'écuyère riding-boots.

édenté [edɑ̃te] *a* toothless.

édenter [edɑ̃te] *vt* to break the teeth of.

édicter [edikte] *vt* to decree, enact.

édification [edifikasjɔ̃] *nf* building, erection; edification.

édifice [edifis] *nm* edifice, building, structure.

édifier [edifje] *vt* to build, erect, edify.

édit [edi] *nm* edict.

éditer [edite] *vt* to edit, publish.

éditeur, -trice [editœːr, tris] *n* editor, editress, publisher.

édition [edisjɔ̃] *nf* edition, publishing trade; maison d'— publishing house.

éditorial [editɔrjal] *a* editorial; *nm* editorial.

édredon [edrədɔ̃] *nm* eiderdown, quilt.

éducation [edykasjɔ̃] *nf* training, rearing, breeding, upbringing.

éduquer [edyke] *vt* to educate, bring up.

effacé [efase] *a* unobtrusive, un-assuming, retiring.

effacement [efasmɑ̃] *nm* oblitera-tion, wearing out, unobtrusiveness.

effacer [efase] *vt* to efface, blot out, delete; *vr* to wear away, fade, remain in the background.

effarement [efarmɑ̃] *nm* alarm, fright.

effarer [efare] *vt* to scare, alarm; *vr* to be scared, take fright.

effaroucher [efaruʃe] *vt* to scare away; *vr* to be startled.

effectif, -ive [efɛktif, iːv] *a* effective, actual, real; *nm* total strength, manpower.

effectivement [efɛktivmɑ̃] *ad* actual-ly, as a matter of fact, exactly.

effectuer [efɛktɥe] *vt* to bring about, carry out, execute.

efféminé [efemine] *a* effeminate.

effervescence [efɛrvɛssɑ̃ːs] *nf* excite-ment, ebullience, turmoil.

effet [efɛ] *nm* effect, result, impres-sion, operation; *pl* effects, posses-sions, stocks; à cet — for this purpose; en — indeed, as a matter of fact; manquer son — to fall flat; faire de l'— to be effective; mettre à l'— to put into operation.

effeuiller [efœje] *vt* to remove the leaves from; *vr* to shed its leaves.

efficace [efikas] *a* effective, efficaci-ous, effectual.

efficacité [efikasite] *nf* efficacy, effectiveness, efficiency.

effigie [efiʒi] *nf* image, likeness.

effilé [efile] *a* fringed, slender, slim, tapering.

effiler [efile] *vt* to unravel, taper; *vr* to fray, taper.

effilocher [efiloʃe] *vt* to unravel; *vr* to fray.

efflanqué [eflɑ̃ke] *a* lean.

effleurer [eflœre] *vt* to graze, brush, skim, touch upon.

effondrement [efɔ̃drəmɑ̃] *nm* col-lapse, falling in, subsidence, slump, breakdown.

effondrer [efɔ̃dre] *vt* to break down, smash in; *vr* to collapse, fall in, slump.

s'efforcer [seforse] *vr* to strive, en-deavor.

effort [efoːr] *nm* endeavor, exertion, strain.

effraction [efraksjɔ̃] *nf* housebreak-ing.

effrayer [efreje] *vt* to frighten, terrify, scare, daunt; *vr* to get a fright, be frightened.

effréné [efrene] *a* unbridled, frantic, frenzied.

effriter [efrite] *vt* to wear away; *vr* to crumble.

effroi [efrwa] *nm* fright, dread, terror.

effronté [efrɔ̃te] *a* shameless, im-pudent, cheeky, saucy.

effronterie [efrɔ̃tri] *nf* effrontery, impudence.

effroyable [efrwajabl] *a* frightful, dreadful, appalling.

effusion [efyzjɔ̃] *nf* effusion, outpouring, effusiveness; — **de sang** bloodshed.

égailler [egaje] vt to flush, scatter; vr to scatter.

égal [egal] a equal, level, even; **cela lui est** — it is all the same to him.

également — [egalmã] ad equally, likewise, as well.

égaler [egale] vt to be equal to, compare with.

égaliser [egalize] vt to equalize, regulate, level.

égalitaire [egalitɛːr] an equalitarian.

égalité [egalite] nf equality, evenness, smoothness; **être à** — to be all square, equal.

égard [egaːr] nm regard, respect, consideration; pl esteem, attentions, consideration; **avoir** — **à** to take into account; **à cet** — in this respect; **à tous les** —**e** in every respect; **à l'**— **de** with regard to, toward.

égaré [egare] a lost, stray, distracted.

égarement [egarmã] nm loss, mislaying; aberration, frenzy; pl disorderly conduct.

égarer [egare] vt to lead astray, mislead, mislay; vr to go astray, lose one's way.

égayer [egeje] vt to cheer up, brighten (up).

égide [eʒid] nf shield, aegis.

églantier [eglãtje] nm wild rose, sweet brier.

églantine [eglãtin] nf wild rose (flower).

église [egliːz] nf church.

égoïsme [egɔism] nm selfishness, egoism.

égoïste [egɔist] a selfish; n egoist, egotist.

égorger [egɔrʒe] vt to cut the throat of, butcher.

s'égosiller [segozije] vr to shout oneself hoarse.

égout [egu] nm drain, sewer, gutter; **eaux d'**— sewage.

égoutter [egute] vt to drain; vr drip, drop, drain.

égratigner [egratiɲe] vt to scratch, graze.

égratignure [egratiɲyːr] nf scratch, graze.

égrener [egrəne] vt to pick out, pick off; vr to drop (one by one); — **son chapelet** to tell one's beads.

égrillard [egrijaːr] a ribald, daring, spicy.

Égypte [eʒipt] nf Egypt.

égyptien, -enne [eʒipsjɛ̃, jɛn] an Egyptian.

éhonté [eɔ̃te] a shameless, brazenfaced.

éjaculer [eʒakyle] vt to ejaculate.

élaborer [elabɔre] vt to elaborate, draw up, labor.

élaguer [elage] vt to lop off, prune, cut down.

élan [elã] nm spring, bound, dash,

impetus, abandon, (out)burst; moose.

élancé [elãse] a slender, slim, tapering.

élancement [elãsmã] nm twinge, stabbing pain.

s'élancer [selãse] vr to dash forward, rush, spring.

élargir [elarʒiːr] vt to widen, enlarge, broaden, release, discharge; vr to broaden out, extend.

élargissement [elarʒismã] nm broadening, extension, release, discharge.

élasticité [elastisite] nf elasticity, resilience, spring.

élastique [elastik] a elastic, springy, resilient; nm elastic, rubber band.

électeur, -trice [elɛktœːr, tris] n voter, constituent.

électif, -ive [elɛktif, iːv] a elective.

élection [elɛksjɔ̃] nf election, choice; **se présenter aux** —**e** to run in an election.

électoral [elɛktɔral] a electoral; **collège** — constituency; **campagne** —**e** electioneering; **corps** — electorate.

électorat [elɛktɔra] nm electorate.

électricien [elɛktrisjɛ̃] nm electrician.

électricité [elɛktrisite] nf electricity.

électrique [elɛktrik] a electric.

électriser [elɛktrize] vt to electrify.

électrocuter [elɛktrɔkyte] vt to electrocute.

électronique [elɛktrɔnik] a electronic; nf electronics.

élégance [elegãːs] nf stylishness, smartness.

élégant [elegã] a well-dressed, fashionable.

élégiaque [eleʒjak] a elegiac.

élégie [eleʒi] nf elegy.

élément [elemã] nm component, element, ingredient; pl rudiments.

élémentaire [elemãtɛːr] a elementary, rudimentary.

éléphant [elefã] nm elephant.

élevage [ɛlvaːʒ] nm raising, rearing, breeding.

élévation [elevasjɔ̃] nf elevation, raising, rise, height, grandeur.

élève [elɛːv] n pupil, boy, girl.

élevé [elve] a elevated, high, lofty, exalted; **bien (mal)** — well- (ill-) bred, well (badly) behaved.

élever [elve] vt to elevate, erect, raise; vr to rise up, arise.

éleveur, -euse [elvœːr, øːz] n stockbreeder, grower, keeper.

élider [elide] vt to elide.

éligibilité [eliʒibilite] nf eligibility.

éligible [eliʒibl] a eligible.

élimer [elime] vt to wear threadbare; vr to wear, be worn threadbare.

éliminatoire [eliminatwaːr] a eliminatory, preliminary.

éliminer [elimine] vt to eliminate, weed out.

élire [eliːr] vt to elect, choose, appoint, return.

élision [elizjɔ̃] nf elision.

élite [elit] *nf* élite, pick, flower; *a d'—* crack.

ellipse [elips] *nf* ellipse, ellipsis.

élocution [elɔkysjɔ̃] *nf* elocution.

éloge [elɔʒ] *nm* eulogy, commendation, praise.

élogieux, -euse [elɔʒjø, jø:z] *a* laudatory, glowing.

éloigné [elwaɲe] *a* distant, far (away, off).

éloignement [elwaɲmɑ̃] *nm* absence, removal, isolation, postponement, distance.

éloigner [elwaɲe] *vt* to remove, get out of the way, alienate, postpone; *vr* to withdraw, stand farther away.

éloquence [elɔkɑ̃:s] *nf* eloquence.

éloquent [elɔkɑ̃] *a* eloquent.

élu [ely] *a* chosen; *nm pl* the elect, the elected members.

élucider [elyside] *vt* to elucidate.

éluder [elyde] *vt* to elude, evade.

émacié [emasje] *a* emaciated.

émail [ema:j] *nm* enamel, glaze.

émailler [emaje] *vt* to enamel, glaze, fleck, besprinkle.

émancipé [emɑ̃sipe] *a* full-fledged, having advanced ideas, emancipated.

émanciper [emɑ̃sipe] *vt* to emancipate; *vr* to become emancipated, kick over the traces.

émaner [emane] *vi* to emanate, come, originate (from).

émasculer [emaskyle] *vt* to emasculate, weaken.

emballage [ɑ̃bala:ʒ] *nm* packing, wrapping.

emballement [ɑ̃balmɑ̃] *nm* (*of machine*) racing, enthusiasm, boom, craze.

emballer [ɑ̃bale] *vt* to pack, wrap up, (*car engine*) race, fill with enthusiasm; *vr* (*horse*) to bolt, be carried away, rave (with enthusiasm), fly into a temper.

emballeur [ɑ̃balœ:r] *nm* packer.

embarcadère [ɑ̃barkade:r] *nm* landing-stage, wharf, platform.

embarcation [ɑ̃barkasjɔ̃] *nf* boat, craft.

embardée [ɑ̃barde] *nf* lurch, swerve, skid.

embargo [ɑ̃bargo] *nm* embargo.

embarquement [ɑ̃barkəmɑ̃] *nm* loading, embarking, shipping, entrainment.

embarquer [ɑ̃barke] *vt* to embark, take aboard, entrain; *vir* to go abroad, entrain.

embarras [ɑ̃bara] *nm* embarrassment, difficulty, quandary, superfluity; *pl* fuss.

embarrassé [ɑ̃barase] *a* embarrassed, involved.

embarrasser [ɑ̃barase] *vt* to embarrass, perplex, confound, hamper, obstruct.

embaucher [ɑ̃boʃe] *vt* to engage, take on, employ.

embauchoir [ɑ̃boʃwa:r] *nm* shoe-tree.

embaumer [ɑ̃bome] *vt* to embalm, perfume; *vi* to have a lovely perfume, smell of.

embellir [ɑ̃beli:r] *vt* to embellish, improve, beautify.

embellissement [ɑ̃belismɑ̃] *nm* embellishment.

embêtant [ɑ̃bɛtɑ̃] *a* (*fam*) annoying.

embêter [ɑ̃bete] *vt* to annoy.

emblée [ɑ̃ble] *ad d'—* right away.

emblème [ɑ̃blɛ:m] *nm* emblem, badge, sign.

embobeliner [ɑ̃bɔbline] *vt* to coax, get round.

emboîtement [ɑ̃bwatmɑ̃] *nm* joint, fitting, encasing.

emboîter [ɑ̃bwate] *vt* to joint, fit together, dovetail, encase; *— le pas à* to fall into step with.

embolie [ɑ̃bɔli] *nf* embolism, stroke.

embonpoint [ɑ̃bɔ̃pwɛ̃] *nm* corpulence, stoutness.

embouché [ɑ̃buʃe] *a mal —* coarse-tongued.

emboucher [ɑ̃buʃe] *vt* to put to one's mouth, blow.

embouchure [ɑ̃buʃy:r] *nf* mouth-piece. (*river, volcano*) mouth.

embourber [ɑ̃burbe] *vt* to bog; *vr* to be bogged, stuck in the mud.

embout [ɑ̃bu] *nm* ferrule, tip.

embouteillage [ɑ̃butɛja:ʒ] *nm* bottling (up), bottleneck, traffic-jam.

embouteiller [ɑ̃butɛje] *vt* to bottle (up), jam, block; *vr* to get jammed.

embranchement [ɑ̃brɑ̃ʃmɑ̃] *nm* branching off, junction, branch-line.

embrancher [ɑ̃brɑ̃ʃe] *vt* to join up, together.

embrasement [ɑ̃brazmɑ̃] *nm* conflagration.

embraser [ɑ̃braze] *vt* to set fire to, fire; *vr* to catch fire.

embrassade [ɑ̃brasad] *nf* embrace, hug.

embrasser [ɑ̃brase] *vt* to embrace, hug, kiss, enfold, take up, include.

embrasure [ɑ̃brazy:r] *nf* recess, embrasure.

embrayage [ɑ̃brɛja:ʒ] *nm* connecting, coupling-gear, putting into gear.

embrayer [ɑ̃brɛje] *vt* to connect, couple, throw into gear; *vi* to let in the clutch.

embrocher [ɑ̃brɔʃe] *vt* to spit, put on the spit.

embrouillement [ɑ̃brujmɑ̃] *nm* entanglement, intricacy, muddle, confusion.

embrouiller [ɑ̃bruje] *vt* to tangle, muddle, embroil, complicate, confuse; *vr* to become entangled, complicated, confused.

embrun [ɑ̃brœ̃] *nm* spray, spindrift.

embryon [ɑ̃briɔ̃] *nm* embryo.

embûche [ãby(:)ʃ] *nf* ambush; dresser une — à to waylay.

embuer [ãbɥe] *vt* to cloud, cover with vapor.

embuscade [ãbyskad] *nf* ambush, ambuscade.

embusqué [ãbyske] *nm* shirker, dodger, sharpshooter.

embusquer [ãbyske] *vt* to place in ambush, put under cover; *vr* to lie in ambush, take cover, shirk war service.

éméché [emeʃe] *a* slightly tipsy, rather merry.

émeraude [emro:d] *nf* emerald.

émerger [emerʒe] *vi* to emerge, come out.

émeri [emri] *nm* emery.

émérite [emerit] *a* emeritus, retired, experienced.

émerveillement [emɛrvɛjmã] *nm* amazement.

émerveiller [emɛrveje] *vt* to amaze, astonish; *vr* to marvel, wonder.

émétique [emetik] *nm* emetic.

émetteur, -trice [emetœːr, tris] *a* issuing, transmitting, broadcasting; *n* issuer transmitter.

émettre [emɛtr] *vt* to emit, issue, utter, give out, express, transmit, broadcast.

émeute [emøːt] *nf* riot, disturbance.

émeutier [emøtje] *nm* rioter.

émietter [emjete] *vtr* to crumble.

émigrant [emigrã] *a* emigrating, migratory; *n* emigrant.

émigré [emigre] *n* political exile.

émigrer [emigre] *vi* to emigrate, migrate.

éminence [eminãːs] *nf* eminence, height, prominence.

éminent [eminã] *a* distinguished.

émissaire [emisɛːr] *nm* emissary; bouc — scapegoat.

émission [emisjɔ̃] *nf* issue transmission, broadcast; poste d'— broadcasting station.

emmagasinage [ãmagazinaːʒ] *nm* storing, storage.

emmagasiner [ãmagazine] *vt* to store (up).

emmailloter [ãmajote] *v.* to swaddle, swathe.

emmancher [ãmãʃe] *vt* to put a handle on; joint; *vr* to fit (into dans), get going.

emmanchure [ãmãʃyːr] *nf* armhole.

emmêler [ãmɛle] *vt* to mix up, muddle, implicate.

emménager [ãmenaʒe] *vt* to move in, furnish; *vi* to move in.

emmener [ãmne] *vt* to lead, take away, take.

emmitoufler [ãmitufle] *vt* to muffle up.

émoi [emwa] *nm* emotion, excitement, stir, flutter; en — agog, astir, in a flutter.

émoluments [emolymã] *nm pl* emoluments, fees.

émonder [emɔ̃de] *vt* to prune, trim.

émotion [emosjɔ̃] *nf* emotion, feeling, excitement.

émotionnable [emosjɔnabl] *a* emotional, excitable.

émotionner [emosjɔne] *vt* to excite, stir, thrill; *vr* to get excited.

émoudre [emudr] *vt* to grind.

émoulu [emuly] *a* sharpened; frais — de just out of, fresh from.

émousser [emuse] *vt* to blunt, deaden; *vr* to become blunt, dulled.

émoustillant [emustijã] *a* piquant, exhilarating.

émoustiller [emustije] *vt* to stir (up), rouse, titillate, stimulate; *vr* to come to life, sparkle.

émouvant [emuvã] *a* moving, exciting, thrilling.

émouvoir [emuvwaːr] *vt* to move, stir up, excite; *vr* to be moved, get excited.

empailler [ãpaje] *vt* to pack, cover in straw, stuff.

empailleur, -euse [ãpajœːr, øːz] *n* taxidermist.

empaler [ãpale] *vt* to impale.

empaqueter [ãpakte] *vt* to pack up, parcel up, bundle.

s'emparer [sãpare] *vr* to seize, take possession (of de), secure.

empâté [ãpate] *a* coated, clogged, thick.

empâter [ãpate] *vt* to cover with paste, make sticky, fatten; *vr* to put on fat.

empêchement [ãpɛʃmã] *nm* impediment, obstacle, hindrance.

empêcher [ãpeʃe] *vt* to prevent, impede, hamper; *vr* to refrain; je ne peux m'— de rire I cannot help laughing.

empeigne [ãpɛɲ] *nf* upper (of shoe).

empennage [ãpenaːʒ] *nm* feathers, feathering, fur, vanes.

empereur [ãprœːr] *nm* emperor.

empesé [ãpəze] *a* starched, stiff, starchy.

empeser [ãpəze] *vt* to starch, stiffen.

empester [ãpɛste] *vt* to 'infect, create a stink in.

empêtrer [ãpetre] *vt* to hobble, entangle, hamper; *vr* to get entangled, involved.

emphase [ãfaːz] *nf* grandiloquence, bombast.

emphatique [ãfatik] *a* bombastic, grandiloquent.

empierrer [ãpjere] *vt* to ballast, metal.

empiétement [ãpjetmã] *nm* encroachment, trespassing, infringement.

empiéter [ãpjete] *vi* to encroach, infringe.

empiffrer [ãpifre] *vt* to stuff; *vr* to stuff oneself, guzzle.

empiler [ãpile] *vt* to pile, stack.

empire [ãpiːr] *nm* empire, sway,

dominion; — **sur soi-même** self-control.

empirer [ɑ̃pire] vt to make worse, aggravate; vr to get worse.

empirique [ɑ̃pirik] a empirical.

emplacement [ɑ̃plasmɑ̃] nm site, location.

emplâtre [ɑ̃plɑːtr] nm plaster, poultice.

emplette [ɑ̃plɛt] nf purchase; **faire ses** —**s** to go shopping.

emplir [ɑ̃pliːr] vt to fill; vr to fill (up).

emploi [ɑ̃plwa] nm use, employment, job, post.

employé [ɑ̃plwaje] n employee, clerk, attendant.

employer [ɑ̃plwaje] vt to employ, use; vr to spend one's time, occupy oneself.

employeur, -euse [ɑ̃plwajœːr, øːz] n employer.

empocher [ɑ̃pɔʃe] vt to pocket.

empoignant [ɑ̃pwaɲɑ̃] a thrilling, gripping.

empoigner [ɑ̃pwaɲe] vt to grasp, grab, grip, hold.

empois [ɑ̃pwa] nm starch.

empoisonnant [ɑ̃pwazɔnɑ̃] a poisonous, rotten.

empoisonnement [ɑ̃pwazɔnmɑ̃] nm poisoning.

empoisonner [ɑ̃pwazɔne] vt to poison, infect, corrupt.

empoisonneur, -euse [ɑ̃pwazɔnœːr, øːz] n poisoner.

emporté [ɑ̃pɔrte] a hot-tempered, fiery, hasty.

emportement [ɑ̃pɔrtəmɑ̃] nm outburst, anger, rapture, passion.

emporte-pièce [ɑ̃pɔrtəpjɛs] nm punch; réponse à l'— caustic reply.

emporter [ɑ̃pɔrte] vt to carry away, off, sweep along, away, remove; vr to fly into a rage, bolt; l'— to carry the day, prevail, have the best of it; — **la balance** to turn the scale.

empoté [ɑ̃pɔte] a clumsy, unathletic; n bungler, duffer.

empoter [ɑ̃pɔte] vt to pot.

empourprer [ɑ̃purpre] vt to tinge with crimson; vr to turn crimson, grow red.

empreindre [ɑ̃prɛ̃ːdr] vt to imprint, stamp.

empreinte [ɑ̃prɛ̃t] nf stamp, mark, imprint, print, impression, mold; — **digitale** fingerprint.

empressé [ɑ̃prese] a eager, solicitous, ardent, sedulous.

empressement [ɑ̃presmɑ̃] nm eagerness, alacrity, haste, zeal.

s'empresser [sɑ̃prese] vr to hurry, be eager, be attentive, dance attendance.

emprise [ɑ̃priːz] nf expropriation, hold, power.

emprisonnement [ɑ̃prizɔnmɑ̃] nm imprisonment.

emprisonner [ɑ̃prizɔne] vt to imprison, put in prison, confine.

emprunt [ɑ̃prœ̃] nm borrowing, loan.

emprunté [ɑ̃prœ̃te] a borrowed, assumed, embarrassed, self-conscious.

emprunter [ɑ̃prœ̃te] vt to borrow, take, assume.

emprunteur, -euse [ɑ̃prœ̃tœːr, øːz] n borrower.

ému [emy] a moved, touched, excited, nervous.

émulation [emylasjɔ̃] nf emulation, rivalry.

émule [emyl] n rival.

en [ɑ̃] prep in, into, to, as, like, while; pn of it, of them, about it, about them, for that, because of that, some, any.

encadrement [ɑ̃kadrəmɑ̃] nm framing, framework, setting, commanding.

encadrer [ɑ̃kadre] vt to frame, set, surround, command.

encaisse [ɑ̃kɛs] nf cash in hand, cash-balance.

encaissé [ɑ̃kɛse] a boxed-in, sunken, steeply embanked, blind (corner).

encaissement [ɑ̃kɛsmɑ̃] nm encasing, packing in boxes, collection, embankment.

encaisser [ɑ̃kɛse] vt to pack in boxes, collect cash, embank, take (blow).

encaisseur [ɑ̃kɛsœːr] nm collector, cashier, payee.

encan [ɑ̃kɑ̃] nm **mettre à l'**— to put up for auction.

encanailler [ɑ̃kanaje] vr to keep bad company, go to the dogs.

encapuchonner [ɑ̃kapyʃɔne] vt to put a hood on, put the cover over.

encart [ɑ̃kaːr] nm inset.

en-cas [ɑ̃kɑ] nm reserve, something to fall back on.

encastrer [ɑ̃kastre] vt to fit in, embed, dovetail.

encaustique [ɑ̃kostik] nf floor, furniture polish.

encaustiquer [ɑ̃kostike] vt to polish, beeswax.

enceindre [ɑ̃sɛ̃ːdr] vt to encircle, gird, surround.

enceinte [ɑ̃sɛ̃t] a pregnant; nf wall, fence, enclosure, circumference.

encens [ɑ̃sɑ̃] nm incense, flattery.

encenser [ɑ̃sɑ̃se] vt to cense, burn incense before, flatter.

encenseur [ɑ̃sɑ̃sœːr] nm censer-bearer, flatterer.

encensoir [ɑ̃sɑ̃swaːr] nm censer.

encercler [ɑ̃sɛrkle] vt to encircle, surround.

enchaînement [ɑ̃ʃɛnmɑ̃] nm chaining, series, putting together.

enchaîner [ɑ̃ʃɛne] vt to chain, link up, hold in check.

enchantement [ɑ̃ʃɑ̃tmɑ̃] nm magic, enchantment, charm, spell.

enchanter [ɑ̃ʃɑ̃te] vt to enchant, delight, bewitch.

enchanteur, -eresse [ɑ̃ʃɑ̃tœːr, rɛːs]

a bewitching, entrancing; *n* enchanter, enchantress.

enchâsser [ɑ̃ʃase] *vt* to enshrine, set, mount.

enchère [ɑ̃ʃɛːr] *nf* bid(ding); **vente à l'—** auction sale.

enchérir [ɑ̃ʃeriːr] *vt* to raise the price of; *vi* to go up in price, make a higher bid; **— sur qn** to outbid, outdo s.o.

enchérissement [ɑ̃ʃerismɑ̃] *nm* rise, increase.

enchérisseur, -euse [ɑ̃ʃerisœːr, øːz] *n* bidder.

enchevêtrement [ɑ̃ʃvetrəmɑ̃] *nm* tangling up, confusion.

enchevêtrer [ɑ̃ʃvetre] *vt* to halter, confuse, mix up; *vr* to get entangled, mixed up.

enclaver [ɑ̃klave] *vt* to enclose, dovetail.

enclencher [ɑ̃klɑ̃ʃe] *vt* to put into gear, engage.

enclin [ɑ̃klɛ̃] *a* inclined, prone.

enclore [ɑ̃klɔːr] *vt* to enclose, fence in.

enclos [ɑ̃klo] *nm* enclosure, paddock.

enclume [ɑ̃klym] *nf* anvil.

encoche [ɑ̃kɔʃ] *nf* notch, last, slot; **avec —s** with thumb index.

encocher [ɑ̃kɔʃe] *vt* to notch, nick.

encoignure [ɑ̃kɔɲyːr] *nf* corner, corner cupboard.

encoller [ɑ̃kɔle] *vt* to gum, glue, paste.

encolure [ɑ̃kɔlyːr] *nf* neck and shoulders, (*dress*) neck, (*collar*) size.

encombrant [ɑ̃kɔ̃brɑ̃] *a* clumsy, bulky, cumbersome.

encombre [ɑ̃kɔ̃br] *nm* obstacle, hindrance, mishap.

encombrement [ɑ̃kɔ̃brəmɑ̃] *nm* obstruction, congestion, jam, litter, overcrowding, glut, bulkiness.

encombrer [ɑ̃kɔ̃bre] *vt* to encumber, burden, congest, crowd, glut, litter.

encontre [ɑ̃kɔ̃tr] *ad* **à l'—** to the contrary; *prep* **à l'—.de** contrary to, unlike.

encore [ɑ̃kɔːr] *ad* still, yet, again, furthermore, even, even at that; **— que** although.

encouragement [ɑ̃kuraʒmɑ̃] *nm* encouragement, incentive, inducement.

encourager [ɑ̃kuraʒe] *vt* to encourage, hearten, foster, abet, egg on.

encourir [ɑ̃kuriːr] *vt* to incur, draw upon oneself.

encrasser [ɑ̃krase] *vt* to dirty, clog, choke; *vr* to become dirty, clog.

encre [ɑ̃ːkr] *nf* ink.

encrier [ɑ̃krie] *nm* inkwell, inkstand.

encroûter [ɑ̃krute] *vt* to encrust, cake; *vr* to become caked, stagnate.

encyclopédie [ɑ̃siklɔpedi] *nf* encyclopedia.

endetter [ɑ̃dɛte] *vt* to run into debt; *vr* to get into debt.

endiablé [ɑ̃djable] *a* reckless, wild, boisterous.

endiguer [ɑ̃dige] *vt* to dam up, bank, dike.

s'endimancher [sɑ̃dimɑ̃ʃe] *vr* to dress in one's Sunday best.

endive [ɑ̃diːv] *nf* chicory.

endolori [ɑ̃dɔlɔri] *a* painful, tender.

endommager [ɑ̃dɔmaʒe] *vt* to damage, injure.

endormi [ɑ̃dɔrmi] *a* asleep, sleeping, drowsy, sluggish, numb; *n* sleepyhead.

endormir [ɑ̃dɔrmiːr] *vt* to put to sleep, make numb, give an anesthetic to; *vr* to fall asleep, drop off.

endosser [ɑ̃dose] *vt* to put on, endorse.

endroit [ɑ̃drwa] *nm* place, spot, aspect, right side; **à l'— de** with regard to.

enduire [ɑ̃dɥiːr] *vt* to coat, smear, daub.

enduit [ɑ̃dɥi] *nm* coating, coat, plaster.

endurance [ɑ̃dyrɑ̃ːs] *nf* endurance, long-suffering.

endurant [ɑ̃dyrɑ̃] *a* patient, long-suffering.

endurcir [ɑ̃dyrsiːr] *vt* to harden, inure; *vr* to harden, become hard, obdurate.

endurcissement [ɑ̃dyrsismɑ̃] *nm* hardening, inuring, obduracy, callousness.

endurer [ɑ̃dyre] *vt* to endure, put up with, bear.

énergie [enɛrʒi] *nf* energy, vigor, power, efficacy, drive.

énergique [enɛrʒik] *a* energetic, vigorous, drastic, strong-willed.

énergumène [enɛrgymɛn] *nm* madman.

énervant [enɛrvɑ̃] *a* enervating, annoying, nerve-racking.

énerver [enɛrve] *vt* to enervate, get on one's nerves; *vr* to grow soft, become irritable, get excited.

enfance [ɑ̃fɑ̃ːs] *nf* childhood, boyhood, children.

enfant [ɑ̃fɑ̃] *n* child, little boy, girl; **— trouvé** foundling; *a* **bon —** easy-going.

enfantement [ɑ̃fɑ̃tmɑ̃] *nm* childbirth, production.

enfanter [ɑ̃fɑ̃te] *vt* to bear, give birth to.

enfantillage [ɑ̃fɑ̃tijaːʒ] *nm* childishness.

enfantin [ɑ̃fɑ̃tɛ̃] *a* childish, childlike, children's.

enfer [ɑ̃fɛːr] *nm* hell.

enfermer [ɑ̃fɛrme] *vt* to shut in, lock up, enclose, sequester; *vr* to shut, lock oneself in.

enferrer [ɑ̃fɛre] *vt* to transfix, run s.o. through; *vr* to transfix oneself, swallow the hook, get caught out.

s'enfiévrer [sɑ̃fjevre] *vr* to grow feverish, get excited.

enfilade [ɑ̃filad] *nf* succession, string, raking fire.

enfiler [ãfile] *vt* to thread, string, pierce, go along, slip on.

enfin [ãfɛ̃] *ad* at last, finally, at length, in a word, after all.

enflammé [ãflame] *a* burning, fiery, blaze.

enflammer [ãflame] *vt* to inflame, set on fire, stir up; *vr* to catch fire, become inflamed.

enflé [ãfle] *a* swollen, inflated, grandiloquent.

enfler [ãfle] *vt* to swell, puff out, bloat; *vr* to swell.

enflure [ãfly:r] *nf* swelling, puffiness, grandiloquence.

enfoncement [ãfɔ̃smã] *nm* driving in, smashing in, depression, recess, bay.

enfoncer [ãfɔ̃se] *vt* to drive in, thrust, smash in; *vi* to sink, settle; *vr* to plunge, dive, sink.

enfouir [ãfwi:r] *vt* to bury, hide.

enfourcher [ãfurʃe] *vt* to stick a fork into, mount.

enfourchure [ãfurʃy:r] *nf* fork, bifurcation.

enfourner [ãfurne] *vt* to put in the oven, shovel in.

enfreindre [ãfrɛ̃:dr] *vt* to infringe, break, contravene.

s'enfuir [sãfɥi:r] *vr* to flee, escape, fly, run away, elope.

enfumé [ãfyme] *a* smoky, smoke-blackened.

enfumer [ãfyme] *vt* to fill (blacken) with smoke.

engagé [ãgaʒe] *a* pledged; *n* volunteer.

engageant [ãgaʒã] *a* winning, prepossessing, inviting, ingratiating.

engagement [ãgaʒmã] *nm* appointment, commitment, pawning, pledge, bond, engagement, enlistment.

engager [ãgaʒe] *vt* to engage, sign on, pawn, pledge, enter into, urge; *vr* to undertake, get involved, commit oneself, enlist, fit, jam, foul.

engainer [ãgɛne] *vt* to sheathe, envelop.

engeance [ãʒã:s] *nf* breed, race.

engelure [ãʒly:r] *nf* chilblain.

engendrer [ãʒãdre] *vt* to beget, engender, breed.

engin [ãʒɛ̃] *nm* engine, machine, device; *pl* tackle, appliances.

englober [ãglobe] *vt* to include, embrace, take in.

engloutir [ãgluti:r] *vt* to swallow up, gulp down, engulf; *vr* to be engulfed.

engoncé [ãgɔ̃se] *a* bunched-up, hunched-up.

engorgement [ãgɔrʒmã] *nm* choking up, clogging, stoppage.

engorger [ãgɔrʒe] *vt* to choke up, clog, obstruct; *vr* to get choked up.

engouement [ãgumã] *nm* infatuation, craze.

engouer [ãgwe] *vt* to obstruct; *vr* to become infatuated, go crazy, mad

(about de), have a passion (for de).

engouffrer [ãgufre] *vt* to engulf, swallow up; *vr* to be engulfed, rush.

engourdi [ãgurdi] *a* numb, cramped, sluggish, lethargic; *n* dullard, sluggard.

engourdir [ãgurdi:r] *vt* to benumb, cramp, chill, dull; *vr* to grow numb, sluggish.

engourdissement [ãgurdismã] *nm* numbness, sluggishness.

engrais [ãgrɛ] *nm* fattening food, manure, fertilizer.

engraissement [ãgrɛsmã] *nm* fattening, growing fat, corpulence.

engraisser [ãgrɛse] *vt* to fatten, fertilize, manure; *vi* to grow fat, put on weight.

engranger [ãgrãʒe] *vt* (corn) to get in, to garner.

engrenage [ãgrəna:ʒ] *nm* gearing, gear, mesh; *pl* gear-wheels, works.

engrener [ãgrəne] *vt* to connect, engage; *vr* to interlock.

enhardir [ãardi:r] *vt* to make bolder, encourage; *vr* to venture, grow bolder.

enharnacher [ãarnaʃe] *vt* to put the harness on.

énigmatique [enigmatik] *a* enigmatic(al).

énigme [enigm] *nf* enigma, riddle, conundrum.

enivrement [ãnivrəmã] *nm* intoxication, rapture.

enivrer [ãnivre] *vt* to intoxicate, send into raptures; *vr* to get drunk, be carried away, be uplifted.

enjambée [ãʒãbe] *nf* stride.

enjambement [ãʒãbmã] *nm* enjambment.

enjamber [ãʒãbe] *vt* to step over, bestride; *vi* to stride along, encroach.

enjeu [ãʒø] *nm* (betting) stake.

enjoindre [ãʒwɛ̃:dr] *vt* to enjoin, exhort, call upon.

enjôler [ãʒole] *vt* to wheedle, cajole, coax.

enjoliver [ãʒɔlive] *vt* to embellish, embroider upon.

enjoué [ãʒwe] *a* playful, sportive, vivacious.

enjouement [ãʒumã] *nm* playfulness.

enlacement [ãlasmã] *nm* entwining, embrace.

enlacer [ãlase] *vt* to entwine, intertwine, clasp, embrace; *vr* to intertwine, twine, embrace each other.

enlaidir [ãlɛdi:r] *vt* to make ugly; *vi* to grow ugly.

enlèvement [ãlɛvmã] *nm* removal, carrying off, kidnapping, storming.

enlever [ãlve] *vt* to remove, carry off (away), storm, perform brilliantly, kidnap, abduct; *vr* to come off, boil over; **s'enlaisser — to elope.

enliser [ãlize] *vt* to draw in, engulf; *vr* to sink, get bogged.

enluminer [ãlymine] *vt* to illumin-ate, color.

enluminure [ãlyminy:r] *nf* illumin-ating, coloring, illumination.

ennemi [ɛnmi] *a* enemy, hostile; *n* enemy, foe.

ennoblir [ãnɔbli:r] *vt* to ennoble, exalt, elevate.

ennui [ãnyi] boredom, tediousness, worry, trouble.

ennuyer [ãnyije] *vt* to bore, bother, worry, annoy; *vr* to weary, be bored.

ennuyeux, -euse [ãnyijø, ø:z] *a* tedious, irksome, tiresome, dull, drab, annoying.

énoncé [enɔ̃se] *nm* statement, word-ing, enunciation.

énoncer [enɔ̃se] *vt* to state, express, articulate.

énonciation [enɔ̃sjasjɔ̃] *nf* stating, articulation.

enorgueillir [ãnɔrgœji:r] *vt* to make proud; *vr* to become proud, pride oneself.

énorme [enɔrm] *a* huge, enormous, excessive, heinous.

énormément [enɔrmemã] *ad* enor-mously, awfully, a great many, a great deal.

énormité [enɔrmite] *nf* hugeness, enormity, incredible lie, excessive-ness.

s'enquérir [sãkeri:r] *vr* to inquire, ask, make inquiries.

enquête [ãkɛt] *nf* inquiry, investiga-tion, inquest.

enquêter [ãkɛte] *vi* to make investi-gations, hold an inquiry.

enraciner [ãrasine] *vt* to plant securely, establish; *vr* to take root, become ingrained.

enragé [ãr.ʒe] *a* mad, enthusiastic, rabid; *n* fan.

enrager [ãraʒe] *vt* to enrage, madden; *vi* to be mad, be in a rage.

enrayer [ãreje] *vt* to lock, check, stop, foul.

enregistrement [ãrəʒistrəmã] *nm* registration, recording; **bureau d'—** cloakroom; **bureau des bagages** checkroom.

enregistrer [ãrəʒistre] *vt* to register, record enroll, enter.

enregistreur, -euse [ãrəʒistrœ:r, ø:z] *a* recording; *nm* registrar.

enrhumer [ãryme] *vt* to give s.o. a cold; *vr* to catch a cold.

enrichir [ãriʃi:r] *vt* to enrich, make wealthy, augment, increase; *vr* to grow wealthy, make money.

enrober [ãrɔbe] *vt* to cover, coat.

enrôler [ãrole] *vtr* to enroll, enlist.

enrouement [ãrumã] *nm* hoarseness, huskiness.

enroué [ãrwe] *a* hoarse, husky.

enrouer [ãrwe] *vt* to make hoarse; *vr* to become hoarse, husky.

enrouler [ãrule] *vt* to roll up, wind, wrap; *vr* to wind, coil.

enrubanner [ãrybane] *vt* to decorate with ribbon.

ensabler [ãsable] *vt* to sand, silt up.

ensanglanter [ãsãglãte] *vt* to stain, cover, with blood.

enseignant [ãseɲã] *a* teaching; **corps —** teaching profession.

enseigne [ãsɛɲ] *nf* mark, sign, token, shop-sign, ensign, (sub-) lieutenant; **logés à la même —** in the same boat.

enseignement [ãsɛɲmã] *nm* teach-ing, education, lesson.

enseigner [ãsɛɲe] *vt* to teach.

ensemble [ãsã:bl] *ad* together, at the same time; *nm* general effect, whole, set; **vue d'—** general view; **dans l'—** on the whole.

ensemencer [ãsmãse] *vt* to sow.

ensevelir [ãsəvli:r] *vt* to bury, entomb, cover.

ensevelissement [ãsəvlismã] *nm* burial, entombment.

ensoleillé [ãsɔleje] *a* sunny.

ensommeillé [ãsɔmeje] *a* sleepy, drowsy.

ensorceler [ãsɔrsəle] *vt* to bewitch, cast a spell upon.

ensorcellement [ãsɔrselmã] *nm* witchcraft, sorcery, spell.

ensuite [ãsyit] *ad* then, afterward, next.

s'ensuivre [sãsyi:vr] *vr* to follow, ensue.

entablement [ãtabləmã] *nm* coping, copestone.

entaille [ãta:j] *nf* notch, nick, slot, dent, gash.

entailler [ãtaje] *vt* to nick, notch, slot, gash.

entamer [ãtame] *vt* to cut, open, break, start.

entassement [ãtasmã] *nm* piling up stacking.

entasser [ãtase] *vt* to heap (up), stack, accumulate, pack together; *vr* to accumulate, pile up, crowd together.

entendement [ãtãdmã] *nm* under-standing reason.

entendre [ãtã:dr] *vt* to hear, under-stand, mean, intend; *vr* to agree, know (about en), be good (at à); **—parler de** to hear of; **dire que** to hear that; **laisser —** to imply.

entendu [ãtãdy] *a* capable, knowing, sensible, shrewd; *ad* **bien —** of course; **c'est — all right, agreed.**

entente [ãtã:t] *nf* agreement, under-standing, knowledge.

entérite [ãterit] *nf* enteritis.

enterrement [ãtɛrmã] *nm* burial, funeral.

enterrer [ãtɛre] *v* to bury, inter.

en-tête [ãtɛ:t] *nm* heading.

entêté [ãtɛte] *a* obstinate, stubborn.

entêtement [ãtɛtmã] *nm* obstinacy, doggedness.

s'entêter [sãtɛte] *vr* to be obstinate, persist.

enthousiasme [ãtuzjasm] nm enthusiasm.

enthousiasmer [ãtuzjasme] vt to fill with enthusiasm, send into raptures; vr to be, become, enthusiastic, rave (about pour).

enthousiaste [ãtuzjast] a enthusiastic; n enthusiast.

entiché [ãtiʃe] a infatuated, keen, mad; — du théâtre stage-struck.

entichement [ãtiʃmã] nm infatuation, craze.

s'enticher [sãtiʃe] vr to become infatuated (with de), take a fancy (to de).

entier, -ière [ãtje, jɛːr] a whole, entire, intact, downright, straightforward, possessive, whole-hearted.

entièrement [ãtjɛrmã] ad entirely, completely, quite.

entomologie [ãtɔmɔlɔʒi] nf entomology.

entonner [ãtɔne] vt to put into casks, strike up, intone; vr to rush, sweep.

entonnoir [ãtɔnwaːr] nm tunnel, crater, shell-hole.

entorse [ãtɔrs] nf sprain, twist, wrench.

entortiller [ãtɔrtije] vt to twine, twist, wind, coax, get around; vr to coil, wind.

entour [ãtuːr] nm pl neighborhood, surroundings; ad à l'— round about, around.

entourage [ãturaːʒ] nm circle of friends, following, environment.

entourer [ãture] vt to surround, encircle, encompass.

entournure [ãturnyːr] nf armhole.

entracte [ãtrakt] nm interval.

entraide [ãtrɛ(ː)d] nf mutual aid.

s'entraider [sãtrɛde] vr to help one another.

entrailles [ãtraːj] nf pl entrails, bowels, feeling.

entrain [ãtrɛ̃] nm spirit, dash, zest, whole-heartedness.

entraînant [ãtrɛnã] a stirring, rousing, catchy.

entraînement [ãtrɛnmã] nm dragging away, enticing away, enthusiasm, catchiness, training.

entraîner [ãtrɛne] vt to drag, carry away, entail, involve, lead astray, train, coach; vr to train, get into training.

entraîneur [ãtrɛnœːr] nm trainer, coach.

entrave [ãtraːv] nf fetter, shackle, obstacle, hobble.

entraver [ãtrave] vt to fetter, shackle, hobble, hamper, clog.

entre [ãːtr] prep between, among(st).

entrebâillement [ãtrəbajmã] nm chink, gap, slit, narrow opening.

entrebâiller [ãtrəbaje] vt to half-open, set ajar.

s'entrechoquer [sãtrəʃɔke] vr to clash, collide, clink.

entrecôte [ãtrəkɔt] nf (rib-)steak.

entrecouper [ãtrəkupe] vt to intersect, interrupt; vr to intersect, be interrupted.

entrecroiser [ãtrəkrwaze] vt to intersect, cross; vr to intersect.

entre-deux [ãtrədø] nm space between, partition, insertion.

entrée [ãtre] nf entry, entrance, way in, admission, inlet, import duty, entrée; — interdite no admittance.

entrefaite [ãtrəfɛt] nf sur ces —s meanwhile.

entrefilet [ãtrəfile] nm paragraph.

entregent [ãtrəʒã] nm tact, gumption.

entrelacement [ãtrəlasmã] nm interlacing, interweaving, intertwining.

entrelacer [ãtrəlase] vtr to interlace, intertwine.

entrelarder [ãtrəlarde] vt to lard, interlard.

entremêler [ãtrəmele] vt to intermingle, intervene.

entremets [ãtrəmɛ] nm side dish.

entremetteur, -euse [ãtrəmɛtœːr, øːz] n intermediary, go-between, procurer.

s'entremettre [sãtrəmɛtr] vr to intervene, act as a go-between.

entremise [ãtrəmiːz] nf intervention, mediation, medium, agency.

entrepont [ãtrəpɔ̃] nm between-decks.

entreposer [ãtrəpoze] vt to bond, warehouse, store.

entreposeur [ãtrəpozœːr] nm warehouseman.

entrepôt [ãtrəpo] nm bonded warehouse, mart, emporium.

entreprendre [ãtrəprɑ̃ːdr] vt to undertake, contract for, take on.

entrepreneur, -euse [ãtrəprənœːr, øːz] n contractor; — en bâtiments builder, building contractor; — de pompes funèbres undertaker.

entreprise [ãtrəpriːz] nf enterprise, undertaking, concern.

entrer [ãtre] vt to bring in; vi to enter, come in, go in.

entresol [ãtrəsɔl] nm entresol, mezzanine.

entre-temps [ãtrətã] nm interval.

entretenir [ãtrətniːr] vt to maintain, keep (up), support, talk to, entertain; vr to keep oneself, converse; s'— la main to keep one's hand in.

entretien [ãtrətjɛ̃] nm maintenance, (up)keep, support, conversation, interview.

entrevoir [ãtrəvwaːr] vt to catch a glimpse of, glimpse, begin to see, foresee vaguely.

entrevue [ãtrəvy] nf interview, conference.

entr'ouvert [ãtruver] a half-open, ajar, (chasm) gaping.

entr'ouvrir [ãtruvriːr] vt to half-open; vr to gape.

énumération [enymerasjɔ̃] *nf* enumeration, counting up.

énumérer [enymere] *vt* to enumerate, count up, detail.

envahir [ɑ̃vaiːr] *vt* to invade, overrun, spread over.

envahisseur [ɑ̃vaisœːr] *nm* invader.

envaser [ɑ̃vaze] *vt* to silt up, choke up; *vr* to silt up, settle down in the mud.

enveloppe [ɑ̃vlɔp] *nf* envelope, cover, wrapping, sheath, outward appearance.

envelopper [ɑ̃vlɔpe] *vt* to envelop, wrap, cover, surround, shroud.

envenimer [ɑ̃vnime] *vt* to poison, inflame, embitter, aggravate; *vr* to fester, grow more bitter.

envergure [ɑ̃vergyːr] *nf* breadth, span, scope; **de grande —** far-reaching.

envers [ɑ̃veːr] *prep* toward; *nm* reverse, wrong side; **à l'—** inside out, wrong way up.

envi [ɑ̃vi] *nm* **à l'—** vying with one another.

enviable [ɑ̃vjabl] *a* enviable.

envie [ɑ̃vi] *nf* desire, longing, inclination, envy; **avoir — de** to want (to); **porter — à** to envy.

envier [ɑ̃vje] *vt* to envy, begrudge, long for, covet, be envious of.

envieux, -euse [ɑ̃vjø, øːz] *a* envious, jaundiced.

environ [ɑ̃virɔ̃] *ad* about; *nm pl* neighborhood, outskirts, surroundings.

environner [ɑ̃virɔne] *vt* to surround.

envisager [ɑ̃vizaʒe] *vt* to look at, face, view, foresee, anticipate.

envoi [ɑ̃vwa] *nm* sending, forwarding, consignment.

envol [ɑ̃vɔl] *nm* taking wing, taking off, take-off.

s'envoler [sɑ̃vɔle] *vr* to fly away, off, take flight.

envoûtement [ɑ̃vutmɑ̃] *nm* (casting of a) spell, hoodoo, passion, craze.

envoûter [ɑ̃vute] *vt* to put a spell, a hoodoo on, hold enthralled.

envoyé [ɑ̃vwaje] *nm* envoy, representative.

envoyer [ɑ̃vwaje] *vt* to send, dispatch; **— chercher** to send for; **— dire** to send word; **— promener** to send about one's business.

épagneul [epaɲœl] *n* spaniel.

épais, -aisse [epɛ, ɛːs] *a* thick, dense.

épaisseur [epesœːr] *nf* thickness, density.

épaissir [epesiːr] *vt* to thicken, make dense; *vr* to thicken grow dense, stout.

épanchement [epɑ̃ʃmɑ̃] *nm* pouring out, effusion, outpouring.

épancher [epɑ̃ʃe] *vt* to pour out, pour forth; *vr* to pour out one's heart, expand, unburden oneself.

épandre [epɑ̃dr] *vt* to spread, shed; *vr* to spread.

épanoui [epanwi] *a* in full bloom, beaming, wreathed in smiles.

épanouir [epanwiːr] *vt* to make (sth) open, bring forth, **— out**; *vr* to open out, bloom, light up, beam.

épanouissement [epanwismɑ̃] *nm* opening up, blossoming.

épargne [eparɲ] *nf* economy, thrift, saving.

épargner [eparɲe] *vt* to save, economize, be sparing of, spare.

éparpiller [eparpije] *vtr* to scatter, disperse.

épars [epaːr] *a* scattered, stray, scant.

épatant [epatɑ̃] *a* (*fam*) great, splendid, terrific.

épate [epat] *nf* **faire de l'—** to show off.

épater [epate] *vt* to astound, startle, stagger; to break the foot of.

épaule [epoːl] *nf* shoulder; **hausser les —s** to shrug one's shoulders.

épauler [epole] *vt* to shoulder; *vi* (*rifle*) to aim.

épaulette [epolɛt] *nf* shoulder-strap, epaulette.

épave [epaːv] *nf* wreck, waif, unclaimed object; *pl* flotsam, jetsam, wreckage.

épée [epe] *nf* sword.

épeler [eple] *vt* to spell.

éperdu [eperdy] *a* distracted, mad.

éperon [eprɔ̃] *nm* spur, buttress.

éperonner [eprɔne] *vt* to spur, urge on.

épervier [epervje] *nm* sparrow-hawk, fishing net.

éphémère [efemɛːr] *a* ephemeral, short-lived, fleeting; *nf* mayfly.

épi [epi] *nm* (*corn*) ear, cluster.

épice [epis] *nf* spice; **pain d'—** (type of) gingerbread.

épicé [epise] *a* spiced, seasoned, spicy.

épicer [epise] *vt* to spice, season.

épicerie [episri] *nf* spices, groceries, grocer's shop.

épicier, -ière [episje, jɛːr] *n* grocer.

épicurien, -ienne [epikyrjɛ̃, jɛn] *a* epicurean; *n* epicure, sybarite.

épicurisme [epikyrism] *nm* epicureanism.

épidémie [epidemi] *nf* epidemic.

épidémique [epidemik] *a* epidemic (al).

épiderme [epiderm] *nm* epiderm(is).

épier [epje] *vt* to spy upon, watch for, listen for.

épigramme [epigram] *nf* epigram.

épilepsie [epilɛpsi] *nf* epilepsy.

épiler [epile] *vt* to remove superfluous hair from, pluck.

épilogue [epilɔg] *nm* epilogue.

épiloguer [epilɔge] *vt* to criticize, find fault with; *vi* to carp.

épinard [epinaːr] *nm* spinach.

épine [epin] *nf* thorn-bush, thorn, prickle.

épinette [epinɛt] *nf* spruce, virginal, spinet.

épineux, -euse [epinø, ø:z] *a* thorny, prickly, knotty, ticklish, tricky.

épingle [epɛ̃:gl] *nf* pin; — de nourrice safety-pin; — à linge clothespin; tiré à quatre —s spruce, dapper.

épingler [epɛ̃gle] *vt* to pin, fasten with a pin.

épique [epik] *a* epic.

épiscopal [episkɔpal] *a* episcopal.

épiscopat [episkɔpa] *nm* episcopate.

épisode [epizɔd] *nm* episode.

épistolaire [epistɔlɛːr] *a* epistolary.

épitaphe [epitaf] *nf* epitaph.

épithète [epitɛt] *nf* epithet, adjective.

épître [epiːtr] *nf* epistle.

éploré [eplɔre] *a* tearful, in tears, weeping.

éplucher [eplyʃe] *vt* to clean, peel, sift, examine.

épluchures [eplyʃyːr] *nf pl* peelings, refuse.

épointer [epwɛ̃te] *vt* to blunt, break the point of.

éponge [epɔ̃:ʒ] *nf* sponge.

éponger [epɔ̃ʒe] *vt* to mop, sponge, dab, mop up.

épopée [epɔpe] *nf* epic.

époque [epɔk] *nf* epoch, era, age, period, time; faire — to mark an epoch, be a landmark.

s'époumoner [sepumɔne] *vr* to talk, shout, till one is out of breath.

épousailles [epuzɑːj] *nf pl* wedding.

épouser [epuze] *vt* to marry, wed.

épousseter [epuste] *vt* to dust, beat.

époussette [epusɛt] *nf* feather-duster.

épouvantable [epuvɑ̃tabl] *a* dreadful, appalling.

épouvantail [epuvɑ̃taːj] *nm* scarecrow, bogy.

épouvante [epuvɑ̃:t] *nf* terror, dread, fright.

épouvanter [epuvɑ̃te] *vt* to terrify; *vr* to be terror-stricken, take fright.

époux, -ouse [epu, uːz] *n* husband, wife.

s'éprendre [seprɑ̃:dr] *vr* to fall in love (with de), take a fancy (to de).

épreuve [eprœːv] *nf* proof, test, trial, ordeal, print, impression, examination paper; à l'— de proof against; à toute — foolproof.

éprouvé [epruve] *a* well-tried, sorely tried, stricken.

éprouver [epruve] *vt* to test, try, feel, suffer.

éprouvette [epruvɛt] *nf* test-tube, gauge.

épuisement [epɥizmɑ̃] *nm* exhaustion, distress, depletion, using up, emptying.

épuiser [epɥize] *vt* to exhaust, use up, tire out.

épuisette [epɥizɛt] *nf* scoop, landing-net.

épuration [epyrasjɔ̃] *nf* purification,

purging, expurgation, filtering.

épurer [epyre] *vt* to purify, filter.

équarrir [ekariːr] *vt* to square, broach, cut up.

équateur [ekwatœːr] *nm* equator.

équation [ekwasjɔ̃] *nf* equation.

équerre [ekɛːr] *nf* square, angle-iron, bevel.

équerrer [ekɛre] *vt* to square, bevel.

équestre [ekɛstr] *a* equestrian.

équilibre [ekilibr] *nm* equilibrium, balance, stability.

équilibrer [ekilibre] *vtr* to balance.

équilibriste [ekilibrist] *n* equilibrist, acrobat, tight-rope walker.

équinoxe [ekinɔks] *nm* equinox.

équipage [ekipaːʒ] *nm* crew, company, retinue, train, carriage and horses, apparel, rig-out, equipment; maître d'— master of the hounds, coxswain.

équipe [ekip] *nf* squad, gang, team, crew, shift, train (of barges); chef d'— foreman.

équipée [ekipe] *nf* escapade, frolic, lark.

équipement [ekipmɑ̃] *nm* equipment, accoutrement, outfit, fitting out (up).

équiper [ekipe] *vt* to equip, appoint, fit out, man.

équipier [ekipje] *nm* one of a squad, member of a team.

équitable [ekitabl] *a* just, fair.

équitation [ekitasjɔ̃] *nf* horsemanship, riding.

équité [ekite] *nf* equity, fairness, justness.

équivalent [ekivalɑ̃] *a nm* equivalent.

équivaloir [ekivalwaːr] *vi* to be equal, be equivalent, be tantamount.

équivoque [ekivɔk] *a* ambiguous, equivocal, doubtful; *nf* ambiguity.

équivoquer [ekivɔke] *vi* to equivocate, quibble.

érable [erabl] *nm* maple.

érafler [erafle] *vt* to scratch, graze, score.

éraflure [eraflyːr] *nf* scratch, graze.

éraillement [erɑjmɑ̃] *nm* fraying, grazing, hoarseness.

érailler [erɑje] *vt* to unravel, graze, roughen; *vr* to fray, become hoarse.

ère [ɛːr] *nf* era, period, epoch.

érection [erɛksjɔ̃] *nf* putting up.

éreintant [erɛ̃tɑ̃] *a* back-breaking, killing.

éreinter [erɛ̃te] *vt* to break the back of, wear out, knock about, slate; *vr* to wear oneself out, slave.

ergot [ergo] *nm* spur, dewclaw, ergot; se dresser sur ses —s to get on one's high horse.

ergotage [ergotaːʒ] *nm* cavilling, quibbling.

ergoter [ergote] *vi* to cavil, quibble, haggle.

ergoteur, -euse [ergotœːr, øːz] *a* cavilling, quibbling; *n* quibbler.

ériger [eriʒe] vt to erect, put up, set up; vr to set oneself up (as en).

ermitage [ermita:ʒ] nm hermitage.

ermite [ermit] nm hermit.

éroder [erɔde] vt to erode, eat away.

erosion [erɔzjɔ̃] nf erosion.

érotique [erɔtik] a erotic.

érotisme [erɔtism] nm eroticism.

errements [ermɑ̃] nm pl erring ways.

errer [ere] vt to wander, roam, ramble.

erreur [erœ:r] nf error, mistake, slip, fallacy.

erroné [erɔne] a erroneous, false, mistaken.

éructer [erykte] vi to belch.

érudit [erydi] a learned, scholarly, erudite; nm scholar scientist

érudition [erydisjɔ̃] nf learning, scholarship.

éruption [erypsjɔ̃] nf eruption.

ès [ɛs] = en + les; docteur — sciences, doctor of science.

escabeau [eskabo] nm stool, steps.

escadre [eska:dr] nf (naut) squadron.

escadrille [eskadri:j] nf (naut) flotilla, (av) squadron.

escadron [eskadrɔ̃] nm (cavalry) squadron.

escalade [eskalad] nf climb(ing), scaling.

escalader [eskalade] vt to climb, scale.

escale [eskal] nf port of call, call; faire — à to put in at; sans — non-stop.

escalier [eskalje] nm staircase, stairs; — de service backstairs; — roulant escalator; il a l'esprit de l'— he has never a ready answer.

escalope [eskalɔp] nf cutlet.

escamotable [eskamɔtabl] a concealable, retractable.

escamotage [eskamɔta:ʒ] nm sleight of hand, conjuring, theft, pinching.

escamoter [eskamɔte] vt to conjure away, whisk away, hide, evade, pinch; (av) retract undercarriage.

escamoteur [eskamɔtœ:r] nm conjurer.

escampette [eskɑ̃pet] nf prendre la poudre d'— to clear off, decamp.

escapade [eskapad] nf escapade, adventure, prank.

escarbille [eskarbi:j] nf cinder, clinker.

escarbot [eskarbo] nm cockchafer, blackbeetle.

escarboucle [eskarbukl] nf carbuncle.

escargot [eskargo] nm snail.

escarmouche [eskarmuʃ] nf skirmish.

escarpé [eskarpe] a steep, sheer, precipitous.

escarpement [eskarpəmɑ̃] nm escarpment.

escarpin [eskarpɛ̃] nm dancing-shoe, pump.

escarpolette [eskarpɔlet] nf swing.

escarre [eska:r] nf bedsore, scab.

escient [esjɑ̃] nm knowledge; à mon — to my knowledge; à son — wittingly.

s'esclaffer [sesklafe] vr to burst out laughing, guffaw.

esclandre [esklɑ̃:dr] nm scandal.

esclavage [esklava:ʒ] nm slavery, bondage.

esclave [eskla:v] n slave.

escompte [eskɔ̃:t] nm discount, rebate.

escompter [eskɔ̃te] vt to discount, allow for, anticipate.

escorte [eskɔrt] nf escort, convoy.

escorter [eskɔrte] vt to escort.

escouade [eskwad] nf squad, section.

escrime [eskrim] nf fencing, swordsmanship, skirmishing.

escrimer [eskrime] vi to fence; vr to try hard, spar.

escrimeur [eskrimœ:r] nm fencer, swordsman.

escroc [eskro] nm swindler, crook.

escroquer [eskrɔke] vt to rob, swindle, cheat.

escroquerie [eskrɔkri] nf swindling, swindle.

ésotérique [esɔterik] a esoteric.

espace [espas] nm space, interval.

espacer [espase] vt to space (out); vr to become more and more isolated, grow fewer and fewer.

espadrille [espadri:j] nf rope-soled canvas shoe.

Espagne [espaɲ] nf Spain.

espagnol [espaɲɔl] a Spanish; n Spaniard.

espagnolette [espaɲɔlet] nf window-catch.

espèce [espes] nf kind, sort, species; pl cash.

espérance [esperɑ̃:s] nf hope, expectation.

espérer [espere] vt to hope (for).

espiègle [espjegl] a mischievous, arch, roguish.

espièglerie [espjegləri] nf mischievousness, roguishness, trick, prank.

espion, -onne [espjɔ̃, ɔn] n spy.

espionnage [espjɔna:ʒ] nm espionage, spying.

espionner [espjɔne] vt to spy (on).

esplanade [esplanad] nf esplanade, parade.

espoir [espwa:r] nm hope.

esprit [espri] nm spirit, ghost, soul, mind, wit.

esquif [eskif] nm skiff.

esquimau, -aude [eskimo] an Eskimo.

esquinter [eskɛ̃te] vt to exhaust, run down, slate.

esquisse [eskis] nf sketch, draft, outline.

esquisser [eskise] vt to sketch, draft, outline.

esquiver [eskive] vt to evade, dodge, shirk; vr to slip away, dodge (off), abscond.

essai [ɛsɛ] nm trial, test, experiment, attempt, try, sample, essay; à l'— on trial, on approval; coup d'— first attempt, trial shot.

essaim [ɛsɛ̃] nm swarm, cluster, hive.

essaimer [eseme] vi to swarm.

essayage [esejaːʒ] nm fitting.

essayer [eseje] vt to test, try, try on, fit, attempt, assay; vr to try one's hand.

essence [ɛsɑ̃ːs] nf essence, extract, gasoline; poste d'— filling-station.

essentiel, -elle [esɑ̃sjɛl] a essential, crucial, key; n the main thing, burden.

essieu [esjø] nm axle.

essor [esɔːr] nm flight, rise, scope.

essoreuse [esɔrøːz] nf wringer, spin-drier.

essoufflé [esufle] a breathless, out of breath.

essoufflement [esufləmɑ̃] nm breathlessness.

essouffler [esufle] vt to wind, put out of breath; vr to get breathless, winded.

essuie-glace [esɥiglas] nm windshield wiper.

essuie-mains [esɥimɛ̃] nm towel.

essuie-pieds [esɥipje] nm doormat.

essuyer [esɥije] vt to wipe (up), clean, meet with.

est [ɛst] nm east.

estacade [ɛstakad] nf line of piles, pier, boom, stockade.

estafette [ɛstafɛt] nf courier, dispatch-rider.

estafilade [ɛstafilad] nf slash, gash, rent.

estaminet [ɛstaminɛ] nm café, bar, public-house.

estampe [ɛstɑ̃ːp] nf print, engraving.

estamper [ɛstɑ̃pe] vt to stamp, emboss, punch, sting.

estampille [ɛstɑ̃piːj] nf stamp, trade-mark, endorsement.

esthète [ɛstɛt] n aesthete.

esthétique [ɛstetik] a aesthetic.

estimateur -trice [ɛstimatœːr, tris] n estimator.

estimation [ɛstimasjɔ̃] nf valuation, valuing, estimate.

estime [ɛstim] nf esteem, regard, estimation, reckoning.

estimer [ɛstime] vt to estimate, valuate, calculate, guess, consider, deem, value, esteem.

estival [ɛstival] a summer, estival.

estivant [ɛstivɑ̃] n summer visitor, holiday-maker.

estoc [ɛstɔk] nm stock, point of sword.

estocade [ɛstɔkad] nf thrust.

estomac [ɛstɔma] nm stomach.

estomaquer [ɛstɔmake] vt to take s.o.'s breath away, stagger.

estompé [ɛstɔ̃pe] a blurred, soft, hazy.

estomper [ɛstɔ̃pe] vt to stump, shade off, soften the outlines of.

estrade [ɛstrad] nf platform, stage, dais.

estropier [ɛstrɔpje] vt to maim, cripple, spoil, murder.

estuaire [ɛstɥɛːr] nm estuary, firth.

estudiantin [ɛstydjɑ̃tɛ̃] a student.

et [e] cj and; et . . . et both . . . and; et vous? what about you? do you? are you?; — alors! so what!

étable [etabl] nf cattle-shed, byre.

établi [etabli] nm (work-)bench.

établir [etabliːr] vt to establish, put up, set up, install, fix, draw up, lay down; vr to establish oneself, settle.

établissement [etablismɑ̃] nm establishment, setting up, installing, drawing up, laying down.

étage [etaːʒ] nm story, floor, tier, layer, rank.

étager [etaʒe] vt to arrange in tiers, terrace, stagger; vr to be tiered, terraced.

étagère [etaʒɛːr] nf rack, shelves.

étai [etɛ] nm stay, prop, strut, mainstay.

étain [etɛ̃] nm tin, pewter.

étal [etal] nm butcher's stall, shop.

étalage [etalaːʒ] nm show, display, window-dressing, show-window; faire — de to display, show off, flaunt.

étaler [etale] vt to display, spread out, lay out, exhibit, show off, air; vr to stretch (oneself out), sprawl, enlarge (upon), expatiate (on).

étalon [etalɔ̃] nm standard, stallion.

étalonner [etalɔne] vt to stamp, mark, standardize.

étamer [etame] vt to tinplate, silver, galvanize.

étameur [etamœːr] nm tinsmith.

étamine [etamin] nf coarse muslin, gauze, bunting, sieve, strainer, stamen.

étampe [etɑ̃ːp] nf stamp, die, punch·

étamper [etɑ̃pe] vt to stamp, mark, punch.

étanche [etɑ̃ːʃ] a impervious, tight, insulated; — à l'air (à l'eau) air- (water)tight.

étancher [etɑ̃ʃe] vt to stanch, stop (flow of), quench, make water(air) tight.

étançonner [etɑ̃sɔne] vt to prop up, shore up.

étang [etɑ̃] nm pond, pool.

étape [etap] nf stage, stopping-place, a day's march.

état [eta] nm state, condition, order, list statement, profession; mettre qn en — de to enable s.o. to; être dans 'ous ses — to be in a great state.

étatisme [etatism] nm state control.

état-major [etamaʒɔːr] nm general staff, headquarters.

étau [eto] nm (tec) vise.

étayer [eteje] vt to prop up, shore up, support; vr to brace oneself.

été [ete] nm summer

éteignoir [etɛɲwaːr] nm damper, extinguisher.

éteindre [etɛ̃:dr] vt to extinguish, put out, switch off, dim; vr to go out, die (out, away, down), fade (away).

éteint [etɛ̃] a extinguished, extinct, dim, faint, dull, dead.

étendard [etɑ̃daːr] nm standard, flag, colors.

étendre [etɑ̃:dr] vt to stretch, spread, extend, enlarge; vr to stretch oneself out, lie down, extend, spread, dwell (upon), hold forth (on).

étendu [etɑ̃dy] a extensive, wide, far-reaching.

étendue [etɑ̃dy] nf extent, size, expanse, stretch.

éternel, -elle [etɛrnɛl] a eternal, everlasting, endless.

éterniser [etɛrnize] vt to perpetuate, drag (out, on); vr to drag on and on.

éternité [etɛrnite] nf eternity.

éternuement [etɛrnymɑ̃] nm sneeze, sneezing.

éternuer [etɛrnɥe] vt to sneeze.

éthéré [etere] a ethereal.

éthique [etik] a ethical; nf ethics.

ethnique [ɛtnik] a ethnical, ethnological.

étinceler [etɛ̃sle] vi to sparkle, glitter, flash.

étincelle [etɛ̃sɛl] nf spark, flash.

étincellement [etɛ̃sɛlmɑ̃] nm sparkling, glittering, twinkling.

étioler [etjɔle] vt to blanch, make wilt, weaken; vr to blanch, wilt.

étique [etik] a emaciated, skinny, gaunt.

étiqueter [etikte] vt to label, ticket, docket.

étiquette [etikɛt] nf label, ticket, docket, etiquette, ceremonial; — à œillets tie-on label; — gommée stick-on label.

étoffe [etɔf] nf material, cloth, fabric, stuff, makings.

étoffé [etɔfe] a ample, rich, stuffed, stout, meaty.

étoile [etwal] nf star, asterisk; dormir à la belle — to sleep in the open.

étole [etɔl] nf stole.

étonnement [etɔnmɑ̃] nm surprise, astonishment.

étonner [etɔne] vt to surprise, astonish, amaze; vr to be surprised.

étouffant [etufɑ̃] a stifling, stuffy, sultry, airless.

étouffement [etufmɑ̃] nm choking, suffocation, attack of breathlessness.

étouffer [etufe] vti to suffocate, choke; vi damp, stifle, deaden, smother, hush up.

étoupe [etup] nf tow, oakum.

étourderie [eturdəri] nf thoughtlessness, giddiness.

étourdi [eturdi] a scatterbrained, hare-brained, dizzy, giddy; n scatterbrain.

étourdir [eturdiːr] vt to daze, bemuse, make one's head reel, deafen, astound.

étourdissement [eturdismɑ̃] nm giddiness, dizziness.

étourneau [eturno] nm starling, scatterbrain.

étrange [etrɑ̃:ʒ] a strange, queer, odd.

étranger, -ère [etrɑ̃ʒe, ɛːr] a foreign, alien, unfamiliar, irrelevant; n foreigner, alien, stranger; nm abroad.

étranglement [etrɑ̃gləmɑ̃] nm strangulation, constriction, narrows, narrowing, bottleneck.

étrangler [etrɑ̃gle] vt to throttle, strangle, choke, constrict; vi to choke; vr to narrow, gulp.

étrave [etraːv] nf (naut) bow, stem.

être [ɛːtr] vi to be, exist; nm being, existence, creature; il est à écrire he is busy writing; où en êtes-vous? how far have you got? il n'en est rien nothing of the kind; le chapeau est à lui the hat is his; comme si de rien n'était as if nothing had happened.

étreindre [etrɛ̃:dr] vt to embrace, clasp, grasp, wring.

étreinte [etrɛ̃:t] nf embrace, hug, clasp, grip, clutch.

étrenne [etrɛn] nf New Year's gift.

étrenner [etrɛne] vt to be the first to buy from, use for the first time, handsel.

étrier [etrie] nm stirrup; coup de l'— stirrup-cup.

étrille [etriːj] nf curry-comb.

étriller [etrije] vt to curry-comb, thrash, give a drubbing to.

étriper [etripe] vt to gut, clean, disembowel.

étriqué [etrike] a tight, skimped, cramped.

étroit [etrwa] a narrow, tight, close, hidebound.

étroitesse [etrwatɛs] nf narrowness, tightness, closeness.

étude [etyd] nf study, research, prep. (lessons), office, chambers; à l'— under consideration; faire ses —e à to be educated at.

étudiant [etydjɑ̃] n student, undergraduate.

étudié [etydje] a studied, affected, deliberate.

étudier [etydje] vt to study, read, investigate; vr to strive, make a point (of).

étui [etɥi] nm case, box.

étuve [etyːv] nf sweating-room, drying-room.

étuver [etyve] vt to dry, heat, stew, steam, jug.

étymologie [etimɔlɔʒi] nf etymology.

étymologique [etimɔlɔʒik] a etymological.

étymologiste [etimɔlɔʒist] n etymologist.

eucharistie [økaristi] *nf* Eucharist, Lord's Supper.

eunuque [ønyk] *nm* eunuch.

euphémisme [øfemism] *nm* euphemism.

euphonie [øfɔni] *nf* euphony.

Europe [ørɔp] *nf* Europe.

européen, -enne [ørɔpeɛ̃ ɛn] *an* European.

euthanasie [øtanazi] *nf* euthanasia.

évacuation [evakyasjɔ̃] *nf* clearing, withdrawal, vacating.

évacué [evakye] *n* evacuee.

évacuer [evakye] *vt* to evacuate, empty, withdraw, vacate.

évadé [evade] *a* escaped; *n* escaped prisoner.

s'évader [sevade] *vr* to escape, run away, break out.

évaluation [evalyasjɔ̃] *nf* valuation, assessment, estimate, appraisal.

évaluer [evalye] *vt* to evaluate, assess, appraise.

évangile [evɑ̃ʒil] *nm* gospel.

évanouir [evanwi:r] *vr* to vanish, disappear, faint.

évanouissement [evanwismɑ̃] *nm* disappearance, fading away, swoon.

évaporation [evapɔrasjɔ̃] *nf* evaporation, frivolousness.

évaporé [evapɔre] *a* giddy, light-headed.

évaporer [evapɔre] *vr* to evaporate, pass off, become silly and frivolous.

évasement [evazmɑ̃] *nm* widening out, flare, bell-mouth.

évaser [evaze] *vtr* to open out, widen, flare.

évasif, -ive [evazif, i:v] *a* evasive.

évasion [evazjɔ̃] *nf* escape, evasion.

évêché [eveʃe] *nm* bishopric, bishop's palace.

éveil [eve:j] *nm* awakening, wide-awake state, alert, alarm.

éveillé [eveje] *a* awake, alert, bright, alive.

éveiller [eveje] *vt* to wake up, awake, arouse; *vr* to wake up, awaken.

événement [evɛnmɑ̃] *nm* event, incident, happening, occurrence; **dans l'—** as it transpired; **attendre l'—** to await the outcome.

éventail [evɑ̃ta:j] *nm* fan.

éventaire [evɑ̃tɛ:r] *nm* flat basket.

éventé [evɑ̃te] *a* flat, stale, musty.

éventer [evɑ̃te] *vt* to air, fan, catch the scent of, get wind of; *vr* to fan oneself, go flat, go stale.

éventrer [evɑ̃tre] *vt* to disembowel, gut, smash open.

éventualité [evɑ̃tyalite] *nf* eventuality, contingency, possibility.

éventuel, -elle [evɑ̃tyɛl] *ad* contingent, possible.

éventuellement [evɑ̃tyɛlmɑ̃] *ad* possibly, should the occasion arise.

évêque [eve:k] *nm* bishop.

s'évertuer [severtye] *vr* to strive, make every effort.

éviction [eviksjɔ̃] *nf* eviction.

évidemment [evidamɑ̃] *ad* evidently, obviously.

évidence [evidɑ̃:s] *nf* obviousness, conspicuousness; **se rendre à l'—** to accept the facts; **être en — l'** to be to the fore, in the limelight.

évident [evidɑ̃] *a* evident, obvious, clear.

évider [evide] *vt* to hollow out, groove, cut away.

évier [evje] *nm* sink.

évincer [evɛ̃se] to evict, turn out.

évitement [evitmɑ̃] *nm* avoiding, shunting, loop.

éviter [evite] *vt* to avoid, shun, evade, save (from).

évocateur, -trice [evɔkatœ:r, tris] *a* evocative, picturesque.

évocation [evɔkasjɔ̃] *nf* evocation, conjuring up, calling to mind.

évoluer [evɔlye] *vi* to maneuver, evolve, revolve.

évolution [evɔlysjɔ̃] *nf* evolution, maneuver.

évoquer [evɔke] *vt* to evoke, call forth, conjure up, call to mind.

exacerber [ɛgzasɛrbe] *vt* to exacerbate.

exact [ɛgzakt] *a* accurate, punctual, strict, express.

exactitude [ɛgzaktityd] *nf* exactness, accuracy, punctuality.

exagération [ɛgzaʒerasjɔ̃] *nf* exaggeration, overstatement.

exagérer [ɛgzaʒere] *vt* to exaggerate, overrate, magnify, overdo, go too far.

exaltation [ɛgzaltasjɔ̃] *nf* exaltation, extolling, excitement.

exalté [ɛgzalte] *a* passionate, elated, impassioned, hot-headed, quixotic.

exalter [ɛgzalte] *vt* to exalt, extol, excite, uplift; *vr* to grow enthusiastic, excited.

examen [ɛgzamɛ̃] *nm* examination, inspection, scrutiny; **se présenter à un —** to take an examination.

examinateur, -trice [ɛgzaminatœ:r, tris] *n* examiner.

examiner [ɛgzamine] *vt* to examine, inspect, scrutinize.

exaspération [ɛgzasperasjɔ̃] *nf* annoyance, aggravation.

exaspérer [ɛgzaspere] *vt* to exasperate, aggravate; *vr* to become exasperated.

exaucer [ɛgzose] *vt* to fulfill, grant.

excavation [ɛkskavasjɔ̃] *nf* excavation, digging out.

excédent [ɛksedɑ̃] *nm* surplus, excess.

excéder [ɛksede] *vt* to exceed, go beyond, overstrain, tire out, exasperate.

excellence [ɛksɛlɑ̃:s] *nf* excellence.

excellent [ɛksɛlɑ̃] *a* excellent.

exceller [ɛksɛle] *vi* to excel.

excentricité [ɛksɑ̃trisite] *nf* eccentricity, oddity.

excentrique [ɛksɑ̃trik] *a* eccentric, odd, outlying; *n* eccentric character.

excepté [ɛksɛpte] *prep* except, but barring.

excepter [ɛksɛpte] *vt* to except, exclude.

exception [ɛksɛpsjɔ̃] *nf* exception; **sauf —** with certain exceptions.

exceptionnel, -elle [ɛksɛpsjɔnɛl] *a* exceptional.

excès [ɛksɛ] *nm* excess; **à l'—** to excess, to a fault, over-.

excessif, -ive [ɛksɛsif, iːv] *a* excessive, undue.

excessivement [ɛksɛsivmɑ̃] *a* exceedingly, over-.

excitabilité [ɛksitabilite] *nf* excitability.

excitant [ɛksitɑ̃] *a* stimulating, exciting, hectic; *nm* stimulant.

excitation [ɛksitasjɔ̃] *nf* excitation, stimulation, incitement.

exciter [ɛksite] *vt* to excite, stimulate, arouse, urge, incite, spur (on); *vr* to get worked up, roused.

exclamatif, -ive [ɛksklamatif, iːv] *a* exclamative, exclamatory.

exclamation [ɛksklamasjɔ̃] *nf* exclamation.

s'exclamer [sɛksklame] *vr* to exclaim.

exclure [ɛksklyːr] *vt* to exclude, leave out, debar.

exclusif, -ive [ɛksklyzif, iːv] *a* exclusive, sole.

exclusion [ɛksklyzjɔ̃] *nf* exclusion.

exclusivité [ɛksklyzivite] *nf* exclusiveness, sole rights.

excommunier [ɛkskɔmynje] *vt* to excommunicate.

excrément [ɛskremɑ̃] *nm* excrement, scum.

excursion [ɛkskyrsjɔ̃] *nf* excursion, trip, outing, raid.

excursionniste [ɛkskyrsjɔnist] *nm* excursionist, tourist.

excusable [ɛkskyzabl] *a* pardonable.

excuse [ɛkskyːz] *nf* excuse, apology.

excuser [ɛkskyze] *vt* to excuse, pardon, make excuses for; *vr* to apologize, excuse oneself; **se faire —** to withdraw, call off.

exécrable [ɛgzekrabl] *a* execrable, abominable.

exécration [ɛgzekrasjɔ̃] *nf* execration, loathing.

exécrer [ɛgzekre] *vt* to execrate, loathe.

exécutable [ɛgzekytabl] *a* feasible, practicable.

exécutant [ɛgzekytɑ̃] *n* executant, performer.

exécuter [ɛgzekyte] *vt* to execute, carry out, perform, enforce; *vr* to comply.

exécuteur, -trice [ɛgzekytœːr, tris] *n* executor, -trix.

exécutif, -ive [ɛgzekytif, iːv] *a* executive.

exécution [ɛgzekysjɔ̃] *nf* execution, accomplishment, performance, en-

forcement; **mettre à —** to put into effect, carry out.

exemplaire [ɛgzɑ̃plɛːr] *a* exemplary; *nm* specimen, copy.

exemple [ɛgzɑ̃ːpl] *nm* example, precedent, instance, lesson; **par —** for example, fancy that!

exempt [ɛgzɑ̃] *a* exempt, free.

exempter [ɛgzɑ̃te] *vt* to exempt, excuse; *vr* to get out (of).

exemption [ɛgzɑ̃sjɔ̃] *nf* exemption, immunity.

exercé [ɛgzɛrse] *a* trained, practiced.

exercer [ɛgzɛrse] *vt* to exercise, exert, carry on, drill, train; *vr* to be exerted, practice.

exercice [ɛgzɛrsis] *nm* drill, training, practice, exercise, carrying out; financial year; **entrer en —** to take up one's duties; **en —** practicing, acting.

exhalaison [ɛgzalɛzɔ̃] *nf* exhalation, odor.

exhalation [ɛgzalasjɔ̃] *nf* exhalation, exhaling.

exhaler [ɛgzale] *vt* to exhale, emit, vent, pour forth.

exhaustif [ɛgzostif] *a* exhaustive.

exhiber [ɛgzibe] *vt* to exhibit, show, flaunt; *vr* to make an exhibition of oneself.

exhibition [ɛgzibisjɔ̃] *nf* show, showing.

exhorter [ɛgzɔrte] *vt* to exhort, urge.

exhumer [ɛgzyme] *vt* to disinter, unearth, exhume.

exigeant [ɛgziʒɑ̃] *a* exacting, hard to please.

exigence [ɛgziʒɑ̃ːs] *nf* demand, requirement.

exiger [ɛgziʒe] *vt* to exact, demand, require, call for.

exigu, -uë [ɛgzigy] *a* tiny, slender, scant, exiguous.

exiguïté [ɛgziguite] *nf* smallness, scantiness, exiguity.

exil [ɛgzil] *nm* exile.

exilé [ɛgzile] *n* exile.

exiler [ɛgzile] *vt* to exile, banish.

existence [ɛgzistɑ̃ːs] *nf* existence, life, subsistence; *pl* stock on hand.

exister [ɛgziste] *vi* to exist, live, be extant.

exode [ɛgzɔd] *nm* exodus.

exonérer [ɛgzɔnere] *vt* to exonerate, exempt.

exorbitant [ɛgzɔrbitɑ̃] *a* exorbitant, extortionate.

exorciser [ɛgzɔrsize] *vt* to exorcize.

exotique [ɛgzɔtik] *a* exotic.

expansif, -ive [ɛkspɑ̃sif] *a* expansive, effusive, forthcoming.

expansion [ɛkspɑ̃sjɔ̃] *nf* expansion, expansiveness.

expatriation [ɛkspatriasjɔ̃] *nf* expatriation.

expatrier [ɛkspatrie] *vt* to expatriate; *vr* to leave one's country.

expectative [ɛkspɛktativ] *nf* expectation, expectancy.

xpectorer [ɛkspɛktɔre] vi to ex-pectorate, spit.

expédient [ɛkspedjɑ̃] a nm expedient; nm device, way.

expédier [ɛkspedje] vt to dispatch, send off, expedite, hurry through, get rid of.

expéditeur, -trice [ɛkspeditœːr, tris] n sender shipper, consigner.

expédition [ɛkspedisjɔ̃] nf dispatch, shipping, consignment, expedition.

expéditionnaire [ɛkspedisjɔnɛːr] a expeditionary; nm forwarding agent.

expérience [ɛksperjɑ̃ːs] nf experi-ence, experiment, test.

expérimental [ɛksperimɑ̃tal] a ex-perimental, applied.

expérimentateur, -trice [ɛksperi-mɑ̃tatœːr, tris] n experimenter.

expérimentation [ɛksperimɑ̃tasjɔ̃] nf experimenting.

expérimenté [ɛksperimɑ̃te] a ex-perienced, skilled.

expérimenter [ɛksperimɑ̃te] vt to test, try; vi to experiment.

expert [ɛkspɛːr] a expert, skilled; nm expert, valuator.

expert-comptable [ɛkspɛrkɔ̃tabl] nm certified public accountant.

expertise [ɛkspertiːz] nf survey, valuation, assessment.

expertiser [ɛkspertize] vt to value, assess, survey.

expiation [ɛkspjasjɔ̃] nf expiation.

expier [ɛkspje] vt to expiate, atone for.

expiration [ɛkspirasjɔ̃] nf breathing out, expiration.

expirer [ɛkspire] vi to expire, to die.

explicatif, -ive [ɛksplikatif, iːv] a explanatory.

explication [ɛksplikasjɔ̃] nf explana-tion.

explicite [ɛksplisit] a explicit, clear.

expliquer [ɛksplike] vt to explain, expound, elucidate, account for; vr to explain oneself, have it out (with avec).

exploit [ɛksplwa] nm deed, feat, writ.

exploitation [ɛksplwatasjɔ̃] nf ex-ploitation, cultivation, working, trading upon; — des mines mining

exploiter [ɛksplwate] vt to exploit, cultivate, work, take advantage of.

explorateur, -trice [ɛksplɔratœːr, tris] a exploring; n explorer.

exploration [ɛksplɔrasjɔ̃] nf explora-tion.

explorer [ɛksplɔre] vt to explore.

exploser [ɛksploze] vi to explode, blow up.

explosible [ɛksplozibl] a (high) explosive.

explosif, -ive [ɛksplozif, iːv] a nm explosive.

explosion [ɛksplozjɔ̃] nf explosion.

exportateur, -trice [ɛkspɔrtatœːr, tris] a exporting; n exporter.

exportation [ɛkspɔrtasjɔ̃] nf ex-portation; pl exports, export trade.

exporter [ɛkspɔrte] vt to export.

exposant [ɛkspozɑ̃] n exhibitor, petitioner.

exposé [ɛkspoze] a exposed, open; nm account, statement.

exposer [ɛkspoze] vt to exhibit, display, show, explain, expose, expound, lay bare.

exposition [ɛkspozisjɔ̃] nf exhibition, display, show, exposure, statement.

exprès, -esse [ɛksprɛ, ɛːs] a express, clear, explicit; ad expressly, on purpose.

expressément [ɛkspresemɑ̃] ad ex-pressly.

express [ɛksprɛːs] nm express train, repeating rifle.

expressif, -ive [ɛkspresif, iːv] a expressive, emphatic.

expression [ɛkspresjɔ̃] nf expression, squeezing, manifestation (of feeling), (turn of) phrase.

exprimer [ɛksprime] vt to express, voice, show, squeeze, press; vr to express oneself.

expropriation [ɛksprɔpriasjɔ̃] nf expropriation.

exproprier [ɛksprɔprie] vt to ex-propriate, dispossess.

expulser [ɛkspylse] vt to expel, drive out, evict, eject.

expulsion [ɛkspylsjɔ̃] nf expulsion, eviction, ejection.

expurger [ɛkspyrge] vt to expurgate, bowdlerize.

exquis [ɛkski] a exquisite.

exsangue [ɛksɑ̃ːg] a bloodless.

extase [ɛkstɑːz] nf ecstasy, rapture, trance.

s'extasier [sɛkstazje] vr to go into raptures.

extatique [ɛkstatik] a ecstatic, rapturous.

extensible [ɛkstɑ̃sibl] a extensible, expanding.

extension [ɛkstɑ̃sjɔ̃] nf stretching, spread, extent.

exténuation [ɛkstenyasjɔ̃] nf ex-tenuation, exhaustion.

exténuer [ɛkstenye] vt to extenuate, exhaust, wear out; vr to wear oneself out.

extérieur [ɛksterjœːr] a exterior, outer, external; nm outside, ex-terior, outward appearance.

exterminer [ɛkstɛrmine] vt to ex-terminate, wipe out, annihilate; vr to kill oneself.

externat [ɛkstɛrna] nm day-school, out-patients' department.

externe [ɛkstɛrn] a external, outside, outward; n day-pupil, non-resident medical student.

extincteur, -trice [ɛkstɛ̃ktœːr, tris] a extinguishing; nm fire-extinguisher.

extinction [ɛkstɛ̃ksjɔ̃] nf extinction, putting out, suppression, quenching, loss.

extirper [ɛkstirpe] vt to extirpate,

eradicate, root out, (corn) remove.

extorquer [ɛkstɔrke] *vt* to extort, squeeze (out of).

extorsion [ɛkstɔrsjɔ̃] *nf* extortion.

extra [ɛkstra] *a* nm extra.

extraction [ɛkstraksjɔ̃] *nf* extraction, getting (out), origin.

extradition [ɛkstradisjɔ̃] *nf* extradition.

extraire [ɛkstrɛːr] *vt* to extract, draw (out).

extrait [ɛkstrɛ] *nm* extract, abstract, excerpt, essence; — **de mariage, de naissance** marriage, birth, certificate.

extraordinaire [ɛkstr(a)ɔrdinɛːr] *a* extraordinary, unusual; **par** — for a wonder.

extra-sensoriel [ɛkstrasɑ̃sɔrjɛl] *a* extrasensory.

extravagance [ɛkstravagɑ̃ːs] *nf* folly, wild act or statement, fantasy.

extravagant [ɛkstravagɑ̃] *a* extravagant, foolish, immoderate, far-fetched, tall.

extrême [ɛkstrɛːm] *a* extreme, far, farthest, drastic, dire; *nm* extreme limit.

extrême-onction [ɛkstrɛmɔ̃ksjɔ̃] *nf* extreme unction.

extrémiste [ɛkstremist] *n* extremist.

extrémité [ɛkstremite] *nf* extremity, end, point, tip.

exubérance [ɛgzyberɑ̃ːs] *nf* exuberance, boisterousness, superabundance, ebullience.

exubérant [ɛgzyberɑ̃] *a* exuberant, high spirited, buoyant, ebullient, superabundant.

exultation [ɛgzyltasjɔ̃] *nf* exultation, elation.

exulter [ɛgzylte] *vi* to exult, rejoice, be elated.

F

fable [faːbl] *nf* fable, tale; **la** — **de la ville** laughing-stock.

fabricant [fabrikɑ̃] *n* manufacturer, maker.

fabricateur, -trice [fabrikatœːr, tris] *n* fabricator, forger.

fabrication [fabrikasjɔ̃] *nf* making, manufacture, forging, fabrication; — **en série** mass production.

fabrique [fabrik] *nf* factory, works; **marque de** — trade-mark; **conseil de** — church council.

fabriquer [fabrike] *vt* to manufacture, make, fabricate, invent; **qu'est-ce qu'il fabrique là?** what is he up to?

fabuleux, -euse [fabylø, øːz] *a* fabulous, prodigious.

façade [fasad] *nf* façade, front, face, figurehead; **de** — sham, superficial.

face [fas] *nf* face, aspect; **faire** — **à** to face up to, cope with; **en** — **de** opposite; — **à** facing.

face-à-main [fasamɛ̃] *nm* lorgnette.

facétie [fasesi] *nf* joke, jest.

facétieux, -euse [fasesjø, øːz] *a* facetious, jocular.

facette [fasɛt] *nf* facet, aspect.

fâché [faʃe] *a* angry, cross, annoyed, sorry.

fâcher [faʃe] *vt* to anger, make angry; grieve; *vr* to get angry.

fâcherie [faʃri] *nf* tiff, bickering.

fâcheux, -euse [faʃø, øːz] *a* annoying, tiresome, unfortunate, unwelcome.

facile [fasil] *a* easy, facile, ready, accommodating.

facilité [fasilite] *nf* easiness, ease, readiness, facility.

faciliter [fasilite] *vt* to facilitate, make easier.

façon [fasɔ̃] *nf* manner, fashion, way, making, workmanship; *pl* fuss, ado, ceremony; **on travaille à** — customer's own materials made up; **à** — bespoke, made to measure; **de** — **à** so as to; **de** — **que** so that.

faconde [fakɔ̃d] *nf* gift of the gab, glibness.

façonner [fasɔne] *vt* to shape, fashion, work, mold.

façonnier, -ière [fasɔnje, jɛːr] *a* ceremonious, fussy; *nm* jobbing tailor.

fac-similé [faksimile] *nm* facsimile.

factage [faktaːʒ] *nm* transport, carriage, delivery.

facteur, -trice [faktœːr, tris] *n* maker of musical instruments, carrier, postman; *nm* factor.

factice [faktis] *a* artificial, imitation, sham, dummy.

factieux, -euse [faksjø, øːz] *a* factious, seditious.

faction [faksjɔ̃] *nf* guard, 'sentry-duty, faction; **faire** — to be on guard.

factionnaire [faksjɔnɛːr] *nm* sentry, guard.

factorerie [faktɔrəri] *nf* trading station.

facture [faktyːr] *nf* bill, invoice, workmanship, treatment.

facturer [faktyre] *vt* to invoice.

facultatif, -ive [fakyltatif, iːv] *a* optional.

faculté [fakylte] *nf* option, power, property, ability, faculty, university.

fadaise [fadɛːz] *nf* silly remark; *pl* nonsense.

fade [fad] *a* insipid, tasteless, wishy-washy, tame.

fadeur [fadœːr] *nf* insipidity, colorlessness, lifelessness, tameness.

fagot [fago] *nm* faggot, bundle of firewood; **sentir le** — to smack of heresy.

fagoté [fagɔte] *a* **mal** — shabbily dressed, dowdy.

faiblard [fɛblaːr] *a* weakish.

faible [fɛbl] *a* feeble, weak, faint,

slender, scanty; nm weakness, liking.

faiblesse [fɛblɛs] nf feebleness, weakness, frailty, failing.

faiblir [fɛbliːr] vi to weaken, grow weak(er), fail, faulter.

faïence [fajɑ̃ːs] nf crockery, delft, earthenware.

failli [faji] nm bankrupt.

faillibilité [fajibilite] nf fallibility.

faillible [fajibl] a fallible.

faillir [fajiːr] vi to fail; **il faillit tomber** he almost fell.

faillite [fajit] nf failure, bankruptcy; **faire** — to go bankrupt, fail.

faim [fɛ̃] nf hunger; **avoir** — to be hungry.

fainéant [fɛneɑ̃] a idle, lazy; n lazybones.

fainéanter [fɛneɑ̃te] vi to idle, laze about, loaf.

fainéantise [fɛneɑ̃tiːz] nf idleness, sloth.

faire [fɛːr] vt to make, do, get, be etc; **il n'y a rien à** — there is nothing can be done about it; **cela ne fait rien** it does not matter; **c'est bien fait** it serves you right; **c'en est fait de lui** he is done for; **il ne fait que de partir** he has just gone; **faites-le monter** show him up; **je lui ai fait écrire la lettre** I got him to write the letter; **cela fait très chic** that looks very smart; vr to become, to form, get accustomed, to mature; **il se fit un silence** silence fell, ensued; **comment se fait-il que vous ne l'ayez pas fait?** how does it come about that you did not do it?

faire-part [fɛrpaːr] nm card, letter.

faisable [fəzabl] a feasible.

faisan [fəzɑ̃] nm pheasant.

faisandé [fəzɑ̃de] a (meat) high.

faisceau [fɛso] nm bundle, pile, cluster, (light) beam.

faiseur, -euse [fəzœːr, øːz] n maker, doer, boaster.

fait [fɛ] a fully grown, developed; nm deed, act, fact, exploit; **—s et gestes doings; prendre sur le** — to catch in the act; **dire son** — à qn to give s.o. some home-truths; **arriver au** — to come to the point; **mettre qn au** — to give s.o. all the facts; **de** — actual(ly); **en** — as a matter of fact, actually; **en** — **de** as regards, in the way of.

fait-divers [fɛdivɛːr] nm news item.

faîte [fɛt] nm top, summit, ridge, cope.

falaise [falɛːz] nf cliff.

falbalas [falbala] nm pl furbelows, flounces.

fallacieux, -euse [falasjø, øːz] a fallacious, deceitful, deceptive.

falloir [falwaːr] v imp to be necessary, must, need, take, require; vr **en** — to be lacking, be far from; **il lui faut une voiture** he needs a car; **il m'a fallu une heure pour le faire** it took me an hour to do it; **il nous faut le faire** we must do it; **tant s'en faut qu'il ait tort** he is far from being wrong.

falot [falo] nm lantern; a dull, tame.

falsificateur, -trice [falsifikatœːr, tris] n falsifier, forger.

falsification [falsifikasjɔ̃] nf forgery, forging, adulteration.

falsifier [falsifje] vt to falsify, adulterate, debase, doctor.

famé [fame] a bien (mal) — of good (evil) repute.

famélique [famelik] a starving; n starveling.

fameux, -euse [famø, øːz] a famous, first-rate, rare, tiptop.

familial [familjal] a family.

familiariser [familjarize] vt to familiarize, acquaint; vr to make oneself become familiar (with avec).

familiarité [familjarite] nf familiarity.

familier, -ière [familje] a familiar, well-known, conversant; n regular visitor.

famille [famiːj] nf family.

famine [famin] nf famine, starvation.

fanal [fanal] nm lantern, beacon.

fanatique [fanatik] a fanatical; n fanatic.

fanatisme [fanatism] nm fanaticism.

faner [fane] vt to wither, (hay) toss; vr to wither, wilt, fade.

faneur, -euse [fanœːr, øːz] n haymaker.

faneuse [fanøːz] nf tedder.

fanfare [fɑ̃faːr] nf flourish, brass band.

fanfaron, -onne [fɑ̃farɔ̃, ɔn] a boasting; n braggart.

fanfaronnade [fɑ̃farɔnad] nf brag, bluster.

fange [fɑ̃ːʒ] nf mud, mire, filth.

fangeux [fɑ̃ʒø] a filthy, abject.

fanion [fanjɔ̃] nm flag.

fanon [fanɔ̃] nm dewlap, wattle, fetlock.

fantaisie [fɑ̃tɛzi] nf imagination, fancy, whim, freak, fantasia; **de** — fanciful; **articles de** — fancy goods.

fantaisiste [fɑ̃tɛzist] a fanciful, whimsical.

fantasmagorique [fɑ̃tasmagɔrik] a weird, fantastic.

fantasque [fɑ̃task] a capricious, quaint, odd, temperamental.

fantassin [fɑ̃tasɛ̃] nm infantryman.

fantastique [fɑ̃tastik] a fanciful, fantastic, eerie.

fantoche [fɑ̃tɔʃ] nm puppet, marionette.

fantôme [fɑ̃toːm] nm ghost, phantom.

faon [fɑ̃] nm fawn.

faraud [faro] a dressed up, cocky.

farce [fars] nf farce, trick, joke, stuffing, forcemeat.

farceur, -euse [farsœːr, øːz] n wag, humorist, practical joker.

farcir [farsiːr] vt to stuff.

fard [faːr] nm rouge, make-up, paint, deceit, pretense.

fardeau [fardo] nm load, burden.

farder [farde] vt to rouge, make up, disguise; vr to make up.

farfouiller [farfuje] vti to rummage (in, about), fumble.

faribole [faribɔl] nf idle story, nonsense.

farine [farin] nf flour, meal; **fleur de —** wheat flour; **— de manioc** garri, cassava flour.

farineux, -euse [farinø, øːz] a floury, mealy.

farouche [faruʃ] a fierce, wild, grim, shy, unsociable.

fascicule [fasikyl] nm fascicle, installment, part, bunch.

fascinateur, -trice [fasinatœːr, tris] a fascinating, glamorous.

fascination [fasinasjɔ̃] nf charm.

fasciner [fasine] vt to fascinate, bewitch.

fascisme [fas(s)ism] nm fascism.

fasciste [fas(s)ist] an fascist.

faste [fast] nm pomp, show, ostentation.

fastidieux, -euse [fastidjø, øːz] a boring, tedious, dull.

fastueux, -euse [fastɥø, øːz] a showy, ostentatious.

fat [fat] a foppish; nm fop.

fatal [fatal] a fatal, fateful, inevitable; **femme —e** vamp.

fatalisme [fatalism] nm fatalism.

fatalité [fatalite] nf fatality, fate, calamity.

fatidique [fatidik] a fateful, prophetical.

fatigant [fatigɑ̃] a tiring, tiresome, irksome.

fatigue [fatig] nf fatigue, weariness, wear and tear.

fatiguer [fatige] vt to tire, fag, strain; vr to get tired, tire oneself; **— un poisson** to play a fish.

fatras [fatra] nm jumble, rubbish.

fatuité [fatɥite] nf fatuity, self-conceit, foppishness.

faubourg [fobuːr] nm suburb, outskirts.

faubourien, -ienne [foburjɛ̃, jɛn] a suburban.

fauché [foʃe] a stony-broke.

faucher [foʃe] vt to mow, reap, cut.

faucheur, -euse [foʃœːr, øːz] n reaper, mower.

faucheuse [foʃøːz] nf reaper, mowing-machine.

faucille [fosiːj] nf sickle.

faucon [fokɔ̃] nm falcon, hawk.

fauconnerie [fokɔnri] nf falconry, hawking, hawk-house.

faufiler [fofile] vt to baste, tack (on), insert, slip in; vr to pick one's way, slip (in, out), sneak (in, out).

faune [toːn] nm faun; nf fauna.

faussaire [fosɛːr] n forger.

fausser [fose] vt to buckle, warp, falsify, pervert.

fausset [fose] nf falsetto, spigot.

fausseté [foste] nf falsity, duplicity, falsehood.

faute [foːt] nf mistake, fault, offense, lack, want, foul; **— de** for want of failing.

fauteuil [fotœːj] nm easy-chair, armchair.

fauteur, -trice [fotœːr, tris] n abettor, instigator.

fautif, -ive [fotif, iːv] a faulty, wrong, at fault.

fauve [foːv] a fawn-colored, tawny; nm fawn (color), deer, wild beast.

fauvette [fovɛt] nf warbler.

faux, fausse [fo, foːs] a false, wrong, inaccurate, insincere, treacherous, sham, bogus; ad false(ly); nm false, fake, forgery, fabrication; nf scythe.

faux-filet [fofile] nm sirloin.

faux-fuyant [fofɥijɑ̃] nm subterfuge, dodge.

faux-monnayeur [fomɔnɛjœːr] nm coiner, forger.

faveur [favœːr] nf favor, boon, kindness, grace; **billet de —** complimentary ticket.

favorable [favɔrabl] a favorable, auspicious.

favori, -ite [favɔri, it] a favorite; nm pl whiskers.

favoriser [favɔrize] vt to favor, encourage, promote.

fébrile [febril] a febrile, feverish.

fécond [fekɔ̃] a fertile, fruitful, prolific, rich.

féconder [fekɔ̃de] vt to fecundate.

fécondité [fekɔ̃dite] nf fertility, fruitfulness.

fécule [fekyl] nf starch.

fédération [federasjɔ̃] nf federation.

fédérer [federe] vtr to federate.

fée [fe] nf fairy.

féerie [feri] nf fairyland, enchantment.

féerique [ferik] a fairylike.

feindre [fɛ̃ːdr] vt to pretend, simulate, sham, feign.

feinte [fɛ̃t] nf feint, pretense, sham.

fêlé [fele] a cracked, mad.

fêler [fele] vtr to crack.

félicitations [felisitasjɔ̃] nf pl congratulations.

félicité [felisite] nf bliss, happiness, felicity.

féliciter [felisite] vt to congratulate, compliment; vr to be pleased (about, with de).

félin [felɛ̃] a feline, catlike.

fêlure [felyːr] nf crack, split, rift, flaw.

femelle [fəmɛl] a nf female, she-, hen-, cow-.

féminin [feminɛ̃] a feminine, female; nm feminine gender.

femme [fam] nf woman, female, wife; **— de ménage** cleaning lady.

fémur [femy:r] nm femur.
fenaison [fənɛzɔ̃] nf haymaking.
fendre [fɑ̃:dr] vtr to split, cleave, rend.
fenêtre [f(ə)nɛ:tr] nf window.
fenouil [fənu:j] nm fennel.
fente [fɑ̃:t] nf crack, split, cleft, chink, crevice, slot.
féodal [feɔdal] a feudal.
féodalité [feɔdalite] nf feudal system.
fer [fɛ:r] nm iron, sword, shoe; pl chains, irons, fetters; (fig) de — hard, inflexible; — rouge brand; — à repasser flat-iron; — à friser curling tongs.
fer-blanc [fɛrblɑ̃] nm tin.
ferblanterie [fɛrblɑ̃tri] nf tinplate, tinsmith's shop.
ferblantier [fɛrblɑ̃tje] nm tinsmith.
férié [ferje] a jour — holiday.
férir [feri:r] vt to strike.
fermage [fɛrma:ʒ] nm rent.
ferme [fɛrm] a firm, solid, steady; ad firmly, hard; nf farm, lease.
fermé [fɛrme] a closed, exclusive, expressionless, hidebound, blind; être — à qch to have no appreciation of sth.
fermentation [fɛrmɑ̃tasjɔ̃] nf fermentation, unrest.
fermenter [fɛrmɑ̃te] vi to ferment, be in a ferment.
fermer [fɛrme] vt to close, shut, fasten, turn off, switch off; vir to shut, to close.
fermeté [fɛrməte] nf firmness, steadiness, resolution.
fermeture [fɛrməty:r] nf shutting, close, closing(-down); — éclair zipper.
fermier, -ière [fɛrmje, jɛ:r] n farmer, farmer's wife, tenant, lessee.
fermoir [fɛrmwa:r] nm clasp, fastener, hasp.
féroce [ferɔs] a wild, savage, fierce, ferocious.
férocité [ferɔsite] nf ferocity, fierceness, savagery.
ferraille [fɛrɑ:j] nf scrap-iron.
ferrant [fɛrɑ̃] a maréchal — blacksmith.
ferré [fɛre] a iron-shod, hob-nailed, good (at en); voie —e railway line.
ferrer [fɛre] vt to bind with iron, shoe, (fish) strike.
ferronnerie [fɛrɔnri] nf iron-foundry, ironmongery.
ferronnier [fɛrɔnje] nm ironworker, ironmonger.
ferroviaire [fɛrɔvjɛ:r] a railway; réseau — railway system.
ferrure [fɛry:r] nf piece of iron work, iron fitting, shoeing.
fertile [fɛrtil] a fruitful, rich.
fertiliser [fɛrtilize] vt to fertilize, make fruitful.
fertilité [fɛrtilite] nf fertility, fruitfulness.
féru [fery] a enamored, struck (with de).

férule [feryl] nf ferrule, rod.
fervent [fɛrvɑ̃] a fervent, ardent; n enthusiast, fan.
ferveur [fɛrvœ:r] nf fervor, ardor, enthusiasm.
fesse [fɛs] nf buttock.
fessée [fɛse] nf spanking, flogging, thrashing, whipping.
fesser [fɛse] vt to spank, whip.
festin [fɛstɛ̃] nm banquet, feast.
feston [fɛstɔ̃] nm festoon, scallop.
festonner [fɛstɔne] vt to festoon, scallop.
festoyer [fɛstwaje] vti to feast.
fêtard [fɛta:r] n reveler.
fête [fɛ:t] nf feast, festival, holiday, festivity, treat, entertainment; faire la — to celebrate, go on a spree.
Fête-Dieu [fɛtdjø] nf Corpus Christi.
fêter [fɛte] vt to observe as a holiday, celebrate, entertain.
fétiche [fetiʃ] nm fetish, mascot.
fétide [fetid] a fetid, stinking.
fétu [fety] nm straw, wisp, jot.
feu [fø] nm fire, heat, light, beacon, ardor, spirit; a late, deceased, dead; — roulant drum-fire; donner du — à qn to give a light to s.o.; faire long — to peter out; n'y voir que du — to be taken in; — d'artifice fireworks.
feuillage [fœja:ʒ] nm foliage.
feuille [fœ:j] nf leaf, sheet; — de présence time-sheet.
feuillée [fœje] nf foliage.
feuillet [fœjɛ] nm (book) leaf, sheet, plate.
feuilleter [fœjte] vt to divide into sheets, turn over, thumb.
feuilleton [fœjtɔ̃] nm feuilleton, article, serial story.
feuillu [fœjy] a leafy.
feutre [fø:tr] nm felt, felt hat, padding.
feutrer [føtre] vt to felt, cover with felt.
fève [fɛ:v] nf bean, broad-bean.
février [fevrie] nm February.
fiacre [fjakr] nm cab, hackney-carriage.
fiançailles [fjɑ̃sɑ:j] nf pl engagement, betrothal.
fiancé [fjɑ̃se] n fiancé(e), betrothed.
fiancer [fjɑ̃se] vt to betroth; vr to become engaged.
fiasco [fjasko] nm fiasco; faire — to fizzle out, flop.
fibre [fibr] nf fiber, grain.
fibreux, -euse [fibrø, ø:z] a fibrous, stringy.
ficeler [fisle] vt to tie up.
ficelle [fisɛl] nf string.
fiche [fiʃ] nf pin, slip of paper, form, index-card, chit.
ficher [fiʃe] vt to fix, drive in, do, give; — le camp to clear out; vr se — de qn to pull s.o.'s leg; je m'en fiche I don't give a damn.
fichier [fiʃje] nm card-index, card-index cabinet.

fichu [fiʃy] nm neckerchief, shawl, fichu.

fictif, -ive [fiktif, i:v] a fictitious, imaginary.

fiction [fiksjɔ̃] nf fiction, invention.

fidèle [fidɛl] a faithful, true, loyal.

fidélité [fidelite] nf fidelity, loyalty, allegiance.

fiduciaire [fidysjɛ:r] a fiduciary; nm trustee.

fieffé [fjɛfe] a given in fief, double-dyed, arrant, arch.

fiel [fjɛl] nm gall, malice.

fier, fière [fjɛ:r] a proud, haughty, fine, arrant.

se fier [səfje] vr to trust, rely, confide in (à).

fierté [fjɛrte] nf pride, haughtiness.

fièvre [fjɛ:vr] nf fever, heat; avoir un peu de — to have a slight temperature; — paludéenne ague, malaria.

fiévreux, -euse [fjevrø, ø:z] a feverish, fevered, hectic.

fifre [fifr] nm fife.

figer [fiʒe] vt to congeal, coagulate, clot, fix; vr to curdle, congeal, set; il resta figé he stood rooted to the spot.

fignoler [fiɲɔle] vt to fiddle, dawdle over; vi to fiddle about.

figue [fig] nf fig.

figuier [figje] nm fig-tree.

figurant [figyrɑ̃] n walker-on, extra.

figuratif, -ive [figyratif, i:v] a figurative.

figure [figy:r] nf figure, shape, face; faire — to cut a figure, figure (as de).

figuré [figyre] a figured, figurative; ad au — figuratively.

figurer [figyre] vt to represent; vi to look, appear, put on a show; vr to fancy, imagine, picture.

fil [fil] nm thread, yarn, wire, grain, edge, current, clue; — de la vierge gossamer; de — en aiguille bit by bit, gradually; au — de l'eau with the stream.

filage [fila:ʒ] nm spinning.

filament [filamɑ̃] nm filament, fiber.

filandreux, -euse [filɑ̃drø, ø:z] a stringy, long-winded.

filant [filɑ̃] a gluey, ropy; étoile —e shooting-star.

filasse [filas] nf tow, oakum.

filateur [filatœ:r] nm mill-owner, spinner, shadower.

filature [filaty:r] nf spinning-mill, spinning, shadowing.

file [fil] nf file, rank; chef de — leader; à la — in single file.

filer [file] vt to spin, prolong, pay out, shadow; vi to flow gently, fly, tear along, buzz off; — à l'anglaise to take French leave; — vingt nœuds do twenty knots.

filet [filɛ] nm thread, fillet, net, thin stream, streak.

fileur, -euse [filœ:r, ø:z] n spinner.

filial [filjal] a filial.

filiale [filjal] nf branch, branch-store, -company.

filière [filjɛ:r] nf draw-plate, die; — à vis screw-plate; passer par la — to work one's way up; — administrative official channels.

filigrane [filigran] nm filigree, water-mark.

fille [fi:j] nf daughter; jeune — girl; petite — little girl; vieille — spinster, old maid; — d'honneur bridesmaid; — de salle waitress; — (publique) prostitute.

fillette [fijɛt] nf little girl.

filleul [fijœl] n godchild.

film [film] nm film, picture; tourner un — to make a film; — sonore talkie.

filmer [filme] vt to film.

filon [filɔ̃] nm vein, seam.

filou [filu] nm pickpocket, thief, rogue.

filouterie [filutri] nf cheating, swindle.

fils [fis] nm son, boy.

filtration [filtrasjɔ̃] nf filtration, percolation.

filtre [filtr] nm filter, strainer.

filtrer [filtre] vt to strain, filter; vi to percolate, filter, seep; — un poste to skip a station.

fin [fɛ̃] a fine, delicate, keen, subtle, choice; nf end, conclusion, close, aim, purpose, object; mener à bonne — to bring to a successful conclusion; en — de compte finally.

final, -als [final] a final, last; nm finale.

finale [final] nf end syllable, final (round).

finalité [finalite] nf finality.

finance [finɑ̃:s] nf finance; ministre des —s Secretary of the Treasury; ministère des —s Treasury Department.

financer [finɑ̃se] vt to finance.

financier, -ière [finɑ̃sje, jɛ:r] a financial; nm financier.

finasser [finase] vi to dodge, fox, finesse.

finaud [fino] a wily, cunning, foxy; n wily bird.

finesse [finɛs] nf fineness, delicacy, astuteness, discrimination, artful dodge.

fini [fini] a finished, ended, over, accomplished, done for, gone, finite; nm finish, perfection.

finir [fini:r] vt to finish, conclude, end; cela n'en finit pas there is no end to it; en — avec to have done with.

finlandais [fɛ̃lɑ̃dɛ] a Finnish; n Finn.

Finlande [fɛ̃lɑ̃:d] nf Finland.

fiole [fjɔl] nf phial, flask.

fioritures [fjɔrity:r] nf pl flourish(es), ornamentation.

firmament [firmamã] nm firmament, heavens.

firme [firm] nf firm.

fisc [fisk] nm treasury, exchequer, internal revenue.

fiscal [fiskal] a fiscal.

fission [fisjɔ̃] nf — nucléaire nuclear fission.

fissure [fis(s)y:r] nf fissure, cleft.

fissurer [fis(s)yre] vtr to crack, split.

fixage [fiksa:ʒ] nm fixing, fastening.

fixatif [fiksatif] nm fixative, hair cream.

fixe [fiks] a fixed, firm, steady, settled.

fixé [fikse] a fixed, stated, fast; **être — sur** to be clear about.

fixe-chaussettes [fiks(ə)ʃoset] nm garter.

fixement [fiksəmã] ad fixedly, steadily, hard.

fixer [fikse] vt to fix, fasten, hold, determine, gaze at, stare at; vr to settle down.

flacon [flakɔ̃] nm bottle, flask, flagon.

flageller [flaʒelle] vt to scourge, flog.

flageoler [flaʒɔle] vi to tremble, shake.

flageolet [flaʒɔle] nm flageolet, kidney-bean.

flagorner [flagɔrne] vt to flatter, toady to.

flagorneur, -euse [flagɔrnœ:r, ø:z] n flatterer, toady.

flagrant [flagrã] a flagrant, glaring; **pris en — délit** caught redhanded.

flair [flɛ:r] nm scent, flair.

flairer [flɛre] vt to scent, smell (out), sniff.

flamant [flamã] nm flamingo.

flambant [flãbã] a blazing, roaring, flaming; **— neuf** brand new.

flambeau [flãbo] nm torch, candlestick.

flambée [flãbe] nf blazing fire, blaze.

flamber [flãbe] vt to singe; vi to blaze, flame, kindle.

flamboyant [flãbwajã] a flaming, blazing, flashing, brilliant.

flamboyer [flãbwaje] vi to blaze, flash, glow.

flamme [fla:m] nf flame, passion, fire, pennant.

flammèche [flamɛʃ] nf spark.

flan [flã] nm flan, custard, **(tec)** mold.

flanc [flã] nm flank, side; **tirer au — to** goof off, shirk, goldbrick.

flancher [flãʃe] vi to flinch, falter.

flanelle [flanɛl] nf flannel.

flâner [flane] vi to stroll, dawdle, lounge about, idle.

flânerie [flanri] nf stroll, idling, dawdling.

flâneur, -euse [flanœ:r, ø:z] n stroller, idler, dawdler.

flanquer [flãke] vt to flank, support, throw, chuck.

flaque [flak] nf puddle, pool.

flasque [flask] a flabby, backboneless, spineless, limp.

flatter [flate] vt to flatter, blandish, stroke, delight; vr to flatter oneself, pride oneself.

flatterie [flatri] nf flattery.

flatteur, -euse [flatœ:r, ø:z] a flattering, pleasing, fond; n flatterer.

flatueux, -euse [flatyø, ø:z] a flatulent, windy.

flatulence [flatylã:s] nf flatulence.

fléau [fleo] nm flail, scourge, plague, beam.

flèche [flɛʃ] nf arrow, dart, spire, pole, indicator; **faire — de tout bois** to make use of every means.

fléchir [fleʃi:r] vt to bend, bow, move to pity; vi to give way, sag, falter.

flegmatique [flɛgmatik] a phlegmatic, stolid.

flegme [flɛgm] nm phlegm, stolidness.

flemmard [flɛma:r] a lazy; n slacker, loafer, sluggard.

flemme [flɛm] nf laziness.

flétrir [fletri:r] vt to fade, wither, brand, sully; vr to wither, fade.

flétrissure [fletrisy:r] nf fading, withering; stigma.

fleur [flœ:r] nf flower, bloom, blossom, heyday; **fine — flower, pick; à — de** on the surface of.

fleurer [flœre] vi to smell of, be redolent of.

fleuret [flœrɛ] nm foil.

fleuri [flœri] a in bloom, flower, flowery, florid.

fleurir [flœri:r] vt to adorn with flowers; vi to flower, bloom, flourish.

fleuriste [flœrist] n florist.

fleuve [flœ:v] nm river.

flexible [flɛksibl] a flexible, pliant, pliable; nm flex.

flexion [flɛksjɔ̃] nf bending, buckling.

flibustier [flibystje] nm buccaneer, pirate.

flic [flik] nm **(sl)** cop.

flirt [flœrt] nm flirtation, flirting, flirt, boy-, girlfriend.

flirter [flœrte] vi to flirt.

flocon [flɔkɔ̃] nm flake, tuft.

floconneux, -euse [flɔkɔnø, ø:z] a fleecy, fluffy.

floraison [flɔrɛzɔ̃] nf blossoming, flowering (time).

floral [flɔral] a floral.

flore [flɔ:r] nf flora.

florissant [flɔrisã] a flourishing, prosperous.

flot [flo] nm wave, billow, surge, flood; pl sea; **à — afloat; à —s in** streams, in torrents.

flottaison [flɔtɛzɔ̃] nf water-line.

flottant [flɔtã] a floating, full, wide, irresolute.

flotte [flɔt] nf fleet, float, **(fam)** water.

flottement [flɔtmã] nm floating, swaying, fluctuation, hesitation.

flotter [flɔte] vi to float, wave, waft, waver, fluctuate.

flotteur [flɔtœ:r] nm raftsman, float.

flotille [flɔti:j] nf flotilla.

flou [flu] a blurred, hazy, fluffy.

fluorescent [flyɔrɛs(s)ɑ̃] a fluorescent.

fluctuer [flyktɥe] vi to fluctuate.

fluet, -ette [flyɛ, ɛt] a slender, thin, delicate, spindly.

fluide [flɥid] a nm fluid, liquid.

fluidité [flɥidite] nf fluidity.

flûte [fly:t] nf flute, flutist, long loaf, tall champagne glass.

flûté [flyte] a flute-like, reed-like.

flûtiste [flytist] nm flautist.

flux [fly] nm flow, flood, rush.

fluxion [flyksjɔ̃] nf inflammation, swelling; — de poitrine pneumonia.

foc [fɔk] nm jib, stay-sail.

foi [fwa] nf faith, trust, belief, confidence, credit.

foie [fwa] nm liver; crise de — bilious attack.

foin [fwɛ̃] nm hay.

foire [fwa:r] nf fair, market.

foireux [fwarø] a cowardly.

fois [fwa] nf time, occasion; à la — at a time, at the same time, both.

foison [fwazɔ̃] nf plenty, abundance.

foisonner [fwazɔne] vi to abound, multiply.

folâtre [fɔlɑ:tr] a playful, frisky, sportive.

folâtrer [fɔlɑtre] vi to romp, gambol, frisk.

folichon, -onne [fɔliʃɔ̃, ɔn] a playful, frisky.

folie [fɔli] nf folly, piece of folly, madness, craze.

follet, -ette [fɔlɛ, ɛt] a merry, gay; feu — will o' the wisp.

fomenter [fɔmɑ̃te] vt to foment, stir up.

foncé [fɔ̃se] a (color) dark, deep.

foncer [fɔ̃se] vt to sink (shaft), drive in, bottom, darken; vi to rush, charge.

foncier, -ière [fɔ̃sje, jɛ:r] a land(ed), fundamental, ground.

fonction [fɔ̃ksjɔ̃] nf function, office; faire — de to act as.

fonctionnaire [fɔ̃ksjɔnɛ:r] nm civil servant.

fonctionnement [fɔ̃ksjɔnmɑ̃] nm functioning, working, behavior.

fonctionner [fɔ̃ksjɔne] vi to function, work, act, run.

fond [fɔ̃] nm bottom, back, far end, depth, foundation, background, substance; à — thoroughly, up to the hilt; au — at heart, at bottom; article de — editorial; course de — long-distance run.

fondamental [fɔ̃damɑ̃tal] a basic, fundamental.

fondateur, -trice [fɔ̃datœ:r, tris] n founder, promoter.

fondation [fɔ̃dasjɔ̃] nf foundation, founding.

fondement [fɔ̃dmɑ̃] nm foundation, base, grounds, reliance.

fondé [fɔ̃de] a founded, entitled, justified; nm — de pouvoir proxy, attorney.

fonder [fɔ̃de] vt to institute, found, lay the foundations of, base, set up; vr to place reliance (on sur), base one's reasons (on sur), be based.

fonderie [fɔ̃dri] nf foundry, smelting works, smelting.

fondeur [fɔ̃dœ:r] nm smelter, founder.

fondre [fɔ̃:dr] vt to smelt, cast, melt, fuse, dissolve; vi melt, dissolve, pounce, fall upon; vr to blend, melt.

fondrière [fɔ̃drjɛ:r] nf bog, quagmire.

fonds [fɔ̃] nm land, stock, fund, means; acheter un — to buy a business; — publics government stocks; — consolidés consols; rentrer dans ses — to get one's money back.

fondu [fɔ̃dy] nm fading in and out (of film), melted (butter), molten (metal), cast (bronze), well-blended (colors); —e nf fondue.

fontaine [fɔ̃tɛn] nf fountain, spring.

fonte [fɔ̃:t] nf smelting, casting, cast iron, melting; — brute pig-iron.

fonts [fɔ̃] nm pl font.

football [futbol] nm football.

footing [futiŋ] nm walking, hiking.

for [fɔ:r] nm dans son — intérieur in his inmost heart.

forage [fɔra:ʒ] nm sinking, boring, (min) drilling.

forain [fɔrɛ̃] a itinerant, traveling, n peddler, stall-keeper, traveling showman.

forçat [fɔrsa] nm convict.

force [fɔrs] nf power, might, strength, prime, compulsion; pl strength, spring, shears; ad many, a lot of; à — de by (means of); — leur fut d'accepter they could do nothing but agree.

forcé [fɔrse] a forced, strained; travaux —s penal servitude.

forcément [fɔrsemɑ̃] ad necessarily, perforce.

forcené [fɔrsəne] a frenzied, frantic, desperate.

forcer [fɔrse] vt to force, compel, break open, strain.

forcir [fɔrsi:r] vi to fill out.

forer [fɔre] vt to sink bore, (min) drill.

forestier, -ière [fɔrɛstje, jɛ:r] a forest, forestry; n forester, ranger.

foret [fɔrɛ] nm drill, broach, bracebit, gimlet.

forêt [fɔrɛ] nf forest.

foreuse [fɔrø:z] nf drill.

forfait [fɔrfɛ] nm serious crime; contract; forfeit; déclarer — to scratch, call off.

forfaiture [fɔrfɛty:r] nf maladministration, breach.

forfanterie [fɔrfɑ̃tri] nf bragging, boasting.

forge [fɔrʒ] nf forge, smithy, iron-works.

forger [fɔrʒe] vt to forge, counterfeit, invent, coin.

forgeron [fɔrʒərɔ̃] nm blacksmith.

forgeur, -euse [fɔrʒœːr, øːz] n forger, inventor, fabricator (of news), coiner (of words).

formaliser [fɔrmalize] vt to give offense to; vr to take offense (at de).

formalisme [fɔrmalism] nm conventionality.

formaliste [fɔrmalist] a formal, stiff, ceremonious, conventional.

formalité [fɔrmalite] nf formality, (matter of) form, ceremony, ceremoniousness.

format [fɔrma] nm format, size.

formation [fɔrmasjɔ̃] nf formation, molding, forming, training.

forme [fɔrm] nf form, shape, figure, mold, last, shoetree; **pour la —** as a matter of form; **être en —** to be in form, be fit.

formel, -elle [fɔrmɛl, ɛl] a strict, formal, definite.

former [fɔrme] vt to shape, form, create, mold, train; vr to take shape, set; **le train se forme à Dijon** the train starts from Dijon.

formidable [fɔrmidabl] a fearsome, terrific, stupendous.

formule [fɔrmyl] nf formula, form.

formuler [fɔrmyle] vt to formulate, draft, put into words, state.

forniquer [fɔrnike] vi to fornicate.

fort [fɔːr] a strong, large, stout, solid, loud, violent; ad very, hard, loud, fast; nm strong part, strong man, fort; **c'est plus — que moi I can't help it; le plus — c'est que the best (worst) of it is . . .; se faire — de** to undertake to; **vous y allez un peu —** you are going a bit too far; **au — de l'hiver** in the dead of winter.

forteresse [fɔrtərɛs] nf fortress, stronghold.

fortifiant [fɔrtifjɑ̃] a fortifying, invigorating, bracing; nm tonic.

fortification [fɔrtifikasjɔ̃] nf fortification, fortifying.

fortifier [fɔrtifje] vt to fortify, strengthen, invigorate; vr to grow stronger.

fortuit [fɔrtɥi] a chance, fortuitous, casual, accidental.

fortuité [fɔrtɥite] nf fortuitousness, casual nature.

fortune [fɔrtyn] nf fortune, (piece of) luck; **de — makeshift; dîner à la — du pot** to take pot luck; **homme à bonnes —s** lady's man, ladykiller.

fortuné [fɔrtyne] a fortunate, well-off, wealthy.

fosse [foːs] nf hole, pit, grave; **— d'aisances** cesspool.

fossé [fose] nm ditch, drain, moat.

fossette [fosɛt, fosɛt] nf dimple.

fossile [fosil] nm fossil.

fossoyer [foswaje, foswaje] vt to trench, ditch.

fossoyeur [foswajœːr, foswajœːr] nm grave-digger.

fou, fol, folle [fu, fɔl, fɔl] a mad, insane, foolish, silly, frantic, frenzied; n lunatic, madman, madwoman, fool, (chess) bishop; **être — de** to be beside oneself with; **succès — terrific success, hit; monde —** enormous crowd.

foudre [fudr] nf thunderbolt, lightning; **coup de — thunderbolt, bolt** from the blue, love at first sight.

foudroyant [fudrwajɑ̃] a crushing, overwhelming, smashing, lightning.

foudroyé [fudrwaje] a blasted, dumbfounded.

foudroyer [fudrwaje] vt to blast, strike down.

fouet [fwɛ] nm whip, lash, whisk; **coup de — cut, fillip.**

fouetter [fwete] vt to whip, flog, whisk, lash; vi to batter (against), flap.

fougère [fuʒɛːr] nf fern, bracken.

fougue [fug] nf dash, fire.

fougueux, -euse [fugø, øːz] a spirited, dashing, mettlesome, fiery.

fouille [fuːj] nf excavation, searching.

fouiller [fuje] vt to excavate, dig, search, ransack, rifle; vi to rummage.

fouillis [fuji] nm confusion, jumble, muddle.

fouine [fwin] nf stone-marten.

fouiner [fwine] vi to ferret, nose about, interfere.

fouir [fwiːr] vt to dig, burrow.

foulard [fulaːr] nm silk handkerchief, foulard, neckerchief, scarf.

foule [ful] nf crowd, throng, mob.

foulée [fule] nf tread, stride; pl spoor, track.

fouler [fule] vt to crush, tread on, (ankle) sprain.

foulure [fulyːr] nf sprain, wrench.

four [fuːr] nm oven, kiln; failure; **faire — to be a flop.**

fourbe [furb] a crafty; n rascal, knave, double-dealer.

fourberie [furbəri] nf double-dealing, deceit, cheating, treachery.

fourbir [furbir] vt to polish, rub up.

fourbu [furby] a foundered, dead-beat, done.

fourche [furʃ] nf fork, pitchfork; **faire — (of roads)** to fork.

fourcher [furʃe] vt to fork; vi to branch off, fork; **la langue lui a fourché** he made a slip of the tongue.

fourchette [furʃɛt] nf (table) fork, wishbone; **c'est une bonne — he is** fond of his food.

fourchu [furʃy] a forked, cloven.

fourgon [furgɔ̃] nm baggage car, truck, wagon, poker, rake.

fourgonner [furgɔne] *vti* to poke, rake.

fourmi [furmi] *nm* ant; **avoir des —s dans le bras** to have pins and needles in one's arm.

fourmilier [furmilje] *nm* anteater.

fourmilière [furmilje:r] *nf* anthill, ants' nest.

fourmillement [furmijmɑ̃] *nm* tingling, prickly feeling, swarming.

fourmiller [furmije] *vi* to swarm, teem, tingle.

fournaise [furnɛ:z] *nf* furnace.

fourneau [furno] *nm* furnace, stove, (pipe) bowl; **haut —** blast furnace.

fournée [furne] *nf* batch (of loaves).

fourni [furni] *a* stocked, plentiful, thick.

fournil [furni] *nm* bakery.

fourniment [furnimɑ̃] *nm* equipment, accoutrement.

fournir [furni:r] *vt* to supply, provide, furnish; *vr* to provide oneself (with de).

fournisseur, -euse [furnisœ:r, ø:z] *n* purveyor, supplier, caterer, tradesman.

fourniture [furnity:r] *nf* supplying, providing; *pl* supplies, requisites.

fourrage [fura:ʒ] *nm* fodder, forage.

fourrager [furaʒe] *vt* to pillage; *vi* to forage, rummage.

fourragère [furaʒɛ:r] *nf* lanyard; forage wagon.

fourré [fure] *a* fur-lined; *n* thicket.

fourreau [furo] *nm* scabbard, case, sheath, sleeve.

fourrer [fure] *vt* to line with fur, cram, stuff, poke, stick; *vr* to thrust oneself, butt (into dans).

fourre-tout [furtu] *nm* hold-all.

fourreur [furœ:r] *nm* furrier.

fourrier [furje] *nm* quarter-master.

fourrure [fury:r] *nf* fur, lining.

fourvoyer [furvwaje] *vt* to mislead, lead astray; *vr* to lose one's way, go wrong.

foyer [fwaje] *nm* hearth, firebox, seat, home, center.

frac [frak] *nm* dress-coat.

fracas [fraka] *nm* din, uproar, crash, clash.

fracasser [frakase] *vtr* to shatter, smash.

fraction [fraksjɔ̃] *nf* fraction.

fracture [frakty:r] *nf* fracture, break, breaking open.

fracturer [fraktyre] *vt* to fracture, force; *vr* to break, fracture.

fragile [fraʒil] *a* fragile, flimsy, frail, breakable, brittle.

fragilité [fraʒilite] *nf* fragility, frailty, weakness.

fragment [fragmɑ̃] *nm* fragment, chip, snatch.

fragmentaire [fragmɑ̃tɛ:r] *a* fragmentary.

fragmenter [fragmɑ̃te] *vt* to divide into fragments.

frai [frɛ] *nm* spawn(ing).

fraîcheur [frɛʃœ:r] *nf* cool(ness), chilliness, freshness.

fraîchir [frɛʃi:r] *vi* to grow cooler, freshen.

frais, fraîche [frɛ, frɛʃ] *a* cool, fresh, recent, new, new-laid; *nm* coolness, cool air; **prendre le —** to take the air.

frais [frɛ] *nm* *pl* expenses, charge, outlay, cost; **faux —** incidental expenses; **— divers** sundries.

fraise [frɛ:z] *nf* strawberry; ruff; milling cutter.

fraiser [frɛze] *vt* to plait, frill, mill.

framboise [frɑ̃bwa:z] *nf* raspberry.

franc, franche [frɑ̃, frɑ̃:ʃ] *a* free, frank, downright, open, honest, candid, above-board; *ad* frankly, candidly; *nm* (coin) franc; **jouer — jeu** to play fair, play the game; **corps —** volunteer corps.

français [frɑ̃sɛ] *a* French; *n* Frenchman, Frenchwoman.

France [frɑ̃:s] *nf* France.

franchement [frɑ̃ʃmɑ̃] *ad* frankly, candidly, really, downright.

franchir [frɑ̃ʃi:r] *vt* to jump (over), clear, cross.

franchise [frɑ̃ʃi:z] *nf* freedom, immunity, frankness, straightforwardness.

franciser [frɑ̃size] *vt* to Gallicize, Frenchify.

franc-maçon [frɑ̃masɔ̃] *nm* freemason.

franc-maçonnerie [frɑ̃masɔ̃nri] *nf* freemasonry.

franco [frɑ̃ko] *ad* free, carriage-free, duty paid.

franc-parler [frɑ̃parle] *nm* frankness, plain-speaking.

franc-tireur [frɑ̃tirœ:r] *nm* sniper, sharpshooter, freelance (journalist).

frange [frɑ̃:ʒ] *nf* fringe.

franquette [frɑ̃kɛt] *nf* **à la bonne —** simply, without fuss.

frappant [frapɑ̃] *a* striking, impressive.

frappe [frap] *nf* minting, striking, impression.

frapper [frape] *vt* to strike, smite, knock, insist, stamp, mint; **— le champagne** to ice champagne.

frasque [frask] *nf* escapade, prank, trick.

fraternel, -elle [fratɛrnɛl, ɛl] *a* fraternal, brotherly.

fraterniser [fratɛrnize] *vi* to fraternize.

fraternité [fratɛrnite] *nf* fraternity, brotherhood.

fratricide [fratrisid] *a* fratricidal; *nm* fratricide.

fraude [fro:d] *nf* fraud, fraudulence, deceit, deception; **passer en —** to smuggle in, out.

frauder [frode] *vt* to defraud, swindle; *vi* to cheat.

fraudeur, -euse [frodœ:r, ø:z] *n* smuggler, defrauder.

frauduleux, -euse [frodylø, øːz] *a* fraudulent.

frayer [freje] *vt* open up, clear; *vi* to spawn, associate (with **avec**).

frayeur [frejœːr] *nf* fear, fright, dread.

fredaine [frɛdɛn] *nf* escapade, prank.

fredonner [frɛdɔne] *vt* to hum.

frégate [fregat] *nf* frigate.

frein [frɛ̃] *nm* bit, brake, curb; **serrer (desserrer) le —** to put on (release) the brake; **ronger son —** to champ at the bit, fret; **sans —** unbridled.

freiner [frɛne] *vt* to brake, check; *vi* to brake.

frelater [frɛlate] *vt* to adulterate, water down.

frêle [frɛːl] *a* frail, delicate, weak, spare.

frelon [frɔlɔ̃] *nm* hornet, drone.

frémir [fremiːr] *vi* to quiver, rustle, tremble, flutter.

frémissement [fremismɑ̃] *nm* quivering, rustling, shaking, quaking.

frêne [frɛːn] *nm* ash-tree.

frénésie [frenezi] *nf* frenzy, madness.

frénétique [frenetik] *a* frantic, frenzied.

fréquence [frekɑ̃ːs] *nf* frequency, prevalence, rate.

fréquent [frekɑ̃] *a* frequent, quick.

fréquentation [frekɑ̃tasjɔ̃] *nf* frequenting.

fréquenter [frekɑ̃te] *vt* to frequent, haunt, associate with; *vi* to visit, go to.

frère [frɛːr] *nm* brother, friar.

fresque [frɛsk] *nf* fresco.

fret [frɛ] *nm* freight, chartering, load.

fréter [frete] *vt* to freight, charter.

frétillant [fretijɑ̃] *a* frisky, lively.

frétiller [fretije] *vi* to wag, wriggle, quiver.

fretin [frɔtɛ̃] *nm* (*of fish*) fry; **menu —** small fry.

frette [frɛt] *nf* hoop, band.

fretter [frete] *vt* to hoop.

friable [friabl] *a* crumbly, friable.

friand [friɑ̃] *a* fond of (good things); **morceau —** titbit.

friandise [friɑ̃diːz] *nf* fondness for good food, titbit; *pl* sweets.

fricassée [frikase] *nf* fricassee, hash.

friche [friʃ] *nf* waste land, fallow land.

fricoter [frikɔte] *vti* to stew, cook.

friction [friksjɔ̃] *nf* friction, rubbing, massage, rub-down, dry shampoo.

frictionner [friksjɔne] *vt* to rub, massage, rub down, give a dry shampoo to.

frigide [friʒid] *a* frigid.

frigo [frigo] *nm* (*sl*) frozen meat.

frigorifier [frigɔrifje] *vt* to chill, refrigerate.

frigorifique [frigɔrifik] *a* chilling, refrigerating; *nm* deepfreeze, frozen meat, refrigerator.

frileux, -euse [frilø, øːz] *a* sensitive to the cold, chilly.

frimas [frima] *nm* hoarfrost, rime.

frime [frim] *nf* pretense, sham, eyewash.

frimousse [frimus] *nf* face of child, girl, cat.

fringale [frɛ̃gal] *nf* **avoir la —** to be ravenous.

fringant [frɛ̃gɑ̃] *a* lively, frisky, spruce, smart.

friper [fripe] *vt* to crush, crumple; *vr* to get crushed.

fripier, -ière [fripje, jɛːr] *n* old-clothes dealer.

fripon, -onne [fripɔ̃, ɔn] *a* roguish; *n* rogue, rascal, hussy.

friponnerie [fripɔnri] *nf* roguery.

fripouille [fripuːj] *nf* rotter, bad egg, cad.

frire [friːr] *vti* to fry.

frise [friz] *nf* frieze.

frisé [frize] *a* curly, frizzy.

friser [frize] *vt* to curl, frizz, skim, graze, verge on; *vi* to curl, be curly.

frisoir [frizwaːr] *nm* curling-tongs, curler.

frisson [frisɔ̃] *nm* shudder, thrill, shiver, tremor.

frissonnement [frisɔnmɑ̃] *nm* shudder(ing), shiver(ing).

frissonner [frisɔne] *vt* to shudder, shiver, quiver.

frit [fri] *a* fried; (**pommes de terres**) **—es** chips, French fried (potatoes).

friture [frityːr] *nf* frying, fry; *pl* crackling noises, static.

frivole [frivɔl] *a* frivolous, empty, flimsy.

frivolité [frivɔlite] *nf* frivolity, emptiness, trifle.

froc [frɔk] *nm* monk's cowl, habit, gown.

froid [frwa] *a* cold, chilly, cool, frigid, unimpressed; *nm* cold, chill, coldness, coolness; **il fait —** it is cold; **il a —** he is cold; **— de loup** bitter cold; **prendre —** to catch cold; **battre — à** to cold-shoulder.

froideur [frwadœːr] *nf* coldness, chilliness, frigidity.

froissement [frwasmɑ̃] *nm* crumpling, bruising, rustle, causing offense.

froisser [frwase] *vt* to bruise, crumple, jostle, offend, ruffle; *vr* to take offense, become crumpled.

frôler [frole] *vt* to graze, brush (against).

fromage [frɔmaːʒ] *nm* cheese; **— de tête** headcheese.

fromager [frɔmaʒe] *nm* silk cotton tree.

froment [frɔmɑ̃] *nm* wheat.

fronce [frɔ̃ːs] *nf* gather, pucker.

froncement [frɔ̃smɑ̃] *nm* puckering, wrinkling.

froncer [frɔ̃se] *vt* to pucker, wrinkle, gather; **— les sourcils** to knit one's brows, frown, scowl.

frondaison [frɔ̃dɛz5] *nf* foliation, foliage.

fronde [frɔ̃:d] *nf* catapult, sling, Fronde.

fronder [frɔ̃de] *vt* to sling, criticize, jeer at.

frondeur, -euse [frɔ̃dœ:r, ø:z] *a* critical, always against authority; *n* slinger, critic, scoffer.

front [frɔ̃] *nm* brow, forehead, face, front, cheek, effrontery; **de —** abreast.

frontière [frɔ̃tjɛ:r] *nf* frontier, border, line, boundary.

frontispice [frɔ̃tispis] *nm* title page, frontispiece.

fronton [frɔ̃t5] *nm* pediment, fronton, ornamental front.

frottement [frɔtmɑ̃] *nm* rubbing, chafing, friction.

frotter [frɔte] *vt* to rub, polish, chafe, (*match*) strike; *vi* to rub; *vr* to rub, come up (against **à**), keep company (with **à**).

frottoir [frɔtwa:r] *nm* polisher, scrubbing brush.

frou-frou [frufru] *nm* rustle, swish.

frousse [frus] *nf* funk.

fructifier [fryktifje] *vi* to fructify, bear fruit.

fructueux, -euse [fryktɥø, ø:z] *a* fruitful, profitable.

frugal [frygal] *a* frugal, thrifty.

frugalité [frygalite] *nf* frugality.

fruit [frɥi] *nm* fruit; *pl* fruits, advantages, benefits; **— sec** (*person*) failure.

fruiterie [frɥitri] *nf* fruit trade, fruiterer's, greengrocer's shop.

fruitier, -ière [frɥitje, jɛ:r] *a* fruit; *n* fruiterer, greengrocer.

frusques [frysk] *nf pl* togs, clothes.

fruste [fryst] *a* worn, defaced, rough, coarse.

frustrer [frystre] *vt* to frustrate, deprive, do (out of **de**).

fugace [fygas] *a* fleeting, transient.

fugacité [fygasite] *nf* transience.

fugitif, -ive [fyʒitif, i:v] *a* fleeting, passing; *n* fugitive.

fugue [fyg] *nf* fugue, escapade, flying visit, jaunt.

fuir [fɥi:r] *vt* to run away from, shun, avoid; *vi* to flee, run away, recede, leak.

fuite [fɥit] *nf* flight, escape, leak(age).

fulgurant [fylgyrɑ̃] *a* flashing, striking.

fuligineux, -euse [fyliʒinø, ø:z] *a* soot-colored, sooty.

fulminer [fylmine] *vt* to fulminate; *vi* to inveigh.

fume-cigarette [fymsigarɛt] *nm* cigarette-holder.

fumée [fyme] *nf* smoke, steam; *pl* fumes.

fumer [fyme] *vt* to smoke, cure, manure; *vi* to smoke, fume, steam.

fumet [fymɛ] *nm* smell, bouquet, aroma, scent.

fumeur, -euse [fymœ:r, ø:z] *n* smoker, curer.

fumeux, -euse [fymø, ø:z] *a* smoky, smoking, heady, hazy.

fumier [fymje] *nm* dung, manure, dunghill, stable-litter.

fumigation [fymigasj5] *nf* fumigation.

fumiger [fymiʒe] *vt* to fumigate.

fumiste [fymist] *nm* stove-setter, practical joker, hoaxer, leg-puller.

fumisterie [fymistri] *nf* stove-setting, hoax, practical joke, leg-pulling.

fumoir [fymwa:r] *nm* smoking room.

funambule [fynɑ̃byl] *n* tight-rope walker.

funambulesque [fynɑ̃bylɛsk] *a* fantastic, queer.

funèbre [fynɛbr] *a* funeral, funereal, dismal.

funérailles [fyneraːj] *nf pl* funeral.

funéraire [fynerɛ:r] *a* funeral, funerary.

funeste [fynɛst] *a* fatal, deadly, disastrous, baleful.

funiculaire [fynikylɛ:r] *a* funicular; *nm* cable-railway.

fur [fy:r] *cj* **au — et à mesure que** (gradually) as, in proportion as; **ad au — et à mesure** gradually, as one goes along.

furet [fyrɛ] *nm* ferret, Nosy Parker.

fureter [fyrte] *vi* to ferret, pry, cast about.

fureur [fyrœ:r] *nf* fury, rage, madness, passion, craze; **faire —** to be all the rage.

furibond [fyribɔ̃] *a* furious.

furie [fyri] *nf* fury, rage, passion.

furieux, -euse [fyrjø, jø:z] *a* furious, wild, raging, in a rage.

furoncle [fyrɔ̃:kl] *nm* boil.

furtif, -ive [fyrtif, i:v] *a* stealthy, covert, furtive, secret, sneaking.

fusain [fyzɛ̃] *nm* spindletree, charcoal sketch.

fuseau [fyzo] *nm* spindle, bobbin.

fusée [fyze] *nf* spindle, fuse, rocket; **— à pétard** firework; **— éclairante** flare; **— porte-amarre** rocket apparatus.

fuselage [fyzlaːʒ] *nm* fuselage.

fuseler [fyzle] *vt* to taper.

fuser [fyze] *vi* to fuse, melt, run, spread.

fusible [fyzibl] *a* fusible, easily melted.

fusil [fyzi] *nm* gun, rifle, steel; **coup de —** gunshot, report; **attraper un coup de —** to get stung, overcharged.

fusilier [fyzilje] *nm* fusilier; **— marin** marine.

fusillade [fyzijad] *nf* firing, volley.

fusiller [fyzije] *vt* to shoot, execute.

fusion [fyzj5] *nf* fusion, melting, smelting, union, amalgamation.

fusionner [fyzjɔne] *vti* to merge, unite, amalgamate.

fustiger [fystiʒe] *vt* to flog, thrash.
fût [fy] *nm* stock, shaft, handle, barrel, cask, bole.
futaie [fytɛ] *nf* wood, forest, very large tree.
futaille [fytɑːj] *nf* cask, barrel, tun.
futé [fyte] *a* crafty, smart.
futile [fytil] *a* futile, frivolous, trivial.
futilité [fytilite] *nf* futility, triviality.
futur [fytyːr] *a* future, to come; *nm* future tense; *n* future husband, wife.
fuyant [fɥijɑ̃] *a* fleeing, fleeting, receding, elusive, shifty.
fuyard [fɥijaːr] *n* fugitive, runaway.

G

gabardine [gabardin] *nf* raincoat, gabardine.
gabarit [gabari] *nm* gauge, templet, model, mold, stamp.
gabegie [gabʒi] *nf* dishonesty, underhand dealings, muddle, mismanagement.
gabier [gabje] *nm* topman, seaman.
gâche [gɑːʃ] *nf* staple, wall-hook.
gâcher [gɑʃe] *vt* to mix, waste, spoil, bungle, make a mess of.
gâchette [gɑʃɛt] *nf* trigger.
gâchis [gɑʃi] *nm* wet mortar, mud, slush, mess.
gaffe [gaf] *nf* boat-hook, gaff, blunder, boner.
gaffer [gafe] *vt* to hook, gaff; *vi* blunder.
gaga [gaga] *a* doddering; *nm* dodderer.
gage [gɑːʒ] *nm* pledge, pawn, security, token, forfeit; *pl* wages, pay.
gager [gaʒe] *vt* to wager, bet, pay, hire.
gageure [gaʒyːr] *nf* wager, bet.
gagnant [gaɲɑ̃] *a* winning; *n* winner.
gagne-pain [gaɲpɛ̃] *nm* livelihood, bread-winner.
gagner [gaɲe] *vt* to earn, gain, win (over), get, reach, overtake, catch up (on); *vr* to be catching, be infectious.
gai [ge, gɛ] *a* gay, merry, blithe, cheerful, bright.
gaieté [gete, gɛte] *nf* gaiety, mirth, merriment, cheerfulness.
gaillard [gajaːr] *a* strong, stalwart, hearty, merry, spicy; *nm* fellow, fine, jolly fellow; — d'avant forecastle; — d'arrière quarter-deck; —e *nf* wench, strapping, bold young woman.
gaillardise [gajardiːz] *nf* jollity, gaiety; *pl* broad humor, suggestive stories.
gain [gɛ̃] *nm* gain, profit, earnings, winning(s); — de cause decision in one's favor.

gaine [gɛːn] *nf* case, cover, sheath, corset.
gala [gala] *nm* gala, fête.
galamment [galamɑ̃] *ad* gallantly, courteously, bravely.
galant [galɑ̃] *a* attentive to women, gay, amatory; **intrigue** —e love-affair; — **homme** gentleman; *nm* lover, ladies' man.
galanterie [galɑ̃tri] *nf* attention to women, love affair, compliment, gift.
galbe [galb] *nm* contour, outline, figure.
gale [gal] *nf* itch, scabies, mange, scab.
galère [galɛːr] *nf* galley.
galerie [galri] *nf* gallery, arcade, balcony, circle.
galet [galɛ] *nm* pebble, shingle, roller, pulley.
galette [galɛt] *nf* cake, ship's biscuit; (*fam*) money, dough.
galeux, -euse [galø, øːz] *a* itchy, mangy, scabby; **brebis** —se black sheep.
galimatias [galimatjɑ] *nm* nonsense, gibberish.
Galles [gal] *nm* pays de — Wales.
gallois [galwa] *a nm* Welsh; *n* Welshman.
galon [galɔ̃] *nm* braid, stripe, band.
galonner [galɔne] *vt* to trim with braid, lace.
galop [galo] *nm* gallop.
galoper [galɔpe] *vti* to gallop.
galopin [galɔpɛ̃] *nm* urchin, young scamp.
galvaniser [galvanize] *vt* to galvanize.
galvauder [galvode] *vt* to botch, besmirch; *vr* to sully one's name.
gambade [gɑ̃bad] *nf* gambol, caper.
gambader [gɑ̃bade] *vi* to gambol, caper, romp.
gamelle [gamɛl] *nf* tin-can, mess-tin.
gamin [gamɛ̃] *nm* urchin, youngster; —e *nf* (pert) little girl.
gamme [gam] *nf* gamut, scale, range.
gammée [game] *a* **croix** — swastika.
ganache [ganaʃ] *nf* lower jaw; duffer, old fogey.
gangrène [gɑ̃grɛn] *nf* gangrene, canker.
gangrener [gɑ̃grəne] *vt* to gangrene, canker; *vr* to mortify, become cankered.
gangreneux, -euse [gɑ̃grənø, øːz] *a* gangrenous, cankerous.
ganse [gɑ̃ːs] *nf* braid, gimp, piping, loop.
gant [gɑ̃] *nm* glove, gauntlet.
gantelé [gɑ̃tle] *a* gauntleted, mailed.
ganter [gɑ̃te] *vt* to glove, *vr* to put on one's gloves.
ganterie [gɑ̃tri] *nf* glove-making, -factory, -shop.
gantier [gɑ̃tje] *nm* glover.

garage [gara:ʒ] nm garage, shed, depot, storage, parking, shunting; **voie de —** siding.

garagiste [garaʒist] nm garage owner, proprietor.

garant [garɑ̃] nm guarantor, surety, bail, authority, warrant, guarantee.

garantie [garɑ̃ti] nf guarantee, pledge, security, safeguard, underwriting.

garantir [garɑ̃ti:r] vt to guarantee, warrant, vouch for, underwrite, shield, insure.

garçon [garsɔ̃] nm boy, lad, son, young man, chap, fellow, bachelor, servant, assistant, waiter; **— d'honneur** usher, best man; **— manqué** tomboy.

garçonnet [garsɔnɛ] nm little boy.

garçonnière [garsɔnjɛ:r] nf bachelor's, single man's flat.

garde [gard] nf guardianship, care, gnard, watch(ing), keeping, charge, flyleaf, the Guards; **prendre —** to take care, beware (à of), be careful (à of), to take good care (à to), be careful not (de to); **sans y prendre — inadvertently;** nm keeper, guard, watchman, guardsman.

garde-à-vous [gardavu] nm **au —** at attention.

garde-barrière [gardbarjɛ:r] n (grade crossing) gatekeeper.

garde-boue [gardəbu] nm mudguard, fender.

garde-champêtre [gardʃɑ̃pɛtr] nm village policeman.

garde-chasse [gardəʃas] nm gamekeeper.

garde-corps [gardəkɔr] nm parapet, balustrade, rail.

garde-feu [gardəfø] nm fireguard, fender.

garde-fou [gardəfu] nm parapet, rail(ing).

garde-malade [gardmalad] n nurse.

garde-manger [gardmɑ̃ʒe] nm larder, pantry.

garder [garde] vt to guard, protect, lock after, preserve, keep, remain in, observe, respect; vr to protect oneself, beware (de of), take care not (de to), refrain (de from).

garde-robe [gardərɔb] nf wardrobe, clothes.

gardeur, -euse [gardœ:r, ø:z] n keeper, herdsman.

gardien, -ienne [gardjɛ̃, jɛn] n guardian, caretaker, warder, attendant, goalkeeper; **— de la paix** policeman.

gare [ga:r] excl look out! take care! mind!; nf station; **—** maritime harbor station.

garer [gare] vt to shunt, garage, park; vr to stand aside, take cover, pull to one side, shunt.

se gargariser [səgargarize] vr to gargle.

gargarisme [gargarism] nm gargle.

gargouille [gargu:j] nf gargoyle.

garnement [garnəmɑ̃] nm mauvais **—** scamp, rascal.

garni [garni] a well-filled, garnished, furnished; nm furnished room(s).

garnir [garni:r] vt to furnish, provide, fill, stock, fit out, trim, garnish, garrison.

garnison [garnizɔ̃] nf garrison.

garniture [garnity:r] nf fittings, furnishings, trimming(s), decoration, lining, lagging, packing.

garrotter [garɔte] vt to strangle, to bind tightly.

gars [gɑ] nm boy, lad, young fellow.

Gascogne [gaskɔɲ] nf Gascony.

gascon, -onne [gaskɔ̃, ɔn] an Gascon.

gaspiller [gaspije] vt to waste, squander, spoil.

gastrique [gastrik] a gastric.

gastronome [gastrɔnɔm] nm gastronome.

gastronomie [gastrɔnɔmi] nf gastronomy.

gastronomique [gastrɔnɔmik] a gastronomical.

gâteau [gato] nm cake, tart; **— de miel** honeycomb.

gâter [gate] vt to spoil, pamper, damage, taint, mar; vr to deteriorate; **enfant gâté** spoiled child.

gâterie [gatri] nf excessive indulgence, spoiling; pl treats, dainties, delicacies.

gâteux, -euse [gatø, ø:z] a senile, in one's dotage; n dotard.

gauche [go:ʃ] a left, warped, clumsy, awkward; nf left.

gaucher [goʃe] a left-handed; n left-hander.

gaucherie [goʃri] nf clumsiness, awkwardness.

gauchir [goʃi:r] vti to warp, buckle.

gaudriole [godriɔl] nf broad joke.

gaufre [go:fr] nf waffle.

gaufrer [gofre] vt to crimp, emboss, crinkle.

gaufrette [gofrɛt] nf water biscuit.

gaule [go:l] nf pole, stick, fishingrod.

gaulois [golwa] a Gallic; **esprit —** free, broad, Gallic wit; n Gaul.

gauloiserie [golwazri] nf broad, free joke.

se gausser [səgose] vr to poke fun (de at), taunt.

gaver [gave] vt to cram, stuff; vr to gorge.

gaz [ga:z] nm gas; pl flatulence, wind; **à pleins —** flat out.

gaze [ga:z] nf gauze.

gazelle [gazɛl] nf gazelle.

gazer [gaze] vt to cover with gauze, gloss over, tone down, veil, gas; vi to speed, go well.

gazeux, -euse [gazø, ø:z] a gaseous, aerated, gassy.

gazogène [gazɔʒɛn] a gas-producing; nm gazogene, gas-generator.

gazomètre [gazɔmɛtr] nm gaso-meter.

gazon [gazɔ̃] nm grass, turf, sod, lawn, green.

gazouillement [gazujmɑ̃] nm twittering, warbling, babbling, prattling.

gazouiller [gazuje] vi to twitter, warble, babble, prattle.

geai [ʒɛ] nm jay.

géant [ʒeɑ̃] a gigantic, giant; n giant, giantess.

geignard [ʒɛɲaːr] a whining, fretful; nm whiner, sniveler.

geindre [ʒɛ̃dr] vi to whine, whimper.

gélatine [ʒelatin] nf gelatin.

gelé [ʒ(ə)le] a frozen, frostbitten.

gelée [ʒ(ə)le] nf frost, jelly.

geler [ʒ(ə)le] vti to freeze; vr to freeze, solidify.

gelure [ʒəlyːr] nf frostbite.

gémir [ʒemiːr] vi to moan, groan, wail.

gémissement [ʒemismɑ̃] nm moan (ing), groan(ing), wail(ing).

gênant [ʒɛnɑ̃] a in the way, awkward, embarrassing.

gencive [ʒɑ̃siːv] nf gum.

gendarme [ʒɑ̃darm] nm gendarme, policeman.

gendre [ʒɑ̃dr] nm son-in-law.

gêne [ʒɛn] nf embarrassment, discomfort, constraint, want, straitened circumstances; sans — free and easy.

gêné [ʒene] a embarrassed, ill at ease, awkward, hard up.

généalogie [ʒenealɔʒi] nf genealogy, pedigree.

généalogique [ʒenealɔʒik] a genealogical, family.

gêner [ʒene] vt to cramp, constrain, pinch, hamper, inconvenience, embarrass; vr to inconvenience oneself; ne pas se — not to put oneself out, to make oneself at home.

général [ʒeneral] a general, prevailing; nm general; — de division major-general; — de brigade brigadier-general.

généralement [ʒeneralmɑ̃] ad generally.

généralisation [ʒeneralizasjɔ̃] nf generalization.

généraliser [ʒeneralize] vt to generalize; vr to become general, spread.

généralissime [ʒeneralisim] nm generalissimo, commander-in-chief.

généralité [ʒeneralite] nf generality.

générateur, -trice [ʒeneratœːr, tris] a generating, generative; nm generator.

génération [ʒenerasjɔ̃] nf generation.

généreux, -euse [ʒenerø, øːz] a generous.

générique [ʒenerik] a generic; nm (film) credits.

générosité [ʒenerozite] nf generosity.

genèse [ʒənɛːz] nf genesis.

genêt [ʒ(ə)nɛ] nm (bot) broom.

genévrier [ʒənevrie] nm juniper.

génial [ʒenjal] a inspired, bright, brilliant.

génie [ʒeni] nm genius, spirit, (army) engineers; — civil engineering.

genièvre [ʒənjɛːvr] nm juniper, gin.

génisse [ʒenis] nf heifer.

genou [ʒənu] nm knee.

genre [ʒɑ̃ːr] nm kind, sort, type, genus, family, style.

gens [ʒɑ̃] n pl people, folk(s), men, servants.

gentiane [ʒɑ̃sjan] nf gentian.

gentil, -ille [ʒɑ̃ti, iːj] a nice, pretty, kind, sweet, good.

gentilhomme [ʒɑ̃tijɔm] nm nobleman.

gentillesse [ʒɑ̃tijɛs] nf prettiness, graciousness, kindness; pl nice things.

gentiment [ʒɑ̃timɑ̃] ad nicely, prettily, sweetly.

géographie [ʒeɔgrafi] nf geography.

géographique [ʒeɔgrafik] a geographical.

geôle [ʒoːl] nf jail, prison.

geôlier [ʒolje] nm jailer, warder.

géologie [ʒeɔlɔʒi] nf geology.

géologue [ʒeɔlɔg] nm geologist.

géométrie [ʒeɔmetri] nf geometry.

géométrique [ʒeɔmetrik] a geometrical.

gérance [ʒerɑ̃ːs] nf management, managership.

géranium [ʒeranjɔm] nm geranium.

gérant [ʒerɑ̃] n manager(ess), director, managing-.

gerbe [ʒɛrb] nf sheaf, spray, shower.

gerçure [ʒɛrsyːr] nf chap, crack, fissure.

gérer [ʒere] vt to manage.

germain [ʒɛrmɛ̃] a full, first.

germanique [ʒɛrmanik] a Germanic.

germe [ʒɛrm] nm germ, (potato) eye, seed.

germer [ʒɛrme] vi to germinate, sprout, shoot.

germination [ʒɛrminasjɔ̃] nf germination.

gésier [ʒezje] nm gizzard.

gésir [ʒeziːr] vi to lie.

geste [ʒɛst] nm gesture, movement, motion, wave.

gesticuler [ʒɛstikyle] vi to gesticulate.

gestion [ʒɛstjɔ̃] nf management, administration, care.

gibecière [ʒipsjɛːr] nf game-bag, satchel.

giberne [ʒibɛrn] nf wallet, pouch, satchel.

gibier [ʒibje] nm game.

giboulée [ʒibule] nf (hail) shower.

giboyeux, -euse [ʒibwajø, øːz] a well stocked with game.

giclement [ʒikləmɑ̃] nm splashing, spurting.

gicler [ʒikle] vi to splash (up), squelch, spurt (out).

gicleur [ʒiklœːr] nm spray, jet.

gifle [ʒifl] nf slap, smack, cuff.

gifler [ʒifle] vt to slap, smack.

gigantesque [ʒigɑ̃tɛsk] a gigantic, huge.

gigot [ʒigo] nm leg of mutton.

gigue [ʒig] nf jig.

gilet [ʒilɛ] nm waistcoat, vest, jacket; — tricoté cardigan.

gingembre [ʒɛ̃ʒɑ̃:br] nm ginger.

girafe [ʒiraf] nf giraffe.

giratoire [ʒiratwa:r] a gyratory, roundabout.

girofle [ʒirɔfl] nm clove.

giroflée [ʒirɔfle] nf stock, wall-flower.

giron [ʒirɔ̃] nm lap.

girouette [ʒirwɛt] nf weathercock, turncoat.

gisant [ʒizɑ̃] a lying, recumbent.

gisement [ʒizmɑ̃] nm layer, seam, stratum, bearing.

gîte [ʒit] nm resting-place, lair, home, shelter, bed, seam, leg of beef.

givre [ʒi:vr] nm hoarfrost.

glabre [gla:br] a smooth, hairless, clean-shaven.

glace [glas] nf ice, glass, mirror, window, icing, ice-cream.

glacé [glase] a frozen, icy, chilled, stony, iced, glossy.

glacer [glase] vt to freeze, chill, ice, glaze.

glacial [glasjal] a icy, frozen, frigid, stony.

glacier [glasje] nm glacier, ice-cream vendor, manufacturer of mirrors.

glacière [glasjɛ:r] nf ice-house, ice-box, freezer.

glacis [glasi] nm slope, bank, glaze.

glaçon [glasɔ̃] nm block of ice, ice-floe, icicle.

gladiateur [gladjatœ:r] nm gladiator.

glaïeul [glajœl] nm gladiolus.

glaise [glɛ:z] nf clay.

glaive [glɛv] nm sword, sword-fish.

gland [glɑ̃] nm acorn, tassel.

glande [glɑ̃:d] nf gland.

glaner [glane] vt to glean.

glaneur, -euse [glanœ:r, ø:z] n gleaner.

glapir [glapi:r] vi to yelp, yap, (fox) bark.

glas [gla] nm knell, death bell.

glauque [glo:k] a glaucous, sea-green.

glissade [glisad] nf slip, slide, sliding.

glissant [glisɑ̃] a slippery, sliding.

glissement [glismɑ̃] nm sliding, slip, gliding, glide.

glisser [glise] vi to slip, skid, slide, glide, pass over; vt to slip; vr to glide, creep, steal into (dans).

glisseur, -euse [glisœ:r, ø:z] n slider; nm speedboat, glider.

glissière [glisjɛ:r] nf groove, slide, shoot; à —s sliding.

global [glɔbal] a total, inclusive, lump.

globe [glɔb] nm globe, orb, ball.

globulaire [glɔbylɛ:r] a globular.

globule [glɔbyl] nm globule.

gloire [glwa:r] nf glory, fame, boast, pride, halo.

glorieux, -euse [glɔrjø, ø:z] a glorious, proud, conceited, boastful; nm braggart.

glorifier [glɔrifje] vt to glorify, praise; vr to boast.

gloriole [glɔrjɔl] nf notoriety, vain-glory, credit.

glose [glo:z] nf gloss, note, comment, criticism.

gloser [gloze] vt to gloss, criticize.

glossaire [glɔsɛ:r] nm glossary.

glouglou [gluglu] nm gurgle, gobble-gobble.

glousser [gluse] vi to cluck, gobble, gurgle, chuckle.

glouton, -onne [glutɔ̃, ɔn] a greedy, gluttonous; n glutton.

gloutonnerie [glutɔnri] nf gluttony.

glu [gly] nf bird-lime.

gluant [glyɑ̃] a gluey, sticky.

glutineux [glytinø] a glutinous.

glycérine [gliserin] nf glycerine.

glycine [glisin] nf wisteria.

go [go] ad tout de — straight off.

gobelet [gɔblɛ] nm goblet, cup, tumbler.

gobe-mouches [gɔbmuʃ] nm fly-catcher, ninny, wiseacre.

gober [gɔbe] vt to swallow, gulp down; vr to fancy oneself.

gobeur, -euse [gɔbœ:r, ø:z] n conceited person.

godasses [gɔdas] nf pl boots.

godet [gɔde] nm mug, cup, flare, gore.

godille [gɔdij] nf scull.

godiller [gɔdije] vi to scull.

goéland [gɔelɑ̃] nm seagull.

goélette [gɔelɛt] nf schooner.

goémon [gɔemɔ̃] nm seaweed.

goguenard [gɔgna:r] a bantering, joking, jeering.

goinfre [gwɛ̃:fr] nm glutton.

goinfrerie [gwɛ̃frəri] nf gluttony, guzzling.

goitre [gwa:tr] nm goiter.

golf [gɔlf] nm golf, golf-course.

golfe [gɔlf] nm gulf, bay.

gombo [gɔ̃bo] nm okra.

gomme [gɔm] nf gum, (india)rubber, eraser.

gommeux, -euse [gɔmø, ø:z] a gummy, sticky; nm pretentious man, dude.

gond [gɔ̃] nm hinge.

gondolant [gɔ̃dɔlɑ̃] a funny, killing.

gondole [gɔ̃dɔl] nf gondola.

gondoler [gɔ̃dɔle] vi to warp, buckle, sag; vr to warp, buckle, shake with laughter.

gondolier [gɔ̃dɔlje] nm gondolier.

gonflage [gɔ̃fla:ʒ] nm inflation, tire pressure.

gonflement [gɔ̃fləmɑ̃] nm inflating, inflation, distension.

gonfler [gɔ̃fle] vt to swell, inflate, blow up; vir to swell, become distended.

gonfleur [gɔ̃flœːr] nm inflator, air-pump.

goret [gɔrɛ] nm piglet.

gorge [gɔrʒ] nf throat, gullet, breast, gorge, (mountain) pass; **rire à —** déployée to laugh heartily; **rendre —** to disgorge; **faire des —s chaudes de** to laugh heartily at the expense of.

gorgée [gɔrʒe] nf mouthful, gulp.

gorger [gɔrʒe] vt to stuff, gorge.

gorille [gɔriːj] nm gorilla.

gosier [gozje] nm throat, gullet.

gosse [gɔs] n youngster, child, kid.

gothique [gɔtik] a gothic.

goudron [gudrɔ̃] nm tar.

goudronner [gudrɔne] vt to tar, spray with tar.

gouffre [gufr] nm gulf, abyss, chasm.

goujat [guʒa] nm boor, cad, black-guard.

goujaterie [guʒatri] nf boorishness, churlish act.

goujon [guʒɔ̃] nm gudgeon, stud, pin.

goulet [gulɛ] nm gully, narrows, narrow channel.

goulot [gulo] nm (bottle)neck.

goulu [guly] a greedy, gluttonous.

goupille [gupiːj] nf (linch)pin.

goupillon [gupijɔ̃] nm holy-water sprinkler.

gourde [gurd] nf gourd, water-bottle, flask, fool.

gourdin [gurdɛ̃] nm cudgel.

gourmand [gurmɑ̃] a greedy, very fond (of); n gourmand, glutton.

gourmander [gurmɑ̃de] vi to guzzle; vt to scold.

gourmandise [gurmɑ̃diːz] nf greedi-ness, gluttony; pl sweet things.

gourme [gurm] nf impetigo, wild oats.

gourmet [gurmɛ] nm epicure.

gousse [gus] nf pod, shell; **— d'ail** clove of garlic.

gousset [gusɛ] nm waistcoat pocket, gusset.

goût [gu] nm taste, flavor, relish, liking, style, manner.

goûter [gute] vt to taste, enjoy, relish, take a snack between meals; nm (afternoon) snack, tea.

goutte [gut] nf drop, drip, dram, splash, spot, sip, gout.

goutteux, -euse [gutø, øːz] a gouty.

gouttière [gutjɛːr] nf gutter, rain-pipe, spout.

gouvernail [guvɛrnaːj] nm rudder, helm.

gouvernante [guvɛrnɑ̃ːt] nf gover-ness, housekeeper.

gouverne [guvɛrn] nf guidance, direction, steering; pl controls.

gouvernement [guvɛrnəmɑ̃] nm government.

gouverner [guvɛrne] vt to govern, control, steer.

gouverneur [guvɛrnœːr] nm gover-nor.

goyavier [gwajavje] nm guava tree.

grabuge [graby:ʒ] nm quarrel, row.

grâce [grɑs] nf grace, gracefulness, favor, pardon, mercy; **de bonne, de mauvaise —** willingly, un-willingly; **— à** thanks to.

gracier [grasje] vt to pardon, reprieve.

gracieux, -euse [grasjø, øːz] a graceful, gracious, free.

gracile [grasil] a slim, slender.

gradation [gradasjɔ̃] nf gradation.

grade [grad] nm grade, rank, degree.

gradé [grade] nm noncommissioned officer.

gradin [gradɛ̃] nm step, tier.

graduel, -elle [graduɛl] a gradual.

graduer [gradue] vt to graduate, grade.

grain [grɛ̃] nm grain, corn, berry, bean, particle, speck, squall; **— de beauté** beauty spot, mole; **— de plomb** pellet; **— de raisin** grape.

graine [grɛn] nf seed.

grainetier [grɛntje] nm seedsman, corn-chandler.

graissage [grɛsaːʒ] nm greasing, lubrication.

graisse [grɛs] nf grease, fat; **— de rognon** suet; **— de rôti** drippings.

graisser [grɛse] vt to grease, lubricate.

graisseux, -euse [grɛsø, øːz] a greasy, oily, fatty.

grammaire [gramɛːr] nf grammar.

grammairien, -ienne [grammɛrjɛ̃, jɛn] nm grammarian.

grammatical [grammatikal] a gram-matical.

gramme [gram] nm gram.

gramophone [gramofɔn] nm gramo-phone, phonograph.

grand [grɑ̃] a tall, large, big, main, great, noble, high, grown up, grand; **en —** on a large scale, full size; nm grandee; pl grown-ups, great ones.

grand'chose [grɑ̃ʃoːz] pr much.

grandement [grɑ̃dmɑ̃] ad greatly, largely, grandly, ample, high.

grandeur [grɑ̃dœːr] nf size, height, magnitude, grandeur, Highness.

grandiloquence [grɑ̃dilɔkɑ̃ːs] nf grandiloquence.

grandiose [grɑ̃djoːz] a grandiose, imposing.

grandir [grɑ̃diːr] vi to grow (up, tall); vt to increase, make taller, magnify.

grand'mère [grɑ̃mɛːr] nf grand-mother.

grand'messe [grɑ̃mɛs] nf high mass.

grand'peine [grɑ̃pɛn] ad **à —** with great difficulty.

grand-père [grɑ̃pɛːr] nm grand-father.

grand'route [grɑ̃rut] nf highway, high road, main road.

grand'rue [grɑ̃ry] nf main street, high street.

grands-parents [grɑ̃parɑ̃] nm pl grandparents.

grange [grɑ̃ːʒ] nf barn.

granit [grani(t)] nm granite.

graphique [grafik] a graphic; nm diagram, graph.

graphite [grafit] nm graphite, plumbago.

grappe [grap] nf bunch, cluster.

grappin [grapɛ̃] nm grapnel, hook, grab; pl climbing-irons.

gras, -se [gra, gras] a fat(ty), fatted, rich, oily, greasy, thick, ribald, heavy; faire — to eat meat; jour — meat day; nm fat.

grassement [grasmɑ̃] ad generously.

grasset, -ette [grasɛ, ɛt] a plump, fattish, chubby.

grasseyer [graseje] vi to burr, roll one's 'r's.

grassouillet, -ette [grasuje, ɛt] a plump, chubby.

gratification [gratifikasjɔ̃] nf bonus, gratuity.

gratifier [gratifje] vt to bestow, confer.

gratin [gratɛ̃] nm browned part, smart set; au — with bread-crumbs and grated cheese.

gratiné [gratine] a with bread-crumbs.

gratis [gratis] ad gratis, free (of charge).

gratitude [gratityd] nf gratitude, gratefulness.

gratte-ciel [gratsjɛl] nm skyscraper.

gratte-pieds [gratpje] nm scraper.

gratter [grate] vt to scratch, scrape (out).

gratuit [gratɥi] a gratuitous, free, uncalled for.

gratuité [gratɥite] nf gratuitousness.

grave [gra:v] a grave, solemn, serious, low-pitched.

graveleux, -euse [gravlø, ø:z] a gritty, ribald.

graver [grave] vt to engrave, cut, carve; — à l'eau-forte to etch.

graveur [gravœ:r] nm engraver, carver.

gravier [gravje] nm gravel, grit.

gravir [gravi:r] vt to climb .

gravitation [gravitasjɔ̃] nf gravitation.

gravité [gravite] nf gravity, severity, seriousness, weight, low pitch.

graviter [gravite] vi to gravitate, revolve.

gravure [gravy:r] nf engraving, print, illustration; — à l'eau-forte etching; — sur bois wood-cut.

gré [gre] nm liking, taste, will; au — de according to, at the mercy of; bon —, mal — willy-nilly; de — à — by mutual consent; de — ou de force by fair means or foul; savoir — à to be grateful to; savoir mauvais — à to be angry with.

grec, grecque [grɛk] a nm Greek; n Greek.

Grèce [grɛs] nf Greece.

gredin [grədɛ̃] nm rogue.

gréement [gremɑ̃] nm rigging, gear.

gréer [gree] vt to rig, sling.

greffe [grɛf] nf graft, grafting.

greffer [grɛfe] vt to graft.

greffier [grɛfje] nm clerk of court.

grêle [grɛ:l] a small, slender, thin, high-pitched; nf hail, shower.

grêlé [grɛle] a pock-marked.

grêler [grɛle] v imp to hail.

grêlon [grɛlɔ̃] nm hailstone.

grelot [grəlo] nm bell.

grelotter [grəlɔte] vi to tremble, shake, shiver.

grenade [grənad] nf pomegranate, grenade; — à main hand-grenade; — sous-marine depth-charge.

grenadine [grənadin] nf grenadine.

grenier [grənje] nm granary, loft, attic, garret.

grenouille [grənu:j] nf frog, funds.

grès [grɛ] nm sandstone.

grésiller [grezije] vi to crackle, sputter, sizzle.

grève [grɛ:v] nf beach, shore, strand, strike; se mettre en — to go on strike; faire — to be on strike; — de solidarité strike in sympathy; — perlée slowdown; — sur le tas sit-down strike; — de zèle work to rule.

grever [grəve] vt to burden, mortgage

gréviste [grevist] n striker.

gri(s)-gri(s) [grigri] nm amulet.

gribouillage [gribuja:ʒ] nm scrawl, scribble.

gribouiller [gribuje] vt to scrawl, scribble.

grief [grief] nm grievance.

grièvement [grievmɑ̃] ad severely, seriously, deeply.

griffe [grif] nf claw, talon, clip, facsimile signature, writing; pl clutches.

griffer [grife] vt to scratch, claw, stamp.

griffonnage [grifɔna:ʒ] nm scrawl, scribble.

griffonner [grifɔne] vt to scrawl, scribble.

grignoter [griɲɔte] vt nibble, pick at.

grigou [grigu] nm skinflint, miser.

gril [gri] nm gridiron, grill.

grillade [grijad] nf grilled meat, grill.

grillage [grija:ʒ] nm grilling, toasting, roasting, grating, netting, lattice-work.

grille [gri:j] nf grating, railings, iron-barred gate, entrance gate, grid.

griller [grije] vt to grill, toast, roast, scorch, rail in, grate.

grillon [grijɔ̃] nm (insect) cricket.

grimace [grimas] nf grimace, wry face.

grimacer [grimase] vi to grimace, make faces.

grimacier, -ière [grimasje, jɛ:r] a grimacing, grinning, simpering.

se grimer [səgrime] vr to make up (one's face).

imper [grɛ̃pe] *vti* to climb.
impeur, -euse [grɛ̃pœːr, øːz] *a* climbing; *n* climber.
grincer [grɛ̃se] *vi* to grate, grind, gnash, creak.
grincheux, -euse [grɛ̃ʃø, øːz] *a* grumpy, surly; *n* grumbler.
griot [grio] *nm* storyteller, praise singer.
grippe [grip] *nf* dislike, influenza.
grippé [gripe] *a* suffering from influenza.
grippe-sou [gripsu] *nm* skinflint, miser.
gris [gri] *a* gray, dull, cloudy, intoxicated.
grisâtre [grizaːtr] *a* grayish.
griser [grize] *vt* to make tipsy, intoxicate; *vr* to become intoxicated, be carried away (with de).
griserie [grizri] *nf* tipsiness, intoxication, rapture.
grisonner [grizɔne] *vi* to turn gray.
grisou [grizu] *nm* firedamp.
grive [griːv] *nf* thrush.
grivois [grivwa] *a* broad, ribald, licentious.
grivoiserie [grivwazri] *nf* ribald, broad joke.
grog [grɔg] *nm* grog, toddy.
grognard [grɔɲaːr] *a* grumbling; *n* grumbler.
grognement [grɔɲəmɑ̃] *nm* grunt (ing), growl(ing), grumbling.
grogner [grɔɲe] *vi* to grunt, growl, snarl, grumble.
grognon [grɔɲɔ̃] *a* grumbling, querulous; *n* grumbler.
groin [grwɛ̃] *nm* snout.
grommeler [grɔmle] *vi* to grumble, mutter.
grondement [grɔ̃dmɑ̃] *nm* growl (ing), snarl(ing), rumble, roaring.
gronder [grɔ̃de] *vi* to growl, snarl, rumble, mutter, roar, grumble; *vt* to scold, rebuke.
gronderie [grɔ̃dri] *nf* scolding.
grondeur, -euse [grɔ̃dœːr, øːz] *a* grumbling, scolding; *n* grumbler, scold.
groom [grum] *nm* groom, page(boy).
gros, -se [gro, groːs] *a* big, large, heavy, stout, thick, coarse, plain, rough, loud, gruff, gross, pregnant; — **bonnets bigwigs**; — **mots** bad language; *nm* bulk, mass, chief part, hardest part; **en** — in bulk, wholesale.
groseille [grozɛːj] *nf* currant (red, white); — **à maquereau** gooseberry.
groseillier [grozɛje] *nm* currant-bush.
grossesse [grosɛs] *nf* pregnancy.
grosseur [grosœːr] *nf* size, bulk, thickness, swelling.
grossier, -ière [grosje, jɛːr] *a* coarse, rough, gross, vulgar, rude.
grossièreté [grosjɛrte] *nf* coarseness, roughness, rudeness, offensive remark.

grossir [grosiːr] *vt* to enlarge, magnify; *vi* to increase, swell, grow bigger.
grossissement [grosismɑ̃] *nm* increase, swelling, magnifying, enlargement.
grotesque [grɔtɛsk] *a* ludicrous.
grotte [grɔt] *nf* grotto.
grouiller [gruje] *vi* to swarm, be alive (with de); *vr* to get a move on, hurry up.
groupe [grup] *nm* group, clump, cluster, party.
groupement [grupmɑ̃] *nm* grouping, group.
grouper [grupe] *vt* to group, arrange; *vr* to form a group, gather.
gruau [gryo] *nm* wheat flour; — **d'avoine** oatmeal, gruel.
grue [gry] *nf* crane, prostitute.
gruger [gryʒe] *vt* to fleece, plunder, sponge on.
grumeau [grymo] *nm* clot, lump.
gué [ge] *nm* ford.
guenille [gəniːj] *nf* rag, tatter.
guenon [gənɔ̃] *nf* she-monkey, ugly woman.
guêpe [gɛːp] *nf* wasp; — **maçonne** mason wasp.
guêpier [gepje] *nm* wasps' nest, hornets' nest.
guère [gɛːr] *ad* hardly (any, ever), barely, not much, not many, but little, but few.
guéridon [geridɔ̃] *nm* pedestal table, occasional table.
guérilla [gerija, -illa] *nf* guerrilla.
guérir [geriːr] *vt* to cure, heal; *vi* to recover, heal.
guérison [gerizɔ̃] *nf* recovery, cure, healing.
guérissable [gerisabl] *a* curable.
guérite [gerit] *nf* sentry-box, signal-box.
guerre [gɛːr] *nf* war(fare), fighting, strife, quarrel, feud; — **d'usure** war of attrition; — **de mouvement** open warfare; — **de position** trench warfare; — **éclair** blitz war; **de bonne** — quite fair; **de** — **lasse** for the sake of peace.
guerrier, -ière [gɛrje, jɛːr] *a* warlike, war-; *nm* warrior.
guerroyer [gɛrwaje] *vi* to wage war.
guet [gɛ] *nm* watch, look-out.
guet-apens [gɛtapɑ̃] *nm* ambush, trap.
guêtre [gɛːtr] *nf* gaiter, spat.
guetter [gete] *vt* to lie in wait for, watch, be on the look-out for, listen for.
guetteur [gɛtœːr] *nm* lookout (man).
gueule [gœl] *nf* mouth, muzzle, face, mug; **ta** — ! shut up! **casser la** — **à qn** to knock s.o.'s face in; **avoir la** — **de bois** to feel parched after excess of alcohol.
gueuler [gœle] *vti* to bawl, shout.
gueuleton [gœltɔ̃] *nm* blow-out, binge.

gueux, -euse [gø, ø:z] *a* poor, beggarly; *n* beggar.

gui [gi] *nm* mistletoe.

guichet [giʃɛ] *nm* wicket-gate, grating, turnstile, barrier, pay-desk, booking-office window.

guide [gid] *nm* guide, conductor, guidebook; *nf* rein.

guider [gide] *vt* to guide, conduct, drive, steer.

guidon [gidɔ̃] *nm* handlebar, marker flag, pennant, (on gun) bead.

guigne [giɲ] *nf* gean; bad luck.

guigner [giɲe] *vt* to peep at, cast an eye over, to leer, ogle.

guignol [giɲɔl] *nm* Punch and Judy show, Punch.

guillemets [gijmɛ] *nm pl* inverted commas, quotation marks.

guilleret, -ette [gijrɛ, ɛt] *a* lively, gay, perky, broad.

guillotine [gijɔtin] *nf* guillotine.

guillotiner [gijɔtine] *vt* to guillotine.

guimauve [gimo:v] *nf* marshmallow.

guimbarde [gɛ̃bard] *nf* jew's-harp, ramshackle vehicle.

guimpe [gɛ̃:p] *nf* wimple, blouse front.

guindé [gɛ̃de] *a* stiff, strained, starchy.

guingois [gɛ̃gwa] *nm* crookedness, skew, twistedness; **de —** askew, awry.

guinguette [gɛ̃gɛt] *nf* suburban tavern with music and dancing.

guipure [gipy:r] *nf* guipure, pointlace, pillow-lace.

guirlande [girlɑ̃:d] *nf* garland, festoon.

guirlander [girlɑ̃de] *vt* to garland, festoon.

guise [gi:z] *nf* way, manner; **à sa —** as one pleases; **en — de** by way of.

guitare [gita:r] *nf* guitar.

guttural [gytyral] *a* guttural.

gymnaste [ʒimnast] *nm* gymnast.

gymnastique [ʒimnastik] *a* gymnastic; **au pas —** on the double; *nf* gymnastics.

gynécologue [ʒinekɔlɔg] *n* gynecologist.

gypse [ʒips] *nm* gypsum, plaster of Paris.

gyroscope [ʒirɔskɔp] *nm* gyroscope.

H

The asterisk denotes that the initial h, which is never pronounced, is aspirate, i.e. there is no liaison or elision.

habile [abil] *a* clever, skillful, smart.

habileté [abilte] *nf* cleverness, skill, skillfulness, capability, smartness.

habillé [abije] *a* dressed (up), clad, smart, dressy.

habillement [abijmɑ̃] *nm* clothing, clothes, dress.

habiller [abije] *vt* to dress, clothes

vr to dress, put one's clothes on.

habilleuse, -euse [abijœ:r, ø:z] *n* dresser (theater).

habit [abi] *nm* dress, coat, evening-dress; *pl* clothes.

habitable [abitabl] *a* (in)habitable.

habitant [abitɑ̃] *nm* inhabitant, dweller, resident, occupier; **loger chez l'—** to billet privately.

habitation [abitasjɔ̃] *nf* dwelling, residence, abode.

habiter [abite] *vt* to inhabit, live in, occupy; *vi* to live, reside, dwell.

habitude [abityd] *nf* habit, custom, use, practice, wont, knack; **d'—** usually; **comme d'—** as usual.

habitué [abitɥe] *nm* regular attendant, frequenter, regular customer.

habituel, -elle [abitɥɛl] *a* usual, habitual, customary.

habituer [abitɥe] *vt* to accustom, get into the habit; *vr* to get used, grow accustomed.

*°**hâbleur** [ablœ:r] *nm* braggart, boaster.

*°**hache** [aʃ] *nf* ax, hatchet.

*°**haché** [aʃe] *a* staccato, jerky, minced.

*°**hacher** [aʃe] *vt* to chop (up), hash, hack, mince.

*°**hachis** [aʃi] *nm* minced meat, mince, hash.

*°**hachoir** [aʃwa:r] *nm* chopper, mincer, chopping-board.

*°**hagard** [aga:r] *a* haggard, wild, drawn.

*°**haie** [ɛ] *nf* hedge(row), hurdle, line.

*°**haillon** [ajɔ̃] *nm* rag, tatter.

*°**haine** [ɛn] *nf* hatred, aversion.

*°**haineux, -euse** [ɛnø, ø:z] *a* full of hatred.

*°**haïr** [ai:r] *vt* to hate, detest, loathe.

*°**haïssable** [aisabl] *a* hateful, detestable.

*°**halage** [ala:ʒ] *nm* towing.

*°**hâle** [a:l] *nm* sunburn, tan.

*°**hâlé** [ale] *a* sunburnt, tanned, weather-beaten.

haleine [alɛn] *nf* breath, wind; **travail de longue —** work requiring a long effort; **tenir en —** to keep in suspense.

*°**haler** [ale] *vt* to tow, pull, heave, haul up, in.

*°**hâler** [ale] *vt* to sunburn, tan, brown.

*°**haleter** [alte] *vi* to pant, gasp for breath.

*°**hall** [al, ɔl] *nm* (entrance) hall, hotel lounge.

*°**halle** [al] *nf* (covered) market.

*°**hallebarde** [albard] *nf* halberd; **il pleut des —e** it's raining cats and dogs.

*°**hallier** [alje] *nm* thicket.

hallucination [al(l)ysinasjɔ̃] *nf* hallucination.

*°**halte** [alt] *nf* stop, halt.

haltère [altɛ:r] *nm* dumb-bell.

*°**hamac** [amak] *nm* hammock.

ameau [amo] nm hamlet.
ameçon [ams5] nm hook, bait.
ampe [ɑ:p] nf staff, pole, handle, haft.
anche [ɑ̃:ʃ] nf hip, haunch.
andicaper [ɑ̃dikape] vt to handicap.
angar [ɑ̃gɑːr] nm shed, outhouse.
anneton [ant5] nm cockchafer.
anter [ɑ̃te] vt to frequent, haunt.
antise [ɑ̃tiːz] nf obsession.
apper [ape] vt to snap up, catch, seize.
aranguer [arɑ̃ge] vt to harangue, lecture.
aras [arɑ] nm stud farm, stud.
arasser [arase] vt to exhaust, wear out.
arceler [arsəle] vt to harass, worry, harry, pester.
ardes [ard] nf pl old clothes, getup, gear.
ardi [ardi] a bold, daring, fearless, rash, forward.
ardiesse [ardjɛs] nf boldness, daring, fearlessness, forwardness, impudence.
areng [arɑ̃] nm herring; — salé = fumé kipper; — saur red herring.
argneux [arɲø] a snarling, ill-tempered, peevish, snappish.
aricot [ariko] nm kidney bean, haricot bean; —s verts string beans.
rmonie [armɔni] nf harmony, accord, band; en — harmoniously, in keeping.
rmonieux, -euse [armɔnjø, øːz] a harmonious, melodious.
rmonique [armɔnik] a nm harmonic.
rmoniser [armɔnize] vt to harmonize, attune; vr to be in keeping, one in.
ernachement [arnaʃmɑ̃] nm harnessing, trappings.
arnais [arnɛ] nm harness, gear, tackle.
arpe [arp] nf harp.
arpie [arpi] nf harpy, shrew.
arpiste [arpist] n harpist.
arpon [arp3] nm harpoon.
arponner [arpɔne] vt to harpoon.
asard [azaːr] nm chance, luck, accident, risk, hazard; au — at random; à tout — on the off chance.
asarder [azarde] vt to hazard, risk, venture; vr to take risks, venture.
asardeux, -euse [azardø, øːz] a hazardous, risky, daring.
ate [ɑːt] nf haste, hurry; avoir — to be in a hurry to, be eager to; la — hastily, hurriedly.
ater [ɑte] vt to hasten, hurry on, quicken; vr to hurry, make haste.
atif, -ive [ɑtif, iːv] a hasty, hurried, early, premature.
ausse [oːs] nf rise, rising, elevation, range, sight; jouer à la — to sell themarket.

•**haussement** [osmɑ̃] nm raising, lifting, shrug(ging). .
•**hausser** [ose] vt to raise, lift, shrug; vi to rise.
•**haussier** [osje] nm (Stock Exchange) bull.
•**haut** [o] a high, tall, lofty, raised, loud, upper, higher, important, remote; ad high, up, above, aloud, back; — les mains hands up; nm height, top, head; en — above, aloft, upstairs; de — en bas from top to bottom, downward, up and down; les —e et les bas ups and downs.
•**hautain** [otɛ̃] a haughty.
•**hautbois** [obwa] nm oboe.
•**hauteur** [otœːr] nf height, elevation, altitude, eminence, hill(top), haughtiness, loftiness, pitch (of note); à la — de level with, equal to.
•**haut-le-cœur** [olɔkœːr] nm heave, retch.
•**haut-le-corps** [olɔkɔːr] nm start, jump.
•**haut-parleur** [oparlœːr] nm loudspeaker.
•**hauturier, -ière** [otyrje, jɛːr] a of the high seas; pilote — deep-sea pilot.
•**hâve** [ɑːv] a hollow, gaunt.
•**havre** [ɑːvr] nm haven, harbor.
•**havresac** [ɑvrəsak] nm knapsack.
•**hé** [e] excl hi! hullo! hey!
hebdomadaire [ɛbdɔmadɛːr] a nm weekly.
héberger [ebɛrʒe] vt to harbor, lodge, put up, shelter.
hébéter [ebete] vt to daze, dull, stupefy, bewilder.
hébreu [ebrø] a nm Hebrew.
hécatombe [ekat3:b] nf hecatomb, slaughter.
hégémonie [eʒemɔni] nf hegemony.
•**hein** [ɛ̃] excl eh! what!
•**hélas** [elɑːs] excl alas!
•**héler** [ele] vt to hail, call.
hélice [elis] nf spiral, propeller, (of ship) screw.
hélicoptère [elikɔptɛːr] nm helicopter.
héliotrope [eljɔtrɔp] a nm heliotrope, sunflower.
hellénique [ɛlenik] a Hellenic.
helvétique [ɛlvetik] a Swiss.
hémicycle [emisikl] nm hemicycle.
hémisphère [emisfɛːr] nm hemisphere.
hémorragie [emɔraʒi] nf hemorrhage, bleeding.
hémorroïdes [emɔrɔid] nf pl piles.
•**hennir** [ɛniːr] vi to neigh, whinny.
héraldique [eraldik] a heraldic; nf heraldry.
•**héraut** [ero] nm herald.
herbage [ɛrbaːʒ] nm grassland, pasture, greens.
herbe [ɛrb] nf herb, plant, weed, grass; en — budding, in embryo.
herbeux, -euse [ɛrbø, øːz] a grassy.
herbivore [ɛrbivɔːr] a herbivorous.

herboriser [ɛrbɔrize] vi to herborize, botanize.

herboriste [ɛrbɔrist] n herbalist.

herculéen, -enne [ɛrkyleɛ̃, ɛn] a herculean.

héréditaire [eredite:r] a hereditary.

hérédité [eredite] nf heredity, right of inheritance.

hérésie [erezi] nf heresy.

hérétique [eretik] a heretical; n heretic.

*ꞏ**hérissé** [erise] a bristly, prickly, bristling.

*ꞏ**hérisser** [erise] vt to bristle (up), ruffle; vr to bristle, stand on end.

*ꞏ**hérisson** [erisɔ̃] nm hedgehog, (sea)urchin.

héritage [erita:ʒ] nm inheritance, heritage.

hériter [erite] vti to inherit.

héritier, -ière [eritje, jɛ:r] n heir, heiress.

hermétique [ɛrmetik] a hermetically sealed, tight.

hermine [ɛrmin] nf stoat, ermine.

herniaire [ɛrnjɛ:r] a hernial; bandage — truss.

*ꞏ**hernie** [ɛrni] nf hernia, rupture.

héroïne [erɔin] nf heroine.

héroïque [erɔik] a heroic.

héroïsme [erɔism] nm heroism.

*ꞏ**héron** [erɔ̃] nm heron.

*ꞏ**héros** [ero] nm hero.

*ꞏ**herse** [ɛrs] nf harrow, portcullis.

hésitation [ezitasjɔ̃] nf hesitation.

hésiter [ezite] vi to hesitate, falter.

hétéroclite [eterɔklit] a odd, queer.

hétérodoxe [eterɔdɔks] a heterodox.

hétérogène [eterɔʒɛn] a heterogeneous, mixed.

*ꞏ**hêtre** [ɛ:tr] nm beech.

heure [œ:r] nf hour, time, o'clock; la dernière — stop-press news; de bonne — early, in good time; sur l'— at once; tout à l'— just now, a few minutes ago, presently; à tout à l'— see you later; à la bonne — that's right, well done!

heureusement [œrøzmɑ̃] ad happily, luckily.

heureux, -euse [œrø, ø:z] a happy, pleased, lucky, successful, blessed.

*ꞏ**heurt** [œ:r] nm knock, shock, bump; sans heurt smoothly.

*ꞏ**heurter** [œrte] vt to knock against, run against, shock; vr to run (into), knock up (against), collide.

*ꞏ**heurtoir** [œrtwa:r] nm doorknocker, buffer.

hévéa [evea] nm rubber tree.

hexagone [ɛksagɔn] a hexagonal; nm hexagon.

*ꞏ**hibou** [ibu] nm owl.

*ꞏ**hideur** [idœ:r] nf hideousness.

*ꞏ**hideux, -euse** [idø, ø:z] a hideous.

hier [jɛ:r] ad yesterday.

*ꞏ**hiérarchie** [jɛrarʃi] nf hierarchy.

*ꞏ**hiérarchique** [jɛrarʃik] a hierarchical; par voie — through official channels.

hiéroglyphe [jerɔglif] nm hieroglyph.

hilarité [ilarite] nf hilarity, merriment.

hindou [ɛ̃du] an Hindu.

hippique [ippik] a horse, equin concours — horse-show.

hippodrome [ip(p)ɔdrom] nm rac course.

hippopotame [ippɔpɔtam] n hippopotamus.

hirondelle [irɔ̃dɛl] nf swallow.

hirsute [irsyt] a hairy, hirsut shaggy.

*ꞏ**hisser** [ise] vt to hoist (up), pull u run up; vr to pull oneself up, rai oneself.

histoire [istwa:r] nf history, stor tale; faire des —s to make a fus — de s'amuser just for a lark.

historien, -ienne [istɔrjɛ̃, jɛn] historian.

historique [istɔrik] a historic(a nm statement, account.

hiver [ive:r] nm winter.

hivernant [ivɛrnɑ̃] a wintering; n winter visitor.

hiverner [ivɛrne] vi to (lie up fo winter, hibernate.

*ꞏ**hocher** [ɔʃe] vt to shake, nod.

hoirie [wari] nf succession, inher ance.

*ꞏ**hollandais** [ɔlɑ̃dɛ] a nm Dutch; Dutchman, Dutchwoman.

*ꞏ**Hollande** [ɔlɑ̃:d] nf Holland.

holocauste [ɔlɔkɔst] nm holocaus sacrifice.

*ꞏ**homard** [ɔma:r] nm lobster.

homicide [ɔmisid] a homicidal; homicide; nm homicide (crime).

hommage [ɔma:ʒ] nm tribute, tok of esteem; pl respects.

hommasse [ɔmas] a masculin mannish.

homme [ɔm] nm man, mankin husband

homogène [ɔmɔʒɛn] a homogeneou

homologuer [ɔmɔloge] vt to confir endorse, ratify, prove, record.

homonyme [ɔmɔnim] nm homonyr namesake.

homosexuel [ɔmɔsɛksɥɛl] a hom sexual.

*ꞏ**Hongrie** [ɔ̃gri] nf Hungary.

*ꞏ**hongrois** [ɔ̃grwa] a nm Hungaria

honnête [ɔnɛt] a honest uprigh decent, well-bred, seemly, reaso able.

honnêteté [ɔnɛtte] nf honesty, u rightness, decency, courtesy.

honneur [ɔnœ:r] nm honor, cred faire — à to honor, meet.

honorable [ɔnɔrabl] a honorab respectable.

honoraire [ɔnɔrɛ:r] a honorar nm pl fees, honorarium.

honorer [ɔnɔre] vt to honc respect, favor, do credit to.

honorifique [ɔnɔrifik] a honorar honorific.

•**honte** [ɔːt] nf shame, disgrace, scandal; avoir — to be ashamed; **faire** — à to put to shame, disgrace.
•**honteux, -euse** [ɔ̃tø, øːz] a ashamed, shamefaced, bashful, disgraceful.
•**hôpital** [ɔpital] nm hospital, infirmary.
•**hoquet** [ɔkɛ] nm hiccup, gasp.
•**horaire** [ɔrɛːr] nm timetable.
•**horde** [ɔrd] nf horde.
•**horizon** [ɔrizɔ̃] nm horizon.
•**horizontal** [ɔrizɔ̃tal] a horizontal.
•**horloge** [ɔrlɔːʒ] nf clock.
•**horloger** [ɔrlɔʒe] nm clock and watchmaker.
•**horlogerie** [ɔrlɔʒri] nf clock and watchmaking, clockwork.
•**hormis** [ɔrmi] prep except, but, save.
•**hormone** [ɔrmɔn] nf hormone.
•**horreur** [ɔrrœːr] nf horror, abhorrence; pl horrid things, atrocities.
•**horrible** [ɔrribl] a horrid, frightful.
•**horrifier** [ɔrrifje] vt to horrify.
•**horrifique** [ɔrrifik] a horrific, hairraising.
•**horripilant** [ɔrripilɑ̃] a hair-raising.
•**horripiler** [ɔrripile] vt to make someone's flesh creep, irritate.
•**hors** [ɔːr] prep out of, outside, except, all but; — de out(side) of; — de combat out of action, disabled; être — de soi to be beside oneself.
•**hors-bord** [ɔrbɔːr] nm outboard motor boat.
•**hors-d'œuvre** [ɔrdøːvr] nm extraneous matter, hors-d'œuvre.
•**hortensia** [ɔrtɑ̃sja] nm hydrangea.
•**horticole** [ɔrtikɔl] a horticultural, flower-.
•**horticulteur** [ɔrtikyltœːr] nm horticulturist.
•**horticulture** [ɔrtikylty:r] nf horticulture.
•**hospice** [ɔspis] nm hospice, home, asylum, poorhouse.
•**hospitalier, -ière** [ɔspitalje, jɛːr] a hospitable.
•**hospitaliser** [ɔspitalize] vt to send, admit to a hospital, a poorhouse.
•**hospitalité** [ɔspitalite] nf hospitality.
•**hostie** [ɔsti] nf (Eucharistic) host.
•**hostile** [ɔstil] a adverse, inimical, unfriendly.
•**hostilité** [ɔstilite] nf hostility, enmity.
•**hôte, -esse** [oːt, otɛs] n host, hostess, landlord, landlady, guest, visitor, inmate, dweller.
•**hôtel** [otɛl] nm hotel, mansion, townhouse; — de ville town hall; — des postes general post office; — des ventes auction rooms; — meublé, garni lodging house, furnished apartments.
•**hôtel-Dieu** [otɛldjø] nm hospital.
•**hôtelier, -ière** [otəlje, jɛːr] n hotelkeeper, landlord.
•**hôtellerie** [otɛlri] nf inn, restaurant, hotel trade.

•**hotte** [ɔt] nf basket (carried on back), hod.
•**houblon** [ublɔ̃] nm (bot) hop(s).
•**houblonnière** [ublɔnjɛːr] nf hopfield.
•**houe** [u] nf hoe.
•**houille** [uːj] nf coal; — blanche hydro-electric power.
•**houiller, -ère** [uje, jɛːr] a coal (bearing).
•**houillère** [ujɛːr] nf coalmine, pit, colliery.
•**houle** [ul] nf swell, surge, hearing.
•**houlette** [ulɛt] nf crook (shepherd's, of umbrella), crozier, trowel.
•**houleux, -euse** [ulø, øːz] a stormy, surging.
•**houppe** [up] nf tuft, bunch, crest, powder-puff.
•**houppé** [upe] a tufted, crested.
•**houppette** [upɛt] nf small tuft, powder-puff.
•**houspiller** [uspije] vt to hustle, jostle, maul, abuse.
•**housse** [us] nf cover(ing), dustsheet, horse-cloth.
•**houx** [u] nm holly.
•**hoyau** [wajo] nm hoe.
•**hublot** [yblo] nm scuttle, porthole.
•**huche** [yʃ] nf trough, bin.
•**hue** [y] excl gee-up!
•**huée** [ye] nf boo(ing), hoot(ing), jeer(ing).
•**huer** [ye] vi to shout, whoop; vt to boo, hoot.
•**huile** [yil] nf oil; — de copra coconut oil.
huiler [yile] vt to oil.
huileux, -euse [yilø, øːz] a oily, greasy.
huilier [yilje] nm oilcan, oil and vinegar cruet.
huis [yi] nm à — clos in camera, behind closed doors.
huissier [yisje] nm usher, bailiff, sheriff's officer.
•**huit** [yit] a eight; — jours week; d'aujourd'hui en — a week from today; donner ses — jours to give a week's notice; nm eight, eighth.
•**huitaine** [yitɛn] nf (about) eight, week.
•**huitième** [yitjɛm] a nm eighth.
huître [yi:tr] nf oyster.
humain [ymɛ̃] a human, humane.
humaniser [ymanize] vt to humanize; vr to become more humane.
humanitaire [ymanitɛːr] a humanitarian, humane.
humanité [ymanite] nf humanity.
humble [œ̃bl] a humble, lowly.
humecter [ymɛkte] vt to moisten, damp, wet.
•**humer** [yme] vt to suck in, (up), breathe in, sniff.
humeur [ymœːr] nf humor, mood, temper, ill-humor.
humide [ymid] a damp, humid, moist, wet.
humidité [ymidite] nf damp(ness),

humidity, moisture, moistness; craint l'— to be kept dry.

humiliation [ymiljasjɔ̃] nf affront.

humilier [ymilje] vt to humiliate, humble.

humilité [ymilite] nf humility, humbleness.

humoriste [ymɔrist] a humorous; nm humorist.

humoristique [ymɔristik] a humorous.

humour [ymu:r] nm humor.

*°**hune** [yn] nf top; — de vigie crow's nest.

*°**hunier** [ynje] nm topsail.

*°**huppe** [yp] nf tuft, crest.

*°**huppé** [ype] a tufted, crested, (fam) well-dressed.

*°**hure** [y:r] nf head, brawn, head-cheese.

*°**hurlement** [yrləmɑ̃] nm howl(ing), yell(ing).

*°**hurler** [yrle] vi to howl, yell, roar; vt to bawl out.

*°**hutte** [yt] nf hut, shed.

hybride [ibrid] a nm hybrid.

hydrate [idrat] nm hydrate.

hydraulique [idrolik] a hydraulic, water-; nf hydraulics.

hydravion [idravjɔ̃] nm sea-plane.

hydrogène [idrɔʒɛn] nm hydrogen; bombe à — hydrogen bomb.

hydroglisseur [idroglisœ:r] nm speed-boat.

hydrophile [idrɔfil] a absorbent.

hydrophobie [idrɔfɔbi] nf hydrophobia, rabies.

hydropisie [idrɔpizi] nf dropsy.

hyène [jɛn] nf hyena.

hygiène [iʒɛn] nf hygiene, health, sanitation.

hygiénique [iʒjenik] a hygienic, healthy, sanitary; papier — toilet paper.

hymne [im(n)] nm song, (national) anthem; nf hymn.

hyperbole [iperbɔl] nf hyperbole, exaggeration.

hypnose [ipno:z] nf hypnosis, trance.

hypnotiser [ipnɔtize] vt to hypnotize.

hypnotisme [ipnɔtism] nm hypnotism.

hypocondriaque [ipɔkɔ̃driak] an hypochondriac.

hypocrisie [ipɔkrizi] nf hypocrisy, cant.

hypocrite [ipɔkrit] a hypocritical; n hypocrite.

hypodermique [ipɔdermik] a hypodermic.

hypothécaire [ipotekɛ:r] a mortgage; nm mortgagee.

hypothèque [ipɔtɛk] nf mortgage.

hypothéquer [ipɔteke] vt to mortgage.

hypothèse [ipɔtɛ:z] nf hypothesis, assumption.

hystérie [isteri] nf hysteria.

hystérique [isterik] a hysteric(al).

I

ici [isi] ad here, now; par — thi way; d'— huit jours a week today d'— là between now and then; d'— peu before long; jusqu'— hitherto as far as this; — bas here below.

iconoclaste [ikɔnɔklast] a icono clastic; nm iconoclast.

idéal [ideal] a nm ideal.

idéaliser [idealize] vt to idealize.

idéalisme [idealism] nm idealism.

idéaliste [idealist] a idealistic; idealist.

idée [ide] nf idea, thought, notion fancy, mind; il lui est venu à l'— que it occurred to him that; — fix obsession.

identification [idɑ̃tifikasjɔ̃] n identification.

identifier [idɑ̃tifje] vt to identify.

identique [idɑ̃tik] a identical.

identité [idɑ̃tite] nf identity.

idéologie [ideɔlɔʒi] nf ideology.

idéologue [ideɔlɔg] a ideological nm ideologue.

idiomatique [idjɔmatik] a idiomatic

idiome [idjɔm] nm language, idiom

idiosyncrasie [idjɔsɛ̃krazi] nf idio syncrasy.

idiot [idjo] a idiot(ic), senseless; r idiot, silly ass.

idiotie [idjɔsi] nf idiocy, imbecility stupidity.

idiotisme [idjɔtism] nm idiom idiomatic expression, idiocy.

idolâtre [idola:tr] a idolatrous; r idolater, idolatress.

idolâtrer [idolatre] vt to idolize worship.

idolâtrie [idolatri] nf idolatry.

idole [idɔl] nf idol, image, god.

idylle [idil] nf idyll.

idyllique [idilik] a idyllic.

if [if] nm yew(tree).

igname [iɲam] nf yam.

ignare [iɲa:r] a ignorant, uneducat ed; n ignoramus.

ignoble [iɲɔbl] a vile, base.

ignominie [iɲɔmini] nf ignominy shame.

ignominieux, -euse [iɲɔminjø, ø:z] a ignominious, disgraceful.

ignorance [iɲɔrɑ̃s] nf ignorance.

ignorant [iɲɔrɑ̃] a ignorant; ignoramus.

ignorer [iɲɔre] vt to be ignorant of not to know, to be unaware of.

il, **ils** [il] pn he, it, they, there.

île [il, i:l] nf island, isle.

illégal [illegal] a illegal.

illégalité [illegalite] nf illegality unlawfulness.

illégitime [illeʒitim] a illegitimate unlawful, unreasonable.

illégitimité [illeʒitimite] nf illegitim acy, unlawfulness.

illettré [illetre] a illiterate, un educated.

illicite [illisit] a illicit, unlawful.

limité [illimite] *a* unlimited, bound-
ess.

lisibilité [illizibilite] *nf* illegibility.

lisible [illizibl] *a* illegible, unread-
able.

logique [illɔʒik] *a* illogical, inconsistent.

logisme [illɔʒism] *nm* illogicality,
inconsistency.

lumination [illyminasjɔ̃] *nf* illumination, lighting, understanding; *pl*
lights, illuminations.

luminer [illymine] *vt* to illuminate,
enlighten, throw light on.

lusion [illyzjɔ̃] *nf* illusion, delusion.

lusionniste [illyzjɔnist] *n* illusion-
st, conjurer.

lusoire [illyzwaːr] *a* illusory.

lustration [illystrasjɔ̃] *nf* illustrat-
ng, illustration.

lustre [illystr] *a* illustrated, made
amous, renowned.

lustré [illystre] *nm* picture-paper,
illustrated newspaper.

lustrer [illystre] *vt* to make famous,
illustrate; *vr* to win renown.

ot [ilo] *nm* islet.

nage [imaːʒ] *nf* image, picture,
likeness, simile, metaphor, reflection; **faire —** to be vivid.

nagé [imaʒe] *a* full of imagery,
picturesque.

naginaire [imaʒineːr] *a* imaginary.

nagination [imaʒinasjɔ̃] *nf* imagination, fancy, invention.

naginer [imaʒine] *vtr* to imagine,
ancy, picture; *vt* invent, devise.

nbattable [ɛ̃batabl] *a* unbeatable,
invincible.

nbécile [ɛ̃besil] *a* imbecile, half-
witted, silly; *n* fool, half-wit.

nbécilité [ɛ̃besilite] *nf* imbecility,
silliness.

nberbe [ɛ̃berb] *a* beardless.

nbiber [ɛ̃bibe] *vt* to imbibe, absorb,
soak, impregnate, steep; *vr* to
become absorbed, soak in, absorb.

nbrissable [ɛ̃brizabl] *a* unbreakable.

nbu [ɛ̃by] *a* soaked, steeped (de in).

nbuvable [ɛ̃byvabl] *a* undrinkable;
of person) unbearable.

nitateur, -trice [imitatœːr, tris] *a*
imitative; *n* imitator.

nitation [imitasjɔ̃] *nf* copy, copy-
ing, mimicking, impersonation.

niter [imite] *vt* to imitate, copy,
mimic.

nmaculé [imakyle] *a* immaculate,
pure, spotless.

nmangeable [imɑ̃ʒabl] *a* uneatable.

nmanquablement [imɑ̃kabləmɑ̃]
ad inevitably, without fail.

nmatériel, -elle [immaterjɛl] *a*
immaterial, incorporeal.

nmatriculation [immatrikylasjɔ̃]
nf matriculation, enrolling, registration; **plaque d'—** license plate.

nmatriculer [immatrikyle] *vtr* to
register, enroll, matriculate.

immaturité [immatyrite] *nf* im-
maturity.

immédiat [immedja] *a* immediate,
direct, urgent.

immémorial [immemɔrjal] *a* immemorial.

immense [immɑ̃ːs] *a* immense, vast,
huge.

immensité [immɑ̃site] *nf* vastness.

immerger [immɛrʒe] *vt* to immerse,
plunge, dip.

immérité [immerite] *a* unmerited,
undeserved.

immersion [immɛrsjɔ̃] *nf* immersion,
dipping, submersion.

immeuble [immœbl] *a* real, fixed;
nm real estate, house, tenement,
premises.

immigrant [immigrɑ̃] *an* immigrant.

immigré [immigre] *n* immigrant,
settler.

imminence [imminɑ̃ːs] *nf* imminence.

imminent [imminɑ̃] *a* imminent.

immiscer [immise] *vt* to mix up,
involve; *vr* to get involved, interfere.

immixtion [immiksjɔ̃] *nf* interference.

immobile [immɔbil] *a* motionless,
still, immovable.

immobilier, -ière [immɔbilje, jɛːr]
a real (*estate*), building (*society*).

immobiliser [immɔbilize] *vt* to
immobilize, tie up, convert into real
estate.

immobilité [immɔbilite] *nf* immobility.

immodéré [immɔdere] *a* immoderate, excessive.

immodeste [immɔdest] *a* immodest,
shameless.

immoler [immɔle] *vt* to sacrifice,
immolate.

immonde [immɔ̃ːd] *a* filthy, foul.

immondices [immɔ̃dis] *nf pl* dirt,
refuse, filth.

immoral [immɔral] *a* immoral.

immoralité [immɔralite] *nf* immorality, immoral act.

immortaliser [immɔrtalize] *vt* to
immortalize.

immortalité [immɔrtalite] *nf* immortality.

immortel, -elle [immɔrtɛl] *a* immortal, undying.

immuable [immɥabl] *a* unalterable,
unchanging.

immuniser [immɥnize] *vt* to immunize.

immunité [immɥnite] *nf* immunity.

immutabilité [immytabilite] *nf*
immutability.

impact [ɛ̃pakt] *nm* impact.

impair [ɛ̃pɛːr] *a* odd, uneven; *nm*
blunder, bloomer.

impalpable [ɛ̃palpabl] *a* intangible.

impardonnable [ɛ̃pardɔnabl] *a* unpardonable, unforgivable.

imparfait [ɛ̃parfɛ] *a* imperfect,
defective, incomplete.

impartial [ɛparsjal] *a* impartial, unprejudiced.
impassable [ɛpasabl] *a* impassable, unfordable.
impasse [ɛpɑ:s] *nf* blind-alley, dilemma, fix, deadlock, (*cards*) finesse.
impassibilité [ɛpasibilite] *nf* impassiveness.
impassible [ɛpasibl] *a* impassive, unmoved, callous.
impatience [ɛpasjɑ̃:s] *nf* impatience, eagerness.
impatient [ɛpasjɑ̃] *a* impatient, anxious, eager.
impatienter [ɛpasjɑ̃te] *vt* to make impatient; *vr* to lose patience.
impayable [ɛpɛjabl] *a* invaluable, priceless, terribly funny.
impeccable [ɛpɛkabl] *a* faultless, flawless.
impécunieux [ɛpekynjø] *a* impecunious.
impénétrable [ɛpenetrabl] *a* impenetrable, impervious, inscrutable.
impénitence [ɛpenitɑ̃:s] *nf* impenitence, obduracy.
impénitent [ɛpenitɑ̃] *a* obdurate, unrepentant.
impératif, -ive [ɛperatif, i:v] *a* imperative, imperious; *nm* imperative.
impératrice [ɛperatris] *nf* empress.
imperceptible [ɛpɛrsɛptibl] *a* imperceptible, inaudible.
imperfection [ɛpɛrfɛksjɔ̃] *nf* imperfection, defectiveness, incompleteness, flaw.
impérial [ɛperjal] *a* imperial.
impériale [ɛperjal] *nf* top-deck, top, imperial, double-decker bus.
impérialisme [ɛperjalism] *nm* imperialism.
impérieux [ɛperjø, ø:z] *a* imperious, peremptory, domineering, urgent.
impérissable [ɛperisabl] *a* imperishable.
imperméabiliser [ɛpɛrmeabilize] *vt* to proof, make waterproof.
imperméable [ɛpɛrmeabl] *a* impervious; *nm* waterproof.
impersonnel, -elle [ɛpɛrsɔnɛl] *a* impersonal.
impertinence [ɛpɛrtinɑ̃:s] *nf* impertinence.
impertinent [ɛpɛrtinɑ̃] *a* impertinent, rude.
imperturbable [ɛpɛrtyrbabl] *a* cool, calm and collected.
impétueux [ɛpetyø, -ø:z] *a* impetuous, impulsive.
impétuosité [ɛpetyozite] *nf* impetuosity, impulsiveness.
impie [ɛpi] *a* impious, blasphemous.
impiété [ɛpjete] *nf* impiety, ungodliness, blasphemy.
impitoyable [ɛpitwajabl] *a* pitiless, ruthless.
implacabilité [ɛplakabilite] *nf* implacability, relentlessness.

implacable [ɛplakabl] *a* implacable, relentless.
implanter [ɛplɑ̃te] *vt* to plant, implant; *vr* to take root, take hold.
implicite [ɛplisit] *a* implicit, absolute.
impliquer [ɛplike] *vt* to implicate, involve.
implorer [ɛplɔre] *vt* to implore, entreat, beseech.
impoli [ɛpɔli] *a* impolite, unmannerly.
impolitesse [ɛpɔlitɛs] *nf* unmannerliness, rude act, word.
impolitique [ɛpɔlitik] *a* impolitic, ill-advised.
impondérable [ɛpɔ̃derabl] *a* imponderable.
impopulaire [ɛpɔpylɛ:r] *a* unpopular.
impopularité [ɛpɔpylarite] *nf* unpopularity.
importance [ɛpɔrtɑ̃:s] *nf* importance, moment, magnitude.
important [ɛpɔrtɑ̃] *a* important, large, extensive, considerable, self-important; *nm* the main thing.
importateur, -trice [ɛpɔrtatœ:r tris] *a* importing; *n* importer.
importation [ɛpɔrtasjɔ̃] *nf* importing, import.
importer [ɛpɔrte] *vt* to import; *vi* to be important, matter; **n'importe** never mind, it does not matter **n'importe qui, quoi, comment quand** anyone, anything, anyhow anytime.
importun [ɛpɔrtœ̃] *a* importunate, tiresome, unwelcome; *n* intruder, nuisance.
importuner [ɛpɔrtyne] *vt* to importune, bother, trouble, dun.
importunité [ɛpɔrtynite] *nf* importunity.
imposable [ɛpozabl] *a* taxable, ratable, assessable.
imposant [ɛpozɑ̃] *a* imposing, impressive.
imposé [ɛpoze] *n* ratepayer, taxpayer.
imposer [ɛpoze] *vt* to impose, set prescribe, enforce, tax, rate; *vi* to command respect; *vr* to assert oneself, force oneself, itself (upon) be imperative; **en —** à to impose upon, take in, overawe.
imposition [ɛpozisjɔ̃] *nf* imposition, imposing, setting, prescribing, taxation, rates.
impossibilité [ɛpɔsibilite] *nf* impossibility.
impossible [ɛpɔsibl] *a* impossible.
imposteur [ɛpɔstœ:r] *nm* impostor, hypocrite.
imposture [ɛpɔsty:r] *nf* imposture, sham, swindle.
impôt [ɛpo] *nm* tax, duty; **frapper d'un —** to tax.
impotence [ɛpɔtɑ̃:s] *nf* helplessness, infirmity.

impotent [ɛ̃pɔtɑ̃] *a* infirm, helpless, crippled; *n* cripple, invalid.

impracticable [ɛ̃pratikabl] *a* impracticable, unfeasible, (*road*) impassable.

imprécation [ɛ̃prekasjɔ̃] *nf* imprecation, curse.

imprécis [ɛ̃presi] *a* vague, inaccurate.

imprécision [ɛ̃presizjɔ̃] *nf* vagueness, inaccuracy.

imprégner [ɛ̃preɲe] *vt* to impregnate, saturate; *vr* to become saturated, soak up.

imprenable [ɛ̃prənabl] *a* impregnable.

impression [ɛ̃presjɔ̃] *nf* impression, stamp(ing), print(ing).

impressionnable [ɛ̃presjɔnabl] *a* impressionable, nervous, sensitive.

impressionnant [ɛ̃presjɔnɑ̃] *a* impressive.

impressionner [ɛ̃presjɔne] *vt* to impress, make an impression on, move; *vr* to be moved, get nervous.

impressionisme [ɛ̃presjɔnism] *nm* impressionism.

imprévoyable [ɛ̃prevwajabl] *a* unforeseeable.

imprévoyance [ɛ̃prevwajɑ̃:s] *n* lack of foresight.

imprévoyant [ɛ̃prevwajɑ̃] *a* short-sighted, improvident.

imprévu [ɛ̃prevy] *a* unforeseen, unexpected; *nm* unexpected, emergency.

imprimé [ɛ̃prime] *nm* printed matter, paper, form, leaflet; **envoyer en —** to send by book-post.

imprimer [ɛ̃prime] *vt* to (im)print, impress, stamp.

imprimerie [ɛ̃primri] *nf* printing, printing house, press.

imprimeur [ɛ̃primœ:r] *nm* printer.

improbabilité [ɛ̃prɔbabilite] *nf* improbability, unlikelihood.

improbable [ɛ̃prɔbabl] *a* improbable, unlikely.

improbité [ɛ̃prɔbite] *nf* dishonesty.

improductif, -ive [ɛ̃prɔdyktif, i:v] *a* unproductive.

impromptu [ɛ̃prɔ̃(p)ty] *a* extempore; *ad* without preparation; *nm* impromptu.

impropriété [ɛ̃prɔprjete] *nf* impropriety, unsuitableness, incorrectness.

improvisation [ɛ̃prɔvizasjɔ̃] *nf* improvisation, extemporization.

improvisé [ɛ̃prɔvize] *a* improvised, extempore, makeshift.

improviser [ɛ̃prɔvize] *vt* to improvise, put together, make up; *vi* to speak extempore.

improviste (à l') [alɛ̃prɔvist] *ad* unexpected(ly).

imprudence [ɛ̃prydɑ̃:s] *nf* rashness, indiscretion.

impudence [ɛ̃pydɑ̃:s] *nf* insolence, (piece of) impudence.

impudent [ɛ̃pydɑ̃] *a* impudent, insolent, shameless.

impudicité [ɛ̃pydisite] *nf* lewdness, immodesty.

impudique [ɛ̃pydik] *a* lewd, immodest, unchaste.

impuissance [ɛ̃pɥisɑ̃:s] *nf* helplessness, powerlessness, impotence.

impuissant [ɛ̃pɥisɑ̃] *a* helpless, powerless, impotence, futile.

impulsif, -ive [ɛ̃pylsif, i:v] *a* impulsive.

impulsion [ɛ̃pylsjɔ̃] *nf* impulse, impetus.

impunément [ɛ̃pynemɑ̃] *ad* with impunity.

impunité [ɛ̃pynite] *nf* impunity.

impur [ɛ̃py:r] *a* impure, unchaste, unclean, foul.

impureté [ɛ̃pyrte] *nf* impurity, foulness.

imputable [ɛ̃pytabl] *a* imputable, attributable, chargeable.

imputation [ɛ̃pytasjɔ̃] *nf* imputation, charge, attribution.

imputer [ɛ̃pyte] *vt* to impute, ascribe, charge.

inabordable [inabɔrdabl] *a* inaccessible, prohibitive.

inacceptable [inakseptabl] *a* unacceptable.

inaccessible [inaksɛsibl] *a* inaccessible, unapproachable.

inaccoutumé [inakutyme] *a* unaccustomed, unusual, unwonted.

inachevé [inaʃve] *a* unfinished, incomplete.

inactif, -ive [inaktif, i:v] *a* inactive, inert.

inaction [inaksjɔ̃] *nf* inaction, inertia.

inactivité [inaktivite] *nf* inactivity, inertness.

inadmissible [inadmisibl] *a* inadmissible, who has failed in written examination.

inadvertance [inadvertɑ̃:s] *nf* inadvertence, oversight, mistake.

inadvertant [inadvertɑ̃] *a* careless.

inaliénable [inaljenabl] *a* inalienable, untransferable.

inaltérable [inalterabl] *a* unalterable, unfailing.

inamovible [inamɔvibl] *a* irremovable, fixed, held for life.

inanimé [inanime] *a* lifeless, inanimate, unconscious.

inanité [inanite] *nf* inanity, inane remark.

inanition [inanisjɔ̃] *nf* starvation, inanition.

inaperçu [inapɛrsy] *a* unnoticed, unseen.

inapparent [inaparɑ̃] *a* unapparent.

inapplication [inaplikasjɔ̃] *nf* lack of diligence, of assiduity.

inappliqué [inaplike] *a* inattentive, careless, unapplied.

inappréciable [inapresjabl] *a* inappreciable, not perceptible, invaluable.

inapprivoisé [inaprivwaze] *a* untamed, wild.
inapte [inapt] *a* unfit, unsuited, inapt, unemployable.
inaptitude [inaptityd] *nf* unfitness.
inarticulé [inartikyle] *a* inarticulate, not jointed.
inassouvi [inasuvi] *a* unappeased, unsatisfied.
inassouvissable [inasuvisabl] *a* insatiable.
inattaquable [inatakabl] *a* unassailable, unquestionable.
inattendu [inatādy] *a* unexpected, unlooked for.
inattentif, -ive [inatātif, i:v] *a* inattentive, careless, unobservant.
inattention [inatāsjɔ̃] *nf* inattention, carelessness.
inaugural [inogyral] *a* inaugural, opening.
inauguration [inogyrasjɔ̃] *nf* opening, unveiling.
inaugurer [inogyre] *vt* to inaugurate, open, unveil.
inavouable [inavwabl] *a* shameful, foul, low.
incalculable [ɛ̃kalkylabl] *a* incalculable, countless.
incandescence [ɛ̃kādessā:s] *nf* white heat.
incantation [ɛ̃kātasjɔ̃] *nf* incantation.
incapable [ɛ̃kapabl] *a* inefficient, unfit, unable.
incapacité [ɛ̃kapasite] *nf* incapacity, inefficiency, inability, disablement.
incarcérer [ɛ̃karsere] *vt* to incarcerate, imprison.
incarnadin [ɛ̃karnadɛ̃] *a* incarnadine, rosy, pink.
incarnat [ɛ̃karna] *a* rosy, pink, flesh colored; *nm* rosiness, rosy hue.
incarnation [ɛ̃karnasjɔ̃] *nf* embodiment.
incarné [ɛ̃karne] *a* incarnate, ingrowing.
incarner [ɛ̃karne] *vt* to incarnate, embody, be the incarnation of.
incartade [ɛ̃kartad] *nf* outburst, tirade, prank.
incendiaire [ɛ̃sādjɛ:r] *a* incendiary, inflammatory; *n* incendiary.
incendie [ɛ̃sādi] *nm* fire, conflagration, burning; **échelle à —** fire-escape; **pompe à —** fire-engine; **poste d'—** fire-station.
incendier [ɛ̃sādje] *vt* to set on fire, burn down.
incertain [ɛ̃sertɛ̃] *a* uncertain, doubtful, unreliable.
incertitude [ɛ̃sertityd] *nf* uncertainty, doubt.
incessamment [ɛ̃sesamā] *ad* immediately.
incessant [ɛ̃sesā] *a* unceasing, ceaseless.
inceste [ɛ̃sɛst] *nm* incest.
incestueux, -euse [ɛ̃sɛstyø, ø:z] *a* incestuous.

incidence [ɛ̃sidā:s] *nf* incidence.
incident [ɛ̃sidā] *a* parenthetical, incidental; *nm* incident, occurrence.
incinérateur [ɛ̃sineratœ:r] *nm* incinerator.
incinérer [ɛ̃sinere] *vt* to incinerate, cremate.
incisif [ɛ̃sisif] *a* incisive.
incision [ɛ̃sizjɔ̃] *nf* incision, cutting, lancing, tapping.
inciter [ɛ̃site] *vt* to incite, urge.
incivilisé [ɛ̃sivilize] *a* uncivilized.
incivilité [ɛ̃sivilite] *nf* incivility, (piece of) rudeness.
inclassable [ɛ̃klasabl] *a* unclassifiable, nondescript.
inclémence [ɛ̃klemā:s] *nf* inclemency.
inclinaison [ɛ̃klinɛzɔ̃] *nf* inclination, incline, gradient, tilt, slope.
inclination [ɛ̃klinasjɔ̃] *nf* inclination, bending, bow, nod, bent.
incliner [ɛ̃kline] *vt* to incline, slope, bow, tilt, dip, predispose; *vi* to be predisposed, inclined; *vr* to slope, slant, bow, give way.
inclure [ɛ̃kly:r] *vt* to enclose.
inclus [ɛ̃kly] *a* including.
inclusif, -ive [ɛ̃klyzif, i:v] *a* inclusive.
inclusion [ɛ̃klyzjɔ̃] *nf* inclusion, enclosing.
incohérence [ɛ̃kɔerā:s] *nf* incoherence, disjointedness.
incohérent [ɛ̃kɔerā] *a* incoherent, disjointed.
incolore [ɛ̃kɔlɔ:r] *a* colorless.
incomber [ɛ̃kɔ̃be] *vi* to fall, devolve, be incumbent.
incombustible [ɛ̃kɔ̃bystibl] *a* incombustible, uninflammable.
incomestible [ɛ̃kɔmɛstibl] *a* inedible.
incommensurable [ɛ̃kɔm(m)āsyrabl] *a* incommensurable, incommensurate, immeasurable.
incommode [ɛ̃kɔmɔd] *a* inconvenient, uncomfortable, awkward, tiresome.
incommoder [ɛ̃kɔmɔde] *vt* to inconvenience, upset, disagree with.
incommodité [ɛ̃kɔmɔdite] *nf* inconvenience, discomfort.
incomparable [ɛ̃kɔ̃parabl] *a* incomparable, matchless.
incompatible [ɛ̃kɔ̃patibl] *a* incompatible.
incompétence [ɛ̃kɔ̃petā:s] *nf* incompetence, inefficiency.
incompétent [ɛ̃kɔ̃petā] *a* incompetent, inefficient, unqualified.
incompréhensible [ɛ̃kɔ̃preāsibl] *a* incomprehensible.
incompréhension [ɛ̃kɔ̃preāsjɔ̃] *nf* obtuseness, want of understanding.
incompris [ɛ̃kɔ̃pri] *a* misunderstood, not appreciated.
inconcevable [ɛ̃kɔ̃s(ə)vabl] *a* inconceivable, unthinkable.
inconciliable [ɛ̃kɔ̃siljabl] *a* irreconcilable, incompatible.

inconduite [ɛ̃kɔ̃dɥit] *nf* bad living, misconduct.

incongru [ɛ̃kɔ̃gry] *a* incongruous, unseemly, stupid.

incongruité [ɛ̃kɔ̃grɥite] *nf* incongruity, unseemliness, stupid remark.

inconnu [ɛ̃kɔny] *a* unknown; *n* stranger, unknown person; *nm* (the) unknown.

inconscience [ɛ̃kɔ̃sjɑ̃:s] *nf* unconsciousness, want of principle.

inconscient [ɛ̃kɔ̃sjɑ̃] *a* unconscious, unaware; *nm* subconscious mind.

inconséquent [ɛ̃kɔ̃sekɑ̃] *a* inconsistent, irresponsible, illogical.

inconsidéré [ɛ̃kɔ̃sidere] *a* inconsiderate, thoughtless, heedless.

inconsistant [ɛ̃kɔ̃sistɑ̃] *a* soft, flabby.

inconsolable [ɛ̃kɔ̃sɔlabl] *a* inconsolable.

inconstance [ɛ̃kɔ̃stɑ̃:s] *nf* inconstancy, fickleness, changeableness.

inconstant [ɛ̃kɔ̃stɑ̃] *a* inconstant, fickle, changeable.

incontestable [ɛ̃kɔ̃testabl] *a* indisputable, beyond question.

incontesté [ɛ̃kɔ̃teste] *a* undisputed.

incontinent [ɛ̃kɔ̃tinɑ̃] *a* incontinent; *ad* straightway, forthwith.

incontrôlable [ɛ̃kɔ̃trolabl] *a* not verifiable, unable to be checked.

inconvenance [ɛ̃kɔ̃vnɑ̃:s] *nf* unsuitability, impropriety, unseemliness, improper act or word.

inconvenant [ɛ̃kɔ̃vnɑ̃] *a* improper, unseemly.

inconvénient [ɛ̃kɔ̃venjɑ̃] *nm* disadvantage, drawback, objection.

incorporer [ɛ̃kɔrpɔre] *vt* to incorporate, embody.

incorrect [ɛ̃kɔr(r)ɛkt] *a* wrong, ill-mannered.

incorrection [ɛ̃kɔr(r)ɛksjɔ̃] *nf* incorrectness, inaccuracy, ill-bred act.

incorrigible [ɛ̃kɔr(r)iʒibl] *a* incorrigible, hopeless.

incorruptible [ɛ̃kɔr(r)yptibl] *a* incorruptible.

incrédibilité [ɛ̃kredibilite] *nf* incredibility.

incrédule [ɛ̃kredyl] *a* incredulous; *n* unbeliever.

incrédulité [ɛ̃kredylite] *nf* incredulity.

incriminer [ɛ̃krimine] *vt* to incriminate, accuse.

incroyable [ɛ̃krwajabl] *a* incredible, unbelievable.

incroyant [ɛ̃krwajɑ̃] *a* unbelieving; *n* unbeliever.

incrustation [ɛ̃krystasjɔ̃] *nf* encrustation, inlaying, inlaid work, furring.

incruster [ɛ̃kryste] *vt* to encrust, fur, inlay; *vr* to become encrusted, furred up.

incubation [ɛ̃kybasjɔ̃] *nf* incubation, hatching.

inculpable [ɛ̃kylpabl] *a* chargeable, indictable.

inculpation [ɛ̃kylpasjɔ̃] *nf* charge, indictment.

inculpé [ɛ̃kylpe] *n* accused, defendant.

inculper [ɛ̃kylpe] *vt* to charge, indict.

inculquer [ɛ̃kylke] *vt* to inculcate, instill.

inculte [ɛ̃kylt] *a* uncultivated, wild, uncultured.

incurable [ɛ̃kyrabl] *a* incurable.

incurie [ɛ̃kyri] *nf* carelessness, negligence.

incuriosité [ɛ̃kyrjozite] *nf* want of curiosity.

incursion [ɛ̃kyrsjɔ̃] *nf* inroad, raid.

Inde [ɛ̃:d] *nf* India; *pl* Indies.

indébrouillable [ɛ̃debrujabl] *a* tangled, inextricable.

indécence [ɛ̃desɑ̃:s] *nf* immodesty, indecency.

indécent [ɛ̃desɑ̃] *a* immodest, indecent, improper.

indéchiffrable [ɛ̃deʃifrabl] *a* undecipherable, illegible, unintelligible.

indécis [ɛ̃desi] *a* undecided, irresolute, doubtful, open, vague.

indécision [ɛ̃desizjɔ̃] *nf* indecision, irresolution.

indéfendable [ɛ̃defɑ̃dabl] *a* indefensible.

indéfini [ɛ̃defini] *a* indefinite, undefined.

indéfinissable [ɛ̃definisabl] *a* indefinable.

indélébile [ɛ̃delebil] *a* indelible.

indélicat [ɛ̃delika] *a* indelicate, tactless.

indélicatesse [ɛ̃delikatɛs] *nf* indelicacy, tactlessness, coarse act or remark.

indémaillable [ɛ̃demajabl] *a* runproof.

indemne [ɛ̃demn] *a* undamaged, unhurt.

indemniser [ɛ̃demnize] *vt* to compensate, indemnify.

indemnité [ɛ̃demnite] *nf* indemnity, compensation, grant, allowance; — de chômage unemployment benefit.

indéniable [ɛ̃denjabl] *a* undeniable.

indépendance [ɛ̃depɑ̃dɑ̃:s] *nf* independence.

indépendant [ɛ̃depɑ̃dɑ̃] *a* independent, unattached, self-contained.

indescriptible [ɛ̃deskriptibl] *a* indescribable.

indésirable [ɛ̃dezirabl] *a* undesirable, objectionable.

indestructible [ɛ̃destryktibl] *a* indestructible.

indéterminé [ɛ̃determine] *a* irresolute, indefinite, indeterminate.

index [ɛ̃dɛks] *nm* forefinger, index, indicator.

indicateur, -trice [ɛ̃dikatœ:r, tris] *a* indicatory; *nm* time-table, gauge, indicator, detector, informer; poteau — signpost.

indicatif, -ive [ɛ̃dikatif, i:v] *a*

indicative; nm indicative (mood), signature tune.

indication [ɛ̃dikasjɔ̃] nf indication, information, sign, clue, pointing out; pl instructions, directions.

indice [ɛ̃dis] nm sign, mark, indication, clue.

indicible [ɛ̃disibl] a unspeakable, indescribable.

indien, -ienne [ɛ̃djɛ̃, jɛn] an Indian.

indienne [ɛ̃djɛn] nf chintz, print, overarm stroke.

indifférence [ɛ̃diferɑ̃:s] nf indifference, apathy.

indifférent [ɛ̃diferɑ̃] a apathetic, immaterial, all the same.

indigence [ɛ̃diʒɑ̃:s] nf want, poverty.

indigène [ɛ̃diʒɛn] a indigenous, native; n native.

indigent [ɛ̃diʒɑ̃] a indigent, needy.

indigeste [ɛ̃diʒɛst] a indigestible, heavy, undigested.

indigestion [ɛ̃diʒɛstjɔ̃] nf attack of indigestion.

indignation [ɛ̃diɲasjɔ̃] nf indignation.

indigne [ɛ̃diɲ] a unworthy, undeserving, vile.

indigné [ɛ̃diɲe] a indignant.

indigner [ɛ̃diɲe] vt to make indignant; vr to be, to become, indignant.

indignité [ɛ̃diɲite] nf indignity, unworthiness, infamy.

indiquer [ɛ̃dike] vt to indicate, point (to, out), show, appoint; c'était indiqué it was the obvious thing to do.

indirect [ɛ̃dirɛkt] a indirect, devious.

indiscipliné [ɛ̃disipline] a unruly, undisciplined.

indiscret, -ète [ɛ̃diskrɛ, ɛt] a indiscreet, unguarded, tactless, prying.

indiscrétion [ɛ̃diskresjɔ̃] nf indiscretion, tactless remark or action.

indiscutable [ɛ̃diskytabl] a unquestionable, indisputable.

indispensable [ɛ̃dispɑ̃sabl] a indispensable, necessary, essential, requisite.

indisponibilité [ɛ̃disponibilite] nf unavailability.

indisposé [ɛ̃dispoze] a indisposed, unwell, ill-disposed.

indisposer [ɛ̃dispoze] vt to upset, disagree with, make unwell, antagonize.

indisposition [ɛ̃dispozisjɔ̃] nf indisposition.

indissoluble [ɛ̃dissolybl] a insoluble (chem), indissoluble.

indistinct [ɛ̃distɛ̃(:)kt] a indistinct, faint, blurred.

individu [ɛ̃dividy] nm individual, fellow, character.

individualiser [ɛ̃dividyalize] vt to individualize, specify.

individuel, -elle [ɛ̃dividyɛl] a individual, personal.

indivisible [ɛ̃divizibl] a indivisible.

Indochine [ɛ̃dɔʃin] nf Indochina.

indocile [ɛ̃dɔsil] a intractable, willful, disobedient.

indolence [ɛ̃dɔlɑ̃:s] nf apathy.

indolent [ɛ̃dɔlɑ̃] a indolent, slack, slothful.

indomptable [ɛ̃dɔ̃tabl] a untamable, ungovernable, unmanageable, invincible.

Indonésie [ɛ̃dɔnezi] nf Indonesia.

indu [ɛ̃dy] a not due, undue, unwarranted, unreasonable.

indubitable [ɛ̃dybitabl] a unquestionable.

induire [ɛ̃dɥi:r] vt to induce, tempt.

indulgence [ɛ̃dylʒɑ̃:s] nf indulgence, forbearance, leniency.

indulgent [ɛ̃dylʒɑ̃] a forbearing, lenient.

indûment [ɛ̃dymɑ̃] ad unduly.

industrialiser [ɛ̃dystrialize] vt to industrialize.

industrialisme [ɛ̃dystrialism] nm industrialism.

industrie [ɛ̃dystri] nf industry, trade, activity, industriousness; vivre d'— to live by one's wits.

industriel, -ielle [ɛ̃dystriɛl] a industrial; nm industrialist, manufacturer.

industrieux, -euse [ɛ̃dystriø, ø:z] a industrious, active.

inébranlable [inebrɑ̃labl] a unshakable, steadfast, unswerving.

inédit [inedi] a unpublished, new.

ineffable [inefabl] a ineffable, unutterable.

ineffaçable [inefasabl] a indelible.

inefficace [inefikas] a ineffective, ineffectual.

inefficacité [inefikasite] nf inefficacy, ineffectiveness, ineffectualness.

inégal [inegal] a unequal, uneven, irregular, unsteady.

inégalité [inegalite] nf inequality, unevenness, roughness, unsteadiness.

inéligible [ineliʒibl] a ineligible.

inéluctable [inelyktabl] a inevitable.

inénarrable [inenarabl] a indescribable, beyond words.

inepte [inɛpt] a inept, foolish.

ineptie [inɛpsi] nf ineptitude, stupid remark.

inépuisable [inepɥizabl] a inexhaustible, abundant.

inéquitable [inekitabl] a unfair.

inerte [inɛrt] a inert, dull, sluggish, listless.

inespéré [inespere] a unexpected, unhoped-for.

inestimable [inestimabl] a priceless, invaluable.

inévitable [inevitabl] a inevitable.

inexact [inɛgzakt] a inexact, inaccurate, unpunctual.

inexactitude [inɛgzaktityd] nf inaccuracy, unpunctuality.

inexcusable [inɛkskyzabl] a unpardonable, unwarranted.

inexécutable [inɛgzekytabl] a impracticable.

inexercé [inɛgzɛrse] a unexercised, unpracticed.

inexistant [inɛgzistɑ̃] a non-existent.

inexorable [inɛgzɔrabl] a inexorable.

inexpérience [inɛksperjɑ̃:s] nf inexperience.

inexpérimenté [inɛksperimɑ̃te] a inexperienced, unpracticed, untried, raw.

inexplicable [inɛksplikabl] a inexplicable, unaccountable.

inexpliqué [inɛksplike] a unexplained, unaccounted for.

inexploité [inɛksplwate] a unworked, undeveloped.

inexpressif, -ive [inɛkspresif, i:v] a expressionless.

inexprimable [inɛksprimabl] a inexpressible, beyond words.

inextricable [inɛkstrikabl] a inextricable.

infaillibilité [ɛ̃fajibilite] nf infallibility.

infaillible [ɛ̃fajibl] a infallible, sure, unerring.

infâme [ɛ̃fɑ:m] a infamous, foul.

infamie [ɛ̃fami] nf infamy, foul deed or word.

infanterie [ɛ̃fɑ̃tri] nf infantry.

infatigable [ɛ̃fatigabl] a tireless, untiring, indefatigable.

infatuation [ɛ̃fatɥasjɔ̃] nf self-conceit, infatuation.

infécond [ɛ̃fekɔ̃] a barren, sterile, unfruitful.

infécondité [ɛ̃fekɔ̃dite] nf sterility, barrenness.

infect [ɛ̃fɛkt] a stinking, tainted, rotten, foul.

infecter [ɛ̃fɛkte] vt to infect, taint, stink of.

infectieux, -euse [ɛ̃fɛksjø, ø:z] a infectious.

infection [ɛ̃fɛksjɔ̃] nf infection, contamination, stink.

s'inféoder [sɛ̃feɔde] vr to give one's support, join.

inférer [ɛ̃fere] vt to infer.

inférieur [ɛ̃ferjœ:r] a inferior, lower; n inferior.

infériorité [ɛ̃ferjɔrite] nf inferiority.

infernal [ɛ̃fɛrnal] a infernal, devilish, diabolical.

infertile [ɛ̃fɛrtil] a barren, infertile, unfruitful.

infester [ɛ̃fɛste] vt to infest, overrun.

infidèle [ɛ̃fidɛl] a unfaithful, faithless, false; n infidel, unbeliever.

infidélité [ɛ̃fidelite] nf infidelity, unfaithfulness.

infiltration [ɛ̃filtrasjɔ̃] nf infiltration, percolation.

s'infiltrer [sɛ̃filtre] vr to infiltrate, seep, soak in.

infime [ɛ̃fim] a lowly, mean, tiny.

infini [ɛ̃fini] a infinite, endless, boundless, countless; nm infinite, infinity.

infiniment [ɛ̃finimɑ̃] ad infinitely.

infinité [ɛ̃finite] nf infinity, infinitude, countless number.

infirme [ɛ̃firm] a infirm, disabled, crippled, feeble; n cripple, invalid.

infirmer [ɛ̃firme] vt to weaken, invalidate, quash.

infirmerie [ɛ̃firməri] nf infirmary, sick-room.

infirmier, -ière [ɛ̃firmje, ɛ:r] n (male) nurse, hospital orderly.

infirmité [ɛ̃firmite] nf infirmity, weakness, disability.

inflammation [ɛ̃flamasjɔ̃] nf inflammation.

inflation [ɛ̃flasjɔ̃] nf inflation.

inflexible [ɛ̃flɛksibl] a inflexible, unbending, rigid.

inflexion [ɛ̃flɛksjɔ̃] nf inflection, modulation.

infliger [ɛ̃fliʒe] vt to inflict.

influence [ɛ̃flyɑ̃:s] nf influence, effect, sway.

influencer [ɛ̃flyɑ̃se] vt to influence, sway.

influent [ɛ̃flyɑ̃] a influential.

influer [ɛ̃flye] vi to have an influence, an effect.

informateur, -trice [ɛ̃fɔrmatœ:r, tris] n informant.

information [ɛ̃fɔrmasjɔ̃] nf inquiry, preliminary investigation; pl news bulletin.

informe [ɛ̃fɔrm] a shapeless, illformed, misshapen; (jur) irregular.

informer [ɛ̃fɔrme] vt to inform, apprise; vi to inform (against contre); vr to make inquiries.

infortune [ɛ̃fɔrtyn] nf misfortune.

infortuné [ɛ̃fɔrtyne] a unfortunate, unlucky.

infraction [ɛ̃fraksjɔ̃] nf infringement, breach.

infranchissable [ɛ̃frɑ̃ʃisabl] a impassable, insuperable.

infructueux, -euse [ɛ̃fryktɥø, ø:z] a unsuccessful, barren, fruitless.

infuser [ɛ̃fyse] vt to infuse, steep; vr to infuse, brew.

infusion [ɛ̃fyzjɔ̃] nf infusion.

ingambe [ɛ̃gɑ̃b] a active.

s'ingénier [sɛ̃ʒenje] vr to contrive, use all one's wits.

ingénieur [ɛ̃ʒenjœ:r] nm engineer.

ingénieux, -euse [ɛ̃ʒenjø, ø:z] a ingenious, clever.

ingéniosité [ɛ̃ʒenjozite] nf ingenuity, ingeniousness.

ingénu [ɛ̃ʒeny] a ingenuous, simple, artless, unsophisticated.

ingénuité [ɛ̃ʒenɥite] nf ingenuousness, simplicity.

s'ingérer [sɛ̃ʒere] vr to interfere, meddle (with dans).

ingouvernable [ɛ̃guvɛrnabl] a unmanageable, uncontrollable.

ingrat [ɛ̃gra] an ungrateful, thankless, unprofitable, barren.

ingratitude [ɛ̃gratityd] nf ingratitude, thanklessness.

ingrédient [ɛ̃gredjɑ̃] nm ingredient.

inguérissable [ɛ̃gerisabl] a incurable.

ingurgiter [ɛ̃gyrʒite] vt to gulp down, swallow.

inhabile [inabil] a awkward, unskilled, clumsy.

inhabitable [inabitabl] a uninhabitable.

inhabité [inabite] a uninhabited, untenanted, vacant.

inhabituel(le) [inabituɛl] a unusual, unwonted.

inharmonieux, -euse [inarmɔnjø, øːz] a discordant, unmusical.

inhérent [inerɑ̃] a inherent.

inhibition [inibisjɔ̃] nf inhibition.

inhospitalier, -ière [inɔspitalje, jeːr] a inhospitable.

inhumain [inymɛ̃] a inhuman, heartless.

inhumer [inyme] vt to bury, inter.

inimaginable [inimaʒinabl] a unimaginable, unthinkable.

inimitable [inimitabl] a inimitable, peerless.

inimitié [inimitje] nf enmity, ill-will, ill-feeling.

ininflammable [inɛ̃flamabl] a fireproof.

inintelligent [inɛ̃tɛliʒɑ̃] a unintelligent, obtuse.

inintelligible [inɛ̃tɛliʒibl] a unintelligible.

ininterrompu [inɛ̃terɔ̃py] a uninterrupted, unbroken.

iniquité [inikite] nf injustice, wickedness.

initial [inisjal] a initial, starting.

initiale [inisjal] nf initial (letter).

initiateur, -trice [inisjatœːr, tris] n initiator.

initiative [inisjatiːv] nf initiative, push; **syndicat d'—** information bureau.

initier [inisje] vt to initiate.

injecter [ɛ̃ʒekte] vt to inject; vr to become bloodshot.

injection [ɛ̃ʒeksjɔ̃] nf injection.

injonction [ɛ̃ʒɔ̃ksjɔ̃] nf injunction, behest.

injudicieux, -euse [ɛ̃ʒydisjø, øːz] a injudicious.

injure [ɛ̃ʒyːr] nf insult, wrong.

injurier [ɛ̃ʒyrje] vt to insult, call names, abuse.

injurieux, -euse [ɛ̃ʒyrjø, øːz] a insulting, abusive.

injuste [ɛ̃ʒyst] a unfair, unjust.

injustice [ɛ̃ʒystis] nf injustice, unfairness, wrong.

injustifiable [ɛ̃ʒystifjabl] a unjustifiable.

inlassable [ɛ̃lasabl] a untiring, tireless.

innavigable [inavigabl] a unnavigable, unseaworthy.

inné [inne] a innate, inborn.

innocence [inɔsɑ̃ːs] nf innocence, harmlessness.

innocent [inɔsɑ̃] a innocent, simple,

guileless, harmless; n half-wit, idiot.

innocenter [inɔsɑ̃te] vt to clear, declare innocent.

innocuité [innɔkɥite] nf innocuousness, harmlessness.

innombrable [innɔ̃brabl] a countless, innumerable.

innover [innɔve] vi to innovate; vi to break new ground.

inobservation [inɔpsɛrvasjɔ̃] nf disregard, breach.

inobservé [inɔpsɛrve] a unnoticed, unobserved.

inoccupé [inɔkype] a unoccupied, idle, vacant.

inoculer [inɔkyle] vt to inoculate, inject.

inodore [inɔdɔr] a odorless, scentless.

inoffensif, -ive [inɔfɑ̃sif, iːv] a inoffensive, harmless.

inondation [inɔ̃dasjɔ̃] nf flood.

inonder [inɔ̃de] vt to flood, inundate; **être inondé de** to be flooded with, soaked in.

inopiné [inɔpine] a unexpected, unforeseen.

inopportun [inɔpɔrtœ̃] a inopportune, unseasonable, ill-timed.

inopportunité [inɔpɔrtynite] nf inopportuneness, unseasonableness.

inoubliable [inubliabl] a unforgettable.

inouï [inui, -w-] a unheard of, outrageous.

inoxydable [inɔksidabl] a rustproof, stainless; nm stainless steel.

inqualifiable [ɛ̃kalifjabl] a unspeakable.

inquiet, -ète [ɛ̃kje, ɛt] a anxious, uneasy, concerned.

inquiéter [ɛ̃kjete] vt to make anxious, disturb, disquiet, alarm; vr to worry, grow anxious.

inquiétude [ɛ̃kjetyd] nf anxiety, misgivings.

insaisissable [ɛ̃sezisabl] a elusive, imperceptible.

insalissable [ɛ̃salisabl] a dirtproof.

insalubre [ɛ̃salybr] a unhealthy, insanitary.

insanité [ɛ̃sanite] nf insanity; pl (fam) nonsense.

insatiable [ɛ̃sasjabl] a insatiable, unquenchable.

inscription [ɛ̃skripsjɔ̃] nf inscription, writing down, enrollment; **droit d'—** entrance fee, registration fee.

inscrire [ɛ̃skriːr] vt to inscribe, write down, enroll, register; vr to enroll, put down one's name.

insecte [ɛ̃sekt] nm insect.

insécurité [ɛ̃sekyrite] nf insecurity.

insensé [ɛ̃sɑ̃se] a mad, senseless, wild, crazy.

insensibiliser [ɛ̃sɑ̃sibilize] vt to anesthetize.

insensibilité [ɛ̃sɑ̃sibilite] nf insensibility, callousness, lack of feeling.

insensible [ɛ̃sɑ̃sibl] a insensitive, callous, unfeeling, imperceptible.

inséparable [ɛ̃separabl] a inseparable.

insérer [ɛ̃sere] vt to insert.

insidieux, -euse [ɛ̃sidjø, ø:z] a insidious.

insigne [ɛ̃siɲ] a distinguished, signal, notorious; nm badge, emblem; pl insignia.

insignifiance [ɛ̃siɲifjɑ̃:s] nf insignificance.

insignifiant [ɛ̃siɲifjɑ̃] a insignificant, trivial, meaningless.

insinuation [ɛ̃sinɥasjɔ̃] nf insinuation, innuendo, insertion.

insinuer [ɛ̃sinɥe] vt to insinuate, hint at, insert; vr to steal, slip, creep (into dans).

insipide [ɛ̃sipid] a insipid, tasteless, dull, flat.

insistance [ɛ̃sistɑ̃:s] nf insistence, persistence.

insister [ɛ̃siste] vi to insist, persist; — sur stress.

insociable [ɛ̃sɔsjabl] a unsociable.

insolation [ɛ̃sɔlasjɔ̃] nf insolation, sunstroke.

insolence [ɛ̃sɔlɑ̃:s] nf insolence, impertinence.

insolent [ɛ̃sɔlɑ̃] an insolent, impudent, impertinent.

insolite [ɛ̃sɔlit] a unusual, strange.

insoluble [ɛ̃sɔlybl] a insoluble, unsolvable.

insolvabilité [ɛ̃sɔlvabilite] nf insolvency.

insolvable [ɛ̃sɔlvabl] a insolvent.

insomnie [ɛ̃sɔmni] nf insomnia, sleeplessness.

insondable [ɛ̃sɔ̃dabl] a fathomless, bottomless, unfathomable.

insonore [ɛ̃sɔnɔ:r] a soundproof.

insouciance [ɛ̃susjɑ̃:s] nf unconcern, casualness.

insouciant [ɛ̃susjɑ̃] a care-free, heedless.

insoucieux -euse [ɛ̃susjø, ø:z] a heedless, regardless.

insoumis [ɛ̃sumi] a unsubdued, unruly, refractory.

insoumission [ɛ̃sumisjɔ̃] nf insubordination.

insoupçonnable [ɛ̃supsɔnabl] a beyond suspicion.

insoutenable [ɛ̃sutnabl] a untenable, indefensible.

inspecter [ɛ̃spɛkte] vt to inspect, examine.

inspecteur, -trice [ɛ̃spɛktœ:r, tris] n inspector, inspectress, examiner, overseer.

inspection [ɛ̃spɛksjɔ̃] nf inspection, examination, survey.

inspiration [ɛ̃spirasjɔ̃] nf inspiration, breathing in.

inspirer [ɛ̃spire] vt to inspire, breathe in, prompt; vr to find inspiration (in de).

instabilité [ɛ̃stabilite] nf instability,

unsteadiness, uncertainty, fickleness.

instable [ɛ̃stabl] a unstable, unsteady, unreliable.

installation [ɛ̃stalasjɔ̃] nf setting up, fittings, plant.

installer [ɛ̃stale] vt to install, fit up, equip; vr to settle down, move in.

instamment [ɛ̃stamɑ̃] ad earnestly, urgently.

instance [ɛ̃stɑ̃:s] nf solicitation, lawsuit; pl entreaties, requests.

instant [ɛ̃stɑ̃] a urgent, pressing; nm instant, moment; à l'— at once, a moment ago; par —s off and on.

instantané [ɛ̃stɑ̃tane] a instantaneous; nm snapshot.

instar [ɛ̃sta:r] prep à l'— de after the manner of, like.

instigateur, -trice [ɛ̃stigatœ:r, tris] n instigator.

instigation [ɛ̃stigasjɔ̃] nf instigation, incitement.

instinct [ɛ̃stɛ̃] nm instinct.

instinctif, -ive [ɛ̃stɛ̃ktif, i:v] a instinctive.

instituer [ɛ̃stitɥe] vt to institute, set up, appoint.

institut [ɛ̃stity] nm institute, institution.

instituteur, -trice [ɛ̃stitytœ:r, tris] n primary school-teacher, founder.

institution [ɛ̃stitysjɔ̃] nf setting up, institution, establishment.

instructeur [ɛ̃stryktœ:r] nm instructor; sergent — drill sergeant.

instructif, -ive [ɛ̃stryktif, i:v] a instructive.

instruction [ɛ̃stryksjɔ̃] nf education, training, (jur) preliminary investigation; pl directions, orders.

instruire [ɛ̃strɥi:r] vt to instruct, train, (jur) investigate, inform.

instruit [ɛ̃strɥi] a educated, learned, trained.

instrument [ɛ̃strymɑ̃] nm instrument, tool.

instrumentation [ɛ̃strymɑ̃tasjɔ̃] nf instrumentation, orchestration.

instrumenter [ɛ̃strymɑ̃te] vt to score, orchestrate; vi to order proceedings to be taken.

insu [ɛ̃sy] nm à l'— de without the knowledge of; à son — without his knowing.

insubmersible [ɛ̃sybmɛrsibl] a unsinkable.

insubordination [ɛ̃sybɔrdinasjɔ̃] nf insubordination.

insuccès [ɛ̃syksɛ] nm failure.

insuffisance [ɛ̃syfizɑ̃:s] nf insufficiency, shortage, inadequacy, incompetence.

insuffisant [ɛ̃syfizɑ̃] a insufficient, inadequate, incompetent.

insulaire [ɛ̃syle:r] a insular; n islander.

insularité [ɛ̃sylarite] nf insularity.

insulte [ɛ̃sylt] nf insult.

insulter [ɛ̃sylte] vt to insult; vi to be an insult to.

insupportable [ɛsyportabl] *a* unbearable, insufferable, intolerable.

insurgé [ɛsyrʒe] *n* rebel, insurgent.

s'insurger [sɛsyrʒe] *vr* to revolt, rise in revolt.

insurmontable [ɛsyrmɔ̃tabl] *a* insuperable.

insurrection [ɛsyrrɛksjɔ̃] *nf* rebellion, insurrection.

intact [ɛtakt] *a* intact, whole, undamaged.

intangible [ɛtɑ̃ʒibl] *a* intangible, inviolable.

intarissable [ɛtarisabl] *a* inexhaustible, endless.

intégral [ɛtegral] *a* integral, full, complete.

intégrant [ɛtegrɑ̃] *a* integral.

intègre [ɛtegr] *a* upright, honest, just.

intégrer [ɛtegre] *vt* integrate.

intégrité [ɛtegrite] *nf* integrity, honesty, entirety.

intellectuel, -elle [ɛtel(l)ɛktɥel] *a* intellectual, mental; *n* intellectual, highbrow.

intelligence [ɛtel(l)iʒɑ̃:s] *nf* intelligence, intellect, understanding; **vivre en bonne — avec** to live on good terms with; **être d'— avec** to be in league with.

intelligent [ɛtel(l)iʒɑ̃] *a* intelligent, clever.

intelligible [ɛtel(l)iʒibl] *a* audible, understandable.

intempérance [ɛtɑ̃perɑ̃:s] *nf* intemperance, license.

intempérant [ɛtɑ̃perɑ̃] *a* intemperate.

intempérie [ɛtɑ̃peri] *nf* inclemency (of weather).

intempestif, -ive [ɛtɑ̃pestif, i:v] *a* unseasonable, inopportune.

intenable [ɛtnabl] *a* untenable.

intendance [ɛtɑ̃dɑ̃:s] *nf* stewardship, commissariat, Army Service Corps, supply depot, finance office.

intendant [ɛtɑ̃dɑ̃] *nm* steward (of household); bursar; **— général** quartermaster general.

intense [ɛtɑ̃:s] *a* intense, intensive, severe.

intensité [ɛtɑ̃site] *nf* intensity, strength.

intenter [ɛtɑ̃te] *vt* **— un procès to** bring an action.

intention [ɛtɑ̃sjɔ̃] *nf* intention, purpose; **à votre —** for you, meant for you.

intentionné [ɛtɑ̃sjɔne] *a* intentioned, meaning, disposed.

intentionnel, -elle [ɛtɑ̃sjɔnel] *a* intentional.

inter [ɛtɛ:r] *nm* (*telephone*) trunks.

intercaler [ɛtɛrkale] *vt* to insert, add.

intercéder [ɛtɛrsede] *vi* to intercede.

intercepter [ɛtɛrsɛpte] *vt* to intercept, cut off.

interception [ɛtɛrsɛpsjɔ̃] *nf* interception, tackle.

intercession [ɛtɛrsɛsjɔ̃] *nf* intercession.

interchangeable [ɛtɛrʃɑ̃ʒabl] *a* interchangeable.

interdiction [ɛtɛrdiksjɔ̃] *nf* interdiction, prohibition.

interdire [ɛtɛrdi:r] *vt* to prohibit, forbid, ban, suspend, nonplus, take aback.

interdit [ɛtɛrdi] *a* suspended, forbidden, taken aback, nonplused; *nm* interdict; **sens — no entry**.

intéressant [ɛtɛresɑ̃] *a* interesting.

intéressé [ɛtɛrese] *a* interested, concerned, selfish.

intéresser [ɛtɛrese] *vt* to interest, concern; *vr* to be interested, take an interest.

intérêt [ɛtɛrɛ] *nm* interest, advantage, stake; **avoir — à faire** to be to one's interest to do it; **porter — à** to take an interest in.

interférer [ɛtɛrfere] *vi* to interfere.

intérieur [ɛtɛrjœ:r] *a* interior, inward, home, domestic, inland; *nm* inside, interior, home, house, **à l'—** inside.

intérim [ɛterim] *nm* interim.

interjection [ɛtɛrʒɛksjɔ̃] *nf* interjection.

interligne [ɛtɛrliɲ] *nm* space between two lines.

interlocuteur, -trice [ɛtɛrlɔkytœ:r, tris] *n* interlocutor, speaker.

interloquer [ɛtɛrlɔke] *vt* to disconcert, take aback; *vr* to become embarrassed.

intermède [ɛtɛrmɛd] *nm* interlude.

intermédiaire [ɛtɛrmedjɛ:r] *a* intermediate, intervening, middle; *nm* intermediary, agency, agent, gobetween, middleman.

interminable [ɛtɛrminabl] *a* neverending, endless.

intermittent [ɛtɛrmittɑ̃] *a* intermittent, irregular.

internat [ɛtɛrna] *nm* boarding-school.

international, -e, -aux [ɛtɛrnasjonal, o] *a* international; *nf* the International.

interne [ɛtɛrn] *a* internal, interior, inner, inward; *n* boarder, resident doctor, intern.

interner [ɛtɛrne] *vt* to intern, confine.

interpellation [ɛtɛrpel(l)asjɔ̃] *nf* question, interruption, challenge.

interpeller [ɛtɛrpel(l)e] *vt* to call upon s.o. for an explanation, challenge.

interplanétaire [ɛtɛrplanetɛ:r] *a* interplanetary.

interpoler [ɛtɛrpole] *vt* to interpolate.

interposer [ɛtɛrpoze] *vt* to interpose, place between; *vr* to intervene.

interprétation [ɛtɛrpretasjɔ̃] *nf* interpretation, rendering.

interprète [ɛtɛrprɛt] *n* interpreter, player, actor.

interpréter [ɛ̃terprete] vt to interpret, expound, render.

interrogateur, -trice [ɛ̃terɔgatœːr, tris] a inquiring, questioning; n interrogator, examiner.

interrogatif, -ive [ɛ̃terɔgatif, iːv] a interrogative.

interrogation [ɛ̃terɔgasjɔ̃] nf interrogation, question(ing), oral test; point d'— question mark.

interrogatoire [ɛ̃terɔgatwaːr] nm interrogation, cross-examination.

interroger [ɛ̃terɔʒe] vt to interrogate, question.

interrompre [ɛ̃terɔ̃ːpr] vt to interrupt, break (off), stop.

interrupteur [ɛ̃teryptœːr] nm switch, cut-out.

interruption [ɛ̃terypsjɔ̃] nf interruption, breaking off, switching off.

intersection [ɛ̃terseksjɔ̃] nf intersection.

interstice [ɛ̃terstis] nm chink.

interurbain [ɛ̃teryrbɛ̃] a interurban, trunk (call).

intervalle [ɛ̃terval] nm· interval, space, distance, period.

intervenir [ɛ̃tervəniːr] vi to intervene, interfere.

intervention [ɛ̃tervɑ̃sjɔ̃] nf intervention.

interversion [ɛ̃terversjɔ̃] nf inversion.

intervertir [ɛ̃tervertiːr] vt to invert, reverse.

interviewer [ɛ̃tervju(v)e] vt to interview.

intestin [ɛ̃testɛ̃] a internal, civil; nm intestine.

intimation [ɛ̃timasjɔ̃] nf notification, notice.

intime [ɛ̃tim] a intimate, inner, inmost.

intimer [ɛ̃time] vt to notify.

intimider [ɛ̃timide] vt to intimidate, frighten.

intimité [ɛ̃timite] nf intimacy, privacy.

intituler [ɛ̃tityle] vt to entitle.

intolérable [ɛ̃tɔlerabl] a intolerable, unbearable.

intolérance [ɛ̃tɔlerɑ̃ːs] nf intolerance.

intolérant [ɛ̃tɔlerɑ̃] a intolerant.

intonation [ɛ̃tɔnasjɔ̃] nf intonation, pitch.

intoxication [ɛ̃tɔksikasjɔ̃] nf poisoning.

intoxiquer [ɛ̃tɔksike] vt to poison.

intraduisible [ɛ̃tradɥizibl] a untranslatable.

intraitable [ɛ̃tretabl] a unmanageable, uncompromising.

intransigeance [ɛ̃trɑ̃siʒɑ̃ːs] nf strictness, intolerance.

intransigeant [ɛ̃trɑ̃siʒɑ̃] a uncompromising, unbending, adamant.

intransportable [ɛ̃trɑ̃spɔrtabl] a not fit to travel.

intrépide [ɛ̃trepid] a intrepid, fearless, dauntless.

intrépidité [ɛ̃trepidite] nf fearlessness, dauntlessness.

intrigant [ɛ̃trigɑ̃] a intriguing, scheming; n intriguer, schemer.

intrigue [ɛ̃trig] nf intrigue, scheme, plot.

intriguer [ɛ̃trige] vt to intrigue, puzzle; vi to plot, scheme.

intrinsèque [ɛ̃trɛ̃sɛk] a intrinsic.

introduction [ɛ̃trɔdyksjɔ̃] nf introduction, bringing in, admission.

introduire [ɛ̃trɔdɥiːr] vt to introduce, put in, show in; vr to enter, get in.

introniser [ɛ̃trɔnize] vt to enthrone, establish.

introspection [ɛ̃trɔspɛksjɔ̃] nf introspection.

introuvable [ɛ̃truvabl] a not to be found, untraceable.

intrus [ɛ̃try] a intruding; n intruder.

intrusion [ɛ̃tryzjɔ̃] nf intrusion, trespass.

intuition [ɛ̃tɥisjɔ̃] nf intuition.

inusité [inyzite] a unusual.

inutile [inytil] a useless, vain, unavailing, needless.

inutilisable [inytilizabl] a useless, unserviceable.

inutilité [inytilite] nf uselessness.

invalide [ɛ̃valid] a infirm, disabled, invalid; nm disabled soldier.

invalider [ɛ̃valide] vt to invalidate, declare void, (elected member) unseat.

invalidité [ɛ̃validite] nf disablement, disability, invalidity.

invariable [ɛ̃varjabl] a invariable, unchanging.

invasion [ɛ̃vazjɔ̃] nf invasion.

invective [ɛ̃vɛktiːv] nf invective.

invectiver [ɛ̃vɛktive] vt to abuse, call s.o. names; vi to revile (contre).

invendable [ɛ̃vɑ̃dabl] a unsalable.

inventaire [ɛ̃vɑ̃tɛːr] nm inventory; dresser l'— to take stock.

inventer [ɛ̃vɑ̃te] vt to invent, devise, discover, make up.

inventeur [ɛ̃vɑ̃tœːr] nm inventor, discoverer.

invention [ɛ̃vɑ̃sjɔ̃] nf invention, inventiveness, device, made-up story.

inventorier [ɛ̃vɑ̃tɔrje] vt to make a list of, inventory.

inverse [ɛ̃vɛrs] a inverse, inverted, opposite; nm opposite, reverse.

inversion [ɛ̃versjɔ̃] nf inversion, reversal.

invertir [ɛ̃vertiːr] vt to invert, reverse.

investigateur, -trice [ɛ̃vestigatœːr, tris] a investigating, searching; n investigator.

investir [ɛ̃vestiːr] vt to invest, entrust; beleaguer.

investiture [ɛ̃vestityːr] nf nomination, induction.

invétéré [ɛ̃vetere] a inveterate, deep-rooted, hardened, confirmed.

invincible [ɛ̃vɛ̃sibl] a invincible, insuperable.

inviolable [ɛ̃vjɔlabl] *a* inviolable, sacred.
invisibilité [ɛ̃vizibilite] *nf* invisibility.
invisible [ɛ̃vizibl] *a* invisible, never to be seen.
invitation [ɛ̃vitasjɔ̃] *nf* invitation.
invite [ɛ̃vit] *nf* invitation, inducement, (*cards*) lead.
invité [ɛ̃vite] *n* guest.
inviter [ɛ̃vite] *vt* to invite, ask, call for.
involontaire [ɛ̃vɔlɔ̃tɛːr] *a* involuntary, unintentional.
invoquer [ɛ̃vɔke] *vt* to invoke, call upon, bring forward.
invraisemblable [ɛ̃vrɛsɑ̃blabl] *a* unlikely, improbable, extraordinary.
invraisemblance [ɛ̃vrɛsɑ̃blɑ̃ːs] *nf* unlikelihood, improbability.
invulnérable [ɛ̃vylnerabl] *a* invulnerable.
iode [jɔd, iɔd] *nm* iodine.
irascible [irassibl] *a* crusty, quick-tempered.
iris [iris] *nm* iris.
irisé [irize] *a* iridescent, rainbow-colored.
irlandais [irlɑ̃dɛ] *an* Irish, Irishman, Irishwoman.
Irlande [irlɑ̃d] *nf* Ireland.
ironie [irɔni] *nf* irony.
ironique [irɔnik] *a* ironical.
irradier [irradje] *vi* to radiate, spread, irradiate.
irraisonnable [irrɛzɔnabl] *a* irrational.
irrecevable [irrəsəvabl] *a* inadmissible.
irréconciliable [irrekɔ̃siljabl] *a* irreconcilable.
irrécusable [irrekyzabl] *a* irrefutable, unimpeachable.
irréel, -elle [irreɛl] *a* unreal.
irréfléchi [irrefleʃi] *a* unconsidered, thoughtless.
irréflexion [irreflɛksjɔ̃] *nf* thoughtlessness.
irréfutable [irrefytabl] *a* irrefutable, indisputable.
irrégularité [irregylarite] *nf* irregularity, unsteadiness, unpunctuality.
irrégulier, -ière [irregylje, jɛːr] *a* irregular, loose (*life*).
irrémédiable [irremedjabl] *a* irremediable, irreparable.
irremplaçable [irrɑ̃plasabl] *a* irreplaceable.
irréparable [irreparabl] *a* irreparable, irretrievable.
irrépressible [irrepresibl] *a* irrepressible.
irréprochable [irreprɔʃabl] *a* irreproachable, faultless, impeccable.
irrésistible [irrezistibl] *a* irresistible.
irrésolu [irrezɔly] *a* irresolute, unsteady, unsolved.
irrésolution [irrezɔlysjɔ̃] *nf* hesitancy, uncertainty, wavering.

irrespectueux, -euse [irrespɛktɥø, øːz] *a* disrespectful.
irresponsable [irrespɔ̃sabl] *a* irresponsible.
irrévérencieux, -euse [irreverɑ̃sjø, øːz] *a* irreverent, disrespectful.
irrévocable [irrevɔkabl] *a* irrevocable, binding.
irrigation [irrigasjɔ̃] *nf* irrigation.
irriguer [irrige] *vt* to irrigate.
irritable [irritabl] *a* irritable, short-tempered, sensitive, jumpy.
irritation [irritasjɔ̃] *nf* irritation.
irriter [irrite] *vt* to irritate, annoy, rouse, inflame; *vr* to become angry, inflamed.
irruption [irrypsjɔ̃] *nf* irruption, inrush, raid.
islandais [islɑ̃dɛ] *a* Icelandic; *n* Icelander.
Islande [islɑ̃d] *nf* Iceland.
isolateur, -trice [izɔlatœːr, tris] *a* insulating; *nm* insulator.
isolement [izɔlmɑ̃] *nm* isolation, loneliness, insulation.
isolé [izɔle] *a* isolated, lonely, insulated.
isoler [izɔle] *vt* to isolate, insulate.
Israël [israɛl] *nf* Israel.
israélien [israeljɛ̃] *an* Israeli.
issu [isy] *a* sprung (from), descended (from).
issue [isy] *nf* issue, outlet, exit, end, conclusion.
isthme [ism] *nm* isthmus.
Italie [itali] *nf* Italy.
italien, -ienne [italjɛ̃, jɛn] *an* Italian.
italique [italik] *a* italic; *nm* italics.
item [itɛm] *ad* likewise.
itinéraire [itinerɛːr] *nm* itinerary, route.
itinérant [itinerɑ̃] *a* itinerant.
ivoire [ivwaːr] *nm* ivory.
ivraie [ivrɛ] *nf* tares, chaff.
ivre [ivr] *a* drunk, tipsy, intoxicated, wild, mad.
ivresse [ivrɛs] *nf* intoxication, rapture.
ivrogne [ivrɔɲ] *a* drunken; *nm* drunkard, drunken man, sot.
ivrognerie [ivrɔɲri] *nf* drunkenness.

J

jabot [ʒabo] *nm* jabot, ruffle, frill.
jacasser [ʒakase] *vi* · to chatter, jabber.
jachère [ʒaʃɛːr] *nf* untilled land, fallow.
jacinthe [ʒasɛ̃t] *nf* hyacinth.
Jacques [ʒaːk] James.
jacquet [ʒakɛ] *nm* backgammon.
jactance [ʒaktɑ̃ːs] *nf* boasting, brag, boastfulness.
jadis [ʒadis] *ad* once, formerly, in bygone days.
jaillir [ʒajiːr] *vi* to spout, gush (out), spurt, flash.

jaillissement [ʒɑjismɑ̃] nm spouting, gushing.

jais [ʒɛ] nm jet.

jalon [ʒalɔ̃] nm surveyor's staff, rod; landmark.

jalonner [ʒalɔne] vt to stake out, mark out, blaze.

jalouser [ʒaluze] vt to be jealous of, envy.

jalousie [ʒaluzi] nf jealousy, venetian blind, shutter.

jaloux, -ouse [ʒalu, uːz] a jealous, anxious.

jamais [ʒamɛ] ad ever, never; ne . . . jamais never.

jambage [ʒɑ̃baːʒ] nm jamb, leg, downstroke.

jambe [ʒɑ̃ːb] nf leg, strut; prendre ses —s à son cou to take to one's heels; à toutes —s as fast as one can.

jambière [ʒɑ̃bjɛːr] nf elastic stocking; pl leggings, shin-guards, waterproof overtrousers.

jambon [ʒɑ̃bɔ̃] nm ham.

jansénisme [ʒɑ̃senism] nm Jansenism.

jante [ʒɑ̃ːt] nf rim.

janvier [ʒɑ̃vje] nm January.

Japon [ʒapɔ̃] nm Japan.

japonais [ʒapɔnɛ] an Japanese.

jappement [ʒapmɑ̃] nm yelping, yapping.

japper [ʒape] vi to yelp, yap.

jaquette [ʒakɛt] nf (woman's) jacket, morning coat.

jardin [ʒardɛ̃] nm garden; — public public park; — potager kitchen garden; — d'enfants kindergarten.

jardinage [ʒardinaːʒ] nm gardening.

jardiner [ʒardine] vi to garden.

jardinière [ʒardinjɛːr] nf flowerstand, window box, market-gardener's cart, mixed vegetables.

jargon [ʒargɔ̃] nm jargon, gibberish.

jarre [ʒaːr] nf earthenware jar.

jarret [ʒarɛ] nm hough, ham, hock.

jarretelle [ʒartɛl] nf suspender, garter; porte-jarretelles nm suspender belt, garter belt.

jars [ʒaːr] nm gander.

jaser [ʒaze] vi to chatter.

jaseur, -euse [ʒazœːr, øːz] a talkative; n chatterbox.

jasmin [ʒasmɛ̃] nm jasmine.

jaspe [ʒasp] nm jasper.

jasper [ʒaspe] vt to mottle, marble.

jatte [ʒat] nf bowl, basin, pan.

jauge [ʒoːʒ] nf gauge, tonnage, dipstick.

jauger [ʒoʒe] vt to gauge, measure, draw.

jaunâtre [ʒonɑːtr] a yellowish.

jaune [ʒoːn] a nm yellow; (slang) blackleg; — d'œuf yolk (of an egg); rire — to smile wryly.

jaunir [ʒoniːr] vt to make yellow; vi to turn yellow.

jaunisse [ʒonis] nf jaundice.

javel [ʒavɛl] nm eau de — (type of) bleach.

javelle [ʒavɛl] nf bundle, swath.

javelot [ʒavlo] nm javelin.

je [ʒə] pn I.

jésuite [ʒezɥit] nm Jesuit.

jet [ʒɛ] nm throw(ing), cast, jet, spurt, ray, shoot; — d'eau fountain; d'un seul — in one piece, at one attempt.

jetée [ʒəte] nf jetty, pier.

jeter [ʒəte] vt to throw (away), cast, fling, utter; vr to throw oneself, attack, fall (upon sur), flow (into dans).

jeton [ʒətɔ̃] nm counter, token.

jeu [ʒø] nm game, playing, acting, gambling, stake(s), child's play; — de cartes pack of cards; — de mot pun; — de société parlor game; ce n'est pas de — it is not fair (play); prendre du — to work loose; hors — offside.

jeudi [ʒødi] nm Thursday.

jeun [ʒœ̃] ad à — fasting, on an empty stomach.

jeune [ʒœn] a young, youthful, junior.

jeûne [ʒøːn] nm fast(ing).

jeûner [ʒøne] vi to fast.

jeunesse [ʒœnɛs] nf youth, boyhood, girlhood, youthfulness, young people.

joaillerie [ʒwajri] nf jeweler's trade, jewelry.

joaillier, -ière [ʒwaje, jɛːr] n jeweler.

jobard [ʒɔbaːr] nm simpleton, dupe, mug.

joie [ʒwa] nf joy, gladness, mirth, merriment; à cœur — to one's heart's content; feu de — bonfire.

joindre [ʒwɛ̃ːdr] vtr to join, unite, combine, add.

joint [ʒwɛ̃] nm joint, join.

jointoyer [ʒwɛ̃twaje] vt to point.

jointure [ʒwɛ̃tyːr] nf join, joint.

joli [ʒɔli] a pretty, fine, nice; c'est du —! what a mess!

joliment [ʒɔlimɑ̃] ad prettily, nicely, awfully.

jonc [ʒɔ̃] nm rush, reed, cane.

joncher [ʒɔ̃ʃe] vt to strew, litter.

jonction [ʒɔ̃ksjɔ̃] nf junction, joining.

jongler [ʒɔ̃gle] vi to juggle.

jonglerie [ʒɔ̃gləri] nf jugglery, juggling.

jongleur [ʒɔ̃glœːr] nm juggler, tumbler.

jonquille [ʒɔ̃kiːj] nf jonquil, daffodil.

joue [ʒu] nf cheek; mettre en — to aim (at).

jouer [ʒwe] vt to play, stake, back, act, feign, cheat; vi to play, gamble, work, be loose; vr to make fun (of de); faire — to work, set in motion.

jouet [ʒwɛ] nm toy, plaything.

joueur, -euse [ʒwœːr, øːz] a fond of play, fond of gambling; n player, performer, gambler; être beau — to be a (good) sport.

jouffiu [ʒufly] a chubby.

joug [ʒug] nm yoke.

jouir [ʒwiːr] vi (de) to enjoy.

jouissance [ʒwisɑ̃ːs] nf pleasure, enjoyment, possession.

jouisseur, -euse [ʒwisœːr, øːz] n pleasure-seeker, sensualist.

joujou [ʒuʒu] nm toy.

jour [ʒuːr] nm day, daylight, light, opening; **en plein —** in broad daylight; **mettre au —** to bring to light; **sous un autre —** in another light; **de — en —** from day to day.

journal [ʒurnal] nm newspaper, diary; **— de bord** logbook.

journalier, -ière [ʒurnalje, jɛːr] a daily; n day-laborer.

journalisme [ʒurnalism] nm journalism.

journaliste [ʒurnalist] n journalist, reporter.

journée [ʒurne] nf day, day's work, day's pay.

journellement [ʒurnɛlmɑ̃] ad daily, every day.

joute [ʒut] nf joust, tilting.

jouter [ʒute] vi to tilt, joust, fight.

jovial [ʒɔvjal] a jovial, jolly.

jovialité [ʒɔvjalite] nf joviality, jollity.

joyau [ʒwajo] nm jewel.

joyeux, -euse [ʒwajø, øːz] a joyous, joyful, merry.

jubilation [ʒybilasjɔ̃] nf glee.

jubilé [ʒybile] nm jubilee.

jubiler [ʒybile] vi to be gleeful, to gloat.

jucher [ʒyʃe] vti to perch; vr to roost, perch.

juchoir [ʒyʃwaːr] nm perch, roosting-place.

judas [ʒyda] nm traitor, spy-hole.

judiciaire [ʒydisjɛːr] a judicial, legal.

judicieux, -euse [ʒydisjø, øːz] a judicious, sensible.

juge [ʒyːʒ] nm judge, umpire; **— d'instruction** examining magistrate; **— de paix** magistrate.

jugé [ʒyʒe] nm **au —** by guesswork.

jugement [ʒyʒmɑ̃] nm judgment, trial, sentence, opinion, discrimination.

jugeote [ʒyʒɔt] nf common sense, gumption.

juger [ʒyʒe] vt to judge, try, sentence, deem, imagine; vi to form an opinion of, imagine.

jugulaire [ʒygylɛːr] a jugular; nf jugular vein, chin-strap.

juif, -ive [ʒɥif, ʒɥiːv] a Jewish; n Jew, Jewess.

juillet [ʒɥije] nm July.

juin [ʒɥɛ̃] nm June.

juiverie [ʒɥivri] nf Jewry, ghetto.

jujube [ʒyʒyb] nm jujube.

jumeau, -elle [ʒymo, ɛl] an twin.

jumeler [ʒymle] vt to arrange in pairs.

jumelles [ʒymɛl] nf pl opera-glasses, field-glasses, binoculars.

jument [ʒymɑ̃] nf mare.

jungle [ʒɔ̃ːgl] nf jungle.

jupe [ʒyp] nf skirt.

jupe-culotte [ʒypkylɔt] nf divided skirt.

jupon [ʒypɔ̃] nm petticoat, underskirt.

juré [ʒyre] a sworn; nm juryman, juror; pl jury.

jurer [ʒyre] vt to vow, pledge, swear; vi to curse, swear, (colors) clash.

juridiction [ʒyridiksjɔ̃] nf jurisdiction.

juridique [ʒyridik] a juridical, legal, judicial.

juriste [ʒyrist] nm jurist.

juron [ʒyrɔ̃] nm oath, curse, swearword.

jury [ʒyri] nm jury, examining board, selection committee.

jus [ʒy] nm juice, gravy.

jusque [ʒysk(ə)] prep up to, as far as, until, even; **jusqu'ici** so far, until now; **—là** up to that point, until then; **jusqu'à ce que** until.

juste [ʒyst] a just, fair, right, righteous, accurate, tight, scanty; ad just, exactly, accurately, barely; **au —** exactly; **comme de —** as is only right.

justement [ʒystəmɑ̃] ad justly, precisely, just; as a matter of fact.

justesse [ʒystɛs] nf correctness, accuracy, exactness, soundness; **de —** only just, just in time.

justice [ʒystis] nf justice, fairness, law; **se faire —** to take the law into one's own hands, to kill oneself.

justicier [ʒystisje] nm justiciary.

justifiable [ʒystifjabl] a justifiable.

justification [ʒystifikasjɔ̃] nf justification, vindication.

justifier [ʒystifje] vt to justify, warrant, vindicate, clear; vr to justify, vindicate, clear oneself.

jute [ʒyt] nm jute.

juteux, -euse [ʒytø, øːz] a juicy.

juvénile [ʒyvenil] a juvenile, youthful.

juxtaposer [ʒykstapoze] vt to place side by side.

K

kangourou [kɑ̃guru] nm kangaroo.

kapokier [kapɔkje] nm silk cotton tree.

karité [karite] nm shea butter.

képi [kepi] nm peaked cap.

kermesse [kɛrmɛs] nf fair.

kif-kif [kifkif] a inv (fam) likewise.

kilogramme [kilɔgram] nm kilogram.

kilomètre [kilɔmɛtr] nm kilometer.

kilométrique [kilɔmetrik] a kilometric; **borne —** milestone.

kiosque [kjɔsk] nm kiosk, stall, stand, conning-tower.

klaxon [klaksɔ̃] nm auto horn.

klaxonner [klaksɔne] *vi* to sound the horn.

kleptomane [kleptɔman] *an* kleptomaniac.

kolatier [kɔlatje] *nm* kola nut tree.

krach [krak] *nm* (financial) crash, failure.

kyrielle [kirjɛl] *nf* rigmarole, string.

L

l' see le.

la [la] *def art pn f* see le.

la [la] *nm* musical note A.

là [la] *ad* there, then, that; *excl* there now! c'est — la question that is the question; d'ici — in the meantime; oh — ! oh, dear!

là-bas [labɑ] *ad* over there, yonder.

labeur [labœːr] *nm* labor, hard work.

labial [labjal] *a* labial.

laboratoire [labɔratwaːr] *nm* laboratory.

laborieux, -euse [labɔrjø, øːz] *a* laborious, hard-working, arduous, hard, slow.

labour [labuːr] *nm pl* plowed land.

labourable [laburabl] *a* arable.

labourage [laburaːʒ] *nm* plowing, tilling.

labourer [labure] *vt* to till, plow (up), furrow.

laboureur [laburœːr] *nm* plowman.

labyrinthe [labirɛ̃ːt] *nm* labyrinth, maze.

lac [lak] *nm* lake, (Scot) loch.

lacer [lase] *vt* to lace (up); *vr* to lace oneself up.

lacérer [lasere] *vt* to lacerate, slash, tear.

lacet [lasɛ] *nm* lace, noose, snare; en — winding.

lâchage [laʃaːʒ] *nm* releasing, dropping.

lâche [laːʃ] *a* cowardly, loose, lax, slack; *n* coward.

lâchement [laʃmɑ̃] *ad* in a cowardly way.

lâcher [laʃe] *vt* to release, drop, let go, let fly, let loose, let out, set free, divulge, blab out; — pied to give ground, give way; — prise to let go (one's hold); *nm* release.

lâcheté [laʃte] *nf* cowardice, craven, cowardly action.

lacis [lasi] *nm* network.

laconique [lakɔnik] *a* laconic.

lacrymogène [lakrimɔʒɛn] *a* gaz — tear gas.

lacté [lakte] *a* milky, lacteal.

lacune [lakyn] *nf* lacuna, gap, break, blank.

là-dedans [ladədɑ̃] *ad* in there, within, in it, in them.

là-dehors [ladəɔːr] *ad* outside, without.

là-dessous [latsu] *ad* under there,

under that, under it, under them, underneath.

là-dessus [latsy] *ad* on that, on it, on them, thereupon.

ladre [laːdr] *a* mean, stingy; *nm* miser, skinflint.

ladrerie [ladrəri] *nf* meanness, niggardliness.

lagune [lagyn] *nf* lagoon.

là-haut [lao] *ad* up there.

laïciser [laisize] *vt* to secularize.

laid [lɛ] *a* ugly, despicable.

laideron, -onne [lɛdrɔ̃, ɔn] *n* plain person.

laideur [lɛdœːr] *nf* ugliness, meanness.

lainage [lɛnaːʒ] *nm* woolen article, fleece; *pl* woolen goods.

laine [lɛn] *nf* wool; — filée yarn; — peignée worsted.

lainerie [lɛnri] *nf* woolen mill, -trade, wool-shop.

laineux, -euse [lɛnø, øːz] *a* woolly, fleecy.

lainier, -ière [lenje, jɛːr] *a* industrie lainière wool trade; *n* woolen-goods manufacturer.

laïque [laik] *a* lay, secular; *nm* layman.

laisse [lɛs] *nf* leash, lead.

laissé-pour-compte [lɛsepuːrkɔ̃ːt] *nm* returned goods, rejects, unsold stock.

laisser [lɛse] *vt* to leave, let, allow; se — faire to submit; — là quelque-chose to give up doing something; ne pas — de faire not to fail to do, to do nevertheless.

laisser-aller [lɛseale] *nm* untidiness, carelessness, neglect.

laisser-faire [lɛsefɛːr] *nm* non-interference, non-resistance.

laissez-passer [lɛsepase] *nm* pass, permit.

lait [lɛ] *nm* milk; frère, sœur de — foster-brother, sister.

laitage [lɛtaːʒ] *nm* dairy produce, milk foods.

laiterie [lɛtri] *nf* dairy.

laiteux, -euse [lɛtø, øːz] *a* milky.

laitier, -ière [lɛtje, jɛːr] *a* dairy-, milk-; *n* dairyman, milkman, milk-maid, dairymaid; *nm* slag, dross.

laiton [lɛtɔ̃] *nm* brass.

laitue [lɛty] *nf* lettuce.

laïus [lajyːs] *nm* (fam) speech.

lama [lama] *nm* (animal) llama; (priest) lama.

lambeau [lɑ̃bo] *nm* scrap, shred, rag, tatter.

lambin [lɑ̃bɛ̃] *a* (fam) slow, sluggish; *n* slow-coach.

lambris [lɑ̃bri] *nm* wainscoting, paneling, paneled ceiling.

lambrissage [lɑ̃brisaːʒ] *nm* wainscoting, paneling.

lame [lam] *nf* blade, strip, slat, wave; — de fond groundswell.

lamé [lame] *a* spangled.

lamentable [lamɑ̃tabl] *a* pitiful

woeful, lamentable, deplorable.

lamentation [lamᾱtasjɔ] nf lament (ation), wail(ing).

se lamenter [sǝlamᾱte] vr to lament, wail.

laminer [lamine] vt to laminate, roll, calender.

laminoir [laminwa:r] nm rolling-mill, roller, calender.

lampadaire [lᾱpade:r] nm standard lamp, candelabrum.

lampe [lᾱ:p] nf lamp, light, torch, valve.

lamper [lᾱpe] vt to gulp, swig.

lampion [lᾱpjɔ] nm fairy light, Chinese lantern.

lampiste [lᾱpist] n lampman.

lampisterie [lᾱpistǝri] nf lamp-room, lamp works.

lance [lᾱ:s] nf spear, lance, nozzle.

lancé [lᾱse] a under way, flying; un homme — a man who has made his name.

lance-bombes [lᾱsbɔ:b] nm trench mortar, bomb rack.

lance-flammes [lᾱsfla:m] nm flame-thrower.

lancement [lᾱsmᾱ] nm throwing, putting, launching, floating, promoting.

lance-pierres [lᾱspjɛ:r] nm catapult.

lancer [lᾱse] vt to throw, cast, drop (bombs), launch, float, start, set (on, going, on one's feet), put on the market; vr to rush, dash, launch (out), plunge.

lance-torpille [lᾱstɔrpi:j] nm torpedo-tube.

lancette [lᾱsɛt] nf lancet.

lancier [lᾱsje] nm lancer.

lancinant [lᾱsinᾱ] a shooting, throbbing.

lande [lᾱ:d] nf heath, moor.

langage [lᾱga:ʒ] nm language, speech, talk.

lange [lᾱ:ʒ] nf baby's diaper; pl swaddling-clothes.

langoureux, -euse [lᾱgurø, ø:z] a languorous, languid.

langouste [lᾱgust] nf (spiny) lobster.

langue [lᾱ:g] nf tongue, language, speech; — vivante modern language; — verte slang; mauvaise — mischief-maker, slandermonger; donner sa — aux chats to give it up.

languette [lᾱgɛt] nf strip, tongue.

langueur [lᾱgœ:r] nf languor, listlessness.

languir [lᾱgi:r] vi to languish, pine.

languissant [lᾱgisᾱ] a listless, languid, dull.

lanière [lanjɛ:r] nf strip, strap, thong, lash.

lanterne [lᾱtɛrn] nf lantern, lamp, light.

lapalissade [lapalisad] nf truism, obvious remark.

laper [lape] vt to lap (up).

lapidaire [lapide:r] a lapidary, concise; nm lapidary.

lapider [lapide] vt to throw stones at, vilify.

lapin [lapɛ̃] nm rabbit, coney; — de garenne wild rabbit; poser un — to fail to turn up.

laps [laps] nm lapse, space of time.

lapsus [lapsy:s] nm lapse, mistake, slip.

laquais [lakɛ] nm lackey, footman.

laque [lak] nf lake, hair-lacquer; — en écailles shellac; nm lacquer.

laquer [lake] vt to lacquer, japan, enamel.

laquelle rel pn see lequel.

larbin [larbɛ̃] nm flunky.

larcin [larsɛ̃] nm larceny, petty theft.

lard [la:r] nm fat, bacon.

larder [larde] vt to lard, inflict, shower, interlard.

large [larʒ] a broad, wide, ample, liberal, generous; nm space, open sea, breadth; au — out at sea; prendre le — to put to sea, make off; au — de off.

largesse [larʒɛs] nf liberality, generosity, largess(e).

largeur [larʒœ:r] nf breadth, broadness, width.

larguer [large] vt to loose, cast off, unfurl, release.

larme [larm] nf tear, drop.

larmoyant [larmwajᾱ] a tearful, maudlin.

larmoyer [larmwaje] vi to snivel, shed tears, (eyes) water.

larron [larɔ̃] nm thief.

larve [larv] nf larva, grub.

laryngite [larɛ̃ʒit] nf laryngitis.

larynx [larɛ̃:ks] nm larynx.

las, lasse [la, la:s] a tired, weary.

lascif, -ive [lasif, i:v] a lewd.

lasser [lase] vt to tire, weary; vr to grow tired, weary.

lassitude [lasityd] nf weariness.

latent [latᾱ] a latent.

latéral [lateral] a lateral, side-cross-.

latin [latɛ̃] a nm Latin; — de cuisine pig Latin.

latitude [latityd] nf latitude, scope.

latte [lat] nf lath, slat.

lattis [lati] nm lathing, lattice-work.

lauréat [lorea, -at] nm laureate, prize-winner.

laurier [lɔrje] nm laurel, bay.

laurier-rose [lɔrjero:z] nm oleander.

lavabo [lavabo] nm wash-hand basin, lavatory.

lavande [lavᾱ:d] nf lavender.

lavandière [lavᾱdjɛ:r] nf washer-woman.

lave [la:v] nf lava.

lavement [lavmᾱ] nm rectal injection, enema.

laver [lave] vt to wash, bathe; vr to wash (oneself), have a wash; — la tête à qn to give s.o. a good dressing-down.

lavette [lavɛt] nf mop, dish-cloth.

laveur, -euse [lavœːr, øːz] n washer, washerwoman, washer-up.

lavis [lavi] nm washing, wash-tint, wash-drawing.

lavoir [lavwaːr] nm wash-house, washboard.

laxatif, -ive [laksatif, iːv] a nm laxative, aperient.

layette [lɛjɛt] nf layette, outfit of baby linen.

lazzi [lazi, ladzi] nm pl jeers.

le, la, l', les [lə, la, l, lɛ] def art the, a (often untranslated); pn him, her, it, them; neut pn so (often untranslated).

léché [leʃe] a finicking, over-polished.

lécher [leʃe] vt to lick.

lécheur, -euse [leʃœːr, øːz] n toady, parasite.

leçon [ləsɔ̃] nf lesson; — de choses object-lesson; faire la — à qn to lecture, drill s.o.

lecteur, -trice [lɛktœːr, tris] n reader, (foreign) assistant in French university.

lecture [lɛktyːr] nf reading, perusal; salle de — reading room.

ledit, ladite, lesdits, lesdites [lədi, ladit, ledi, ledit] a the aforesaid.

légal [legal] a legal, lawful.

légaliser [legalize] vt to attest, authenticate, legalize.

légalité [legalite] nf legality, lawfulness.

légataire [legateːr] nm legatee, heir.

légation [legasjɔ̃] nf legation.

légendaire [leʒɑ̃deːr] a legendary.

légende [leʒɑ̃ːd] nf legend, inscription, caption, key.

léger, -ère [leʒe, ɛːr] a light, agile, flighty, frivolous, slight, mild, weak; ad à la légère lightly, scantily, without due reflection.

légèreté [leʒɛrte] nf lightness, fickleness, levity, agility, mildness, weakness.

légion [leʒjɔ̃] nf legion.

législateur, -trice [leʒislatœːr, tris] a legislative; n legislator, lawgiver.

législatif, -ive [leʒislatif, iːv] a legislative.

législation [leʒislasjɔ̃] nf legislation, laws.

législature [leʒislatyːr] nf legislature, legislative body.

légitime [leʒitim] a legitimate, lawful, justifiable, sound.

légitimer [leʒitime] vt to legitimate, legitimatize, justify.

legs [lɛ] nm legacy, bequest.

léguer [lege] vt to bequeath, leave, will.

légume [legym] nm vegetable; grosse — bigwig.

lendemain [lɑ̃dmɛ̃] nm next day, day after, morrow; sans — short-lived; du jour au — very quickly, from one day to the next.

lénifiant [lenifjɑ̃] a soothing, relaxing.

lent [lɑ̃] a slow, lingering.

lenteur [lɑ̃tœːr] nf slowness, dilatoriness.

lentille [lɑ̃tiːj] nf lentil, lens.

léopard [leopaːr] nm leopard.

lèpre [lɛpr] nf leprosy.

lépreux, -euse [leprø, øːz] a leprous; n leper.

lequel, laquelle, lesquels, lesquelles [ləkɛl, lakɛl, lekɛl] rel pn who, whom, which; inter pn which (one).

léser [leze] vt to injure, wrong.

lésiner [lezine] vi to be mean, close-fisted, haggle (over).

lésion [lezjɔ̃] nf lesion, injury, wrong.

lessive [lɛsiːv] nf wash(ing).

lessiver [lɛsive] vt to wash, scrub.

lessiveuse [lɛsivøːz] nf clothes boiler, washing machine.

lest [lɛst] nm ballast.

leste [lɛst] a light, nimble, smart, flippant, free, spicy (humor).

léthargie [letarʒi] nf lethargy.

léthargique [letarʒik] a lethargic, dull.

lettre [lɛtr] nf letter, note; pl literature, letters; — de change bill of exchange; — de voiture consignment note; au pied de la — literally; écrire quelque chose en toutes —s to write something out in full.

lettré [lɛtre] a lettered, literate, well-read; nm scholar.

leu [lø] nm à la queue — — in single file.

leur [lœ(ː)r] pos a their; pos pn le, la —, les —s theirs; nm their own; pl their own people; pn dat (to) them.

leurre [lœːr] nm lure, decoy, bait, allurement, catch.

leurrer [lœre] vt to lure, decoy, allure, entice; vr to be taken in.

levain [ləvɛ̃] nm leaven, yeast.

levant [ləvɑ̃] a rising (sun); nm East, Orient.

levé [ləve] a raised, up, out of bed; voter à main —e vote by show of hands; nm survey.

levée [ləve] nf lifting, adjourning, collection, levy, embankment, (cards) trick.

lever [ləve] vt to raise, lift (up), collect, levy, remove, cut off, (camp) strike, adjourn, (anchor) weigh, (survey) effect; vi to shoot, rise; vr to stand up, get up, rise, (day) dawn; nm rising, levee, survey; — de rideau curtain-raiser; — du soleil sunrise.

levier [ləvje] nm lever, crowbar; — de commande control lever.

lèvre [lɛvr] nf lip, rim; du bout des —e forced, disdainful.

lévrier [levrie] nm greyhound.

levure [ləvyːr] nf yeast.

lexicographe [lɛksikɔgraf] nm lexicographer.

lexique [lɛksik] nm lexicon, glossary.

lézard [lezaːr] nm lizard; **faire le —** to bask in the sun.

lézarde [lezard] nf crevice, crack, chink.

lézarder [lezarde] vt to crack, split; vir to lounge, sun oneself.

liaison [ljɛzɔ̃] nf joining, binding, connection, linking, liaison, slur, (mus) tie.

liant [ljɑ̃] a friendly, engaging, responsive, flexible, pliant; nm friendly disposition, flexibility.

liasse [ljas] nf bundle, wad.

libation [libasjɔ̃] nf libation, drinking.

libelle [libɛl] nm lampoon, libel.

libeller [libɛlle] vt to draw up.

libellule [libɛllyl] nf dragonfly.

libéral [liberal] an liberal, broad, generous.

libéralité [liberalite] nf liberality, generosity.

libérateur, -trice [liberatœːr, tris] a liberating; n liberator.

libération [liberasjɔ̃] nf liberation, release, discharge.

libérer [libere] vt to liberate, release, free, discharge.

liberté [libɛrte] nf liberty, freedom.

libertin [libɛrtɛ̃] a licentious, dissolute, wayward; n libertine, rake, free-thinker.

libertinage [libɛrtinaːʒ] nm dissolute ways.

libraire [librɛːr] nm bookseller.

librairie [librɛri] nf book-trade, bookshop.

libre [libr] a free, clear, open, disengaged, unoccupied, vacant, for hire.

libre-échange [libreʃɑ̃ːʒ] nm free-trade.

libre-service [librəsɛrvis] nm self-service.

licence [lisɑ̃ːs] nf license, excessive liberty, permission, certificate, bachelor's degree.

licencié [lisɑ̃sje] nm licentiate, licensee, license-holder; **— ès lettres** (approx) B.A.; **— en droit** (approx) L.L.B.; **— ès sciences** (approx) B.Sc.

licencier [lisɑ̃sje] vt to disband, sack, dismiss.

licencieux, -euse [lisɑ̃sjø, øːz] a licentious.

licite [lisit] a licit, lawful.

licorne [likɔrn] nf unicorn.

licou [liku] nm halter.

lie [li] nf lees, dregs.

lié [lje] a bound, tied, friendly, intimate.

liebig [libig] nm beef extract.

liège [ljɛːʒ] nm cork.

lien [ljɛ̃] nm bond, tie.

lier [lje] vt to bind, tie (up), link, join, (sauce) thicken; **— amitié avec qn** to strike up an acquaintance with s.o.; **vr to become friendly, intimate (with avec).**

lierre [ljɛːr] nm ivy.

lieu [ljø] nm place, spot, scene; pl premises; **en premier, dernier —** firstly, lastly; **avoir —** to take place, have every reason (to); **donner —** to give rise (to à); **tenir —** to take the place (of de); **au —** de instead of.

lieue [ljø] nf league.

lieuse [ljøːz] nf (mechanical) binder.

lieutenant [ljøtnɑ̃] nm lieutenant, mate; **— de vaisseau** lieutenant-commander.

lièvre [ljɛːvr] nm hare; **mémoire de — memory like a sieve.**

liftier, -ière [liftje, jɛːr] n elevator man, boy, girl, operator.

ligaturer [ligatyre] vt to tie up, bind, ligature.

ligne [liɲ] nf line, cord, row; **hors —** outstanding, out of the common; **à la —** new paragraph.

lignée [liɲe] nf issue, stock, descendants.

lignite [liɲit] nf lignite.

ligoter [ligote] vt to bind, tie up.

ligue [lig] nf league.

liguer [lige] vt to league; vr to form a league.

lilas [lila] a nm lilac.

limace [limas] nf slug.

limaçon [limasɔ̃] nm snail; **en —** spiral.

limande [limɑ̃ːd] nf dab.

lime [lim] nf file.

limer [lime] vt to file (up, off, down), (verses) polish.

limier [limje] nm bloodhound.

limitation [limitasjɔ̃] nf restriction.

limite [limit] nf limit, boundary; pl bounds; a maximum.

limiter [limite] vt to limit, mark the bounds of.

limitrophe [limitrɔf] a adjacent, bordering.

limoger [limɔʒe] vt to relegate.

limon [limɔ̃] nm mud, silt, lime.

limonade [limɔnad] nf lemonade.

limoneux, -euse [limɔnø, øːz] a muddy.

limpide [lɛ̃pid] a limpid.

limpidité [lɛ̃pidite] nm limpidity, clarity.

lin [lɛ̃] nm flax, linseed, linen.

linceul [lɛ̃sœl] nm shroud.

linéaire [lineɛːr] a linear.

linéal [lineal] a lineal.

linéament [lineamɑ̃] nm lineament, feature.

linge [lɛ̃ːʒ] nm linen.

lingère [lɛ̃ʒɛːr] nf seamstress.

lingerie [lɛ̃ʒri] nf underwear, linen-room.

linguiste [lɛ̃ɡɥist] n linguist.

linguistique [lɛ̃ɡɥistik] a linguistic; nf linguistics.

linoléum [linɔleɔm] nm linoleum.

linon [linɔ̃] nm lawn, buckram.

linotte [linɔt] nf linnet; **tête de —** feather-brained person.

linteau [lɛ̃to] nm lintel.

lion. -onne [ljɔ̃, ɔn] n lion, lioness.

lionceau [ljɔ̃so] nm lion cub.
lippu [lipy] a thick-lipped.
liquéfier [likefje] vt to liquefy.
liqueur [likœːr] nm liquor, drink, liqueur, liquid.
liquidation [likidasjɔ̃] nf liquidation, settlement, clearing, selling off.
liquide [likid] a liquid, ready; nm liquid.
liquider [likide] vt to liquidate, settle, sell off, finish off.
liquoreux, -euse [likɔrø, øːz] a liqueur-like, sweet.
lire [liːr] vt to read.
lis [lis] nm lily.
liséré [lizere] nm border, edge, piping, binding.
liséer [lizere] vt to border, edge, pipe.
liseron [lizrɔ̃] nm bindweed.
liseur, -euse [lizœːr, øːz] a reading; n reader.
liseuse [lizøːz] nf dust-jacket, bookmarker, bed-jacket.
lisibilité [lizibilite] nf legibility.
lisible [lizibl] a legible.
lisière [lizjɛːr] nf edge, border, selvage, list, leading-strings.
lisse [lis] a smooth, polished.
lisser [lise] vt to smooth, polish, preen.
liste [list] nf list, roster, register.
lit [li] nm bed, layer, bottom; — de sangle camp-bed; — enfant du second — child of the second marriage.
litanie [litani] nf litany, rigmarole.
lit-armoire [liarmwaːr] nm box-bed.
literie [litri] nf bedding.
lithographie [litɔɡrafi] nf lithograph(y).
litière [litjɛːr] nf litter.
litige [litiːʒ] nm litigation, lawsuit; en — under dispute.
litigieux, -euse [litiʒjø, øːz] a litigious.
litre [litr] nm liter.
littéraire [literɛːr] a literary.
littéral [literal] a literal, written.
littérateur [literatœːr] nm man of letters.
littérature [literatyːr] nf literature.
littoral [litɔral] a littoral, coastal; nm seaboard.
liturgie [lityrʒi] nf liturgy.
liturgique [lityrʒik] a liturgical.
livide [livid] a livid, ghastly.
livraison [livrɛzɔ̃] nf delivery, part, installment; à — on delivery.
livre [liːvr] nf pound; nm book; — de poche paperback.
livrée [livre] nf livery.
livrer [livre] vt to deliver, surrender, give up, hand over; — bataille to give, join battle; vr to give oneself up, confide (in à), indulge (in), take (to).
livresque [livrɛsk] a book, bookish.
livret [livre] nm small book, booklet, handbook, libretto.

livreur, -euse [livrœːr, øːz] n delivery-man, -boy, -girl.
lobe [lɔb] nm lobe, flap.
local [lɔkal] a local; nm premises, building, quarters.
localiser [lɔkalize] vt to localize, locate.
localité [lɔkalite] nf locality, place, spot.
locataire [lɔkatɛːr] n tenant, lessee, lodger.
location [lɔkasjɔ̃] nf hiring, letting, renting, booking; en — on hire; agent de — renting agent.
locomotive [lɔkɔmɔtiv] nf locomotive, engine.
locomotion [lɔkɔmosjɔ̃] nf locomotion.
locution [lɔkysjɔ̃] nf expression, phrase.
lof [lɔf] nm (naut) windward side.
logarithme [lɔɡaritm] nm logarithm.
loge [lɔːʒ] nf lodge, box, dressing-room.
logement [lɔʒmɑ̃] nm lodging(s), accommodation, billet(ing), housing.
loger [lɔʒe] vi to lodge, live, be billeted; vt to lodge, house, billet, stable, put, place; vr to lodge, find a home, a place.
logeur, -euse [lɔʒœːr, øz] n land-lord -lady.
logique [lɔʒik] a logical, reasoned; nf logic.
logis [lɔʒi] nm dwelling, home, lodgings, accommodations.
loi [lwa] nf law, act, rule; projet de — bill.
loin [lwɛ̃] ad far, a long way off; au — in the distance, far and wide; de — from a distance; de — en — at long intervals, now and then.
lointain [lwɛ̃tɛ̃] a distant, far-off; nm distance.
loir [lwaːr] nm dormouse.
loisible [lwazibl] a permissible, convenient.
loisir [lwaziːr] nm leisure, spare time.
londonien, -enne [lɔ̃dɔnjɛ̃, jɛn] n Londoner.
Londres [lɔ̃dr] nm London.
long [lɔ̃] a long, lengthy, slow; nm length; à la longue in the long run; de — en large up and down, to and fro; le — de along(side); tout le — du jour the whole day long; en dire — to speak volumes; en savoir — to know a lot.
longe [lɔ̃ːʒ] nf halter.
longer [lɔ̃ʒe] vt to skirt, hug, run alongside.
longeron [lɔ̃ʒrɔ̃] nm girder, beam, tail-boom, spar.
longévité [lɔ̃ʒevite] nf longevity, expectation of life.
longitude [lɔ̃ʒityd] nf longitude.
longtemps [lɔ̃tɑ̃] ad long, a long time.
longuement [lɔ̃ɡmɑ̃] ad for a long time, at length.

longueur [l5gœːr] nf length; pl tedious passages; **tirer en —** to drag on, spin out.

longue-vue [l5gvy] nf telescope, field-glass.

looping [lupiŋ] nm **faire du —** to loop the loop.

lopin [lɔpɛ̃] nm plot, allotment.

loquace [lɔkwas] a loquacious, talkative.

loquacité [lɔkwasite] nf loquacity, talkativeness.

loque [lɔk] nf rag.

loquet [lɔkɛ] nm latch.

loqueteux, -euse [lɔktø, øːz] a tattered, ragged.

lorgnade [lɔrɲad] nf sidelong glance.

lorgner [lɔrɲe] vt to cast a (sidelong) glance at, have a covetous eye on, make eyes at, ogle.

lorgnette [lɔrɲɛt] nf opera-glasses.

lorgnon [lɔrɲ5] nm eyeglasses, pince-nez.

loriot [lɔrjo] nm oriole.

lors [lɔːr] ad depuis, dès — from that time, ever since then; — **même que** even when; — **de** at the time of.

lorsque [lɔrsk(ə)] cj when.

losange [lɔzɑ̃ːʒ] nm lozenge; **en —** diamond-shaped.

lot [lo] nm share, portion, lot, prize; **gros —** first prize.

loterie [lɔtri] nf lottery, raffle, draw.

lotion [losj5] nf lotion.

lotir [lɔtiːr] vt to divide into lots, sort out, allot.

lotissement [lɔtismɑ̃] nm dividing into lots, selling in lots, building site, housing estate.

lotte [lɔt] nf burbot.

louable [lwabl, lu-] a praiseworthy, commendable.

louage [lwaːʒ, lu-] nm hire, hiring, letting out.

louange [lwɑ̃ːʒ] nf praise.

louche [luʃ] a ambiguous, suspicious, queer; nf ladle.

loucher [luʃe] vi to squint, (fam) to look enviously (at sur).

louer [lwe, lue] vt to hire (out), let (out), rent, reserve, praise, commend; vr to engage, hire oneself, be pleased, satisfied (with), congratulate oneself (upon **de**).

loueur, -euse [lwœːr, lu-, øːz] n hirer, renter.

loufoque [lufɔk] a cracked, crazy.

loulou [lulu] nm Pomeranian dog.

loup [lu] nm wolf, black velvet mask, flaw, error; **à pas de —** stealthily; **avoir une faim de —** to be ravenously hungry; **un froid de —** bitter cold; **quand on parle du —, on en voit la queue** talk of the devil and he's sure to appear; **— de mer** old salt, sea dog.

loup-cervier [lusɛrvje] nm lynx.

loupe [lup] nf lens, magnifying glass, wen.

louper [lupe] vt to bungle, make a mess of.

loup-garou [lugaru] nm werewolf.

lourd [luːr] a heavy, ponderous, ungainly, dull(witted), close, sultry.

lourdaud [lurdo] a loutish, clumsy, dullwitted; n lout, blockhead.

lourdeur [lurdœːr] nf heaviness, ponderousness, ungainliness, dullness, sultriness.

loustic [lustik] nm joker, wag.

loutre [lutr] nf otter.

louve [luːv] nf she-wolf.

louveteau [luvto] nm wolf-cub.

louvoyer [luvwaje] vi to tack, maneuver.

loyal [lwajal] a loyal, true, upright, fair.

loyauté [lwajote] nf loyalty, fidelity, uprightness, honesty, fairness.

loyer [lwaje] nm rent.

lubie [lybi] nf whim, fad.

lubricité [lybrisite] nf lewdness.

lubrifiant [lybrifjɑ̃] a lubricating; nm lubricant.

lubrique [lybrik] a lewd.

lucarne [lykarn] nf attic window, skylight.

lucide [lysid] a lucid, clear.

lucidité [lysidite] nf lucidity, clearness.

luciole [lysjɔl] nf fire-fly.

lucratif, -ive [lykratif, iːv] a lucrative, profitable.

luette [lɥɛt] nf uvula.

lueur [lɥœːr] nf gleam, glimmer, light.

luge [lyːʒ] nf toboggan.

lugubre [lygyːbr] a lugubrious, gloomy, dismal.

lui [lɥi] pers pn dat (to) him, her, it, from him, her, it; disj pn he, him; **—même** himself.

luire [lɥiːr] vi to shine, gleam.

luisant [lɥizɑ̃] a shining, gleaming; nm gloss, sheen.

lumière [lymjɛːr] nf light; pl understanding, knowledge, enlightenment.

lumignon [lymiɲ5] nm candle-end, dim light.

lumineux, -euse [lyminø, øːz] a luminous, bright.

luminosité [lyminozite] nf luminosity.

lunaire [lynɛːr] a lunar.

lunatique [lynatik] a whimsical, capricious, moody.

lundi [lœ̃di] nm Monday.

lune [lyn] nf moon; **clair de —** moonlight; **être dans la —** to be wool-gathering; **— de miel** honeymoon.

lunetier [lyntje] nm spectacle-maker, optician.

lunette [lynɛt] nf telescope, wishbone, (toilet) seat; pl spectacles, goggles; **— de soleil** sunglasses.

lupin [lypɛ̃] nm lupin.

lurette [lyrɛt] nf **il y a belle — que** a long time ago.

luron, -onne [lyrɔ̃, ɔn] n strapping lad (lass), lively fellow, tomboy.

lustre [lystr] nm polish, gloss, chandelier, period of five years.

lustrer [lystre] vt to polish (up), gloss, glaze.

lustrine [lystrin] nf cotton luster.

luth [lyt] nm lute.

luthier [lytje] nm violin-maker.

lutin [lytɛ̃] a mischievous; nm sprite, imp.

lutiner [lytine] vt to tease, torment.

lutrin [lytrɛ̃] nm lectern.

lutte [lyt] nf struggle, contest, strife, wrestling; **de haute — by force** (of arms), hard-won.

lutter [lyte] vi to struggle, compete, fight, wrestle.

luxe [lyks] nm luxury, profusion, superfluity; **de — first-class, luxury.

luxer [lykse] vt to dislocate, put out of joint.

luxueux, -euse [lyksɥø, ø:z] a luxurious, sumptuous.

luxure [lyksy:r] nf lewdness.

luxurieux, -euse [lyksyrjø, ø:z] a lewd, lustful.

luzerne [lyzɛrn] nf lucerne, alfalfa.

lycée [lise] nm secondary school.

lycéen, -enne [liseɛ̃, ɛn] n pupil, schoolboy, -girl.

lymphatique [lɛ̃fatik] a lymphatic.

lyncher [lɛ̃ʃe] vt to lynch.

lynx [lɛ̃ks] nm lynx.

lyre [li:r] nf lyre.

lyrique [lirik] a lyric(al); nm lyric poet.

lyrisme [lirism] nm lyricism, enthusiasm.

lys [lis] nm lily.

M

ma [ma] af see mon.

maboul [mabul] a crazy, cracked, mad.

macabre [maka:br] a grim, gruesome; **danse — Dance of Death.

macadamiser [makadamize] vt to macadamize.

macaron [makarɔ̃] nm macaroon, rosette.

macaroni [makarɔni] nm macaroni.

macédoine [masedwan] nf salad, hodgepodge.

macérer [masere] vt to macerate, steep, mortify.

mâchefer [maʃfɛ:r] nm clinker, slag, dross.

mâché [maʃe] a chewed, worn, ragged, frayed.

mâcher [maʃe] vt to chew, munch, champ; **ne pas — ses mots** not to mince one's words.

machiavélique [makjavelik] a Machiavellian.

mâchicoulis [maʃikuli] nm machicolation.

machin [maʃɛ̃] nm thing, contraption, thingummy.

machinal [maʃinal] a mechanical.

machinateur, -trice [maʃinatœ:r, tris] n machinator, schemer, intriguer.

machination [maʃinasjɔ̃] nf machination, plot.

machine [maʃin] nf machine, engine, contraption; pl machinery; — **à écrire** typewriter; **fait à la — machine made.

machiner [maʃine] vt to plot, scheme.

machinerie [maʃinri] nf machine construction, machinery, plant, engine-room.

machinisme [maʃinism] nm mechanism, (use of) machinery.

machiniste [maʃinist] nm stage-hand.

mâchoire [maʃwa:r] nf jaw, jaw-bone.

mâchonner [maʃɔne] vt to chew, munch, mumble.

maçon [masɔ̃] nm mason, brick-layer.

maçonner [masɔne] vt to build, face with stone, brick up.

maçonnerie [masɔnri] nf masonry, stonework.

maçonnique [masɔnik] a masonic.

macule [makyl] nf stain, blemish, spot.

maculer [makyle] vti to stain, spot, blur.

madame [madam] nf Mrs, madam.

madeleine [madlɛn] nf sponge-cake.

mademoiselle [madmwazɛl] nf Miss.

madone [madɔn] nf Madonna.

madré [madre] a wily, mottled; n wily bird.

madrier [madrie] nm beam, joist, thick plank.

madrigal [madrigal] nm madrigal.

madrilène [madrilɛn] a of Madrid.

magasin [magazɛ̃] nm shop, store, warehouse, (mil) magazine.

magasinage [magazina:ʒ] nm storing, warehouse dues.

magasinier [magazinje] nm warehouseman, storekeeper.

magazine [magazin] nm magazine.

mage [ma:ʒ] nm seer; pl wise men.

magicien, -ienne [maʒisjɛ̃, ɛn] n magician, wizard.

magie [maʒi] nf magic, wizardry.

magique [maʒik] a magic(al).

magistral [maʒistral] a magisterial, masterly.

magistrat [maʒistra] nm magistrate, judge.

magistrature [maʒistraty:r] nf magistracy.

magnanerie [mananri] nf rearing-house for silkworms, sericulture.

magnanime [mananim] a magnanimous, great-hearted.

magnanimité [maɲanimite] *nf* magnanimity.

magnésie [maɲezi] *nf* magnesia.

magnétique [maɲetik] *a* magnetic.

magnétiser [maɲetize] *vt* to magnetize, hypnotize, mesmerize.

magnétisme [maɲetism] *nm* magnetism, hypnotism, mesmerism.

magnéto [maɲeto] *nm* magneto.

magnétophone [maɲetɔfɔn] *nm* tape-recorder.

magnificence [maɲifisɑ̃:s] *nf* magnificence, splendor, liberality, munificence.

magnifier [maɲifje] *vt* to glorify, exalt.

magnifique [maɲifik] *a* magnificent, sumptuous, grand.

magot [mago] *nm* small ape, grotesque porcelain figure, ugly man, (*money*) hoard.

mahométan [maɔmetɑ̃] *a* Mohammedan, Moslem.

mai [mɛ] *nm* May.

maigre [mɛːgr] *a* thin, lean, scanty, frugal, meager, poor; *nm* lean (*of meat*); **faire** — to fast; **jour** — fast-day; **repas** — meatless meal.

maigreur [mɛgrœːr] *nf* leanness, thinness, scantiness.

maigrir [mɛgriːr] *vt* to make thin (ner), thin down; *vi* to grow thin, lose weight.

mail [maːj] *nm* avenue, public walk, mall.

maille [maːj] *nf* mesh, link, stitch, speckle; **cotte de** —**s** coat of mail.

maillet [maje] *nm* mallet.

maillon [majɔ̃] *nm* link, shackle; — **tournant** swivel.

maillot [majo] *nm* swaddling-clothes, jersey, singlet, tights; — **de bain** bathing suit.

main [mɛ̃] *nf* hand, handwriting, (*cards*) hand, quire; — **courante** handrail; **coup de** — surprise attack, helping hand; **sous la** — to, at hand; **à pleines** —**s** liberally, in handfuls; **fait à la** — handmade; **se faire la** — to get one's hand in; **avoir perdu la** — to be out of practice; **gagner haut la** — to win hands down; **ne pas y aller de** — **morte** to go at it; **avoir la** — **dure** to be a martinet; **en venir aux** —**s** to come to blows; **mettre la dernière** — **à** to put the finishing touch to.

main d'œuvre [mɛ̃dœːvr] *nf* manpower, labor.

main-forte [mɛ̃fɔrt] *nf* help, assistance.

mainmise [mɛ̃miːz] *nf* seizure.

mainmorte [mɛ̃mɔrt] *nf* mortmain.

maint [mɛ̃] *a* many a; **à** —**es reprises** many a time.

maintenant [mɛ̃tnɑ̃] *ad* now; **dès** — from now on, even now.

maintenir [mɛ̃tniːr] *vt* to support, hold up, maintain, uphold; *vr* to keep, continue, hold one's own.

maintien [mɛ̃tjɛ̃] *nm* maintenance, keeping, demeanor, bearing.

maire [mɛːr] *nm* mayor.

mairie [meri] *nf* town hall, municipal buildings.

mais [mɛ] *but*; *excl* **why!** *ad* more; **je n'en peux** — I can't help it.

maïs [mais] *nm* maize, Indian corn.

maison [mɛzɔ̃] *nf* house, household, family, dynasty, firm; — **de santé** nursing-home; — **de fous** lunatic asylum; — **de correction** reformatory; **garder la** — to stay indoors, at home.

maisonnée [mɛzɔne] *nf* household, family.

maisonnette [mɛzɔnɛt] *nf* cottage, small house.

maître, -esse [mɛːtr, mɛtrɛs] *a* principal, main, chief, out and out, utter; *n* master, mistress; — **de conférences** lecturer; — **d'équipage** boatswain; **premier** — chief petty officer; — **d'hôtel** butler, head-waiter, chief steward; **maîtresse femme** capable woman.

maître-autel [mɛtrotɛl] *nm* high altar.

maîtrise [mɛtriːz] *nf* command, mastery, control, self-control; choir-school.

maîtriser [mɛtrize] *vt* to master, curb, subdue; *vr* to keep control of oneself.

majesté [maʒɛste] *nf* majesty, grandeur.

majestueux, -euse [maʒɛstɥø, øːz] *a* majestic, stately.

majeur [maʒœːr] *a* major, greater, chief, important, of age; **force** —**e** absolute necessity, compulsion.

major [maʒɔːr] *nm* regimental adjutant, medical officer.

majoration [maʒɔrasjɔ̃] *nf* overvaluation, increase, additional charge.

majordome [maʒɔrdɔm] *nm* major-domo, steward.

majorer [maʒɔre] *vt* to overvalue, raise, put up the price of, make an additional charge.

majorité [maʒɔrite] *nf* majority, coming of age.

majuscule [maʒyskyl] *a nf* capital (letter).

mal [mal] *nm* evil, wrong, harm, hurt, ache, malady, difficulty, trouble; *ad* badly, ill; — **lui en a pris** he had cause to rue it; **prendre en** — to take amiss; **avoir** — **au cœur** to feel sick; **avoir** — **à la tête** to have a headache; **se trouver** — to feel faint; **avoir le** — **du pays** to be homesick; **se donner du** — **pour** to take pains to; **tant bien que** — somehow or other; **pas** — **de** a good lot of, a good many; **elle n'est pas** — she is not bad looking; **on est très** — **ici** we are very uncomfortable here.

malade [malad] *a* ill, sick, upset, sore, painful; *n* invalid, sick person, patient; **se faire porter —** to report sick.

maladie [maladi] *nf* illness, complaint, ailment, disease, disorder.

maladif, -ive [maladif, i:v] *a* sickly, unhealthy.

maladresse [maladrɛs] *nf* awkwardness, clumsiness, lack of skill, slip, blunder.

maladroit [maladrwa] *a* clumsy, unskilful; *n* blunderer.

malaise [malɛ:z] *nm* discomfort, faintness, indisposition, uneasiness.

malappris [malapri] *a* uncouth; *n* ill-bred person.

malavisé [malavize] *a* indiscreet, unwise, rash.

malchance [malʃɑ̃:s] *nf* (piece of) bad luck.

malchanceux, -euse [malʃɑ̃sø, ø:z] *a* unlucky, unfortunate.

maldonne [maldɔn] *nf* misdeal.

mâle [mɑ:l] *a* male, manly, he-, dog-, cock-, buck-; *nm* male.

malédiction [malediksjɔ̃] *nf* curse.

maléfice [malefis] *nm* evil spell.

maléfique [malefik] *a* evil, baleful, maleficent.

malencontreux, -euse [malɑ̃kɔ̃trø, ø:z] *a* untoward, unlucky, tiresome.

malentendu [malɑ̃tɑ̃dy] *nm* misunderstanding.

malfaçon [malfasɔ̃] *nf* bad workmanship.

malfaisant [malfəzɑ̃] *a* evil, harmful.

malfaiteur, -trice [malfɛtœ:r, tris] *n* malefactor, evil-doer.

malfamé [malfame] *a* of ill repute.

malgache [malgaʃ] *an* Madagascan.

malgré [malgre] *prep* in spite of, notwithstanding; *cj* **— que** in spite of, although.

malhabile [malabil] *a* awkward, clumsy.

malheur [malœ:r] *nm* misfortune, ill luck; **jouer de —** to be out of luck.

malheureux, -euse [malœrø, ø:z] *a* unhappy, wretched, unfortunate, unlucky.

malhonnête [malɔnɛt] *a* dishonest, rude, improper.

malhonnêteté [malɔnɛtte] *nf* dishonesty, dishonest action, rudeness, rude remark.

malice [malis] *nf* malice, spitefulness, mischievousness, roguishness, trick; **n'y pas entendre —** to mean no harm.

malicieux, -euse [malisjø, ø:z] *a* mischievous, naughty.

malignité [maliɲite] *nf* spite, malignancy.

malin, -igne [malɛ̃, iɲ] *a* malicious, mischievous, sly, shrewd, malignant; **ce n'est pas —** that's easy enough.

malingre [malɛ̃:gr] *a* sickly, weakly, puny.

malintentionné [malɛ̃tɑ̃sjɔne] *a* ill-disposed, evil-minded.

malle [mal] *nf* trunk, box; **faire sa —** to pack one's trunk.

malléable [maleabl] *a* malleable, pliable, soft.

malle-poste [malpɔst] *nf* mail car.

mallette [malɛt] *nf* small trunk.

malmener [malməne] *vt* to ill-treat, ill-use, treat roughly, put through it.

malodorant [malɔdɔrɑ̃] *a* evil-smelling.

malotru [malɔtry] *a* ill-bred, coarse; *nm* boor, lout.

malpeigné [malpeɲe] *n* slut, slovenly person.

malpropre [malprɔpr] *a* dirty, untidy, indecent, dishonest.

malpropreté [malprɔprəte] *nf* dirtiness, untidiness, unsavoriness, dishonesty.

malsain [malsɛ̃] *a* unhealthy, unwholesome, corrupting.

malséant [malseɑ̃] *a* unseemly, unbecoming.

malt [malt] *nm* malt.

maltraiter [maltrɛte] *vt* to ill-treat.

malveillance [malvɛjɑ̃:s] *nf* malevolence, spitefulness, foul play.

malveillant [malvɛjɑ̃] *a* malevolent, spiteful.

malvenu [malvəny] *a* ill-advised, unjustified.

malversation [malvɛrsasjɔ̃] *nf* embezzlement.

maman [mamɑ̃] *nf* mummy, mama.

mamelle [mamɛl] *nf* breast, udder.

mamelon [mamlɔ̃] *nf* nipple, teat, rounded hillock.

mammifère [mamifɛ:r] *nm* mammal.

mamour [mamu:r] *nm* my love; *pl* **faire des — à quelqu'un** to cuddle, coax someone.

manche [mɑ̃:ʃ] *nf* sleeve, hose-pipe, game, set, round, heat; **la Manche** the English Channel; *nm* handle, shaft, stock, joy-stick.

mancheron [mɑ̃ʃrɔ̃] *nm* handle (of plow), short sleeve.

manchette [mɑ̃ʃɛt] *nf* cuff, wristband, newspaper headline, marginal note; *pl* handcuffs.

manchon [mɑ̃ʃɔ̃] *nm* muff, socket, sleeve, casing, gas-mantle.

manchot [mɑ̃ʃo] *an* one-armed (person); penguin.

mandarine [mɑ̃darin] *nf* tangerine.

mandat [mɑ̃da] *nm* mandate, commission, money order, warrant; **— de comparution** summons.

mandataire [mɑ̃datɛ:r] *n* mandatory, agent, proxy.

mandat-poste [mɑ̃dapɔst] *nm* postal money order.

mander [mɑ̃de] *vt* to send for, summon, send word to; *vi* to report.

mandibule [mɑ̃dibyl] *nf* mandible.

mandoline [mɑ̃dɔlin] *nf* mandolin.

mandragore [mãdragɔːr] *nf* man-dragora, mandrake.

manège [manɛːʒ] *nm* training of horses, horsemanship, riding-school, trick, little game; — **de chevaux de bois** roundabout, merry-go-round.

manette [manɛt] *nf* hand lever, handle.

manganèse [mãganɛːz] *nm* man-ganese.

mangeable [mãʒabl] *a* eatable, edible.

mangeaille [mãzaːj] *nf* food, grub.

mangeoire [mãʒwaːr] *nf* manger, trough.

manger [mãʒe] *vt* to eat (up, away, into), squander; *nm* food; **donner à — à** to feed, give sth to eat to.

mange-tout [mãʒtu] *nm* spend-thrift, string-bean.

mangouste [mãgust] *nf* mongoose.

mangue [mãːg] *nf* mango.

maniable [manjabl] *a* manageable, easily handled, handy.

maniaque [manjak] *a* raving mad, faddy; *n* maniac, crank.

manie [mani] *nf* mania, craze, fad.

maniement [manimã] *nm* handling; — **d'armes** rifle drill.

manier [manje] *vt* to handle, ply, wield, control, feel.

manière [manjɛːr] *nf* manner, way; *pl* manners, affected airs; **à sa —** in his own way; **à la —** de after, in the manner of; **de cette —** in this way; **d'une — ou d'une autre** somehow or other; **en — de** by way of; **arranger qn de la belle —** to give s.o. a thorough dressing-down.

maniéré [manjere] *a* affected, mincing.

maniérisme [manjerism] *nm* man-nerism.

manifestant [manifɛstã] *n* demon-strator.

manifestation [manifɛstasjɔ̃] *nf* (public) demonstration, manifesta-tion.

manifeste [manifɛst] *a* manifest, obvious, evident, patent; *nm* mani-festo.

manifester [manifɛste] *vt* to mani-fest, display, reveal, show, express; *vi* to demonstrate; **se —** to show, reveal itself, appear, become appar-ent.

manigance [manigãːs] *nf* intrigue, scheme, game; *pl* underhand work, trickery.

manigancer [manigãse] *vt* to plot, scheme, arrange, be up to.

manille [maniːj] *nf* ankle-ring, shackle, manille.

manioc [manjɔk] *nm* cassava.

manipulateur, -trice [manipylat-œːr, tris] *n* manipulator.

manipuler [manipyle] *vt* to mani-pulate, operate, handle, arrange.

manitou [manitu] *nm* **le grand —** the big boss.

manivelle [manivɛl] *nf* handle, crank, starting-handle.

manne [man] *nf* manna, basket, hamper.

mannequin [mankɛ̃] *nm* small hamper, manikin, dummy, manne-quin.

manœuvrable [manœvrabl] *a* easily handled.

manœuvre [manœːvr] *nf* working, handling, maneuver, drill, shunting, scheme, move; *nm* laborer.

manœuvrer [manœvre] *vt* to work, operate, handle, maneuver, shunt; *vi* to maneuver, scheme.

manoir [manwaːr] *nm* manor, country house.

manomètre [manɔmɛtr] *nm* pressure-gauge.

manquant [mãkã] *a* missing, want-ing, absent; *n* absentee.

manque [mãːk] *nm* lack, want, shortage, deficiency, breach; — **de mémoire** forgetfulness; **à la —** dud.

manqué [mãke] *a* unsuccessful, missed, wasted; **un garçon —** tomboy.

manquement [mãkmã] *nm* failure, omission, breach, oversight, lapse.

manquer [mãke] *vt* to miss, waste; *vi* to be short (of de), lack, run short, be missing, fail; **il manqua (de) tomber** he almost fell; — **à sa parole** to break one's word; **il leur manque** they miss him; **ne pas —** de to be sure to.

mansarde [mãsard] *nf* attic, garret.

mansardé [mãsarde] *a* with sloping ceiling, roof.

mansuétude [mãsyetyd] *nf* gentle-ness.

mante [mãːt] *nf* mantis; — **religieuse** praying mantis.

manteau [mãto] *nm* coat, cloak, mantle; mantelpiece.

manucure [manykyːr] *n* manicurist.

manuel, -elle [manɥɛl] *a* manual; *nm* handbook.

manufacture [manyfaktyːr] *nf* factory, works.

manufacturer [manyfaktyre] *vt* to manufacture.

manufacturier, -ière [manyfaktyr-je, jɛːr] *a* manufacturing; *n* manu-facturer.

manuscrit [manyskri] *nm* manu-script.

manutention [manytãsjɔ̃] *nf* admin-istration, handling, stores.

mappemonde [mapmɔ̃ːd] *nf* map of the world.

maquereau [makro] *nm* mackerel.

maquette [makɛt] *nf* clay model, model, dummy, mock-up.

maquignon, -onne [makiɲɔ̃, ɔn] *n* horse-dealer, shady dealer, jobber.

maquignonnage [makiɲɔnaːʒ] *nm* horse-dealing, faking, shady dealing.

maquignonner [makiɲɔne] *vt* to doctor, arrange, fix.

maquillage [makija:ʒ] nm make-up, making-up.

maquiller [makije] vt to make up, fake, doctor, cook up; vr to make up.

maquis [maki] nm bush, scrub; Resistance Movement.

maquisard [makiza:r] n member of the Resistance Movement.

maraîcher, -ère [marɛʃe, ɛːr] a market-gardening; n market gardener.

marais [marɛ] nm marsh, bog; floating vote; — **salant** salt-pan.

marasme [marasm] nm wasting, stagnation, depression.

marâtre [marɑːtr] nf stepmother, hard-hearted mother.

maraude [maro:d] nf marauding, looting, plundering; être en — to be on the prowl.

marbre [marbr] nm marble.

marbrer [marbre] vt to marble, vein, mottle, blotch.

marbrier [marbrie] nm marble cutter.

marbrure [marbry:r] nf marbling, veining, mottling, blotch.

marc [ma:r] nm residue; — **de café** coffee grounds.

marcassin [markasɛ̃] nm young wild boar.

marchand [marʃɑ̃] a commercial, trading, merchant; n shopkeeper, tradesman, dealer; **valeur —e** market value; — **des quatre saisons** hawker, huckster.

marchander [marʃɑ̃de] vt to bargain, haggle over, be sparing of, grudge.

marchandise [marʃɑ̃di:z] nf merchandise, commodity, wares, goods.

marche [marʃ] nf walk(ing), gait, march(ing), working, running, progress, course, step, stair; en — moving, running, under way; mettre en — to get going, start up; faire — arrière to reverse, go astern.

marché [marʃe] nm market, bargain, deal(ing), contract; (à) bon — cheap(ly); par-dessus le — into the bargain; faire bon — de to attach little value to.

marchepied [marʃəpje] nm step, running-board.

marcher [marʃe] vi to walk, tread, go, run, work, get along; il ne marche pas he is not having any, he won't do as he is told; faire — qn to make s.o. do as he is told, pull s.o.'s leg.

marcheur, -euse [marʃœ:r, ø:z] n walker; vieux — old rake.

mardi [mardi] nm Tuesday; — **gras** Shrove Tuesday.

mare [ma:r] nf pool, pond.

marécage [marɛka:ʒ] nm marsh (land), swamp.

marécageux, -euse [marɛkaʒø, ø:z] a marshy, swampy, boggy.

maréchal [mareʃal] nm marshal; — **ferrant** farrier, blacksmith; — **des logis** sergeant; — **de France** field-marshal.

marée [mare] nf tide, fresh fish; — **montante** flood tide; — **descendante** ebb tide; **arriver comme** — **en carême** to come at the right time.

marelle [marɛl] nf hopscotch.

mareyeur, -euse [marɛjœ:r, ø:z] n fish merchant, fish porter.

margarine [margarin] nf margarine.

marge [marʒ] nf margin, edge, border, fringe.

margelle [marʒɛl] nf edge.

marguerite [margərit] nf daisy, marguerite.

marguillier [margije] nm churchwarden.

mari [mari] nm husband.

mariage [marja:ʒ] nm marriage, matrimony.

Marie [mari] Mary.

marié [marje] a married; n bridegroom, bride.

marier [marje] vt to marry, give in marriage, unite, blend, cross; vr to get married, marry, harmonize.

marie-salope [marisalɔp] nf dredger, slut.

marigot [marigo] nm small stream.

marin [marɛ̃] a marine, sea-; nm sailor, seaman, seafaring man; **avoir le pied** — to be a good sailor; **se faire** — to go to sea; — **d'eau douce** landlubber.

marinade [marinad] nf pickle, brine.

marine [marin] nf navy, seamanship, seascape; — **marchande** merchant marine; **bleu** — navy blue.

mariner [marine] vt to pickle, souse, marinate; vi to be in a pickle.

marinier, -ière [marinje, jɛːr] a naval, marine; nm bargeman, boatman.

marionnette [marjɔnɛt] nf marionnette, puppet.

maritime [maritim] a maritime, naval, seaside, sea(borne); **agent** — shipping agent; **courtier** — shipbroker.

marivaudage [marivoda:ʒ] nm affected, flippant conversation, mild flirtation.

marlou [marlu] nm pimp.

marmaille [marma:j] nf (fam) brats, children.

marmelade [marməlad] nf compote, marmalade.

marmite [marmit] nf pot, pan, camp-kettle, heavy shell; — **de géants** pothole.

marmiter [marmite] vt to shell, bombard.

marmiton [marmitɔ̃] nm cook's boy, scullion.

marmonner [marmɔne] vt to mutter, mumble.

marmot [marmo] nm brat, child.

marmotte [marmɔt] *nf* marmot, kerchief.
marmotter [marmɔte] *vt* to mumble, mutter.
marne [marn] *nf* marl.
Maroc [marɔk] *nm* Morocco.
marocain [marɔkɛ̃] *a* Moroccan.
maroquinerie [marɔkinri] *nf* (morocco-) leather trade, goods, shop.
marotte [marɔt] *nf* cap and bells, bauble, hobby, fad.
marquant [markɑ̃] *a* outstanding, notable.
marque [mark] *nf* mark, stamp, make, token, proof, marker, tally, score, scoring; — de fabrique trademark; — déposée registered trademark; vin de — first class wine; personnage de — prominent person.
marqué [marke] *a* marked, pronounced, appointed.
marquer [marke] *vt* to mark, put a mark on, show, note down, record, score; *vi* to stand out, make one's mark; elle marque bien she is a good-looker; — son âge to look one's age; — les points to keep the score; — le pas to mark time.
marqueter [markəte] *vt* to speckle, spot, inlay.
marqueterie [markətri] *nf* marquetry, inlaid-work.
marqueur, -euse [markœːr, øːz] *n* marker, stamper, scorer.
marquis [marki] *nm* marquis, marquess.
marquise [markiːz] *nf* marchioness, awning, glass porch, marquee.
marraine [marɛn] *nf* godmother, sponsor.
marrant [marɑ̃] *a* terribly funny, killing.
marre [maːr] *nf* j'en ai — I'm fed up.
marrer [mare] *vr* to split one's sides laughing.
marron, -onne [marɔ̃, ɔn] *a* chestnut-colored; unlicensed, quack, sham; *nm* chestnut.
marronnier [marɔnje] *nm* chestnut-tree.
mars [mars] *nm* March, Mars; champ de — parade-ground.
marsouin [marswɛ̃] *nm* porpoise, colonial infantry soldier.
marteau [marto] *nm* hammer, doorknocker.
marteler [martəle] *vt* to hammer (out); *vi* to knock.
martial [marsjal] *a* martial, warlike, soldierlike.
martinet [martinɛ] *nm* strap, whip, swift.
martingale [martɛ̃gal] *nf* martingale, half-belt.
martin-pêcheur [martɛ̃pɛʃœːr] *nm* kingfisher.
martre [martr] *nm* marten, sable.
martyr [martiːr] *n* martyr.
martyre [martiːr] *nm* martyrdom.

martyriser [martirize] *vt* to martyr, torture.
marxisme [marksism] *nm* Marxism.
mascarade [maskarad] *nf* masquerade.
mascaret [maskarɛ] *nm* bore, tidal wave.
mascotte [maskɔt] *nf* mascot, charm.
masculin [maskylɛ̃] *a* masculine, male, mannish; *nm* masculine gender.
masque [mask] *nm* mask, features, expression, masque.
masquer [maske] *vt* to mask, hide, screen, disguise; virage masqué blind corner.
massacre [masakr] *nm* massacre, slaughter; jeu de — Aunt Sally (game).
massacrer [masakre] *vt* to massacre, slaughter, butcher, spoil; être d'une humeur massacrante to be in a vile temper.
massage [masaːʒ] *nm* massage, rubbing down.
masse [mas] *nf* mass, bulk, crowd, mace, sledge-hammer.
masser [mase] *vt* to mass, massage, rub down; *vr* to mass, throng together.
masseur, -euse [masœːr, øːz] *n* masseur, masseuse.
massif, -ive [masif, iːv] *a* solid, massive, bulky; *nm* clump, group, range.
massue [masy] *nf* club, bludgeon.
mastic [mastik] *nm* mastic, putty, cement.
mastication [mastikasjɔ̃] *nf* mastication, chewing.
mastiquer [mastike] *vt* to masticate, chew, putty, fill with cement.
m'as-tu-vu [matyvy] *nm* smart aleck, show-off.
masure [mazyːr] *nf* hovel, tumbledown house.
mat [mat] *a* a dull, unpolished, mat checkmated; *nm* checkmate.
mât [mɑ] *nm* mast, pole, strut; — de cocagne greasy pole.
match [matʃ] *nm* match; — de sélection trial match.
matelas [matla] *nm* mattress.
matelasser [matlase] *vt* to pad cushion; porte matelassée baize covered door.
matelot [matlo] *nm* sailor, seaman — de première (deuxième) classe leading (able) seaman.
mater [mate] *vt* to dull, mat, check mate, humble.
matérialiser [materjalize] *vtr* to materialize.
matérialiste [materjalist] *a* materialistic; *n* materialist.
matériaux [materjo] *nm* material(s).
matériel, -elle [materjel] *a* material sensual, physical; *nm* material plant, implements, equipment — roulant rolling stock.

maternel, -elle [maternɛl] *a* maternal, mother(ly); **école —le** infant school.

maternité [maternite] *nf* maternity, motherhood, maternity hospital.

mathématicien, -ienne [matematisjɛ̃, jɛn] *n* mathematician.

mathématique [matematik] *a* mathematical; *nf pl* mathematics.

matière [matjɛ:r] *nf* matter, substance, material, subject.

matin [matɛ̃] *nm* morning; **de grand, de bon —** early in the morning.

mâtin [matɛ̃] *nm* mastiff.

matinal [matinal] *a* morning, early rising; **il est —** he is up early.

matinée [matine] *nf* morning, matinee; **faire la grasse —** to lie late in bed.

matines [matin] *nf pl* matins.

matineux, -euse [matinø, ø:z] *a* early rising; **il est —** he gets up early.

matois [matwa] *a* sly, crafty, cunning; *n* cunning person; **fin —** sly, wily, bird.

matou [matu] *nm* tom-cat.

matraque [matrak] *nf* bludgeon.

matrice [matris] *nf* matrix, womb, mold, die.

matricide [matrisid] *a* matricidal; *n* matricide.

matricule [matrikyl] *nf* register, roll, registration (certificate); *nm* (registration) number; **plaque —** license plate.

matriculer [matrikyle] *vt* to enroll, enter in a register, stamp a number on.

matrimonial [matrimɔnjal] *a* matrimonial.

maturation [matyrasjɔ̃] *nf* maturation, ripening.

mâture [maty:r] *nf* masts; **dans la —** aloft.

maturément [matyremɑ̃] *ad* after due deliberation.

maturité [matyrite] *nf* maturity, ripeness, mellowness.

maudire [modi:r] *vt* to curse.

maudit [modi] *a* cursed, damned, damnable, confounded.

maugréer [mogree] *vi* to curse, (fret and) fume.

mausolée [mozole] *nm* mausoleum.

maussade [mosad] *a* glum, sullen, dismal, dull.

mauvais [movɛ] *a* bad, wrong, poor, nasty; *ad* **sentir —** to have a bad smell; **il fait —** the weather is bad.

mauve [mo:v] *a nm* mauve.

mauviette [movjɛt] *nf* chit, softy.

maxime [maksim] *nf* maxim.

maximum [maksimɔm] *a nm* maximum.

mazout [mazu] *nm* fuel oil.

ne [m(ə)] *pn* me, to me, myself, to myself.

méandre [meɑ̃dr] *nm* meander, bend, winding.

mécanicien, -ienne [mekanisjɛ̃, jɛn] *a* mechanical; *n* mechanic, machinist, engineer, engine-driver.

mécanique [mekanik] *a* mechanical, clockwork; *nf* mechanics, machinery, mechanism.

mécanisation [mekanizasjɔ̃] *nf* mechanization.

mécaniser [mekanize] *vt* to mechanize.

mécanisme [mekanism] *nm* mechanism, machinery, works, technique.

mécano [mekano] *nm* (*fam*) mechanic.

méchanceté [meʃɑ̃ste] *nf* wickedness, spitefulness, naughtiness, ill-natured word or act.

méchant [meʃɑ̃] *a* wicked, bad, naughty, ill-natured, spiteful, vicious, wretched, sorry.

mèche [mɛʃ] *nf* wick, fuse, match, (hair) lock, wisp, gimlet, spindle, drill; **éventer la —** to give the game away; **être de — avec** to be in league with.

mécompte [mekɔ̃:t] *nm* miscalculation, error, misjudgment, disappointment.

méconnaissable [mekɔnɛsabl] *a* unrecognizable.

méconnaissance [mekɔnɛsɑ̃:s] *nf* refusal to recognize or appreciate, ignoring, disavowal.

méconnaître [mekɔnɛ:tr] *vt* to fail (refuse) to recognize, not to appreciate, to ignore, misunderstand, disavow.

mécontent [mekɔ̃tɑ̃] *a* discontented, displeased, dissatisfied.

mécontentement [mekɔ̃tɑ̃tmɑ̃] *nm* discontent, dissatisfaction.

mécontenter [mekɔ̃tɑ̃te] *vt* to displease, dissatisfy, annoy.

mécréant [mekreɑ̃] *a* misbelieving, unbelieving; *n* infidel.

médaille [medɑ:j] *nf* medal, badge; **revers de la —** other side of the coin.

médaillon [medɑjɔ̃] *nm* medallion, locket, inset.

médecin [medsɛ̃] *nm* doctor, physician.

médecine [medsin] *nf* medicine.

médiateur, -trice [medjatœ:r, tris] *a* mediatory, mediating; *n* mediator.

médiation [medjasjɔ̃] *nf* mediation.

médical [medikal] *a* medical.

médicament [medikamɑ̃] *nm* medicine, medicament.

médicinal [medisinal] *a* medicinal.

médiéval [medjeval] *a* medieval.

médiocre [medjɔkr] *a* mediocre, moderate, second-rate; *nm* mediocrity.

médiocrité [medjɔkrite] *nf* mediocrity, feebleness, nonentity.

médire [medi:r] *vi* to slander, speak ill of.

médisance [medizɑ̃:s] *nf* calumny, scandal.

médisant [medizã] *a* slanderous, calumnious, backbiting; *n* slanderer.
méditatif, -ive [meditatif, i:v] *a* meditative.
méditation [meditasjɔ̃] *nf* meditation, contemplation.
méditer [medite] *vt* to contemplate, ponder; *vi* to meditate, muse.
Méditerranée [mediterane] *nf* Mediterranean.
méditerranéen, -enne [mediterraneɛ̃, ɛn] *a* Mediterranean.
médium [medjɔm] *nm* medium.
médius [medjys] *nm* middle finger.
méduse [medy:z] *nf* jellyfish.
méduser [medyze] *vt* to petrify, paralyze.
méfait [mefɛ] *nm* misdeed; *pl* damage.
méfiance [mefjã:s] *nf* distrust, mistrust, suspicion.
méfiant [mefjã] *a* distrustful, suspicious.
se méfier [səmefje] *vr* to distrust, mistrust, be watchful, be on one's guard.
mégalomanie [megalɔmani] *nf* megalomania.
mégaphone [megafɔn] *nm* megaphone.
mégarde [megard] *ad* par — inadvertently.
mégère [meʒɛ:r] *nf* shrew.
mégot [mego] *nm* cigarette-end.
méhari [meari] *nm* racing camel.
meilleur [mejœ:r] *a* better, best; *comp sup* of **bon**; *nm* best, best thing.
mélancolie [melãkɔli] *nf* melancholy, dejection, melancholia, sadness.
mélange [melã:ʒ] *nm* mixing, mingling, blending, mixture, blend, mélange.
mélanger [melãʒe] *vt* to mix, mingle, blend.
mélasse [melas] *nf* molasses, treacle.
mêlée [mele] *nf* conflict, fray, scuffle, scrimmage.
mêler [mele] *vt* to mix, mingle, blend, tangle, involve, implicate, shuffle; *vr* to mix, mingle, interfere, meddle.
mélèze [melɛ:z] *nm* larch.
méli-mélo [melimelo] *nm* jumble.
mélodie [melɔdi] *nf* melody, tune, harmony, song.
mélodieux, -euse [melɔdjø, ø:z] *a* melodious, tuneful, harmonious.
mélodique [melɔdik] *a* melodic.
mélodramatique [melɔdramatik] *a* melodramatic.
mélodrame [melɔdram] *nm* melodrama.
mélomane [melɔman] *a* music-loving; *n* music-lover.
melon [məlɔ̃] *nm* melon, bowler hat.
mélopée [melɔpe] *nf* art of recitative, chant, singsong.
membrane [mãbran] *nf* membrane, web.
membre [mã:br] *nm* member, limb.

membré [mã:bre] *a* -limbed.
membrure [mãbry:r] *nf* limbs framework.
même [mɛm] *a* same, very, -self; *ad* even; **de lui —** of his own accord; **de —** likewise; **il en est de — de lui** it is the same with him; **tout de —** all the same; **à — la bouteille** out of the bottle; **revenir au —** come to the same thing; **à — de** in a position to.
mémento [memɛ̃to] *nm* memorandum, notebook, memento, synopsis.
mémoire [memwa:r] *nm* memoir, paper, memorial, bill, account; *nf* memory, recollection.
mémorable [memɔrabl] *a* memorable, eventful.
mémorandum [memɔrãdɔm] *nm* memorandum, notebook.
mémorial [memɔrjal] *nm* memorial, memoirs, daybook.
menaçant [mənasã] *a* threatening, menacing.
menace [mənas] *nf* threat, menace; *pl* intimidation.
menacer [mənase] *vt* to threaten, menace; **— ruine** to be falling to pieces; **— qn du poing** to shake one's fist at s.o.
ménage [mena:ʒ] *nm* household, family, married couple, housekeeping, housework; **se mettre en —** to set up house; **faire bon — ensemble** to get on well together; **femme de —** housekeeper, cleaning woman.
ménagement [menaʒmã] *nm* consideration, caution, care.
ménager [menaʒe] *vt* to be sparing of, save, humor, spare, arrange, contrive; *vr* to take care of oneself; to spare oneself.
ménager, -ère [menaʒe, ʒɛ:r] *a* domestic, house-, thrifty, careful, housewifely; *nf* housewife, housekeeper.
ménagerie [menaʒri] *nf* menagerie.
mendiant [mãdjã] *a* begging, mendicant; *n* beggar.
mendicité [mãdisite] *nf* begging, beggary.
mendier [mãdje] *vt* to beg (for); *vi* to beg.
menée [məne] *nf* track, intrigue; *pl* maneuvers.
mener [məne] *vt* to lead, take, drive, steer, manage, control; **— à bonne fin** to carry through; **n'en pas — large** to feel small.
ménétrier [menetrie] *nm* (strolling) fiddler.
meneur, -euse [mənœ:r, ø:z] *n* leader, agitator, ringleader.
méningite [menɛ̃ʒit] *nf* meningitis.
menotte [mənɔt] *nf* tiny hand; *pl* handcuffs, manacles.
menotter [mənɔte] *vt* to manacle, handcuff.
mensonge [mãsɔ̃:ʒ] *nm* lie, falsehood, illusion.

nensonger, -ère [mãsɔ̃ʒe, ɛːr] *a* lying, deceitful, illusory.

nensualité [mãsɥalite] *nf* monthly payment.

nensuel, -elle [mãsɥɛl] *a* monthly.

nensuration [mãsyrasjɔ̃] *nf* measurement, measuring, mensuration.

nental [mãtal] *a* mental.

nentalité [mãtalite] *nf* mentality.

nenterie [mãtri] *nf* fib, tale, story.

nenteur, -euse [mãtœːr, øːz] *a* lying, deceptive, false; *n* liar.

nenthe [mãːt] *nf* mint, peppermint.

nention [mãsjɔ̃] *nf* endorsement; reçu avec — passed with distinction; faire — de to mention.

nentionner [mãsjone] *vt* to mention, speak of.

nentir [mãtiːr] *vi* to lie, tell lies.

nenton [mãtɔ̃] *nm* chin.

nentonnière [mãtonjɛːr] *nf* chin-strap, chinpiece, chinrest.

nentor [mãtɔːr] *nm* mentor, tutor, guide.

nenu [məny] *a* small, tiny, fine, minute, slight, trifling, petty; *ad* small, fine; *nm* menu, bill of fare; par le — in detail.

nenuet [mənɥɛ] *nm* minuet.

nenuiserie [mənɥizri] *nf* carpentry, woodwork.

nenuisier [mənɥizje] *nm* joiner, carpenter.

néplat [mepla] *a* flat; *nm* flat part, plane.

méprendre [səmeprãːdr] *vr* to be mistaken, make a mistake (about sur); il n'y a pas à s'y — there is no mistake about it.

népris [mepri] *nm* scorn, contempt.

néprisable [meprizabl] *a* contemptible, despicable.

néprisant [meprizã] *a* contemptuous, scornful.

néprise [mepriːz] *nf* error, mistake, misapprehension.

népriser [meprize] *vt* to despise, scorn.

ner [mɛːr] *nf* sea; en pleine — on the high seas; prendre la — to put out to sea; mettre à la — to lower *a boat*).

nercantile [mɛrkãtil] *a* commercial, money-grabbing, mercenary.

nercantilisme [mɛrkãtilism] *nm* profiteering, commercialism.

nercenaire [mɛrsənɛːr] *an* mercenary.

nercerie [mɛrsəri] *nf* haberdashery.

nerci [mɛrsi] *nf* mercy; *ad* thanks, thank you, no thanks, no thank you.

nercier, -ière [mɛrsje, jɛːr] *n* haberdasher.

nercredi [mɛrkrədi] *nm* Wednesday; — des Cendres Ash Wednesday.

nercure [mɛrkyːr] *nm* mercury, quicksilver.

nercuriale [mɛrkyrjal] *nf* market price-list, reprimand.

merde [mɛrd] *nf* shit, excrement.

mère [mɛːr] *nf* mother, source; *a* main.

méridien, -ienne [meridjɛ̃, jɛn] *a* meridian, meridional; *nm* meridian; *nf* meridian line.

méridional [meridjonal] *a* meridional, Southern; *n* Southerner.

meringue [mərɛ̃g] *nf* meringue.

mérinos [merinos] *nm* merino.

merisier [mərizje] *nm* wild cherry-tree.

méritant [meritã] *a* deserving, meritorious, worthy.

mérite [merit] *nm* merit, worth, credit, ability.

mériter [merite] *vt* to deserve, merit, earn.

méritoire [meritwaːr] *a* deserving, worthy, meritorious.

merlan [mɛrlã] *nm* whiting; (*fam*) barber.

merle [mɛrl] *nm* blackbird.

merluche [mɛrlyʃ] *nf* hake, dried cod.

merrain [mɛrɛ̃] *nm* caskwood.

merveille [mɛrvɛːj] *nf* marvel, wonder; à — wonderfully well, excellently.

merveilleux, -euse [mɛrvɛjø, øːz] *a* marvelous, wonderful; *nm* supernatural.

mes [me] *a pl see* mon.

mésalliance [mezaljãːs] *nf* misalliance, unsuitable marriage.

se mésallier [səmezalje] *vr* to marry beneath one.

mésange [mezãːʒ] *nf* tit; — charbonnière tomtit, great tit.

mésaventure [mezavãtyːr] *nf* misadventure, mishap.

mésentente [mezãtãt] *nf* misunderstanding, disagreement.

mésestime [mezɛstim] *nf* low esteem, poor opinion.

mésestimer [mezɛstime] *vt* to underestimate, have a poor opinion of.

mésintelligence [mezɛtɛliʒãːs] *nf* misunderstanding, disagreement, discord.

mesquin [mɛskɛ̃] *a* mean, petty, shabby, paltry.

mesquinerie [mɛskinri] *nf* meanness, pettiness, shabbiness, paltriness, stinginess, mean action.

mess [mɛs] *nm* officers' mess.

message [mesaːʒ] *nm* message.

messager, -ère [mesaʒe, ɛr] *n* messenger, carrier.

messagerie [mesaʒri] *nf* freight trade; les —s central newsagency; — maritime shipping office.

messe [mɛs] *nf* mass; — des morts requiem mass.

messie [mesi] *nm* Messiah.

mesure [məzyːr] *nf* measure, standard (size), gauge, extent, bounds, moderation; *pl* measures, steps; en — de in a position to; donner sa — to show what one can

do; **dépasser la —** to overstep the mark; **fait sur —** made to measure; **à —** que as.
mesure-étalon [məzyretalɔ̃] nf standard measure.
mesuré [məzyre] a measured, moderate, restrained.
mesurer [məzyre] vt to measure (out, off), judge, calculate; vr to measure oneself (with), tackle; **— qn des yeux** to eye s.o. up and down.
métairie [meteri] nf small farm.
métal [metal] nm metal.
métallique [metalik] a metallic; **toile —** wire gauze.
métalliser [metalize] vt to metalize, plate.
métallurgie [metalyrʒi] nf metallurgy.
métallurgiste [metalyrʒist] nm metallurgist, metal-worker.
métamorphose [metamɔrfoz] nf metamorphosis, transformation.
métaphore [metafɔːr] nf metaphor.
métaphorique [metafɔrik] a metaphorical.
métaphysicien, -ienne [metafizisjɛ̃, jɛn] n metaphysician.
métaphysique [metafizik] a metaphysical; nf metaphysics.
métayer, -ère [metɛje, jɛːr] n farmer, share-cropper.
métempsychose [metɑ̃psikoːz] nf metempsychosis, transmigration of souls.
météore [meteɔːr] nm meteor.
météorologie [meteɔrɔlɔʒi] nf meteorology.
météorologique [meteɔrɔlɔʒik] a meteorological; **bulletin —** weather report.
métèque [metɛk] nm (pej) foreigner.
méthode [metɔd] nf method, system, orderliness, primer.
méthodique [metɔdik] a methodical.
méticuleux, -euse [metikylø, øːz] a meticulous, particular, punctilious.
métier [metje] nm trade, profession, craft(smanship), loom; **homme de — craftsman; — manuel** handicraft; **sur le —** on the stocks, in preparation.
métis, -isse [metis] a half-bred, cross-bred, mongrel; n half-cast, half-breed, mongrel.
métisser [metise] vt to cross(breed).
métrage [metraːʒ] nm measuring, metric area or volume, length; **(film à) court —** a short.
mètre [metr] nm meter, rule; **— à ruban** tape-measure.
métrique [metrik] a metric(al); nf metrics, prosody.
métro [metro] nm underground (railway), subway.
métropole [metrɔpɔl] nf metropolis, mother country.
métropolitain [metrɔpɔlitɛ̃] a metropolitan, home-; nm underground (railway), subway.

mets [mɛ] nm dish, food.
mettable [metabl] a wearable.
metteur, -euse [metœːr, øːz] n — **en scène** producer, director.
mettre [metr] vt to put (up, on) place, set (up), lay, wear; vr to go stand, sit, put on; **se — à** to begin set about; **mettons qu'il l'ait fai** suppose he did do it; **se — en colère** to get angry; **—en scène** to produce (a play).
meuble [mœbl] a movable; nm piece or suite of furniture; pl furniture.
meublé [mœble] a furnished, stocked; nm furnished room(s).
meubler [mœble] vt to furnish, stock; vr to furnish (one's house).
meugler [mœgle] vi to low.
meule [møːl] nf millstone, stack, rick.
meuler [møle] vt to grind.
meulière [møljeːr] nf millstone, -quarry.
meunerie [mønri] nf milling, milling-trade.
meunier, -ière [mønje, jeːr] n miller.
meurtre [mœrtr] nm murder.
meurtrier, -ière [mœrtrie, ieːr] a murderous, deadly; n murderer, murderess.
meurtrière [mœrtrieːr] nf loophole.
meurtrir [mœrtriːr] vt to bruise, batter.
meurtrissure [mœrtrisyːr] nf bruise.
meute [møːt] nf pack, mob, crowd.
mexicain [mɛksikɛ̃] an Mexican.
Mexique [mɛksik] nm Mexico.
mi [mi] ad half, semi, mid-; **à la — -septembre** in mid-September; **à — -chemin** half way; **à — -côte** half way up; **à — -corps** to the waist; nm note E.
miasme [mjasm] nm miasma.
miauler [mjole] vi to mew, cater-waul.
mi-carême [mikarɛm] nm Mid-Lent.
miche [miʃ] nf round loaf.
Michel [miʃɛl] Michael.
micmac [mikmak] nm trickery, scheming.
micocoulier [mikɔkuljej] nm nettle-tree.
micro [mikro] nm mike, microphone.
microbe [mikrɔb] nm microbe, germ.
microbicide [mikrɔbisid] a germ-killing; nm germ-killer.
microcosme [mikrɔkɔsm] nm micro-cosm.
microscope [mikrɔskɔp] nm micro-scope.
microsillon [mikrɔsijɔ̃] nm long playing record.
midi [midi] nm noon, midday south; **chercher — à quatorze heures** to see difficulties when there are none.

midinette [midinɛt] *nf* workgirl, young dressmaker.

mie [mi] *nf* crumb, soft part of a loaf.

miel [mjɛl] *nm* honey.

mielleux, -euse [mjɛlø, ø:z] *a* honeyed, sugary, bland.

mien, mienne [mjɛ̃, mjɛn] *pos pn* le(s) —(s), la mienne, les miennes mine; *nm* my own; *pl* my own people.

miette [mjɛt] *nf* crumb, morsel, tiny bit, atom.

mieux [mjø] *ad* better, (the) best, *comp sup of bien*; *nm* best thing, improvement; de — en — better and better; à qui — — one more than the other; c'est on ne peut — it could not be better; faire de son — to do one's best; être au — avec to be on the best terms with; tant —! all the better!

mièvre [mjɛ:vr] *a* affected, pretty-pretty, delicate.

mièvrerie [mjɛvrəri] *nf* affectation, insipid prettiness.

mignard [miɲaːr] *a* affected, simpering, mincing, pretty-pretty.

mignardise [miɲardiːz] *nf* affectation, mincing manner, prettiness, garden pink.

mignon, -onne [miɲɔ̃, ɔn] *a* dainty, sweet, tiny; *n* darling, pet, favorite; péché — besetting sin.

mignonnette [miɲɔnɛt] *nf* mignonette lace, coarsely ground pepper, London pride.

migraine [migrɛn] *nf* migraine, sick headache.

migrateur, -trice [migratœ:r, tris] *a* migratory, migrant.

migration [migrasjɔ̃] *nf* migration.

mijaurée [miʒɔre] *nf* affected woman.

mijoter [miʒɔte] *vt* to stew slowly, let simmer, plot; *vi* to stew, simmer; *vr* to simmer.

mil [mil] *a* thousand.

milan [milɑ̃] *nm* kite.

milice [milis] *nf* militia.

milieu [miljø] *nm* middle, midst, environment, circle, set, class, mean, middle course; au beau — de right in the middle of; juste — happy medium.

militaire [milite:r] *a* military, soldierlike; *nm* soldier.

militant [militɑ̃] *an* militant (supporter).

militariser [militarize] *vt* to militarize.

militer [milite] *vi* to militate, tell.

mille [mil] *a* thousand; *nm* thousand; mile; avoir des — et des cents to have tons of money.

mille-feuille [milfœːj] *nf* flaky pastry, yarrow.

millénaire [millenɛːr] *a* millenial; *nm* thousand years.

millénium [millenjɔm] *nm* millenium.

mille-pattes [milpat] *nm* centipede.

millésime [mil(l)ezim] *nm* date (coin), year of manufacture, of vintage.

millet [mijɛ] *nm* millet.

milliardaire [miljardɛːr] *a nm* multimillionaire.

millier [milje] *nm* thousand.

milligramme [milligram] *nm* milligram.

millimètre [mil(l)imɛtr] *nm* millimeter.

million [miljɔ̃] *nm* million.

millionnaire [miljɔnɛːr] *an* millionaire(ss).

mime [mim] *nm* mimic, mime.

mimique [mimik] *a* mimic; *nf* mimicry.

mimosa [mimoza] *nm* mimosa.

minable [minabl] *a* shabby, seedy-looking, pitiable.

minaret [minarɛ] *nm* minaret.

minauder [minode] *vi* to smirk, simper, mince.

minaudier, -ière [minodje, jɛːr] *a* smirking, simpering, mincing, affected.

mince [mɛ̃ːs] *a* thin, slim, slight, scanty; *excl* — alors! hang it all, well I never!

minceur [mɛ̃sœːr] *nf* thinness, slimness.

mine [min] *nf* appearance, look, mine, lead; — de plomb graphite; de bonne (mauvaise) — prepossessing (evil-looking); avoir bonne (mauvaise) — to look well (ill); faire — de to make as if to; faire bonne — à to be pleasant to; cela ne paie pas de — it is not much to look at.

miner [mine] *vt* to (under)mine, sap.

minerai [minrɛ] *nm* ore.

minéral [mineral] *a nm* mineral.

minet, -ette [minɛ, ɛt] *n* pussy.

mineur, -eure [minœːr] *a* minor, underage, lesser; *n* minor; *nm* miner, sapper.

miniature [minjatyːr] *nf* miniature, small scale.

minier, -ière [minje, jɛːr] *a* mining.

minime [minim] *a* small, trifling, trivial.

minimum [minimɔm] *a nm* minimum.

ministère [ministɛːr] *nm* ministry, office, government; — des Affaires Etrangères State Department; — de l'Intérieur Interior Department; — de la Guerre Defense Department.

ministériel, -elle [ministerjɛl] *a* ministerial, cabinet.

ministre [ministr] *nm* minister, clergyman; premier — Prime Minister; — des Affaires Etrangères Secretary of State; — de l'Intérieur Secretary of the Interior; — des Finances Secretary of The Treasury

minois [minwa] *nm* pretty face.

minorité [minɔrite] *nf* minority, infancy.

minoterie [minɔtri] *nf* flour-mill, -milling.

minotier [minɔtje] *nm* miller.

minuit [minɥi] *nm* midnight.

minuscule [minyskyl] *a* small, tiny, diminutive, minute.

minute [minyt] *nf* minute, record, draft; *excl* not so fast! hold on! **réparations à la —** repairs while you wait.

minuter [minyte] *vt* to minute, record, enter, draw up.

minuterie [minytri] *nf* time switch.

minutie [minysi] *nf* minute detail, trifle, fussiness over detail, thoroughness.

minutieux, -euse [minysjø, øːz] *a* minute, detailed, thorough, meticulous.

mioche [mjɔʃ] *n* (*fam*) small child, kid.

mi-parti [miparti] *a* half and half, parti-colored.

mirabelle [mirabɛl] *nf* mirabelle plum.

miracle [mirakl] *nm* miracle, wonder.

miraculeux, -euse [mirakylø, øːz] *a* miraculous, marvelous, wonderful.

mirage [miraːʒ] *nm* mirage.

mire [miːr] *nf* aiming, sight, surveyor's pole, (TV) test pattern; **point de —** cynosure.

mirer [mire] *vt* to sight, aim at, have one's eye on, examine; *vr* to look at oneself admire oneself.

mirifique [mirifik] *a* amazing, wonderful.

mirobolant [mirɔbɔlɑ̃] *a* amazing, astounding.

miroir [mirwaːr] *nm* mirror, looking-glass, speculum; **œufs au —** eggs cooked in butter.

miroiter [mirwate] *vi* to gleam, sparkle, shimmer; **faire — qch** to dazzle, entice with sth.

misaine [mizɛn] *nf* foresail; **mât de —** foremast.

misanthrope [mizɑ̃trɔp] *a* misanthropic; *nm* misanthrope, misanthropist.

misanthropie [mizɑ̃trɔpi] *nf* misanthropy.

mise [miz] *nf* putting, setting, placing, stake, bid, dress; **— à l'eau** launching; **— en scène** setting, staging; **— en retraite** pensioning; **— en plis** setting (of hair); **— en marche** starting up; **cela n'est pas de —** that is not done, (worn, permissible).

miser [mize] *vt* to stake, gamble, lay, bid.

misérable [mizerabl] *a* wretched, miserable, despicable; *n* wretch, scoundrel.

misère [mizɛːr] *nf* misery, poverty, want, distress, trouble, worry wretchedness, shabbiness, trifle **crier —** to plead poverty, be shabby **faire des — à** to tease unmercifully

miséreux, -euse [mizerø, øːz] *a* destitute, poverty-stricken (person)

miséricorde [mizerikɔrd] *nf* mercy *excl* goodness gracious!

miséricordieux, -euse [mizerikɔrdjø, øːz] *a* merciful.

misogyne [mizɔʒin] *a* misogynous *nm* misogynist, woman-hater.

misogynie [mizɔʒini] *nf* misogyny.

missel [misɛl] *nm* missal.

missile [misil] *nm* missile.

mission [misjɔ̃] *nf* mission; **en —** on a mission.

missionnaire [misjɔnɛːr] *nm* missionary.

missive [misiːv] *nf* missive.

mistral [mistral] *nm* mistral (wind)

mitaine [mitɛn] *nf* mitten.

mite [mit] *nf* moth, mite.

mité [mite] *a* moth-eaten.

mi-temps [mitɑ̃] *nf* half-time, interval, half.

miteux, -euse [mitø, øːz] *a* shabby seedy-looking.

mitigation [mitigasjɔ̃] *nf* mitigation

mitiger [mitiʒe] *vt* to mitigate.

mitonner [mitɔne] *vt* to let simmer concoct; *vi* to simmer.

mitoyen, -enne [mitwajɛ̃, ɛn] *a* dividing, intermediate.

mitraille [mitraːj] *nf* grapeshot (*fam*) change (*money*).

mitrailler [mitraje] *vt* to machine gun, (*fam*) take shots of; **— d** questions to fire questions at.

mitraillette [mitrajɛt] *nf* tommy gun.

mitrailleur [mitrajœːr] *nm* machine gunner; **fusil —** automatic rifle **bren-gun; fusilier —** bren-gunner.

mitrailleuse [mitrajøːz] *nf* machine gun.

mitre [mitr] *nf* miter, chimney-pot chimney-cowl.

mi-vitesse [mivitɛs] *ad* **à —** at half speed.

mi-voix [mivwa] *ad* **à —** under one' breath, in an undertone.

mixte [mikst] *a* mixed, composite joint.

mixture [mikstyːr] *nf* mixture.

mnémonique [mnemɔnik] *a* mnemonic; *nf* mnemonics.

mobile [mɔbil] *a* mobile, moving movable, detachable, changeable unstable; *nm* moving body, motive motive power.

mobilier, -ière [mɔbilje, jɛːr] *a* movable, personal; *nm* (suite of furniture.

mobilisable [mɔbilizabl] *a* mobiliz able, available.

mobilisation [mɔbilizasjɔ̃] *nf* mobil ization, liquidation.

mobiliser [mɔbilize] *vt* to mobilize call up, liquidate.

nobilité [mɔbilite] *nf* mobility, instability.

nocassin [mɔkasɛ̃] *nm* moccasin.

noche [mɔʃ] *a* (*fam*) ugly, lousy, rotten.

nodalité [mɔdalite] *nf* modality; *pl* clauses, terms.

node [mɔd] *nf* fashion, manner, vogue; *pl* millinery, fashions; *nm* mood, mode, method; **à la —** in fashion; **magasin de —s** milliner's shop; **— d'emploi** directions for use.

nodèle [mɔdɛl] *a* model, exemplary; *nm* model, pattern; **prendre — sur** to model oneself on.

nodelé [mɔdle] *nm* relief, modeling.

nodeler [mɔdle] *vt* to model, fashion, shape, mold; *vr* to model oneself.

nodérateur, -trice [mɔderatœ:r, tris] *a* moderating, restraining; *n* moderator; *nm* regulator, governor, control.

nodération [mɔderasjɔ̃] *nf* moderation, temperance, restraint, mitigation, reduction.

nodéré [mɔdere] *a* moderate, restrained temperate.

nodérer [mɔdere] *vt* to moderate, restrain, temper, control, regulate, mitigate, reduce; *vr* to control oneself, calm down, abate.

noderne [mɔdɛrn] *a* modern.

noderniser [mɔdɛrnize] *vt* to modernize.

nodeste [mɔdɛst] *a* modest, quiet, retiring, unpretentious.

nodestie [mɔdɛsti] *nf* modesty, unpretentiousness.

nodicité [mɔdisite] *nf* moderateness, reasonableness, slenderness (of means).

nodificateur, -trice [mɔdifikatœ:r, tris] *a* modifying; *n* modifier.

nodificatif, -ive [mɔdifikatif, i:v] *a* modifying, modal.

nodification [mɔdifikasjɔ̃] *nf* modification, change, alteration.

nodifier [mɔdifje] *vt* to modify, change, alter.

nodique [mɔdik] *a* moderate, slender, reasonable.

nodiste [mɔdist] *n* milliner, modiste.

nodulation [mɔdylasjɔ̃] *nf* modulation, inflexion.

nodule [mɔdyl] *nm* module, unit, modulus.

noduler [mɔdyle] *vti* to modulate.

noelle [mwal] *nf* marrow, substance, pith, medulla; **jusqu'à la —** to the backbone, to the core.

noelleux, -euse [mwalø, ø:z] *a* mellow, velvety, soft; *nm* mellowness, velvetiness, softness.

noellon [mwalɔ̃] *nm* quarry stone.

nœurs [mœrs] *nf pl* customs, habits, manners, morals.

noi [mwa] *pn* I, me; *nm* self, ego; **moi-même** myself; **à moi** help! **un ami à —** a friend of mine; **de vous à —** between you and me.

moignon [mwaɲɔ̃] *nm* stump.

moindre [mwɛ̃:dr] *a* lesser, least, *comp sup* of petit.

moine [mwan] *nm* monk, friar.

moineau [mwano] *nm* sparrow.

moins [mwɛ̃] *ad* less, not so (much, many), (the) least, *comp sup* of peu; *prep* less, minus; **— de** less than; **au — at** least; **du — at** least, at any rate; **pas le — du monde** not in the least; **en — de rien** in no time, in a jiffy; **à — de** unless, barring; **à — que** unless; **rien — que** anything but, nothing less than.

moins-value [mwɛ̃valy] *nf* depreciation.

moire [mwa:r] *nf* watered silk.

moiré [mware] *a* moiré, watered.

mois [mwa] *nm* month.

moise [mwa:z] *nm* wicker cradle.

moisir [mwazi:r] *vt* to mildew, make moldy; *vi* to mildew, go moldy, vegetate.

moisi [mwazi] *a* mildewed, moldy, musty, fusty; *nm* mildew, mold; **sentir le —** to have a musty smell.

moisissure [mwazisy:r] *nf* mildew, moldiness, mustiness.

moisson [mwasɔ̃] *nf* harvest, harvest-time, crop.

moissonner [mwasɔne] *vt* to harvest, gather (in), reap.

moissonneur, -euse [mwasɔnœ:r, ø:z] *n* harvester, reaper.

moissonneuse [mwasɔnø:z] *nf* reaping-machine; **—-batteuse** combine-harvester.

moite [mwat] *a* moist, damp, clammy.

moiteur [mwatœ:r] *nf* moistness, clamminess.

moitié [mwatje] *nf* half, (*fam*) better half; **plus grand de —** half as big again; **se mettre de — avec** to go halves with; **couper par —** to cut in halves; **— — fifty-fifty.**

molaire [mɔlɛ:r] *a nf* molar.

môle [mol] *nm* mole, breakwater.

molécule [mɔlekyl] *nf* molecule.

moleskine [mɔlɛskin] *nf* imitation leather.

molester [mɔlɛste] *vt* to molest.

molette [mɔlɛt] *nf* small pestle, knob, (*of spur*) rowel, trimmer.

mollasse [mɔlas] *a* soft, flabby, spineless, apathetic.

mollesse [mɔlɛs] *nf* softness, flabbiness, indolence, apathy.

mollet, -ette [mɔlɛ, ɛt] *a* softish; *nm* (*leg*) calf; **œuf —** soft-boiled egg.

molletière [mɔltjɛ:r] *nf* puttee.

molleton [mɔltɔ̃] *nm* flannel, swansdown.

mollir [mɔli:r] *vt* to ease, slacken; *vi* to become soft, abate, slacken, weaken.

mollusque [mɔlysk] *nm* mollusk, spineless person, vegetable.

môme [mo:m] *n* (*fam*) kid.

moment [mɔmɑ̃] *nm* moment,

momentum; **en ce —** at the moment,
just now; **sur le —** on the spur of
the moment, for a moment; **d'un —
à l'autre** any moment; **à tout —**
constantly; **du — que** from the time
when, seeing that.

momentané [mɔmãtane] *a* momentary.

momie [mɔmi] *nf* mummy.

mon, ma, mes [mɔ̃, ma, me] *a* my;
un de mes amis a friend of mine.

monacal [mɔnakal] *a* monastic,
monkish.

monarchie [mɔnarʃi] *nf* monarchy.

monarchiste [mɔnarʃist] *an* mon-
archist.

monarque [mɔnark] *nm* monarch.

monastère [mɔnastɛːr] *nm* monastery.

monastique [mɔnastik] *a* monastic.

monceau [mɔ̃so] *nm* heap, pile.

mondain [mɔ̃dɛ̃] *a* worldly, society,
fashionable; *n* man about town,
society woman.

mondanité [mɔ̃danite] *nf* worldliness, mundaneness; *pl* social events,
society news.

monde [mɔ̃d] *nm* world, society,
company, crowd, people; **tout le —**
everybody; **homme du —** society
man, society; **beau — society;
aller dans le —** to move in society,
go out; **avoir du —** to have company; **être le mieux du — avec** to
be on the best of terms with;
savoir son — to know how to
behave in company.

mondial [mɔ̃djal] *a* world-, world-
wide.

monégasque [mɔnegask] *an* of
Monaco.

monétaire [mɔnetɛːr] *a* monetary,
financial.

monétiser [mɔnetize] *vt* to mint.

moniteur, -trice [mɔnitœːr, tris] *n*
monitor, instructor, supervisor,
coach.

monnaie [mɔnɛ] *nf* money, currency,
change; — **du pape** honesty
(*flower*); **rendre à qn la — de sa
pièce** to pay s.o. back in his own
coin.

monnayer [mɔnɛje] *vt* to coin, mint,
exploit.

monnayeur [mɔnɛjœːr] *nm* minter;
faux — counterfeiter, coiner.

monocle [mɔnɔkl] *nm* monocle.

monogame [mɔnɔgam] *a* mono-
gamous.

monogramme [mɔnɔgram] *nm*
monogram.

monographie [mɔnɔgrafi] *nm*
monograph.

monolithe [mɔnɔlit] *a* monolithic;
nm monolith.

monologue [mɔnɔlɔg] *nm* monologue,
soliloquy.

monologuer [mɔnɔlɔge] *vi* to solilo-
quize.

monôme [mɔnoːm] *nm* monomial,

procession of students in single file.

monoplan [mɔnɔplã] *nm* monoplane.

monopole [mɔnɔpɔl] *nm* monopoly

monopoliser [mɔnɔpɔlize] *vt* t
monopolize.

monoprix [mɔnɔpri] *nm* a depart
ment store chain.

monorail [mɔnɔraːj] *a nm* monorai

monosyllabe [mɔnɔsillab] *a* mono
syllabic; *nm* monosyllable.

monosyllabique [mɔnɔsillabik]
monosyllabic.

monotone [mɔnɔtɔn] *a* monotonous
dreary, dull.

monotonie [mɔnɔtɔni] *nf* monotony
sameness, dullness.

monseigneur [mɔ̃sɛnjœːr] *nm* H
(Your) Grace, His (Your) Lordship
His (Your) Royal Highness, m
Lord; **pince — nf** jimmy, crowbar.

monsieur [m(ə)sjø] *nm* Mr, master
sir, gentleman.

monstre [mɔ̃ːstr] *a* (*fam*) huge
monstrous, colossal; *nm* monster
monstrosity.

monstrueux, -euse [mɔ̃stryø, øːz]
monstrous, colossal, gigantic, un
natural, scandalous.

mont [mɔ̃] *nm* mount mountain
par —s et par vaux up hill an
down dale.

montage [mɔ̃taːʒ] *nm* carrying up
assembling, equipping, fitting u
(on, out), setting, staging, producing
editing.

montagnard [mɔ̃tanaːr] *a* highland
mountain; *n* highlander, mountain
dweller.

montagne [mɔ̃tan] *nf* mountain(s)
—s russes scenic railway.

montagneux, -euse [mɔ̃tanø, øːz]
mountainous.

montant [mɔ̃tã] *a* rising, climbing
uphill, high-necked; *nm* post, up
right, pole, amount, total, pun
gency.

mont-de-piété [mɔ̃dəpjete] *nr*
pawnbroker's office, shop.

monte [mɔ̃ːt] *nf* mating (season)
mount(ing), horsemanship.

monte-charge [mɔ̃tʃarʒ] *nm* hoist.

monte-plats [mɔ̃tpla] *nm* service
elevator.

monté [mɔ̃te] *a* mounted, fitted
equipped, stocked; **coup —** put-u
job, frame-up; **être — contre** hav
a grudge against.

montée [mɔ̃te] *nf* rise, gradient
slope, climb(ing).

monter [mɔ̃te] *vt* to climb, go up
mount, ride, bring up, carry up
take up, assemble, fit up (out, on
set (up), produce, stage; *vi* t
climb, go (come) up, ascend, com
(to), rise, get in; *vr* to amount; **se —
la tête** to get excited; **je l'ai fait —
à côté de moi** I gave him a lif

monteur, -euse [mɔ̃tœːr, øːz]
mounter, setter, fitter, produce
editor.

monticule [mɔ̃tikyl] *nm* hillock, hummock.

montrable [mɔ̃trabl] *a* presentable, fit to be seen.

montre [mɔ̃:tr] *nf* watch, display, show, show-case; — **-bracelet** wrist-watch; **faire** — **de** to display, show; **mettre qch en** — to display sth. in the window.

montrer [mɔ̃tre] *vt* to show (how to), display, point out, **prove**; *vr* to appear, prove, turn out (to be).

montreur, -euse [mɔ̃trœːr, øːz] *n* showman, -woman.

montueux, -euse [mɔ̃tɥø, øːz] *a* hilly.

monture [mɔ̃tyːr] *nf* mount, setting, frame, handle.

monument [mɔnymɑ̃] *nm* monument, memorial, historic building.

monumental [mɔnymɑ̃tal] *a* monumental, colossal.

se moquer [səmɔke] *vr* to make fun (of **de**), laugh at; **il s'en moque** he doesn't care.

moquerie [mɔkri] *nf* mockery, derision, scoffing.

moquette [mɔkɛt] *nf* moquette.

moqueur, -euse [mɔkœːr, øːz] *a* mocking, derisive, scoffing; *n* scoffer.

moral [mɔral] *a* ethical, moral, intellectual, mental; *nm* morale, mind; **remonter le** — **à qn** to raise s.o.'s spirits, buck s.o. up.

morale [mɔral] *nf* moral, morals, ethics, moral philosophy, preachifying; **faire la** — **à qn** to sermonize, lecture.

moralisateur, -trice [mɔralizatœːr, tris] *a* moralizing, edifying; *n* moralizer.

moraliser [mɔralize] *vt* to sermonize, raise the morals of, lecture; *vi* to moralize.

moraliste [mɔralist] *n* moralist.

moralité [mɔralite] *nf* morality, morals, moral (lesson).

moratoire [mɔratwaːr] *a* moratory.

morbide [mɔrbid] *a* morbid.

morbidité [mɔrbidite] *nf* morbidity, morbidness.

morceau [mɔrso] *nm* morsel, piece, bit, scrap.

morceler [mɔrsəle] *vt* to cut into small pieces, break up.

morcellement [mɔrsɛlmɑ̃] *nm* cutting up, breaking up, dismemberment.

mordant [mɔrdɑ̃] *a* caustic, biting, pungent, piercing, corrosive; *nm* mordancy, pungency.

mordicus [mɔrdikys] *ad* tenaciously, stoutly.

mordiller [mɔrdije] *vt* to nibble, snap playfully at.

mordoré [mɔrdɔre] *a* bronze; *nm* bronze color.

mordre [mɔrdr] *vt* to bite; *vi* to bite, catch, take (to **à**); **s'en** — **les doigts** to be sorry for it.

mordu [mɔrdy] *a* mad (about); *n* fan.

morfondre [mɔrfɔ̃:dr] *vt* to chill to the bone; *vr* to freeze, be bored, wait impatiently.

morganatique [mɔrganatik] *a* morganatic.

morgue [mɔrg] *nf* pride, arrogance, mortuary.

moribond [mɔribɔ̃] *a* moribund, dying.

moricaud [mɔriko] *a* dark-skinned, swarthy; *n* blackamoor.

morigéner [mɔriʒene] *vt* to lecture, haul over the coals.

morne [mɔrn] *a* dismal, dreary, gloomy, dull.

morose [mɔroːz] *a* morose, surly, gloomy.

morosité [mɔrɔzite] *nf* surliness, gloominess.

morphine [mɔrfin] *nf* morphia, morphine.

morphinomane [mɔrfinɔman] *n* morphia addict, drug addict.

morphologie [mɔrfɔlɔʒi] *nf* morphology.

mors [mɔ:r] *nm* bit, chap, joint.

morse [mɔrs] *nm* walrus, Morse code.

morsure [mɔrsyːr] *nf* bite.

mort [mɔ:r] *a* dead, deceased, spent; *nf* death; *n* dead man, dead woman, dummy; **arrêt de** — death-sentence; **avoir la** — **dans l'âme** to be sick at heart; **se donner la** — to take one's life; **point** — neutral, deadlock; **nature** —**e** still life; **eau** —**e** stagnant water; **faire le** — to pretend to be dead, lie low, (*bridge*) be dummy.

mortadelle [mɔrtadɛl] *nf* bologna sausage.

mortaise [mɔrtɛːz] *nf* slot, mortise.

mortalité [mɔrtalite] *nf* mortality.

morte-eau [mɔrto] *nf* neap tide.

mortel, -elle [mɔrtɛl] *a* mortal, fatal, deadly, (*fam*) deadly dull.

morte-saison [mɔrtsɛzɔ̃] *nf* slack season, off season.

mortier [mɔrtje] *nm* mortar, mortar-board.

mortifier [mɔrtifje] *vt* to hang (*game*), mortify, hurt.

mort-né [mɔrne] *a* stillborn.

mortuaire [mɔrtɥɛːr] *a* mortuary, burial, funeral; **drap** — pall.

morue [mɔry] *nf* cod.

morutier [mɔrytje] *nm* cod-fishing boat, cod-fisher.

morve [mɔrv] *nf* glanders, nasal mucus.

morveux, -euse [mɔrvø, øːz] *a* glandered, snotty; *n* (*fam*) brat.

mosaïque [mɔzaik] *a nf* mosaic.

mosquée [mɔske] *nf* mosque.

mot [mo] *nm* word, term, saying; **bon** — witticism; — **de passe** (ralliement) pass word, catchword; — **d'ordre** watchword, directive; — **pour** — word for word; —**s croisés** crossword puzzle; **comprendre à demi**—— to take the hint.

motard [mɔtaːr] nm motorcycle policeman.

motet [mɔtɛ] nm motet, anthem.

moteur, -trice [mɔtœːr, tris] a motive, driving; nm motor, engine.

motif, -ive [mɔtif, iːv] a motive; nm reason, motive, cause, grounds, theme, pattern, design.

motion [mɔsjɔ̃] nf motion, proposal.

motiver [mɔtive] vt to motivate, warrant, give cause for, give the reason for.

moto [mɔto] nf motorcycle, motor-bike.

motocycliste [mɔtɔsiklist] nm motor cyclist.

motorisé [mɔtɔrize] a fitted with a motor, motorized.

motte [mɔt] nf mound, lump, clod, pat; — de gazon turf.

motus [mɔtys] excl mum's the word!

mou, molle [mu, mɔl] a soft, flabby, feeble, limp, slack, close; nm slack (of rope), lights (animal lungs).

mouchard [muʃar] nm sneak, spy, informer, telltale.

moucharder [muʃarde] vt to spy on, inform against, squeal; vi to spy.

mouche [muʃ] nf fly, speck, spot, bull's eye, beauty-spot; — bleue blue-bottle; bateau — river steamer; faire — to hit the bull's-eye; prendre la — to get into a huff.

moucher [muʃe] vt to wipe (s.o.'s) nose, snuff, trim, (fam) tell off; vr to blow one's nose; il ne se mouche pas du pied he thinks a lot of himself.

moucheron [muʃrɔ̃] nm gnat, midge.

moucheté [muʃte] a speckled, flecked, brindle(d).

moucheture [muʃtyːr] nf speckle, spot, fleck.

mouchoir [muʃwaːr] nm handkerchief, kerchief.

moudre [mudr] vt to grind, mill.

moue [mu] nf pout; faire la — to pout.

mouette [mwɛt] nf seagull.

mouffard [mufaːr] n fat-faced, heavy-jowled person.

moufle [mufl] nf mitten, pulley-block, clamp, muffle-furnace.

mouflon [muflɔ̃] nm moufflon, wild sheep.

mouillage [mujaːʒ] nm wetting, damping, moistening, mooring, anchorage, watering-down.

mouiller [muje] vt to wet, damp, moisten, anchor, moor, lay (mines); vr to get wet, fill (eyes); poule mouillée cissy, milksop.

mouilleur [mujœːr] nm damper; — de mines minelayer.

moulage [mulaːʒ] nm milling, grinding, molding, casting.

moule [mul] nm mold, cast, matrix, shape, cake pan; nf mussel, blockhead.

moulé [mule] a molded, well-proportioned, copperplate; nm print.

mouler [mule] vt to mold, cast, fit closely.

mouleur [mulœːr] nm molder, caster.

moulin [mulɛ̃] nm mill; jeter son bonnet par-dessus les —s to throw propriety to the winds.

moulinet [mulinɛ] nm turnstile, current-meter, (fishing) reel; faire le — to twirl one's stick.

moulure [mulyːr] nf molding.

mourant [murɑ̃] a dying, feeble; n dying person.

mourir [muriːr] vi to die (away); vr to be dying, fade (away, out); c'était à — de rire it was killingly funny.

mouron [murɔ̃] nm chickweed; — rouge scarlet pimpernel.

mousquetaire [muskətɛːr] nm musketeer.

mousse [mus] nm ship's boy, cabin-boy; nf moss, froth, foam, cream, lather.

mousseline [muslin] nf muslin; — de soie chiffon; gâteau — sponge cake; pommes — mashed potatoes.

mousser [muse] vi to froth, foam, effervesce, lather.

mousseux, -euse [musø, øːz] a foaming, frothy, sparkling, fizzy.

mousson [musɔ̃] nm monsoon.

moussu [musy] a mossy, moss-grown.

moustache [mustaʃ] nf mustache; pl whiskers.

moustachu [mustaʃy] a having a mustache, whiskered.

moustiquaire [mustikɛːr] nf mosquito net.

moustique [mustik] nm mosquito, gnat.

moutard [mutaːr] nm small boy, youngster, kid.

moutarde [mutard] nf mustard.

moutardier [mutardje] nm mustard-pot, mustard-maker.

mouton [mutɔ̃] nm sheep, mutton, sheepskin, (fam) spy; pl white-caps (waves).

moutonnant [mutɔnɑ̃] a foam-flecked.

moutonner [mutɔne] vi foam, be covered with whitecaps.

moutonneux, -euse [mutɔnø, øːz] a foaming.

mouture [mutyːr] nf milling, grinding, milling dues, (cereals, coffee) ground mixture, rehash.

mouvant [muvɑ̃] a moving, unstable, changeable; sables —s quicksands.

mouvement [muvmɑ̃] nm movement, motion, change, action, impulse, outburst, thrill, stir, traffic; de son propre — of one's own accord; être dans le — to be in the swim.

mouvementé [muvmɑ̃te] a lively,

exciting, thrilling, eventful, animated.

mouvoir [muvwa:r] *vt* to move, drive, propel, move to action, prompt; *vr* to move.

moyen, -enne [mwajẽ, jɛn] *a* medium, average, mean, middle; *nm* means, way, course; *pl* resources, ability; — **âge** Middle Ages; **il n'y a pas —** it can't be done; **au — de** by means of; **employer les grands —s** to take drastic measures.

moyennant [mwajenã] *prep* for, at (price); — **que** on condition that; — **argent** for a consideration.

moyenne [mwajen] *nf* average, mean, passing mark; **en —** on an average.

moyeu [mwajø] *nm* hub, nave, boss.

mû [my] *a* driven, propelled.

muable [myabl] *a* changeable, unstable.

mue [my] *nf* molting, slough(ing), casting of skin or coat, molting time, breaking of the voice, coop.

muer [mɥe] *vi* to molt, cast skin or coat, slough, break; *vr* **se — en** to change into.

muet, -ette [mɥɛ, ɛt] *a* mute, dumb, silent, unsounded; *n* mute, dumb person.

mufle [myfl] *nm* muzzle, snout, nose, mug, fathead, swine.

muflerie [myfləri] *nf* vulgar behavior, mean trick.

mugir [myʒi:r] *vi* to low, bellow, roar, moan, howl.

mugissement [myʒismã] *nm* lowing, bellowing, roaring, moaning.

muguet [mygɛ] *nm* lily of the valley.

muid [mɥi] *nm* hogshead.

mulâtre [myla:tr] *a* mulatto, half-cast; *n* (*f* **mulâtresse**) mulatto.

mule [myl] *nf* (she-)mule; bedroom slipper, mule.

mulet [mylɛ] *nm* (he-)mule; gray mullet.

muletier [myltje] *nm* muleteer, mule-driver.

mulot [mylo] *nm* field mouse.

multicolore [myltikɔlɔ:r] *a* multicolored.

multiple [myltipl] *a* multiple, multifarious, manifold; *nm* multiple.

multiplicateur, -trice [myltiplikatœ:r, tris] *a* multiplying; *nm* multiplier.

multiplication [myltiplikasjɔ̃] *nf* multiplication.

multiplicité [myltiplisite] *nf* multiplicity, multifariousness.

multiplier [myltiplie] *vti* to multiply; *vr* to be on the increase, be everywhere at once.

multitude [myltityd] *nf* multitude, crowd.

municipal [mynisipal] *a* municipal; **conseil —** town-council; **conseiller — town-councilor; loi —e** bylaw.

municipalité [mynisipalite] *nf* municipality, town-council.

munificence [mynifisã:s] *nf* munificence, bounty.

munificent [mynifisã] *a* munificent, bountiful.

munir [myni:r] *vt* to provide, supply, furnish, fit.

munition [mynisjɔ̃] *nf* munitioning, provisioning; *pl* ammunition, munitions.

munitionner [mynisjɔne] *vt* to munition, supply.

muqueux, -euse [mykø, ø:z] *a* mucous.

mur [my:r] *nm* wall; **mettre qn au pied du —** to corner s.o.

mûr [my:r] *a* ripe, mature, mellow.

mûraie [myrɛ] *nf* mulberry plantation.

muraille [myra:j] *nf* wall, rampart, barrier, (*of ship*) side.

mural [myral] *a* mural, wall-.

mûre [my:r] *nf* mulberry; — **sauvage** blackberry.

murer [myre] *vt* to wall in, brick up, block up.

mûrier [myrje] *nm* mulberry bush; — **sauvage** blackberry bush, bramble bush.

mûrir [myri:r] *vt* to ripen, mature, develop; *vi* to grow ripe, reach maturity.

murmure [myrmy:r] *nm* murmur (ing), whisper, babbling.

murmurer [myrmyre] *vti* to murmur, whisper.

musaraigne [myzarɛɲ] *nf* shrewmouse.

musarder [myzarde] *vi* to idle, moon about, dawdle.

musc [mysk] *nm* musk.

muscade [myskad] *nf* nutmeg.

muscat [myska] *nm* muscat grape, muscatel (wine).

muscle [myskl] *nm* muscle.

musclé [myskle] *a* muscular, brawny.

musculature [myskylaty:r] *nf* musculature.

muse [my:z] *nf* muse.

museau [myzo] *nm* muzzle, snout; (*fam*) mug.

musée [myze] *nm* museum; — **de peinture** picture-gallery.

museler [myzle] *vt* to muzzle.

muselière [myzəlje:r] *nf* muzzle.

muser [myze] *vi* to idle, moon about, trifle.

muserolle [myzrɔl] *nf* noseband.

musette [myzɛt] *nf* bagpipe, nosebag, haversack, school-bag; **bal —** popular dance hall.

musical [myzikal] *a* musical.

musicien, -enne [myzisjẽ, jɛn] *a* musical; *n* musician, bandsman.

musicomane [myzikɔman] *n* music-lover.

musique [myzik] *nf* music, band.

musqué [myske] *a* musk-scented, affected.

musulman [myzylmã] *an* Moslem, Mohammedan.

mutabilité [mytabilite] *nf* mutability.

mutation [mytasjɔ̃] *nf* mutation, change, transfer.

mutilation [mytilasjɔ̃] *nf* mutilation, defacement.

mutilé [mytile] *a* mutilated, maimed; *nm* disabled soldier.

mutiler [mytile] *vt* to mutilate, maim, deface.

mutin [mytɛ̃] *a* unruly, roguish, arch, *nm* mutineer.

se mutiner [səmytine] *vr* to rebel, mutiny, refuse to obey.

mutinerie [mytinri] *nf* unruliness, mutiny.

mutisme [mytism] *nm* muteness, dumbness.

mutualité [mytɥalite] *nf* mutuality, (system of) friendly societies.

mutuel, -elle [mytɥɛl] *a* mutual; **société de secours —** friendly society.

myope [mjɔp] *a* short-sighted.

myopie [mjɔpi] *nf* short-sightedness.

myosotis [mjɔzɔtis] *nm* forget-me-not.

myriade [mirjad] *nf* myriad.

myrrhe [miːr] *nf* myrrh.

myrte [mirt] *nm* myrtle.

mystère [mistɛːr] *nm* mystery, mystery play; **il n'en fait pas —** he makes no bones about it, no secret of it.

mystérieux, -euse [misterjø, øːz] *a* mysterious, weird, eerie, uncanny.

mysticisme [mistisism] *nm* mysticism.

mystificateur, -trice [mistifikatœːr, tris] *a* mystifying; *n* hoaxer, leg-puller.

mystification [mistifikasjɔ̃] *nf* mystification, hoax, leg-pull.

mystifier [mistifje] *vt* to mystify, hoax, pull s.o.'s leg.

mystique [mistik] *a* mystical; *n* mystic.

mythe [mit] *nm* myth, legend.

mythique [mitik] *a* mythical, legendary.

mythologie [mitɔlɔʒi] *nf* mythology.

mythologique [mitɔlɔʒik] *a* mythological.

N

nabot [nabo] *n* midget, dwarf.

nacelle [nasɛl] *nf* skiff, gondola.

nacre [nakr] *nf* mother of pearl.

nacré [nakre] *a* pearly.

naevus [nevyːs] *nm* birthmark, mole.

nage [naːʒ] *nf* swimming, rowing, sculling, stroke; **en —** bathed in perspiration.

nageoire [naʒwaːr] *nf* fin, float.

nager [naʒe] *vi* to swim, float, row, scull.

nageur, -euse [naʒœːr, øːz] *n* swimmer, oarsman.

naguère [nagɛːr] *ad* not long since, a little while ago.

naïf, -ïve [naif, iːv] *a* artless, ingenuous, unaffected.

nain [nɛ̃] *an* dwarf.

naissance [nɛsɑ̃ːs] *nf* birth, descent, root, rise, dawn.

naissant [nɛsɑ̃] *a* newborn, dawning, budding, incipient, nascent.

naître [nɛːtr] *vi* to be born, spring up, grow, originate; **faire —** to give rise to, arouse; **à —** unborn.

naïveté [naivte] *nf* artlessness, ingenuousness.

nantir [nɑ̃tiːr] *vt* to give security to, provide.

naphtaline [naftalin] *nf* mothballs, naphthalene.

nappe [nap] *nf* tablecloth, cover, cloth, sheet (of water).

napperon [naprɔ̃] *nm* traycloth, napkin.

narcisse [narsis] *nm* narcissus.

narcotique [narkɔtik] *a nm* narcotic.

narguer [narge] *vt* to flout.

narine [narin] *nf* nostril.

narquois [narkwa] *a* quizzical, waggish.

narrateur, -trice [narratœːr, tris] *n* narrator, teller.

narratif, -ive [narratif, iːv] *a* narrative.

narration [narrasjɔ̃] *nf* narration, story, narrative.

nasal [nazal] *a* nasal.

naseau [nazo] *nm* nostril.

nasillard [nazijaːr] *a* nasal, through one's nose, with a nasal twang.

nasiller [nazije] *vi* to speak through one's nose.

nasse [nas] *nf* net, trap, eel-pot.

natal [natal] *a* native, natal, birth-.

natalité [natalite] *nf* birth-rate.

natation [natasjɔ̃] *nf* swimming.

natif, -ive [natif, iːv] *a* native, inborn.

nation [nasjɔ̃] *nf* nation.

national [nasjɔnal] *a nm* national; **route—e** main road.

nationaliser [nasjɔnalize] *vt* to nationalize.

nationalisme [nasjɔnalism] *nm* nationalism.

nationalité [nasjɔnalite] *nf* nationality.

nativité [nativite] *nf* nativity.

natte [nat] *nf* mat(ting), plait, braid.

naturalisation [natyralizasjɔ̃] *nf* naturalisation.

naturaliser [natyralize] *vt* to naturalize.

naturaliste [natyralist] *a* naturalistic; *n* naturalist.

nature [natyːr] *nf* nature, kind, character, disposition; **— morte** still-life; **grandeur —** life-size; *a* plain, natural; **café —** black coffee.

naturel, -elle [natyrɛl] *a* natural, unaffected, illegitimate; *nm* disposition, naturalness, simplicity.

naufrage [nofra:ʒ] *nm* shipwreck; **faire —** to be shipwrecked.

naufragé [nofraʒe] *a* shipwrecked; *n* castaway.

nauséabond [nozeabɔ̃] *a* nauseous, foul.

nausée [noze] *nf* nausea, sickness, disgust.

nautique [notik] *a* nautical, aquatic.

naval [naval] *a* naval, sea-.

navet [navɛ] *nm* turnip; (*fam*) rubbish, daub.

navette [navɛt] *nf* shuttle, incense box; rape seed; **faire la —** go to and fro.

navigable [navigabl] *a* navigable, seaworthy.

navigateur [navigatœ:r] *nm* navigator, seafarer; *a* seafaring.

navigation [navigasjɔ̃] *nf* navigation, sailing, shipping.

naviguer [navige] *vti* to navigate, sail.

navire [navi:r] *nm* ship, vessel, boat.

navrant [navrɑ̃] *a* heartbreaking, -rending.

navrer [navre] *vt* to break one's heart, grieve.

ne [n(ə)] *neg ad used mostly with pas, point, etc,* not.

néanmoins [neɑ̃mwɛ̃] *ad* nevertheless, notwithstanding, yet, still.

néant [neɑ̃] *nm* nothing(ness), worthlessness, naught.

nébuleux, -euse [nebylø, ø:z] *a* nebulous, cloudy, hazy.

nécessaire [nesɛsɛ:r] *a* necessary, needful, required, requisite; *nm* necessaries, what is necessary, bag, case, outfit.

nécessité [nesesite] *nf* necessity, straitened circumstances.

nécessiter [nesesite] *vt* to necessitate, entail.

nécessiteux, -euse [nesesitø, ø:z] *a* necessitous, needy.

nécrologie [nekrɔlɔʒi] *nf* obituary notice.

nécromancien, -ienne [nekrɔmɑ̃sjɛ̃, jɛn] *n* necromancer.

nectarine [nɛktarin] *nf* nectarine peach.

nef [nɛf] *nf* nave.

néfaste [nefast] *a* luckless, baneful, ill-fated, evil.

nèfle [nɛfl] *nf* medlar.

négatif, -ive [negatif, i:v] *a nm* negative.

négligé [negliʒe] *a* neglected, careless, slovenly; *nm* undress, negligee, dishabille.

négligeable [negliʒabl] *a* negligible.

négligence [negliʒɑ̃:s] *nf* negligence, neglect, carelessness.

négligent [negliʒɑ̃] *a* negligent, careless, neglectful, off-hand.

négliger [negliʒe] *vt* to neglect, be neglectful of, disregard, leave undone; *vr* to neglect oneself, be careless of one's appearance.

négoce [negɔs] *nm* trade, business.

négociable [negɔsjabl] *a* negotiable, transferable.

négociant [negɔsjɑ̃] *n* trader, merchant.

négociation [negɔsjasjɔ̃] *nf* negotiation, transaction, treaty, dealing.

négocier [negɔsje] *vt* to negotiate.

nègre [nɛ:gr] *nm* Negro, black; hackwriter; *a* Negro; **parler petit —** to speak pidgin.

négresse [negrɛs] *nf* negress.

neige [nɛ:ʒ] *nf* snow; **— fondue** sleet, slush; **œufs à la —** floating islands; **tempête de — snowstorm.**

neiger [neʒe] *vi* to snow.

neigeux, -euse [neʒø, ø:z] *a* snowy, snow-covered.

nénufar, nénuphar [nenyfa:r] *nm* water-lily.

néologisme [neɔlɔʒism] *nm* neologism.

néophyte [neɔfit] *nm* neophyte, beginner.

néo-zélandais [neozelɑ̃dɛ] *an* New Zealander, from New Zealand.

néphrite [nefrit] *nf* nephritis.

népotisme [nepotism] *nm* nepotism.

nerf [nɛ:r] *nm* nerve, sinew, (*fig*) energy, stamina; *pl* hysterics; **porter sur les —** à qn to get on s.o.'s nerves.

nerveux, -euse [nɛrvø, ø:z] *a* excitable, highly-strung, sinewy, nervous.

nervosité [nɛrvozite] *nf* irritability, nerves.

nervure [nɛrvy:r] *nf* rib, nervure, vein.

net, nette [nɛt] *a* clean, clear, distinct, plain, sharp, fair, (*of prices*) net; **mettre au —** to make a fair copy of; **faire place nette** to clear out; *ad* plainly, flatly, clearly, dead.

netteté [nɛt(ə)te] *nf* cleanness, cleanliness, distinctness, downrightness.

nettoyage [nɛtwaja:ʒ] *nm* cleaning, cleansing.

nettoyer [nɛtwaje] *vt* to clean (out), clear, mop up.

nettoyeur, -euse [nɛtwajœ:r, ø:z] *n* cleaner.

neuf [nœf] *a nm* nine, ninth.

neuf, neuve [nœf, nœ:v] *a* new; **à — anew**, like new; **quoi de —** what is the news? what's new?

neurasthénie [nørasteni] *nf* neurasthenia.

neutraliser [nøtralize] *vt* to neutralize, counteract.

neutralité [nøtralite] *nf* neutrality.

neutre [nø:tr] *a nm* neuter; *a* neutral; **zone —** no man's land.

neuvième [nœvjɛm] *a nm* ninth.

neveu [n(ə)vø] *nm* nephew.

névralgie [nevralʒi] *nf* neuralgia.

névrite [nevrit] *nf* neuritis.

névrose [nevro:z] *nf* neurosis.

névrosé [nevroze] *an* neurotic, neurasthenic.

nez [ne] *nm* nose, face, nose-piece, sense of smell.

ni [ni] *cj* nor, or, neither ... nor.

niais [niɛ, njɛ] *a* simple, foolish, silly; *n* fool, simpleton.

niaiserie [niɛzri, njɛ-] *nf* silliness, foolishness; *pl* nonsense.

niche [niʃ] *nf* niche, recess, dog-kennel, trick, prank.

nichée [niʃe] *nf* nest(ful), brood.

nicher [niʃe] *vi* to nest; *vt* to put, lodge; *vr* to build a nest, lodge.

nid [ni] *nm* nest.

nièce [njɛs] *nf* niece.

nier [nie, nje] *vt* to deny, plead not guilty.

nigaud [nigo] *a* silly; *n* simpleton, booby, fool.

nimbe [nɛ̃:b] *nm* nimbus, halo.

se nipper [sənipe] *vr* to rig oneself out.

nippes [nip] *nf pl* (old) clothes, things.

nique [nik] *nf* faire la — à to pull a face at, turn up one's nose.

nitouche [nituʃ] *nf* sainte — little prude.

nitrate [nitrat] *nm* nitrate.

niveau [nivo] *nm* level, standard; passage à — grade crossing.

niveler [nivle] *vt* to level, even up, survey.

nobiliaire [nɔbiljɛːr] *n* peerage (-book, -list).

noble [nɔbl] *a* noble, lofty, high-minded; *n* noble(man, woman).

noblesse [nɔblɛs] *nf* nobility, noble birth, nobleness.

noce [nɔs] *nf* wedding, wedding-party; voyage de — s honeymoon; faire la — to live it up.

noceur, -euse [nɔsœːr, øːz] *n* fast liver, dissolute man, rake.

nocif, -ive [nɔsif, iːv] *a* noxious, injurious.

noctambule [nɔktãbyl] *nm* sleep-walker, night-prowler.

nocturne [nɔktyrn] *a* nocturnal, night-; *nm* nocturne.

Noël [nɔɛl] *nm* Christmas, Christmas carol.

nœud [nø] *nm* knot, bow, bond, crux.

noir [nwaːr] *a* black, swarthy, dark, gloomy, dirty, base, foul; *nm* black, black man, bull's eye; broyer du — to be in the dumps.

noire [nwaːr] *nf* quarter note, black-ball.

noirâtre [nwaraːtr] *a* blackish, darkish.

noirceur [nwarsœːr] *nf* blackness, darkness, smut, base action.

noircir [nwarsiːr] *vi* to grow black; *vt* to blacken, darken, sully.

noisetier [nwaztje] *nm* hazel tree.

noisette [nwazet] *nf* hazel-nut; *a* hazel, nut-brown.

noix [nwa] *nf* walnut, nut.

nom [nɔ̃] *nm* name, noun; — de famille surname; petit — Christian

pet name; — de guerre assumed name; qui n'a pas de — beyond words, unspeakable.

nomade [nɔmad] *a* nomadic, wandering.

nombre [nɔ̃:br] *nm* number.

nombrer [nɔ̃bre] *vt* to count, number.

nombreux, -euse [nɔ̃brø, øːz] *a* numerous, many.

nombril [nɔ̃bri] *nm* navel.

nominatif, -ive [nɔminatif, iːv] *a* nominal, registered; *nm* nominative.

nomination [nɔminasjɔ̃] *nf* appointment, nomination.

nommément [nɔmemã] *ad* namely, by name.

nommer [nɔme] *vt* to name, call, mention by name, appoint, nominate, elect; *vr* to be called, give one's name.

non [nɔ̃] *ad* no, not; non-, un-, in-; *nm* no; faire signe que — to shake one's head.

nonagénaire [nɔnaʒenɛːr] *n* nonagenarian.

nonchalance [nɔ̃ʃalãːs] *nf* nonchalance, unconcern.

non-lieu [nɔ̃ljø] *nm* no case.

nonne [nɔn] *nf* nun.

nonobstant [nɔnɔbstã] *prep* notwithstanding; *ad* nevertheless.

nonpareil, -eille [nɔ̃parɛːj] *a* matchless.

non-sens [nɔ̃sãːs] *nm* meaningless sentence, remark.

non-valeur [nɔ̃valœːr] *nf* valueless object, bad debt, worthless security, unproductiveness, inefficient person, non-effective unit.

nord [nɔːr] *nm* north; *a* north, northern; perdre le — be all at sea.

nord-est [nɔr(d)ɛst] *nm* north-east.

nordique [nɔrdik] *a* Nordic.

nord-ouest [nɔr(d)west] *nm* north-west.

normal [nɔrmal] *a* normal, standard, average.

normalien, -ienne [nɔrmaljɛ̃, jen] *n* student at the *Ecole Normale Supérieure*.

normand [nɔrmã] *a* Norman, non-committal, shrewd; *n* Norman.

Normandie [nɔrmãdi] *nf* Normandy.

norme [nɔrm] *nf* norm, standard.

Norvège [nɔrvɛːʒ] *nf* Norway.

norvégien, -ienne [nɔrveʒjɛ̃, jen] *an* Norwegian.

nostalgie [nɔstalʒi] *nf* nostalgia, home-sickness.

notable [nɔtabl] *a* notable, considerable, eminent.

notaire [nɔtɛːr] *nm* notary, solicitor.

notamment [nɔtamã] *ad* notably, especially, among others.

note [nɔt] *nf* note, memorandum, mark, bill, account; changer de — to change one's tune; forcer la — to lay it on, overdo it.

noté [nɔte] *a* **bien, mal — of** good, bad, reputation.

noter [nɔte] *vt* to note, take a note of, write down.

notice [nɔtis] *nf* notice, account, review.

notification [nɔtifikasjɔ̃] *nf* notification, intimation.

notifier [nɔtifje] *vt* to notify, intimate.

notion [nɔsjɔ̃] *nf* notion, idea.

notoire [nɔtwa:r] *a* well-known, notorious.

notoriété [nɔtɔrjete] *nf* notoriety, repute; **— publique common knowledge.**

notre, nos [nɔtr, no] *pos a* our.

nôtre [no:tr] *pos pn* **le, la —, les —s** ours; *nm* ours, our own; *pl* our own people *etc.*

nouer [nwe, nue] *vt* to tie (up), knot; *vr* to become knotted, become stiff; **— conversation avec** to enter into conversation with.

noueux, -euse [nue, ø:z] *a* knotty, gnarled, stiff.

nougat [nuga] *nm* nougat.

nouilles [nu:j] *nf pl* ribbon vermicelli, noodles.

nounou [nunu] *nf* nanny, children's nurse.

nourri [nuri] *a* fed, nourished, furnished, copious, full, sustained, prolonged.

nourrice [nuris] *nf* (wet) nurse; auxiliary tank, feed-pipe.

nourricier, -ière [nurisje, jɛːr] *a* nutritious, nutritive, foster-.

nourrir [nuri:r] *vt* to nourish, feed, suckle, nurse, rear, maintain, board, foster, cherish, fill out.

nourrissant [nurisɑ̃] *a* nourishing, nutritious.

nourrisson [nurisɔ̃] *nm* baby at the breast, infant, foster-child.

nourriture [nurity:r] *nf* food, board, feeding.

nous [nu] *pn* we, us, ourselves, each other; **à — ours.**

nouveau, -elle [nuvo, ɛl] *a* new, recent, fresh, another, further, second; **du — something** new; **de — again; à — afresh, anew.**

nouveau-né [nuvone] *an* new-born (child).

nouveauté [nuvote] *nf* novelty, change, innovation, new publication, play *etc*; *pl* new styles, latest fashions; **magasin de —s** drapery store.

nouvelle [nuvɛl] *nf* piece of news, short story.

nouvellement [nuvɛlmɑ̃] *ad* newly, lately.

Nouvelle-Zélande [nuvɛlzelɑ̃d] *nf* New Zealand.

nouvelliste [nuvɛlist] *nm* short-story writer.

novateur, -trice [nɔvatœːr, tris] *n* innovator.

novembre [nɔvɑ̃:br] *nm* November.

novice [nɔvis] *a* inexperienced, new, fresh, unpracticed; *n* novice, beginner, probationer, apprentice.

noviciat [nɔvisja] *nm* novitiate, probationary period, apprenticeship.

noyade [nwajad] *nf* drowning.

noyau [nwajo] *nm* stone, kernel, nucleus, cell, hub, core.

noyautage [nwajota:ʒ] *nm* (communist) infiltration.

noyé [nwaje] *a* drowned, flooded, sunken, choked, suffused; *n* drowned, drowning man, woman.

noyer [nwaje] *nm* walnut-tree.

noyer [nwaje] *vt* to drown, sink, flood, swamp, (fish) play; *vr* to drown, be drowned.

nu [ny] *a* naked, nude, bare, plain; *nm* nude; **à — uncovered, exposed, bareback.**

nuage [nɥaːʒ] *nm* cloud, haze, drop (of milk in tea).

nuageux, -euse [nɥaʒe, ø:z] *a* cloudy, overcast, hazy.

nuance [nɥɑ̃:s] *nf* shade, hue, tinge, slight suggestion.

nuancer [nɥɑ̃se] *vt* to blend, shade, vary.

nubile [nybil] *a* nubile; **âge — age of consent.**

nucléaire [nyklɛɛːr] *a* nuclear.

nudisme [nydism] *nm* nudism.

nudité [nydite] *nf* nudity, nakedness, bareness.

nue [ny] *nf* cloud.

nuée [nɥe] *nf* (large) cloud, swarm, host, shower.

nuire [nɥiːr] *vt* to harm, hurt, injure, prejudice.

nuisible [nɥizibl] *a* harmful, injurious.

nuit [nɥi] *nf* night, dark(ness); **cette — last** night, tonight; **à la — tombante at nightfall.**

nul, nulle [nyl] *a* no, not one, not any, worthless, of no account, null, invalid, non-existent; **course nulle dead heat; partie nulle tie, tie game; nulle part nowhere;** *pn* no one, none, nobody.

nullement [nylmɑ̃] *ad* not at all, by no means, in no way.

nullité [nyllite] *nf* nullity, invalidity, emptiness, incapacity, nonentity.

nûment [nymɑ̃] *ad* frankly; without embellishment.

numéral [nymeral] *a nm* numeral.

numérique [nymerik] *a* numerical.

numéro [nymero] *nm* number, item, turn; **c'est un — he is a** character.

nuptial [nypsjal] *a* nuptial, bridal, wedding-.

nuque [nyk] *nf* nape of the neck.

nutritif, -ive [nytritif, iːv] *a* nutritious, nourishing, food-.

nymphe [nɛ̃:f] *nf* nymph.

o

obéir [ɔbeiːr] vt to obey, comply (with à).

obéissance [ɔbeisãːs] nf obedience, submission.

obéissant [ɔbeisã] a obedient, dutiful.

obélisque [ɔbelisk] nm obelisk.

obèse [ɔbeːz] a fat, corpulent, stout.

obésité [ɔbezite] nf obesity, corpulence.

objecter [ɔbʒekte] vt to raise (as) an objection.

objecteur [ɔbʒektœːr] nm (conscientious) objector.

objectif, -ive [ɔbʒektif, iːv] a objective; nm objective, target, lens.

objection [ɔbʒeksjɔ̃] nf objection.

objet [ɔbʒɛ] nm object, thing, aim, purpose, subject.

obligation [ɔbligasjɔ̃] nf obligation, duty, agreement, bond, debenture.

obligatoire [ɔbligatwaːr] a obligatory, compulsory, binding.

obligé [ɔbliʒe] a obliged, bound, indispensable, inevitable, grateful.

obligeance [ɔbliʒãːs] nf obligingness, kindness.

obliger [ɔbliʒe] vt to oblige, compel, do (s.o.) a favor.

oblique [ɔblik] a oblique, slanting, indirect, underhand.

obliquer [ɔblike] vi to edge, slant, turn off (direction).

oblitération [ɔbliterasjɔ̃] nf obliteration, canceling.

oblitérer [ɔblitere] vt to obliterate, cancel.

obole [ɔbɔl] nf mite.

obscène [ɔpsɛ(ː)n] a obscene.

obscénité [ɔpsenite] nf obscenity.

obscur [ɔpskyːr] a obscure, indistinct, unknown, dark.

obscurcir [ɔpskyrsiːr] vt to obscure, darken, dim, make unintelligible; vr to grow dark, become obscure, dim.

obscurcissement [ɔpskyrsismã] nm darkening, growing dim, blackout.

obscurité [ɔpskyrite] nf obscurity, darkness, dimness, unintelligibility.

obséder [ɔpsede] vt to obsess, haunt, worry.

obsèques [ɔpsɛk] nf pl obsequies, funeral.

obséquieux, -euse [ɔpsekjø, øːz] a obsequious.

observance [ɔpsɛrvãːs] nf observance.

observateur, -trice [ɔpsɛrvatœːr, tris] a observant, observing; n observer.

observation [ɔpsɛrvasjɔ̃] nf observation, remark, comment, reprimand, observance.

observatoire [ɔpsɛrvatwaːr] nm observatory.

observer [ɔpsɛrve] vt to observe, keep (to), watch, note; **faire —** to

point out; vr to be careful, discreet.

obsession [ɔpsesjɔ̃] nf obsession.

obstacle [ɔpstakl] nm obstacle, impediment.

obstination [ɔpstinasjɔ̃] nf obstinacy.

obstiné [ɔpstine] a obstinate, stubborn.

obstruction [ɔpstryksjɔ̃] nf obstruction, blocking, choking.

obstruer [ɔpstrɥe] vt to obstruct, block, choke; vr to become blocked, choked.

obtempérer [ɔptãpere] vt to comply (with à).

obtenir [ɔptəniːr] vt to obtain, get, procure, achieve.

obtention [ɔptãsjɔ̃] nf obtaining.

obtus [ɔpty] a obtuse, dull, blunt.

obus [ɔby(ːs)] nm shell.

obusier [ɔbyzje] nm howitzer.

oc [ɔk] ad **langue d'—** dialect of South of France.

occasion [ɔkazjɔ̃, -ka-] nf occasion, opportunity, motive, bargain; **à l'—** when the opportunity occurs, in case of need, once in a while, on the occasion (of de), with regard (to de), **d'—** second-hand.

occasionner [ɔkazjɔne, -ka-] vt to occasion, give rise to.

occident [ɔksidã] nm West.

occidental [ɔksidãtal] a West(ern).

occlusion [ɔklyzjɔ̃] nf occlusion, closing, obstruction.

occulte [ɔkylt] a occult, hidden.

occupant [ɔkypã] a occupying; n occupying (power, army etc), occupier.

occupation [ɔkypasjɔ̃] nf occupation, occupancy, business, employment.

occupé [ɔkype] a occupied, busy, engaged.

occuper [ɔkype] vt to occupy, inhabit, fill, hold, employ; vr to keep oneself busy, go in (for de), turn one's attention (to de), attend (to de); **occupez-vous de ce qui vous regarde** mind your own business.

occurrence [ɔkyrãːs] nf occurrence, event; **en l'—** under the circumstances.

océan [ɔseã] nm ocean.

océanique [ɔseanik] a ocean(ic).

ocre [ɔkr] nf ochre.

octave [ɔktaːv] nf octave.

octobre [ɔktɔbr] nm October.

octogénaire [ɔktɔʒeneːr] an octogenarian.

octogone [ɔktɔgɔn] a octagonal; nm octagon.

octroi [ɔktrwa] nm concession, tollhouse.

octroyer [ɔktrwaje] vt to concede, grant, allow, bestow.

oculaire [ɔkyleːr] a ocular, eye-; nm eyepiece.

oculiste [ɔkylist] nm oculist.

ode [ɔd] nf ode.

odeur [ɔdœːr] nf odor, smell, scent.

odieux, -euse [ɔdjø, ø:z] *a* odious, hateful, heinous; *nm.* odiousness, odium.

odorant [ɔdɔrã] *a* sweet-smelling.

odorat [ɔdɔra] *nm* sense of smell.

œil [œ:j] *nm, pl* **yeux** [jø] eye, sight, look; **regarder dans le blanc des yeux** to look full in the face; **cela saute aux yeux** it is obvious; **coûter les yeux de la tête** to cost an outrageous price; **à l'—** on credit, free; **à vue d'—** visibly, at a glance; **coup d'—** view, glance; **faire de l'—à** to give the glad eye to, wink at.

œillade [œjad] *nf* glance; *pl* sheep's eyes.

œillère [œjɛ:r] *nf* blinker, eyecup, eye-tooth.

œillet [œje] *nm* eyelet, pink, carnation; **— de poète** sweet-william.

œsophage [ezɔfa:ʒ] *nm* esophagus, gullet.

œuf [œf] *nm* egg; *pl* spawn, roe; **— dur** hard-boiled egg; **— sur le plat** egg fried in butter; **faire d'un — un bœuf** to make a mountain out of a molehill.

œuvre [œ:vr] *nf* work; **— de bienfaisance** charitable society, charity; **mettre en —** to put in hand, bring into play; *nm* works.

offensant [ɔfɑ̃sã] *a* offensive, objectionable.

offense [ɔfɑ̃:s] *nf* offense.

offenser [ɔfɑ̃se] *vt* to offend, injure, be offensive to; *vr* to take offense.

offensif, -ive [ɔfɑ̃sif, i:v] *a* offensive.

office [ɔfis] *nm* office, functions, service, worship, department; **faire — de** to act as; **d'—** officially, automatically; **des morts** burial-service; *nf* pantry, servants' hall.

officiel, -elle [ɔfisjɛl] *a* official, formal.

officier [ɔfisje] *nm* officer; **— de l'état civil** registrar; *vi* to officiate.

officieux, -euse [ɔfisjø, ø:z] *a* officious, semi-official; **à titre —** unofficially; *n* busybody.

officine [ɔfisin] *nf* drugstore, den, hotbed.

offrande [ɔfrɑ̃:d] *nf* offering.

offrant [ɔfrã] *a nm* **le plus —** the highest bidder.

offre [ɔfr] *nf* offer, tender; **l'— et la demande** supply and demand.

offrir [ɔfri:r] *vt* to offer, proffer, stand, bid, afford, put up; *vr* to offer oneself, present itself.

offusquer [ɔfyske] *vt* to offend, shock; *vr* to take offense (at de).

ogival [ɔʒival] *a* pointed, ogival, gothic.

ogive [ɔʒi:v] *nf* ogive, pointed arch.

ogre, -esse [ɔgr, ɔgrɛs] *n* ogre, ogress.

oie [wa] *nf* goose.

oignon [ɔɲɔ̃] *nm* onion, bulb, bunion.

oindre [wɛ̃:dr] *vt* to oil, anoint.

oiseau [wazo] *nm* bird, individual; **à vol d'—** as the crow flies.

oiseau-mouche [wazomuʃ] *nm* humming-bird.

oiselet [wazlɛ] *nm* small bird.

oiseleur [wazlœ:r] *nm* bird-catcher.

oiseux, -euse [wazø, ø:z] *a* idle, useless, trifling.

oisif, -ive [wazif, i:v] *a* idle; *n* idler.

oisillon [wazijɔ̃] *nm* fledgling.

oisiveté [wazivte] *nf* idleness.

oison [waz5] *nm* gosling, simpleton.

oléagineux, -euse [ɔleaʒinø, ø:z] *a* oleaginous, oily, oil.

olfactif, -ive [ɔlfaktif, i:v] *a* olfactory.

oligarchie [ɔligarʃi] *nf* oligarchy.

olivâtre [ɔliva:tr] *a* olive-hued, sallow.

olive [ɔli:v] *a* olive-green, -shaped; *nf* olive.

olivier [ɔlivje] *nm* olive-tree, -wood.

Olympe [ɔlɛ̃:p] *nm* Olympus.

olympique [ɔlɛ̃pik] *a* Olympic.

ombilical [5bilikal] *a* umbilical, navel.

ombrage [5bra:ʒ] *nm* shade, umbrage.

ombrager [5braʒe] *vt* to shade, overshadow.

ombrageux, -euse [5braʒø, ø:z] *a* touchy, (horse) shy.

ombre [5:br] *nf* shade, shadow, darkness, ghost.

ombrelle [5brɛl] *nf* sunshade, parasol.

ombreux, -euse [5brø, ø:z] *a* shady.

omelette [ɔmlɛt] *nf* omelet; **— aux fines herbes** savory omelet.

omettre [ɔmɛtr] *vt* to omit.

omission [ɔmisjɔ̃] *nf* omission.

omnibus [ɔmniby:s] *nm* (omni)bus; **train —** local, milk train.

omnipotence [ɔmnipɔtɑ̃:s] *nf* omnipotence.

omnivore [ɔmnivɔ:r] *a* omnivorous.

omoplate [ɔmɔplat] *nf* shoulder-blade.

on [5] *pn* one, people, a man, we, you, they; **— demande** wanted; **— dit** it is said; **— ne passe pas** no thoroughfare.

oncle [5:kl] *nm* uncle.

onction [5ksj5] *nf* oiling, anointing, unction, unctuousness.

onctueux, -euse [5ktɥø, ø:z] *a* unctuous, oily, greasy.

onde [5:d] *nf* wave, ocean, water.

ondé [5de] *a* wavy, waved, watered.

ondée [5de] *nf* heavy shower.

on-dit [5di] *nm pl* hearsay, idle talk.

ondoyant [5dwajã] *a* undulating, waving.

ondoyer [5dwaje] *vi* to undulate, wave, sway.

ondulant [5dylã] *a* undulating, waving, flowing.

ondulation [5dylasj5] *nf* undulation, wave.

ondulé [5dyle] *a* wavy, undulating, corrugated.

onduler [5dyle] *vi* to undulate; *vt*

to corrugate, wave; **se faire —** to have one's hair waved.

onéreux, -euse [ɔnerø, øːz] a onerous, heavy.

ongle [5ːgl] nm nail, claw, talon; **se faire les —s** to trim one's nails.

onglée [5gle] nf numbness, tingling (of the fingers).

onglet [5glɛ] nm guard, tab.

onguent [5gɑ̃] nm ointment, salve.

onomatopée [ɔnɔmatɔpe] nf onomatopœia.

onyx [ɔniks] nm onyx.

onze [5ːz] a nm eleven, eleventh.

onzième [5zjɛm] an eleventh.

opacité [ɔpasite] nf opacity.

opale [ɔpal] nf opal.

opaque [ɔpak] a opaque.

opéra [ɔpera] nm opera, opera-house.

opérateur [ɔperatœːr] nm operator, cameraman.

opération [ɔperasj5] nf operation, process, transaction; **salle d'—** operating room.

opératoire [ɔperatwaːr] a operative.

opéré [ɔpere] n person operated upon, surgical case.

opérer [ɔpere] vt to operate, perform an operation on, effect, work, carry out, make; **se faire —** to undergo an operation.

opérette [ɔperɛt] nf operetta, light opera, musical comedy.

ophtalmique [ɔftalmik] a ophthalmic.

opiner [ɔpine] vi to express an opinion, vote; **— du bonnet** to nod approval.

opiniâtre [ɔpinjaːtr] a obstinate, opinionated, stubborn, dogged, persistent.

opiniâtrer [ɔpinjatre] vr to be obstinate, persist (in à).

opiniâtreté [ɔpinjatrəte] nf obstinacy.

opinion [ɔpin5] nf opinion, view.

opium [ɔpjɔm] nm opium.

opportun [ɔpɔrtœ̃] a opportune, timely, advisable.

opportunisme [ɔpɔrtynism] nm opportunism.

opportuniste [ɔpɔrtynist] n opportunist, time-server.

opportunité [ɔpɔrtynite] nf opportuneness, timeliness, advisability.

opposé [ɔpoze] a opposed, opposite, opposing; nm contrary, opposite, reverse; **à l'—** de contrary to.

opposition [ɔpozisj5] nf opposition, objection, injunction, contrast; **par — à** as opposed to, in contradiction to.

oppresser [ɔprese] vt to oppress.

oppresseur [ɔpresœːr] a oppressive, tyrannical; nm oppressor.

oppressif, -ive [ɔpresif, iv] a oppressive.

oppression [ɔpresj5] nf oppression.

opprimer [ɔprime] vt to oppress.

opprobre [ɔprɔbr] nm opprobrium, disgrace.

opter [ɔpte] vt to choose, decide (in favor of pour).

opticien [ɔptisjɛ̃] nm optician.

optimisme [ɔptimism] nm optimism.

optimiste [ɔptimist] a optimistic; n optimist.

option [ɔpsj5] nf choice, option.

optique [ɔptik] a optic, visual, optical; nf optics.

opulence [ɔpylɑ̃ːs] nf opulence, affluence.

opulent [ɔpylɑ̃] a opulent, affluent, rich.

opuscule [ɔpyskyl] nm pamphlet.

or [ɔːr] nm gold; **à prix d'—** at an exorbitant price; **affaire d'—** good bargain, good thing; cj now.

oracle [ɔraːkl] nm oracle.

orage [ɔraːʒ] nm (thunder)storm.

orageux, -euse [ɔraʒø, øːz] a stormy, thundery.

oraison [ɔrɛz5] nf oration, prayer.

oral [ɔral] a oral, verbal; nm oral examination.

orange [ɔrɑ̃ːʒ] nf orange.

orangé [ɔrɑ̃ʒe] a orange(-colored).

orangeade [ɔrɑ̃ʒad] nf orangeade.

oranger [ɔrɑ̃ʒe] nm orange-tree; **fleur(s) d'—** orange-flower, -blossom.

orangerie [ɔrɑ̃ʒri] nf orange-grove, -greenhouse.

orang-outan(g) [ɔrɑ̃utɑ̃] nm orang-outang.

orateur [ɔratœːr] nm orator, speaker.

oratoire [ɔratwaːr] a oratorical; nm chapel, oratory.

orbe [ɔrb] nm orb, globe, heavenly body.

orbite [ɔrbit] nf orbit, socket.

orchestration [ɔrkɛstrasj5] nf orchestration.

orchestre [ɔrkɛstr] nm orchestra; **chef d'—** conductor.

orchestrer [ɔrkɛstre] vt to orchestrate, score.

orchidée [ɔrkide] nf orchid.

ordinaire [ɔrdinɛːr] a usual, common, ordinary, vulgar; **vin —** table wine; nm custom, wont, normal habit, daily fare; **d'—** as a rule; **comme d'—** as usual.

ordinal [ɔrdinal] a ordinal.

ordinateur [ɔrdinatœːr] nm computer.

ordonnance [ɔrdɔnɑ̃ːs] nf order, arrangement, ordinance, regulation, ruling, orderly, batman, medical prescription; **officier d'—** orderly officer, aide-de-camp.

ordonné [ɔrdɔne] a orderly, tidy, methodical.

ordonner [ɔrdɔne] vt to arrange, order, command, prescribe, ordain.

ordre [ɔrdr] nm order, method, discipline, class, character, command, warrant; **mettre en —** to put in order; **à l'—!** order! **— du jour**

order of the day, agenda; **cité à l'— du jour** mentioned in dispatches; **passer à l'— du jour** to proceed with the business; **jusqu'à nouvel —** until further notice; **billet à —** promissory note.

ordure [ɔrdy:r] nf dirt, filth(iness); pl rubbish, refuse; **boîte à —s** trash, garbage can.

ordurier, -ière [ɔrdyrje, jɛ:r] a filthy, obscene.

oreille [ɔrɛ:j] nf ear, lug; **avoir l'—dure** to be hard of hearing; **avoir de l'—** to have a good ear; **dresser l'—** to prick up one's ears; **se faire tirer l'—** to have to be asked twice; **faire la sourde —** to turn a deaf ear; **rebattre les —s à qn** to din in s.o.'s ears.

oreiller [ɔrɛje] nm pillow.

oreillon [ɔrɛjɔ̃] nm earflap; pl mumps.

ores [ɔ:r] ad **d'— et déjà** here and now.

orfèvre [ɔrfɛ:vr] nm goldsmith.

orfèvrerie [ɔrfɛvrəri] nf goldsmith's craft, shop, (gold, silver) plate.

orfraie [ɔrfrɛ] nf sea-hawk.

organdi [ɔrgɑ̃di] nm organdy.

organe [ɔrgan] nm organ, agency, mouthpiece.

organique [ɔrganik] a organic.

organisateur, -trice [ɔrganizatœ:r, tris] a organizing; n organizer.

organisation [ɔrganizasjɔ̃] nf organization, organizing, constitution, body.

organiser [ɔrganize] vt to organize, arrange.

organisme [ɔrganism] nm organism, constitution, system.

organiste [ɔrganist] nm organist.

orge [ɔrʒ] nf barley.

orgelet [ɔrʒəlɛ] nm sty.

orgie [ɔrʒi] nf orgy, riot.

orgue [ɔrg] nm (pl is f) organ; **— de Barbarie** barrel-organ.

orgueil [ɔrgœj] nm pride.

orgueilleux, -euse [ɔrgœjø, ø:z] a proud.

orient [ɔrjɑ̃] nm Orient, East.

oriental [ɔrjɑ̃tal] a Eastern, East, Oriental; n Oriental.

orientation [ɔrjɑ̃tasjɔ̃] nf orientation, guidance, direction, trend.

orienter [ɔrjɑ̃te] vt to orient, guide, direct, point, take the bearings of; vr to find one's bearings, turn (to).

orifice [ɔrifis] nm opening, orifice.

originaire [ɔriʒinɛ:r] a original, native, originating.

originairement [ɔriʒinɛrmɑ̃] ad originally.

original [ɔriʒinal] a original, first, novel, odd; nm original, top copy, eccentric.

originalement [ɔriʒinalmɑ̃] ad in an original manner, oddly.

originalité [ɔriʒinalite] nf originality, eccentricity.

origine [ɔriʒin] nf origin, beginning, extraction, source; **à l'—** originally.

originel, -elle [ɔriʒinɛl] a original, primordial; **péché —** original sin.

oripeau [ɔripo] nm tinsel; pl gaudy finery.

orme [ɔrm] nm elm-tree.

ornement [ɔrnəmɑ̃] nm ornament, adornment.

ornemental [ɔrnəmɑ̃tal] a ornamental, decorative.

ornementer [ɔrnəmɑ̃te] vt to ornament.

orner [ɔrne] vt to ornament, adorn.

ornière [ɔrnjɛ:r] nf rut, groove.

ornithologie [ɔrnitɔlɔʒi] nf ornithology.

orphelin [ɔrfəlɛ̃] a orphan(ed); n orphan; **— de mère** motherless.

orphelinat [ɔrfəlina] nm orphanage.

orteil [ɔrtɛj] nm toe.

orthodoxe [ɔrtɔdɔks] a orthodox, conventional.

orthodoxie [ɔrtɔdɔksi] nf orthodoxy.

orthographe [ɔrtɔgraf] nf spelling.

orthographier [ɔrtɔgrafje] vt to spell.

ortie [ɔrti] nf nettle.

os [ɔs; pl o] nm bone; **trempé jusqu'aux —** soaked to the skin.

oscillateur [ɔsil(l)atœ:r] nm oscillator.

oscillation [ɔsil(l)asjɔ̃] nf oscillation, fluctuation.

osciller [ɔsije, ɔsile] vi to oscillate, swing, flicker, fluctuate, waver.

osé [oze] a daring, bold.

oseille [ɔzɛ:j, o-] nf sorrel.

oser [oze] vt to dare.

osier [ozje] nm osier; **panier d'—** wicker-basket.

ossature [ɔssaty:r] nf frame(work), skeleton.

osselet [ɔslɛ] nm knuckle-bone.

ossements [ɔsmɑ̃, os-] nm pl bones.

osseux, -euse [ɔsø, ø:z] a bony.

ossifier [ɔssifje] vt to ossify; vr to harden.

ossuaire [ɔssɥɛ:r] nm charnel-house.

ostensible [ɔstɑ̃sibl] a ostensible.

ostensoir [ɔstɑ̃swar] nm monstrance.

ostentation [ɔstɑ̃tasjɔ̃] nf ostentation, show.

ostraciser [ɔstrasize] vt to ostracize.

ostréiculture [ɔstreikylty:r] nf oyster-breeding.

otage [ɔta:ʒ] nm hostage.

ôter [ote] vt to remove, take away, take off; vr to remove oneself.

otite [ɔtit] nf otitis.

ottomane [ɔt(t)ɔman] nf divan, ottoman.

ou [u] cj or; **— . . . —** either . . . or.

où [u] ad inter where?; rel where, in which, to which, when; **n'importe —** anywhere; **d'—?** whence? where? where from? **d'— vient que . . .?** how does it happen that . . .? **jusqu'—?** how far? **partout —** wherever.

ouailles [wa:j] nf pl flock.
ouate [wat] nf wadding, cotton wool.
ouaté [wate] a padded, quilted, fleecy, soft.
ouater [wate] vt to pad, line with wadding, quilt.
oubli [ubli] nm forgetfulness, oblivion, omission, oversight; **par —** inadvertently.
oublie [ubli] nf cone, wafer.
oublier [ublie] vt to forget, neglect, overlook; vr to be unmindful of oneself, forget oneself.
oubliettes [ubliɛt] nf pl dungeon.
oublieux, -euse [ublio, ø:z] a forgetful, oblivious.
oued [wɛd] nm watercourse, wadi.
ouest [wɛst] a west(ern); nm west.
ouf [uf] excl ah! phew!
oui [wi] ad yes, ay(e); **je crois que —** I think so.
oui-dire [widi:r] nm hearsay.
ouïe [wi] nf (sense of) hearing; pl gills.
ouïr [wi:r, ui:r] vt to hear.
ouragan [uragɑ̃] nm hurricane.
ourdir [urdi:r] vt to warp, hatch, (plot) weave.
ourler [urle] vt to hem.
ourlet [urlɛ] nm hem, edge.
ours [urs] nm bear; **— blanc** polar bear; **— en peluche** teddy-bear; **— mal léché** unlicked cub, boorish fellow; **il ne faut pas vendre la peau de l'— avant de l'avoir tué** don't count your chickens before they are hatched.
oursin [ursɛ̃] nm sea-urchin.
ourson [ursɔ̃] nm bear's cub.
ouste [ust] excl **allez —!** off you go! clear out!
outil [uti] nm tool.
outillage [utija:ʒ] nm tools, gear, plant; **— national** national capital equipment.
outiller [utije] vt to equip, fit out; provide with tools, equip with plant.
outrage [utra:ʒ] nm outrage, offense, contempt.
outrageant [utraʒɑ̃] a outrageous, insulting.
outrager [utraʒe] vt to outrage, insult, offend.
outrance [utrɑ̃:s] nf excess; **à —** to the utmost, to the bitter end.
outre [u:tr] prep beyond, in addition to, ultra-; ad **passer —** to go on, take no notice (of), disregard; **en — besides**, over and above; **en — de** in addition to; **d'— en — through** and through; **— que** apart from the fact that.
outré [utre] a exaggerated, overdone.
outrecuidance [utrəkɥidɑ̃:s] nf presumptuousness.
outre-Manche [utrəmɑ̃:ʃ] ad across the Channel.
outre-mer [utrəmɛ:r] ad beyond the sea(s), oversea(s).

outrepasser [utrəpase] vt to exceed, go beyond.
outrer [utre] vt to exaggerate, overdo, carry to excess, revolt, provoke beyond measure.
ouvert [uvɛ:r] a open, gaping, unfortified, frank; **grand —** wide open.
ouvertement [uvɛrtəmɑ̃] ad openly, frankly.
ouverture [uvɛrty:r] nf opening, outbreak, overture, aperture, gap, width, span; **heures d'— business** hours, visiting hours.
ouvrable [uvrabl] a workable, working.
ouvrage [uvra:ʒ] nm work, workmanship.
ouvragé [uvraʒe] a worked, wrought.
ouvrager [uvraʒe] vt to work, figure.
ouvrant [uvrɑ̃] a opening; nm leaf (of door).
ouvre-boîtes [uvrəbwat] nm can opener.
ouvre-bouteilles [uvrəbutɛ:j] nm bottle-opener, can opener.
ouvrer [uvre] vt to work.
ouvreuse [uvrø:z] nf usher(ette).
ouvrier, -ière [uvrie, ɛ:r] a working, labor; n worker, workman, operative, laborer, hand; f factory girl.
ouvrir [uvri:r] vt to open, turn (on), draw back, cut (through, open), lance, begin, start; vi to open (onto sur); vr to open, begin, open one's heart.
ovaire [ɔvɛ:r] nm ovary.
ovale [ɔval] a nm oval.
ovation [ɔvasjɔ̃] nf ovation, acclamation.
oxydable [ɔksidabl] a oxidizable, liable to rust.
oxyde [ɔksid] nm oxide.
oxygène [ɔksiʒɛn] nm oxygen.
oxygéné [ɔksiʒene] a oxygenated; **eau — e** hydrogen peroxide; **cheveux — s** peroxided hair.
ozone [ɔzɔn, -o:n] nm ozone.

P

pacage [paka:ʒ] nm pasture, grazing.
pachyderme [paʃidɛrm, paki-] a thick-skinned; nm pachyderm.
pacificateur, -trice [pasifikatœ:r, tris] a pacifying; n peace-maker.
pacification [pasifikasjɔ̃] nf pacification, peace-making.
pacifier [pasifje] vt to pacify, appease, quiet, calm down.
pacifique [pasifik] a pacific, peaceful.
pacifisme [pasifism] nm pacifism.
pacotille [pakɔti:j] nf cheap goods; **de —** tawdry.
pacte [pakt] nm pact.
pactiser [paktize] vi to come to terms, treat.
pagaie [pagɛ] nf paddle.

pagaïe [pagaːj] nf rush, disorder, chaos.

paganisme [paganism] nm paganism.

pagayer [pageje] vti to paddle.

page [paːʒ] nf page; nm page(boy); **à la —** up to date.

pagination [paʒinasjɔ̃] nf paging, pagination.

pagne [paɲ] nm loincloth, (Africa) cloth (toga).

païen, -enne [pajɛ̃, jɛn] a nf pagan, heathen.

paillard [pajaːr] a lewd, ribald.

paillardise [pajardiːz] nf ribaldry, ribald joke.

paillasse [pajas] nf straw mattress, palliasse.

paillasson [pajasɔ̃] nm (door)mat, matting.

paille [paːj] nf straw, chaff, mote, flaw; **feu de —** flash in the pan; **homme de —** figurehead.

pailleter [pajte] vt to spangle.

paillette [pajɛt] nf spangle, flaw, flash, flake.

paillotte [pajɔt] nf straw, reed hut.

pain [pɛ̃] nm bread, loaf; **petit —** roll; **— de savon** cake of soap; **cela se vend comme du — frais** that sells like hot cakes; **pour une bouchée de —** for a mere song.

pair [peːr] a equal, even; nm equal, peer, par; **être au —** to have board and lodging but unpaid; **aller de — avec** to be in keeping with; **marcher de — avec** to keep abreast of; **traiter qn de — à égal** to treat someone as an equal.

paire [peːr] nf pair, brace.

pairie [peri] nf peerage.

paisible [pezibl] a peaceful, quiet.

paître [peːtr] vt to pasture, graze, crop; vi to browse, graze; **envoyer — qn** to send s.o. about his business.

paix [pɛ] nf peace(fulness), quiet (ness).

palabrer [palabre] vi to palaver.

palace [palas] nm magnificent hotel.

palais [palɛ] nm palace, palate; **P— de Justice** law-courts.

palan [palɑ̃] nm pulley-block, tackle.

palatal [palatal] a palatal.

pale [pal] nf blade, sluice.

pâle [paːl] a pale, pallid, wan.

palefrenier [palfrənje] nm groom, ostler.

palet [palɛ] nm quoit, puck.

paletot [palto] nm coat, overcoat.

palette [palɛt] nf palette, bat, blade; **roue à —e** paddle-wheel.

pâleur [palœːr] nf pallor, paleness.

palier [palje] nm (stair) landing, stage, level stretch.

pâlir [paliːr] vt to make pale; vi to turn pale, grow dim.

palissade [palisad] nf palisade, fence, stockade.

palissandre [palisɑ̃ːdr] nm rose-wood.

palliatif, -ive [palljatif, iːv] a nm palliative.

palmarès [palmareːs] nm prize list, honors list.

palme [palm] nf palm(-branch); **noix de —** palm nut.

palmier [palmje] nm palm-tree.

palonnier [palɔnje] nm swing-bar, rudder-bar.

pâlot, -otte [palo, ɔt] a palish, drawn.

palpable [palpabl] a palpable, obvious.

palpabilité [palpabilite] nf palpability, obviousness.

palper [palpe] vt to feel, finger.

palpitant [palpitɑ̃] a quivering, throbbing, fluttering, exciting.

palpiter [palpite] vi to palpitate, quiver, throb, flutter.

paludéen, -enne [palydeɛ̃, ɛn] a marsh.

paludisme [palydism] nm malaria.

pâmer [pame] vir to faint, swoon; **se — d'admiration devant** to go into raptures over.

pâmoison [pamwazɔ̃] nf swoon, faint.

pamphlet [pɑ̃flɛ] nm pamphlet, lampoon.

pamphlétaire [pɑ̃fleteːr] nm pamphleteer.

pamplemousse [pɑ̃pləmus] nf grapefruit.

pampre [pɑ̃ːpr] nm vine-branch.

pan [pɑ̃] nm skirt, tail, flap, side, bit.

pan! [pɑ̃] excl bang!

panacée [panase] nf panacea.

panache [panaʃ] nm plume, tuft, trail, wreath, somersault; **avoir du — to** have style; **avoir son — to** be slightly intoxicated.

panaché [panaʃe] a plumed, mixed, motley; **bière —e** shandygaff.

panade [panad] nf **être dans la — to** be in a fix, to be in want.

panard [panaːr] nm (fam) foot.

panaris [panari] nm whitlow.

pancarte [pɑ̃kart] nf bill, placard.

panégyrique [paneʒirik] a eulogistic; nm panegyric.

paner [pane] vt to cover with breadcrumbs.

panier [panje] nm basket, hamper; **— à salade** salad shaker, black Maria; **— percé** spendthrift.

panique [panik] a nf panic.

panne [pan] nf plush, fat, breakdown; **en — hove** to, stranded, broken down; **rester en — d'essence** to run out of gas.

panneau [pano] nm panel, board, hoarding, trap.

panoplie [panɔpli] nf panoply, suit of armor.

panorama [panɔrama] nm panorama.

panoramique [panɔramik] a panoramic.

panse [pɑ̃ːs] nf paunch.

pansement [pãsmã] nm dressing.

panser [pãse] vt to dress, groom, rub down.

pansu [pãsy] a pot-bellied.

pantalon [pãtalɔ̃] nm trousers, knickers.

pantelant [pãtlã] a panting.

panthéisme [pãteism] nm pantheism.

panthère [pãtɛːr] nf panther.

pantin [pãtɛ̃] nm jumping-jack, puppet, nobody.

pantois [pãtwa] a flabbergasted, speechless.

pantomime [pãtɔmim] nf pantomime, dumb show.

pantoufle [pãtufl] nf slipper.

panure [panyːr] nf bread-crumbs.

paon, -onne [pã, pan] n peacock, -hen.

papa [papa] nm daddy, papa; à la — unhurriedly; de — old-fashioned.

papauté [papote] nf papacy.

papaye [papaj] nf pawpaw.

pape [pap] nm Pope.

papelard [paplaːr] a nmf sanctimonious (person).

paperasse [papras] nf official paper, old paper, red tape.

paperassier, -ière [paprasje, jɛːr] a who likes to accumulate papers, bureaucratic.

papeterie [paptri] nf paper manufacture, trade, mill, stationer's shop.

papetier, -ière [paptje, jɛːr] n paper-manufacturer, stationer.

papier [papje] nm paper, document; — à lettres notepaper; — de soie tissue paper; — peint wallpaper; — hygiénique toilet paper.

papillon [papijɔ̃] nm butterfly, moth, leaflet, inset, ticket.

papillonner [papijɔne] vi to flit, flutter about.

papillote [papijɔt] nf curl paper, oiled paper for cooking.

papilloter [papijɔte] vt to put into curl papers; vi to flicker, blink.

papyrus [papiryːs] nm papyrus.

pâque [paːk] nf Passover.

paquebot [pakbo] nm steamer, liner, packet-boat.

pâquerette [pakrɛt] nf daisy.

Pâques [paːk] nm Easter; nf pl Easter sacrament; — fleuries Palm Sunday.

paquet [pakɛ] nm parcel, package, bundle; — de mer mass of sea water, heavy sea.

par [par] prep by, through, for, with, in, from, out, over, about, on, out of; — où a-t-il passé? which way did he go? — ici (là) this way (that way); — trop difficile far too difficult; —ci, —là here and there.

parabole [parabɔl] nf parable, parabola.

parabolique [parabɔlik] a parabolic.

parachever [paraʃve] vt to finish off, complete.

parachute [paraʃyt] nm parachute.

parachutiste [paraʃytist] n parachutist, paratrooper.

parade [parad] nf parade, show, display, parry.

paradis [paradi] nm paradise, heaven, gallery.

paradoxal [paradɔksal] a paradoxical.

paradoxe [paradɔks] nm paradox.

paraffine [parafin] nf (liquid) paraffin.

parage [paraːʒ] nm trimming, birth, lineage; pl regions, parts, latitudes.

paragraphe [paragraf] nm paragraph.

paraître [parɛːtr] vi to appear, seem, look, be published, show; il y paraît that is quite obvious; à ce qu'il me paraît as far as I can judge.

parallèle [paralɛl] a nm parallel, comparison.

parallélogramme [paralelɔgram] nm parallelogram.

paralyser [paralize] vt to paralyze, cripple.

paralysie [paralizi] nf paralysis.

paralytique [paralitik] a nmf paralytic.

parangon [parãgɔ̃] nm paragon, flawless gem.

parapet [parapɛ] nm parapet.

paraphe [paraf] nm flourish, initial.

parapher [parafe] vt to initial.

paraphrase [parafraːz] nf paraphrase.

paraphraser [parafraze] vt to paraphrase.

parapluie [paraplɥi] nm umbrella.

parasite [parazit] a parasitic; nm parasite; pl (radio) interference.

parasol [parasɔl] nm sunshade, parasol.

paratonnerre [paratɔnɛːr] nm lightning conductor.

paratyphoïde [paratifɔid] a nf paratyphoid.

paravent [paravã] nm folding-screen.

parbleu [parblø] excl I should think so! you bet!

parc [park] nm park, pen, paddock, parking lot; — à huîtres oyster bed.

parcage [parkaːʒ] nm penning, (cars) parking.

parcelle [parsɛl] nf particle, scrap, plot.

parce que [pars(ə)kə] cj because.

parchemin [parʃəmɛ̃] nm parchment, vellum.

parcimonie [parsimɔni] nf parsimony, meanness.

parcimonieux, -euse [parsimɔnjø, øːz] a parsimonious, niggardly.

parcourir [parkuriːr] vt to go through, travel over (through), read through, glance through, cover.

parcours [parkuːr] nm distance, mileage, run, course.

par-dessous [pardəsu] prep under, beneath; ad underneath, under it, them.

par-dessus [pardəsy] prep over; ad over it, them, on top (of it, them); nm overcoat.

par-devant [pardəvã] prep before, in the presence of.

pardon [pardɔ̃] nm pardon, forgiveness, pilgrimage.

pardonner [pardɔne] vt to forgive, pardon, excuse.

pare-boue [parbu] nm fender.

pare-brise [parbriz] nm windscreen, windshield.

pare-chocs [parʃɔk] nm bumper.

pareil, -eille [parɛj] a similar, like, same, equal, such; nmf peer, equal, match; rendre la —le à qn to get even with s.o.

pareillement [parɛjmã] ad likewise, also.

parement [parmã] nm cuff, altar cloth, facing, curbstone.

parent [parã] nm relative, kinsman; pl parents, relations.

parenté [parãte] nf relationship, kinship.

parenthèse [parãtɛːz] nf parenthesis, digression, bracket; entre —s in parentheses, by the way.

parer [pare] vt to adorn, deck out, trim, pare, ward off; vi — à qch to guard against sth.

paresse [parɛs] nf laziness, sloth, sluggishness.

paresser [parɛse] vi to idle, laze.

paresseux, -euse [parɛsø, øːz] a lazy, idle, sluggish; n lazybones.

parfaire [parfɛːr] vt to finish off, complete.

parfait [parfɛ] a perfect, real; nm perfect tense.

parfaitement [parfɛtmã] ad perfectly, absolutely, exactly, quite so.

parfois [parfwa] ad sometimes, occasionally, at times.

parfum [parfœ̃] nm perfume, scent, flavor.

parfumé [parfyme] a perfumed, scented, fragrant, flavored.

parfumerie [parfymri] nf perfumery.

pari [pari] nm bet, wager; — mutuel totalizator.

paria [parja] nm outcast.

parier [parje] vt to bet, lay wager.

parieur, -euse [parjœːr, øːz] n backer, punter.

parisien, -ienne [parizjɛ̃, jɛn] nmf Parisian, from Paris.

paritaire [paritɛːr] a représentation — equal representation.

parité [parite] nf parity, equality, evenness.

parjure [parʒyːr] a perjured; n perjurer; nm perjury.

parlant [parlã] a talking; film — talkie.

parlement [parləmã] nm parliament.

parlementaire [parləmãtɛːr] a parliamentary; drapeau — flag of truce.

parlementer [parləmãte] vi to parley.

parler [parle] vti to speak, talk; nm speech, speaking; façon de — manner of speaking.

parleur, -euse [parlœːr, øːz] n speaker, talker.

parloir [parlwaːr] nm parlour.

parmi [parmi] prep among(st), amid(st).

Parnasse [parnaːs] nf Parnassus.

parodie [parɔdi] nf parody, skit.

parodier [parɔdje] vt to parody, do a skit on.

paroi [parwa] nf partition, wall, lining.

paroisse [parwas] nf parish.

paroissial [parwasjal] a parochial.

paroissien, -enne [parwasjɛ̃, jɛn] a parochial; n parishioner; nm prayerbook.

parole [parɔl] nf word, remark, parole, promise, (power of) speech; porter la — to be the spokesman.

paroxysme [parɔksism] nm paroxysm, fit, outburst.

parquer [parke] vt to pen up, imprison, park.

parquet [parkɛ] nm floor(ing), public prosecutor's department.

parqueter [parkəte] vt to parquet, floor.

parqueterie [parkətri] nf laying of floors, parquetry.

parrain [parɛ̃] nm godfather, sponsor.

parricide [parisid] a parricidal; nm parricide.

parsemer [parsəme] vt to sprinkle, strew, dot.

part [paːr] nf share, portion, part; billet de faire — invitation, announcement (wedding, funeral): prendre — à to take part in, join in; faire — de qch à qn to acquaint s.o. with sth; de — en — through and through; de — et d'autre on both sides; d'une —, d'autre — on the one hand, on the other hand; à — aside, except for.

partage [partaːʒ] nm sharing, portion, allotment.

partager [partaʒe] vt to divide, share (out), apportion.

partance [partãːs] nf departure; en — (outward) bound, outgoing.

partant [partã] a departing; nm pl departing guests, starters; ad therefore.

partenaire [partənɛːr] nmf partner.

parterre [partɛːr] nm flower-bed, pit.

parti [parti] nm party, side, advantage, decision, course, match; se ranger du — de to side with; en prendre son — to make the best of it; tirer — de to take advantage of;

— **pris** prejudice; *a* gone, away tipsy.

partial [parsjal] *a* partial, prejudiced.

partialité [parsjalite] *nf* partiality, prejudice.

participation [partisipasjɔ̃] *nf* participation, share.

participe [partisip] *nm* participle.

participer [partisipe] *vi* to participate, share; — **de** to partake of, have something of.

particulariser [partikylarize] *vt* to particularize, specify; *vr* to be different from others.

particularité [partikylarite] *nf* particularity, peculiarity.

particule [partikyl] *nf* particle.

particulier, -ière [partikylje, jɛːr] *a* particular, peculiar, special, personal, private; *n* private individual.

partie [parti] *nf* part, party, game; **faire** — **de** to belong to, be part of; **se mettre de la** — to join in; **prendre à** — to call to account.

partiel [parsjel] *a* partial.

partir [partiːr] *vi* to depart, leave, set off, go away, start; — **(d'un éclat) de rire** to burst out laughing.

partisan [partizɑ̃] *nm* partisan, supporter, follower, guerrilla soldier.

partition [partisjɔ̃] *nf* partition, score.

partout [partu] *ad* everywhere; — **où** wherever.

parure [paryːr] *nf* adorning, ornament, dress, set of jewelry.

parution [parysjɔ̃] *nf* appearance, publication.

parvenir [parvəniːr] *vi* to arrive, reach, attain, manage, succeed.

parvenu [parvəny] *n* upstart.

parvis [parvi] *nm* parvis, square.

pas [pɑ] *ad* not; *nm* step, pace, tread, threshold, strait, pass; **mauvais** — awkward predicament; **à deux** — **d'ici** nearby, just round the corner; **au** — at walking pace, dead slow; **prendre le** — **sur** to take precedence over.

passable [pasabl] *a* passable, fair.

passage [pɑsaːʒ] *nm* passage, way through, passing, crossing, transition; **être de** — to be passing through; — **interdit** no thoroughfare.

passager, -ère [pasaʒe, ɛːr] *a* fleeting, short-lived; *n* passenger.

passant [pasɑ̃] *a* busy; *n* passer-by.

passe [pɑːs] *nf* pass(ing), channel, permit, thrust; **en** — **de** in a fair way to.

passementerie [pasmɑ̃tri] *nf* lace (trade), trimmings.

passe-montagne [pasmɔ̃taɲ] *nm* Balaclava (helmet).

passe-partout [paspartu] *nm* master-, (skeleton-)key.

passe-passe [paspas] *nm* sleight of hand.

passeport [paspɔːr] *nm* passport.

passé [pase] *a* past, over, faded; *nm* past.

passer [pase] *vt* to pass, hand, cross, ferry across, exceed, excuse, spend, strain, slip on; *vi* to pass (on, over, off, by, through), fade, call, to be shown, be promoted; *vr* to happen, take place, go off, be spent; — **un examen** to take an examination; **faire** — to hand around; **se faire** — **pour** to pose as; **se** — **de** to do without.

passereau [pasro] *nm* sparrow.

passerelle [pasrel] *nf* foot-bridge, (ship) bridge, gangway.

passe-temps [pastɑ̃] *nm* pastime.

passeur, -euse [pasœːr, øːz] *n* ferryman (woman).

passible [pasibl] *a* liable.

passif, -ive [pasif, iːv] *a* passive; *nm* debit, liabilities, passive voice.

passion [pasjɔ̃] *nf* passion.

passionnel, -elle [pasjɔnel] *a* concerning the passions, caused by jealousy.

passionné [pasjɔne] *a* passionate, enthusiastic; *nmf* enthusiast.

passionner [pasjɔne] *vt* to impassion, thrill, excite, fill with enthusiasm; *vr* to become passionately fond (of **pour**), be enthusiastic (over **pour**).

passivité [pasivite] *nf* passivity.

passoire [paswaːr] *nf* strainer.

pastel [pastel] *nm* crayon, pastel (drawing).

pastèque [pastɛk] *nf* water-melon.

pasteur [pastœːr] *nm* shepherd, pastor, minister.

pasteuriser [pastœrize] *vt* to pasteurize.

pastiche [pastiʃ] *nm* pastiche, parody.

pastille [pastiːj] *nf* lozenge, drop, (rubber) patch.

pastis [pastis] *nm* aniseed aperitif, a muddle.

pastoral [pastɔral] *a* pastoral.

pat [pat] *a nm* stalemate.

pataquès [patakɛːs] *nm* faulty liaison.

patate [patat] *nf* (sweet) potato, (*fam*) spud.

patati [patati] **et** — **et patata** and so on and so forth.

pataud [pato] *a* clumsy, boorish.

patauger [patoʒe] *vi* to splash, flounder, paddle.

pâte [paːt] *nf* paste, dough, fufu (W. African); *pl* noodles, spaghetti *etc*; **être de la** — **des héros** to be of the stuff that heroes are made of; **quelle bonne** — **d'homme** what a good guy.

pâté [pate] *nm* pie, blot, block.

pâtée [pate] *nf* mash, food.

patelin [patlɛ̃] *a* glib, wheedling; *nm* village.

patenôtre [patnoːtr] *nf* Lord's prayer.

patent [patɑ̃] *a* patent, obvious.
patente [patɑ̃t] *nf* license.
patenter [patɑ̃te] *vt* to license; **faire —** to patent.
patère [patɛːr] *nf* (hat-) coat-peg.
paterne [patɛrn] *a* patronizing.
paternel, -elle [patɛrnɛl] *a* paternal, fatherly.
paternité [patɛrnite] *nf* paternity, fatherhood.
pâteux, -euse [patø, øːz] *a* doughy, thick, coated.
pathétique [patetik] *a* pathetic, touching; *nm* pathos.
pathologie [patɔlɔʒi] *nf* pathology.
pathos [patɔs] *nm* bathos.
patibulaire [patibylɛːr] *a* of the gallows, hangdog.
patiemment [pasjamɑ̃] *ad* patiently.
patience [pasjɑ̃ːs] *nf* patience.
patient [pasjɑ̃] *a* patient, long-suffering; *n* patient.
patienter [pasjɑ̃te] *vi* to have patience.
patin [patɛ̃] *nm* skate, runner, skid; **—s à roulettes** roller skates.
patine [patin] *nf* patina.
patiner [patine] *vi* to skate, slip.
patineur, -euse [patinœːr, øːz] *n* skater.
patinoire [patinwaːr] *nf* skating-rink.
pâtir [pɑtiːr] *vi* to suffer.
pâtisserie [pɑtisri] *nf* pastry (-making), pastry-shop, tea-room; *pl* cakes.
pâtissier, -ière [pɑtisje, jɛːr] *n* pastry-cook, tea-room proprietor.
patois [patwa] *nm* patois, dialect, lingo.
patraque [patrak] *a* out of sorts, seedy, rotten.
pâtre [pɑːtr] *nm* herdsman, shepherd.
patriarche [patriarʃ] *nm* patriarch.
patrie [patri] *nf* native land, fatherland.
patrimoine [patrimwan] *nm* patrimony, heritage.
patriote [patriɔt] *a* patriotic; *nmf* patriot.
patriotique [patriɔtik] *a* patriotic.
patriotisme [patriɔtism] *nm* patriotism.
patron, -onne [patrɔ̃, ɔn] *n* patron, patron saint, protector, head, boss, skipper; *nm* pattern, model.
patronal [patrɔnal] *a* of a patron saint, of employers.
patronat [patrɔna] *nm* (body of) employers.
patronner [patrɔne] *vt* to patronize, support.
patrouille [patruːj] *nf* patrol.
patrouiller [patruje] *vi* to patrol.
patte [pat] *nf* paw, foot, leg, tab, flap; **— de mouches** scrawl.
patte-d'oie [patdwa] *nf* crossroads; *pl* crow's feet, wrinkles.
pattemouille [patmuːj] *f* damp cloth (*for ironing*).

pâturage [pɑtyraːʒ] *nm* grazing, pasture.
pâture [pɑtyːr] *nf* food, pasture.
paturon [patyrɔ̃] *nm* pastern.
paume [poːm] *nf* palm (of hand), tennis.
paupière [popjɛːr] *nf* eyelid.
paupiette [popjet] *nf* (veal) bird.
pause [poːz] *nf* pause, interval, rest; **—café** coffee-break.
pauvre [poːvr] *a* poor, scanty, sorry, wretched, shabby; *n* poor **man, woman.**
pauvresse [povrɛs] *nf* poor woman.
pauvreté [povrəte] *nf* poverty, want.
se pavaner [səpavane] *vr* to strut (about).
pavé [pave] *nm* pavement, paved road, paving-stone, slab; **battre le —** to walk the streets; **prendre le haut du —** to assume lordly airs.
pavillon [pavijɔ̃] *nm* pavilion, lodge, flag, ear- (mouth)piece, bell (of brass instrument); **— de jardin** summer-house.
pavoiser [pavwaze] *vt* to deck with flags, bunting.
pavot [pavo] *nm* poppy.
payable [pɛjabl] *a* payable.
payant [pɛjɑ̃] *a* paying; *n* payer.
paye [pɛːj] *nf* pay, wages.
payement [pɛjmɑ̃] *nm* payment.
payer [pɛje] *vt* to pay (for), stand, treat; *vi* to pay; **—d'audace** to brazen it out, put a bold face on it; **— de mots** to put off with fine talk; **— la tête de qn** to get a rise out of s.o.; **il est payé pour le savoir** he knows it to his cost.
payeur, -euse [pɛjœːr, øːz] *n* payer, teller, paymaster.
pays [pe(j)i] *nm* country, land, district, locality; *n* (*f* **payse**) fellow-countryman, -woman.
paysage [peizaːʒ] *nm* landscape, scenery.
paysagiste [peizaʒist] *nm* landscape painter.
paysan, -anne [peizɑ̃, an] *a* peasant; *n* countryman.
péage [peaːʒ] *nm* toll.
peau [po] *nf* skin, hide, peel; **avoir qn dans la —** to be head over heels in love with s.o.; **faire — neuve** to cast its skin, turn over a new leaf.
peau-rouge [poruːʒ] *nm* redskin, Red Indian.
peccadille [pekadiːj] *nf* peccadillo.
pêche [pɛʃ] *nf* fishing, fishery, catch, peach.
péché [peʃe] *nm* sin.
pécher [peʃe] *vi* to sin.
pêcher [peʃe] *vt* to fish for, fish up; *vi* to fish.
pêcherie [pɛʃri] *nf* fishery, fishing-ground.
pécheur, -eresse [peʃœːr, peʃrɛs] *a* sinning; *n* sinner.
pêcheur, -euse [pɛʃœːr, øːz] *a* fishing; *n* fisher, fisherman, -woman; **— à la ligne** angler.

péculateur [pekylatœːr] nm peculator, embezzler.

pécule [pekyl] nf savings, nest-egg, gratuity.

pécuniaire [pekynjɛːr] a pecuniary.

pédagogie [pedagɔʒi] nf pedagogy.

pédagogique [pedagɔʒik] a pedagogic.

pédale [pedal] nf pedal, treadle.

pédaler [pedale] vi to pedal, cycle.

pédant [pedɑ̃] a pedantic; n pedant.

pédicure [pediky:r] n chiropodist.

pègre [pɛːgr] nf underworld.

peigne [pɛɲ] nm comb, card.

peigné [peɲe] a combed; **bien —** well-groomed; **mal —** unkempt, tousled.

peignée [peɲe] nf drubbing.

peigner [peɲe] vt to comb (out), card, dress down.

peignoir [peɲwaːr] nm (woman's) dressing-gown, wrap.

peindre [pɛ̃ːdr] vt to paint, depict.

peine [pɛn] nf penalty, punishment, affliction, sorrow, trouble, difficulty; **homme à — laborer; en être pour sa —** to have one's trouble for nothing; **à — hardly, scarcely.

peiner [pɛne] vt to vex, grieve, pain; vi toil, drudge.

peintre [pɛ̃ːtr] nm painter, artist.

peinture [pɛ̃ty:r] nf painting, picture, paint.

péjoratif, -ive [peʒɔratif, iːv] a pejorative.

pelage [pəlaːʒ] nm coat, fur, wool.

pêle-mêle [pɛlmɛl] ad pell-mell, helter-skelter; nm jumble.

peler [p(ə)le] vt to peel, skin; vi to peel off.

pèlerin [pɛlrɛ̃] n pilgrim.

pèlerine [pɛlrin] nf cape.

pèlerinage [pɛlrinaːʒ] nm pilgrimage.

pélican [pelikɑ̃] nm pelican.

pelisse [p(ə)lis] nf pelisse, fur-lined coat.

pelle [pɛl] nf shovel, scoop.

pelleter [pɛlte] vt to shovel.

pelleterie [pɛltri] nf fur-trade, furriery.

pelletier, -ière [pɛltje, jɛːr] n furrier.

pellicule [pelikyl] nf pellicle, skin, film; pl dandruff.

pelote [plɔt] nf ball, wad, pincushion, pelota.

peloton [plɔtɔ̃] nm ball, group, squad, platoon.

pelotonner [plɔtɔne] vt to wind into a ball; vr to curl up, huddle together.

pelouse [pluːz] nf lawn, green, public enclosure.

peluche [plyʃ] nf plush, shag.

pelure [plyːr] nf peel, skin, rind; **papier —** onionskin paper.

pénal [penal] a penal.

pénalité [penalite] nf penalty.

penaud [pəno] a crestfallen, sheepish, abashed.

penchant [pɑ̃ʃɑ̃] nm slope, tendency.

penché [pɑ̃ʃe] a leaning, stooping.

pencher [pɑ̃ʃe] vt to bend, tilt; vi to lean, incline; vr to stoop, bend, lean.

pendable [pɑ̃dabl] a hanging, abominable.

pendaison [pɑ̃dɛzɔ̃] nf hanging.

pendant [pɑ̃dɑ̃] a hanging, pending, baggy; nm pendant, counterpoint; prep during, for; cj **— que** while, whilst.

pendeloque [pɑ̃dlɔk] nf pendant, drop, shred.

penderie [pɑ̃dri] nf wardrobe.

pendre [pɑ̃ːdr] vt to hang, hang up; vi to hang (down).

pendu [pɑ̃dy] a hanged, hanging.

pendule [pɑ̃dyl] nf clock; nm pendulum, balancer.

pêne [pɛn] nm bolt, latch.

pénétrable [penetrabl] a penetrable.

pénétrant [penetrɑ̃] a penetrating, piercing, keen.

pénétration [penetrasjɔ̃] nf penetration, shrewdness, insight, perspicacity.

pénétré [penetre] a penetrated, imbued, full, earnest.

pénétrer [penetre] vt to penetrate, pierce, imbue, see through; vi to penetrate, enter, break (into); vr to become imbued, impregnated.

pénible [penibl] a painful, distressing, hard.

péniche [peniʃ] nf barge, lighter.

péninsule [penɛ̃syl] nf peninsula.

pénitence [penitɑ̃ːs] nf penitence, repentance, penance, disgrace.

pénitencier [penitɑ̃sje] nm penitentiary.

pénitent [penitɑ̃] an penitent.

pénitentiaire [penitɑ̃sjɛːr] a penitentiary.

penne [pɛn] nf quill, feather.

pénombre [penɔ̃ːbr] nf half-light, semi-darkness.

pensant [pɑ̃sɑ̃] a thinking; **bien —** orthodox, right-thinking, moral; **mal —** unorthodox, evil-thinking.

pensée [pɑ̃se] nf thought, idea, pansy.

penser [pɑ̃se] vti to think; **— à faire qch** to remember to do sth; **— le voir** to expect to see him; **il pensa mourir** he almost died; **vous n'y pensez pas** you don't mean it.

penseur, -euse [pɑ̃sœːr, øːz] n thinker.

pensif, -ive [pɑ̃sif, iːv] a pensive, thoughtful.

pension [pɑ̃sjɔ̃] nf pension, allowance, board and lodging, boardinghouse, -school; **prendre — chez** to board, lodge with; **— de famille** residential hotel.

pensionnaire [pɑ̃sjɔnɛːr] n pensioner, boarder, inmate.

pensionnat [pɑ̃sjɔna] nm boardingschool, hostel.

pensum [pɛ̃sɔm] nm imposition, unpleasant task.

pentagonal [pɛ̃tagɔnal] *a* pentagonal.

pentagone [pɛ̃tagɔn] *a* pentagonal; *nm* pentagon.

pente [pɑ̃:t] *nf* slope, gradient, bent.

Pentecôte [pɑ̃tko:t] *nf* Pentecost.

pénurie [penyri] *nf* scarcity, shortage, poverty.

pépère [pepe:r] *a* first-class, easy; *nm* granddad, old chap.

pépier [pepje] *vi* to peep, chirp.

pépin [pepɛ̃] *nm* pip, stone, umbrella, (*fam*) hitch, trouble.

pépinière [pepinjɛ:r] *nf* nursery.

pépiniériste [pepinjerist] *nm* nurseryman.

pépite [pepit] *nf* nugget.

percale [pɛrkal] *nf* percale, chintz.

perçant [pɛrsɑ̃] *a* piercing, keen, shrill.

perce-neige [pɛrsnɛ:ʒ] *nm or f inv* snowdrop.

perce-oreille [pɛrsɔrɛ:j] *nm* earwig.

percepteur, -trice [pɛrsɛptœ:r, tris] *n* tax-collector.

perceptible [pɛrsɛptibl] *a* perceptible, audible, collectible.

perceptif, -ive [pɛrsɛptif, i:v] *a* perceptive.

perception [pɛrsɛpsjɔ̃] *nf* perception, collection, tax-office.

percée [pɛrse] *nf* cutting, opening, vista, break(through).

percer [pɛrse] *vt* to pierce, hole, go through, break through, broach, bore; *vi* to come through, break through.

perceuse [pɛrsø:z] *nf* drill.

percevable [pɛrsəvabl] *a* perceivable, leviable.

percevoir [pɛrsəvwa:r] *vt* to perceive, discern, collect.

perche [pɛrʃ] *nf* pole, rod, perch, lanky person.

percher [pɛrʃe] *vi* to roost, perch; *vr* to perch, alight.

percheron [pɛrʃərɔ̃] *nm* Percheron, draft horse.

perchoir [pɛrʃwa:r] *nm* perch, roost.

perclus [pɛrkly] *a* stiff, crippled, paralyzed.

perçoir [pɛrswa:r] *nm* gimlet, awl, broach.

percolateur [pɛrkɔlatœ:r] *nm* percolator.

percussion [pɛrkysjɔ̃] *nf* percussion.

percutant [pɛrkytɑ̃] *a* percussive, percussion.

percuter [pɛrkyte] *vt* to strike, tap.

perdant [pɛrdɑ̃] *a* losing; *n* loser.

perdition [pɛrdisjɔ̃] *nf* perdition; en — sinking, on the road to ruin.

perdre [pɛrdr] *vt* to lose, waste, ruin, *vi* to lose, deteriorate; *vr* to get lost, go to waste, disappear; il s'y perd he can't make anything of it.

perdu [pɛrdy] *a* lost, ruined, doomed, wasted, spare, distracted; à corps — recklessly.

perdreau [pɛrdro] *nm* young partridge.

perdrix [pɛrdri] *nf* partridge.

père [pɛr] *nm* father, senior.

péremptoire [perɑ̃ptwa:r] *a* peremptory, final.

pérennité [perennite] *nf* perenniality.

perfectible [pɛrfɛktibl] *a* perfectible.

perfection [pɛrfɛksjɔ̃] *nf* perfection, faultlessness.

perfectionnement [pɛrfɛksjɔnmɑ̃] *nm* perfecting, improving.

perfectionner [pɛrfɛksjɔne] *vt* to perfect, improve.

perfide [pɛrfid] *a* perfidious, treacherous.

perfidie [pɛrfidi] *nf* (act of) perfidy, perfidiousness.

perforant [pɛrfɔrɑ̃] *a* perforating, armor-piercing.

perforateur, -trice [pɛrfɔratœ:r, tris] *a* perforating.

perforatrice [pɛrfɔratris] *nf* drill.

perforation [pɛrfɔrasjɔ̃] *nf* perforation, drilling.

performance [pɛrfɔrmɑ:s] *nf* performance.

péricliter [periklite] *vi* to be shaky, in jeopardy.

péril [peril] *nm* peril, risk, danger.

périlleux, -euse [perijø, ø:z] *a* perilous, hazardous; saut — somersault.

périmé [perime] *a* out of date, not valid, expired.

périmètre [perimetr] *nm* perimeter.

période [perjɔd] *nf* period, era, spell.

périodique [perjɔdik] *a* periodical, recurring; *nm* periodical.

péripétie [peripesi] *nf* vicissitude, change.

périphérie [periferi] *nf* periphery, circumference.

périphrase [perifra:z] *nf* periphrasis.

périr [peri:r] *vi* to perish, die, be lost.

périscope [periskɔp] *nm* periscope.

périssable [perisabl] *a* perishable, mortal.

périssoire [periswa:r] *nf* canoe, skiff.

péristyle [peristil] *nm* peristyle.

péritonite [peritɔnit] *nf* peritonitis.

perle [pɛrl] *nf* pearl, bead, drop.

perler [pɛrle] *vt* to pearl, husk; *vi* to form in beads.

permanence [pɛrmanɑ:s] *nf* permanence; en — continuous, permanent(ly).

permanent [pɛrmanɑ̃] *a* continuous, standing.

permanente [pɛrmanɑ̃t] *nf* permanent wave.

perméable [pɛrmeabl] *a* permeable, pervious.

permettre [pɛrmetr] *vt* to permit, allow, enable; *vr* to take the liberty, indulge (in de).

permis [pɛrmi] *a* permitted, allowed, permissible; *nm* permit, license.

permission [pɛrmisjɔ̃] *nf* permission, leave, pass.

permissionnaire [permisjɔnɛːr] nm person, soldier on leave.

permutation [pɛrmytasjɔ̃] nf permutation, exchange.

permuter [pɛrmyte] vt to exchange, permute.

pernicieux, -euse [pɛrnisjø, øːz] a pernicious, hurtful.

pérorer [perɔre] vi to deliver a harangue, expatiate.

perpendiculaire [pɛrpɑ̃dikylɛːr] a nf perpendicular.

perpétrer [pɛrpetre] vt to perpetrate.

perpétuel, -elle [pɛrpetɥɛl] a perpetual, endless.

perpétuer [pɛrpetɥe] vt to perpetuate; vr to last.

perpétuité [pɛrpetɥite] nf perpetuity; à — in perpetuity, for life.

perplexe [pɛrplɛks] a perplexed, at a loss, perplexing.

perplexité [pɛrplɛksite] nf perplexity, confusion.

perquisition [pɛrkizisjɔ̃] nf search, inquiry.

perquisitionner [pɛrkizisjɔne] vi to search.

perron [pɛrɔ̃] nm (flight of) steps.

perroquet [pɛrɔkɛ] nm parrot.

perruche [pɛryʃ] nf hen-parrot, parakeet.

perruque [pɛryk] nf wig.

perruquier, -ière [pɛrykje, jɛːr] n wigmaker.

pers [pɛːr] a bluish-green.

persan [pɛrsɑ̃] an Persian.

Perse [pɛrs] nf Persia.

persécuter [pɛrsekyte] vt to persecute, plague, dun.

persécution [pɛrsekysjɔ̃] nf persecution, pestering.

persévérance [pɛrseverɑ̃ːs] nf perseverance, doggedness, steadfastness.

persévérant [pɛrseverɑ̃] a persevering, dogged.

persévérer [pɛrsevere] vi to persevere, persist.

persienne [pɛrsjɛn] nf venetian blind, shutter.

persiflage [pɛrsiflaːʒ] nm persiflage, banter, chaff.

persil [pɛrsi] nm parsley.

persillé [pɛrsije] a blue-molded, spotted with fat.

persistance [pɛrsistɑ̃ːs] nf persistence, continuance, doggedness.

persistant [pɛrsistɑ̃] a persistent, dogged, steady.

persister [pɛrsiste] vi to persist, continue.

personnage [pɛrsɔnaːʒ] nm personage, character, individual, notability.

personnalité [pɛrsɔnalite] nf personality, personal remark, person of note.

personne [pɛrsɔn] nf person, individual; pn anyone, anybody, no one, nobody.

personnel, -elle [pɛrsɔnɛl] a person-al, not transferable; nm personnel, staff.

personnification [pɛrsɔnifikasjɔ̃] nf personification.

personnifier [pɛrsɔnifje] vt to personify.

perspective [pɛrspektiːv] nf perspective, prospect, outlook, vista.

perspicace [pɛrspikas] a perspicacious, astute.

perspicacité [pɛrspikasite] nf perspicacity, insight, astuteness.

persuader [pɛrsɥade] vt to persuade, convince, induce.

persuasif, -ive [pɛrsɥazif, iːv] a persuasive.

persuasion [pɛrsɥazjɔ̃] nf persuasion, conviction.

perte [pɛrt] nf loss, waste, ruin; à — de vue as far as the eye can see.

pertinence [pɛrtinɑ̃ːs] nf pertinence, pertinency, relevancy.

pertinent [pɛrtinɑ̃] a pertinent, relevant.

perturbation [pɛrtyrbasjɔ̃] nf perturbation, disturbance, trepidation.

pervenche [pɛrvɑ̃ːʃ] nf periwinkle.

pervers [pɛrvɛr] a perverse, depraved.

perversion [pɛrvɛrsjɔ̃] nf perversion, corruption.

perversité [pɛrvɛrsite] nf perversity, depravity.

pervertir [pɛrvɛrtiːr] vt to pervert, corrupt; vr to become depraved, corrupted.

pesage [pəzaːʒ] nm weighing, paddock.

pesant [pəzɑ̃] a heavy, ponderous; nm weight.

pesanteur [pəzɑ̃tœːr] nf weight, heaviness.

pesée [pəze] nf weighing, leverage.

pèse-lettres [pɛzlɛtr] nm postage scale.

peser [pəze] vt to weigh, ponder; vi to weigh, hang heavy, be a burden (to sur), stress.

pessimisme [pesimism] nm pessimism, despondency.

pessimiste [pesimist] a pessimistic; n pessimist.

peste [pɛst] nf plague, pestilence, pest.

pester [pɛste] vi to curse, storm (at contre).

pestifère [pɛstifɛːr] a pestiferous, pestilential.

pet [pɛ] nm fart; — de nonne fritter.

pétale [petal] nm petal.

pétarade [petarad] nf crackling, backfire, succession of bangs.

pétarader [petarade] vi to make a succession of bangs, backfire.

pétard [petaːr] nm detonator, blast, firecracker, torpedo (railroad).

péter [pete] vi to fart, pop, bang, crackle.

pétiller [petije] vi to spark(le), fizz, bubble, crackle.

etit [pəti] *a* small, little, tiny, petty; *n* little boy, girl, pup, kitten, cub, whelp.

etit-beurre [pətibœ:r] *nm* biscuit.

etite-fille [pətitfi:j] *nf* granddaughter.

etitement [pətitmɑ̃] *ad* in a limited way, pettily, half-heartedly.

etitesse [pətitɛs] *nf* smallness, tininess, pettiness, mean act, thing.

etit-fils [pətifis] *nm* grandson.

etit-gris [pətigri] *nm* squirrel (fur).

étition [petisjɔ̃] *nf* petition.

étitionner [petisjɔne] *vi* to make a petition.

etit-lait [pətilɛ] *nm* whey.

etit-maître [pətimɛtr] *nm* fop, dandy.

etits-enfants [pətizɑ̃fɑ̃] *nm pl* grandchildren.

étrifier [petrifje] *vt* to petrify; *vr* to be petrified, turn into stone.

étrin [petrɛ̃] *nm* kneading-trough; dans le — in the soup, in a fix.

étrir [petri:r] *vt* to knead, mold, shape; **pétri d'orgueil** bursting with pride.

étrole [petrɔl] *nm* petroleum, kerosene.

étrolier [petrɔlje] *a* oil; *nm* oiltanker.

étrolifère [petrɔlifɛ:r] *a* oil(bearing).

étulance [petylɑ̃:s] *nf* liveliness, impulsiveness.

eu [pə] *ad* little, not much, few, not many, not very, dis-, un-, -less; un — a little, rather, just; — à little by little; **avant** —, **d'ici** — before long; **à** — **près** almost; **quelque** — not a little, somewhat; **pour** — **que** however little.

euplade [pœplad] *nf* tribe.

euple [pœpl] *nm* people, nation, masses; **petit** — lower classes.

eupler [pœple] *vt* to populate, stock, throng; *vr* to become populous, peopled.

euplier [pœplie] *nm* poplar.

eur [pœ:r] *nf* fear, fright; **avoir une** — **bleue** to be in a blue funk; **à faire** — frightfully; **faire** — **à** to frighten; **de** — **que** lest, for fear that.

eureux, -euse [pœrø, ø:z] *a* timorous, timid.

eut-être [pøtɛtr] *ad* perhaps, maybe.

hacochère [fakɔʃɛ:r] *nm* warthog.

halange [falɑ̃:ʒ] *nf* phalanx, finger, toe-joint; host.

halène [falɛn] *nf* moth.

haramineux, -euse [faraminø, ø:z] *a* colossal, terrific.

hare [fa:r] *nm* lighthouse, beacon, headlight.

harmaceutique [farmasøtik] *a* pharmaceutic(al).

harmacie [farmasi] *nf* pharmacy,

drugstore, dispensary; **armoire à** — medicine-chest.

pharmacien, -enne [farmasjɛ̃, jɛn] *n* chemist, druggist.

pharyngite [farɛ̃ʒit] *nf* pharyngitis.

phase [fɑ:z] *n* phase, stage, phasis.

phénique [fenik] *a* carbolic.

phénix [feniks] *nm* phœnix, paragon.

phénoménal [fenɔmenal] *a* phenomenal.

phénomène [fenɔmɛn] *nm* phenomenon, freak, marvel.

philanthrope [filɑ̃trɔp] *nm* philanthropist.

philanthropie [filɑ̃trɔpi] *nf* philanthropy.

philatéliste [filatelist] *n* philatelist, stamp-collector.

philistin [filistɛ̃] *an* Philistine.

philologie [filɔlɔʒi] *nf* philology.

philosophe [filɔzɔf] *a* philosophical; *n* philosopher.

philosophie [filɔzɔfi] *nf* philosophy.

philosophique [filɔzɔfik] *a* philosophical.

phobie [fɔbi] *nf* phobia.

phonétique [fɔnetik] *a* phonetic; *nf* phonetics.

phonologie [fɔnɔlɔʒi] *nf* phonology, phonemics.

phoque [fɔk] *nm* seal.

phosphate [fɔsfat] *nm* phosphate.

phosphore [fɔsfɔ:r] *nm* phosphorus.

phosphorescence [fɔsfɔressɑ̃:s] *nf* phosphorescence.

photo [fɔto] *nf* photo.

photogénique [fɔtɔʒenik] *a* photogenic.

photographe [fɔtɔgraf] *nm* photographer.

photographie [fɔtɔgrafi] *nf* photography, photograph.

photographier [fɔtɔgrafje] *vt* to photograph.

phrase [frɑ:z] *nf* sentence, phrase; **faire des** —**s** to use flowery language.

phraseur, -euse [frazœ:r, ø:z] *n* wordy speaker, empty talker.

phtisie [ftizi] *nf* phthisis, consumption.

phtisique [ftizik] *an* consumptive.

physicien, -enne [fizisjɛ̃, jɛn] *n* physicist, natural philosopher.

physiologie [fizjɔlɔʒi] *nf* physiology.

physiologique [fizjɔlɔʒik] *a* physiological.

physionomie [fizjɔnɔmi] *nf* physiognomy, countenance.

physique [fizik] *a* physical, bodily; *nm* physique; *nf* physics, natural philosophy.

piaffer [pjafe] *vi* to prance, paw the ground, swagger.

piailler [pjaje] *vi* to cheep, squeal, squall.

pianiste [pjanist] *n* pianist.

piano [pjano] *nm* piano; — **à queue** grand piano.

pianoter [pjanɔte] *vi* to strum, drum, tap.

piauler [pjole] vi to cheep, whimper.

piaule [pjol] nf lodgings, rooms.

pic [pik] nm pick(ax), peak, woodpecker; à — sheer, steep(ly), at the right moment.

pichenette [piʃnɛt] nf flick, fillip.

picorer [pikɔre] vt to steal, pilfer; vi to scratch about for food, pick.

picoter [pikɔte] vt to peck (at), prick, sting; vi prickle, smart, tingle.

pic-vert [pivɛːr] nm green woodpecker.

pie [pi] a piebald; n piebald horse; nf magpie.

pièce [pjɛs] nf piece, part, patch, room, coin, document, cask; — de théâtre play; — d'eau ornamental lake; de toutes —s completely, out of nothing; travailler à la — to do piece-work; trois francs la — three francs a piece.

pied [pje] nm foot(ing), base, leg (chair), stem, scale; — de laitue head of lettuce; au — levé offhand, at a moment's notice; sur — afoot, up; perdre — to lose one's footing, to get out of one's depth; lever le — to clear out, elope.

pied-à-terre [pjetatɛːr] nm occasional residence.

pied-d'alouette [pjedalwɛt] nm larkspur.

piédestal [pjedɛstal] nm pedestal.

piège [pjɛʒ] nm snare, trap; tendre un — to set a trap.

pierraille [pjɛraːj] nf rubble, gravel for road making.

pierre [pjɛr] nf stone; c'est une — dans votre jardin it is a dig at you.

Pierre [pjɛr] Peter.

pierreries [pjɛrəri] nf pl jewels, gems.

pierreux, -euse [pjɛrø, øːz] a stony, gritty.

piété [pjete] nf piety, godliness.

piétiner [pjetine] vt to trample (down), tread, stamp on; vi to stamp; — sur place to mark time.

piéton [pjetɔ̃] nm pedestrian.

piètre [pjɛtr] a poor, paltry, sorry.

pieu [pjø] nm post, stake, pile, (fam) bed.

pieuvre [pjœːvr] nf octopus.

pieux, -euse [pjø, øːz] a pious, religious, reverent.

pige [piːʒ] nf measuring rod.

pigeon, -onne [piʒɔ̃, ɔn] n pigeon, greenhorn.

pigeonnier [piʒɔnje] nm dovecote.

piger [piʒe] vt to look at, twig, understand, catch; vi to understand, get it.

pigment [pigmɑ̃] nm pigment.

pignon [piɲɔ̃] nm gable, pinion.

pignouf [piɲuf] nm lout, skinflint.

pile [pil] nf pile, heap, battery, pier, thrashing; — ou face heads or tails; s'arrêter — to stop dead.

piler [pile] vt to crush, pound.

pilier [pilje] nm pillar, column, shaft.

pillage [pijaːʒ] nm pillage, looting, ransacking.

piller [pije] vt to pillage, loot, plunder, ransack, rifle.

pilon [pilɔ̃] nm pestle, steam hammer, (fam) drumstick.

pilori [pilɔri] nm pillory.

pilot [pilo] nm pile.

pilotage [pilɔtaːʒ] nm pile-driving, piloting, driving.

pilote [pilɔt] nm pilot.

piloter [pilɔte] vt to pilot, fly, drive.

pilotis [pilɔti] nm pile (foundation).

pilule [pilyl] nf pill.

pimbêche [pɛ̃bɛʃ] nf unpleasant, supercilious woman, sour puss, catty woman.

piment [pimɑ̃] nm spice, red pepper.

pimenter [pimɑ̃te] vt to season, spice.

pimpant [pɛ̃pɑ̃] a spruce.

pin [pɛ̃] nm pine, fir-tree.

pinacle [pinakl] nm pinnacle.

pinard [pinaːr] nm wine.

pince [pɛ̃s] nf pincers, tongs, pliers, forceps, tweezers, clip, peg, claw, grip; — monseigneur jimmy.

pinceau [pɛ̃so] nm (paint)brush.

pincé [pɛ̃se] a supercilious, huffy, prim; nm pizzicato.

pincée [pɛ̃se] nf pinch.

pince-nez [pɛ̃sne] nm eye-glasses, pince-nez.

pincer [pɛ̃se] vt to pinch, nip (off), pluck, nab, grip; — les lèvres to purse one's mouth.

pince-sans-rire [pɛ̃sɑ̃riːr] nm person with a dry sense of humor.

pingouin [pɛ̃gwɛ̃] nm penguin, auk.

pingre [pɛ̃gr] a stingy, mean; n skinflint, miser.

pinson [pɛ̃sɔ̃] nm finch, chaffinch.

pintade [pɛ̃tad] nf guinea-fowl.

pioche [pjɔʃ] nf pickaxe, mattock.

piocher [pjɔʃe] vt to dig (with pick).

piocheur, -euse [pjɔʃœːr, øːz] n pickman, digger.

piolet [pjɔlɛ] nm ice ax.

pion [pjɔ̃] nm pawn, (checkers) piece, monitor.

pioncer [pjɔ̃se] vi to sleep, snooze.

pionnier [pjɔnje] nm pioneer.

pipe [pip] nf pipe, tube.

pipeau [pipo] nm reed-pipe, bird-call.

piper [pipe] vt to lure, decoy.

pipi [pipi] nm faire — to piddle, pee.

piquant [pikɑ̃] a stinging, prickly, cutting, pungent, piquant, spicy, tart; nm prickle, quill, pungency, point.

pique [pik] nm spade(s) (cards); pike, spite.

piqué [pike] a quilted, padded, (worm)eaten, spotted, dotty, staccato; nm piqué, quilting, nose-dive; bombarder en — to dive-bomb; pas — des vers first rate.

pique-assiette [pikasjɛt] nm sponger, parasite.

pique-nique [piknik] nm picnic; faire (un) — to picnic

piquer [pike] vt to prick, bite, sting, make smart, excite, spur, stitch, nettle, dive, give an injection to; — une tête to take a header; vr to prick oneself, to get nettled, become eaten up (with de), to pride oneself (on de).

piquet [pikɛ] nm stake, peg, picket, (cards) piquet.

piqueter [pikte] vt to stake (out), peg out, picket, spot, dot.

piquette [pikɛt] nf poor wine.

piqueur, -euse [pikœːr, øːz] n whipper-in, huntsman.

piqûre [pikyːr] nf sting, bite, prick, injection, stitching.

pirate [pirat] nm pirate.

pire [piːr] a worse, worst; comp sup of mauvais; nm worst; worst of it.

pirogue [pirɔg] nf canoe, surf boat.

pirouette [pirwɛt] nf pirouette, whirligig.

pirouetter [pirwɛte] vi to pirouette.

pis [pis] nm udder, dug, pap; ad worse, worst; comp sup of mal; de mal en — from bad to worse.

pis-aller [pizale] nm makeshift, last resource; au — at the worst.

piscine [pisin] nf swimming pool.

pisé [pize] nm puddled clay.

pissenlit [pisɑ̃li] nm dandelion.

pissotière [pisɔtjɛːr] nf public urinal.

pistache [pistaʃ] nf pistachio (nut).

piste [pist] nf track, trail, race-track, rink, floor; — de décollage runway; route à double — divided highway; — sonore sound track; faire fausse — to be on the wrong track.

pistolet [pistolɛ] nm pistol.

piston [pistɔ̃] nm piston, ram, valve, influence.

pistonner [pistɔne] vt to push (on), use one's influence for, help on.

pitance [pitɑ̃ːs] nf allowance pittance.

piteux, -euse [pitø, øːz] a piteous, sorry; faire piteuse mine to look woe-begone.

pitié [pitje] nf pity, mercy, compassion; avec — compassionately; elle lui fait — he is sorry for her; prendr qn en — to take pity on s.o.

piton [pitɔ̃] nm eyebolt, peak.

pitoyable [pitwajabl] a pitiful, piteous, wretched.

pitre [pitr] nm clown.

pittoresque [pitɔrɛsk] a picturesque, graphic; nm picturesqueness.

pivert [pivɛr] nm green woodpecker.

pivoine [pivwan] nf peony.

pivot [pivo] nm pivot, pin, swivel.

pivoter [pivɔte] vi to pivot, swivel, hinge, turn.

placage [plakaːʒ] nm plating, veneering.

placard [plakaːr] nm cupboard, bill, poster, panel.

placarder [plakarde] vt to post up, stick bills on.

place [plas] nf place, seat, post, job, room, square; faire — à to make room, way, for; — forte fortress.

placement [plasmɑ̃] nm investing, investment, placing, sale, employment.

placer [plase] vt to place, put, find a seat (a post) for, invest, sell; vr to take up one's position, take a seat, get a post.

placet [plasɛ] nm petition.

placidité [plasidite] nf placidity.

plafond [plafɔ̃] nm ceiling, maximum.

plafonnier [plafɔnje] nm ceiling light.

plage [plaːʒ] nf beach, shore, seaside resort.

plagiaire [plaʒjɛːr] a nm plagiarist.

plagiat [plaʒja] nm plagiarism.

plagier [plaʒje] vt to plagiarize.

plaid [plɛ] nm plaid, traveling-rug.

plaider [plede] vti to plead, argue.

plaideur, -euse [plɛdœr, øːz] n suitor, litigant.

plaidoirie [plɛdwari] nf pleading, speech.

plaidoyer [plɛdwaje] nm speech for the defense.

plaie [plɛ] nf wound, sore, evil.

plaignant [plɛɲɑ̃] n plaintiff, prosecutor.

plain-chant [plɛ̃ʃɑ̃] nm plainsong.

plaindre [plɛ̃ːdr] vt to pity, be sorry for; vr to complain.

plaine [plɛn] nf plain, flat country, open country.

plain-pied [plɛ̃pje] ad de — level, on one floor, smoothly, straight.

plainte [plɛ̃ːt] nf complaint, moan, lament; porter — contre to make a complaint against.

plaintif, -ive [plɛ̃tif, iːv] a plaintive, doleful, mournful.

plaire [plɛːr] vt to please, appeal to; vr to take pleasure, thrive, like it, be happy; s'il vous plaît please; plaît-il? I beg your pardon?

plaisance [plɛzɑ̃ːs] nf maison de — country seat; bateau de — pleasure boat.

plaisant [plɛzɑ̃] a funny, amusing; nm joker, wag; mauvais — practical joker.

plaisanter [plɛzɑ̃te] vi to joke, jest; vt to banter, chaff.

plaisanterie [plɛzɑ̃tri] nf joke, jest(ing); entendre la — to be able to take a joke.

plaisir [plɛziːr] nm pleasure, enjoyment, favor; à — without reason, freely; au — I hope we shall meet again; par — for the fun of the thing; partie de — pleasure-trip, -party, outing, picnic.

plan [plɑ̃] a even, flat, level; nm plane, plan scheme, draft; gros —

close-up; **premier —** foreground; **en —** in the lurch.

planche [plɑ̃:ʃ] *nf* plank, board, shelf, plate, engraving; *pl* boards, stage; **— de bord** dashboard; **— de salut** sheet-anchor, last hope; **faire la —** to float on one's back.

planchéier [plɑ̃ʃeje] *vt* to floor, board (over).

plancher [plɑ̃ʃe] *nm* floor(ing), floorboard.

planer [plane] *vt* to plane; smooth; *vi* to hover, glide, soar.

planète [planɛt] *nf* planet.

planeur [planœ:r] *nm* glider.

planquer [plɑ̃ke] (*fam*) *vt* to hide; *vr* to take cover.

plant [plɑ̃] *nm* plantation, patch, sapling, seedling.

plantain [plɑ̃tɛ̃] *nm* plantain.

plantation [plɑ̃tasjɔ̃] *nf* planting, plantation.

plante [plɑ̃:t] *nf* plant, sole (of foot); **jardin des —s** botanical gardens.

planter [plɑ̃te] *vt* to plant, set, fix, stick; *vr* to station oneself, stand; **— là** to leave in the lurch.

planteur [plɑ̃tœ:r] *nm* planter, grower.

planton [plɑ̃tɔ̃] *nm* orderly.

plantureux, -euse [plɑ̃tyrø, ø:z] *a* abundant, copious, rich, lush.

plaquage [plaka:ʒ] *nm* throwing over, tackle.

plaque [plak] *nf* sheet, plate, slab, tablet, plaque, disk.

plaqué [plake] *a* plated, veneered; *nm* veneered wood, plated metal, electroplate.

plaquer [plake] *vt* to plate, veneer, plaster, throw over, drop, tackle, lay flat; *vr* to lie down flat, pancake.

plaquette [plakɛt] *nf* tablet, booklet.

plastique [plastik] *a* plastic; *nf* (art of) modeling, plastic art, plastic.

plastron [plastrɔ̃] *nm* breast-plate, shirt-front.

plastronner [plastrɔne] *vi* to swagger, strut, pose.

plat [pla] *a* flat, level, dull, tame; *nm* flat, dish, course, flat-racing; **à — flat**, run down, all in; **faire du — à —** to toady to, fawn upon; **à — ventre** flat on the ground.

platane [platan] *nm* plane-tree.

plat-bord [plabɔ:r] *nm* gunwale.

plateau [plato] *nm* tray, plateau, platform, turntable.

plate-bande [platbɑ̃:d] *nf* flowerbed.

plate-forme [platfɔrm] *nf* platform, footplate.

platine [platin] *nm* platinum.

platiner [platine] *vt* to platinum-plate.

platitude [platityd] *nf* platitude, dullness.

plâtras [platra] *nm* broken plaster, rubbish.

plâtre [plɑ:tr] *nm* plaster; *pl* plaster-work.

plâtrer [platre] *vt* to plaster (up).

plausible [plozibl] *a* plausible.

plébiscite [plebissit] *nm* plebiscite.

plein [plɛ̃] *a* full, big, solid; **en — right** in the middle (of), out and out; *nm* avoir son **— to** be fully loaded; **battre son — to** be in full swing; **faire le — to** fill up (with de).

plénière [plenjɛ:r] *a* plenary, full, complete.

plénipotentiaire [plenipɔtɑ̃sjɛ:r] *a nm* plenipotentiary.

plénitude [plenityd] *nf* plenitude, fullness.

pléonastique [pleɔnastik] *a* pleonastic.

pleurard [plœra:r] *a* tearful, sniveling; *n* sniveler.

pleurer [plœre] *vt* to weep for, mourn (for); *vi* weep, cry, drip.

pleurésie [plœrezi] *nf* pleurisy.

pleureur, -euse [plœrœ:r, ø:z] *a* tearful, whimpering; *n* whimperer, mourner.

pleurnicher [plœrniʃe] *vi* to whine, snivel.

pleutre [pløtr] *nm* coward.

pleuvoir [plœvwa:r] *vi* to rain; **— à verse** to pour.

pli [pli] *nm* fold, pleat, crease, pucker, envelope, cover, note, habit, trick.

pliant [pliɑ̃] *a* pliant, flexible, collapsible; *nm* camp-stool, folding chair.

plie [pli] *nf* plaice.

plier [plie] *vt* to fold (up), bend; *vi* to bend, give way; *vr* to submit, yield.

plinthe [plɛ̃:t] *nf* plinth, baseboard.

plissé [plise] *a* pleated; *nm* pleats, pleating.

plissement [plismɑ̃] *nm* pleating, creasing, crumpling.

plisser [plise] *vt* to pleat, crumple, crease, corrugate.

plomb [plɔ̃] *nm* lead, shot, fuse; **de — leaden; à — vertical(ly); fil à — plumbline; faire sauter les —s** to blow the fuses.

plombage [plɔ̃ba:ʒ] *nm* leading, (tooth) filling.

plombagine [plɔ̃baʒin] *nf* blacklead, graphite.

plomber [plɔ̃be] *vt* to (cover with) lead, fill (tooth).

plomberie [plɔ̃bri] *nf* plumbing, plumber's shop, lead-works.

plombier [plɔ̃bje] *nm* plumber, leadworker.

plongeoir [plɔ̃ʒwa:r] *nm* divingboard.

plongeon [plɔ̃ʒɔ̃] *nm* dive, plunge, diver.

plongée [plɔ̃ʒe] *nf* dive, plunge.

plonger [plɔ̃ʒe] *vt* to plunge, immerse, thrust; *vi* to dive, plunge, dip; *vr* to immerse oneself, devote oneself (to **dans**).

plongeur, -euse [plɔ̃ʒœːr, øːz] a diving; n diver, bottlewasher, dish-washer.

ploutocrate [plutɔkrat] nm pluto-crat.

ployer [plwaje] vt to bend; vi to give way, bow.

pluie [plɥi] nf rain.

plumage [plymaːʒ] nm plumage, feathers.

plumard [plymaːr] nm (fam) bed.

plume [plym] nf feather, quill, pen, nib.

plumeau [plymo] vt feather duster.

plumer [plyme] vt to pluck, fleece.

plumet [plymɛ] nm plume, ostrich feather.

plumier [plymje] nm pencil-case.

plupart (la) [(la)plypaːr] nf (the) most, greatest or greater part, majority; pour la — mostly.

plural [plyral] a plural.

pluralité [plyralite] nf plurality, multiplicity.

pluriel, -elle [plyrjɛl] a nm plural.

plus [ply(s)] ad more, most, plus, in addition; nm more, most; — (et) — the more... the more; tant et — any amount; — de more, more than, no more; ne... plus no more, no longer, not now, not again; de — more, besides; en — extra, into the bargain; en — de over and above; non — either; tout au — at the very most.

plusieurs [plyzjœːr] a pn several.

plus-que-parfait [plyskəparfɛ] nm pluperfect.

plus-value [plyvaly] nf apprecia-tion, increase (in value).

plutôt [plyto] ad rather, sooner, on the whole.

pluvier [plyvje] nm plover.

pluvieux, -euse [plyvjø, øːz] a rainy, wet.

pneu [pnø] nm tire.

pneumatique [pnømatik] a pneu-matic, air-; nm tire, express letter.

pneumonie [pnømɔni] nf pneu-monia.

pochard [pɔʃaːr] n boozer.

poche [pɔʃ] nf pocket, pouch, bag; acheter chat en — to buy a pig in a poke; y être de sa — to be out of pocket.

pocher [pɔʃe] vt to poach, dash off; vi to get baggy, to crease; — l'œil à qn to give s.o. a black eye.

pochette [pɔʃɛt] nf small pocket, handbag, fancy handkerchief, small fiddle.

pochoir [pɔʃwaːr] nm stencil.

poêle [pwaːl, pwal] nm stove, pall; nf frying pan.

poème [pɔɛːm] nm poem.

poésie [pɔezi] nf poetry, poem.

poète [pɔɛt] a poetic; nm poet.

poétique [pɔetik] a poetic(al); nf poetics.

pognon [pɔɲɔ̃] nm money, dough.

poids [pwa] nm weight, burden, importance; prendre du — to put on weight.

poignant [pwaɲɑ̃] a poignant, soul-stirring.

poignard [pwaɲaːr] nm dagger.

poignarder [pwaɲarde] vt to stab.

poigne [pwaɲ] nf grip, energy, firmness, drive.

poignée [pwaɲe] nf handful, handle; — de main handshake.

poignet [pwaɲɛ] nm wrist, cuff, wrist-band.

poil [pwal] nm hair, fur, coat, bristle, nap; à — naked, hairy; au —! wonderful! reprendre du — de la bête to take a hair of the dog that bit you.

poilu [pwaly] a hairy, shaggy; nm soldier, tommy.

poinçon [pwɛ̃sɔ̃] nm awl, piercer, punch, stamp.

poinçonner [pwɛ̃sɔne] vt to pierce, punch, stamp.

poindre [pwɛ̃ːdr] vi to dawn, break, come up.

poing [pwɛ̃] nm fist, hand; coup de — punch; dormir à —s fermés to sleep like a log.

point [pwɛ̃] ad not, not at all; nm point, speck, dot, mark, stitch, full stop; à — done to a turn; à — nommé in the nick of time; de tous —s in all respects; mettre au — to focus, tune up, adjust, clarify, perfect; mise au — focusing, tuning up, clarification; faire le — to take one's bearings, take stock of one's position.

pointage [pwɛ̃taːʒ] nm checking, ticking off, sighting.

pointe [pwɛ̃ːt] nf point, tip, top, head, touch, tinge, twinge, quip; — sèche etching-needle, dry-point etching; — du jour daybreak; heures de — rush hours; pousser une — jusqu'à to push on to, take a walk over to; en — pointed.

pointer [pwɛ̃te] vt to prick, stab, sharpen, tick off, check, point, aim; vi to appear, soar, rise, sprout.

pointeur [pwɛ̃tœːr] nm checker, time-keeper, scorer.

pointillé [pwɛ̃tije] a dotted, stippled; nm dotted line, stippling.

pointiller [pwɛ̃tije] vt to dot, stipple, pester, annoy; vi to cavil, quibble.

pointilleux, -euse [pwɛ̃tijø, øːz] a captious, critical.

pointu [pwɛ̃ty] a pointed, sharp, angular.

pointure [pwɛ̃tyːr] nf size.

poire [pwaːr] nf pear, bulb; (fam) oaf; garder une — pour la soif to put something by for a rainy day.

poireau [pwaro] nm leek.

poireauter [pwarote] vi to hang about (waiting).

poirier [pwarje] nm pear-tree.

pois [pwa] nm pea, spot; **petits —** green peas; **— de senteur** sweet peas; **— chiches** chick peas.

poison [pwazɔ̃] nm poison.

poissard [pwasaːr] a vulgar, coarse.

poisse [pwas] nf bad luck.

poisser [pwase] vt to coat with pitch, wax, make sticky.

poisson [pwasɔ̃] nm fish; **— rouge** goldfish; **— d'avril** April fool.

poissonnerie [pwasɔnri] nf fish-market, fish-shop.

poissonneux, -euse [pwasɔnø, øːz] a full of fish, stocked with fish.

poissonnier, -ière [pwasɔnje, jeːr] n fishmonger, fishwife.

poissonnière [pwasɔnjeːr] nf fish-kettle.

poitevin, -e [pwatvɛ̃, in] a from Poitou or Poitiers.

poitrail [pwatraːj] nm chest, breast (strap).

poitrinaire [pwatrineːr] an consumptive.

poitrine [pwatrin] nf chest, breast, bosom, brisket.

poivre [pwaːvr] nm pepper, spiciness.

poivré [pwavre] a peppery, spicy.

poivrier [pwavrie] nm pepper-pot, pepper-plant.

poivron [pwavrɔ̃] nm Jamaica pepper, capsicum.

poivrot [pwavro] nm boozer, drunkard.

poix [pwa] nf pitch, wax.

polaire [pɔleːr] a polar.

polariser [pɔlarize] vt to polarize; vr to have a one-track mind.

pôle [poːl] nm pole.

polémique [pɔlemik] a polemic(al); nf controversy.

polémiste [pɔlemist] nm polemist.

poli [pɔli] a polished, glossy, polite; nm polish, gloss.

policer [pɔlise] vt to organize, establish order in.

police [pɔlis] nf police, policing, policy; **salle de —** guard-room; **faire la —** to keep order.

polichinelle [pɔliʃinɛl] nf punch, turncoat, puppet, buffoon; **théâtre de —** Punch and Judy show; **secret de —** open secret.

policier, -ière [pɔlisje, jeːr] a police; nm detective; **roman —** detective story.

polir [pɔliːr] vt to polish.

polisson, -onne [pɔlisɔ̃, ɔn] a ribald, naughty; n scamp, rascal, scapegrace.

polissonnerie [pɔlisɔnri] nf naughtiness, smutty remark.

politesse [pɔlitɛs] nf politeness, courtesy, manners.

politicien, -enne [pɔlitisjɛ̃, jɛn] n politician.

politique [pɔlitik] a political, politic, diplomatic; nm politician; nf politics, policy.

pollen [pɔlɛn] nm pollen.

polluer [pɔlɥe] vt to pollute, defile.

pollution [pɔlysjɔ̃] nf pollution, defilement.

Pologne [pɔlɔɲ] nf Poland.

polonais [pɔlɔnɛ] a nm Polish; n Pole.

poltron, -onne [pɔltrɔ̃, ɔn] a cowardly, timid; n coward.

polycopié [pɔlikɔpje] nm mimeographed lecture.

polycopier [pɔlikɔpje] vt to mimeograph, stencil.

polygame [pɔligam] a polygamous; n polygamist.

polyglotte [pɔliglɔt] an polyglot.

polygone [pɔligɔn] nm polygon, experimental range.

polype [pɔlip] nm polyp, polypus.

polytechnicien [pɔliteknisjɛ̃] nm student of the *Ecole polytechnique*.

pombe [pɔ̃b] nf millet beer.

pommade [pɔmad] nf pomade, hair-cream, ointment, lip-salve.

pomme [pɔm] nf apple, knob, head; **— de terre** potato; **— d'arrosoir** rose of a watering-can; **— de pin** fir-cone; **tomber dans les —** to pass out.

pommeau [pɔmo] nm pommel.

pommeler [pɔmle] vr to become dappled, mottled.

pommette [pɔmɛt] nf knob, cheek-bone.

pommier [pɔmje] nm apple-tree.

pompe [pɔ̃p] nf pump, pomp, display; **— à incendie** fire-engine; **entrepreneur de —s funèbres** undertaker.

pomper [pɔ̃pe] vt to pump, suck up.

pompette [pɔ̃pɛt] a slightly tipsy.

pompeux, -euse [pɔ̃pø, øːz] a pompous, turgid.

pompier [pɔ̃pje] nm fireman, pump-maker; a uninspired.

pomponner [pɔ̃pɔne] vt to adorn, titivate; vr to deck oneself out, titivate.

ponce [pɔ̃s] nf **pierre —** pumice-stone.

poncer [pɔ̃se] vt to pumice, sand-paper, pounce.

poncif [pɔ̃sif] nm pounced drawing, conventional work, commonplace effect, image etc.

ponctionner [pɔ̃ksjɔne] vt to tap, puncture.

ponctualité [pɔ̃ktɥalite] nf punctuality.

ponctuation [pɔ̃ktɥasjɔ̃] nf punctuation.

ponctuel, -elle [pɔ̃ktɥɛl] a punctual.

ponctuer [pɔ̃ktɥe] vt to punctuate, emphasize, dot.

pondération [pɔ̃derasjɔ̃] nf balance, level-headedness.

pondéré [pɔ̃dere] a thoughtful, level-headed.

pondre [pɔ̃dr] vt to lay, produce.

pont [pɔ̃] nm bridge, deck, axle; **— levis** drawbridge; **— roulant** gantry;

faire le — to take the intervening day(s) off.

ponte [pɔ̃t] nf laying, eggs laid.

pontife [pɔ̃tif] nm pontiff, pundit.

pontifier [pɔ̃tifje] vi to lay down the law, dogmatize.

ponton [pɔ̃tɔ̃] nm landing-stage, ramp.

popote [pɔpɔt] nf kitchen, restaurant, cooking, mess.

populace [pɔpylas] nf riff-raff, rabble, mob.

populacier, -ière [pɔpylasje. jɛːr] a vulgar, common.

populaire [pɔpylɛːr] a popular, vulgar; chanson — folksong, street song.

populariser [pɔpylarize] vt to popularize.

popularité [pɔpylarite] nf popularity.

population [pɔpylasjɔ̃] nf population.

populeux, -euse [pɔpylø, øːz] a populous.

porc [pɔːr] nm pig, swine, pork.

porcelaine [pɔrsəlɛn] nf porcelain, china.

porc-épic [pɔrkepik] nm porcupine.

porche [pɔrʃ] nm porch.

porcherie [pɔrʃəri] nf pigsty, piggery.

pore [pɔːr] nm pore.

poreux, -euse [pɔrø, øːz] a porous.

pornographie [pɔrnɔgrafi] nf pornography.

porphyre [pɔrfiːr] nm porphyry, slab.

port [pɔːr] nm port, harbor, haven, carriage, postage, carrying, bearing; se mettre au — d'armes to shoulder arms; — dû carriage forward.

portable [pɔrtabl] a portable, presentable, wearable.

portage [pɔrtaːʒ] nm porterage, carrying, transport, portage.

portail [pɔrtaːj] nm portal, door.

portant [pɔrtɑ̃] a carrying, bearing; être bien (mal) portant to be well (ill).

portatif, -ive [pɔrtatif, iːv] a portable.

porte [pɔrt] nf door, gate(way); — battante swing-door; — tambour revolving door; — cochère carriage entrance; mettre à la — to turn (put) s.o. out; écouter aux —s to eavesdrop.

porte-affiches [pɔrtafiʃ] nm bulletin board.

porte-amarre [pɔrtamaːr] nm line-rocket.

porte-avions [pɔrtavjɔ̃] nm aircraft carrier.

porte-bagages [pɔrtbagaːʒ] nm luggage-rack.

porte-bonheur [pɔrtbɔnœːr] nm charm, mascot.

porte-clefs [pɔrtkle] nm keyring.

porte-documents [pɔrtdɔkymɑ̃] nm attaché-case.

portée [pɔrte] nf litter, brood, range, reach, scope, span; à — de la voix within call; d'une grande — far-reaching.

portefaix [pɔrtafɛ] nm porter.

porte-fenêtre [pɔrtfənɛːtr] nf french window.

portefeuille [pɔrtafœːj] nm portfolio, pocket-book, wallet, letter-case.

porte-flambeau [pɔrtflɑ̃bo] nm torch-bearer.

portemanteau [pɔrtmɑ̃to] nm clothes tree.

porte-mine [pɔrtəmin] nm mechanical pencil.

porte-monnaie [pɔrtmɔnɛ] nm purse.

porte-parole [pɔrtparɔl] nm spokesman, mouthpiece

porte-plume [pɔrtəplym] nm pen (holder).

porter [pɔrte] vt to carry, bear, wear, take, inscribe, produce, bring (in), induce; vi bear, carry, hit (home), tell; vr to go, proceed, be; — un coup to deal, aim a blow; — manquant to post as missing; il me porte sur les nerfs he gets on my nerves; se — candidat to stand as candidate; se — bien to be well.

porte-serviettes [pɔrtsɛrvjɛt] nm towel rack.

porteur, -euse [pɔrtœːr, øːz] n porter, bearer, carrier.

porte-voix [pɔrtavwa] nm megaphone.

portier, -ière [pɔrtje, jɛːr] n door keeper, gate-keeper.

portière [pɔrtjɛːr] nf door.

portillon [pɔrtijɔ̃] nm sidegate, wicket-gate.

portion [pɔrsjɔ̃] nf portion, helping, share.

portique [pɔrtik] nm porch, portico.

porto [pɔrto] nm port (wine).

portrait [pɔrtrɛ] nm portrait, likeness; — en pied full-length portrait.

portraitiste [pɔrtrɛtist] nm portrait-painter.

portugais [pɔrtygɛ] an Portuguese.

Portugal [pɔrtygal] nm Portugal.

pose [poːz] nf pose, attitude, posing, affectation, (time) exposure, laying, posting.

posé [poze] a sitting, sedate, staid, steady.

poser [poze] vt to put (down), place, lay (down), set, fix up, admit, suppose; vi to pose, sit, rest; vr to settle, alight, set oneself up (as en).

poseur, -euse [pozœːr, øːz] n poseur, snob, layer.

positif, -ive [pozitif, iːv] a positive, actual, matter-of-fact; nm positive.

position [pozisjɔ̃] nf position, situation, site, status, posture, post.

possédant [posedɑ̃] a classes —es propertied classes.

possédé [posede] a possessed; n person possessed, maniac.

posséder [pɔsede] *vt* to possess, own, know thoroughly; *vr* to contain oneself.

possesseur [pɔsɛsœːr] *nm* possessor, owner.

possessif, -ive [pɔsɛsif, iːv] *a nm* possessive.

possession [pɔsɛsjɔ̃] *nf* possession, ownership.

possibilité [pɔsibilite] *nf* possibility, feasibility.

possible [pɔsibl] *a* possible, feasible; *nm* possible, utmost; **pas —** not really! well I never!

postal [pɔstal] *a* postal.

poste [pɔst] *nm* post, job, appointment, station; **— de T.S.F.** radio set, -station; *nf* post, post office; **mettre une lettre à la —** to mail a letter.

poster [pɔste] *vt* to post, station; *vr* to take up a position.

postérieur [pɔsterjœːr] *a* posterior, subsequent, rear, back; *nm* posterior, bottom.

postérité [pɔsterite] *nf* posterity, issue.

posthume [pɔstym] *a* posthumous.

postiche [pɔstiʃ] *a* false, imitation, sham, dummy.

postillon [pɔstijɔ̃] *nm* postilion; **envoyer des —s** to splutter.

postscolaire [pɔstskɔlɛːr] *a* further (education), after-school.

postulant [pɔstylɑ̃] *n* applicant, candidate.

postuler [pɔstyle] *vt* to apply for, solicit.

posture [pɔstyːr] *nf* posture, position, attitude.

pot [po] *nm* pot, jar, jug, mug, tankard; **payer les —s cassés** to pay the damage.

potable [pɔtabl] *a* drinkable.

potache [pɔtaʃ] *nm* schoolboy, pupil.

potage [pɔtaːʒ] *nm* soup.

potager, -ère [pɔtaʒe, ɛːr] *a* for the pot; *nm* kitchen-garden.

potasse [pɔtas] *nf* potash.

potasser [pɔtase] *vt* to bone up on; *vi* to bone up.

pot-au-feu [pɔtofø] *a* homely, plain; *nm* stock-pot, soup with boiled beef.

pot-de-vin [pɔdvɛ̃] *nm* bribe.

poteau [pɔto] *nm* post, pole; **— d'arrivée** finish line; **— de départ** starting-post.

potelé [pɔtle] *a* chubby, plump.

potence [pɔtɑ̃s] *nf* gibbet, gallows, jib, derrick.

potentiel, -elle [pɔtɑ̃sjɛl] *a* potential; *nm* potentialities.

poterie [pɔtri] *nf* pottery.

poterne [pɔtɛrn] *nf* postern.

potiche [pɔtiʃ] *nf* (Chinese) porcelain vase.

potier, -ière [pɔtje, jɛːr] *n* potter.

potin [pɔtɛ̃] *nm* piece of gossip, (*fam*) noise; *pl* tittle-tattle.

potiron [pɔtirɔ̃] *nm* pumpkin.

pou [pu] *nm* louse.

poubelle [pubɛl] *nf* trash can.

pouce [pus] *nm* thumb, big toe, inch; **manger sur le —** to take a snack.

poucet [pusɛ] *nm* **le petit —** Tom Thumb.

poucier [pusje] *nm* thumb-stall, -piece.

poudre [puːdr] *nf* powder, dust; **— aux yeux** bluff, eyewash.

poudrer [pudre] *vt* to powder, dust; *vr* to put on powder.

poudreux, -euse [pudrø, øːz] *a* dusty, powdery.

poudrier [pudrie] *nm* powder-box, compact.

poudrière [pudriɛːr] *nf* powder-horn, magazine.

poudroyer [pudrwaje] *vt* to cover with dust; *vi* to form clouds of dust.

pouf [puf] *nm* pouf, puff.

pouffer [pufe] *vir* (se) **— de rire** to roar with laughter.

pouilleux, -euse [pujø, øːz] *a* lousy, verminous.

poulailler [pulaje] *nm* hen-house, -roost, (*theater fam*) peanut gallery.

poulain [pulɛ̃] *nm* colt, foal, pony-skin, skid.

poularde [pulard] *nf* fowl.

poule [pul] *nf* hen, fowl, pool, sweepstake; tart; **— d'eau** moorhen; **— mouillée** coward, chicken.

poulet [pulɛ] *nm* chick(en), love-letter.

poulette [pulɛt] *nf* pullet.

pouliche [puliʃ] *nf* filly.

poulie [puli] *nf* pulley, block.

poulpe [pulp] *nm* octopus.

pouls [pu] *nm* pulse.

poumon [pumɔ̃] *nm* lung; **crier à pleins —s** to shout at the top of one's voice; **respirer à pleins —s** to take a deep breath.

poupe [pup] *nf* poop, stern.

poupée [pupe] *nf* doll, (tailor's) dummy, puppet.

poupon, -onne [pupɔ̃, ɔn] *n* baby, baby-faced boy, girl.

pouponnière [puponjɛːr] *nf* day-nursery.

pour [puːr] *prep* for, on behalf of, in favor of, because of, for the sake of, instead of, as, to, by, in order to, with regard to, although; **— que** in order that, so that; **— dix francs (de)** ten francs worth (of); **je n'y suis — rien** I have nothing to do with it; **il en a — une heure** it will take him an hour; **— ce qui est de l'argent** as far as the money is concerned.

pourboire [purbwaːr] *nm* tip gratuity.

pourceau [purso] *nm* hog, swine, pig.

pour-cent [pursɑ̃] *nm* (rate) per cent.

pourcentage [pursɑ̃taːʒ] *nm* percentage.

pourchasser [purʃase] vt to pursue.
pourlécher [purleʃe] vt to lick around; vr to run one's tongue over one's lips.
pourparler [purparle] nm parley, negotiation.
pourpoint [purpwɛ̃] nm doublet.
pourpre [purpr] a nm deep red, crimson; nf purple.
pourquoi [purkwa] cj adv why?
pourri [puri] a rotten, bad.
pourrir [puri:r] vt to rot; vir to decay, rot, go bad.
pourriture [purity:r] nf rotting, rot(tenness).
poursuite [pursɥit] nf pursuit, tracking (down); pl proceedings, prosecution, suing.
poursuivant [pursɥivã] n prosecutor, plaintiff.
poursuivre [pursɥi:vr] vt to pursue, chase, prosecute, carry on, continue, dog; vr to continue, go on.
pourtant [purtã] ad however, yet, still.
pourtour [purtu:r] nm circumference, periphery, precincts, area.
pourvoir [purvwa:r] vt to provide (for, with de,) make provision (for à), furnish, supply, equip.
pourvoyeur, -euse [purvwajœ:r, ø:z] n purveyor, caterer, provider.
pousse [pus] nf growth, shoot.
poussé [puse] a thorough, exhaustive, deep.
pousse-café [puskafe] nm liqueur (after coffee), chaser.
poussée [puse] nf push(ing), shove, thrust, pressure.
pousse-pousse [puspus] nm rickshaw, go-cart (of child).
pousser [puse] vt to push (on), thrust, shove, urge (on), drive, impel, prompt, utter; vi to grow, shoot, push (on, forward); vr to push oneself forward.
poussier [pusje] nm coal-dust.
poussière [pusjɛ:r] nf dust.
poussiéreux, -euse [pusjerø, ø:z] a dusty.
poussif, -ive [pusif, i:v] a broken-winded, wheezy.
poussin [pusɛ̃] nm chick.
poutre [pu:tr] nf beam, joist, girder.
poutrelle [putrel] nf small beam, girder, spar.
pouvoir [puvwa:r] nm power, influence, authority, power of attorney; vt to be able, can, manage, to be allowed, may, might etc; vr to be possible; il n'en peut plus he is worn out; on n'y peut rien it can't be helped, nothing can be done about it; c'est on ne peut plus difficile nothing could be more difficult.
prairie [preri] nf meadow, field, grassland.
praline [pralin] nf burnt almond.
praliner [praline] vt to bake in sugar, crust.

praticabilité [pratikabilite] nf practicability, feasibility.
praticable [pratikabl] a practicable, feasible, passable.
praticien, -enne [pratisjɛ̃, jɛn] n practitioner, expert; a practicing.
pratiquant [pratikã] a practicing.
pratique [pratik] a practical, useful; nf practice, practical knowledge, experience, association, custom; pl practices, dealings.
pratiquer [pratike] vti to practice; vt put into practice, employ, make, associate with.
pré [pre] nm meadow.
préalable [prealabl] a previous, preliminary; au — previously, to begin with.
préambule [preãbyl] nm preamble (to de).
préau [preo] nm yard, covered playground.
préavis [preavi] nm (previous) notice, warning.
précaire [prekɛ:r] a precarious, shaky.
précaution [prekosjɔ̃] nf (pre)caution, care, wariness.
précautionneux, -euse [prekosjɔnø, ø:z] a cautious, wary, guarded.
précédent [presedã] a preceding, previous; nm precedent.
précéder [presede] vt to precede, take precedence over; vi to have precedence.
précepte [presept] nm precept.
précepteur, -trice [preseptœ:r, tris] n tutor, governess.
prêche [prɛ:ʃ] nm sermon.
prêcher [preʃe] vt to preach (to), recommend; vi to preach; — d'exemple to practice what one preaches; — pour son saint to talk in one's own interests.
prêchi-prêcha [preʃipreʃa] nm going on and on, preachifying.
précieux, -euse [presjø, ø:z] a precious, valuable, affected.
préciosité [presjosite] nf preciosity, affectation.
précipice [presipis] nm precipice.
précipitamment [presipitamã] ad precipitately, hurriedly, headlong.
précipitation [presipitasjɔ̃] nf precipitancy, overhastiness, precipitation.
précipité [presipite] a precipitate, rushed, hurried, headlong; nm precipitate.
précipiter [presipite] vt to precipitate, rush, hurry, hurl down, into; vr to rush, dash, bolt.
précis [presi] a precise, definite, accurate; nm précis, summary.
précisément [presizemã] ad precisely, just, exactly, as a matter of fact.
préciser [presize] vt to state exactly, specify; vi to be precise, more explicit.

précision [presizjɔ̃] nf precision, accuracy, preciseness; pl fuller particulars.

précoce [prekɔs] a precocious, early.

précocité [prekɔsite] nf precociousness, earliness.

préconçu [prekɔ̃sy] a preconceived.

préconiser [prekɔnize] vt to advocate.

précurseur [prekyrsœ:r] nm forerunner, precursor.

prédécesseur [predesesœ:r] nm predecessor.

prédestiner [predɛstine] vt to predestine, foredoom, fix beforehand.

prédicateur [predikatœ:r] nm preacher.

prédiction [prediksjɔ̃] nf prediction, foretelling.

prédilection [predilɛksjɔ̃] nf liking, fondness.

prédire [predi:r] vt to predict, foretell, forecast.

prédisposer [predispoze] vt to predispose, prejudice.

prédisposition [predispozisjɔ̃] nf predisposition, prejudice, propensity.

prédominance [predɔminã:s] nf predominance, prevalence, supremacy.

prédominer [predɔmine] vi to predominate, prevail.

prééminence [preeminã:s] nf preeminence, superiority.

prééminent [preeminã] a pre-eminent, outstanding.

préface [prefas] nf preface.

préfacer [prefase] vt to write a preface for.

préfectoral [prefektɔral] a prefectoral, of a prefect.

préfecture [prefɛkty:r] nf prefecture, prefect's house or office; — de police Paris police headquarters.

préférable [preferabl] a preferable, better.

préférence [preferã:s] nf preference, priority.

préférer [prefere] vt to prefer, like better.

préfet [prefɛ] nm prefect; — de police chief commissioner of the Paris police.

préfixe [prefiks] nm prefix.

préfixer [prefikse] vt to settle beforehand, prefix.

préhistorique [preistɔrik] a prehistoric.

préjudice [preʒydis] nm injury, detriment, prejudice; porter — à qn to harm, injure, hurt.

préjudiciable [preʒydisjabl] a prejudicial, injurious, detrimental.

préjugé [preʒyʒe] nm prejudice, preconceived idea.

préjuger [preʒyʒe] vti to judge beforehand.

se prélasser [səprelase] vr to lounge, loll, laze.

prélat [prela] nm prelate.

prélèvement [prelɛvmã] nm deduction, levy.

prélever [prelve] vt to deduct, levy.

préliminaire [prelimine:r] a nm preliminary.

prélude [prelyd] nm prelude.

prématuré [prematyre] a premature, untimely.

préméditer [premedite] vt to premeditate.

prémices [premis] nf pl first fruits.

premier, -ière [prəmje, jɛ:r] a first, foremost, early, original; — rôle leading part, lead; — venu first comer, anybody; du — coup first shot, at the first attempt; nm au — first floor; jeune — juvenile lead.

première [prəmjɛ:r] nf first night, first performance, first class, sixth form.

prémisse [premis] nf premise, premiss.

prémonition [premɔnisjɔ̃] nf premonition.

prémunir [premyni:r] vt to (fore)warn; vr to provide.

prendre [prã:dr] vt to take (up, on, in), pick up, grasp, catch, assume; vi to freeze, seize, congeal, set, catch on; vr to catch, get caught, begin, clutch, cling; à tout — on the whole; bien lui en a pris de partir it was a good thing for him that he left; s'en — à to attack, blame; se — d'amitié pour to take a liking to; cela ne prend pas that won't take a trick; s'y prendre to set about it.

prénom [prenɔ̃] nm first name, Christian name.

préoccupation [preɔkypasjɔ̃] nf preoccupation, anxiety, concern, care.

préoccuper [preɔkype] vt to preoccupy, worry, engross; vr to attend, see (to de).

préparatif [preparatif] nm preparation.

préparation [preparasjɔ̃] nf preparing, preparation.

préparatoire [preparatwa:r] a preparatory.

préparer [prepare] vt to prepare, get ready, read for; vr to get ready, prepare, brew.

prépondérance [prepɔ̃derã:s] nf preponderance, prevalency.

prépondérant [prepɔ̃derã] a preponderant, predominant; voix — deciding vote.

préposé [prepoze] n person in charge.

préposer [prepoze] vt to appoint.

préposition [prepozisjɔ̃] nf preposition.

prérogative [prerɔgati:v] nf prerogative, privilege.

près [prɛ] ad near, near-by, close by; prep — de near, close to, by, on, about; à beaucoup — by far; à peu — nearly, about; à cela — with that exception; **de** — closely, at a short distance; **il n'est pas à cent francs** — 100 francs more or less does not matter to him.

présage [preza:3] *nm* presage, foreboding, omen.

présager [prezaʒe] *vt* to presage, predict, portend.

pré-salé [presale] *nm* mutton, sheep (fattened in fields near the sea).

presbyte [prezbit] *a* far-sighted.

presbytère [prezbite:r] *nm* presbytery, rectory, manse.

prescience [presjɑ̃:s] *nf* prescience, foreknowledge.

prescription [preskripsjɔ̃] *nf* prescription, regulation, direction.

prescrire [preskri:r] *vt* to prescribe, stipulate, ordain.

préséance [preseɑ̃:s] *nf* precedence, priority.

présence [prezɑ̃:s] *nf* presence, attendance; **faire acte de** — to put in an appearance.

présent [prezɑ̃] *a* present, ready; *nm* present (time or tense), gift.

présentable [prezɑ̃tabl] *a* presentable.

présentation [prezɑ̃tasjɔ̃] *nf* presentation, introduction, get-up.

présenter [prezɑ̃te] *vt* to present, introduce, show; *vr* to introduce oneself, appear, call, arise, occur; **le livre présente bien** the book is attractively got up; **se bien** — to look promising, well.

préservatif, -ive [prezervatif, i:v] *a nm* preservative, preventive.

préservation [prezervasjɔ̃] *nf* preservation, protection, saving.

préserver [prezerve] *vt* to preserve, protect, save.

présidence [prezidɑ̃:s] *nf* presidency, president's house, chairmanship.

président [prezidɑ̃] *n* president, chairman.

présidentiel, -elle [prezidɑ̃sjel] *a* presidential, of the president.

présider [prezide] *vt* to preside over; *vi* to preside, be in the chair.

présomptif, -ive [prezɔ̃ptif, i:v] *a* presumptive, apparent.

présomption [prezɔ̃psjɔ̃] *nf* presumption, presumptuousness.

présomptueux, -euse [prezɔ̃ptɥø, ø:z] *a* presumptuous, presuming, forward.

presque [presk] *ad* nearly, almost, hardly.

presqu'île [preskil] *nf* peninsula.

pressant [presɑ̃] *a* pressing, urgent.

presse [pre:s] *nf* crowd, throng, hurry, press(ing-machine), press, newspapers; **sous** — printing; **heures de** — rush hours.

pressé [prese] *a* pressed, squeezed, crowded, hurried, in a hurry, urgent.

pressentiment [presɑ̃timɑ̃] *nm* presentiment, forewarning, feeling.

presser [prese] *vt* to press, squeeze hasten, hurry (on), quicken, beset; *vi* to be urgent, press; *vr* to hurry (up), crowd.

pression [presjɔ̃] *nf* pressure, tension; **bière à la** — draft beer; **bouton** — push button.

pressoir [preswa:r] *nm* wine-, cider-press.

pressurer [presyre] *vt* to press (out), squeeze.

prestance [prestɑ̃:s] *nf* fine presence.

prestation [prestasjɔ̃] *nf* loan, lending, prestation; — **de serment** taking an oath.

preste [prest] *a* nimble, alert, quick.

prestidigitateur [prestidiʒitatœ:r] *nm* conjuror.

prestidigitation [prestidiʒitasjɔ̃] *nf* conjuring, sleight of hand.

prestige [presti:ʒ] *nm* prestige, fascination.

prestigieux, -euse [prestiʒjø, ø:z] *a* amazing, marvelous, spellbinding.

présumer [prezyme] *vt* to presume, assume; **trop** — **de** to overrate.

présupposer [presypoze] *vt* to presuppose, take for granted.

prêt [pre] *a* ready, prepared; *nm* loan, lending.

prêt-bail [prebaj] *nm* lend-lease.

prétendant [pretɑ̃dɑ̃] *n* candidate, applicant, claimant; *nm* suitor.

prétendre [pretɑ̃:dr] *vt* to claim, require, intend, state, maintain, aspire.

prétendu [pretɑ̃dy] *a* alleged, so-called, would-be; *n* intended.

prétentieux, -euse [pretɑ̃sjø, ø:z] *a* pretentious, snobbish, conceited.

prétention [pretɑ̃sjɔ̃] *nf* pretension, claim, aspiration, self-conceit.

prêter [prete] *vt* to lend, ascribe, attribute; *vi* lend itself (to à), give scope (for à); *vr* to fall in (with à), be a party (to à), indulge (in à).

prêteur, -euse [pretœ:r, ø:z] *a* (given to) lending; *n* lender; — **sur gages** pawnbroker.

prétexte [pretekst] *nm* pretext, excuse; **sous aucun** — on no account.

prétexter [pretekste] *vt* to pretext, plead, make the excuse of.

prêtre [pre:tr] *nm* priest.

prêtrise [pretri:z] *nf* priesthood.

preuve [prœ:v] *nf* proof, token, evidence; **faire** — **de** to show, display; **faire ses** — **s** to survive the test, show what one can do.

prévaloir [prevalwa:r] *vi* to prevail; *vr* to avail oneself, take advantage (of **de**).

prévenance [prevnɑ̃:s] *nf* attention, kindness.

prévenant [prevnɑ̃] *a* attentive, considerate, prepossessing.

prévenir [prevni:r] *vt* to prevent, avert, anticipate, inform, warn, tell, prejudice.

prévenu [prevny] *a* prejudiced, biased; *n* accused.

préventif, -ive [prevātif, i:v] *a* preventive, deterrent.

prévention [prevāsjɔ̃] *nf* prejudice, detention.

prévision [previzjɔ̃] *nf* forecast(ing), expectation, anticipation, likelihood.

prévoir [prevwa:r] *vt* to foresee, forecast, provide for.

prévoyance [prevwajā:s] *nf* foresight, forethought.

prévoyant [prevwajā] *a* foreseeing, far-sighted.

prie-Dieu [pridjø] *nm* prayer-stool.

prier [prie] *vt* to pray, beg, request, ask, invite; **sans se faire** — without having to be coaxed, readily; **je vous en prie** please do, don't mention it.

prière [prie:r] *nf* prayer, entreaty, request; — **de ne pas fumer** please do not smoke.

prieur [priœ:r] *n* prior, prioress.

prieuré [priœre] *nm* priory.

primaire [prime:r] *a* primary.

primat [prima] *nm* primate.

primauté [primote] *nf* primacy, pre-eminence.

prime [prim] *a* first, earliest; *nf* premium, bonus, option, subsidy, reward, free gift; **de** — **saut on the first impulse**; **faire** — to be at a premium.

primer [prime] *vt* to surpass, outdo, award a prize, bonus to, to give a subsidy, bounty, to.

prime-sautier, -ière [primsotje, je:r] *a* impulsive, spontaneous.

primeur [primœ:r] *nf* newness, freshness; *pl* early vegetables.

primevère [primvɛ:r] *nf* primrose, primula.

primitif, -ive [primitif, i:v] *a* primitive, earliest, original; **les** —**s** the early masters.

primordial [primɔrdjal] *a* primordial, primeval, of prime importance.

prince [prɛ̃:s] *nm* prince.

princesse [prɛ̃ses] *nf* princess; **aux frais de la** — at the expense of the state, free, gratis.

princier, -ière [prɛ̃sje, je:r] *a* princely.

principal [prɛ̃sipal] *a* principal, chief; *nm* chief, head(master), main thing.

principauté [prɛ̃sipote] *nf* principality.

principe [prɛ̃sip] *nm* principle; **sans** —**s** unscrupulous; **dès le** — from the beginning.

printanier, -ière [prɛ̃tanje, je:r] *a* spring(-like).

printemps [prɛ̃tā] *nm* spring(time).

priorité [priɔrite] *nf* priority.

prise [pri:z] *nf* hold, grip, capture, taking, pinch, prize, setting; — **d'air** air-intake; — **d'eau** hydrant, cock; — **de courant** plug; — **de**

vues filming, shooting; **donner** — **à** to leave oneself open to; **en venir aux** —**s** to come to grips; **lâcher** — to let go.

priser [prize] *vt* to snuff (up), value, prize; *vi* to take snuff.

prisme [prism] *nm* prism.

prison [prizɔ̃] *nf* prison, jail, imprisonment.

prisonnier, -ière [prizɔnje, je:r] *a* captive; *n* prisoner.

privation [privasjɔ̃] *nf* (de)privation, hardship.

privé [prive] *a* private, privy; *nm* private life.

priver [prive] *vt* to deprive; *vr* to deny oneself.

privilège [privilɛ:3] *nm* privilege, prerogative, preference.

privilégié [privilejie] *a* privileged licensed, preference.

prix [pri] *nm* price, prize, reward, value, cost; — **de revient** cost price; — **du trajet** fare; **au** — **de** at the price of, compared with; **de** — expensive; **attacher beaucoup de** — **à** to set a high value on.

probabilité [prɔbabilite] *nf* probability, likelihood.

probable [prɔbabl] *a* probable, likely.

probant [prɔbā] *a* conclusive, convincing.

probe [prɔb] *a* upright, honest.

probité [prɔbite] *nf* integrity, probity.

problématique [prɔblematik] *a* problematical.

problème [prɔblɛm] *nm* problem.

procédé [prɔsede] *nm* process, method, proceeding, conduct, dealing, tip; **bons** —**s** civilities, fair dealings.

procéder [prɔsede] *vi* to proceed, originate (in de), take proceedings.

procédure [prɔsedy:r] *nf* procedure, proceedings.

procès [prɔsɛ] *nm* (legal) action, proceedings, case; **sans autre forme de** — without further ado, at once.

procession [prɔsesjɔ̃] *nf* procession.

processus [prɔsesy:s] *nm* process, method.

procès-verbal [prɔseverbal] *nm* minutes, report, particulars; **dresser un** — **à qn** to take s.o.'s name and address.

prochain [prɔʃɛ̃] *a* next, nearest, neighboring, approaching; *n* neighbor.

prochainement [prɔʃɛnmā] *ad* shortly.

proche [prɔʃ] *a* near, at hand; *ad* near.

proclamation [prɔklamasjɔ̃] *nf* proclamation.

proclamer [prɔklame] *vt* to proclaim, declare.

procréer [prɔkree] *vt* to procreate beget.

procurer [prɔkyre] *vtr* to procure, get, obtain.

procureur, -atrice [prɔkyrœːr, prɔkyratris] *n* procurator, proxy, agent; *nm* attorney.

prodigalité [prɔdigalite] *nf* prodigality, extravagance, lavishness.

prodige [prɔdiːʒ] *nm* prodigy, marvel.

prodigieux, -euse [prɔdiʒjø, øːz] *a* prodigious.

prodigue [prɔdig] *a* prodigal, lavish, profuse, thriftless; *n* waster, prodigal.

prodiguer [prɔdige] *vt* to be prodigal of, be lavish of, waste; *vr* to strive to please, make o.s. cheap.

producteur, -trice [prɔdyktœːr, tris] *a* productive; *n* producer.

productif, -ive [prɔdyktif, iːv] *a* productive.

production [prɔdyksjɔ̃] *nf* product (ion), generation, yield, output.

productivité [prɔdyktivite] *nf* productivity, productiveness.

produire [prɔdɥiːr] *vt* to produce, bear, yield, bring out, forward; *vr* to occur.

produit [prɔdɥi] *nm* product, produce, takings; — **secondaire** by-product.

proéminence [prɔeminɑ̃ːs] *nf* prominence, protuberance.

profane [prɔfan] *a* profane, lay; *n* layman, outsider.

profaner [prɔfane] *vt* to desecrate, misuse.

proférer [prɔfere] *vt* to utter, speak.

professer [prɔfese] *vt* to profess, teach.

professeur [prɔfesœːr] *nm* professor, teacher.

profession [prɔfesjɔ̃] *nf* profession, occupation, trade.

professionnel, -elle [prɔfesjɔnɛl] *an* professional; *a* vocational; **enseignement** — vocational training.

professorat [prɔfesɔra] *nm* teaching profession, professorship, body of teachers.

profil [prɔfil] *nm* profile, section.

profiler [prɔfile] *vt* to draw in profile, in section, shape; *vr* to be outlined, stand out.

profit [prɔfi] *nm* profit, advantage, benefit.

profiter [prɔfite] *vi* to profit, be profitable, take advantage (of **de**).

profiteur [prɔfitœːr] *nm* profiteer.

profond [prɔfɔ̃] *a* deep, profound, deep-seated; *nm* depth.

profondeur [prɔfɔ̃dœːr] *nf* depth, profundity.

profusion [prɔfyzjɔ̃] *nf* profusion, abundance.

progéniture [prɔʒenityːr] *nf* progeny, offspring.

programme [prɔgram] *nm* program, syllabus, curriculum.

progrès [prɔgrɛ] *nm* progress, improvement, headway.

progresser [prɔgrese] *vi* to progress, make headway.

progressif, -ive [prɔgresif, iːv] *a* progressive, gradual.

progression [prɔgresjɔ̃] *nf* progress (ion).

prohiber [prɔibe] *vt* to prohibit, forbid.

prohibitif, -ive [prɔibitif, iːv] *a* prohibitive.

proie [prwa] *nf* prey, quarry; **en** — **à** a prey to.

projecteur [prɔʒɛktœːr] *nm* projector, searchlight, spotlight.

projectile [prɔʒɛktil] *nm* projectile, missile.

projection [prɔʒɛksjɔ̃] *nf* projection, throwing out, beam, lantern slide.

projet [prɔʒɛ] *nm* project, scheme, plan, draft; — **de loi** bill.

projeter [prɔʒəte] *vt* to project, throw, plan; *vr* to be thrown, stand out.

prolétaire [prɔletɛːr] *an* proletarian.

prolifique [prɔlifik] *a* prolific.

prolixe [prɔliks] *a* prolix, verbose.

prolixité [prɔliksite] *nf* prolixity, wordiness.

prologue [prɔlɔg] *nm* prologue.

prolongation [prɔlɔ̃gasjɔ̃] *nf* prolongation, protraction, extension; *pl* extra time.

prolongement [prɔlɔ̃ʒmɑ̃] *nm* prolongation, lengthening, extension.

prolonger [prɔlɔ̃ʒe] *vt* to prolong, protract, extend; *vr* to be prolonged, continue.

promenade [prɔmnad] *nf* walk(ing), outing, ramble, public walk; — **en auto** car ride, drive; — **en bateau** sail; **emmener en** — to take for a walk.

promener [prɔmne] *vt* to take for a walk, a sail, a run, take about; *vr* to go for a walk *etc*; **envoyer** — **qn** to send s.o. about his business.

promeneur, -euse [prɔmnœːr, øːz] *nmf* walker, rambler.

promenoir [prɔm(ə)nwaːr] *nm* lounge, lobby, promenade.

promesse [prɔmɛs] *nf* promise.

prometteur, -euse [prɔmetœːr, øːz] *a* promising, full of promise(s).

promettre [prɔmɛtr] *vt* to promise, look promising.

promiscuité [prɔmiskɥite] *nf* promiscuity.

promontoire [prɔmɔ̃twaːr] *nm* promontory, headland.

promoteur, -trice [prɔmɔtœːr, tris] *a* promoting; *n* promoter.

promotion [prɔmɔsjɔ̃] *nf* promotion.

prompt [prɔ̃] *a* prompt, quick, hasty, ready.

promptitude [prɔ̃tityd] *nf* promptitude, readiness.

promulguer [prɔmylge] *vt* to promulgate, issue.

prôner [prone] *vt* to praise, extol.

pronom [prɔnɔ̃] *nm* pronoun.

prononcer [prɔnɔ̃se] vt to pronounce, say, mention, deliver; vr to declare one's opinion, decision, speak out.

prononciation [prɔnɔ̃sjasjɔ̃] nf pronunciation, utterance, delivery.

pronostic [prɔnɔstik] nm prognostic (ation), forecast.

pronostiquer [prɔnɔstike] vt to forecast.

propagande [prɔpagɑ̃:d] nf propaganda, publicity.

propagation [prɔpagasjɔ̃] nf propagation, spreading.

propager [prɔpaʒe] vtr to propagate, spread.

propension [prɔpɑ̃sjɔ̃] nf propensity within limits.

prophète, prophétesse [prɔfɛt, prɔfetɛs] n prophet, prophetess.

prophétie [prɔfesi] nf prophecy, prophesying.

prophétiser [prɔfetize] vt to prophesy, foretell.

propice [prɔpis] a propitious, favorable.

proportion [prɔpɔrsjɔ̃] nf proportion, ratio; pl size; toute — gardée within limits.

proportionné [prɔpɔrsjɔne] a proportionate, proportioned.

proportionnel, -elle [prɔpɔrsjɔnɛl] a proportional.

proportionner [prɔpɔrsjɔne] vt to proportion, adapt.

propos [prɔpo] nm purpose, remark, matter, subject; pl talk; à — by the way, appropriate(ly), opportune(ly); mal à — untimely.

proposer [prɔpoze] vt to propose, suggest; vr to come forward, propose (to).

proposition [prɔpozisjɔ̃] nf proposition, proposal, motion, clause.

propre [prɔpr] a own, very; suitable (for à); peculiar (to à); proper; clean, neat; nm characteristic, peculiarity; au — in the literal sense.

proprement [prɔprəmɑ̃] ad properly, nicely, neatly, appropriately.

propreté [prɔprəte] nf clean(li)ness, tidiness.

propriétaire [prɔprietɛ:r] n owner, proprietor, landlord, -lady.

propriété [prɔpriete] nf property, estate, ownership, propriety.

propulser [prɔpylse] vt to propel.

propulseur [prɔpylsœ:r] a propelling; nm propeller.

propulsion [prɔpylsjɔ̃] nf propulsion, drive.

prorogation [prɔrɔgasjɔ̃] nf prorogation, delay, extension

proroger [prɔrɔʒe] vt to adjourn, extend, delay.

prosaïque [prɔzaik] a prosaic, pedestrian.

prosateur, -trice [prɔzatœ:r, tris] n prose writer.

proscription [prɔskripsjɔ̃] nf proscription, outlawing, banishment.

proscrire [prɔskri:r] vt to proscribe, outlaw, banish.

proscrit [prɔskri] a outlawed; n outlaw.

prose [pro:z] nf prose.

prospecter [prɔspɛkte] vt to prospect, circularize.

prospectus [prɔspɛkty:s] nm prospectus, handbill.

prospère [prɔspɛ:r] a prosperous, flourishing, favorable.

prospérer [prɔspere] vi to prosper, thrive.

prospérité [prɔsperite] nf prosperity.

prosterné [prɔstɛrne] a prostrate, prone.

se prosterner [səprɔstɛrne] vr to prostrate oneself, grovel.

prostituée [prɔstitɥe] nf prostitute, whore.

prostré [prɔstre] a prostrate(d), exhausted.

protagoniste [prɔtagɔnist] nm protagonist.

protecteur, -trice [prɔtɛktœ:r, tris] a protective, patronizing; n protector, protectress, patron(ess).

protection [prɔtɛksjɔ̃] nf protection, patronage.

protégé [prɔteʒe] n protégé(e), ward.

protéger [prɔteʒe] vt to protect, patronize, be a patron of.

protéine [prɔtein] nf protein.

protestant [prɔtɛstɑ̃] n Protestant.

protestation [prɔtɛstasjɔ̃] nf protestation, protest.

protester [prɔtɛste] vti to protest.

protêt [prɔtɛ] nm protest.

protocole [prɔtɔkɔl] nm protocol, correct procedure, etiquette.

protubérance [prɔtyberɑ̃:s] nf protuberance, projection, bump.

proue [pru] nf prow, bows.

prouesse [prues] nf prowess, exploit.

prouver [pruve] vt to prove, give proof of.

provenance [prɔvnɑ̃:s] nf origin, produce; en — de coming from.

provençal [prɔvɑ̃sal] an Provençal.

Provence [prɔvɑ̃:s] nf Provence.

provende [prɔvɑ̃:d] nf provender, fodder, supplies.

provenir [prɔvni:r] vi to originate, come, arise.

proverbe [prɔvɛrb] nm proverb.

proverbial [prɔvɛrbjal] a proverbial.

providence [prɔvidɑ̃:s] nf providence.

providentiel, -elle [prɔvidɑ̃sjɛl] a providential.

province [prɔvɛ̃:s] nf province(s).

provincial [prɔvɛ̃sjal] a provincial.

proviseur [prɔvizœ:r] nm headmaster (of lycée).

provision [prɔvizjɔ̃] nf provision, supply, reserve, stock.

provisoire [prɔvizwa:r] a temporary, provisional; à titre — provisionally, temporarily.

provocant [prɔvɔkɑ̃] a provocative.

provocateur, -trice [prɔvɔkatœːr, tris] *a* provocative; *n* instigator, inciter.

provocation [prɔvɔkasjɔ̃] *nf* provocation, instigation, inciting, challenge.

provoquer [prɔvɔke] *vt* to provoke, arouse, cause, incite, challenge.

proxénète [prɔksenɛt] *n* procurer, procuress.

proximité [prɔksimite] *nf* proximity, nearness.

prude [pryd] *a* prudish; *nf* prude.

prudence [prydɑ̃ːs] *nf* prudence, caution, carefulness.

prudent [prydɑ̃] *a* prudent, careful, cautious.

prune [pryn] *nf* plum; **jouer pour des —s** to play for the fun of the thing.

pruneau [pryno] *nm* prune.

prunelle [prynɛl] *nf* sloe, pupil, apple (of eye).

prunier [prynje] *nm* plum-tree.

Prusse [prys] *nf* Prussia.

prussien, -enne [prysjɛ̃, jɛn] *an* Prussian.

psalmodier [psalmɔdje] *vt* to intone, chant, drone; *vi* to chant.

psaume [psoːm] *nm* psalm.

psautier [psɔtje] *nm* psalter.

pseudonyme [psødɔnim] *a* pseudonymous; *nm* pseudonym, assumed name.

psychanalyse [psikanaliːz] *nf* psychoanalysis.

psyché [psiʃe] *nf* psyche, cheval glass.

psychiatrie [psikjatri] *nf* psychiatry.

psychique [psiʃik] *a* psychic.

psychologie [psikɔlɔʒi] *nf* psychology.

psychologique [psikɔlɔʒik] *a* psychological.

psychologue [psikɔlɔg] *nm* psychologist.

psychose [psikoːz] *nf* psychosis.

puanteur [pɥɑ̃tœːr] *nf* stink, stench.

puberté [pybɛrte] *nf* puberty.

public, -ique [pyblik] *a nm* public.

publication [pyblikasjɔ̃] *nf* publication, publishing.

publiciste [pyblisist] *nm* publicist.

publicité [pyblisite] *nf* publicity, advertising; **faire de la —** to advertise.

publier [pyblie] *vt* to publish, proclaim.

puce [pys] *nf* flea; **mettre la — à l'oreille de qn** to arouse s.o.'s suspicions, start s.o. thinking.

pucelle [pysɛl] *nf* virgin, maid(en).

pudeur [pydœːr] *nf* modesty, decorousness, decency.

pudibond [pydibɔ̃] *a* prudish, easily shocked.

pudibonderie [pydibɔ̃dri] *nf* prudishness.

pudique [pydik] *a* modest, chaste, virtuous.

puer [pɥe] *vi* to stink, smell.

puéril [pɥeril] *a* puerile, childish.

puérilité [pɥerilite] *nf* puerility, childishness, childish statement.

pugilat [pyʒila] *nm* boxing, fight.

pugiliste [pyʒilist] *nm* pugilist, boxer.

puîné [pɥine] *a* younger.

puis [pɥi] *ad* then, next, afterwards; **et — après** what about it, what next?

puisard [pɥizaːr] *nm* cesspool, sump.

puiser [pɥize] *vt* to draw, take.

puisette [pɥizɛt] *nf* scoop, ladle.

puisque [pɥisk(ə)] *cj* as, since.

puissance [pɥisɑ̃ːs] *nf* power, strength, force.

puissant [pɥisɑ̃] *a* powerful, strong, mighty, potent.

puits [pɥi] *nm* well, shaft, pit, fount.

pulluler [pyllyle] *vi* to multiply rapidly, teem, swarm.

pulmonaire [pylmɔnɛːr] *a* pulmonary.

pulpe [pylp] *nf* pulp.

pulper [pylpe] *vt* to pulp.

pulpeux, -euse [pylpø, øːz] *a* pulpy.

pulsation [pylsasjɔ̃] *nf* pulsation, throb(bing).

pulvérisateur [pylverizatœːr] *nm* pulverizer, atomizer.

pulvériser [pylverize] *vt* to pulverize, grind (down), spray, atomize.

punaise [pynɛːz] *nf* bug, thumbtack.

punir [pyniːr] *vt* to punish.

punition [pynisjɔ̃] *nf* punishment, punishing.

pupille [pypil] *n* ward; *nf* pupil (of eye).

pupitre [pypiːtr] *nm* desk, stand, rack.

pur [pyːr] *a* pure, clear, sheer, mere, genuine.

purée [pyre] *nf* purée, thick soup, mash; **— de pommes de terre** mashed potatoes; **être dans la —** to be hard-up.

pureté [pyrte] *nf* pureness, purity, clearness.

purgatif, -ive [pyrgatif, iːv] *a nm* purgative.

purgatoire [pyrgatwaːr] *nm* purgatory.

purge [pyrʒ] *nf* purge, purgative, draining, cleaning.

purger [pyrʒe] *vt* to purge, clean (out), cleanse, clear; *vr* to take medicine; **— sa peine** to serve one's sentence.

purificateur, -trice [pyrifikatœːr, tris] *a* purifying, cleansing; *n* purifier, cleanser.

purification [pyrifikasjɔ̃] *nf* purification.

purifier [pyrifje] *vt* to purify, cleanse, refine; *vr* to clear, become pure.

purin [pyrɛ̃] *nm* liquid manure.

puritanisme [pyritanism] *nm* puritanism.

pur-sang [pyrsɑ̃] nm thoroughbred.
pus [py] nm pus, matter.
pusillanime [pyzillanim] a pusillanimous, faint-hearted.
pustule [pystyl] nf pustule, pimple.
putain [pytɛ̃] nf whore.
putatif, -ive [pytatif, iːv] a putative, supposed.
putois [pytwa] nm pole-cat, skunk.
putréfaction [pytrefaksjɔ̃] nf putrefaction.
putréfier [pytrefye] vtr to putrefy, rot.
putride [pytrid] a putrid, tainted.
pygmée [pigme] n pygmy.
pyjama [piʒama] nm pajamas.
pylône [pɨloːn] nm pylon, mast, pole.
pyorrhée [pjɔre] nf pyorrhea.
pyramide [piramid] nf pyramid.
pyromane [pirɔman] n pyromaniac.
python [pitɔ̃] nm python.

Q

quadragénaire [kwadraʒenɛːr] an quadragenarian.
quadrangulaire [kwadrɑ̃gylɛːr] a quadrangular.
quadrilatéral [kwadrilateral] a quadrilateral.
quadriller [kadrije] vt to rule in squares, cross-rule.
quadrupède [kwadryped] a four-footed; nm quadruped.
quadrupler [kwadryple] vt to quadruple.
quai [ke] nm quay, wharf, embankment, platform.
qualificatif, -ive [kalifikatif, iːv] a qualifying.
qualification [kalifikasjɔ̃] nf qualifying, title.
qualifier [kalifje] vt to qualify, call, describe.
qualité [kalite] nf quality, property, capacity, qualification, rank; en — de as, in the capacity of.
quand [kɑ̃] cj ad when; — même cj even if; ad all the same.
quant [kɑ̃t] ad — à as for, as to, as regards.
quantième [kɑ̃tjɛm] nm day of the month.
quantité [kɑ̃tite] nf quantity, amount, lot.
quarantaine [karɑ̃tɛn] nf (about) forty, quarantine.
quarante [karɑ̃ːt] anm forty.
quarantième [karɑ̃tjɛm] anm fortieth.
quart [kaːr] nm quarter, quarter of a liter, watch; être de —, to be on watch, on duty.
quarteron [kart(ə)rɔ̃] an quadroon.
quartier [kartje] nm quarter, part, portion, district, ward, quarters; — général headquarters.
quartier-maître [kartjemɛːtr] nm quartermaster, leading seaman.

quasi [kazi] ad quasi, almost, all but.
quasiment [kazimɑ̃] ad as it were.
quatorze [katɔrz] anm fourteen, fourteenth.
quatorzième [katɔrzjɛm] anm fourteenth.
quatrain [katrɛ̃] nm quatrain.
quatre [katr] anm four, fourth; se mettre en quatre, to do all one can.
quatre-vingt-dix [katrəvɛ̃dis] anm ninety.
quatre-vingts [katrəvɛ̃] anm eighty.
quatrième [katriɛm] fourth.
quatuor [kwatɥɔːr] nm (mus) quartet.
que [k(ə)] cj that, but; as than, how, how many; ne ... que, only; (soit) — ... (soit) — ... whether ... or; qu'il parle, let him speak; pr that, whom, which, what; qu'est-ce qui? qu'est-ce que? what?
Québec [kebek] nm Quebec.
quel, -le [kɛl] a what, which, who, what a; — que whoever, whatever.
quelconque [kɛlkɔ̃k] a any, some, whatever, commonplace, ordinary.
quelque [kɛlk(ə)] a some, any; pl some, a few; — ... qui, que whatever, whatsoever; ad some, about; — ... que ad however
quelque chose [kɛlkəʃoːz] pn something, anything.
quelquefois [kɛlkəfwa] ad sometimes.
quelque part [kɛlkəpaːr] ad somewhere.
quelqu'un, quelqu'une [kɛlkœ̃, kɛlkyn] pn someone, anyone, one; pl some, a few.
quémander [kemɑ̃de] vi to beg; vt to solicit, beg for.
qu'en dira-t-on [kɑ̃diratɔ̃] nm what people will say, gossip.
quenelle [kənɛl] nf fish ball, forcemeat ball.
quenouille [kənuːj] nf distaff.
querelle [kərɛl] nf quarrel, row.
quereller [kərɛle] vt to quarrel with; vr to quarrel.
querelleur, -euse [kərɛlœːr, øːz] a quarrelsome; n quarreler, wrangler.
question [kɛstjɔ̃] nf question, query, matter, point.
questionnaire [kɛstjɔnɛːr] nm list of questions.
questionner [kɛstjɔne] vt to question.
quête [kɛːt] nf search, quest, collection.
quêter [kete] vt to search for, collect.
queue [kø] nf tail, end, train, stalk, stem, rear, queue, file, cue; finir en — de poisson to peter out; piano à — grand piano; en, à la — in the rear.
queue d'aronde [kødarɔ̃ːd] nf dovetail.
queue-de-pie [kødpi] nf tails, evening dress.
queue-de-rat [kødra] nf small taper.
qui [ki] pn who, whom, which, that;

— que who(so)ever, whom(so)ever;
— que ce soit anyone; — est-ce
que? whom?

quiconque [kik5:k] *pn* who(so)ever,
anyone who.

quiétude [kчietyd, kje] *nf* quietude.

quignon [kiɲ5] *nm* hunk, chunk.

quille [ki:j] *nf* skittle, ninepin, keel.

quincaillerie [kɛ̃kajri] *nf* hardware store.

quincaillier [kɛ̃kaje] *nm* hardware dealer.

quinine [kinin] *nf* quinine.

quinquennal [kчɛ̃kчɛnnal] *a* quinquennial, five-year.

quintal [kɛ̃tal] *nm* 100 kilograms.

quinte [kɛ̃:t] *nf* (*mus*) fifth; fit of
bad temper; — de toux fit of
coughing.

quintessence [kɛ̃tɛssɑ̃:s] *nf* quintessence.

quintette [k(ч)ɛ̃tet] *nm* quintet.

quinteux, -euse [kɛ̃tø, ø:z] *a* fitful,
restive, fretful.

quintupler [k(ч)ɛ̃typle] *vti* to
increase fivefold.

quinzaine [kɛ̃zɛn] *nf* (about) fifteen,
fortnight, two weeks.

quinze [kɛ̃:z] *a nm* fifteen, fifteenth;
— jours fortnight, two weeks.

quinzième [kɛ̃zjem] *a nm* fifteenth.

quiproquo [kiprɔko] *nm* mistake,
misunderstanding.

quittance [kitɑ̃:s] *nf* receipt, discharge.

quitte [kit] *a* quit, rid, free (of); en
être — pour la peur to get off with
a fright; — à even though, at the
risk of.

quitter [kite] *vt* to quit, leave; ne
quittez pas! hold the line!

qui-vive [kivi:v] *nm* challenge; sur
le — on the alert.

quoi [kwa] *pn* what, which; avoir
de — vivre to have enough to live
on; il n'y a pas de — don't mention
it; de — écrire writing materials;
sans — otherwise; — qui, que
whatever; — qu'il en soit be that
as it may; — que ce soit anything
whatever; à — bon? what's the use?

quoique [kwak(ə)] *cj* (al)though.

quolibet [kɔlibe] *nm* gibe.

quotidien, -enne [kɔtidjɛ̃, jɛn] *a*
daily, everyday; *nm* daily paper.

R

rabâcher [rabaʃe] *vti* to repeat over
and over again.

rabais [rabe] *nm* reduction, rebate,
allowance; au — at a reduced price.

rabaisser [rabese] *vt* to lower,
reduce, belittle, humble.

rabat-joie [rabaʒwa] *n* killjoy,
spoilsport.

rabatteur, -euse [rabatœ:r, ø:z] *n*
tout; *nm* beater (*hunting*).

rabattre [rabatr] *vt* to lower, bring
down, turn down, take down,
reduce, beat (up); *vi* to turn of
en — to climb down; *vr* to fol
(down), fall back.

rabbin [rabɛ̃] *nm* rabbi.

rabiot [rabjo] *nm* surplus, bucksheε
extra (work).

râble [rɑ:bl] *nm* back, saddle (c
hare).

râblé [rable] *a* broadbacked, stra
ping.

rabot [rabo] *nm* plane.

raboter [rabɔte] *vt* to plane, polish.

raboteux, -euse [rabɔtø, øz]
rough, bumpy.

rabougrir [rabugri:r] *vt* to stunt
vir to become stunted.

rabougrissement [rabugrismɑ̃] *n*
stuntedness.

rabrouer [rabrue] *vt* to scolc
rebuke, rebuff, snub.

racaille [rakɑ:j] *nf* rabble, riff-raf
trash.

raccommodage [rakɔmɔda:ʒ] *n*
mend(ing), repair(ing), darn(ing).

raccommodement [rakɔmɔdmɑ̃] *n*
reconciliation.

raccommoder [rakɔmɔde] *vt* t
mend, repair, darn, reconcile; *vr* t
make it up.

raccord [rakɔ:r] *nm* join, joint, lin
connection.

raccorder [rakɔrde] *vt* to join, lin
up, connect, bring into line; *vr* t
fit together.

raccourci [rakursi] *a* short(ened
abridged; à bras —(s) with migh
and main, with a vengeance; *n*
abridgement, foreshortening, sho
cut; en — in miniature, in short.

raccourcir [rakursi:r] *vt* to shorter
curtail, foreshorten; *vir* to gro
shorter, draw in.

raccroc [rakro] *nm* fluke.

raccrocher [rakrɔʃe] *vt* to hook up
hang up, get hold of again; *vr* t
clutch, catch on, recover, cling.

race [ras] *nf* race, descent, strain
stock, breed; avoir de la — to b
pure-bred, pedigreed; bon chie
chasse de — what's bred in th
bone comes out in the flesh.

racé [rase] *a* thoroughbred.

rachat [raʃa] *a* repurchase, redemp
tion.

rachetable [raʃtabl] *a* redeemable.

racheter [raʃte] *vt* to repurchase, bu
back, redeem, ransom, retrieve
atone for.

rachitique [raʃitik] *a* rachitic
rickety.

racine [rasin] *nf* root.

racisme [rasism] *nm* color ba
prejudice, race, racism.

raclée [rakle] *nf* thrashing.

racler [rakle] *vt* to scrape, rake
rasp; se — la gorge to clear one
throat.

racloir [raklwa:r] *nf* scraper.

racoler [rakɔle] *vt* to recruit, enlist, tout for.

racoleur [rakɔlœːr] *nm* recruiting-sergeant, tout.

racontars [rakɔ̃taːr] *nm pl* gossip, tittle-tattle.

raconter [rakɔ̃te] *vt* to relate, tell (about), recount; *vi* to tell a story; **en —** to exaggerate, spin a yarn.

raconteur, -euse [rakɔ̃tœːr, øːz] *n* (story-)teller, narrator.

racornir [rakɔrniːr] *vtr* to harden, toughen.

rade [rad] *nf* roadstead, roads.

radeau [rado] *nm* raft.

radiateur [radjatœːr] *a* radiating; *nm* radiator.

radiation [radjasjɔ̃] *nf* erasure, cancellation, striking off, radiation.

radical [radikal] *a nm* radical.

radier [radje] *vt* to erase, cancel, strike off, radiate.

radieux, -euse [radjø, øːz] *a* radiant, beaming.

radio [radjo] *nf* radio, X-rays; **par —** broadcast; *nm* radio message, radio operator.

radio-actif [radjoaktif, iːv] *a* radio-active.

radio-diffusion [radjɔdifyzjɔ̃] *nf* broadcast(ing).

radiogramme [radjɔgram] *nm* radiogram, X-ray photograph.

radiographie [radjɔgrafi] *nf* radiography.

radiologie [radjɔlɔ3i] *nf* radiology.

radio-reportage [radjɔrəpɔrtaːʒ] *nm* running commentary.

radiotélégraphie [radjɔtelegrafi] *nf* radiotelegraphy.

radiothérapie [radjɔterapi] *nf* radiotherapy.

radis [radi] *nm* radish.

radium [radjɔm] *nm* radium.

radotage [radɔtaːʒ] *nm* drivel, twaddle.

radoter [radɔte] *vi* to drivel, talk nonsense.

radoteur, -euse [radɔtœːr, øːz] *n* dotard.

radoub [radu] *nm* repair, refitting; **en —** in dry dock.

radoucir [radusiːr] *vt* to calm, soften, mollify; *vr* to grow milder.

rafale [rafal] *nf* squall, gust, burst.

raffermir [rafermiːr] *vt* to harden, strengthen, fortify; *vr* to harden, improve, be restored.

raffiné [rafine] *a* refined, subtle, fine, polished.

raffiner [rafine] *vt* to refine; *vi* to be too subtle; *vr* to become refined.

raffinerie [rafinri] *nf* refinery.

raffoler [rafɔle] *vi* to be very fond (of **de**), dote (upon **de**), be mad (about **de**).

rafistoler [rafistɔle] *vt* to patch up, do up.

rafle [rɑːfl] *nf* raid, clean sweep, round-up.

rafler [rɑfle] *vt* to make a clean sweep of, round up, comb out.

rafraîchir [rafreʃiːr] *vt* to refresh, cool, freshen up, touch up, trim, brush up; *vr* to turn cooler, have sth to drink, rest.

rafraîchissement [rafreʃismɑ̃] *nm* refreshing, cooling, freshening up, brushing up; *pl* refreshments.

ragaillardir [ragajardiːr] *vtr* to cheer up, revive.

rage [raːʒ] *nf* rage, madness, rabies, mania, passion; **— de dents** violent attack of toothache; **faire —** to rage.

rager [raʒe] *vi* to rage; **faire — qn** to make s.o. wild.

rageur, -euse [raʒœːr, øːz] *a* hot-tempered, passionate.

ragot [rago] *nm* gossip.

ragoût [ragu] *nm* stew.

rahat-loukoum [raatlukum] *nm* Turkish delight.

raid [red] *nm* raid, long-distance flight, l.-d. run.

raide [red] *a* stiff, taut, unbending, steep; **coup —** stinging blow; **c'est un peu —!** that's too much! **— mort** stone-dead.

raideur [redœːr] *nf* stiffness, tightness, steepness; **avec —** stiffly, arrogantly.

raidir [rediːr] *vt* to stiffen, tighten; *vr* to stiffen, brace oneself, steel oneself.

raie [re] *nf* line, stroke, streak, stripe, parting, ridge, ray, (*fish*) skate.

railler [raje] *vt* to jeer at, laugh at; *vi* to joke; *vr* to make fun (of **de**), scoff (at **de**).

raillerie [rajri] *nf* raillery, banter, joke.

railleur, -euse [rajœːr, øːz] *a* bantering, mocking; *n* joker, scoffer.

rainure [renyːr] *nf* groove, slot, channel.

rais [re] *nm* spoke.

raisin [rezɛ̃] *nm* grape; **—s** sec raisins; **—s de Corinthe** currants.

raison [rezɔ̃] *nf* reason, motive, right mind, sense(s), satisfaction, ratio; **avoir —** to be right; **avoir — de qn, de qch** to get the better of s.o., sth; **se faire une —** to make the best of it; **à — de** at the rate of.

raisonnable [rezɔnabl] *a* reasonable, fair, adequate.

raisonnement [rezɔnmɑ̃] *nm* reasoning, argument.

raisonner [rezɔne] *vi* to reason, argue; *vt* to reason with, study.

raisonneur, -euse [rezɔnœːr, øːz] *a* reasoning, argumentative; *n* reasoner, arguer.

rajeunir [raʒœniːr] *vt* to rejuvenate, make (s.o. look) younger, renovate; *vi* to look younger.

rajuster [raʒyste] *vt* to readjust, put straight.

râle [ra:l] nm rattle (in the throat).

ralenti [ralăti] a slow(er); nm slow motion; au — dead slow; mettre au — to slow down, throttle down.

ralentir [ralăti:r] vti to slacken, slow down.

râler [rale] vi to rattle, be at one's last gasp, be furious.

ralliement [ralimă] nm rally(ing); mot de — password.

rallier [ralje] vt to rally, rejoin, win over; vr to rally, join.

rallonge [ralɔ:ʒ] nf extension piece, extra leaf.

rallonger [ralɔ̃ʒe] vt to lengthen, let down.

rallye [rali] nm auto race, rally.

ramage [rama:ʒ] nm floral design, warbling, singing.

ramassé [ramase] a thickset, stocky, compact.

ramasser [ramase] vt to gather, collect, pick up; vr to gather, crouch.

rame [ram] nf oar, ream, string, train.

rameau [ramo] nm branch, bough; le dimanche des R—x Palm Sunday.

ramener [ramne] vt to bring back, bring around, reduce, pull down, restore.

ramer [rame] vi to row, pull.

rameur [ramœ:r] n rower, oarsman.

ramier [ramje] nm wood pigeon.

ramification [ramifikasjɔ̃] nf ramification, branch(ing).

se ramifier [səramifje] vr to branch out.

ramollir [ramɔli:r] vt to soften, enervate; vr to soften, grow soft (-headed).

ramollissement [ramɔlismã] nm softening.

ramoner [ramɔne] vt to sweep, rake out.

ramoneur [ramɔnœ:r] nm (chimney-) sweep.

rampe [rã:p] nf slope, gradient, handrail, footlights, ramp.

ramper [rãpe] vi to creep, crawl, grovel, cringe.

rancart [rãka:r] nm mettre au — to cast aside.

rance [rã:s] a rancid.

rancir [rãsi:r] vi to become rancid.

rancœur [rãkœr] nf rancor, bitterness, resentment.

rançon [rãsɔ̃] nf ransom.

rancune [rãkyn] nf rancor, grudge, spite, ill-feeling.

rancunier, -ière [rãkynje, jɛ:r] a vindictive, spiteful.

randonnée [rãdɔne] nf tour, run, excursion.

rang [rã] nm row, line, rank, status; rompre les —s to disperse, dismiss; de premier — first-class.

rangé [rãʒe] a orderly, well-ordered, steady, staid; bataille —e pitched battle.

rangée [rãʒe] nf row, line.

ranger [rãʒe] vt to arrange, draw up, put away, tidy, keep back, rank, range; vr to draw up, settle down, fall in (with à); se — du côté de to side with; se — de côté to stand aside.

ranimer [ranime] vt to revive, rekindle, stir up; vr to come to life again.

rapace [rapas] a rapacious.

rapacité [rapasite] nf rapaciousness.

rapatrier [rapatrie vt to repatriate.

râpe [ra:p] nf rasp, file, grater.

râpé [rape] a grated, shabby, threadbare.

râper [rape] vt to rasp, grate, wear out.

rapetasser [raptase] vt to patch (up).

rapetisser [raptise] vt to shorten, make smaller; vir to shrink, shorten.

rapide [rapid] a rapid, quick, swift, steep; nm express train.

rapidité [rapidite] nf rapidity, swiftness, steepness.

rapiécer [rapjese] vt to patch.

rapin [rapɛ̃] nm (fam) art student.

rappareiller [raparɛje] vt to match.

rapparier [raparje] vt to match.

rappel [rapɛl] nm recall, call(ing), reminder, repeal.

rappeler [raple] vt to recall, call back, remind, repeal; vr to recall, remember; rappelez-moi à son bon souvenir remember me kindly to him.

rapport [rapɔ:r] nm return, yield, profit, report, relation, connection, contact; pl relations, terms; en — avec in keeping with; par — à with regard to; sous ce — in this respect.

rapporter [raporte] vt to bring back, bring in, yield, report, tell tales, revoke, refer; vr to agree, tally, fit together, refer, relate; s'en — à to rely on, to leave it to, go by.

rapporteur, -euse [raportœr, ø:z] n tale bearer; nm reporter, recorder, protractor.

rapproché [raprɔʃe] a near, close (-set), related.

rapprochement [raprɔʃmã] nm bringing together, reconciling, comparing, nearness, reconciliation.

rapprocher [raprɔʃe] vt to bring together, bring near(er), draw up, compare, reconcile; vr to draw near(er) become reconciled.

rapt [rapt] nm kidnapping, abduction.

raquette [rakɛt] nf racket, snowshoe, prickly pear.

rare [ra:r] a rare, unusual, sparse.

rarement [rarmã] ad seldom, rarely.

rareté [rarte] nf rarity, scarcity, unusualness, rare happening, curiosity.

ras [ra] a close-cropped, close-shaven, bare; en —e campagne in the open country; faire table —e

de to make a clean sweep of; **à, au — de** level with, flush with, up to.

rasade [razad] nf bumper.

rase-mottes [razmɔt] nm **voler à —** to hedge-hop.

raser [raze] vt to shave, bore, raze to the ground, skim (over, along), hug; vr to shave, be bored; **se faire — to** have a shave.

rasoir [razwaːr] nm razor; **qu'il est —!** how boring, tiresome he is!

rassasier [rasazje] vt to satisfy, satiate, surfeit; vr to eat one's fill.

rassemblement [rasɑ̃bləmɑ̃] nm assembling, gathering, fall-in, crowd.

rassembler [rasɑ̃ble] vtr to assemble, gather together, muster.

rasséréner [raserene] vt to clear (up); vr to clear up, brighten up.

rassis [rasi] a settled, staid, sane, stale.

rassurer [rasyre] vt to reassure, strengthen; vr to feel reassured, set one's mind at rest.

rat [ra] nm rat, miser; **— de bibliothèque** bookworm; **— de cave** exciseman, wax taper; **— d'église** excessively pious person; **— d'hôtel** hotel thief; **mort aux —s** rat-poison.

ratatiné [ratatine] a shriveled, wizened.

rate [rat] nf spleen; **ne pas se fouler la —** to take things easy.

raté [rate] a miscarried, bungled, muffed; n failure, misfire.

râteau [rɑto] nm rake, cue-rest.

râteler [rɑtle] vt to rake up.

râtelier [rɑtəlje] nm rack, denture.

rater [rate] vi to miscarry, misfire, fail; vt to miss, fail, bungle, muff.

ratière [ratjɛːr] nf rat-trap.

ratifier [ratifje] vt to ratify.

ration [rasjɔ̃] nf ration, allowance.

rationnel, -elle [rasjonɛl] a rational.

rationnement [rasjɔnmɑ̃] nm rationing.

rationner [rasjone] vt to ration (out).

ratisser [ratise] vt to rake.

ratissoire [ratiswaːr] nf rake, hoe, scraper.

rattacher [rataʃe] vt to (re)fasten, tie up, bind, connect; vr to be connected (with **à**), fastened (to **à**).

rattraper [ratrape] vt to recapture, catch (again, up), overtake, recover; vr to save oneself, recoup oneself, make it up.

rature [ratyːr] nf erasure.

raturer [ratyre] vt to erase, cross out.

rauque [roːk] a raucous, hoarse, harsh.

ravage [ravaːʒ] nm (usu pl) havoc.

ravager [ravaʒe] vt to devastate, lay waste.

ravaler [ravale] vt to swallow (again, down), disparage, roughcast; vr to lower oneself; **— ses paroles** to eat one's words.

ravauder [ravode] vt to mend, darn.

ravi [ravi] a delighted, overjoyed, enraptured.

ravigoter [ravigɔte] vtr to revive, buck up.

ravin [ravɛ̃] nm ravine.

raviner [ravine] vt to gully, cut up, rut.

ravir [raviːr] vt to ravish, carry off, enrapture, delight; **à —** ravishingly, delightfully.

se raviser [səravize] vr to change one's mind.

ravissant [ravisɑ̃] a lovely, delightful, bewitching, ravishing.

ravitaillement [ravitajmɑ̃] nm revictualing, supply(ing); **service du —** Army Service Corps.

ravitailler [ravitaje] vtr to revictual; vt to supply.

ravitailleur [ravitajœːr] nm carrier, supply-ship.

raviver [ravive] vtr to revive, brighten.

rayer [rɛje] vt to scratch, rule, stripe, delete, strike off.

rayon [rɛjɔ̃] nm ray, beam, radius, drill, row, shelf, counter, department; **— visuel** line of sight; **— de miel** honeycomb; **chef de —** floorwalker, buyer.

rayonne [rɛjɔn] nf rayon.

rayonnement [rɛjɔnmɑ̃] nm radiation, radiance.

rayonner [rɛjone] vi to radiate, beam, be radiant.

rayure [rɛjyːr] nf scratch, stripe, erasure, striking off.

raz [rɑ] nm strong current; **— de marée** tide-race, tidal wave.

ré [re] nm the note D, D string.

réactif [reaktif, iːv] a **papier —** litmus paper.

réacteur [reaktœːr] nm reactor, (aut) choke.

réaction [reaksjɔ̃] nf reaction; **avion à —** jet-plane.

réactionnaire [reaksjonɛːr] an reactionary.

réagir [reaʒiːr] vi to react.

réalisation [realizasjɔ̃] nf realization, carrying into effect, selling out.

réaliser [realize] vt to realize, carry out, sell out; vr to materialize, be realized.

réalisme [realism] nm realism.

réaliste [realist] a realistic; n realist.

réalité [realite] nf reality.

réarmement [rearməmɑ̃] nm rearming, refitting.

réassurer [reasyre] vt to reassure, reinsure.

rébarbatif, -ive [rebarbatif, iːv] a forbidding, grim, crabbed, repulsive.

rebattre [rəbatr] vt to beat again, reshuffle; **— les oreilles à qn** to repeat the same thing over and over again to s.o.

rebattu [rəbaty] a hackneyed, trite.

rebelle [rəbɛl] a rebellious, obstinate; n rebel.

rébellion [rebeljɔ̃] nf rebellion, rising.

reboiser [rəbwaze] vt to retimber, (re)afforest.

rebondi [rəbɔ̃di] a plump, chubby, rounded.

rebondir [rəbɔ̃diːr] vi to rebound, bounce, start up all over again.

rebord [rəbɔːr] nm edge, hem, border, rim, flange.

rebours [rəbuːr] nm wrong way, contrary; à, au — against the grain, backward, the wrong way.

rebouteur [rəbutœːr] nm bone-setter.

rebrousse-poil [rəbruspwal] ad à — the wrong way, against the nap or hair.

rebuffade [rəbyfad] nf rebuff.

rébus [rebyːs] nm puzzle, riddle.

rebut [rəby] nm scrap, waste, rubbish, scum; pl rejects; bureau des —s dead-letter office.

rebutant [rəbytɑ̃] a discouraging, irksome, repulsive, forbidding

rebuter [rəbyte] vt to rebuff, repulse, discourage; vr to become discouraged, jib.

récalcitrant [rekalsitrɑ̃] a recalcitrant, refractory.

recaler [rəkale] vt to fail.

récapituler [rekapityle] vt to recapitulate.

receler [rəsele] vt to conceal, hide, receive (stolen goods).

receleur, -euse [rəslœːr, øːz] n receiver, fence.

récemment [resamɑ̃] ad recently, lately.

recensement [rəsɑ̃smɑ̃] nm census, counting.

recenser [rəsɑ̃se] vt to take the census of, count, check off.

récent [resɑ̃] a recent, fresh, late.

récépissé [resepise] nm receipt.

réceptacle [reseptakl] nm receptacle.

récepteur, -trice [reseptœːr, tris] a receiving; nm receiver.

réception [resepsjɔ̃] nf receipt, reception, admission, welcome, receiving desk; accuser — de to acknowledge receipt of; avis, (accusé) de — notice (acknowledgment) of delivery; jour de — at-home day.

recette [rəsɛt] nf receipt(s), takings, gate-money, recipe.

receveur, -euse [rəsəvœːr, øːz] n receiver, addressee, tax-collector, conductor, -tress; — des Postes postmaster.

recev r [rəsəvwaːr] vt to receive, get, tain, welcome, take in (board s accept, admit; vi be at home.

rechan [rəʃɑ̃ʒ] nm replacement, pare ange, refill; a de — spare.

réchapper [reʃape] vi to escape, recov r

r charge [rəʃarʒe] vt to recharge,

réchaud [reʃo] nm portable stov (gas-)ring, hot-plate.

réchauffé [reʃofe] nm warmed-u dish, rehash.

réchauffer [reʃofe] vt to rehea warm up, stir up.

rêche [rɛʃ] a harsh, rough, crabbe sour.

recherche [rəʃɛrʃ] nf search, pursui studied refinement; pl research.

recherché [rəʃɛrʃe] a in grea demand, choice, mannered, affected

rechercher [rəʃɛrʃe] vt to searc (for, into), seek.

rechigner [rəʃiɲe] vi to look surly jib (at à, devant).

rechute [rəʃyt] nf relapse.

récidiver [residive] vi to offen again, recur.

récidiviste [residivist] n old offende

récif [resif] nm reef.

récipient [resipjɑ̃] nm receive container, vessel.

réciprocité [resiprɔsite] nf recipr city.

réciproque [resiprɔk] a reciproca mutual; nf the like.

réciproquement [resiprɔkmɑ̃] a reciprocally, vice-versa, mutually.

récit [resi] nm recital, account, stor narrative.

récitation [resitasjɔ̃] nf recitin recitation.

réciter [resite] vt to recite, say.

réclamation [reklamasjɔ̃] nf com plaint, claim.

réclame [reklɑːm] nf publicity advertising, advertisement, sign.

réclamer [reklame] vi to complair protest; vt to claim, demand back beg for, call (out) for; vr — de q to quote s.o. as one's authority, t use s.o.'s name.

reclus [rəkly] n recluse.

réclusion [reklyzjɔ̃] nf reclusion seclusion.

recoin [rəkwɛ̃] nm nook, recess.

récolte [rekɔlt] nf harvest(ing crop(s).

récolter [rekɔlte] vt to harvest gather (in).

recommandation [rəkɔmɑ̃dasjɔ̃] n recommendation, advice; lettre d — letter of introduction, testimonia

recommander [rəkɔmɑ̃de] vt t (re)commend, advise, register.

recommencer [rəkɔmɑ̃se] vti t recommence, begin again.

récompense [rekɔ̃pɑ̃ːs] nf recom pense, reward, prize.

récompenser [rekɔ̃pɑ̃se] vt to recom pense, reward, requite.

réconciliation [rekɔ̃siljasjɔ̃] nf re conciliation.

réconcilier [rekɔ̃silje] vt to reconcile vr to make it up, make one's peac become friends again.

reconduire [rəkɔ̃dɥiːr] vt to accom pany back escort, see home, sho out

récon ort [rekɔ̃fɔːr] nm comfort, consolation.

réconforter [rekɔ̃fɔrte] vt to comfort, console, fortify, refresh; vr to cheer up.

reconnaissance [rəkɔnɛsɑ̃ːs] nf recognition, acknowledgment, admission, reconnoitering, reconnaissance, gratitude, thankfulness.

reconnaissant [rəkɔnɛsɑ̃] a grateful, thankful.

reconnaître [rəkɔnɛːtr] vt to recognize, acknowledge, reconnoiter; vr to acknowledge, get one's bearings; ne plus s'y — to be quite lost, bewildered.

reconstituant [rəkɔ̃stityɑ̃] a nm restorative.

record [rəkɔːr] nm record.

recourbé [rəkurbe] a bent (back, down, round), curved, crooked.

recour r [rəkuriːr] vi to run (again, back), have recourse (to à), appeal (to à).

recours [rəkuːr] nm recourse, resort, claim, appeal.

recouvrement [rəkuvrəmɑ̃] nm recovery, collection, recovering, cover(ing), overlapping.

recouvrer [rəkuvre] vt to recover, regain, collect.

recouvrir [rəkuvriːr] vt to recover, cover (over), overlap; vr to become overcast.

récréation [rekreasjɔ̃] nf recreation, amusement, relaxation, playtime; cour de — playground; en — at play.

récréer [rekree] vt to enliven, refresh, entertain, amuse; vr to take some recreation.

se récrier [sərekrie] vr to cry out, exclaim, protest.

récriminer [rekrimine] vi to recriminate.

se recroqueviller [sərəkrɔkvije] vr to curl (up, in), shrivel (up).

recru [rəkry] a — de fatigue worn out, dead tired.

recrudescence [rəkrydɛssɑ̃ːs] nf recrudescence.

recrue [rəkry] nf recruit.

recruter [rəkryte] vt to recruit, enlist.

rectangle [rɛktɑ̃ːgl] a right-angled; nm rectangle.

rectangulaire [rɛktɑ̃gylɛːr] a rectangular.

recteur [rɛktœːr] nm rector.

rectification [rɛktifikasjɔ̃] nf rectification, rectifying, straightening, (re)adjustment.

rectifier [rɛktifje] vt to rectify, straighten, adjust.

rectiligne [rɛktiliɲ] a rectilinear.

rectitude [rɛktityd] nf straightness, rectitude.

reçu [rəsy] pp of recevoir; nm receipt.

recueil [rəkœːj] nm collection.

recueillement [rəkœːjmɑ̃] nm meditation, composure, concentration.

recueilli [rəkœji] a meditative, rapt, concentrated, still.

recueillir [rəkœjiːr] vt to gather, collect, take in; vr to collect one's thoughts, commune with oneself.

recul [rəkyl] nm recoil, backward movement, room to move back.

reculade [rəkylad] nf backward movement, withdrawal.

reculé [rəkyle] a remote.

reculer [rəkyle] vi to move back, draw back; vt to move back, postpone.

reculons [rəkylɔ̃] ad à — backward.

récupérer [rekypere] vt to recover, recoup, salvage; vr to recuperate.

récurer [rekyre] vt to scour.

récuser [rekyze] vt to challenge, take exception to; vr to refuse to give an opinion, disclaim competence, decline.

rédacteur, -trice [redaktœːr, tris] n writer, editor.

rédaction [redaksjɔ̃] nf writing, editing, editorial staff, newspaper office, composition, wording.

reddition [rɛddisjɔ̃] nf surrender.

rédempteur, -trice [redɑ̃ptœːr, tris] a redeeming; n redeemer.

rédemption [redɑ̃psjɔ̃] nf redemption.

redevable [rədvabl] a indebted, obliged.

redevance [rədvɑ̃ːs] nf rent, tax, due.

rédiger [rediʒe] vt to draft, write, edit.

redingote [rədɛ̃gɔt] nf frock-coat.

redire [rədiːr] vt to repeat; trouver à — à to find fault with.

redite [rədit] nf repetition.

redondance [rədɔ̃dɑ̃ːs] nf redundance.

redoubler [rəduble] vt to redouble, reline, repeat (a class); vi to redouble.

redoutable [rədutabl] a formidable.

redoute [rədut] nf redoubt.

redouter [rədute] vt to dread.

redressement [rədrɛsmɑ̃] nm setting up again, righting, rectifying, straightening, redress.

redresser [rədrɛse] vt to set upright again, right, rectify, straighten; vr to sit up again, draw oneself up, right oneself.

réductible [redyktibl] a reducible.

réduction [redyksjɔ̃] nf reduction, cut, conquest.

réduire [reduiːr] vt to reduce; vr to be reduced, confine oneself to, boil down.

réduit [redui] nm retreat, hovel, redoubt.

rééducation [reedykasjɔ̃] nf centre de — reformatory.

réel, -elle [reɛl] a real, actual; nm reality.

réexpédier [reɛkspedje] *vt* to forward, retransmit.

réfaction [refaksjɔ̃] *nf* rebate, allowance.

refaire [rəfɛ:r] *vt* to remake, do again, make again, repair, take in; *vr* to recuperate.

réfection [refɛksjɔ̃] *nf* remaking, repairing.

réfectoire [refɛktwa:r] *nm* dining-hall.

référence [referɑ̃:s] *nf* reference.

référer [refere] *vt* to refer, ascribe; *vir* to refer (to à).

refiler [rəfile] *vt* to fob off, pass on.

réfléchi [reflefi] *a* thoughtful, considered, reflexive.

réfléchir [reflefi:r] *vt* to reflect, throw back; *vi* to reflect, consider; *vr* to be reflected.

reflet [rəflɛ] *nm* reflection, gleam.

refléter [rəflete] *vt* to reflect, throw back.

réflexe [reflɛks] *a nm* reflex.

réflexion [reflɛksjɔ̃] *nf* reflection, thought, remark.

refluer [rəflye] *vi* to ebb, surge back.

reflux [rəfly] *nm* ebb(-tide), surging back.

refondre [rəfɔ̃:dr] *vt* to recast, reorganize.

refonte [rəfɔ̃:t] *nf* recasting, reorganization.

réformateur, -trice [reformatœ:r, tris] *a* reforming; *n* reformer.

réformation [reformasjɔ̃] *nf* reformation.

réforme [reform] *nf* reform, reformation, discharge.

réformé [reforme] *n* Protestant, disabled soldier.

réformer [reforme] *vt* to reform, discharge (as unfit).

refoulement [rəfulmɑ̃] *nm* forcing back, repression.

refouler [rəfule] *vt* to drive back, repress.

réfractaire [refraktɛ:r] *an* refractory, insubordinate.

réfracter [refrakte] *vt* to refract; *vr* to be refracted.

refrain [rəfrɛ̃] *nm* refrain, theme, chorus.

refréner [rəfrene] *vt* to restrain, curb.

réfrigérant [refriʒerɑ̃] *nm* refrigerator, cooler.

réfrigérer [refriʒere] *vt* to refrigerate, cool, chill.

refroidir [rəfrwadi:r] *vt* to chill, cool, damp; *vir* to grow cold, cool down.

refroidissement [rəfrwadismɑ̃] *nm* cooling (down), chill.

refuge [rəfy:ʒ] *nm* shelter, refuge, traffic island.

réfugié [refyʒje] *n* refugee.

e réfugier [sərefyʒje] *vr* to take refuge.

refus [rəfy] *nm* refusal; ce n'est pas de — it is not to be refused.

refuser [rəfyze] *vtr* to refuse; *vt* to reject, fail, turn away, grudge.

réfuter [refyte] *vt* to refute, disprove.

regagner [rəgaɲe] *vt* to regain, recover, get back to.

regain [rəgɛ̃] *nm* aftercrop, renewal, fresh lease.

régal [regal] *nm* feast, treat.

régaler [regale] *vt* to entertain, treat.

regard [rəga:r] *nm* look, glance, gaze; au — de compared with; en — de opposite.

regardant [rəgardɑ̃] *a* particular, mean, stingy.

regarder [rəgarde] *vt* to look at, consider, concern, watch; *vi* to look (on to sur), be particular (about à).

régate [regat] *nf* regatta, boater.

régence [reʒɑ̃:s] *nf* regency, fob chain, necktie.

régénérer [reʒenere] *vt* to regenerate.

régent [reʒɑ̃] *n* regent, governor.

régenter [reʒɑ̃te] *vt* to lord it over, domineer.

régie [reʒi] *nf* management, stewardship, excise.

regimber [rəʒɛ̃be] *vi* to kick, jib (at contre).

régime [reʒim] *nm* diet, government, administration, system, rules, flow, bunch, object.

régiment [reʒimɑ̃] *nm* regiment.

région [reʒjɔ̃] *nf* region, district.

régional [reʒjonal] *a* regional, local.

régir [reʒi:r] *vt* to govern, manage.

régisseur [reʒisœ:r] *nm* agent, steward, stage-manager.

registre [rəʒistr] *nm* register, account-book.

réglage [regla:ʒ] *nm* ruling, adjusting, turning.

règle [rɛgl] *nf* rule, ruler; en — in order; *pl* menses, period.

réglé [regle] *a* ruled, regular, steady.

règlement [rɛgləmɑ̃] *nm* regulation, settlement, rule.

réglementaire [rɛgləmɑ̃tɛ:r] *a* statutory, regulation.

réglementer [rɛgləmɑ̃te] *vt* to make rules for, regulate.

régler [regle] *vt* to rule, order, adjust, settle; *vr* to model oneself (on sur).

réglisse [reglis] *nf* licorice.

règne [rɛɲ] *nm* reign, sway, kingdom.

régner [reɲe] *vi* to reign, prevail.

regorger [rəgɔrʒe] *vt* to disgorge; *vi* to overflow (with de), abound (in de).

régression [regresjɔ̃] *nf* regression, recession, drop.

regret [rəgrɛ] *nm* regret, sorrow; à — regretfully; être au — (de) to be sorry.

regretter [rəgrete] *vt* to regret, be sorry (for), miss.

régulariser [regylarize] *vt* to regularize, put in order.

régularité [regylarite] *nf* regularity, steadiness, punctuality.

régulateur, -trice [regylatœːr, tris] *a* regulating; *nm* regulator, governor, throttle.

régulier, -ière [regylje, ɛːr] *a* regular, steady, punctual.

réhabiliter [reabilite] *vt* to rehabilitate, discharge.

rehausser [raose] *vt* to raise, heighten, enhance, accentuate, bring out.

rein [rɛ̃] *nm* kidney; *pl* back.

reine [rɛn] *nf* queen.

reine-claude [rɛnkloːd] *nf* greengage.

réintégrer [reɛ̃tegre] *vt* to reinstate, take up again.

réitérer [reitere] *vt* to repeat, reiterate.

rejaillir [rəʒajiːr] *vi* to gush out, be reflected come back (upon **sur**).

rejet [rəʒɛ] *nm* rejection, throwing up (out).

rejeter [rəʒ(ə)te] *vt* to reject, throw (back, out); *vr* to fall back (on **sur**).

rejeton [rəʒtɔ̃] *nm* shoot, offspring.

rejoindre [rəʒwɛ̃ːdr] *vt* to (re)join, overtake; *vr* to meet (again).

réjouir [reʒwiːr] *vt* to delight, hearten, amuse; *vr* to rejoice, be delighted.

réjouissance [reʒwisɑ̃ːs] *nf* rejoicing, merrymaking.

relâche [rəlɑːʃ] *nm* relaxation, respite, no performance; *nf* (port of) call.

relâchement [rəlɑʃmɑ̃] *nm* slackening, relaxing, relaxation, looseness.

relâcher [rəlɑʃe] *vt* to slacken, loosen, relax, release; *vr* to slacken, get loose, abate, grow lax, milder.

relais [rəlɛ] *nm* relay, stage, shift, posthouse.

relancer [rəlɑ̃se] *vt* to throw back; to go after (s.o.); to be at (s.o.); restart.

relater [rəlate] *vt* to relate, report.

relatif, -ive [rəlatif, iːv] *a* relative, relating (to **à**).

relation [rəlasjɔ̃] *nf* relation, contact, connection, account.

relaxer [rəlakse] *vt* to release; *vr* to relax.

relayer [rəleje] *vt* to relay, relieve; *vi* to change horses.

relent [rəlɑ̃] *nm* stale smell, mustiness.

relève [rəlɛːv] *nf* relief, changing (of guard).

relevé [rəlve] *a* lofty, spicy; *nm* statement, account.

relever [rəlve] *vt* to raise up (again), turn up, pick up, relieve, set off, point out; *vi* to be dependent (on **de**); *vi* to rise (again), recover.

relie [rəljef] *nm* relief, prominence.

relier [rəlje] *vt* to bind (again), join, connect.

relieur, -euse [rəljœːr, øːz] *n* bookbinder.

religieux, -euse [rəliʒjø, øːz] *a* religious; *n* monk, nun.

religion [rəliʒjɔ̃] *nf* religion.

reliquaire [rəlikɛːr] *nm* shrine.

reliquat [rəlika] *nm* remainder, after-effects.

relique [rəlik] *nf* relic.

reliure [rəljyːr] *nf* (book)binding.

reluire [rəlyiːr] *vi* to shine, gleam.

reluquer [rəlyke] *vt* to eye.

remailler [rəmaje] *vt* to remesh, mend.

remanier [rəmanje] *vt* to rehandle, recast.

remarquable [rəmarkabl] *a* remarkable (for **par**).

remarque [rəmark] *nf* remark.

remarquer [rəmarke] *vt* to remark, notice.

rembarrer [rɑ̃bare] *vt* to tell off, snub.

remblai [rɑ̃blɛ] *nm* embankment.

rembourrer [rɑ̃bure] *vt* to stuff, pad.

rembourser [rɑ̃burse] *vt* to refund, repay.

rembrunir [rɑ̃bryniːr] *vtr* to darken, become sad; *vt* to sadden.

remède [rəmɛd] *nm* remedy, cure.

remédier [rəmedje] *vt* — **à** to remedy.

remembrement [rəmɑ̃brəmɑ̃] *nr* reallocation of land.

remémorer [rəmemɔre] *vt* to remind (of); *vr* to remember.

remerciement [rəmɛrsimɑ̃] *nr* thanks.

remercier [rəmɛrsje] *vt* to thank, dismiss, decline.

remettre [rəmɛtr] *vt* to put back (again), hand (over, in), remit, postpone; *vr* to recover, begin; s'e — **à qn** to rely on s.o., leave it t s.o.

remise [rəmiːz] *nf* putting back, off remittance, delivery, rebate, shed.

rémission [remisjɔ̃] *nf* remission, pardon.

remonter [rəmɔ̃te] *vt* to go u (again), carry up, pull up, wind up buck up; *vi* to go up again, remoun go back (to **à**); *vr* to cheer up, regai strength.

remonte-pente [rəmɔ̃tpɑ̃ːt] *nm* sk lift.

remontoir [rəmɔ̃twaːr] *nm* winde key.

remontrance [rəmɔ̃trɑ̃ːs] *nf* remor strance.

remontrer [rəmɔ̃tre] *vt* to sho again; **en — à** to remonstrate wit outdo.

remords [rəmɔːr] *nm* remorse.

remorque [rəmɔrk] *nf* tow(ing tow-line, trailer.

remorqueur [rəmɔrke] *nm* tu (-boat).

rémouleur [remulœːr] *nm* knif grinder.

remous [rəmu] *nm* eddy, backwas

rempart [rɑ̃paːr] *nm* rampart.

remplaçant [rãplasã] n substitute.
remplacement [rãplasmã] nm replacing, substitution.
remplacer [rãplase] vt to replace, deputize for.
rempli [rãpli] nm tuck.
remplir [rãpliːr] vtr to fill (up, in); vt fulfill, occupy.
remporter [rãporte] vt to carry away, gain, win.
remuant [rəmyã] a stirring, restless.
remue-ménage [rəmymena:ʒ] nm bustle, stir.
remuer [rəmųe] vti to move, stir.
rémunérateur, -trice [remynerat œːr, tris] a remunerative, paying.
rémunération [remynerasjɔ̃] nf remuneration.
renâcler [rənakle] vi to snort, hang back.
renaissance [rənɛsã:s] nf rebirth, revival.
renaître [rənɛːtr] vi to be born again, revive, reappear.
renard [rənaːr] n fox, vixen.
renchérir [rãʃeriːr] vt to raise the price of; vi to rise in price, outbid, outdo.
rencontre [rãkɔ̃:tr] nf meeting, encounter, collision, occasion; de — chance.
rencontrer [rãkɔ̃tre] vt to meet (with), run across; vr to meet, collide, agree.
rendement [rãdmã] nm yield, output, profit, efficiency.
rendez-vous [rãdevu] nm appointment, meeting-place.
rendre [rã:dr] vt to give back (up, out), yield, deliver, surrender, make; vr to proceed, go, surrender, yield.
rêne [rɛn] nf rein.
renégat [rənega] n renegade.
renfermé [rãferme] a uncommunicative, reticent; nm musty smell.
renfermer [rãferme] vt to shut up (again), lock up, include, contain.
renfler [rãfle] vti to swell (out).
renflouer [rãflue] vt to refloat.
renfoncement [rãfɔ̃smã] nm cavity, recess, knocking in.
renfoncer [rãfɔ̃se] vt to drive in, pull down.
renforcer [rãfɔrse] vt to reinforce, strengthen; vir to become stronger.
renfort [rãfɔːr] nm reinforcement(s).
se renfrogner [sərãfrɔɲe] vr to frown, scowl.
rengaine [rãgeːn] nf old story, old refrain, catchword.
rengainer [rãgene] vt to sheathe.
se rengorger [sərãgɔrʒe] vr to puff oneself out, swagger.
renier [rənje] vt to disown, repudiate.
renifler [rənifle] vti to sniff.
renne [rɛn] nm reindeer.
renom [rənɔ̃] nm renown, fame, repute.
renommé [rənɔme] a celebrated, famous.

renommée [rənɔme] nf fame, good name.
renoncement [rənɔ̃smã] nm renouncing, self-denial.
renoncer [rənɔ̃se] vt to renounce.
renoncule [rənɔ̃kyl] nf buttercup.
renouer [rənwe] vt to join again; to resume, renew.
renouveau [rənuvo] nm springtime, renewal.
renouveler [r(ə)nuvle] vt to renew, renovate; vr to be renewed, recur.
rénovation [renɔvasjɔ̃] nf renovation, revival.
renseignement [rãsɛɲmã] nm (piece of) information.
renseigner [rãsɛɲe] vt to inform; vr to inquire (about sur), find out.
rente [rã:t] nf unearned income, pension.
rentier, -ière [rãtje, jeːr] n person of private means, stock-holder.
rentrée [rãtre] nf return, reopening, gathering (in).
rentrer [rãtre] vt to bring (take, get, pull) in; vi to come (go) in (again), come (go) home, reopen.
renverse [rãvers] nf change, turn; à la — backward.
renversement [rãvɛrsəmã] nm overturning, overthrow, reversal, inversion.
renverser [rãverse] vt to knock over (down), overthrow, spill, reverse, invert, flabbergast; vr to overturn, recline.
renvoi [rãvwa] nm sending back, reflecting, dismissal, reference, putting-off, belch.
renvoyer [rãvwaje] vt to send back, reflect, dismiss, refer, defer.
repaire [rəpeːr] nm lair, den, haunt.
repaître [rəpeːtr] vtr to feed.
répandre [repã:dr] vt to spread, pour out, shed, scatter; vr to (be) spread, spill.
répandu [repãdy] a widespread, well-known.
réparation [reparasjɔ̃] nf repair(ing), reparation, amends.
réparer [repare] vt to mend, repair, redress, restore.
repartie [rəparti] nf repartee, retort.
repartir [rəpartiːr] vi to set out again, retort.
répartir [repartiːr] vi to distribute, divide, allot.
répartition [repartisjɔ̃] nf distribution, sharing out, allotment.
repas [rəpɑ] nm meal.
repasser [rəpɑse] vt to pass again, cross again, go over, iron, sharpen; vi to pass again, call back.
repêcher [rəpeʃe] vt to fish out (again), pick up, rescue; vr to get another chance (examination).
repentir [rəpãtiːr] nm repentance; vr to repent, rue.
répercussion [reperkysjɔ̃] nf repercussion.

répercuter [reperkyte] *vtr* to reverberate, reflect.

repère [rəpɛ:r] *nm* point de — reference, guide, landmark.

repérer [rəpere] *vt* to locate, spot; *vr* to take one's bearings.

répertoire [repertwa:r] *nm* repertory, list, collection.

répéter [repete] *vt* to repeat, rehearse; *vr* to recur.

répétiteur, -trice [repetitœ:r, tris] *n* assistant-teacher, private tutor, chorus master.

répétition [repetisjɔ̃] *nf* repetition, rehearsal, private lesson; — générale dress rehearsal.

répit [repi] *nm* respite.

repli [rəpli] *nm* fold, crease, bend, coil, withdrawal.

replier [rəplie] *vtr* to fold up, turn in (back), coil up; *vr* to wind. withdraw.

réplique [replik] *nf* ready answer, cue, replica.

répliquer [replike] *vi* to retort.

répondre [repɔ̃:dr] *vt* to answer, reply, respond, comply; *vi* to answer, be answerable (for de), correspond (to à), come up (to à).

réponse [repɔ̃:s] *nf* answer.

report [rəpɔ:r] *nm* carrying-forward, amount brought forward.

reportage [rəpɔrta:ʒ] *nm* report(ing).

reporter [rəpɔrte] *vt* to carry (take) back, bring forward; *vr* to refer.

repor'er [rəpɔrtœ:r, tɛ:r] *nm* reporter.

repos [rəpo] *nm* rest, peace.

reposé [rəpoze] *a* refreshed, calm; à tête —e at leisure, quietly.

reposer [rəpoze] *vt* to replace, put back, rest; *vi* to rest, lie; *vr* to rest, alight again, rely (on sur).

reposoir [rəpozwa:r] *nm* resting-place, temporary altar.

repoussant [rəpusɑ̃] *a* repulsive.

repousser [rəpuse] *vt* to push away (back, off), reject, repel; *vi* to grow again, recoil.

repoussoir [rəpuswa:r] *nm* foil, punch.

répréhensible [repreɑ̃sibl] *a* reprehensible.

reprendre [rəprɑ̃:dr] *vt* to recapture, take back, recover, resume, reprove, correct; *vi* to begin again, set (in) again; *vr* to correct oneself, pull oneself together.

représailles [rəpreza:j] *nf pl* reprisals.

représentant [rəprezɑ̃tɑ̃] *an* representative.

représentatif, -ive [rəprezɑ̃tatif, i:v] *a* representative.

représentation [rəprezɑ̃tasjɔ̃] *nf* representation, performance, agency, protest.

représenter [rəprezɑ̃te] *vt* to represent, portray, perform, act, reintroduce; *vi* to put up a show, have a

fine appearance; *vr* to present oneself again, recur, describe oneself (as comme).

répression [represjɔ̃] *nf* repression.

réprimande [reprimɑ̃:d] *nf* reproof, reprimand.

réprimander [reprimɑ̃de] *vt* to reprove, reprimand.

réprimer [reprime] *vt* to repress, quell, curb.

repris [rəpri] *n* — de justice old offender.

reprise [rəpri:z] *nf* recapture, taking back, resumption, revival, acceleration, darn(ing), round; à plusieurs — several times.

repriser [rəprize] *vt* to darn, mend.

réprobateur, -trice [reprɔbatœ:r, tris] *a* reproachful, reproving.

réprobation [reprɔbasjɔ̃] *nf* reprobation.

reproche [rəprɔʃ] *nm* reproach, blame.

reprocher [rəprɔʃe] *vt* to reproach (with), begrudge, cast up.

reproduction [rəprɔdyksjɔ̃] *nf* reproduction, copy.

reproduire [rəprɔdɥi:r] *vt* to reproduce; *vr* to breed, recur.

réprouver [repruve] *vt* to disapprove of, reprobate.

reptile [rɛptil] *a nm* reptile.

repu [rəpy] *a* satiated.

républicain [repyblikɛ̃] *an* republican.

république [repyblik] *nf* republic.

répudier [repydje] *vt* to repudiate, renounce.

répugnance [repynɑ̃:s] *nf* repugnance, loathing, reluctance.

répugnant [repynɑ̃] *a* repugnant, loathsome.

répugner [repyne] *vi* to be repugnant, loathe, be reluctant.

répulsion [repylsjɔ̃] *nf* repulsion.

réputation [repytasjɔ̃] *nf* reputation, repute, name.

réputé [repyte] *a* of repute, well-known.

requérir [rəkeri:r] *vt* to ask (for), demand, summon.

requête [rəkɛ:t] *nf* request, petition.

requin [rəkɛ̃] *nm* shark.

requinquer [rəkɛ̃ke] *vt* to smarten up, repair; *vr* to smarten oneself up, recover.

requis [rəki] *a* requisite, necessary.

réquisition [rekizisjɔ̃] *nf* requisition (ing).

réquisitionner [rekizisjɔne] *vt* to requisition.

réquisitoire [rekizitwa:r] *nm* indictment, charge.

rescapé [rɛskape] *a* rescued; *n* survivor.

rescinder [rɛssɛ̃de] *vt* to annul, rescind.

rescousse [rɛskus] *nf* rescue.

réseau [rezo] *nm* net(work), system.

réséda [reseda] *nm* mignonette.

réservation [rezɛrvasjɔ̃] nf reservation.

réserve [rezɛrv] nf reserve, reservation, aloofness, caution; de — spare, reserve.

réservé [rezɛrve] a reserved, cautious, aloof, private.

réserver [rezɛrve] vt to reserve, save, set aside.

réserviste [rezɛrvist] nm reservist.

réservoir [rezɛrvwa:r] nm reservoir, tank.

résidence [rezidɑ̃:s] nf residence, abode.

résider [rezide] vi to reside, live, lie.

résidu [rezidy] nm residue, balance.

résignation [rezinasjɔ̃] nf resignation.

résigner [rezine] vt to resign, give up.

résilier [rezilje] vt to cancel, annul.

résille [rezi:j] nf hair-net, snood.

résine [rezin] nf resin.

résistance [rezistɑ̃:s] nf resistance, opposition, endurance, strength; pièce de — main dish, feature.

résistant [rezistɑ̃] a resistant, strong, fast.

résister [reziste] vt to resist, withstand; vi to be fast.

résolu [rezɔly] a resolute.

résolution [rezɔlysjɔ̃] nf resolve, determination, solution, canceling.

résonance [rezɔnɑ̃:s] nf resonance.

résonner [rezɔne] vi to resound, clang, ring.

résoudre [rezu:dr] vt to resolve, decide, (dis)solve, settle; vr to decide, dissolve.

respect [rɛspɛ] nm respect.

respectable [rɛspɛktabl] a respectable.

respecter [rɛspɛkte] vt to respect, have regard for.

respectif, -ive [rɛspɛktif, i:v] a respective.

respectueux, -euse [rɛspɛktɥø, ø:z] a respectful.

respiration [rɛspirasjɔ̃] nf breathing.

respirer [rɛspire] vt to breathe (in), inhale; vi to breathe.

resplendir [rɛsplɑ̃di:r] vi to shine, glow, be resplendent.

responsabilité [rɛspɔ̃sabilite] nf responsibility, liability.

responsable [rɛspɔ̃sabl] a responsible.

resquilleur, -euse [rɛskijœ:r, ø:z] n gatecrasher, wangler.

ressac [rəsak] nm undertow, surf.

ressaisir [rəsezi:r] vt to seize again; vr to pull oneself together, recover one's self-control.

ressasser [rəsase] vt repeat, harp on, resift.

ressemblance [rəsɑ̃blɑ̃:s] nf resemblance, likeness.

ressemblant [rəsɑ̃blɑ̃] a (a)like.

ressembler [rəsɑ̃ble] vt to resemble, be like.

ressentiment [rəsɑ̃timɑ̃] nm resentment.

ressentir [rəsɑ̃ti:r] vt to feel; vr to feel the effects (of de).

resserrement [rəsɛrmɑ̃] nm contraction, tightness; — du cœur pang.

resserrer [rəsɛre] vt to contract, tighten, draw tight; vr to contract, shrink, narrow, retrench.

ressort [rəsɔ:r] nm spring, resilience, line, province, resort.

ressortir [rəsɔrti:r] vt to bring out again; vi to come, (go) out again, stand out, follow (from de), belong (to à); faire — to bring out.

ressortissant [rəsɔrtisɑ̃] nm national.

ressource [rəsurs] nf resource(fulness), expedient; en dernière — in the last resort.

ressusciter [resysite] vti to resuscitate, revive.

restant [rɛstɑ̃] a remaining, left; nm rest, remainder.

restaurant [rɛstɔrɑ̃] nm restaurant.

restaurateur, -trice [rɛstɔratœ:r, tris] n restorer; nm restaurant-keeper.

restauration [rɛstɔrasjɔ̃] nf restoring, restoration.

restaurer [rɛstɔre] vt to restore, refresh; vr to take refreshment, build oneself up.

reste [rɛst] nm remainder, rest; pl remains, traces, scraps; au (du) — moreover; de — left.

rester [rɛste] vi to remain, stay, keep, stand, be left.

restituer [rɛstitɥe] vt to restore, return.

restitution [rɛstitysjɔ̃] nf restitution, restoration, refunding.

restreindre [rɛstrɛ̃:dr] vt to restrict, limit; vr to restrict oneself, retrench.

restriction [rɛstriksjɔ̃] nf restriction, limitation.

résultat [rezylta] nm result, outcome.

résulter [rezylte] vi to result, be the result (of de).

résumé [rezyme] nm summary; en — in brief.

résumer [rezyme] vtr to sum up.

résurrection [rezyrɛksjɔ̃] nf resurrection, revival.

rétablir [retabli:r] vt to re-establish, restore, reinstate; vr to recover, re-establish oneself.

rétablissement [retablismɑ̃] nm re-establishment, restoration, reinstatement, recovery.

retaper [rətape] vt to do up, mend; vr to recover.

retard [rəta:r] nm delay, lateness; en — in arrears.

retardataire [rətardatɛ:r] a late, backward; n laggard, straggler.

retarder [rətarde] vt to delay, make late, put back; vi to be lat . lag.

retenir [rətni:r] vt to hold (back), retain, detain, restrain, reserve; vr

to refrain (from de), restrain oneself.
retentir [rətãti:r] *vi* to echo, reverberate, resound.
retentissement [rətãtismã] *nm* reverberation, repercussion.
retenue [rətny] *nf* withholding, deduction, restraint, detention, discretion.
réticence [retisã:s] *nf* reserve, reticence.
rétif, -ive [retif, i:v] *a* stubborn.
retiré [rətire] *a* retired, remote.
retirer [rətire] *vt* to withdraw, obtain, remove; *vr* to retire, recede.
retomber [rət5be] *vi* to fall back, droop, hang down.
rétorquer [retɔrke] *vt* to retort, cast back.
retors [rətɔ:r] *a* twisted, bent, crafty, sly.
retouche [rətuʃ] *nf* retouch(ing), small alteration.
retoucher [rətuʃe] *vt* to touch up.
retour [rətu:r] *nm* return, turn, recurrence, change.
retourner [rəturne] *vt* to turn (inside out), turn (back, down, over, round, up), return; *vi* to return, go back; *vr* to turn around, over.
retracer [rətrase] *vt* to retrace, recall.
rétracter [retrakte] *vtr* to retract, withdraw.
retrait [rətrɛ] *nm* withdrawal, shrinkage, recess.
retraite [rətrɛt] *nf* retreat, retirement, refuge, (*mil*) tattoo.
retraité, -e [rətrete] *nmf* pensioner.
retranchement [rətrãʃmã] *nm* cutting off (down, out), entrenchment.
retrancher [rətrãʃe] *vt* to cut off (out, down); *vr* to entrench oneself, cut down one's expenses.
rétrécissement [retresismã] *nm* narrowing, shrinking.
rétrécir [retresi:r] *vtir* to narrow, shrink, contract.
rétribuer [retribɥe] *vt* to remunerate, pay.
rétribution [retribysj5] *nf* remuneration, reward.
rétrograde [retrɔgrad] *a* retrograde, backward.
rétrograder [retrɔgrade] *vt* to reduce in rank; *vi* to go back, change down.
rétrospectif, -ive [retrɔspektif, i:v] *a* retrospective.
retrousser [rətruse] *vt* to turn up, roll up, tuck up; **nez retroussé** snub nose.
rétroviseur [retrɔvizœ:r] *nm* driving-mirror.
réunion [reynj5] *nf* reunion, meeting, joining.
réunir [reyni:r] *vt* to reunite, collect, gather; *vr* to unite, meet.
réussi [reysi] *a* successful.
réussir [reysi:r] *vt* to make a success of; *vi* to succeed, be successful.

réussite [reysit] *nf* success, outcome, (*cards*) patience.
revaloir [rəvalwa:r] *vt* to pa[y] back.
revanche [rəvãːʃ] *nf* revenge, return game; **en —** in return, on the other hand.
rêvasser [rɛvase] *vi* to daydream.
rêve [rɛːv] *nm* dream.
revêche [rəvɛʃ] *a* rough, difficult, cantankerous.
réveil [revɛ:j] *nm* awakening.
réveille-matin [revɛjmatɛ̃] *nm* alarm-clock.
réveiller [reveje] *vtr* to wake (up), revive.
réveillon [revɛj5] *nm* midnight party (at Christmas, New Year).
révélateur, -trice [revelatœːr, tris] *a* revealing, telltale.
révélation [revelasj5] *nf* revelation, disclosure.
révéler [revele] *vt* to reveal, disclose.
revenant [rəvnã] *nm* ghost.
revendeur, -euse [rəvãdœːr, øːz] *n* retailer, second-hand dealer.
revendication [rəvãdikasj5] *nf* claim(ing).
revendiquer [rəvãdike] *vt* to claim.
revenir [rəvni:r] *vi* to come back, amount (to à), recover (from de); **go back on; en — to get over it; faire —** (*cooking*) to brown.
revenu [rəvny] *nm* income, revenue.
rêver [reve] *vt* to dream (of); *vi* to dream, ponder.
réverbère [reverbe:r] *nm* street lamp, reflector.
réverbérer [reverbere] *vt* to reverberate, reflect; *vi* to be reverberated, reflected.
révérence [reverã:s] *nf* reverence, bow, curtsy.
révérencieux, -euse [reverãsjø, øːz] *a* ceremonious, deferential.
révérer [revere] *vt* to revere.
rêverie [rɛvri] *nf* dreaming, musing.
revers [rəvɛːr] *nm* reverse, back, lapel, turn-up; backhand.
revêtement [rəvɛtmã] *nm* coating, facing, casing, surface, revetment.
revêtir [rəvɛti:r] *vt* to (re)clothe, dress, invest, coat, face, put on.
rêveur, -euse [rɛvœːr, øːz] *a* dreaming, dreamy; *n* dreamer.
revient [rəvjɛ̃] *nm* **prix de —** cost price.
revirement [rəvirmã] *nm* veering, sudden change.
réviser [revize] *vt* to revise, examine, overhaul.
révision [reviz5] *nf* revision, inspection, overhaul(ing); **conseil de —** draft board.
revivre [rəvi:vr] *vt* to relive; *vi* to live again, revive.
révocation [revɔkasj5] *nf* revocation, repeal, dismissal.
revoir [rəvwa:r] *vt* to see again, revise; **au — good-bye.**

révolte [revɔlt] nf revolt,
révolté [revɔlte] n rebel.
révolter [revɔlte] vt to revolt,
shock, disgust; vr to revolt, rebel.
révolu [revɔly] a completed, past,
ended.
révolution [revɔlysjɔ̃] nf revolution,
complete change.
révolutionnaire [revɔlysjɔnɛːr] an
revolutionary.
révolutionner [revɔlysjɔne] vt to
revolutionize.
revolver [revɔlvɛːr] nm revolver.
révoquer [revɔke] vt to revoke,
repeal, dismiss.
revue [rəvy] nf revue, inspection.
rez-de-chaussée [redʃose] nm
ground floor.
rhabiller [rabije] vt to reclothe,
repair; vr to dress oneself again,
buy new clothes.
rhénan [renɑ̃] a Rhenish, of the
Rhine.
rhétorique [retɔrik] nf rhetoric.
rhinocéros [rinɔserɔs] nm rhinoceros, rhinoceros beetle.
rhubarbe [rybarb] nf rhubarb.
rhum [rɔm] nm rum.
rhumatisant [rymatizɑ̃] an
rheumatic(ky) (person).
rhumatisme [rymatism] nm
rheumatism.
rhume [rym] nm cold; — de cerveau
cold in the head.
riant [rjɑ̃] a laughing, smiling,
pleasant.
ribambelle [ribɑ̃bɛl] nf (fam) long
string.
ricaner [rikane] vi to sneer, laugh
derisively.
riche [riʃ] a rich, wealthy, valuable.
richesse [riʃes] nf richness, wealth,
fertility.
ricin [risɛ̃] nm castor-oil plant;
huile de — castor oil.
ricocher [rikɔʃe] vi to ricochet,
glance off, rebound.
ricochet [rikɔʃe] nm rebound, ricochet.
rictus [riktyːs] nm grin.
ride [rid] nf wrinkle, ripple.
ridé [ride] a wrinkled, shriveled,
corrugated.
rideau [rido] nm curtain, screen,
veil.
ridelle [ridɛl] nf rail, rack.
rider [ride] vtr to wrinkle, pucker,
shrivel, ripple.
ridicule [ridikyl] a ridiculous, ludicrous; nm ridiculousness, absurdity.
ridiculiser [ridikylize] vt to ridicule.
rien [rjɛ̃] pn nothing, not anything;
nm trifle, just a little; comme si de
— n'était as if nothing had happened; il n'en fera — he will do nothing
of the kind; il n'y est pour — he
has (had) nothing to do with it;
cela ne fait — it does not matter.
rieur, -euse [rjœːr, øːz] a laughing,
gay; n laughter.

riflard [riflaːr] nm paring chisel, file.
rigide [riʒid] a tense, rigid, stiff.
rigidité [riʒidite] nf tenseness, rigidity, stiffness.
rigolade [rigɔlad] nf fun, joke, lark.
rigole [rigɔl] nf gutter, drain,
channel.
rigoler [rigɔle] vi to laugh, have
some fun.
rigolo, -ote [rigɔlo, ɔt] a funny,
comical, queer; n wag.
rigoureux, -euse [rigurø, øːz] a
rigorous, harsh, severe, strict.
rigueur [rigœːr] nf rigor, severity,
harshness, strictness; à la — if need
be, at a pinch; être de — to be
obligatory.
rillettes [rijet] nf pl potted minced
pork.
rime [rim] nf rhyme.
rimer [rime] vt to put into rhyme;
vi to rhyme, write verse; cela ne
rime à rien there is no sense in it.
rinçage [rɛ̃saːʒ] nm rinse, rinsing.
rincée [rɛ̃se] nf drubbing.
rincer [rɛ̃se] vt to rinse (out); se —
la dalle to wet one's whistle.
riquiqui [rikiki] a undersized (pers
or thing), runt, shrimp.
ripaille [ripɑːj] nf feasting, carous-
ing.
riposte [ripɔst] nf retort, counter
(stroke), riposte.
riposter [ripɔste] vi to retort,
counter, riposte.
rire [riːr] vi to laugh, joke, smile;
vr to laugh (at de); nm laughter,
laugh(ing); vous voulez —! you are
joking! pour — for fun, make-
believe; fou — nm wi d lːugh.
ris [ri] nm laugh(ter), reef; — de
veau sweetbread.
risée [rize] nf laughing-stock, jeer.
risible [rizibl] a laughable, comical,
ludicrous.
risque [risk] nm risk; à ses —s et
périls at one's own risk.
risquer [riske] vt to risk, venture;
vr to take a risk, venture.
ristourner [risturne] vt to repay,
return.
rite [rit] nm rite.
rituel, -elle [ritɥel] a nm ritual.
rivage [rivaːʒ] nm bank, shore, side.
rival [rival] an rival.
rivaliser [rivalize] vi to vie (with),
emulate.
rivalité [rivalite] nf rivalry.
rive [riːv] nf shore, bank, side, edge.
river [rive] vt to rivet, clinch.
riverain [rivrɛ̃] a water-, river-,
wayside; n riverside resident.
rivet [rive] nm rivet.
rivière [rivjɛːr] nf river, stream.
rixe [riks] nf brawl, scuffle.
riz [ri] nm rice.
rizière [rizjɛːr] nf rice-field.
robe [rɔb] nf dress, frock, gown,
coat, skin; — de chambre dressing-
gown.

robinet [rɔbinɛ] *nm* tap, cock, faucet.

robot [rɔbo] *nm* robot; *(aviation)* pilotless plane.

robuste [rɔbyst] *a* robust, strong, hardy, sturdy.

roc [rɔk] *nm* rock.

rocaille [rɔkɑːj] *nf* rock.

rocailleux, -euse [rɔkajø, øːz] *a* rocky, stony, rugged.

roche [rɔʃ] *nf* rock, boulder.

rocher [rɔʃe] *nm* rock, crag.

rochet [rɔʃɛ] *nm* ratchet.

rocheux, -euse [rɔʃø, øːz] *a* rocky, stony.

rococo [rɔkɔko] *a nm* rococo, baroque.

rodage [rɔdaːʒ] *nm* running in.

rôder [rode] *vi* to prowl, roam.

rôdeur, -euse [rodœr, øːz] *a* prowling; *n* prowler, vagrant.

rogatons [rɔgatɔ̃] *nm pl* scraps.

rogner [rɔɲe] *vt* to clip, trim, pare.

rognon [rɔɲɔ̃] *nm* kidney.

rognures [rɔɲyːr] *nf pl* clippings, trimmings, parings.

rogomme [rɔgɔm] *nm* liquor; **voix de —** husky, throaty voice.

rogue [rɔg] *a* haughty, arrogant.

roi [rwa] *nm* king; **fêtes des —s** Twelfth Night; **tirer les —s** to celebrate Twelfth Night.

roide, roideur, roidir [rwad] *see* **raide, raideur, raidir.**

roitelet [rwatlɛ] *nm* wren.

rôle [roːl] *nm* rôle, part, register, roster; **à tour de —** in turn.

romain [rɔmɛ̃] *a* Roman.

romaine [rɔmɛn] *nf* romaine lettuce.

roman [rɔmɑ̃] *a* Romanic, Romanesque; *nm* novel, romance; **— feuilleton** serial story.

romance [rɔmɑ̃ːs] *nf* sentimental song, ballad.

romancier, -ière [rɔmɑ̃sje, jeːr] *n* novelist.

romanesque [rɔmanɛsk] *a* romantic.

romanichel, -elle [rɔmaniʃɛl] *n* gipsy, vagrant.

romantique [rɔmɑ̃tik] *a* romantic; *n* romanticist.

romantisme [rɔmɑ̃tism] *nm* romanticism.

romarin [rɔmarɛ̃] *nm* rosemary.

rompre [rɔ̃ːpr] *vt* to break (off, up, in, into), snap, burst; *vi* to break (off, up); *vr* to break (off, up), break oneself (in, to à).

rompu [rɔ̃py] *a* broken (in), tired out.

ronce [rɔ̃ːs] *nf* bramble, blackberry bush; *pl* thorns.

ronchonner [rɔ̃ʃɔne] *vi* to grouse, grumble, growl.

rond [rɔ̃] *a* round(ed), plump; *nm* ring, circle, round, disc, bean.

rond-de-cuir [rɔ̃dkɥiːr] *nm* clerk, bureaucrat.

ronde [rɔ̃ːd] *nf* round, beat, whole note; **à la —** around.

rondeau [rɔ̃do] *nm* rondeau, rondo.

rondelet, -ette [rɔ̃dlɛ, ɛt] *a* plump, roundish, tidy.

rondelle [rɔ̃dɛl] *nf* slice, small round, ring, disc.

rondement [rɔ̃dmɑ̃] *ad* roundly, smartly, frankly.

rondeur [rɔ̃dœːr] *nf* roundness, plumpness, frankness.

rond-point [rɔ̃pwɛ̃] *nm* traffic circle, rotary.

ronflement [rɔ̃fləmɑ̃] *nm* snore, snoring, rumbling, throbbing, hum.

ronfler [rɔ̃fle] *vi* to snore, roar, throb, whir, hum.

ronger [rɔ̃ʒe] *vt* to gnaw, corrode, erode; **se —** le cœur to eat one's heart out.

rongeur, -euse [rɔ̃ʒœːr, øːz] *a* rodent, gnawing; *nm* rodent.

rônier [ronje] *nm* fan-palm.

ronronnement [rɔ̃rɔnmɑ̃] *nm* purr(ing), hum(ming).

ronronner [rɔ̃rɔne] *vi* to purr, hum.

roquet [rɔkɛ] *nm* pug-dog, cur.

rosace [rozas] *nf* rose-window.

rosaire [rozɛːr] *nm* rosary.

rosâtre [rozɑːtr] *a* pinkish.

rosbif [rɔsbif] *nm* roast beef.

rose [roːz] *nf* rose; *a* pink, rosy; **— des vents** compass-card; **découvrir le pot aux —s** to discover the secret.

rosé [roze] *a* rosy, roseate, *(wine)* rosé.

roseau [rozo] *nm* reed.

rosée [roze] *nf* dew.

roseraie [rozrɛ] *nf* rose-garden.

rosette [rozɛt] *nf* rosette, bow.

rosier [rozje] *nm* rose-bush.

rosir [roziːr] *vi* to turn pink, rosy.

rosse [rɔs] *nf* nag, nasty person, beast; *a* nasty, spiteful.

rossée [rɔse] *nf* thrashing, drubbing, licking.

rosser [rɔse] *vt* to thrash, beat.

rosserie [rɔsri] *nf* nasty remark, dirty trick, nastiness.

rossignol [rɔsiɲɔl] *nm* nightingale, skeleton-key, bit of junk.

rot [ro] *nm* belch.

rotatif, -ive [rɔtatif, iːv] *a* rotary.

rotation [rɔtasjɔ̃] *nf* rotation.

rotatoire [rɔtatwaːr] *a* rotative, rotatory.

roter [rɔte] *vi* to belch.

rotin [rɔtɛ̃] *nm* rattan, cane.

rôti [roti] *nm* roast (meat).

rôtir [rotiːr] *vti* to roast, toast, scorch.

rôtisserie [rotisri] *nf* restaurant.

rotonde [rɔtɔ̃ːd] *nf* rotunda, circular hall.

rotondité [rɔtɔ̃dite] *nf* roundness, rotundity, stoutness.

rotule [rɔtyl] *nf* knee-cap, ball-and-socket joint.

roturier, -ière [rɔtyrje] *a* of the common people; *n* commoner.

rouage [rwaːʒ] *nm* wheel(s), works.

roublard [rublaːr] *an* crafty, wily (person).

roublardise [rublardiːz] *nf* craftiness, wily trick.
roucouler [rukule] *vi* to coo.
roue [ru] *nf* wheel; **faire la —** to
turn cartwheels, spread its tail,
strut.
roué [rwe] *a* sly, wily; *nm* rake.
rouennerie [rwanri] *nf* printed
cotton goods.
rouer [rwe] *vt* to break on the wheel;
— de coups to beat unmercifully.
rouet [rwɛ] *nm* spinning-wheel,
pulley-wheel.
rouf(le) [rufl] *nm* deck-house.
rouge [ruːʒ] *a* red; *nm* red, rouge;
bâton de — lipstick.
rougeâtre [ruʒɑːtr] *a* reddish.
rouge-gorge [ruʒɡɔrʒ] *nm* robin.
rougeole [ruʒɔl] *nf* measles.
rougeoyer [ruʒwaje] *vi* to glow, turn
red.
rouget [ruʒe] *nm* gurnard, red mullet.
rougeur [ruʒœːr] *nf* redness, flush,
blush.
rougir [ruʒiːr] *vt* to redden; *vi* blush,
flush, turn red.
rouille [ruːj] *nf* rust, blight, mildew.
rouillé [ruje] *a* rusted, rusty.
rouiller [ruje] *vt* to rust, blight,
mildew; *vr* to rust, be blighted,
mildewed.
rouillure [rujyːr] *nf* rustiness, blight.
roulage [rulaːʒ] *nm* rolling, haulage,
cartage.
roulant [rulɑ̃] *a* rolling, moving,
sliding, smooth, killingly funny.
rouleau [rulo] *nm* roller, roll, coil,
spool; **— compresseur** steamroller.
roulement [rulmɑ̃] *nm* rolling,
rumbling, running, rotation; **— à
billes** ball-bearing.
rouler [rule] *vt* to roll (up), haul,
trick, take in, turn over; *vi* to roll
(along, down, over), roam, rumble,
run, turn (upon **sur**); *vr* to roll.
roulette [rulɛt] *nf* roller, caster,
roulette.
roulier [rulje] *nm* truck driver.
roulis [ruli] *nm* rolling, lurching.
roulotte [rulɔt] *nf* caravan.
roumain [rumɛ̃] *an* Rumanian.
Roumanie [rumani] *nf* Rumania.
roupie [rupi] *nf* drop, rupee.
roupiller [rupije] *vi* (*fam*) to sleep.
rouquin [rukɛ̃] *a* red-haired, carroty;
n ginger-head, red-head.
rouspéter [ruspete] *vi* (*fam*) to
protest, cut up rough, kick.
roussâtre [rusɑːtr] *a* reddish.
rousseur [rusœːr] *nf* redness; **tache
de —** freckle.
roussir [rusiːr] *vti* to redden, turn
brown, singe.
route [rut] *nf* road, track, course,
route; **— nationale** main road; **se
mettre en —** to set out.
routier, -ière [rutje, jɛːr] *a* road-;
café — roadside diner; *nm* long
distance truck driver, road racer;
vieux — old campaigner.

routine [rutin] *nf* routine.
routinier, -ière [rutinje, jɛːr] *a*
routine, unenterprising.
rouvrir [ruvriːr] *vti* to reopen.
roux, rousse [ru, rus] *a* reddish-
brown, russet, red; *nm* reddish-
brown, russet, (*sauce*) roux.
royal [rwajal] *a* royal, regal, crown.
royaliste [rwajalist] *an* royalist.
royaume [rwajoːm] *nm* kingdom,
realm.
royauté [rwajote] *nf* royalty.
ruade [rɥad] *nf* kicking.
ruban [rybɑ̃] *nm* ribbon, band, tape.
rubis [rybi] *nm* ruby; **payer — sur
l'ongle** to pay on the nail.
rubrique [rybrik] *nf* heading, rubric,
column, imprint, red ocher.
ruche [ryʃ] *nf* hive, ruche.
rude [ryd] *a* coarse, rough, harsh,
uncouth, gruff, hard.
rudesse [rydɛs] *nf* coarseness, roughness, harshness, uncouthness, gruffness.
rudiments [rydimɑ̃] *nm pl* rudiments, first principles.
rudoyer [rydwaje] *vt* to treat
roughly, bully, browbeat.
rue [ry] *nf* street.
ruée [rɥe] *nf* (on)rush.
ruelle [rɥɛl] *nf* lane, alley, space
between bed and wall.
ruer [rɥe] *vi* to kick, lash out; *vr* to
hurl oneself (upon **sur**).
rugir [ryʒiːr] *vi* to roar, howl.
rugissement [ryʒismɑ̃] *nm* roar(ing),
howling.
rugosité [rygozite] *nf* ruggedness,
wrinkle.
rugueux, -euse [rygø, øːz] *a* rough,
rugged, wrinkled.
ruine [rɥin] *nf* ruin(ation), downfall;
menacer — to be falling to pieces.
ruiner [rɥine] *vt* to ruin, undo,
destroy; *vr* to fall to ruin, ruin
oneself.
ruisseau [rɥiso] *nm* stream, brook,
gutter.
ruisseler [rɥisle] *vi* to stream, run,
trickle.
rumeur [rymœːr] *nf* rumor, hum,
confused murmur, din.
ruminant [ryminɑ̃] *a nm* ruminant.
ruminer [rymine] *vti* to chew the
cud, ruminate, ponder.
rupture [ryptyːr] *nf* breaking (off,
down), fracture, rupture.
rural [ryral] *a* rural, country.
ruse [ryːz] *nf* trick, dodge, ruse,
stratagem.
rusé [ryze] *a* sly, crafty, artful.
russe [rys] *an* Russian.
Russie [rysi] *nf* Russia.
rustaud [rysto] *a* uncouth, boorish;
n boor.
rustique [rystik] *a* rustic, robust.
rustre [rystr] *a* boorish, churlish;
nm boor, bumpkin.
rut [ryt] *nm* rut(ting).
rutabaga [rytabaga] *nm* swede.

rutilant [rytilɑ̃] *a* gleaming, glowing red.
rythme [ritm] *nm* rhythm.
rythmé [ritme] *a* rhythmic(al).
rythmique [ritmik] *a* rhythmic(al).

S

sa [sa] *see* son.
sable [saːbl] *nm* sand, gravel; **—s mouvants** quicksands.
sablé [sable] *a* sanded, graveled; *nm* shortbread.
sabler [sable] *vt* to sand, cover with gravel, drink.
sableux, -euse [sablø, øːz] *a* sandy.
sablier [sablie] *nm* hour-glass, egg-timer, sand-dealer.
sablière [sabliɛːr] *nf* sand-, gravel-pit.
sablonneux, -euse [sablɔnø, øːz] *a* sandy, gritty.
sablonnière [sablɔnjɛːr] *nf* sandpit.
sabord [sabɔːr] *nm* porthole.
saborder [sabɔrde] *vt* to scuttle.
sabot [sabo] *nm* clog, hoof.
sabotage [sabotaːʒ] *nm* clog-making, sabotage.
saboter [sabɔte] *vt* to shoe, bungle, scamp, sabotage.
saboteur, -euse [sabɔtœːr, øːz] *n* saboteur, bungler.
sabotier [sabɔtje] *nm* clog-maker.
sabre [saːbr] *nm* saber, sword, swordfish.
sabrer [sabre] *vt* to saber, cut (down), scamp.
sac [sak] *nm* sack, bag, pouch, knapsack, sackcloth, sacking; **— de couchage** sleeping-bag; **— à main** handbag.
saccade [sakad] *nf* jerk, jolt; **par —s** by fits and starts.
saccadé [sakade] *a* jerky.
saccager [sakaʒe] *vt* to pillage, sack, ransack.
saccharine [sakarin] *nf* saccharin.
sacerdoce [saserdɔs] *nm* priesthood, ministry.
sacerdotal [saserdɔtal] *a* sacerdotal, priestly.
sachet [saʃɛ] *nm* small bag, sachet.
sacoche [sakɔʃ] *nf* satchel, wallet, tool-bag, saddle-bag.
sacre [sakr] *nm* coronation, consecration.
sacrement [sakrəmɑ̃] *nm* sacrament.
sacré [sakre] *a* sacred, holy, damned, confounded.
sacrer [sakre] *vt* to crown, consecrate, anoint; *vi* to swear.
sacrifice [sakrifis] *nm* sacrifice.
sacrifier [sakrifje] *vt* to sacrifice, give up.
sacrilège [sakrilɛːʒ] *a* sacrilegious; *nm* sacrilege.
sacristain [sakristɛ̃] *nm* sexton, sacristan.
sacristie [sakristi] *nf* vestry, sacristy.

sadique [sadik] *a* sadistic.
sadisme [sadism] *nm* sadism.
safran [safrɑ̃] *a* saffron-colored; *nm* crocus, saffron.
sagace [sagas] *a* sagacious, shrewd.
sagacité [sagasite] *nf* sagacity, shrewdness.
sagaie [sage] *nf* assegai, spear.
sage [saːʒ] *a* wise, sensible, discreet, good, well-behaved.
sage-femme [saʒfam] *nf* midwife.
sagesse [saʒɛs] *nf* wisdom, discretion, good behavior.
sagou [sagu] *nm* sago.
saignant [sɛɲɑ̃] *a* bleeding, raw, red, underdone.
saignée [sɛɲe] *nf* bleeding, blood-letting, bend of the arm, irrigation ditch.
saigner [sɛɲe] *vt* to bleed, let blood from; *vi* to bleed.
saillant [sajɑ̃] *a* projecting, jutting out, prominent, salient; *nm* salient.
saillie [saji] *nf* projection, protrusion, ledge, spring, bound, flash of wit.
saillir [sajiːr] *vi* to jut out, project, spurt out, stand out.
sain [sɛ̃] *a* healthy, wholesome, sound.
saindoux [sɛ̃du] *nm* lard.
saint [sɛ̃] *a* holy, hallowed, godly, saintly, blessed; *n* saint; **il ne sait plus à quel — se vouer** he does not know where to turn.
Saint-Esprit [sɛ̃tɛspri] *nm* Holy Ghost.
sainteté [sɛ̃təte] *nf* holiness, sanctity.
Saint-Martin [sɛ̃martɛ̃] *nf* Martinmas.
Saint-Michel [sɛ̃miʃɛl] *nf* Michaelmas.
Saint-Siège [sɛ̃sjɛːʒ] *nm* Holy See.
Saint-Sylvestre [sɛ̃silvɛstr] *nf* New Year's Eve, (*Scot*) Hogmanay.
saisie [sezi] *nf* seizure, distraint, foreclosure.
saisir [seziːr] *vt* to seize, grasp, catch hold of, grip, understand, perceive; *vr* to seize, lay hands (on de).
saisissant [sezisɑ̃] *a* thrilling, striking, keen, biting, piercing.
saisissement [sezismɑ̃] *nm* seizure, shock, thrill, chill.
saison [sezɔ̃] *nf* season.
saisonnier, -ière [sezɔnje, jɛːr] *a* seasonal.
salacité [salasite] *nf* salaciousness.
salade [salad] *nf* salad, lettuce, hodgepodge, mess.
saladier [saladje] *nm* salad-bowl.
salaire [salɛːr] *nm* wage(s), pay, reward, retribution.
salaison [salɛzɔ̃] *nf* salting, curing.
salamandre [salamɑ̃ːdr] *nf* salamander, stove.
salant [salɑ̃] *a* **marais —** salt-pans, salt-marsh.
salarié [salarje] *a* paid, wage-earning; *n* wage-earner.

salaud [salo] *n* dirty dog, rotter, swine, slattern.

sale [sal] *a* dirty, soiled, filthy, foul; — type rotter.

salé [sale] *a* salt(y), salted, spicy, exorbitant, stiff; *nm* pickled pork.

saler [sale] *vt* to salt, pickle, overcharge, fleece, punish severely.

saleté [salte] *nf* dirt, trash, dirtiness, dirty trick (act, remark).

salière [saljɛːr] *nf* saltcellar, salt shaker.

saligaud [saligo] *n* rotter, skunk, dirty person.

salin [salɛ̃] *a* saline, salty, briny; *nm* salt-marsh.

saline [salin] *nf* salt-pan, rock-salt mine.

salir [saliːr] *vt* to dirty, soil, defile, tarnish; *vr* to get dirty, soil, besmirch one's reputation.

salive [saliːv] *nf* saliva, spittle.

salle [sal] *nf* room, hall, ward, house, audience; — à manger dining-room; — d'opérations operating theater; — d'attente waiting room.

salon [salɔ̃] *nm* drawing-room, saloon, cabin; — de l'automobile au o show; — de beauté beauty parlor; — de coiffure hairdressing-salon; — de thé tea-room.

saloperie [salɔpri] *nf* filth(iness), trash, dirty trick.

salopette [salɔpet] *nf* overalls, dungarees.

salpêtre [salpɛːtr] *nm* saltpeter, niter.

saltimbanque [saltɛ̃bɑ̃ːk] *nm* acrobat; (fig) mountebank, charlatan.

salubre [salybr] *a* salubrious, wholesome, healthy.

salubrité [salybrite] *nf* salubrity, wholesomeness, healthiness.

saluer [salɥe] *vt* to salute, bow to, greet, acclaim.

salure [salyːr] *nf* saltness, tang.

salut [saly] *nm* greeting, bow, salute, safety, salvation; — à tout le monde! hello, everybody!

salutaire [salytɛːr] *a* salutary, beneficial, wholesome.

salutation [salytasjɔ̃] *nf* salutation, bow, salute, greeting; *pl* kind regards.

salutiste [salytist] *n* member of the Salvation Army.

salve [salv] *nf* salvo, volley, round, salute.

samara [samara] *nm* sandal.

samedi [samdi] *nm* Saturday.

sanatorium [sanatɔrjɔm] *nm* sanatorium convalescent home.

sanctification [sɑ̃ktifikasjɔ̃] *nf* sanctification.

sanctifier [sɑ̃ktifje] *vt* to sanctify, hallow.

sanction [sɑ̃ksjɔ̃] *nf* sanction, assent, penalty.

sanctionner [sɑ̃ksjɔne] *vt* to sanction, ratify, approve, penalize.

sanctuaire [sɑ̃ktɥɛːr] *nm* sanctuary, sanctum.

sandale [sɑ̃dal] *nf* sandal, gym-shoe.

sandwich [sɑ̃dwitʃ] *nm* sandwich.

sang [sɑ̃] *nm* blood, gore, kin(ship); race; effusion de — bloodshed; coup de — apoplectic fit, stroke; se faire du mauvais — to worry, fret; son — n'a fait qu'un tour it gave him an awful shock.

sang-froid [sɑ̃frwa] *nm* composure, coolness, self-possession; de — coolly.

sanglade [sɑ̃glad] *nf* lash, cut.

sanglant [sɑ̃glɑ̃] *a* bloody, gory, bloodstained, cutting, scathing.

sangle [sɑ̃gl] *nf* strap, band; lit de — camp bed.

sangler [sɑ̃gle] *vt* to girth, strap (up); *vr* to lace (button) oneself up tightly.

sanglier [sɑ̃glie] *nm* wild boar.

sanglot [sɑ̃glo] *nm* sob.

sangloter [sɑ̃glɔte] *vi* to sob.

sangsue [sɑ̃sy] *nf* leech, bloodsucker.

sanguin [sɑ̃gɛ̃] *a* blood, full-blooded.

sanguinaire [sɑ̃ginɛːr] *a* bloodthirsty, bloody.

sanguine [sɑ̃gin] *nf* red chalk, drawing in red chalk, bloodstone, blood orange.

sanguinolent [sɑ̃ginɔlɑ̃] *a* tinged with blood.

sanitaire [sanitɛːr] *a* sanitary, medical, ambulance-, hospital-.

sans [sɑ̃] *prep* without, but for, were it not for, had it not been for, un-, less, -lessly; — que *cj* without.

sans-culotte [sɑ̃kylɔt] *nm* sans-culotte, rabid republican.

sans-façon [sɑ̃fasɔ̃] *a* homely, down-right, outspoken, unceremonious, over-familiar, free and easy; *nm* homeliness, outspokenness, over-familiarity.

sans-fil [sɑ̃fil] *nm* radio message, radiogram.

sans-filiste [sɑ̃filist] *n* radio fan, radio operator.

sans-gêne [sɑ̃ʒɛn] *a* offhanded, unceremonious; *nm* offhandedness, over-familiarity, cheek; *nm pl* il est — he is a cool customer.

sans-logis [sɑ̃lɔʒi] *nm pl* homeless.

sansonnet [sɑ̃sɔne] *nm* starling.

sans-souci [sɑ̃susi] *a* carefree, unconcerned; *n* easy-going person; *nm* unconcern.

sans-travail [sɑ̃travaːj] *nm pl* unemployed, workless.

santal [sɑ̃tal] *nm* sandalwood.

santé [sɑ̃te] *nf* health; service de — medical service.

sape [sap] *nf* sap(ping), undermining.

saper [sape] *vt* to sap, undermine.

sapeur [sapœːr] *nm* sapper, pioneer.

sapeur-pompier [sapœrpɔ̃pje] *nm* fireman.

sapeur-télégraphiste [sapœrtele-

grafist] nm telegraph operator; pl signal corps, signals.
saphir [safiːr] nm sapphire.
sapin [sapɛ̃] nm fir (tree), coffin.
sapinière [sapinjɛːr] nf fir plantation.
sapristi [sapristi] excl good heavens!
sarbacane [sarbakan] nf blowpipe, pea-shooter.
sarcasme [sarkasm] nm (piece of) sarcasm, taunt.
sarcastique [sarkastik] a sarcastic.
sarcler [sarkle] vt to hoe, weed, clean.
sarcloir [sarklwaːr] nm hoe.
sarcophage [sarkɔfaːʒ] nm sarcophagus.
sardine [sardin] nf sardine.
sardonique [sardɔnik] a sardonic, sarcastic.
sarment [sarmɑ̃] nm vine-shoot, -branch, bine.
sarrasin [sarazɛ̃] nm buckwheat, Saracen.
sarrau [saro] nm overall, smock.
sasser [sɑse] vt to sieve, riddle, sift.
satané [satane] a confounded, abominable.
satanique [satanik] a satanic, diabolical, fiendish.
satellite [satellit] nm satellite, henchman, planet.
satiété [sasjete] nf satiety, surfeit, repletion.
satin [satɛ̃] nm satin.
satiner [satine] vt to satin, make glossy, glaze.
satinette [satinɛt] nf sateen.
satire [satiːr] nf satire, satirizing.
satirique [satirik] a satiric(al); nm satirist.
satiriser [satirize] vt to satirize.
satisfaction [satisfaksjɔ̃] nf satisfaction, gratification, atonement, amends.
satisfaire [satisfɛːr] vt to satisfy, gratify, fulfill, meet.
satisfait [satisfɛ] a satisfied, contented, pleased.
satisfaisant [satisfəzɑ̃] a satisfactory, satisfying.
saturation [satyrasjɔ̃] nf saturation.
saturer [satyre] vt to saturate; vr to become saturated.
satyre [satiːr] nm satyr.
sauce [sos] nf sauce, soft black crayon.
saucée [sose] nf (fam) drenching, soaking, telling-off.
saucer [sose] vt to dip into sauce, drench, souse, tell off; se faire — to get soaked, get a scolding.
saucière [sosjɛːr] nf sauce-boat.
saucisse [sosis] nf sausage, observation or barrage balloon.
saucisson [sosisɔ̃] nm large dry sausage.
sauf, sauve [sof, soːv] a safe, saved, unhurt; prep but, except, save, barring; — que except that.

sauf-conduit [sofkɔ̃dɥi] nm safeconduct, pass.
sauge [soːʒ] nf sage.
saugrenu [sogrəny] a ridiculous, absurd.
saule [soːl] nm willow.
saumâtre [somaːtr] a briny, brackish, bitter.
saumon [somɔ̃] a salmon-pink; nm salmon.
saumure [somyːr] nf pickle, brine.
saupoudrer [sopudre] vt to sprinkle, dust, powder.
saupoudroir [sopudrwaːr] nm sugarsifter, castor.
saur [sɔːr] a hareng — red herring.
saut [so] nm leap, jump, bound, vault, falls, jerk; — périlleux somersault; — d'obstacles hurdling; —-de-mouton overpass.
saute [soːt] nf sudden rise, jump, change.
saute-mouton [sotmutɔ̃] nm leapfrog.
sauter [sote] vt to jump (over), leap (over), leave out, miss, skip; vi jump, leap, blow up, explode, crash, come off, change, veer, blow out; faire — to explode, burst, blow up, blow out.
sauterelle [sotrɛl] nf grasshopper, locust.
sauterie [sotri] nf dance, hop.
saute-ruisseau [sotrɥiso] nm errandboy.
sauteur, -euse [sotœːr, øːz] a jumping; n jumper, turncoat, weathercock.
sautiller [sotije] vi to hop (about), skip, jump about.
sautoir [sotwaːr] nm St Andrew's cross, neck-chain, jumping lathe; en — crosswise, over one's shoulder.
sauvage [sovaːʒ] a wild, savage, barbarous, uncivilized, shy, unsociable; n savage, unsociable person.
sauvagerie [sovaʒri] nf savagery, barbarousness, unsociability.
sauvegarde [sovgard] nf safeguard, safe-keeping, safe-conduct.
sauvegarder [sovgarde] vt to safeguard, protect.
sauve-qui-peut [sovkipø] nm stampede, rout, everyone for himself.
sauver [sove] vt to save, rescue; vr to escape, run away, be off.
sauvetage [sovtaːʒ] nm rescue, salvage; canot de — lifeboat.
sauveteur [sovtœːr] nm rescuer, lifesaver.
sauveur [sovœːr] nm deliverer, Savior, Redeemer.
savamment [savamɑ̃] ad learnedly, knowingly, expertly, ably, cleverly.
savane [savan] nf savanna.
savant [savɑ̃] a learned, scholarly, skillful; n scholar, scientist; chien— performing dog.
savate [savat] nf old shoe, French

boxing; **traîner la — ** to be down at heel.

savetier [savtje] nm cobbler.

saveur [savœːr] nf savor, flavor, taste, raciness, zest.

savoir [savwaːr] nm knowledge, learning; vt to know (how, of), be able, contrive, manage; **faire — ** qch à qn to let s.o, know about sth, inform s.o of sth; **à — ** to wit, namely; **sachez que** I would have you know that; **sans le — ** unconsciously, unwittingly; **(au)tant que je le le sache** as far as I know, to the best of my knowledge; **pas que je sache** not that I am aware of; **je ne sache pas l'avoir dit** I am not aware of having said so; **il n'a rien voulu — he** would not hear of it; **je ne sais qui** someone or other.

savoir-faire [savwarfɛːr] nm tact, cleverness, ability.

savoir-vivre [savwarviːvr] nm good-breeding, (good) manners, art of living.

savon [sav5] nm soap, dressing down; **pain de — ** cake of soap.

savonner [savɔne] vt to soap, wash, dress down.

savonnerie [savɔnri] nf soap-factory, soap-trade.

savonnette [savɔnɛt] nf cake of toilet soap.

savonneux, -euse [savɔnø, øːz] a soapy.

savonnier, -ière [savɔnje, jɛːr] a soap-; nm soap-manufacturer.

savourer [savure] vt to relish, enjoy.

savoureux, -euse [savurø, øːz] a savory, tasty, racy.

saxophone [saksɔfɔn] nm saxophone.

saynète [sɛnɛt] nf sketch.

sbire [zbiːr] nm policeman, hired ruffian.

scabreux, -euse [skabrø, øːz] a scabrous, smutty, dangerous, difficult, rough.

scalper [skalpe] vt to scalp.

scandale [skɑ̃dal] nm scandal, disgrace.

scandaleux, -euse [skɑ̃dalø, øːz] a scandalous, disgraceful.

scandaliser [skɑ̃dalize] vt to scandalize, shock; vr to be shocked, scandalized.

scander [skɑ̃de] vt to scan, stress, mark.

scaphandrier [skafɑ̃drie] nm diver.

scarabée [skarabe] nm beetle.

scarlatine [skarlatin] nf scarlet fever.

sceau [so] nm seal, stamp, mark.

scélérat [selera] a wicked, cunning, nefarious; n scoundrel, villain.

scélératesse [seleratɛs] nf wickedness, low cunning.

scellé [sele] a sealed, under seal; nm seal.

sceller [sele] vt to seal (up), fix, fasten, confirm.

scène [sɛn] nf stage, scene, row; **mettre en — ** to produce.

scénique [senik] a scenic, stage.

scepticisme [sɛptisism] nm skepticism.

sceptique [sɛptik] a skeptical; n skeptic.

sceptre [sɛptr] nm scepter.

schéma [ʃema] nm diagram, outline.

schématique [ʃematik] a diagrammatic, schematic.

schisme [ʃism] nm schism.

sciatique [sjatik] a sciatic; nm sciatic nerve; nf sciatica.

scie [si] nf saw, catchword, bore.

science [sjɑ̃ːs] nf knowledge, learning, science.

scientifique [sjɑ̃tifik] a scientific.

scier [sje] vt to saw (off).

scierie [siri] nf sawmill.

scinder [sɛ̃de] vt to split up.

scintillation [sɛ̃tijasjɔ̃, -tilla-] nf scintillation, twinkling, sparkling.

scintiller [sɛ̃tije, -tille] vi to scintillate, twinkle, sparkle.

scission [sissjɔ̃] nf scission, split, division, secession.

sciure [sjyːr] nf — **de bois** sawdust; **— de fer** iron filings.

sclérose [skleroːz] nf sclerosis.

sclérosé [skleroze] a hardened, (fig) in a rut.

scolaire [skɔlɛːr] a school.

scolastique [skɔlastik] a scholastic; nf scholasticism.

scolopendre [skɔlɔpɑ̃ːdr] nf centipede.

scorbut [skɔrby] nm scurvy.

scorie [skɔri] nf slag, cinders, dross.

scoutisme [skutism] nm scouting, Boy Scout movement.

scrofule [skrɔfyl] nf scrofula.

scrupule [skrypyl] nm scruple; **se faire un — ** de to have scruples about.

scrupuleux, -euse [skrypylø, øːz] a scrupulous.

scrutateur, -trice [skrytatœːr, tris] a searching, keen, scrutinizing; n scrutinizer, teller.

scruter [skryte] vt to scrutinize, scan.

scrutin [skrytɛ̃] nm poll, ballot, voting; **— de liste** multiple voting; **procéder au — ** to take the vote; **voter au — ** to ballot; **dépouiller le — ** to count the votes.

sculpter [skylte] vt to carve, sculpture.

sculpteur [skyltœːr] nm sculptor, carver.

sculptural [skyltyral] a sculptural, statuesque.

sculpture [skyltyːr] nf sculpture, carving.

se [s(ə)] pn oneself, himself, herself, itself, themselves, each other, one another.

séance [seɑ̃ːs] nf session, sitting,

meeting, performance, séance.
séant [seã] *a* becoming, seemly, proper, sitting; *nm* bottom, behind; **se dresser sur son —** to sit up.
seau [so] *nm* pail, bucket
sec, sèche [sɛk, sɛʃ] *a* dry, dried, harsh, unfeeling, gaunt, spare, curt, tart, sharp; **boire —** to drink liquor straight, drink heavily; **parler —** to clip one's words; **à pied —** dryshod; **à —** dry, dried-up, aground, hard-up.
sécateur [sekatœr] *nm* pruning shears.
sécession [sesesjɔ̃] *nf* secession.
sèche [sɛʃ] *nf (fam)* fag, (*cigarette*).
sèchement [sɛʃmã] *ad* dryly, boldly, curtly.
sécher [seʃe] *vt* to dry (up), fail, cut, skip; *vi* to become or run dry, dry up, be stumped, stick; *vr* to dry oneself, dry up, run dry; **faire — qn** to stump s.o.; **— sur pied** to pine for.
sécheresse [seʃrɛs] *nf* dryness, drought, harshness, unfeelingness, gauntness, barrenness, curtness.
séchoir [seʃwar] *nm* drying place, drier, airer.
second [səɡɔ̃, zɡɔ̃] *a* second; *nm* first mate, chief officer, second in command; second floor.
secondaire [səɡɔ̃dɛr, zɡɔ̃-] *a* secondary, subordinate, minor.
seconde [səɡɔ̃d, zɡɔ̃d] *nf* second, second class, eleventh grade.
seconder [səɡɔ̃de, zɡɔ̃-] *vt* to second, support, assist, promote, further.
secouer [səkwe] *vt* to shake (up, down, off), rouse, stir; *vr* to shake oneself, bestir oneself.
secourable [səkurabl] *a* helpful, ready to help, helping.
secourir [səkurir] *vt* to help, aid, succor, relieve.
secours [s(ə)kur] *nm* help, aid, succor, relief, assistance; **porter — à** to lend assistance to; **apporter les premiers — à** to apply first-aid to; **poste de —** first-aid station; **de —** spare, emergency, relief; **au —!** help!
secousse [səkus] *nf* shake, shaking, shock, jolt.
secret [səkrɛ] *a* secret; *nm* secret, secrecy; **au —** in solitary confinement.
secrétaire [səkretɛr] *n* secretary; *nm* writing-desk.
secrétariat [səkretarja] *nm* secretaryship, secretariat.
sécréter [sekrete] *vt* to secrete.
sectaire [sɛktɛr] *n* sectarian.
secte [sɛkt] *nf* sect.
secteur [sɛktœr] *nm* sector, beat (of policeman).
section [sɛksjɔ̃] *nf* cutting, section, division, branch, stage, platoon.
sectionner [sɛksjɔne] *vt* to divide into sections, cut into pieces.

séculaire [sekylɛr] *a* century-old, venerable, secular.
séculier, -ière [sekylje, jɛr] *a* secular; *n* layman, -woman.
sécurité [sekyrite] *nf* security, safety, safeness.
sédatif, -ive [sedatif, iːv] *a nm* sedative.
sédentaire [sedɑ̃tɛr] *a* sedentary, fixed.
sédiment [sedimã] *nm* sediment, deposit.
séditieux, -euse [sedisjø, øːz] *a* seditious; *nm* mutineer, rebel.
sédition [sedisjɔ̃] *nf* sedition, mutiny.
séducteur, -trice [sedyktœr, tris] *a* seductive, tempting, alluring, enticing; *n* seducer, enticer, tempter.
séduction [sedyksjɔ̃] *nf* seduction, enticement, bribing, seductiveness, charm.
séduire [sedɥir] *vt* to seduce, (al)lure, captivate, charm, suborn, lead astray.
séduisant [sedɥizã] *a* tempting, captivating, attractive, fascinating, alluring.
ségrégation [segregasjɔ̃] *nf* segregation, separation.
seiche [sɛʃ] *nf* cuttle-fish.
seigle [sɛgl] *nm* rye.
seigneur [sɛɲœr] *nm* lord, nobleman, God, the Lord.
seigneurie [sɛɲœri] *nf* lordship, manor.
sein [sɛ̃] *nm* bosom, breast.
séisme [seism] *nm* seism, earthquake.
seize [sɛːz] *a nm* sixteen, sixteenth.
seizième [sɛzjɛm] *a nm* sixteenth.
séjour [seʒur] *nm* sojourn, stay, residence, abode.
séjourner [seʒurne] *vi* to stay, sojourn, reside.
sel [sɛl] *nm* salt, spice, wit; *pl* smelling salts.
sélection [seleksjɔ̃] *nf* selection.
selle [sɛl] *nf* saddle, stool, movement of bowels.
seller [sele] *vt* to saddle.
sellette [sɛlɛt] *nf* stool of repentance, small stool; **tenir qn sur la —** to have s.o. on the carpet.
sellier [selje] *nm* saddler.
selon [s(ə)lɔ̃] *prep* according to, after; **c'est —** it depends.
Seltz [sɛls] *nm* **eau de S—** soda-water.
semailles [s(ə)maːj] *nf pl* sowing(s).
semaine [s(ə)mɛn] *nf* week, working-week, week's pay; **faire la — anglaise** to stop work on Saturdays at midday.
semblable [sãblabl] *a* similar, like, alike, such; *n* fellow-man, like.
semblant [sãblã] *nm* semblance, show, sham, appearance; **faire — de** to pretend.
sembler [sãble] *vi* to seem, appear, look; **à ce qu'il me semble** as far as I can see, to my mind.

semelle [s(ə)mɛl] *nf* sole, foot, tread; **battre la —** to stamp one's feet (for warmth).

semence [s(ə)mɑ̃:s] *nf* seed, (tin) tacks.

semer [s(ə)me] *vt* to sow, scatter, spread, dot, outpace, shake off.

semestre [s(ə)mɛstr] *nm* term, half-year, semester.

semestriel, -elle [s(ə)mɛstriɛl] *a* half-yearly.

semeur, -euse [s(ə)mœːr, øːz] *n* sower, spreader.

sémillant [semijɑ̃] *a* sprightly, lively, brisk.

séminariste [seminarist] *nm* seminarist.

semis [səmi] *nm* sowing, seed-bed, seedling.

sémitique [semitik] *a* Semitic.

semonce [səmɔ̃:s] *nf* rebuke, scolding, dressing-down.

semoncer [səmɔ̃se] *vt* to scold, rebuke, lecture.

semoule [s(ə)mul] *nf* semolina.

sénat [sena] *nm* senate.

sénateur [senatœːr] *nm* senator.

sénile [senil] *a* senile.

sénilité [senilite] *nf* senility.

sens [sɑ̃:s] *nm* sense, intelligence, meaning, direction; **bon —** common sense; **rue à —** unique one-way street; **— interdit** no entry; **— dessus dessous** upside down.

sensation [sɑ̃sasjɔ̃] *nf* sensation, feeling, stir.

sensationnel, -elle [sɑ̃sasjɔnɛl] *a* sensational, super.

sensé [sɑ̃se] *a* sensible, judicious.

sensibilisateur, -trice [sɑ̃sibilizatœːr, tris] *a* sensitizing; *nm* sensitizer.

sensibilité [sɑ̃sibilite] *nf* sensibility, sensitiveness, feeling, tenderness.

sensible [sɑ̃sibl] *a* sensitive, susceptible, tender, sore, palpable, perceptible.

sensiblerie [sɑ̃sibləri] *nf* mawkish sentiment.

sensitif, -ive [sɑ̃sitif] *a* sensitive, sensory.

sensualisme [sɑ̃syalism] *nm* sensualism.

sensualité [sɑ̃syalite] *nf* sensuality.

sensuel, -elle [sɑ̃syɛl] *a* sensual, sensuous, voluptuous; *n* sensualist.

sentence [sɑ̃tɑ̃:s] *nf* maxim, sentence.

sentencieux, -euse [sɑ̃tɑ̃sjø, øːz] *a* sententious.

senteur [sɑ̃tœːr] *nf* perfume, scent.

senti [sɑ̃ti] *a* heartfelt, genuine.

sentier [sɑ̃tje] *nm* path.

sentiment [sɑ̃timɑ̃] *nm* feeling, sense, sensation, sentiment, opinion; **faire du —** to play on the emotions.

sentimental [sɑ̃timɑ̃tal] *a* sentimental.

sentimentalité [sɑ̃timɑ̃talite] *nf* sentimentality.

sentine [sɑ̃tin] *nf* bilge.

sentinelle [sɑ̃tinɛl] *nf* sentry,

sentinel; **en —** on sentry duty.

sentir [sɑ̃tiːr] *vt* to feel, smell, be aware (of); *vi* to smell (of) taste of, smack of; *vr* to feel; **je ne peux pas le —** I can't stand him; **ne pas se — de joie** to be beside oneself with joy, overjoyed.

seoir [swaːr] *vi* to become, suit.

séparable [separabl] *a* separable.

séparation [separasjɔ̃] *nf* separation, breaking up, parting.

séparatisme [separatism] *nm* separatism.

séparé [separe] *a* separate, apart, distinct.

séparément [separemɑ̃] *ad* separately, apart, singly.

séparer [separe] *vt* to separate, divide, part, be between; *vr* to part, separate, divide, break up.

sept [se(t)] *a nm* seven, seventh.

septembre [sɛptɑ̃:br] *nm* September.

septentrional [sɛptɑ̃triɔnal] *a* northern; *n* Northerner.

septième [sɛtjɛm] *a nm* seventh.

septique [sɛptik] *a* septic.

septuagénaire [sɛptyaʒenɛːr] *an* septuagenarian.

septuor [sɛptyɔːr] *nm* septet.

sépulcral [sepylkral] *a* sepulchral.

sépulcre [sepylkr] *nm* sepulcher, tomb.

sépulture [sepyltyːr] *nf* burial-place, tomb, interment.

séquelle [sekɛl] *nf* gang, string; *pl* after-effects.

séquence [sekɑ̃:s] *nf* sequence, run.

séquestration [sekɛstrasjɔ̃] *nf* sequestration, seclusion, isolation.

séquestre [sekɛstr] *nm* sequestrator, trustee, sequestration, embargo; **sous —** sequestered.

séquestrer [sekɛstre] *vt* to sequester, sequestrate, confine, isolate.

séraphin [serafɛ̃] *nm* seraph.

séraphique [serafik] *a* seraphic, angelic

serein [sərɛ̃] *a* serene, calm, quiet.

sérénade [serenad] *nf* serenade.

sérénité [serenite] *nf* serenity, calmness.

serf, serve [sɛrf, sɛrv] *a* in bondage; *n* serf.

serge [sɛrʒ] *nm* serge.

sergent [sɛrʒɑ̃] *nm* sergeant; **— major** quartermaster-sergeant; **— de ville** policeman.

série [seri] *nf* series, succession, line, set, run, break; **fin de —** remnant; **article hors —** specially made article, outsize; **voiture de —** car of standard model.

sérieux, -euse [serjø, øːz] *a* serious, grave, solemn, earnest, genuine; *nm* seriousness, gravity; **manque de — **levity; **prendre qch au —** to take sth seriously; **garder son —** to keep a straight face.

serin [s(ə)rɛ̃] *nm* canary, simpleton.

seringue [sərɛ̃:g] *nf* syringe.

serment [sɛrmɑ̃] nm oath; **prêter —** to take an oath, be sworn in; **sous —** on oath.

sermon [sɛrmɔ̃] nm sermon, talking-to.

sermonner [sɛrmɔne] vt to lecture; vi to preachify, lay down the law.

sermonneur, -euse [sɛrmɔnœːr, øːz] a sermonizing; n sermonizer.

serpe [sɛrp] nf bill-hook.

serpent [sɛrpɑ̃] nm snake, serpent; **— à sonnettes** rattlesnake.

serpenter [sɛrpɑ̃te] vi to wind, meander.

serpentin [sɛrpɑ̃tɛ̃] a serpentine; nm worm (of still), coil, streamer.

serpette [sɛrpet] nf bill-hook, pruning-knife.

serpillière [sɛrpijɛːr] nf sacking, apron.

serpolet [sɛrpɔle] nm wild thyme.

serrage [sɛraːʒ] nm tightening, clamping, grip; **— des freins** braking.

serre [sɛːr] nf greenhouse, pressing, talon, claw, grip, clip; **— chaude** hothouse.

serré [sɛre] a tight, close, serried, packed, closely-woven, compact, close-fisted.

serrement [sɛrmɑ̃] nm squeezing, pressure; **— de cœur** pang; **— de main(s)** handshake.

serre-papiers [sɛrpapje] nm file, paper-clip, -weight.

serrer [sɛre] vt to press, squeeze, clasp, shake (hands), clench, close (up), tighten, condense, put away; vr to stand or sit closer, huddle together, crowd, tighten.

serre-tête [sɛrtɛːt] nm head-band, crash-helmet.

serrure [sɛryːr] nf lock; **trou de la — keyhole.**

serrurerie [sɛryr(ə)ri] nf lock, locksmith's (shop), locksmithing, metal work.

serrurier [sɛryrje] nm locksmith, ironsmith.

sertir [sɛrtiːr] vt to set.

servage [sɛrvaːʒ] nm bondage, serf-dom.

serval [sɛrval] nm bush-cat, serval.

servant [sɛrvɑ̃] a serving; nm server; pl gun crew.

servante [sɛrvɑ̃ːt] nf maid-servant, dumb-waiter, tea wagon.

serveur, -euse [sɛrvœːr, øːz] n carver, barman, barmaid, waitress, server; f coffee pot.

serviable [sɛrvjabl] a obliging, helpful.

service [sɛrvis] nm service, disposition, attendance, good turn, department, course, set; **escalier de —** backstairs; **porte de —** tradesmen's entrance; **entrer en —** to go into service; **entrer au —** to go into the army; **être de —** to be on duty; **assurer le — entre . . . et . . .** to run

between **. . . and . . .;** bon pour le — fit for service, serviceable; **libre —** self-service.

serviette [sɛrvjet] nf napkin, towel, brief-case.

servile [sɛrvil] a slavish, servile.

servilité [sɛrvilite] nf servility, slavishness.

servir [sɛrviːr] vt to serve (up, out), attend to, wait on, help, work, operate; vi to serve, be in use, be useful, be used; vr to help oneself, shop, deal, use; **— de** to be used as, serve as; **cela ne sert à rien** that is no use.

serviteur [sɛrvitœːr] nm servant.

servitude [sɛrvityd] nf servitude, slavery, bondage.

ses [se] see son.

session [sesjɔ̃] nf session, sitting.

séton [setɔ̃] nm **blessure en —** flesh wound.

seuil [sœːj] nm threshold, doorstep.

seul [sœl] a single, alone, sole, one, only, by oneself.

seulement [sœlmɑ̃] ad only, merely, solely, even.

sève [sɛːv] nf sap, pith, vigor.

sévère [sevɛːr] a severe, stern, harsh, strict.

sévérité [severite] nf severity, sternness, harshness, strictness.

sévices [sevis] nm pl brutality, maltreatment, cruelty.

sévir [seviːr] vi to be rife, severe, to rage, deal severely (with contre).

sevrer [sevre] vt to wean, deprive.

sexagénaire [sɛksaʒenɛːr] an sexagenarian.

sexe [sɛks] nm sex.

sextant [sɛkstɑ̃] nm sextant.

sexualité [sɛksyalite] nf sexuality.

sexuel, -elle [sɛksyɛl] a sexual.

seyant [sejɑ̃] a becoming.

shampooing [ʃɑ̃pwɛ̃] nm shampoo.

si [si] ad so, as, such, yes; cj if, whether, how, what about; nm B (mus); **si . . . que** however; **si ce n'était** were it not for.

siamois [sjamwa] an Siamese.

sidéré [sidere] a struck dumb, dazed, dumbfounded.

sidérurgie [sideryrʒi] nf metallurgy, iron smelting.

siècle [sjɛkl] nm century, age, period.

siège [sjɛːʒ] nm seat, chair, bottom (of chair), center, siege; **déclarer l'état de —** to declare martial law.

siéger [sjeʒe] vi to sit, be seated, be centered.

sien, sienne [sjɛ̃, sjɛn] pos pn **le(s) —(s), la sienne, les siennes** his, hers, its, one's; nm his, her, its, one's own; pl one's own people; **y mettre du —** to do one's share; **faire des siennes** to be up to one's tricks.

sieste [sjest] nf siesta, nap.

sifflant [siflɑ̃] a whistling, hissing, sibilant.

ier [sifle] *vt* to whistle (for, to, :er) pipe, boo, hiss, swig; *vi* to istle, hiss, sizzle, whiz, wheeze.
let [sifle] *nm* whistle, pipe, hiss, call.
eur, -euse [siflœːr, øːz] *a* istling, hissing, wheezy; *n* istler, booer.
loter [siflɔte]· *vti* to whistle tly.
e [sigl] *nm* initials, trade-name, de-mark.
ial [sinal] *nm* signal.
ialement [sinalmã] *nm* descrip-n, particulars.
ialé [sinale] *a* signal, well-own, conspicuous.
ialer [sinale] *vt* to signal, dis-guish, point out, report, give a scription of; *vr* to distinguish eself.
ialeur [sinalœːr] *nm* signaler, nalman.
ialisateur [sinalizatœːr] *nm* naling apparatus, traffic indica-r.
ialisation [sinalizasjɔ̃] *nf* signal-.
ataire [sinateːr] *n* signatory.
ature [sinatyːr] *nf* signature, ning.
ie [sin] *nm* sign, mark, symptom, dication, gesture; — de tête nod; ire — à qn to beckon, motion to.
ier [sine] *vt* to sign, stamp; *vr* cross oneself.
iet [sine] *nm* bookmark(er).
ificatif, -ive [sinifikatif, iːv] *a* nificant.
ification [sinifikasjɔ̃] *nf* significa-n, significance, meaning, notifica-n.
iifier [sinifje] *vt* to signify, mean, tify.
nce [silɑ̃ːs] *nm* silence, stillness, sh, rest; passer sous — to ignore.
ncieux, -euse [silɑ̃sjø, øːz] *a* ent, still, noiseless; *nm* silencer.
x [sileks] *nm* silex, flint.
ouette [silwɛt] *nf* silhouette.
ouetter [silwɛte] *vt* to silhouette, tline, figure; *vr* to stand out, show up.
age [sijaːʒ] *nm* wake, wash, ck.
on [sijɔ̃] *nm* furrow, track, trail, inkle, groove, streak.
onner [sijɔne] *vt* to furrow, w, cleave, wrinkle.
agrée [simagre] *nf usu pl* ectation, affected airs.
iesque [simjɛsk] *a* ape-like, nkey-like.
ilaire [simileːr] *a* similar, like.
ilarité [similarite] *nf* similarity, eness.
ili [simili] *nm* imitation.
ilitude [similityd] *nf* similitude, ilarity, likeness.

simple [sɛ̃ːpl] *a* simple, easy, mere, ordinary, plain, homely, guileless, single; *nm* single (game); *pl* herbs; — soldat private (soldier).
simplicité [sɛ̃plisite] *nf* simplicity, plainness, naturalness, simple-mindedness.
simplificateur, -trice [sɛ̃plifikatœːr, tris] *a* simplifying.
simplification [sɛ̃plifikasjɔ̃] *nf* simplification.
simplifier [sɛ̃plifje] *vt* to simplify.
simpliste [sɛ̃plist] *a* over-simple.
simulacre [simylakr] *nm* semblance, sham, show, image.
simulateur, -trice [simylatœːr, tris] *n* simulator, shammer.
simulation [simylasjɔ̃] *nf* simula-tion, shamming.
simuler [simyle] *vt* to simulate, sham, feign.
simultané [simyltane] *a* simultane-ous.
sinapisme [sinapism] *nm* mustard plaster.
sincère [sɛ̃seːr] *a* sincere, genuine, frank, candid.
sincérité [sɛ̃serite] *nf* sincerity, genuineness, candor.
singe [sɛ̃ːʒ] *nm* monkey, ape, mimic, (sl) bully-beef.
singer [sɛ̃ʒe] *vt* to ape, mimic.
singerie [sɛ̃ʒri] *nf* grimace, antic, affected airs, monkey-house.
singulariser [sɛ̃gylarize] *vt* to make conspicuous.
singularité [sɛ̃gylarite] *nf* peculiarity, unusualness, oddness, eccentricity.
singulier, -ière [sɛ̃gylje, jɛːr] *a* peculiar, singular, unusual, remark-able, queer, odd; *nm* singular; combat — single combat.
sinistre [sinistr] *a* sinister, ominous, fatal; *nm* catastrophe, disaster, calamity.
sinistré [sinistre] *a* damaged (by fire *etc*); *n* victim.
sinon [sinɔ̃] *cj* if not, otherwise, except.
sinueux, -euse [sinyø, øːz] *a* sinuous, winding, meandering.
sinuosité [sinyozite] *nf* winding, meander, bend.
sinusite [sinyzit] *nf* sinusitis.
siphon [sifɔ̃] *nm* siphon, trap.
sire [siːr] *nm* sire; triste — sorry fellow.
sirène [siren] *nf* siren, vamp, buzzer, hooter, foghorn.
sirop [siro] *nm* syrup.
siroter [sirɔte] *vt* to sip; *vi* to tipple.
sis [si] *pp* situated.
sismique [sismik] *a* seismic.
site [sit] *nm* beauty spot, site.
sitôt [sito] *ad* — dit, — fait no sooner said than done; nous ne le reverrons pas de — we will not see him for some time to come.
situation [sitɥasjɔ̃] *nf* situation, site, position, post, state.

situer [sitɥe] vt to situate, locate, place.

six [si(s)] a nm six, sixth.

sixième [sizjɛm] an sixth; nm sixth (part).

ski [ski] nm ski, skiing; — nautique water-skiing.

skieur, -euse [skiœːr, øːz] n skier.

slip [slip] nm slip, slipway, briefs, underpants.

smoking [smɔkiŋ] nm dinner jacket.

snob [snɔb] nm snob, slavish imitator of popular fashion or opinion; a smart, snobbish.

snob∙sme [snɔbism] nm snobbery, slavish imitation of popular fashion or ⌐ pinion.

s⌐⌐ [sɔbr] a temperate, moderate, s⌐ ing, quiet.

s⌐b⌐iété [sɔbriete] nf sobriety, temperateness, moderation.

s⌐b 'quet [sɔbrikɛ] nm nickname.

s⌐ ⌐k] nm plowshare.

s⌐⌐abilité [sɔsjabilite] nf sociability, sociableness.

sociable [sɔsjabl] a sociable.

social [sɔsjal] a social; **raison —e** name of a firm.

socialisme [sɔsjalism] nm socialism.

socialiste [sɔsjalist] a socialist(ic); n socialist.

sociétaire [sɔsjetɛːr] n member, shareholder.

société [sɔsjete] nf society, association, club, companionship, company, partnership; S — des Nations League of Nations.

sociologie [sɔsjɔlɔʒi] nf sociology.

socle [sɔkl] nm pedestal, plinth, base, stand.

socque [sɔk] nm clog, patten, sock.

socquette [sɔkɛt] nf ankle sock.

sodium [sɔdjɔm] nm sodium.

sœur [sœːr] nf sister, nun.

sofa [sɔfa] nm sofa, settee.

soi [swa] pn oneself, him-, her-, it-; — même oneself.

soi-disant [swadizã] a would-be, so-called, self-styled; ad supposedly.

soie [swa] nf silk, bristle; **papier de — tissue paper.

soierie [swari] nf silk-fabric, silks, silk-trade, -factory.

soif [swaf] nf thirst; **avoir —** to be thirsty, eager (for de).

soigné [swaɲe] a neat, careful, carefully done, well-groomed, trim.

soigner [swaɲe] vt to take care of, attend (to), look after, nurse, take pains with; vr to take care of o.s., look after o.s.

soigneux, -euse [swaɲø, øːz] a careful, tidy, neat.

soin [swɛ̃] nm care, trouble, attention, pains, task; pl solicitude, attention(s), aid, treatment; **avoir — to take care; **être aux petits —s auprès de qn** to be most attentive to.

soir [swaːr] nm evening, night.

soirée [sware] nf evening, pa reception.

soit [swa] excl right! agreed! ⌐ l'un — l'autre either one or other; — aujourd'hui ou der either today or tomorrow; — le fasse ou qu'il ne le fasse whether he does it or not.

soixantaine [swasãtɛn] nf a sixty.

soixante [swasãːt] a nm sixty.

soixantième [swasãtjɛm] a sixtieth.

sol [sɔl] nm ground, soil, earth (mus).

solaire [sɔlɛːr] a solar.

soldat [sɔlda] nm soldier; **simpl** private; — de première cl lance-corporal; — de plomb soldier.

solde [sɔld] nm balance, settlem job lot, surplus stock, clear sale; nf pay; prix de — bar price; **être à la — de** to be in pay of.

solder [sɔlde] vt to balance, se clear off, sell off.

sole [sɔl] nf sole.

solécisme [sɔlesism] nm solecism

soleil [sɔlɛːj] nm sun, sunsh sunflower, monstrance, Cathe wheel; **coup de — sunburn, stroke, sunny interval; **il fait d it is sunny.

solennel, -elle [sɔlanɛl] a sole grave, official.

solenniser [sɔlanize] vt to solem celebrate.

solennité [sɔlanite] nf solemn solemn ceremony.

solfège [sɔlfɛːʒ] nm sol-fa.

solidaire [sɔlidɛːr] a interdepend jointly responsible, binding, b⌐ up (with de).

solidariser [sɔlidarize] vt to n responsible.

solidarité [sɔlidarite] nf responsibility, interdepende solidarity; **faire la grève de — strike in sympathy.

solide [sɔlid] a solid, secure, so strong, hefty, staunch; nm s⌐ viser au — to have an eye to main chance.

solidifier [sɔlidifje] vtr to solidif

solidité [sɔlidite] nf solidity, so ness, stability, strength, stau ness.

soliloque [sɔlilɔk] nm soliloquy.

soliste [sɔlist] a solo; n soloist.

solitaire [sɔlitɛːr] a solitary, lo⌐ nm hermit, recluse, solitaire.

solitude [sɔlityd] nf solitude, lo⌐ ness, wilderness.

solive [sɔliːv] nf beam, joist, raf⌐

sollicitation [sɔllisitasjɔ̃] nf soli⌐ tion, entreaty, canvassing.

solliciter [sɔllisite] vt to solicit, for, canvass, apply for, attract.

solliciteur, -euse [sɔllisitœːr, ø⌐

etitioner, canvasser, applicant.
llicitude [sɔllisityd] *nf* solicitude, oncern, care, anxiety.
lo [sɔlo] *a nm* solo.
lstice [sɔlstis] *nm* solstice.
luble [sɔlybl] *a* soluble, solvable.
lution [sɔlysjɔ̃] *nf* solution, answer, ettlement.
lvabilité [sɔlvabilite] *nf* solvency.
lvable [sɔlvabl] *a* solvent.
mbre [sɔ̃:br] *a* somber, dark, ismal, gloomy, dull.
mbrer [sɔ̃bre] *vi* to sink, founder, o down.
mmaire [sɔmmɛ:r] *a* summary, uccinct, hasty, scant; *nm* summary, ynopsis.
mmation [sɔmasjɔ̃] *nf* notice, ummons.
mme [sɔm] *nf* sum, amount, pack-addle; *nm* nap, snooze; **bête de —** east of burden; **— toute, en —** on he whole, in short.
mmeil [sɔmɛ:j] *nm* sleep, slumber, leepiness; **avoir —** to be sleepy, drowsy; **avoir le — léger (profond)**, o be a light (heavy) sleeper.
mmeiller [sɔmeje] *vi* to slumber, e asleep, nod.
mmelier [sɔmǝlje] *nm* wine-waiter.
mmer [sɔme] *vt* to summon, call pon.
mmet [sɔmɛ] *nm* summit, top, rown, crest, apex; **conférence au —** ummit conference.
mmier [sɔmje] *nm* bed-springs, egister.
mmité [sɔmmite] *nf* summit, top, eading figure.
mnambule [sɔmnɑ̃byl] *a* omnambulistic; *n* somnambulist, leep-walker.
mnifère [sɔmnifɛ:r] *a nm* sleeping-ill, soporific.
mnolence [sɔmnɔlɑ̃:s] *nf* somno-ence, drowsiness.
mnolent [sɔmnɔlɑ̃] *a* somnolent, rowsy, sleepy.
mnoler [sɔmnɔle] *vi* to doze, nod, rowse.
mptueux, -euse [sɔ̃ptɥø, ø:z] *a* umptuous.
n, sa, ses [sɔ̃, sa, se] *a* his, her, its, ne's.
n [sɔ̃] *nm* sound, bran; **tache de —** eckle.
nate [sɔnat] *nf* sonata.
ndage [sɔ̃da:ʒ] *nm* sounding, oring, probing, bore-hole.
nde [sɔ̃:d] *nf* plummet, sounding-ne, -rod, boring-machine, probe, aster.
nder [sɔ̃de] *vt* to sound, bore, robe, investigate, fathom.
ndeuse [sɔ̃dø:z] *nf* drilling-achine.
nge [sɔ̃:ʒ] *nm* dream.
nge-creux [sɔ̃ʒkrø] *nm* dreamer, isionary.

songer [sɔ̃ʒe] *vi* to dream, muse, imagine, remember, think.
songerie [sɔ̃ʒri] *nf* reverie, musing, daydream(ing), brown study.
songeur, -euse [sɔ̃ʒœ:r, ø:z] *a* dreamy, pensive; *n* dreamer.
sonnaille [sonaj] *nf* cowbell.
sonnant [sonɑ̃] *a* ringing, striking; **à une heure —e** on the stroke of one; **espèces —es** hard cash.
sonner [sone] *vt* to ring (for), strike; *vi* to ring, sound, toll, strike.
sonnerie [sonri] *nf* ringing, chimes, bell, system of bells, bugle call; **— électrique** electric bell; **— aux morts** last post.
sonnet [sonɛ] *nm* sonnet.
sonnette [sonɛt] *nf* small bell, housebell, handbell; **coup de —** ring.
sonneur [sonœ:r] *nm* bell-ringer.
sonore [sonɔ:r] *a* sonorous, resounding, resonant, ringing, voiced, with good acoustics; **bande —** sound-track.
sonoriser [sonɔrize] *vt* to add the sound effects to (a film), to install amplifiers.
sonorité [sonɔrite] *nf* sonority, resonance.
sophisme [sofism] *nm* sophism, fallacy.
sophiste [sofist] *nm* sophist.
sophistiqué [sofistike] *a* sophisticated, adulterated.
soporifique [sopɔrifik] *a* soporific, tiresome.
sorbier [sɔrbje] *nm* service-tree, rowan-tree.
sorcellerie [sɔrsɛlri] *nf* witchcraft, sorcery.
sorcier, -ière [sɔrsje, jɛ:r] *n* sorcerer, sorceress, wizard, witch, hag.
sordide [sɔrdid] *a* squalid, sordid, mean, dirty.
sornettes [sɔrnɛt] *nf pl* nonsense, trash.
sort [sɔ:r] *nm* fate, chance, lot, spell; **tirer au —** to draw lots, ballot.
sortable [sɔrtabl] *a* suitable, eligible, presentable.
sortant [sɔrtɑ̃] *a* outgoing, retiring.
sorte [sɔrt] *nf* kind, sort, way, manner; **de la —** in that way; **de — que** so that; **en quelque —** in a way.
sortie [sɔrti] *nf* going out, coming out, exit, way out, leaving, sortie, trip, outburst; **— de secours** emergency exit; **jour de —** day out; **— de bain** bathing wrap.
sortilège [sɔrtileʒ] *nm* charm, spell.
sortir [sɔrti:r] *vt* to take (put, bring, pull) out; *vi* to go (come, walk) out, protrude, stand out, spring, descend; *nm* coming out; **— de table** to rise from table; **faire —** to put out, take out; **il est sorti** he is out; **au — de l'école** on coming out of school, on leaving school.

sosie [sɔzi] nm double.

sot, sotte [so, sɔt] a stupid, foolish, silly; n fool, dolt.

sottise [sɔtiːz] nf stupidity, folly, silliness, foolish thing.

sou [su] nm sou; cent —s five francs; il n'a pas le — he is penniless; il n'a pas pour deux —s de curiosité he is not the least bit curious.

soubassement [subasmã] nm base, basement, substructure.

soubresaut [subrəso] nm leap, start, jump, jolt, gasp; pl spasmodic movements, convulsions.

soubrette [subrɛt] nf soubrette, lady's maid.

souche [suʃ] nf stump, log, dolt, counterfoil, origin; faire — to found a family; de bonne — of good stock, pedigree.

souci [susi] nm care, worry, anxiety, solicitude, marigold.

se soucier [səsusje] vr to concern o.s., worry, trouble, care, mind, bother.

soucieux, -euse [susjø, øːz] a anxious, mindful, worried.

soucoupe [sukup] nf saucer.

soudain [sudɛ̃] a sudden; ad suddenly.

soudaineté [sudɛnte] nf suddenness.

soudard [sudaːr] nm old soldier.

soude [sud] nf soda; bicarbonate de — bicarbonate of soda, baking soda.

souder [sude] vt to solder, weld; vr to weld, knit; lampe à — blowtorch.

soudoyer [sudwaje] vt to hire, bribe.

soudure [sudyːr] nf soldering, welding, soldered joint, solder.

soufflage [sufla:ʒ] nm blowing, blast.

souffle [sufl] nm breath, breathing, blast, puff, inspiration; couper le — à qn to take s.o.'s breath away; à bout de — out of breath.

soufflé [sufle] a unvoiced; nm soufflé.

souffler [sufle] vt to blow (out, off, up), breathe, utter, filch, pinch; vi to blow, pant, puff, recover one's breath; — (son rôle à) qn to prompt s.o.

soufflet [suflɛ] nm bellows, gore, insult, box on the ear, slap.

souffleter [suflǝte] vt to slap, box s.o.'s ears, insult.

souffleur, -euse [suflœːr, øːz] n prompter; nm blower.

souffrance [sufrãːs] nf suffering, pain; en — in suspense, awaiting delivery.

souffrant [sufrã] a suffering, unwell, ailing.

souffre-douleur [sufrǝdulœːr] nm butt, drudge.

souffreteux, -euse [sufrǝtø, øːz] a sickly, seedy, needy.

souffrir [sufriːr] vt to suffer, endure, bear, allow (of); vi to be in pain, suffer.

soufre [sufr] nm sulphur, brimstone.

soufrer [sufre] vt to sulphurate.

souhait [swɛ] nm wish, desire; à to one's liking.

souhaitable [swetabl] a desirable.

souhaiter [swete] vt to wish (fo desire.

souiller [suje] vt to soil, pollu stain, sully.

souillon [sujɔ̃] n sloven, slut; scullery maid.

souillure [sujyːr] nf stain, sp blemish, blot.

soûl [su] a drunk, surfeited; tout — one's fill.

soulagement [sulaʒmã] nm reli comfort, alleviation.

soulager [sulaʒe] vt to relie alleviate, ease; vr to relieve on feelings, relieve oneself.

soûlard [sulaːr] nm drunkard.

soûler [sule] vt to stuff with fo make drunk; vr to gorge, get dru

soûlerie [suiri] nf drinking bo drunken orgy.

soulèvement [sulɛvmã] nm risi upheaval, revolt, indignant o burst.

soulever [sulve] vt to raise, l rouse, stir up; vr to revolt, heave

soulier [sulje] nm shoe.

souligner [suliɲe] vt to underli stress, emphasize.

soumettre [sumɛtr] vt to subd subject, refer, lay, submit; vr submit, comply, yield, defer.

soumis [sumi] a submissive, am able, biddable, liable, subject.

soumission [sumisjɔ̃] nf submissi submissiveness, compliance, tend

soupape [supap] nf valve.

soupçon [supsɔ̃] nm suspicion, tou dash, flavor.

soupçonner [supsɔne] vt to suspe guess, conjecture, surmise.

soupçonneux, -euse [supsɔnø, ø a suspicious, distrustful.

soupe [sup] nf soup.

soupente [supãːt] nf garret, lo recess, brace, strap.

souper [supe] vi to have supper; supper; j'en ai soupé I am fed (with it).

soupeser [supǝze] vt to weigh in hand, feel the weight of.

soupière [supjɛːr] nf soup-tureen.

soupir [supiːr] nm sigh.

soupirail [supira:j] nm ventilat air-hole.

soupirant [supirã] nm suitor.

soupirer [supire] vi to sigh, ga long (for après).

souple [supl] a supple, flexi adaptable, pliant.

souplesse [suplɛs] nf suppiene pliability, flexibility, litheness; d'esprit adaptability.

source [surs] nf source, spring, w fount(ain), origin, root; de bonne on good authority.

sourci -ière [sursje, jeːr] n wat divir·

urcil [sursi] nm eyebrow.

urciller [sursije] vi to frown, nch wince.

urcilleux, -euse [sursijø, ø:z] a owning, supercilious.

ard [su:r] a deaf, muffled, dull, eiled, muted, sound-proof, unoiced; **bruit —** thud; **lanterne —e** ark-lantern; **— comme un pot** as af as a door post.

ardement [surdəmã] ad with a ull hollow sound, dully, secretly.

ardine [surdin] nf mute, damper, mmer; **en —** on the sly.

ard-muet, sourde-muette [surue, surdmµet] a deaf-and-dumb; deaf-mute.

ardre [surdr] vi to well up, spring, lse.

ricière [surisje:r] nf mousetrap, ap.

rire [suri:r] vi to smile, appeal; n smile.

ris [suri] nf mouse; nm smile.

rnois [surnwa] a sly, crafty, tful, underhand; n sneak, shifty aracter, sly boots.

rnoiserie [surnwazri] nf craftiss, underhand piece of work.

s [su] prep under(neath), below, neath, within (time), sub-; **— la uie in the rain; — peine de mort** , pain of death.

s-alimentation [suzalimãtasjõ] malnutrition.

s-bois [subwa] nm underwood, dergrowth.

s-chef [suʃef] nm deputy chief, sistant manager, chief assistant.

scription [suskripsjõ] nf subription, contribution, signi ig, gnature; **verser une —** to make a ntribution.

scrire [suskri:r] vt to subscribe), sign.

s-développé [sudevləpe] a underveloped.

s-directeur, -trice [sudirektœ:r, s] n assistant-manager(ess), vicencipal.

s-entendre [suzãtã:dr] vt to ply, understand.

s-entendu [suzãtãdy] nm imcation; **parler par —s** to hint, inuate.

s-entente [suzãtãt] nf mental ervation.

s-estimer [suzɛstime] vt to der-estimate.

s-gouverneur [suguvɛrnœ:r] nm puty-, vice-governor.

s-jacent [suʒasã] a subjacent, derlying.

s-lieutenant [suljøtnã] nm ond-, sub-lieutenant.

s-location [suləkasjõ] nf sublet ng).

s-louer [sulwe] vt to sub-let, -lease.

s-main [sumɛ̃] nm writing-pad,

blotting-pad; **en — behind the scenes.**

sous-marin [sumarɛ̃] a submarine, submerged; nm submarine.

sous-officier [suzɔfisje] nm noncommissioned officer, (naut) petty officer.

sous-pied [supje] nm under-strap.

sous-préfecture [suprefɛkty:r] nf sub-prefecture.

sous-produit [suprɔdµi] nm byproduct.

sous-secrétaire [susəkretɛ:r] n under-secretary.

sous-seing [susɛ̃] nm private contract, agreement.

soussigner [susiɲe] vt to sign, undersign.

sous-sol [susɔl] nm basement, subsoil.

sous-titre [suti:tr] nm sub-title, caption.

soustraction [sustraksjõ] nf subtraction, removal.

soustraire [sustre:r] vt to subtract, remove, take away, shield, screen; vr to elude, avoid, dodge, get out (of à); **se — à la justice** to abscond.

sous-ventrière [suvãtrje:r] nf bellyband, saddle-girth.

sous-vêtement [suvetmã] nm undergarment.

soutache [sutaʃ] nf braid.

soutane [sutan] nf cassock.

soute [sut] nf store-room, coalbunker; **— à eau** water-tank; **— à munitions** magazine.

soutenable [sutnabl] a bearable, tenable, arguable.

soutenance [sutnã:s] nf maintaining (thesis).

souteneur [sutnœ:r] nm upholder, pimp.

soutenir [sutni:r] vt to sustain, support, withstand, maintain, keep, back (up), assert; vr to support oneself, keep up, be maintained.

soutenu [sutny] a sustained, unflagging, constant, continued, steady, elevated.

souterrain [sutɛrɛ̃] a subterranean, underground; nm tunnel, underground passage.

soutien [sutjɛ̃] nm support, prop, supporter.

soutien-gorge [sutjɛ̃gɔrʒ] nm brassière.

soutier [sutje] nm trimmer.

soutirer [sutire] vt to rack, draw off, squeeze.

souvenance [suvnã:s] nf recollection.

souvenir [suvni:r] v imp to come to mind; vr to remember, recall; nm memory, recollection, remembrance, memento, souvenir, memorial, keepsake.

souvent [suvã] ad often.

souverain [suvrɛ̃] a sovereign, supreme; n sovereign, ruler.

souveraineté [suvrɛnte] nf sovereignty.

soviétique [sɔvjetik] *a* soviet; *n* Soviet citizen.

soyeux, -euse [swajø, ø:z] *a* silky, silken.

spacieux, -euse [spasjø, ø:z] *a* spacious, roomy.

sparadrap [sparadra] *nm* sticking-plaster.

sparte [spart] *nm* esparto grass.

spartiate [sparsjat] *a* spartan.

spasme [spasm] *nm* spasm.

spasmodique [spasmɔdik] *a* spas-modic.

spatule [spatyl] *nf* spatula.

speaker, -ine [spikœ:r, krin] *n* (radio) announcer.

spécial [spesjal] *a* special, particular.

se spécialiser [səspesjalize] *vr* to specialize.

spécialiste [spesjalist] *n* specialist, expert.

spécialité [spesjalite] *nf* specialty, special feature.

spécieux, -euse [spesjø, ø:z] *a* specious.

spécification [spesifikasjɔ̃] *nf* specification.

spécifier [spesifje] *vt* to specify, determine.

spécifique [spesifik] *a* specific, precise.

spécimen [spesimɛn] *a nm* specimen.

spéciosité [spesjozite] *nf* specious-ness.

spectacle [spektakl] *nm* spectacle, scene, sight, display, theater, show; **salle de —** theater; **pièce à grand — spectacular play; se donner en —** to make an exhibition of o.s.

spectaculaire [spektakylɛːr] *a* spec-tacular.

spectateur, -trice [spektatœːr, tris] *n* spectator, onlooker, bystander.

spectral [spektral] *a* spectral, ghost-ly, ghostlike, of the spectrum.

spectre [spektr] *nm* ghost, specter, apparition, spectrum.

spéculaire [spekylɛːr] *a* specular.

spéculateur, -trice [spekylatœːr, tris] *n* speculator, theorizer.

spéculatif, -ive [spekylatif, iːv] *a* speculative.

spéculation [spekylasjɔ̃] *nf* specula-tion, theorizing, conjecture.

spéculer [spekyle] *vi* to speculate, theorize, cogitate; **— à la baisse (hausse)** to speculate on a rise (fall).

spermatozoïde [spɛrmatɔzɔid] *nm* spermatozoon.

sperme [spɛrm] *nm* sperm.

sphère [sfɛr] *nf* sphere, orb, globe.

sphérique [sferik] *a* spherical.

sphéroïde [sferɔid] *nm* spheroid.

sphinx [sfɛ̃:ks] *nm* sphinx.

spider [spidɛːr] *nm* trunk (of car), rumble seat.

spinal [spinal] *a* spinal.

spiral [spiral] *a* spiral.

spirale [spiral] *nf* spiral; **escalier en — winding staircase.**

spirite [spirit] *a* spiritualistic *n* spiritualist.

spiritisme [spiritism] *nm* spirit-ism.

spiritualiste [spiritɥalist] *a* sp-ualistic; *n* spiritualist.

spirituel, -elle [spiritɥɛl] *a* spirit sacred, witty.

spiritueux, -euse [spiritɥø, ø:] spirituous, alcoholic; *nm pl* spir

spleen [splin] *nm* spleen, depress **avoir le —** to have the blues.

splendeur [splɑ̃dœːr] *nf* splen grandeur, magnificence, brillia pomp.

splendide [splɑ̃did] *a* splen magnificent, grand, gorge glorious.

spoliateur, -trice [spɔljatœːr, *a* spoliatory, despoiling; *n* despo plunderer.

spoliation [spɔljasjɔ̃] *nf* spoliat despoiling, plundering.

spolier [spɔ.je] *vt* to despoil, plunder.

spongieux, -euse [spɔ̃ʒø, ø:z spongy.

spontané [spɔ̃tane] *a* spontane involuntary.

spontanéité [spɔ̃taneite] *nf* s taneity.

sporadique [spɔradik] *a* sporadi

spore [spɔːr] *nf* spore.

sport [spɔːr] *nm* sport(s), game sporting, casual.

sportif, -ive [spɔrtif, iːv] *a* s (ing), athletic; *n* sportsman, -wor lover of games; **réunion spo** sports, athletic meeting.

sportsman [spɔrt(s)man] *nm* sp man, race-goer.

spumeux, -euse [spymø, ø:z spumy, frothy, foamy.

square [skwɛːr, skwaːr] *nm* s public garden.

squelette [skəlɛt] *nm* skele framework, outline.

squelettique [skəlɛtik] *a* skele like.

stabilisateur, -trice [stabiliza tris] *a* stabilizing, steadying; stabilizer.

stabiliser [stabilize] *vt* to stab steady; *vr* to become steady, st

stabilité [stabilite] *nf* stabi steadiness, firmness, bala durability.

stable [stabl] *a* stable, steady, durable.

stade [stad] *nm* stadium, sp ground, stage.

stage [staːʒ] *nm* probationary pe course.

stagiaire [staʒjɛːr] *a* probation *n* probationer.

stagnant [stagnɑ̃] *a* stagnant, d

stagnation [stagnasjɔ̃] *nf* stagna stagnancy, standstill.

stalactite [stalaktit] *nf* stalactite

stalagmite [stalagmit] *nf* stalag

talle [stal] nf stall, box, seat, pew.

tance [stɑ̃:s] nf stanza.

tand [stɑ̃:d] nm stand, shooting-gallery.

tandard [stɑ̃da:r] nm switchboard, standard.

tandardisation [stɑ̃dardizasjɔ̃] nf standardization.

tandardiser [stɑ̃dardize] vt to standardize.

tation [stasjɔ̃] nf stop, station, stage, taxi-stand, position, post, standing; — **centrale** power-house; — **balnéaire** seaside resort, spa; — **thermale** spa, watering place; — **d'hiver** winter resort; **faire une** — à to halt at.

tationnaire [stasjɔnɛ:r] a stationary, fixed.

tationnement [stasjɔnmɑ̃] nm standing, stopping, stationing, taxi-stand; **parc de** — parking place; — **interdit** no parking.

tationner [stasjɔne] vi to stand, park, stop, be stationed.

atique [statik] a static.

atistique [statistik] a statistical; nf statistics.

atuaire [statɥɛ:r] a statuary; n sculptor; nf statuary.

atue [staty] nf statue.

atuer [statɥe] vt to ordain, decree, enact; — **sur une affaire** to decide, give a decision on a matter.

ature [staty:r] nf stature, height.

atut [staty] nm statute, regulation, article, ordinance, bylaw.

atutaire [statytɛ:r] a statutory.

énodactylo(graphe) [stenɔdaktilɔgraf] n shorthand-typist.

énodactylographie [stenɔdaktilɔrafi] nf shorthand and typing.

énographe [stenɔgraf] n stenographer, shorthand writer.

énographie [stenɔgrafi] nf stenography, shorthand.

énographier [stenɔgrafje] vt to ake down in shorthand.

entor [stɑ̃tɔ:r] nm **voix de** — tentorian voice.

eppe [stɛp] n steppe.

ère [stɛ:r] nm stere, cubic meter.

éréophonie [stereɔfɔni] nf stereophony.

éréotype [stereɔtip] a stereotype(d); nm stereotype plate.

érile [steril] a sterile, barren, ruitless.

érilisation [sterilizasjɔ̃] nf sterilization.

ériliser [sterilize] vt to sterilize.

érilité [sterilite] nf sterility, barrenness, fruitlessness.

ernum [stɛrnɔm] nm sternum, reastbone.

igmate [stigmat] nm stigma, scar, rand.

igmatiser [stigmatize] vt to tigmatize, brand (with infamy), ock-mark.

stimulant [stimylɑ̃] a stimulating; nm stimulant, stimulus, incentive.

stimulation [stimylasjɔ̃] nf stimulation.

stimuler [stimyle] vt to stimulate, incite, rouse.

stipulation [stipylasjɔ̃] nf stipulation.

stipuler [stipyle] vt to stipulate, lay down.

stock [stɔk] nm stock; — **en magasin** stock in hand.

stockiste [stɔkist] nm stocker, wholesale warehouseman, agent; **agence** — **service-station**.

stoïcien, -enne [stɔisjɛ̃, jɛn] a stoïc(al); n stoïc.

stoïcisme [stɔisism] nm stoïcism.

stoïque [stɔik] a stoïc(al).

stomacal [stɔmakal] a gastric.

stomachique [stɔmaʃik] a stomach-, stomachic.

stoppage [stɔpa:ʒ] nm stopping, stoppage, invisible mending.

stopper [stɔpe] vt to stop, fine-darn; vi to (come to a) stop.

store [stɔ:r] nm blind, window shade.

strabisme [strabism] nm squinting.

strangulation [strɑ̃gylasjɔ̃] nf strangulation, throttling, constriction.

strapontin [strapɔ̃tɛ̃] nm folding-seat, jump seat.

strass [stras] nm strass, paste jewelry.

stratagème [strataʒɛm] nm stratagem.

stratégie [strateʒi] nf strategy, generalship, craft.

stratégique [strateʒik] a strategic (al).

stratosphère [stratɔsfɛ:r] nf stratosphere.

strict [strikt] a strict, severe; **le** — **nécessaire** the bare necessities.

strident [stridɑ̃] a strident, harsh, grating.

strie [stri] nf score, streak.

strier [strie] vt to score, scratch, streak, groove.

striure [striy:r] nf score, scratch, streak, groove, striation.

strophe [strɔf] nf stanza, verse.

structure [strykty:r] nf structure.

strychnine [striknin] nf strychnine.

stuc [styk] nm stucco.

studieux, -euse [stydjø, ø:z] a studious.

studio [stydjo] nm (film) studio, artist's studio.

stupéfaction [stypefaksjɔ̃] nf stupefaction, amazement, bewilderment.

stupéfait [stypefɛ] a stupefied, amazed, astounded.

stupéfiant [stypefjɑ̃] a stupefying, astounding; nm narcotic, drug.

stupéfier [stypefje] vt to stupefy, bemuse, astound.

stupeur [stypœ:r] nf stupor, astonishment, amazement.

stupide [stypid] *a* stupid, foolish, silly.

stupidité [stypidite] *nf* stupidity, foolishness, stupid thing.

stupre [stypr] *nm* debauchery.

style [stil] *nm* style, pin, etching-needle; **robe de —** period dress.

styler [stile] *vt* to train, school.

stylet [stilɛ] *nm* stiletto.

styliser [stilize] *vt* to stylize, conventionalize.

stylo(graphe) [stilɔ(graf)] *nm* fountain-pen, stylograph.

styptique [stiptik] *a nm* styptic, astringent.

su [sy] *nm* **au — de** to the knowledge of; **à mon vu et —** to my certain knowledge.

suaire [sɥɛːr] *nm* shroud, winding-sheet.

suave [sɥaːv] *a* bland, suave, sweet, mild, soft, mellow.

suavité [sɥavite] *nf* blandness, suavity, sweetness, mildness, mellowness.

subalterne [sybaltɛrn] *a* subordinate, junior; *nm* subaltern, underling.

subdiviser [sybdivize] *vtr* to subdivide.

subdivision [sybdivizjɔ̃] *nf* subdivision.

subir [sybiːr] *vt* to undergo, go through, sustain, suffer.

subit [sybi] *a* sudden, unexpected.

subjacent [sybʒasɑ̃] *a* subjacent, underlying.

subjectif, -ive [sybʒɛktif, iːv] *a* subjective.

subjonctif, -ive [sybʒɔ̃ktif, iːv] *a nm* subjunctive.

subjuguer [sybʒyge] *vt* to subjugate, subdue, overcome, captivate.

sublime [syblim] *a* sublime, exalted, lofty; *nm* sublime.

sublimer [syblime] *vt* to sublimate, purify.

submerger [sybmɛrʒe] *vt* to submerge, immerse.

submersible [sybmɛrsibl] *a* submersible, sinkable; *nm* submersible, submarine.

submersion [sybmɛrsjɔ̃] *nf* submersion, immersion.

subordination [sybɔrdinasjɔ̃] *nf* subordination.

subordonné [sybɔrdɔne] *a* subordinate, dependent; *n* subordinate, underling.

subordonner [sybɔrdɔne] *vt* to subordinate.

subornation [sybɔrnasjɔ̃] *nf* subornation, bribing.

suborner [sybɔrne] *vt* to suborn, bribe.

subreptice [sybrɛptis] *a* surreptitious, stealthy.

subrogation [sybrɔgasjɔ̃] *nf* subrogation, substitution, delegation.

subroger [sybrɔʒe] *vt* to subrogate, appoint as deputy.

subséquent [sypsekɑ̃] *a* subsequent, ensuing.

subside [sypsid] *nm* subsidy.

subsidence [sypsidɑ̃ːs] *nf* subsidence.

subsidiaire [sypsidjɛːr] *a* subsidiary, accessory.

subsistance [sypsistɑ̃ːs] *nf* subsistence, keer sustenance.

subsister [sypsiste] *vi* to subsist, exist, hold good.

substance [sypstɑ̃ːs] *nf* substance, matter, material.

substantiel, -elle [sypstɑ̃sjɛl] *a* substantial.

substantif, -ive [sypstɑ̃tif, iːv] substantive; *nm* noun.

substituer [sypstitɥe] *vt* to substitute, entail; *vr* to take the place (of à).

substitut [sypstity] *nm* deputy, assistant, delegate.

substitution [sypstitysjɔ̃] *nf* substitution.

subterfuge [sybtɛrfyːʒ] *nm* subterfuge, dodge.

subtil [sybtil] *a* subtle, shrewd, discerning, fine, tenuous, thin.

subtiliser [sybtilize] *vt* to subtilize, refine, make too subtle, pinch.

subtilité [sybtilite] *nf* subtlety, rarity, shrewdness, acuteness.

subvenir [sybvəniːr] *vi* to provide for, supply; **— aux frais d'un voyage** to defray the expenses of a journey.

subvention [sybvɑ̃sjɔ̃] *nf* subsidy, grant.

subventionner [sybvɑ̃sjɔne] *vt* subsidize; **théâtre subventionné par l'état** state-aided theater.

subversif, -ive [sybvɛrsif, iːv] subversive.

subversion [sybvɛrsjɔ̃] *nf* subversion, overthrow.

suc [syk] *nm* juice, sap, pith, essence, substance.

succédané [syksedane] *nm* substitute.

succéder [syksede] *vt* to follow, succeed.

succès [syksɛ] *nm* success, (favorable) outcome, result; **remporter un —** to bring the house down.

successeur [syksesœːr] *nm* successor.

successif, -ive [syksesif, iːv] successive.

succession [syksesjɔ̃] *nf* succession, sequence, estate, inheritance; **prendre la — de** to take over (from).

succinct [syksɛ̃] *a* succinct, concise, brief.

succion [syksjɔ̃] *nf* suction, sucking.

succomber [sykɔ̃be] *vi* to succumb, die, yield.

succulent [sykylɑ̃] *a* succulent, juicy, tasty.

succursale [sykyrsal] *nf* branch office.

sucer [syse] *vt* to suck.

sucette [sysɛt] *nf* pacifier, lollipop.

suçoir [syswaːr] *nm* sucker.

sucre [sykr] nm sugar; — en pain loaf sugar; — en poudre powdered sugar.

sucré [sykre] a sugared, sweet(ened), sugary.

sucrer [sykre] vt to sugar, sweeten.

sucrerie [sykrəri] nf sugar refinery; pl confectionery, sweets.

sucrier [sykrie] nm sugar bowl.

sud [syd] a south, southern, southerly; nm south.

sudation [sydasjɔ̃] nf sweating.

sud-est [sydɛst] a south-east(ern), south-easterly; nm south-east.

sud-ouest [sydwɛst] a south-west (ern), south-westerly; nm south-west.

Suède [sqɛd] nf Sweden.

suédois [sqedwa] a Swedish; n Swede.

suer [sqe] vi to sweat, perspire, exude, toil.

sueur [sqœːr] nf sweat, perspiration; en — sweating.

suffire [syfiːr] vi to suffice, be enough, be adequate, meet, cope (with à); vr to be self-sufficient.

suffisance [syfizɑ̃s] nf sufficiency, adequacy, (self-)conceit, priggishness.

suffisant [syfizɑ̃] a sufficient, enough, adequate, conceited, self-satisfied.

suffixe [syfiks] nm suffix.

suffocation [syfɔkasjɔ̃] nf choking, suffocation.

suffoquer [syfɔke] vt to suffocate, choke, stifle; vi to choke.

suffrage [syfraːʒ] nm suffrage, franchise, vote.

suffusion [syfyzjɔ̃] nf suffusion, blush.

suggérer [sygʒere] vt to suggest, hint (at).

suggestif, -ive [sygʒestif, iːv] a suggestive.

suggestion [sygʒestjɔ̃] nf suggestion, hint.

suicide [sqisid] a suicidal; nm suicide.

suicidé [sqiside] n suicide.

se suicider [səsqiside] vr to commit suicide.

suie [sqi] nf soot.

suif [sqif] nm tallow, candle-grease.

suinter [sqɛ̃te] vi to ooze, sweat, run, seep, leak.

Suisse [sqis] nf Switzerland.

suisse [sqis] an Swiss; nm church officer; petit — cream cheese.

suite [sqit] nf continuation, succession, series, suite, retinue, train, sequel, result, consequence, coherence; donner — à to follow up, execute; faire — à to be a continuation of, a sequel to; dans la — subsequently; par la — afterwards, later on; par — (de) as a result (of); tout de suite immediately; de — in succession, one end; sans — disconnected, incoherent.

suivant [sqivɑ̃] a following, next; nm follower, attendant; prep according to, following; — que according as.

suivi [sqivi] a coherent, steady, continuous, popular.

suivre [sqiːvr] vt to follow (up), pursue, act upon, observe, escort; — des cours to attend lectures; faire — to forward; à — to be continued.

sujet, -ette [syʒe, ɛt] a subject, dependent, prone, liable, open; n subject; nm subject, topic, ground, theme, reason, fellow; bon — steady person; mauvais — bad lot, worthless character; au — de about, with regard to.

sujétion [syʒesjɔ̃] nf subjection, servitude.

sulfate [sylfat] nm sulphate.

sulfater [sylfate] vt to sulphate, dress with copper sulphate.

sulfure [sylfyːr] nm sulphide.

sulfureux, -euse [sylfyrø, øːz] a sulphurous.

sulfurique [sylfyrik] a sulphuric.

sultan [syltɑ̃] nm sultan.

sultane [syltan] nf sultana.

superbe [syperb] a superb, splendid, magnificent, stately, arrogant, haughty; nf arrogance, haughtiness.

super(carburant) [syperkarbyrɑ̃] nm high-grade gasoline.

supercherie [syperʃəri] nf fraud, hoax, deceit.

superficie [syperfisi] nf area, surface.

superficiel, -elle [syperfisjel] a superficial, shallow.

superflu [syperfly] a superfluous, unnecessary; nm superfluity, overabundance.

superfluité [syperflyite] nf superfluity.

supérieur [syperjœːr] a superior, upper, higher; n superior, head.

supériorité [syperjɔrite] nf superiority, supremacy, superiorship.

superlatif, -ive [syperlatif, iːv] a nm superlative.

superposer [syperpoze] vt to super-(im)pose.

superstitieux, -euse [syperstisjø, øːz] a superstitious.

superstition [syperstisjɔ̃] nf superstition.

supplanter [syplɑ̃te] vt to supplant, supersede.

suppléance [sypleɑ̃ːs] nf deputyship, substitution.

suppléant [sypleɑ̃] a temporary, acting; n deputy, substitute.

suppléer [syplee] vt to deputize for, make up, make good; — à to compensate for.

supplément [syplemɑ̃] nm supplement, extra, addition, extra fare; en — additional, extra.

supplémentaire [syplemɑ̃tɛːr] a supplementary, extra, additional.

suppliant [sypliɑ̃] *a* suppliant, pleading, beseeching; *n* supplicant, suppliant.

supplication [syplikasjɔ̃] *nf* supplication.

supplice [syplis] *nm* torture, punishment, anguish, torment, agony.

supplier [syplie] *vt* to implore, beseech, beg.

support [sypɔːr] *nm* support, prop, stand, bracket, rest, holder.

supportable [sypɔrtabl] *a* bearable, tolerable.

supporter [sypɔrte] *vt* to hold up, support, prop, endure, suffer, put up with, tolerate.

supposé [sypoze] *a* supposed, alleged, fictitious, assumed, forged; — **que** supposing that.

supposer [sypoze] *vt* to suppose, assume, imply.

supposition [sypozisjɔ̃] *nf* supposition, assumption.

suppositoire [sypozitwaːr] *nm* suppository.

suppôt [sypo] *nm* tool.

suppression [sypresjɔ̃] *nf* suppression, canceling, discontinuance.

supprimer [syprime] *vt* to suppress, abolish, cancel, discontinue, omit.

suppurer [sypyre] *vi* to suppurate, run.

supputer [sypyte] *vt* to calculate, compute.

suprématie [sypremasi] *nf* supremacy.

suprême [sypreːm] *a* supreme, crowning, paramount, last.

sur [syːr] *prep* (up)on, over, above, about, towards, along, over-, super-; **un homme — dix** one man out of ten; **dix mètres — huit** ten yards by eight; — **ce (quoi)** whereupon.

sûr [syr] *a* sure, certain, unerring, unfailing, safe, reliable, staunch; **à coup —** without fail, for certain.

surabondant [syrabɔ̃dɑ̃] *a* superabundant.

surabonder [syrabɔ̃de] *vi* to superabound, be surfeited (with **de**).

suraigu, -uë [syregy] *a* high-pitched, overshrill.

suralimenter [syralimɑ̃te] *vt* to feed up, overfeed.

suranné [syrane] *a* old-fashioned, out of date.

surcharge [syrʃarʒ] *nf* overload(ing), extra load, excess weight, surcharge, overtax.

surcharger [syrʃarʒe] *vt* to overload, overcharge, surcharge, overtax.

surchauffer [syrʃofe] *vt* to overheat, superheat.

surclasser [syrklase] *vt* to outclass.

surcomprimé [syrkɔ̃prime] *a* supercharged.

surcontrer [syrkɔ̃tre] *vt* to redouble.

surcroissance [syrkrwasɑ̃ːs] *nf* overgrowth.

surcroît [syrkrwa] *nm* increase, addition; **par —** in addition, into the bargain.

surdité [syrdite] *nf* deafness.

sureau [syro] *nm* elder (tree).

surélever [syrelve] *vt* to raise, heighten.

sûrement [syrmɑ̃] *ad* surely, certainly, safely, securely.

surenchère [syrɑ̃ʃeːr] *nf* higher bid.

surenchérir [syrɑ̃ʃeriːr] *vi* to bid higher; *vt* — **sur** outbid.

surestimer [syrestime] *vt* to overestimate.

sûreté [syrte] *nf* sureness, soundness, safety, security, guarantee; **la Sûreté** the Criminal Investigation Department; **pour plus de —** to be on the safe side.

surexcitation [syreksitasjɔ̃] *nf* (over) excitement.

surexciter [syreksite] *vt* to excite, over-stimulate.

surexposer [syrekspoze] *vt* to overexpose.

surface [syrfas] *nf* surface, area.

surfaire [syrfeːr] *vt* to overcharge, overrate; *vi* to overcharge.

surgir [syrʒiːr] *vi* to (a)rise, loom up, come into sight, crop up.

surhausser [syrose] *vt* to raise, heighten, increase.

surhumain [syrymɛ̃] *a* superhuman.

surimposer [syrɛ̃poze] *vt* to superimpose, increase the tax on.

suriner [syrine] *vt* (*fam*) to knife, do in.

surintendant [syrɛ̃tɑ̃dɑ̃] *nm* superintendent, steward.

surjet [syrʒe] *nm* overcasting, whipping (*of seams*).

sur-le-champ [syrləʃɑ̃] *ad* immediately.

surlendemain [syrlɑ̃dmɛ̃] *nm* next day but one, day after tomorrow; **le — de son départ** the second day after his departure.

surmenage [syrmənaːʒ] *nm* overworking, overdriving, strain.

surmené [syrməne] *a* overworked, jaded, fagged.

surmener [syrməne] *vt* to overwork, overexert; *vr* to overwork, overdo it.

surmontable [syrmɔ̃tabl] *a* surmountable.

surmonter [syrmɔ̃te] *vt* to surmount, top, overcome, get over; *vr* to master one's feelings.

surnaturel, -elle [syrnatyrel] *a* supernatural, uncanny; *nm* supernatural.

surnom [syrnɔ̃] *nm* nickname.

surnombre [syrnɔ̃ːbr] *nm* excessive number; **en —** supernumerary.

surnommer [syrnɔme] *vt* to nickname, call.

suroît [syrwa] *nm* sou'wester.

surpasser [syrpase] *vt* to surpass, outdo, outshine, exceed, excel, pass one's understanding.

surpayer [syrpeje] *vt* to overpay, pay too much for.

surpeuplement [syrpœpləmɑ̃] nm overcrowding.

surplis [syrpli] nm surplice.

surplomb [syrplɔ̃] nm overhang; **en —** overhanging.

surplomber [syrplɔ̃be] vti to overhang.

surplus [syrply] nm surplus, excess; **au —** besides.

surpoids [syrpwa] nm overweight; **en —** in excess.

surprenant [syrprənɑ̃] a surprising, astonishing.

surprendre [syrprɑ̃:dr] vt to surprise, astonish, catch unawares, overtake, overhear, intercept, catch, detect.

surprise [syrpri:z] nf surprise, astonishment, grab bag.

surproduction [syrprɔdyksjɔ̃] nf overproduction.

sursaut [syrso] nm start, jump; **en — with a start.

sursauter [syrsote] vi to start, jump.

surseoir [syrswa:r] vt to postpone, delay, suspend.

sursis [syrsi] nm postponement, reprieve, deferment.

surtaux [syrto] nm overassessment.

surtaxe [syrtaks] nf surtax, supertax, surcharge.

surtout [syrtu] ad above all, particularly, especially.

surveillance [syrvɛjɑ̃:s] nf supervision, vigilance, watching.

surveillant [syrvɛjɑ̃] n supervisor, overseer, watchman, usher, invigilator.

surveiller [syrvɛje] vt to supervise, superintend, invigilate, look after, watch; vr to watch one's step.

survenir [syrv(ə)ni:r] vi to happen, arise, crop up.

survêtement [syrvɛtmɑ̃] nm tracksuit.

survie [syrvi] nf survival, survivorship, after-life.

survivance [syrvivɑ̃:s] nf survival.

survivant [syrvivɑ̃] a surviving; n survivor.

survivre [syrvi:vr] vi to survive; vt **— à** to outlive.

survoler [syrvɔle] vt to fly over.

survolté [syrvɔlte] a worked up, het up.

sus [sys] ad against, upon; excl come on! **courir — à** qn to rush at s.o.; **en —** in addition, besides.

susceptibilité [syseptibilite] nf susceptibility, touchiness.

susceptible [syseptibl] a susceptible, touchy, likely, liable, apt.

susciter [syssite] vt to arouse, stir up, raise up, give rise to, bring on.

susdit [sydi] a aforesaid, abovementioned.

suspect [syspɛ(kt)] a suspect, suspicious, doubtful; nm suspect.

suspecter [syspɛkte] vt to suspect, doubt.

suspendre [syspɑ̃:dr] vt to suspend, hang, stop, defer; vr to hang (on).

suspendu [syspɑ̃dy] a suspended, hanging, sprung; **pont —** suspension bridge.

suspens [syspɑ̃] ad **en —** in suspense, undecided, in abeyance.

suspension [syspɑ̃sjɔ̃] nf suspension, hanging, interruption, springing, hanging lamp.

suspicion [syspisjɔ̃] nf suspicion.

sustenter [systɑ̃te] vt to sustain, support.

susurrer [sysyre] vi to murmur, rustle, sough.

suture [syty:r] nf suture, join; **point de —** stitch.

suturer [sytyre] vt to stitch.

suzerain [syzrɛ̃] a paramount, sovereign; n suzerain.

suzeraineté [syzrɛnte] nf suzerainty.

svelte [svɛlt] a slim, slender, slight.

sveltesse [svɛltɛs] nf slimness, slenderness.

sycomore [sikɔmɔ:r] nm sycamore.

syllabe [sillab] nf syllable.

sylphe [silf] nm sylph.

sylphide [silfid] nf sylph.

sylvestre [silvɛstr] a woodland, sylvan.

sylviculture [silvikylty:r] nf forestry.

symbole [sɛ̃bɔl] nm symbol, sign.

symbolique [sɛ̃bɔlik] a symbolic(al).

symboliser [sɛ̃bɔlize] vt to symbolize.

symétrie [simetri] nf symmetry.

symétrique [simetrik] a symmetrical.

sympathie [sɛ̃pati] nf liking, sympathy; **avoir de la — pour** qn to like s.o.

sympathique [sɛ̃patik] a likable, congenial, sympathetic; **encre — invisible ink.

sympathiser [sɛ̃patize] vi to sympathize, have a fellow feeling (for **avec**).

symphonie [sɛ̃fɔni] nf symphony, orchestra.

symphonique [sɛ̃fɔnik] a symphonic.

symptomatique [sɛ̃ptɔmatik] a symptomatic.

symptôme [sɛ̃pto:m] nm symptom, sign.

synagogue [sinagɔg] nf synagogue.

synchroniser [sɛ̃krɔnize] vt to synchronize.

synchronisme [sɛ̃krɔnism] nm synchronism.

syncope [sɛ̃kɔp] nf faint, syncope.

syncoper [sɛ̃kɔpe] vt to syncopate.

syndic [sɛ̃dik] nm syndic, assignee, trustee.

syndical [sɛ̃dikal] a syndical, trade union.

syndicalisme [sɛ̃dikalism] nm trade unionism.

syndicaliste [sɛ̃dikalist] nm trade unionist.

syndicat [sɛ̃dika] *nm* syndicate, trusteeship, trade union, federation.
syndiquer [sɛ̃dike] *vt* to syndicate, unite in a trade union; *vr* to form a trade union, combine.
synonyme [sinɔnim] *a* synonymous; *nm* synonym.
syntaxe [sɛ̃taks] *nf* syntax.
synthèse [sɛ̃tɛːz] *nf* synthesis.
synthétique [sɛ̃tetik] *a* synthetic.
synthétiser [sɛ̃tetize] *vt* to synthesize
Syrie [siri] *nf* Syria.
systématique [sistematik] *a* systematic, stereotyped, hidebound.
systématiser [sistematize] *vt* to systematize.
système [sistɛm] *nm* system, type; esprit de — hidebound mentality, unimaginativeness; **employer le —** D (*fam*) to wangle it.

T

ta [ta] *see* ton.
tabac [taba] *nm* tobacco; — à priser snuff.
tabagie [tabaʒi] *nf* place smelling (full) of tobacco-smoke, smoking room.
tabatière [tabatjɛːr] *nf* snuff-box.
tabernacle [tabɛrnakl] *nm* tabernacle.
table [tabl] *nf* table, board, slab; **mettre la —** to set the table.
tableau [tablo] *nm* board, picture, scene, panel, roster; — **de bord** dashboard.
tabler [table] *vi* to reckon, count (on sur).
tablette [tablɛt] *nf* tablet, cake, slab, shelf, notebook; **inscrire sur ses —s** to make a note of.
tabletterie [tablɛtri] *nf* fancy-goods (industry).
tablier [tablie] *nm* apron, pinafore, footplate, floor (of bridge), dashboard.
tabouret [taburɛ] *nm* stool.
tac au tac [takotak] *ad* tit for tat.
tache [taʃ] *nf* spot, stain, blot.
tâche [taːʃ] *nf* task, job; **travail à la —** piecework, jobbing; **prendre à — de** to make a point of.
tacher [taʃe] *vt* to stain, spot; *vr* to stain (one's clothes).
tâcher [taʃe] *vi* to try.
tâcheron [taʃrɔ̃] *nm* pieceworker, jobber.
tacheter [taʃte] *vt* to speckle, mottle, fleck.
tacite [tasit] *a* tacit, understood.
taciturne [tasityrn] *a* taciturn, silent.
taciturnité [tasityrnite] *nf* taciturnity.
tacot [tako] *nm* ramshackle automobile, jalopy.

tact [takt] *nm* touch, feel, tact.
tacticien [taktisjɛ̃] *nm* tactician.
tactile [taktil] *a* tactile.
tactique [taktik] *a* tactical; *nf* tactics.
taffetas [tafta] *nm* taffeta.
taie [tɛ] *nf* pillowcase.
taillade [tajad] *nf* slash, gash, cut.
taillant [tajɑ̃] *nm* (cutting) edge.
taille [taːj] *nf* cut(ting), hewing, clipping, figure, waist, height, tax; **être de —** à to be fit to.
tailler [taje] *vt* to cut (out), hew, clip, carve, sharpen.
tailleur, -euse [tajœːr, øːz] *n* cutter, hewer, tailor(ess); *nm* (woman's) costume, suit.
taillis [taji] *nm* copse, brushwood.
tain [tɛ̃] *nm* silvering, foil.
taire [tɛːr] *vt* to say nothing about, keep dark; *vr* to be silent, hold one's tongue.
talent [talɑ̃] *nm* talent, gift, ability.
taloche [talɔʃ] *nf* cuff, (builder's) mortar-board.
talon [talɔ̃] *nm* heel, counterfoil, beading, flange, butt; **marcher sur les — de qn** to follow close on s.o.'s heels, close behind s.o.
talonner [talɔne] *vt* to follow, dog, spur on, dun, heel.
talus [taly] *nm* slope, bank, ramp.
tambour [tɑ̃buːr] *nm* drum, drummer, barrel, spool, revolving door; — **de ville** town crier.
tambourin [tɑ̃burɛ̃] *nm* tambourine, tabor.
tambouriner [tɑ̃burine] *vi* to drum, knock.
tambour-major [tɑ̃burmaʒɔːr] *nm* drum-major.
tamis [tami] *nm* sifter, sieve, riddle.
tamiser [tamize] *vt* to sift, strain, filter, screen; *vi* to filter through.
tampon [tɑ̃pɔ̃] *nm* stopper, bung, plug, buffer, pad, stamp.
tamponnement [tɑ̃pɔnmɑ̃] *nm* collision, plugging.
tamponner [tɑ̃pɔne] *vt* to plug, dab, pad, collide with.
tam-tam [tamtam] *nm* African drum, dance.
tancer [tɑ̃se] *vt* to scold, chide.
tandis que [tɑ̃di(s)kə] *cj* while, whereas.
tangage [tɑ̃gaːʒ] *nm* pitching.
tangent [tɑ̃ʒɑ̃] *a* tangent.
tangible [tɑ̃ʒibl] *a* tangible.
tanguer [tɑ̃ge] *vi* to pitch.
tanière [tanjɛːr] *nf* lair, den, hole.
tanin [tanɛ̃] *nm* tannin.
tanner [tane] *vt* to tan.
tannerie [tanri] *nf* tannery.
tanneur [tanœːr] *nm* tanner.
tant [tɑ̃] *ad* so much, so many, as much, so; — **que** as much as, as long as; **si — est que** if it is true that, if it is the case that; — **soit peu** somewhat, ever so little; **en — que** in so far as, as; — **pis** so much

the worse, can't be helped, too bad.
tante [tɑ̃:t] *nf* aunt.
tantième [tɑ̃tjɛm] *nm* percentage, quota.
tantinet [tɑ̃tinɛ] *nm* tiny bit, spot.
tantôt [tɑ̃to] *ad* presently, soon, a little while ago; tantôt ... tantôt ... now ... now; à —I see you later!
taon [tɑ̃] *nm* horse-fly.
tapage [tapaːʒ] *nm* din, row.
tapageur, -euse [tapaʒœːr, øːz] *a* rowdy, noisy, showy, flashy.
tape [tap] *nf* stopper, tap, pat, slap.
tape-à-l'œil [tapalœːj] *nm* flashy article; *a* flashy.
tapecul [tapky] *nm* pillion-seat, jalopy.
taper [tape] *vt* to tap, pat, hit, touch, type; — dans l'œil à qn to catch, fill s.o.'s eye; — sur qn to slate s.o.; (*fam*) ça tape it's hot.
tapinois [tapinwa] *ad* en — on the sly, slyly.
se tapir [sətapiːr] *vr* to crouch, cower, squat, take cover.
tapis [tapi] *nm* carpet, cloth, cover; mettre qch sur le — to bring sth up for discussion; — roulant conveyer belt, moving sidewalk.
tapisser [tapise] *vt* to paper, line, cover.
tapisserie [tapisri] *nf* tapestry (making), wallpaper; faire — to be a wallflower.
tapissier, -ière [tapisje, jɛːr] *n* tapestry-worker, upholsterer.
tapoter [tapote] *vt* to tap, strum.
taquin [takɛ̃] *a* teasing; *n* tease.
taquiner [takine] *vt* to tease.
taquinerie [takinri] *nf* teasing.
tarabiscoté [tarabiskote] *a* ornate, grooved.
tard [taːr] *ad* late; sur le — late in the day, late in life; tôt ou — sooner or later.
tarder [tarde] *vi* to delay, loiter, be long (in à); il leur tarde de vous revoir they are longing to see you.
tardif, -ive [tardif, iːv] *a* late, backward, belated, tardy, slow.
tare [taːr] *nf* blemish, defect, depreciation, tare.
tarer [tare] *vt* to damage, blemish, spoil.
se targuer [sətarge] *vr* to pride oneself (on de).
tarière [tarjɛːr] *nf* auger, drill.
tarif [tarif] *nm* tariff, price list, fare.
tarifer [tarife] *vt* to price.
tarir [tariːr] *vti* to dry up.
tarte [tart] *nf* tart.
tartine [tartin] *nf* slice of bread and butter, long story, rigmarole.
tartre [tartr] *nm* tartar, fur, scale.
tartufe [tartyf] *nm* hypocrite, impostor.
tas [tɑ] *nm* heap, pile, pack, lot(s); grève sur le — sit-down strike.
tasse [tɑːs] *nf* cup.
tassé [tɑse] *a* full, heaped, squat.

tasser [tɑse] *vt* to squeeze, pack, cram; *vr* to crowd together, squeeze up, settle.
tâter [tate] *vt* to feel, taste, try; *vr* to hesitate.
tatillonner [tatijɔne] *vi* to interfere, meddle, fuss, be fussy.
tâtonner [tatɔne] *vi* to feel one's way, grope (about).
tâtons (à) [tatɔ̃] *ad* groping(ly), warily.
tatouer [tatwe] *vt* to tattoo.
taudis [todi] *nm* hovel; *pl* slums.
taupe [toːp] *nf* mole(skin).
taupinière [topinjɛːr] *nf* molehill.
taureau [tɔro] *nm* bull.
tautologie [tɔtɔlɔʒi] *nf* tautology.
taux [to] *nm* rate, scale.
taverne [tavɛrn] *nf* tavern, public house.
taxe [taks] *nf* tax, duty, rate, charge.
taxer [takse] *vt* to tax, charge, fix the price of, accuse.
taxi [taksi] *nm* taxi.
Tchécoslovaquie [tʃekɔslɔvaki] *nf* Czechoslovakia.
tchèque [tʃɛk] *an* Czech.
te [t(ə)] *pn* you, to you, yourself, thee, to thee, thyself.
technicien [tɛknisjɛ̃] *nm* technician.
technique [tɛknik] *a* technical; *nf* technique, technics, engineering.
technologie [tɛknɔlɔʒi] *nf* technology.
technologique [tɛknɔlɔʒik] *a* technological.
teigne [tɛɲ] *nf* moth, scurf, ringworm, vixen.
teigneux, -euse [tɛɲø, øːz] *a* scurfy.
teindre [tɛ̃:dr] *vt* to dye, tinge, stain; *vr* to be tinged, dye one's hair.
teint [tɛ̃] *nm* dye, color, complexion.
teinte [tɛ̃:t] *nf* shade, hue, tint, tinge, touch.
teinter [tɛ̃te] *vt* to tint, tinge.
teinture [tɛ̃tyːr] *nf* dye(ing), tinting, hue, tincture, smattering.
teinturier, -ière [tɛ̃tyrje, jɛːr] *n* dyer.
tek [tɛk] *nm* teak.
tel, telle [tɛl] *a* such, like; *pn* such a one; — que such as, like; — quel as it (she, he) is, ordinary; monsieur un — Mr So-and-so.
télécinéma [telesinema] *nm* televised movie.
télécommander [telekɔmɑ̃de] *vt* to operate by remote control.
télégramme [telegram] *nm* telegram.
télégraphe [telegraf] *nm* telegraph.
télégraphie [telegrafi] *nf* telegraphy; — sans fil radiotelegraphy.
télégraphier [telegrafje] *vti* to telegraph, cable, wire.
téléguider [telegide] *vt* to radio-control.
télépathie [telepati] *nf* telepathy.
téléphérique [teleferik] *a nm* cable railway.

téléphone [telefɔn] nm (tele)phone.
téléphoner [telefɔne] vti to (tele)phone, ring up.
téléphonique [telefɔnik] a telephonic; cabine — telephone booth.
téléphoniste [telefɔnist] n telephone operator.
télescope [teleskɔp] nm telescope.
télescoper [teleskɔpe] vti to telescope, crumple up.
télésiège [telesjɛʒ] nm chair-lift.
télévision [televizjɔ̃] nf television.
tellement [tɛlmɑ̃] ad so, in such a way.
téméraire [temerɛːr] a rash, reckless, bold.
témérité [temerite] nf rashness, temerity, rash act.
témoignage [temwaɲaʒ] nm evidence, testimony, token, mark.
témoigner [temwaɲe] vt to show, display, prove, testify to; vi to give evidence.
témoin [temwɛ̃] nm witness, second, baton.
tempe [tɑ̃p] nf temple.
tempérament [tɑ̃peramɑ̃] nm constitution, nature; vente à — hire-purchase.
tempérance [tɑ̃perɑ̃s] nf moderation.
tempérant [tɑ̃perɑ̃] a temperate, moderate.
température [tɑ̃peratyːr] nf temperature.
tempéré [tɑ̃pere] a moderate, temperate.
tempérer [tɑ̃pere] vt to moderate, temper; vr to moderate, abate.
tempête [tɑ̃pɛːt] nf storm.
tempêter [tɑ̃pete] vi to storm, rage.
tempétueux, -euse [tɑ̃petɥø, øːz] a stormy.
temple [tɑ̃pl] nm temple, (Protestant) church.
temporaire [tɑ̃pɔrɛːr] a provisional, temporary.
temporel, -elle [tɑ̃pɔrɛl] a temporal.
temporiser [tɑ̃pɔrize] vi to temporize, procrastinate.
temps [tɑ̃] nm. time, period, age, weather, tense; à — in time; de tout — at all times; quel — fait-il? what is the weather like?
tenable [tənabl] a tenable, bearable.
tenace [tənas] a tenacious, adhesive, retentive, rooted.
ténacité [tenasite] nf tenacity, adhesiveness, retentiveness.
tenaille [tənɑːj] nf tongs; pl pincers.
tenancier, -ière [tənɑ̃sje, jɛːr] n keeper, lessee, tenant.
tenant [tənɑ̃] a séance —e forthwith; —e et aboutissants adjoining properties, ins and outs; d'un seul — in one piece.
tendance [tɑ̃dɑ̃s] nf tendency, trend.
tendancieux, -euse [tɑ̃dɑ̃sjø, øːz] a tendentious.

tendre [tɑ̃ːdr] vt to stretch (out), strain, hang, set, tighten, spread, hold out; vi to lead, tend; vr to become tight, strained, taut, tense.
tendre [tɑ̃ːdr] a tender, delicate, loving.
tendresse [tɑ̃drɛs] nf tenderness, love.
ténèbres [tenɛːbr] nf pl darkness.
ténébreux, -euse [tenebrø, øːz] a dark, sinister.
teneur [tənœːr, øːz] n holder, keeper, taker; nf tenor, purport, content.
ténia [tenja] nm tapeworm.
tenir [təniːr] vt to hold, keep, run, occupy, contain; vi to hold, stick, stand, last; vr to stand, sit, remain, stay; contain oneself, behave oneself; — à to be close to, be the result of; s'il ne tient qu'à cela if that is all; qu'à cela ne tienne never mind that; je n'y tiens plus I can't stand it any longer; — de to have sth of, take after, get from; — pour to consider as, be in favor of; tiens, tiens, well, well! indeed! tiens, tenez (look) here; on tient quatre dans cette voiture this car holds four; se — à to keep to, hold on to; s'en — à to abide by, be content with.
tennis [tenis] nm tennis (court).
ténor [tenɔːr] nm tenor.
tension [tɑ̃sjɔ̃] nf tension, pressure, stretching.
tentacule [tɑ̃takyl] nm feeler, tentacle.
tentateur, -trice [tɑ̃tatœːr, tris] a tempting; n tempter, temptress.
tentation [tɑ̃tasjɔ̃] nf temptation.
tentative [tɑ̃tatiːv] nf attempt.
tente [tɑ̃ːt] nf tent, canvas, awning.
tenter [tɑ̃te] vt to tempt, try.
tenture [tɑ̃tyːr] nf tapestry, hangings, wallpaper.
tenu [təny] a kept, bound.
ténu [teny] a fine, tenuous, slender, subtle.
tenue [təny] nf holding, sitting, upkeep, behavior, dress, seat; avoir de la — to behave oneself; en grande — in full dress.
ténuité [tenɥite] nf fineness, slenderness, tenuousness.
térébenthine [terebɑ̃tin] nf turpentine.
tergiverser [tɛrʒiverse] vi to beg the question, hesitate.
terme [tɛrm] nm term, expression, end, limit, quarter; mener qch à bon — to carry sth through.
terminaison [tɛrminɛzɔ̃] nf termination, ending.
terminer [tɛrmine] vtr to terminate, finish, end.
terminologie [tɛrminɔlɔʒi] nf terminology.
terminus [tɛrminyːs] nm terminus.
terne [tɛrn] a dull, lifeless, flat.

ternir [tɛrniːr] vt to tarnish, dim, dull; vr to become dim, dull.

terrain [tɛrɛ̃] nm land, (piece of) ground, course.

terrasse [tɛras] nf terrace, bank.

terrassement [tɛrasmɑ̃] nm digging, banking, earthwork.

terrasser [tɛrase] vt to bank up, lay low, fell.

terrassier [tɛrasje] nm digger.

terre [tɛːr] nf earth, world, land, soil, estate; par — on the ground, on the floor; descendre à — to go ashore; — à — commonplace.

Terre-Neuve [tɛrnœːv] nf Newfoundland; nm -dog.

terre-neuvien, **-enne** [tɛrnœvjɛ̃, jɛn] a Newfoundland; n Newfoundlander; nm fisherman, boat that goes to fishing grounds off Newfoundland.

terrestre [tɛrɛstr] a terrestrial, earthly.

terreur [tɛrœːr] nf terror, dread.

terrible [tɛribl] a terrible, dreadful.

terrien, **-enne** [tɛrjɛ̃, jɛn] a landed; landowner, landsman.

terrier [tɛrje] nm hole, burrow, terrier.

terrifier [tɛr(r)ifje] vt to terrify.

terrine [tɛrin] nf earthenware pot, pan, potted meat.

territoire [tɛritwaːr] nm territory.

territorial [tɛritɔrjal] a territorial.

terroir [tɛrwaːr] nm soil.

terroriser [tɛr(r)ɔrize] vt to terrorize.

tertre [tɛrtr] nm mound, hillock.

tes [te] see ton.

tesson [tɛsɔ̃] nm fragment, broken end.

testament [tɛstamɑ̃] nm testament, will.

testateur, **-trice** [tɛstatœːr, tris] n testator, testatrix.

testicule [tɛstikyl] nm testicle.

tétanos [tetanɔs] nm lockjaw, tetanus.

têtard [tetaːr] nm tadpole.

tête [tɛːt] nf head, face, top, front; calcul de — mental arithmetic; mauvaise — unruly person; femme de — capable woman; forte — self-willed person; faire une — to pull a long face; en faire à sa — to have one's own way; monter la — à qn to rouse s.o., work s.o. up.

tête-à-queue [tɛtako] nm faire — to swing right round.

tête-à-tête [tɛtatɛːt] nm private conversation, tête-à-tête..

tête-bêche [tɛtbɛʃ] ad head to foot, head to tail.

tétée [tete] nf suck.

téter [tete] vt to suck.

tétière [tetjɛːr] nf baby's cap, head-stall (of harness).

tétin [tetɛ̃] nm nipple, dug.

tétine [tetin] nf udder, dug, (rubber) teat.

téton [tetɔ̃] nm breast.

têtu [tety] a obstinate, stubborn.

teuton, **-onne** [tøtɔ̃, ɔn] a Teuton(ic); n Teuton.

teutonique [tøtɔnik] a Teutonic.

texte [tɛkst] nm text.

textile [tɛkstil] a nm textile.

textuel, **-elle** [tɛkstɥɛl] a textual.

texture [tɛkstyːr] nf texture.

thé [te] nm tea, tea-party.

théâtral [teatral] a theatrical.

théâtre [teaːtr] nm theater, stage, drama, scene.

théière [tejɛːr] nf teapot.

thème [tɛm] nm theme, topic, prose composition.

théologie [teɔlɔʒi] nf theology, divinity.

théologique [teɔlɔʒik] a theological.

théorème [teɔrɛm] nm theorem.

théoricien, **-enne** [teɔrisjɛ̃, jɛn] n theorist.

théorie [teɔri] nf theory.

théorique [teɔrik] a theoretical.

théoriser [teɔrize] vti to theorize.

thermal [tɛrmal] a thermal; station —e spa; eaux —es hot springs.

thermomètre [tɛrmɔmɛtr] nm thermometer.

thésauriser [tezɔrize] vt to hoard.

thèse [tɛːz] nf thesis, argument.

Thierry [tjɛri] n pr Theodore.

thon [tɔ̃] nm tuna fish.

thorax [tɔraks] nm thorax, chest.

thuriféraire [tyrifeːr] nm incense-bearer, flatterer.

thym [tɛ̃] nm thyme.

tibia [tibja] nm shin-bone, tibia.

tic [tik] nm twitching, mannerism.

ticket [tikɛ] nm ticket, check, slip.

tic-tac [tiktak] nm tick-tock, ticking, pit-a-pat.

tiède [tjɛd] a lukewarm, tepid.

tiédeur [tjedœːr] nf lukewarmness, tepidity, half-heartedness, coolness.

tiédir [tjediːr] vt to make tepid, cool; vi to become tepid, cool down, off.

tien, **tienne** [tjɛ̃, tjɛn] poss pn le(s) —(s), la tienne, les tiennes yours, thine; nm your own; pl your own people.

tierce [tjɛrs] nf tierce, third.

tiercé [tjɛrse] nm betting (on horses).

tiers, **tierce** [tjɛːr, tjɛrs] a third; nm third (part), third person, -party.

tige [tiːʒ] nf stalk, stem, trunk, shank, shaft.

tignasse [tiɲas] nf mop, shock.

tigre, **tigresse** [tigr, tigrɛs] n tiger, tigress.

tilleul [tijœl] nm lime-tree, infusion of lime-flowers.

timbale [tɛ̃bal] nf kettledrum, metal drinking mug, raised piedish.

timbre [tɛ̃ːbr] nm stamp, stamp-duty, bell, timbre.

timbré [tɛ̃bre] a stamped, post-marked, sonorous, (fam) crazy, cracked.

timbre-poste [tɛ̃brəpɔst] nm postage-stamp.

timbre-quittance [tɛ̃brəkitɑ̃:s] nm receipt-stamp.

timbrer [tɛ̃bre] vt to stamp.

timide [timid] a timid, coy, shy, diffident.

timidité [timidite] nf timidity, shyness, diffidence.

timon [timɔ̃] nm shaft, pole, helm.

timonerie [timɔnri] nf steering (-gear), signaling.

timonier [timɔnje] nm helmsman, signalman.

timoré [timɔre] a timorous, fearful.

tintamarre [tɛ̃tamaːr] nm noise, racket, din.

tinter [tɛ̃te] vti to toll, ring; vi to clink, jingle, tinkle, tingle.

tir [tiːr] nm shooting, gunnery, firing, rifle-range, shooting-gallery.

tirade [tirad] nf (long) speech, tirade.

tirage [tiraːʒ] nm pulling, hauling, draft, drawing, printing, circulation.

tiraillement [tirɑjmɑ̃] nm pulling, tugging, friction, pang, twinge.

tirailler [tiraje] vt to pull about, tug; vi to fire away.

tirailleur [tirajœːr] nm sharpshooter, freelance.

tirant [tirɑ̃] nm purse-string, stay, ship's draft; — d'air headroom.

tire [tiːr] nf pull; voleur à la — pickpocket.

tiré [tire] a drawn, certificated.

tire-bouchon [tirbuʃɔ̃] nm corkscrew.

tire-bouchonner [tirbuʃɔne] vi to curl up, wrinkle; vt to screw up.

tire-bouton [tirbutɔ̃] nm buttonhook.

tire-d'aile [tirdɛl] ad à — swiftly.

tire-larigot [tirlarigo] ad boire à — to drink heavily.

tirelire [tirliːr] nf money-box.

tirer [tire] vt to haul, draw, tug, pull off, out, fire, shoot, let off, print; vi to tug, pull, incline, verge (oh sur); vr to extricate o.s., get out; se — d'affaire, s'en — to get out of trouble, manage.

tiret [tirɛ] nm dash, hyphen.

tireur, -euse [tirœːr, øːz] n drawer, marksman, shot.

tiroir [tirwaːr] nm drawer, slide (-valve).

tisane [tizan] nf infusion.

tison [tizɔ̃] nm brand, half-burned log.

tisonner [tizɔne] vt to poke, stir, fan.

tisonnier [tizɔnje] nm poker.

tisser [tise] vt to weave.

tisserand [tisrɑ̃] n weaver.

tissu [tisy] nm cloth, fabric, tissue.

titre [tiːtr] nm title, heading, qualification, right, claim, title-deed, diploma, bond; pl securities; en — titular; à — d'office ex officio; à quel —? on what grounds? à — gratuit free of charge.

titré [titre] a titled, certificated.

titrer [titre] vt to give a title to.

tituber [titybe] vi to stagger, reel.

titulaire [titylɛːr] a titular; n holder.

toaster [toste] vt to toast.

toc [tɔk] nm faked stuff, imitation, rap, knock.

tocsin [tɔksɛ̃] nm alarm-signal, tocsin.

tohu-bohu [tɔybɔy] nm hubbub, hurly-burly.

toi [twa] pn you, thou, thee.

toile [twal] nf linen, cloth, canvas, painting; — cirée oilcloth, oilskin; — d'araignée spider's web, cobweb; — de fond back-cloth, -drop.

toilette [twalɛt] nf toilet; dress(ing), dressing-table, wash-stand, lavatory.

toise [twaːz] nf fathom, measuring apparatus.

toiser [twaze] vt to measure, look (s.o.) up and down.

toison [twazɔ̃] nf fleece.

toit [twa] nm roof, home.

toiture [twatyːr] nf roof(ing).

tôle [toːl] nf sheet-iron.

tolérance [tɔlerɑ̃:s] nf tolerance, toleration, allowance.

tolérer [tɔlere] vt to tolerate, suffer.

tolet [tɔlɛ] nm oarlock.

tollé [tɔlle] nm outcry; crier — contre to raise a hue and cry after.

tomate [tɔmat] nf tomato.

tombe [tɔ̃:b] nf tomb, grave, tombstone.

tombeau [tɔ̃bo] nm tomb, tombstone.

tombée [tɔ̃be] nf fall.

tomber [tɔ̃be] vi to fall, drop, die down, hang; vt to throw, take off; — sur to come across, fall upon; — juste to arrive, (happen), at the right time, guess right; laisser — to drop.

tombereau [tɔ̃bro] nm dump cart, tumbrel.

tombola [tɔ̃bɔla] nf tombola.

tome [toːm] nm volume, tome.

ton, ta, tes [tɔ̃, ta, te] a your, thy.

ton [tɔ̃] nm tone, color, key, pitch, fashion; le bon — good form.

tonalité [tɔnalite] nf tonality.

tondeuse [tɔ̃døːz] nf shears, lawnmower.

tondre [tɔ̃:dr] vt to clip, shear, mow, fleece.

tonifier [tɔnifje] vt to tone up, brace.

tonique [tɔnik] a nm tonic; a bracing.

tonitruant [tɔnitryɑ̃] a thunderous, blustering.

tonne [tɔn] nf tun, cask, ton.

tonneau [tɔno] nm barrel, cask, ton.

tonnelier [tɔnəlje] nm cooper.

tonnelle [tɔnɛl] nf arbor, bower.

tonnellerie [tɔnɛlri] nf cooper's shop, cooperage.

tonner [tɔne] vi to thunder.

tonnerre [tɔnɛːr] nm thunder; **du —** marvelous, terrific.

tonsure [tɔ̃syːr] nf tonsure.

tonte [tɔ̃ːt] nf clipping, shearing.

topaze [tɔpaːz] nf topaz.

toper [tɔpe] vi to agree, shake hands on it; **tope-là!** done!

topinambour [tɔpinãbuːr] nm Jerusalem artichoke.

topo [tɔpo] nm lecture, demonstration, plan.

topographie [tɔpɔgrafi] nf topography, surveying.

topographique [tɔpɔgrafik] a topographic(al), ordnance.

toquade [tɔkad] nf craze, fancy.

toque [tɔk] nf toque, cap.

toqué [tɔke] a cracked, crazy, infatuated.

toquer [tɔke] vt to infatuate; vr to become infatuated (with de).

torche [tɔrʃ] nf torch pad.

torchon [tɔrʃɔ̃] nm duster, dishcloth, floor-cloth.

tordant [tɔrdã] a screamingly funny.

tordre [tɔrdr] vt to twist, wring, distort; vr to twist, writhe; **se — de rire** to split one's sides with laughter.

tornade [tɔrnad] nf tornado.

torpédo [tɔrpedo] nm open touring-car.

torpeur [tɔrpœːr] nf torpor.

torpille [tɔrpiːj] nf torpedo.

torpiller [tɔrpije] vt to torpedo.

torréfier [tɔrrefje] vt to roast, scorch.

torrent [tɔr(r)ã] nm torrent, stream.

torrentiel, -elle [tɔr(r)ãsjɛl] a torrential.

torride [tɔrrid] a torrid, broiling.

tors [tɔːr] a twisted, crooked.

torse [tɔrs] nm torso.

torsion [tɔrsjɔ̃] nf twist(ing), torsion.

tort [tɔːr] nm wrong, fault, harm, injury, injustice; **avoir —** to be wrong; **donner — à** to decide against; **à — et à travers** at random.

torticolis [tɔrtikɔli] nm stiff neck.

tortillard [tɔrtijaːr] nm small locomotive, railway.

tortiller [tɔrtije] vt to twist, twirl; vi to wriggle, shilly-shally; vr to wriggle.

tortue [tɔrty] nf tortoise.

tortueux, -euse [tɔrtɥø, øːz] a tortuous, winding.

torture [tɔrtyːr] nf torture, torment.

torturer [tɔrtyre] vt to torture, rack, twist.

tôt [to] ad soon, early; **— ou tard** sooner or later.

total [tɔtal] a nm total, whole.

totalisateur, -trice [tɔtalizatœːr, tris] a adding; nm pari-mutuel.

totaliser [tɔtalize] vt to total up.

totalitaire [tɔtalitɛːr] a totalitarian.

totalité [tɔtalite] nf totality, whole.

touchant [tuʃã] a touching, moving; prep with regard to, concerning.

touche [tuʃ] nf touch, manner, key, bite, hit, look.

touche-à-tout [tuʃatu] n meddler.

toucher [tuʃe] vt to touch (on), hit, draw, cash, move, concern; vi **— à** to be close to, be in contact with, affect, meddle; vr to adjoin; nm touch, feel.

touer [twe] vt to tow, warp.

touffe [tuf] nf tuft, cluster, clump.

touffu [tufy] a thick, bushy, involved, intricate.

toujours [tuʒuːr] ad always, ever, still, all the same.

toupet [tupɛ] nm forelock, tuft, cheek.

toupie [tupi] nf top.

tour [tuːr] nf tower; nm turn, course, shape, revolution, round, circuit, feat, trick, stroll; **— à —** in turn; **à — de bras** with all one's might; **mon sang n'a fait qu'un —** it gave me an awful shock.

tourangeau, -elle [turãʒo, ɛl] an (inhabitant) of Touraine.

tourbe [turb] nf peat, rabble.

tourbière [turbjɛːr] nf peat-bog.

tourbillon [turbijɔ̃] nm whirlwind, -pool, eddy, whirl, giddy round.

tourbillonner [turbijɔne] vi to whirl, swirl, eddy.

tourelle [turɛl] nf turret.

tourisme [turism] nm touring, travel.

touriste [turist] n tourist, traveler.

tourment [turmã] nm torment, anguish.

tourmente [turmãːt] nf gale, turmoil.

tourmenter [turmãte] vt to torment, torture, worry, pester, tease, fiddle with; vr to worry, fret.

tournant [turnã] nm bend, corner, turning-point.

tournebroche [turnəbrɔʃ] nm roasting spit, turnspit.

tournedos [turnədo] nm filet steak.

tourné [turne] a turned, sour; **bien —** shapely, neat.

tournée [turne] nf circuit, round, tour.

tourner [turne] vt to turn, wind, dodge, get round; vi to turn (out), revolve, result, curdle; vr to turn; **— un film** to make a film, act in a film; **— autour du pot** to beat about the bush.

tournesol [turnəsɔl] nm sunflower.

tournevis [turnəvis] nm screwdriver.

tourniquet [turnikɛ] nm turnstile, tourniquet.

tournoi [turnwa] nm tournament.

tournoyer [turnwaje] vi to whirl, wheel, swirl.

tournure [turnyːr] nf shape, figure, turn, course bustle.

tourte [turt] nf pie, tart.

tourterelle [turtərɛl] nf turtle dove.

Toussaint [tusɛ̃] nf **la —** All Saints' day.

tousser [tuse] vi to cough.

tout [tu] *a* all, whole, every, any; *pr* everything, all, anything; *nm* whole, all, main thing; *ad* very, completely, entirely, quite, right, however, while; **pas du —** not at all; **— à vous yours truly; — au plus** at the very most; **— à fait** quite, entirely; **— fait** ready made.

toutefois [tutfwa] *ad* yet, however, nevertheless.

toutou [tutu] *nm* doggie.

tout-puissant [tupqisã] *a* omnipotent, all-powerful.

toux [tu] *nf* cough.

toxique [tɔksik] *a* toxic, poisonous.

trac [trak] *nm* funk, stage-fright.

tracas [trakɑ] *nm* worry, bother.

tracasser [trakase] *vtr* to bother, worry.

tracasserie [trakasri] *nf* worry, fuss.

tracassier, -ière [trakasje, jɛːr] *a* meddlesome, fussy.

trace [tras] *nf* trace, track, trail, mark.

tracé [trase] *nm* outline, graph, lay-out, tracing, marking out, plotting.

tracer [trase] *vt* to outline, draw, sketch, plot, lay-out, mark out.

tractation [traktasjɔ̃] *nf* underhand deal(ing).

tracteur [traktœːr] *nm* tractor.

traction [traksjɔ̃] *nf* traction, pulling; **— avant** front-wheel drive (car).

tradition [tradisjɔ̃] *nf* tradition.

traditionnel, -elle [tradisjɔnɛl] *a* traditional.

traducteur, -trice [tradyktœːr, tris] *n* translator.

traduction [tradyksjɔ̃] *nf* translation, translating.

traduire [tradɥiːr] *vt* to translate, express; **— en justice** to prosecute.

trafic [trafik] *nm* traffic, trade, trading.

trafiquant [trafikã] *nm* trafficker, black-marketeer.

trafiquer [trafike] *vi* to trade, deal, traffic.

tragédie [traʒedi] *nf* tragedy.

tragique [traʒik] *a* tragic; *nm* tragic element, poet.

trahir [traiːr] *vt* to betray, give away, reveal.

trahison [traizɔ̃] *nf* betrayal, treachery, treason.

train [trɛ̃] *nm* train, line, string, suite, mood, movement, pace; **à fond de —** at full speed; **être en — de** to be busy, engaged in; **être en — —** to be in the mood, in good form; **mener grand —** to live in great style; **mettre en —** to set going.

traînant [trɛnã] *a* dragging, drawling, listless.

traînard [trɛnaːr] *nm* laggard, straggler.

traîne [trɛːn] *nf* drag-net, train (*dress*); **à la —** in tow, behind.

traîneau [trɛno] *nm* sleigh, sled.

traînée [trɛne] *nf* trail, train.

traîner [trɛne] *vt* to drag (out, on), trail, haul, drawl; *vi* to trail, straggle, lag (behind), lie about, drag (on); *vr* to crawl, shuffle along.

train-train [trɛ̃trɛ̃] *nm* routine; **aller son —** to jog along.

traire [trɛːr] *vt* to milk.

trait [trɛ] *nm* dart, shaft, gibe, feature, characteristic, stroke; **— d'union** hyphen; **d'un —** at one gulp, go; **avoir — à** to refer to; **cheval de —** draft horse.

traitable [trɛtabl] *a* tractable, docile.

traite [trɛt] *nf* trade, slave-trade, draft, stage, stretch, milking; **d'une — at** a stretch.

traité [trɛte] *nm* treaty, treatise.

traitement [trɛtmã] *nm* treatment, salary.

traiter [trɛte] *vt* to treat, entertain, discuss, call; *vi* to negotiate; **— de** to deal with, treat for, with.

traiteur [trɛtœːr] *nm* caterer, restaurateur.

traître, -tresse [trɛːtr, trɛtrɛs] *a* treacherous; *n* traitor, traitress.

traîtrise [trɛtriːz] *nf* treachery.

trajectoire [traʒɛktwaːr] *nf* trajectory.

trajet [traʒɛ] *nm* journey, way, passage, course.

trame [tram] *nf* woof, web, plot.

tramer [trame] *vt* to weave.

tramontane [tramɔ̃tan] *nf* north wind, North.

tranchant [trãʃã] *a* sharp, keen, peremptory, contrasting; *nm* edge.

tranche [trãːʃ] *nf* slice, round, slab, edge, series, chisel.

tranchée [trãʃe] *nf* trench.

trancher [trãʃe] *vt* to cut (off, short), slice, settle; *vi* to contrast (with); **— le mot** to speak bluntly.

tranquille [trãkil] *a* calm, quiet, easy; **laisser —** to leave alone.

tranquillisant [trãkilizã] *nm* tranquilizer.

tranquilliser [trãkilize] *vt* to soothe, set at rest; *vr* to set one's mind at rest.

tranquillité [trãkilite] *nf* peace, calm, quiet.

transaction [trãzaksjɔ̃] *nf* transaction, compromise.

transatlantique [trãzatlãtik] *a* transatlantic; *nm* liner, deck-chair.

transborder [trãsbɔrde] *vt* to transship.

transbordeur [trãsbɔrdœːr] *nm* (pont) — transporter-bridge.

transcription [trãskripsjɔ̃] *nf* transcription, copy.

transcrire [trãskriːr] *vt* to transcribe, write out.

transe [trãːs] *nf* trance; *pl* fear.

transférer [trãsfere] *vt* to transfer, remove.

transfert [trãsfeːr] *nm* transfer(ence).

transformateur [trãsfɔrmatœːr, tris] nm transformer.
transformer [trãsfɔrme] vt to transform; vr to change, turn.
transfuge [trãsfyːʒ] nm deserter, turncoat.
transfuser [trãsfyze] vt to transfuse.
transgresser [trãsgrɛse] vt to transgress, break.
transi [trãsi] a frozen, paralyzed.
transiger [trãsiʒe] vi to (come to a) compromise.
transir [trãsiːr] vt to benumb, chill.
transition [trãzisjɔ̃] nf transition.
transitoire [trãzitwaːr] a transitory, temporary.
transmettre [trãsmɛtr] vt to transmit, convey, hand down.
transmission [trãsmisjɔ̃] nf transfer, transmission, handing down; — **directe** live broadcast.
transparaître [trãsparɛːtr] vi to show through.
transparent [trãsparã] a transparent, clear.
transpercer [trãspɛrse] vt to pierce, transfix.
transpirer [trãspire] vi to perspire, transpire.
transplanter [trãsplãte] vt to transplant.
transport [trãspɔːr] nm transport, carriage, rapture.
transporter [trãspɔrte] vt to transport, convey, assign, enrapture.
transporteur [trãspɔrtœːr] nm carrier, conveyer.
transposer [trãspoze] vt to transpose.
transversal [trãsvɛrsal] a transversal, cross-, side-.
trapèze [trapɛːz] nm trapezium, trapeze.
trappe [trap] nf trap(door).
trapu [trapy] a squat, stocky, thickset.
traquenard [traknaːr] nm trap, pitfall.
traquer [trake] vt to track down, run to earth, hunt, beat.
travail [travaːj] nm (piece of) work, labor, craftsmanship; **travaux forcés** hard labor.
travaillé [travaje] a wrought, elaborate.
travailler [travaje] vt to work (at, upon), obsess, torment; vi to work, toil.
travailleur, -euse [travajœːr, øːz] a hard-working; n worker.
travailliste [travajist] a Labour (Party); nm member of the Labour Party.
travée [trave] nf girder, bay, span.
travers [travɛːr] nm breadth, fault, failing; **à —, au — de** across, through; **en —** across, crosswise; **par le —** amidships; **de —** awry, askance.
traverse [travɛrs] nf cross-beam, -bar, rung, sleeper; **chemin de —** crossroad, side-road.
traversée [travɛrse] nf crossing.
traverser [travɛrse] vt to cross, go through; thwart.
traversin [travɛrsɛ̃] nm crossbar, bolster.
travestir [travɛstiːr] vt to disguise, misrepresent; **bal travesti** fancy-dress ball.
travestissement [travɛstismã] nm disguise, disguising, travesty.
trébucher [trebyʃe] vi to stumble, trip.
trèfle [trɛfl] nm clover, trefoil, clubs.
treillage [trɛjaːʒ] nm trellis, lattice-work.
treille [trɛːj] nf climbing vine, vine-arbor.
treillis [trɛji] nm lattice, trellis, dungarees; — **métallique** wire-netting, -screening.
treize [trɛːz] a nm thirteen, thirteenth.
treizième [trɛzjɛm] an thirteenth.
tréma [trema] nm diaeresis.
tremble [trãːbl] nm aspen.
tremblement [trãbləmã] n trembling, tremor, quivering, quavering; — **de terre** earthquake.
trembler [trãble] vi to tremble, shake, quiver, quaver.
trembloter [trãblɔte] vi to quiver, quaver, flicker.
trémière [tremjɛːr] a **rose —** hollyhock.
trémousser [tremuse] vir to flutter; vr to fidget; go to a lot of trouble.
trempe [trãːp] nf steeping, temper (ing), stamp.
tremper [trãpe] vt to steep, soak, drench, temper; vi to steep, have a hand (in).
trempette [trãpɛt] nf bread etc, dipped in coffee etc; quick bath.
tremplin [trãplɛ̃] nm spring-, diving-board.
trentaine [trãtɛn] nf about thirty.
trente [trãːt] a nm thirty, thirtieth.
trente-six [trãtsi, -sis, -siz] a nm thirty-six; **ne pas y aller par — chemins** not to beat about the bush; **voir — chandelles** to see stars.
trentième [trãtjɛm] an thirtieth.
trépaner [trepane] vt to drill, bore, trepan.
trépas [trepa] nm death.
trépasser [trepase] vi to die, pass away.
trépidation [trepidasjɔ̃] nf shaking, vibration, trepidation.
trépied [trepje] nm tripod.
trépigner [trepiɲe] vi to stamp, dance.
très [trɛ] ad very, (very) much, most.
trésor [trezɔːr] nm treasure, riches, treasury.
trésorerie [trezɔrri] nf treasury, treasurer's office.

trésorier, -ière [trezɔrje, jɛːr] n treasurer, paymaster, -mistress.

tressaillement [tresajmɑ̃] nm start, thrill.

tressaillir [tresajiːr] vi to start, shudder, bound, thrill.

tressauter [tresote] vi to start, jump.

tresse [tres] nf plait, tress.

tresser [trese] vt to plait, braid, weave.

tréteau [treto] nm trestle, stand; pl boards, stage.

treuil [trœːj] nm windlass, winch.

trêve [trɛːv] nf truce, respite; — de no more of.

tri [tri] nm sorting.

triage [triaːʒ] nm sorting; **gare de —** marshalling yard.

triangle [triɑ̃ːgl] nm triangle, set-square.

tribord [tribɔːr] nm starboard.

tribu [triby] nf tribe.

tribulation [tribylasjɔ̃] nf tribulation, trouble.

tribunal [tribynal] nm tribunal, (law) court, bench.

tribune [tribyn] nf tribune, platform, grandstand.

tribut [triby] nm tribute.

tricher [triʃe] vti to cheat, trick.

tricherie [triʃri] nf cheating, trickery.

tricheur, -euse [triʃœːr, øːz] n cheat, trickster.

tricolore [trikɔlɔːr] a tricolored.

tricorne [trikɔrn] a nm three-cornered (hat).

tricot [triko] nm knitting, cardigan, jumper, jersey.

tricoter [trikɔte] vt to knit.

triennal [triɛnnal] a triennial.

trier [trie] vt to sort (out), pick out.

trigonométrie [trigɔnɔmetri] nf trigonometry.

trimbaler [trɛ̃bale] vt to lug, trail, drag about.

trimer [trime] vi to toil, drudge.

trimestre [trimɛstr] nm quarter, term.

trimestriel, -elle [trimɛstriɛl] a quarterly.

tringle [trɛ̃ːgl] nf (curtain-) rod, bar.

trinquer [trɛ̃ke] vi to clink glasses, toast.

triomphal [triɔ̃fal] a triumphal.

triomphe [triɔ̃ːf] nm triumph.

triompher [triɔ̃fe] vi to triumph (over de), surmount.

tripatouiller [tripatuje] vt to tinker, tamper with.

tripes [trip] nf pl tripe, intestines, guts.

triple [tripl] a nm treble, triple, threefold.

tripler [triple] vt to treble.

tripot [tripo] nm gambling house.

tripotage [tripɔtaːʒ] nm fiddling about, jobbery.

tripoter [tripɔte] vt to fiddle with, tamper with, finger, paw; vi to

potter, fiddle, mess about, dabble.

trique [trik] nf cudgel.

triste [trist] a sad, mournful, dismal, bleak, wretched.

tristesse [tristɛs] nf sadness, gloom, sorrow, mournfulness.

triturer [trityre] vt to grind.

trivial [trivjal] a vulgar, commonplace, trite.

trivialité [trivjalite] nf vulgarity, coarse word, triteness.

troc [trɔk] nm barter, exchange, swap(ping).

troène [trɔɛn] nm privet.

troglodyte [trɔglɔdit] nm cave-dweller.

trogne [trɔɲ] nf face, dial.

trognon [trɔɲɔ̃] nm core, stump.

trois [trwa] a three, third.

troisième [trwazjɛm] an third.

trombe [trɔ̃ːb] nf water-spout, cloudburst, whirlwind.

trombone [trɔ̃bɔn] nm trombone, paper-clip.

trompe [trɔ̃ːp] nf trumpet, horn, (elephant) trunk.

trompe-l'œil [trɔ̃plœːj] nm sham, eyewash, window-dressing (fig).

tromper [trɔ̃pe] vt to deceive, cheat, beguile; vr to be mistaken, be wrong.

tromperie [trɔ̃pri] nf (piece of) deceit, fraud.

trompette [trɔ̃pet] nf trumpet, trumpeter.

trompeur, -euse [trɔ̃pœːr, øːz] a deceitful, deceptive, misleading; n deceiver, cheat.

tronc [trɔ̃] nm trunk, bole, collection-box.

tronçon [trɔ̃sɔ̃] nm stump, fragment, section.

tronçonner [trɔ̃sɔne] vt to cut into pieces.

trône [troːn] nm throne.

trôner [trone] vi to sit enthroned, lord it, queen it.

tronquer [trɔ̃ke] vt to truncate, mutilate.

trop [tro] ad too, too much, over-; **de —** too much, too many, unwanted.

trophée [trɔfe] nm trophy.

tropical [trɔpikal] a tropical.

tropiques [trɔpik] nm pl tropics.

trop-plein [trɔplɛ̃] nm overflow, excess.

troquer [trɔke] vt to barter, exchange, swap.

trot [tro] nm trot.

trotte [trɔt] nf stretch, bit, distance, walk.

trotter [trɔte] vi to trot, scamper.

trotteuse [trɔtøːz] nf go-cart.

trottiner [trɔtine] vi to scamper, toddle, jog along.

trottinette [trɔtinet] nf scooter.

trottoir [trɔtwaːr] nm pavement, footpath, platform.

trou [tru] nm hole, gap, dead-and-alive place; — **d'air** air-pocket; — **du souffleur** prompter's box.

trouble [trubl] *a* muddy, dim, cloudy; *nm* confusion, uneasiness; *pl* disturbances.

trouble-fête [trubləfɛːt] *nm* spoil-sport, killjoy.

troubler [truble] *vt* to disturb, upset, excite, blur, make muddy; *vr* to get upset, become excited, muddy, dim.

trouée [true] *nf* gap.

trouer [true] *vt* to hole, make holes in.

troupe [trup] *nf* troop, gang, company, flock, herd, other ranks; *pl* troops.

troupeau [trupo] *nm* flock, herd, drove.

troupier [trupje] *nm* soldier, seasoned campaigner.

trousse [trus] *nf* outfit, kit, bundle, truss; **à mes —s** after me, at my heels.

trousseau [truso] *nm* bunch, outfit, trousseau.

trousser [truse] *vt* to turn up, tuck up, truss.

trouvaille [truvaːj] *nf* find, windfall, godsend.

trouver [truve] *vt* to find, hit upon, think; *vr* to be, be found, happen, feel.

truc [tryk] *nm* knack, dodge, gadget, thingummy.

truchement [tryʃmã] *nm* inter-mediary, interpreter.

truculence [trykylãːs] *nf* truculence.

truelle [tryɛl] *nf* trowel, fish-slice.

truffe [tryf] *nf* truffle, dog's nose.

truie [trɥi] *nf* sow.

truite [trɥit] *nf* trout.

trumeau [trymo] *nm (archit)* pier; pier-glass; leg of beef.

truquer [tryke] *vt* to fake, cook, rig.

tsé-tsé [tsetse] *nf* tsetse fly.

T.S.F. *nf* radio.

tu [ty] *pn* you, thou.

tube [tyb] *nm* tube, pipe; *(song)* hit.

tuberculeux, -euse [tybɛrkylø, øːz] *a* tubercular, tuberculous, con-sumptive.

tuberculose [tybɛrkyloːz] *nf* tuber-culosis.

tuer [tɥe] *vt* to kill, slay.

tuerie [tyri] *nf* slaughter, carnage.

tue-tête [tytɛt] *ad* **à —** at the top of one's voice.

tueur [tɥœːr] *nm* killer, slaughter-man.

tuile [tɥil] *nf* tile, bit of bad luck.

tulipe [tylip] *nf* tulip.

tulle [tyl] *nm* tulle.

tuméfier [tymefje] *vt* to make swell.

tumulte [tymylt] *nm* tumult, up-roar.

tumultueux, -euse [tymyltɥø, øːz] *a* tumultuous, noisy.

tunique [tynik] *nf* tunic.

tunnel [tynɛl] *nm* tunnel.

turbine [tyrbin] *nf* turbine.

turbulence [tyrbylãːs] *nf* turbulence, boisterousness.

turbulent [tyrbylã] *a* turbulent, unruly.

turc, turque [tyrk] *a* Turkish; *n* Turk.

turf [tyrf] *nm* racing, racetrack.

turfiste [tyrfist] *nm* racegoer.

turpitude [tyrpityd] *nf* turpitude, baseness, base act.

Turquie [tyrki] *nf* Turkey.

turquoise [tyrkwaːz] *a nm* turquoise (color); *nf* turquoise.

tutelle [tytɛl] *nf* guardianship, pro-tection.

tuteur, -trice [tytœːr, tris] *n* guardian; *nm* stake, trainer.

tutoyer [tytwaje] *vt* to address as 'tu', be familiar with.

tuyau [tɥijo] *nm* tube, (hose-) pipe, stem, goffer, tip, hint.

tuyauter [tɥijote, tɥijote] *vt* to goffer, frill, give a tip, hint to.

tympan [tɛ̃pã] *nm* eardrum, tym-panum.

type [tip] *nm* type, fellow.

typhoïde [tifɔid] *a* typhoid.

typique [tipik] *a* typical.

typo(graphe) [tipɔgraf] *nm* printer, typographer.

typographie [tipɔgrafi] *nf* printing.

tyran [tirã] *nm* tyrant.

tyrannie [tirani] *nf* tyranny.

tyrannique [tiranik] *a* tyrannical, tyrannous.

tyranniser [tiranize] *vt* to tyrannize, oppress.

tzigane [tsigan] *n* gipsy.

U

ubiquité [ybikɥite] *nf* ubiquity.

ulcère [ylsɛːr] *nm* ulcer, sore.

ulcérer [ylsere] *vt* to ulcerate, hurt, embitter; *vr* to fester, grow em-bittered.

ultérieur [ylterjœːr] *a* ulterior, subsequent, further.

ultimatum [yltimatɔm] *nm* ultimat-um.

ultime [yltim] *a* ultimate, last, final.

un, une [œ̃, yn] *indef art* a; *a* one; *nm* one; *nf* first page; **— à —** one by one; **en savoir plus d'une** to know a thing or two.

unanime [ynanim] *a* unanimous.

unanimité [ynanimite] *nf* unanim-ity; **à l'—** unanimously.

uni [yni] *a* united, smooth, self-colored, plain.

unième [ynjɛm] *a (in compound numbers only)* first.

unification [ynifikasjɔ̃] *nf* unifica-tion, amalgamation.

unifier [ynifje] *vt* to unify, amalgam-ate.

uniforme [ynifɔrm] *a nm* uniform.

uniformiser [yniformize] *vt* to make uniform, standardize.
uniformité [yniformite] *nf* uniformity.
unilatéral [ynilateral] *a* unilateral, one-sided.
union [ynjɔ̃] *nf* union, unity, association.
uniprix [ynipri] *a* **magasin —** dime store.
unique [ynik] *a* single, only, sole, one, unique; **rue à sens —** one-way street.
unir [yn:ir] *vt* to unite, join, make, smooth; *vr* to unite, join, become smooth.
unisson [ynisɔ̃] *nm* unison.
unité [ynite] *nf* unity, consistency, unit.
univers [ynivε:r] *nm* universe.
universalité [yniversalite] *nf* universality.
universel, -elle [yniversel] *a* universal, world-wide, versatile.
universitaire [yniversite:r] *a* university; *n* university teacher.
université [yniversite] *nf* university.
uranium [yranjɔm] *nm* uranium.
urbain [yrbɛ̃] *a* urban, town; *n* city-dweller.
urbanisme [yrbanism] *nm* town-planning.
urbanité [yrbanite] *nf* urbanity.
urgence [yrʒɑ̃:s] *nf* urgency, emergency; **d'—** urgently, emergency.
urgent [yrʒɑ̃] *a* urgent, pressing.
urine [yrin] *nf* urine.
uriner [yrine] *vi* to urinate, make water.
urinoir [yrinwa:r] *nm* urinal.
urne [yrn] *nf* urn.
URSS *nf* USSR.
urticaire [yrtikε:r] *nf* nettle-rash.
us [y] *nm pl* **les — et coutumes** ways and customs.
usage [yza:ʒ] *nm* use, using, service, wear, practice, custom, breeding; **d'—** usual, for everyday use.
usagé [yzaʒe] *a* used, worn.
usager, -ère [yzaʒe, ε:r] *a* for personal use, of everyday use; *n* user.
usé [yze] *a* worn (out, away), threadbare, shabby, stale.
user [yze] *vt* to wear out (away); **— de** to use; *vr* to wear out (away, down); **en bien (mal) — avec qn** to treat s.o. well (badly).
usine [yzin] *nf* factory, mill, works.
usiner [yzine] *vt* to machine(-finish).
usité [yzite] *a* used, current.
ustensile [ystɑ̃sil] *nm* utensil, tool.
usuel, -elle [yzɥel] *a* usual, customary; **nm** reference book.
usufruit [yzyfrɥi] *nm* life interest, usufruct.
usure [yzy:r] *nf* wear (and tear), wearing away, attrition, usury, interest.

usurier, -ière [yzyrje, jε:r] *a* usurious; *n* usurer.
usurpateur, -trice [yzyrpatœ:r, tris] *a* usurping; *n* usurper.
usurper [yzyrpe] *vti* to usurp.
ut [yt] *nm* musical note C, do.
utile [ytil] *a* useful, handy, serviceable, effective, due.
utilisation [ytilizasjɔ̃] *nf* utilization, using.
utiliser [ytilize] *vt* to utilize, use.
utilitaire [ytilite:r] *an* utilitarian.
utilité [ytilite] *nf* utility, use(fulness), service.
utopie [ytɔpi] *nf* utopia.
utopique [ytɔpik] *a* utopian.
utopiste [ytɔpist] *an* utopian.
uvule [yvyl] *nf* uvula.

V

vacance [vakɑ̃:s] *nf* vacancy; *pl* holidays, vacation; **en —s** on vacation; **grandes —s** summer vacation.
vacant [vakɑ̃] *a* vacant.
vacarme [vakarm] *nm* din, uproar, hullabaloo.
vaccin [vaksɛ̃] *nm* vaccine, lymph.
vaccination [vaksinasjɔ̃] *nf* vaccination, inoculation.
vacciner [vaksine] *vt* to vaccinate, inoculate.
vache [vaʃ] *nf* cow, cowhide, nasty person, beast; **manger de la — enragée** to have a hard time of it; **parler français comme une — espagnole** to murder the French language.
vachement [vaʃmɑ̃] *ad* damn(ed), terribly.
vacher, -ère [vaʃe, ε:r] *n* cowherd.
vacherie [vaʃri] *nf* cowshed, dirty trick.
vacillant [vasillɑ̃, -ijɑ̃] *a* wavering, flickering, unsteady, wobbling, uncertain.
vaciller [vasille, -ije] *vi* to waver, flicker, stagger, wobble.
va-comme-je-te-pousse [vakɔm-ʒətpus] *a* easy-going; *ad* any old way.
vacuité [vakɥite] *nf* emptiness.
vacuum [vakɥɔm] *nm* vacuum.
vadrouille [vadru:j] *nf* spree, swab, mop.
vadrouiller [vadruje] *vi* to rove, roam, gallivant.
vadrouilleur, -euse [vadrujœ:r, ø:z] *n* gadabout, rake.
va-et-vient [vaevjɛ̃] *nm* coming and going, movement to and fro.
vagabond [vagabɔ̃] *a* vagabond, roving, wandering; *n* vagrant, vagabond, tramp.
vagabondage [vagabɔ̃da:ʒ] *nm* vagabondage, vagrancy.
vagabonder [vagabɔ̃de] *vi* to wander, roam, rove.

vagin [vaʒɛ̃] nm vagina.

vagir [vaʒiːr] vi to wail.

vague [vag] a vague, hazy, indefinite, empty; nm vagueness, space; nf wave; **terrains —s** vacant land.

vaguemestre [vagmɛstr] nm postman, mail clerk.

váguer [vage] vi to roam, ramble, wander.

vaillance [vajɑ̃ːs] nf valor, bravery.

vaillant [vajɑ̃] a valiant, gallant, brave, stout; **n'avoir pas un sou —** not to have a cent.

vain [vɛ̃] a vain, useless, empty, futile.

vaincre [vɛ̃ːkr] vt to vanquish, defeat, conquer.

vainqueur [vɛ̃kœːr] a inv victorious, conquering; nm victor, conqueror, winner.

vairon [vɛrɔ̃] nm minnow.

vaisseau [vɛso] nm vessel, ship, receptacle.

vaisselier [vɛsəlje] nm dresser.

vaisselle [vɛsɛl] nf plates and dishes, table-service; **faire la —** to wash up.

val [val] nm valley, vale; **par monts et par vaux** up hill and down dale.

valable [valabl] a valid, available, good.

valet [valɛ] nm valet, footman, knave, jack, servant, farm-hand.

valeur [valœːr] nf value, worth, valor, merit, asset; pl securities, bills; **objets de —** valuables; **mettre en —** to bring out, emphasize, develop; **—s actives** assets; **—s passives** liabilities.

valeureux, -euse [valœrø, øːz] a valorous, gallant.

valide [valid] a valid, able-bodied, fit.

valider [valide] vt to ratify, validate.

validité [validite] nf validity.

valise [valiːz] nf suitcase, bag, valise.

vallée [vale] nf valley.

vallon [valɔ̃] nm (small) valley, vale, dale.

vallonné [valɔne] a undulating.

valoir [valwaːr] vti to be worth, be as good (bad) as, deserve, be equivalent to, win, bring (in); **faire —** to assert, make the most of, develop, show off; **se faire —** to show off, push o.s. forward; **cela vaut la peine d'être vu** it is worth seeing; **cela vaut le coup** it is worth while; **il vaut mieux le vendre** it is better to sell it; **ne pas — grand'chose** not to be up to much; **vaille que vaille** at all costs.

valorisation [valɔrizasjɔ̃] nf valorization, stabilization.

valoriser [valɔrize] vt to valorize, stabilize.

valse [vals] nf waltz.

valser [valse] vi to waltz.

valve [valv] nf valve.

vampire [vɑ̃piːr] nm vampire.

vandale [vɑ̃dal] nm vandal.

vandalisme [vɑ̃dalism] nm vandalism.

vanille [vaniːj] nf vanilla.

vanité [vanite] nf vanity, conceit, futility; **tirer — de** to take pride in.

vaniteux, -euse [vanitø, øːz] a vain, conceited.

vanne [van] nf sluice-gate, floodgate.

vanneau [vano] nm lapwing, plover, peewit.

vanner [vane] vt to winnow, sift, tire out.

vannerie [vanri] nf basket-making, basket-, wicker-work.

vanneuse [vanøːz] nf winnowing-machine.

vannier [vanje] nm basket-maker.

vantail [vɑ̃taːj] nm leaf (of door etc).

vantard [vɑ̃taːr] a boastful, bragging; n boaster, braggart.

vantardise [vɑ̃tardiːz] nf boast(fulness), bragging.

vanter [vɑ̃te] vt to praise, extol; vr to brag, boast, pride o.s.

vanterie [vɑ̃tri] nf boast(ing), brag(ging).

va-nu-pieds [vanypje] n barefoot beggar, ragamuffin.

vapeur [vapœːr] nm steamer, steamship; nf steam, vapor, haze, dizziness; **à toute —** full steam (ahead).

vaporeux, -euse [vapɔrø, øːz] a vaporous, steamy, hazy.

vaporisateur [vapɔrizatœːr] nm atomizer, (scent-)spray, evaporator.

vaporisation [vapɔrizasjɔ̃] nf evaporation, atomization, vaporization.

vaporiser [vapɔrize] vt to atomize, vaporize, volatilize, spray; vr to vaporize, spray oneself.

vaquer [vake] vi to be vacant, (jur) not to be sitting; **— à** to attend to, look after.

varech [varɛk] nm seaweed, wrack, kelp.

vareuse [varøːz] nf (sailor's) jersey, pea-jacket, short tunic.

variable [varjabl] a variable, changeable, unsettled.

variante [varjɑ̃ːt] nf variant.

variation [varjasjɔ̃] nf variation, change.

varice [varis] nf varicose vein.

varicelle [varisɛl] nf chicken-pox.

varié [varje] a varied, miscellaneous, variegated.

varier [varje] vt to vary, change; vi to vary, differ, fluctuate.

variété [varjete] nf variety, diversity.

variole [varjɔl] nf smallpox.

vase [vaːz] nm vase, receptacle; **— de nuit** chamber-pot; **en — clos** in isolation; nf mud, slime.

vaseline [vazlin] nf vaseline.

vaseux, -euse [vazø, øːz] a muddy, slimy, off-color, woolly.

vasistas [vazistɑːs] nm transom.

vassal [vasal] an vassal.

vaste [vast] a vast, wide, spacious.

vau [vo] ad à — l'eau downstream, to rack and ruin, to the dogs.

vaurien, -enne [vorjɛ̃, jɛn] n good-for-nothing, waster, black-guard, scamp.

vautour [votuːr] nm vulture.

vautrer [votre] vr to wallow, sprawl.

veau [vo] nm calf, veal, calf-skin.

vécu [veky] a true to life, realistic.

vedette [vədɛt] nf mounted sentry, motor launch, small steamer, scout, star; être en — to be in the lime-light, in large type; être mis en — sur l'affiche to top the bill.

végétal [veʒetal] a vegetable, plant-; nm plant.

végétarien, -enne [veʒetarjɛ̃, jɛn] an vegetarian.

végétarisme [veʒetarism] nm vegetarianism.

végétation [veʒetasjɔ̃] nf vegetation; pl adenoids.

végéter [veʒete] vi to vegetate.

véhémence [veemɑ̃ːs] nf vehemence.

véhément [veemɑ̃] a vehement, violent.

véhicule [veikyl] nm vehicle.

veille [vɛːj] nf vigil, wakefulness, watch(ing), late night, sitting up, eve, day before; à la — de on the brink of.

veillée [veje] nf social evening, vigil, wake, night-nursing.

veiller [veje] vt to sit up with, look after; vi to watch, be on the look-out, keep awake, sit up; — à to see to, look after.

veilleur, -euse [vejœːr, øːz] n watcher, keeper of a vigil; — de nuit night-watchman.

veilleuse [vejøːz] nf night-light, pilot-light; mettre en — to dim, turn down.

veinard [venaːr] an lucky (fellow).

veine [vɛn] nf vein, mood, luck; coup de — stroke of luck, fluke.

veineux, -euse [vɛnø, øːz] a venous, veined.

vêler [vele] vi to calve.

vélin [velɛ̃] nm vellum.

velléité [velleite] nf inclination, slight desire.

vélo [velo] nm bike, cycle; faire du — to go in for cycling.

vélocité [velosite] nf velocity, speed.

vélodrome [velodroːm] nm cycle-racing track.

velours [v(ə)luːr] nm velvet; — de coton velveteen.

velouté [v(ə)lute] a velvety, smooth, soft; nm velvetiness, bloom, soft-ness.

velu [vəly] a hairy.

venaison [vɛnɛzɔ̃] nf venison, game.

vénal [venal] a venal, corrupt(ible).

vénalité [venalite] nf venality.

venant [vənɑ̃] a thriving; nm à tout

— to all comers, to anyone at all.

vendable [vɑ̃dabl] a salable, marketable.

vendange [vɑ̃dɑ̃ːʒ] nf grape-gather-ing, wine harvest, vintage.

vendanger [vɑ̃dɑ̃ʒe] vti to gather in the grapes.

vendangeur, -euse [vɑ̃dɑ̃ʒœːr, øːz] n vintager, grape-gatherer.

vendeur, -euse [vɑ̃dœːr, øːz] n seller, salesman, -woman, sales-clerk, vendor.

vendredi [vɑ̃drədi] nm Friday; le — saint Good Friday.

vendre [vɑ̃dr] vt to sell, betray.

vendu [vɑ̃dy] nm traitor.

vénéneux, -euse [venenø, øːz] a poisonous.

vénérable [venerabl] a venerable.

vénération [venerasjɔ̃] nf veneration, reverence.

vénérer [venere] vt to venerate, revere, worship.

vénérien, -ienne [venerjɛ̃, jɛn] a venereal.

vengeance [vɑ̃ʒɑ̃ːs] nf vengeance, revenge, retribution; tirer — de to be avenged on.

venger [vɑ̃ʒe] vt to avenge; vr to revenge oneself, take vengeance.

vengeur, -eresse [vɑ̃ʒœːr, ərɛs] a avenging; n avenger.

véniel, -elle [venjɛl] a venial.

venimeux, -euse [vənimø, øːz] a venomous, poisonous, spiteful.

venin [vənɛ̃] nm venom, poison, spite.

venir [v(ə)niːr] vi to come, reach, grow, be the result (of de); — à apparaître to happen, chance to appear; — de sortir to have just gone out; faire — send for; — chercher to come for; en — à to come to the point of, be reduced to; l'idée me vient que it occurs to me that.

vent [vɑ̃] nm wind, blast, flatulence, vent, scent; coup de — gust of wind; il fait du — it is windy; avoir — de to get wind of; mettre au — to hang out to air.

vente [vɑ̃ːt] nf sale, selling; en — on sale; — de charité charity bazaar.

venter [vɑ̃te] vi to be windy, blow.

venteux, -euse [vɑ̃tø, øːz] a windy, windswept.

ventilateur [vɑ̃tilatœːr] nm ventilat-or, fan.

ventiler [vɑ̃tile] vt to ventilate.

ventouse [vɑ̃tuːz] nf cupping-glass, sucker, vent-hole.

ventre [vɑ̃tr] nm abdomen, belly, stomach, paunch, bulge; prendre du — to grow stout; n'avoir rien dans le — to be starving, have no guts; se mettre à plat — to lie flat, grovel.

ventriloque [vɑ̃trilɔk] a ventrilo-quous; nm ventriloquist.

ventru [vɑ̃try] a stout, portly, pot-bellied.

venu [vəny] n comer.

venue [vəny] nf coming, arrival, advent, growth.

vêpres [vɛːpr] nf pl vespers, evensong.

ver [vɛːr] nm worm, maggot; — luisant glow-worm; — solitaire tapeworm; — à soie silkworm; tirer les —s du nez de qn to worm it out of s.o.

véracité [vɛrasite] nf veracity, truth (fulness).

véranda [vɛrɑ̃da] nf veranda.

verbal [vɛrbal] a verbal.

verbaliser [vɛrbalize] vi to make out an official report.

verbe [vɛrb] nm verb, word; avoir le — haut to be loud-mouthed.

verbeux, -euse [vɛrbø, øːz] a verbose, long-winded.

verbiage [vɛrbjaːʒ] nm verbiage.

verbosité [vɛrbozite] nf verbosity, long-windedness.

verdâtre [vɛrdɑːtr] a greenish.

verdeur [vɛrdœːr] nf greenness, tartness, vigor.

verdict [vɛrdikt] nm verdict, finding.

verdier [vɛrdje] nm greenfinch.

verdir [vɛrdiːr] vt to paint or make green; vi to turn green, become covered with verdigris.

verdoyant [vɛrdwajɑ̃] a green, verdant.

verdure [vɛrdyːr] nf verdure, greenery, greenness, greens.

véreux, -euse [vɛrø, øːz] a wormeaten, maggoty, shady.

verge [vɛrʒ] nf rod, switch, wand.

verger [vɛrʒe] nm orchard.

verglas [vɛrgla] nm ice, black ice.

vergogne [vɛrgɔɲ] nf shame; sans — shameless.

vergue [vɛrg] nf yard.

véridicité [veridisite] nf truth(fulness).

véridique [veridik] a veracious, truthful.

vérificateur [verifikatœːr] nm inspector, examiner, gauge, auditor.

vérification [verifikasjɔ̃] nf inspection, verification, overhauling, checking, auditing.

vérifier [verifje] vt to inspect, verify, check, overhaul, audit.

véritable [veritabl] a real, true, genuine, downright.

vérité [verite] nf truth(fulness), sincerity, fact.

vermeil, -eille [vɛrmɛːj] a vermilion, bright red, ruby; nm silver-gilt.

vermicelle [vɛrmisɛl] nm vermicelli.

vermillon [vɛrmijɔ̃] nm vermilion, bright red.

vermine [vɛrmin] nf vermin.

vermoulu [vɛrmuly] a wormeaten, decrepit.

verni [vɛrni] a varnished, patent (leather), lucky.

vernir [vɛrniːr] vt to varnish, glaze, polish, japan.

vernis [vɛrni] nm varnish, glaze, polish, gloss.

vernissage [vɛrnisaːʒ] nm varnishing, glazing, polishing, preview.

vernisseur, -euse [vɛrnisœːr] n varnisher, glazer, japanner.

vérole [verɔl] nf pox; petite — smallpox.

verrat [vɛra] nm boar.

verre [vɛːr] nm glass; — de lunettes lens; papier de — sandpaper; tempête dans un — d'eau tempest in a teapot.

verrerie [vɛr(ə)ri] nf glassmaking, glassware, glass-factory.

verrier [vɛrje] nm glassmaker, -blower.

verrière [vɛrjɛːr] nf glass casing, stained glass window.

verroterie [vɛrɔtri] nf small glassware, beads.

verrou [vɛru] nm bolt, bar, breechbolt; pousser (tirer) le — to bolt (unbolt) the door; sous les —s under lock and key.

verrouiller [vɛruje] vt to bolt, lock up.

verrue [vɛry] nf wart.

vers [vɛːr] nm line; pl poetry, verse; prep toward, to, about.

versant [vɛrsɑ̃] nm slope, side.

versatile [vɛrsatil] a changeable, unstable, fickle.

versatilité [vɛrsatilite] nf instability, fickleness.

verse [vɛrs] ad à — in torrents.

versé [vɛrse] a versed, conversant, well up.

versement [vɛrs(ə)mɑ̃] nm pouring (out), payment, installment, deposit; bulletin de — deposit slip.

verser [vɛrse] vt to pour (out), shed, deposit, assign, lay, overturn; vi to be laid flat, overturn; — à boire to pour out a drink.

verset [vɛrsɛ] nm verse.

versification [vɛrsifikasjɔ̃] nf versification.

versifier [vɛrsifje] vt to put into verse; vi to write poetry.

version [vɛrsjɔ̃] nf version, account, translation.

verso [vɛrso] nm back, verso; voir au — see overleaf.

vert [vɛːr] a green, unripe, spicy, sharp, vigorous, hale; nm green.

vert-de-gris [vɛrdəgri] nm verdigris.

vertébral [vɛrtebral] a vertebral; colonne —e spine.

vertèbre [vɛrtɛːbr] nf vertebra.

vertement [vɛrtəmɑ̃] ad sharply, severely.

vertical [vɛrtikal] a vertical, perpendicular, upright.

verticale [vɛrtikal] nf vertical.

vertige [vɛrtiːʒ] nm giddiness, dizziness, vertigo; avoir le — to be giddy.

vertigineux, -euse [vɛrtiʒinø, øːz] a giddy, dizzy.

vertu [verty] *nf* virtue chastity, property, quality; **en — de** by virtue of.

vertueux, -euse [vertɥø, øːz] *a* virtuous, chaste.

verve [verv] *nf* verve, zest, go, vigor, high spirits; **être en —** to be in fine fettle.

verveine [verven] *nf* verbena, vervain.

vesce [ves] *nf* vetch, tare.

vésicatoire [vezikatwaːr] *a nm* vesicatory.

vésicule [vezikyl] *nf* vesicle, blister, air-cell; **— biliaire** gall-bladder.

vespasienne [vespazjen] *nf* street urinal.

vespéral [vesperal] *a* evening.

vessie [vesi] *nf* bladder; **prendre des —s pour des lanternes** to think the moon is made of green cheese.

veste [vest] *nf* jacket.

vestiaire [vestjeːr] *nm* cloakroom, changing-room, robing-room.

vestibule [vestibyl] *nm* (entrance-) hall, lobby, vestibule.

vestige [vestiːʒ] *nm* trace, mark, vestige.

vestimentaire [vestimɑ̃teːr] *a* vestimentary.

veston [vestɔ̃] *nm* jacket.

vêtement [vetmɑ̃] *nm* garment; *pl* clothing, clothes; **—s de dessous** underwear.

vétéran [veterɑ̃] *nm* veteran.

vétérinaire [veterineːr] *a* veterinary; *nm* veterinarian.

vétille [vetiːj] *nf* trifle.

vétilleux, -euse [vetijø, øːz] *a* captious, finicky.

vêtir [vetiːr] *vt* to dress, clothe; *vr* to dress oneself.

veto [veto] *nm* veto; **mettre son — à** to veto.

vétusté [vetyste] *nf* decrepitude, old age.

veuf, veuve [vœf, vœːv] *a* widowed; *n* widower, widow.

veule [vœl] *a* weak, soft, flabby, inert, drab.

veulerie [vœlri] *nf* weakness, flabbiness, drabness.

veuvage [vœvaːʒ] *nm* widow(er)-hood.

vexation [veksasjɔ̃] *nf* vexation, annoying word or deed.

vexatoire [veksatwaːr] *a* vexatious.

vexer [vekse] *vt* to vex, annoy, pester, upset, irritate; *vr* to get annoyed.

viable [viabl, vjabl] *a* strong enough to live, viable, fit for traffic.

viaduc [vjadyk] *nm* viaduct.

viager, -ère [vjaʒe, ɛ:r] *a* for life; *nm* life interest; **rente viagère** life annuity.

viande [vjɑ̃ːd] *nf* meat, flesh.

viatique [vjatik] *nm* viaticum.

vibrant [vibrɑ̃] *a* vibrant, ringing, rousing, vibrating.

vibration [vibrasjɔ̃] *nf* vibration, resonance.

vibratoire [vibratwaːr] *a* vibratory, oscillatory.

vibrer [vibre] *vi* to vibrate, throb; **faire —** to thrill, rouse.

vicaire [vikeːr] *nm* curate.

vice [vis] *nm* vice, flaw, defect.

vice-consul [viskɔ̃syl] *nm* vice-consul.

vice-roi [visrwa] *nm* viceroy.

vicier [visje] *vt* to vitiate, contaminate, corrupt, taint; *vr* to become corrupted, tainted, foul, spoiled.

vicieux, -euse [visjø, øːz] *a* vicious, depraved, bad-tempered, faulty.

vicinal [visinal] *a* **route —e** back road, by-road.

vicissitude [visisityd] *nf* vicissitude; *pl* ups and downs.

vicomte [vikɔ̃ːt] *nm* viscount.

vicomtesse [vikɔ̃tes] *nf* viscountess.

victime [viktim] *nf* victim, sacrifice.

victoire [viktwaːr] *nf* victory.

victorieux, -euse [viktɔrjø, øːz] *a* victorious.

victuailles [viktɥaːj] *nf pl* victuals, eatables.

vidange [vidɑ̃ːʒ] *nf* emptying, draining, clearing; *nf pl* night-soil.

vidanger [vidɑ̃ʒe] *vt* to empty, drain.

vidangeur [vidɑ̃ʒœːr] *nm* scavenger, cesspool clearer.

vide [vid] *a* empty, unoccupied, blank; *nm* empty space, emptiness, blank, gap, vacuum.

vider [vide] *vt* to empty, drain (off), blow, clean, gut, core, stone, bale, settle; *vr* to empty; **— une question** to settle a question; **— les arçons** to be unsaddled.

vie [vi] *nf* life, existence, lifetime (way of) living, livelihood, vitality; **à —** for life; **avoir la — dure** to die hard, be hard to kill.

vieillard [vjejaːr] *nm* old man.

vieilleries [vjejri] *nf pl* old things, dated ideas.

vieillesse [vjejes] *nf* (old) age, oldness.

vieillissement [vjejismɑ̃] *nm* aging, growing old.

vieillir [vjejiːr] *vt* to age, make look older; *vi* to age, grow old, become antiquated.

vieillot, -otte [vjejo, ɔt] *a* oldish, old-fashioned.

vierge [vjerʒ] *a* virgin(al), pure, blank; *nf* virgin, maiden.

vieux, vieil, vieille [vjø, vjɛ(ː)j] *a* old, ancient, stale; *nm pl* old people; **il est —** jeu he is old-fashioned, antiquated; **mon — old man; un — de la vieille** one of the old brigade, an old-timer.

vif, vive [vif, viːv] *a* lively, brisk, sharp, keen, quick, alive, high-spirited, vivid, bright; *nm* living flesh, quick heart; **haie vive** quickset hedge; **peindre sur le —** to paint from life.

vif-argent [vifarzã] nm quicksilver, mercury.

vigie [viʒi] nf look-out (man), watch-tower.

vigilance [viʒilãːs] nf vigilance, care.

vigilant [viʒilã] a vigilant, watchful.

vigne [viɲ] nf vine, vineyard; **— vierge** Virginia creeper; **être dans les —s du Seigneur** to be in one's cups.

vigneron, -onne [viɲrɔ̃, ɔn] n vinegrower, vineyard worker.

vignette [viɲɛt] nf excise stamp, Internal Revenue stamp, vignette.

vignoble [viɲɔbl] nm vineyard.

vigoureux, -euse [viguro, øːz] a vigorous, sturdy, strong, hardy.

vigueur [vigœːr] nf vigor, sturdiness, strength, effect; **entrer en —** to come into effect, force; **mettre en —** to enforce.

vil [vil] a vile, base, low(ly), cheap.

vilain [vilɛ̃] a bad, naughty, nasty, dirty, mean, scurvy, ugly, wretched; nm rascal, villain.

vilebrequin [vilbrəkɛ̃] nm brace, drill; **arbre à —** crankshaft.

vilenie [viləni] nf nastiness, meanness, foul word, low action.

vilipender [vilipɑ̃de] vt to abuse, run down.

villa [vil(l)a] nf villa.

village [vilaːʒ] nm village.

villageois [vilaʒwa, waːz] a country, boorish; n villager.

ville [vil] nf town, city; **— d'eau** spa.

villégiateur [vil(l)eʒjatœːr] nm visitor, holiday-maker.

villégiature [vil(l)eʒjatyːr] nf holiday, stay in the country.

vin [vɛ̃] nm wine; **— de Bordeaux** claret; **— de Bourgogne** burgundy; **— de Xérès** sherry; **— en cercle** wine in the cask; **— millésimé** vintage wine; **avoir le — triste** to be maudlin in drink.

vinaigre [vinɛgr] nm vinegar.

vinaigrette [vinɛgrɛt] nf oil and vinegar dressing.

vinaigrier [vinɛgrie] nm vinegarmaker, vinegar-cruet.

vindicatif, -ive [vɛ̃dikatif, iːv] a vindictive, revengeful.

vineux, -euse [vinø, øːz] a wineflavored, wine-stained, full-bodied, strong, rich in wine.

vingt [vɛ̃] a nm twenty, twentieth.

vingtaine [vɛ̃tɛn] nf about twenty, a score.

vingtième [vɛ̃tjɛm] a nm twentieth.

vinicole [vinikɔl] a wine-growing.

viol [vjɔl] nm rape.

violacé [vjɔlase] a purplish-blue.

violateur, -trice [vjɔlatœːr, tris] n violator, transgressor.

violation [vjɔlasjɔ̃] nf violation, breach, breaking, infringement.

violence [vjɔlãːs] nf violence, force, vehemence.

violent [vjɔlã] a violent, fierce, strong, high.

violenter [vjɔlãte] vt to do violence to.

violer [vjɔle] vt to violate, break, transgress, rape.

violet, -ette [vjɔlɛ, ɛt] a nm purple, violet.

violette [vjɔlɛt] nf violet.

violon [vjɔlɔ̃] nm violin, fiddle, violinist, jail, clink.

violoncelle [vjɔlɔ̃sɛl] nm violoncello, cello (player).

violoniste [vjɔlɔnist] n violinist.

vipère [vipɛːr] nf viper, adder.

virage [viraːʒ] nm turn(ing), swinging round, tacking, cornering, bend.

virement [virmã] nm turn(ing), transfer; **banque de —** clearing-bank.

virer [vire] vt to turn over, clear, transfer; vi to turn, swing round, tack, veer, corner, bank, change color.

virevolte [virvɔlt] nf quick circling, sudden change.

virevolter [virvɔlte] vi to circle, spin round.

virginal [virʒinal] a virginal.

virginité [virʒinite] nf virginity, maidenhood.

virgule [virgyl] nf comma, decimal point; **point et —** semi-colon.

viril [viril] a virile, manly, male; **l'âge —** manhood.

virilité [virilite] nf virility, manliness.

virole [virɔl] nf ferrule, binding-ring.

virtuel, -elle [virtɥɛl] a virtual, potential.

virtuose [virtɥoːz] n virtuoso.

virtuosité [virtɥozite] nf virtuosity.

virulence [virylãːs] nf virulence.

vis [vis] nf screw, thread.

visa [viza] nm visa, initials.

visage [vizaːʒ] nm face, visage, countenance; **trouver — de bois** to find nobody at home, the door shut.

vis-à-vis [vizavi] ad opposite; prep **— de** opposite, facing, with regard to, towards; nm person opposite, partner.

viscère [visɛːr] nm viscus; pl viscera.

viscosité [viskozite] nf viscosity, stickiness.

visée [vize] nf aim(ing), sight(ing), design.

viser [vize] vt to aim at, sight, allude to, initial, countersign; vi to aim, aspire.

viseur, -euse [vizœːr, øːz] n aimer; nm view-finder, sights, sighting-tube.

visibilité [vizibilite] nf visibility.

visible [vizibl] a visible, obvious, perceptible, open; **il n'est pas —** he is not at home.

visière [vizjɛːr] *nf* visor, eye-shade, peak; **rompre en — avec** to quarrel openly with, attack openly.

vision [vizjɔ̃] *nf* vision, (eye)sight, fantasy.

visionnaire [vizjɔnɛːr] *a* visionary; *n* dreamer.

visite [vizit] *nf* visit, call, inspection, visitor, caller; **faire (rendre) — à** to visit, call on; **rendre à qn sa —** to return s.o.'s visit; **— des bagages** customs inspection.

visiter [vizite] *vt* to visit, attend, inspect, examine, go over, search; **faire — la maison à qn** to show s.o. over the house.

visiteur, -euse [vizitœːr, øːz] *n* visitor, caller, inspector.

vison [vizɔ̃] *nm* vison, mink.

visqueux, -euse [viskø, øːz] *a* viscous, sticky, gluey, thick.

visser [vise] *vt* to screw (down, in, on, up), put the screw on, keep down.

visuel, -elle [vizɥɛl] *a* visual; **champ —** field of vision.

vital [vital] *a* vital.

vitalité [vitalite] *nf* vitality.

vitamine [vitamin] *nf* vitamin.

vite [vit] *a* speedy, fast, fleet, swift; *ad* quickly, fast, soon; **avoir — fait de** to be quick about; **faites vite!** hurry up!

vitesse [vitɛs] *nf* speed, rapidity, rate; **à toute — at** full speed; **en petite — by** freight train; **gagner qn de — to** outstrip s.o., outrun, steal a march on s.o.; **prendre de la — to** gather speed.

viticole [vitikɔl] *a* wine.

viticulteur [vitikyltœːr] *nm* vine-grower.

viticulture [vitikyltyːr] *nf* wine-growing.

vitrage [vitraːʒ] *nm* glazing, windows.

vitrail [vitraːj] *nm* stained glass window.

vitre [vitr] *nf* (window) pane.

vitrer [vitre] *vt* to glaze.

vitreux, -euse [vitrø, øːz] *a* vitreous, glazed, glassy.

vitrier [vitrie] *nm* glazier.

vitrine [vitrin] *nf* shop-window, glass-case, showcase, cabinet.

vitriol [vitrjɔl] *nm* vitriol.

vitupération [vityperasjɔ̃] *nf* vituperation.

vitupérer [vitypere] *vt* to blame.

vivace [vivas] *a* long-lived, undying, hardy, perennial.

vivacité [vivasite] *nf* vivacity, vivaciousness, vividness, intensity, hastiness, burst of temper.

vivant [vivɑ̃] *a* living, alive, lively, lifelike, vivid; **langues —es** modern languages; *nm* living person, lifetime; **bon — person** who enjoys life, boon companion; **de mon — in** my lifetime.

vivat [vivat] *nm* hurrah.

vive-eau [vivo] *nf* spring-tide.

vivement [vivmɑ̃] *ad* briskly, sharply, warmly.

viveur, -euse [vivœːr, øːz] *n* rake, fast liver.

vivier [vivje] *nm* fish-pond.

vivifiant [vivifjɑ̃] *a* vivifying, bracing, invigorating.

vivisection [viviseksjɔ̃] *nf* vivisection.

vivoter [vivɔte] *vi* to live from hand to mouth.

vivre [vivr] *vi* to live; *nm* food, living; *pl* provisions, supplies; **avoir de quoi — to** have enough to live on; **apprendre à — à qn** to teach s.o. manners; **être commode à — to** be easy to get on with.

vlan [vlɑ̃] *excl* whack! bang!

vocable [vɔkabl] *nm* vocable, word.

vocabulaire [vɔkabylɛːr] *nm* vocabulary.

vocal [vɔkal] *a* vocal.

vocalise [vɔkaliːz] *nf* exercise in vocalization.

vocation [vɔkasjɔ̃] *nf* vocation, bent, call(ing).

vociférant [vɔsiferɑ̃] *a* vociferous.

vociférer [vɔsifere] *vi* to vociferate, yell, shout.

voeu [vø] *nm* vow, wish.

vogue [vɔg] *nf* vogue, fashion; **être en — to** be popular; **c'est la grande — it's** all the rage.

voguer [vɔge] *vi* to sail.

voici [vwasi] *prep* here is, here are, this is, these are; **me — here** I am; **le — qui arrive** here he comes.

voie [vwa] *nf* way, track(s), thoroughfare, passage; **— d'eau** leak; **— ferrée** railway line; **— de garage** siding; **être en — de** to be in a fair way to.

voilà [vwala] *prep* there is, there are, that is, those are; **le — there** he is; **— un an a** year ago; **en — une idée** what an idea! **ne —t-il pas qu'il pleure** there now, if he isn't crying.

voile [vwal] *nm* veil, cloak; *nf* sail; **mettre à la — to** set sail.

voiler [vwale] *vt* to veil, muffle, cloud, shade, hide; *vr* to cloud over.

voilette [vwalɛt] *nf* (hat) veil, half-veil.

voilier [vwalje] *nm* sailing ship, sail-maker.

voilure [vwalyːr] *nf* sails.

voir [vwaːr] *vt* to see, notice, imagine, look into; *vr* to be seen, show, be obvious; **faire — to** show, reveal; **faites — let's** see it; **— sur** to look out on; **à ce que je vois** as far as I can see; **il ne peut pas me — he** can't stand the sight of me; **il n'y voit pas** he can't see; **se faire bien — to** get into s.o.'s good books; **vous n'avez rien à — là-dedans** it is none of your business; **cela n'a rien à — à l'affaire** that has nothing to do with it.

voire [vwaːr] *ad* nay, in truth; — même and indeed.

voirie [vwari] *nf* roads, refuse (-heap); le service de — Highways Department.

voisin [vwazɛ̃] *a* neighboring, next, adjoining, bordering; *n* neighbor.

voisinage [vwazinaːʒ] *nm* neighborhood, vicinity, nearness, proximity.

voisiner [vwazine] *vi* to adjoin, be side by side, visit neighbors.

voiturage [vwatyraːʒ] *nm* carriage, cartage.

voiture [vwatyːr] *nf* automobile, vehicle, carriage, cart, van; — à bras hand-cart, barrow; — d'enfant perambulator, baby carriage; — de malade wheelchair; — de place cab taxi; aller en — to drive; en —! all aboard!

voiturer [vwatyre] *vt* to transport, convey.

voiturier, -ière [vwatyrje, jɛːr] *a* carriage(able); *nm* carter, carrier.

voix [vwa] *nf* voice, vote; à haute — aloud; à mi- — under one's breath; avoir — au chapitre to have a say in the matter; de vive — by word of mouth, viva voce; mettre aux — to put to the vote.

vol [vɔl] *nm* flight, flying, flock, theft, robbery, stealing, stolen goods; à — d'oiseau as the crow flies; — à la roulotte theft from an automobile; — à l'étalage shop-lifting; — à la tire pocket-picking, bag-snatching; — à l'américaine confidence trick.

volage [vɔlaːʒ] *a* fickle, flighty.

volaille [vɔlaːj] *nf* poultry, fowl.

volailler [vɔlaːje] *nm* poultry-yard, poultry dealer.

volant [vɔlɑ̃] *a* flying, detachable, loose, fluttering; *nm* shuttlecock, flywheel, steering-wheel, flounce.

volatil [vɔlatil] *a* volatile.

volatile [vɔlatil] *nm* winged creature, bird.

volatiliser [vɔlatilize] *vt* to volatilize; *vr* to volatilize, vanish, disappear into thin air.

vol-au-vent [vɔlovɑ̃] *nm* vol-au-vent, puff pastry pie.

volcan [vɔlkɑ̃] *nm* volcano.

volcanique [vɔlkanik] *a* volcanic.

volée [vɔle] *nf* flight, flock, volley, shower, thrashing; à la — in flight, on the wing; semer à la — to broadcast; sonner à toute — to ring a full peal; de la première — of the first rank, crack.

voler [vɔle] *vt* to steal, rob, swindle; *vi* to fly, soar; il ne l'a pas volé he deserved it.

volet [vɔlɛ] *nm* shutter, sorting-board; trié sur le — select, hand-picked.

voleter [vɔlte] *vi* to flutter, flit.

voleur, -euse [vɔlœːr, øːz] *a* flying, thievish, thieving; *nm* thief, robber; au —! stop thief!

volière [vɔljɛːr] *nf* aviary.

volontaire [vɔlɔ̃tɛːr] *a* voluntary, willful, determined, self-willed; *n* volunteer.

volonté [vɔlɔ̃te] *nf* will; *pl* caprices, whims; dernières —s de last will and testament of; de bonne — with a good grace, with a will; à — at will, at lib, ad lib; de sa propre — of one's own accord; faire ses quatre —s to do as one pleases.

volontiers [vɔlɔ̃tje] *ad* willingly, gladly, readily.

volt [vɔlt] *nm* volt.

voltage [vɔltaːʒ] *nm* voltage.

voltampere [vɔltɑ̃pɛːr] *nm* watt.

volte-face [vɔltfas] *nf* volte-face, turning-around, about-face faire — to face about, reverse one's opinions.

voltige [vɔltiːʒ] *nf* slack-rope, flying trapeze exercises, trick-riding, vaulting.

voltiger [vɔltiʒe] *vi* to flutter, flit, flap, perform on the flying trapeze or on horseback.

voltigeur, -euse [vɔltiʒœːr, øːz] *n* trapeze artist, trick-rider, equestrian performer; *nm* light infantryman.

volubilité [vɔlybilite] *nf* volubility, fluency.

volume [vɔlym] *nm* volume, bulk, capacity, tome.

volumineux, -euse [vɔlyminø, øːz] *a* voluminous, bulky.

volupté [vɔlypte] *nf* pleasure, delight, sensuousness.

voluptueux, -euse [vɔlyptɥø, øːz] *a* sensuous, voluptuous; *n* sensualist.

volute [vɔlyt] *nf* volute, scroll, wreath.

vomir [vɔmiːr] *vti* to vomit; *vt* bring up, belch forth.

vomissement [vɔmismɑ̃] *nm* vomit (ing).

vomitif, -ive [vɔmitif, iːv] *a nm* emetic.

vorace [vɔras] *a* voracious.

voracité [vɔrasite] *nf* voraciousness, voracity.

votant [vɔtɑ̃] *a* voting, having a vote; *n* voter.

vote [vɔt] *nm* vote, voting, poll, passing; bulletin de — voting-paper; droit de — franchise.

voter [vɔte] *vt* to vote, pass, carry; *vi* to vote; — à main levée to vote by show of hands.

votre, vos [vɔtr, vo] *pos a* your.

vôtre, vos [voːtr] *pos pn* le, la —, les —s yours; *nm* yours, your own; *pl* your own people *etc*; vous avez encore fait des —s you have been up to your tricks again.

vouer [vwe] *vt* to vow, devote, pledge, dedicate; je ne sais à quel saint me — I don't know what to do next.

vouloir [vulwaːr] *vt* to want, wish, like, will, be willing, consent, be determined, insist, intend, require, need, try; *vr* to try to be; **nm** will; **que voulez-vous?** what can you expect? what do you want? **il ne veut pas de nous** he won't have anything to do with us; **en — à to bear** (s.o.) a grudge, be angry with; **je veux bien** I don't mind; **sans le —** unintentionally.

voulu [vuly] *a* required, due, intentional, deliberate.

vous [vu] **pn** you, to you, (to) yourself, (to) each other, one another; **—même(s)** yourself, yourselves.

voussoir [vuswaːr] **nm** arch-stone.

voussure [vusyːr] *nf* curve, arching.

voûte [vut] *nf* arch, vault, dome, canopy, roof.

voûter [vute] *vt* to arch, vault, bow; *vr* to become bent.

vouvoyer [vuvwaje] *vt* to address as 'vous'.

voyage [vwajaːʒ] **nm** journey, voyage, trip; **pl** travel; **compagnon de —** fellow-traveler, traveling companion; **— de noces** honeymoon.

voyager [vwajaʒe] *vi* to travel, journey, migrate.

voyageur, -euse [vwajaʒœːr, øːz] *a* traveling, migratory; *n* traveler, passenger, fare; **pigeon —** homing pigeon.

voyant [vwajã] *a* gaudy, conspicuous, loud, showy, clairvoyant; *n* seer, clairvoyant.

voyelle [vwajel] *nf* vowel.

voyer [vwaje] **nm** road surveyor.

voyou, -oute [vwaju, ut] *n* hooligan, guttersnipe.

vrac [vrak] **nm** en — in bulk, loose, wholesale, pell-mell.

vrai [vrɛ] *a* true, real, genuine, downright; *ad* really, truly; **nm** truth; **à — dire** as a matter of fact; **pour de —** in earnest; **il y a du —** there is something in it.

vraiment [vrɛmã] *ad* truly, really, indeed, is that so?

vraisemblable [vrɛsãblabl] *a* likely, probable; **nm** what is probable.

vraisemblance [vrɛsãblãːs] *nf* likelihood, probability.

vrille [vriːj] *nf* tendril, gimlet, borer; **descente en —** spiral dive, spin.

vriller [vrije] *vt* to bore; *vi* to twist, corkscrew.

vrombir [vrɔ̃biːr] *vi* to throb, buzz, hum.

vrombissement [vrɔ̃bismã] **nm** throbbing, buzzing, drone, humming.

vu [vy] *a* seen; **prep** in view of, considering; **cj — que** seeing that, whereas; **nm** sight, presentation; **mal —** unpopular, disliked; **bien —** well thought of; **ni — ni connu** nobody is any the wiser for it; **au — de tous** openly; **au — et au su de tous** as everyone knows.

vue [vy] *nf* (eye)sight, view, prospect, purpose, intention, design, slide; **de — by sight; en — de** in sight of, with a view to; **perdre qn de — to** lose sight of s.o.

vulcaniser [vylkanize] *vt* to vulcanize.

vulcanite [vylkanit] *nf* ebonite, vulcanite.

vulgaire [vylgɛːr] *a* vulgar, common, coarse, low; **nm** common people, vulgarity.

vulgarisation [vylgarizasjɔ̃] *nf* popularization.

vulgariser [vylgarize] *vt* to popularize, vulgarize; *vr* to become popular, vulgar.

vulgarité [vylgarite] *nf* vulgarity.

vulnérabilité [vylnerabilite] *nf* vulnerability.

vulnérable [vylnerabl] *a* vulnerable.

W

wagon [vagɔ̃] **nm** carriage, coach, truck, wagon.

wagon-couloir [vagɔ̃kulwaːr] **nm** corridor-coach.

wagon-lit [vagɔ̃li] **nm** sleeping-car, sleeper.

wagon-poste [vagɔ̃pɔst] **nm** mail-car.

wagon-restaurant [vagɔ̃restɔrã] **nm** dining-car.

watt [wat] **nm** watt.

wattman [watman] **nm** driver.

wolfram [vɔlfram] **nm** tungsten ore, wolfram.

X

xérès [keres, gzeres] **nm** sherry.

xylographe [ksilɔgraf] **nm** wood-engraver.

xylographie [ksilɔgrafi] *nf* wood-engraving, wood-cut.

xylophone [ksilɔfɔn] **nm** xylophone.

Y

y [i] *ad* here, there; **pn** at, to, on, in, by, of it or them; **j'y suis** I've got it, I understand; **ça y est** that's it, there you are, right!; **il y a** there is, there are; **il n'y est pour rien** he had nothing to do with it.

yacht [jak(t), jat, jɔt] **nm** yacht.

yaourt [jaurt] **nm** yoghourt.

yeuse [jøːz] *nf* holm-oak.

yole [jɔl] *nf* yawl, skiff.

yougoslave [jugɔslaːv] *an* Yugoslav.

Yougoslavie [jugɔslavi] *nf* Yugoslavia.

youyou [juju] **nm** dinghy.

ypérite [iperit] *nf* mustard-gas.

Z

zazou [zazu] nm weirdie, crank.

zèbre [zɛbr] nm zebra.

zébré [zebre] a striped.

zélateur, -trice [zɛlatœːr, tris] a zealous; n zealot, enthusiast.

zèle [zɛːl] nm zeal, enthusiasm; **faire du —** to be over-eager, bustle about.

zélé [zele] a zealous.

zénith [zenit] nm zenith, height.

zéphyr [zefiːr] nm zephyr, light breeze.

zéro [zero] nm zero, cipher, nought.

zest [zɛst] nm être entre le zist et le — to be betwixt and between, be so-so.

zeste [zɛst] nm peel.

zézayement [zezɛmɑ̃] nm lisp(ing).

zézayer [zezɛje] vi to lisp.

zibeline [ziblin] nf sable.

zigouiller [ziguje] vt to kill, knife.

zigzag [zigzag] nm zigzag; **faire des —s** to zigzag, stagger along; **éclair en —** forked lightning.

zigzaguer [zigzage] vi to zigzag.

zinc [zɛ̃ːg] nm zinc, bar, counter.

zinguer [zɛ̃ge] vt to (cover with) zinc, galvanize.

zodiaque [zɔdjak] nm zodiac.

zona [zɔna] nm (med) shingles.

zone [zoːn] nf zone, area, belt; **— neutre** no man's land.

zoologie [zɔɔlɔʒi] nf zoology.

zoologique [zɔɔlɔʒik] a zoological; **jardin —** zoological gardens, zoo.

zoologiste [zɔɔlɔʒist] nm zoologist.

zut [zyt] excl darn it! hang it all!

zyeuter [zjøte] vt to take a squint at.

English — French

A

a [ei, ə] *indef art* un, une.

aback [ə'bæk] *ad* en arrière, par derrière (surprise), abasourdi, interdit.

abandon [ə'bændən] *vt* abandonner, délaisser.

abandoned [ə'bændənd] *a* dissolu, abandonné.

abandonment [ə'bændənmənt] *n* abandon *m*, dévergondage *m*.

abase [ə'beis] *vt* abaisser, humilier.

abasement [ə'beismənt] *n* abaissement *m*, dégradation *f*.

abash [ə'bæʃ] *vt* déconcerter.

abashment [ə'bæʃmənt] *n* ébahissement *m*, confusion *f*.

abate [ə'beit] *vt* diminuer, rabattre; *vi* se calmer.

abatement [ə'beitmənt] *n* apaisement *m*, diminution *f*, rabais *m*.

abbess ['æbis] *n* abbesse *f*.

abbey ['æbi] *n* abbaye *f*.

abbot ['æbət] *n* abbé *m*.

abbreviate [ə'bri:vieit] *vt* abréger.

abbreviation [ə.bri:vi'eiʃən] *n* abréviation *f*.

abdicate ['æbdikeit] *vti* abdiquer.

abdication [.æbdi'keiʃən] *n* abdication *f*.

abduct [æb'dʌkt] *vt* enlever.

abduction [æb'dʌkʃən] *n* enlèvement *m*, rapt *m*.

abed [ə'bed] *ad* au lit.

aberration [.æbə'reiʃən] *n* aberration *f*, égarement *m*.

abet [ə'bet] *vt* encourager, assister.

abetment [ə'betmənt] *n* instigation *f*.

abettor [ə'betə] *n* fauteur, -trice, complice *mf*.

abeyance [ə'beiəns] *n* suspens *m*, souffrance *f*, sommeil *m*, carence *f*, vacance *f*.

abhor [əb'hɔ:] *vt* abhorrer.

abhorrence [əb'hɔrəns] *n* horreur *f*.

abhorrent [əb'hɔrənt] *a* odieux.

abide [ə'baid] *vt* attendre, souffrir; *vi* rester fidèle (à by), demeurer.

abiding [ə'baidiŋ] *a* permanent.

ability [ə'biliti] *n* capacité *f*, talent *m*, moyens *m pl*; **to the best of my — de mon mieux.**

abject ['æbdʒekt] *a* abject.

abjection [æb'dʒekʃən] *n* abjection *f*.

abjuration [.æbdʒuə'reiʃən] *n* abjuration *f*.

abjure [əb'dʒuə] *vt* abjurer, renoncer à.

ablaze [ə'bleiz] *a ad* enflammé, en feu.

able ['eibl] *a* capable, en état (de to); **—bodied** *a* valide.

ablution [ə'blu:ʃən] *n* ablution *f*.

abnegation [.æbni'geiʃən] *n* abnégation *f*, renoncement *m*, répudiation *f*.

abnormal [æb'nɔ:məl] *a* anormal.

aboard [ə'bɔ:d] *ad* à bord; *prep* à bord de.

abode [ə'boud] *n* demeure *f*.

abolish [ə'bɔliʃ] *vt* abolir.

abolition [.æbə'liʃən] *n* abolition *f*.

abominable [ə'bɔminəbl] *a* abominable.

abominate [ə'bɔmineit] *vt* avoir en abomination.

abortion [ə'bɔ:ʃən] *n* avortement *m*, avorton *m*.

abound [ə'baund] *vi* abonder, foisonner.

about [ə'baut] *ad* à peu près, environ, çà et là; *prep* autour de, près de, sur le point de, au sujet de.

above [ə'bʌv] *prep* au dessus de, en amont de; *ad* plus que (de), cidessus, en amont, au-dessus.

above-board [ə'bʌv'bɔ:d] *ad* net, loyal; *ad* loyalement.

above-named [ə'bʌv'neimd] *a* susnommé.

abrasion [ə'breiʒən] *n* écorchure *f*.

abreast [ə'brest] *ad* de front.

abridge [ə'bridʒ] *vt* abréger, restreindre.

abridgment [ə'bridʒmənt] *n* raccourcissement *m*, abrégé *m*.

abroad [ə'brɔ:d] *ad* à l'étranger, au large, dehors.

abrogate ['æbrougeit] *vt* abroger.

abrogation [.æbrou'geiʃən] *n* abrogation *f*.

abrupt [ə'brʌpt] *a* brusque.

abruptness [ə'brʌptnis] *n* brusquerie *f*, escarpement *m*.

abscess ['æbsis] *n* abcès *m*.

abscond [əb'skɔnd] *vi* s'esquiver, décamper.

absence ['æbsəns] *n* absence *f*.

absent [æb'sent] *vi* to **— oneself** s'absenter.

absent ['æbsənt] *a* absent.

absently ['æbsəntli] *ad* d'un air absent, distraitement.

absolute ['æbsəlu:t] *an* absolu *m*.

absolutely ['æbsəlu:tli] *ad* absolument.

absolution [.æbsə'lu:ʃən] *n* absolution *f*, acquittement *m*.

absolutism ['æbsəluːtizəm] n absolutisme m.

absolutist ['æbsəluːtist] n absolutiste mf.

absolve [əb'zɔlv] vt absoudre, dispenser.

absorb [əb'zɔːb] vt absorber.

absorption [əb'zɔːpʃən] n absorption f.

abstain [əb'stein] vi s'abstenir.

abstemious [æb'stiːmjəs] a sobre, abstinent.

abstention [æb'stenʃən] n abstention f.

abstinence ['æbstinəns] n abstinence f.

abstinent ['æbstinənt] a abstinent.

abstract [æb'strækt] n précis m, extrait m; a abstrait.

abstract [æb'strækt] vt faire abstraction de, soustraire, distraire, résumer.

abstracted [æb'stræktid] a distrait.

abstraction [æb'strækʃən] n abstraction f.

absurd [əb'səːd] a absurde.

absurdity [əb'səːditi] n absurdité f.

abundance [ə'bʌndəns] n abondance f.

abundant [ə'bʌndənt] a abondant.

abundantly [ə'bʌndəntli] ad abondamment.

abuse [ə'bjuːs] n abus m, insulte f.

abuse [ə'bjuːz] vt abuser de, mésuser de, insulter, injurier.

abusive [ə'bjuːsiv] a abusif, outrageant, injurieux.

abut [ə'bʌt] vi se toucher.

abyss [ə'bis] n abîme m.

academy [ə'kædəmi] n académie f, institution f, école f.

accede [æk'siːd] vi arriver (à to), adhérer (à to).

accelerate [æk'seləreit] vti accélérer, activer.

acceleration [æk͵selə'reiʃən] n accélération f.

accelerator [ək'seləreitə] n accélérateur m.

accent ['æksənt] n accent m.

accent [æk'sent] vt accentuer.

accentuate [æk'sentjueit] vt faire ressortir, souligner, accentuer.

accentuation [æk͵sentju'eiʃən] n accentuation f.

accept [ək'sept] vt accepter, agréer, admettre.

acceptance [ək'septəns] n bienvenue f acceptation f.

access ['ækses] n accès m, abord m.

accessible [æk'sesəbl] a accessible.

accessory [æk'sesəri] n complice mf; an accessoire m.

accident ['æksidənt] n accident m, avarie f; ——prone sujet aux accidents.

accidental [͵æksi'dentl] a accidentel, fortuit.

accidentally [͵æksi'dentəli] ad par accident.

acclaim [ə'kleim] vt acclamer.

acclamation [͵æklə'meiʃən] n acclamation f.

acclimatization [ə'klaimətai'zeiʃən] n acclimatation f.

acclimatize [ə'klaimətaiz] vt acclimater.

acclivity [ə'kliviti] n montée f, rampe f.

accommodate [ə'kɔmədeit] vt adapter, arranger, fournir, obliger, loger.

accommodating [ə'kɔmədeitiŋ] a accommodant, serviable, complaisant.

accommodation [ə͵kɔmə'deiʃən] n adaptation f, accommodement m, commodités f pl, logement m, prêt m.

accompaniment [ə'kʌmpənimənt] n accompagnement m.

accompanist [ə'kʌmpənist] n accompagnateur, -trice.

accompany [ə'kʌmpəni] vt accompagner.

accomplice [ə'kɔmplis] n complice mf.

accomplish [ə'kʌmpliʃ] vt accomplir, parachever, faire.

accomplishment [ə'kʌmpliʃmənt] n accomplissement m, exécution f; pl talents m, grâces f pl.

accord [ə'kɔːd] n accord m, assentiment m; with one — d'une seule voix; of one's own — de son propre mouvement; vt accorder; vi s'accorder.

accordance [ə'kɔːdəns] n conformité f, accord m.

according [ə'kɔːdiŋ] ad — to prep selon; — as cj selon que.

accordingly [ə'kɔːdiŋli] ad en conséquence.

accost [ə'kɔst] vt accoster, aborder.

account [ə'kaunt] n compte m, importance f, compte-rendu m; vt regarder (comme); to — for rendre compte de, répondre de, expliquer; — rendered rappel; on one's own — à ses risques et périls, de sa propre initiative; on — of en raison (vue) de; on no — à aucun prix.

accountable [ə'kauntəbl] a responsable, explicable.

accountancy [ə'kauntənsi] n tenue f des livres, comptabilité f.

accountant [ə'kauntənt] n comptable m.

accouterment [ə'kuːtrəmənt] n équipement m, fourniment m, caparaçon m.

accredit [ə'kredit] vt (ac)créditer.

accrue [ə'kruː] vi résulter, s'ajouter (à to), s'accumuler.

accumulate [ə'kjuːmjuleit] vt accumuler; vi s'accumuler.

accumulation [ə͵kjuːmju'leiʃən] n accumulation f, amas m.

accumulative [ə'kjuːmjulətiv] a cumulatif.

accumulator [ə'kjuːmjuleitə] n (*motor etc*) accu(mulateur) m, accumulateur, -trice.
accuracy ['ækjurəsi] n exactitude f, précision f.
accurate ['ækjurit] a exact, correct, précis.
accursed [ə'kəːsid] a maudit.
accusation [,ækju(ː)'zeiʃən] n accusation f.
accuse [ə'kjuːz] vt accuser.
accuser [ə'kjuːzə] n accusateur, -trice.
accustom [ə'kʌstəm] vt habituer; to — oneself se faire (à), s'habituer.
ace [eis] n un m, as m; within an — of à deux doigts de.
acerbity [ə'səːbiti] n acerbité f.
ache [eik] n mal m; vi avoir mal, souffrir, faire mal.
achieve [ə'tʃiːv] vt exécuter, acquérir, atteindre.
achievement [ə'tʃiːvmənt] n exécution f, succès m.
aching ['eikiŋ] a douloureux.
acid ['æsid] an acide m.
acidity [ə'siditi] n acidité f.
acidulous [ə'sidjuləs] a acidulé.
acknowledge [ək'nɔlidʒ] vt reconnaître, accuser réception de, répondre à.
acknowledgment [ək'nɔlədʒmənt] n reconnaissance f, accusé m de réception.
acme ['ækmi] n apogée m.
acne [ækni] n acné m.
acorn ['eikɔːn] n gland m.
acquaint [ə'kweint] vt informer; to — oneself with se familiariser avec, faire connaissance avec, prendre connaissance de.
acquainted [ə'kweintid] a en relation (avec), versé (dans).
acquaintance [ə'kweintəns] n connaissance f.
acquiesce [,ækwi'es] vi acquiescer.
acquiescence [,ækwi'esns] n assentiment m.
acquire [ə'kwaiə] vt acquérir, prendre.
acquirement [ə'kwaiəmənt] n acquisition f; pl talents m pl.
acquisition [,ækwi'ziʃən] n acquisition f.
acquit [ə'kwit] vti acquitter, s'acquitter (de).
acquittal [ə'kwitl] n quittance f, acquittement m, accomplissement m.
acquittance [ə'kwitəns] n paiement m, décharge f, reçu m.
acre ['eikə] n acre f.
acrid ['ækrid] a âcre, acerbe.
acridity [æ'kriditi] n âcreté f.
acrimonious [,ækri'mounjəs] a acrimonieux.
acrimony ['ækriməni] n acrimonie f.
acrobat ['ækrəbæt] n acrobate mf.
acrobatics [,ækrə'bætiks] n acrobatie f.

across [ə'krɔs] prep à travers; ad en travers, en croix.
act [ækt] n acte m; vti jouer; vt représenter; vi agir, servir.
acting ['æktiŋ] n action f, représentation f, jeu m; a qui joue, qui fait semblant, en exercice, suppléant par intérim.
action ['ækʃən] n action f.
actionable ['ækʃnəbl] a sujet à poursuites.
activate ['æktiveit] vt activer, organiser.
active ['æktiv] a actif, ingambe.
actively ['æktivli] ad to be — involved in prendre une part active à.
activity [æk'tiviti] n activité f, animation f.
actor ['æktə] n acteur m.
actress ['æktris] n actrice f.
actual ['æktjuəl] a réel, de fait, actual.
actuality [,æktju'æliti] n réalité f.
actually ['æktjuəli] ad en fait, présentement.
actuate ['æktjueit] vt actionner, mettre en marche, motiver, pousser.
acumen ['ækjumen] n sagacité f, perspicacité f.
acute [ə'kjuːt] a aigu, -uë.
acuteness [ə'kjuːtnis] n acuité f, vivacité f.
adage ['ædidʒ] n adage m.
adamant ['ædəmənt] a inflexible, intransigeant.
adapt [ə'dæpt] vt adapter.
adaptability [ə,dæptə'biliti] n faculté f d'adaptation, souplesse f.
adaptable [ə'dæptəbl] a adaptable, souple.
adaptation [,ædæp'teiʃən] n adaptation f.
A.D.C. ['ei'diː'siː] n aide de camp m.
add [æd] vt ajouter, additionner.
adder ['ædə] n vipère f.
addict ['ædikt] n action f, personne adonnée à, -mane mf, morphinomane mf etc.
addicted [ə'diktid] a adonné (à to); to be — to s'adonner à.
addiction [ə'dikʃən] n besoin m, habitude f, goût m.
addition [ə'diʃən] n addition f; in — par surcroît.
additional [ə'diʃənl] a additionnel, supplémentaire.
addle ['ædl] a pourri, couvi; confus; vt brouiller, pourrir.
address [ə'dres] n adresse f, tenue f, allocution f; pl avances f pl, cour f; vt s'adresser à, adresser.
addressee [,ædre'siː] n destinataire mf.
adduce [ə'djuːs] vt alléguer.
adept ['ædept] a expert (en at), n passé maître m.
adequate ['ædikwit] a adéquat, suffisant.
adhere [əd'hiə] vi adhérer, se coller, maintenir (to à).

adherence [əd'hiərəns] n adhérence f, adhésion f.

adherent [əd'hiərənt] an adhérent(e) mf.

adhesion [əd'hiːʒən] n adhésion f.

adhesive [əd'hiːsiv] a collant.

adjacent [ə'dʒeisənt] a adjacent, attenant.

adjective ['ædʒiktiv] n adjectif m.

adjoin [ə'dʒɔin] vt joindre, attenir à; vi se toucher.

adjoining [ə'dʒɔiniŋ] a contigu, -uë, attenant.

adjourn [ə'dʒəːn] vt ajourner, remettre.

adjournment [ə'dʒəːnmənt] n ajournement m.

adjudge [ə'dʒʌdʒ] vt décider, condamner, adjuger.

adjudicate [ə'dʒuːdikeit] vti juger.

adjudication [ə.dʒuːdi'keiʃən] n jugement m.

adjudicator [ə'dʒuːdikeitə] n juge m.

adjunct ['ædʒʌŋkt] n accessoire m, auxiliaire mf.

adjuration [.ædʒuə'reiʃən] n adjuration f.

adjure [ə'dʒuə] vt adjurer, conjurer.

adjust [ə'dʒʌst] vt ajuster, régler.

adjustment [ə'dʒʌstmənt] n ajustement m, réglage m.

ad-lib [æd'lib] vi improviser.

administer [əd'ministə] vt administrer, (oath) déférer, gérer.

administration [əd.minis'treiʃən] n administration f, gérance f.

administrative [əd'ministrativ] a administratif.

administrator [əd'ministreitə] n administrateur m, gérant m.

admirable ['ædmərəbl] a admirable.

admiral ['ædmərəl] n amiral m; rear—— contre-amiral m; vice—— vice-amiral m.

admiralty ['ædmərəlti] n Amirauté f; First Lord of the A—— Ministre de la Marine.

admiration [.ædmə'reiʃən] n admiration f.

admire [əd'maiə] vt admirer.

admirer [əd'maiərə] n admirateur, -trice.

admiring [əd'maiəriŋ] a admiratif.

admiringly [əd'maiəriŋli] ad avec admiration.

admissible [əd'misəbl] a admissible.

admission [əd'miʃən] n confession f, admission f, aveu m, entrée f.

admit [əd'mit] vt admettre, avouer, laisser entrer; to —— of permettre, comporter.

admittance [əd'mitəns] n entrée f, accès m.

admittedly [əd'mitidli] ad sans conteste.

admonish [əd'mɔniʃ] vt admonester, avertir, exhorter.

admonishment [əd'mɔniʃmənt] n admonestation f, exhortation f, avertissement m.

ado [ə'duː] n affaire f, embarras m, bruit m.

adolescence [.ædə'lesns] n adolescence f.

adolescent [.ædə'lesnt] a adolescent.

adopt [ə'dɔpt] vt adopter, suivre, embrasser.

adoption [ə'dɔpʃən] n adoption f, choix m.

adoptive [ə'dɔptiv] a adoptif.

adorable [ə'dɔːrəbl] a adorable.

adoration [.ædɔː'reiʃən] n adoration f.

adore [ə'dɔə] vt adorer.

adorer [ə'dɔːrə] n adorateur, -trice.

adorn [ə'dɔːn] vt orner.

adornment [ə'dɔːnmənt] n ornement m, parure f.

adrift [ə'drift] ad à la dérive.

adroit [ə'drɔit] a adroit.

adroitness [ə'drɔitnis] n adresse f.

adulation [.ædju'leiʃən] n adulation f.

adult ['ædʌlt] an adulte mf.

adulterate [ə'dʌltəreit] vt frelater, falsifier.

adulteration [ə.dʌltə'reiʃən] n falsification f.

adulterer [ə'dʌltərə, —ess, is] n homme, femme adultère.

adulterine [ə'dʌltərain] a adultérin.

adultery [ə'dʌltəri] n adultère m.

adumbrate ['ædʌmbreit] vt esquisser, ébaucher.

advance [əd'vaːns] n avance f, hausse f, progrès m; vti avancer, pousser; vi faire des progrès, hausser.

advancement [əd'vaːnsmənt] n avancement m, progrès m.

advantage [əd'vaːntidʒ] n avantage m, dessus m; to take —— of profiter de; vt avantager.

advantageous [.ædvən'teidʒəs] a avantageux.

advent ['ædvənt] n Avent m, arrivée f, venue f.

adventure [əd'ventʃə] n aventure f, hasard m; vt risquer; vi s'aventurer (à, dans upon).

adventurer [əd'ventʃərə, —ess, is] a aventurier, -ière, chevalier d'industrie m.

adventurous [əd'ventʃərəs] a aventureux.

adverb ['ædvəːb] n adverbe m.

adversary ['ædvəsəri] n adversaire mf.

adverse ['ædvəːs] a adverse, hostile, contraire.

adversity [əd'vəːsiti] n adversité f.

advert [æd'vəːt] vi faire allusion (à to).

advertise ['ædvətaiz] vt annoncer, faire valoir, faire de la réclame pour; vi faire de la publicité.

advertisement [əd'vəːtismənt] n publicité f, réclame f, affiche , annonce f.

advertising ['ædvətaiziŋ] n publicité f.

advice [əd'vais] n avis m, conseil(s) m (pl).

advisable [əd'vaizəbl] a recommendable, sage.

advisability [əd.vaizə'biliti] n convenance f, sagesse f.

advise [əd'vaiz] vt conseiller.

advised [əd'vaizd] a (bien, mal) avisé.

advisedly [əd'vaizidli] ad sagement, en connaissance de cause.

adviser [əd'vaizə] n conseiller, -ère.

advisory [əd'vaizəri] a consultatif.

advocacy ['ædvəkəsi] n plaidoyer (en faveur de) m.

advocate ['ædvəkit] n avocat m.

advocate ['ædvəkeit] vt defendre, préconiser.

aerate ['eiəreit] vt aérer.

aerated ['eiəreitid] a gazeux.

aeration [.eiə'reiʃən] n aération f.

aerial ['eəriəl] n antenne f; a aérien, de l'air.

aerobatics [.eərə'bætiks] n acrobatie aérienne f.

aerodrome ['eərədroum] n aérodrome m.

aeronaut ['eərənɔːt] n aéronaute m.

aeronautics [.eərə'nɔːtiks] n aéronautique f.

aeroplane ['eərəplein] n avion m.

aesthete ['iːsθiːt] n esthète mf.

aesthetics [iːs'θetiks] n esthétique f.

afar [ə'faː] ad de loin, au loin.

affability [.æfə'biliti] n affabilité f.

affable ['æfəbl] a affable.

affair [ə'feə] n affaire f.

affect [ə'fekt] vt affecter, poser à, attaquer, toucher.

affectation [.æfek'teiʃən] n affectation f, simagrées f pl.

affection [ə'fekʃən] n affection f, disposition f.

affectionate [ə'fekʃnit] a affectueux.

affianced [ə'faiənst] a fiancé.

affidavit [.æfi'deivit] n déclaration assermentée f.

affiliate [ə'filieit] vt (s')affilier.

affiliation [ə.fili'eiʃən] n attribution de paternité f, affiliation f.

affinity [ə'finiti] n affinité f.

affirm [ə'fəːm] vt affirmer.

affirmation [.æfə'meiʃən] n affirmation f.

affirmative [ə'fəːmətiv] n affirmative f; a affirmatif.

affix [ə'fiks] vt apposer.

afflict [ə'flikt] vt affliger.

affliction [ə'flikʃən] n affliction f.

afflictive [ə'fliktiv] a affligeant.

affluence ['æfluəns] n affluence f, richesse f.

affluent ['æfluənt] a riche.

afford [ə'fɔːd] vt s'offrir, se permettre, fournir.

affray [ə'frei] n bagarre f, rixe f.

affright [ə'frait] n effroi m; vt effrayer.

affront [ə'frʌnt] n affront m; vt offenser, faire honte à.

afloat [ə'flout] ad à flot; to get — lancer; to get — again renflouer.

afoot [ə'fut] ad à (sur) pied.

aforesaid [ə'fɔːsed] a susdit.

aforethought [ə'fɔːθɔːt] a with malice — avec préméditation.

afraid [ə'freid] a effrayé; to be — avoir peur.

Africa ['æfrikə] n Afrique f.

African ['æfrikən] a africain.

aft [aːft] ad à l'arrière.

after ['aːftə] prep (d')après, selon; ad ensuite; cj après que, quand.

aftermath ['aːftəmæθ] n regain m, suites f pl.

afternoon ['aːftə'nuːn] n après-midi m or f inv.

afterthought ['aːftəθɔːt] n réflexion f après coup, second mouvement m.

afterwards ['aːftəwədz] ad ensuite, plus tard.

again [ə'gen] ad encore, de plus, de nouveau; re—; — and — à maintes reprises; now and — de temps à autre; as much — as deux fois autant (plus, aussi).

against [ə'genst] prep contre, sur, à, en vue de.

agape [ə'geip] ad grand ouvert, bouche bée.

age [eidʒ] n âge m, génération f; of — majeur; under — mineur; pl siècles m pl; vti vieillir.

aged ['eidʒid] a âgé, vieux.

agency ['eidʒənsi] n opération f, entremise f, agence f, bureau m.

agenda [ə'dʒendə] n ordre m du jour, agenda m.

agent ['eidʒənt] n agent m, cause f, représentant m.

agglomerate [ə'gləmereit] n agglomérat m; vt agglomérer.

agglomeration [ə.gləmə'reiʃən] n agglomération f.

aggravate ['ægrəveit] vt aggraver, exaspérer.

aggravation [.ægrə'veiʃən] n aggravation f, exaspération f, envenimement m.

aggregate ['ægrigit] n agrégat m, ensemble m, total m.

aggregate ['ægrigeit] vt aggréger; v se monter à.

aggression [ə'greʃən] n agression f.

aggressive [ə'gresiv] a agressif.

aggressor [ə'gresə] n agresseur m.

aggrieved [ə'griːvd] a affligé, blessé.

aghast [ə'gaːst] a terrifié, stupéfait, interdit.

agile ['ædʒail] a agile.

agility [ə'dʒiliti] n agilité f.

agitate ['ædʒiteit] vt agiter, débattre; vi faire de l'agitation.

agitator ['ædʒiteitə] n agitateur m, meneur m.

aglow [ə'glou] a luisant, rayonnant, embrasé.

ago [ə'gou] ad il y a.

agog [ə'gɔg] *a* ardent, en émoi, impatient.

agonize ['ægənaiz] *vt* torturer.

agony ['ægəni] *n* agonie *f*, angoisse *f*, supplice *m*.

agree [ə'griː] *vi* consentir (à to), être d'accord, convenir (de to), accepter.

agreeable [ə'griəbl] *a* agréable, disposé, qui consent, qui convient, d'accord.

agreed [ə'griːd] *a* d'accord.

agreement [ə'griːmənt] *n* accord *m*, convention *f*.

agricultural [,ægri'kʌltʃərəl] *a* agricole.

agriculture ['ægrikʌltʃə] *n* agriculture *f*.

aground [ə'graund] *ad* à la côte, échoué, par le fond.

ague ['eigjuː] *n* fièvre paludéenne *f*.

ahead [ə'hed] *ad* en tête, l'avant, de l'avant, en avant.

aid [eid] *n* aide *mf*, assistance *f*; *vt* aider, contribuer à.

ail [eil] *vt* tracasser; *vi* avoir mal, souffrir.

ailment ['eilmənt] *n* indisposition *f*.

aim [eim] *n* but *m*, visée *f*; *vt* viser, pointer; **to — at** viser.

aimless ['eimlis] *a* sans but.

aimlessly ['eimlisli] *ad* au hasard, sans but.

air [ɛə] *n* air *m*; *vt* aérer, sécher, étaler, mettre à l'évent; *vi* prendre l'air.

air- (**cushion** *etc*) gonflé d'air.

airborne ['ɛəbɔːn] *a* aéroporté.

air-brake ['ɛəbreik] *n* frein *m* pneumatique.

aircraft ['ɛəkrɑːft] *n* avion; **—carrier** *n* porte-avions *m*; **—man** *n* mécanicien *m*.

air-cushion ['ɛə,kuʃin] *m* coussin à air *m*.

Air Force ['ɛəfɔːs] *n* Armée de l'Air *f*.

airhole ['ɛəhoul] *n* soupirail *m*.

air-hostess ['ɛə'houstis] *n* hôtesse de l'air.

airily ['ɛərili] *ad* d'un air dégagé.

airing ['ɛəriŋ] *n* aération *f*, éventage *m*, tour *m*.

airless ['ɛəlis] *a* sans air, renfermé, étouffant.

airliner ['ɛəlainə] *n* avion de ligne *m*.

airmail ['ɛəmeil] *n* courrier *m* aérien; **by —** par avion.

airman ['ɛəmən] *n* aviateur *m*.

airplane ['ɛə,plein] *n* avion *m*.

airport ['ɛə,pɔːt] *n* aéroport *m*.

air-pump ['ɛə'pʌmp] *n* pompe *f*.

air-raid ['ɛəreid] *n* raid aérien *m*.

airship ['ɛəʃip] *n* aérostat *m*, (ballon) dirigeable *m*.

airtight ['ɛətait] *a* étanche, hermétique.

airworthy ['ɛə,wəːði] *a* qui tient l'air, bon pour voler, navigable.

airy ['ɛəri] *a* aéré, aérien, gracieux, désinvolte.

aisle [ail] *n* bas-côté *m*.

ajar [ə'dʒɑː] *ad* entr'ouvert.

akimbo [ə'kimbou] *ad* les poings sur les hanches.

akin [ə'kin] *a* parent (de to), analogue, qui tient (de to).

alacrity [ə'lækriti] *n* vivacité *f*, empressement *m*.

Alan ['ælən] Alain *m*.

alarm [ə'lɑːm] *n* alarme *f*, alerte *f*; *vt* alarmer, alerter.

alarm-bell [ə'lɑːmbel] *n* cloche, sonnette d'alarme *f*, tocsin *m*.

alarm-clock [ə'lɑːmklɔk] *n* réveille-matin *m*.

alarmist [ə'lɑːmist] *n* alarmiste *mf*.

alas [ə'læs] *excl* hélas!

albeit [ɔːl'biːit] *cj* bien que, quoique.

album ['ælbəm] *n* album *m*.

alchemy ['ælkimi] *n* alchimie *f*.

alcohol ['ælkəhɔl] *n* alcool *m*.

alcoholic [,ælkə'hɔlik] *an* alcoolique.

alcoholism ['ælkəhɔlizəm] *n* alcoolisme *m*.

alcove ['ælkouv] *n* niche *f*, retrait *m*, renfoncement *m*.

alder ['ɔːldə] *n* aune *m*.

alderman ['ɔːldəmən] *n* adjoint au maire *m*.

ale [eil] *n* bière *f*.

ale-house ['eilhaus] *n* brasserie *f*, cabaret *m*.

alert [ə'ləːt] *n* alerte *f*, qui-vive *m*; *a* vigilant, alerte, vif.

alertness [ə'ləːtnis] *n* vigilance *f*, promptitude *f*, vivacité *f*.

algebra ['ældʒibrə] *n* algèbre *f*.

alias ['eiljəs] *n* autre nom *m*, faux nom *m*; *ad* autrement dit, connu sous le nom de.

alibi ['ælibai] *n* alibi *m*.

alien ['eiljən] *n* étranger, -ère; *a* étranger, différent, répugnant (à to).

alienate ['eiljəneit] *vt* (s')aliéner, détourner.

alienation [,eiljə'neiʃən] *n* aliénation *f*.

alight [ə'lait] *a* allumé, éclairé, en feu; *vi* descendre, atterrir, se poser.

align [ə'lain] *vt* aligner.

alignment [ə'lainmənt] *n* alignement *m*.

alike [ə'laik] *a* pareil, ressemblant; *ad* de même, de la même manière.

alimony ['æliməni] *n* pension alimentaire *f*.

alive [ə'laiv] *a* en vie, vif, éveillé, grouillant; **to be — and kicking** être plein de vie; **to keep —** entretenir, soutenir.

all [ɔːl] *n* tous *m pl*, tout *m*, tout le monde *m*; *a* tout, tous, toute(s); *ad* tout, entièrement; **— but** à peu près, autant dire; **I — but fell** j'ai failli tomber; **— clear** fin d'alerte *f*; **All Fools' Day** le premier avril; **All Hallows' Day** (le jour de) la Toussaint; **— in** tout compris, à tout prendre; **— of you** vous tous; **— one** tout un; **— out** total, complètement, à plein rendement, à toute vitesse; — **powerful** tout-puissant; — **right** très bien, ça va bien, entendu, soit!; **All Saints' Day** (le jour de) la Toussaint; **All Souls' Day** le jour des Morts m; **at** — du tout; **one and** — tous sans exception; **to stake one's** — jouer son va-tout.

allay [ə'lei] vt soulager, apaiser.

allegation [,æle'geiʃən] n allégation f.

allege [ə'ledʒ] vt alléguer.

allegiance [ə'liːdʒəns] n hommage m, foi f, fidélité f.

allegory ['æligəri] n allégorie f.

alleviate [ə'liːvieit] vt alléger, adoucir.

alleviation [ə,liːvi'eiʃən] n soulagement m, allègement m.

alley ['æli] n allée f, ruelle f; **blind** — impasse f, cul de sac m.

alliance [ə'laiəns] n alliance f.

allied ['ælaid] a allié, connexe.

allocate ['æləkeit] vt allouer, assigner, distribuer.

allocation [,ælə'keiʃən] n allocation f, attribution f.

allot [ə'lɔt] vt lotir, assigner, répartir, destiner, attribuer.

allotment [ə'lɔtmənt] n attribution f, répartition f, lot m, lopin m, lotissement m.

allow [ə'lau] vt laisser, permettre, admettre, allouer; **to** — **for** tenir compte de, compter, faire la part de, prévoir.

allowance [ə'lauəns] n permission f, pension f, remise f, concession f, indemnité f, ration f; **to make** — **for** tenir compte de, faire la part de, se montrer indulgent pour.

alloy ['æloi] n titre m, aloi m, alliage m; vt allier, dévaloriser, modérer.

allude [ə'luːd] vi faire allusion (à to).

allure [ə'ljuə] vt tenter, attirer, aguicher, séduire.

allurement [ə'ljuəmənt] n attrait m, charme m.

alluring [ə'ljuəriŋ] a séduisant, attrayant.

allusion [ə'luːʒən] n allusion f.

ally ['ælai] n allié.

ally [ə'lai] vt allier, unir; vi s'allier.

almanac ['ɔːlmənæk] n almanach m, annuaire m.

almighty [ɔːl'maiti] an tout-puissant m; a (fam) formidable.

almond ['ɑːmənd] n amande f; **burnt** — praline f; **sugared** — dragée f; — **tree** n amandier m.

almoner ['ɑːmənə] n aumônier m.

almost ['ɔːlmoust] ad presque, à peu près; **he** — **fell** il faillit tomber.

alms [ɑːmz] n aumône f; —**house** n hospice m, asile m.

aloft [ə'lɔft] ad (en) haut, en l'air.

alone [ə'loun] a seul, tranquille; **to let, leave s.o., sth** — laisser tranquille, laisser en paix; **leave me** —

laissez-moi, fichez-moi la paix; **let** — encore moins, loin de, sans compter, sans parler de.

along [ə'lɔŋ] prep le long de; ad tout au (du) long; **all** — tout le temps; **all** — **the line** sur toute la ligne.

alongside [ə'lɔŋ'said] prep le long de, au bord de, à côté de; ad côte à côte; **to come** — accoster, aborder.

aloof [ə'luːf] a distant; ad à l'écart.

aloofness [ə'luːfnis] n réserve f, quant à soi m.

aloud [ə'laud] ad à haute voix, tout haut.

alphabet ['ælfəbit] n alphabet m.

alphabetical [,ælfə'betikəl] a alphabétique.

already [ɔːl'redi] ad déjà.

also ['ɔːlsou] ad aussi, en outre.

altar ['ɔːltə] n autel m.

alter ['ɔːltə] vt altérer, changer (de), remanier, transformer, déplacer; **to** — **for the better** s'améliorer; **to** — **for the worse** s'altérer.

alteration [,ɔːltə'reiʃən] n retouche f, changement m, modification f.

altercation [,ɔːltə'keiʃən] n altercation f, dispute f.

alternate [ɔːl'təːnit] a alterne, alternatif; **on** — **days** tous les deux jours.

alternate ['ɔːltəːneit] vt faire alterner; vi alterner.

alternately [ɔːl'təːnitli] ad alternativement, tour à tour.

alternation [,ɔːltəː'neiʃən] n alternance f, alternative f.

alternative [ɔːl'təːnətiv] n alternative f, choix m.

although [ɔːl'ðou] cj bien que, quoique.

altitude ['æltitjuːd] n altitude f, hauteur f, profondeur f.

altogether [,ɔːltə'geðə] ad tout compte fait, en tout, entièrement, absolument.

aluminum [,ælju'minjəm] n aluminium m.

alumnus [ə'lʌmnəs] n élève mf, pensionnaire mf.

always ['ɔːlweiz] ad toujours.

amalgam [ə'mælgəm] n amalgame m.

amalgamate [ə'mælgəmeit] vt amalgamer; vi s'amalgamer.

amass [ə'mæs] vt amasser.

amateur ['æmətə] n amateur m.

amaze [ə'meiz] vt stupéfier, confondre, renverser.

amazement [ə'meizmənt] n stupéfaction f, stupeur f.

amazing [ə'meiziŋ] a renversant.

ambassador [æm'bæsədə] n ambassadeur m.

ambassadress [æm'bæsədris] n ambassadrice f.

amber ['æmbə] n ambre m; a ambre; — **light** feu jaune m.

ambidextrous ['æmbi'dekstrəs] a ambidextre.

ambiguity [ˌæmbiˈgjuiti] n ambiguïté f.

ambiguous [æmˈbigjuəs] a ambigu, -uë, équivoque, obscur.

ambition [æmˈbiʃən] n ambition f.

ambitious [æmˈbiʃəs] a ambitieux.

amble [ˈæmbl] vi aller (à) l'amble; to — along marcher d'un pas tranquille, à la papa.

ambulance [ˈæmbjuləns] n ambulance f.

ambush [ˈæmbuʃ] n embuscade f; vt attirer dans un piège, dans un guet-apens; to lie in — vi s'embusquer.

ameliorate [əˈmiːljəreit] vt améliorer; vi s'améliorer, s'amender.

amelioration [əˌmiːljəˈreiʃən] n amélioration f.

amen [ˈɑːmen] excl amen, ainsi soit-il.

amenable [əˈmiːnəbl] a responsable, sensible (à to), soumis, maniable, passable, docile; — to reason raisonnable.

amend [əˈmend] vt amender, modifier, corriger; vi s'amender, se corriger.

amendment [əˈmendmənt] n modification f, rectification f, amendement m.

amends [əˈmendz] n dédommagement m, réparation f; to make — for dédommager, réparer

amenity [əˈmiːniti] n agrément m, aménité f; pl commodités f pl.

America [əˈmerikə] n Amérique f; North —, South — l'Amérique du Nord, l'Amérique du Sud.

American [əˈmerikən] a américain n Américain(e) m(f).

amiability [ˌeimjəˈbiliti] n amabilité f, cordialité f, concorde f.

amiable [ˈeimjəbl] a aimable.

amicable [ˈæmikəbl] a amical, à l'amiable.

amid(st) [əˈmid(st)] prep au milieu de, parmi.

amidships [əˈmidʃips] ad par le travers.

amiss [əˈmis] a insuffisant, fâcheux, qui cloche; ad (en) mal, de travers.

amity [ˈæmiti] n amitié f, bonne intelligence f.

ammonia [əˈmounjə] n ammoniaque f.

ammunition [ˌæmjuˈniʃən] n munitions f pl; a de munition, réglementaire.

amnesia [æmˈniːzjə] n amnésie f.

amnesty [ˈæmnəsti] n amnistie f; vt amnistier.

among(st) [əˈmʌŋ(st)] prep parmi, au milieu de, (d')entre.

amorous [ˈæmərəs] a porté à l'amour, amoureux.

amorousness [ˈæmərəsnis] n penchant à l'amour m.

amorphous [əˈmɔːfəs] a amorphe.

amount [əˈmaunt] n montant m, compte m, somme f, quantité f; vi (se) monter (à to), s'élever (à to), revenir (à to).

amour [əˈmuə] n liaison f, intrigue galante f.

ample [ˈæmpl] a ample, vaste, abondant.

ampleness [ˈæmplnis] n ampleur f, abondance f.

amplification [ˌæmplifiˈkeiʃən] n amplification f.

amplifier [ˈæmplifaiə] n amplificateur m.

amplify [ˈæmplifai] vt amplifier, développer.

amplitude [ˈæmplitjuːd] n ampleur f, abondance f, dignité f.

amputate [ˈæmpjuteit] vt amputer.

amputation [ˌæmpjuˈteiʃən] n amputation f.

amuck [əˈmʌk] ad comme un fou, furieux.

amulet [ˈæmjulit] n amulette f, gri(s)-gri(s) m.

amuse [əˈmjuːz] vt amuser, divertir.

amusement [əˈmjuːzmənt] n amusement m, divertissement m, distraction f.

Amy [ˈeimi] Aimée f.

an [æn, ən, n] art un, une.

analogous [əˈnæləgəs] a analogue.

analogy [əˈnælədʒi] n analogie f.

analysis [əˈnæləsis] n analyse f.

analyst [ˈænəlist] n analyste m.

analytic(al) [ˌænəˈlitik(əl)] a analytique.

analyze [ˈænəlaiz] vt analyser, faire l'analyse de.

anarchist [ˈænəkist] n anarchiste mf.

anarchy [ˈænəki] n anarchie f.

anathema [əˈnæθəmə] n anathème m.

anathematize [əˈnæθəmətaiz] vt jeter l'anathème sur.

anatomist [əˈnætəmist] n anatomiste m.

anatomize [əˈnætəmaiz] vt disséquer.

anatomy [əˈnætəmi] n anatomie f.

ancestor [ˈænsistə] n ancêtre m, aïeul, -eux m.

ancestral [ænˈsestrəl] a ancestral.

ancestry [ˈænsistri] n race f, lignée f.

anchor [ˈæŋkə] n ancre f; vt ancrer, mettre au mouillage; vi jeter l'ancre, mouiller; to cast — jeter l'ancre; to weigh — lever l'ancre.

anchovy [ˈæntʃəvi] n anchois m.

ancient [ˈeinʃənt] a ancien, antique.

ancientness [ˈeinʃəntnis] n ancienneté f.

and [ænd, ənd, ən] cj et; — so on et ainsi de suite; wait — see attendez voir.

andiron [ˈændaiən] n chenet m.

Andrew [ˈændruː] André m.

anecdote [ˈænikdout] n anecdote f.

anecdotic(al) [ˌænekˈdɔtik(əl)] a anecdotique.

anemia [ə'niːmjə] n anémie f.
anemic [ə'niːmik] a anémique.
anemone [ə'nemənɪ, n anémone f.
anesthesia [ˌænɪs'θiːzjə] n anesthésie f.
anesthetic [ˌænɪs'θetik] n anesthétique m.
anesthetize [æ'niːsθətaɪz] vt anesthésier, insensibiliser, endormir.
aneurysm ['ænjuərɪzəm] n anévrisme m.
anew [ə'njuː] ad de nouveau, autrement.
angel ['eɪndʒəl] n ange m.
Angela ['ændʒələ] Angèle f.
angelic [æn'dʒelik] a angélique, d'ange.
anger ['æŋgə] n colère f; vt mettre en colère, irriter.
angina [æn'dʒaɪnə] n angine f; — pectoris angine de poitrine.
angle ['æŋgl] n angle m, coin m; vt pêcher à la ligne.
angler ['æŋglə] n pêcheur m à la ligne.
Anglicanism ['æŋglikənizəm] n anglicanisme m.
angling ['æŋglɪŋ] n pêche f.
angry ['æŋgri] a en colère, fâché, enflammé, douloureux; to get — se mettre en colère, se fâcher, s'irriter; to get — with s.o. se fâcher contre qn; I am — with myself for doing it je m'en veux de l'avoir fait.
anguish ['æŋgwiʃ] n angoisse f, supplice m.
angular ['æŋgjulə] a angulaire, anguleux.
animal ['ænɪməl] an animal m.
animate ['ænimeit] vt animer, inspirer, inciter.
animated ['ænimeitid] a animé, vif.
animation [ˌæni'meiʃən] n animation f, entrain m, vivacité f, vie f, encouragement m.
animator ['ænimeitə] n animateur, -trice.
animosity [ˌæni'mɔsiti] n animosité f.
ankle ['æŋkl] n cheville f.
Ann [æn] Anne f.
annals ['ænlz] n annales f pl.
anneal [ə'niːl] vt tremper, tempérer.
annex ['æneks] n annexe f; [ə'neks] vt annexer.
annexation [ˌænek'seiʃən] n annexion f.
annihilate [ə'naɪəleit] vt annihiler, anéantir.
annihilation [ə.naɪə'leiʃən] n anéantissement m.
anniversary [ˌæni'vəːsəri] n anniversaire m.
annotate ['ænouteit] vt annoter, commenter.
annotation [ˌænou'teiʃən] n annotation f, commentaire m.

annotator ['ænouteitə] n annotateur m, commentateur m.
announce [ə'nauns] vt annoncer, faire part de.
announcement [ə'naunsmənt] n annonce f, avis n, faire-part m.
announcer [ə'naunsə] n annonceur m, speaker m.
annoy [ə'nɔi] vt contrarier, ennuyer.
annoyance [ə'nɔiəns] n contrariété f, dégoût m, ennui m.
annoying [ə'nɔiɪŋ] a contrariant, fâcheux, ennuyeux.
annual ['ænjuəl] n annuaire m, plante annuelle f; a annuel.
annuity [ə'njuː(ː)iti] n annuité f, rente f; life — rente viagère f.
annul [ə'nʌl] vt annuler, abroger, résilier.
annulment [ə'nʌlmənt] n annulation f, abrogation f.
annunciate [ə'nʌnsieit] vt annoncer.
annunciation [ə.nʌnsi'eiʃən] n annonce f, annonciation f.
anoint [ə'nɔint] vt oindre.
anointing [ə'nɔintɪŋ] n onction f, sacre m.
anomalous [ə'nɔmələs] a anormal, irrégulier.
anomaly [ə'nɔməli] n anomalie f.
anon [ə'nɔn] ad tantôt; ever and — de temps à autre.
anonymity [ˌænə'nimiti] n anonymat m.
anonymous [ə'nɔniməs] a anonyme.
another [ə'nʌðə] a pron un (une) autre; encore (un, une); one — l'un l'autre, les uns les autres; one way or — d'une façon ou d'une autre; that's — matter c'est tout autre chose.
answer ['aːnsə] n réponse f; vt répondre; to — for répondre de (vouch), répondre pour (instead of).
answerable ['aːnsərəbl] a responsable.
answering ['aːnsəriŋ] a sympathique, qui répond à, qui correspond à.
ant [ænt] n fourmi f; —eater fourmilier m; —hill n fourmilière f.
antagonism [æn'tægənizəm] n antagonisme m.
antagonist [æn'tægənist] n adversaire m.
antagonize [æn'tægənaiz] vt contrecarrer, se faire un ennemi de.
antecedent [ˌænti'siːdənt] n antécédent m; a antérieur.
antedate [ˌænti'deit] vt antidater.
antenatal [ˌænti'neitl] a prénatal.
antenna [æn'tenə] n antenne f.
anterior [æn'tiəriə] a antérieur.
anteriority [æntiəri'ɔriti] n antériorité f.
anthem ['ænθəm] n antienne f hymne m.
Anthony ['æntəni] Antoine m.
anti-aircraft ['ænti'ɛəkrɑːft] contre-avions, anti-aérien.

antibiotic ['æntibai'ɔtik] n antibiotique f.

antibody ['ænti.bɔdi] n anticorps m.

Antichrist ['æntikraist] n Antéchrist m.

anticipate [æn'tisipeit] vt anticiper (sur), prévenir, devancer, s'attendre à.

anticipation [æn.tisi'peiʃən] n anticipation f, prévision f, attente f; in — d'avance, par avance.

antics ['æntiks] n pl pitreries f pl, singeries f pl, cabrioles f pl.

antidote ['æntidout] n antidote m.

anti-glare [.ænti'gleə] a anti-aveuglant; — **headlights** phares-code m pl.

antipathetic(al) [.æntipə'θetik(l)] a antipathique.

antipathy [æn'tipəθi] n antipathie f.

antipodes [æn'tipədiːz] n antipodes m pl.

antiquarian [.ænti'kweəriən] n antiquaire m; —'s shop magasin d'antiquités m.

antiquated ['æntikweitid] a suranné, vieilli, désuet.

antique [æn'tiːk] a antique, ancien; n antique m, objet antique m; — dealer antiquaire m; — shop magasin m d'antiquités.

antiquity [æn'tikwiti] n antiquité f.

antiseptic [.ænti'septik] an antiseptique m.

antitheft [ænti'θeft] a antivol.

antithesis [æn'tiθəsis] n antithèse f, contraire m.

antithetic(al) [.ænti'θetik(əl)] a antithétique.

antler ['æntlə] n andouiller m; pl bois m pl.

anvil ['ænvil] n enclume f.

anxiety [æŋ'zaiəti] n anxiété f, inquiétude f, désir m.

anxious ['æŋkʃəs] a anxieux, inquiet, soucieux, désireux, inquiétant.

any ['eni] a du, de la, des; quelque, tout, un, en; not — ne . . . aucun, nul; pn quiconque; ad en rien.

anybody, **anyone** ['enibɔdi, 'eniwʌn] pn quelqu'un, n'importe qui, tout le monde, quiconque; not — ne . . . personne.

anyhow ['enihau] ad n'importe comment, de toute façon, en tout cas; — you can try vous pouvez toujours essayer.

anyone see **anybody**.

anything ['eniθiŋ] pn quelque chose, n'importe quoi, tout; not — ne . . . rien; — else, sir? et avec cela, monsieur? — you like tout ce que vous voudrez; I would give — to know je donnerais gros pour savoir; to run like — courir à toutes jambes.

anyway ['eniwei] ad n'importe comment, de toute façon, en tout cas; en fait, en fin de compte.

anywhere ['eniwɛə] ad n'importe où,

dans quelque endroit que ce soit; not — ne . . . nulle part.

apace [ə'peis] ad vite, vivement, à grands pas.

apart [ə'paːt] ad à part, de côté, à l'écart, indépendamment (de from); to come — se détacher; a espace; they are 10 miles — ils sont à 10 milles l'un de l'autre.

apartment [ə'paːtmənt] n chambre f, pièce f, logement m, appartement m.

apathetic [.æpə'θetik] a apathique, indifférent.

apathy ['æpəθi] n apathie f.

ape [eip] n singe m; vt singer.

aperient [ə'piəriənt] n laxatif m, purge f.

aperture ['æpətjuə] n orifice m, ouverture f.

apex ['eipeks] n sommet m.

apiary ['eipjəri] n rucher m.

apiece [ə'piːs] ad (la) pièce, chaque, chacun, par tête.

apish ['eipiʃ] a simiesque, de singe, sot.

apogee ['æpoudʒiː] n apogée m.

apologetic(al) [ə.pɔlə'dʒetik(əl)] a apologétique, d'excuse.

apologetics [ə.pɔlə'dʒetiks] n apologétique f.

apologist [ə'pɔlədʒist] n apologiste m.

apologize [ə'pɔlədʒaiz] vi s'excuser, demander pardon.

apology [ə'pɔlədʒi] n excuses f pl, apologie f.

apoplectic [.æpə'plektik] a apoplectique; an — fit, stroke une attaque (d'apoplexie).

apoplexy ['æpəpleksi] n apoplexie f, congestion cérébrale f.

apostasy [ə'pɔstəsi] n apostasie f.

apostate [ə'pɔstit] n apostat m.

apostle [ə'pɔsl] n apôtre m.

apostleship [ə'pɔslʃip] n apostolat m.

apostolic [.æpəs'tɔlik] a apostolique.

apothecary [ə'pɔθikəri] n apothicaire m, pharmacien m.

appalling [ə'pɔːliŋ] a effroyable, épouvantable.

apparatus [.æpə'reitəs] n dispositif m, appareil m, attirail m.

apparel [ə'pærəl] n habit m, vêtement(s) m(pl); vt habiller, vêtir.

apparent [ə'pærənt] a manifeste, évident; (heir) présomptif.

apparently [ə'pærəntli] ad apparemment.

apparition [.æpə'riʃən] n apparition f, fantôme m.

appeal [ə'piːl] n appel m; vi interjeter appel; to — to recourir à, en appeler à, faire appel à, plaire à, s'adresser à; that doesn't — to me cela ne me dit rien; the idea —s to me l'idée me sourit.

appear [ə'piə] vi apparaître, paraître, sembler, se présenter.

appearance [ə'piərəns] *n* apparition *f*, apparence *f*, mine *f*, tournure *f*; to put in an — faire acte de présence; for the sake of —(s) pour la forme; to, by all —(s) selon toute apparence.

appease [ə'piːz] *vt* apaiser, calmer.

appeasement [ə'piːzmənt] *n* apaisement *m*, conciliation *f*.

append [ə'pend] *vt* attacher, ajouter, apposer, joindre.

appendage [ə'pendidʒ] *n* addition *f*, apanage *m*.

appendicitis [ə,pendi'saitis] *n* appendicite *f*.

appendix [ə'pendiks] *n* appendice *m*, annexe *f*.

appertain [,æpə'tein] *vi* appartenir, se rapporter.

appertaining [,æpə'teiniŋ] *a* relatif, qui incombent.

appetite ['æpitait] *n* appétit *m*, soif *f*; to whet someone's — mettre qn en appétit.

appetizer ['æpitaizə] *n* apéritif *m*.

appetizing ['æpitaiziŋ] *a* appétissant.

applaud [ə'plɔːd] *vti* applaudir.

applause [ə'plɔːz] *n* applaudissements *m pl*.

apple ['æpl] *n* pomme *f*, (of the eye) pupille *f*, prunelle *f*.

apple-dumpling ['æpl'dʌmpliŋ] *n* chausson *m*.

apple-pie ['æpl'pai] *n* tourte aux pommes *f*; in — order en ordre parfait; — bed *n* lit en porte-feuille *m*.

apple tree ['æpltriː] *n* pommier *m*.

appliance [ə'plaiəns] *n* moyen *m*, dispositif *m*, machine *f*, appareil *m*.

applicable ['æplikəbl] *a* applicable, approprié.

applicant ['æplikənt] *n* postulant *m*, requérant *m*.

application [,æpli'keiʃən] *n* application *f*, demande *f*.

apply [ə'plai] *vt* appliquer; *vi* s'appliquer (à to), s'addresser (à to), se présenter; to — for demander, solliciter.

appoint [ə'point] *vt* fixer, nommer, équiper, meubler.

appointment [ə'pointmənt] *n* rendez-vous *m*, nomination *f*, emploi *m*; *pl* équipement *m*, installation *f*; to make an — with donner un rendez-vous à.

apportion [ə'pɔːʃən] *vt* répartir, assigner.

apportionment [ə'pɔːʃənmənt] *n* répartition *f*, distribution *f*, allocation *f*.

apposite ['æpəzit] *a* approprié, à propos.

appositeness ['æpəzitnis] *n* convenance *f*, justesse *f*.

apposition [,æpə'ziʃən] *n* apposition *f*.

appraisal [ə'preizəl] *n* évaluation *f*, mise à prix *f*.

appraise [ə'preiz] *vt* évaluer.

appraiser [ə'preizə] *n* commissaire-priseur *m*.

appreciate [ə'priːʃieit] *vt* évaluer, apprécier, faire cas de, goûter; *vi* prendre de la valeur, augmenter de valeur.

appreciation [ə,priːʃi'eiʃən] *n* évaluation *f*, hausse *f*, appréciation *f*; compte-rendu *m*, critique *f*.

apprehend [,æpri'hend] *vt* appréhender, comprendre.

apprehension [,æpri'henʃən] *n* compréhension *f*, appréhension *f*, crainte *f*, arrestation *f*.

apprehensive [,æpri'hensiv] *a* intelligent, inquiet, craintif.

apprentice [ə'prentis] *n* apprenti *m*; *vt* mettre en apprentissage.

apprenticeship [ə'prentiʃip] *n* apprentissage *m*.

apprise [ə'praiz] *vt* informer, apprendre, prévenir.

approach [ə'proutʃ] *n* approche *f*, approximation *f*, accès *m*; *pl* avances *f pl*; *vt* approcher de, aborder, faire des offres à; *vi* (s')approcher.

approachable [ə'proutʃəbl] *a* abordable.

approbation [,æprə'beiʃən] *n* approbation *f*; on — à condition, à l'essai.

appropriate [ə'proupriit] *a* propre (à to), approprié; [ə'prouprieit] *vt* s'approprier, destiner.

approval [ə'pruːvəl] *n* approbation *f*; on — à condition, à l'examen, à l'essai.

approve [ə'pruːv] *vt* approuver.

approver [ə'pruːvə] *n* approbateur, -trice.

approximate [ə'prɔksimit] *a* approximatif, proche.

approximation [ə,prɔksi'meiʃən] *n* approximation *f*.

appurtenance [ə'pəːtinəns] *a* appartenance *f*; *pl* dépendances *f pl*, accessoires *m pl*.

apricot ['eiprikɔt] *n* abricot *m*; — tree abricotier *m*.

April ['eiprəl] *n* avril *m*; to make an — fool of s.o. donner un poisson d'avril à qn.

apron ['eiprən] *n* tablier *m*; to be tied to one's mother's — strings être pendu aux jupes de sa mère.

apt [æpt] *a* approprié, juste, porté (à to), sujet (à to), prompt d'esprit, doué, habile.

aptitude ['æptitjuːd] *n* aptitude *f*, disposition *f*.

aptly ['æptli] *ad* (avec) à propos habilement.

aptness ['æptnis] *n* justesse *f*, tendance *f*, propriété *f*.

aqualung ['ækwə'lʌŋ] *n* scaphandre *m*.

aqueduct ['ækwidʌkt] *n* aqueduc *m*.

aqueous ['eikwiəs] *a* aqueux.

aquiline ['ækwilain] *a* aquilin.
Arab ['ærəb] *an* arabe.
Arabic ['ærəbik] *a* arabique.
arable ['ærəbl] *a* arable.
arbitrage ['ɑːbitridʒ] *n* arbitrage *m*.
arbitrary ['ɑːbitrəri] *a* arbitraire.
arbitrate ['ɑːbitreit] *vti* arbitrer.
arbitration [,ɑːbi'treiʃən] *n* arbitrage *m*.
arbitrator ['ɑːbitreitə] *n* arbitre *m*.
arbor ['ɑːbə] *n* bosquet *m*, berceau *m* de verdure, tonnelle *f*.
arc [ɑːk] *n* arc *m*.
arcade [ɑː'keid] *n* arcade *f*.
arch [ɑːtʃ] *n* arche *f*, voûte *f*, cintre *m*; *vt* voûter, cintrer, arquer; *vi* former voûte; *a* espiègle, malicieux.
arch- ['ɑːtʃ] *a* maître, fieffé, archi-, consommé.
archaeologist [,ɑːki'ɔlədʒist] *n* archéologue *m*.
archaeology [,ɑːki'ɔlədʒi] *n* archéologie *f*.
archaic [ɑː'keiik] *a* archaïque.
archaism ['ɑːkeiizəm] *n* archaïsme *m*.
archangel ['ɑːk,eindʒəl] *n* archange *m*.
archbishop ['ɑːtʃ'biʃəp] *n* archevêque *m*.
archbishopric [ɑːtʃ'biʃəprik]' *n* archevêché *m*.
archdeacon ['ɑːtʃ'diːkən] *n* archidiacre *m*.
archdeaconship [ɑːtʃ'diːkənʃip] *n* archidiaconat *m*.
archduchess ['ɑːtʃ'dʌtʃis] *n* archiduchesse *f*.
archduke ['ɑːtʃ'djuːk] *n* archiduc *m*.
arched [ɑːtʃt] *ad* en arc, voûté, arqué, cintré, busqué, cambré.
archer ['ɑːtʃə] *n* archer *m*.
archery ['ɑːtʃəri] *n* tir à l'arc *m*.
archetype ['ɑːkitaip] *n* archétype *m*.
archipelago [,ɑːki'peligou] *n* archipel *m*.
architect ['ɑːkitekt] *n* architecte *m*.
architecture ['ɑːkitektʃə] *n* architecture *f*.
archives ['ɑːkaivz] *n* archives *f pl*.
archivist ['ɑːkivist] *n* archiviste *m*.
archness ['ɑːtʃnis] *m* malice *f*, espièglerie *f*.
archway ['ɑːtʃwei] *n* arcades *f pl*.
arctic ['ɑːktik] *a* arctique.
ardent ['ɑːdənt] *a* ardent, fervent.
ardently ['ɑːdəntli] *ad* ardemment, avec ardeur.
ardor ['ɑːdə] *a* ardeur *f*.
arduous ['ɑːdjuəs] *a* ardu, pénible, escarpé, énergique.
area ['eəriə] *n* aire *f*, cour en sous-sol *f*, surface *f*, étendue *f*, zone *f*.
arena [ə'riːnə] *n* arène *f*.
arguable ['ɑːgjuəbl] *a* soutenable, discutable.
argue ['ɑːgju] *vt* prouver, soutenir; *vi* argumenter, discuter, raisonner, se disputer.
argument ['ɑːgjumənt] *n* argument *m*, débat *m*, discussion *f*, argumentation *f*.
arid ['ærid] *a* aride.
aridity [æ'riditi] *n* aridité *f*.
aright [ə'rait] *ad* à juste titre, à bon droit.
arise [ə'raiz] *vi* se lever, s'élever, survenir, surgir, se présenter.
arisen [ə'rizen] *pp of* **arise**.
aristocracy [,æris'tɔkrəsi] *n* aristocratie *f*.
aristocrat ['æristəkræt] *n* aristocrate *mf*.
aristocratic [,æristə'krætik] *a* aristocratique, aristocrate.
arithmetic [ə'riθmətik] *n* arithmétique *f*.
ark [ɑːk] *n* coffre *m*, arche *f*.
arm [ɑːm] *n* bras *m*; arme *f*: *pl* armoiries *f pl*; **fore—** avant-bras *m*; **— in —** bras dessus bras dessous; **with open —s** à bras ouverts; **at —'s length** à longueur de bras; **fire—** arme à feu *f*; **to lay down one's —s** mettre bas les armes; *vt* armer.
armament ['ɑːməmənt] *n* armement *m*, artillerie *f*.
armature ['ɑːmətjuə] *n* armature *f*.
armband ['ɑːmbænd] *n* brassard *m*.
armchair ['ɑːm'tʃeə] *n* fauteuil *m*.
armful ['ɑːmful] *n* brassée *f*.
armhole ['ɑːmhoul] *n* emmanchure *f*.
armistice ['ɑːmistis] *n* armistice *m*.
armlet ['ɑːmlit] *n* brassard *m*, bracelet *m*.
armor ['ɑːmə] *n* armure *f*, blindage *m*, les blindés *m pl*; **—clad** *a* cuirassé, blindé; **— plates** *n* (plaques de) blindage *f pl*.
armorer ['ɑːmərə] *n* armurier *m*.
armory ['ɑːməri] *n* armurie *f*, arsenal *m*.
armpit ['ɑːmpit] *n* aisselle *f*.
army ['ɑːmi] *n* armée *f*.
aroma [ə'roumə] *n* arome *m*, bouquet *m*.
arose [ə'rouz] *pt of* **arise**.
around [ə'raund] *prep* autour de; *ad* à l'entour, à la ronde.
arouse [ə'rauz] *vt* soulever, exciter, éveiller.
arraign [ə'rein] *vt* mettre en accusation *f*, attaquer.
arraignment [ə'reinmənt] *n* mise en accusation *f*.
arrange [ə'reindʒ] *vt* ranger; *vi* (s')arranger (pour to).
arrangement [ə'reindʒmənt] *n* arrangement *m*, dispositions *f pl*.
arrant ['ærənt] *a* insigne, fieffé, pur.
array [ə'rei] *n* ordre *m*, cortège *m*, atours *m pl*; *vt* rassembler, disposer, parer.
arrear [ə'riə] *n* arrière *m*; *pl* arriéré *m*, arrérages *m pl*; **in —s** en retard, arriéré.
arrearage [ə'riəridʒ] *n* arrérages *m pl*.

arrest [ə'rest] n arrêt m, saisie f, arrestation f; vt arrêter, suspendre, captiver.

arrival [ə'raivəl] n arrivée f, arrivage m.

arrive [ə'raiv] vi arriver.

arrogance [ˈærəgəns] n arrogance f.

arrogant [ˈærəgənt] a arrogant, rogue.

arrogantly [ˈærəgəntli] ad arrogamment.

arrogate [ˈærəgeit] vt s'arroger, attribuer.

arrow [ˈærou] n flèche f.

arson [ˈɑːsn] n incendie volontaire m.

art [ɑːt] n art m, artifice m; **black—** magie noire f.

arterial [ɑːˈtiəriəl] a artériel.

artery [ˈɑːtəri] n artère f.

artful [ˈɑːtful] a rusé, habile, malin.

artfulness [ˈɑːtfulnis] n ingéniosité f, art(ifice) m.

artichoke [ˈɑːtitʃouk] n (Jerusalem) topinambour m; (globe) artichaut m.

article [ˈɑːtikl] n article m, objet m, pièce f; vt passer un contrat d'apprentissage à.

articulate [ɑːˈtikjuleit] vti articuler.

articulation [ɑːˌtikjuˈleiʃən] n articulation f.

artifice [ˈɑːtifis] n artifice m, habileté f, ruse f.

artificial [ˌɑːtiˈfiʃəl] a artificiel, simili-, faux, factice.

artillery [ɑːˈtiləri] n artillerie f; **—man** artilleur m.

artisan [ˌɑːtiˈzæn] n artisan m; ouvrier qualifié m.

artist [ˈɑːtist] n artiste mf.

artistic [ɑːˈtistik] a artistique, artiste.

artless [ˈɑːtlis] a sans art, naturel, ingénu, innocent.

Aryan [ˈɛəriən] an aryen.

as [æz, əz] ad aussi, si, comme, en (qualité de); cj que, comme, tout . . . que, si . . . que, pendant que, puisque; **so good — to** assez bon pour; **— for, — to** quant à; **— from** à dater de, provenant de; **— though** comme si; **— it were** pour ainsi dire; **— yet** jusqu'ici.

asbestos [æsˈbestɔs] n asbeste m.

ascend [əˈsend] vt gravir; vi s'élever; vti (re)monter.

ascendancy [əˈsendənsi] n ascendant m, suprématie f.

ascension [əˈsenʃən] n ascension f.

ascent [əˈsent] n escalade f, montée f, ascension f.

ascertain [ˌæsəˈtein] vt constater, s'assurer, savoir.

ascetic [əˈsetik] an ascétique mf.

asceticism [əˈsetisizəm] n ascétisme m.

ascribe [əsˈkraib] vt attribuer, imputer.

asepsis [æˈsepsis] n asepsie f.

aseptic [æˈseptik] a aseptique.

ash [æʃ] n frêne m; cendre f; **—bin** n boite f à ordures; **—tray** n cendrier m.

ashamed [əˈʃeimd] a honteux; **to be —** avoir honte.

ashen [ˈæʃn] a en bois de frêne, en cendres, cendré; **—faced** blême.

ashore [əˈʃɔː] ad à terre, à la côte; **to go —** débarquer; **to run —** s'échouer.

aside [əˈsaid] n aparté m; ad de côté, à part, à l'écart.

ask [ɑːsk] vti demander; vt inviter, (question) poser; **to — for** chercher, demander; **to — about** se renseigner sur; **to — after** s'informer de; **for the asking** sur demande, pour rien.

askance [əsˈkæns] ad de travers, avec méfiance.

askew [əsˈkjuː] ad obliquement, de biais, de travers.

aslant [əsˈlɑːnt] ad obliquement, de biais.

asleep [əsˈliːp] a endormi; **to be —** dormir.

asp [æsp] n tremble m, aspic m.

asparagus [əsˈpærəgəs] n asperge f.

aspect [ˈæspekt] n aspect m, mine f, exposition f.

aspen [ˈæspən] n tremble m.

asperity [æsˈperiti] n rudesse f, aspérité f.

asperse [əsˈpəːs] vt calomnier, éclabousser.

aspersion [əsˈpəːʃən] n aspersion f, calomnie f.

asphalt [ˈæsfælt] n asphalte m.

asphyxia [æsˈfiksiə] n asphyxie f.

asphyxiate [æsˈfiksieit] vt asphyxier.

aspirate [ˈæspərit] vt aspirer.

aspiration [ˌæspəˈreiʃən] n aspiration.

aspire [əsˈpaiə] vi aspirer.

aspirin [ˈæspərin] n aspirine f.

aspiring [əsˈpaiəriŋ] a ambitieux, qui aspire (à to).

ass [æs] n âne m; **she —** ânesse f; **young — ** ânon m; **to behave like an —** faire l'âne, le sot, l'idiot.

assail [əˈseil] vt assaillir.

assailable [əˈseiləbl] a attaquable.

assailant [əˈseilənt] n assaillant m.

assassin [əˈsæsin] n assassin m.

assassinate [əˈsæsineit] vt assassiner.

assassination [əˌsæsiˈneiʃən] n assassinat m.

assault [əˈsɔːlt] n assaut m, agression f, attentat m; **by —** d'assaut vt attaquer, donner l'assaut à, attenter (à la pudeur).

assay [əˈsei] n essai m; vt essayer, titrer.

assegai [ˈæsigai] n sagaie f.

assemblage [əˈsemblidʒ] n assemblage m, réunion f.

assemble [əˈsembl] vt assembler; vi s'assembler, se rassembler.

assembly [əˈsembli] n assemblée f, rassemblement m.

assent [əˈsent] n assentiment m

consentement m; vt consentir, déférer (à to), convenir (de to).

assert [ə'sɜːt] vt revendiquer, affirmer, faire valoir.

assertion [ə'sɜːʃən] n revendication f, affirmation f.

assertive [ə'sɜːtiv] a péremptoire, autoritaire.

assertiveness [ə'sɜːtivnis] n ton péremptoire m.

assess [ə'ses] vt imposer, taxer, évaluer, estimer.

assessable [ə'sesəbl] a imposable, évaluable.

assessment [ə'sesmənt] n répartition f, évaluation f, taxation f, imposition f.

assessor [ə'sesə] n répartiteur m, assesseur m, contrôleur m.

assets ['æsets] n actif m, biens m pl.

asseverate [ə'sevəreit] vt attester, affirmer.

asseveration [ə,sevə'reiʃən] n attestation f.

assiduity [,æsi'dju(ː)iti] n assiduité f.

assiduous [ə'sidjuəs] a assidu.

assign [ə'sain] vt assigner, attribuer, fixer, transférer.

assignation [,æsig'neiʃən] n assignation f, transfert m, rendez-vous m, attribution f.

assignment [ə'sainmənt] n assignation f, attribution f, allocation f.

assimilable [ə'similəbl] a assimilable.

assimilate [ə'simileit] vt assimiler.

assimilation [ə,simi'leiʃən] n assimilation f.

assist [ə'sist] vt assister, aider; vi assister (à at).

assistance [ə'sistəns] n assistance f, aide f.

assistant [ə'sistənt] a adjoint, sous-; n aide mf, assistant(e) mf, adjoint(e) mf, employé(e) mf.

assize [ə'saiz] n assises f pl.

associate [ə'souʃiit] an associé m, camarade mf.

associate [ə'souʃieit] vt associer, mettre en contact; vi fréquenter, frayer (avec with) s'associer, s'allier (à with).

association [ə,sousi'eiʃən] n association f, fréquentation f, société f, amicale f.

assort [ə'sɔːt] vt classer, assortir; vi s'associer.

assortment [ə'sɔːtmənt] n assortiment m, classement m.

assuage [ə'sweidʒ] vt apaiser.

assuagement [ə'sweidʒmənt] n apaisement m.

assume [ə'sjuːm] vt prendre, assumer, affecter, présumer.

assuming [ə'sjuːmiŋ] a arrogant, prétentieux; cj en admettant que.

assumption [ə'sʌmpʃən] n hypothèse f, arrogance f, Assomption f; — of office entrée en fonctions f.

assurance [ə'ʃuərəns] n assurance f.

assure [ə'ʃuə] vt assurer.

assuredly [ə'ʃuəridli] ad assurément

asterisk ['æstərisk] n astérisque m.

astern [əs'tɜːn] ad (naut) à l'arrière, derrière.

asthma ['æsmə] n asthme m.

astir [ə'stɜː] ad en mouvement, en émoi, levé, debout.

astonish [əs'tɔniʃ] vt étonner.

astonishing [əs'tɔniʃiŋ] a étonnant.

astonishingly [əs'tɔniʃiŋli] ad étonnamment.

astonishment [əs'tɔniʃmənt] n étonnement m.

astound [əs'taund] vt stupéfier, abasourdir.

astraddle [ə'strædl] ad à califourchon, à cheval.

astray [əs'trei] a égaré; ad hors du droit chemin; to go — s'égarer, faire fausse route, se dévoyer; to lead — égarer, dévoyer.

astride [əs'traid] ad à califourchon, à cheval.

astrologer [əs'trɔledʒə] n astrologue m.

astrology [əs'trɔledʒi] n astrologie f.

astronaut ['æstrənɔːt] n astronaute m.

astronautics [,æstrə'nɔːtiks] n astronautique f.

astronomer [əs'trɔnəmə] n astronome m.

astronomy [əs'trɔnəmi] n astronomie f.

astute [əs'tjuːt] a sagace, astucieux, fin.

astuteness [əs'tjuːtnis] n finesse f, astuce f.

asunder [ə'sʌndə] ad à part, en pièces, en deux.

asylum [ə'sailəm] n asile m.

at [æt] prep à, chez qn; — one d'accord; — that et de plus, tel quel; — hand sous la main; — all events en tout cas; to be — s.o. s'en prendre à qn.

ate [et] pt of eat.

atheism ['eiθiizm] n athéisme m.

atheist ['eiθiist] n athée mf.

athlete ['æθliːt] n athlète m.

athletic [æθ'letik] a athlétique, sportif, bien taillé.

athleticism [æθ'letisizəm] n athlétisme m.

athletics [æθ'letiks] n pl sports m pl, culture physique f.

at-home [ət'houm] n réception f, jour m.

athwart [ə'θwɔːt] prep en travers de; ad en travers, par le travers.

atmosphere ['ætməsfiə] n atmosphère f, ambiance f.

atmospheric [,ætməs'ferik] a atmosphérique; n pl parasites m pl, fritures f pl, perturbations f pl.

atom ['ætəm] n atome m.

atomic [ə'tɔmik] a atomique.

atomize ['ætəmaiz] vt vaporiser, pulvériser.

atone [ə'toun] vti expier.

atonement [ə'tounmənt] n expiation f, réparation f.

atrocious [ə'trouʃəs] a atroce, exécrable, affreux.

atrocity [ə'trɔsiti] **atrociousness** [ə'trouʃəsnis] n atrocité f.

attach [ə'tætʃ] vt attacher, fixer, lier, saisir.

attaché [ə'tæʃei] n attaché m; — **case** serviette f, mallette f, porte-documents m.

attachment [ə'tætʃmənt] n attachement m, attache f, saisie f.

attack [ə'tæk] n attaque f, assaut m, accès m, crise f; vt attaquer, s'attaquer à.

attain [ə'tein] vt atteindre.

attainable [ə'teinəbl] a accessible, à portée.

attainder [ə'teində] n mort civile f.

attainment [ə'teinmənt] n réalisation f, arrivée f; pl talents m pl, succès m pl, connaissances f pl.

attempt [ə'tempt] n tentative f, coup de main m, essai m, attentat m; vt tenter, essayer, attaquer.

attend [ə'tend] vt s'occuper de, soigner, assister à; vi faire attention; to — to se charger de, s'occuper de.

attendance [ə'tendəns] n présence f, service m, assistance f.

attendant [ə'tendənt] n employé(e) mf, appariteur m, gardien, -ienne, ouvreuse f; a présent, qui sui(ven)t.

attention [ə'tenʃən] n attention f, garde-à-vous m.

attentive [ə'tentiv] a attentif, plein d'attentions, prévenant, soucieux.

attenuate [ə'tenjueit] vt atténuer.

attenuation [ə.tenju'eiʃən] n atténuation f.

attest [ə'test] vt attester, déférer le serment à.

attestation [.ætes'teiʃən] n attestation f, déposition f.

attic ['ætik] n mansarde f, grenier m, combles m pl.

attire [ə'taiə] n habit m, atours m pl, costume m; vt habiller, parer.

attitude ['ætitjuːd] n attitude f, pose f.

attorney [ə'təːni] n fondé de pouvois m, procureur (général) m, avoué m; power of — procuration f.

attract [ə'trækt] vt attirer.

attraction [ə'trækʃən] n attraction f, séduction f.

attractive [ə'træktiv] a attrayant, séduisant.

attractiveness [ə'træktivnis] n attrait m, charme m.

attribute ['ætribjuːt] n attribut m, apanage m, qualité f.

attribute [ə'tribjuːt] vt attribuer, prêter.

attribution [.ætri'bjuːʃən] n attribution f.

attrition [ə'triʃən] n attrition f, usure f.

attune [ə'tjuːn] vt accorder.

auburn ['ɔːbən] a châtain, auburn (no f).

auction ['ɔːkʃən] n vente aux enchères f; vt mettre aux enchères.

auctioneer [.ɔːkʃə'niə] n commissaire-priseur m, crieur m.

audacious [ɔː'deiʃəs] a audacieux, hardi.

audacity [ɔː'dæsiti] n audace f.

audible ['ɔːdəbl] a qui s'entend, intelligible, perceptible.

audibly ['ɔːdəbli] ad distinctement.

audience ['ɔːdjəns] n audience f, auditoire m, assistance f.

audio-visual ['ɔːdiou'vizjuəl] a audio-visuel.

audit ['ɔːdit] n apurement de comptes m; vt apurer, vérifier.

audition [ɔː'diʃən] n ouïe f, audition f, séance f.

auditor ['ɔːditə] n expert-comptable m.

auger ['ɔːgə] n tarière f.

aught [ɔːt] n for — I know autant que je sache.

augment [ɔːg'ment] vti augmenter.

augmentation [.ɔːgmen'teiʃən] n augmentation f.

augur ['ɔːgə] n augure m; vti augurer.

augury ['ɔːgjuri] n augure m, présage m.

August ['ɔːgəst] n août m.

august [ɔː'gʌst] a auguste.

aunt [ɑːnt] n tante f.

aurora [ɔː'rɔːrə] n aurore f, aube f.

auspices ['ɔːspisiz] n pl auspices m pl.

auspicious [ɔːs'piʃəs] a favorable, propice.

austere [ɔs'tiə] a austere, âpre.

austerity [ɔs'teriti] n austérité f.

Australia [ɔs'treiljə] n Australie f.

Austria ['ɔstriə] n Autriche f.

Austrian ['ɔstriən] a autrichien.

authentic [ɔː'θentik] a authentique.

authenticate [ɔː'θentikeit] vt authentiquer, certifier, légaliser.

authenticity [.ɔːθen'tisiti] n authenticité f.

author ['ɔːθə] n auteur m.

authoritative [ɔː'θɔritətiv] a qui fait autorité, autorisé, péremptoire autoritaire.

authority [ɔː'θɔriti] n autorité f mandat m.

authorization [.ɔːθərai'zeiʃən] n autorisation f, mandat m.

authorize ['ɔːθəraiz] vt autoriser.

authorship ['ɔːθəʃip] n paternité f.

autocracy [ɔː'tɔkrəsi] n autocratie f.

autocrat ['ɔːtəkræt] n autocrate m.

autograph ['ɔːtəgrɑːf] n autograph m; vt signer, autographier.

automatic [.ɔːtə'mætik] a automatique, machinal.

automation [.ɔːtə'meiʃən] n auto matisation f.

automaton [ɔː'tɔmətən] n automat m.

automobile [ˈɔːtəməbiːl] n automobile f.

autonomous [ɔːˈtɒnəməs] a autonome.

autonomy [ɔː tɒnəmi] n autonomie f.

autumn [ˈɔːtəm] n automne m.

autumnal [ɔː tʌmnəl] a automnal, d'automne.

auxiliary [ɔːg ziljəri] an auxiliaire mf.

avail [əˈveil] n utilité f; without — sans effet; vi servir à, être utile à; to — oneself of profiter de.

available [əˈveiləbl] a utile, accessible, disponible, existant, valable.

avarice [ˈævəris] n cupidité f.

avaricious [ævə riʃəs] a cupide, avaricieux, avare.

avenge [əˈvendʒ] vt venger.

avenger [əˈvendʒə] n vengeur, -eresse.

avenue [ævinjuː] n avenue f.

aver [əˈvəː] vt affirmer.

average [ˈævəridʒ] n moyenne f; a moyen, courant; vt compter (faire) en moyenne, établir la moyenne de.

averse [əˈvəːs] a opposé, hostile (à to).

aversion [əˈvəːʃən] n aversion f; pet — bête f noire.

avert [əˈvəːt] vt détourner, écarter, prévenir.

aviary [ˈeivjəri] n volière f.

aviation [eivi eiʃən] n aviation f.

aviator [eivieitə] n aviateur, -trice.

avid [ævid] a avide.

avidity [əˈviditi] n avidité f.

avocation [ævou keiʃən] n vocation f, métier m.

void [ə vɔid] vt éviter.

avoidable [ə vɔidəbl] a évitable.

avoirdupois [ævədə pɔiz] n système m des poids et mesures.

avow [ə vau] vt avouer.

avowal [ə vauəl] n aveu m.

avowedly [ə vauidli] ad franchement.

await [əˈweit] vt attendre.

awake [ə weik] vi s'éveiller, se réveiller; vt éveiller, réveiller; a éveillé, vigilant, averti, informé (de to).

awakening [ə weikniŋ] n (r)éveil m.

award [ə wɔːd] n jugement m, attribution f; vt adjuger, accorder, décerner.

aware [ə wɛə] a instruit (de of), informé (de of); to be — of savoir, avoir conscience de.

awash [ə wɔʃ] a baigné, lavé, inondé, à fleur d'eau.

away [ə wei] ad à distance, au loin; go —! sortez!; out and — de loin, sans arrêter; to make — with détruire, enlever; far and — de beaucoup; right — sur-le-champ, tout de suite.

awe [ɔː] n stupeur sacrée f, respect craintif m, effroi m, terreur f; — stricken, —struck frappé de terreur, intimidé.

awful [ˈɔːful] a terrible, affreux solennel.

awfully [ˈɔːfuli] ad terriblement, infiniment; thanks — merci mille fois.

awhile [ə wail] ad un moment.

awkward [ˈɔːkwəd] a gauche, gêné, embarrassant, peu commode.

awkwardness [ˈɔːkwədnis] n gaucherie f, embarras m, inconvénient m, gêne f.

awl [ɔːl] n alène f.

awn [ɔːn] n barbe f.

awning [ˈɔːniŋ] n marquise f, tente f, bâche f, abri m.

awoke [ə wouk] pt of awake.

awry [əˈrai] a tortueux, pervers; ad de travers.

ax [æks] n hache f; vt porter la hache dans; to have an — to grind avoir un intérêt au jeu.

axiom [ˈæksiəm] n axiome m.

axis [ˈæksis] n axe m.

axle [ˈæksl] n essieu m.

ay(e) [ai] n oui; [ei] ad toujours.

azure [ˈeiʒə] n azur m; a d'azur, azure.

B

babble [ˈbæbl] n babil m; vi babiller.

baboon [bə buːn] n babouin m, cynocéphale m.

baby [ˈbeibi] n bébé m; — carriage voiture f d'enfant.

babyhood [ˈbeibihud] n enfance f, bas âge m.

babyish [ˈbeibiiʃ] a enfantin, puéril.

bachelor [ˈbætʃələ] n célibataire m, garçon m, bachelier, -ière.

bachelorhood [ˈbætʃələhud] n célibat m.

back [bæk] n dos m, arrière m, dossier m, envers m, verso m, fond m; vt (faire) reculer, appuyer, parier pour, endosser; vi reculer, faire marche arrière; to — down descendre à reculons, en rabattre; to — out sortir à reculons, se dégonfler, s'excuser; a arrière, de derrière; ad en arrière, à l'arrière, dans le sens contraire, de retour; there and — aller et retour.

backbite [ˈbækbait] vt médire de.

backbiter [ˈbæk baitə] n mauvaise langue f.

backbiting [ˈbækbaitiŋ] n médisance f.

backbone [ˈbækboun] n épine dorsale f; to the — jusqu'à la moelle des os.

backdate [ˈbæk deit] vt antidater.

backdoor [ˈbæk dɔː] n porte de service f, porte basse f; a souterrain.

backfiring [ˈbæk faiəriŋ] n retour de flamme m, (aut) pétarade f.

backgammon [bæk gæmən] n tric-trac m.

background ['bækgraund] n arrière-plan m, fond m.

backing ['bækiŋ] n recul m, appui m, soutien m.

back-scratcher ['bæk'skrætʃə] n scratch m.

backsliding ['bæk'slaidiŋ] n rechute f.

backstairs ['bæk'stɛəz] n escalier de service m.

backward ['bækwəd] a rétrograde, arriéré, en retard, en arrière.

backwardness ['bækwədnis] n lenteur f, retard m, état m arriéré.

backwards ['bækwədz] ad à reculons, à la renverse, à rebours, en arrière.

bacon ['beikən] n lard m, bacon m.

bad [bæd] n mauvais m, ruine f; a mauvais, méchant, malade, fort, gros.

bade [beid] pt of bid.

badge [bædʒ] n (in)signe m.

badger ['bædʒə] n blaireau m.

badly ['bædli] ad mal, gravement; — off gêné.

badness ['bædnis] n méchanceté f, pauvreté f, maladie f.

baffle ['bæfl] vt déjouer, contre-carrer, défier.

bag [bæg] n sac m, gibecière f, tableau m, (cows) pis m, (eyes) poche f; pl pantalon m; vt mettre en sac, empocher, chiper, prendre; vi bouffer, s'enfler.

bagful ['bægful] n sac m, sachée f.

baggage ['bægidʒ] n bagage m; donzelle f.

baggy ['bægi] a bouffant.

bagpipe ['bægpaip] n cornemuse f, biniou m.

bail [beil] n caution f; batflanc m, anse f; vt se porter (donner) caution pour, vider, écoper.

bailiff ['beilif] n bailli m, huissier m, régisseur m.

bait [beit] n amorce f; vt amorcer, tourmenter.

baize [beiz] n serge f.

bake [beik] vt (faire) cuire au four, rissoler; vi cuire, se rôtir.

bakehouse ['beikhaus] n fournil m.

baker ['beikə] n boulanger, -ère.

baker's (shop) ['beikəz] n boulangerie f.

baking ['beikiŋ] n cuisson m; — powder levure f, poudre f à lever.

balance ['bæləns] n équilibre m, balance f, bilan m; — in hand avoir; — due manque m; vt peser, équilibrer, balancer; vi osciller, s'équilibrer, se faire contre-poids.

balance-sheet ['bælənsʃiːt] n bilan m.

balance-wheel ['bælənswiːl] n balancier m.

balcony ['bælkəni] n balcon m.

bald [bɔːld] a chauve, pelé, dégarni.

balderdash ['bɔːldədæʃ] n balivernes f pl.

baldness ['bɔːldnis] n calvitie f.

bale [beil] n ballot m, paquet m, malheur m.

baleful ['beilful] a funeste.

balk [bɔːk] n obstacle m, poutre f; vt contrecarrer, contrarier, esquiver; vi se dérober, reculer (devant at).

ball [bɔːl] n bal m, boule f, bille f, ballon m, balle f, boulet m, peloton m.

ballad [bæ'lɑːd] n ballade f.

ballast ['bæləst] n lest m, ballast m; vt lester, empierrer.

ball-bearing ['bɔːl'bɛəriŋ] n roulement à billes m.

balloon [bə'luːn] n ballon m.

ballot ['bælət] n boule f, scrutin m, bulletin m; vote à main levée m; vt voter; vti tirer au sort.

ballot-box ['bælətbɔks] n urne f.

balm [bɑːm] n baume m.

balmy ['bɑːmi] a embaumé, toqué.

baluster ['bæləstə] n rampe f, balustre m.

balustrade [.bæləs'treid] n balustrade f.

bamboo [bæm'buː] n bambou m.

bamboozle [bæm'buːzl] vt mystifier, filouter.

bamboozlement [bæm'buːzlmənt] n mystification f.

ban [bæn] n ban m, interdit m, mise hors la loi f, malédiction f; vt mettre au ban, interdire, mettre à l'index.

banana [bə'nɑːnə] n banane f.

band [bænd] n bande f, musique f, orchestre m; vt bander; vi to — together s'associer, se bander.

bandage ['bændidʒ] n bandage m, bandeau m.

bandbox ['bændbɔks] n carton à chapeaux m.

bandmaster ['bænd.mɑːstə] n chef m de musique.

bandstand ['bændstænd] n kiosque m, estrade f.

bandy ['bændi] vt échanger; a bancal arqué.

bane [bein] n poison m, ruine f.

baneful ['beinful] a empoisonné ruineux, funeste.

bang [bæŋ] n coup sonore m, claquement m, détonation f; vti claquer frapper; excl pan! v'lan!

bangle ['bæŋgl] n anneau m, bracelet m.

banish ['bæniʃ] vt bannir, proscrire exiler.

banishment ['bæniʃmənt] n bannissement m, exil m.

banister ['bænistə] n rampe f.

bank [bæŋk] n rive f, berge f, bor m, banque f, talus m, banc m; vt endiguer, relever, mettre en banque vi virer, miser (sur on).

banker ['bæŋkə] n banquier m.

banknote ['bæŋknout] n billet d banque m.

bankrupt ['bæŋkrəpt] n banque

routier, -ière, failli(e) m; vt réduire à la faillite.

bankruptcy ['bæŋkrəptsi] n banqueroute f, faillite f.

banner ['bænə] n bannière f, étandard m.

banns [bænz] n bans m pl.

banquet ['bæŋkwit] n banquet m; vt traiter; vi banqueter.

banter ['bæntə] n plaisanterie f; vti plaisanter.

baptism ['bæptizəm] n baptême m.

baptismal [bæp'tizməl] a baptismal, de baptême.

baptize [bæp'taiz] vt baptiser.

bar [ba:] n barre f, bar m, comptoir m, barrière f, (law) barreau m; vt barrer, exclure; prep moins, sauf.

barb [ba:b] n barbe f, pointe f.

barbarian [ba:'beəriən] an barbare mf.

barbarism ['ba:bərizəm] n barbarie f.

barbarous ['ba:bərəs] a cruel, grossier.

barbed [ba:bd] a barbelé, acéré.

barbed-wire ['ba:bd'waiə] n fil de fer barbelé m.

barber ['ba:bə] n barbier m, coiffeur m.

bard [ba:d] n barde f.

bare [bεə] a nu, vide, seul, simple; vt mettre à nu, dégainer, dépouiller.

bareback [bεəbæk] ad à cru.

barefaced [beəfeist] a impudent, cynique, effronté.

barefooted [beə'futid] a nu-pieds.

bareheaded [beə hedid] a nu-tête, découvert.

barely ['beəli] ad à peine, tout juste.

bareness ['beənis] n nudité f, dénuement m.

bargain ['ba:gin] n marché m, occasion f; into the — par dessus le marché; vi traiter, négocier; to — over, with marchander.

barge [ba:dʒ] n chaland m, barque f, péniche f.

bargee [ba:'dʒi:] n batelier m.

baritone ['bæritoun] n (mus) baryton m.

bark [ba:k] n écorce f, aboiement m, trois-mâts m; vt écorcer, écorcher; vi aboyer.

barley ['ba:li] n orge m.

barm [ba:m] n levure f.

barmaid [ba:meid] n serveuse f.

barman [ba:mən] n garçon m de comptoir, barman m.

barn [ba:n] n grange f, écurie f, étable f, hangar m.

barometer [bə'rɔmitə] n baromètre m.

baron ['bærən] n baron m.

baroness ['bærənis] n baronne f.

baronet ['bærənit] n baronnet m.

baronetcy [bærənitsi] n baronnie f.

barrack(s) ['bærəks) n caserne f, baraque f.

barrage [bæru:ʒ] n barrage m.

barrel ['bærəl] n baril m, barrique f, canon de fusil m, barillet m; **double-barreled** à deux coups.

barren ['bærən] a stérile, aride.

barrenness ['bærənnis] n stérilité f, aridité.

barricade [,bæri'keid] n barricade f; vt barricader.

barrier ['bæriə] n barrière f; **sound** — mur m du son.

barring ['ba:riŋ] prep excepté.

barrister ['bæristə] n avocat m.

barrow ['bærou] n brouette f, charrette f à bras.

bartender ['ba:tendə] n barman m.

barter ['ba:tə] n troc m, échange m; vt troquer.

base [beis] n base f; vt baser, fonder; a bas, vil.

baseless ['beislis] a sans fondement, sans base.

basement ['beismənt] n soubassement m, sous-sol m.

baseness ['beisnis] n bassesse f.

bash [bæʃ] vt cogner; to — in enfoncer.

bashful ['bæʃful] a timide.

bashfulness ['bæʃfulnis] n timidité f, fausse honte f.

basic ['beisik] a fondamental, de base.

basin ['beisn] n cuvette f, bassine f, bassin m, jatte f.

basis ['beisis] n see base.

bask [ba:sk] vi se chauffer.

basket ['ba:skit] n panier m, corbeille f; éventaire m; vt mettre dans un (au) panier.

bass [beis) n basse f, bar m; a de basse, grave.

bastard ['bæstəd] an bâtard(e) mf.

bastardy ['bæstədi] n bâtardise f.

baste [beist] vt faufiler, bâtir, arroser, rosser.

bat [bæt] n chauve-souris f, crosse f.

batch [bætʃ] n fournée f; tas m.

bath [ba:θ] n bain m, baignoire f.

bathe [beið] vt baigner; vi se baigner.

bather ['beiðə] n baigneur, -euse.

bathos ['beiθɔs] n chute f, dégringolade f.

bathroom ['ba:θrum] n salle de bain f.

batman ['bætmən] n ordonnance f, brosseur m.

battalion [bə'tæljən] n bataillon m.

batten ['bætn] vi s'empiffrer, s'engraisser, se repaître.

batter [bætə] n pâte f; vt battre, malmener, cabosser.

battering-ram ['bætəriŋræm] n bélier m.

battery [bætəri] n batterie f, pile f, voies de fait f pl.

battle [bætl] n bataille f; vi se battre, lutter.

battle-ax ['bætlæks] n hache f d'armes.

battledore ['bætldɔ:] n raquette f.

battlement ['bætlmənt] ·n créneau m.

battleship ['bætlʃip] n cuirassé m.

bauble ['bɔːbl] n babiole f, (fool's) marotte f.

bawdiness ['bɔːdinis] n obscénité f.

bawdy ['bɔːdi] a obscène.

bawl [bɔːl] vi vociférer, gueuler, brailler; vt — out engueuler.

bay [bei] n laurier m, baie f; entre-deux m; aboiement m, abois m pl; vi aboyer, hurler; a bai, en saillie.

bayonet ['beiənit] n baïonnette f; vt embrocher.

bazaar [bə'zɑː] n bazar m.

be [biː] vi être, exister, avoir, aller, faire (froid etc).

beach [biːtʃ] n plage f, grève f; vt atterrir, échouer.

beacon ['biːkən] n balise f, feu m, poteau m.

bead [biːd] n grain m, perle f, bulle f; pl chapelet m.

beadle ['biːdl] n bedeau m, appariteur m.

beak [biːk] n bec m, éperon m, magistrat m.

beaker ['biːkə] n coupe f.

beam [biːm] n poutre f, fléau m, rayon m; vi rayonner.

bean [biːn] n haricot m; broad — fève f; French — haricot vert m.

bear ['beə] n ours m; baissier m; vi jouer à la baisse; vt (em-, rem-, sup-, se com-)porter, souffrir, endurer, mettre au jour; to — out confirmer.

bearable ['beərəbl] a supportable.

beard [biəd] n barbe f; vt défier, narguer.

bearded ['biədid] a barbu.

beardless ['biədlis] a imberbe, sans barbe.

bearer ['beərə] n porteur, -euse.

bearing ['beəriŋ] n conduite f; rapport m, aspect m, maintien m, port m, position f.

beast [biːst] n bête f, bétail m, brute f, porc m.

beastliness ['biːstlinis] n gloutonnerie f, bestialité f.

beastly ['biːstli] a bestial, répugnant; ad terriblement.

beat [biːt] n coup de baguette m, cadence f; battement m, ronde f, tournée f; (mus) mesure f; vti battre; to — about the bush tourner autour du pot; to — one's brains se creuser la cervelle.

beaten ['biːtn] a (re)battu.

beater ['biːtə] n rabatteur m, battoir m, fléau m.

beatification [bi(ː)ætifi'keiʃən] n béatification f.

beatify [bi(ː)'ætifai] vt béatifier.

beatitude [bi(ː)'ætitjuːd] n béatitude f.

beau [bou] n dandy m.

beautiful ['bjuːtəful] a beau, (before vowels) bel, belle.

beauty ['bjuːti] n beauté f; — spot n mouche f, site m.

beaver ['biːvə] n castor m.

becalm [bi'kɑːm] vt déventer.

became [bi'keim] pt of become.

because [bi'kɔz] cj parce que; prep — of à cause de.

beck [bek] n signe m, ordre m.

beckon ['bekən] vt faire signe à, appeler; vi faire signe.

become [bi'kʌm] vi devenir; vt aller bien à.

becoming [bi'kʌmiŋ] a seyant, convenable.

becomingly [bi'kʌmiŋli] ad avec grâce, convenablement.

bed [bed] n lit m, plate-bande f, banc m, gisement m; a de lit; vt coucher, repiquer, dépoter, sceller.

bed-chamber ['bed.tʃeimbə] n chambre f.

bedclothes ['bedklouðz] n pl draps m pl de lit.

bedding ['bediŋ] n literie f.

bedizen [bi'daizn] vt pomponner, affubler.

bed-ridden ['bed.ridn] a alité.

bedroom ['bedrum] n chambre f à coucher.

bedside ['bedsaid] n chevet m.

bedsore ['bedsɔː] n escarre f.

bedspread ['bedspred] n couvre-lit m.

bedstead ['bedsted] n bois de lit m.

bedtime ['bedtaim] n heure f d'aller au lit.

bee [biː] n abeille f.

beech [biːtʃ] n hêtre m.

beef [biːf] n bœuf m, bifteck m.

beehive ['biːhaiv] n ruche f.

beekeeper ['biːkiːpə] n apiculteur m.

beeline ['biːlain] n ligne f droite.

been [biːn] pp of be.

beer [biə] n bière f; millet — pombe m.

beerhouse ['biəhaus] n brasserie f.

beet [biːt] n bette f.

beetle ['biːtl] n (tool) maillet m, masse f, demoiselle f, (insect) blatte f, scarabée m; vi surplomber.

beetling ['biːtliŋ] a saillant, menaçant, bombé, broussailleux, en surplomb.

beetroot ['biːtruːt] n betterave f.

befall [bi'fɔːl] vti arriver (à), advenir, survenir.

befit [bi'fit] vt aller à, convenir à.

befitting [bi'fitiŋ] a seyant, convenable.

before [bi'fɔː] prep avant, devant, par-devant; ad (aupar)avant, devant, en avant; cj avant que, plutôt que.

beforehand [bi'fɔːhænd] ad d'avance, au préalable, par avance, déjà.

befriend [bi'frend] vt traiter (etc) en ami, protéger, venir en aide à.

beg [beg] vt prier, supplier, demander, solliciter, mendier; vi faire le beau, mendier.

began [bi'gæn] pt of begin.

beget [bi'get] *vt* engendrer, procréer, enfanter.

begetter [bi'getə] *n* père *m*.

beggar ['begə] *n* mendiant(e) *mf*, gueux, -se, quémandeur, -euse; *vt* réduire à la misère, mettre sur la paille, défier.

beggarliness ['begəlinis] *n* misère *f*, mesquinerie *f*.

beggarly ['begəli] *a* miséreux, misérable, mesquin.

beggary ['begəri] *n* misère *f*, mendicité *f*.

begin [bi'gin] *vti* commencer; to — with pour commencer; *vt* amorcer, entamer, se mettre à.

beginner [bi'ginə] *n* débutant(e) *mf*, novice *mf*, auteur *m*.

beginning [bi'giniŋ] *n* commencement *m*, début *m*, origine *f*.

begone [bi'gɔn] *excl* sortez! allez-vous en!

begot(ten) [bi'gɔt(n)] *pt of* beget.

begrudge [bi'grʌdʒ] *vt* mesurer, envier, donner à contre-cœur.

beguile [bi'gail] *vt* tromper, charmer, distraire, séduire.

begun [bi'gʌn] *pp of* begin.

behalf [bi'hɑːf] *n* in, on — of au nom de, de la part de, au compte de.

behave [bi'heiv] *vi* se conduire, se comporter, fonctionner.

behaved [bi'heivd] *a* well —sage, bien élevé; **badly** — mal élevé.

behavior [bi'heivjə] *n* conduite *f*, maintien *m*, tenue *f*, manières *f pl*, fonctionnement *m*.

behead [bi'hed] *vt* décapiter.

beheading [bi'hediŋ] *n* décapitation *f*, décollation *f*.

beheld [bi'held] *pt of* behold.

behest [bi'hest] *n* commandement *m*, ordre *m*.

behind [bi'haind] *prep* derrière, en arrière de, en retard sur; *ad* (par) derrière, en arrière.

behold [bi'hould] *vt* apercevoir, voir, regarder.

beholden [bi'houldən] *a* obligé, redevable.

beholder [bi'houldə] *n* spectateur, -trice, témoin *m*.

behoof [bi'huːf] *n* bien *m*; on s.o.'s — à l'intention de, à l'avantage de.

behoove [bi'huːv] *vt* incomber à, seoir à, appartenir à.

being ['biːiŋ] *n* être *m*.

belabor [bi'leibə] *vt* rosser, rouer de coups.

belated [bi'leitid] *a* retardé, en retard, attardé, tardif.

belch [beltʃ] *n* rot *m*, renvoi *m*, grondement *m*, jet de flamme *m*; *vi* roter, éructer; *vt* vomir.

beleaguer [bi'liːgə] *vt* assiéger.

belfry ['belfri] *n* beffroi *m*.

Belgian ['beldʒən] *a n* belge *mf*.

Belgium ['beldʒəm] *n* Belgique *f*.

belie [bi'lai] *vt* démentir, donner un démenti à.

belief [bi'liːf] *n* foi *f*, croyance *f*, conviction *f*.

believe [bi'liːv] *vti* croire; *vt* ajouter foi à; to make — faire semblant.

believer [bi'liːvə] *n* croyant(e) *mf*, partisan *m*.

belittle [bi'litl] *vt* diminuer, décrier, rabaisser.

bell [bel] *n* cloche *f*, sonnette *f*, sonnerie *f*, timbre *m*, grelot *m*, clochette *f*.

bellboy ['belbɔi], **bellhop** ['belhɔp] *n* groom *m*.

bellied ['belid] *a* ventru.

belligerency [bi'lidʒərənsi] *n* état de guerre *m*.

belligerent [bi'lidʒərənt] *a n* belligérant(e) *mf*.

bellow ['belou] *n* mugissement *m*, beuglement *m*, grondement *m*; *vi* mugir, gronder; *vti* beugler, brailler.

bellows ['belouz] *n* soufflet *m*.

belly ['beli] *n* ventre *m*, panse *f*, bedaine *f*; *vt* gonfler; *vi* se gonfler, s'enfler.

bellyful ['beliful] *n* ventrée *f*; to have had one's — en avoir plein le dos.

belong [bi'lɔŋ] *vi* appartenir (à to), être (à to).

belongings [bi'lɔŋiŋz] *n* biens *m pl*, affaires *f pl*, effets *m pl*.

beloved [bi'lʌvd] *a n* (bien-)aimé(e) *mf*, chéri(e) *mf*.

below [bi'lou] *prep* au dessous de, en aval de; *ad* (au, en, là-) dessous, ci-dessous, plus loin, en bas, en aval.

belt [belt] *n* ceinture *f*, ceinturon *m*, courroie *f*, bande *f*, zone *f*; *vt* ceindre, entourer.

bemoan [bi'moun] *vt* pleurer, se lamenter de.

bemuse [bi'mjuːz] *vt* étourdir, stupéfier.

bench [bentʃ] *n* banc *m*, banquette *f*, gradin *m*; établi *m*, tribunal *m*, magistrature *f*.

bend [bend] *n* nœud *m*, courbe *f*, virage *m*, tournant *m*, coude *m*; *pl* mal *m* des caissons; *vti* courber, ployer, plier, fléchir, pencher, arquer; *vi* se courber, s'incliner, tourner, faire un coude (*road etc*); to — back *vt* replier, recourber; *vi* se replier, se recourber; to — down *vi* se baisser, se courber.

beneath [bi'niːθ] *prep* au dessous de, sous; *ad* (au-)dessous, en bas.

Benedictine [ˌbeni'diktin] *a n* bénédictin(e) *mf*; *n* (*liqueur*) bénédictine.

benediction [ˌbeni'dikʃən] *n* bénédiction *f*.

benefaction [ˌbeni'fækʃən] *n* bienfait *m*, don *m*.

benefactor, -tress ['benifæktə, tris] *n* bienfaiteur, -trice, donateur, -trice.

beneficence [bi'nefisəns] *n* bienfaisance *f*.

beneficent [bi'nefisənt] *a* bienfaisant, salutaire.

beneficently [bi'nefisəntli] *ad* généreusement, salutairement.

beneficial [,beni'fiʃəl] *a* avantageux, salutaire.

beneficiary [,beni'fiʃəri] *n* bénéficiaire *m*, bénéficier, -ière.

benefit ['benifit] *n* bénéfice *m*, bien *m*, gouverne *f*, secours (mutuels) *m pl*; *vt* profiter à; *vi* bénéficier, profiter (de by).

benevolence [bi'nevələns] *n* bienveillance *f*, bienfait *m*.

benevolent [bi'nevələnt] *a* bienveillant; — **society** société *f* de secours mutuels.

benighted [bi'naitid] *a* surpris par la nuit, aveuglé, plongé dans l'ignorance.

benign [bi'nain] *a* bénin, -igne, affable, heureux, doux.

benignity [bi'nigniti] *n* bénignité *f*; bienveillance *f*.

bent [bent] *pt of* bend; *n* pli *m*, tour *m*, penchant *m*, dispositions *f pl*; *a* courbé, plié, voûté, arqué, résolu.

benumb [bi'nʌm] *vt* engourdir, transir, frapper de stupeur.

benzine [benzi:n] *n* benzine *f*.

bequeath [bi'kwi:ð] *vt* léguer.

bequest [bi'kwest] *n* legs *m*.

bereave [bi'ri:v] *vt* enlever, ravir, priver.

bereaved [bi'ri:vd] *pp a* affligé, en deuil.

bereavement [bi'ri:vmənt] *n* perte *f*, deuil *m*.

bereft [bi'reft] *pp of* bereave.

berry ['beri] *n* baie *f*, grain *m*.

berth [bə:θ] *n* cabine *f*, couchette *f*; mouillage *m*, place *f*; *vi* mouiller; *vt* amarrer à quai.

beseech [bi'si:tʃ] *vt* supplier, implorer, conjurer.

beset [bi'set] *vt* cerner, entourer, assaillir, obséder.

besetting [bi'setiŋ] — **sin** *n* péché mignon *m*.

beside [bi'said] *prep* à côté de, près de; to be — o.s. être hors de soi.

besides [bi'saidz] *ad* d'ailleurs, en outre, en plus, du reste; *prep* en outre de, sans compter.

besiege [bi'si:dʒ] *vt* assiéger.

besieger [bi'si:dʒə] *n* assiégeant *m*.

besmear [bi'smiə] *vt* graisser, tacher, barbouiller.

besmirch [bi'smə:tʃ] *vt* salir, obscurcir, ternir, souiller.

besom ['bi:zəm] *n* balai de bruyère *m*.

besot [bi'sɔt] *vt* abrutir.

besought [bi'sɔ:t] *pt of* beseech.

bespatter [bi'spætə] *vt* éclabousser.

bespeak [bi'spi:k] *vt* commander, retenir, annoncer.

bespoke [bi'spouk] *a* sur mesure, à façon.

best [best] *a* le meilleur; *ad* le mieux; *n* le mieux *m*; to do one's — faire de son mieux; to look one's — être

à son avantage; to the — of one's ability de son mieux; to get the — of it avoir le dessus; to make the — of it en prendre son parti; to the — of my knowledge autant que je sache; the — of it is that ... le plus beau de l'affaire, c'est que...; — **man** garçon d'honneur.

best-seller ['best'selə] *n* best-seller *m*, livre à succès *m*, grand favori *m*.

bestir [bi'stə:] *vi* to — o.s. se remuer.

bestow [bi'stou] *vt* conférer, octroyer.

bestowal [bi'stouəl] *n* octroi *m*, don *m*.

bestrew [bi'stru:] *vt* joncher, parsemer.

bestride [bi'straid] *vt* enfourcher, enjamber, se mettre à califourchon sur.

bet [bet] *n* pari *m*; *vt* parier; *pt of* bet.

betake [bi'teik] *vt* to — o.s. se rendre.

betimes [bi'taimz] *ad* de bonne heure, à temps.

betoken [bi'toukən] *vt* indiquer, annoncer, révéler.

betray [bi'trei] *vt* livrer, vendre, trahir, montrer.

betrayal [bi'treiəl] *n* trahison *f*, révélation *f*.

betrayer [bi'treiə] *n* traître, -esse.

betrothal [bi'trouðəl] *n* fiançailles *f pl*.

betrothed [bi'trouðd] *an* fiancé(e) *mf*.

better ['betə] *n* parieur *m*; *a* meilleur; *ad* mieux; *vt* améliorer, surpasser; to be — aller mieux, valoir mieux; to get — s'améliorer, se rétablir, guérir; to get the — of l'emporter sur; to think — se raviser; — **and** — de mieux en mieux.

betterment ['betəmənt] *n* amélioration *f*.

between [bi'twi:n] *prep* entre; **far** — clairsemé, rare.

bevel ['bevəl] *n* équerre *f*, biais *m*, biseau *m*; *vt* biseauter, tailler en biais, chanfreiner.

beveled ['bevəld] *a* biseauté, de biais.

beverage ['bevəridʒ] *n* breuvage *m*, boisson *f*.

bevy ['bevi] *n* compagnie *f*, troupe *f*, bande *f*.

bewail [bi'weil] *vt* se lamenter sur, pleurer.

bewailing [bi'weiliŋ] *n* lamentation *f*.

beware [bi'weə] *vi* prendre garde; *vt* to — of prendre garde à (de), se garder de, se méfier de.

bewilder [bi'wildə] *vt* abasourdir, ahurir, dérouter, désorienter, confondre.

bewilderment [bi'wildəmənt] *n* ahurissement *m*, confusion *f*.

bewitch [bi'witʃ] *vt* ensorceler, charmer, enchanter.

bewitchment [bi'wit∫mənt] n ensorcellement m.

beyond [bi'jɔnd] n l'au-delà m; prep au-delà de, après, par-delà, derrière, outre; ad au-delà, plus loin, pardelà.

bias ['baiəs] n biais m, penchant m, tendance f, prévention f, parti-pris m.

biased ['baiəst] a prévenu, tendancieux, partial.

bib [bib] n bavette f, bavoir m.

bibber ['bibə] n soiffard m, buveur m.

Bible ['baibl] n bible f.

biblical ['biblikəl] a biblique.

bibliographer [,bibli'ɔgrəfə] n bibliographe m.

bibliographical [,biblia'græfikəl] a bibliographique.

bibliography [,bibli'ɔgrəfi] n bibliographie f.

bibliophile ['bibliuofail] n bibliophile m.

bicker ['bikə] vi se quereller, se chamailler, murmurer, crépiter, briller.

bickering ['bikəriŋ] n prise de bec f, chamailleries f pl, bisbille f.

bicycle ['baisikl] n bicyclette f.

bid [bid] n offre f, enchère f, demande f; vti commander, dire, inviter, offrir, demander; to — for faire une offre pour; to — s.o. good-day donner le bonjour à qn.

bidden ['bidn] pp of bid.

bidder ['bidə] n enchérisseur m; to the highest — au plus offrant.

bide [baid] vt attendre.

biennial [bai'eniəl] a bisannuel, biennal.

bier [biə] n brancard m, civière f.

big [big] a gros(se), grand.

bigamist ['bigəmist] n bigame mf.

bigamous ['bigəməs] a bigame mf.

bigamy ['bigəmi] n bigamie f.

bight [bait] n baie f, anse f, crique f.

bigness ['bignis] n grosseur f, importance f, grandeur f.

bigot ['bigət] n bigot(e) mf, fanatique mf.

bigotry ['bigətri] n bigoterie f, fanatisme f.

bigwig ['bigwig] n gros bonnet m.

bike [baik] n bécane f, vélo m.

bile [bail] n bile f.

bilge [bildʒ] n sentine f, fond de cale m; vi faire eau; to talk — dire des balivernes.

bilious ['biljəs] a bilieux, cholérique; — attack, crise f de foie.

bilk [bilk] vt filouter, éluder, tromper.

bill [bil] n bec m, facture f, note f, traite f, effet m, addition f; — of fare carte f, affiche f; hand — prospectus m; vt annoncer, afficher, placarder; vi se becqueter; to — and coo faire les tourtereaux.

billet ['bilit] n bûche f, (billet m de) logement m, place f; vt loger, cantonner.

billiard-ball ['biljədbɔ:l] n bille f.

billiard-cloth ['biljədklɔθ] n drap m.

billiard-cue ['biljədkju:] n queue f.

billiard-room ['biljədrum] n salle de billard f.

billiards ['biljədz] n billard m.

billiard-table ['biljəd,teibl] n billard m.

billion ['biljən] n milliard m, billion m.

billow ['bilou] n grande vague f, houle f, lame f; vi se soulever, s'enfler.

billowy ['biloui] a houleux.

bill-poster, -sticker ['bil,poustə, ,stikə] n afficheur m.

bill-posting ['bil,poustiŋ] n affichage m.

billy-goat ['biligout] n bouc m.

bin [bin] n seau m, huche f, boîte à ordures f, panier m, coffre m.

bind [baind] vt lier, attacher, ligoter, bander, obliger, relier, engager.

binder ['baində] n (re)lieur, -euse, botteleur, -euse, bandage m, lieuse f, ceinture f.

binding ['baindiŋ] n reliure f, bordure f, bandage m, liséré m; a obligatoire.

binoculars [bi'nɔkjuləz] n pl jumelle(s) f pl.

biographer [bai'ɔgrəfə] n biographe m.

biographical [,baiou'græfikəl] a biographique.

biography [bai'ɔgrəfi] n biographie f.

biological [baiə'lɔdʒikəl] a biologique.

biologist [bai'ɔlədʒist] n biologue m.

biology [bai'ɔlədʒi] n biologie f.

biped ['baiped] an bipède m.

biplane ['baiplein] n biplan m.

birch [bə:t∫] n bouleau m, verges f pl; vt donner les verges à, flageoler.

bird [bə:d] n oiseau m, perdreau m, volaille f, type m; a — in the hand is worth two in the bush un 'tiens' vaut mieux que deux 'tu l'auras'; to give s.o. the — siffler qn, envoyer promener qn; bird's-eye view vue à vol d'oiseau.

bird-call ['bə:dkɔ:l] n appeau m.

bird-catcher ['bə:d,kæt∫ə] n oiseleur m.

bird-lime ['bə:dlaim] n glu f.

bird-seed ['bə:dsi:d] n mouron m.

birth [bə:θ] n naissance f, origine f, lignée f; to give — to donner le jour à, enfanter, mettre bas; — certificate acte m de naissance.

birthday ['bə:θdei] n anniversaire m, fête f.

birthplace ['bə:θpleis] n lieu natal m, lieu de naissance, berceau m.

birth-rate ['bə:θreit] n natalité f.

birthright ['bə:θrait] n droit m d'aînesse, de naissance.

biscuit ['biskit] n biscuit m, gateau sec m.

bishop ['biʃəp] n évêque m, (chess) fou m.

bishopric ['biʃəprik] n évêché m.

bison ['baisn] n bison m.

bissextile [bi'sekstail] a bissextile.

bit(ten) [bit, 'bitn] pt (pp) of bite.

bit [bit] n mors m, frein m; morceau m, brin m, miette f, bout m, two—a pièce f de ¼ dollar.

bitch [bitʃ] n chienne f etc, femelle f.

bite [bait] n morsure f, piqûre f, bouchée f, touche f, coup de dent m, mordant m; vt mordre, piquer, sucer, prendre, donner un coup de dent à, attraper; vi mordre.

biting ['baitiŋ] a mordant, piquant, cuisant, cinglant, âpre.

bitter ['bitə] a amer, aigre, âpre, rude, cruel, acharné; — cold n froid de loup m; to the — end jusqu'au bout.

bittern ['bitə(:)n] n butor m.

bitterness ['bitənis] n amertume f, acrimonie f, aigreur f, âpreté f, rancune f.

bitumen ['bitjumin] n bitume m.

bituminous [bi'tjuːminəs] a bitumineux.

bivouac ['bivuæk] n bivouac m; vi bivouaquer.

blab [blæb] vt révéler; vi parler au bout vendre la mèche.

blabber ['blæbə] n bavard(e) mf, indiscret, -ète mf.

black [blæk] a noir, triste, sombre; to be — and blue être couvert de bleus; — eye œil poché m, œil au beurre noir m; — Maria panier m à salade; — pudding boudin m; — sheep brebis f galeuse; n noir(e) mf, nègre, négresse; vt noircir, cirer.

blackball ['blækbɔːl] n boule f noire; vt blackbouler.

blackbeetle ['blækbiːtl] n cafard m.

blackberry ['blækbəri] n mûre f; — bush ronce f, mûrier m.

blackbird ['blækbəːd] n merle m.

blackboard ['blækbɔːd] n tableau noir m.

blackcurrant(s) ['blæk'kʌrənt(s)] n cassis m.

blacken ['blækən] vt noircir, assombrir, obscurcir; vi (se) noircir, s'assombrir.

Blackfriar ['blæk'fraiə] n dominicain m.

blackguard ['blægɑːd] n canaille f, vaurien m.

blacking ['blækiŋ] n cirage noir m.

blackish ['blækiʃ] a noirâtre.

blacklead ['blæk'led] n mine f de plomb, plombagine f.

blackleg ['blækleg] n escroc m, renard m, jaune m.

blackmail ['blækmeil] n chantage m; vt faire chanter.

blackmailer ['blækmeilə] n maître chanteur m.

blackness ['blæknis] n noirceur f, obscurité f.

blackout ['blækaut] n couvre-feu m, obscurcissement m, black-out m; vt obscurcir.

blacksmith ['blæksmiθ] n forgeron m, maréchal ferrant m; —'s forge f.

blackthorn ['blækθɔːn] n prunellier m, épine noire f.

bladder ['blædə] n vessie f, outre f gonflée de vent, vésicule f.

blade [bleid] n feuille f, brin m, plat m, pale f, lame f; tranchant m, omoplate f, épaule f, boute-en-train m, luron m.

blame [bleim] n blâme m, faute f; vt blâmer, reprocher, attribuer.

blameless ['bleimlis] a irréprochable, innocent.

blameworthy ['bleim,wəːði] a blâmable, répréhensible.

blanch [blɑːntʃ] vti blanchir, pâlir; vi blêmir.

bland [blænd] a aimable, flatteur, doux, affable, doucereux, suave.

blandish ['blændiʃ] vt flatter, cajoler, amadouer.

blandishment ['blændiʃmənt] n flatterie f, cajolerie f.

blank [blæŋk] n blanc m, billet blanc m, vide m, trou m; a blanc, en (à) blanc, inexpressif, vide, confondu, net.

blanket ['blæŋkit] n couverture f; to toss s.o. in a — verner qn; wet —, rabat-joie m.

blankly ['blæŋkli] ad vaguement, d'un air déconcerté.

blare [blɛə] n sonnerie f, accents cuivrés m pl; vi sonner, retentir; vt faire retentir, brailler.

blarney ['blɑːni] n eau f bénite de cour, boniments m pl, flagornerie f, pommade f.

blaspheme [blæs'fiːm] vti blasphémer.

blasphemer [blæs'fiːmə] n blasphémateur, -trice.

blasphemous ['blæsfiməs] a blasphématoire, blasphémateur, impie.

blasphemy ['blæsfimi] n blasphème m.

blast [blɑːst] n souffle m, coup de vent m, charge explosive f, rafale f, sonnerie f; vt faire sauter, foudroyer flétrir, brûler, détruire, anéantir.

blast-furnace ['blɑːst,fəːnis] n haut-fourneau m.

blasting ['blɑːstiŋ] n sautage m coups m pl de mine, foudroiement m, anéantissement m.

blast-off ['blɑːstɔːf] n mise f à feu.

blatant ['bleitənt] a bruyant, criard criant.

blaze [bleiz] n flamme f, flambée f éclat m, conflagration f; go to — allez au diable! vi trompeter; flamber, flamboyer, resplendir; to — up s'enflammer, s'emporter, s révolter.

blazon ['bleizn] n blason m, armoirie f pl; vt blasonner; to — fort proclamer, publier, crier du haut des toits.

bleach [bli:tʃ] vti blanchir; vi décolorer; n décolorant m, agent de blanchiment m.

bleak [bli:k] n ablette f; a blème, battu des vents, désolé, glacial, désert.

bleary [bliəl] a confus, vague, chassieux; vt brouiller, estomper, rendre trouble.

bleat [bli:t] n bêlement m; vi bêler.

bleed [bli:d] vti saigner.

bleeding ['bli:diŋ] n saignement m, saignée f; a saignant, ensanglanté.

blemish ['blemiʃ] n tache f, défaut m, tare f; vt gâter, (en)tacher, souiller.

blench [blentʃ] vi broncher, pâlir, blêmir.

blend [blend] n mélange m, alliance f; vt mêler, mélanger, fondre, marier; vi se mêler, se mélanger, se marier, se confondre.

bless [bles] vt bénir, consacrer, accorder.

blessed ['blesid] a béni, comble, bienheureux, saint, fichu.

blessedness ['blesidnis] n félicité f.

blessing ['blesiŋ] n bénédiction f, bénédicité m.

blew [blu:] pt of blow.

blight [blait] n mildiou m, rouille f, nielle f, brouissure f, fléau m; vt frapper de mildiou, rouiller, nieller, brouir, moisir, flétrir.

blind [blaind] n store m, jalousie f, feinte f; a aveugle, invisible, masqué; sans issue; vt aveugler, crever les yeux à, éblouir.

blindfold ['blaindfould] a ad les yeux bandés; vt bander les yeux à.

blindly ['blaindli] ad aveuglément, à l'aveugle(tte).

blindman's buff ['blaindmænz'bʌf] n colin-maillard m.

blindness ['blaindnis] n cécité f, aveuglement m.

blink [bliŋk] n lueur f, coup d'œil m, clignement d'yeux m, échappée f; vi ciller, cligner, clignoter, papilloter; to — at fermer les yeux sur.

blinkers ['bliŋkəz] n œillères f pl.

bliss [blis] n félicité f, béatitude f.

blister ['blistə] n ampoule f, cloque f, boursuflure f.

blithe [blaið] a joyeux.

blitz [blits] n guerre-éclair f; bombardement m.

blizzard ['blizəd] n tempête f, tourmente de neige f.

bloat [blout] vt saler et fumer, enfler, gonfler, bouffir.

bloated ['bloutid] a bouffi, gonflé, congestionné.

bloater ['bloutə] n hareng saur m.

blob [blɔb] n tache f, pâté d'encre m.

block [blɔk] n bûche f, souche f, billot m, bloc m, obstruction f, tronçon m; **traffic —** embouteillage

m; **— of houses** pâté de maisons m; **— of flats** immeuble m; vt bloquer, obstruer, boucher, encombrer, barrer.

blockade [blɔ'keid] n blocus m; **to run the —** braver le blocus; vt bloquer, obstruer, faire le blocus de.

blockhead ['blɔkhed] n tête f de bois, bûche f.

blockhouse ['blɔkhaus] n blokhaus m.

bloke [blouk] n (fam) type m, individu m, coco m.

blood [blʌd] n sang m; **in cold —** de sang-froid; **his — was up** il était monté.

blood-donor ['blʌd'dounə] n donneur de sang m.

bloodhound ['blʌdhaund] n limier m, détective m.

bloodless ['blʌdlis] a exsangue, anémié, sans effusion de sang.

bloodletting ['blʌd'letiŋ] n saignée f.

blood poisoning ['blʌd'pɔizniŋ] n empoisonnement m du sang, toxémie f.

bloodshed ['blʌdʃed] n massacre m, carnage m.

bloodshot ['blʌdʃɔt] a injecté de sang.

bloodsucker ['blʌd'sʌkə] n sangsue f.

bloodthirsty ['blʌd'θə:sti] a sanguinaire, assoiffé de sang.

bloodvessel ['blʌd'vesl] n vaisseau sanguin m.

bloody ['blʌdi] a sanglant, en (de, du) sang, ensanglanté, sanguinaire; ad rudement, diablement.

bloom [blu:m] n fleur f, épanouissement m, duvet m, velouté m; vi fleurir, être dans sa, en, fleur.

bloomer ['blu:mə] n gaffe f, bévue f, bourde f.

blooming ['blu:miŋ] n fleuraison f; a en fleur, fleurissant, florissant, sacré.

blossom ['blɔsəm] n fleur f; vi fleurir; to — out s'épanouir.

blot [blɔt] n tache f, pâté m, défaut m; vt faire des taches sur, noircir (du papier), sécher, boire; to — out effacer, anéantir.

blotch [blɔtʃ] n pustule f, tache f; vt marbrer, couvrir de taches.

blotchy ['blɔtʃi] a marbré, couperosé.

blotting-paper ['blɔtiŋ.peipə] n buvard m.

blouse [blauz] n blouse f, chemisette f; camisole f, chemisier m.

blow [blou] n coup m, souffle m d'air, floraison f; vi souffler, venter, fleurir, fondre, sauter; vt souffler, essoufler, chasser, faire sauter; to — a kiss envoyer un baiser; to — one's nose se moucher; to — away emporter; to — down (r)abattre, renverser; to — out souffler, éteindre, enfler; vi s'éteindre; to — up vi sauter; vt faire sauter, gonfler.

blower ['blouə] n souffleur m, tablier de cheminée m.

blowfly ['blouflai] n mouche f à viande.

blown [bloun] pp of blow.

blowpipe ['bloupaip] n chalumeau m, canne f, sarbacane f.

blowy ['bloui] a venteux, balayé par le vent.

blubber ['blʌbə] n graisse f de baleine, vi pleurer bruyamment, pleurnicher, pleurer comme un veau.

blubberer ['blʌbərə] n pleurnicheur, -euse, pleurard(e) mf.

bludgeon ['blʌdʒən] n trique f, matraque f; vt assommer, asséner un coup de matraque à.

blue [blu:] a bleu; n bleu m, ciel m, la grande bleue f; to have the —s avoir le cafard, les papillons noirs; light — bleu clair; dark — bleu foncé; navy — bleu marine; Prussian — bleu de Prusse; sky — bleu de ciel; vt bleuir, passer au bleu, gaspiller.

bluebell ['blu:bel] n clochette f, campanule f.

bluebottle ['blu: bɔtl] n bluet m, mouche bleue f.

bluejacket ['blu:.dʒækit] n matelot m.

blue-stocking ['blu:'stɔkin] n bas-bleu m.

bluff [blʌf] n cap escarpé m, bluff m; vti bluffer; vi faire du bluff; a à pic, brusque, cordial.

bluffness ['blʌfnis] n brusquerie f cordiale, franc-parler m.

bluish ['blu:iʃ] a bleuâtre, bleuté.

blunder ['blʌndə] n bévue f, gaffe f; vi faire une gaffe, gaffer; to — into heurter; to — along marcher à l'aveuglette.

blunderbuss ['blʌndəbʌs] n tromblon m.

blundering ['blʌndərin] a maladroit, brouillon.

blunt [blʌnt] a émoussé, brusque, franc; vt émousser.

bluntly ['blʌntli] ad rudement, carrément.

bluntness ['blʌntnis] n rudesse f, brusquerie f, état émoussé m.

blur [blə:] n tache f, macule f, buée f, effet confus m; vt tacher, obscurcir, troubler, brouiller, voiler, estomper.

blurb [blə:b] n annonce f, fadaises f pl.

blurt [blə:t] vt to — out lâcher, raconter de but en blanc.

blush [blʌʃ] n rougeur f; vi rougir.

blushingly ['blʌʃinli] ad en rougissant.

bluster ['blʌstə] n fracas m, rodomontades f pl, jactance f, menaces f pl; vi faire rage, s'emporter, le prendre de haut, fanfaronner, faire du fracas.

blusterer ['blʌstərə] n fanfaron m, rodmont m.

blustering ['blʌstərin] a soufflant en rafales, bravache.

boa ['bouə] n boa m.

boar [bɔ:] n verrat m, sanglier m.

board [bɔ:d] n planche f, madrier m, tableau m, carton m, pension f, commission f, ministère m, conseil m, comité m; above — franc, net; on — à bord (de); vi être en pension, prendre pension; vt planchéier, prendre en pension, aborder, aller à bord de, s'embarquer sur; to — out mettre en pension; to — up condamner, boucher.

boarder ['bɔ:də] n pensionnaire mf.

boarding-house ['bɔ:diŋhaus] n pension f.

boarding-school ['bɔ:diŋsku:l] n pensionnat m, internat m.

boast [boust] n hâblerie f, vanterie f; vi se vanter, se faire gloire (de about).

boaster ['boustə] n vantard m, fanfaron m, hâbleur m.

boastful ['boustful] a vantard, glorieux.

boat [bout] n bateau m, barque f, canot m, embarcation f; to be in the same — être logés à la même enseigne; vi aller, se promener en bateau, faire du canotage.

boater ['boutə] n (hat) canotier m.

boat-hook ['bouthuk] n gaffe f.

boating ['boutiŋ] n canotage m, partie de canotage f.

boatman ['boutmən] n batelier m, loueur de canots m.

boat-race ['boutreis] n course de bateaux f, match d'aviron m, régate f.

boatswain ['bousn] n maître d'équipage m.

bob [bɔb] n bouche f, bonchon m, plomb m, coiffure f à la Ninon, courbette f, petit bond m; vt couper court, écourter; vi danser, s'agiter, faire la courbette.

bobbin ['bɔbin] n bobine f.

bobby ['bɔbi] n (fam) sergot m, flic m.

bode [boud] vt présager.

bodice ['bɔdis] n corsage m, cachecorset m.

bodily ['bɔdili] a corporel, physique; ad corporellement, en corps.

boding ['boudiŋ] n présage m, pressentiment m.

bodkin ['bɔdkin] n passelacet m, épingle f.

body ['bɔdi] n corps m, cadavre m, carrosserie f, fuselage m, substance f, consistance f.

bog [bɔg] n marais m, bourbier m, fondrière f, marécage m; v: enliser, embourber; to get bogged s'enliser.

bogey ['bougi] n épouvantail m, lutin m, croquemitaine m, le Père Fouettard m.

boggle ['bɔgl] vi to — at, over réchigner à, devant, reculer, hésiter devant.

boggy ['bɔgi] a marécageux, tourbeux.

bogle ['bougl] n fantôme m, épouvantail m.

bogus ['bougəs] a faux, véreux.

boil [bɔil] n furoncle m, clou m; vi bouillir, bouillonner; vt faire bouillir, faire cuire; to — down vt condenser, réduire; vi se réduire; to — over déborder.

boiler ['bɔilə] n chaudière f, bouilloire f, lessiveuse f.

boiler-maker ['bɔiləmeikə] n chaudronnier m.

boiling ['bɔiliŋ] n ébullition f, remous m, bouillonnement m.

boisterous ['bɔistərəs] a violent, exubérant, tapageur, bruyant, tempétueux.

boisterousness ['bɔistərəsnis] n violence f, exubérance f, turbulence f.

bold [bould] a hardi, téméraire, audacieux, effronté; to make — to se permettre de, oser.

boldness ['bouldnis] n hardiesse f, effronterie f, audace f.

bole [boul] n tronc m, fût m.

Bolshevism ['bɔlʃivizəm] n bolchevisme m.

Bolshevist ['bɔlʃivist] n bolcheviste mf.

bolster ['boulstə] n traversin m, coussinet m; vt soutenir, préserver, appuyer.

bolt [boult] n verrou m, pêne m, boulon m, coup de foudre m, culasse f; vt verrouiller, enfermer, boulonner, avaler tout rond, gober, bouffer; vi s'emballer, détaler, déguerpir, décamper, filer, lever le pied.

bolter ['boultə] n blutoir m; vt bluter.

bolting ['boultiŋ] n blutage m.

bomb [bɔm] n bombe f; time — bombe f à retardement; —proof à l'abri des bombes.

bombard [bɔm'bɑːd] vt bombarder, pilonner.

bombast ['bɔmbæst] n emphase f, grandiloquence f.

bombastic [bɔm'bæstik] a ampoulé, emphatique.

bomb-crater ['bɔmkreitə] n entonnoir m.

bomber ['bɔmə] n bombardier m.

bond [bɔnd] n attache f, lien m, engagement m, obligation f, dépôt m, bon m, entrepôt m, douane f; pl fers m pl; vt assembler, entreposer, mettre en dépôt.

bondage ['bɔndidʒ] n servitude f, esclavage m, emprisonnement m.

bondholder ['bɔnd,houldə] n obligataire m, porteur m de bons.

bondsman ['bɔndzmən] n esclave m.

bone [boun] n os m, (fish) arêt: f; ossements m pl; vt désosser, escamoter.

boneless ['bounlis] a mou, désossé, sans arêtes.

bonfire ['bɔn,faiə] n feu m de joie.

bonnet ['bɔnit] n bonnet m, béguin m, capot m; bee in the — araignée dans le plafond.

bonny ['bɔni] a beau, joli.

bonus ['bounəs] n boni m, prime f, gratification f.

bony ['bouni] a osseux, décharné, anguleux, tout os, plein d'arêtes.

boo [buː] n huée; vt huer.

booby ['buːbi] n niais(e) mf, nigaud(e) mf.

booby-trap ['buːbitræp] n attrape-nigaud m.

book [buk] n livre m, bouquin m, livret m, cahier m, carnet m; vt entrer, inscrire, enregistrer, louer.

bookbinder ['buk,baində] n relieur m.

bookbinding ['buk,baindiŋ] n reliure f.

bookcase ['bukkeis] n bibliothèque f.

book-ends ['bukendz] n pl serre-livres m inv.

booking ['bukiŋ] n location f, inscription f, réservation f.

booking-office ['bukiŋ,ɔfis] n bureau m de location, guichet m.

bookish ['bukiʃ] a livresque.

book-keeper ['buk,kiːpə] n teneur m de livres, comptable m.

book-keeping ['buk,kiːpiŋ] n tenue f de livres, comptabilité f.

booklet ['buklit] n livret m, brochure f.

bookmaker ['buk,meikə] n bookmaker m.

bookmark ['bukmɑːk] n signet m.

bookseller ['buk,selə] n libraire m.

book-sewer ['buk,souə] n brocheur m.

bookshop ['bukʃɔp] n librairie f.

bookstall ['bukstɔːl] n étalage m de livres, (station) bibliothèque f.

bookworm ['bukwəːm] n rat de bibliothèque m.

boom [buːm] n emballement m, vogue f, hausse rapide f, boom m, grondement m, ronflement m, barrage m; vt faire de la réclame pour, faire du tapage, du battage, autour de; vi entrer en hausse, s'emballer, trouver la grande vente, retentir, ronfler, tonner.

boon [buːn] n faveur f, don m, bénédiction f, avantage m; — companion bon vivant m, bon compagnon m.

boor [buə] n rustre m, goujat m, paysan m.

boorishness ['buəriʃnis] n rusticité f, grossièreté f.

boost [buːst] vt faire du tapage autour de, faire de la réclame pour, lancer, chauffer.

boot [buːt] n bottine f, botte f, brodequin m, coffre m.

bootblack ['buːtblæk] n cireur m.

booth [buːð] n tente f, baraque f, salle f de scrutin.

boot-jack ['buːtdʒæk] n tirebottes m.

bootleg ['buːt.leg] vi faire la contrebande des boissons alcooliques.

bootmaker ['buːt.meikə] n bottier m, cordonnier m.

boot polish ['buːt.pɔliʃ] v cirage m, crème f à chaussures.

boots [buːts] n garçon m d'étage, cireur m de chaussures.

booty ['buːti] n butin m.

booze [buːz] n (fam) boisson f; vi chopiner, être en ribote.

bopeep [bou'piːp] n cache-cache m.

border ['bɔːdə] n bord m, bordure f, marge f, lisière f, frontière f; vt border; to — upon frôler, toucher à, tirer sur, friser, côtoyer.

borderer ['bɔːdərə] n frontalier, -ière.

borderline ['bɔːdəlain] n ligne de démarcation f; — case cas limite m.

bore [bɔː] pt of bear; n (gun) âme f, calibre m, trou m, mascaret m, raseur m, importun(e) mf, corvée f, scie f; vt forer, percer, assommer, ennuyer; vi (horse) encenser.

boredom ['bɔːdəm] n ennui m.

boring ['bɔːriŋ] a ennuyeux, assommant.

born [bɔːn] pp né; to be — naître; **he was** — il est né, il naquit; **to be — again** renaître.

borne [bɔːn] pp of bear.

borough ['bʌrə] n bourg m.

borrow ['bɔrou] vt emprunter.

borrower ['bɔrouə] n emprunteur, -euse.

borrowing ['bɔrouiŋ] n emprunt m.

bosh [bɔʃ] n blague f, fariboles f pl, chansons f pl.

bosom ['buzəm] n sein m, giron m, poitrine f, cœur m, surface f; a intime.

boss [bɔs] n bosse f, patron, -onne.

bossy ['bɔsi] a autoritaire.

botanist ['bɔtənist] n botaniste mf.

botany ['bɔtəni] n botanique f.

botch [bɔtʃ] n travail malfait m, ravaudage m; vt ravauder, saboter; to — up retaper, rafistoler.

both [bouθ] pn tous (les) deux, l'un et l'autre; a deux; ad à la fois, tant . . . que . . .

bother ['bɔðə] n ennui m, tracas m, embêtement m; vt ennuyer, tourmenter, tracasser, embêter; vi s'inquiéter, se faire de la bile; excl zut!

bottle ['hɔtl] n bouteille f, flacon m, bocal m, (hay) botte f, (baby's) biberon m; hot-water — bouillote f, moine m; vt mettre en bouteilles, botteler; to — up ravaler, refouler, étouffer, embouteiller.

bottleneck ['bɔtlnek] n étranglement m, goulot m, embouteillage m.

bottle-washer ['bɔtl.wɔʃə] n plongeur m.

bottom ['bɔtəm] n fond m, derrière m, siège m, lit m, bas bout m, queue f, bas m, dessous m; vt mettre un fond, siège, à; vi toucher le fond; **to get to the** — of approfondir.

bottomless ['bɔtəmlis] a sans fond, insondable.

bough [bau] n rameau m, branche f.

boulder ['bouldə] n gros galet m, roche f, pierre f roulée.

bounce [bauns] n bond m, vantardise f, épate f; vt faire rebondir; vi (re)bondir, se vanter, faire de l'épate.

bouncer ['baunsə] n hâbleur m, épateur m, mensonge impudent m, expulseur m, videur m.

bound [baund] pt pp of bind; n limite f, bornes f pl, saut m, bond m; vt borner, limiter; vi (re)bondir, (sur)sauter; a à destination de, en route (pour), lié (à to), tenu (de to); **he is** — **to come** il ne peut pas manquer de venir.

boundary ['baundəri] n frontière f, limite f, bornes f pl.

bounden ['baundən] a sacré, impérieux.

boundless ['baundlis] a illimité, infini, sans bornes.

bounteous ['bauntiəs] a abondant, généreux.

bountiful ['bauntiful] a généreux, bienfaisant.

bounty ['baunti] n générosité f, munificence f, fondation f, prime f, subvention f.

bouquet [bu'kei] n bouquet m.

bout [baut] n tour m, orgie f, crise f, accès m, lutte f.

bow [bou] n courbe f, arc m, (coup d')archet m, nœud m; a arqué, cintré.

bow [bau] n révérence f, salut m, avant m, étrave f; vt courber, incliner, baisser, plier, voûter; vi s'incliner, faire une révérence.

bowels ['bauəlz] n boyaux m pl, entrailles f pl, intestins m pl.

bower ['bauə] n charmille f, tonnelle f.

bowl [boul] n bol m, jatte f, coupe f, (pipe) fourneau m, boule f; pl (jeu de) boules f pl; vt rouler, lancer; vi jouer aux boules; to — over renverser.

bowler ['boulə] n joueur m de boules, (hat) melon m.

bowling-green ['bouliŋgriːn] n boulingrin m, jeu m de boules.

bowman ['boumən] n archer m.

bowsprit ['bousprit] n beaupré m.

bow-window ['bou'windou] n fenêtre cintrée f, en saillie.

box [bɔks] n boîte f, caisse f, coffre m, carton m, tirelire f, tronc m, loge f, barre f, siège m du cocher, guérite f, pavillon m de chasse, (*horse*) box m, stalle *f*; — **on the ear** gifle *f*, claque *f*; vt to — s.o.'s ears gifler qn, calotter; vi boxer, faire de la boxe.

boxer ['bɔksə] n boxeur m.

boxing ['bɔksiŋ] n boxe *f*.

box-office ['bɔks'ɔfis] n bureau m de location.

box-room ['bɔksrum] n (chambre *f* de) débarras m.

boxwood ['bɔkswud] n buis m.

boy [bɔi] n enfant m, garçon m, gars m, élève m, gamin m, boy m.

boycott ['bɔikət] vt boycotter.

boycotting ['bɔikɔtiŋ] n boycottage m.

boyhood ['bɔihud] n enfance *f*, adolescence *f*.

boyish ['bɔiiʃ] a garçonnier, puéril, enfantin, de garçon, d'enfant.

brace [breis] n attache *f*, croisillon m, acolade *f*, vilebrequin m, paire *f*, couple *f*; pl bretelles *f* pl; vt attacher, armer, ancrer, tendre, coupler, fortifier; to — up ravigoter, remonter, retremper; to — o.s. se raidir.

bracelet ['breislit] n bracelet m.

bracing ['breisiŋ] a fortifiant, tonique, tonifiant.

bracken ['brækən] n fougère *f*.

bracket ['brækit] n applique *f*, console *f*, tasseau m, (*gas*) bras m, parenthèse *f*, crochet m; vt mettre entre parenthèses, accoler.

bracket-seat ['brækit ̩siːt] n strapontin m.

brackish ['brækiʃ] a saumâtre.

brag [bræg] n vantardise *f*, fanfaronnade *f*; vi se vanter.

braggart ['brægət] n vantard m, fanfaron m.

braid [breid] n natte *f*, tresse *f*, galon m, lacet m, ganse *f*, soutache *f*; vt natter, border, soutacher galonner, passementer.

brain [brein] n cerveau m, cervelle *f*; to rack one's —s se creuser la cervelle; a cérébral; vt assommer, casser la tête à.

brain-child ['breintʃaild] n conception personnelle *f*.

brain-drain ['breindrein] n brain-drain m.

brain-fever ['brein̩fiːvə] n fièvre cérébrale *f*.

brainless ['breinlis] a idiot, stupide.

brainwave ['breinweiv] n idée géniale *f*, trouvaille *f*, inspiration *f*.

brainy ['breini] a (*fam*) intelligent; to be — avoir de la tête.

braise [breiz] vt braiser.

brake [breik] n fourré m, hallier m, frein m; vti freiner; vi serrer le frein.

brakeman ['breikmən] n serre-frein m.

bramble ['bræmbl] n ronce *f*, mûrier m des haies; — berry mûre sauvage *f*.

bran [bræn] n son m.

branch [braːntʃ] n branche *f*, rameau m, bras m, embranchement m, filiale *f*, succursale *f*; vi to — out se ramifier; to — off bifurquer.

branch-line, -road ['braːntʃlain, roud] n embranchement m, bifurcation *f*.

brand [brænd] n tison m, brandon m, marque *f*, fer rouge m; vt marquer au fer rouge, cautériser, stigmatiser, flétrir.

brandish ['brændiʃ] vt brandir.

brand-new ['brænd'njuː] a flambant neuf.

brandy ['brændi] n cognac m, eau *f* de vie; liqueur — fine champagne *f*.

brass [braːs] n cuivre jaune m, laiton m, les cuivres m pl, toupet m, (sl) galette *f*.

brass-band ['braːs'bænd] n fanfare *f*.

brass-hat ['braːs'hæt] n officier d'état-major m, galonnard m.

brassière ['bræsiə] n soutien-gorge m.

brass-plate ['braːs'pleit] n plaque *f*.

brassware ['braːsweə] n dinanderie *f*.

brat [bræt] n mioche mf, moutard m.

bravado [brə'vaːdou] n crânerie *f*, bravade *f*.

brave [breiv] a brave, courageux, beau, élégant; vt braver, affronter.

bravery ['breivəri] n bravoure *f*, courage m, élégance *f*, atours m pl.

brawl [brɔːl] n dispute *f*, rixe *f*, bagarre *f*, murmure m, bruissement m; vi se chamailler, se bagarrer, brailler, bruire, murmurer.

brawn [brɔːn] n muscle m, fromage m de tête.

brawny ['brɔːni] a musclé, costaud.

bray [brei] n braiment m; vti braire; vt broyer.

braze [breiz] vt souder, braser.

brazen ['breizn] a d'airain, effronté, cynique; to — it out payer d'audace.

brazier ['breizjə] n chaudronnier m, braséro m.

breach [briːtʃ] n brèche *f*, rupture *f*, contravention *f*, violation *f*, infraction *f*; vt faire (une) brèche dans, percer.

bread [bred] n pain m; fresh — pain frais; stale — pain rassis; brown — pain bis; whole-wheat — pain complet; — bin huche *f* au pain, maie *f*.

bread-crumbs ['bredkrʌmz] n pl chapelure *f*, gratin m.

breadth [bredθ] n largeur *f*, ampleur *f*.

break [breik] n fracture *f*, cassure *f*, rupture *f*, alinéa m, percée *f*, trouée *f*, lacune *f*, trou m, arrêt m, répit m; — of day point du jour m; vt (inter)rompre, casser, briser, entamer, violer, manquer à, amortir, résilier; vi (se) briser, (se) rompre, (se) casser, poindre, muer, s'altérer, déferler; to — **down** vt démolir, supprimer; venir à bout de; vi s'effondrer, échouer, demeurer court, fondre en larmes, rester en panne; to — **in** vt défoncer, enfoncer, dresser; vi intervenir, entrer par effraction, faire irruption; to — **off** vt détacher, casser, (inter) rompre; vi se détacher, s'(inter) rompre; to — **out** s'évader, se déclarer, éclater; to — **through** vt enfoncer, percer, trouer; vi faire une percée, se frayer un passage; to — **up** vt démolir, séparer, désarmer, démembrer, morceler, disperser, rompre; vi se désagréger, se séparer, se disperser, se démembrer, entrer en vacances.

breakable ['breikəbl] a fragile.
breakage ['breikidʒ] n casse f, fracture f.
breakdown ['breikdaun] n panne f, effondrement nerveux m, rupture f, insuccès m, interruption f.
breaker ['breikə] n dresseur, -euse, dompteur, -euse, brisant m, violateur, -trice.
breakfast ['brekfəst] n petit déjeuner m; vi déjeuner.
breakneck ['breiknek] a à se rompre le cou.
break-through ['breik'θru:] n percée f, trouée f.
break-up ['breik'ʌp] n dissolution f dispersion f, affaissement m, entrée f en vacances.
breakwater ['breik,wɔ:tə] n brise-lames m, môle m.
bream [brirm] n brème f.
breast [brest] n poitrine f, sein m, poitrail m, blanc m, devant m.
breastbone ['brestboun] n sternum m.
breasted ['brestid] a **single—** droit; **double—** croisé.
breastplate ['brestpleit] n cuirasse f, plastron m.
breast-stroke ['breststrouk] n brasse f (sur le ventre).
breath [breθ] n souffle m, haleine f, bouffée f; last — dernier soupir m, âme f; under one's — à mi-voix, en sourdine.
breathe [bri:ð] vti souffler, respirer; vt exhaler, murmurer; to — **in** aspirer; to — **out** exhaler.
breather ['bri:ðə] n moment de répit m; to give a — to s.o. laisser souffler qn; to go for a — aller prendre l'air.
breathing ['bri:ðiŋ] n respiration f.
breathless ['breθlis] a essoufflé.
breathlessness ['breθlisnis] n essoufflement m.
bred [bred] pp pt of **breed**.
breech [bri:tʃ] n culasse f, derrière m; pl culotte f.
breed [bri:d] n race f, lignée f, couvée f, espèce f; vt porter, élever,

produire, engendrer, procréer; vi multiplier, se reproduire, faire de l'élevage.
breeder ['bri:də] n éleveur m, reproducteur, -trice.
breeding ['bri:diŋ] n élevage m, reproduction f, éducation f, savoir vivre m.
breeze [bri:z] n brise f, grabuge m.
breezy ['bri:zi] a venteux, désinvolte, bruyant.
brethren ['breðrin] n pl frères m pl.
Breton ['bretən] an Breton, -onne.
breviary ['bri:vjəri] n bréviaire m.
brevity ['breviti] n brièveté f.
brew [bru:] vt brasser, faire infuser, fomenter; vi fermenter, s'infuser, se préparer, se mijoter, se tramer.
brewer ['bru:ə] n brasseur m.
brewery ['bru:əri] n brasserie f.
brewing ['bru:iŋ] n brassage m.
briar ['braiə] n ronce f, bruyère f, églantier m; — **rose** églantine f.
bribe [braib] n pot-de-vin m; vt acheter, soudoyer, graisser la patte à.
bribery ['braibəri] n corruption f.
bribing ['braibiŋ] n corruption f, subornation f.
brick [brik] n brique f; to drop a — faire une gaffe.
brick-kiln ['brikkiln] n four m à briques.
bricklayer ['brikleiə] n maçon m.
brickwork ['brikwə:k] n maçonnerie f.
bridal ['braidl] a de noce, de mariée, nuptial, de mariage.
bride [braid] n mariée f, jeune mariée f.
bridegroom ['braidgrum] n marié m.
bridesmaid ['braidzmeid] n demoiselle d'honneur f.
bridge [bridʒ] n pont m, passerelle f, (nose) dos m, (violin) chevalet m, (cards) bridge m; vt jeter un pont sur, relier, combler.
bridgehead ['bridʒhed] n tête de pont f, point d'appui m.
Bridget ['bridʒit] Brigitte f.
bridge-train ['bridʒtrein] n les pontonniers m pl, train de pontons m.
bridle ['braidl] n bridon m, bride f, frein m; vt brider, refréner; vi se rebiffer, se redresser, regimber.
brief [bri:f] n bref m, dossier m, exposé m, cause f; vt engager, constituer, rédiger; a bref, court; in — bref, en résumé.
briefless ['bri:flis] a sans cause.
briefly ['bri:fli] ad brièvement.
brig [brig] n brick m.
brigade [bri'geid] n brigade f.
brigadier [brigə'diə] n général m de brigade.
brigand ['brigənd] n bandit m, brigand m.
bright ['brait] a clair, vif, éclatant, lumineux, brillant, éveillé.

brighten ['braitn] *vt* animer, éclairer, égayer, dérider, fourbir; *vi* s'animer, s'éclairer, se dérider, s'épanouir, s'éclaircir.

brightness ['braitnis] *n* éclat *m*, splendeur *f*, vivacité *f*.

brilliant ['briljənt] *a* brillant.

brilliantly ['briljəntli] *ad* brillamment, avec brio.

brim [brim] *n* bord *m*, *vt* remplir jusqu'au bord; to — over déborder.

brimstone ['brimstən] *n* soufre *m*.

brine [brain] *n* saumure *f*; *vt* saler.

bring [briŋ] *vt* apporter, amener, faire venir; to — about causer, amener, produire, effectuer, opérer, entraîner, occasionner; to — down abattre, (r)abaisser, terrasser, faire crouler, descendre; to — forth produire, mettre au monde, mettre bas, provoquer; to — forward avancer, reporter; to — in introduire, faire entrer, rapporter, faire intervenir; to — off mener à bien, réussir, sauver, renflouer; to — out faire (res)sortir, faire valoir, mettre en relief, lancer; to — round ranimer, (r)amener; to — together réunir, réconcilier; to — up élever, (faire) monter, avancer, mettre sur le tapis, rendre.

brink [briŋk] *n* bord *m*; on the — of près de, à la veille de.

briny ['braini] *a* salé, saumâtre; *n* (fam) mer *f*.

brisk [brisk] *a* vif, actif, fringant, animé, gazeux, vivifiant, frais.

brisket ['briskit] *n* poitrine *f* (de bœuf).

briskness ['brisknis] *n* vivacité *f*, activité *f*.

bristle ['brisl] *n* soie *f*, crin *m*, poil *m*; *vt* faire dresser, hérisser; *vi* se hérisser, se rebiffer, regimber.

bristling ['brisliŋ] *a* hérissé.

Britain ['britn] *n* Angleterre *f*; Great — Grande Bretagne *f*.

British ['britiʃ] *a* anglais, britannique.

Briton ['britn] *n* Anglais(e) *mf*.

Brittany ['britəni] *n* Bretagne *f*.

brittle ['britl] *a* fragile, cassant.

brittleness ['britlnis] *n* fragilité *f*.

broach [broutʃ] *n* broche *f*, flèche *f*, perçoir *m*, foret *m*; *vt* percer, mettre en perce, entamer, embrocher.

broad [brɔːd] *a* large, plein, grivois, hardi, libre, marqué; *n* (sl) poupée *f*.

broadcast ['brɔːdkɑːst] *vt* radiodiffuser, répandre, disséminer; *n* émission *f*, radio-reportage *m*, audition *f*.

broadcaster ['brɔːdkɑːstə] *n* microphoniste *mf*, artiste *mf* de la radio.

broadcasting ['brɔːdkɑːstiŋ] *n* radiodiffusion *f*; — station poste émetteur *m*.

broaden ['brɔːdn] *vt* élargir; *vi* s'élargir, s'évaser.

broadening ['brɔːdniŋ] *n* élargissement *m*.

broad-minded ['brɔːdmaindid] *a* tolérant, aux idées larges.

broadness ['brɔːdnis] *n* largeur *f*, grossièreté *f*.

broadside ['brɔːdsaid] *n* bordée *f*, flanc *m*, travers *m*.

brocade [brə'keid] *n* brocart *m*.

broil [brɔil] *n* dispute *f*, rixe *f*; *vti* (faire) griller.

broiling ['brɔiliŋ] *a* ardent, torride.

broke [brouk] *pt* of break; *a* sans le sou, dans la dèche.

broken ['broukən] *pp* of break; *a* brisé, détraqué, raboteux, incertain, en pièces, (entre)coupé, agité, décousu.

brokenly ['broukənli] *ad* sans suite, par à-coups.

broken-winded ['broukən'windid] *a* poussif.

broker ['broukə] *n* revendeur, -euse, courtier *m*, agent *m* de change, brocanteur *m*.

brokerage ['broukəridʒ] *n* courtage *m*.

bronchitis [brɔŋ'kaitis] *n* bronchite *f*.

bronze [brɔnz] *n* bronze *m*; *vt* bronzer; *vi* se bronzer.

brooch [broutʃ] *n* broche *f*.

brood [bruːd] *n* couvée *f*, nichée *f*, volée *f*; *vi* couver, méditer, rêver; to — over remâcher, ruminer.

brook [bruk] *n* ruisseau *m*; *vt* souffrir.

brooklet ['bruklit] *n* ruisselet *m*.

broom [bruːm] *n* genêt *m*; balai *m*; —stick manche *m* à balai.

broth [brɔθ] *n* bouillon *m*, potage *m*.

brother ['brʌðə] *n* frère *m*, confrère *m*.

brotherhood ['brʌðəhud] *n* confrérie *f*, société *f*, fraternité *f*.

brother-in-law ['brʌðərinlɔː] *n* beau-frère *m*.

brotherly ['brʌðəli] *a* fraternel.

brought [brɔːt] *pt* of bring.

brow [brau] *n* sourcil *m*, front *m*, surplomb *m*, crête *f*.

browbeat ['braubiːt] *vt* malmener, intimider, rabrouer.

brown [braun] *an* brun *m*, marron *m*; *a* châtain, fauve; *vt* brunir, faire dorer, rissoler.

brownish ['brauniʃ] *a* brunâtre.

browse [brauz] *vti* brouter, bouquiner.

bruise [bruːz] *n* meurtrissure *f*, contusion *f*, bleu *m*, noir *m*; *vt* meurtrir, contusionner.

brunette [bruː'net] *an* brune *f*.

brunt [brʌnt] *n* choc *m*, poids *m*, fort *m*.

brush [brʌʃ] *n* brosse *f*, balai *m*, pinceau *m*, coup *m* de brosse, (fox) queue *f*; échauffourée *f*; *vt* brosser, balayer; to — aside écarter; to — out balayer; to — up, down donner un coup de brosse à;

to — **up** repolir, rafraîchir, dérouiller; to — **against** frôler, effleurer.

brushwood ['brʌʃwud] n broussailles f pl, fourré m, brindilles f pl.

brusque [brusk] a brusque, bourru, rude.

Brussels ['brʌsɪz] n Bruxelles; — **sprouts** choux m pl de Bruxelles.

brutal ['bruːtl] a brutal, de brute, sensuel.

brutality [bruːˈtæliti] n brutalité f.

brutalize ['bruːtəlaiz] vt abrutir.

brute [bruːt] n bête f, brute f; a brut, stupide.

brutish ['bruːtiʃ] a bestial, de brute, abruti.

bubble ['bʌbl] n bulle f, bouillon m, chimère f; vi bouillonner, pétiller, glouglouter; to — **over** déborder.

buccaneer [ˌbʌkəˈniə] n flibustier m, pirate m.

buck [bʌk] n daim m, chevreuil m, mâle m, dandy m; to — **off** désarçonner; vt to — **up** remonter le courage à, ravigoter; vi reprendre courage, se remuer.

bucket ['bʌkit] n seau m, baquet m.

buckle ['bʌkl] n boucle f, agrafe f, voile m, benne f; vt boucler, agrafer, serrer, voiler; vi se mettre (à to), s'appliquer (à to); to — **up** se voiler, se gondoler.

buckler ['bʌklə] n bouclier m.

buckram ['bʌkrəm] n bougran m.

buckshee ['bʌkʃiː] ad à l'œil, gratis.

buckskin ['bʌkskin] n peau f de daim.

buckwheat ['bʌkwiːt] n sarrasin m.

bud [bʌd] n bourgeon m, bouton m; vi bourgeonner, boutonner.

budding ['bʌdiŋ] a qui bourgeonne, qui boutonne, en herbe.

budge [bʌdʒ] vi bouger, remuer, reculer.

budget ['bʌdʒit] n sac m, budget m; to — **for** sth porter qch au budget.

buff [bʌf] n buffle m; a couleur buffle; vt polir; to **strip to the** — se mettre à poil.

buffalo ['bʌfəlou] n buffle m.

buffer ['bʌfə] n tampon m, amortisseur m; —**state** état-tampon m.

buffer-stop ['bʌfəstɔp] n butoir m.

buffet ['bʌfit] n soufflet m; vt souffleter, ballotter, secouer; vi lutter.

buffet ['bufei] n buffet m.

buffoon [bʌˈfuːn] n bouffon m.

buffoonery [bʌˈfuːnəri] n bouffonnerie f.

bug [bʌg] n punaise f, insecte m; big — grosse légume.

bugbear ['bʌgbɛə] n épouvantail m, cauchemar m, bête noire f, loupgarou m.

bugle ['bjuːgl] n clairon m; vi sonner du clairon.

bugler ['bjuːglə] n clairon m.

build [bild] vt construire, bâtir, fonder; to — **up** échafauder,

affermir, créer; n construction f, charpente f.

builder ['bildə] n entrepreneur m, constructeur m, fondateur, -trice.

building ['bildiŋ] n bâtiment m, édifice m, construction f.

built [bilt] pp pt of build; —**up area** agglomération urbaine f.

bulb [bʌlb] n bulbe m, ampoule f, poire f, oignon m.

Bulgaria [bʌlˈgɛəriə] n Bulgarie f.

Bulgarian [bʌlˈgɛəriən] a bulgare; n Bulgare mf.

bulge [bʌldʒ] n gonflement m, renflement m, bombement m; vti bomber, ballonner; vi faire saillie.

bulk [bʌlk] n chargement m, grande carcasse f, masse f, gros m, volume m, grandeur f; in — en vrac, en gros; vt empiler, grouper; to — **large** occuper une place importante.

bulkhead ['bʌlkhed] n cloison f étanche.

bulky ['bʌlki] a volumineux, encombrant.

bull [bul] n taureau m, mâle m, haussier m, bulle f, bourde f, mouche f.

bulldog ['buldɔg] n bouledogue m.

bulldozer ['bulˌdouzə] n niveleuse f, bulldozer m.

bullet ['bulit] n balle f.

bulletin ['bulitin] n bulletin m, communiqué m; news — informations f pl, journal parlé m.

bullfight ['bulfait] n course f de taureaux.

bullfinch ['bulfintʃ] n bouvreuil m.

bullheaded ['bulˈhedid] a têtu, gaffeur, impétueux.

bullion ['buljən] n lingot m.

bullock ['bulək] n bœuf m.

bull's eye ['bulzai] n noir m, mouche f, hublot m, œil de bœuf m, lanterne sourde f, lentille f.

bully ['buli] n brute f, brimeur m, souteneur m; vt rudoyer, brutaliser, malmener.

bully-beef ['buliˈbiːf] n (fam) singe m.

bulwark ['bulwək] n rempart m, bastingage m.

bumble-bee ['bʌmblbiː] n bourdon m.

bump [bʌmp] n heurt m, secousse f, cahot m, bosse f; vt heurter, cogner, secouer; vi (se) heurter, (se) cogner, buter; to — **along** cahoter; to — **into** tamponner, buter contre; excl pan!

bumper ['bʌmpə] n (aut) pare-chocs m; rasade f; a monstre, comble etc.

bumpkin ['bʌmpkin] n rustre m.

bumptious ['bʌmpʃəs] a arrogant, présomptueux.

bumptiousness ['bʌmpʃəsnis] n arrogance f, suffisance f, outrecuidance f.

bumpy ['bʌmpi] a en creux et en bosses, cahoteux, inégal.

bunch [bʌntʃ] n bouquet m, (grapes)

grappe *f*, (*radishes*) botte *f*, (*bananas*) régime *m*, (*keys*) trousseau *m*, (*people*) bande *f*, groupe *m*, peloton *m*; *vt* lier, attacher, botteler, réunir, grouper; *vi* se pelotonner, se serrer.

bundle ['bʌndl] *n* paquet *m*, fagot *m*, liasse *f*, ballot *m*, faisceau *m*; *vt* mettre en paquet, empaqueter, fourrer; to — off envoyer paître; to — out flanquer à la porte.

bungle ['bʌŋgl] *n* gâchis *m*; *vt* gâcher, bousiller, rater, massacrer.

bungler ['bʌŋglə] *n* maladroit(e) *mf*, bousilleur *m*.

bunion ['bʌnjən] *n* oignon *m*.

bunk [bʌŋk] *n* couchette *f*; *vi* décamper, filer.

bunker ['bʌŋkə] *n* soute *f*, banquette *f*, (*golf*) bunker *m*.

bunkum ['bʌŋkəm] *n* blague *f*, balivernes *f pl*.

bunting ['bʌntiŋ] *n* étamine *f*, drapeaux *m pl*.

buoy [bɔi] *n* bouée *f*.

buoyancy ['bɔiənsi] *n* insubmersibilité *f*, élasticité *f*, entrain *m*, ressort *m*.

buoyant ['bɔiənt] *a* élastique, exubérant, flottable, insubmersible, qui a du ressort.

burble ['bə:bl] *n* murmure *m*, gloussement *m*; *vi* murmurer, glousser.

burden ['bə:dn] *n* charge *f*, fardeau *m*, tonnage *m*, poids *m*, refrain *m*, essentiel *m*, fond *m*; *vt* charger, encombrer.

burdensome ['bə:dnsəm] *a* pesant, encombrant, fâcheux, onéreux.

bureau ['bjuərou] *n* bureau *m*, secrétaire *m*.

bureaucracy [bjuə'rɔkrəsi] *n* bureaucratie *f*.

bureaucrat ['bjuəroukræt] *n* bureaucrate *m*, rond-de-cuir *m*.

burgess ['bə:dʒis] *n* bourgeois *m*, citoyen *m*.

burgh ['bʌrə] *n* (*Scot*) bourg *m*.

burglar ['bə:glə] *n* cambrioleur *m*.

burglary ['bə:gləri] *n* cambriolage *m*.

burgle ['bə:gl] *vt* cambrioler.

burgomaster ['bə:gə,ma:stə] *n* bourgmestre *m*.

Burgundian [bə:'gʌndjən] *a* bourguignon; *n* Bourguignon, -onne.

Burgundy ['bə:gəndi] *n* Bourgogne *f*, (*wine*) bourgogne *m*.

burial ['beriəl] *n* enterrement *m*.

burlesque [bə:'lesk] *an* burlesque *m*; *n* parodie *f*; *vt* parodier.

burly ['bə:li] *a* massif, solide, costaud.

Burma ['bə:mə] *n* Birmanie *f*.

Burmese [bə:'mi:z] *an* birman.

burn [bə:n] *n* brûlure *f*; *vti* brûler.

burner ['bə:nə] *n* brûleur, -euse, bec *m*, brûleur *m*.

burnish ['bə:niʃ] *vt* polir.

burnt [bə:nt] *pp of* **burn**; — offering holocauste *m*.

burrow ['bʌrou] *n* terrier *m*; *vt* creuser; *vi* se terrer, fouiller.

bursar ['bə:sə] *n* économe *mf*, boursier, -ière.

burst [bə:st] *n* éclatement *m*, explosion *f*, salve *f*, éclat *m*; *vi* éclater, crever; *vt* faire éclater, faire sauter, percer, rompre; *vi* faire explosion, exploser, sauter, se rompre, éclore, regorger; to — in *vt* enfoncer; *vi* faire irruption; to — out jaillir, éclater, s'exclamer, sortir en coup de vent.

bury ['beri] *vt* enterrer, enfouir, ensevelir, enfoncer, plonger.

bus [bʌs] *n* autobus *m*, (auto)car *m*; to miss the — manquer l'autobus, manquer le coche.

bush [buʃ] *n* arbuste *m*, arbrisseau *m*, buisson *m*, brousse *f*, coussinet *m*, bague *f*; —cat serval *m*.

bushel ['buʃl] *n* boisseau *m*.

bushy ['buʃi] *a* touffu, broussailleux, épais.

busily ['bizili] *ad* activement, avec affairement.

business ['biznis] *n* affaire(s) *f pl*, occupation *f*, établissement *m*; it is none of your — cela ne vous regarde pas; to make it one's — to se faire un devoir de; to send *s.o.* about his — envoyer promener qn; big —man brasseur d'affaires; —man homme d'affaires.

businesslike ['biznislaik] *a* actif, pratique, sérieux.

buskin ['bʌskin] *n* cothurne *m*.

bust [bʌst] *n* buste *m*, gorge *f*.

bustle ['bʌsl] *n* agitation *f*, remue-ménage *m*; *vi* s'agiter, s'affairer, faire l'empressé; *vt* bousculer.

busy ['bizi] *a* occupé, actif, affairé; *vt* occuper.

busybody ['bizibɔdi] *n* mouche *f* du coche, officieux, -euse *mf*.

but [bʌt] *cj* mais, sans (que), que . . . ne (*after a negative*); *ad* seulement, ne . . . que, excepté, autre que, sinon, si ce n'est; — for sans, à part; all — presque, autant dire; anything — riens moins que.

butcher ['butʃə] *n* boucher *m*; *vt* massacrer, égorger; —'s boucherie *f*.

butchery ['butʃəri] *n* boucherie *f*, massacre *m*, tuerie *f*.

butler ['bʌtlə] *n* sommelier *m*, dépensier *m*, maître d'hôtel *m*.

butt [bʌt] *n* crosse *f*, gros bout *m*, mégot *m*, butte *f*, coup *m* de tête, tête *f* de turc, souffre-douleur *m*, cible *f*; *pl* champ *m* de tir; *vt* donner un coup de tête à; *vi* fourrer le nez (dans into), foncer (dans into), donner de la tête (contre against).

butter ['bʌtə] *n* beurre *m*; shea — karité *f*; *vt* beurrer; — would not melt in his mouth c'est une sainte nitouche.

butter-bean ['bʌtəbi:n] *n* haricot beurre *m*.

buttercup ['bʌtəkʌp] n bouton m d'or.

butter-dish ['bʌtədiʃ] n beurrier m.

butter-fingers ['bʌtə,fiŋgəz] n empoté(e) mf, maladroit(e) mf.

butterfly ['bʌtəflai] n papillon m.

buttermilk ['bʌtəmilk] n petit-lait m, babeurre m.

buttock ['bʌtək] n fesse f.

button ['bʌtn] n bouton m; vt boutonner; — -hook tire-bouton m.

buttonhole ['bʌtnhoul] n boutonnière f; vt accrocher, cueillir.

buttress ['bʌtris] n contrefort m, arc-boutant m; vt soutenir, renforcer, étayer.

buxom ['bʌksəm] a rebondi, avenant

buy [bai] vt acheter; to — back rachetet; to — off acheter; to — out désintéresser; to — up accaparer.

buyer ['baiə] n acheteur, -euse, chef m de rayon.

buzz [bʌz] n bourdonnement m, brouhaha m, fritures f pl; vi bourdonner, tinter; to — off déguerpir, filer.

buzzard ['bʌzəd] n buse f.

by [bai] prep par, près de, à côté de, à, en, pour, avec, de, sur, envers; ad près, à (de) côté; — and — avant peu, tout à l'heure.

bygone ['baigɔn] an passé m.

bylaw ['bailɔː] n arrêté municipal m.

by-name ['baineim] n sobriquet m.

by-pass ['baipɑːs] n route f d'évitement m; vt éviter, contourner, filtrer.

by-product ['bai.prɔdəkt] n sous-produit m.

by-road ['bairoud] n rue écartée f.

bystander ['bai,stændə] n spectateur, -trice, curieux -euse.

byway ['baiwei] n chemin détourné m, raccourci m; pl à-côtés m pl.

byword ['baiwəːd] n proverbe m, risée f, fable f.

C

cab [kæb] n flacre m., voiture de place f, cabine f.

cabbage ['kæbidʒ] n chou m.

cabbage-patch ['kæbidʒpætʃ] n plant m, carré de choux m.

cabin ['kæbin] n cabane f, cabine f, case f, poste m de conduite.

cabinet ['kæbinit] n vitrine f, bonheur du jour m, coffret m, ministère m; a ministériel, d'état.

cabinet-maker ['kæbinit,meikə] n ébéniste m.

cabinet-work ['kæbinit.wəːk] n ébénisterie f.

cabin-trunk ['kæbin.trʌŋk] n malle f (de) paquebot.

cable ['keibl] n câble m, chaîne f, câblogramme m; vt câbler, aviser par câble.

cable-railway ['keibl'reilwei] n funiculaire m.

cabman ['kæbmən] n cocher m, chauffeur m.

caboodle [kə'buːdl] n the whole — tout le bazar, tout le fourbi.

caboose [kə'buːs] n wagon m de queue.

cabstand ['kæbstænd] n station f de voitures.

ca' canny [kɔ'kæni] a tout doux, hésitant; vi faire la grève perlée.

cackle ['kækl] n caquet m; vi caqueter.

cacophony [kæ'kɔfəni] n cacophonie f.

cad [kæd] n goujat m, mufle m, canaille f.

caddie ['kædi] n cadet m, caddie m.

caddishness ['kædiʃnis] n goujaterie f, muflerie f.

caddy ['kædi] n boîte f à thé.

cadence ['keidəns] n cadence f, rythme m.

cadet [kə'det] n cadet m, élève officier, m membre m d'un bataillon scolaire.

cadge [kædʒ] vti colporter, mendier, écornifler.

cadger ['kædʒə] n colporteur m, camelot m, mendiant(e) mf, écornifleur m.

cage [keidʒ] n cage f.

cahoot [kə'huːt] n to be in — with (sl) être de mèche avec.

cajole [kə'dʒoul] vt cajoler, enjôler.

cajolery [kə'dʒouləri] n cajolerie f, enjôlement m.

cajoling [kə'dʒouliŋ] a enjôleur.

cake [keik] n gâteau m, tablette f, morceau m, pain m; to sell like hot — s se vendre comme du pain frais.

cake-shop ['keikʃɔp] n pâtisserie f.

calabash ['kæləbæʃ] n calebasse f, gourde f.

calamitous [kə'læmitəs] a désastreux.

calamity [kə'læmiti] n calamité f, désastre m, malheur m.

calculate ['kælkjuleit] vti calculer, estimer, évaluer; vi faire un (des) calcul(s).

calculated ['kælkjuleitid] a délibéré, calculé, propre (à to).

calculating ['kælkjuleitiŋ] a calculateur, avisé, réfléchi.

calculation [,kælkju'leiʃən] n calcul m.

calendar ['kælində] n calendrier m, répertoire m.

calf [kɑːf] n veau m, mollet m.

calibrate ['kælibreit] vt calibrer, étalonner, graduer.

caliber ['kælibə] n calibre m, alésage m.

call [kɔːl] n appel m, cri m, rappel m, visite f, invitation f, demande f, invite f, communication f, coup de téléphone m; on — sur demande; **within** — à portée de la voix; vti crier, appeler; vt héler, convoquer, ordonner, déclarer; vi faire escale, toucher (à at); to — aside prendre à part; to — back vt rappeler; vi repasser; to — for demander, venir chercher; to — forth évoquer, provoquer, faire appel à; to — off vt décommander, rompre, rappeler; vi s'excuser, se retirer; to — on faire une visite à, passer chez, se présenter chez; to — out vti appeler; vt provoquer, réquisitionner; to — together réunir, convoquer; to — up évoquer, appeler au téléphone, mobiliser; to — upon sommer.

callbox ['kɔːlbɔks] n cabine téléphonique f.

caller ['kɔːlə] n visiteur, -euse, visite f.

calling ['kɔːliŋ] n appel m, vocation f, profession f, état m.

callosity [kæ'lɔsiti] n callosité f, durillon m.

call-up ['kɔːlʌp] n mobilisation f.

callous ['kæləs] a calleux, brutal, dur, endurci.

callousness ['kæləsnis] n dureté f, manque m de cœur.

callow ['kælou] a sans plumes, novice, inexpérimenté; a — youth un blancbec.

calm [kɑːm] a calme, tranquille; n calme m, tranquillité f; vt calmer, tranquilliser, apaiser; to — down s'apaiser, se calmer.

calumniate [kə'lʌmnieit] vt calomnier.

calumniator [kə'lʌmnieitə] n calomniateur, -trice.

calumny ['kæləmni] n calomnie f.

calvary ['kælvəri] n calvaire m.

calve [kɑːv] vi vêler.

cam [kæm] n came f.

camber ['kæmbə] n cambrure f, bombement m.

Cambodia [kæm'boudjə] n Cambodge m.

cambric ['keimbrik] n batiste f.

came [keim] pt of come.

camel ['kæməl] n chameau m.

cameo ['kæmiou] n camée m.

camera ['kæmərə] n appareil m photographique; in — à huis clos; movie — caméra f.

cameraman ['kæmərəmæn] n photographe m, opérateur m.

cami-knickers ['kæminikəz] n chemise-culotte f.

camouflage ['kæməflɑːʒ] n camouflage m; vt camoufler.

camp [kæmp] n camp m, campement m; vti camper; to go —ing faire du camping.

campaign [kæm'pein] n campagne f; vi faire campagne.

camper ['kæmpə] n amateur (-trice) de camping, campeur m.

camphor ['kæmfə] n camphre m.

can [kæn] n broc m, pot m, bidon m, boîte f, (oil) burette f, (beer)

canette f; vt mettre, conserver, en boîte.

can [kæn] vi pouvoir, savoir; all one — de son mieux; he cannot but do it il ne peut pas ne pas le faire.

Canada ['kænədə] n Canada m.

Canadian [kə'neidjən] a canadien; n Canadien, -ienne.

canal [kə'næl] n canal m.

canalization [,kænəlai'zeiʃən] n canalisation f.

canalize ['kænəlaiz] vt canaliser.

canary [kə'neəri] n canari m, serin m.

cancel ['kænsəl] vt annuler, biffer, révoquer, résilier, supprimer, décommander, contremander; to — out s'éliminer.

cancellation [,kænse'leiʃən] n annulation f, résiliation f, révocation f, contre-ordre m.

cancer ['kænsə] n cancer m.

cancerous ['kænsərəs] a cancéreux.

candid ['kændid] a franc, sincère, impartial, sans malice.

candidate ['kændidit] n candidat(e) mf, aspirant m, pretendant(e) mf.

candidature ['kændiditʃə] n candidature f.

candle ['kændl] n bougie f, chandelle f, cierge f.

candlestick ['kændlstik] n chandelier m, bougeoir m.

candor ['kændə] n franchise f, impartialité f, bonne foi f.

candy ['kændi] n sucre candi m; vt glacer, faire candir, confire.

cane [kein] n tige f, canne f, badine f, rotin m; — chair chaise cannée f; vt bâtonner, fouetter.

canine ['keinain] n canine f; a canin.

caning ['keiniŋ] n bastonnade f, correction f.

canister ['kænistə] n boîte f.

canker ['kæŋkə] n chancre m, fléau m, plaie f; vt ronger, corrompre.

canned [kænd] a en boîte; en conserve.

cannibal ['kænibəl] an cannibale mf.

cannibalism ['kænibəlizəm] n cannibalisme m.

cannon ['kænən] n canon m, pièce f, carambolage m; vi caramboler, se heurter.

cannonade [,kænə'neid] n canonnade f; vt canonner.

cannon-ball ['kænənbɔːl] n boulet m.

cannon-fodder ['kænənfɔdə] n chair à canon f.

canny ['kæni] a avisé, sûr, rusé, finaud, économe.

canoe [kə'nuː] n canoë m, pirogue f, périssoire f.

canon ['kænən] n canon m, chanoine m, règle f.

canoness ['kænənis] n chanoinesse f.

canonize ['kænənaiz] vt canoniser.

canonry ['kænənri] n canonicat m.

can-opener ['kænoupnə] n ouvre-boîte m.

canopy ['kænəpi] n dais m, baldaquin m, ciel m, marquise f.

cant [kænt] n argot m, pharisaïsme m, tartuferie f, plan incliné m; vt incliner.

cantankerous [kən'tæŋkərəs] a revêche, batailleur, acariâtre.

canteen [kæn'tiːn] n cantine f, gamelle f, bidon m, caisse f; — of cutlery service m de table en coffre.

canter ['kæntə] n petit galop m; vi aller au petit galop.

canticle ['kæntikl] n cantique m.

cantilever ['kæntiliːvə] n encorbellement m, cantilever m.

canto ['kæntou] n chant m.

canvas ['kænvəs] n toile f, tente f, voile f; under — sous voile, sous la tente.

canvass ['kænvəs] vt discuter, solliciter, briguer; vi (com) faire la place, faire une tournée électorale.

canvasser ['kænvəsə] n agent électoral m, solliciteur, -euse, placier m.

cap [kæp] n bonnet m, casquette f, toque f, calotte f; vt coiffer, couronner, surpasser, saluer; to — it pour comble; if the — fits, wear it qui se sent morveux, se mouche.

capability [.keipə'biliti] n pouvoir m, moyens m pl, capacité f, faculté f.

capable ['keipəbl] a capable, : compétent, susceptible (de).

capacious [kə'peiʃəs] a spacieux, ample, grand.

capacity [kə'pæsiti] n capacité f, contenance f, débit m, rendement m, aptitude f, qualité f, mesure f; to — à plein, comble.

cape [keip] n cap m, collet m, pèlerine f, cape f.

caper ['keipə] n câpre f, cabriole f; vi cabrioler, gambader.

capital ['kæpitl] n capitale f, majuscule f, capital m, chapiteau m; a capital, fameux.

capitalism ['kæpitəlizəm] n capitalisme m.

capitalist ['kæpitəlist] n capitaliste mf.

capitalize ['kæpitəlaiz] vt capitaliser.

capitulate [kə'pitjuleit] vi capituler.

capitulation [kə.pitju'leiʃən] n capitulation f.

capon ['keipən] n chapon m.

caprice [kə'priːs] b caprice m.

capricious [kə'priʃəs] a capricieux.

capriciousness [kə'priʃəsnis] n humeur capricieuse f, inconstance f.

capsize [kæp'saiz] vi chavirer, capoter; vt faire chavirer.

capstan ['kæpstən] n cabestan m.

capsule ['kæpsjuːl] n capsule f, (of spaceship) cabine f.

captain ['kæptin] n capitaine m, chef m (d'équipe); vt commander, diriger.

caption ['kæpʃən] n arrestation f,

légende f, soustitre m, rubrique f, manchette f.

captious ['kæpʃəs] a captieux, chicaneur, pointilleux.

captivate ['kæptiveit] vt séduire, captiver, charmer.

captive ['kæptiv] an prisonnier, -ière, captif, -ive.

captivity [kæp'tiviti] n captivité f.

capture ['kæptʃə] n capture f, prise f; vt prendre, capturer, capter.

car [kaː] n char m, wagon m, voiture f, auto f; dining — wagon-restaurant m; sleeping — wagon-lit m.

carafe [kə'raːf] n carafe f.

caramel ['kærəmel] n caramel m, bonbon m au caramel.

caravan ['kærəvæn] n caravane f, roulotte f.

carbide ['kaːbaid] n carbure m.

carbine ['kaːbain] n carabine f.

carbon ['kaːbən] n (papier) carbone m.

carbonize ['kaːbənaiz] vt carboniser, carburer.

carboy ['kaːbɔi] n bonbonne f.

carbuncle ['kaːbʌŋkl] n anthrax m, escarboucle f.

carburetor ['kaːbjuretə] n carburateur m.

carcass ['kaːkəs] n corps m, cadavre m, carcasse f.

card [kaːd] n carte f; visiting — carte f de visite; he is a — c'est un numéro; a queer — un drôle de type.

cardboard ['kaːdbɔːd] n carton m.

card-case ['kaːdkeis] n porte-cartes m.

cardigan ['kaːdigən] n tricot m, cardigan m.

cardinal ['kaːdinl] an cardinal m.

card-index ['kaːd'indeks] n classeur m, fichier m.

card-sharper ['kaːd.ʃaːpə] n bonneteur m, tricheur, -euse, escroc m.

care [kɛə] n soin m, souci m, attention f, peine f, solicitude f, préoccupation f, entretien m; vi s'inquiéter, se soucier; c/o (care of) aux bons soins de; with — fragile; to take — prendre garde; to take — not to se garder de, prendre garde de; to take — of prendre soin de, se charger de; to — for si aimer, soigner; I don't — a rap je m'en fiche, je m'en moque pas mal; I don't — for this tobacco ce tabac ne me dit rien.

career [kə'riə] n course f, cours m, carrière f; vi marcher (courir) comme un fou.

careerist [kə'riərist] n arriviste mf.

careful ['kɛəful] a soigneux, prudent, attentif.

carefulness ['kɛəfulnis] n soin m, attention f, prudence f, circonspection f.

careless ['kɛəlis] a sans soin, négligent, insouciant.

carelessness ['keəlisnis] n négligence f, insouciance f.

caress [kə'res] n caresse f; vt caresser.

caretaker ['kɛə,teikə] n concierge mf, gardien, -ienne.

cargo ['ka:gou] n cargaison f.

cargo-boat ['ka:goubout] n cargo m.

caricature [,kærikə'tjuə] n caricature f, charge f; vt caricaturer, charger.

carmine ['ka:main] an carmin m; a carminé.

carnage ['ka:nidʒ] n carnage m, tuerie f.

carnal ['ka:nl] a charnel, sensuel, de la chair.

carnation [ka:'neiʃən] n œillet m; an incarnat m.

carnival ['ka:nivəl] n carnaval m.

carnivore ['ka:nivɔ:] n carnassier m.

carnivorous [ka:'nivərəs] a carnassier, carnivore.

carol ['kærəl] n chant m; **Christmas —** (chant de) Noël m; vti chanter, tirelirer.

carousal [kə'rauzəl] n buverie f, orgie f, bombe f.

carouse [kə'rauz] vi faire la noce, faire la bombe.

carp [ka:p] n carpe f; vi mordre sur tout; **to — at** crier après, gloser sur, chicaner.

carpenter ['ka:pintə] n charpentier m.

carpet ['ka:pit] n tapis m; **to be on the —** être sur la sellette; vt poser un (des) tapis sur, recouvrir d'un tapis.

carping ['ka:piŋ] a mordant, chicanier, malveillant, pointilleux.

carport ['ka:pɔ:t] n abri m.

carriage ['kæridʒ] n (trans)port m, voiture f, wagon m, affût m, allure f, maintien m; **— free** franco; **— forward** en port dû; **— paid** franco de port.

carriageway ['kæridʒwei] n **dual —** route jumelée f.

carrier ['kæriə] n camionneur m, roulier m, porteur, -euse, porte-avions m, porte-bagages m.

carrion ['kæriən] n charogne f.

carrot ['kærət] n carotte f.

carroty ['kærəti] a rouquin, roux, rouge de carotte.

carry ['kæri] n trajet m, trajectoire f, portée f; vti porter, vt transporter, rouler, amener, conduire, emporter, enlever, supporter, voter, adopter; **to — away** emporter, enlever, entraîner; **to — back** rapporter, ramener, reporter; **to — down** descendre; **to — forward** avancer, reporter; **to — off** enlever, (r)emporter; **to — on** vt soutenir, entretenir, poursuivre; vi continuer, persister, se conduire; **to — out** exécuter, mettre à exécution, appliquer, réussir, exercer, porter dehors; **to — through** mener à bonne fin;

to — weight peser, avoir de l'influence, avoir du poids, être handicapé.

cart [ka:t] n charrette f, tombereau m, camion m; vt transporter, charroyer, charrier; **to — about** trimbaler.

cartage ['ka:tidʒ] n charroi m, charriage m, transport m.

carter ['ka:tə] n charretier m, roulier m, camionneur m.

cart-horse ['ka:thɔ:s] n cheval m de trait.

cart-load ['ka:tloud] n charretée f, tombereau m.

cart-shed ['ka:tʃed] n remise f, hangar m.

Carthusian [ka:'θju:zjən] an chartreux m.

cartilage ['ka:tilidʒ] n cartilage m.

cartoon [ka:'tu:n] n carton m, dessin m (satirique, humoristique, animé), portrait caricaturé m.

cartridge ['ka:tridʒ] n cartouche f.

cartwright ['ka:trait] n charron m.

carve [ka:v] vt tailler, sculpter (sur bois), ciseler, découper.

carver ['ka:və] n ciseleur m, serveur m, découpeur m, couteau m à découper.

carving ['ka:viŋ] n sculpture f, découpage m.

cascade [kæs'keid] n cascade f, chute f d'eau; vi tomber en cascade.

case [keis] n cas m, affaire f, cause f, boîte f, caisse f, trousse f, fourreau m, étui m, vitrine f, vitrine f, boîtier m; **in —** au cas où; **in any (no) —** en tout (aucun) cas; vt emballer, encaisser, envelopper.

casement ['keismənt] n battant m, croisée f.

cash [kæʃ] n monnaie f, argent comptant m, espèces f pl; vt encaisser, toucher; **— account** compte m en banque; **petty —** argent m de poche, petite caisse f; **— down** comptant; **— on delivery** paiement m à la livraison; **— book** livre m de caisse; **— box** n caisse f.

cashier [kæ'ʃiə] n caissier, -ière; vt casser.

cashmere ['kæʃmiə] n cachemire m.

casino [kə'si:nou] n casino m.

cask [ka:sk] n tonneau m, fût m.

casket ['ka:skit] n écrin m, boîte f, coffret m, cassette f.

cassava [kə'sa:və] n manioc m.

cassock ['kæsək] n soutane f.

cast [ka:st] n lancement m, jet m, calcul m, moule m, moulage m, modèle m, coulée f, bas de ligne m, (dice) coup m, (eye) faux-trait m, (mind) type m, trempe f, qualité f, (theatre) troupe f, distribution f des rôles; vt lancer, (pro)jeter, ôter, couler, mouler, fondre, assigner un rôle à; **to — about** fureter; **to — aside** rejeter, se débarrasser de, mettre de côté; **to — away** jeter (au loin); to — **back** renvoyer, reporter; to — **down** déprimer, abattre, jeter bas; to — **off** rejeter, larguer, renier; to — **up** rejeter, reprocher.

castaway ['kɑːstəwei] n naufragé(e) mf, réprouvé(e) mf, proscrit(e) mf.

caste [kɑːst] n caste f; **half——** an, metis, -isse.

castigate ['kæstigeit] vt corriger, châtier.

castigation [ˌkæsti'geiʃən] n correction f, châtiment m.

casting ['kɑːstiŋ] n jet m, fronte f, moulage m, modelage m, distribution des rôles; f a (vote) qui départage.

cast-iron ['kɑːst'aiən] n fonte f; a de fer, de fonte.

castle ['kɑːsl] n château m; — **s in the air** des châteaux en Espagne; vi (chess) roquer.

castor ['kɑːstə] n saupoudrier m, poivrière f, roulette f.

castor-oil ['kɑːstər'ɔil] n huile f de ricin.

castrate [kæs'treit] vt châtrer, émasculer.

casual ['kæʒjuəl] a fortuit, accidentel, banal, désinvolte, insouciant.

casually ['kæʒjuəli] ad en passant, avec désinvolture.

casualty ['kæʒjuəlti] n accident m, blessé(e) mf, mort(e) mf, malheur m; pl pertes f pl.

cat [kæt] n chat, -tte; **tom——** matou m.

cataclysm ['kætəklizm] n cataclysme m.

catacombs ['kætəkoumz] n catacombes f pl.

catalepsy ['kætəlepsi] n catalepsie f.

catalogue ['kætəlɔg] n catalogue m, liste f, prix-courant m; vt cataloguer.

catapult ['kætəpʌlt] n lance-pierres m inv, fronde f, catapulte f; vt lancer.

cataract ['kætərækt] n cataracte f.

catarrh [kə'tɑː] n catarrhe m.

catastrophe [kə'tæstrəfi] n catastrophe f, désastre m, dénouement m.

catcalls ['kætkɔːlz] n pl miaulements m pl, sifflets m pl, huées f pl.

catch [kætʃ] n prise f, capture f, pêche f, attrape f, piège m, agrafe f, loquet m, déclic m, cran d'arrêt m; vti prendre; vt attraper, saisir, accrocher, surprendre; vi se prendre, s'engager, mordre; to — **on** prendre, réussir; to — **up** saisir, rattraper, rejoindre.

catching ['kætʃiŋ] a séduisant, contagieux, communicatif.

catchword ['kætʃwəːd] n mot m d'ordre, mot m de ralliement, slogan m scie f.

catchy ['kætʃi] a entraînant, insidieux.

catechism ['kætikizm] n catéchisme m.

categorical [ˌkæti'gɔ. ˈəl] a catégorique.

category ['kætigəri] n catégorie f.

cater ['keitə] vi pourvoir; to — **for** pourvoir à, approvisionner.

caterer ['keitərə] n fournisseur, -euse, pourvoyeur, -euse, traiteur m.

catering ['keitəriŋ] n approvisionnement m; to do the — fournir le buffet.

caterpillar ['kætəpilə] n chenille f.

caterwaul ['kætəwɔːl] vi miauler, faire du tapage.

caterwauling ['kætəwɔːliŋ] n miaulements m pl, tapage m, sabbat m de chats.

catgut ['kætgʌt] n catgut m.

cathedral [kə'θiːdrəl] n cathédrale f.

catholic ['kæθəlik] an catholique mf; a universel, tolérant.

Catholicism [kə'θɔlisizəm] n catholicisme m.

catholicity [ˌkæθə'lisiti] n catholicité f, orthodoxie f, universalité f, tolérance f.

cat-o'-nine-tails ['kætə'nainteilz] n garcette f.

cat's-paw ['kætspɔː] n instrument m, dupe f.

cattish ['kætiʃ] a méchant, rosse.

cattle ['kætl] n bétail m, bestiaux m pl; — **show** comice agricole m.

cattle-drover ['kætldrouvə] n bouvier m.

cattle-shed ['kætlʃed] n étable f.

caucus ['kɔːkəs] n comité m, clique politique f.

caught [kɔːt] pt pp of **catch**.

cauldron ['kɔːldrən] n chaudron m, chaudière f.

cauliflower ['kɔliflauə] n chou-fleur m.

caulk [kɔːk] vt calfater, calfeutrer, mater.

cause [kɔːz] n cause f, motif m, occasion f, raison f, sujet m; vt causer, occasionner, provoquer.

causeway ['kɔːzwei] n chaussée f, digue f.

caustic ['kɔːstik] a caustique, mordant.

cauterize ['kɔːtəraiz] vt cautériser.

caution ['kɔːʃən] n prudence f, précaution f, circonspection f, réprimande f, avertissement m; vt avertir, mettre sur ses gardes.

cautious ['kɔːʃəs] a prudent, circonspect.

cautiousness ['kɔːʃəsnis] n prudence f, circonspection f.

cavalier [ˌkævə'liə] n cavalier m, gentilhomme m, cavalier servant m, galant m; a cavalier, désinvolte.

cavalry ['kævəlri] n cavalerie f.

cavalryman ['kævəlrimən] n cavalier m, soldat m de cavalerie.

cave [keiv] n caverne f, grotte f; to — **in** s'affaisser, s'effondrer, s'enfoncer, céder.

cavern ['kævən] n souterrain m, caverne f.

cavil ['kævil] vi ergoter, chicaner.

caviling ['kæviliŋ] n argutie f, ergotage m, chicanerie f; a ergoteur.

cavity ['kæviti] n cavité f, creux m, trou m, fosse f.

caw [kɔ:] vi croasser.

cease [si:s] n cesse f; vti cesser.

cease-fire [si:s'faiə] n cessez-le-feu m.

ceaseless ['si:slis] a incessant.

ceaselessly ['si:slisli] ad incessamment, sans cesse.

Cecilia [si'siljə] Cécile f.

cedar ['si:də] n cèdre m.

ceiling ['si:liŋ] n plafond m.

celebrate ['selibreit] vt célébrer, fêter, commémorer; vi faire la fête.

celebration [.seli'breiʃən] n fête f, commémoration f.

ce'ebrity [si'lebriti] n célébrité f, renommée f, sommité f.

celeriac [sə'leriæk] n céleri-rave m.

celery ['seləri] n céleri m.

celestial [si'lestjəl] a céleste.

celibacy ['selibəsi] n célibat m.

celibate ['selibit] n célibataire mf.

cell [sel] n cellule f, cachot m.

cellar ['selə] n cave f, caveau m.

cellophane ['seləfein] n cellophane f.

celluloid ['seljulɔid] n celluloïde m.

cellulose ['seljulous] n cellulose f.

Celtic ['keltik] a celtique, celte.

cement [si'ment] n ciment m; vt cimenter.

cemetery ['semitri] n cimetière m.

cense [sens] vt encenser.

censer ['sensə] n encensoir m.

censor ['sensə] n censeur m, vt interdire, supprimer, contrôler; to be —ed passer par la censure.

censoring ['sensəriŋ] n censure f.

censorious [sen'sɔ:riəs] a réprobateur, dénigrant, sévère.

censorship ['sensəʃip] n censure f, contrôle m.

censurable ['senʃərəbl] a répréhensible, censurable.

censure ['senʃə] n censure f, blâme m; vt censurer, condamner, critiquer

census ['sensəs] n recensement m.

cent [sent] n cent m; he hasn't a — il n'a pas le sou.

centenarian [.senti'nɛəriən] an centenaire mf.

centenary [sen'ti:nəri] an centenaire m.

center ['sentə] n centre m, milieu m, foyer m; vt centrer, concentrer; vi se centrer, se concentrer.

center-forward [.sentə'fɔ:wəd] n avant-centre m.

center-half [.sentə'hɑ:f] n demi-centre m.

centigram ['sentigræm] n centi-gramme m.

centimeter ['senti.mitə] n centi-mètre m.

centipede ['sentipi:d] n mille-pattes m inv.

central ['sentrəl] a central.

centralize ['sentrəlaiz] vt centraliser.

centrifugal [sen'trifjugəl] a centri-fuge.

centripetal [sen'tripitl] a centripète.

centuple ['sentjupl] an centuple m; vt centupler.

century ['sentʃuri] n siècle m.

cereal ['siəriəl] an céréale f.

cerebral ['seribrəl] a cérébral.

ceremonial [.seri'mounjəl] n céré-monial m, étiquette f; a de céré-monie.

ceremonious [.seri'mounjəs] a céré-monieux.

ceremony ['seriməni] n cérémonie f, façon(s) f pl.

certain ['sə:tn] a certain, sûr; to make — s'assurer.

certainly ['sə:tnli] ad certainement, certes, assurément, à coup sûr; — not! non, par example.

certainty ['sə:tnti] n certitude f.

certificate [sə'tifikit] n certificat m, attestation f, titre m, diplôme m; diplômer.

certify ['sə:tifai] vt certifier, déclarer, attester.

certifying ['sə:tifaiiŋ] n attestation f, homologation f, approbation f.

certitude ['sə:titju:d] n certitude f.

cessation [se'seiʃən] n cessation f, arrêt m.

cession ['seʃən] n cession f, abandon m.

cesspool ['sespu:l] n fosse f, puisard m.

chafe [tʃeif] vt frotter, irriter, écorcher, frictionner, érailler; vi se frotter, s'irriter, s'énerver, s'agiter.

chaff [tʃɑ:f] n balle f, paille f, blague f, persiflage m; vt blaguer, railler.

chaffinch ['tʃæfintʃ] n pinson m.

chafing ['tʃeifiŋ] n irritation f, frottement m, friction f, écorche-ment m.

chagrin ['ʃægrin] n chagrin m, dépit m; vt chagriner, mortifier.

chain [tʃein] n chaîne f, enchaîne-ment m, série f, suite f; vt enchaîner, attacher; —gang chaîne de galé-riens.

chair [tʃɛə] n chaise f, siège m, fauteuil m, chaire f; to be in the — présider.

chairman ['tʃɛəmən] n président m.

chalice ['tʃælis] n calice m.

chalk [tʃɔ:k] n craie f, pastel m, blanc m; vt marquer, tracer etc à la craie.

chalky ['tʃɔ:ki] a crayeux.

challenge ['tʃælindʒ] n défi m, provocation f, qui vive m, inter-pellation f, récusation f; vt défier, crier qui vive à, porter un défi à, provoquer (en duel), mettre en question, récuser.

chamber ['tʃeimbə] n chambre f, cabinet m, salle f, étude f.

chamberlain ['tʃeimbəlin] n chambellan m.

chambermaid ['tʃeimbəmeid] n femme f de chambre.

chamber-pot ['tʃeimbəpot]ɲn pot m de chambre.

champ [tʃæmp] vt mâcher, ronger.

Champagne [ʃæm'pein] n Champagne f; (wine) champagne m.

champion ['tʃæmpjən] n champion, -onne; vt soutenir.

championship ['tʃæmpjənʃip] n championnat m.

chance [tʃɑːns] n chance f, sort m, occasion f, hasard m; a fortuit, de rencontre; vt risquer; vi venir (à to); to — upon rencontrer (par hasard), tomber sur.

chancel ['tʃɑːnsəl] n chœur m.

chancellor ['tʃɑːnsələ] n chancelier m.

chancellory ['tʃɑːnsələri] n chancellerie f.

chancy ['tʃɑːnsi] a chanceux, incertain, risqué.

chandelier [.ʃændi'liə] n lustre m, candélabre m.

change [tʃeindʒ] n changement m, change f, revirement m, monnaie f; vt changer, transformer, modifier; vi (se) changer, se modifier, se transformer.

changeable ['tʃeindʒəbl] a changeant, variable.

changeableness ['tʃeindʒəblnis] n mobilité f, inconstance f, variabilité f.

channel ['tʃænl] n lit m, canal m, rainure f, voie f; the Channel la Manche; Irish Channel mer d'Irlande f.

chant [tʃɑːnt] n (plain-)chant m, psalmodie f; vt chanter, psalmodier.

chanty ['tʃɑːnti] n chanson de bord f.

chaos ['keiɔs] n chaos m.

chaotic [kei'ɔtik] a chaotique, sans ordre, désorganisé.

chap [tʃæp] n gerçure f, crevasse f, bajoue f, type m; vt gercer, crevasser.

chapel ['tʃæpl] n chapelle f, oratoire m.

chaperon ['ʃæpəroun] n chaperon m; vt chaperonner.

chaplain ['tʃæplin] n aumônier m; army chaplain, aumônier (mil).

chaplet ['tʃæplit] n guirlande f, chapelet m.

chapter ['tʃæptə] n chapitre m, suite f; branche d'une société f.

char [tʃɑː] vt carboniser.

character ['kæriktə] n caractère m, moralité f, certificat m (de moralité), réputation f, numéro m, original(e) mf, personnage m, individu m; a bad — un mauvais sujet.

characteristic [.kæriktə'ristik] n trait m (de caractère), particularité f; a caractéristique.

characterize ['kæriktəraiz] vt caractériser, être caractéristique de.

charcoal ['tʃɑːkoul] n charbon m de bois, fusain m.

charcoal-burner ['tʃɑːkoul.bəːnə] n charbonnier m.

charge [tʃɑːdʒ] vti charger; vt accuser, demander; n charge f, prix m, frais m pl, fonction f, emploi m, soin m, garde f, accusation f; to — s.o. with sth accuser qn de qch, reprocher qch à qn; to — sth to s.o. mettre qch au compte de qn; on a — of sous l'inculpation de; free of — franco, gratuitement, gratis.

chargeable ['tʃɑːdʒəbl] a imputable, inculpable.

charger ['tʃɑːdʒə] n chargeur m, plateau m, cheval m de bataille.

charily ['tʃɛərili] ad prudemment, chichement.

chariness ['tʃɛərinis] n prudence f, parcimonie f.

chariot ['tʃæriət] n char m.

charitable ['tʃæritəbl] a charitable, de bienfaisance.

charity ['tʃæriti] n charité f, bienfaisance f, aumônes f pl.

charm [tʃɑːm] n charme m, agrément m, sort m, sortilège m, portebonheur m, fétiche m; vt charmer, enchanter, jeter un sort sur.

charnel-house ['tʃɑːnlhaus] n charnier m.

chart [tʃɑːt] n carte f, diagramme m; vt relever la carte de, porter sur une carte, établir le graphique de, l'hydrographie de, explorer.

charter ['tʃɑːtə] n charte f; vt accorder une charte à, affréter, louer.

chartering ['tʃɑːtəriŋ] n nolisement m, affrètement m.

charwoman ['tʃɑːwumən] n femme de ménage f.

chary ['tʃɛəri] a prudent, chiche, avare.

chase [tʃeis] n chasse f, poursuite f; vt poursuivre, (pour)chasser, ciseler, repousser.

chaser ['tʃeisə] n chasseur m, pousse-café m.

chasing ['tʃeisiŋ] n ciselure f, repoussage m.

chasm ['kæzəm] n crevasse f, abîme m, gouffre m, vide m.

chassis ['ʃæsi] n chassis m.

chaste [tʃeist] a chaste, pudique, pur.

chasten ['tʃeisn] vt châtier, assagir, dégonfler.

chastise [tʃæs'taiz] vt châtier, corriger.

chastisement ['tʃæstizmənt] n châtiment m.

chastity ['tʃæstiti] n chasteté f, pureté f, sobriété f.

chat [tʃæt] n (brin de) causerie f, causette f; vi bavarder, causer.

chattel ['tʃætl] n propriété f, bien

m, mobilier m; **goods and —s** biens et effets m pl.
chatter ['tʃætə] n babil m, caquetage m, bavardage m, claquement m; vi bavarder, jaser, caqueter, claquer.
chatterbox ['tʃætəbɒks] n moulin m à paroles, bavard m.
chatty ['tʃæti] a bavard, causant, causeur.
chauffeur ['ʃoufə] n chauffeur m.
cheap [tʃiːp] a bon marché, (à prix) réduit, trivial, facile; **it's dirt —** c'est donné.
cheapen ['tʃiːpən] vt déprécier, baisser le prix de.
cheaply ['tʃiːpli] ad (à) bon marché, à peu de frais, à bon compte.
cheat [tʃiːt] n tricheur, -euse, escroc m, filou m; vti tricher; vt tromper, voler.
cheating ['tʃiːtiŋ] n tricherie f, tromperie f, fourberie f.
check [tʃek] n échec m, arrêt (brusque) m, contrôle m, contremarque f, rebuffade f, bulletin m, ticket m, étoffe à carreaux f; vt tenir en échec, arrêter, retenir, contenir, freiner, réprimer, réprimander, contrôler, vérifier, réviser, compulser; n (bank) chèque m; **blank —** chèque en blanc; **traveler's — chèque** de voyage; **to cross a —** barrer un chèque.
checkbook ['tʃekbuk] n carnet m de chèques, chéquier m.
checker ['tʃekə] n contrôleur m, pointeur m, damier m; pl carreaux m pl, quadrillage m; vt disposer en damier, quadriller, diaprer, varier.
checker-board ['tʃekəbɔːd] n damier m.
checkered ['tʃekəd] a varié, diapré, inégal, quadrillé, en damier, à carreaux, accidenté.
checkmate ['tʃek'meit] vt faire échec et mat à, déjouer, contrecarrer.
cheek [tʃiːk] n joue f, toupet m, effronterie f.
cheekbone ['tʃiːkboun] n pommette f.
cheekiness ['tʃiːkinis] n effronterie f.
cheeky ['tʃiːki] a effronté.
cheep [tʃiːp] vi piauler, pépier.
cheer [tʃiə] n belle humeur f, bonne chère f, acclamations f pl, applaudissements m pl, vivats m pl; vt réconforter, égayer, acclamer; **to give three —s for** accorder un ban à; vti applaudir; **to — up** vi reprendre courage, se regaillardir; vt réconforter, remonter le moral à; **— up!** courage!
cheerful ['tʃiəful] a joyeux, gai, réconfortant, égayant.
cheerfully ['tʃiəfuli] ad gaiment, de bon cœur.
cheerfulness ['tʃiəfulnis] n gaieté f, belle humeur f, entrain m.

cheering ['tʃiəriŋ] n applaudissements m pl, acclamation f; a réjouissant, encourageant, réconfortant.
cheerio ['tʃiəri'ou] excl à bientôt! à tantôt! à la vôtre!
cheerless ['tʃiəlis] a sombre, morne, triste.
cheery ['tʃiəri] a gai, joyeux.
cheese [tʃiːz] n fromage m.
chef [ʃef] n chef m (de cuisine).
chemical ['kemikəl] a chimique; n pl produits chimiques m pl.
chemist ['kemist] n chimiste m, pharmacien m; **—'s shop** pharmacie f.
chemistry ['kemistri] n chimie f.
cherish ['tʃeriʃ] vt chérir, soigner, caresser.
cherry ['tʃeri] n cerise f.
cherry tree ['tʃeritri] n cerisier m.
cherub ['tʃerəb] n chérubin m.
chervil ['tʃɔːvil] n cerfeuil m.
chess [tʃes] n échecs m pl.
chessboard ['tʃesbɔːd] n échiquier m.
chest [tʃest] n poitrine f, poitrail m, coffre m, caisse f; **— of drawers** commode f.
chestnut ['tʃesnʌt] n châtaigne f, marron m; a châtain, marron, alezan.
chestnut tree ['tʃesnʌttri] n châtaignier m, marronnier m.
chew [tʃuː] vt (re)mâcher, mastiquer, chiquer, ruminer.
chicanery [ʃi'keinəri] n chicanerie f, arguties f pl.
chick [tʃik] n poussin m.
chicken ['tʃikin] n poulet m.
chicken-pox ['tʃikinpɒks] n varicelle f.
chickweed ['tʃikwiːd] n mouron m des oiseaux.
chicory ['tʃikəri] n endive f.
chidden ['tʃidn] pp of chide.
chide [tʃaid] vti gronder.
chief [tʃiːf] n chef m, patron m; a en chef, principal.
chiefly ['tʃiːfli] ad notamment.
chilblain ['tʃilblein] n engelure f.
child [tʃaild] n enfant mf.
childbed ['tʃaildbed] n couches f pl.
childbirth ['tʃaildbəːθ] n accouchement m.
childhood ['tʃaildhud] n enfance f.
childish ['tʃaildiʃ] a enfantin, d'enfant, puéril.
childishness ['tʃaildiʃnis] n puérilité f, enfantillage m.
childless ['tʃaildlis] a sans enfant, stérile.
childlike ['tʃaildlaik] a enfantin, d'enfant.
children ['tʃildrən] pl of child.
chill [tʃil] n froid m, refroidissement m, chaud et froid m, frisson m; a glacial, froid; vt glacer, refroidir; vi se glacer, se refroidir.
chilled [tʃild] a transi de froid, glacé, frigorifié.

chilly ['tʃili] a froid, frileux, glacial, frisquet.

chime [tʃaim] n carillon m; vti sonner, carillonner; vi s'harmoniser (avec with); to — in placer son mot, intervenir.

chimera [kai'miərə] n chimère f.

chimney ['tʃimni] n cheminée f.

chimney-pot ['tʃimnipɔt] n cheminée f.

chimney-sweep ['tʃimniswiːp] n ramoneur m.

chin [tʃin] n menton m.

chinstrap ['tʃinstræp] n jugulaire f.

china ['tʃainə] n porcelaine f.

China ['tʃainə] n Chine f.

Chinese [tʃai'niːz] an chinois m; n Chinois(e) mf.

chink [tʃink] n fente f, crevasse f, lézarde f, entrebâillement m, tintement m; vi sonner, tinter; vt faire sonner, faire tinter.

chintz [tʃints] n perse f.

chip [tʃip] n copeau m, éclat m, tranche f, écornure f, écaille f, jeton m; vt couper, ébrécher, écorner; vi s'ébrécher, s'écorner; to — in intervenir, placer son mot.

chips [tʃips] n pl (pommes f pl de terre) frites f pl.

chiropodist [ki'rɔpədist] n pédicure m.

chirp [tʃəːp] **chirrup** ['tʃirəp] n pépiement m, gazouillement m; vi pépier, gazouiller, grésiller; —ing pépiement.

chisel ['tʃizl] n ciseau m, burin m; vt ciseler, sculpter.

chit [tʃit] n marmot m, mioche mf.

chit-chat ['tʃittʃæt] n commérages m pl.

chivalrous ['ʃivəlrəs] a chevaleresque.

chivalry ['ʃivəlri] n chevalerie f, courtoisie f.

chive [tʃaiv] n ciboulette f.

chlorine ['klɔːriːn] n chlore m.

chloroform ['klɔrəfɔːm] n chloroforme m.

chock [tʃɔk] n cale f; vt caler, mettre sur cale, bourrer.

chock-full ['tʃɔkful] a bourré, bondé.

chocolate ['tʃɔkəlit] n chocolat m; — button, candy crotte de chocolat f.

choice [tʃɔis] n choix m, préférence f, élection f; a de choix, choisi.

choir ['kwaiə] n chœur m, maîtrise f.

choke [tʃouk] n étranglement m, étrangleur m, (aut) starter m; vti étrangler, suffoquer, étouffer; vt boucher, obstruer; vi se boucher, obstruer; vi se boucher, s'obstruer; to — back refouler; to — down avaler.

choking ['tʃoukiŋ] n suffocation f, étranglement m, étouffement m, obstruction f.

cholera ['kɔlərə] n choléra m.

choleric ['kɔlərik] a cholérique, irascible.

choose [tʃuːz] vt choisir, opter, élire, adopter.

choosy ['tʃuːzi] a difficile, chipoteur.

chop [tʃɔp] n coup m (de hache), côtelette f, clapotis m; vt hacher, tailler, couper, fendre; vi clapoter; to — down abattre; to — off couper, trancher.

chopper ['tʃɔpə] n hachoir m, couperet m; hélicoptère m.

choppy ['tʃɔpi] a agité, haché.

chopstick ['tʃɔpstik] n baguette f.

chord [kɔːd] n corde f, accord m.

chorister ['kɔristə] n choriste m, chantre m, enfant de chœur m.

chorus ['kɔːrəs] n chœur m, refrain m; —girl girl f.

chose [tʃouz] pt of choose.

Christ [kraist] n le Christ.

christen ['krisn] vt baptiser.

Christendom ['krisndəm] n chrétienté f.

christening ['krisniŋ] n baptême m.

Christian ['kristjən] an chrétien, -ienne.

Christianity [,kristi'æniti] n christianisme m.

Christmas ['krisməs] n Noël m; **Father** — le Père Noël.

Christmas-box ['krisməsbɔks] n étrennes f pl.

Christmas-carol ['krisməs'kærəl] n noël m.

Christopher ['kristəfə] Christophe m.

chromium ['kroumjəm] n chrome m.

chromium-plated ['kroumjəm,pleitid] a chromé.

chronic ['krɔnik] a chronique, constant.

chronicle ['krɔnikl] n chronique f; vt relater, faire la chronique de.

chronicler ['krɔniklə] n chroniqueur m.

chronological [,krɔnə'lɔdʒikl] a chronologique.

chronology [krə'nɔlədʒi] n chronologie f.

chronometer [krə'nɔmitə] n chronomètre m.

chrysalis ['krisəlis] n chrysalide f.

chrysanthemum [kri'sænθəməm] n chrysanthème m.

chubby ['tʃʌbi] a joufflu, potelé.

chuck [tʃʌk] n tape f; vt jeter, plaquer; to — out flanquer à la porte; to — up abandonner, balancer.

chuckle ['tʃʌkl] n rire étouffé m, gloussement m; vi rire sous cape, glousser.

chum [tʃʌm] n copain m, copine f, camarade mf.

chunk [tʃʌŋk] n gros morceau m, (bread) quignon m.

church [tʃəːtʃ] n église f, temple m.

churchwarden ['tʃɜːtʃ'wɔːdn] n marguillier m.
churchyard ['tʃɜːtʃ'jɑːd] n cimetière
m.
churl [tʃɜːl] n rustre m, ladre m.
churlish ['tʃɜːliʃ] a grossier, mal
élevé, grincheux, hargneux, bourru.
churlishness ['tʃɜːliʃnis] n rusticité
f, grossièreté f.
churn [tʃɜːn] n baratte f; vt battre;
vi (sea) bouillir, bouillonner.
cicada [si'kɑːdə] n cigale f.
cider ['saidə] n cidre m.
cigar [si'gɑː] n cigare m.
cigarette [ˌsigə'ret] n cigarette f.
cigarette-case [ˌsigɑː'retkeis] n étui
m à cigarettes.
cigarette-holder [ˌsigɑː'ret.houldə] n
fume-cigarette m.
cinder ['sində] n cendre f; pl cendres
f pl, escarbilles f pl.
Cinderella [ˌsində'relə] n Cendrillon.
cine-camera ['sini'kæmərə] n
caméra f.
cinema ['sinimə] n cinéma m.
cine-projector ['siniprə.dʒektə] n
ciné-projecteur m.
cinnamon ['sinəmən] n canelle f.
cipher ['saifə] n zéro m, chiffre m,
clé f; vt chiffrer.
circle ['sɜːkl] n cercle m, milieu m;
vicious — cercle vicieux; vt encercler,
entourer, faire le tour de; vi tourner
en rond, tournoyer.
circuit ['sɜːkit] n circuit m, ressort
m, tournée f, tour m, enceinte f,
parcours m, pourtour m, détour m.
circuitous [sə'kjuitəs] a tournant,
détourné.
circular ['sɜːkjulə] an circulaire f.
circularize ['sɜːkjuləraiz] vt envoyer des circulaires à.
circulate ['sɜːkjuleit] vi circuler; vt
faire circuler.
circulation [ˌsɜːkju'leiʃən] n circulation f, (of newspaper) tirage m.
circumcise ['sɜːkəmsaiz] vt circoncire.
circumcision [ˌsɜːkəm'siʒən] n cir-
concision f.
circumference [sə'kʌmfərəns] n circonférence f.
circumflex ['sɜːkəmfleks] an circonflexe m.
circumlocution [ˌsɜːkəmlə'kjuːʃən]
n circonlocution f, ambages f pl.
circumscribe ['sɜːkəmskraib] vt circonscrire.
circumspect ['sɜːkəmspekt] a circonspect.
circumspection [ˌsɜːkəm'spekʃən] n
circonspection f.
circumstance ['sɜːkəmstəns] n circonstance f, situation f, cérémonie f.
circumstantial [ˌsɜːkəm'stænʃəl] a
indirect, circonstancié, circonstan-
ciel.
circumvent [ˌsɜːkəm'vent] vt circonvenir.

circus ['sɜːkəs] n cirque m, rond-
point m.
cistern ['sistən] n réservoir m,
citerne f.
citadel ['sitədl] n citadelle f.
citation [sai'teiʃən] n citation f.
cite [sait] vt citer, assigner.
citizen ['sitizn] n citoyen, citadin(e)
mf bourgeois(e) mf.
citizenship ['sitiznʃip] n civisme m.
citron ['sitrən] n cédrat m.
city ['siti] n (grande)ville f, cité f;
garden — cité jardin f.
civic ['sivik] a civique, municipal.
civics ['siviks] n instruction civique
f.
civil ['sivil] a civil, poli, honnête;
C— Service n administration f;
— servant n fonctionnaire m; in —
life dans le civil; C— War Guerre
f de sécession.
civilian [si'viljən] n civil m, pékin m.
civility [si'viliti] n politesse f,
civilité f.
civilization [ˌsivilai'zeiʃən] n civilisation f.
civilize ['sivilaiz] vt civiliser.
clack [klæk] n claquement m; vi
claquer, caqueter.
clad [klæd] pt pp of clothe.
claim [kleim] n revendication f,
réclamation f, titre m, droit m,
demande f, prétention f; vt réclamer, revendiquer, prétendre (à),
demander.
claimant ['kleimənt] n demandeur,
-eresse, réclamant(e) mf, prétendant
(e) mf, revendicateur m.
clairvoyant [kleə'vɔiənt] a clairvoyant, doué de seconde vue; n
voyant(e) mf.
clam [klæm] n palourde f.
clamant ['kleimənt] a bruyant,
criant, urgent.
clamber ['klæmbə] vi grimper; n
escalade f.
clammy ['klæmi] a moite, humide,
gluant.
clamor ['klæmə] n clameur f; vi
pousser des cris, vociférer; to — for
demander, réclamer, à grand cris.
clamorous ['klæmərəs] a bruyant,
braillard.
clamp [klæmp] n crampon m,
mordache f, patte f d'attache,
(potato) silo m; vt consolider, brider,
agrafer.
clan [klæn] n clan m.
clandestine [klæn'destin] a clandestin.
clang [klæŋ] n bruit m retentissant,
son m métallique; vt résonner,
retentir; vt faire résonner.
clank [klæŋk] n cliquetis m; vi
sonner; vt faire sonner.
clap [klæp] n éclat m, battement m,
applaudissements m pl, tape f; vi
battre (des mains); vti applaudir;
vt camper, fourrer.
clapper ['klæpə] n battant m,

crécelle f, claquet m, claqueur m.
claptrap ['klæptræp] n tape-à-l'œil m, boniment m.
claret ['klærət] n bordeaux m rouge.
clarify ['klærifai] vt clarifier, éclaircir; vi se clarifier, s'éclaircir.
clarinet [,klæri'net] n clarinette f.
clarion ['klæriən] n clairon m; a claironnant.
clarity ['klæriti] n clarté f, lucidité f.
clash [klæʃ] n choc m, heurt m, fracas m, cliquetis m, confit m; vi faire du fracas, se heurter, s'entrechoquer, jurer; vt faire résonner.
clasp [klɑːsp] n agrafe f, fermoir m, fermeture f, étreinte f; vt agrafer, serrer, étreindre.
clasp-knife ['klɑːspnaif] n couteau fermant, pliant m.
class [klɑːs] n classe f, catégorie f, type m, sorte f; vt classer.
classic ['klæsik] an classique m.
classicism ['klæsisizəm] n classicisme m.
classification [,klæsifi'keiʃən] n classement m.
classify ['klæsifai] vt classer.
clatter ['klætə] n bruit m, fracas m, brouhaha m, ferraillement m.
clause [klɔːz] n clause f, article m, proposition f.
clavicle ['klævikl] n clavicule f.
claw [klɔː] n serre f, pince f, griffe f; vt gratter, griffer, déchirer, égratigner.
clay [klei] n argile f, glaise f, pisé m.
clean [kliːn] a propre, net, bien fait, complet; vt nettoyer, vider, mettre en ordre, balayer, (re)curer, décrotter, décrasser.
cleaner ['kliːnə] n teinturier m, nettoyeur, -euse, décrotteur m, balayeur, -euse.
cleaning ['kliːniŋ] n nettoyage m, dégraissage m.
clean(li)ness ['klenlinis] n propreté f, nettété f.
cleanse [klenz] vt purifier, laver, curer, assainir.
clear [kliə] a clair, net, évident, libre, dégagé, sûr; all — fin d'alerte f; vt éclaircir, disculper, déblayer, dégager, franchir, solder, acquitter, gagner net, desservir, (forest, bush) débrousser; vi s'éclaircir, se dégager, se dissiper; to — away vt écarter, enlever; vi se dissiper; to — off enlever, solder; to — out vt nettoyer, balayer, vider; vi filer, ficher le camp, se sauver; to — up vt tirer au clair, éclaircir; vi s'éclaircir.
clearance ['kliərəns] n déblayage m, liquidation f, congé m, jeu m.
clear-cut ['kliə'kʌt] a distinct, net ciselé.
clear-headed ['kliə'hedid] a lucide, perspicace.
clearing ['kliəriŋ] n clairière f, levée f, dégagement m, déblaiement m, évacuation f, défrichement m.

clearness ['kliənis] n clarté f, nettété f.
clear-sighted ['kliə'saitid] a clairvoyant.
cleavage ['kliːvidʒ] n division f, scission f, (fam) décolleté m.
cleave [kliːv] vt fendre; vi se fendre, s'attacher.
cleaver ['kliːvə] n couperet m, fendoir m.
cleft [kleft] pt pp of **cleave**; n fente f, crevasse f, fissure f; a fourchu, (palate) fendu; **in a — stick** dans une impasse, mal pris.
clemency ['klemənsi] n clémence f, douceur f, indulgence f.
clement ['klemənt] a clément, indulgent, doux.
clench [klentʃ] see **clinch**; vt serrer; vi se serrer.
clergy ['kləːdʒi] n clergé m.
clergyman ['kləːdʒimən] n ecclésiastique m, pasteur m.
clerical ['klerikəl] a de clerc, d'écriture, de copiste.
clerk [klɑːk] n clerc m, commis m, employé(e) de bureau mf.
clever ['klevə] a habile, adroit, intelligent, ingénieux.
cleverness ['klevənis] n habileté f, adresse f, intelligence f, ingéniosité f.
click [klik] n (dé)clic m, cliquetis m; vti cliqueter, claquer; vi avoir de la veine, avoir des touches, cadrer.
client ['klaiənt] n client(e) mf.
clientele [,kliː̃aːn'tel] n clientèle f.
cliff [klif] n falaise f, paroi f rocheuse, rochers m pl.
climate ['klaimit] n climat m.
climatic [klai'mætik] a climat(ér)que.
climax ['klaimæks] n gradation f, comble m, apogée f.
climb [klaim] n escalade f, montée f, ascension f, côte f; vti monter, grimper; vt escalader, gravir, monter à, sur, grimper à, sur, faire l'ascension de; vi prendre de l'altitude; to — down vti descendre; vi baisser pavillon, en rabattre, se dégonfler; to — over escalader, franchir.
climber ['klaimə] n grimpeur m, alpiniste, plante grimpante f, arriviste mf.
clinch [klintʃ] n crampon m, corps à corps m; vt river, serrer, conclure.
clincher ['klintʃə] n argument décisif m.
cling [kliŋ] vi se cramponner, s'accrocher, se prendre, coller.
clinging ['kliŋiŋ] a étroit, collant.
clinic ['klinik] n clinique f.
clink [kliŋk] n tintement m, cliquetis m; prison f; vi tinter, s'entrechoquer; vt faire tinter, choquer; to — glasses trinquer.
clip [klip] n agrafe f, pince f, attache f; vt agrafer, pincer, tondre, rogner, tailler.

clippers ['klipəz] n tondeuse f.
clipping ['klipiŋ] n tonte f, tondage m, taille f, coupure f; pl rognures f pl.
cloak [klouk] n manteau m, masque m; vt couvrir, masquer.
cloakroom ['kloukrum] n consigne f, vestiaire m.
clock [klɔk] n pendule f, horloge f, baguette f; vt chronométrer.
clock-maker ['klɔk'meikə] n horloger m.
clock-making ['klɔk'meikiŋ] n horlogerie f.
clockwise ['klɔkwaiz] a dans le sens des aiguilles d'une montre, à droite.
clockwork ['klɔkwə:k] n mouvement d'horlogerie m, rouage m d'horloge; to go like — marcher comme sur des roulettes.
clod [klɔd] n motte f de terre, rustre m.
clog [klɔg] n entrave f, galoche f, sabot m; vt entraver, obstruer, arrêter, boucher; vi s'obstruer, se boucher.
cloister ['klɔistə] n cloître m; pl ambulatoire m.
close [klous] n (en)clos m, clôture f, enceinte f; a fermé, clos, confiné, lourd, compact, serré, secret, proche, étroit, exact, intime, avare; ad de près, étroitement; — by tout près; — to prep tout près de.
close [klouz] n clôture f, fermeture f, conclusion f, fin f; to draw to a — tirer à sa fin; vt fermer, clore, conclure, terminer, (res)serrer; vi (se) fermer, se terminer, faire relâche, en venir aux prises; to — down vti fermer; to — up vt boucher, barrer, obturer; vi s'obturer, se serrer.
closely ['klousli] ad de près.
closeness ['klousnis] n proximité f, rapprochement m, étroitesse f, intimité f, lourdeur f, avarice f, exactitude f, réserve f.
closet ['klɔzit] n cabinet m, armoire f; vt enfermer.
close-up ['klousʌp] n gros, premier plan m.
closing ['klouziŋ] n fermeture f, clôture f.
closure ['klouʒə] n clôture f.
clot [klɔt] n caillot m, grumeau m; vi se prendre, se coaguler, se figer, se cailler.
cloth [klɔθ] n toile f, étoffe f, nappe f, napperon m, linge m, torchon m, drap m, tapis m, habit ecclésiastique m; to lay the — mettre la nappe, le couvert.
clothe [klouð] vt (re)vêtir, habiller, couvrir.
clothes [klouðz] n pl habits m pl, vêtements m pl, effets m pl.
clothes-horse ['klouðzhɔːs] n séchoir m.
clothes-peg ['klouðzpeg] n patère f.
clothier ['klouðiə] n drapier m.

clothing ['klouðiŋ] n habillement m, vêtements m pl.
cloud [klaud] n nuage m, nue f, nuée f, buée f; vt assombrir, couvrir, obscurcir, voiler, ternir, embuer, troubler; vi s'assombrir, se couvrir, s'obscurcir, se voiler, se troubler, se ternir.
cloudy ['klaudi] a nuageux, couvert, trouble.
clout [klaut] n torchon m, linge m, chiffon m, taloche f.
clove [klouv] pt of cleave; n clou m de girofle; — of garlic gousse f d'ail.
cloven ['klouvn] pp of cleave; a fendu, fourchu.
clover ['klouvə] n trèfle m; to be in — être comme un coq en pâte.
clown [klaun] n clown m, bouffon m, pitre m; vi faire le clown.
cloy [klɔi] vt rassasier, affadir.
club [klʌb] n massue f, crosse f, gourdin m, club m, cercle m, (cards) trèfle m; vt frapper avec un gourdin, assommer; vi s'associer; to — together se cotiser.
club-foot ['klʌb'fut] n pied-bot m.
cluck [klʌk] n gloussement m; vi glousser.
clue [kluː] n indice m, indication f.
clump [klʌmp] n massif m, bouquet m, masse f; vi sonner, marcher lourdement.
clumsiness ['klʌmzinis] n gaucherie f, balourdise f, maladresse f.
clumsy ['klʌmzi] a gauche, maladroit.
clung [klʌŋ] pt pp of cling.
cluster ['klʌstə] n groupe m, grappe f, essaim m, bouquet m; vt grouper; vi se grouper.
clutch [klʌtʃ] n prise f, étreinte f, poigne f, griffes f pl, couvée f, (cheville d')embrayage f; to let in (out) the — embrayer, (débrayer); vt empoigner, étreindre, saisir; to — at s'agripper à, se raccrocher à.
clutter ['klʌtə] n encombrement m, pagaïe f; to — up encombrer.
coach [koutʃ] n coche m, carrosse m, voiture f, autocar m, répétiteur m, entraîneur m; vt donner des leçons à, entraîner.
coach-builder ['koutʃ'bildə] n carrossier m.
coach-building ['koutʃ'bildiŋ] n carrosserie f.
coach-house ['koutʃhaus] n remise f.
coaching ['koutʃiŋ] n leçons f pl, répétitions f pl, dressage m, entraînement m.
coachman ['koutʃmən] n cocher m.
coachwork ['koutʃwəːk] n carrosserie f.
coagulate [kou'ægjuleit] vt (faire) coaguler, figer; vi se coaguler, se figer.
coal [koul] n charbon m, houille f; to haul s.o. over the —s laver la tête à qn; vi faire le charbon.

coal-bed ['koul'bed] n banc m, couche f de houille.

coalesce [.kouə'les] vi s'unir, fusionner.

coalfield ['koulfi:ld] n bassin houiller m.

coalition [.koulə'liʃən] n coalition f.

coalmine ['koulmain] n mine f de houille, houillère f.

coalminer ['koulmainə] n mineur m, houilleur m.

coal-tar ['koul'ta:] n goudron m.

coarse [ko:s] a gros(sier), rude, rêche.

coarseness ['ko:snis] n grossièreté f, rudesse f, grosseur f, brutalité f.

coast [koust] n côte f, rivage m, littoral m; vi côtoyer le rivage, faire le cabotage; to — down a hill descendre une côte en roue libre, le moteur débrayé.

coastal ['koustəl] a côtier.

coaster ['koustə] n caboteur m.

coasting ['koustiŋ] n cabotage m, navigation côtière.

coat [kout] n pardessus m, manteau m, habit m, robe f, poil m, couche f, revêtement m; vt couvrir, enduire, revêtir.

coat-hanger ['kout,hæŋə] n porte-vêtements m.

coat-peg ['koutpeg] n patère f.

coax [kouks] vt amadouer, câliner, cajoler, amener (à to).

coaxing ['kouksiŋ] n cajoleries f pl, enjôlement m; a cajoleur, câlin.

cob [kɔb] n cygne m, bidet m, torchis m, (bread) miche f, (nut) aveline f.

cobble ['kɔbl] n galet m, caillou m; vt paver, rapiécer.

cobbler ['kɔblə] n savetier m, cordonnier m.

cobra ['koubrə] n cobra m, serpent à lunettes m.

cobweb ['kɔbweb] n toile d'araignée f.

cock [kɔk] n coq m, mâle m, robinet m, (gun) chien m, (hay) meule f, (scales) aiguille f, retroussis m; vt dresser, retrousser, mettre de travers, armer.

cockade [kɔ'keid] n cocarde f.

cock-a-doodle-doo ['kɔkədu:dl'du:] excl cocorico!

cock-and-bull story ['kɔkən'bul 'stɔ:ri] n coq à l'âne m.

cockatoo [.kɔkə'tu:] n cacatoès m.

cockchafer ['kɔk,tʃeifə] n hanneton m.

cockle ['kɔkl] n coque f, bucarde f.

cockney ['kɔkni] an londonien, -ienne.

cockpit ['kɔkpit] n arène f, carlingue f.

cockroach ['kɔkroutʃ] n cafard m, blatte f, cancrelet m.

cockscomb ['kɔkskoum] n crête f de coq.

cocksure ['kɔk'ʃuə] a qui ne doute de rien, outrecuidant, très assuré.

cocky ['kɔki] a faraud, outrecuidant.

cocoa ['koukou] n cacao m; — tree cacaoyer m; — plantation cacaotière f.

coconut ['koukənʌt] n noix de coco f; — palm cocotier m; — plantation cocoteraie f; — oil huile f de copra.

cocoon [kə'ku:n] n cocon m.

cod [kɔd] n morue f, cabillaud m.

coddle ['kɔdl] vt dorloter, choyer.

code [koud] n code m, chiffre m; vt codifier, chiffrer.

codicil ['kɔdisil] n codicille m.

codliver-oil ['kɔdlivər'ɔil] n huile f de foie de morue.

coerce [kou'ə:s] vt forcer, contraindre.

coercion [kou'ə:ʃən] n coercition f, contrainte f.

coercive [kou'ə:siv] a coercitif.

coffee ['kɔfi] n café m; — bean grain m de café; — grounds marc m de café black — café noir; light — café au lait, café crème.

coffee-mill ['kɔfimil] n moulin à café m.

coffee plant ['kɔfiplɑ:nt] n caféier m.

coffee plantation ['kɔfiplæn,teiʃən] n caféière f.

coffeepot ['kɔfipɔt] n cafetière f.

coffer ['kɔfə] n coffre m.

coffin ['kɔfin] n cercueil m, bière f.

cog [kɔg] n dent f; he's only a — in the wheel il n'est qu'un rouage de la machine.

cogency ['koudʒənsi] n force f, puissance f, urgence f.

cogent ['koudʒənt] a décisif, valable, urgent.

cogitate ['kɔdʒiteit] vi réfléchir; vti méditer.

cogitation [.kɔdʒi'teiʃən] n réflexion f, délibération f.

cognate ['kɔgneit] a parent, connexe, analogue, qui a du rapport, de même origine.

cognizance ['kɔgnizəns] n connaissance f, compétence f, ressort m.

cogwheel ['kɔgwi:l] n roue dentée f.

cohabit [kou'hæbit] vi cohabiter.

cohabitation [.kouhæbi'teiʃən] n cohabitation f.

coheir ['kou'eə] n cohéritier, -ière.

cohere [kou'hiə] vi se tenir ensemble, adhérer, s'agglomérer, être conséquent, se tenir.

coherence [kou'hiərəns] n cohésion f, cohérence f, suite f.

coherent [kou'hiərənt] a cohérent, qui a de la suite, conséquent.

cohesion [kou'hi:ʒən] n cohésion f.

cohesive [kou'hi:siv] a adhérent, cohésif.

coil [kɔil] n rouleau m, bobine f, anneau m, repli m; vt embobiner, (en)rouler; to — up vi s'enrouler, se lover, se mettre en rond, serpenter; vt enrouler.

coin [kɔin] n pièce f, monnaie f; vt frapper, forger, inventer.

coinage ['kɔinidʒ] n frappe f monnaie f.

coincide [ˌkouin'said] *vi* coincider, s'accorder.

coincidence [kou'insidəns] *n* co-incidence *f*, concours *m*.

coiner ['kɔinə] *n* faux-monnayeur, *m*, forgeur *m*, inventeur *m*.

coke [kouk] *n* coke *m*.

colander ['kɔləndə] *n* passoire *f*.

cold [kould] *a* froid, insensible; *n* froid *m*, rhume *m*; — **in the head** rhume de cerveau *m*; **it is** — il fait froid; **he is** — il a froid; **to catch** — prendre froid, s'enrhumer, attraper un rhume; **to grow** — se refroidir.

coldness ['kouldnis] *n* froideur *f*, froid *m*, froidure *f*.

cold-shoulder ['kould'ʃouldə] *vt* battre froid à.

colic ['kɔlik] *n* colique *f*.

collaborate [kə'læbəreit] *vi* collaborer.

collaboration [kə,læbə'reiʃən] *n* collaboration *f*.

collaborator [kə'læbəreitə] *n* collaborateur, -trice.

collapse [kə'læps] *n* effondrement *m*, écroulement *m*, dégringolade *f*, débâcle *f*; *vi* s'effondrer, s'écrouler, s'affaisser, se rabattre.

collapsible [kə'læpsəbl] *a* pliant, démontable, rabattable.

collar ['kɔlə] *n* (faux-)col *m*, collier *m*, collerette *f*, collet *m*; *vt* prendre au collet, saisir.

collarbone ['kɔləboun] *n* clavicule *f*.

colleague ['kɔli:g] *n* collègue *mf*.

collect [kə'lekt] *vt* rassembler, réunir, percevoir, ramasser; *vi* se rassembler, s'amasser, faire la quête.

collected [kə'lektid] *a* froid, posé, recueilli, de sang-froid.

collection [kə'lekʃən] *n* collecte *f*, quête *f*, levée *f*, collection *f*, rassemblement *m*, collectionnement *m*, recueil *m*, perception *f*.

collective [kə'lektiv] *a* collectif.

collector [kə'lektə] *n* collecteur, -trice, collectionneur, -euse, quêteur, -euse, percepteur, -trice, receveur, -euse, encaisseur *m*; **ticket** — contrôleur *m*.

college ['kɔlidʒ] *n* collège *m*, école *f*.

collide [kə'laid] *vi* se heurter.

collier ['kɔliə] *n* mineur *m* (de charbon), (navire) charbonnier *m*.

colliery ['kɔljəri] *n* mine *f* de houille.

collision [kə'liʒən] *n* collision *f*, tamponnement *m*.

colloquial [kə'loukwiəl] *a* familier, parlé.

colloquy ['kɔləkwi] *n* colloque *m*.

collusion [kə'lu:ʒən] *n* collusion *f*, connivence *f*.

colon ['koulən] *n* deux-points *m*.

colonel ['kə:nl] *n* colonel *m*.

colonial [kə'lounjəl] *a* colonial.

colonist ['kɔlənist] *n* colon *m*.

colonization [ˌkɔlənai'zeiʃən] *n* colonisation *f*.

colonize ['kɔlənaiz] *vt* coloniser.

colony ['kɔləni] *n* colonie *f*.

colossal [kə'bɔsl] *a* colossal.

colossus [kə'bɔsəs] *n* colosse *m*.

color ['kʌlə] *n* couleur *f*, coloris *m*, teint *m*; *pl* drapeau *m*, cocarde *f*, livrée *f*; *vt* colorer, colorier, présenter sous un faux jour; *vi* rougir, se colorer; **in its true** —**s** sous son vrai jour; **to be off** — n'être pas dans son assiette; **with flying** —**s** haut la main.

color-bar ['kʌləbɑ:] *n* racisme *m*.

color-blind ['kʌləblaind] *a* daltonien.

color-blindness ['kʌləblaindnis] *n* daltonisme *m*.

colored ['kʌləd] *a* coloré, de couleur.

colorful ['kʌləful] *a* pittoresque, coloré.

coloring ['kʌləriŋ] *n* coloris *m*, coloration *f*, teint *m*.

colorless ['kʌləlis] *a* incolore, terne, pâle.

colt [koult] *n* poulain *m*, pouliche *f*.

column ['kɔləm] *n* colonne *f*.

comb [koum] *n* peigne *m*, étrille *f*, carde *f*, crête *f*; *vt* peigner, étriller, carder, fouiller; *vi* déferler; **to** — **out** démêler, faire une rafle dans.

combat ['kɔmbæt] *n* combat *m*; *vt* combattre, lutter contre, s'opposer à.

combatant ['kɔmbətənt] *n* combattant *m*.

combative ['kɔmbətiv] *a* combatif, batailleur.

combination [ˌkɔmbi'neiʃən] *n* combinaison *f*, mélange *m*, combiné *m*.

combine ['kɔmbain] *n* combinaison *f*, cartel *m*; [kəm'bain] *vt* combiner, unir, joindre, allier; *vi* se combiner, s'unir, fusionner, se syndiquer.

combined [kəm'baind] *a* combiné, joint (**a** with).

combustible [kəm'bʌstibl] *a* inflammable; *an* combustible *m*.

combustion [kəm'bʌstʃən] *n* combustion *f*.

come [kʌm] *vi* venir, arriver, en venir (à), en arriver (à); **to** — **about** arriver, se passer, se faire; **to** — **across** tomber sur, rencontrer, trouver; **to** — **along** s'en venir, s'amener, se dépêcher; **to** — **away** partir, se détacher; **to** — **back** revenir, en revenir (à); **to** — **by** *vi* passer par; *vt* obtenir; **to** — **down** *vi* descendre; *vi* baisser, s'abaisser, s'écrouler; **to** — **forward** (s')avancer; **to** — **in** entrer; **to** — **off** descendre, se détacher, s'effacer, avoir lieu, réussir, aboutir; **to** — **out** sortir, débuter, paraître, se montrer, s'effacer, se mettre en grève; **to** — to revenir à soi, reprendre connaissance; **to** — **up to** s'approcher de, venir à, répondre à, s'élever à; **to** — **up against** entrer en conflit avec.

se heurter avec; **to — upon** tomber sur, surprendre.

come-back ['kʌmbæk] n retour m (à la charge), réplique f, réapparition f.

comedian [kə'mi:djən] n auteur m, (acteur) comique, comédien, -ienne.

comedy ['kɔmidi] n comédie f.

comeliness ['kʌmlinis] n grâce f.

comely ['kʌmli] a gracieux, avenant.

comer ['kʌmə] n (premier, -ière, nouveau, -elle) venu(e) mf arrivant(e) mf, venant(e) mf.

comet ['kɔmit] n comète f.

comfit ['kʌmfit] n dragée f, bonbon m.

comfort ['kʌmfət] n (ré)confort m, aisance f, bienêtre m, confortable m, consolation f, soulagement m; pl douceurs f pl, gâteries f pl; vt réconforter, consoler, soulager, mettre à l'aise.

comfortable ['kʌmfətəbl] a à l'aise, bien, confortable, aisé, commode.

comforter ['kʌmfətə] n consolateur, -trice, cache-nez m, écharpe f, tétine f, sucette f.

comic ['kɔmik] an comique m.

comical ['kɔmikəl] a comique, drôle.

coming ['kʌmiŋ] a prochain, à venir, futur, d'avenir; n venue f, arrivée f, approche f, avènement m; — **of age** majorité f.

comity ['kɔmiti] n affabilité f.

comma ['kɔmə] n virgule f; **inverted —s** guillemets m pl.

command [kə'mɑ:nd] n ordre m, commandement m, maîtrise f; vt ordonner, commander (à), dominer.

commandeer [.kɔmən'diə] vt réquisitionner.

commander [kə'mɑ:ndə] n commandeur m, commandant m (en chef), capitaine de frégate m.

commanding [kə'mɑ:ndiŋ] a imposant, dominateur, dominant.

commandment [kə'mɑ:ndmənt] n commandement m.

commemorate [kə'meməreit] vt commémorer.

commemoration [kə,memə'reiʃən] n commémoration f.

commemorative [kə'memərətiv] a commémoratif.

commence [kə'mens] vti commencer.

commencement [kə'mensmənt] n commencement m.

commend [kə'mend] vt confier, recommander, louer.

commendable [kə'mendəbl] a recommandable, louable.

commendation [.kɔmen'deiʃən] n recommandation f, éloge m, louange f.

commensurate [kə'menʃərit] a proportionné, commensurable.

comment ['kɔment] vi commenter, faire des observations; n commentaire m, observation f.

commentary ['kɔmentəri] n com-

mentaire m, glose f; **running —** radio-reportage m.

commentator ['kɔmenteitə] n commentateur, -trice, radio-reporter m.

commerce ['kɔmə:s] n commerce m, les affaires f pl.

commercial [kə'mə:ʃəl] a commercial, mercantile; n annonce publicitaire f; — **traveler** n commis-voyageur m.

commiserate [kə'mizəreit] vt compatir (à **with**), s'apitoyer (sur **with**).

commiseration [kə,mizə'reiʃən] n commisération f.

commissary ['kɔmisəri] n délégué m, intendant m.

commission [kə'miʃən] n commission f, courtage m, guelte f, délégation f, mandat m, brevet m, nomination f, perpétration f; vt mandater, nommer, charger (de), commissionner, déléguer, (**ship**) armer.

commissionaire [kə,miʃə'nɛə] n commissionnaire m, chasseur m.

commissioned [kə'miʃənd] a commissionné; **non— officer** sous-officier m.

commissioner [kə'miʃənə] n commissaire m, délégué m.

commit [kə'mit] vt confier, remettre, commettre, compromettre, renvoyer, engager; — **to memory** apprendre par cœur; — **suicide** se suicider.

commitment [kə'mitmənt] n engagement m.

committal [kə'mitl] n engagement m, perpétration f.

committee [kə'miti] n comité m, commission f, conseil m.

commode [kə'moud] n commode f, chaise percée f.

commodious [kə'moudjəs] a spacieux, ample.

commodiousness [kə'moudjəsnis] n grandeur f.

commodity [kə'mɔditi] n denrée f, marchandise f, article m.

common ['kɔmən] a commun, public, vulgaire, ordinaire, courant, coutumier, (mil) simple, communal.

commonalty ['kɔmənəlti] n commun m des hommes, les roturiers m pl.

commoner ['kɔmənə] n bourgeois(e) mf, homme du peuple, roturier, -ière.

commonly ['kɔmənli] ad. communément, vulgairement.

commonness ['kɔmənnis] n vulgarité f, trivialité f, fréquence f.

commonplace ['kɔmənpleis] n lieu commun m; a banal, terre à terre.

commons ['kɔmənz] n peuple m; **the House of Commons** = la Chambre des Députés.

commonsense ['kɔmən,sens] n bon sens m, sens commun m.

commonweal ['kɔmənwi:l] n bien public m, chose publique f.

commonwealth ['kɔmənwelθ] n république f, commonwealth m.
commotion [kə'mouʃən] n commotion f, émoi m, agitation f, ébranlement m, brouhaha m, troubles m pl.
communal ['kɔmjuːnl] a communal,
public, (life) collectif.
commune [kə'mjuːn] vi communier
s'entretenir; to — with oneself se
recueillir, vivre en soi.
communicable [kə'mjuːnikəbl] a
communicable, contagieux.
communicant [kə'mjuːnikənt] n
communiant(e) mf, informateur,
-trice.
communicate [kə'mjuːnikeit] vti
communiquer; vi communier, faire
part de.
communication [kə,mjuːni'keiʃən]
n communication f, rapports m pl.
communicative [kə'mjuːnikətiv] a
communicatif, expansif.
communion [kə'mjuːnjən] n communion f, relations f pl.
communism ['kɔmjunizəm] n communisme m.
communist ['kɔmjunist] an communiste mf.
community [kə'mjuːniti] n communauté f, solidarité f, société f.
communize ['kɔmjunaiz] vt
socialiser, communiser.
commutable [kə'mjuːtəbl] a
échangeable, permutable, commu-
able.
commutation [,kɔmjuː'teiʃən] n
commutation f.
commute [kə'mjuːt] vt (é)changer,
commuer.
compact ['kɔmpækt] n contrat m,
accord m, pacte m, poudrier m;
[kəm'pækt] a compact, tassé, serré,
concis.
compactness [kəm'pæktnis] n compacité f, concision f.
companion [kəm'pænjən] n compagnon m, compagne f, demoiselle
(dame) de compagnie f.
companionable [kəm'pænjənəbl] a
sociable.
companionship [kəm'pænjənʃip] n
camaraderie f.
company ['kʌmpəni] n compagnie f,
(ship) équipage m, société f, corporation f, bande f, troupe f; to have —
for dinner avoir du monde à dîner.
comparable ['kɔmpərəbl] a comparable.
comparative [kəm'pærətiv] a comparatif, relatif.
comparatively [kəm'pærətivli] ad
par comparaison, relativement.
compare [kəm'pɛə] vt comparer,
confronter, collationner, échanger.
compared [kəm'pɛəd] pt pp of
compare; — with prep à côte de,
par rapport à, au prix de, par comparaison à.
comparison [kəm'pærisn] n comparaison f.

compartment [kəm'pɑːtmənt] n
compartiment m, case f.
compass ['kʌmpəs] n compas m,
boussole f, portée f, limites f pl,
détour m; vt faire le tour de,
entourer, saisir, tramer, exécuter.
compassion [kəm'pæʃən] n compassion f, pitié f.
compassionate [kəm'pæʃənit] a
compatissant.
compatibility [kəm,pæti'biliti] n
compatibilité f.
compatible [kəm'pætibl] a compatible.
compatriot [kəm'pætriət] n compatriote mf.
compel [kəm'pel] vt contraindre,
forcer, obliger, imposer.
compendious [kəm'pendiəs] a succinct.
compendium [kəm'pendiəm] n
abrégé m.
compensate ['kɔmpenseit] vt (ré)
compenser, rémunérer, dédommager; to — for racheter, compenser.
compensation [,kɔmpen'seiʃən] n
dédommamgeent m, indemnité f.
compete [kəm'piːt] vi rivaliser,
concourir, faire concurrence, disputer.
competence ['kɔmpitəns] n compétence f, aisance f.
competent ['kɔmpitənt] a compétent, capable.
competition [,kɔmpi'tiʃən] n concurrence f, concours m.
competitive [kəm'petitiv] a de
concours, de concurrence.
competitor [kəm'petitə] n com-
pétiteur, -trice, concurrent(e) mf,
émule mf.
compilation [,kɔmpi'leiʃən] n compilation f.
compile [kəm'pail] vt compiler,
dresser.
compiler [kəm'pailə] n compilateur,
-trice.
complacency [kəm'pleisnsi] n contentement m (de soi), suffisance f.
complacent [kəm'pleisnt] a suffisant,
content de soi-même.
complain [kəm'plein] vi se plaindre,
porter plainte.
complainer [kəm'pleinə] n récla-
mant(e) mf, mécontent(e) mf.
complaint [kəm'pleint] n plainte f,
grief m, maladie f.
complaisance [kəm'pleizəns] n complaisance f.
complaisant [kəm'pleizənt] a complaisant, obligeant.
complement ['kɔmplimənt] n complément m; [,kɔmpli'ment] vt compléter.
complete [kəm'pliːt] a complet,
entier, total, absolu, accompli,
achevé, au complet; vt compléter,
accomplir, achever, mettre le comble
à.

completion [kəm'pli:ʃən] n achèvement m, accomplissement m, satisfaction f.

complex ['kɔmpleks] an complexe m.

complexion [kəm'plekʃən] n teint m, jour m, couleur f, caractère m.

complexity [kəm'pleksíti] n complexité f.

compliance [kəm'plaiəns] n déférence f, acquiescement m; in — with conformément à.

compliant [kəm'plaiənt] a obligeant, docile.

complicate ['kɔmplikeit] vt compliquer.

complication [.kɔmpli'keiʃən] n complication f.

complicity [kəm'plisiti] n complicité f.

compliment ['kɔmplimənt] n compliment m; [.kɔmpli'ment] vt féliciter, complimenter.

complimentary [.kɔmpli'mentəri] a flatteur, (ticket) de faveur, (book) en hommage.

comply [kəm'plai] vi se conformer (à with), accéder (à with), obéir (à with), observer, se soumettre (à with), s'exécuter.

component [kəm'pounənt] n élément m, composant m; a constitutif, constituant.

compose [kəm'pouz] vt composer, arranger; to — oneself se calmer, se remettre.

composed [kəm'pouzd] a calme, posé, composé.

composer [kəm'pouzə] n compositeur, -trice.

composite ['kɔmpəzit] a composite, composé.

composition [.kɔmpə'zišən] n composition f, constitution f, arrangement m, composé m, mélange m, rédaction f, dissertation f.

compositor [kəm'pɔzitə] n typographe m, compositeur m.

composure [kəm'pouʒə] n calme m, maîtrise de soi f, sang-froid m.

compound ['kɔmpaund] an composé m, concession f; — interest intérêts composés; a complexe; n mastic m.

compound [kəm'paund] vt mélanger, combiner, arranger, composer; vi s'arranger, transiger.

comprehend [.kɔmpri'hend] vt comprendre.

comprehensible [.kɔmpri'hensəbl] a compréhensible.

comprehension [.kɔmpri'henʃən] n compréhension f.

comprehensive [.kɔmpri'hensiv] a compréhensive; — school collège pilote (mixte) f.

comprehensiveness [.kɔmpri'hensivnis] n étendue f, portée f.

compress ['kɔmpres] n compresse f.

compress [kəm'pres] vt comprimer, bander, condenser, concentrer.

comprise [kəm'praiz] vt comprendre, comporter, renfermer.

compromise ['kɔmprəmaiz] n compromis m; vt transiger; vti compromettre; to — oneself se compromettre.

compulsion [kəm'pʌlʃən] n force f, contrainte f.

compulsory [kəm'pʌlsəri] a obligatoire, coercitif.

compunction [kəm'pʌŋkʃən] n remords m, regret m, componction f.

computation [.kɔmpju'teiʃən] n calcul m, estimation f.

compute [kəm'pju:t] vt calculer, estimer.

computer [kəm'pju:tə] n ordinateur m, calculateur m.

comrade ['kɔmrid] n camarade m, compagnon m.

comradeship ['kɔmridʃip] n camaraderie f.

con [kɔn] vt étudier, diriger, escroquer.

concave ['kɔn'keiv] a concave, incurvé.

conceal [kən'si:l] vt cacher, dissimuler, céler, voiler, dérober, masquer.

concealment [kən'si:lmənt] n dissimulation f, réticence f.

concede [kən'si:d] vt accorder, concéder, admettre.

conceit [kən'si:t] n vanité f, suffisance f, pointe f, jugement m.

conceited [kən'si:tid] a vaniteux, suffisant, glorieux.

conceivable [kən'si:vəbl] a concevable.

conceive [kən'si:v] vt concevoir; vi s'imaginer.

concentrate ['kɔnsəntreit] vt concentrer; vi se concentrer.

concentration [.kɔnsən'treiʃən] n concentration f, application f, rassemblement m.

conception [kən'sepʃən] n conception f, idée f.

concern [kən'sə:n] n intérêt m, sympathie f, affaire f, souci m, sollicitude f, maison f de commerce, entreprise f; the whole — toute la boutique; vt regarder, concerner, intéresser, importer; to — oneself with s'occuper de, s'intéresser à.

concerned [kən'sə:nd] a préoccupé (de with), intéressé, (à with), inquiet, soucieux.

concerning [kən'sə:niŋ] prep quant à, au sujet de, en ce qui concerne, pour ce qui est de.

concert ['kɔnsət] n concert m, accord m, unisson m; — hal salle f de concert; in — with d concert avec.

concert [kən'sə:t] vt concerter; vi s concerter.

concession [kən'seʃən] n concession f.

conciliate [kən'silieit] v t (ré)concilie

conciliation [kən,sili'eiʃən] n conciliation f.

conciliatory [kən'siliətəri] a conciliant, conciliatoire.

concise [kən'sais] a concis.

concision [kən'siʒən] n concision f.

conclude [kən'klu:d] vti conclure; vi se terminer; vt terminer, achever, régler.

conclusion [kən'klu:ʒən] n conclusion f, fin f.

conclusive [kən'klu:siv] a concluant, décisif.

conclusiveness [kən'klu:sivnis] n force décisive f.

concoct [kən'kɔkt] vt confectionner, composer, combiner, imaginer, concevoir.

concoction [kən'kɔkʃən] n pot-pourri m, boisson f, confectionnement m, conception f, tissu m.

concord [ˈkɔŋkɔ:d] n harmonie f, accord m.

concordance [kən'kɔ:dəns] n concordance f, harmonie f, accord m.

concordant [kən'kɔ:dənt] a concordant.

concourse [ˈkɔŋkɔ:s] n concourse m, affluence f, foule f.

concrete [ˈkɔnkri:t] n ciment m, béton m; **reinforced —** béton armé; a concret m.

concrete [kən'kri:t] vt solidifier, cimenter, bétonner; vi se solidifier.

concur [kən'kə:] vi s'accorder, contribuer, concourir, être d'accord.

concurrence [kən'kʌrəns] n concours m, approbation f, assentiment m.

concurrent [kən'kʌrənt] a concurrent, simultané.

concurrently [kən'kʌrəntli] ad concurremment.

concussion [kən'kʌʃən] n commotion f, secousse f, ébranlement m, choc m.

condemn [kən'dem] vt condamner, censurer.

condemnation [,kɔndem'neiʃən] n condamnation f, censure f.

condensation [,kɔnden'seiʃən] n condensation f.

condense [kən'dens] vt condenser, concentrer, serrer; vi se condenser.

condenser [kən'densə] n condenseur m, distillateur m.

condescend [,kɔndi'send] vi condescendre, s'abaisser.

condescending [,kɔndi'sendiŋ] a condescendant.

condescension [,kɔndi'senʃən] n condescendance f, déférence f.

condign [kən'dain] a juste, mérité, exemplaire.

condiment [ˈkɔndimənt] n assaisonnement m, condiment m.

condition [kən'diʃən] n condition f, situation f, état m; vt conditionner.

conditional [kən'diʃənl] a conditionnel, dépendant.

condolatory [kən'doulətəri] a de condoléance.

condole [kən'doul] vi sympathiser (avec **with**), exprimer ses condoléances (à **with**).

condolence [kən'douləns] n condoléances f pl.

condone [kən'doun] vt pardonner.

conduce [kən'dju:s] vi aboutir, contribuer.

conducive [kən'dju:siv] a qui conduit (à **to**), qui contribue (à **to**), favorable (à **to**).

conduct [ˈkɔndəkt] n conduite f, gestion f.

conduct [kən'dʌkt] vt conduire, mener, diriger, gérer; **to — oneself** se conduire, se comporter.

conduction [kən'dʌkʃən] n conduction f, transmission f.

conductor [kən'dʌktə] n guide m, conducteur m, chef m d'orchestre, (bus) receveur m.

conductress [kən'dʌktris] n conductrice f, receveuse f.

conduit [ˈkɔndit] n conduit m.

cone [koun] n cône m, pomme de pin f.

confection [kən'fekʃən] n confection f; bonbons m pl, confits m pl.

confectioner [kən'fekʃənə] n confiseur m.

confectioner's [kən'fekʃənəz] n confiserie f.

confectionery [kən'fekʃnəri] n confiserie f.

confederacy [kən'fedərəsi] n confédération f, conspiration f.

confederate [kən'fedərit] an confédéré m; n complice m, comparse m.

confer [kən'fə:] vti conférer; vt accorder, octroyer.

conference [ˈkɔnfərəns] n conférence f, congrès m, consultation f.

conferment [kən'fə:mənt] n octroi m, attribution f.

confess [kən'fes] vt confesser, avouer; vi se confesser, faire des aveux.

confession [kən'feʃən] n confession f, aveu m; **to go to —** aller à confesse.

confessional [kən'feʃənl] n confessional m; a confessionnel.

confessor [kən'fesə] n confesseur m.

confide [kən'faid] vt confier, avouer en confidence; vi se fier (à **in**).

confidence [ˈkɔnfidəns] n confidence f, confiance f (en soi), assurance f; **— game** fraude f.

confident [ˈkɔnfidənt] a confiant, assuré, sûr.

confidential [,kɔnfi'denʃəl] a confidentiel, de confiance.

confidentially [,kɔnfi'denʃəli] ad en confidence, à titre confidentiel.

confidently [ˈkɔnfidəntli] ad avec confiance.

confine [kən'fain] vt limiter, confiner, borner, emprisonner, renfermer.

confined [kən'faind] *a* (space) resserré; — **to bed** alité, (woman) en couches.

confinement [kən'fainmənt] *n* réclusion *f*, emprisonnement *m*, restriction *f*, accouchement *m*, couches *f pl*.

confines ['kɔnfainz] *n pl* confins *m pl*.

confirm [kən'fəːm] *vt* confirmer, fortifier, raffermir.

confirmation [ˌkɔnfə'meiʃən] *n* confirmation *f*, raffermissement *m*.

confirmed [kən'fəːmd] *a* invétéré, enduri, incorrigible.

confiscate ['kɔnfiskeit] *vt* confisquer.

confiscation [ˌkɔnfis'keiʃən] *n* confiscation *f*.

conflagration [ˌkɔnflə'greiʃən] *n* conflagration *f*, incendie *m*, embrasement *m*.

conflict ['kɔnflikt] *n* conflit *m*, lutte *f*.

conflict [kən'flikt] *vi* être en conflit, jurer, se heurter.

confluent ['kɔnfluənt] *n* confluent *m*, affluent *m*.

conform [kən'fɔːm] *vt* conformer; *vi* se conformer, obéir, s'adapter.

conformation [ˌkɔnfɔː'meiʃən] *n* conformation *f*, structure *f*.

conformity [kən'fɔːmiti] *n* conformité *f*; **in — with** conformément à.

confound [kən'faund] *vt* confondre, embarrasser, déconcerter.

confounded [kən'faundid] *a* maudit, sacré.

confraternity [ˌkɔnfrə'təːniti] *n* confrérie *f*, bande *f*.

confront [kən'frʌnt] *vt* affronter, confronter, faire face à, se trouver en présence de.

confuse [kən'fjuːz] *vt* mettre en désordre, confondre, embrouiller, (em)mêler.

confused [kən'fjuːzd] *a* confus, interdit, ahuri, bouleversé, trouble.

confusedly [kən'fjuːzidli] *ad* confusément.

confusion [kən'fjuːʒən] *n* confusion *f*, désordre *m*, désarroi *m*, remueménage *m*.

confutation [ˌkɔnfjuː'teiʃən] *n* réfutation *f*.

confute [kən'fjuːt] *vt* :éfuter, démolir les arguments de.

congeal [kən'dʒiːl] *vt* (con)geler, coaguler, figer; *vi* se congeler, se coaguler, se figer, se prendre.

congenial [kən'dʒiːnjəl] *a* du même caractère que, au goût de, sympathique, agréable, convenable.

congeniality [kənˌdʒiːni'æliti] *n* sympathie *f*, caractère agréable *m*, accord *m* de sentiments.

congest [kən'dʒest] *vt* congestionner, encombrer, embouteiller.

congestion [kən'dʒestʃən] *n* congestion *f*, encombrement *m*, embouteillage *m*, surpeuplement *m*.

conglomerate [kən'glɔməreit] *vt* conglomérer; *vi* se conglomérer, s'agglomérer.

congratulate [kən'grætjuleit] *vt* féliciter.

congratulation [kənˌgrætju'leiʃən] *n* félicitation *f*.

congregate ['kɔngrigeit] *vt* rassembler, réunir; *vi* se réunir, se rassembler.

congregation [ˌkɔngri'geiʃən] *n* congrégation *f*, assemblée *f*, amas *m*, rassemblement *m*.

congress ['kɔngres] *n* congrès *m*, réunion *f*.

congruency ['kɔngruənsi] *n* accord *m*, conformité *f*.

congruous ['kɔngruəs] *a* approprié, conforme.

conifer ['kɔnifə] *n* conifère *m*.

conjecture [kən'dʒektʃə] *n* conjecture *f*; *vt* conjecturer.

conjugal ['kɔndʒugəl] *a* conjugal.

conjugate ['kɔndʒugeit] *vt* conjuguer.

conjugation [ˌkɔndʒu'geiʃən] *n* conjugaison *f*.

conjunction [kən'dʒʌnkʃən] *n* connexion *f*, jonction *f*, coïncidence *f*; **in — with** conjointement avec.

conjuncture [kən'dʒʌnktʃə] *n* conjoncture *f*, circonstance *f*.

conjuration [ˌkɔndʒuə'reiʃən] *n* conjuration *f*, évocation *f*.

conjure [kən'dʒuə] *vt* conjurer, évoquer.

conjure ['kʌndʒə] *vi* faire des tours de prestidigitation; **to — away** escamoter.

conjurer ['kʌndʒərə] *n* prestidigitateur *m*.

connect [kə'nekt] *vt* (re)lier, rattacher, réunir, associer; *vi* se (re)lier, se réunir, faire correspondance.

connection [kə'nekʃən] *n* lien *m*, rapport *m*, sens *m*, égard *m*, parenté *f*, clientèle *f*, correspondance *f*, prise *f* de courant.

conning-tower ['kɔniŋ.tauə] *n* (sous-marin **submarine**) capot *m*.

connivance [kə'naivəns] *n* connivence *f*, complicité *f*.

connive [kə'naiv] *vi* être de connivence (avec **with**), fermer les yeux (sur **at**).

connubial [kə'njuːbjəl] *a* conjugal.

conquer ['kɔŋkə] *vt* conquérir, vaincre.

conqueror ['kɔŋkərə] *n* conquérant *m*, vainqueur *m*.

conquest ['kɔŋkwest] *n* conquête *f*.

conscience ['kɔnʃəns] *n* conscience *f*.

conscientious [ˌkɔnʃi'enʃəs] *a* consciencieux, scrupuleux.

conscientiousness [ˌkɔnʃi'enʃəsnis] *n* conscience *f*.

conscious ['kɔnʃəs] *a* conscient; **to be — of** sentir, avoir conscience de, s'apercevoir de; **to become —** reprendre connaissance.

consciously ['kɔnʃəsli] *ad* consciement.

consciousness ['kɔnʃəsnis] *n* conscience *f*, connaissance *f*, sens *m*.

conscript ['kɔnskript] *an* conscrit *m*.

conscript [kən'skript] *vt* engager, enrôler.

conscription [kən'skripʃən] *n* conscription *f*.

consecrate ['kɔnsikreit] *vt* consacrer, bénir.

consecration [.kɔnsi'kreiʃən] *n* consécration *f*.

consecutive [kən'sekjutiv] *a* consécutif, de suite.

consensus [kən'sensəs] *n* accord *m*, unanimité *f*, consensus *m*.

consent [kən'sent] *n* consentement *m*, assentiment *m*, agrément *m*; *vi* consentir.

consequence ['kɔnsikwəns] *n* conséquence *f*, importance *f*.

consequent ['kɔnsikwənt] *a* résultant.

consequential [.kɔnsi'kwenʃəl] *a* conséquent, consécutif, important, plein de soi.

consequently ['kɔnsikwəntli] *ad* conséquemment, en conséquence.

conservation [.kɔnsə'veiʃən] *n* conservation *f*.

conservative [kən'sɔːvətiv] *an* conservateur, -trice.

conservatory [kən'sɔːvətri] *n* serre *f*, jardin *m* d'hiver.

conserve [kən'sɔːv] *vt* conserver, préserver.

conserves [kən'sɔːvz] *n pl* confitures *f pl*, conserves *f pl*.

consider [kən'sidə] *vt* considérer, réfléchir à, regarder, estimer, examiner, envisager, avoir égard à.

considerable [kən'sidərəbl] *a* considérable.

considerate [kən'sidərit] *a* attentif, prévenant.

considerately [kən'sidəritli] *ad* avec égards, avec prévenance.

consideration [kən,sidə'reiʃən] *n* considération *f*, réflexion *f*, récompense *f*, importance *f*; **in — of** eu égard à; **under — à** l'étude, en délibération; **after due — tout** bien considéré, après mûre réflexion; **for a — moyennant** finance; **on no — pour** rien au monde, à aucun prix.

considering [kən'sidəriŋ] *ad* somme toute; *prep* étant donné, vu, eu égard à; *cj* vu que, attendu que.

consign [kən'sain] *vt* livrer, expédier, déposer, consigner.

consignment [kən'sainmənt] *n* expédition *f*, envoi *m*, dépôt *m*; **— note** récépissé *m*, lettre de voiture *f*.

consist [kən'sist] *vi* consister (en, à **of**), se composer (de **of**).

consistence [kən'sistəns] *n* consistance *f*.

consistency [kən'sistənsi] *n* suite *f*,

logique *f*, uniformité *f*, régularité *f*.

consistent [kən'sistənt] *a* compatible, fidèle (à **with**), conséquent, logique, régulier.

consolation [.kɔnsə'leiʃən] *n* consolation *f*.

console [kən'soul] *vt* consoler.

console ['kɔnsoul] *n* console *f*.

consolidate [kən'sɔlideit] *vt* consolider, raffermir, unifier.

consolidation [kən,sɔli'deiʃən] *n* consolidation *f*, raffermissement *m*.

consols [kən'sɔlz] *n pl* fonds consolidés *m pl*.

consonance ['kɔnsənəns] *n* consonance *f*, accord *m*.

consonant ['kɔnsənənt] *n* consonne *f*; *a* compatible, harmonieux, qui s'accorde.

consort ['kɔnsɔːt] *n* consort(e) *mf*, époux, -se *mf*.

consort [kən'sɔːt] *vi* to **— with** fréquenter, frayer avec.

conspicuous [kən'spikjuəs] *a* marquant, insigne, remarquable, en vue, en évidence; **to make oneself — se** faire remarquer, se signaler.

conspiracy [kən'spirəsi] *n* conspiration *f*, conjuration *f*.

conspirator [kən'spirətə] *n* conspirateur, -trice, conjuré *m*.

conspire [kən'spaiə] *vi* conspirer, comploter, agir de concert, concourir.

constable ['kʌnstəbl] *n* agent *m* de police, gendarme *m*; **chief — commissaire** *m* de police.

constabulary [kən'stæbjuləri] *n* police *f*, gendarmerie *f*.

constancy ['kɔnstənsi] *n* constance *f*, régularité *f*, fidelité *f*, fermeté *f*.

constant ['kɔnstənt] *a* constant, continuel, fidèle, invariable.

constantly ['kɔnstəntli] *ad* constamment, toujours.

constellation [.kɔnstə'leiʃən] *n* constellation *f*.

consternation [.kɔnstə'neiʃən] *n* consternation *f*.

constipate ['kɔnstipeit] *vt* constiper.

constipation [.kɔnsti'peiʃən] *n* constipation *f*.

constituency [kən'stitjuənsi] *n* circonscription *f*, collège électoral *m*.

constituent [kən'stitjuənt] *n* électeur, -trice, élément *m*; *a* constituant, constitutif.

constitute ['kɔnstitjuːt] *vt* constituer.

constitution [.kɔnsti'tjuːʃən] *n* constitution *f*, composition *f*, santé *f*.

constitutional [.kɔnsti'tjuːʃənl] *a* constitutionnel.

constrain [kən'strein] *vt* contraindre, forcer.

constraint [kən'streint] *n* contrainte *f*, retenue *f*.

constrict [kən'strikt] *vt* rétrécir, (res)serrer, étrangler.

constriction [kən'strikʃən] *n* étranglement *m*, resserrement *m*.

construct ['kən'strʌkt] vt' construire, établir, charpenter.

construction [kən'strʌkʃən] n construction f, établissement m, édifice m, interprétation f.

construe [kən'struː] vt traduire, interpréter, expliquer, analyser.

consul ['kɔnsəl] n consul m.

consular ['kɔnsjulə] a consulaire.

consulate ['kɔnsjulit] n consulat m.

consult [kən'sʌlt] vti consulter.

consultation [.kɔnsəl'teiʃən] n consultation f, délibération f.

consume [kən'sjum] vt consumer, consommer, épuiser, perdre.

consumer [kən'sjumə] n consommateur, -trice.

consummate [kən'sʌmit] a consommé, achevé.

consummate ['kɔnsʌmeit] vt consommer.

consummation [.kɔnsʌ'meiʃən] n consommation f, comble m.

consumption [kən'sʌmpʃən] n consomption f, phtisie f, consommation f.

consumptive [kən'sʌmptiv] a phtisique, tuberculeux.

contact ['kɔntækt] n contact m, rapport m; vt se mettre en rapport avec, contacter.

contagion [kən'teidʒən] n contagion f.

contagious [kən'teidʒəs] a contagieux, communicatif.

contain [kən'tein] vt contenir, comporter, renfermer, retenir.

container [kən'teinə] n récipient m.

contaminate [kən'tæmineit] vt contaminer, vicier, corrompre.

contamination [kən.tæmi'neiʃən] n contamination f.

contemplate ['kɔntempleit] vt contempler, considérer, envisager; vi méditer, se recueillir.

contemplation [.kɔntem'pleiʃən] n contemplation f, recueillement m.

contemplative ['kɔntempleitiv] a contemplatif, recueilli.

contemporary [kən'tempərəri] an contemporain(e) mf.

contempt [kən'tempt] n mépris m.

contemptible [kən'temptəbl] a méprisable.

contemptuous [kən'temptjuəs] a méprisant, de mépris.

contend [kən'tend] vi lutter, disputer, rivaliser; vt soutenir, prétendre.

content [kən'tent] n contentement m, contenance f; a content; vt contenter.

contentedly [kən'tentidli] ad avec plaisir.

contention [kən'tenʃən] n discussion f, rivalité f, idée f, prétention f.

contentious [kən'tenʃəs] a disputeur, chicanier, discutable.

contentment [kən'tentmənt] n contentement m.

contents ['kɔntents] n pl contenu m, table des matières f.

contest ['kɔntest] n lutte f, concours m.

contest [kən'test] vt contester, disputer, débattre.

contestation [.kɔntes'teiʃən] n contestation f.

context ['kɔntekst] n contexte m.

contiguous [kən'tigjuəs] a contigu, -uë.

continence ['kɔntinəns] n continence f.

continent ['kɔntinənt] an continent m.

continental [.kɔnti'nentl] a continental.

contingent [kən'tindʒənt] n contingent m; a éventuel, subordonné.

continual [kən'tinjuəl] a continuel, sans cesse.

continuation [kən.tinju'eiʃən] n continuation f, durée f, suite f.

continue [kən'tinju] vti continuer vt maintenir, poursuivre, prolonger vi se prolonger.

continuity [.kɔnti'njuiti] n continuité f.

continuous [kən'tinjuəs] a continu, permanent.

continuously [kən'tinjuəsli] ad continûment, sans arrêt, sans désemparer.

contort [kən'tɔːt] vt tordre, crisper.

contortion [kən'tɔːʃən] n contorsion f, crispation f.

contour ['kɔntuə] n contour m, profil m, tracé m.

contraband ['kɔntrəbænd] n contrebande f.

contraceptive [.kɔntrə'septiv] n préservatif m; a anticonceptionnel.

contract ['kɔntrækt] n contrat m, entreprise f.

contract [kən'trækt] vt contracter resserrer, crisper; vi s'engager, s rétrécir, se crisper, se contracter.

contraction [kən'trækʃən] n contraction f, rétrécissement m, crispement m.

contractor [kən'træktə] n entrepreneur m, (mil) fournisseur m.

contradict [.kɔntrə'dikt] vt démentir contredire.

contradiction [.kɔntrə'dikʃən] contradiction f, démenti m.

contradictory [.kɔntrə'diktəri] contradictoire.

contraption [kən'træpʃən] n machi m, truc m, dispositif m.

contrary ['kɔntrəri] a contraire opposé; on the —— au contraire.

contrast ['kɔntraːst] n contraste m.

contrast [kən'raːst] vi contraster vt mettre en contraste, opposer.

contravene [.kɔntrə'viːn] vt en freindre, contrevenir à, s'opposer à

contravention [.kɔntrə'venʃən] violation f, contravention f.

contribute [kən'tribjut] vti con

tribuer (à to), souscrire; to — to a newspaper collaborer à un journal.

contribution [ˌkɔntri'bjuːʃən] n contribution f.

contrite ['kɔntrait] a contrit.

contrivance [kən'traivəns] n invention f, manigance f, ingéniosité f, dispositif m.

contrive [kən'traiv] vt inventer, combiner; vi s'arranger (pour to), trouver moyen (de to).

control [kən'troul] n contrôle m, maîtrise f, autorité f; vt contrôler, maîtriser, diriger.

controller [kən'troulə] n contrôleur, -euse, commande f.

controversial [ˌkɔntrə'vəːʃəl] a controversé, (person) disputeur.

controversy ['kɔntrəvəːsi] n controverse f.

contumacious [ˌkɔntju'meiʃəs] a rebelle, contumace.

contuse [kən'tjuːz] vt contusionner.

contusion [kən'tjuːʒən] n contusion f.

conundrum [kə'nʌndrəm] n énigme f, problème m, devinette f.

convalesce [ˌkɔnvə'les] vi être en convalescence, relever de maladie.

convalescence [ˌkɔnvə'lesns] n convalescence f.

convalescent [ˌkɔnvə'lesnt] a convalescent.

convector [kən'vektə] n appareil m de chauffage par convection.

convene [kən'viːn] vt convoquer; vi se réunir.

convenience [kən'viːnjəns] n convenance f, commodité f, avantage m; pl commodités f pl, agréments m pl.

convenient [kən'viːnjənt] a commode.

conveniently [kən'viːnjəntli] ad commodément, sans inconvénient.

convent ['kɔnvənt] n couvent m.

convention [kən'venʃən] n convention f, convocation f, usage m; pl bienséances f pl.

conventional [kən'venʃənl] a conventionnel, normal, ordinaire, classique, stylisé.

conventionality [kən,venʃə'næliti] n formalisme m, bienséances f pl.

converge [kən'vəːdʒ] vi converger.

convergence [kən'vəːdʒəns] n convergence f.

conversant [kən'vəːsənt] a familiar, versé, au courant (de with).

conversation [ˌkɔnvə'seiʃən] n conversation f, entretien m.

converse ['kɔnvəːs] an réciproque f, converse f.

converse [kən'vəːs] vi causer, s'entretenir.

conversely ['kɔnvəːsli] ad réciproquement.

conversion [kən'vəːʃən] n conversion f.

convert ['kɔnvəːt] n converti(e) mf.

convert [kən'vəːt] vt convertir, transformer.

convex ['kɔn'veks] a convexe, bombé.

convey [kən'vei] vt (trans)porter, transmettre, communiquer.

conveyance [kən'veiəns] n transport m, voiture f, transmission f.

convict ['kɔnvikt] n forçat m.

convict [kən'vikt] vt convaincre, condamner.

conviction [kən'vikʃən] n conviction f, condamnation f.

convince [kən'vins] vt convaincre, persuader.

convivial [kən'viviəl] a plein d'entrain, jovial, de fête.

convocation [ˌkɔnvə'keiʃən] n convocation f, assemblée f.

convoke [kən'vouk] vt convoquer.

convoy ['kɔnvɔi] n convoi m, escorte f.

convoy ['kɔnvɔi] vt convoyer, escorter.

convulse [kən'vʌls] vt bouleverser, décomposer, tordre, convulser.

convulsion [kən'vʌlʃən] n convulsion f, bouleversement m.

convulsive [kən'vʌlsiv] a convulsif.

coo [kuː] vi roucouler.

cook [kuk] n cuisinier, -ière; vti cuire, cuisiner; vt faire cuire; maquiller, truquer.

cooker ['kukə] n réchaud m, cuisinière f.

cookery ['kukəri] n cuisine f.

cool [kuːl] n frais m, fraîcheur f; a frais, rafraîchissant, impudent; vt rafraîchir, refroidir; vi se rafraîchir, se refroidir.

cooler ['kuːlə] n seau m à glace, refroidisseur m, taule f.

coolly ['kuːli] ad froidement, avec sang-froid.

coolness ['kuːlnis] n fraîcheur f, sang-froid m.

coop [kuːp] n mue f; vt enfermer, claustrer.

co-operate [kou'ɔpəreit] vi coopérer, collaborer.

co-operation [kou,ɔpə'reiʃən] n collaboration f, coopération f, concours m.

co-operative stores [kou'ɔpərətiv 'stɔːz] n coopérative f.

co-opt [kou'ɔpt] vt coopter.

co-ordinate [kou'ɔːdineit] vt coordonner.

co-ordination [kou,ɔːdi'neiʃən] n coordination f.

cop [kɔp] n fuseau m, flic m; vt pincer, attraper, écoper.

cope [koup] to — with faire face à, tenir tête à, venir à bout de.

copious ['koupjəs] a copieux, abondant.

copiousness ['koupjəsnis] n abondance f.

copper ['kɔpə] n cuivre m, billon m, sou m, lessiveuse f, sergot m.

copse [kɔps] n taillis m.

copy ['kɔpi] n copie f, exemplaire m, numéro m; vt copier, imiter, se modeler sur.

copyist ['kɔpiist] n copiste mf.

copyright ['kɔpirait] n propriété littéraire f, droit d'auteur m.

coral ['kɔrəl] n corail m.

cord [kɔːd] n cordelette f, cordon m, (vocal) cordes f pl, étoffe f à côtes, ganse f; vt corder.

corded ['kɔːdid] a côtelé, à côtes.

cordial ['kɔːdjəl] an cordial m; a chaleureux.

cordiality [,kɔːdi'æliti] n cordialité f.

cordon ['kɔːdn] n cordon m; to — off vt isoler, entourer d'un cordon.

corduroy ['kɔːdərɔi] n velours côtelé m.

core [kɔː] n cœur m, trognon m.

co-respondent ['kouris,pɔndənt] n complice mf (d'adultère).

cork [kɔːk] n liège m, bouchon m; vt boucher.

corked [kɔːkt] a qui sent le bouchon.

corkscrew ['kɔːkskruː] n tire-bouchon m.

corn [kɔːn] n grain m, blé m, maïs m; (foot) cor m.

cornea ['kɔːniə] n cornée f.

corned [kɔːnd] a salé, de conserve.

corner ['kɔːnə] n coin m, angle m, tournant m, virage m, accaparement m; vt acculer, mettre au pied du mur, accaparer; vi virer.

corner-stone ['kɔːnəstoun] n pierre angulaire f.

cornet ['kɔːnit] n cornet m (à piston).

corn exchange ['kɔːniks'tʃeindʒ] n halle f aux blés.

cornflower ['kɔːnflauə] n bluet m.

cornice ['kɔːnis] n corniche f.

cornstarch ['kɔːnstaːtʃ] n farine f de maïs.

coronation [,kɔrə'neiʃən] n couronnement m, sacre m.

corporal ['kɔːpərəl] n caporal m, brigadier m; a corporel.

corporate ['kɔːpərit] a constitué; — spirit esprit de corps m, solidarité.

corporation [,kɔːpə'reiʃən] n corporation f, conseil municipal m, bedaine f.

corpse [kɔːps] n cadavre m.

corpuscle ['kɔːpʌsl] n corpuscle m.

Corpus Christi ['kɔːpəs'kristi] n Fête-Dieu f.

correct [kə'rekt] a correct, juste, exact; vt corriger, reprendre, rectifier.

correction [kə'rekʃən] n correction f, redressement m.

corrector [kə'rektə] n correcteur, -trice.

correspond [,kɔris'pɔnd] vi correspondre (à with, to).

correspondence [,kɔris'pɔndəns] n correspondance f.

correspondent [,kɔris'pɔndənt] n correspondant(e) mf, envoyé m.

corridor ['kɔridɔː] n couloir m, corridor m.

corroborate [kə'rɔbəreit] vt corroborer, confirmer.

corroboration [kə,rɔbə'reiʃən] n corroboration f.

corrode [kə'roud] vt corroder, ronger; vi se corroder.

corrosion [kə'rouʒən] n corrosion f.

corrosive [kə'rousiv] an corrosif m.

corrugated ['kɔrugeitid] a ondulé, cannelé, gaufré.

corrupt [kə'rʌpt] vt corrompre, altérer; a corrompu.

corruption [kə'rʌpʃən] n corruption f, subornation f.

corsair ['kɔːsɛə] n corsaire m.

corset ['kɔːsit] n corset m.

Corsica ['kɔːsikə] n la Corse f.

Corsican ['kɔːsikən] a nm corse; n Corse mf.

cosmic ['kɔzmik] a cosmique.

cosmonaut ['kɔzmənɔːt] n cosmonaute mf.

cosmopolitan [,kɔsmə'pɔlitən] an cosmopolite mf.

cosmopolitanism [,kɔzmə'pɔlitənizəm] n cosmopolitisme m.

cost [kɔst] n prix m, coût m, dépens m pl, frais m pl; vi coûter; vt établir le prix de.

costermonger ['kɔstə,mʌŋgə] n marchand m des quatre saisons.

costly ['kɔstli] a coûteux, dispendieux, précieux, somptueux.

cot [kɔt] n abri m, berceau m, couchette f, hutte f.

cottage ['kɔtidʒ] n chaumière f.

cotton ['kɔtn] n coton m, fil m; — plant cotonnier m; — plantation cotonneraie f.

cotton-wool ['kɔtn'wul] n ouate f, coton hydrophile m.

couch [kautʃ] n lit m, divan m; vt coucher; vi se tapir, s'embusquer.

cough [kɔf] n toux f; vi tousser.

could [kud] pt of can.

council ['kaunsl] n concile m, conseil m.

councilor ['kaunsilə] n conseiller m (municipal).

counsel ['kaunsəl] n conseil m délibération f, avocat m; vt conseiller, recommande.

counselor ['kaunsələ] n conseiller m.

count [kaunt] n compte m, calcul m comte m; vti compter.

countdown ['kauntdaun] n compte à rebours m.

countenance ['kauntinəns] n expression f, visage m, sérieux m contenance f, appui m; vt sanctionner, appuyer, approuver.

counter ['kauntə] n comptoir m jeton m, contre m; a opposé; v contrarier, contredire, aller à l'en contre de; vi riposter; ad en sen contraire.

counteract [,kauntə'rækt] vt neutraliser.

counterbalance [ˌkauntəˈbæləns] n contre-poids m; vt contrebalancer, faire contrepoids à, compenser.

countercharge [ˈkauntətʃɑːdʒ] n contre-accusation f.

counterfeit [ˈkauntəfit] contrefaçon f; — coin pièce fausse f; vt feindre, contrefaire, forger.

counterfoil [ˈkauntəfɔil] n talon m, souche f.

countermand [ˌkauntəˈmɑːnd] vt contremander, rappeler, décommander.

counterpane [ˈkauntəpein] n couvre-pied m, courtepointe f.

counterpart [ˈkauntəpɑːt] n contre-partie f, pendant m.

countersign [ˈkauntəsain] n mot m de passe, mot m d'ordre; vt viser, contresigner.

countess [ˈkauntis] n comtesse f.

countless [ˈkauntlis] a innombrable.

country [ˈkʌntri] n contrée f, pays m, campagne f, province f, patrie f.

country-house [ˈkʌntriˈhaus] n maison de campagne f.

countryman [ˈkʌntrimən] n campagnard m, compatriote m.

countryside [ˈkʌntrisaid] n campagne f, pays m.

county [ˈkaunti] n comté m.

couple [ˈkʌpl] n couple mf, laisse f; vt (ac)coupler, unir, associer.

coupon [ˈkuːpɔn] n coupon m, ticket m, estampille officielle f, bon(-prime) m.

courage [ˈkʌridʒ] n courage m.

courageous [kəˈreidʒəs] a courageux.

courier [ˈkuriə] n courrier m.

course [kɔːs] n course f, cours m, champ de courses m, carrière f, série f, marche f, direction f, route f, plat m, service m; of — naturellement; matter of — chose qui va de soi, positif, prosaïque.

court [kɔːt] n cour f, terrain de jeux m, court m (tennis); vt courtiser, inviter, chercher, solliciter, aller au-devant de.

courteous [ˈkəːtiəs] a courtois.

courtesy [ˈkəːtisi] n courtoisie f, politesses f pl.

courtesan [ˌkəːtiˈzæn] n courtisane f.

courtier [ˈkɔːtjə] n courtisan m.

courtliness [ˈkɔːtlinis] n élégance f, affinement m.

courtly [ˈkɔːtli] a élégant, courtois.

courtship [ˈkɔːtʃip] n cour f.

courtyard [ˈkɔːtjɑːd] n cour f.

cousin [ˈkʌzn] n cousin(e) mf; first — cousin germain; second — issu de germain; third — au 3ᵉ degré etc.

cove [kouv] n (sea) anse f, crique f, type m.

covenant [ˈkʌvinənt] n pacte m, alliance f, contrat m.

cover [ˈkʌvə] n couverture f, housse f, bâche f, dessus m, couvercle m, abri m; couvert m, voile m, masque m; compte-rendu m; vt (re)couvrir,

revêtir, embrasser; faire un compte-rendu.

covering [ˈkʌvəriŋ] a de couverture, confirmatif.

coverlet [ˈkʌvəlit] n couvre-pied m, dessus m de lit, couvre-lit m.

covert [ˈkʌvət] a couvert, furtif, voilé, indirect.

covet [ˈkʌvit] vt convoiter.

covetous [ˈkʌvitəs] a convoiteux, avide.

covetousness [ˈkʌvitəsnis] n convoitise f, cupidité f.

covey [ˈkʌvi] n couvée f, compagnie f, vol m, troupe f.

cow [kau] n vache f, femelle f; vt intimider.

coward [ˈkauəd] an lâche mf.

cowardice [ˈkauədis] n lâcheté f.

cowardly [ˈkauədli] a lâche, poltron; ad lâchement.

cower [ˈkauə] vi s'accroupir, se blottir, se faire petit.

cowl [kaul] n capuchon m, capot m, mitre f, champignon m.

cowrie-shell [ˈkauriʃel] n cauri m.

coxcomb [ˈkɔkskoum] n poseur m, fat m, petit-maître m.

coxswain [ˈkɔksn] n homme de barre m, maître m d'équipage.

coy [kɔi] a timide, réservé, écarté.

coyness [ˈkɔinis] n timidité f, réserve f.

cozy [ˈkouzi] n couvre-théière m; a tiède, douillet, bon.

crab [kræb] n crabe m, (apple) pomme sauvage f, (tool) chèvre f.

crabbed [ˈkræbd] a revêche, raboteux, grincheux, aigre.

crack [kræk] n craquement m, coup sec m, fêlure f, lézarde f, fente f; a (fam) d'élite; —brained fêlé, timbré, toqué; vi craquer, claquer, se casser, se gercer, se fêler, muer; vt faire craquer (claquer), casser, fêler, (joke) faire.

cracker [ˈkrækə] n pétard m, casse-noix m, diablotin m.

crackle [ˈkrækl] n craquement m, crépitement m, friture f, craquelure f; vi crépiter, craqueter, grésiller, pétiller.

cracksman [ˈkræksmən] n (sl) cambrioleur m.

cradle [ˈkreidl] n berceau m; —song berceuse f; vt coucher, bercer.

craft [krɑːft] n habileté f, ruse f, art m, métier m, vaisseau m, avion m.

craftsman [ˈkrɑːftsmən] n ouvrier qualifié m, artisan m.

crafty [ˈkrɑːfti] a rusé, cauteleux, fin.

crag [kræg] n rocher m.

craggy [ˈkrægi] a rocheux, rocailleux.

cram [kræm] vt remplir, gaver, fourrer, enfoncer, bourrer, chauffer; vi se gaver, s'empiffrer, s'entasser.

cramming [ˈkræmiŋ] n gavage m, bourrage m, chauffage m.

cramp [kræmp] n crampe f, crampon m; vt donner des crampes à, engourdir.

cramped [kræmpt] a crispé, gêné, à l'étroit.

crane [krein] n grue f; vt tendre, soulever.

crank [krænk] n manivelle f, coude m, meule f, original(e) mf, toque(e) mf.

crape [kreip] n crêpe m.

crash [kræʃ] n fracas m, crac m, krach m, accident m; vt briser, fracasser, écraser; vi dégringoler, s'abattre, s'écraser, casser du bois; **to —** into heurter, tamponner, accrocher.

crass [kræs] a grossier, crasse.

crate [kreit] n manne f, cageot m.

crater ['kreitə] n cratère m, entonnoir m.

crave [kreiv] vt solliciter; **to — for** désirer violemment, avoir soif de.

craven ['kreivən] an lâche mf.

craving ['kreiviŋ] n besoin m, faim f, soif f.

crawl [krɔ:l] vi se traîner, ramper, grouiller; n rampement m, (swimming) crawl m.

crawler ['krɔ:lə] n (cab) maraudeur m, reptile m.

crayfish ['kreifiʃ] n langouste f, écrevisse f.

crayon ['kreiən] n fusain m, pastel m.

craze [kreiz] n folie f, manie f, toquade f.

crazy ['kreizi] a branlant, toqué, affolé, insensé, fou.

creak [kri:k] n grincement m; vi grincer, craquer, crier.

cream [kri:m] n crème f; vi crêmer, mousser; vt écrémer.

creamery ['kri:məri] n crèmerie f.

creamy ['kri:mi] a crèmeux.

crease [kri:s] n pli m; vt plisser, froisser; vt se plisser, prendre un faux pli, se froisser.

create [kri:'eit] vt créer.

creation [kri:'eiʃən] n création f.

creator [kri:'eitə] n créateur, -trice.

creature ['kri:tʃə] n créature f, être m, homme m.

credentials [kri'denʃəlz] n lettres de créance f, certificat m.

credibility [ˌkredi'biliti] n crédibilité f.

credible ['kredibl] a croyable, digne de foi.

credibly ['kredibli] ad vraisemblablement.

credit ['kredit] n foi f, mérite m, honneur m, crédit m; **tax —s** déductions fiscales; vt croire, ajouter foi à, créditer, accorder, reconnaître.

creditable ['kreditəbl] a honorable, qui fait honneur (à to).

creditor ['kreditə] n créancier, -ière.

credulity [kri'dju:liti] n crédulité f.

credulous ['kredjuləs] a crédule.

creed [kri:d] n crédo m, foi f.

creek [kri:k] n crique f, anse f.

creep [kri:p] vi ramper, se glisser, grimper.

creeper ['kri:pə] n plante rampante f, grimpante.

creeps [kri:ps] n chair f de poule.

cremate [kri'meit] vt brûler, incinérer.

cremation [kri'meiʃən] n incinération f.

crematorium [ˌkremə'tɔ:riəm] n four crématoire m.

crept [krept] pt pp of creep.

crescent ['kresnt] n croissant m.

cress [kres] n cresson m.

crest [krest] n crête f, huppe f, plumet m, cimier m, armoiries f pl.

crestfallen ['krest,fɔ:lən] a penaud, découragé.

crevice ['krevis] n crevasse f, fente f, fissure f.

crew [kru:] n équipage m, équipe f, bande f.

crib [krib] n mangeoire f, crèche f, lit d'enfant m, poste m; **to — from** plagier, copier sur.

crick [krik] n torticolis m.

cricket ['krikit] n cricket m, grillon m.

crier ['kraiə] n crieur m.

crime [kraim] n crime m, délit m.

criminal ['kriminl] an criminel, -elle.

criminality [ˌkrimi'næliti] n criminalité f.

crimp [krimp] vt plisser, onduler, friser, racoler.

crimson ['krimzn] an cramoisi m, pourpre m.

cringe [krindʒ] n courbette obséquieuse f; vi s'aplatir, se tapir, faire le chien couchant.

crinkle ['kriŋkl] n pli m, ride f; vt chiffonner, froisser; vi se froisser.

cripple ['kripl] n estropié(e) m, infirme mf; vt estropier, paralyser.

crisis ['kraisis] n crise f.

crisp [krisp] a cassant, croquant, vif, brusque, bouclé; vti boucler; crêper.

criss-cross ['kriskrɔs] n entrecroisement m; a entrecroisé, revêche; vt entrecroiser; vi .'entrecroiser.

criterion [krai'tiəriən] n critérium m, critère m.

critic ['kritik] n critique m.

critical ['kritikəl] a critique.

criticism ['kritisizəm] n critique f.

criticize ['kritisaiz] vt critiquer, censurer.

croak [krouk] n c(r)oassement m; c(r)oasser.

crochet ['krouʃei] n crochet m.

crockery ['krɔkəri] n faïence vaisselle f.

crocodile ['krɔkədail] n crocodile m caïman m.

crocus ['kroukəs] n crocus m, safran m.

croft [krɔft] n clos m.

crook [kruk] n houlette f, crosse f.

croc m, crochet m, courbe f, escroc m; vt (re)courber.

crooked ['krukid] a courbé, tordu, tortueux, malhonnête.

croon [kru:n] n bourdonnement m, fredonnement m, plainte f; vi bourdonner, fredonner.

crop [krɔp] n récolte f, jabot m, manche f de fouet, cravache f, coupe f de cheveux (à ras); vt récolter, brouter, écourter, tondre, couper ras, planter; to — up vi affleurer, surgir, se présenter.

cross [krɔs] n croix f, barre f, croisement m; a croisé, fâché; vt croiser, traverser, barrer; vi se croiser; to — out vt biffer; to — oneself se signer.

crossbar ['krɔsba:] n traverse f.

cross-belt ['krɔsbelt] n cartouchière f, bandoulière f.

crossbreed ['krɔsbri:d] n hybride m, métis, -isse.

cross-examination ['krɔsig,zæmi'neiʃən] n contre-interrogatoire m.

cross-eyed ['krɔsaid] a louche.

cross-grained ['krɔsgreind] a à contre-fil, revêche, grincheux.

crossing ['krɔsiŋ] n croisement m, traversée f.

cross-legged ['krɔs'legd] a les jambes croisées.

crossroads ['krɔsroudz] n carrefour m.

cross-section ['krɔs'sekʃən] n coupe f, tranche f, catégorie f.

crossword ['krɔswə:d] n mots croisés m pl.

crotchet ['krɔtʃit] n noire f, caprice m.

crotchety ['krɔtʃiti] a fantasque, difficile.

crouch [krautʃ] vi s'accroupir, se blottir, se ramasser.

croup [kru:p] n croupe f, croup m.

crow [krou] n corneille f, corbeau m, cri du coq m; as the — flies à vol d'oiseau; vi chanter, crier de joie, chanter victoire, crâner.

crowbar ['kroubɑ:] n levier m, pince f.

crowd [kraud] n foule f, affluence f, bande f, monde m; vt remplir, tasser, serrer; vi se presser, s'entasser, s'empiler, affluer, s'attrouper.

crowded ['kraudid] a comble, bondé, encombré.

crown [kraun] n couronne f; vt couronner.

crucial ['kru:ʃəl] a essentiel, décisif, critique.

crucible ['kru:sibl] n creuset m.

crucifix ['kru:sifiks] n crucifix m.

crucifixion [,kru:si'fikʃən] n crucifiement m.

crucify ['kru:sifai] vt crucifier.

crude [kru:d] a cru, mal digéré, vert, rude, sommaire, brutal, frustre.

crudely ['kru:dli] ad crûment, rudement, grossièrement.

crudity ['kru:diti] n crudité f, grossièreté f.

cruel ['kruəl] a cruel.

cruelty ['kruəlti] n cruauté f.

cruet ['kru:it] n burette f.

cruet-stand ['kru:itstænd] n huilier m.

cruise [kru:z] n croisière f; vi croiser, marauder.

cruiser ['kru:zə] n croiseur m.

crumb [krʌm] n mie f, miette f.

crumble ['krʌmbl] vt briser en morceaux, émietter, effriter; vi s'écrouler, s'émietter, s'effriter.

crumple ['krʌmpl] vt froisser, chiffonner; vi se froisser, se friper, se télescoper.

crunch [krʌntʃ] vt croquer, écraser; vi craquer, grincer, crier.

crusade [kru:'seid] n croisade f, campagne f.

crush [krʌʃ] n écrasement m, cohue f, béguin m; vt écraser, froisser, terrasser, broyer.

crust [krʌst] n croûte f, croûton m, dépôt m.

crutch [krʌtʃ] n béquille f.

crux [krʌks] n nœud m.

cry [krai] n cri m, crise f de larmes; vi crier, pleurer; to — down décrier; to — off renoncer, se faire excuser; to — out s'écrier; to — up louer.

crypt [kript] n crypte f.

crystal ['kristl] n cristal m, boule de cristal f; a cristallin, limpide.

cub [kʌb] n petit m, ourson m, ours mal léché, louveteau m.

Cuba ['kju:bə] n Cuba m.

Cuban ['kju:bən] an cubain.

cube [kju:b] n cube m.

cubic ['kju:bik] a cubique.

cuckoo ['kuku] n coucou m.

cucumber ['kju:kʌmbə] n concombre m.

cud [kʌd] to chew the — ruminer.

cuddle ['kʌdl] vt mignoter, peloter; to — into se pelotonner contre.

cudgel ['kʌdʒəl] n gourdin m; vt rosser.

cue [kju:] n queue f, invite f, indication f, mot m.

cuff [kʌf] n taloche f, claque f, manchette f; vt gifler, calotter.

cull [kʌl] vt (re)cueillir.

culling ['kʌliŋ] n cueillette f; pl glanures f pl.

culminant ['kʌlminənt] a culminant.

culminate ['kʌlmineit] vi s'achever (en in), se couronner (par in).

culmination [,kʌlmi'neiʃən] n point culminant m.

culpability [,kʌlpə'biliti] n culpabilité f.

cult [kʌlt] n culte m.

cultivate ['kʌltiveit] vt cultiver.

cultivation [,kʌlti'veiʃən] n cultivation f.

cultivator ['kʌltiveitə] n cultivateur, motoculteur m.

culture ['kʌltʃə] n culture f.

culvert ['kʌlvət] n canal m, canalisation f, tranchée f, cassis m.

cumbersome ['kʌmbəsəm] a encombrant, gênant.

cumbrous ['kʌmbrəs] a encombrant, gênant.

cumulate ['kju:mjuleit] vt (ac)cumuler.

cumulation [‚kju:mju'leiʃən] n accumulation f, cumul m.

cumulative ['kju:mjulətiv] a cumulatif.

cunning ['kʌniŋ] n finesse f, ruse f, habileté f, rouerie f; a entendu, retors, rusé, cauteleux.

cup [kʌp] n tasse f, coupe f, calice m.

cupboard ['kʌbəd] n buffet m, armoire f, placard m.

cupidity [kju'piditi] n cupidité f.

cur [kə:] n roquet m, cuistre m.

curable ['kjuərəbl] a guérissable.

curate ['kjuərit] n vicaire m, abbé m.

curator [kjuə'reitə] n curateur m, conservateur m.

curb [kə:b] n gourmette f, margelle f, bordure f, frein m; vt refréner, brider.

curd [kə:d] n lait caillé m.

curdle ['kə:dl] vi se cailler, se figer, tourner.

cure [kjuə] n guérison f, remède m, cure f, soin m; vt guérir, saler, fumer, mariner.

curfew ['kə:fju:] n couvre-feu m.

curio ['kjuəriou] n pièce rare f, bibelot m, curiosité f.

curiosity [‚kjuəri'ɔsiti] n curiosité f.

curious ['kjuəriəs] a curieux, singulier, indiscret.

curl [kə:l] n boucle f, (lips) ouriet m; vt (en)rouler, friser; vi déferler, monter en spirale, friser.

curlew ['kə:lu:] n courlis m.

curling-tongs ['kə:liŋtɔŋz] n fer m à friser.

curl-paper ['kə:lpeipə] n papillotte f.

curly ['kə:li] a bouclé, frisé.

currant ['kʌrənt] n groseille f, raisin de Corinthe m.

currency ['kʌrənsi] n cours m, circulation monétaire f, monnaie (courante) f.

current ['kʌrənt] n courant m, cours m, tendance f; a courant, en cours.

currently ['kʌrəntli] ad couramment.

curry ['kʌri] n cari m; to — favor with amadouer, se mettre bien avec.

curse [kə:s] n malédiction f, fléau m, juron f; vt maudire; vi sacrer, blasphémer, jurer, pester.

cursory ['kə:səri] a superficiel, rapide.

curt [kə:t] a bref, sec.

curtail [kə:'teil] vt écourter, restreindre, réduire.

curtailment [kə:'teilmənt] n retranchement m, restriction f, réduction f.

curtain ['kə:tn] n rideau m; excl tableau! fireproof — rideau de fer m; —raiser lever de rideau m.

curtly ['kə:tli] ad brièvement, sèchement.

curtness ['kə:tnis] n sécheresse f, brièveté f, rudesse f.

curtsy ['kə:tsi] n révérence f; vi faire une révérence.

curve [kə:v] n courbe f; vt (re)courber; vi se courber.

cushion ['kuʃən] n coussin m, (billiards) bande f.

cushy ['kuʃi] a (fam) moelleux, pépère, de tout repos.

custard ['kʌstəd] n flan de lait m, crème cuite f.

custody ['kʌstədi] n garde f, prison f.

custom ['kʌstəm] n usage m, coutume f, clientèle f; pl (droits de) douane f.

customary ['kʌstəməri] a d'usage, habituel.

customarily ['kʌstəmərili] ad d'habitude.

customer ['kʌstəmə] n client(e) mf, chaland(e) mf, type m, coco m.

custom-house ['kʌstəmhaus] n bureau m de la douane.

customs-officer ['kʌstəmz'ɔfisə] n douanier m.

cut [kʌt] n coupure f, coupe f, tranche f, incision f, coup m; vti couper; vt blesser, (teeth) faire, percer, (lecture) sécher, couper (au) court; to — down réduire; to — off amputer, trancher; to — up tailler en pièces.

cute [kju:t] a rusé, malin, coquet, mignon.

cutlass ['kʌtləs] n coutelas m, coupe-coupe m.

cutler ['kʌtlə] n coutelier m.

cutlery ['kʌtləri] n coutellerie f.

cutlet ['kʌtlit] n côtelette f.

cut-throat ['kʌtθrout] n coupe-jarret m.

cutting ['kʌtiŋ] n taille f, (dé)coupage m, incision f, coupure f, bouture f; a tranchant, mordant.

cycle ['saikl] n cycle m, bicyclette f; —motor — motocyclette f; vi faire de la (aller à) bicyclette.

cycling ['saikliŋ] n cyclisme m.

cyclist ['saiklist] n cycliste mf.

cyclone ['saikloun] n cyclone m.

cygnet ['signit] n jeune cygne m.

cylinder ['silində] n cylindre m.

cylindrical [si'lindrikəl] a cylindrique.

cynic ['sinik] n cynique m, sceptique m.

cynical ['sinikəl] a cynique, sceptique.

cynicism ['sinisizəm] n cynisme m, scepticisme m.

cynosure ['sinəzjuə] n point de mir m.

cypress ['saipris] n cyprès m.

Cyprus ['saiprəs] n Chypre f.

cyst [sist] n kyste m.
czar [zɑː] n czar m, tsar m.
czarina [zɑːˈriːnə] n tsarine f.

D

D-Day [ˈdiːdei] n Jour J. m.
dab [dæb] n limande f, tape f, coup d'éponge m; vt tamponner, éponger, tapoter.
dabble [ˈdæbl] vt mouiller; vi patauger, jouer (à in), faire, s'occuper (de in).
dabbler [ˈdæblə] n amateur, -trice.
dad(dy) [ˈdædi] n papa m.
daddy-long-legs [ˈdædiˈbɒŋlegz] n faucheux m.
daffodil [ˈdæfədil] n narcisse des bois m, jonquille f.
daft [dɑːft] a toqué, entiché.
dagger [ˈdægə] n poignard m; at —s drawn à couteaux tirés; to look —s at s.o. foudroyer qn du regard.
daily [ˈdeili] an quotidien m; a journalier; ad tous les jours.
daintiness [ˈdeintinis] n délicatesse f, beauté fine f.
dainty [ˈdeinti] n morceau m de choix, friandise f; a délicat, mignon, exquis.
dairy [ˈdɛəri] n laiterie f.
dairymaid [ˈdɛərimeid] n laitière f.
dairyman [ˈdɛərimən] n laitier m.
dais [ˈdeiis] n estrade f, dais m.
daisy [ˈdeizi] n marguerite f, pâquerette f.
dale [deil] n vallée f, combe f.
dalliance [ˈdæliəns] n coquetteries f pl, flânerie f, badinage m, délai m.
dally [ˈdæli] vi jouer, coqueter, badiner, tarder.
dam [dæm] n barrage m, digue f; vt barrer, endiguer.
damage [ˈdæmidʒ] n dégâts m pl, dommages m pl, préjudice m; pl dommages-intérêts m pl; vt endommager, nuire à, abîmer, faire tort à.
damaging [ˈdæmidʒiŋ] a dévastateur, nuisible.
dame [deim] n dame f.
damn [dæm] vt (con)damner, perdre, maudire, envoyer au diable; excl zut!; I don't give a — je m'en fiche.
damnable [ˈdæmnəbl] a damnable, maudit.
damnation [dæmˈneiʃən] n damnation f.
damned [dæmd] a damné, perdu, sacré; ad vachement.
damp [dæmp] n humidité f; a humide, moite; vt mouiller, étouffer, décourager, refroidir.
damper [ˈdæmpə] n éteignoir m, sourdine f, rabat-joie m.
damson [ˈdæmzən] n prune f de Damas.
dance [dɑːns] n danse f, bal m, (African) tam-tam; vti danser; vi sauter, trépigner; vt faire danser.

dance-hall [ˈdɑːnshɔːl] n dancing m, salle f de danse.
dancer [ˈdɑːnsə] n danseur, -euse.
dandelion [ˈdændilaiən] n pissenlit m.
dandle [ˈdændl] vt dodeliner, dorloter.
dandruff [ˈdændrəf] n pellicules f pl.
dandy [ˈdændi] n dandy m.
Dane [dein] n Danois(e) mf.
danger [ˈdeindʒə] n danger m, péril m, risque m.
dangerous [ˈdeindʒrəs] a dangereux, périlleux.
dangle [ˈdæŋgl] vi pendre, se balancer, agiter, pendiller; vt faire balancer.
Danish [ˈdeiniʃ] an danois m.
dapper [ˈdæpə] a net, soigné, tiré à quatre épingles.
dappled [ˈdæpld] a pommelé, tacheté.
dare [dɛə] vt oser, risquer, défier, braver.
dare-devil [ˈdɛə.devil] n casse-cou m.
daring [ˈdɛəriŋ] n audace f; a hardi, audacieux.
dark [dɑːk] n noir m, nuit f, obscurité f; a sombre, noir, foncé.
darken [ˈdɑːkən] vt assombrir, obscurcir, attrister; vi s'assombrir, s'obscurcir.
darkness [ˈdɑːknis] n obscurité f, ténèbres f pl.
darling [ˈdɑːliŋ] n chéri(e) mf, amour m.
darn [dɑːn] n reprise f; vt repriser, ravauder.
dart [dɑːt] n flèche f, dard m, fléchette f, ancement m; vt lancer, darder; vi s'élancer, foncer.
dash [dæʃ] n fougue f, allant m, brio m, trait m, tiret m, pointe f, (fig) goutte f, filet m; vt lancer, éclabousser, diluer, étendre, décevoir; vi se précipiter, s'élancer; to — off vt bâcler; vi filer en vitesse, se sauver.
dashboard [ˈdæʃbɔːd] n tablier m.
dashing [ˈdæʃiŋ] a fougueux, impétueux, tapageur, plein d'entrain, galant.
dastardly [ˈdæstədli] a infâme, lâche.
date [deit] n date f, rendezvous m, datte f; vti dater; out of — démodé, périmé; up to — au courant, à la page.
dating [ˈdeitiŋ] dating from à dater de.
daub [dɔːb] n barbouillage m, croûte f, navet m; vt enduire, barbouiller.
daughter [ˈdɔːtə] n fille f.
daughter-in-law [ˈdɔːtərinlɔː] n belle-fille f.
daunt [dɔːnt] vt effrayer, intimider, décourager.
dauntless [ˈdɔːntlis] a intrépide, courageux.
dawdle [ˈdɔːdl] vi traîner, flâner; to — away gaspiller

dawdler ['dɔːdlə] n lambin(e) mf, flâneur, -euse.

dawn [dɔːn] n aube f, aurore f; vi poindre, naître, se faire jour.

day [dei] n jour m, journée f; — **before** veille f; — **after** lendemain m; **a week today** d'aujourd'hui en huit.

day-boarder ['dei,bɔːdə] n demi-pensionnaire mf.

day-boy ['deibɔi] n externe m.

daybreak ['deibreik] n point du jour m.

daydream ['deidriːm] n rêve (éveillé) m, rêverie f; n rêver, rêvasser.

day-laborer ['dei'leibərə] n ouvrier m à la journée.

daylight ['deilait] n (lumière f du) jour m, publicité f, notoriété f.

day-nursery ['dei,nəːsri] n crèche f, garderie f.

daze [deiz] vt ébahir, ahurir, étourdir, hébéter.

dazzle ['dæzl] vt éblouir, aveugler.

dazzling ['dæzliŋ] n éblouissement m; a éblouissant.

deacon ['diːkən] n diacre m.

deaconess ['diːkənis] n diaconesse f.

dead [ded] n morts m pl; a mort, défunt, feu, funèbre, éteint, amorti, (loss) net, sec, plat; ad droit, en plein, à fond; **in the — of** au cœur de, au plus fort de, au milieu de.

deaden ['dedn] vt étouffer, amortir, émousser, feutrer.

dead-end ['ded'end] n cul de sac m, impasse f.

dead-letter ['ded'letə] n lettre morte f, mise au rebut f.

deadline ['dedlain] n dernière limite f, date limite f.

deadlock ['dedlɔk] n point mort m, impasse f.

deadly ['dedli] a mortel.

deaf [def] a sourd.

deafen ['defn] vt rendre sourd, assourdir.

deafness ['defnis] n surdité f.

deal [diːl] n planche f, bois blanc m, sapin m, quantité f, nombre m, affaire f, (cards) donne f; vt donner, distribuer, asséner; vi avoir affaire (à, avec with), s'occuper (de with), traiter (de with), faire le commerce (de in), se conduire.

dealer ['diːlə] n marchand(e) mf, fournisseur m, donneur m.

dealing(s) ['diːliŋz] n relations f pl, affaire f, agissements m pl, menées f pl.

dean [diːn] n doyen m.

deanery ['diːnəri] n doyenné m.

dear ['diə] a cher, coûteux.

dearly ['diəli] ad cher, chèrement.

dearness ['diənis] n cherté f.

dearth [dəːθ] n disette f, pénurie f.

death [deθ] n mort f, décès m; — **certificate** acte m de décès.

deathbed ['deθbed] n lit m de mort.

death-bell ['deθbel] n glas m.

death-rate ['deθreit] n taux de mortalité m.

death-trap ['deθtræp] n souricière f, casse-cou m.

death-warrant ['deθwɔrənt] n ordre m d'exécution, arrêt m de mort.

debar [di'bɑː] vt exclure.

debase [di'beis] vt avilir, altérer.

debatable [di'beitəbl] a discutable.

debate [di'beit] n débat m, discussion f; vt débattre; vti discuter.

debauch [di'bɔːtʃ] n débauche f; vt débaucher, corrompre.

debauchee [,debɔː'tʃiː] n débauché(e) mf.

debilitate [di'biliteit] vt débiliter.

debility [di'biliti] n débilité f.

debit ['debit] n débit m, doit m; vt porter au débit (de with), débiter.

debouch [di'bautʃ] vi déboucher.

debt [det] n dette f, passif m.

debt-collector ['detkəlektə] n huissier m.

debtor ['detə] n débiteur, -trice.

debunk [di'bʌŋk] vt dégonfler.

debut [deibuː] n début m.

decade [dekeid] n décade f.

decadence ['dekədəns] n décadence f.

decadent ['dekədənt] a décadent.

decamp [di'kæmp] vi décamper, filer.

decant [di'kænt] vt décanter.

decanter [di'kæntə] n carafe f.

decapitate [di'kæpiteit] vt décapiter.

decapitation [di,kæpi'teiʃən] n décapitation f.

decay [di'kei] n déclin m, décadence f, décomposition f; vi tomber en décadence, décliner, pourrir.

decease [di'siːs] n décès m; vi décéder.

deceased [di'siːst] an défunt(e) mf.

deceit [di'siːt] n fourberie f, apparence trompeuse f.

deceitful [di'siːtful] a trompeur, faux, perfide.

deceitfulness [di'siːtfulnis] n fausseté f, perfidie f.

deceive [di'siːv] vt tromper, décevoir.

December [di'sembə] n décembre m.

decency ['diːsnsi] n bienséance f, décence f.

decent ['diːsnt] a décent, passable, honnête.

decently ['diːsntli] ad décemment.

decentralization [diː,sentrəlai'zeiʃn] n décentralisation f.

decentralize [diː'sentrəlaiz] vt décentraliser.

deception [di'sepʃən] n tromperie f, déception f, fraude f.

deceptive [di'septiv] a trompeur.

decide [di'said] vti décider; vt régler, trancher; vi se décider.

decided [di'saidid] a décidé, net, arrêté.

decidedly [di'saididli] ad catégoriquement, incontestablement.

decimal ['desiməl] n décimale f; a décimal.

decimate ['desimeit] vt décimer.
decipher [di'saifə] vt déchiffrer.
deciphering [di'saifəriŋ] n déchiffrement m.
decision [di'siʒən] n décision f, arrêt m.
decisive [di'saisiv] a décisif, net, tranchant.
deck [dek] n pont m; vt orner, couvrir, pavoiser.
deck-chair ['dek'tʃɛə] n transatlantique m.
deck-house ['dekhaus] n (naut) rouf m.
decisim [di'kleim] vti déclamer.
declamation [.deklə'meiʃən] n déclamation f.
declamatory [di'klæmətəri] a déclamatoire.
declaration [.deklə'reiʃən] n déclaration f, (pol) proclamation f, annonce f.
declare [di'klɛə] vt déclarer, annoncer.
decline [di'klain] n déclin m, baisse f, phtisie f; vti décliner; vt refuser, repousser; vi baisser, s'incliner, descendre.
declivity [di'kliviti] n pente f.
decode [di:'koud] vt déchiffrer.
decompose [.di:kəm'pouz] vt décomposer; vi se décomposer, pourrir.
decomposition [.di:kɔmpə'ziʃən] n décomposition f, putréfaction f.
decontrol [di:kən'troul] vt décontrôler.
decorate ['dekəreit] vt décorer, pavoiser.
decoration [.dekə'reiʃən] n décoration f, décor m.
decorator ['dekəreitə] n décorateur m.
decorative ['dekərətiv] a décoratif.
decorous ['dekərəs] a séant.
decorum [di'kɔ:rəm] n décorum m, bienséance f.
decoy [di'kɔi] n piège m, amorce f, appeau m, appât m, agent provocateur m; vt attraper, induire (à into), leurrer, attirer.
decrease ['di:kri:s] n diminution f, décroissance f.
decrease [di:'kri:s] vti diminuer; vi décroître.
decree [di'kri:] n décret m, arrêt m, édit m; vt décréter; — nisi divorce m sous conditions.
decrepit [di'krepit] a décrépit, caduc, délabré.
decrepitude [di'krepitju:d] n décrépitude f, caducité f.
decry [di'krai] vt décrier, dénigrer, huer.
dedication [.dedi'keiʃən] n consécration f, dédicace f.
dedicate ['dedikeit] vt consacrer, dédier.
deduce [di'dju:s] vt déduire, conclure.
deduct [di'dʌkt] vt retrancher, rabattre.

deduction [di'dʌkʃən] n déduction f, rabais m, conclusion f.
deed [di:d] n acte m, (haut) fait m, exploit m.
deem [di:m] vt estimer, juger.
deep [di:p] n fond m, profondeur f, mer f, abîme m, gouffre m; a profond, (mourning) grand, (colour) chaud, foncé, (sound) riche, bas.
deepen ['di:pən] vt approfondir, creuser, augmenter; vi devenir plus profond etc.
deepening ['di:pniŋ] n approfondissement m.
deeply ['di:pli] ad profondément.
deer [diə] n daim m, cerf m.
deerskin ['diəskin] n peau f de daim.
deface [di'feis] vt défigurer, discréditer, mutiler, oblitérer.
defalcation [.di:fæl'keiʃən] n défalcation f, détournement m.
defalcate ['di:fælkeit] vi défalquer, détourner des fonds.
defamation [.defə'meiʃən] n diffamation f.
defamatory [di'fæmətəri] a diffamatoire.
defame [di'feim] vt diffamer.
default [di'fɔ:lt] n défaut m, forfait m; vi faire défaut.
defaulter [di'fɔ:ltə] n défaillant m, contumace mf.
defeat [di'fi:t] n défaite f, annulation f; vt déjouer, battre, vaincre, contrarier.
defeatism [di'fi:tizəm] n défaitisme m.
defeatist [di'fi:tist] n défaitiste mf.
defect [di'fekt] n défaut m, manque m.
defection [di'fekʃən] n défection f.
defective [di'fektiv] a défectueux, anormal.
defend [di'fend] vt défendre, protéger.
defendant [di'fendənt] n défendeur, -eresse.
defender [di'fendə] n défenseur m.
defense [di'fens] n défense f.
defensible [di'fensəbl] a défendable.
defensive [di'fensiv] n défensive f; a défensif.
defer [di'fə:] vt différer, ajourner; vi déférer (à to).
deference ['defərəns] n déférence f.
deferment [di'fə:mənt] n ajournement m, remise f.
defiance [di'faiəns] n défi m, révolte f.
defiant [di'faiənt] a rebelle, défiant, provocant.
deficiency [di'fiʃənsi] n insuffisance f, manque m, défaut m, manquant m.
deficient [di'fiʃənt] a qui manque de, déficitaire, défectueux.
deficit ['defisit] n déficit m.
defile ['di:fail] n défilé m; [di'fail] vi marcher par files, défiler; vt souiller, profaner.

defilement [di'failmənt] n souillure f, profanation f.
definable [di'fainəbl] a définissable.
define [di'fain] vt définir, (dé)limiter.
definite ['definit] a défini, net, précis, définitif.
definiteness ['definitnis] n netteté f, précision f.
definition [‚defi'nifən] n définition f.
definitive [di'finitiv] a définitif.
deflate [di'fleit] vt dégonfler; vi pratiquer la déflation.
deflect [di'flekt] vt (faire) dévier, détourner.
deflection [di'flekfən] n déviation f, déjettement m.
deform [di'fɔ:m] vt déformer, défigurer.
deformed [di'fɔ:md] a difforme.
deformity [di'fɔ:miti] n difformité f.
deformation [‚di:fɔ:'meifən] n déformation f.
defraud [di'frɔ:d] vt voler, frauder, frustrer.
defray [di'frei] vt défrayer, couvrir.
deft [deft] a adroit.
deftness ['deftnis] n adresse f.
defunct [di'fʌŋkt] a défunt.
defy [di'fai] vt défier.
degenerate [di'dʒenəreit] an dégénéré(e) mf; vi dégénérer.
degeneration [di‚dʒenə'reifən] n dégénérescence f.
degradation [‚degrə'deifən] n dégradation f, abrutissement m.
degrade [di'greid] vt avilir, dégrader, casser.
degree [di'gri:] n degré m, grade m, titre m, échelon m, condition f; to a — au dernier point.
dehydrate [di:'haidreit] vt déshydrater.
deign [dein] vi daigner.
deity ['di:iti] n divinité f.
dejected [di'dʒektid] a déprimé, abattu.
dejection [di'dʒekfən] n abattement m.
delay [di'lei] n délai m, retard m; vt remettre, retarder, différer.
delegate ['deligit] n délégué(e) mf.
delegate ['deligeit] vt déléguer.
delegation [‚deli'geifən] n délégation f.
delete [di'li:t] vt effacer, rayer.
deleterious [‚deli'tiəriəs] a délétère, nuisible.
deletion [di'li:fən] n radiation f, rature f, suppression f.
deliberate [di'libərit] a délibéré, voulu, réfléchi.
deliberate [di'libəreit] vti délibérer.
deliberately [di'libəritli] ad délibérément, exprès.
deliberation [di‚libə'reifən] n délibération f.
delicacy ['delikəsi] n délicatesse f, finesse f, friandise f.
delicate ['delikit] a délicat, fin, raffiné, épineux.

delicious [di'lifəs] a délicieux, exquis.
delight [di'lait] n délices f, pl joie f; vt enchanter, ravir.
delightful [di'laitful] a délicieux, ravissant.
delineate [di'linieit] vt tracer, esquisser.
delineation [di‚lini'eifən] n délinéation f, description f, tracé m.
delinquency [di'liŋkwənsi] n délit m, faute f, négligence f.
delinquent [di'liŋkwənt] an délinquant(e) mf, coupable mf.
delirious [di'liriəs] a délirant, en délire.
delirium [di'liriəm] n délire m.
deliver [di'livə] vt (dé)livrer, remettre, (letters) distribuer, (blow) asséner, (ball) lancer, (lectures) faire.
deliverance [di'livərəns] n délivrance f, libération f.
deliverer [di'livərə] n libérateur, -trice, livreur, -euse.
delivery [di'livəri] n livraison f, distribution f, remise f, débit m.
dell [del] n vallon m, combe f.
delude [di'lu:d] vt tromper, duper.
deluge ['delju:dʒ] n déluge m; vt inonder.
delusion [di'lu:ʒən] n leurre m, illusion f, hallucination f.
demand [di'ma:nd] n requête f, (com) demande f, revendication f; vt requérir, exiger, réclamer.
demarcation [di:ma:'keifən] n démarcation f.
demarcate ['di:ma:keit] vt délimiter.
demean [di'mi:n] vi to — oneself s'abaisser.
demeanor [di'mi:nə] n conduite f, tenue f.
demented [di'mentid] a (tombé) en démence, fou.
demise [di'maiz] n transfert m, carence f, mort f; vt transférer, céder.
demobilization ['di:‚moubilai'zeifən] n démobilisation f.
demobilize [di:'moubilaiz] vt démobiliser.
democracy [di'mɔkrəsi] n démocratie f.
democrat ['deməkræt] n démocrate mf; membre mf du parti démocrate.
democratic [‚demə'krætik] a démocratique, démocrate.
demolish [di'mɔlif] vt démolir.
demolition [‚demə'lifən] n démolition f.
demon ['di:mən] n démon m.
demonetize [di:'mʌnitaiz] vt 'démonétiser.
demonstrate ['demənstreit] vt démontrer; vi manifester.
demonstration [‚deməns'treifən] n démonstration f, manifestation f.
demonstrative [di'mɔnstrətiv] a démonstratif, expansif.
demonstrator ['demənstreitə] n dé-

monstrateur *m*, préparateur *m*, manifestant *m*.

demoralization [di͵mɔrəlai'zeiʃən] *n* démoralisation *f*.

demoralize [di'mɔrəlaiz] *vt* démoraliser.

demur [di'məː] *n* objection *f*; *vi* objecter, hésiter.

demure [di'mjuə] *a* réservé, composé, faussement modeste, prude.

demureness [di'mjuənis] *n* ingénuité feinte *f*, air prude *m*.

den [den] *n* tanière *f*, antre *m*, retraite *f*, turne *f*, cagibi *m*; (*fam*) cabinet *m* de travail.

denial [di'naiəl] *n* refus *m*, démenti *m*, désaveu *m*, reniement *m*.

denizen ['denizn] *n* habitant(e) *mf*, hôte *m*.

Denmark ['denmɑːk] *n* Danemark *m*.

denominate [di'nɔmineit] *vt* dénommer.

denote [di'nout] *vt* dénoter, accuser, respirer.

denounce [di'nauns] *vt* dénoncer, déblatérer contre.

dense [dens] *a* dense, épais, lourd, bouché.

density ['densiti] *n* densité *f*, lourdeur *f*.

dent [dent] *n* entaille *f*, bosselure *f*; *vt* entailler, bosseler.

dental ['dentl] *n* dentale *f*; *a* dentaire.

dentifrice ['dentifris] *n* dentifrice *m*.

dentist ['dentist] *n* dentiste *m*.

dentition [den'tiʃən] *n* dentition *f*.

denture ['dentʃə] *n* dentier *m*, denture *f*.

denude [di'njuːd] *vt* dénuder, dépouiller.

denunciation [di͵nʌnsi'eiʃən] *n* dénonciation *f*.

deny [di'nai] *vt* (re)nier, refuser, démentir, désavouer.

depart [di'pɑːt] *vi* partir, trépasser, se départir (de from).

department [di'pɑːtmənt] *n* département *m*, rayon *m*, service *m*, bureau *m*; — **store** bazar *m*, grand magasin *m*.

departmental [͵diːpɑːt'mentl] *a* départemental, de service.

departure [di'pɑːtʃə] *n* départ *m*, déviation *f*.

depend [di'pend] *vi* dépendre (de on), compter (sur on), tenir (à on).

dependable [di'pendəbl] *a* sûr, (digne) de confiance.

dependence [di'pendəns] *n* dépendance *f*, confiance *f*.

dependency [di'pendənsi] *n* dépendance *f*.

dependent [di'pendənt] *a* dépendant, subordonné.

depict [di'pikt] *vt* (dé)peindre.

deplenish [di'pleniʃ] *vt* vider, dégarnir.

deplete [di'pliːt] *vt* vider, épuiser.

depletion [di'pliːʃən] *n* épuisement *m*.

deplorable [di'plɔːrəbl] *a* déplorable, lamentable.

deplore [di'plɔː] *vt* déplorer.

deploy [di'plɔi] *vt* déployer.

deployment [di'plɔimənt] *n* déploiement *m*.

depopulate [diː'pɔpjuleit] *vt* dépeupler.

depopulation [diː͵pɔpju'leiʃən] *n* dépopulation *f*.

deport [di'pɔːt] *vt* déporter, expulser (*aliens*); **to — oneself** se comporter.

deportation [͵diːpɔː'teiʃən] *n* déportation *f*, expulsion *f*.

deportment [di'pɔːtmənt] *n* comportement *m*, tenue *f*.

depose [di'pouz] *vt* déposer.

deposit [di'pɔzit] *n* dépôt *m*, sédiment *m*, gisement *m*, gage *m*; *vt* déposer, verser en gage.

depositary [di'pɔzitəri] *n* dépositaire *m*.

deposition [͵diːpə'ziʃən] *n* déposition *f*.

depository [di'pɔzitəri] *n* garde-meubles *m*, entrepôt *m*.

depot ['depou] *n* dépôt *m*, entrepôt *m*, garage *m*; gare *f*.

depravation [͵deprə'veiʃən] *n* dépravation *f*.

deprave [di'preiv] *vt* dépraver.

deprecate ['deprikeit] *vt* déconseiller (fortement), désapprouver.

depreciate [di'priːʃieit] *vt* déprécier; *vi* se déprécier.

depreciation [di͵priːʃi'eiʃən] *n* dépréciation *f*, amortissement *m*.

depredation [͵depri'deiʃən] *n* déprédation *f*.

depress [di'pres] *vt* (a)baisser, appuyer, déprimer, attrister.

depression [di'preʃən] *n* dépression *f*, abattement *m*.

deprival [di'praivəl] *n* privation *f*.

deprive [di'praiv] *vt* priver.

depth [depθ] *n* profondeur *f*, fond *m*, fort *m*, cœur *m*; **to get out of one's —** perdre pied.

deputation [͵depju'teiʃən] *n* délégation *f*.

depute [di'pjuːt] *vt* déléguer.

deputize ['depjutaiz] **to — for** *vt* représenter, remplacer.

deputy ['depjuti] *n* délégué *m*, suppléant *m*, sous-.

derail [di'reil] *vt* (faire) dérailler.

derailment [di'reilmənt] *n* déraillement *m*.

derange [di'reindʒ] *vt* déranger.

derangement [di'reindʒmənt] *n* dérangement *m*.

derelict ['derilikt] *n* épave *f*; *a* abandonné.

dereliction [͵deri'likʃən] *n* abandon *m*, négligence *f*.

deride [di'raid] *vt* tourner en dérision, bafouer, se gausser de.

derision [di'riʒən] n dérision f, objet m de dérision.

derisive [di'raisiv] a ironique, dérisoire, railleur.

derivation [ˌderi'veiʃən] n dérivation f.

derivative [di'rivətiv] an dérivatif m.

derive [di'raiv] vti tirer; vi dériver, provenir.

derogate ['derəgeit] vi déroger (à from), diminuer.

derogation [ˌderə'geiʃən] n dérogation f, abaissement m.

derogatory [di'rɔgətəri] a dérogatoire.

descend [di'send] vti descendre, dévaler; vi s'abaisser.

descent [di'sent] n descente f, lignage m, parage m, transmission f.

describe [dis'kraib] vt dépeindre, décrire, donner pour, qualifier, signaler.

description [dis'kripʃən] n description f, signalement m, espèce f.

descriptive [dis'kriptiv] a descriptif, de description.

descry [dis'krai] vt apercevoir, aviser.

desecrate ['desikreit] vt profaner.

desert [di'zə:t] n mérite m, dû m; vt abandonner; vti déserter.

desert ['dezət] an désert m.

deserter [di'zə:tə] n déserteur m.

desertion [di'zə:ʃən] n désertion f, abandon m.

deserve [di'zə:v] vt mériter.

deservedly [di'zə:vidli] ad à juste titre.

deserving [di'zə:viŋ] a méritant, méritoire.

desiccate ['desikeit] vt dessécher.

desiccation [ˌdesi'keiʃən] n desiccation f.

design [di'zain] n dess(e)in m, esquisse f, modèle m, projet m; vt désigner, esquisser, projeter, créer, former, destiner.

designate ['dezigneit] vt désigner, nommer.

designation [ˌdezig'neiʃən] n désignation f, nom m.

designedly [di'zainidli] ad à dessein.

designer [di'zainə] n dessinateur, -trice, créateur, -trice, décorateur m.

designing [di'zainiŋ] a intrigant.

desirable [di'zaiərəbl] a désirable, souhaitable.

desire [di'zaiə] n désir m, souhait m; vt désirer, avoir envie de.

desirous [di'zaiərəs] a désireux.

desist [di'zist] vi renoncer (à from), cesser (de from).

desk [desk] n pupitre m, bureau m.

desolate ['desəlit] a solitaire, abandonné, désert, désolé.

desolate ['desəleit] vt dépeupler, dévaster, désoler.

desolation [ˌdesə'leiʃən] n désolation f, solitude f.

despair [dis'pɛə] n désespoir m; vi désespérer.

despairingly [dis'pɛəriŋli] ad désespérément.

desperate ['despərit] a désespéré, forcené, acharné, affreux.

desperation [ˌdespə'reiʃən] n désespoir m.

despicable [dis'pikəbl] a méprisable.

despise [dis'paiz] vt mépriser.

despite [dis'pait] ad malgré.

despoil [dis'pɔil] vt dépouiller, spolier.

despoiler [dis'pɔilə] n spoliateur, -trice.

despoliation [ˌdispɔli'eiʃən] n spoliation f.

despond [dis'pɔnd] vi se décourager.

despondency [dis'pɔndənsi] n découragement m, abattement m.

despondent [dis'pɔndənt] a découragé, abattu.

despot ['despɔt] n despote m.

despotic [des'pɔtik] a despotique, arbitraire.

despotism ['despətizəm] n despotisme m.

dessert [di'zə:t] n dessert m, entremets m.

dessert-spoon [di'zə:tspu:n] n cuiler f à entremets.

destination [ˌdesti'neiʃən] n destination f.

destine ['destin] vt destiner.

destiny ['destini] n destinée f, destin m, sort m.

destitute ['destitju:t] a sans ressources, dénué, indigent.

destitution [ˌdesti'tju:ʃən] n dénuement m, misère f, indigence f.

destroy [dis'trɔi] vt détruire.

destroyer [dis'trɔiə] n destructeur, -trice, (naut) contre-torpilleur m.

destruction [dis'trʌkʃən] n destruction f.

destructive [dis'trʌktiv] a destructeur, destructif.

desultorily ['desəltərili] ad sans suite, à bâtons rompus.

desultoriness ['desəltərinis] n incohérence f, décousu m, manque de suite m.

desultory ['desəltəri] a décousu, sans suite.

detach [di'tætʃ] vt détacher, dételer.

detachedly [di'tætʃədli] ad d'un ton (air) détaché, avec désinvolture.

detachment [di'tætʃmənt] n détachement m, indifférence f.

detail ['di:teil] n détail m, détachement m; vt détailler, affecter (à for).

detailed ['di:teild] a détaillé, circonstancié; — work travail très fouillé.

detain [di'tein] vt retenir, empêcher, détenir.

detect [di'tekt] vt découvrir, apercevoir, repérer, détecter.

detection [di'tekʃən] n découverte f, détection f, repérage m.

detective [di'tektiv] n détective m; — novel roman policier m.

detention [di'tenʃən] n détention f,

arrestation f, arrêts m pl, retard m, retenue f.
deter [di'tə:] vt détourner, décourager, retenir.
deteriorate [di'tiəriəreit] vt détériorer; vi se détériorer, dégénérer, se gâter.
deterioration [di.tiəriə'reiʃən] n détérioration f, dégénération f.
determination [di.tə:mi'neiʃən] n détermination f, résolution f.
determine [di'tə:min] vti déterminer, décider; vt constater.
determined [di'tə:mind] a résolu.
deterrent [di'terənt] n mesure préventive f, arme f de dissuasion.
detest [di'test] vt détester.
detestation [.di:tes'teiʃən] n horreur f, haine f.
detonate ['detəneit] vi détoner; vt faire détoner.
detonation [.detə'neiʃən] n détonation f.
detract [di'trækt] to — from retrancher, déprécier, diminuer.
detraction [di'trækʃən] n dénigrement m, détraction f.
detractor [di'træktə] n détracteur, -trice.
detriment ['detrimənt] n détriment m, préjudice m.
detrimental [.detri'məntl] a préjudiciable, nuisible.
deuce [dju:s] n deux m, diable m, diantre m.
deuced [dju:st] a sacré, satané.
devastate ['devəsteit] vt ravager, dévaster.
devastation [.devəs'teiʃən] n dévastation f.
devastating ['devəsteitiŋ] a dévastateur.
develop [di'veləp] vt exploiter, développer; vi se développer, se produire.
development [di'veləpmənt] n développement m.
deviate ['di:vieit] vi dévier, s'écarter.
deviation [.di:vi'eiʃən] n déviation f, écart m.
device [di'vais] n plan m, ruse f, moyen m, invention f, dispositif m, devise f.
devil ['devl] n diable m.
devilish ['deviliʃ] a diabolique.
devilry ['devlri] n diablerie f, méchanceté f.
devious ['di:vjəs] a détourné, tortueux.
devise [di'vaiz] vt imaginer, combiner, tramer.
deviser [di'vaizə] n inventeur, -trice.
devoid [di'vɔid] a dénué, dépourvu.
devolve [di'vɔlv] vt passer (à upon), rejeter (sur upon), transmettre; vi échoir, incomber.
devote [di'vout] vt vouer, dévouer, consacrer.
devotee [.devou'ti:] n fanatique mf, fervent(e) mf.

devotion [di'vouʃən] n dévotion f, dévouement m, consécration f.
devour [di'vauə] vt dévorer.
devout [di'vaut] an dévôt, fervent, zélé.
dew [dju:] n rosée f.
dewy ['dju:i] a couvert de rosée.
dexterity [deks'teriti] n dextérité f.
dexterous ['dekstrəs] a adroit.
diabetes [.daiə'bi:ti:z] n diabète m.
diabetic [.daiə'betik] an diabétique mf.
diabolic(al) [.daiə'bɔlik(əl)] a diabolique, infernal.
diadem ['daiədem] n diadème m.
diagnose ['daiəgnouz] vt diagnostiquer.
diagnosis [.daiəg'nousis] n diagnostic m.
diagonal [dai'ægənl] n diagonale f; a diagonal.
diagram ['daiəgræm] n diagramme m, tracé m, schéma m.
dial ['daiəl] n cadran m.
dialogue ['daiəlɔg] n dialogue m.
diameter [dai'æmitə] n diamètre m.
diametrical [.daiə'metrikəl] a diamétral.
diamond ['daiəmənd] n diamant m, losange m, (cards) carreau m.
diaper ['daiəpə] n linge damassé m; couches fpl; vt damasser.
diaphragm ['daiəfræm] n diaphragme m, membrane m.
diary ['daiəri] n journal m, agenda m.
dibble ['dibl] n plantoir m.
dice [dais] n dés m pl; — box cornet m.
dicky ['diki] n faux-plastron m, tablier m, (aut) spider m; a flanchard.
dictate ['dikteit] n dictat m, ordre m, voix f; [dik'teit] vt dicter, ordonner; vi faire la loi.
dictation [dik'teiʃən] n dictée f.
dictator [dik'teitə] n dictateur m.
dictatorial [.diktə'tɔ:riəl] a dictatorial.
dictatorship [dik'teitəʃip] n dictature f.
diction ['dikʃən] n diction f, style m.
dictionary ['dikʃənri] n dictionnaire m.
did [did] pt of do.
die [dai] n (pl dice) dé m, (pl dies) coin m, matrice f; vi mourrir, crever; to — away, out s'éteindre, tomber.
diehard ['daiha:d] n jusqu'au boutiste m; the —s le dernier carré m, les irréductibles m pl; a — conservative conservateur intransigeant.
diet ['daiət] n régime m, diète f; vt mettre au régime; vi suivre un régime.
differ ['difə] vi différer.
difference ['difrəns] n différence f, écart m, différend m.
different ['difrənt] a différent, divers.
differentiate [.difə'renʃieit] vt différencier; vi faire la différence.

differently ['difrəntli] *ad* différemment.

difficult ['difikəlt] *a* difficile.

difficulty ['difikəlti] *n* difficulté *f*, ennui *m*, peine *f*, gêne *f*.

diffidence ['difidəns] *n* défiance de soi *f*, timidité *f*.

diffident ['difidənt] *a* modeste, timide, qui manque d'assurance.

diffuse [di'fju:z] *vt* diffuser, répandre.

diffuse [di'fju:s] *a* diffus.

diffusion [di'fju:ʒən] *n* diffusion *f*.

dig [dig] *vt* creuser, bêcher, piocher, piquer; to — up déterrer, déraciner.

digest [dai'dʒest] *vt* digérer, assimiler; *vi* se digérer, s'assimiler.

digestible [di'dʒestəbl] *a* digestible.

digestion [di'dʒestʃən] *n* digestion *f*

digestive [di'dʒestiv] *a* digestif.

dignified ['dignifaid] *a* digne, majestueux.

dignify ['dignifai] *vt* honorer, donner un air de majesté à.

dignity ['digniti] *n* dignité *f*.

digress [dai'gres] *vi* s'écarter (de from), faire une digression.

digression [dai'greʃən] *n* digression *f*.

digs [digz] *n* *pl* garni *m*, logement *m*, piaule *f*.

dike [daik] *n* levée *f*, digue *f*, remblai *m*; *vt* endiguer, remblayer.

dilapidated [di'læpideitid] *a* délabré, décrépit.

dilapidation [di,læpi'deiʃən] *n* délabrement *m*, dégradation *f*.

dilatation [,dailei'teiʃən] *n* dilatation *f*.

dilate [dai'leit] *vt* dilater; *vi* se dilater, s'étendre (sur upon).

dilatoriness ['dilətərinis] *n* temporisation *f*, tergiversation *f*, lenteur *f*.

dilatory ['dilətəri] *a* lent, tardif.

dilemma [dai'lemə] *n* dilemme *m*.

diligence ['dilidʒəns] *n* diligence *f*, application *f*.

diligent ['dilidʒənt] *a* diligent, appliqué.

diligently ['dilidʒəntli] *ad* diligemment.

dilute [dai'lju:t] *a* dilué, atténué; *vt* diluer, arroser, atténuer.

dim [dim] *a* indistinct, voilé, faible, sourd; *vt* assombrir, éclipser, ternir, mettre en veilleuse; *vi* s'affaiblir, baisser.

dime [daim] *n* pièce de dix cents; — store prix unique *m*.

dimension [di'menʃən] *n* dimension *f*.

diminish [di'miniʃ] *vti* diminuer.

diminution [,dimi'nju:ʃən] *n* diminution *f*.

diminutive [di'minjutiv] *an* diminutif *m*.

dimmer ['dimə] *n* phare code *m*.

dimness ['dimnis] *n* pénombre *f*, faiblesse *f*, imprécision *f*.

dim-out ['dimaut] *n* obscurcissement *m*.

dimple ['dimpl] *n* fossette *f*, ride *f*, creux *m*.

din [din] *n* tintamarre *m*, vacarme *m*; *vt* corner, rabattre.

dine [dain] *vi* dîner; to — out dîner en ville.

dinghy ['dingi] *n* canot *m*.

dingy ['dindʒi] *a* sale, crasseux, terne, sombre.

dining-room ['dainiŋrum] *n* salle *f* à manger.

dinner ['dinə] *n* dîner *m*.

dinner-jacket ['dinə,dʒækit] *n* smoking *m*.

dint [dint] by — of à force de.

diocese ['daiəsis] *n* diocèse *m*.

dip [dip] *n* plongeon *m*, pent · *f*, immersion *f*, bain *m*; *vti* plonger, baisser, (*headlights*) basculer; *vt* puiser, tremper, baigner; *vi* pencher.

diphtheria [dip'θiəriə] *n* diphtérie *f*.

diphthong ['difθɔŋ] *n* diphtongue *f*.

diploma [di'ploumə] *n* diplôme *m*.

diplomacy [di'plouməsi] *n* diplomatie *f*.

diplomat ['dipləmæt] *n* diplomate *m*.

diplomatic [,diplə'mætik] *a* diplomatique, prudent.

dire ['daiə] *a* affreux, cruel, dernier, extrême.

direct [dai'rekt] *a* direct, droit, catégorique, formel, franc; *vt* adresser, diriger, attirer, ordonner, indiquer.

direction [di'rekʃən] *n* direction *f*, sens *m*, adresse *f*; *pl* instructions *f* *pl*.

directly [di'rektli] *ad* tout de suite, (tout) droit, directement, tout à l'heure, bientôt, personnellement.

director [di'rektə] *n* directeur *m*, gérant *m*, administrateur *m*.

directorship [di'rektəʃip] *n* directorat *m*.

directory [di'rektəri] *n* indicateur *m*, annuaire *m*, bottin *m*, directoire *m*.

dirge [də:dʒ] *n* misérère *m*, chant funèbre *m*.

dirk [də:k] *n* poignard *m*.

dirt [də:t] *n* boue *f*, saleté *f*, ordure *f*, crasse *f*.

dirtiness ['də:tinis] *n* crasse *f*, saleté *f*.

dirty ['də:ti] *vt* salir; *vi* se salir; *a* sale, malpropre, crasseux, vilain, polisson.

disability [,disə'biliti] *n* incapacité *f* (de travail), infirmité *f*.

disable [dis'eibl] *vt* rendre impropre au travail, mettre hors de combat, désemparer.

disabled [dis'eibld] *a* invalide, estropié, désemparé.

disabuse [,disə'bju:z] *vt* désabuser.

disaffected [,disə'fektid] *a* détaché, refroidi.

disaffection [ˌdisə'fekʃən] n désaffection f.

disagree [ˌdisə'griː] vi n'être pas d'accord, ne pas convenir.

disagreeable [ˌdisə'griːəbl] a désagréable, fâcheux.

disagreement [ˌdisə'griːmənt] n disconvenance f, désaccord m, mésentente f.

disallow ['disə'lau] vt désavouer, interdire, ne pas admettre, rejeter.

disappear [ˌdisə'piə] vi disparaître.

disappearance [ˌdisə'piərəns] n disparition f.

disappoint [ˌdisə'point] vt désappointer, décevoir.

disappointed [ˌdisə'pointəd] a déçu; manqué.

disappointment [ˌdisə'pointmənt] n déception f, désappointement m, déboire m.

disapproval [ˌdisə'pruːvəl] n désapprobation f.

disapprove [ˌdisə'pruːv] vti désapprouver.

disapproving [ˌdisə'pruːviŋ] a désapprobateur.

disarm [dis'aːm] vti désarmer.

disarmament [dis'aːməmənt] n désarmement m.

disarrange ['disə'reindʒ] vt déranger.

disarrangement [ˌdisə'reindʒmənt] n désorganisation f, désordre m, dérangement m.

disarray ['disə'rei] n désarroi m, désordre m, déroute f.

disaster [di'zaːstə] n désastre m, sinistre m, catastrophe f.

disastrous [di'zaːstrəs] a désastreux, funeste.

disavow ['disə'vau] vt désavouer, renier.

disavowal [ˌdisə'vauəl] n désaveu m, reniement m.

disband [dis'bænd] vt licencier; vi se débander.

disbanding [dis'bændiŋ] n licenciement m.

disbelief ['disbi'liːf] n incrédulité f.

disc [disk] n disque m, plaque f; slipped — hernie discale f.

discard [dis'kaːd] n écart m, défausse f; vt se défausser de, écarter, mettre au rancart, laisser de côté.

discern [di'səːn] vt distinguer, discerner.

discernible [di'səːnəbl] a discernable, perceptible.

discerning [di'səːniŋ] a perspicace, judicieux.

discernment [di'səːnmənt] n discernement m.

discharge [dis'tʃaːdʒ] n déchargement m, décharge f, acquittement m, élargissement m, renvoi m, exécution f, paiement m; vt décharger, élargir, renvoyer, (s')acquitter (de), lancer; vi se jeter, se dégorger.

disciple [di'saipl] n disciple m.

disciplinary ['disiplinəri] a disciplinaire.

discipline ['disiplin] n discipline f; vt discipliner, mater, former.

disclaim [dis'kleim] vt répudier, désavouer, renoncer à, dénier.

disclaimer [dis'kleimə] n répudiation f, désaveu m, déni m.

disclose [dis'klouz] vt découvrir, divulguer, révéler.

disclosure [dis'klouʒə] n révélation f, divulgation f.

discolor [dis'kʌlə] vt décolorer, ternir, délaver; vi se décolorer, se ternir.

discoloration [dis.kʌlə'reiʃən] n décoloration f.

discomfit [dis'kʌmfit] vt déconcerter, déconfire.

discomfiture [dis'kʌmfitʃə] n déconfiture f, déconvenue f.

discomfort [dis'kʌmfət] n malaise m, gêne f.

discomposure [ˌdiskəm'pouʒə] n confusion f, trouble m.

disconcert [ˌdiskən'səːt] vt déranger, déconcerter, interloquer.

disconnect [ˌdiskə'nekt] vt couper, décrocher, disjoindre, débrayer.

disconnected ['diskə'nektid] a décousu, sans suite.

disconnection [ˌdiskə'nekʃən] n disjonction f, débrayage m.

disconsolate [dis'kɔnsəlit] a inconsolable, désolé.

discontent ['diskən'tent] n mécontentement m.

discontented ['diskən'tentid] a mécontent, insatisfait (de with).

discontinuance [ˌdiskən'tinjuəns] n discontinuation f, fin f.

discontinue [dis'kən'tinju] vt discontinuer; vti cesser.

discontinuity ['dis.kɔnti'njuiti] n discontinuité f.

discontinuous ['diskən'tinjuəs] a discontinu.

discord ['diskɔːd] n discorde f, discordance f, dissonance f.

discount ['diskaunt] n rabais m, escompte m; [dis'kaunt] vt escompter, laisser hors de compte.

discountenance [dis'kauntinəns] vt désapprouver, décontenancer.

discourage [dis'kʌridʒ] vt décourager, déconseiller.

discouragement [dis'kʌridʒmənt] n découragement m.

discourse ['diskɔːs] n traité m, sermon m, essai m, dissertation f.

discourse [dis'kɔːs] vi causer, discourir.

discourteous [dis'kəːtjəs] a discourtois, impoli.

discourtesy [dis'kəːtisi] n discourtoisie f, impolitesse f.

discover [dis'kʌvə] vt découvrir, révéler, s'apercevoir (de), constater.

discovery [dis'kʌvəri] n révélation f, découverte f, trouvaille f.

discredit [dis'kredit] n déconsidération f, discrédit m, doute m; vt discréditer, déconsidérer, mettre en doute.

discreditable [dis'kreditəbl] a indigne, déshonorant.

discreet [dis'kri:t] a discret, prudent.

discrepancy [dis'krepənsi] n désaccord m, inconsistance f, écart m.

discretion [dis'krefən] n prudence f, discrétion f, choix m.

discriminate [dis'krimineit] vt distinguer.

discriminating [dis'krimineitiŋ] a sagace, avisé, fin.

discrimination [dis,krimi'neifən] n finesse f, goût m, discernement m.

discuss [dis'kʌs] vt discuter, délibérer, débattre.

discussion [dis'kʌfən] n discussion f.

disdain [dis'dein] n dédain m; vt dédaigner.

disdainful [dis'deinful] a dédaigneux.

disease [di'zi:z] n maladie f, affection f.

diseased [di'zi:zd] a malade; — mind esprit morbide m.

disembark ['disim'ba:k] vti débarquer.

disembarkation [,disemba:'keifən] n débarquement m.

disembody ['disim'bɔdi] vt désincarner, désincorporer, licencier.

disembowel [,disim'bauəl] vt éventrer.

disengage ['disin'geidʒ] vt dégager, rompre, débrayer, déclencher; vi se dégager, rompre.

disengaged ['disin'geidʒd] a libre, visible.

disengagement ['disin'geidʒmənt] n dégagement m, rupture f.

disentangle ['disin'tæŋgl] vt débrouiller, démêler, dépêtrer.

disentanglement ['disin'tæŋglmənt] n débrouillement m, démêlage m.

disfavor [dis'feivə] n défaveur f, disgrâce f.

disfigure [dis'figə] vt défigurer, gâter.

disfranchise ['dis'fræntfaiz] vt priver de droits politiques, de représentation parlementaire.

disgorge [dis'gɔ:dʒ] vt rendre, dégorger; vi se jeter.

disgrace [dis'greis] n disgrâce f, honte f; vt disgrâcier, déshonorer.

disgraceful [dis'greisful] a honteux, scandaleux.

disgruntled [dis'grʌntld] a mécontent, bougon.

disguise [dis'gaiz] n déguisement m, feinte f; in — déguisé; vt déguiser, travestir.

disgust [dis'gʌst] n dégoût m; vt dégoûter, écœurer.

disgusting [dis'gʌstiŋ] a dégoûtant, dégueulasse.

dish [dif] n plat m, mets m, récipient m, bol m; vt servir, supplanter, rouler, déjouer.

dish-cloth ['difklɔθ] n lavette f, torchon m.

dish-cover ['dif kʌvə] n couvre-plat m.

dishearten [dis'ha:tn] vt décourager, démoraliser.

disheveled [di'fevəld] a débraillé, dépeigné.

dishonest [dis'ɔnist] a malhonnête, déloyal.

dishonesty [dis'ɔnisti] n malhonnêteté f, improbité f.

dishonor [dis'ɔnə] n déshonneur m; vt déshonorer.

dishonorable [dis'ɔnərəbl] a déshonorant, sans honneur.

dishwasher ['dif wɔfə] n plongeur m.

dishwater ['dif wɔ:tə] n eau de vaisselle f.

disillusion [,disi'lu:ʒən] vt désillusionner, désabuser.

disillusionment [,disi'lu:ʒənmənt] n désenchantement m, désillusionnement m.

disinclination [,disinkli'neifən] n aversion f, répugnance f.

disinfect [,disin'fekt] vt désinfecter.

disinfectant [,disin'fektənt] an désinfectant m.

disinfection [,disin'fekfən] n désinfection f.

disingenuous [,disin'dʒenjuəs] a faux.

disingenuousness [,disin'dʒenjuəsnis] n fausseté f.

disinherit [disin'herit] vt déshériter.

disintegrate [dis'intigreit] vt désintégrer, désagréger; vi se désintégrer, se désagréger.

disintegration [dis,inti'greifən] n désintégration f, désagrégation f.

disinterested [dis'intristid] a désintéressé.

disinterestedness [dis'intristidnis] n désintéressement m.

disjoin [dis'dʒɔin] vt disjoindre, désunir.

disjoint [dis'dʒɔint] vt disjoindre, disloquer, démettre, désarticuler.

disjointed [dis'dʒɔintid] a disloqué, décousu, incohérent.

dislike [dis'laik] n antipathie f; vt ne pas aimer, trouver antipathique, détester.

dislodge [dis'bdʒ] vt déloger, détacher, dénicher.

disloyal ['dis'biəl] a déloyal, infidèle.

disloyalty ['dis'biəlti] n déloyauté f, infidélité f.

dismal [dizməl] a morne, lugubre.

dismantle [dis'mæntl] vt démanteler, démonter.

dismantling [dis'mæntliŋ] n démantèlement m, démontage m.

dismay [dis'mei] n consternation f, épouvante f, gêne f; vt effrayer, consterner, affoler.

dismember [dis'membə] *vt* démembrer.

dismiss [dis'mis] *vt* renvoyer, congédier, révoquer, rejeter, écarter, acquitter.

dismissal [dis'misəl] *n* renvoi *m*, révocation *f*, acquittement *m*.

disobedience [.disə'bi:djəns] *n* désobéissance *f*.

disobedient [.disə'bi:djənt] *a* désobéissant.

disobey [.disə'bei] *vt* désobéir à; *vi* désobéir.

disoblige [.disə'blaidʒ] *vt* désobliger.

disobliging [.disə'blaidʒiŋ] *a* désobligeant.

disorder [dis'ɔ:də] *n* désordre *m*, confusion *f*.

disorderly [dis'ɔ:dəli] *a* désordonné, turbulent, déréglé, en désordre.

disorganization [dis.ɔ:gənai'zeiʃən] *n* désorganisation *f*.

disorganize [dis'ɔ:gənaiz] *vt* désorganiser.

disown [dis'oun] *vt* désavouer, renier.

disparage [dis'pæridʒ] *vt* dénigrer déprécier.

disparagement [dis'pæridʒmənt] *n* dénigrement *m*, dépréciation *f*.

disparity [dis'pæriti] *n* inégalité *f*, différence *f*.

dispassionate [dis'pæʃnit] *a* calme, impartial, désintéressé.

dispatch [dis'pætʃ] *n* envoi *m*, rapidité *f*, dépêche *f*, expédition *f*, promptitude *f*; *vt* expédier, envoyer, dépêcher.

dispatch-rider [dis'pætʃ.raidə] *n* estafette *f*.

dispel [dis'pel] *vt* dissiper, chasser.

dispensary [dis'pensəri] *n* dispensaire *m*, pharmacie *f*.

dispensation [.dispen'seiʃən] *n* distribution *f*, dispensation *f*, dispense *f*.

dispense [dis'pens] *vt* distribuer, administrer; *vi* se dispenser (de with), se passer (de with).

disperse [dis'pə:s] *vt* disperser, dissiper; *vi* se disperser.

dispersion [dis'pə:ʃən] *n* dispersion *f*.

dispirit [dis'pirit] *vt* décourager.

displace [dis'pleis] *vt* déplacer, remplacer.

displacement [dis'pleismənt] *n* déplacement *m*.

display [dis'plei] *n* déploiement *m*, étalage *m*, parade *f*, manifestation *f*, montre *f*; *vt* déployer, faire parade, (montre, preuve) de, manifester, afficher.

displease [dis'pli:z] *vt* déplaire à, mécontenter.

displeasure [dis'pleʒə] *n* déplaisir *m*, mécontentement *m*.

disport [dis'pɔ:t] *vr* se divertir.

disposal [dis'pouzəl] *n* disposition *f*, vente *f*, cession *f*.

dispose [dis'pouz] *vt* disposer,

arranger, expédier; *vi* se disposer (de of), se débarasser (de of).

dispossess [.dispə'zes] *vt* déposséder.

dispossession [.dispə'zeʃən] *n* dépossession *f*.

disproof [dis'pru:f] *n* réfutation *f*.

disproportion [.disprə'pɔ:ʃən] *n* disproportion *f*.

disproportionate [.disprə'pɔ:ʃnit] *a* disproportionné.

disprove [dis'pru:v] *vt* réfuter.

disputable [dis'pju:təbl] *a* discutable, contestable.

dispute [dis'pju:t] *n* dispute *f*, discussion *f*; *vt* discuter, débattre, contester; *vi* se disputer.

disqualification [dis.kwɔlifi'keiʃən] *n* disqualification *f*, inhabilité *f*.

disqualify [dis'kwɔlifai] *vt* disqualifier.

disquiet [dis'kwaiət] *n* inquiétude *f*; *vt* inquiéter.

disregard [.disri'gɑ:d] *n* indifférence *f*, mépris *m*; *vt* laisser de côté, ne tenir aucun compte de, mépriser.

disregarding [.disri'gɑ:diŋ] *prep* sans égard à (pour).

disrepair [.disri'pɛə] *n* délabrement *m*.

disreputable [dis'repjutəbl] *a* déconsidéré, de mauvaise réputation, minable.

disrepute ['disri'pju:t] *n* mauvaise réputation *f*, discrédit *m*.

disrespect ['disris'pekt] *n* manque de respect *m*.

disrespectful [.disris'pektful] *a* irrespectueux, irrévérencieux.

disruption [dis'rʌpʃən] *n* dislocation *f*, scission *f*, démembrement *m*.

dissatisfaction ['dis.sætis'fækʃən] *n* mécontentement *m*.

dissatisfy [dis'sætisfai] *vt* mécontenter.

dissect [di'sekt] *vt* disséquer.

dissection [di'sekʃən] *n* dissection *f*.

dissemble [di'sembl] *vt* dissimuler.

dissembler [di'semblə] *n* hypocrite *mf*.

disseminate [di'semineit] *vt* disséminer.

dissemination [di.semi'neiʃən] *n* dissémination *f*.

dissension [di'senʃən] *n* dissension *f*.

dissent [di'sent] *n* dissentiment *m*, dissidence *f*; *vi* différer.

dissenter [di'sentə] *n* dissident *m*.

dissipate ['disipeit] *vt* dissiper; *vi* se dissiper.

dissipation [.disi'peiʃən] *n* dissipation *f*, dispersion *f*, gaspillage *m*, dérèglement *m*.

dissolute ['disəlu:t] *a* dissolu, débauché.

dissoluteness ['disəlu:tnis] *n* dérèglement *m*, débauche *f*.

dissolution [.disə'lu:ʃən] *n* dissolution *f*, dissipation *f*.

dissolve [di'zɔlv] *vt* dissoudre; *vi* se dissoudre.

dissolvent [di'zɔlvənt] *an* dissolvant m.

distaff ['distɑːf] *n* quenouille *f*.

distance ['distəns] *n* distance *f*, lointain *m*, intervalle *m*, éloignement *m*.

distant ['distənt] *a* éloigné, lointain, distant, réservé.

distaste ['dis'teist] *n* répugnance *f*, aversion *f*.

distasteful [dis'teistful] *a* répugnant, antipathique.

distemper [dis'tempə] *n* maladie *f* (des chiens), badigeon *m*, détrempe *f*; *vt* badigeonner.

distend [dis'tend] *vt* gonfler, dilater; *vi* enfler, se dilater.

distill [dis'til] *vti* distiller; *vi* s'égoutter, se distiller.

distillation [.disti'leiʃən] *n* distillation *f*.

distiller [dis'tilə] *n* distillateur *m*.

distillery [dis'tiləri] *n* distillerie *f*.

distinct [dis'tiŋkt] *a* distinct, net, clair.

distinction [dis'tiŋkʃən] *n* distinction *f*.

distinctive [dis'tiŋktiv] *a* distinctif.

distinctness [dis'tiŋktnis] *n* netteté *f*.

distinguish [dis'tiŋgwiʃ] *vt* distinguer; *vi* faire la distinction.

distinguishable [dis'tiŋgwiʃəbl] *a* perceptible, sensible.

distort [dis'tɔːt] *vt* déformer, travestir, tordre, convulser, fausser.

distract [dis'trækt] *vt* distraire, détourner, diviser, déranger.

distracted [dis'træktid] *a* fou, furieux, affolé.

distraction [dis'trækʃən] *n* distraction *f*, dérangement *m*, folie *f*, affolement *m*.

distress [dis'tres] *n* détresse *f*, dénuement *m*, misère *f*, angoisse *f*; *vt* tourmenter, affliger, épuiser.

distribute [dis'tribjuːt] *vt* distribuer, répartir.

distribution [.distri'bjuːʃən] *n* distribution *f*, répartition *f*.

district ['distrikt] *n* district *m*, région *f*.

distrust [dis'trʌst] *n* méfiance *f*; *vt* se méfier de.

distrustful [dis'trʌstful] *a* méfiant, soupçonneux.

disturb [dis'təːb] *vt* troubler, agiter, déranger.

disturbance [dis'təːbəns] *n* trouble *m*, bagarre *f*, émeute *f*, tapage *m*.

disunion [dis'juːnjən] *n* désunion *f*.

disuse ['dis'juːs] *n* désuétude *f*.

disused [dis'juːzd] *a* hors de service, hors d'usage.

ditch [ditʃ] *n* tranchée *f*, fossé *m*; *vt* creuser, drainer; faire dérailler (train); to — be é échouer, être dans le pétrin.

ditcher ['ditʃə] *n* fossoyeur *m*.

ditto ['ditou] *an* idem, amen.

ditty ['diti] *n* chanson (nette) *f*.

divagate ['daivəgeit] *vi* divaguer.

divagation [.daivə'geiʃən] *n* divagation *f*.

divan [di'væn] *n* divan *m*; —bed divan-lit *m*.

dive [daiv] *n* plongeon *m*, plongée *f*, pique *m*; *vi* se plonger, piquer (une tête, du nez).

diver ['daivə] *n* plongeur *m*, scaphandrier *m*.

diverge [dai'vəːdʒ] *vi* diverger, s'écarter.

divergence [dai'vəːdʒəns] *n* divergence *f*.

diverse [dai'vəːs] *a* divers, différent.

diversify [dai'vəːsifai] *vt* diversifier.

diversion [dai'vəːʃən] *n* diversion *f*, divertissement *m*, détournement *m*.

divert [dai'vəːt] *vt* détourner, divertir, écarter, distraire.

divest [dai'vest] *vt* dévêtir, dépouiller, priver.

divide [di'vaid] *vt* partager, diviser; *vi* aller aux voix, se diviser, se partager, fourcher.

dividend ['dividend] *n* dividende *m*.

dividers [di'vaidəz] *n* compas *m*.

divine [di'vain] *n* théologien *m*, prêtre *m*; *a* divin; *vt* deviner, prédire.

diviner [di'vainə] *n* devin *m*, sourcier *m*.

diving ['daiviŋ] *n* (*sport*) plongeon *m*, (*av*) piqué *m*; — board plongeoire *m*.

divinity [di'viniti] *n* divinité *f*, théologie *f*.

division [di'viʒən] *n* division *f*, partage *m*, répartition *f*, frontière *f*, vote *m*.

divorce [di'vɔːs] *n* divorce *m*; *vt* divorcer.

divulge [dai'vʌldʒ] *vt* divulguer.

divulgement [dai'vʌldʒmənt] *n* divulgation *f*.

dizziness ['dizinis] *n* vertige *m*, étourdissement *m*.

dizzy ['dizi] *a* étourdi, vertigineux.

do [duː] *vt* faire, finir, cuire à point, rouler, refaire; *vi* se porter, aller, s'acquitter; to — away with supprimer, abolir, tuer; to — up remettre à neuf, retaper.

docile ['dousail] *a* docile.

docility [dou'siliti] *n* docilité *f*.

dock [dɔk] *n* bassin *m*, dock *m*, cale *f*, banc *m* des accusés, box *m*; *vt* mettre en bassin; *vi* entrer au bassin.

docker ['dɔkə] *n* débardeur *m*.

docket ['dɔkit] *n* bordereau *m*, fiche *f*, étiquette *f*; *vt* classer, étiqueter.

dockyard ['dɔkjɑːd] *n* chantier maritime *m*.

doctor ['dɔktə] *n* docteur *m*, médecin *m*; *vt* soigner, falsifier, cuisiner, doper, truquer, maquiller.

document ['dɔkjumənt] *n* document *m*; —case porte-documents *m*.

documentary [ˌdɔkju'mentəri] a
documentaire
documentation [ˌdɔkjumen'teiʃən]
n documentation f.
dodge [dɔdʒ] n tour m, faux-fuyant
m, truc m, esquive f; vi se jeter de
côté, s'esquiver, finasser; vt esquiver,
éviter, tourner, éluder.
dodger [dɔdʒə] n finaud m, tire-au-
flanc m.
doe [dou] n daine f, lapine f.
doff [dɔf] vt ôter.
dog [dɔg] n chien m, chenet m,
gaillard m; **dirty——** salaud m;
——-tired (fam) claqué.
dog-days [dɔgdeiz] n canicule f.
dogged [dɔgid] a tenace.
doggedness [dɔgidnis] n ténacité f,
persévérance f.
doggerel [dɔgərəl] n poésie burlesque f; a trivial, boiteux, de
mirliton.
dogma [dɔgmə] n dogme m.
dogmatic [dɔg'mætik] a dogmatique,
tranchant.
dog's ear [dɔgz'iə] n corne f; vt faire
une corne à, corner.
doily [dɔili] n napperon m.
doings [du:iŋz] n pl faits et gestes
m pl, agissements m pl, exploits
m pl.
doldrums [dɔldrəmz] n pl to be in
the — avoir le cafard, être dans le
marasme.
dole [doul] n don m, aumône f,
allocation de chômage f; to — out
vt donner au compte-goutte.
doleful [doulful] a triste sombre,
dolent, lugubre.
doll [dɔl] n poupée f.
dolphin [dɔlfin] n dauphin m.
dolt [doult] n niais m, sot m.
domain [də'mein] n domaine m,
propriété f.
dome [doum] n dôme m, coupole f.
domestic [də'mestik] an domestique
mf; a d'intérieur, national, de
ménage.
domesticate [də'mestikeit] vt do-
mestiquer, apprivoiser.
domesticated [də'mestikeitid] a
soumis, d'intérieur.
domesticity [ˌdɔmes'tisiti] n amour
m du foyer, vie privée f, soumission
f.
domicile [dɔmisail] n domicile m.
dominate [dɔmineit] vti dominer;
vt commander.
domination [ˌdɔmi'neiʃən] n domination f.
domineer [ˌdɔmi'niə] vt tyranniser.
domineering [ˌdɔmi'niəriŋ] a
dominateur, autoritaire.
Dominican [də'minikən] an domini-
cain(e) mf.
dominion [də'minjən] n domination
f, empire m; pl dominions m pl,
colonies f pl.
don [dɔn] vt enfiler, endosser, revêtir;
n professeur m.

donation [dou'neiʃən] n donation f,
don m.
done [dʌn] pp of do; a fourbu, fini,
conclu! tope là, cuit à point; over—
trop cuit; under— saignant; well
—! bravo! bien cuit.
donkey [dɔŋki] n âne m, baudet m.
donor [dounə] n donateur, -trice.
doom [du:m] n jugement m (dernier),
ruine f, malheur m, sort m; vt condamner, vouer, perdre.
door [dɔː] n porte f, portière f.
doorkeeper [dɔːˌki:pə] n concierge
mf, portier m.
doormat [dɔːmæt] n paillasson.
doorstep [dɔːstep] n pas m, seuil m.
dope [doup] n narcotique m, stupéfiant m, tuyau m, bourrage de
crâne m; vt droguer, doper, endormir.
dormer [dɔːmə] n lucarne f.
dormitory [dɔːmitri] n dortoir m.
dormouse [dɔːmaus] n loir m.
Dorothy [dɔrəθi] Dorothée f.
dose [dous] n dose f; vt doser,
droguer.
dot [dɔt] n point m; vt mettre les
points sur, semer, pointiller, piquer.
dotage [doutidʒ] n radotage m,
seconde enfance f.
dotard [doutəd] n gaga m, gâteux
m.
dote [dout] vt radoter, raffoler (de
on).
double [dʌbl] n double m, crochet
m, sosie m; a double; ad double
(ment), deux fois, à double sens, en
partie double; vt doubler, plier en
deux; vi (se) doubler, prendre le pas
de gymnastique.
double-clutch [ˌdʌbl'klʌtʃ] vi (aut)
faire un double débrayage.
double-dealer [ˌdʌbl'di:lə] n fourbe
m.
double-dealing [dʌbl'di:liŋ] m duplicité f.
double-dyed [dʌbl'daid] a fieffé,
achevé.
double-edged [dʌbl'edʒd] a à deux
tranchants.
double-lock [dʌbl'lɔk] vt fermer à
double tour.
double-quick [dʌbl'kwik] ad au pas
de course.
doubt [daut] n doute m; vt douter.
doubtful [dautful] a douteux, incertain.
doubtless [dautlis] ad sans doute.
dough [dou] n pâte f; (sl) fric m.
doughnut [dounʌt] n beignet soufflé
m, pet de nonne m.
doughy [doui] a pâteux.
dour [duə] a sévère, obstiné, buté.
dove [dʌv] n colombe f.
dovecot [dʌvkɔt] n colombier m.
dovetail [dʌvteil] n queue d'aronde
f; vi s'encastrer; vt encastrer,
assembler à queue d'aronde.
dowager [dauədʒə] n douairière f.

dowdy ['daudi] *a* mal fagoté.
down [daun] *n* dune *f*; duvet m; bas m; *a* en bas, en pente, descendant; *prep* au (en) bas de; *ad* en bas, en aval, à bas! comptant, par écrit, en baisse; *vt* abattre, terrasser, descendre.
down-and-outer ['daunǝn'autǝ] *n* pouilleux m, miséreux.
downcast ['daunkɑːst] *a* abattu, déprimé.
downfall ['daunfɔːl] *n* chute *f*, ruine *f*.
downhearted ['daun'hɑːtid] *a* découragé, abattu.
downpour ['daunpɔː] *n* déluge m, forte pluie *f*.
downright ['daunrait] *a* franc, droit, net; *ad* carrément, catégoriquement; tout à fait.
downstairs ['daun'steǝz] *ad* en bas.
downtrodden ['daun'trɔdn] *a* opprimé, foulé aux pieds.
downward ['daunwǝd] *ad* en aval, en descendant.
downy ['dauni] *a* duveté.
dowry ['dauri] *n* dot *f*, douaire m.
doze [douz] *n* somme m; *vi* sommeiller, s'assoupir.
dozen ['dazn] *n* douzaine *f*.
drab [dræb] *a* brunâtre, terne, ennuyeux, prosaïque.
draft [drɑːft] *n* détachement m, traite *f*, effet m, tracé m, brouillon m, projet m; conscription *f*, n traction *f*, courant d'air m, tirant d'eau m, coup m (de vin *etc*), esquisse *f*, traite *f*; *pl* jeu de dames m; on — à la pression; *vt* détacher, désigner, esquisser, rédiger.
draft horse ['drɑːfthɔːs] *n* cheval m de trait.
draftsman ['drɑːftsmǝn] *n* dessinateur m, rédacteur m.
drag [dræg] *n* drague *f*, herse *f*, traineau m, obstacle m, grappin m, sabot m, résistance *f*; *vt* draguer, (en)trainer; *vi* tirer, trainer.
dragon ['drægǝn] *n* dragon m.
dragonfly ['drægǝnflai] *n* libellule *f*.
dragoon [drǝ'guːn] *n* dragon m; *vt* persécuter, contraindre.
drain [drein] *n* fossé m. caniveau m, égout m, perte *f*, (*fig*) saignée *f*; *vt* drainer, assécher, assainir; *vi* s'écouler, s'égoutter.
drake [dreik] *n* canard m.
drama ['drɑːmǝ] *n* drame m, le théâtre m.
dramatic [drǝ'mætik] *a* dramatique.
dramatist ['dræmǝtist] *n* dramaturge m.
dramatize ['dræmǝtaiz] *vt* mettre au théâtre, adapter à la scène, dramatiser.
drank ['dræŋk] *pt* of **drink**.
drape [dreip] *vt* draper.
draper ['dreipǝ] *n* drapier m, marchand m de nouveautés.
drapery ['dreipǝri] *n* draperie *f*.

drastic ['dræstik] *a* radical, énergique.
draw [drɔː] *n* tirage m, partie nulle *f*, question insidieuse *f*, loterie *f*, clou m, attraction *f*; *vt* (at-, re)tirer, trainer, tendre, aspirer, (*tooth*) extraire, (*salary*) toucher, faire parler, dessiner, rédiger; to — **aside** *vt* écarter, tirer; vi s'écarter; to — **back** *vt* retirer; *vi* reculer; to — **up** *vt* (re)lever, approcher; *vi* s'arrêter.
drawback ['drɔːbæk] *n* remise *f*, mécompte m, échec m, inconvénient m.
drawbridge ['drɔːbridʒ] *n* pont-levis m.
drawer ['drɔːǝ] *n* tiroir m; *pl* caleçon m, pantalon m de femme.
drawing ['drɔːiŋ] *n* dessin m.
drawing-board ['drɔːiŋbɔːd] *n* planche *f*.
drawing-pin ['drɔːiŋpin] *n* punaise *f*.
drawing-room ['drɔːiŋrum] *n* salon m.
drawl [drɔːl] *n* voix trainante *f*; *vt* trainer; *vi* parler d'une voix trainante
drawn [drɔːn] *pp* of **draw**; *a* tiré, nul.
dray [drei] *n* camion m, haquet m.
dread [dred] *n* effroi m; *vt* redouter.
dreadful ['dredful] *a* terrible, horrible
dreadnought ['drednɔːt] *n* cuirassé m.
dream [driːm] *n* rêve m, songe m; *vt* rêver.
dreamer ['driːmǝ] *n* rêveur, -euse, songe-creux m.
dreamy ['driːmi] *a* rêveur, songeur, vague.
dreary ['driǝri] *a* lugubre, morne, ennuyeux, terne.
dredge [dredʒ] *n* drague *f*; *vt* draguer, curer, saupoudrer.
dredger ['dredʒǝ] *n* curemôle m, drague *f*.
dregs [dregz] *n* lie *f*.
drench [drentʃ] *vt* tremper, mouiller.
dress [dres] *n* vêtement m, tenue *f*, costume m, robe *f*, toilette *f*; full — grande tenue; badly —ed mal mis m, mal mise *f*; well —ed bien mis m, bien mise *f*; *vt* habiller, vêtir, coiffer, pavoiser, aligner, parer, panser, tailler; *vi* s'habiller, faire sa toilette, se mettre (en habit), s'aligner; to get —ed s'habiller.
dress-circle ['dres'sǝːkl] *n* fauteuils m *pl* de balcon.
dresser ['dresǝ] *n* dressoir m, habilleuse *f*, apprêteur, -euse; commode-toilette *f*.
dressing ['dresiŋ] *n* habillage m, toilette *f*, pansement m, assaisonnement m, apprêt m, alignement m; (*naut*) pavoisement m.
dressing-case ['dresiŋkeis] *n* nécessaire m de toilette.

dressing-down ['dresiŋ'daun] n semonce f, savonnage m.

dressing-gown ['dresiŋgaun] n robe f de chambre, peignoir m.

dressing-room ['dresiŋrum] n cabinet m de toilette.

dressing-table ['dresiŋ‚teibl] n coiffeuse f.

dressmaker ['dres‚meikə] n couturier, -ière.

dressy ['dresi] a élégant, chic, qui aime la toilette.

drew [dru:] pt of draw.

dribble ['dribl] n goutte f, dégouttement m, dribble m; vi dégoutter, baver, dribbler.

drift [drift] n débâcle f, dérive f, laisser-aller m, direction f, portée f, amas m; vi être emporté, dériver, s'amasser, se laisser aller; vt flotter, charrier.

drifter ['driftə] n chalutier m.

drill [dril] n foret m, mèche f, perforateur m, perceuse f, sillon m, semoir m, exercice m, manœuvre f; — sergeant sergent instructeur m; vt forer, semer, instruire, faire faire l'exercice à; vi faire l'exercice, manœuvrer.

drink [driŋk] n boisson f, alcool m, un verre m, ivrognerie f, boire m; vt boire.

drinkable ['driŋkəbl] a buvable, potable.

drinker ['driŋkə] n buveur, -euse, alcoolique mf.

drinking ['driŋkiŋ] n boire m, boisson f; —water eau f potable f.

drip [drip] vt verser goutte à goutte; vi s'égoutter, dégoutter, dégouliner, suinter; n (d)égouttement m, dégoulinement m.

dripping ['dripiŋ] n graisse (à frire) f, (d)égouttement m; — pan lèchefrite f.

drive [draiv] n avance f, poussée f, randonnée f, promenade f, avenue f, tendance f, mouvement m, énergie f; vt pousser, entraîner, conduire, chasser, forcer, surmener, actionner; vi se promener, chasser, conduire; **driving school** auto-école f.

drivel ['drivl] n bave f, roupie f, radotage m; vi radoter, baver.

driver ['draivə] n mécanicien m, conducteur m, chauffeur, -euse.

drizzle ['drizl] n bruine f; vi bruiner.

droll [droul] a drôle.

drollery ['drouləri] n drôlerie f, bouffonnerie f.

dromedary ['drɔmədəri] n dromadaire m.

drone [droun] n bourdon m, bourdonnement m, ronronnement m, fainéant m; vi bourdonner, ronronner.

droop [dru:p] n attitude penchée f, découragement m; vt laisser tomber, pendre, (a)baisser, pencher; vi languir, se pencher, retomber, s'affaisser.

drop [drɔp] n goutte f, pastille f, chute f, baisse f, rideau m, pendant m; vi s'égoutter, se laisser tomber, tomber, plonger, baisser; vt laisser tomber, baisser, lâcher, abandonner, laisser, verser goutte à goutte; to — in entrer en passant; to — off partir, s'endormir.

dropsy ['drɔpsi] n hydropisie f.

drought [draut] n sécheresse f.

drove [drouv] n troupeau m, foule f.

drover ['drouvə] n toucheur de bœufs m.

drown [draun] vt noyer, tremper, inonder, couvrir; vi se noyer.

drowsiness ['drauzinis] n somnolence f.

drowsy ['drauzi] a assoupi, endormi, soporifique.

drubbing ['drʌbiŋ] n (fam) raclée f, tripotée f.

drudge [drʌdʒ] n tâcheron m, femme de peine f, souffre-douleur mf; vi trimer.

drudgery ['drʌdʒəri] n corvée f, travail ingrat m.

drug [drʌg] n drogue f, stupéfiant m, (fig) rossignol m; vt droguer, endormir.

druggist ['drʌgist] n droguiste m, pharmacien m.

drum [drʌm] n tympan m; bonbonne f, tambour m; big — grosse caisse; African — tam-tam m.

drummer ['drʌmə] n tambour m.

drum-fire ['drʌm'faiə] m feu roulant m.

drumming ['drʌmiŋ] n bourdonnement m, battement m, tambourinage m.

drunk [drʌŋk] pp of drink; a ivre, saoûl.

drunkard ['drʌŋkəd] n ivrogne, ivrognesse.

drunkenness ['drʌŋkənnis] n ivresse f, ivrognerie f.

dry [drai] a sec, à sec, tari, caustique; n prohibitionniste m; vt (faire) sécher, essuyer; vi sécher, se dessécher, tarir.

dryness ['drainis] n sécheresse f.

dub [dʌb] vt armer, traiter (de), doubler.

dubious ['dju:bjəs] a douteux, louche, incertain.

duchess ['dʌtʃis] n duchesse f.

duchy ['dʌtʃi] n duché m.

duck [dʌk] n canard m, cane f, plongeon m, courbette f, esquive f, coutil m; vti plonger; vi se baisser, esquiver de la tête.

duckling ['dʌkliŋ] n caneton m.

duct [dʌkt] n conduit m, conduite f.

dud [dʌd] n raté m; pl nippes f pl; a moche, faux.

dudgeon ['dʌdʒən] n colère f.

due [dju:] n dû m, dettes f pl, droits m pl; a dû, attendu.

duel ['djuəl] *n* duel *m*; *vi* se battre en duel.

duelist ['djuəlist] *n* duelliste *m*, bretteur *m*.

duet [dju'et] *n* duo *m*.

duffer ['dʌfə] *n* cancre *m*, empoté(e) *mf*, maladroit(e) *mf*.

dug [dʌg] *pt pp of* **dig**; *n* pis *m*, téton *m*.

dug-out ['dʌgaut] *n* trou *m*, abri *m*, cagna *m*.

duke [dju:k] *n* duc *m*.

dull [dʌl] *a* ennuyeux, stupide, insensible, émoussé, terne, sourd, mat, sombre; *vt* amortir, émousser, ternir, hébéter.

dullard ['dʌləd] *n* balourd(e) *mf*, cancre *m*.

dullness ['dʌlnis] *n* hébétude *f*, lourdeur *f*, monotonie *f*, marasme *m*.

duly ['dju:li] *ad* dûment, à point.

dumb [dʌm] *a* muet, sot; **—bell** haltère *f*; **— show** pantomime *f*.

dumbfounded [dʌm'faundid] *a* éberlué, interdit.

dumbness ['dʌmnis] *n* mutisme *m*.

dummy ['dʌmi] *n* homme de paille *m*, mannequin *m*, silhouette *f*, mort *m*, *(of baby)* sucette *f*, maquette *f*; *a* faux, postiche.

dump [dʌmp] *n* dépôt *m* (de munitions), *(fam)* trou *m*; *vt* décharger, déposer (avec un bruit sourd); *vi* faire du dumping.

dumpling ['dʌmpliŋ] *n* chausson *m*.

dumps [dʌmps] *n pl* cafard *m*; to be in the **—s** avoir le cafard, broyer du noir.

dumpy ['dʌmpi] *a* trapu, replet, boulot.

dun [dʌn] *a* gris-brun; *vt* relancer, importuner.

dunce [dʌns] *n* endormi(e) *mf*, cancre *m*, crétin *m*; **—'s cap** bonnet *m* d'âne.

dung [dʌŋ] *n* bouse *f*, fiente *f*, crottin *m*.

dungeon ['dʌndʒən] *n* cul-de-basse-fosse *m*, cachot *m*.

dunghill ['dʌŋhil] *n* fumier *m*.

dunk ['dʌŋk] *vt* tremper; *vi* faire trempette.

dupe [dju:p] *n* dupe *f*; *vt* duper.

duplex ['dju:pleks] *a* double.

duplicate ['dju:plikit] *n* double *m*; *a* double de rechange.

duplicate ['dju:plikeit] *vt* établir en double.

duplicity [dju'plisiti] *n* duplicité *f*.

durable ['djuərəbl] *a* durable, résistant.

duration [djuə'reiʃən] *n* durée *f*.

duress [djuə'res] *n* contrainte *f*, emprisonnement *m*.

during ['djuəriŋ] *prep* pendant, au cours de.

durst [də:st] *pt (old) of* **dare**.

dusk [dʌsk] *n* crépuscule *m*.

dusky ['dʌski] *a* sombre, brun, foncé, noiraud.

dust [dʌst] *n* poussière *f*; *vt* saupoudrer, couvrir de poussière, épousseter; **— coat** cache-poussière *m*; **—jacket** protège-livre *m*.

dustbin ['dʌstbin] *n* boîte à ordures *f*, poubelle *f*.

duster ['dʌstə] *n* torchon *m*, chiffon à épousseter *m*.

dusty ['dʌsti] *a* poussiéreux, poudreux.

Dutch [dʌtʃ] *a* Hollandais; *n* Hollandais (*language*).

dutiable ['dju:tjəbl] *a* imposable, taxable.

dutiful ['dju:tiful] *a* respectueux, soumis.

duty ['dju:ti] *n* devoir *m*, taxe *f*, droits *m pl*; on **—** de service; **— paid** franco, franc de douane.

dwarf [dwɔ:f] *n* nain *m*.

dwell [dwel] *vi* demeurer, s'étendre (sur on).

dwelling ['dweliŋ] *n* maison *f*, demeure *f*.

dwelt [dwelt] *pt of* **dwell**.

dwindle ['dwindl] *vi* fondre, dépérir.

dye [dai] *n* teinte *f*, teinture *f*, teint *m*; **—works** teinturerie *f*; *vt* teindre, teinter; *vi* se teindre.

dyer ['daiə] *n* teinturier *m*.

dying ['daiiŋ] *a* mourant, de mort.

dynamite ['dainəmait] *n* dynamite *f*; *vt* faire sauter à la dynamite.

dynasty ['dinəsti] *n* dynastie *f*.

dysentery ['disntri] *n* dysenterie *f*.

dyspepsia [dis'pepsiə] *n* dyspepsie *f*.

dyspeptic [dis'peptik] *a* dyspeptique.

E

each [i:tʃ] *a* chaque; *pn* chacun(e); two francs **—** deux francs la pièce; **— other** l'un l'autre, entre eux.

eager ['i:gə] *a* empressé, ardent, avide, impatient.

eagerly ['i:gəli] *ad* ardemment, avec empressement.

eagerness ['i:gənis] *n* ardeur *f*, empressement *m*.

eagle ['i:gl] *n* aigle *m*.

eaglet ['i:glit] *n* aiglon *m*.

ear [iə] *n* oreille *f*, (corn) épi *m*, (tec) anse *f*.

ear-drop ['iədrɔp] *n* pendant d'oreille *m*.

ear-drum ['iədrʌm] *n* tympan *m*.

early ['ə:li] *a* matinal, précoce, prochain, premier; in **— summer** au début de l'été; *ad* de bonne heure, tôt.

ear-mark ['iəmɑ:k] *vt* réserver, assigner.

earn [ə:n] *vt* gagner.

earnest ['ə:nist] *n* présage *m*, (com) arrhes *f pl*, avant-goût *m*; *a* sérieux, sincère, consciencieux; in **—** pour de bon.

earnestly ['ə:nistli] *ad* sérieusement, instamment.

earnestness ['ə:nistnis] n sérieux m, sincérité f, ardeur f, ferveur f.
earnings ['ə:niŋz] n gain(s) m, gages m pl.
earring ['iəriŋ] n boucle f d'oreille.
earshot ['iəʃɔt] n portée f de la voix.
earth [ə:θ] n terre f, terrier m; vt relier au sol.
earthen ['ə:θən] a de (en) terre.
earthenware ['ə:θənwɛə] n faïence f, poterie f; — pot canari m.
earthliness ['ə:θlinis] n mondanité f.
earthly ['ə:θli] a terrestre.
earthquake ['ə:θkweik] n tremblement m de terre.
earthworks ['ə:θwə:ks] n terrassements m pl.
earthworm ['ə:θwə:m] n ver m de terre.
earthy ['ə:θi] a terreux.
ear-trumpet ['iə,trʌmpit] n cornet acoustique m.
earwig ['iəwig] n perce-oreille(s) m.
ease [i:z] n facilité f, tranquillité f, aise f, soulagement m; (mil) repos m; vt soulager, calmer, détendre; to — up ralentir, freiner, se relâcher.
easel ['i:zl] n chevalet m.
easily ['i:zili] ad facilement, aisément, tranquillement.
east [i:st] n est m, levant m, orient m; Near E— proche Orient; Middle E— moyen Orient; Far E— extrême Orient.
Easter ['i:stə] n Pâques f pl.
easterly ['i:stəli] a oriental, d'est; ad vers l'est.
eastern ['i:stən] a oriental, de l'est.
eastward ['i:stwəd] ad vers l'est; a à l'est.
easy ['i:zi] a facile, aisé, à l'aise, tranquille, accommodant, dégagé.
easy-chair ['i:zi'tʃɛə] n fauteuil m.
easy-going ['i:zi,gouiŋ] a débonnaire, qui ne s'en fait pas, accommodant.
eat [i:t] vt manger.
eatable ['i:təbl] a mangeable.
eatables ['i:təblz] n pl comestibles m pl, provisions f pl.
eaten ['i:tn] pp of eat; — up with dévoré de, consumé par, pétri de.
eating ['i:tiŋ] n manger m; a à croquer, de dessert.
eaves [i:vz] n avance f de toit.
eavesdrop ['i:vzdrɔp] vi écouter aux portes.
ebb [eb] n reflux m, déclin m; vi refluer, décliner.
E-boat ['i:bout] n vedette lance-torpilles f.
ebony ['ebəni] n ébène f.
ebullience [i'bʌljəns] n exubérance f, effervescence f.
ebullient [i'bʌljənt] a exubérant, bouillant.
ebullition [,ebə'liʃən] n ébullition f, effervescence f.
eccentric [ik'sentrik] a excentrique, original.

eccentricity [,eksen'trisiti] n excentricité f.
echo ['ekou] n écho m; vt faire écho à, se faire l'écho de, répéter; vi faire écho, retentir.
eclipse [i'klips] n éclipse f; vt éclipser.
economic [,i:kə'nɔmik] a économique.
economical [,i:kə'nɔmikəl] a économe, économique.
economics [,i:kə'nɔmiks] n économie politique f, régime économique m.
economist [i:'kɔnəmist] n économiste m.
economize [i:'kɔnəmaiz] vt économiser; vi faire des économies.
economy [i:'kɔnəmi] n économie f.
ecstasy ['ekstəsi] n extase f, transe f, ravissement m.
ecstatic [eks'tætik] a extatique, en extase.
eddy ['edi] n remous m, volute f, tourbillon m.
edge [edʒ] n bord m, bordure f, fil m, tranchant m; on — agacé, énervé; vt border, aiguiser; to — (in), to — one's way se faufiler (dans); to — away s'écarter tout doucement.
edgeless ['edʒlis] a émoussé.
edgeways ['edʒweiz] ad de côté, de champ; to get a word in — glisser un mot dans la conversation.
edible ['edibl] a mangeable, comestible, bon à manger.
edict ['i:dikt] n édit m.
edify ['edifai] vt édifier.
edit ['edit] vt éditer, rédiger.
edition [i'diʃən] n édition f.
editor ['editə] n éditeur m, rédacteur en chef m, directeur m.
editorial [,edi'tɔ:riəl] an éditorial m; n article de fond m.
educate ['edjukeit] vt instruire, élever, former; he was educated in Paris il a fait ses études à Paris.
education [,edju'keiʃən] n éducation f, instruction f, enseignement m.
educational [,edju'keiʃənl] a d'enseignement, éducateur.
educative ['edjukeitiv] a éducatif.
educator ['edjukeitə] n éducateur, -trice.
Edward ['edwəd] Edouard m.
eel [i:l] n anguille f.
eerie ['iəri] a étrange, fantastique, surnaturel.
efface [i'feis] vt effacer, oblitérer.
effect [i'fekt] n effet m, influence f, conséquence f; of no — inutile, inefficace; to no — en vain; for — à effet; to the same — dans le même sens; in — en fait, en réalité; vt exécuter, accomplir.
effective [i'fektiv] n effectif m; a effectif, efficace, valide.
effectively [i'fektivli] ad en réalité, efficacement.
effectiveness [i'fektivnis] n efficacité f.

effeminate [i'feminit] *a* efféminé.
effervesce [.efə'ves] *vi* bouillonner, mousser.
effervescence [.efə'vesns] *n* effervescence *f*.
effete [e'fi:t] *a* épuisé, caduc.
efficacious [.efi'keiʃəs] *a* efficace.
efficaciousness [.efi'keiʃəsnis] *n* efficacité *f*.
efficacy ['efikəsi] *n* efficacité *f*, rapidité *f*.
efficiency [i'fiʃənsi] *n* efficience *f*, efficacité *f*, rendement *m*, capacité *f*, valeur *f*.
efficient [i'fiʃənt] *a* efficace, compétent, effectif, capable
efficiently [i'fiʃəntli] *ad* efficacement.
effigy ['efidʒi] *n* effigie *f*.
effort ['efət] *n* effort *m*.
effortless ['efətlis] *a* sans effort, passif, facile.
effrontery [e'frʌntəri] *n* effronterie *f*.
effulgence [e'fʌldʒəns] *n* éclat *m*, splendeur *f*.
effulgent [e'fʌldʒənt] *a* resplendissant, éclatant.
effusion [i'fju:ʒən] *n* effusion *f*, épanchement *m*.
effusive [i'fju:siv] *a* expansif, démonstratif.
effusiveness [i'fju:sivnis] *n* exubérance *f*, effusion *f*.
egg [eg] *n* œuf *m*; new-laid — œuf frais; boiled — œuf à la coque; hard-boiled — œuf dur; soft-boiled — œuf mollet; fried — œuf sur le plat; poached — œuf poché; scrambled —s œufs brouillés; *vt* to — on encourager.
egg-cup ['egkʌp] *n* coquetier *m*.
egg-spoon ['egspu:n] *n* petite cuiller *f*.
egg-whisk ['egwisk] *n* fouet *m*.
eglantine ['egləntain] *n* églantine *f*, églantier *m*.
ego ['egou] *n* le moi.
egoist ['egouist] *n* égoïste *mf*.
egregious [i'gri:dʒəs] *a* énorme, insigne.
egret ['i:gret] *n* aigrette *f*.
Egyptian [i'dʒipʃən] *an* égyptien.
eiderdown ['aidədaun] *n* édredon *m*.
eight [eit] *an* huit *m*.
eighteen ['ei'ti:n] *an* dixhuit *m*.
eighteenth ['ei'ti:nθ] *an* dixhuit *m*, dix-huitième *mf*.
eighth [eitθ] *an* huit *m*, huitième *mf*.
eightieth ['eitiiθ] *an* quatre-vingts *m*, quatre-vingtième *mf*.
eighty ['eiti] *an* quatre-vingts *m*.
either ['aiðə] *pn* l'un et (ou) l'autre; *a* chaque; on — side de chaque côté; *cj* ou, soit, non plus; — ... or ou ... ou, soit ... soit; not ... — ne ... non plus.
eject [i'dʒekt] *vt* jeter (dehors), expulser, émettre.
eke out ['i:k 'aut] *vt* ajouter à, compléter, faire durer.
elaborate [i'læbəreit] *vt* élaborer.

elaborate [i'læbərit] *a* compliqué, soigné, tiré, recherché.
elaboration [i.læbə'reiʃən] *n* élaboration *f*.
elapse [i'læps] *vi* s'écouler.
elastic [i'læstik] *an* élastique *m*.
elasticity [.elæs'tisiti] *n* élasticité *f*.
elated [i'leitid] *a* gonflé, transporté, exultant, enivré.
elation [i'leiʃən] *n* orgueil *m*, ivresse *f*, exaltation *f*.
elbow ['elbou] *n* coude *m*; *vt* coudoyer, pousser des coudes; *vi* jouer des coudes; to have — room avoir ses coudées franches.
elder ['eldə] *n* (bot) sureau *m*; aîné(e) *mf*, Ancien *m*; *a* plus âgé, aîné.
elderly ['eldəli] *a* d'un certain âge.
eldest ['eldist] *a* aîné.
elect [i'lekt] *vt* choisir, élire; *a* désigné, élu.
election [i'lekʃən] *n* élection *f*.
electioneer [i.lekʃə'niə] *vi* mener une campagne électorale.
electioneering [i.lekʃə'niəriŋ] *n* campagne *f* (propagande *f*) électorale.
elector [i'lektə] *n* électeur *m*, votant *m*.
electorate [i'lektərit] *n* corps électoral *m*.
electric [i'lektrik] *a* électrique.
electrical [i'lektrikəl] *a* électrique.
electrician [ilek'triʃən] *n* électricien *m*.
electricity [ilek'trisiti] *n* électricité *f*.
electrification [i.lektrifi'keiʃən] *n* électrification *f*.
electrify [i'lektrifai] *vt* électrifier, électriser.
electrocute [i'lektrəkju:t] *vt* électrocuter.
electrocution [i.lektrə'kju:ʃən] *n* électrocution *f*.
electrolier [i.lektrou'liə] *n* lustre électrique *m*.
electron [i'lektrɔn] *n* électron *m*.
electroplate [i'lektroupleit] *n* ruolz *m*, articles *m pl* argentés; *vt* plaquer.
electrotyping [i'lektrou'taipiŋ] *n* galvanoplastie *f*.
elegance ['eligəns] *n* élégance *f*.
elegant ['eligənt] *a* élégant.
elegantly ['eligəntli] *ad* élégamment.
elegy ['elidʒi] *n* élégie *f*.
element ['elimənt] *n* élément *m*, facteur *m*; *pl* rudiments *m pl*.
elementary [.eli'mentəri] *a* élémentaire, primaire.
elephant ['elifənt] *n* éléphant *m*.
elevate ['eliveit] *vt* élever.
elevation [.eli'veiʃən] *n* élévation *f*, altitude *f*.
elevator ['eliveitə] *n* élévateur *m*, ascenseur *m*.
eleven [i'levn] *an* onze *m*.
eleventh [i'levnθ] *n* onze; *an* onzième *mf*.
elf [elf] *n* elfe *m*, lutin *m*.
elicit [i'lisit] *vt* extraire, tirer.
elide [i'laid] *vt* élider.

eligible ['elidʒəbl] *a* éligible, admissible, désirable.

eliminate [i'limineit] *vt* éliminer.

elimination [i,limi'neiʃən] *n* élimination *f*.

elision [i'liʒən] *n* élision *f*.

elixir [i'liksə] *n* élixir *m*.

elk [elk] *n* élan *m*.

ell [el] *n* aûne *f*.

elm [elm] *n* orme *m*.

elongate ['i:lɔŋgeit] *vt* allonger; *vi* s'allonger.

elope [i'loup] *vi* se laisser (se faire) enlever, prendre la fuite.

elopement [i'loupmənt] *n* enlèvement *m*, fuite *f*.

eloquence ['eləkwəns] *n* éloquence *f*.

eloquent ['eləkwənt] *a* éloquent.

eloquently ['eləkwəntli] *ad* éloquemment.

else [els] *a* (d')autre de plus; *ad* autrement, ou bien; **something —** autre chose *m*; **everywhere —** partout ailleurs; **anybody —** quelqu'un d'autre.

elsewhere ['els'weə] *ad* ailleurs, autre part.

elucidate [i'lu:sideit] *vt* élucider, éclaircir.

elucidation [i,lu:si'deiʃən] *n* élucidation *f*.

elude [i'lu:d] *vt* éluder, échapper à, esquiver.

elusive [i'lu:siv] *a* fuyant, insaisissable, évasif, souple.

elusiveness [i'lu:sivnis] *n* souplesse fuyante *f*, intangibilité *f*.

emaciated [i'meiʃieitid] *a* émacié, décharné.

emaciation [i,meisi'eiʃən] *n* maigreur extrême *f*.

emanate ['eməneit] *vi* émaner.

emanation [,emə'neiʃən] *n* émanation *f*.

emancipate [i'mænsipeit] *vt* émanciper.

emancipator [i'mænsipeitə] *n* émancipateur, -trice.

emasculate [i'mæskjuleit] *vt* châtrer, expurger.

embalm [im'ba:m] *vt* embaumer.

embalming [im'ba:miŋ] *n* embaumement *m*.

embank [im'bæŋk] *vt* endiguer, remblayer.

embankment [im'bæŋkmənt] *n* quai *m*, remblai *m*, levée *f*.

embargo [em'ba:gou] *n* embargo *m*, séquestre *m*; **to put an — on** mettre l'embargo sur, interdire.

embark [im'ba:k] *vt* embarquer; *vi* s'embarquer.

embarkation [,emba:'keiʃən] *n* embarquement *m*.

embarrass [im'bærəs] *vt* gêner, embarrasser.

embarrassment [im'bærəsmənt] *n* embarrass *m*, gêne *f*.

embassy ['embəsi] *n* ambassade *f*.

embedded [im'bedid] *a* pris, enfoncé.

embellish [im'beliʃ] *vt* embellir, enjoliver.

embellishment [im'beliʃmənt] *n* embellissement *m*.

ember ['embə] *n* braise *f*; **— days** Quatre-Temps *m pl*.

embezzle [im'bezl] *vt* détourner.

embezzlement [im'bezlmənt] *n* détournement *m*.

embitter [im'bitə] *vt* envenimer, aigrir, aggraver.

embitterment [im'bitəmənt] *n* aigreur *f*, aggravation *f*, envenimement *m*.

emblem ['embləm] *n* emblème *m*, symbole *m*.

emblematic [,embli'mætik] *a* emblématique, figuratif.

embodiment [im'bɔdimənt] *n* incarnation *f*.

embody [im'bɔdi] *vt* incarner, donner corps à, exprimer, incorporer.

embolden [im'bouldən] *vt* enhardir.

embolism ['embəlizəm] *n* embolie *f*.

emboss [im'bɔs] *vt* estamper, repousser.

embossing [im'bɔsiŋ] *n* relief *m*, brochage *m* (d'étoffes), repoussage *m*.

embrace [im'breis] *n* embrassement *m*, étreinte *f*; *vt* embrasser, étreindre, saisir, adopter, comporter.

embrasure [im'breiʒə] *n* embrasure *f*.

embroider [im'brɔidə] *vt* broder.

embroidery [im'brɔidəri] *n* broderie *f*.

embroil [im'brɔil] *vt* (em)brouiller, envelopper, entraîner.

embroilment [im'brɔilmənt] *n* imbroglio *m*.

embryo ['embriou] *n* embryon *m*.

embryonic [,embri'ɔnik] *a* embryonnaire, en herbe.

emend [i:'mend] *vt* corriger.

emendation [,i:men'deiʃən] *n* correction *f*, émendation *f*.

emerald ['emərəld] *n* émeraude *f*.

emerge [i'mə:dʒ] *vi* émerger, sortir.

emergency [i'mə:dʒənsi] *n* crise *f*, éventualité *f*; **— brake, — exit** frein *m*, sortie *f* de secours.

emery ['eməri] *n* émeri *m*; **— cloth** toile *f* d'émeri.

emetic [i'metik] *n* vomitif *m*.

emigrant ['emigrənt] *n* émigrant(e) *mf*, émigré *m*.

emigrate ['emigreit] *vi* émigrer.

emigration [,emi'greiʃən] *n* émigration *f*.

eminence ['eminəns] *n* éminence *f*, distinction *f*.

eminent ['eminənt] *a* éminent.

eminently ['eminəntli] *ad* éminemment, par excellence.

emissary ['emisəri] *n* émissaire *m*.

emission [i'miʃən] *n* émission *f*.

emit [i'mit] *vt* émettre.

emoluments [i'mɔljumənts] *n pl* émoluments *m pl*, traitement *m*, appointements *m pl*.

emotion [i'mouʃən] n émotion f, trouble m.
emotive [i'moutiv] a émotif.
emperor ['empərə] n empereur m.
emphasis ['emfəsis] n accent m, intensité f, insistance f, force f.
emphasize ['emfəsaiz] vt mettre en relief, souligner.
emphatic [im'fætik] a expressif, accentué, significatif, énergique, positif, net.
empire ['empaiə] n empire m.
employ [im'plɔi] n service m: vt employer.
employee [,emplɔi'i:] n employé(e) mf.
employer [im'plɔiə] n patron, -onne, employeur m, maître, -tresse.
employment [im'plɔimənt] n situation f, travail m, emploi m.
empower [im'pauə] vt autoriser, donner pouvoir à.
empress ['empris] n impératrice f.
emptiness ['emptinis] n vide m, néant m.
empty ['empti] a vide, vain, inoccupé; **to come back —handed** revenir bredouille; vt vider; vi se décharger, se vider.
emulate ['emjuleit] vt rivaliser avec, imiter.
emulation [,emju'leiʃən] n émulation f.
enable [i'neibl] vt mettre à même (de to), permettre (à), autoriser.
enact [i'nækt] vt ordonner, décréter, jouer.
enactment [i'næktmənt] n décret m, promulgation f.
enamel [i'næməl] n émail m, vernis m; vt émailler, vernir.
enameler [i'næmələ] n émailleur m.
encamp [in'kæmp] vt (faire) camper; vi camper.
encampment [in'kæmpmənt] n campement m, camp m.
encase [in'keis] vt enfermer, encaisser, revêtir.
enchant [in'tʃɑ:nt] vt enchanter, ensorceler.
enchanting [in'tʃɑ:ntiŋ] a enchanteur, ravissant.
enchantment [in'tʃɑ:ntmənt] n enchantement m, ravissement m.
encircle [in'sə:kl] vt encercler, entourer, cerner.
enclave ['enkleiv] n enclave f.
enclose [in'klouz] vt enclore, entourer, (r)enfermer, insérer.
enclosed [in'klouzd] a ci-inclus, ci-joint.
enclosure [in'klouʒə] n clôture f, enceinte f, (en)clos m, pièce incluse f.
encompass [in'kʌmpəs] vt entourer, contenir, renfermer.
encore [ɔŋ'kɔ:] excl bis m; vt bisser.
encounter [in'kauntə] n rencontre f, combat n, assaut m; vt rencontrer, affronter, essuyer.

encourage [in'kʌridʒ] vt encourager, favoriser.
encouragement [in'kʌridʒmənt] n encouragement m.
encroach [in'kroutʃ] vi empiéter (sur upon).
encroachment [in'kroutʃmənt] n empiètement m, usurpation f.
encrust [in'krʌst] vt incruster, encroûter.
encumber [in'kʌmbə] vt gêner, embarrasser, encombrer, grever.
encumbrance [in'kʌmbrəns] n charge f, encombrement m, embarras m.
encyclic [en'siklik] an encyclique f.
encyclopedia [en'saiklou'pi:djə] n encyclopédie f.
encyclopedic [en,saiklou'pi:dik] a encyclopédique.
end [end] n fin f, bout m, extrémité f; vti finir; vt terminer, achever; **on —** debout, de suite; **in the —** au bout du compte, à la fin; **to the bitter —** jusqu'au bout.
endanger [in'deindʒə] vt mettre en danger, exposer.
endear [in'diə] vt rendre cher, faire aimer.
endeavor [in'devə] n effort m, tentative f; vi s'efforcer, tenter.
ending ['endiŋ] n fin f, conclusion f, dénouement m, terminaison f; a final, dernier.
endive ['endiv] n chicorée f.
endless ['endlis] a sans fin, interminable.
endorse [in'dɔ:s] vt appuyer, endosser, estampiller.
endorsement [in'dɔ:sment] n (fin) endossement m, (passport) mention f, approbation f.
endow [in'dau] vt doter, investir.
endowed [in'daud] a doué, muni.
endowment [in'daumənt] n dotation f, fondation f.
endurable [in'djuərəbl] a supportable.
endurance [in'djuərəns] n résistance f, endurance f.
endure [in'djuə] vt supporter, endurer.
enduring [in'duəriŋ] a durable, qui persiste.
enemy ['enimi] an ennemi(e) mf.
energetic [,enə'dʒetik] a énergique.
energy ['enədʒi] n énergie f, vigueur f, nerf m.
enervate ['enə:veit] vt énerver, amollir.
enervation [,enə:'veiʃən] n énervement m, mollesse f.
enfeeble [in'fi:bl] vt affaiblir.
enfeeblement [in'fi:blmənt] n affaiblissement m.
enfilade [,enfi'leid] n enfilade f; vt prendre d'enfilade.
enforce [in'fɔ:s] vt imposer, faire respecter, mettre en vigueur, appliquer.

enforcement [in'fɔːsmənt] n application f, mise f en vigueur.

enfranchise [in'fræntʃaiz] vt donner le droit de vote à, ériger en circonscription.

engage [in'geidʒ] vt occuper, engager, retenir, embaucher, attirer.

engaged [in'geidʒd] a occupé, retenu, fiancé.

engagement [in'geidʒmənt] n engagement m, fiançailles f pl, combat m.

engender [in'dʒendə] vt engendrer, faire naître.

engine ['endʒin] n engin m, machine f, locomotive f, moteur m.

engine-driver ['endʒin,draivə] n mécanicien m.

engineer [,endʒi'niə] n ingénieur m, mécanicien m; pl (mil) le génie m; vt construire, machiner, combiner.

engineering [,endʒi'niəriŋ] n génie m, construction f, mécanique f.

England ['iŋglənd] n Angleterre f.

English ['iŋgliʃ] n Anglais(e) mf; an anglais m.

Englishman ['iŋgliʃmən] n Anglais m.

engrave [in'greiv] vt graver.

engraver [in'greivə] n graveur m.

engraving [in'greiviŋ] n gravure f.

engross [in'grous] vt accaparer, absorber.

engulf [in'gʌlf] vt engloutir.

enhance [in'hɑːns] vt (re)hausser, relever, mettre en valeur, accroître.

enhancement [in'hɑːnsmənt] n mise f en valeur.

enigma [i'nigmə] n énigme f.

enigmatic [,enig'mætik] a énigmatique.

enjoin [in'dʒɔin] vt enjoindre, recommander.

enjoy [in'dʒɔi] vt aimer, goûter, jouir de, prendre plaisir à; to — oneself s'amuser.

enjoyable [in'dʒɔiəbl] a agréable.

enjoyment [in'dʒɔimənt] n plaisir m, jouissance f.

enlarge [in'lɑːdʒ] vt accroître, agrandir, élargir, développer; vi s'élargir, s'agrandir; to — upon s'étendre sur.

enlargement [in'lɑːdʒmənt] n agrandissement m, accroissement m.

enlighten [in'laitn] vt éclairer.

enlightenment [in'laitnmənt] n lumières f pl.

enlist [in'list] vt enrôler; vi s'engager.

enlistment [in'listmənt] n enrôlement m.

enliven [in'laivn] vt animer, inspirer, égayer.

enmity ['enmiti] n hostilité f, inimitié f.

ennoble [i'noubl] vt anoblir, ennoblir.

enormity [i'nɔːmiti] n énormité f.

enormous [i'nɔːməs] a énorme, gigantesque.

enormously [i'nɔːməsli] ad énormément.

enough [i'nʌf] a n ad assez (de), suffisamment.

enquire [in'kwaiə] vi se renseigner (sur about), s'informer (de about).

enrage [in'reidʒ] vt exaspérer, faire enrager.

enrapture [in'ræptʃə] vt ravir, transporter.

enrich [in'ritʃ] vt enrichir.

enroll [in'roul] vt enrôler, immatriculer, enregistrer.

enrollment [in'roulmənt] n enrôlement m, enregistrement m, embauche f.

ensconce [in'skɔns] to — oneself se nicher, s'installer, se carrer.

enshrine [in'ʃrain] vt enchâsser.

enshroud [in'ʃraud] vt cacher, voiler, envelopper.

ensign ['ensain] n insigne m, pavillon m, porte-drapeau m.

enslave [in'sleiv] vt asservir.

enslavement [in'sleivmənt] n asservissement m.

ensnare [in'snɛə] vt prendre au piège, dans ses filets.

ensue [in'sjuː] vi s'ensuivre.

ensure [in'ʃuə] vt mettre en sûreté, (s')assurer.

entail [in'teil] vt impliquer, entraîner, occasionner.

entangle [in'tæŋgl] vt embrouiller, emmêler, empêtrer.

entanglement [in'tæŋglmənt] n enchevêtrement m; pl complications f pl.

enter ['entə] vt entrer dans; vi entrer, se faire inscrire; vt enregistrer, inscrire.

enterprise ['entəpraiz] n entreprise f, initiative f.

enterprising ['entəpraiziŋ] a entreprenant.

entertain [,entə'tein] vt recevoir, entretenir, caresser, amuser, régaler.

entertaining [,entə'teiniŋ] a amusant, divertissant.

entertainment [,entə'teinmənt] n amusement m, fête f, divertissement m.

enthrall [in'θrɔːl] vt ensorceler, charmer, envoûter.

enthrone [in'θroun] vt mettre sur le trône, introniser.

enthronement [in'θrounmənt] n couronnement m, intronisation f.

enthusiasm [in'θjuːziæzəm] n enthousiasme m.

enthusiast [in'θjuːziæst] n enthousiaste mf, fervent(e) mf.

enthusiastic [in,θjuːzi'æstik] a enthousiaste, passionné.

entice [in'tais] vt attirer, séduire; enticing séduisant.

enticement [in'taismənt] n attrait m, séduction f.

entire [in'taiə] a entier, complet, tout, pur.

entirely [in'taiəli] ad entièrement, tout à fait.

entirety [in'taiəti] n totalité f, intégralité f.

entitle [in'taitl] vt intituler, donner le titre, le droit, à, autoriser.

entomb [in'tu:m] vt enterrer.

entrails ['entreilz] n entrailles f pl.

entrain [en'trein] vt embarquer (dans le train).

entrance ['entrəns] n entrée f, accès m, admission f; — **examination** examen m d'entrée.

entrance [in'tra:ns] vt ravir, transporter.

entreat [in'tri:t] vt supplier.

entreaty [in'tri:ti] n supplication f; pl instances f pl.

entrench [in'trentʃ] vt retrancher.

entrust [in'trʌst] vt charger (de with), confier (à).

entry ['entri] n entrée f, inscription f; by double (single) — en partie double (simple).

entwine [in'twain] vt entrelacer, enlacer; vi s'entrelacer.

enumerate [i'nju:məreit] vt énumérer, dénombrer.

enumeration [i,nju:mə'reiʃən] n énumération f.

enunciate [i'nʌnsieit] vt articuler, énoncer.

enunciation [i,nʌnsi'eiʃən] n énonciation f.

envelop [in'veləp] vt envelopper.

envelope ['envəloup] n enveloppe f.

enviable ['enviəbl] a enviable, digne d'envie.

envious ['enviəs] a envieux, d'envie; **to be — of** porter envie à.

environment [in'vaiərənmənt] n milieu m, entourage m, ambiance f, atmosphère f.

environs [en'vaiərənz] n pl environs m pl.

envisage [in'vizidʒ] vt regarder en face, envisager.

envoy ['envɔi] n envoyé m.

envy ['envi] n envie f; vt envier, porter envie à.

epic ['epic] n épopée f; a épique.

epicure ['epikjuə] n gourmet m.

epidemic [,epi'demik] n épidémie f; a épidémique.

epidermis [,epi'də:mis] n épiderme m.

epigram ['epigræm] n épigramme f.

epigraph ['epigra:f] n épigraphe f.

epilepsy ['epilepsi] n épilepsie f.

epileptic [,epi'leptik] a épileptique.

episcopacy [i'piskəpəsi] n épiscopat m.

episcopal [i'piskəpəl] a épiscopal.

episode ['episoud] n épisode m.

episodic [,epi'sɔdik] a épisodique.

epistle [i'pisl] n épître f.

epistolary [i'pistələri] a épistolaire.

epitaph ['epita:f] n épitaphe f.

epithet ['epiθet] n épithète f.

epitome [i'pitəmi] n abrégé m, résumé m.

epoch ['i:pɔk] n époque f.

equable ['ekwəbl] a égal, uni(forme), régulier.

equal ['i:kwəl] n égal(e) mf, pareil(le) mf; a égal, de taille (à tò); vt égaler.

equality [i:'kwɔliti] n égalité f.

equalization [,i:kwəlai'zeiʃən] n égalisation f.

equalize ['i:kwəlaiz] vt égaliser.

equally ['i:kwəli] ad également, pareillement.

equator [i'kweitə] n équateur m.

equatorial [,ekwə'tɔ:riəl] a équatorial.

equerry ['ekwəri] n écuyer m.

equestrian [i'kwestriən] a équestre.

equilibrate [,i:kwi'laibreit] vt équilibrer.

equilibrium [,i:kwi'libriəm] n équilibre m.

equinox ['i:kwinɔks] n équinoxe m.

equip [i'kwip] vt munir, équiper, monter.

equipage ['ekwipidʒ] n équipage m.

equipment [i'kwipmənt] n équipement m, outillage m, installation f, matériel m.

equipoise ['ekwipɔiz] n équilibre m, contre-poids m.

equitable ['ekwitəbl] a équitable.

equity ['ekwiti] n équité f.

equivalence [i'kwivələns] n équivalance f.

equivalent [i'kwivələnt] an équivalent m.

equivocal [i'kwivəkəl] a équivoque, ambigu -uë, douteux.

equivocate [i'kwivəkeit] vi jouer sur les mots, tergiverser.

era ['iərə] n ère f.

eradicate [i'rædikeit] vt extirper, déraciner.

eradication [i,rædi'keiʃən] n déracinement m.

erase [i'reiz] vt effacer, raturer.

eraser [i'reizə] n gomme f.

erasure [i'reiʒə] n rature f.

ere [eə] prep avant; cj avant que.

erect [i'rekt] a droit; vt dresser, bâtir, ériger.

erection [i'rekʃən] n érection f, construction f, montage m, édifice m.

ermine ['ə:min] n hermine f.

erode [i'roud] vt ronger, éroder, corroder.

erosion [i'rouʒən] n érosion f, usure f.

err [ə:] vi se tromper, faire erreur, être erroné, pécher.

errand ['erənd] n course f, commission f.

errand-boy ['erəndbɔi] n commissionnaire m, chasseur m.

erroneous [i'rouniəs] a erroné, faux.

error ['erə] n erreur f, faute f, méprise f.

erupt [i'rʌpt] vi faire éruption.

eruption [i'rʌpʃən] n éruption f.

escalator ['eskəleitə] n escalier mouvant m.

escapade [ˌeskəˈpeid] n escapade f, frasque f.

escape [isˈkeip] n évasion f, fuite f; vi s'évader, s'esquiver, (s')échapper; vt échapper à.

eschew [isˈtʃuː] vt éviter, s'abstenir de, renoncer à.

escort [ˈeskɔːt] n escorte f, cavalier m.

escort [isˈkɔːt] vt escorter, accompagner, reconduire.

escutcheon [isˈkʌtʃən] n écu(sson) m, blason m.

Eskimo [ˈeskimou] an Esquimau m; — woman femme esquimau.

especial [isˈpeʃəl] a (tout) particulier, propre.

espouse [isˈpauz] vt se marier avec, épouser.

espy [isˈpai] vt apercevoir, aviser.

essay [ˈesei] n tentative f, essai m, dissertation f.

essay [eˈsei] vt essayer, éprouver.

essence [ˈesns] n essence f, extrait m, fond m, suc m.

essential [iˈsenʃəl] an essentiel m, indispensable m.

establish [isˈtæbliʃ] vt fonder, créer, établir.

establishment [isˈtæbliʃmənt] n établissement m, fondation f, pied m (de guerre), train m de maison.

estate [isˈteit] n condition f, rang m, succession f, domaine m, immeuble m.

esteem [isˈtiːm] n estime f; vt estimer, tenir (pour).

estimate [ˈestimit] n estimation f, devis m, appréciation f; [ˈestimeit] vt évaluer, apprécier.

estimation [ˌestiˈmeiʃən] n estime f, jugement m.

estrange [isˈtreindʒ] vt (s')aliéner, indisposer.

estrangement [isˈtreindʒmənt] n désaffection f, refroidissement m, aliénation f.

estuary [ˈestjuəri] n estuaire m.

etch [etʃ] vt graver à l'eau forte.

etching [ˈetʃiŋ] n eau-forte f.

eternal [iˈtəːnl] a éternel.

eternity [iˈtəːniti] n éternité f.

ether [ˈiːθə] n éther m.

ethereal [iˈθiəriəl] a éthéré.

ethical [ˈeθikəl] a moral.

ethics [ˈeθiks] n morale f.

etiquette [ˈetiket] n étiquette f, convenances f pl, cérémonial m, protocole m.

etymology [ˌetiˈmɔlədʒi] n étymologie f.

eucharist [ˈjuːkərist] n eucharistie f.

eulogize [ˈjuːlədʒaiz] vt faire l'éloge de.

eulogy [ˈjuːlədʒi] n éloge m, panégyrique m.

eunuch [ˈjuːnək] n eunuque m.

Europe [ˈjuərəp] n l'Europe f.

European [ˌjuərəˈpiːən] n Européen, -enne mf; a européen.

evacuate [iˈvækjueit] vt évacuer, expulser.

evacuation [iˌvækjuˈeiʃən] n évacuation f.

evade [iˈveid] vt esquiver, déjouer, éviter, tourner.

evaluate [iˈvæljueit] vt évaluer, estimer.

evangelic [ˌiːvænˈdʒelik] a évangélique.

evangelist [iˈvændʒəlist] n évangéliste mf.

evaporate [iˈvæpəreit] vt faire évaporer; vi s'évaporer, se vaporiser. **vaporation** [iˌvæpəˈreiʃən] n évaporation f.

evasion [iˈveiʒən] n subterfuge m, faux-fuyant m, échappatoire f.

evasive [iˈveiziv] a évasif.

eve [iːv] n veille f.

even [ˈiːvən] a égal, uni, plat, pair; ad même, seulement, encore; vt égaliser, aplanir.

evening [ˈiːvniŋ] n soir m, soirée f.

evening-dress [ˈiːvniŋdres] n habit m, robe f de soirée, tenue f de soirée.

evenly [ˈiːvənli] ad également, régulièrement.

evensong [ˈiːvənsɔŋ] n office du soir m, vêpres f pl.

event [iˈvent] n événement m, cas m, chance f, résultat m, épreuve f; in the — of au cas où; at all —s à tout hasard.

eventful [iˈventful] a mouvementé, mémorable, tourmenté.

ever [ˈevə] ad toujours, jamais.

everlasting [ˌevəˈlɑːstiŋ] a éternel.

evermore [ˈevəˈmɔː] ad pour toujours, à jamais.

every [ˈevri] a chaque, tout; — other day tous les deux jours.

everybody [ˈevribɔdi] pn tout le monde, tous, chacun.

everyday [ˈevridei] a quotidien, journalier, banal.

everyone [ˈevriwʌn] pn tout le monde, chacun, tous.

everything [ˈevriθiŋ] pn tout.

everywhere [ˈevriwɛə] ad partout.

evict [iˈvikt] vt expulser.

eviction [iˈvikʃən] n expulsion f, éviction f.

evidence [ˈevidəns] n évidence f, signe m, preuve f, témoignage m; vt indiquer, attester, manifester.

evident [ˈevidənt] a évident.

evil [ˈiːvl] n mal m, péché m; a mauvais, méchant, malin.

evilly [ˈiːvili] ad mal.

evince [iˈvins] vt montrer.

evocation [ˌevouˈkeiʃən] n évocation f.

evoke [iˈvouk] vt évoquer.

evolution [ˌiːvəˈluːʃən] n évolution f, développement m.

evolve [iˈvɔlv] vt dérouler, développer, élaborer; vi évoluer, se dérouler, se développer.

ewe [juː] n brebis f.

ewer ['ju:ə] n aiguière f, pot m à eau, broc m.

exact [ig'zækt] a juste, exact, précis; vt exiger, extorquer.

exacting [ig'zæktiŋ] a exigeant, fatigant.

exaction [ig'zækʃən] n exigence f, exaction f.

exactitude [ig'zæktitju:d] n exactitude f, précision f.

exactly [ig'zæktli] ad précisément, justement, tout juste, juste.

exaggerate [ig'zædʒəreit] vti exagérer.

exaggeration [ig.zædʒə'reiʃən] n exagération f.

exalt [ig'zɔːlt] vt exalter, porter aux nues, élever.

exaltation [.egzɔːl'teiʃən] n exaltation f, élévation f.

examination [ig.zæmi'neiʃən] n examen m, inspection f, visite f, interrogatoire m, (term) composition f.

examine [ig'zæmin] vt examiner, visiter, vérifier.

examiner [ig'zæminə] n examinateur, -trice, inspecteur, -trice.

example [ig'zɑːmpl] n exemple m, précédent m.

exasperate [ig'zæspəreit] vt exaspérer, aggraver.

exasperation [ig.zæspə'reiʃən] n exaspération f.

excavate ['ekskəveit] vt fouiller, creuser, déterrer.

excavation [.ekskə'veiʃən] n excavation f, fouille f.

exceed [ik'siːd] vt dépasser, excéder, aller au-delà de.

exceedingly [ik'siːdiŋli] ad excessivement, extrêmement.

excel [ik'sel] vt surpasser, dépasser; vi exceller.

excellence ['eksələns] n excellence f, mérite m.

excellent ['eksələnt] a excellent, parfait.

except [ik'sept] vt excepter, exclure; prep excepté; cj sauf que.

exception [ik'sepʃən] n exception f, objection f.

exceptionable [ik'sepʃnəbl] a répréhensible.

exceptional [ik'sepʃnl] a exceptionnel.

excerpt ['eksəːpt] n extrait m.

excess [ik'ses] n excès m, surplus m, excédent m, supplément m.

excessive [ik'sesiv] a excessif, immodéré.

excessively [ik'sesivli] ad excessivement, démesurément, à l'excès.

exchange [iks'tʃeindʒ] n échange m, Bourse f, change m; vt (é)changer; vi permuter.

exchangeable [iks'tʃeindʒəbl] a échangeable.

exchequer [iks'tʃekə] n Echiquier m, ministère des finances m, Trésor m, fisc m.

excise ['eksaiz] n contributions indirectes f pl; excise f; vt couper, retrancher.

excision [ek'siʒən] n excision f, coupure f.

excitable [ik'saitəbl] a (sur)excitable, émotionnable.

excitation [.eksi'teiʃən] n excitation f.

excite [ik'sait] vt exciter, susciter, émouvoir, agiter.

excitement [ik'saitmənt] n agitation f, émotion f, surexcitation f, sensation(s) f pl.

exciting [ik'saitiŋ] a passionant, palpitant, mouvementé.

exclaim [iks'kleim] vi (s'é)crier, se récrier.

exclamation [.eksklə'meiʃən] n exclamation f.

exclude [iks'kluːd] vt exclure.

excluding [iks'kluːdiŋ] a sans compter.

exclusion [iks'kluːʒən] n exclusion f.

exclusive [iks'kluːsiv] a non compris, à l'exclusion (de of), exclusif, unique.

exclusively [iks'kluːsivli] ad exclusivement.

excommunicate [.ekskə'mjuːnikeit] vt excommunier.

excommunication ['ekskə.mjuːni'keiʃən] n excommunication f.

excoriate [eks'kɔːrieit] vt écorcher.

excrescence [iks'kresns] n excroissance f.

excruciating [iks'kruːʃieitiŋ] a atroce, déchirant.

excursion [iks'kəːʃən] n sortie f, excursion f.

excusable [iks'kjuːzəbl] a excusable, pardonnable.

excuse [iks'kjuːs] n excuse f, prétexte m.

excuse [iks'kjuːz] vt excuser, dispenser (de from).

executant [ig'zekjutənt] n exécutant(e) mf.

execute ['eksikjuːt] vt exécuter, valider, s'acquitter de.

execution [.eksi'kjuːʃən] n exécution f, validation f, saisie f.

executioner [.eksi'kjuːʃnə] n bourreau m.

executive [ig'zekjutiv] an exécutif m.

executor [ig'zekjutə] n exécuteur, -trice.

exemplar [ig'zemplə] n modèle m, exemplaire m.

exemplary [ig'zempləri] a exemplaire, caractérisque.

exemplify [ig'zemplifai] vt illustrer d'exemples, être l'exemple de.

exempt [ig'zempt] a exempt; vt dispenser.

exemption [ig'zempʃən] n exemption f, dispense f.

exercise ['eksəsaiz] n exercice m, devoir m; vt exercer, pratiquer, éprouver; vi s'entraîner.

exert [ig'zə:t] vt déployer, faire sentir, employer, exercer.

exertion [ig'zə:ʃən] n effort m, efforts m pl, fatigues f pl, emploi m.

exhalation [ˌeksha'leiʃən] n exhalaison f, bouffée f, effluve m.

exhale [eks'heil] vt exhaler; vi se dilater, s'exhaler.

exhaust [ig'zɔ:st] n échappement m; vt épuiser, exténuer.

exhaustion [ig'zɔ:stʃən] n épuisement m.

exhaustive [ig'zɔ:stiv] a qui épuise, complet, minutieux.

exhibit [ig'zibit] n pièce à conviction f, objet exposé m; vt montrer, étaler, exhiber.

exhibition [ˌeksi'biʃən] n exposition f, exhibition f, spectacle m, étalage m.

exhort [ig'zɔ:t] vt exhorter.

exhortation [ˌegzɔ:'teiʃən] n exhortation f.

exhumation [ˌekshju'meiʃən] n exhumation f.

exhume [eks'hju:m] vt exhumer.

exigence ['eksidʒəns] n exigence f, nécessité f.

exigent ['eksidʒənt] a urgent, exigeant.

exiguity [ˌeksi'gju(:)iti] n exiguïté f.

exiguous [eg'zigjuəs] a exigu, -uë.

exile ['eksail] n exil m, exilé(e) mf; vt exiler, bannir.

exist [ig'zist] vi exister.

existence [ig'zistəns] n existence f, vie f.

existing [ig'zistiŋ] a existant, actuel.

exit ['eksit] n sortie f.

exodus ['eksədəs] n exode m, sortie f.

exonerate [ig'zɔnəreit] vt exonérer, décharger.

exoneration [ig.zɔnə'reiʃən] n exonération f.

exorbitance [ig'zɔ:bitəns] n énormité f, exorbitance f.

exorbitant [ig'zɔ:bitənt] a exorbitant, extravagant.

exorcise ['eksɔ:saiz] vt exorciser.

exorcising ['eksɔ:saiziŋ] n exorcisme m.

exotic [ig'zɔtik] a exotique.

expand [iks'pænd] vt étendre, dilater, épancher; vi se dilater, se développer.

expanse [iks'pæns] n étendue f.

expansion [iks'pænʃən] n expansion f, développement m.

expansive [iks'pænsiv] a expansif, étendu.

expatiate [eks'peiʃieit] vi s'étendre (sur on), pérorer.

expatriate [eks'pætrieit] vt expatrier.

expect [iks'pekt] vt (s')attendre (à), compter sur.

expectancy [iks'pektənsi] n attente f, expectative f.

expectation [ˌekspek'teiʃən] n

attente f, espérances f pl, prévision f.

expediency [iks'pi:djənsi] n convenance f, opportunité f.

expedient [iks'pi:djənt] an expédient m.

expedite ['ekspidait] vt hâter, expédier.

expedition [ˌekspi'diʃən] n expédition f, rapidité f.

expeditious [ˌekspi'diʃəs] a expéditif, prompt.

expel [iks'pel] vt chasser, expulser.

expend [iks'pend] vt dépenser, consommer, épuiser.

expenditure [iks'penditʃə] n dépense(s) f pl.

expense [iks'pens] n débours m pl, dépens m pl, frais m pl.

expensive [iks'pensiv] a cher, coûteux, dispendieux.

experience [iks'piəriəns] n expérience f, épreuve f.

experienced [iks'piəriənst] a expérimenté, exercé.

experiment [iks'perimənt] n essai m, expérience f; vi expérimenter, faire une expérience.

experimental [eks.peri'mentl] a expérimental.

experimentally [eks.peri'mentəli] ad expérimentalement, à titre d'essai.

expert ['ekspə:t] an expert m; a habile.

expiate ['ekspieit] vt expier.

expiation [ˌekspi'eiʃən] n expiation f.

expiration [ˌekspaiə'reiʃən] n expiration f, (d)échéance f.

expire [iks'paiə] vti exhaler, expirer; vi s'éteindre.

expiry [iks'paiəri] n fin f, terminaison f.

explain [iks'plein] vt expliquer, éclaircir.

explanation [ˌeksplə'neiʃən] n explication f.

explanatory [iks'plænətəri] a explicatif; explicateur, -trice.

explicable [eks'plikəbl] a explicable.

explicit [iks'plisit] a formel, clair.

explode [iks'ploud] vt faire sauter, dégonfler; vi sauter, faire explosion, éclater.

exploit ['eksplɔit] n exploit m; vt exploiter.

exploitation [ˌeksplɔi'teiʃən] n exploitation f.

exploration [ˌeksplɔ:'reiʃən] n exploration f.

explore [iks'plɔ:] vt explorer.

explorer [iks'plɔ:rə] n explorateur, -trice.

explosion [iks'plouʒən] n explosion f, détonation f.

explosive [iks'plouziv] a explosible, explosif, détonnant.

export [eks'pɔ:t] vt exporter.

export ['ekspɔ:t] n exportation f; pl exportations f pl.

exportation [ˌekspɔ:'teiʃən] n exportation f.

exporter [eks'pɔːtə] n exportateur, -trice.

expose [iks'pouz] vt exposer, mettre à nu, démasquer.

expostulate [iks'pɔstjuleit] vi en remontrer (à with), faire des remontrances (à with).

expostulation [iks,pɔstju'leiʃən] n rémontrance f.

expound [iks'paund] vt exposer, expliquer.

express [iks'pres] n exprès m, rapide m, express m; compagnie f de messageries; a exact, exprès; vt exprimer.

expression [iks'preʃən] n expression f.

expressive [iks'presiv] a expressif.

expressly [iks'presli] ad expressément, formellement.

expropriate [eks'prouprieit] vt exproprier.

expropriation [eks,proupri'eiʃən] n expropriation f.

expulsion [iks'pʌlʃən] n expulsion f.

expunge [iks'pʌndʒ] vt biffer, rayer.

expurgate ['ekspɔːgeit] vt expurger, épurer.

exquisite [eks'kwizit] n élégant m; a exquis, raffiné.

exquisiteness [eks'kwizitnis] n finesse exquise f, raffinement m.

extant [eks'tænt] a subsistant.

extempore [eks'tempəri] a improvisé; ad d'abondance.

extemporization [eks,tempərai'zeiʃən] n improvisation f.

extemporize [iks'tempəraiz] vti improviser.

extend [iks'tend] vt étendre, prolonger, accorder; vi se déployer, s'étendre.

extensible [iks'tensibl] a extensible.

extension [iks'tenʃən] n extension f, prolongement m, prolongation f, agrandissement m.

extensive [iks'tensiv] a extensif, étendu, ample.

extensively [iks'tensivli] ad to use — se servir largement, beaucoup.

extent [iks'tent] n étendue f, mesure f, point m.

extenuate [eks'tenjueit] vt atténuer, excuser.

extenuation [eks,tenju'eiʃən] n atténuation f, affaiblissement m, exténuation f.

exterior [eks'tiəriə] an extérieur m; n dehors m.

exterminate [eks'tɔːmineit] vt exterminer, extirper.

extermination [eks,tɔː'miˈneiʃən] n extermination f, extirpation f.

external [eks'tɔːnl] a externe, extérieur.

extinct [iks'tiŋkt] a éteint.

extinction [iks'tiŋkʃən] n extinction f.

extinguish [iks'tiŋgwiʃ] vt éteindre, éclipser, anéantir.

extinguisher [iks'tiŋgwiʃə] n éteignoir m, extincteur m.

extirpate ['ekstəːpeit] vt extirper.

extol [iks'tɔl] vt porter aux nues, exalter.

extort [iks'tɔːt] vt extorquer, arracher.

extortion [iks'tɔːʃən] n extorsion f, arrachement m.

extortionate [iks'tɔːʃnit] a exorbitant, de pirate.

extra ['ekstrə] a supplémentaire, d'extra, de plus; ad extra, super, ultra, en plus; n supplément m; pl à-côtés m pl.

extract ['ekstrækt] n extrait m.

extract [iks'trækt] vt extraire, (sou) tirer.

extraction [iks'trækʃən] n extraction f, origine f.

extradite ['ekstrədait] vt extrader.

extradition [,ekstrə'diʃən] n extradition f.

extraneous [eks'treinjəs] a étranger, en dehors de.

extraordinary [iks'trɔːdnri] a extraordinaire.

extravagance [iks'trævəgəns] n extravagance f, folle dépense f, gaspillage m.

extravagant [iks'trævəgənt] a extravagant, dépensier.

extreme [iks'triːm] an extrême m.

extremely [iks'triːmli] ad extrêmement, au dernier point.

extremist [iks'triːmist] n extrémiste mf.

extremity [iks'tremiti] n extrémité f, bout m.

extricate ['ekstrikeit] vt tirer, sortir, dégager.

exuberance [ig'zuːbərəns] n exubérance f, luxuriance f.

exuberant [ig'zuːbərənt] a exubérant.

exult [ig'zʌlt] vi exulter.

exultation [,egzʌl'teiʃən] n jubilation f, exultation f.

eye [ai] n œil m, pl yeux m pl (needle) chas m; vt regarder, lorgner.

eyeball ['aibɔːl] n pupille f, prunell f.

eyebrow ['aibrau] n sourcil m.

eyeglass ['aiglɑːs] n monocle m; p lorgnon m.

eyelash ['ailæʃ] n cil m.

eyelet ['ailit] n œillet m.

eyelid ['ailid] n paupière f.

eyeshot ['aiʃɔt] n portée f de vue.

eyesight ['aisait] n vue f.

eyesore ['aisɔːr] n mal m d'yeux tache f, hideur f.

eyetooth ['aituːθ] n canine f.

eyewash ['aiwɔʃ] n poudre aux yeu f.

eyewitness ['ai,witnis] n témoi oculaire m.

F

fable ['feibl] *n* fable *f*, conte *m*.
fabric ['fæbrik] *n* construction *f*, édifice *m*, tissu *m*.
fabricate ['fæbrikeit] *vt* fabriquer, inventer.
fabrication [ˌfæbri'keiʃən] *n* faux *m*, fabrication *f*.
fabulist ['fæbjulist] *n* fabuliste *m*.
fabulous ['fæbjuləs] *a* fabuleux, légendaire, prodigieux.
face [feis] *n* visage *m*, figure *f*, face *f*, air *m*, mine *f*, grimace *f*, toupet *m*, façade *f*, cadran *m*; — **cream** crème *f* de beauté; —**pack** masque *m* anti-ride; — **value** valeur *f* nominale; *vt* regarder en face, faire face à, confronter garnir, couvrir, donner sur; — **up to** affronter.
facet ['fæsit] *n* facette *f*.
facetious [fə'siːʃəs] *a* facétieux, bouffon.
facial ['feiʃəl] *a* facial.
facile ['fæsail] *a* facile.
facility [fə'siliti] *n* facilité *f*.
facing ['feisiŋ] *n* parement *m*, revers *m*, revêt *m*.
fact [fækt] *n* fait *m*; **matter-of-—** (*of person*) pratique; **as a matter of —** en effet, en réalité.
faction ['fækʃən] *n* faction *f*, cabale *f*.
factious ['fækʃəs] *a* factieux.
factitious [fæk'tiʃəs] *a* factice, artificiel.
factor ['fæktə] *n* facteur *m*, agent *m*, régisseur *m*.
factory ['fæktəri] *n* usine *f*, manufacture *f*, fabrique *f*, factorerie.
factotum [fæk'toutəm] *n* factotum *n*.
facultative ['fækəltətiv] *a* facultatif.
faculty ['fækəlti] *n* faculté *f*, pouvoir *n*, liberté *f*.
fad [fæd] *n* lubie *f*, manie *f*, marotte *f*.
faddist ['fædist] *n* maniaque *mf*.
fade [feid] *vi* se faner, se déteindre, s'éteindre; *vt* faner, décolorer.
faded ['feidid] *a* fané, décoloré, défraichi.
fade-out ['feidaut] *n* fondu *m*.
fading ['feidiŋ] *a* pâlissant, estompé; *n* flétrissure *f*, décoloration *f*, (*of sound*) chute *f* d'intensité.
fag [fæg] *n* corvée *f*, (*sl*) sèche *f*; *vi* turbiner, trimer; *vt* fatiguer, éreinter.
fag-end ['fægend] *n* mégot *m*.
faggot ['fægət] *n* fagot *m*.
fail [feil] *vi* manquer, échouer, faire faillite, baisser; *vt* refuser, coller, manquer à; *ad* **without** — sans faute.
failing ['feiliŋ] *prep* faute de; *n* défaut *m*, défaillance *f*.
failure ['feiljə] *n* échec *m*, manque (*ment*) *m*, faillite *f*, raté(e) *mf*, four *n*, panne *f*.
fain [fein] *a* heureux; *ad* volontiers.
faint [feint] *n* défaillance *f*, syncope

f; *vi* s'évanouir; *a* faible, pâle, vague, léger.
fair [feə] *a* beau, blond, clair, loyal, juste, passable, moyen; *n* foire *f*.
fair-copy ['feə'kɔpi] *n* mise au net *f*, copie au net *f*.
fairly ['feəli] *ad* absolument, assez, loyalement.
fairness ['feənis] *n* justice *f*, loyauté *f*, impartialité *f*; *n* blancheur *f*, fraicheur *f*; **in all — en bonne conscience.
fair-play ['feə'plei] *n* franc jeu *m*.
fairy ['feəri] *n* fée *f*.
fairyland ['feərilænd] *n* féerie *f*.
fairy-like ['feərilaik] *a* féerique.
faith [feiθ] *n* foi *f*, parole *f*.
faithful ['feiθful] *a* fidèle.
faithfully ['feiθfuli] *adv* fidèlement; **yours — agréez l'expression de nos sentiments distingués.
faithless ['feiθlis] *a* sans foi.
fake [feik] *n* truquage *m*, faux *m*; *vt* truquer, maquiller.
falcon ['fɔːlkən] *n* faucon *m*.
fall [fɔːl] *n* chute *f*, tombée *f*; automne *m*; *vi* tomber, baisser, échoir.
fallacy ['fæləsi] *n* illusion *f*, fausseté *f*, erreur *f*.
fallacious [fə'leiʃəs] *a* fallacieux, trompeur.
fallen ['fɔːlən] *pp of* **fall**.
fallibility [ˌfæli'biliti] *n* faillibilité *f*.
fallible ['fæləbl] *a* faillible.
fall-out ['fɔːlaut] *n* retombée *f*.
fallow ['fælou] *n* friche *f*, jachère *f*.
false [fɔls] *a* faux, trompeur, perfide.
falsehood ['fɔlshud] *n* fausseté *f*, mensonge *m*.
falseness ['fɔlsnis] *n* duplicité *f*, mauvaise foi *f*.
falsification [ˌfɔlsifi'keiʃən] *n* falsification *f*.
falsify ['fɔlsifai] *vt* falsifier, tromper, rendre faux.
falter ['fɔltə] *vi* trébucher, balbutier, hésiter, flancher.
fame [feim] *n* réputation *f*, renom *m*, renommée *f*.
famed [feimd] *a* célèbre, famé.
familiar [fə'miljə] *a* familier, intime.
familiarity [fəˌmili'æriti] *n* familiarité *f*, connaissance *f*.
familiarize [fə'miljəraiz] *vt* familiariser, habituer.
family ['fæmili] *n* famille *f*.
famine ['fæmin] *n* famine *f*.
famish ['fæmiʃ] *vi* être affamé.
famous ['feiməs] *a* célèbre, fameux.
fan [fæn] *n* éventail *m*, ventilateur *m*, aérateur *m*, fan *m*, fervent(e) *mf*, enragé(e) *mf*; — **palm** rômer *m*; *vt* éventer, souffler (sur), attiser, vanner.
fanatic [fə'nætik] *n* fanatique *mf*, enragé(e) *mf*.
fanatical [fə'nætikəl] *a* fanatique.
fanaticism [fə'nætisizəm] *n* fanatisme *m*.

fanciful ['fænsiful] a capricieux, fantaisiste, chimérique.

fancy ['fænsi] n imagination f, fantaisie f, chimère f, caprice m; vt (s')imaginer, se toquer de; to — oneself se gober.

fang [fæŋ] n croc m, crochet m, défense f, racine f.

fanner ['fænə] n vanneur, -euse.

fantastic [fæn'tæstik] a fantastique, fantasque.

fantasy ['fæntəzi] n imagination f, extravagance f.

far [fɑː] a éloigné, lointain; ad loin, au loin, avant, (de) beaucoup; so — jusqu'ici; in so — as dans la mesure où; — afield très loin.

faraway ['fɑːrəwei] a éloigné, lointain.

far-between ['fɑːbi'twiːn] a espacé.

far-fetched ['fɑː'fetʃt] a outré, tiré par les cheveux, extravagant.

far-off ['fɑːr'ɔf] a éloigné.

far-reaching ['fɑː'riːtʃiŋ] a de longue portée, de grande envergure.

far-sighted ['fɑː'saitid] a presbyte, à longue vue, prévoyant.

farce [fɑːs] n farce f.

farcical ['fɑːsikəl] a grotesque.

fare [fɛə] n prix m (du voyage), places f pl, voyageur, -euse, client(e) mf; **good** — bonne chère f; vi se faire, se porter, se trouver; **single** — aller m; **return** — aller et retour m.

farewell ['fɛə'wel] n adieu m.

farm [fɑːm] n ferme f; vt affermer, cultiver, exploiter; vi être cultivateur.

farmer ['fɑːmə] n fermier m, cultivateur m.

farming ['fɑːmiŋ] n culture f, affermage m, exploitation f.

farrier ['færiə] n maréchal ferrant m, vétérinaire m.

farther ['fɑːðə] see **further**.

farthing ['fɑːðiŋ] n liard m, sou m.

fascinate ['fæsineit] vt séduire, fasciner.

fascination [ˌfæsi'neiʃən] n fascination f, charme m.

fascism ['fæʃizəm] n fascisme m.

fascist ['fæʃist] an fasciste mf.

fashion ['fæʃən] n mode f, façon f, coutume f; vt façonner, former.

fashionable ['fæʃnəbl] a à la mode, élégant.

fast [fɑːst] n jeûne m; vi jeûner; a fixé, confiné, sûr, solide, bon teint, rapide, qui va fort, qui avance; ad solidement, rapidement, fort, vite.

fasten ['fɑːsn] vt attacher, ficeler, fermer, fixer, saisir; vi se cramponner, se fixer.

fastener ['fɑːsnə] n attache f, agrafe f, fermeture f.

fastidious [fæs'tidjəs] a difficile, délicat.

fastidiousness [fæs'tidjəsnis] n goût difficile m.

fastness ['fɑːstnis] n rapidité f

vitesse f, fermeté f, solidité forteresse f.

fat [fæt] n gros m, graisse f; a gras gros.

fatal ['feitl] a fatal, mortel, funeste

fatalism ['feitəlizəm] n fatalisme m

fatalist ['feitəlist] n fataliste mf.

fatality [fə'tæliti] n fatalité sinistre m, accident mortel m.

fate [feit] n destin m, sort m, destiné f.

fateful ['feitful] a décisif, gr d'avenir, fatidique, fatal.

father ['fɑːðə] n père m; —in-la beau-père m; vt reconnaître, avoue imputer, patronner, engendrer.

fatherhood ['fɑːðəhud] n paternité

fatherland ['fɑːðəlænd] n patrie f.

fatherless ['fɑːðəlis] a sans père.

fatherly ['fɑːðəli] a paternel.

fathom ['fæðəm] n toise f, brasse vt sonder, approfondir.

fathomless ['fæðəmlis] a insondabl sans fond.

fatigue [fə'tiːg] n fatigue f, corvée vt fatiguer.

fatten ['fætn] vtn engraisser.

fatty ['fæti] a graisseux, onctueu gras, gros.

fatuous ['fætjuəs] a sot, idiot.

fatuousness ['fætjuəsnis] n stupidi f.

faucet ['fɔːsit] n robinet m.

fault [fɔlt] n défaut m, faute f, fail f; to — jusqu'à l'excès.

faultless ['fɔltlis] a impeccable, sa faute.

faulty ['fɔlti] a fautif, défectueu inexact.

favor ['feivə] n faveur f; vt favoris approuver, appuyer.

favorable ['feivərəbl] a favorabl propice, avantageux.

favorite ['feivərit] an favori, -it a préféré.

favoritism ['feivəritizəm] n favo tisme m.

fawn [fɔːn] n faon m; a fauve; to — upon caresser, flagorner, fa le chien couchant devant.

fear [fiə] n peur f, crainte f; craindre, avoir peur de.

fearful ['fiəful] a terrible, affreu craintif, peureux.

fearless ['fiəlis] a sans peur, intr pide.

fearsome ['fiəsəm] a hideux, doutable.

feasible ['fiːzəbl] a faisable, pra cable, probable.

feasibility [ˌfiːzə'biliti] n possibil f, praticabilité f.

feast [fiːst] n fête f, régal m, festin vt fêter, régaler; vi se régaler, fa festin.

feat [fiːt] n exploit m, prouesse f, ha fait m, tour de force m.

feather ['feðə] n plume f, penne plumage m; vt garnir de plum empenner.

feathery ['feðəri] a léger comme une plume, plumeux.

feather-weight ['feðəweit] n poids plume m.

feature ['fiːtʃə] n trait m (saillant), caractéristique f, spécialité f; grand film m, long-métrage m; vt caractériser, esquisser, mettre en manchette, mettre en vedette.

featureless ['fiːtʃəlis] a terne.

February ['februəri] n février m.

fecund ['fiːkənd] a fécond.

fecundate ['fiːkəndeit] vt féconder.

fecundation [ˌfiːkənˈdeiʃən] n fécondation f.

fecundity [fiˈkʌnditi] n fécondité f.

fed [fed] pt pp of feed; to be — up en avoir assez, marre.

federal ['fedərəl] a fédéral.

federalism [ˌfedərəlizəm] n fédéralisme m.

federate ['fedəreit] vt fédérer; vi se fédérer; a fédéré.

federation [ˌfedeˈreiʃən] n fédération f.

fee [fiː] n fief m, frais m pl, cachet m, honoraires m pl.

feeble ['fiːbl] a faible, infirme, chétif.

feebleness ['fiːblnis] n faiblesse f.

feeblish ['fiːbliʃ] a faiblard.

feed [fiːd] n repas m, tétée f, pâture f, picotin m, alimentation f, fourrage m; vt nourrir, alimenter, donner à manger à, ravitailler; vi manger, se nourrir, s'alimenter, brouter.

feeder ['fiːdə] n mangeur, -euse, biberon m, tétine f, bavette f.

feed-back ['fiːdbæk] n rétroaction f, réaction f.

feel [fiːl] n toucher m, sensation f; vt toucher, tâter, palper, sentir; vi se sentir, tâtonner, fouiller.

feeler ['fiːlə] n antenne f, éclaireur m, sondage m.

feeling ['fiːliŋ] n toucher m, maniement m, sensation f, sentiment m, sensibilité f; a sensible.

feelingly ['fiːliŋli] ad avec émotion.

feign [fein] vt feindre, simuler.

feint [feint] n feinte f; vi faire une fausse attaque, feinter.

felicitous [fiˈlisitəs] a heureux, bien trouvé.

felicity [fiˈlisiti] n félicité f.

fell [fel] n peau f, toison f; vt abattre; a sinistre, cruel.

fellow ['felou] n type m, gars m, individu m, membre m, confrère m, pareil m.

fellowship ['felouʃip] n société f, amitié f, association f, camaraderie f.

felon ['felən] n auteur d'un crime m, criminel, -elle.

felonious [fiˈlounjəs] a criminel.

felt [felt] pp pt of feel; n feutre m, vt feutrer, couvrir de carton goudronné.

female ['fiːmeil] n femelle f, femme f; a féminin.

feminine ['feminin] a féminin, femelle.

fen [fen] n marais m.

fence [fens] n barrière f, clôture f, receleur, -euse; vi faire de l'escrime, s'escrimer; vt enclore, clôturer.

fencing ['fensiŋ] n escrime f, clôture f.

fend [fend] vt to — for oneself se débrouiller; vt to — off parer, écarter.

fender ['fendə] n garde-boue m; garde-feu m.

ferment ['fəːment] n ferment m.

ferment [fəːˈment] vt faire fermenter, fomenter; vi fermenter, travailler.

fermentation [ˌfəːmenˈteiʃən] n fermentation f, travail m, effervescence f.

fern [fəːn] n fougère f.

ferocious [fəˈrouʃəs] a féroce.

ferocity [fəˈrositi] n férocité f.

ferret ['ferit] n furet m; vi fureter; vt to — out débusquer, dénicher.

ferro-concrete ['ferouˈkɔŋkriːt] n ciment armé m.

ferrule ['feruːl] n virole f, embout m.

ferry ['feri] n bac m; vt passer.

ferryman ['ferimən] n passeur m.

fertile ['fəːtail] a fertile.

fertility [fəːˈtiliti] n fertilité f, fécondité f.

fertilize ['fəːtilaiz] vt fertiliser, féconder.

fertilizer ['fəːtilaizə] n engrais m.

fervent ['fəːvənt] a brûlant, fervent, ardent.

fervor ['fəːvə] n chaleur f, ferveur f, zèle m

fester ['festə] n abcès m; vi suppurer; vt empoisonner, ulcérer.

festival ['festəvəl] n festival m, fête f.

festive ['festiv] a joyeux, de fête.

festivity [fesˈtiviti] n festivité f, fête f.

festoon [fesˈtuːn] n feston m; vt festonner.

fetch [fetʃ] vt aller chercher, apporter, atteindre, (blow) envoyer, (sigh) pousser, (breath) reprendre.

fetching ['fetʃiŋ] a intéressant.

fetid ['fetid] a fétide.

fetidness ['fetidnis] n fétidité f, puanteur f.

fetter ['fetə] n lien m; pl fers m pl, entraves f pl; vt enchaîner, entraver.

fettle ['fetl] n état m; in good — en train, en forme.

feud [fjuːd] n vendetta f.

feudal ['fjuːdl] a féodal.

feudalism ['fjuːdəlizəm] n féodalité f.

fever ['fiːvə] n fièvre f.

feverish ['fiːvəriʃ] a fiévreux, fébrile.

few [fjuː] a peu de, un (le) petit nombre; a — quelques.

fewer ['fjuːə] a moins de, moins nombreux.

fewest ['fjuːist] a le moins de, le moins nombreux.

fez [fez] n chéchia m.

fiasco [fi'æskou] n fiasco m, four m.

fib [fib] n petit mensonge m, craque f, colle f; vi enconter (à to).

fiber ['faibə] n fibre f; **staple — fibrane** f.

fibrous ['faibrəs] a fibreux.

fickle ['fikl] a volage, changeant, inconstant.

fickleness ['fiklnis] n inconstance f.

fiction ['fikʃən] n fiction f, romans m pl.

fictitious [fik'tiʃəs] a fictif, imaginaire.

fiddle ['fidl] n violon m, crin-crin m; vi jouer du violon, râcler du violon; to — **with** tripoter, tourmenter.

fiddler ['fidlə] n ménétrier m, violoneux m; violiniste.

fiddlestick ['fidlstik] n archet m; pl sottises f pl.

fidelity [fi'deliti] n fidélité f, loyauté f, exactitude f.

fidget ['fidʒit] n to have the —s avoir la bougeotte; vi s'agiter, se trémousser.

fie [fai] excl fi!

field [fi:ld] n champ m; (mil) campagne f, terrain de jeux m, domaine m, candidatures f pl; a de campagne.

field glasses ['fi:ldglɑːsiz] n jumelles f pl.

field-marshal ['fi:ld'mɑːʃəl] n maréchal m.

field-mouse ['fi:ldmaus] n mulot m.

fiend [fi:nd] n démon m.

fiendish ['fi:ndiʃ] a diabolique, infernal.

fierce [fiəs] a féroce, violent.

fiercely ['fiəsli] ad violemment, âprement.

fierceness ['fiəsnis] n férocité f, sauvagerie f, violence f.

fiery ['faiəri] a de feu, ardent, emporté, fougueux.

fife [faif] n fifre m.

fifteen ['fif'ti:n] an quinze m.

fifteenth ['fif'ti:nθ] an quinzième mf, quinze m.

fifth [fifθ] an cinquième mf, cinq m.

fiftieth ['fiftiəθ] an cinquantième mf.

fifty ['fifti] an cinquante m.

fig [fig] n figue f, tenue f, forme f.

fight [fait] n lutte f, combat m, combat(t)ivité f; vi se battre, lutter, combattre; vt combattre, se battre avec.

fighter ['faitə] n combattant m, militant m, avion de combat m.

figment ['figmənt] n invention f, rêve m.

fig-tree ['figtri:] n figuier m.

figure ['figə] n forme f, corps m, taille f, personne f, ligne f, galbe m, chiffre m, emblème m, figure f; vt (se) figurer, estimer; vi calculer, faire figure, se chiffrer, figurer.

figurehead ['figəhed] n façade f, prête-nom m, figure de proue f.

filbert ['filbə(ː)t] n noisette f.

filch [filtʃ] vt voler, escamoter.

file [fail] n lime f, piquenotes m, classeur m, dossier m, liasse f, file f; vt limer, enfiler, classer, soumettre; vi défiler.

filial ['filjəl] a filial.

filiation [fili'eiʃən] n filiation f.

filibuster ['filibʌstə] n flibustier m; vi flibuster.

filigree ['filigriː] n filigrane m.

filing ['failiŋ] n limaille f, limage m; classement m.

fill [fil] n plein m, soûl m, pipée f; vt remplir, plomber, compléter, combler; vi se remplir, se garnir; to — up vi faire le plein.

filling ['filiŋ] n plombage m, chargement m, remplissage m.

filling-station ['filiŋ,steiʃən] n poste d'essence m.

fillet ['filit] n bandeau m, filet m.

fillip ['filip] n chiquenaude f, stimulant m, coup de fouet m.

filly ['fili] n pouliche f.

film [film] n pellicule f, film m, voile m, (eye) taie f; vt filmer, tourner.

film-star ['filmstɑː] n vedette du cinéma f.

filter ['filtə] n filtre m; vti filtrer; tamiser.

filth [filθ] n saleté f, ordure f.

filthy ['filθi] a sale, crasseux, immonde.

fin [fin] n nageoire f, aileron m.

final ['fainl] a final, dernier, définitif, décisif.

finally ['fainəli] ad enfin, finalement.

finance [fai'næns] n finance f; vt financer.

financial [fai'nænʃəl] a financier.

financier [fai'nænsiə] n financier m.

finch [fintʃ] n pinson m.

find [faind] n trouvaille f, découverte f; vt trouver, constater, pourvoir, fournir; **all found** tout compris.

fine [fain] n amende f; vt mettre l'amende; a beau, bon, fin, délié, élégant.

finely ['fainli] ad habilement, subtilement, magnifiquement, fin.

fineness ['fainnis] n beauté f, élégance f, finesse f, excellence f.

finery ['fainəri] n atours m pl, parure f.

finesse [fi'nes] n finesse f; vi user de finesse, faire une impasse.

finger ['fiŋgə] n doigt m; **fore-index** m; **middle —** médius m; **ring—** annulaire m; **little —** pet doigt m, auriculaire m; vt toucher, manier, jouer, tripoter.

finger-bowl ['fiŋgəboul] n rince doigts m.

fingering ['fiŋgəriŋ] n maniement m, touche f, doigté m.

fingernail ['fiŋgəneil] n ongle de la main m.

fingerprint ['fiŋgəprint] n empreinte digitale f.

finish ['finiʃ] n fini m, dernière touche f; to a — à mort; vti finir, terminer; vt achever; vi prendre fin, se terminer.
finished ['finiʃt] a accompli.
Finland ['finlənd] n Finlande f.
Finn [fin] n Finlandais(e) mf.
Finnish ['finiʃ] an finlandais m.
fir [fə:] n sapin m.
fire ['faiə] n feu m, incendie m, tir m, ardeur f; vt allumer, incendier, mettre le feu à, enflammer; vi faire feu; — away allez!
fire-alarm ['faiərə,lɑːm] n avertisseur d'incendie m.
firearm ['faiərɑːm] n arme à feu f.
firebrand ['faiəbrænd] n incendiaire m, boutefeu m, brandon m.
fire-brigade ['faiəbri,geid] n compagnie de sapeurs-pompiers f.
firedamp ['faiədæmp] n grisou m.
firedog ['faiədɔg] n chenet m.
fire-engine ['faiər,endʒin] n pompe à incendie f.
fire-escape ['faiəris,keip] n échelle de sauvetage f.
fireguard ['faiəgɑːd] n garde-feu m.
fireman ['faiəmən] n pompier m, chauffeur m.
fireplace ['faiəpleis] n cheminée f.
fireproof ['faiəpruːf] a ignifuge.
fireside ['faiəsaid] n coin du feu m.
firework ['faiəwəːk] n feu d'artifice m.
firing-squad ['faiəriŋ,skwɔd] n peloton d'exécution m.
firm [fəːm] n firme f, maison de commerce f; a ferme, solide, résolu.
firmly ['fəːmli] ad fermement.
firmness ['fəːmnis] n fermeté f, solidité f.
first [fəːst] a premier; ad premièrement, primo.
first-aid ['fəːst'eid] n premiers secours m pl.
first-class ['fəːst'klɑːs] a de première classe, qualité.
first-rate ['fəːst'reit] a de premier ordre.
firth [fəːθ] n estuaire m.
fish [fiʃ] n poisson m; vti pêcher.
fishbone ['fiʃboun] n arête f.
fisherman ['fiʃəmən] n pêcheur m.
fishery ['fiʃəri] n pêcherie f.
fishing ['fiʃiŋ] n pêche f.
fishing-ground ['fiʃiŋgraund] n pêcherie f.
fishing-net n ['fiʃiŋnet] n épervier m.
fishing-rod ['fiʃiŋrɔd] n canne à pêche f.
fish-kettle ['fiʃ'ketl] n poissonnière f.
fishmonger ['fiʃ,mʌŋgə] n marchand de poisson m.
fishmonger's ['fiʃ,mʌŋgəz] n poissonnerie f.
fish-pond ['fiʃpɔnd] n vivier m.
fishy ['fiʃi] a poissoneux, louche.
fissionable ['fiʃənəbl] a fissile.
fissure ['fiʃə] n fissure f.

fist [fist] n poing m.
fit [fit] n attaque f, accès m, ajustement m, coupe f; a apte, bon, convenable, en forme; vt aller à, ajuster, garnir, munir, préparer, équiper; vi s'adapter, s'ajuster; to — on monter, essayer; to — out garnir, équiper; to — up monter.
fitful ['fitful] a capricieux.
fitfully ['fitfuli] ad par accès, par à-coups.
fitly ['fitli] ad à propos, à point.
fitness ['fitnis] n parfait état m convenance f, aptitude f.
fitter ['fitə] n ajusteur m, essayeur m.
fitting ['fitiŋ] n ajustage m, essayage m; pl garnitures f pl; a bon, juste, approprié.
five [faiv] an cinq m.
fivefold ['faivfould] a quintuple.
fix [fiks] n embarras m, situation fâcheuse f; vt fixer, établir, arrêter, assujettir.
fixed [fikst] a fixe, arrêté.
fixedly ['fiksidli] ad fixement.
fixity ['fiksiti] n fixité f.
fixture(s) ['fikstʃə(s)] n garniture(s) fixe(s) f (pl), (fig) meuble m, match m.
fizz [fiz] n bruit de fusée m, pétillement m, (fam) champagne m; vi pétiller, siffler.
fizzle ['fizl] n pétillement m, grésillement m; vi fuser, grésiller; to — out faire long feu, faire four.
flabbergast ['flæbəgɑːst] vt renverser, stupéfier.
flabby ['flæbi] a flasque, pendant.
flag [flæg] n drapeau m, pavillon m, dalle f, glaïeul m; vi pendre, languir, fléchir, se relâcher; vt jalonner, signaler, pavoiser.
flagbearer ['flæg'beərə] n porte-drapeau m.
flagging ['flægiŋ] n dallage m, ralentissement m.
flagon ['flægən] n flacon m, burette f.
flagrancy ['fleigrənsi] n éclat m, énormité f.
flagrant ['fleigrənt] a flagrant, énorme, scandaleux.
flagship ['flægʃip] n vaisseau-amiral m.
flagstaff ['flægstɑːf] n mât m.
flail [fleil] n fléau m.
flair [flɛə] n flair m.
flak [flæk] n tir m contre avion, la DCA.
flake [fleik] n flocon m, flammèche f, lamelle f, pelure f, écaille f; vi tomber à flocons, (s')écailler.
flaky ['fleiki] a floconneux, écailleux, feuilleté.
flame [fleim] n flamme f; vi flamber, s'enflammer.
flame-thrower ['fleim,θrouə] n lance-flammes m.
flaming ['fleimiŋ] a flambant.
Flanders ['flɑːndəz] n Flandre f.

flank [flæŋk] n flanc m; vt flanquer, prendre de flanc.

flannel ['flænl] n flanelle f.

flap [flæp] n tape f, battement d'ailes m, patte f, claquement m, pan m, bord m; vti battre; vi s'agiter, claquer.

flare [flɛə] n flambée f, fusée éclairante f, flamme f, feu d'atterrissage m; vi flamber, s'évaser; vt évaser; to — up s'emporter, s'enflammer.

flash [flæʃ] n éclair m, lueur f; in a — en un clin d'œil; vi flamboyer, jeter des éclairs; vt faire étinceler, télégraphier.

flashing ['flæʃiŋ] n éclat m, clignotement m, projection f.

flashy ['flæʃi] a voyant, tapageur.

flask [flɑːsk] n gourde f, fiole f.

flat [flæt] n appartement m; plat m, plaine f, (mus) bémol m; a plat, tout sec, pur, éventé, catégorique, insipide.

flat-iron ['flæt‚aiən] n fer à repasser m.

flatness ['flætnis] n platitude f, monotonie f, égalité f.

flatten ['flætn] vt aplatir, aplanir, niveler, laminer; vi s'aplatir, s'aplanir.

flatter ['flætə] vt flatter.

flatterer ['flætərə] n flatteur m.

flattery ['flætəri] n flatterie f.

flaunt [flɔːnt] vi s'exhiber, se pavaner; vt afficher, faire étalage de, étaler.

flautist ['flɔːtist] n flûtiste mf.

flavor ['fleivə] n saveur f, bouquet m, fumet m, goût m; vt assaisonner, relever, aromatiser.

flavoring ['fleivəriŋ] n assaisonnement m.

flaw [flɔː] n fêlure f, défaut m, paille f, tache f.

flawless ['flɔːlis] a impeccable, sans défaut.

flax [flæks] n lin m.

flaxen ['flæksən] a en (de) lin, blond, filasse.

flay [flei] vt étriller, écorcher, massacrer, rosser.

flea [fliː] n puce f, vétille f.

fleabite ['fliːbait] n morsure de puce f, rien m.

fleck [flek] n tache de son f, grain m, moucheture f; vt tacheter, moucheter.

fled [fled] pt pp of flee.

fledged [fledʒd] a couvert de plumes; fully— a dru, émancipé.

flee [fliː] vi fuir, se sauver.

fleece [fliːs] n toison f; vt tondre, estamper.

fleecy ['fliːsi] a laineux, cotonneux, moutonné.

fleet [fliːt] n flotte f; train m; vi passer, s'enfuir.

fleeting ['fliːtiŋ] a fugitif, éphémère.

flesh [fleʃ] n chair f.

fleshy ['fleʃi] a charnu, pulpeux.

flew [fluː] pt of fly.

flex [fleks] n flexible m; vti fléchir.

flexibility [‚fleksi'biliti] n flexibilité f, souplesse f.

flexible ['fleksəbl] a flexible, souple.

flexion ['flekʃən] n flexion f, courbe f.

flick [flik] n chiquenaude f, pichenette f, petit coup m.

flicker ['flikə] n frémissement m, éclair m, clignement m; vi frémir, vaciller, flotter.

flight [flait] n fuite f, vol m, ligne f, essor m, saillie f, volée f, raid m; — deck pont m d'envol.

flighty ['flaiti] a volage, écervelé, frivole, pauvre.

flimsy ['flimzi] a fragile, trivial, frivole.

flinch [flintʃ] vi broncher, reculer, fléchir.

fling [fliŋ] n jet m, impulsion f; vt (re)jeter, lancer, émettre; vi se jeter, se précipiter.

flint ['flint] n silex m, pierre à briquet f.

flinty ['flinti] a dur comme pierre, caillouteux.

flip [flip] n chiquenaude f, tape f, petit tour de vol m; vt lancer, tapoter, (ear) pincer.

flippancy ['flipənsi] n désinvolture f, irrévérence f.

flippant ['flipənt] a impertinent, désinvolte.

flirt [fləːt] n coquette f, flirt m; vi flirter, conter fleurette (a with).

flit [flit] vi voltiger, passer, déménager; n déménagement m.

float [flout] n radeau m, bouchon m, flotteur m, rampe f; vt lancer, émettre, porter, mettre à flot, flotter; vi flotter, nager, faire la planche.

floatation [flou'teiʃən] n lancement m, émission f.

flock [flɔk] n troupeau m, troupe f, bourre m, flocon m; vi s'assembler, s'attrouper.

floe [flou] n banquise f.

flog [flɔg] vt fouetter, fouailler, bazarder.

flogging ['flɔgiŋ] n fessée f, flagellation f.

flood [flʌd] n inondation f, crue f, déluge m, flux m, marée f; · vt inonder, irriguer, grossir; vi déborder, se noyer, être en crue.

floodgate ['flʌdgeit] n vanne f.

floodlight ['flʌdlait] vt illuminer par projecteurs.

floor [flɔː] n plancher m, parquet m, étage m; vt planchéier, terrasser, renverser.

floorcloth ['flɔːklɔθ] n torchon m.

flop [flɔp] n plouf, bruit m sourd, four m; vi s'affaler, faire four.

florid ['flɔrid] a rubicond, fleuri, flamboyant.

florist ['flɔrist] n fleuriste mf.

floss [flɔs] n bourre f.

flotilla [flə'tilə] n flottille f.

flotsam ['flɔtsəm] n épave f flottante.

flounce [flauns] n sursaut m, volant m; to — out sortir en colère.

flounder ['flaundə] n carrelet m; vi patauger.

flour ['flauə] n farine f; cassava —, garri farine f de manioc.

flourish ['flʌriʃ] n fioritures f pl, parafe m, grand geste m, fanfare f; vi prospérer, embellir; vt brandir.

flourishing ['flʌriʃiŋ] a florissant, prospère.

flout [flaut] vt narguer, se moquer de.

flow [flou] n écoulement m, arrivée f, courant m, flux m, flot m; vi couler, affluer, flotter; résulter, se jeter.

flower ['flauə] n fleur f; vi fleurir; — garden jardin m d'agrément; — shop boutique f de fleuriste.

flowery ['flauəri] a fleuri.

flowing ['flouiŋ] a coulant, flottant, aisé.

flown [floun] pp of fly; a high — ampoulé.

flu [flu:] n see influenza.

fluctuate ['flʌktjueit] vi fluctuer, vaciller, flotter.

fluctuation [,flʌktju'eiʃən] n fluctuation f, variations f pl.

flue [flu:] n tuyau m (de cheminée).

fluency ['flu:ənsi] n aisance f, facilité f.

fluent ['flu:ənt] a coulant, facile.

fluently ['flu:əntli] ad avec facilité, couramment.

fluff [flʌf] n duvet m.

fluffy ['flʌfi] a duveté, pelucheux.

fluid ['flu:id] an fluide m.

fluidity [flu:'iditi] n fluidité f, inconstance f.

fluke [flu:k] n fer m, pointe f, (coup m de) raccroc m.

flung [flʌŋ] pt pp of fling.

flurry ['flʌri] n coup de vent m, excitation f, émoi m, rafale f, vt agiter, étourdir.

flush [flʌʃ] n rougeur f, accès m, transport m, flot m, jet m, vol m d'oiseau, chasse f (d'eau); a débordant, regorgeant, abondant, de niveau; vi jaillir, rougir; vt enivrer, inonder, laver à grande eau.

fluster ['flʌstə] n agitation f; vt énerver, agiter, faire perdre la tête à.

flute [flu:t] n flûte f, cannelure f; vi jouer de la flûte, parler d'une voix flûtée; vt canneler, rainurer.

flutist ['flu:tist] n flûtiste mf.

flutter ['flʌtə] n battement m (d'ailes), émoi m, sensation f, palpitation f, voltigement m; vti battre faiblement; vi palpiter, s'agiter, frémir, trémousser; vt agiter, secouer.

flux [flʌks] n flux m.

fly [flai] n mouche f, fiacre m, braguette f; a malin; vi voler,

courir, se sauver; vti fuir; vt faire voler, piloter; to — away s'envoler.

flyer, flier ['flaiə] n aviateur, -trice.

flying ['flaiiŋ] n vol m, aviation f; a flottant, au vent, volant — visit visite-éclair f.

flying-boat ['flaiiŋbout] n hydravion m.

flying-bomb ['flaiiŋ'bɔm] n bombe volante f.

flying-club ['flaiiŋ,klʌb] n aéro-club m.

flying-squad ['flaiiŋ'skwɔd] n brigade volante f.

flysheet ['flaiʃi:t] n circulaire m, papillon m.

flywheel ['flaiwi:l] n volant m (de commande).

foal [foul] n poulain m.

foam [foum] n écume f; vi écumer, bouillonner, baver.

fob [fɔb] n gousset m, régence f; to — off vt refiler.

focus ['foukəs] n foyer m; vt mettre au point, concentrer; vi converger; out of — brouillé.

fodder ['fɔdə] n fourrage m.

foe [fou] n ennemi m.

fog [fɔg] n brouillard m, voile m; vt embruner, voiler.

foggy ['fɔgi] a épais, brumeux, brouillé.

foghorn ['fɔghɔ:n] n sirène f.

fog-signal ['fɔg,signl] n pétard m.

foil [fɔil] n feuille f, tain m, repoussoir m, fleuret m, piste f; vt donner le change à, tromper, déjouer, faire échouer.

foist [fɔist] vt repasser, refiler.

fold [fould] n parc à bestiaux m, bercail m, troupeau m, (re)pli m, creux m, battant m; vt parquer, plier, envelopper, serrer, croiser; vi se (re)plier.

folding ['fouldiŋ] n (re)pliage m; a pliant, rabattable.

foliage ['fouliidʒ] n feuillage n, feuillée f.

folk(s) [fouk(s)] n gens mf pl.

folksong ['fouksɔŋ] n chanson f populaire.

follow ['fɔlou] vti suivre; vt succéder à; vi s'ensuivre.

follower ['fɔlouə] n partisan m, serviteur m.

following ['fɔlouiŋ] n suite f; a suivant.

folly ['fɔli] n folie f.

foment [fou'ment] vt fomenter.

fond [fɔnd] a tendre, affectueux, indulgent, friand, amateur; to be — of aimer.

fondle ['fɔndl] vt câliner.

font [fɔnt] n fonts baptismaux m pl.

food [fu:d] n nourriture f, alimentation f, vivres m pl, pâture f, pâtée f; a alimentaire, nutritif.

fool [fu:l] n sot, sotte, fou, folle, imbécile mf, idiot(e) mf, bouffon m; vt rouler, duper; vi faire la bête.

foolhardiness ['fuːlˌhɑːdinis] n témérité f.

foolhardy ['fuːlˌhɑːdi] a téméraire, casse-cou.

foolish ['fuːliʃ] a stupide, fou, absurde, insensé.

foolishness ['fuːliʃnis] n folie f, bêtise f.

foolproof ['fuːlpruːf] a de sureté, à toute épreuve.

foot [fut] n pied m, patte f, base f, fond m, bas m, bas-bout m; vt danser, payer.

foot-and-mouth disease ['futənˈmauθdiˈziz] n fièvre aphteuse f.

football ['futbɔːl] n ballon m, football m.

footboard ['futbɔːd] n marchepied m.

footbridge ['futbridʒ] n passerelle f.

foothold ['futhould] n prise f, pied m.

footing ['futiŋ] n pied m, prise f.

footlights ['futlaits] n rampe f.

footman ['futmən] n valet de pied m, laquais m.

footmuff ['futmʌf] n chancelière f.

footnote ['futnout] n note f.

footpath ['futpɑːθ] n sentier m, trottoir m.

footplate ['futpleit] n plateforme f.

footprint ['futprint] n empreinte f.

footslogger ['futslɔgə] n piéton m, fantassin m, biffin m.

footstep ['futstep] n pas m; pl traces f pl, brisées f pl.

footstool ['futstuːl] n tabouret m.

foot-warmer ['futˌwɔːmə] n bouillotte f, chaufferette f.

footwear ['futwɛə] n chaussures f pl.

foozle ['fuːzl] vt rater.

fop [fɔp] n gandin m, fat m.

for [fɔː] prep pour, à, quant à, comme, pendant, malgré; cj car.

forage ['fɔridʒ] n fourrage m; vt fourrager, marauder; vi aller au fourrage.

forage-cap ['fɔridʒˌkæp] n calot m.

forasmuch [fərəzˈmʌtʃ] cj vu que, d'autant que.

foray ['fɔrei] n raid m, incursion f.

forbear [fɔːˈbɛə] vt tolérer, s'abstenir de; vi patienter.

forbearance [fɔːˈbɛərəns] n indulgence f, patience f.

forbid [fəˈbid] vt défendre.

forbidden [fəˈbidn] a interdit, défendu, prohibé; **smoking —** défense de fumer.

forbidding [fəˈbidiŋ] a sévère, rébarbatif, sinistre.

force [fɔːs] n force f, contrainte f, violence f, puissance f, vigueur f; **task —** corps m expéditionnaire; vt forcer.

forced [fɔːst] a forcé, inévitable, faux.

forceful ['fɔːsful] a énergique, puissant.

force-land ['fɔːslænd] vi faire un atterrissage forcé.

forcible ['fɔːsəbl] a puissant, vigoureux.

ford [fɔːd] n gué m; vt passer à gué.

fordable ['fɔːdəbl] a guéable.

fore [fɔː] n avant m, premier plan m; **to the —** en vue.

forearm ['fɔːrɑːm] n avant-bras m.

forebear ['fɔːbɛə] n ancêtre m.

forebode [fɔːˈboud] vt pressentir, augurer.

foreboding [fɔːˈboudiŋ] n pressentiment m, mauvais augure m.

forecast ['fɔːkɑːst] n prévision f, pronostic m; vt prévoir.

forecastle ['fouksl] n gaillard d'avant m.

foreclose [fɔːˈklouz] vt défendre; (law) forclore, saisir.

forefather ['fɔːˌfɑːðə] n ancêtre m, aïeul m.

forefinger ['fɔːˌfiŋgə] n index m.

forefront ['fɔːfrʌnt] n premier rang m, premier plan m.

foregone ['fɔːgɔn] a acquis (couru) d'avance, prévu.

foreground ['fɔːgraund] n premier plan m.

forehead ['fɔrid] n front m.

foreign ['fɔrin] a étranger.

foreigner ['fɔrinə] n étranger, -ère.

foreland ['fɔːlənd] n promontoire m, cap m, pointe f.

forelock ['fɔːlɔk] n mèche f.

foreman ['fɔːmən] n contremaître n, chef d'équipe m, président du jury m.

foremost ['fɔːmoust] a premier, en tête.

forenoon ['fɔːnuːn] n matinée f.

forerunner ['fɔːˌrʌnə] n précurseur m, avant-coureur m, avant-courrier, -ère.

foresee [fɔːˈsiː] vt prévoir.

foreshadow [fɔːˈʃædou] vt laisser prévoir, présager.

foresight ['fɔːsait] n prevoyance f, prévision f, (gun) bouton m de mire.

forest ['fɔrist] n forêt f.

forestall [fɔːˈstɔːl] vt anticiper, devancer, prévenir.

forester ['fɔristə] n garde-forestier m.

foretaste ['fɔːteist] n avant-goût m.

foretell [fɔːˈtel] vt prédire, présager.

forethought ['fɔːθɔːt] n prévoyance f, préméditation f.

forever [fəˈrevə] ad pour toujours, à jamais.

forewarn [fɔːˈwɔːn] vt prévenir, avertir.

foreword ['fɔːwəd] n avant-propos m, préface f.

forfeit ['fɔːfit] n prix m, rançon f, amende f, confiscation f, forfait m; vt perdre, avoir à payer, forfaire à.

forgave [fəˈgeiv] pt of forgive.

forge [fɔːdʒ] n forge f; vt forger, contrefaire, fabriquer; **to — ahead** prendre de l'avance, pousser de l'avant.

forger ['fɔːdʒə] n faussaire mf, forgeron m.

forgery ['fɔːdʒəri] n faux m, contrefaçon f.

forget [fə'get] vt oublier, négliger.

forgetful [fə'getful] a oublieux, négligent.

forgetfulness [fə'getfulnis] n oubli m.

forget-me-not [fə'getminɔt] n myosotis m.

forgivable [fə'givəbl] a pardonnable.

forgive [fə'giv] vt pardonner.

forgiveness [fə'givnis] n pardon m.

forgiving [fə'giviŋ] a indulgent.

forgo [fɔː'gou] vt renoncer à.

forgot, -ten [fə'gɔt, -n] pt pp of forget.

fork [fɔːk] n fourche f, fourchette f, branche f, (em)branchement m; vi fourcher, bifurquer.

forked [fɔːkt] a fourchu.

forlorn [fə'lɔːn] a abandonné, désespéré, désolé.

form [fɔːm] n forme f, formule f, formulaire m, formalité f, manières f pl, classe f, banc m, gite f; vt former, façonner, contracter; vi prendre forme, se former, se faire.

formal ['fɔːməl] a formel, formaliste, gourmé, de cérémonie, protocolaire.

formality [fɔː'mæliti] n formalité f, cérémonie f.

formally ['fɔːməli] ad formellement.

formation [fɔː'meiʃən] n formation f, disposition f.

former ['fɔːmə] a antérieur, ancien, premier, précédent, celui-là, ceux-là, celle(s)-là f.

formerly ['fɔːməli] ad antérieurement, autrefois.

formidable ['fɔːmidəbl] a formidable, redoutable.

formless ['fɔːmlis] a informe.

formula ['fɔːmjulə] n formule f.

formulate ['fɔːmjuleit] vt formuler.

forsake [fə'seik] vt renoncer à, retirer, abandonner.

forsaken [fə'seikən] pp of forsake.

forsook [fə'suk] pt of forsake.

forswear [fɔː'sweə] vt renoncer sous serment à, renier.

fort [fɔːt] n fort m; small — fortin m.

forth [fɔːθ] ad en avant, en route; and so — et ainsi de suite, et caetera.

forthcoming [fɔːθ'kʌmiŋ] a proche, prochain, tout prêt, à venir.

forthright ['fɔːθrait] a droit, franc; ad tout droit.

forthwith ['fɔːθwiθ] ad sur-le-champ.

fortieth ['fɔːtiiθ] an quarantième mf.

fortification [ˌfɔːtifi'keiʃən] n fortification f.

fortify ['fɔːtifai] vt fortifier, affermir, armer.

fortitude ['fɔːtitjuːd] n force d'âme f, courage m.

fortnight ['fɔːtnait] n quinzaine f, today — d'aujourd'hui en quinze.

fortnightly ['fɔːtnaitli] ad tous les quinze jours; a bimensuel.

fortress ['fɔːtris] n forteresse f.

fortuitous [fɔː'tjuːitəs] a fortuit, imprévu.

fortunate [fɔː'tʃənit] a heureux, qui a de la chance.

fortunately ['fɔːtʃənitli] ad heureusement.

fortune ['fɔːtʃən] n fortune f, chance f, hasard m.

fortune-teller ['fɔːtʃən,telə] n diseuse de bonne aventure f.

forty ['fɔːti] an quarante m.

forward ['fɔːwəd] n avant m; a qui va de l'avant, précoce, avancé, effronté, présomptueux; ad en avant; vt promouvoir, hâter, faire suivre, expédier.

forwardness ['fɔːwədnis] n audace f, présomption f.

fossil ['fɔsil] an fossile m.

foster ['fɔstə] vt nourrir, élever, encourager.

foster-brother ['fɔstə,brʌðə] n frère de lait m.

foster-child ['fɔstətʃaild] n nourrisson, -onne.

foster-father ['fɔstə,faːðə] n père nourricier m.

foster-mother ['fɔstə,mʌðə] n nourrice f.

foster-sister ['fɔstə,sistə] n sœur de lait f.

fought [fɔːt] pt pp of fight.

foul [faul] n coup bas m, faute f; a sale, nauséabond, vicié, obscène, traître, ordurier, déloyal, emmêlé, enrayé; vt salir, enrayer, emmêler, obstruer; vi se rencontrer s'enrayer, s'encrasser.

found [faund] pp pt of find; vt fonder, établir.

foundation [faun'deiʃən] n fondation f, fondement m, établissement m, assise f.

founder ['faundə] n fondateur m, fondeur m; vi s'effondrer, sombrer, couler.

foundling ['faundliŋ] n enfant trouvé(e) mf.

foundry ['faundri] n fonderie f.

fountain ['fauntin] n fontaine f, source f, jet d'eau m, réservoir m.

fountain-pen ['fauntinpen] n stylo m.

four [fɔː] an quatre m; —engined quadriréacteur.

fourfold ['fɔːfould] a quadruple.

fourteen [fɔː'tiːn] an quatorze m.

fourteenth [fɔː'tiːnθ] an quatorzième mf, quatorze m.

fourth [fɔːθ] an quatrième mf, quatre m.

fowl [faul] n volaille f, oiseau m.

fox [fɔks] n renard m, rusé m, roublard m.

foxy ['fɔksi] a roublard, rusé.

fraction ['frækʃən] n fraction f, fragment m.

fractious ['frækʃəs] a hargneux, rétif.

fracture ['fræktʃə] n fracture f; vt fracturer, casser; vi se casser, se fracturer.

fragile ['frædʒail] a fragile.

fragility [frə'dʒiliti] n fragilité f.

fragment ['frægmənt] n fragment m.

fragrance ['freigrəns] n parfum m.

fragrant ['freigrənt] a embaumé, odorant, parfumé.

frail [freil] n bannette f; a frêle, éphémère.

frailty ['freilti] n fragilité f.

frame [freim] n cadre m, fuselage m, châssis m, charpente f, corps m, carcasse f; — **house** maison f démontable (en bois); vt encadrer, façonner, ajuster, construire, concevoir, monter un coup contre.

frame-up ['freimʌp] n coup monté m.

framework ['freimwəːk] n cadre m, charpente f.

France [frɑːns] n France f.

franchise ['fræntʃaiz] n droit de vote m, franchise f.

Frances ['frɑːnsis] Françoise f, Francine f.

Francis ['frɑːnsis] Francis m, François m.

frank [fræŋk] a franc.

frankincense ['fræŋkinsens] n encens m.

frantic ['fræntik] a frénétique, effréné.

fraternal [frə'təːnl] a fraternel.

fraternity [frə'təːniti] n amour fraternel m, confrérie f, compagnie f.

fraternize ['frætənaiz] vi fraterniser.

fraternizing ['frætə'naiziŋ] n fraternisation f.

fratricide ['frætrisaid] n fratricide m.

fraud [frɔːd] n fraude f, supercherie f, imposteur m.

fraudulent ['frɔːdjulənt] a frauduleux.

fraught [frɔːt] a gros (de with).

fray [frei] n bagarre f; vt effilocher, effiler; vi s'effilocher, s'effiler.

frayed [freid] a frangeux.

freak [friːk] n caprice m, phénomène m, monstre m.

freakish ['friːkiʃ] a capricieux, fantasque.

freckle ['frekl] n tache de rousseur f.

freckled ['frekld] a couvert de taches de rousseur.

free [friː] a libre, exempt, gratuit, franco; vt affranchir, libérer, élargir.

freedom ['friːdəm] n liberté f.

freehold ['friːhould] n propriété libre f.

freelance ['friːlɑːns] n franc-tireur m, indépendant(e) mf.

freely ['friːli] ad librement, largement, franchement.

freemason ['friːˌmeisn] n franc-maçon m.

freemasonry ['friːˈmeisnri] n franc-maçonnerie f.

free-trade ['friːˈtreid] n libre échange m.

free-will ['friːˈwil] n libre arbitre m; **of one's own** — de son propre gré.

freeze [friːz] vti geler; vi se figer, se congeler; vt glacer, congeler; n austerité f, blocage m des prix.

freezing ['friːziŋ] a de congélation, glacial; n gel m, réfrigération f.

freight [freit] n fret m, cargaison f, marchandises f pl; vt (af)fréter, charger, noliser.

French [frentʃ] an français m.

Frenchman ['frentʃmən] n Français m.

French-speaking ['frentʃ'spiːkiŋ] a francophone.

Frenchwoman ['frentʃ,wumən] n Française f.

frenzied ['frenzid] a fou, affolé, délirant, frénétique.

frenzy ['frenzi] n frénésie f, transport m.

frequency ['friːkwənsi] n fréquence f.

frequent ['friːkwənt] a fréquent, répandu.

frequent [fri'kwent] vt fréquenter, courir, hanter.

frequentation ['friːkwen'teiʃən] n fréquentation f.

frequently ['friːkwəntli] ad fréquemment, souvent.

fresco ['freskou] n fresque f.

fresh [freʃ] a frais, nouveau, novice, récent, (water) doux, (wind) vif, alerte, effronté.

freshen ['freʃn] vi rafraîchir, raviver.

freshness ['freʃnis] n fraîcheur f, vigueur f.

fret [fret] n grecque f, irritation f; vt ronger, irriter; vi s'agiter, se faire du mauvais sang.

fretful ['fretful] a irritable, agité.

fretfulness ['fretfulnis] n irritabilité f.

fretsaw ['fretsɔː] n scie à découper f.

fretwork ['fretwəːk] n découpage m, bois découpé m.

friable ['fraiəbl] a friable.

friar ['fraiə] n moine m, frère m.

friction ['frikʃən] n friction f, frottement m, tirage m.

Friday ['fraidi] n vendredi m; **Good** — vendredi saint.

friend [frend] n ami(e) mf.

friendly ['frendli] a amical.

friendship ['frendʃip] n amitié f.

frieze [friːz] n frise f.

frigate ['frigit] n frégate f.

fright [frait] n frayeur f, épouvante f, peur f.

frighten ['fraitn] vt terrifier, faire peur à.

frightful ['fraitful] a effrayant, affreux.

frightfulness ['fraitfulnis] n terreur f, horreur f.

frigid ['fridʒid] a glacial, froid, réfrigérant.

frill [fril] n ruche f, jabot m. volant m; vt plisser, tuyauter.

fringe [frindʒ] n frange f, bord m, zone f limitrophe.

frippery ['fripəri] n tralala m, fioritures f pl, babioles f pl.

frisk [frisk] vi gambader.

frisky ['friski] a fringant, frétillant, folâtre.

fritter ['fritə] n beignet m; to — away gaspiller.

frivolous ['frivələs] a frivole, futile.

frizz [friz] n frisette f, vti friser.

frizzle ['frizl] vi crépiter, grésiller; vt faire frire.

frock [frɔk] n blouse f, robe f.

frockcoat ['frɔk'kout] n redingote f.

frog [frɔg] n grenouille f.

frolic ['frɔlik] n cabriole f; pl gambades f pl; vi batifoler, s'ébattre.

frolicsome ['frɔliksəm] a espiègle, folâtre.

from [frɔm] prep de, avec, d'après, de chez, à, contre.

front [frʌnt] n front m, façade f, devant m, plastron m, devanture f; in — of devant, en avant de; vt affronter, donner sur.

frontage ['frʌntidʒ] n exposition f, vue f, façade f, devanture f.

frontier ['frʌntjə] n frontière f.

frontispiece ['frʌntispiːs] n frontispice m.

frost [frɔst] n gelée f, gel m, givre m, verglas m; vt geler, glacer, givrer, ferrer à glace.

frostbite ['frɔstbait] n gelure f, congélation f.

frostbitten ['frɔst,bitn] a gelé, brûlé par le froid.

frosty ['frɔsti] a gelé, givré, poudré, glacial.

froth [frɔθ] n écume f, mousse f.

frothy ['frɔθi] a écumeux, mousseux.

frown [fraun] n froncement de sourcils m, vi froncer les sourcils, se renfrogner; to — upon désapprouver.

frowzy ['frauzi] a moisi, renfermé, négligé.

froze, -zen [frouz, -n] pp pt of **freeze**.

fructify ['frʌktifai] vi porter fruit, fructifier; vt faire fructifier.

frugal ['fruːgəl] a frugal, économe, simple.

frugality [fruː'gæliti] n frugalité f, économie f.

fruit [fruːt] n fruit m.

fruiterer ['fruːtərə] n frutier, -ière.

fruiterer's ['fruːtərəz] n fruiterie f.

fruitful ['fruːtful] a fécond, fructueux, fertile.

fruitfulness ['fruːtfulnis] n fécondité f, productivité f.

fruition [fruː'iʃən] n jouissance f, maturation f.

fruitless ['fruːtlis] a stérile.

fruitlessness ['fruːtlisnis] n stérilité f.

fruit-tree ['fruːttriː] n arbre fruitier m.

frustrate [frʌs'treit] vt frustrer, déjouer, faire échouer.

frustration [frʌs'treiʃən] n frustration f, anéantissement m.

fry [frai] n fretin m, frai m; vt faire frire; vi frire.

frying-pan ['fraiŋ,pæn] n poêle f.

fuddle ['fʌdl] n cuite f; vt griser, brouiller, enfumer.

fuel ['fjuəl] n combustible m, carburant m, essence f; — pump pompe à essence.

fugacious [fjuː'geiʃəs] a fugace.

fugitive ['fjudʒitiv] an fugitif, -ive mf; a éphémère.

fulcrum ['fʌlkrəm] m point m d'appui.

fulfill [ful'fil] vt remplir, accomplir, exaucer, exécuter.

fulfillment [ful'filmənt] n accomplissement m, exécution f, réalisation f.

full [ful] a plein, rempli, complet, riche, vigoureux, rond, ample, bouffant.

full-blown ['ful'bloun] a épanoui.

full-dress ['ful'dres] n grande tenue f; — rehearsal répétition générale f.

full-debate ['ful'deit] n débat en règle m.

full-length ['ful'leŋθ] a en pied.

full-speed ['ful'spiːd] ad à toute vitesse, à fond de train.

full-stop ['ful'stɔp] n point m.

fullness ['fulnis] n plénitude f, ampleur f, rondeur f.

fully ['fuli] ad pleinement, en plein.

fulminate ['fulmineit] vi fulminer.

fulsome ['fulsəm] a écœurant, excessif.

fumble ['fʌmbl] vi tâtonner, fouiller; to — with tripoter.

fume [fjuːm] n fumée f, vapeur f; vi fumer (de rage), rager.

fun [fʌn] n plaisanterie f, amusement m; for — pour rire, histoire de rire.

function ['fʌŋkʃən] n fonction f, cérémonie f; vi fonctionner, marcher.

functionary ['fʌŋkʃənəri] n fonctionnaire m.

fund [fʌnd] n fonds m, caisse f, rente f; vt convertir, consolider.

fundamental [,fʌndə'mentl] a fondamental, essentiel, foncier; n pl essentiel m, principe m.

funeral ['fjuːnərəl] n enterrement m, funérailles f pl.

funereal [fjuː'niəriəl] a funéraire, funèbre, sépulcral.

funicular [fjuː'nikjuːlə] n funiculaire m.

funk [fʌnk] n frousse f, trouille f, trac m, froussard(e) mf; vt esquiver; vi avoir la frousse, se dégonfler.

funnel ['fʌnl] n entonnoir m, cheminée f.

funny ['fʌni] a drôle, marrant, comique.

fur [fəː] n fourrure f.

furbish ['fəːbiʃ] vt fourbir, astiquer.

furious ['fjuəriəs] a furieux, furibond, acharné.

furl [fəːl] vt rouler, serrer, plier, ferler.

furlough ['fəːlou] n permission f.

furnace ['fəːnis] n fourneau m, fournaise f, calorifère m, brasier m.

furnish ['fəːniʃ] vt fournir, garnir, meubler.

furniture ['fəːnitʃə] n mobilier m, meubles m pl; piece of — meuble m; — polish encaustique f.

furrier ['fʌriə] n fourreur m, pelletier, -ière.

furrow ['fʌrou] n sillon m, rainure f; vt labourer, sillonner.

furry ['fəːri] a fourré, garni de fourrure, sale, chargé, encrassé.

further ['fəːðə] a nouveau, supplémentaire, plus ample, plus éloigné; ad plus loin, d'ailleurs, davantage; vt appuyer, favoriser, avancer.

furtherance ['fəːðərəns] n avancement m.

furthermore ['fəːðəˈmɔː] ad en outre, de plus.

furtive ['fəːtiv] a furtif.

fury ['fjuəri] n fureur f, rage f, furie f.

furze [fəːz] n genêt m, ajonc m.

fuse [fjuːz] n plomb m, amorce f, fusée f; vti fondre, fusionner; the lights fused les plombs ont sauté.

fuselage ['fjuːzəlɑːʒ] n fuselage m.

fusion ['fjuːʒən] n fusion f.

fuss [fʌs] n bruit m, agitation f, embarras m pl; vt tracasser; vi faire des embarras, faire des histoires.

fussy ['fʌsi] a agité, tracassier, méticuleux, tatillon.

fusty ['fʌsti] a moisi, ranci, renfermé, démodé.

futile ['fjuːtail] a futile, vain.

futility [fjuːˈtiliti] n futilité f, inutilité f.

future ['fjuːtʃə] n avenir m, futur m; a futur.

fuzzy ['fʌzi] a crépu, duveté, frisé, brouillé.

G

gab [gæb] n parole f; gift of the — bagout m, faconde f.

gabble ['gæbl] n bafouillage m; vi bredouiller, jacasser.

gable ['geibl] n pignon m.

gad [gæd] vi to — about courir (la prétentaine), papillonner.

gadfly ['gædflai] n taon m.

gadget ['gædʒit] n truc m, dispositif m.

gaff [gæf] n gaffe f.

gag [gæg] n bâillon m, gag m; vt bâillonner.

sage [geidʒ] n gage m, garantie f, défi m; vt gager, offrir en gage.

gaiety ['geiəti] n gaieté f, allégresse f.

gain [gein] n gain m, bénéfice m, avantage m; vt gagner.

gainer ['geinə] n gagnant(e) mf.

gainsay ['geinˈsei] vt nier, démentir, contredire.

gait [geit] n port m, allure f, démarche f.

gaiter ['geitə] n guêtre f.

galaxy ['gæləksi] n voie f lactée, constellation f.

gale [geil] n rafale f, tempête f.

gall [gɔːl] n fiel m, rancœur f, amertume f, écorchure f; effronterie f, aplomb m; vt écorcher, blesser, irriter.

gallant ['gælənt] n élégant m, galant m; a vaillant, galant, brave, noble.

gallantly ['gæləntli] ad vaillamment, galamment.

gallantry ['gæləntri] n vaillance f, galanterie f.

gall-bladder ['gɔːlˌblædə] n vésicule biliaire f.

gallery ['gæləri] n galerie f, tribune f, musée m.

galley ['gæli] n galère f, cambuse f, placard m.

galley-slave ['gælisleiv] n galérien m.

gallop ['gæləp] n galop m; vi galoper; vt faire galoper.

gallows ['gælouz] n potence f.

gallstone ['gɔːlstoun] n calcul biliaire m.

galore [gəˈlɔː] n abondance f, ad en abondance, à profusion, à gogo.

galosh [gəˈbʃ] n caoutchouc m.

galvanize ['gælvənaiz] vt galvaniser.

gamble ['gæmbl] n jeu m, spéculation f; vti jouer; vt risquer.

gambler ['gæmblə] n joueur, -euse.

gambol ['gæmbəl] n gambade f; vi gambader, s'ébattre.

game [geim] n jeu m, partie f, tour m, manche f, gibier m.

game-bag ['geimbæg] n gibecière f.

gamekeeper ['geimˌkiːpə] n garde-chasse m.

game-licence ['geimˌlaisəns] n permis de chasse m.

gammon ['gæmən] n jambon m, blague f, attrape f; vt saler, fumer, mystifier.

gamp [gæmp] n pépin m, riflard m.

gamut ['gæmət] n gamme f.

gander ['gændə] n jars m.

gang [gæŋ] n équipe f, bande f.

gang-foreman ['gæŋˈfɔːmən] n brigadier m, chef d'équipe m.

gangrene ['gæŋgriːn] n gangrène f; vt gangrener; vi se gangrener.

gangrenous ['gæŋgrənəs] a gangreneux.

gangster ['gæŋstə] n bandit m, gangster m.

gangway ['gæŋwei] n passage m, passerelle f.

gap [gæp] n trou m, trouée f, brèche f, lacune f, différence f, écart m, intervalle f.

gape [geip] vi bâiller, rester bouche bée, être béant, s'ouvrir.

gaping ['geipiŋ] a béant, bouche bée.

garage ['gærɑːʒ] n garage m; vt remiser, garer.

garb [gɑːb] n costume m, tenue f; vt habiller, vêtir.

garbage ['gɑːbidʒ] n ordures f pl, détritus m pl, tripaille f.

garble ['gɑːbl] vt dénaturer, tronquer, mutiler.

garden ['gɑːdn] n jardin m; vi jardiner; — party réception en plein air, f.

gardener ['gɑːdnə] n jardinier m.

gargle ['gɑːgl] n gargarisme m; vi se gargariser.

gargoyle ['gɑːgɔil] n gargouille f.

garish ['gɛəriʃ] a criard, voyant.

garland ['gɑːlənd] n guirlande f, couronne f.

garlic ['gɑːlik] n ail m.

garment ['gɑːmənt] n vêtement m.

garner ['gɑːnə] n grenier m; vt accumuler, rentrer, engranger.

garnet ['gɑːnit] n grenat m.

garnish ['gɑːniʃ] n garniture f, vt parer, garnir; (jur) appeler en justice.

garotte [gə'rɔt] tourniquet m, garotte f; vt étrangler, garrotter.

garret ['gærit] n mansarde f.

garrison ['gærisən] n garnison f; vt tenir garnison à, garnir de troupes.

garrulity [gə'ruːliti] n loquacité f.

garrulous ['gæruləs] a bavard, loquace.

garter ['gɑːtə] n jarretière f.

gas [gæs] n gaz m, (poison-gas) les gaz m pl, essence f; vt gazer, asphyxier.

gas-burner ['gæs,bəːnə] n bec de gaz m.

gaseous ['geisiəs] a gazeux.

gas-fitter ['gæs,fitə] n gazier m.

gash [gæʃ] n balafre f, taillade f, entaille f; vt balafrer, entailler.

gas-holder ['gæshouldə] n gazomètre m.

gasket ['gæskit] n joint m.

gas-lamp ['gæs'læmp] n réverbère m.

gasman ['gæsmæn] n employé du gaz m.

gas-mantle ['gæs,mæntl] n manchon à gaz m.

gas-mask ['gæsmɑːsk] n masque à gaz m.

gas-meter ['gæs,miːtə] n compteur à gaz m, gazomètre m.

gasoline ['gæsəliːn] n essence f.

gasp [gɑːsp] n aspiration f convulsive, dernier soupir m; vi panteler, en rester bouche bée, avoir un hoquet, respirer avec peine.

gassy ['gæsi] a gazeux, mousseux.

gastronomy [gæs'trɔnəmi] n gastronomie f.

gasworks ['gæswəːks] n usine à gaz f.

gate [geit] n porte f, grille f, barrière f, vanne f; — keeper portier, -ière; — money recette f.

gatecrasher ['geitkræʃə] n resquilleur m.

gateway ['geitwei] n portail m, porte f.

gather ['gæðə] vt réunir, rassembler, cueillir, moissonner, amasser, gagner, froncer, imaginer; vi grossir, se réunir, s'accumuler, s'amonceler.

gathering ['gæðəriŋ] n assemblée f, réunion f, amoncellement m, moisson f, cueillette f, quête f, abcès m, froncure f.

gathers ['gæðəz] n pl fronces f pl.

gaudy ['gɔːdi] a criard, voyant, éclatant.

gauge [geidʒ] n jauge f, mesure f, calibre m, indicateur m, (rails) écartement m; vt jauger, mesurer, estimer; narrow — voie étroite; standard — écartement normal.

gaunt [gɔːnt] a hâve, hagard, décharné.

gauntlet ['gɔːntlit] n gantelet m, gant m (à manchette).

gauze [gɔːz] n gaze f.

gave [geiv] pt of give.

gawky ['gɔːki] a dégingandé.

gay [gei] a gai, resplendissant.

gaze [geiz] n regard fixe m; vti regarder fixement; to — at fixer, contempler.

gazette [gə'zet] n gazette f, journal officiel m; vt publier à l'Officiel.

gazetteer [,gæzə'tiə] n gazetier m, dictionnaire m de géographie.

gear [giə] n harnais m, attirail m, ustensiles m pl, engrenage m, marche f, vitesse f; to throw into— embrayer; to put out of — débrayer.

gearbox ['giəbɔks] n boîte de vitesses f, carter m.

gearing ['giəriŋ] n engrenage m, embrayage m.

gearless ['giəles] a sans engrenage.

gear-lever ['giəliːvə] n levier m de vitesse.

gear-shift ['giəʃift] n levier m de vitesse.

gearwheel ['giəwiːl] n roue dentée f, rouage m.

gecko ['gekou] n margouillat m.

gel [dʒel] n gèle m; vi coaguler.

gelatine ['dʒelə'tiːn] n gélatine f; explosive — plastic m.

geld [geld] vt châtrer.

gelding ['geldiŋ] n hougre m, eunuque m.

gem [dʒem] n gemme f, perle f, joyau m.

gender ['dʒendə] n genre m.

general ['dʒenərəl] an général m.

generalissimo [,dʒenəri'lisimou] n généralissime m.

generality [,dʒenə'ræliti] n généralité f, portée générale f.

generalization [.dʒenərəlai'zeiʃən] n
généralisation f.

generalize ['dʒenərəlaiz] vt généraliser.

generalship ['dʒenərəlʃip] n stratégie
f.

generate ['dʒenəreit] vt produire,
générer.

generation [.dʒenə'reiʃən] n génération f, production f.

generosity [.dʒenə'rɔsiti] n générosité f.

generous ['dʒenərəs] a généreux,
copieux.

genesis ['dʒenisis] n genèse f.

genial ['dʒi:njəl] a jovial, cordial,
doux, chaud.

geniality [.dʒi:ni'æliti] n belle
humeur f, cordialité f.

genius ['dʒi:njəs] n génie m, aptitude
f.

genteel [dʒen'ti:l] a distingué,
élégant, qui affecte de la distinction.

Gentile ['dʒentail] n Gentil(e) mf.

gentility [dʒen'tiliti] n bonne société
f.

gentle ['dʒentl] a bien né, doux,
aimable.

gently ['dʒentli] ad doucement.

gentlefolk ['dʒentlfouk] n personnes
de distinction f pl.

gentleman ['dʒentlmən] n monsieur
m, homme comme il faut m,
gentleman m.

gentlemanly ['dʒentlmənli] a comme
il faut, distingué, convenable.

gentleness ['dʒentlnis] n gentillesse
f, douceur f.

gentry ['dʒentri] n haute bourgeoisie
f, petite noblesse f.

genuine ['dʒenjuin] a authentique,
naturel, sincère, franc, véritable.

geographer [dʒi'ɔgrəfə] n géographe
m.

geographical [dʒiə'græfikəl] a géographique.

geography [dʒi'ɔgrəfi] n géographie
f.

geologist [dʒi'ɔlədʒist] n géologue m.

geology [dʒi'ɔlədʒi] n géologie f.

geometric [dʒiə'metrik] a géométrique; — **drawing** dessin m géométrique, linéaire.

geometrician [.dʒioume'triʃən] n
géomètre m.

geometry [dʒi'ɔmitri] n géométrie f.

geomorphic [dʒiou'mɔ:fik] a semblable à la terre.

geophysics ['dʒiou'fiziks] n pl géo-
physique, physique f du globe.

George [dʒɔ:dʒ] Georges m.

germ [dʒə:m] n germe m, bacille m,
microbe m.

German ['dʒə:mən] n Allemand(e)
mf; an allemand m.

Germany ['dʒə:məni] n Allemagne
f.

germinate ['dʒə:mineit] vi germer.

germination [.dʒə:mi'neiʃən] n germination f.

gerrymander ['dʒerimændə] vt
manipuler, truquer.

gesticulate [dʒes'tikjuleit] vi gesticuler.

gesticulation [dʒes.tikju'leiʃən] n
gesticulation f.

gesture ['dʒestʃə] n geste m; vi faire
des gestes.

get [get] vt se procurer, obtenir,
acquérir, chercher, comprendre,
piger, tenir, attraper, avoir, faire; vi
devenir, arriver, aboutir; (fam)
get! fiche le camp!; to — **across** vt
traverser, franchir; vi passer la
rampe; to —**away** partir, s'échapper;
to — **back** revenir, reculer; to — **in**
(r)entrer (dans), monter; to — **on**
monter (sur); to — **up** se lever,
monter.

ghastly ['gɑ:stli] a livide, horrible.

gherkin ['gə:kin] n cornichon m.

ghost [goust] n fantôme m, revenant
m, ombre f, esprit m.

ghostly ['goustli] a spectral, fanto-
matique, spirituel.

ghoul [gu:l] n vampire m, strige f.

giant ['dʒaiənt] n géant m.

gibber ['dʒibə] vi baragouiner.

gibberish ['gibəriʃ] n baragouin m,
charabia m.

gibbet ['dʒibit] n gibet m, potence f.

gibe [dʒaib] n sarcasme m, quolibet
m; vt railler.

giblets ['dʒiblits] n pl abat(t)is m pl.

giddiness ['gidinis] n vertige m.

giddy ['gidi] a étourdi, vertigineux,
volage.

gift [gift] n don m, cadeau m, prime f.

gifted ['giftid] a (pour bien) doué.

gig [gig] n cabriolet m, canot m.

gigantic [dʒai'gæntik] a gigantesque,
colossal.

giggle ['gigl] n gloussement m, petit
rire m; vi glousser, pousser des
petits rires.

gild [gild] vt dorer.

gilder ['gildə] n doreur m.

gilding ['gildiŋ] n dorure f.

gill [gil] n ouïe(s) f pl, branchie(s)
f pl, bajoues f pl.

gilt [gilt] n dorure f; a doré.

gimlet ['gimlit] n vrille f.

gimmick ['gimik] n machin, truc.

gin [dʒin] n trappe f, genièvre m,
gin m, piège m.

ginger ['dʒindʒə] n gingembre m,
énergie f; a roux.

gingerbread ['dʒindʒəbred] n (espèce
de) pain d'épice m.

gingerly ['dʒindʒəli] ad avec précaution.

gingham ['giŋəm] n ginnham m.

gipsy ['dʒipsi] n bohémien, -ienne,
romanichel, -elle.

giraffe [dʒi'rɑ:f] n girafe f.

gird [gə:d] vt ceindre, entourer; to
— **at** railler.

girder ['gə:də] n poutre f, poutrelle f.

girdle ['gə:dl] n gaine f, ceinture f,
cordelière f.

girl [gə:l] n (jeune) fille f, amie f.
girlish ['gə:liʃ] a de jeune fille, efféminé.
girth [gə:θ] n sangle f, tour m.
gist [dʒist] n fin mot m, fond m, essentiel m.
give [giv] vti donner; to — away trahir, conduire à l'autel; — in céder, se laisser faire; — out annoncer, distribuer; — over cesser, abandonner; to — up renoncer à, livrer.
given ['givn] pp of give; cj étant donné que.
giver ['givə] n donneur, -euse, donateur, -trice.
gizzard ['gizəd] n gésier m.
glacial ['gleisjəl] a glacial.
glacier ['glæsjə] n glacier m.
glad [glæd] a content, heureux, joyeux.
gladden ['glædn] vt réjouir.
glade [gleid] n clairière f.
gladly ['glædli] ad volontiers.
gladness ['glædnis] n plaisir m, joie f.
glamorous ['glæmərəs] a fascinant, charmeur, enchanteur.
glamour ['glæmə] n éclat m, charme m, fascination f.
glance [glɑ:ns] n coup d'œil m, regard m; vi jeter un coup d'œil (sur at); to — off glisser, ricocher, dévier.
gland [glænd] n glande f.
glare [glɛə] n lumière aveuglante f, éclat m, regard de défi m; vi flamboyer; to — at vt regarder d'un œil furibond.
glaring ['glɛəriŋ] a aveuglant, flagrant, éclatant, cru.
glass [glɑ:s] n verre m, (beer) bock m, vitre f, baromètre m; pl lunettes f pl.
glassblower ['glɑ:s,blouə] n verrier m.
glasscase ['glɑ:s,keis] n vitrine f.
glasscutter ['glɑ:s,kʌtə] n diamant m, tournette f.
glass-paper ['glɑ:s,peipə] n papier de verre m.
glassware ['glɑ:sweə] n verrerie f.
glassy ['glɑ:si] a vitreux, transparent.
glaze [gleiz] n glacis m, lustre m; vt vitrer, glacer, lustrer, devenir vitreux.
glazier ['gleizjə] n vitrier m.
gleam [gli:m] n rayon m, lueur f, reflet m; vi luire, miroiter.
glean [gli:n] vt glaner.
gleaner ['gli:nə] n glaneur, -euse.
gleaning ['gli:niŋ] n glanage m; pl glanures f pl.
glee [gli:] n joie f, gaîté f.
glen [glen] n vallon m.
glib [glib] a spécieux, qui a de la faconde.
glibness ['glibnis] n faconde f, spéciosité f.
glide [glaid] n glissement m, glissade f, vol plané m; vi glisser, planer.

glider ['glaidə] n avion en remorque m, planeur m.
glimmer ['glimə] n lueur f; vi luire.
glimpse [glimps] n lueur passagère f, coup d'œil m, échappée f, aperçu m; vt entrevoir.
glint [glint] vi entreluire, étinceler; n trait m, meur f.
glisten ['glisn] vi étinceler, scintiller, luire.
glitter ['glitə] n scintillement m; vi scintiller, étinceler.
gloat [glout] to — over manger (couvrer) des yeux, se réjouir de.
globe [gloub] n globe m, sphère f.
gloom [glu:m] n obscurité f, dépression f.
gloomy ['glu:mi] a obscur, sombre, lugubre.
glorification [,glɔ:rifi'keiʃən] n glorification f.
glorify ['glɔ:rifai] vt glorifier.
glorious ['glɔ:riəs] a glorieux.
glory ['glɔ:ri] n gloire f; to — in se faire gloire de.
gloss [glɔs] n lustre m, vernis m; vt lustrer, glacer; to — over glisser sur.
glossary ['glɔsəri] n glossaire m, lexique m.
glossy ['glɔsi] a lustré, brillant, glacé.
glove [glʌv] n gant m; vt ganter.
glow [glou] n rougeur (diffuse) f, ardeur f, éclat m, rougeoiement m; vi briller, luire, rougeoyer, s'embraser, brûler.
glow-worm ['glouwə:m] n luciole f, ver luisant m.
glue [glu:] n colle forte f; vt coller.
glum [glʌm] a renfrogné, maussade.
glut [glʌt] n surabondance f, encombrement m; vt gorger, gaver, encombrer.
glutton ['glʌtn] n goinfre m, gourmand(e) mf.
gluttonous ['glʌtənəs] a vorace, goulu.
gnarled [nɑ:ld] a noueux, tordu.
gnash [næʃ] vt to — one's teeth grincer des dents.
gnashing ['næʃiŋ] n grincement m.
gnat [næt] n cousin m, moustique m.
gnaw [nɔ:] vti grignoter, ronger.
go [gou] n aller m, allant m, affaire f; vi (s'en) aller, marcher, partir, tendre à, passer, faire loi, disparaître, devenir; to — away partir; to — back revenir, retourner, reculer; to — down descendre, se coucher, sombrer; to — for aller chercher; to — in(to) entrer (dans); to — off partir; to — on avancer, continuer; to — out sortir; to — through traverser, parcourir.
goad [goud] n aiguillon m; vt piquer, exciter.
goal [goul] n but m.
goalkeeper ['goul,ki:pə] n goal m, gardien de but m.
goat [gout] n chèvre f; he— bouc m.

go-between ['goubi'twi:n] n entremetteur m, truchement m.

gobble ['gobl] vt bâfrer, bouffer; vi glouglouter, glousser.

goblet ['goblit] n gobelet m, coupe f.

goblin ['goblin] n lutin m.

God [god] n Dieu m.

godchild ['godtʃaild] n filleul(e) mf.

goddess ['godis] n déesse f.

godfather ['god,fɑ:ðə] n parrain m.

godmother ['god,mʌðə] n marraine f.

godless ['godlis] a athée, impie.

godliness ['godlinis] n piété f.

godly ['godli] a pieux, saint.

godsend ['godsend] n aubaine f.

godspeed ['god'spi:d] excl bonne chance! bon voyage!

goggle ['gogl] vi rouler les yeux; n pl lunettes d'automobile f pl; (fam) —box télé(vision) f.

goggle-eyed ['goglaid] a aux yeux saillants, de homard.

going ['gouiŋ] n terrain m, circonstances m pl f.

gold [gould] n or m; — dust poudre f d'or.

gold-digger ['gould,digə] n chercheur d'or m.

golden ['gouldən] a d'or, doré.

goldfinch ['gouldfintʃ] n chardonneret m.

goldfish ['gouldfiʃ] n dorade f, poisson rouge m.

goldsmith ['gouldsmiθ] n orfèvre m.

gold-standard ['gould,stændəd] n étalon-or m.

golf [golf] n golf m; —course (terrain m de) golf m.

gondola ['gondələ] n gondole f, nacelle f.

gone [gon] pp of go; a parti, fini, disparu, épris (de on).

good [gud] n bien m, bon m, profit m; pl marchandises f pl, effets m pl; a bon, sage; — for nothing propre à rien; for — pour de bon; — Heavens! Ciel! — gracious! bonté divine!

good-bye ['gud'bai] excl n au revoir m, adieu m.

good-looking ['gud'lukiŋ] a de bonne mine, bien, beau.

goodly ['gudli] a large, ample.

goodness ['gudnis] n bonté f, vertu f.

goodwill [gud'wil] n bon vouloir m, clientèle f.

goody ['gudi] n commère f; a édifiant; to be a — la faire à la vertu.

goose [gu:s] n oie f.

gooseberry ['guzbəri] n groseille à maquereau f.

gooseflesh ['gu:sfleʃ] n chair de poule f.

goose-step ['gu:sstep] n pas de l'oie m.

gore [go:] n sang m (caillé), pointe f, pièce f, soufflet m, godet m; vt encorner, blesser d'un coup de cornes.

gorge [go:dʒ] n gorge f, défilé m, cœur m; vt rassasier, gorger; vi s'empiffrer, se gorger.

gorgeous ['go:dʒəs] a splendide, superbe.

gorgeousness ['go:dʒəsnis] n splendeur f.

gorilla [gə'rilə] n gorille m.

gormandize ['go:məndaiz] vi bâfrer.

gormandizer ['go:məndaizə] n gourmand(e) mf, goinfre m.

gorse [go:s] n ajonc m, genêt m.

gory ['go:ri] a ensanglanté.

gosling ['gozliŋ] n oison m.

gospel ['gospəl] n évangile m.

gossamer ['gosəmə] n fils de la Vierge m pl, gaze f; a léger, ténu.

gossip ['gosip] n commérage m, mauvaise langue f, bavette f; vi cancaner, bavarder.

gouge [gaudʒ] n gouge f; vt arracher.

gourd [guəd] n potiron m, gourde f, calebasse f.

gourmet ['guəmei] n gourmet m, fine fourchette f.

gout [gaut] n goutte f.

gouty ['gauti] a goutteux.

govern ['gʌvən] vt gouverner, administrer.

governess ['gʌvənis] n gouvernante f.

governing ['gʌvəniŋ] a gouvernant, au pouvoir.

government ['gʌvnmənt] n gouvernement m, régime m, ministère m.

governor ['gʌvənə] n gouverneur m, gouvernant m, patron m.

gown [gaun] n robe f.

grab [græb] n rapacité f; vt saisir, happer, arracher.

grace [greis] n grâce f, bénédicité m; pl grâces f pl; vt orner, honorer.

graceful ['greisful] a gracieux.

graceless ['greislis] a sans grâce.

gracious ['greiʃəs] a gracieux, accueillant, bow; good —! bonté divine! mon Dieu!

gradation [grə'deiʃən] n gradation f.

grade [greid] n degré m, rang m, qualité f, pente f, rampe f; vt graduer, fondre, classer.

grade crossing ['greid'krosiŋ] n passage m à niveau.

gradient ['greidjənt] n pente f, rampe f, variation f.

gradual ['grædjuəl] a graduel.

gradually ['grædjuəli] ad doucement, peu à peu.

graduate ['grædjueit] n licencié(e) mf; vt passer sa licence, recevoir ses diplômes, conférer (un diplôme).

graft [grɑ:ft] n greffe f, tripotage m, gratte f, corruption f; vt greffer; vi tripoter, rabioter.

grain [grein] n grain m; against the — à contre-fil, à contre-cœur; with a — of salt avec réserve.

grammar ['græmə] n grammaire f; — school lycée.

gramophone ['græməfoun] n phonographe m.

granary ['grænəri] n grenier m.

grand [grænd] a grand(iose).

grandchildren ['græn,tʃildrən] n pl petits-enfants m pl.

grand-daughter ['græn,dɔːtə] n petite-fille f.

grandee [,græn'diː] n Grand m.

grandeur ['grændjə] n grandeur f, splendeur f.

grandfather ['grænd,fɑːðə] n grand-père m.

grandiloquence [græn'diləkwəns] n emphase f.

grandiose ['grændiouz] a grandiose, magnifique, pompeux.

grandmother ['græn,mʌðə] n grand'mère f.

grandson ['grænsʌn] n petit-fils m.

grandstand ['grændstænd] n tribune f.

grange [greindʒ] n maison avec ferme f.

granite ['grænit] n granit m; a granitique.

granny ['græni] n bonne-maman f.

grant [grɑːnt] n subvention f, allocation f; vt accorder, admettre, octroyer.

grape [greip] n raisin m.

grapefruit ['greipfruːt] n pamplemousse f.

grape-harvest ['greip,hɑːvist] n vendange f.

grapeshot ['greipʃɔt] n mitraille f.

graphic ['græfik] a graphique, vivant.

grapnel ['græpnəl] n grappin m, ancre f.

grapple ['græpl] n grappin m, prise f, étreinte f; to — with empoigner, colleter, en venir aux prises avec.

grasp [grɑːsp] n prise f, étreinte f, serre f, portée de la main f, compréhension f; vt saisir, serrer, empoigner.

grasping ['grɑːspiŋ] a rapace, cupide.

grass [grɑːs] n herbe f.

grasshopper ['grɑːs,hɔpə] n sauterelle f.

grassy ['grɑːsi] a herbu, herbeux, verdoyant.

grate [greit] vt râper, racler; vi grincer, crier, crisser; to — on choquer, agacer.

grater ['greitə] n râpe f.

grateful ['greitful] n reconnaissant.

gratefully ['greitfuli] ad avec reconnaissance.

gratefulness ['greitfulnis] n reconnaissance f.

grating ['greitiŋ] a grinçant; n grille f, grillage m, râpage m, grincement m.

gratification [,grætifi'keiʃən] n plaisir m, satisfaction f.

gratify ['grætifai] vt contenter, rémunérer, satisfaire.

gratis ['grɑːtis] ad gratis; a gratuit.

gratitude ['grætitjuːd] n gratitude f, reconnaissance f.

gratuitous [grə'tjuːitəs] a gratuit.

gratuity [grə'tjuːiti] n gratification f, pourboire m, pot de vin m.

gravamen [grə'veimən] n poids m, fond m.

grave [greiv] n fosse f, tombe f, tombeau m; a sérieux, grave; vt graver, radouber.

grave-digger ['greiv,digə] n fossoyeur m.

gravel ['grævəl] n gravier m.

gravestone ['greivstoun] n pierre tombale f.

graveyard ['greivjɑːd] n cimetière m.

graving-dock ['greiviŋdɔk] n bassin de radoub m.

graving-tool ['greiviŋtuːl] n burin m.

gravitate ['græviteit] vi graviter.

gravity ['græviti] n gravité f, sérieux m.

gravitation [,grævi'teiʃən] n gravitation f, pesanteur f.

gravy ['greivi] n sauce f, jus m.

gray [grei] an gris m; to grow — grisonner.

grayish ['greiiʃ] a grisâtre.

graze [greiz] n égratignure f; vt égratigner, effleurer; vti brouter, paître.

grease [griːs] n graisse f; vt graisser.

greasy ['griːsi] a graisseux, gras.

great [greit] a grand, gros, fort.

greatcoat ['greitkout] n par-dessus m, capote f.

greatly ['greitli] ad énormément, puissamment, beaucoup.

greatness ['greitnis] n grandeur f, noblesse f.

Greece [griːs] n Grèce f.

greed [griːd] n convoitise f, cupidité f.

greediness ['griːdinis] n cupidité f, gloutonnerie f.

greedy ['griːdi] a gourmand, glouton, cupide, avide.

Greek [griːk] n Grec, Grecque; an grec m.

green [griːn] an vert m; a naïf, sot, inexpérimenté.

greengage ['griːngeidʒ] n reine-claude f.

greengrocer ['griːn,grousə] n fruitier, -ière.

greenhorn ['griːnhɔːn] n blanc-bec m, bleu m.

greenhouse ['griːnhaus] n serre f.

greenish ['griːniʃ] a verdâtre.

Greenland ['griːnlənd] n Groenland m.

greet [griːt] vt saluer, accueillir.

greeting ['griːtiŋ] n salut m, salutation f.

gregarious [gri'gɛəriəs] a grégaire, de troupeau.

grenade [gri'neid] n grenade f.

grenadier [,grenə'diə] n grenadier m.

grew [gruː] pt of grow.

greyhound ['greihaund] n lévrier m, levrette f.

grid [grid] n grille f.

gridiron ['grid.aiən] n gril m, terrain m de football.

grief [gri:f] n chagrin m, mal m, peine f.

grievance ['gri:vəns] n grief m, tort m.

grieve [gri:v] vt affliger, faire de la peine à; vi se désoler, s'affliger.

grievous ['gri:vəs] a affligeant, douloureux.

grill [gril] n gril m, grillade f, grille f, grillage m; vt griller, cuisiner.

grim [grim] a sévère, farouche, sardonique, sinistre.

grimace [gri'meis] n grimace f; vi grimacer, faire la grimace.

grime [graim] n crasse f; vt salir.

grimy ['graimi] a crasseux, encrassé, noir.

grin [grin] n rictus m, sourire épanoui m; vi découvrir ses dents, sourire à belles dents.

grind [graind] vt moudre, broyer, écraser, affiler; vi grincer, (fig) piocher; n grincement m, turbin m.

grinder ['graində] n rémouleur m, broyeur m.

grinding ['graindiŋ] n broyage m, mouture f, grincement m.

grindstone ['graindstoun] n meule f.

grip [grip] n prise f, étreinte f, serre f; pl prises f pl, mains f pl; vt agripper, empoigner, saisir, serrer.

gripe [graip] vi donner la colique à.

grisly ['grizli] a terrifiant, macabre.

grist [grist] n blé m; to bring — to the mill faire venir l'eau au moulin.

gristle ['grisl] n cartilage m, croquant m.

grit [grit] n gravier m, sable m, grès m, cran m; vi grincer; vt sabler.

gritty ['griti] a graveleux, sablonneux.

grizzled ['grizld] a gris, grisonnant.

groan [groun] n gémissement m, grognement m; vi gémir, grogner.

grocer ['grousə] n épicier, -ière.

grocery ['grousəri] n épicerie f.

groggy ['grɔgi] a ivre, étourdi, titubant.

groin [grɔin] n aine f.

groom [gru:m] n palefrenier m, valet d'écurie m; vt panser.

groomed [gru:md] a well—— (bien) soigné, tiré à quatre épingles.

grooming ['gru:miŋ] n pansage m.

groomsman ['gru:mzmən] n garçon d'honneur m.

groove [gru:v] n sillon m, rainure f, glissière f; vt rayer, sillonner; micro—— microsillon m.

grope [group] vi tâtonner; to —— for chercher à tâtons.

gross [grous] n grosse f; a dru, obèse, grossier, brut, gros.

ground [graund] pp of **grind**; a moulu, broyé; n sol m, terrain m,

fond m, fondement m raison f; vt fonder, appuyer, instruire, (arms) reposer, maintenir au sol; vi s'échouer.

ground floor ['graundflɔ:] n rez-de-chaussée m.

groundless ['graundlis] a sans fondement, immotivé.

groundnut ['graundnʌt] n arachide f.

grounds [graundz] n pl lie f, marc m.

groundsheet ['graundʃi:t] n bâche f de campement.

groundswell ['graundswel] n lame f de fond.

groundwork ['graundwə:k] n fond m, base f, assise f, plan m.

group [gru:p] n groupe m; vt grouper; vi se grouper.

grouse [graus] n coq m de bruyère; vi grogner, ronchonner, rouspéter.

grove [grouv] n bosquet m.

grovel ['grɔvl] vi s'aplatir, ramper.

groveler ['grɔvlə] n flagorneur m, sycophante m, piedplat m.

grow [grou] vt cultiver; vi pousser, grandir, croître, devenir.

growl [graul] n grondement m; vi gronder, grommeler, grogner.

grown [groun] pp of **grow**.

grown-up ['groun'ʌp] n adulte mf, grande personne f.

growth [grouθ] n croissance f, accroissement m, tumeur f.

grub [grʌb] n larve f, (sl) boustifaille f; vt bêcher, nettoyer; vi fouiller.

grudge [grʌdʒ] n dent f, rancune f; vt donner à contre-cœur, mesurer.

grudgingly ['grʌdʒiŋli] ad à contre-cœur.

gruel ['gruəl] n gruau m, brouet m.

grueling ['gruəliŋ] a éreintant, épuisant.

gruesome ['gru:səm] a macabre, répugnant.

gruff [grʌf] a bourru, revêche, rude, gros.

gruffly ['grʌfli] ad rudement.

gruffness ['grʌfnis] n rudesse f, ton bourru m.

grumble ['grʌmbl] n grognement m; vti grommeler, bougonner.

grumbler ['grʌmblə] n ronchonneur, -euse, grognard(e) mf, rouspéteur, -euse.

grumpy ['grʌmpi] a maussade, grincheux.

grunt [grʌnt] n grognement m; vi grogner.

guarantee [.gærən'ti:] n garant(e) mf, garantie f, caution f; vt garantir, se porter garant pour.

guard [ga:d] n garde f, chef de train m, geôlier m; vt garder, protéger; vi mettre (se tenir) en garde.

guarded ['ga:did] a circonspect.

guardedly ['ga:didli] ad prudemment, avec réserve.

guardian ['ga:djən] n gardien, -ienne, tuteur, -trice.

guardianship ['gɑːdjənʃip] n garde f, tutelle f.

guava ['gwɑːvə] n goyave f; — tree goyavier m.

gudgeon ['gʌdʒən] n goujon m.

guess [ges] n conjecture f; vti deviner; vt estimer; at a — au jugé.

guesswork ['geswəːk] n hypothèse f, conjecture f.

guest [gest] n invité(e) mf; paying-pensionnaire mf; — house pension f.

guffaw [gʌ'fɔː] n gros rire m; vi s'esclaffer.

guidance ['gaidəns] n conduite f, direction f, gouverne f, orientation f.

guide [gaid] n guide m; vt guider, conduire, diriger.

guidebook ['gaidbuk] n guide m.

guided ['gaidid] a (of rockets) téléguidé.

guidepost ['gaidpoust] n poteau indicateur m.

guild [gild] n corporation f, confrérie f.

guildhall ['gildhɔːl] n hôtel de ville m.

guile [gail] n astuce f.

guileful ['gailful] a retors.

guileless ['gaillis] a sans malice, naïf.

guilt [gilt] n culpabilité f.

guiltless ['giltlis] a innocent.

guilty ['gilti] a coupable.

guinea-fowl ['ginifaul] n pintade f.

guinea-pig ['ginipig] n cobaye m, cochon d'Inde m.

guise [gaiz] n forme f, apparence f, costume m.

guitar [gi'tɑː] n guitare f.

gulf [gʌlf] n golfe m, gouffre m, abîme m.

gull [gʌl] n mouette f, jobard m, gogo m; vt rouler.

gullet ['gʌlit] n œsophage m, gosier m.

gullibility [ˌgʌli'biliti] n crédulité f, jobardise f.

gullible ['gʌlibl] a crédule, jobard.

gully ['gʌli] n ravin m.

gulp [gʌlp] n lampée f, trait m; vti boire, avaler d'un trait; vi s'étrangler.

gum [gʌm] n gencive f, gomme f; vt gommer, coller.

gumboil ['gʌmbɔil] n abcès à la gencive m.

gumption ['gʌmpʃən] n jugeotte f, gingin m.

gun [gʌn] n fusil m, canon m, pièce f.

gunboat ['gʌnbout] n canonnière f.

gun-carriage ['gʌnˌkæridʒ] n affût de canon m.

gunner ['gʌnə] n canonnier m, artilleur m.

gunnery ['gʌnəri] n tir au canon m.

gunpowder ['gʌnˌpaudə] n poudre f.

gunshot ['gʌnʃɔt] n portée de fusil f (canon), coup de feu m.

gunsmith ['gʌnsmiθ] n armurier m.

gurgle ['gəːgl] n glouglou m, gar-gouillement m; vi glouglouter, gargouiller; vti glousser.

gush [gʌʃ] n jaillissement m, jet m, projection f, effusion f; vi jaillir, saillir, se répandre, la faire au sentiment.

gust [gʌst] n rafale f, ondée f, accès m.

gusto ['gʌstou] n brio m, entrain m.

gut [gʌt] n boyau m; pl entrailles f pl, cran m; vt vider, dévaster.

gutter ['gʌtə] n gouttière f, ruisseau m, rigole f.

guy [gai] n corde f, hauban m, type m, épouvantail m; vt railler, travestir.

guzzle ['gʌzl] vt boire à tire-larigot, bouffer; vi s'empiffrer, se gaver.

gymnasium [dʒim'neizjəm] n gymnase m.

gymnast ['dʒimnæst] n gymnaste mf.

gymnastics [dʒim'næstiks] n pl gymnastique f.

haberdasher ['hæbədæʃə] n mercier m.

haberdasher's ['hæbədæʃəz] n mercerie f.

habit ['hæbit] n habitude f, état m, constitution f.

habitable ['hæbitəbl] a habitable.

habitation [ˌhæbi'teiʃən] n habitation f, demeure f.

habitual [hə'bitjuəl] a habituel, invétéré.

hack [hæk] n pioche f, pic m, blessure f, cheval m (de louage), rosse f, corvée f, écrivassier m; vt couper, frapper, hacher, taillader; vi tousser sèchement.

hackneyed ['hæknid] a usé, rebattu, banal.

had [hæd] pp pt of **have**.

haddock ['hædək] n aiglefin m, aigrefin m.

haft [hɑːft] n manche m, poignée f.

hag [hæg] n sorcière f, chipie f.

haggard ['hægəd] a hagard, hâve, décharné, égaré.

haggle ['hægl] vi ergoter, chicaner.

hail [heil] n grêle f, salut m; vi grêler; vt saluer, héler, venir (de from), descendre (de from).

hailstone ['heilstoun] n grêlon m.

hair [hɛə] n cheveu m, chevelure f, poil m, crin m; to comb one's — se peigner.

haircut ['hɛəkʌt] n coupe de cheveux f.

hairdresser ['hɛəˌdresə] n coiffeur, -euse.

hairless ['hɛəlis] a chauve, sans poils, glabre.

hairline ['hɛəlain] n — crack gerçure f; (fig) distinction f subtile.

hairpin ['hɛəpin] n épingle à cheveux f.

hair-raising ['hɛə,reiziŋ] a horrifique, horripilant.

hair's breadth ['hɛəz'bredθ] ad à un cheveu (près).

hair-splitting ['hɛə,splitiŋ] n chinoiserie f, ergotage m.

hairy ['hɛəri] a chevelu, poilu, velu.

hake [heik] n merluche f, colin m.

hale [heil] a robuste; — and **hearty** frais et dispos.

half [hɑ:f] n moitié f; a demi, mi-; ad à moitié, demi, en deux; — as **much again** une fois et demie autant, la moitié en plus; — **hearted** a tiède; at—tide à mi-marée.

half-back ['hɑ:fbæk] n demi(-arrière) m.

half-bred ['hɑ:fbred] a métis, demi-sang.

half-brother ['hɑ:f,brʌðə] n demi-frère m.

half-caste ['hɑ:fkɑ:st] a demi-sang; an métis, -isse, hybride m.

half-dozen ['hɑ:f'dʌzn] n demi-douzaine f.

half-hour ['hɑ:f'auə] n demi-heure f.

half-mast ['hɑ:f'mɑ:st] ad en berne, à mi-mât.

half-measure ['hɑ:f'meʒə] n demi-mesure f.

half-pay ['hɑ:f'pei] n demi-solde f.

halfway ['hɑ:f'wei] ad à mi-chemin.

halibut ['hælibət] n flétan m.

hall [hɔ:l] n salle f, vestibule m, hall m.

hallmark ['hɔ:lmɑ:k] n contrôle m, poinçon m, empreinte f.

hallow ['hælou] vt sanctifier, bénir.

hallucinate [hə'lu:sineit] vt halluciner.

hallucination [hə,lu:si'neiʃən] n hallucination f.

halo ['heilou] n halo m, nimbe m, auréole f.

halt [hɔlt] n halte f; vi s'arrêter, hésiter, boiter; a boiteux.

halter ['hɔltə] n licou m, corde f.

halve [hɑ:v] vt couper en deux, partager.

ham [hæm] n jambon m, jarret m.

hamlet ['hæmlit] n hameau m.

hammer ['hæmə] n marteau m; vt marteler, battre.

hammock ['hæmək] n hamac m.

hamper ['hæmpə] n corbeille f, manne f, banne f; vt gêner, empêcher.

hand [hænd] n main f, (watch) aiguille f, jeu m, ouvrier, -ière; — to — corps à corps; out of — hors de contrôle; on the one — d'une part; old — vieux routier m; vt tendre, passer, remettre.

handbag ['hændbæg] n sac à main m, pochette f.

handbook ['hændbuk] n manuel m, guide m.

handcuff ['hændkʌf] vt passer les menottes à.

handcuffs ['hændkʌfs] n pl menottes f pl.

handful ['hændful] n poignée f.

handicap ['hændikæp] n handicap m, désavantage m; vt handicaper, désavantager.

handicraft ['hændikrɑ:ft] n habileté manuelle f, métier manuel m, travail manuel m.

handiwork ['hændiwə:k] n travail manuel m, ouvrage m.

handkerchief ['hæŋkətʃif] n mouchoir m, pochette f.

handle ['hændl] n poignée f, manche m, anse f, bouton m, bras m; vt manier, traiter, prendre en main.

handlebar ['hændlbɑ:] n guidon m.

handling ['hændliŋ] n maniement m, manœuvre f.

handrail ['hændreil] n rampe f, main courante f.

handshake ['hændʃeik] n poignée de main f.

handsome ['hænsəm] a beau, élégant, généreux.

handsomely ['hænsəmli] ad élégamment, libéralement.

handwriting ['hænd,raitiŋ] n écriture f, main f.

handy ['hændi] a sous la main, commode, adroit, maniable.

hang [hæŋ] vt pendre, accrocher, tapisser, poser; vi pendre, planer, peser, tomber; to — about rôder, flâner; to — back hésiter, rester en arrière.

hangar ['hæŋə] n hangar m.

hanger ['hæŋə] n portemanteau m, cintre m, crochet m.

hanging ['hæŋiŋ] n pose f, tenture f, suspension f, montage m, pendaison f.

hangman ['hæŋmən] n bourreau m.

hanker ['hæŋkə] vi aspirer (à after).

hankering ['hæŋkəriŋ] n aspiration f, forte envie f.

hanky-panky ['hæŋki'pæŋki] n boniment m, tour de passe-passe m.

hansom ['hænsəm] n cabriolet m.

haphazard ['hæp'hæzəd] a fortuit; ad au petit bonheur, à l'aveuglette.

hapless ['hæplis] a malchanceux, infortuné.

happen ['hæpən] vi arriver, se passer, se produire.

happening ['hæpniŋ] n événement m.

happily ['hæpili] ad heureusement, par bonheur.

happiness ['hæpinis] n bonheur m.

happy ['hæpi] a heureux.

harangue [hə'ræŋ] n harangue f, vt haranguer.

harass ['hærəs] vt harceler, tracasser, tourmenter.

harbinger ['hɑ:bindʒə] n précurseur m, avant-coureur m, messager, -ère.

harbor ['ha:bə] n port m, asile m;
vt recéler, nourrir, abriter.
hard [ha:d] a dur, difficile, sévère;
— by tout près; — up à sec; — upon
de près, sur les talons; ad dur, fort,
durement.
harden ['ha:dn] vt (en)durcir,
tremper; vi durcir, s'endurcir, devenir dur.
hardfisted ['ha:d'fistid] a pingre,
radin.
hardhearted ['ha:d'ha:tid] a dur,
inflexible.
hardihood ['ha:dihud] n audace f.
hard labor ['ha:d'leibə] n travaux
forcés m pl.
hardly ['ha:dli] ad à (avec) peine,
ne . . . guère, sévèrement.
hardness ['ha:dnis] n dureté f,
difficulté f.
hardship ['ha:dʃip] n privation f,
épreuve f.
hardware ['ha:dwɛə] n quincaillerie
f.
hardwareman ['ha:dwɛəmən] n
quincailler m.
hardy ['ha:di] a résistant, robuste,
vigoureux.
hare [hɛə] n lièvre m.
hare-brained ['hɛəbreind] a écervelé, insensé.
harelip ['hɛə'lip] n bec-de-lièvre m.
haricot ['hærikou] n — bean haricot
m vert etc; (stew) haricot de
mouton m.
hark [ha:k] vti écouter; to — back to
revenir à.
harm [ha:m] n mal m, tort m; vt
faire tort à, faire (du) mal à, porter
préjudice à.
harmful ['ha:mful] a nuisible, pénible, nocif.
harmless ['ha:mlis] a inoffensif.
harmlessly ['ha:mlisli] ad innocemment.
harmonious [ha:'mounjəs] a harmonieux.
harmonize ['ha:mənaiz] vt harmoniser, concilier; vi s'harmoniser,
s'accorder.
harmony ['ha:məni] n harmonie f,
accord m.
harness ['ha:nis] n harnais m; vt
harnacher, capter, aménager.
harness-maker ['ha:nis,meikə] n
bourrelier m.
Harold ['hærəld] Henri m.
harp [ha:p] n harpe f; vi jouer de la
harpe; to — on ressasser, rabâcher.
harpoon [ha:'pu:n] n harpon m; vt
harponner.
harpsichord ['ha:psikɔ:d] n clavecin
m.
harrow ['hærou] n herse f; vt herser,
blesser, déchirer.
harrowing ['hærouiŋ] a déchirant,
navrant.
harry ['hæri] vt ravager, tracasser,
harceler.
harsh [ha:ʃ] a rèche, âpre, cruel.

harshness ['ha:ʃnis] n rudesse f,
âpreté f, rigueur f.
hart [ha:t] n cerf m.
harum-scarum ['hɛərəm'skɛərəm]
an hurluberlu(e) mf, écervelé(e) mf.
harvest ['ha:vist] n moisson f,
récolte f, vendange f, fenaison f; vt
moissonner, récolter; vi faire la
moisson.
harvester ['ha:vistə] n moissonneur,
-euse, (machine) moissonneuse f.
hash [hæʃ] n hachis m, gâchis m,
compte m; vt hacher, gâcher.
hassock ['hæsək] n coussin m.
haste [heist] n hâte f.
hasten ['heisn] vt presser, hâter,
avancer; vi se presser, se dépêcher
se hâter.
hastily ['heistili] ad à la hâte.
hasty ['heisti] a hâtif, vif, emporté.
hat [hæt] n chapeau m.
hat-box ['hætbɔks] n carton à
chapeau m.
hatch [hætʃ] n écoutille f, couvaison
f, couvée f, éclosion f; vt couver,
tramer; vi éclore, se tramer.
hatchet ['hætʃit] n hachette f,
cognée f.
hatching ['hætʃiŋ] n éclosion f,
machination f.
hate [heit] n haine f, aversion f; vt
haïr, détester.
hateful ['heitful] a haïssable, odieux.
hat-peg ['hætpeg] n patère f.
hatred ['heitrid] n haine f.
hatter ['hætə] n chapelier m.
hatter's ['hætəz] n chapellerie f.
haughtiness ['ho:tinis] n hauteur f,
morgue f.
haughty ['ho:ti] a hautain.
haul [ho:l] n traction f, coup de filet
m, butin m; vt haler, tirer, traîner.
haulage ['ho:lidʒ] n halage m, roulage
m, charriage m.
haunch [ho:ntʃ] n hanche f, cuissot
m, quartier m.
haunt [ho:nt] n rendez-vous m,
repaire m; vt fréquenter, hanter,
obséder.
have [hæv] vt avoir, permettre,
savoir, soutenir, admettre, prendre,
faire, tenir; I had better, rather je
ferais (aimerais) mieux; to — it out
with s'expliquer avec.
haven ['heivn] n port m.
haversack ['hævəsæk] n musette f,
havresac m.
haves [hævz] n pl les possédants
m pl.
havoc ['hævək] n ravage m, dégâts
m pl.
hawk [ho:k] n faucon m; vt colporter;
vi chasser au faucon.
hawker ['ho:kə] n camelot m,
colporteur m, (fruit) marchand des
quatre saisons m.
hawser ['ho:zə] n haussière f, amarre
f.
hawthorn ['ho:θɔ:n] n aubépine f.
hay [hei] n foin m.

hayloft ['heilɔft] n fenil m.
haymaker ['heimeikə] n faneur, -euse.
haymaking ['heimeikiŋ] n fenaison f.
haystack ['heistæk] n meule de foin f.
hazard ['hæzəd] n hasard m; vt hasarder, risquer.
haze [heiz] n brume f (de chaleur), harassement m, brimade f; vt brimer, bizuter.
hazel ['heizl] n noisetier m.
hazel-nut ['heizlnʌt] n noisette f.
hazy ['heizi] a brumeux, vague, estompé.
he [hi:] pr il, lui, celui; an mâle m.
head [hed] n tête f, face f, sommet m, source f, haut bout m, chef m, crise f; a premier, principal, (en) chef; vt conduire, intituler, venir en tête de; to — for se diriger vers, mettre le cap sur.
headache ['hedeik] n mal de tête m.
headdress ['heddres] n coiffure f.
heading ['hediŋ] n titre m, en-tête m, rubrique f.
headland ['hedlənd] n cap m, promontoire m.
headlight ['hedlait] n phare m.
headline ['hedlain] n titre m, manchette f.
headlong ['hedlɔŋ] a impétueux; ad la tête la première, tête baissée.
headman ['hedmən] n chef m.
headmaster ['hed'ma:stə] n proviseur m, directeur m.
headmistress ['hed'mistris] n directrice f.
headphone ['hedfoun] n récepteur m, écouteur m.
headquarters ['hed'kwɔ:təz] n quartier général m, état major m.
headstone ['hedstoun] n pierre angulaire f, pierre tombale f.
headstrong ['hedstrɔŋ] a têtu, volontaire.
headway ['hedwei] n progrès m (pl), erre f.
heady ['hedi] a violent, capiteux.
heal [hi:l] vti guérir; vi se cicatriser.
healing ['hi:liŋ] n guérison f.
health [helθ] n santé f.
healthy ['helθi] a sain, bien portant, salubre.
heap [hi:p] n tas m, monceau m; vt entasser, amonceler, combler.
heaped [hi:pd] a entassé, amoncelé, comble.
hear [hiə] vt entendre, entendre dire, apprendre, faire répéter; to — from recevoir des nouvelles de.
heard [hə:d] pp pt of **hear**.
hearer ['hiərə] n auditeur, -trice.
hearing ['hiəriŋ] n ouïe f, oreille f, audition f, audience f.
hearken ['ha:kən] vi écouter, prêter l'oreille (à to).
hearsay ['hiəsei] n ouï-dire m.
hearse [hə:s] n corbillard m.
heart [ha:t] n cœur m, courage m.

heartbeat ['ha:tbi:t] n battement de cœur m.
heartbreaking ['ha:tbreikiŋ] a navrant, accablant, déchirant.
heartbroken ['ha:t,broukən] a navré, accablé.
heartburn ['ha:tbə:n] n aigreurs f pl.
hearten ['ha:tn] vt réconforter, remonter le moral à.
heartfelt ['ha:tfelt] a sincère, senti.
heartily ['ha:tili] ad de bon cœur, avec appétit.
heartiness ['ha:tinis] n cordialité f, vigueur f.
heartless ['ha:tlis] a sans cœur, cruel.
heartlessness ['ha:tlisnis] n dureté f, manque de cœur m.
hearth [ha:θ] n foyer m.
hearty ['ha:ti] a cordial, copieux, solide.
heat [hi:t] n chaleur f, colère f, épreuve f, manche f; vti chauffer; vt (r)échauffer, enflammer; vi s'échauffer.
heated ['hi:tid] a chaud, chauffé, animé.
heater ['hi:tə] n radiateur m.
heath [hi:θ] n lande f, bruyère f.
heathen ['hi:ðən] an païen, -ienne.
heather ['heðə] n bruyère f.
heating ['hi:tiŋ] n chauffage m, chauffe f.
heave [hi:v] n soulèvement m, effort m; vt soulever, pousser; vi palpiter, avoir des haut-le-cœur, se soulever, battre du flanc; to — to mettre en panne.
heaven ['hevn] n ciel m.
heavenly ['hevnli] a céleste, divin.
heavily ['hevili] ad pesamment, lourdement.
heaviness ['hevinis] n lourdeur f, poids m, lassitude f.
heavy ['hevi] a lourd, (sea) dur, violent, gros, triste.
Hebrew ['hi:bru:] an hébreu.
heckle ['hekl] vt harceler.
hectic ['hektik] a fiévreux, excitant.
hector ['hektə] vt rudoyer.
hedge [hedʒ] n haie f, (fig) mur m; vt enclore; vi se couvrir, esquiver la question.
hedgehog ['hedʒhɔg] n hérisson m.
heed [hi:d] n attention f; vt faire attention à.
heedful ['hi:dful] a attentif.
heedless ['hi:dlis] a inattentif, léger, insouciant.
heedlessly ['hi:dlisli] ad étourdiment.
heel [hi:l] n talon m; vt réparer le talon de; vi talonner; to bring to — mettre au pas; to — l ici! down at — éculé.
hefty ['hefti] a solide, costaud.
heifer ['hefə] n génisse f.
height [hait] n hauteur f, comble m.
heighten ['haitn] vt rehausser, faire ressortir.
heinous ['heinəs] a atroce, odieux.

heinousness ['heinəsnis] n atrocité f, énormité f.
heir [ɛə] n héritier m.
heiress ['ɛəris] n héritière f.
heirloom ['ɛəlu:m] n bien inaliénable m, meuble m de famille.
held [held] pt pp of **hold**.
Helen ['helin] Hélène f.
hell [hel] n enfer m, diable m.
hellish ['heliʃ] a infernal.
helm [helm] n barre f, gouvernail m.
helmet ['helmit] n casque m.
helmsman ['helmzmən] n timonier m, homme de barre m.
help [help] n aide f, secours m, domestique mf, auxiliaire mf, collaborateur, -trice; vt aider, secourir, servir; I can't — laughing je ne peux m'empêcher de rire; I can't — it je n'y peux rien.
helpful ['helpful] a secourable, serviable, utile.
helpfulness ['helpfulnis] n serviabilité f.
helping ['helpiŋ] n portion f, morceau m.
helpless ['helplis] a sans défense désemparé, sans ressource.
helplessness ['helplisnis] n impuissance f, faiblesse f.
helter-skelter ['heltə'skeltə] ad pêle mêle, à la débandade.
hem [hem] n ourlet m; vt ourler; to — in cerner.
hemlock ['hemlɔk] n ciguë f.
hemp [hemp] n chanvre m.
hen [hen] n poule f, femelle f.
hence [hens] ad d'ici.
henceforth ['hens'fɔ:θ] ad à l'avenir dorénavant.
henchman ['hentʃmən] n partisan m, bras droit m.
henhouse ['hen'haus] n poulailler m.
henpecked ['henpekt] a dominé par sa femme.
henroost ['henrust] n perchoir m.
Henry ['henri] Henri m.
her [hə:] a son, sa, ses; pn la, lui, à elle; —self elle-même; —s pn le sien, la sienne, les siens, les siennes.
herald ['herəld] n héraut m, messager, -ère, avant-coureur m, avant-courrier, -ière.
heraldry ['herəldri] n blason m, art héraldique m.
herb [hə:b] n herbe f; pl simples m pl.
herbaceous [hə:'beiʃəs] a herbacé.
herbalist ['hə:bəlist] n herboriste mf.
herd [hə:d] n troupeau m; vi vivre en troupe.
herdsman ['hə:dzmən] n pâtre m, bouvier m.
here [hiə] ad ici.
hereafter [hiər'ɑ:ftə] n vie future f, au-delà m; ad à l'avenir, désormais, ci-dessous.
hereditary [hi'reditəri] a héréditaire.
heredity [hi'rediti] n hérédité f.

herein ['hiərin] ad ici, ci-dedans, ci-inclus.
heresy ['herəsi] n hérésie f.
heretic ['herətik] n hérétique mf.
heritage ['heritidʒ] n héritage m.
hermit ['hə:mit] n ermite m.
hernia ['hə:njə] n hernie f.
hero ['hiərou] n héros m.
heroic [hi'rouik] a héroïque.
heroine ['herouin] n héroïne f.
heron ['herən] n héron m.
herring ['heriŋ] n hareng m; red — (fig) diversion.
hesitate ['heziteit] vi hésiter.
hesitation [.hezi'teiʃən] n hésitation f.
hew [hju:] vt couper, ouvrir, tailler.
hewer ['hju:ə] n bûcheron m, tailleur m.
heyday ['heidei] n fleur f, apogée m, beaux jours m pl.
hiccup ['hikʌp] n hoquet m; vi avoir le hoquet.
hid, hidden [hid, 'hidn] pt pp of **hide**.
hide [haid] n peau f, cuir m; vt cacher; vi se cacher.
hide-and-seek ['haidən'si:k] n cache-cache m.
hidebound ['haidbaund] a étroit, fermé, systématique.
hideous ['hidjəs] a hideux, horrible, affreux, odieux.
hiding ['haidiŋ] n râclée f, dissimulation f.
hiding-place ['haidiŋpleis] n cachette f.
higgledy-piggledy ['higldi'pigldi] ad en confusion, pêle-mêle.
high [hai] a haut (placé), élevé, grand, gros, avancé, faisandé, (of drug addict) parti, en voyage; — altar maître-autel m; — school lycée m, collège m.
highborn ['haibɔ:n] a de haute naissance.
highbrow ['haibrau] n intellectuel, -elle, pontife m, snob m.
highflown ['haifloun] a ampoulé, extravagant.
high-handed ['hai'hændid] a impérieux, arbitraire.
highly ['haili] ad fortement, hautement, fort, très; —strung exalté, nerveux.
highness ['hainis] n Altesse f, hauteur f.
high-pitched ['hai'pitʃt] a aigu, -uë.
high-spirited ['hai'spiritid] a exubérant, courageux, enthousiaste.
highway ['haiwei] n route f nationale, principale, grande route f, grand chemin m, voie f; a routier; divided — route jumelée.
highwayman ['haiweimən] n voleur de grand chemin m.
hike [haik] n excursion f à pied; vi faire du footing, trimarder.
hilarious [hi'lɛəriəs] a hilaire.
hilarity [hi'læriti] n hilarité f.
hill [hil] n colline f, côte f, coteau m, montée f.

hillock ['hilək] n tertre m, butte f.
hilltop ['hiltɔp] n sommet m.
hilly ['hili] a accidenté, montueux.
hilt [hilt] n poignée f, garde f, crosse f.
him [him] pn le, lui; —self lui-même.
hind [haind] n biche f; a de derrière.
hinder ['hində] vt gêner, empêcher, entraver.
hindmost ['haindmoust] a dernier.
hindquarters ['haind'kwɔːtəz] n arrière train m.
hindrance ['hindrəns] n entrave f, obstacle m, empêchement m.
hinge [hindʒ] n gond m, pivot m, charnière f; vi tourner, dépendre.
hint [hint] n allusion f, insinuation f, mot m; vt insinuer, faire entendre; vi faire allusion (à **at**).
hip [hip] n hanche f.
hire ['haiə] n louage m, location f; on, for — à louer; vt louer, embaucher.
hireling ['haiəliŋ] n mercenaire m.
hire-purchase ['haiə'pəːtʃis] n paiements échelonnés m pl, vente à tempérament f.
hirsute ['həːsjuːt] a hirsute, velu.
his [hiz] a son, sa, ses; pn le sien, la sienne, les siens, les siennes, à lui.
hiss [his] n sifflement m, sifflets m pl; vti siffler.
historian [his'tɔːriən] n historien m.
historic [his'tɔrik] a historique.
history ['histəri] n histoire f.
hit [hit] n coup m (au but), succès m; vt frapper, atteindre, mettre le doigt sur; vi se cogner, donner.
hitch [hitʃ] n secousse f, accroc m, nœud m; vt pousser (tirer) brusquement, attacher, accrocher.
hitchhike ['hitʃhaik] vi faire de l'autostop.
hither ['hiðə] ad ici, y, çà.
hitherto ['hiðə'tuː] ad jusqu'ici.
hive [haiv] n ruche f, essaim m.
hoard [hɔːd] n stock m, magot m; vt amasser, thésauriser.
hoarding ['hɔːdiŋ] n palissade f, panneau-réclame m, thésaurisation f, amassage m.
hoarfrost ['hɔːˈfrɔst] n gelée blanche f, givre m.
hoarse [hɔːs] a rauque, enroué.
hoarseness ['hɔːsnis] n enrouement m.
hoary ['hɔːri] a chenu, vénérable, blanchâtre.
hoax [houks] n mystification f, vt mystifier.
hobble ['hɔbl] n boiterie f, entrave f, embarras m; vt entraver; vi aller clopin-clopant.
hobby ['hɔbi] n marotte f, dada m.
hobnail ['hɔbneil] n clou à ferrer m.
hock [hɔk] n jarret m, vin du Rhin m.
hod [hɔd] n hotte f, auge f.
hoe [hou] n houe f, sarcloir m, hoyau m, daba m; vt biner, sarcler.

hog [hɔg] n porc m, pourceau m, cochon m.
hogshead ['hɔgzhed] n barrique f.
hoist [hɔist] n poulie f, treuil m, monte-charge m; vt hisser.
hold [hould] n prise f, mainmise f, influence f, empire m, cale f (con-, dé-, main-, re-, sou-, tenir, porter; vi tenir (bon), se maintenir, persister, subsister; to — **back** vt retenir; vi hésiter, rester en arrière; to — on tenir bon, s'accrocher.
holdall ['houldɔːl] n valise f, fourre-tout m.
holder ['houldə] n manche m, poignée f, récipient m, porteur, -euse, détenteur, -trice, titulaire mf.
holdfast ['houldfɑːst] n crampon m.
holding ['houldiŋ] n propriété f, tenue f, conservation f, tenure f.
hold-up ['houldʌp] n embouteillage m, panne f, attaque f, coup à main armée m.
hole [houl] n trou m; vt trouer, percer.
holiday ['hɔlidei] n jour férié m, congé m, vacances f pl.
holiness ['houlinis] n sainteté f.
Holland ['hɔlənd] n la Hollande f.
hollow ['hɔlou] n creux m, cavité f, cuvette f; a creux, faux, sourd; vt creuser.
holly ['hɔli] n houx m.
hollyhock ['hɔlihɔk] n rose trémière f.
holm [houm] n îlot m, berge f; —**oak** chêne vert m.
holster ['houlstə] n fontes f pl, étui m.
holy ['houli] a saint, bénit, sacré; **the H**— Ghost le Saint-Esprit.
home [houm] n chez-soi m, maison f, foyer m, pays m, asile m, clinique f; a domestique, de famille, indigène, métropolitain, national, (coup) direct, bien appliqué; ad chez soi, de retour; not at — sorti; to **drive** — pousser à fond; to **strike** — frapper juste.
homecoming ['houm,kʌmiŋ] n retour m, rentrée f.
homeless ['houmlis] a sans logis.
homely ['houmli] a simple, commun.
home-made ['houm'meid] a fait chez soi, bricolé.
Home Office ['houm,ɔfis] n (UK) ministère de l'Intérieur m.
home rule ['houm'ruːl] n autonomie f.
Home Secretary ['houm'sekrətri] n (UK) ministre de l'Intérieur m.
homesickness ['houmsiknis] n mal du pays m.
homespun ['houmspʌn] a filé à la maison.
homeward ['houmwəd] ad vers la maison, vers le pays.
homily ['hɔmili] n homélie f.
homogeneity [,hɔmoudʒə'niːiti] n homogénéité f.
homogeneous [,hɔmə'dʒiːnjəs] n homogène.

hone [houn] n pierre f à aiguiser, (razors) cuir m.

honest ['ɔnist] a honnête, probe, loyal.

honestly ['ɔnistli] ad sincèrement, de bonne foi, honnêtement.

honesty ['ɔnisti] n honnêteté f, sincérité f.

honey ['hʌni] n miel m.

honeycomb ['hʌnikoum] n rayon de miel m; vt cribler.

honeydew ['hʌnidju:] n miellée f.

honeymoon ['hʌnimu:n] n lune de miel f, voyage de noces m.

honeysuckle ['hʌni.sʌkl] n chèvre-feuille m.

honor ['ɔnə] n honneur m, distinction f; vt honorer.

honorable ['ɔnərəbl] a honorable, honnête.

honorary ['ɔnərəri] a honoraire, honorifique.

hood [hud] n capuchon m, cape (line) f, capote f, capot m (de moteur).

hooded ['hudid] a encapuchonné, mantelé.

hoodwink ['hudwiŋk] vt égarer, donner le change à.

hoof [hu:f] n sabot m.

hook [huk] n croc m, crochet m, hameçon m, faucille f; —up (radio) combinaison f d'intérêts, conjugaison f de postes; vt (ac)crocher, agrafer, (fish) ferrer.

hookah ['hukə] n narghileh m.

hooked [hukt] a crochu, busqué.

hooligan ['hu:ligən] n voyou m.

hoop [hu:p] n cercle m, cerceau m, arceau m.

hoot [hu:t] n hululement m, huée f, coup de klaxon m; vi hululer, corner, klaxonner; vti huer; vt siffler.

hooter ['hu:tə] n sirène f, corne f.

hop [hɔp] n houblon m, petit saut m, sauterie f; vi saut(ill)er; to — it ficher le camp.

hope [houp] n espoir m, espérance f, attente f; vt espérer; to — for espérer.

hopeful ['houpful] a qui a bon espoir, qui donne espoir.

hopefully ['houpfuli] ad avec confiance.

hopeless ['houplis] a désespéré, incurable.

hop-garden ['hɔp'ga:dn] n houblonnière f.

hopping ['hɔpiŋ] n sautillement m, cueillette du houblon f.

horde [hɔ:d] n horde f.

horizon [hə'raizn] n horizon m.

horizontal [.hɔri'zɔntl] a horizontal.

horn [hɔ:n] n cor m, corne f.

hornbill ['hɔ:nbil] n calao m.

hornet ['hɔ:nit] n frelon m.

horrible ['hɔribl] a horrible, affreux.

horrid ['hɔrid] a affreux.

horrify ['hɔrifai] vt horrifier.

horror ['hɔrə] n horreur f.

horror-struck ['hɔrəstrʌk] a saisi, glacé.

horse [hɔ:s] n cheval m, cavalerie f, chevalet m.

horseback ['hɔ:sbæk] ad on — à cheval.

horse-dealer ['hɔ:s.di:lə] n maquignon m.

horsefly ['hɔ:sflai] n taon m.

horseman ['hɔ:smən] n écuyer m, cavalier m.

horsemanship ['hɔ:smənʃip] n équitation f.

horseplay ['hɔ:splei] n jeu de vilain m, jeu brutal m.

horsepower ['hɔ:s.pauə] n cheval-vapeur m.

horse-radish ['hɔ:s.rædiʃ] n raifort m.

horseshoe ['hɔ:sʃu:] n fer à cheval m.

horsewoman ['hɔ:s.wumən] n cavalière f, écuyère f, amazone f.

hose [houz] n tuyau m, bas m pl.

hosier's ['houʒəz] n bonneterie f.

hospitable [hɔs'pitəbl] a hospitalier.

hospitably [hɔs'pitəbli] ad à bras ouverts.

hospital ['hɔspitl] n hôpital m.

hospitality [.hɔspi'tæliti] n hospitalité f.

host ['houst] n hôte m, hostie f, armée f.

hostage ['hɔstidʒ] n ôtage m.

hostel ['hɔstəl] n foyer m, pension f; youth — auberge de la jeunesse f.

hostess ['houstes] n hôtesse f, maîtresse f de maison.

hostile ['hɔstail] a hostile, ennemi.

hostility [hɔs'tiliti] n hostilité f.

hot [hɔt] a très chaud, brûlant, qui emporte la bouche.

hotch-potch ['hɔtʃpɔtʃ] n salmigondis m, macédoine f.

hotel [hou'tel] n hôtel m.

hot-headed ['hɔt'hedid] a exalté, impétueux, emporté.

hothouse ['hɔthaus] n serre chaude f.

hot-line ['hɔtlain] n téléphone rouge m.

hotpot ['hɔtpɔt] n ragoût m.

hot-water bottle ['hɔt'wɔ:tə.bɔtl] n bouillotte f, moine m.

hough [hɔk] n jarret m.

hound [haund] n chien courant m; pl meute f; vt chasser.

hour ['auə] n heure f; — hand petite aiguille f.

hourly ['auəli] ad à toute heure, à l'heure.

house [haus] n maison f, Chambre f; [hauz] vt loger, abriter, garer; town — hôtel m particulier.

house-agent ['haus.eidʒənt] n agent de location m.

housebreaking ['haus.breikiŋ] n vol m avec effraction, cambriolage m.

household ['haushould] n maisonnée f, ménage m, maison f.

householder ['haus.houldə] n occupant(e) mf.

housekeeper ['haus,ki:pə] n femme de charge f, ménagère f.
housekeeping ['haus,ki:piŋ] n ménage m.
housemaid ['hausmeid] n femme de chambre f, bonne f.
housetop ['haustɔp] n toit m; **to shout from the —s** crier qch sur les toits.
housewarming ['haus,wɔ:miŋ] n **to hold a —** pendre la crémaillère.
housewife ['hauswaif] n ménagère f.
housework ['hauswə:k] n ménage m.
housing ['hauziŋ] n logement m, rentrée f; **— problem** crise de logement f.
hovel ['hɔvəl] n masure f, taudis m.
hover ['hɔvə] vi planer, flâner, hésiter; **—craft** n aéroglisseur m.
how [hau] ad comment, comme, combien.
however [hau'evə] ad cependant; cj quelque (si) . . . que, de quelque manière que.
howitzer ['hauitsə] n obusier m.
howl [haul] n hurlement m; vi hurler, rugir, mugir.
hub [hʌb] n moyeu m, centre m.
huddle ['hʌdl] n tas m, fouillis m; vt entasser, serrer; vi se blottir, s'entasser, se serrer.
hue [hju:] n teinte f, nuance f; **to raise a —** and cry against crier tollé contre.
huff [hʌf] vt offusquer, froisser, souffler; **to take a —** prendre la mouche, s'offusquer; **to be |in a —** être offusqué.
hug [hʌg] n étreinte f; vt étreindre, presser, embrasser, serrer, longer, s'accrocher à.
huge [hju:dʒ] a immense, énorme.
hugeness ['hju:dʒnis] n énormité f, immensité f.
hulk [hʌlk] n carcasse f; pl pontons m pl.
hull [hʌl] n cosse f, coque f.
hullabaloo [,hʌləbə:'lu:] n vacarme m, charivari m.
hum [hʌm] n bourdonnement m, fredonnement m, ronron(nement) m; vi bourdonner, fredonner, ronronner.
human ['hju:mən] a humain.
humane [hju:'mein] a humain, humanitaire.
humanist ['hju:mənist] n humaniste m.
humanity [hju:'mæniti] n humanité f, genre humain m.
humanize ['hju:mənaiz] vt humaniser.
humble ['hʌmbl] a humble; vt humilier, rabattre.
humbug ['hʌmbʌg] n blagueur m, fumiste m, blague f, fumisterie f.
humdrum ['hʌmdrʌm] a plat, assommant, monotone, quotidien.
humid ['hju:mid] a humide.
humidity [hju:'miditi] n humidité f.

humiliate [hju:'milieit] vt humilier.
humiliation [hju:,mili'eifən] n humiliation f.
humility [hju:'militi] n humilité f.
hummock ['hʌmək] n mamelon m, monticule m.
humor ['hju:mə] n humeur f, humour m; vt flatter, se prêter à.
humorist ['hju:mərist] n plaisant m, humoriste m, comique m.
humorous ['hju:mərəs] a humoristique, comique, plaisant, drôle.
hump [hʌmp] n bosse f, cafard m.
humpback(ed) ['hʌmpbæk(t)] an bossu(e) mf.
hunch [hʌntʃ] n bosse f, pressentiment m; vt incurver, voûter.
hundred ['hʌndrid] an cent m.
hundredth ['hʌndridθ] a centième.
hung [hʌŋ] pp pt of hang.
Hungarian [hʌŋ'gɛəriən] a hongrois.
Hungary ['hʌŋgəri] n Hongrie f.
hunger ['hʌŋgə] n faim f; vi avoir faim, être affamé.
hunger-strike ['hʌŋgəstraik] n grève f de la faim.
hungry ['hʌŋgri] a qui a (donne) faim, affamé.
hunt [hʌnt] n chasse f; vti chasser; vi chasser à courre.
hunter ['hʌntə] n chasseur m, monture f.
hunting-box ['hʌntiŋbɔks] n pavillon de chasse m.
hunting-ground ['hʌntiŋgraund] n terrain de chasse m.
hunting-horn ['hʌntiŋhɔ:n] n cor de chasse m.
huntsman ['hʌntsmən] n piqueur m, veneur m, chasseur m.
hurdle ['hə:dl] n claie f, haie f, obstacle m; **— race** course de haies f, steeple-chase m.
hurl [hə:l] vt lancer, précipiter.
hurrah [hu'ra:] int n hourra m.
hurricane ['hʌrikən] n ouragan m; **—lamp** lampe-tempête f.
hurried ['hʌrid] a pressé, hâtif.
hurriedly ['hʌridli] ad précipitamment, à la hâte.
hurry ['hʌri] n hâte f, urgence f; vt hâter, presser; vi (se) presser, se dépêcher; **in a —** pressé, en toute hâte, de si tôt; **there is no — rien** ne presse.
hurt [hə:t] n mal m, blessure f, tort m, préjudice m; vt faire (du) mal à, blesser, faire tort à; vi faire mal.
hurtful ['hə:tful] a préjudiciable, nocif, nuisible.
husband ['hʌzbənd] n mari m; vt ménager, gérer sagement.
husbandman ['hʌzbəndmən] n fermier m, laboureur m.
husbandry ['hʌzbəndri] n culture f, gestion habile f.
hush [hʌʃ] n silence m, accalmie f; vt faire taire, étouffer; vi se taire; excl chut!
husk [hʌsk] n cosse f, gousse f, balle

f. peau f; vt écosser, décortiquer, éplucher.

husky ['hʌski] a enroué, altéré, fort, costaud; n chien esquimau m.

hussar [hu'zɑː] n hussard m.

hussy ['hʌsi] n effrontée f, luronne f.

hustle ['hʌsl] n bousculade f, activité f, vt bousculer, presser; vi jouer des coudes, se hâter.

hut [hʌt] n cabane f, baraque f; (mil) baraquement m; straw — paillotte.

hutch [hʌtʃ] n clapier m.

hyacinth ['haiəsinθ] n jacinthe f, hyacinthe f.

hybrid ['haibrid] an hybride m.

hydrangea [hai'dreindʒə] n hortensia m.

hydrant ['haidrənt] n prise d'eau f.

hydro-electric [,haidroui'lektrik] a hydraulique; —power houille f blanche.

hydrogen ['haidrədʒən] n hydrogène m.

hydrophobia [,haidrə'foubjə] n hydrophobie f, rage f.

hyena [hai'iːnə] n hyène f.

hygiene ['haidʒiːn] n hygiène f.

hygienic [hai'dʒiːnik] a hygiénique.

hymn [him] n hymne m.

hyphen ['haifən] n trait d'union m.

hypnosis [hip'nousis] n hypnose f.

hypnotic [hip'nɔtik] a hypnotique.

hypnotism ['hipnətizəm] n hypnotisme m.

hypnotize ['hipnətaiz] vt hypnotiser.

hypocrisy [hi'pɔkrisi] n hypocrisie f.

hypocrite ['hipəkrit] n hypocrite mf.

hypocritical [,hipə'kritikəl] a hypocrite.

hypothesis [hai'pɔθisis] n hypothèse f.

hypothetical [,haipou'θetikəl] a hypothétique.

hysteria [his'tiəriə] n hystérie f.

hysterical [his'terikəl] a hystérique, sujet à des crises de nerfs.

hysterics [his'teriks] n crise de nerfs f.

I

I [ai] pn je, moi.

Iain ['iən] (Scot) Jean m.

Iberia [ai'biəriə] n Ibérie f.

Iberian [ai'biəriən] a ibérique; an ibérien, -ienne.

ibex ['aibeks] n chamois m.

ice [ais] n glace f; vt (con)geler, glacer, (wine) frapper.

iceberg ['aisbəːg] n iceberg m, glaçon m.

icebound ['aisbaund] a pris par les glaces.

icecream ['ais'kriːm] n glace f.

ice-floe ['aisflou] n banquise f.

ice-house ['aishaus] n glacière f.

icicle ['aisikl] n glaçon m.

icy ['aisi] a glacial, couvert de glace.

idea [ai'diə] n idée f, notion f.

ideal [ai'diəl] an idéal m.

idealize [ai'diəlaiz] vt idéaliser.

identical [ai'dentikəl] a identique, conforme.

identify [ai'dentifai] vt identifier, établir l'identité de.

identity [ai'dentiti] n identité f.

idiocy ['idiəsi] n idiotie f.

idiom ['idiəm] n dialecte m, locution f, idiome m, idiotisme m; —atically ad d'une manière idiomatique.

idiot ['idiət] n idiot(e) mf.

idiotic [,idi'ɔtik] a idiot, bête.

idle ['aidl] a paresseux, désœuvré, perdu, vain; vi paresser, muser, marcher au ralenti.

idleness ['aidlnis] n paresse f, oisiveté f, chômage m, futilité f.

idler ['aidlə] n fainéant(e) mf, flâneur, -euse, désœuvré(e) mf.

idly ['aidli] ad paresseusement, vainement.

idol ['aidl] n idole f.

idolatrous [ai'dɔlatrəs] a idolâtre.

idolatry [ai'dɔlatri] n idolâtrie f.

idolize ['aidəlaiz] vt idolâtrer, adorer.

if [if] cj si.

igloo ['igluː] n igloo m.

ignite [ig'nait] vt allumer, mettre le feu à; vi prendre feu.

ignition [ig'niʃən] n allumage m, ignition f.

ignoble [ig'noubl] a né bas, ignoble, infâme.

ignominious [,ignə'miniəs] a ignominieux.

ignominy ['ignəmini] n ignominie f.

ignorance ['ignərəns] n ignorance f.

ignorant ['ignərənt] a ignorant.

ignore [ig'nɔː] vt passer sous silence, méconnaître, ne pas tenir compte de.

ill [il] n mal m, tort m; a malade, mauvais; ad mal.

ill-bred ['il'bred] a mal élevé.

ill-considered ['ilkən'sidəd] a peu réfléchi, hâtif, -ive.

ill-disposed ['ildis'pouzd] a malveillant.

illegal [i'liːgəl] a illégal.

illegality [,iliː'gæliti] n illégalité f.

illegible [i'ledʒəbl] a illisible.

illegitimacy [,ilidʒi'timəsi] n illégitimité f.

illegitimate [,ilidʒi'timit] a illégitime.

ill-fated ['il'feitid] a malchanceux, néfaste.

ill-feeling ['il'fiːliŋ] m rancune f, ressentiment m.

ill-gotten ['il'gɔtn] a mal acquis.

illiberal [i'libərəl] a borné, grossier, mesquin.

illicit [i'lisit] a illicite.

ill-informed ['ilin'fɔːmd] a mal renseigné.

illiterate [i'litərit] an illettré(e) mf.

illness ['ilnis] n maladie f.

ill-starred ['il'stɑːd] a né sous une mauvaise étoile, néfaste.

ill-timed ['il'taimd] a inopportun, malencontreux.

illuminate [i'luːmineit] vt illuminer, éclairer, enluminer.

illumination [i.luːmi'neiʃən] n illumination f, enluminure f.

ill-used ['il'juːzd] a malmené, maltraité.

illusion [i'luːʒən] n illusion f.

illusionist [i'luːʒənist] n prestidigitateur m.

illusive [i'luːsiv] a trompeur, mensonger.

illustrate ['iləstreit] vt éclairer, illustrer.

illustration [.iləs'treiʃən] n illustration f, explication f, exemple m.

illustrator ['iləstreitə] n illustrateur m.

illustrious [i'lʌstriəs] a illustre, célèbre.

image ['imidʒ] n image f, statuette f.

imagery ['imədʒəri] n images fpl.

imaginable [i'mædʒinəbl] a imaginable.

imaginary [i'mædʒinəri] a imaginaire.

imagination [i.mædʒi'neiʃən] n imagination f.

imaginative [i'mædʒinətiv] a imaginatif.

imagine [i'mædʒin] vt s'imaginer, se figurer, concevoir, croire, imaginer.

imbecile ['imbəsiːl] an imbécile mf; a faible.

imbecility [.imbi'siliti] n imbécillité f.

imbibe [im'baib] vt boire, absorber, imbiber, adopter.

imbue [im'bjuː] vt imprégner, inspirer.

imitate ['imiteit] vt imiter.

imitation [.imi'teiʃən] n imitation f.

imitative ['imitətiv] a imitatif, imitateur.

imitator ['imiteitə] n imitateur, -trice.

immaculate [i'mækjulit] a immaculé, irréprochable.

immaterial [.imə'tiəriəl] a immatériel, sans importance.

immature [.imə'tjuə] a pas mûr.

immeasurable [i'meʒərəbl] a incommensurable, infini.

immediate [i'miːdjət] a immédiat, direct, premier.

immediately [i'miːdjətli] ad aussitôt, tout de suite.

immemorial [.imi'mɔːriəl] a immémorial.

immense [i'mens] a immense, vaste.

immensely [i'mensli] ad énormément, immensément.

immensity [i'mensiti] n immensité f.

immerse [i'məːs] vt immerger, plonger.

immigrant ['imigrənt] an immigrant(e) mf, immigré(e) mf.

immigrate ['imigreit] vi immigrer.

immigration [.imi'greiʃən] n immigration f.

imminence ['iminəns] n imminence f.

imminent ['iminənt] a imminent.

immobility [.imou'biliti] n immobilité f, fixité f.

immoderate [i'mɔdərit] a immodéré, démesuré.

immoderately [i'mɔdəritli] ad démesurément, immodérément.

immoderation [.i.mɔdər'eiʃən] n manque de mesure m.

immoral [i'mɔrəl] a immoral.

immorality [.imɔ'ræliti] n immoralité f.

immortal [i'mɔːtl] a immortel.

immortality [.imɔː'tæliti] n immortalité f.

immortalize [i'mɔːtəlaiz] vt immortaliser.

immovable [i'muːvəbl] a immuable, inébranlable, insensible.

immune [i'mjuːn] a à l'abri (de to), réfractaire (à to).

immunity [i'mjuːniti] n immunité f, exemption f.

immunize ['imjunaiz] vt immuniser.

immutability [i.mjuːtə'biliti] n immutabilité f.

immutable [i'mjuːtəbl] a immuable.

imp [imp] n diablotin m.

impact ['impækt] n choc m, collision f, impression f.

impair [im'peə] vt affaiblir, altérer.

impairment [im'peəmənt] n affaiblissement m, altération f.

impale [im'peil] vt empaler.

impart [im'paːt] vt faire part de, communiquer.

impartial [im'paːʃəl] a impartial, équitable.

impassable [im'paːsəbl] a infranchissable, impraticable.

impassibility [.impaːsə'biliti] n impassibilité f.

impassioned [im'pæʃnd] a passionné.

impassive [im'pæsiv] a impassible.

impatience [im'peiʃəns] n impatience f.

impatient [im'peiʃənt] a impatient.

impeach [im'piːtʃ] vt mettre en accusation, mettre en cause, attaquer, blâmer.

impeccable [im'pekəbl] a impeccable.

impecuniosity [.impikjuːnj'ɔsiti] n dénuement m.

impecunious [.impi'kjuːnjəs] a sans le sou, besogneux.

impede [im'piːd] vt entraver, retarder.

impediment [im'pedimənt] n empêchement m, entrave f, obstacle m, embarras m.

impedimenta [im.pedi'mentə] n pl bagages m pl.

impel [im'pel] vt pousser.

impend [im'pend] vt menacer, être imminent.

impenetrable [im'penitrəbl] *a* impénétrable.

impenitence [im'penitəns] *n* impénitence *f*.

impenitent [im'penitənt] *a* impénitent.

imperative [im'perətiv] *an* impératif *m*; *a* péremptoire, impérieux.

imperceptible [impə'septəbl] *a* imperceptible, insensible, insaisissable.

imperfect [im'pə:fikt] *a* imparfait, défectueux.

imperfection [,impə'fekʃən] *n* imperfection *f*, défectuosité *f*.

imperial [im'piəriəl] *a* impérial, majestueux.

imperialism [im'piəriəlizəm] *n* impérialisme *m*.

imperialist [im'piəriəlist] *an* impérialiste *mf*.

imperil [im'peril] *vt* mettre en danger.

imperious [im'piəriəs] *a* impérieux.

imperishable [im'periʃəbl] *a* impérissable.

impermeable [im'pə:mjəbl] *a* imperméable.

impersonal [im'pə:snl] *a* impersonnel.

impersonate [im'pə:səneit] *vt* se faire passer pour, représenter.

impersonation [im,pə:sə'neiʃən] *n* personnification *f*, incarnation *f*, imitation *f*.

impertinence [im'pə:tinəns] *n* insolence *f*, impertinence *f*.

impertinent [im'pə:tinənt] *a* impertinent, insolent.

imperturbability [,impətə:bə'biliti] *n* flegme *m*, imperturbabilité *f*, sang-froid *m*.

imperturbable [,impə'tə:bəbl] *a* imperturbable, inaltérable, serein.

impervious [im'pə:vjəs] *a* impénétrable, imperméable.

impetuosity [im,petju'ɔsiti] *n* impétuosité *f*.

impetuous [im'petjuəs] *a* impétueux.

impetus ['impitəs] *n* impulsion *f*, élan *m*.

impiety [im'paiəti] *n* impiété *f*.

impinge [im'pindʒ] *vi* to — upon frapper, se heurter à.

impious ['impiəs] *a* impie.

implant [im'plɑ:nt] *vt* implanter, inspirer, inculquer.

implement ['implimənt] *n* instrument *m*, article *m*, outil *m*; *pl* attirail *m*, matériel *m*.

implement ['impliment] *vt* remplir, exécuter.

implicate ['implikeit] *vt* mettre en cause, emmêler, impliquer.

implication [,impli'keiʃən] *n* implication *f*, insinuation *f*, portée *f*.

implicit [im'plisit] *a* implicite, tacite, absolu.

implore [im'plɔ:] *vt* implorer, supplier.

imploring [im'plɔ:riŋ] *a* suppliant.

imply [im'plai] *vt* impliquer, (faire) supposer.

impolite [,impə'lait] *a* impoli.

impolitely [,impə'laitli] *ad* impoliment.

impoliteness [,impə'laitnis] *n* impolitesse *f*.

import ['impɔ:t] *n* portée *f*, signification *f*; *pl* importations *f pl*.

import [im'pɔ:t] *vt* importer, introduire, signifier, dénoter.

importance [im'pɔ:təns] *n* importance *f*, onséquence *f*.

important [im'pɔ:tənt] *a* important.

importing [im'pɔ:tiŋ] *n* importation *f*.

importunate [im'pɔ:tjunit] *a* importun, ennuyeux.

importune [,impɔ:'tjuːn] *vt* importuner, solliciter.

impose [im'pouz] *vt* imposer, infliger; to — upon abuser de, en imposer à.

imposition [,impə'ziʃən] *n* imposition *f*, impôt *m*, imposture *f*, supercherie, pensum *m*.

impossibility [im,pɔsə'biliti] *n* impossibilité *f*.

impossible [im'pɔsəbl] *a* impossible.

impostor [im'pɔstə] *n* imposteur *m*.

imposture [im'pɔstʃə] *n* imposture *f*.

impotence ['impətəns] *n* impuissance *f*.

impotent ['impətənt] *a* impuissant, impotent.

impound [im'paund] *vt* mettre à la fourrière, saisir, confisquer, enfermer.

impoverish [im'pɔvəriʃ] *vt* appauvrir.

impoverishment [im'pɔvəriʃmənt] *n* appauvrissement *m*.

impracticability [im,præktikə'biliti] *n* impossibilité *f*.

impracticable [im'præktikəbl] *a* impraticable, intraitable, infaisable.

impregnable [im'pregnəbl] *a* imprenable, inexpugnable.

impregnate ['impregneit] *vt* saturer, imprégner.

impress ['impres] *n* empreinte *f*.

impress [im'pres] *vt* empreindre, timbrer, imprimer, impressionner, enrôler de force.

impression [im'preʃən] *n* impression *f*, tirage *m*.

impressionable [im'preʃnəbl] *a* impressionnable, susceptible.

impressionism [im'preʃənizəm] *n* impressionnisme *m*.

impressive [im'presiv] *a* frappant, impressionnant.

imprint ['imprint] *n* empreinte *f*, griffe *f*.

imprint [im'print] *vt* imprimer.

imprison [im'prizn] *vt* emprisonner.

imprisonment [im'prizmənt] *n* emprisonnement *m*, prison *f*.

improbability [im,prɔbə'biliti] *n* invraisemblance *f*, improbabilité *f*.

improbable [im'prɔbəbl] a improbable, invraisemblable.

improper [im'prɔpə] a impropre, indécent.

impropriety [,imprə'praiəti] n impropriété f, inconvenance f.

improve [im'pru:v] vt améliorer, profiter de; vi s'améliorer, faire des progrès.

improved [im'pru:vd] a amélioré, perfectionné.

improvement [im'pru:vmənt] n amélioration f, progrès m pl, mieux m.

improvidence [im'prɔvidəns] n imprévoyance f.

improvident [im'prɔvidənt] a imprévoyant.

improvisation [,imprəvai'zeiʃən] n improvisation f.

improvise ['imprəvaiz] vti improviser.

imprudence [im'pru:dəns] n imprudence f.

imprudent [im'pru:dənt] a imprudent.

impudent ['impjudənt] a impudent.

impudently ['impjudəntli] ad impudemment.

impugn [im'pju:n] vt critiquer, contester.

impulse ['impʌls] n impulsion f, mouvement m, poussée f.

impulsive [im'pʌlsiv] a impulsif, prime-sautier.

impulsiveness [im'pʌlsivnis] n impulsivité f.

impunity [im'pjuniti] n impunité f; **with** — impunément.

impure [im'pjuə] a impur, rouillé.

impurity [im'pjuriti] n impureté f.

imputable [im'pju:təbl] a imputable.

imputation [,impju'teiʃən] n imputation f, attribution f.

impute [im'pju:t] vt imputer, attribuer.

in [in] prep en, dans, pendant; à, de, sur, par; ad y, là, rentré, de retour, à la maison.

inability [,inə'biliti] n incapacité f, impuissance f.

inaccessibility ['inæk,sesə'biliti] n inaccessibilité f.

inaccessible [,inæk'sesəbl] a inaccessible, inabordable.

inaccuracy [in'ækjurəsi] n inexactitude f.

inaccurate [in'ækjurit] a inexact.

inaction [in'ækʃən] n inaction f, inertie f.

inactive [in'æktiv] a inactif, inerte.

inactivity [,inæk'tiviti] n inactivité f.

inadequacy [in'ædikwəsi] n insuffisance f.

inadequate [in'ædikwit] a inadéquat, insuffisant.

inadvertency [,inəd'və:tənsi] n inadvertance f.

inadvertent [,inəd'və:tənt] a inattentif, involontaire.

inadvertently [,inəd'və:təntli] ad par mégarde.

inane [i'nein] a vide, stupide, inepte.

inanimate ['inænimit] a inanimé.

inanity [in'æniti] n inanité f, niaiserie f.

inapposite [in'æpəzit] a déplacé.

inappropriate [,inə'proupriit] a déplacé, impropre.

inapt [in'æpt] a impropre, inapte, inexpert.

inarticulate [,inɑ:'tikjulit] a inarticulé, muet.

inasmuch as [inəz'mʌtʃ,æz] cj en tant que, vu que.

inattention [,inə'tenʃən] n inattention f.

inaudible [in'ɔ:dəbl] a insaisissable, imperceptible, faible.

inaugural [i'nɔ:gjurəl] a inaugural.

inaugurate [i'nɔ:gjureit] vt inaugurer, introniser.

inauguration [i,nɔ:gju'reiʃən] n inauguration f.

inauspicious [,inɔ:s'piʃəs] a de mauvais augure, malencontreux.

inborn ['in'bɔ:n] a inné, infus.

incandescent [,inkæn'desənt] a incandescent.

incapable [in'keipəbl] a incapable, incompétent, inaccessible.

incarcerate [in'kɑ:səreit] vt incarcérer, emprisonner.

incarceration [in,kɑ:sə'reiʃən] n incarcération f.

incarnate [in'kɑ:nit] vt incarner; a incarné.

incarnation [,inkɑ:'neiʃən] n incarnation f.

incendiary [in'sendjəri] an incendiaire m.

incense ['insens] n encens m.

incense [in'sens] vt offenser, exaspérer.

incentive [in'sentiv] n encouragement m, stimulant m; a stimulant.

inception [in'sepʃən] n commencement m, début m.

incessant [in'sesnt] a incessant continuel.

incessantly [in'sesntli] ad incessamment, sans cesse.

incest ['insest] n inceste m.

incestuous [in'sestjuəs] a incestueux.

inch [intʃ] n pouce m; vi avancer reculer, peu à peu.

incidence ['insidəns] n incidence f.

incident ['insidənt] n incident m.

incidental [,insi'dentl] a accessoire fortuit, commun (à to); — expense faux frais.

incidentally [,insi'dentəli] ad in cidemment, en passant.

incinerator [in'sinəreitə] n incinérateur m.

incise [in'saiz] vt inciser.

incision [in'siʒən] n incision entaille f.

incisive [in'saisiv] a incisif, mordant pénétrant.

incite [in'sait] vt inciter, pousser, exciter.

incitement [in'saitmənt] n incitation f, instigation f.

incivility [.insi'viliti] n impolitesse f.

inclemency [in'klemənsi] n inclémence f, rigueur f.

inclination [.inkli'neiʃən] n inclinaison f, pente f, inclination f.

incline ['inklain] n pente f, rampe f.

incline [in'klain] vt incliner, pencher.

include [in'klu:d] vt comprendre, englober.

inclusive [in'klu:siv] a inclus, tout compris; — sum somme globale.

inclusively [in'klu:sivli] ad inclusivement.

incoherence [.inkou'hiərəns] n incohérence f.

incoherent [.inkou'hiərənt] a décousu, incohérent.

income ['inkəm] n revenu m; — tax ·impôt m sur le revenu.

incomparable [in'kɔmpərəbl] a incomparable, hors ligne.

incompatible [.inkəm'pætibl] a incompatible, inconciliable.

incompetence [in'kɔmpitəns] n incapacité f, incompétence f.

incomplete [.inkəm'pli:t] a incomplet, inachevé.

incomprehensible [.inkɔmpri'hensibl] a incompréhensible.

incomprehension [.inkɔmpri'henʃən] n inintelligence f, incompréhension f.

inconceivable [.inkən'si:vəbl] a inconcevable.

inconclusive [.inkən'klu:siv] a pas (non) concluant.

incongruity [.inkɔŋ'gru:iti] n incongruité f.

incongruous [in'kɔŋgruəs] a incongru, déplacé.

incongruously [in'kɔŋgruəsli] ad incongrûment.

inconsiderable [.inkən'sidərəbl] a négligeable, insignifiant.

inconsiderate [.inkən'sidərit] a irréflechi, étourdi, sans égard.

inconsistency [.inkən'sistənsi] n inconséquence, inconsistance.

inconsistent [.inkən'sistənt] a décousu, inconsistant, inconséquent, contradictoire.

inconsolable [.inkən'souləbl] a inconsolable.

inconspicuous [.inkən'spikjuəs] a effacé, discret.

inconstancy [in'kɔnstənsi] n inconstance f, instabilité f.

inconstant [in'kɔnstənt] a inconstant, volage.

incontinently [in'kɔntinəntli] ad incontinent, sur-le-champ.

inconvenience [.inkən'vi:njəns] n inconvénient m, incommodité f.

inconvenient [.inkən'vi:njənt] a incommode, inopportun.

incorporate [in'kɔ:pəreit] vt in-

corporer; vi se former en société.

incorrect [.inkə'rekt] a inexact, incorrect.

incorrigible [in'kɔridʒəbl] a incorrigible.

increase ['inkri:s] n augmentation f.

increase [in'kri:s] vt accroître; vti augmenter; vi s'accroître, s'agrandir.

increasingly [in'kri:siŋli] ad de plus en plus.

incredible [in'kredibl] a incroyable.

incredulous [in'kredjuləs] a incrédule, sceptique.

increment ['inkrimənt] n accroissement m, plus-value f.

incriminate [in'krimineit] vt inculper, incriminer.

incriminating [in'krimineitiŋ] a accusateur, à conviction.

incubate ['inkjubeit] vti couver.

incubation [.inkju'beiʃən] n couvaison f, incubation f.

incubator ['inkju.beitə] n couveuse artificielle f.

inculcate ['inkʌlkeit] vt inculquer.

inculpate ['inkʌlpeit] vt inculper.

inculpation [.inkʌl'peiʃən] n inculpation f.

incumbent [in'kʌmbənt] a qui incombe (à upon).

incur [in'kə:] vt encourir, s'attirer, contracter.

incurable [in'kjuərəbl] a incurable.

incursion [in'kə:ʃən] n incursion f.

indebted [in'detid] a endetté, redevable, obligé.

indebtedness [in'detidnis] n dette f, obligation f.

indecent [in'di:snt] a indécent, inconvenant.

indecision [.indi'siʒən] n indécision f, irrésolution f.

indecisive [.indi'saisiv] a indécis(if), peu concluant.

indecorous [in'dekərəs] a inconvenant, malséant.

indecorousness [in'dekərəsnis] n inconvenance f.

indeed [in'di:d] ad vraiment, en vérité, en effet, de fait.

indefatigable [.indi'fætigəbl] a infatigable.

indefensible [.indi'fensibl] a insoutenable, indéfendable.

indefinable [.indi'fainəbl] a indéfinissable.

indefinite [in'definit] a indéfini, vague, indéterminé.

indelible [in'delibl] a indélébile, ineffaçable.

indelicate [in'delikit] a indélicat, inconvenant.

indemnify [in'demnifai] vt indemniser, dédommager.

indemnity [in'demniti] n indemnité f, sécurités f pl.

indent ['indent] n commande f, ordre de requisition m; [in'dent] vt entailler, échancrer; to — for commander, réquisitionner.

indentation [.inden'teiʃən] n échancrure f, entaille f.

indenture [in'dentʃə] n contrat m; vt lier par contrat.

independence [indi'pendəns] n indépendance f.

independent [.indi'pendənt] a indépendant.

independently [.indi'pendəntli] ad indépendamment, séparément.

indescribable [.indis'kraibəbl] a indescriptible, indicible.

indestructible [.indis'trʌktəbl] a indestructible.

index ['indeks] n table f alphabétique, indice m; classeur m; vt classer, répertorier.

index-card ['indeks.kɑːd] n fiche f.

India [indjə] n l'Inde f.

Indian [indjən] an Indien, -ienne.

india-rubber ['indjə'rʌbə] n caoutchouc m, gomme f (à effacer).

indicate ['indikeit] vt indiquer, désigner, dénoter.

indication [.indi'keiʃən] n indication f, signe m, indice m.

indicative [in'dikativ] an indicatif m; a suggestif.

indicator ['indikeitə] n indicateur m, aiguille f.

indict [in'dait] vt accuser, traduire en justice.

indictment [in'daitmənt] n accusation f, inculpation f.

Indies [indiz] n pl Indes f pl; East — les Grandes Indes f; West — les Antilles.

indifference [in'difrəns] n indifférence f, médiocrité f, impartialité.

indifferent [in'difrənt] a indifférent, égal, médiocre, impartial.

indigence ['indidʒəns] n indigence f, misère f.

indigenous [in'didʒinəs] a indigène, du pays, autochtone.

indigent ['indidʒənt] a indigène, nécessiteux.

indigestible [.indi'dʒestəbl] a indigeste.

indigestion [.indi'dʒestʃən] n indigestion f, mauvaise digestion f.

indignant [in'dignənt] a indigné.

indignation [.indig'neiʃən] n indignation f.

indignity [in'digniti] n indignité f, affront m.

indigo ['indigou] n indigo m.

indirect [.indi'rekt] a indirect, détourné.

indiscernible [.indi'sə:nəbl] a imperceptible.

indiscreet [.indis'kriːt] a indiscret, imprudent.

indiscretion [.indis'kreʃən] n indiscrétion f, imprudence f, sottise f.

indiscriminate [.indis'kriminit] a fait au hasard.

indiscriminately [.indis'krim'nitli] ad au petit bonheur, au hasard.

indispensable [.indis'pensəbl] a indispensable, de première nécessité.

indispose [.indis'pouz] vt indisposer (contre), incommoder; to be —d être indisposé, souffrant.

indisposition [.indispə'ziʃən] n indisposition f, aversion f, malaise m.

indisputable [.indis'pjuːtəbl] a indiscutable, incontestable.

indissoluble [.indi'sɔljubl] a indissoluble.

indistinct [.indis'tiŋkt] a confus, vague, h. distinct.

indistinctness [.indis'tiŋktnis] n confusion f.

indistinguishable [.indis'tiŋgwiʃəbl] a impossible à distinguer, imperceptible, insaisissable.

individual [.indi'vidjuəl] n individu m; a individuel, particulier.

individuality [.indi.vidju'æliti] n individualité f.

indivisible [.indi'vizəbl] a indivisible.

Indochina ['indo'tʃainə] n Indochine f.

indoctrinate [in'dɔktrineit] vt endoctriner, instruire.

indolence ['indələns] n indolence f.

indolent ['indələnt] a indolent, paresseux.

indomitable [in'dɔmitəbl] a indomptable.

indoor ['indɔː] a de salon, de société, d'intérieur; ad —s à l'intérieur, à la maison.

induce [in'djus] vt induire, amener, provoquer, décider.

inducement [in'djusmənt] n invite f, encouragement m.

induct [in'dʌkt] vt installer, initier.

induction [in'dʌkʃən] n installation f, induction f.

indulge [in'dʌldʒ] vt satisfaire, nourrir, gâter; to — in s'abandonner à, se livrer à.

indulgence [in'dʌldʒəns] n goût excessif m, indulgence f.

indulgent [in'dʌldʒənt] a faible, indulgent.

industrial [in'dʌstriəl] a industriel.

industrialism [in'dʌstriəlizəm] n industrialisme m.

industrialist [in'dʌstriəlist] n industriel m.

industrialize [in'dʌstriəlaiz] vt industrialiser.

industrious [in'dʌstriəs] a actif, industrieux, laborieux.

industry ['indəstri] n industrie f, activité f, application f.

inebriate [i'niːbrieit] vt griser, enivrer; n ivrogne m.

inebriated [i'niːbrieitid] a ivre, enivré, grisé.

inebriety [.iniː'braiəti] n ébriété f, ivresse f.

ineffable [in'efəbl] a ineffable, indicible.

ineffective [.ini'fektiv] a inefficace, impuissant.

ineffectual [ˌini'fektjuəl] *a* vain, stérile, inefficace.

inefficacious [ˌinefi'keiʃəs] *a* inefficace.

inefficiency [ˌini'fiʃənsi] *n* inefficacité *f*, incapacité *f*.

inefficient [ˌini'fiʃənt] *a* inefficace, incompétent.

inelastic [ˌini'læstik] *a* raide, inélastique, fixe.

inept [i'nept] *a* déplacé, inepte.

ineptitude [i'neptitjuːd] *n* ineptie *f*.

inequality [ˌini'kwɔliti] *n* inégalité *f*, irrégularité *f*.

ineradicable [ˌini'rædikəbl] *a* indéracinable, inextirpable.

inert [i'nəːt] *a* inerte.

inertia [i'nəːʃə] *n* inertie *f*, paresse *f*.

inestimable [in'estiməbl] *a* inestimable, incalculable.

inevitable [in'evitəbl] *a* inévitable, fatal.

inexact [ˌinig'zækt] *a* inexact.

inexcusable [ˌiniks'kjuːzəbl] *a* impardonnable, inexcusable.

inexhaustible [ˌinig'zɔːstəbl] *a* inépuisable, intarissable.

inexorable [in'eksərəbl] *a* inexorable.

inexpedience [ˌiniks'piːdjəns] *n* inopportunité *f*.

inexpedient [ˌiniks'piːdjənt] *a* inopportun, malavisé.

inexpensive [ˌiniks'pensiv] *a* bon marché, pas cher.

inexperienced [ˌiniks'piəriənst] *a* inexpérimenté, inexercé.

inexpert [in'ekspəːt] *a* inexpert, maladroit.

inexpiable [in'ekspiəbl] *a* inexpiable.

inexplicable [ˌiniks'plikəbl] *a* inexplicable.

inexpressible [ˌiniks'presəbl] *a* inexprimable.

inextinguishable [ˌiniks'tiŋgwiʃəbl] *a* inextinguible, inassouvissable.

inextricable [in'ekstrikəbl] *a* inextricable.

infallible [in'fæləbl] *a* infaillible.

infallibility [in'fæli'biliti] *n* infaillibilité *f*.

infamous [ˈinfəməs] *a* infâme, abominable.

infamy [ˈinfəmi] *n* infamie *f*.

infancy [ˈinfənsi] *n* première enfance *f*, minorité *f*.

infant [ˈinfənt] *n* (petit) enfant *mf*, mineur(e) *mf*.

infantile [ˈinfəntail] *a* infantile, enfantin, d'enfant.

infantry [ˈinfəntri] *n* infanterie *f*.

infantryman [ˈinfəntrimən] *n* fantassin *m*.

infatuate [in'fætjueit] *vt* engouer, affoler.

infatuation [inˌfætju'eiʃən] *n* folie *f*, engouement *m*.

infect [in'fekt] *vt* infecter, vicier, contagionner.

infection [in'fekʃən] *n* infection *f*, contagion *f*.

infectious [in'fekʃəs] *a* contagieux, infectieux.

infer [in'fəː] *vt* inférer.

inference [ˈinfərəns] *n* inférence *f*, conclusion *f*.

inferior [in'fiəriə] *an* inférieur(e) *mf*; *n* subalterne *m*, subordonné(e) *mf*.

inferiority [inˌfiəri'ɔriti] *n* infériorité *f*.

infernal [in'fəːnl] *a* infernal.

infest [in'fest] *vt* infester.

infidel [ˈinfidəl] *an* infidèle *mf*.

infidelity [ˌinfi'deliti] *n* infidélité *f*.

infinite [ˈinfinit] *an* infini *m*.

infinity [in'finiti] *n* infinité *f*.

infirm [in'fəːm] *a* faible, infirme.

infirmary [in'fəːməri] *n* infirmerie *f*, hôpital *m*.

infirmity [in'fəːmiti] *n* faiblesse *f*, infirmité *f*.

inflame [in'fleim] *vt* enflammer, mettre le feu à; *vi* s'enflammer.

inflammable [in'flæməbl] *a* inflammable.

inflammation [ˌinflə'meiʃən] *n* inflammation *f*.

inflammatory [in'flæmətəri] *a* inflammatoire, incendiaire.

inflate [in'fleit] *vt* gonfler, grossir, hausser; *vi* faire de l'inflation.

inflated [in'fleitid] *a* enflé, gonflé, bouffi.

inflation [in'fleiʃən] *n* gonflement *m*, inflation *f*, hausse *f*, enflure *f*.

inflect [in'flekt] *vt* courber, fléchir, moduler.

inflexible [in'fleksəbl] *a* inflexible, inébranlable.

inflict [in'flikt] *vt* infliger, imposer.

influence [ˈinfluəns] *n* influence *f*; *vt* influencer.

influential [ˌinflu'enʃəl] *a* influent.

influenza [ˌinflu'enzə] *n* grippe *f*, influenza *f*.

influx [ˈinflʌks] *n* afflux *m*, affluence *f*.

inform [in'fɔːm] *vt* informer, avertir, faire savoir à.

informal [in'fɔːməl] *a* irrégulier, sans cérémonie.

informant [in'fɔːmənt] *n* informateur, -trice.

information [ˌinfə'meiʃən] *n* informations *f pl*, renseignements *m pl*; **a piece of —** un renseignement.

informative [in'fɔːmətiv] *a* instructif.

informer [in'fɔːmə] *n* dénonciateur, -trice, délateur *m*, mouchard *m*.

infraction [in'frækʃən] *n* infraction *f*, violation *f*.

infringe [in'frindʒ] *vt* violer, enfreindre, empiéter sur.

infringement [in'frindʒmənt] *n* infraction *f*, atteinte *f*, violation *f*.

infuriate [in'fjuərieit] *vt* mettre en fureur.

infuriated [in'fjuərieitid] *a* furieux, en fureur.

infuse [in'fjuːz] *vt* infuser.

infusion [in'fju:ʒən] n infusion f, tisane f.

ingenious [in'dʒi:njəs] a ingénieux.

ingeniousness [in'dʒi:njəsnis] n ingéniosité f.

ingenuity [,indʒə'nju:iti] n ingéniosité f.

ingenuous [in'dʒenjuəs] a franc, ingénu, candide.

ingenuousness [in'dʒenjuəsnis] n franchise f, naïveté f.

inglorious [in'glɔ:riəs] a ignominieux.

ingot ['iŋgət] n lingot m.

ingrained [in'greind] a enraciné, encrassé.

ingratiate [in'greiʃieit] vt to — oneself with se pousser dans les bonnes grâces de.

ingratiating [in'greiʃieitiŋ] a insinuant, doucereux.

ingratitude [in'grætitju:d] n ingratitude f.

ingredient [in'gri:djənt] n ingrédient m, élément m.

ingress ['ingres] n entrée f.

ingrowing ['in,grouiŋ] a incarné.

ingrown ['ingroun] a incarné, invétéré.

inhabit [in'hæbit] vt habiter.

inhabitable [in'hæbitəbl] a habitable.

inhabitant [in'hæbitənt] n habitant (e) mf.

inhalation [,inhə'leiʃən] n inhalation f, aspiration f.

inhale [in'heil] vt inhaler, aspirer, avaler.

inherent [in'hiərənt] a inhérent, propre.

inherit [in'herit] vt hériter (de), succéder à.

inheritance [in'heritəns] n héritage m.

inhibit [in'hibit] vt reprimer, inhiber, défendre à.

inhibition [,inhi'biʃən] n inhibition f, défense f.

inhospitable [,inhɔs'pitəbl] a inhospitalier.

inhuman [in'hju:mən] a inhumain.

inhumanity [,inhju:'mæniti] n inhumanité f, cruauté f.

inhume [in'hju:m] vt inhumer, enterrer.

inimical [i'nimikəl] a hostile, ennemi.

inimitable [i'nimitəbl] a inimitable.

iniquitous [i'nikwitəs] a inique.

iniquity [i'nikwiti] n iniquité f.

initial [i'niʃəl] n initiale f; pl parafe m; a initial.

initiate [i'niʃieit] vt initier.

initiation [i,niʃi'eiʃən] n initiation f.

initiative [i'niʃiətiv] n initiative f.

initiator [i'niʃieitə] n initiateur, -trice.

inject [in'dʒekt] vt injecter, faire une piqûre à, piquer.

injection [in'dʒekʃən] n injection f, piqûre f.

injudicious [,indʒu:'diʃəs] a malavisé, peu judicieux.

injunction [in'dʒʌŋkʃən] n injonction f.

injure ['indʒə] vt blesser, faire tort à, léser, offenser.

injurious [in'dʒuəriəs] a préjudiciable, nocif, injurieux.

injury ['indʒəri] n préjudice m, blessure f, mal m, tort m.

injustice [in'dʒʌstis] n injustice f.

ink [iŋk] n encre f.

inkling ['iŋkliŋ] n vague idée f, soupçon m.

inkwell ['iŋkwel] n encrier.

inky ['iŋki] a taché d'encre, noir.

inlaid ['in'leid] a incrusté.

inland ['inlænd] an intérieur m; ad à (de) l'intérieur.

inlay ['in'lei] vt incruster, marqueter, encastrer.

inlaying ['in'leiiŋ] n marqueterie f, incrustation f.

inlet ['inlət] n crique f, arrivée f.

inmate ['inmeit] n habitant(e) mf, pensionnaire mf.

inmost ['inmoust] a le plus profond, intime.

inn [in] n auberge f.

innate [i'neit] a inné.

inner ['inə] a intérieur, intime.

innings ['iniŋz] n manche f.

innkeeper ['inki:pə] n aubergiste mf.

innocence ['inəsns] n innocence f, candeur f.

innocent ['inəsnt] a innocent, pur, vierge.

innocuous [i'nɔkjuəs] a inoffensif.

innovate ['inouveit] vi innover.

innovation [,inou'veiʃən] n innovation f, changement m.

innovator ['inouveitə] n (in)novateur -trice.

innuendo [,inju:'endou] n insinuation f, sous-entendu m.

innumerable [i'nju:mərəbl] a innombrable.

inoculate [i'nɔkjuleit] vt inoculer vacciner.

inoculation [i,nɔkju'leiʃən] n inoculation f.

inodorous [in'oudərəs] a inodore.

inoffensive [,inə'fensiv] a inoffensif.

inoperative [in'ɔpərətiv] a sans action (effet).

inopportune [in'ɔpətju:n] a intempestif, inopportun.

inopportunely [in'ɔpətju:nli] ad hors de propos.

inordinate [i'nɔ:dinit] a démesuré déréglé.

inquest ['inkwest] n enquête f.

inquire [in'kwaiə] vti s'informe (de about), demander, se renseigne (sur about).

inquiry [in'kwaiəri] n question enquête f.

inquisition [,inkwi'ziʃən] n investiga tion f, inquisition f.

inquisitive [in'kwizitiv] a curieux.

inquisitiveness [in'kwizitivnis] n curiosité aiguë f.

inroad ['inroud] n incursion f; to make —s upon entamer.

inrush ['inrʌʃ] n irruption f.

insane [in'sein] a fou, aliéné.

insanity [in'sæniti] n insanité f, démence f, folie f.

insatiable [in'seiʃəbl] a insatiable, inassouvissable.

inscribe [in'skraib] vt inscrire, graver.

inscription [in'skripʃən] n inscription f.

inscrutable [in'skruːtəbl] a impénétrable, fermé.

insect ['insekt] n insecte m.

insecticide [in'sektisaid] n insecticide m.

insecure [,insi'kjuə] a peu sûr, mal affermi, incertain.

insensible [in'sensəbl] a insensible, sans connaissance.

insensibility [in,sensə'biliti] n défaillance f, insensibilité f.

insert [in'səːt] vt insérer, introduire.

insertion [in'səːʃən] n insertion f.

inset ['inset] n médaillon m, hors-texte m.

inside [in'said] an intérieur m; n dedans m; ad à l'intérieur, au dedans; prep à l'intérieur de, au dedans de, dans.

insidious [in'sidiəs] a insidieux, captieux.

insight ['insait] n intuition f, perspicacité f, aperçu m.

insignificance [,insig'nifikəns] n insignifiance f.

insignificant [,insig'nifikənt] a insignifiant.

insincere [,insin'siə] a faux, de mauvaise foi.

insincerity [,insin'seriti] n insincérité f.

insinuate [in'sinjueit] vt insinuer.

insinuation [in,sinju'eiʃən] n insinuation f.

insipid [in'sipid] a insipide, fade.

insipidity [,insi'piditi] n fadeur f, insipidité f.

insist [in'sist] vi insister, appuyer, soutenir, vouloir.

insistence [in'sistəns] n insistance f.

insistent [in'sistənt] a pressant, importun.

insolence ['insələns] n insolence f.

insolent ['insələnt] a insolent.

insolently ['insələntli] ad insolemment.

insoluble [in'sɔljubl] a insoluble.

insolvent [in'sɔlvənt] a insolvable.

insomnia [in'sɔmniə] n insomnie f.

aspect [in'spekt] vt inspecter, examiner, vérifier, visiter.

inspection [in'spekʃən] n inspection f, contrôle m, revue f, visite f.

inspector [in'spektə] n inspecteur m.

inspiration [,inspə'reiʃən] n inspiration f.

inspire [in'spaiə] vt inspirer, aspirer.

inspirit [in'spirit] vt animer, enflammer.

instability [,instə'biliti] n instabilité f.

install [in'stɔːl] vt installer, monter.

installation [,instə'leiʃən] n installation f, montage m.

installment [in'stɔːlmənt] n acompte m, tranche f; on the — system à tempérament.

instance ['instəns] n exemple m, cas m, instance(s) f pl; vt citer en exemple.

instancy ['instənsi] n urgence f, imminence f.

instant ['instənt] n instant m; a pressant, urgent, du courant.

instantaneous [,instən'teinjəs] a instantané.

instantly ['instəntli] ad à l'instant, sur-le-champ.

instead [in'sted] ad au lieu de cela; prep au lieu de (of).

instep ['instep] n cou de pied m, cambrure f.

instigate ['instigeit] vt inciter, provoquer.

instigation [,insti'geiʃən] n instigation f.

instigator ['instigeitə] n instigateur, -trice, fauteur m.

instill [in'stil] vt verser goutte à goutte, infiltrer, inculquer.

instinct ['instiŋkt] n instinct m; a plein.

instinctive [in'stiŋktiv] a instinctif.

institute ['institjuːt] n institut m; vt fonder, ouvrir.

institution [,insti'tjuːʃən] n institution f, établissement m.

instruct [in'strʌkt] vt former, instruire, ordonner.

instruction [in'strʌkʃən] n instruction(s) f pl; pl indications f pl, ordres m pl.

instructive [in'strʌktiv] a instructif.

instructor [in'strʌktə] n instructeur m, précepteur m.

instrument ['instrumənt] n instrument m, mécanisme m, appareil m; — panel tableau de bord m.

instrumental [,instrə'mentl] a qui trouve le moyen de, instrumental, contributif.

insubordinate [,insə'bɔːdinit] a insubordonné, mutin.

insubordination ['insə,bɔːdi'neiʃən] n insubordination f, insoumission f.

insufferable [in'sʌfərəbl] a intolérable, insupportable.

insufficiency [,insə'fiʃənsi] n insuffisance f.

insufficient [,insə'fiʃənt] a insuffisant.

insular ['insjələ] a insulaire.

insularity [,insju'læriti] n insularité f.

insulate ['insjuleit] vt isoler.

insult ['insʌlt] n insulte f, affront m; [in'sʌlt] vt insulter, injurier.

insuperable [in'sju:pərəbl] a insurmontable.

insurance [in'ʃɔ:rəns] n assurance f; **life —** assurance sur la **vie** f; **— company** compagnie f d'assurance(s).

insure [in'ʃɔ:] vt assurer, garantir.

insurer [in'ʃɔ:rə] n assureur m.

insurgent [in'sə:dʒənt] n insurgé(e) mf.

insurrection [insə'rekʃən] n soulèvement m, émeute f.

intact [in'tækt] a intact, indemne.

intangibility [in.tændʒi'biliti] n intangibilité f.

intangible [in'tændʒəbl] a intangible, impalpable.

integral ['intigrəl] a intégral, intégrant.

integrate ['intigreit] vt compléter, intégrer.

integrity [in'tegriti] n intégrité f, probité f.

intellect ['intilekt] n intellect m, intelligence f.

intellectual [.inti'lektjuəl] a intellectuel.

intelligence [in'telidʒəns] n intelligence f, esprit m, sagacité f.

intelligent [in'telidʒənt] a intelligent.

intelligible [in'telidʒəbl] a intelligible, compréhensible.

intemperance [in'tempərəns] n intempérance f, alcoolisme m.

intemperate [in'tempərit] a immodéré, intempérant.

intend [in'tend] vt avoir l'intention (de to), entendre, projeter (de to), vouloir (dire), destiner (à to).

intended [in'tendid] n futur(e) mf, prétendu(e) mf; a voulu, projeté.

intense [in'tens] a intense, vif, profond.

intensity [in'tensiti] n intensité f, violence f.

intent [in'tent] n intention f; a appliqué, absorbé, profond.

intention [in'tenʃən] n intention f, dessein m, but m.

intentional [in'tenʃənl] a intentionnel, voulu, fait exprès.

inter [in'tə:] vt enterrer.

interaction [.intər'ækʃən] n interaction f.

intercede [.intə:'si:d] vi intercéder.

intercept [.intə:'sept] vt intercepter, arrêter, couper, capter.

interception [.intə'sepʃən] n interception f.

intercession [.intə'seʃən] n intercession f.

interchange [.intə'tʃeindʒ] n échange m, communication f; vt échanger.

intercourse ['intəkɔ:s] n commerce m, relations f pl.

interdict ['intədikt] n interdit m, interdiction f; vt interdire (à).

interdiction [.intə'dikʃən] n interdiction f.

interest ['intrist] n intérêt m; **participation** f, crédit m; vt intéresser; **to be —ed in** s'intéresser à, s'occuper de.

interesting ['intristiŋ] a intéressant.

interfere [.intə'fiə] vi se mêler (de in, with), s'immiscer (dans in), toucher (à with), intervenir; **don't — mêlez-vous** de vos affaires.

interference [.intə'fiərəns] n ingérence f, intervention f, brouillage m.

interfering [.intə'fiəriŋ] a indiscret, fouinard, importun.

interim ['intərim] n intérim m; a intérimaire; ad en attendant.

interior [in'tiəriə] an intérieur m; a interne.

interject [.intə'dʒekt] vt interjeter; vi s'écrier.

interjection [.intə'dʒekʃən] n interjection f.

interlace [.intə'leis] vt entrelacer, entrecroiser.

interlard [.intə'lɑ:d] vt bigarrer, entremêler.

interlinear [.intə'liniə] a interlinéaire.

interlock [.intə'lɔk] vt emboîter, enclencher; vi s'emboîter, s'enclencher, s'engrener.

interlocutor [.intə'lɔkjutə] n interlocuteur m.

interloper ['intələupə] n intrus(e) mf, courtier marron m, resquilleur, -euse.

interlude ['intəlu:d] n intermède m.

intermediary [.intə'mi:djəri] an intermédiaire m.

intermediate [.intə'mi:djət] a intermédiaire, intermédiat.

interment [in'tə:mənt] n enterrement m.

intermission [.intə'miʃən] n interruption f, relache f, pause f, entr'acte m, (school) récréation f.

intermit [.intə'mit] vt arrêter, suspendre.

intermittence [.intə'mitəns] n intermittence f.

intermittent [.intə'mitənt] a intermittent.

intern [in'tə:n] vt interner; ['intə:n] n interne.

internal [in'tə:nl] a interne, intérieur, intime; **— revenue** n fisc m.

international [.intə'næʃnəl] a international; n match international m.

internecine [.intə'ni:sain] a **— war** guerre f d'extermination réciproque.

internee [.intə'ni:] n interné(e) mf.

interplay ['intəplei] n jeu croisé m, effet m réciproque (combiné).

interpolate [in'tə:pəleit] vt intercaler, interpoler.

interpose [.intə'pouz] vt interposer; vi s'interposer.

interpret [in'tə:prit] vt interpréter; vi faire l'interprète.

interpretation [in.tə:pri'teiʃən] n interprétation f.

interpreter [in'tə:pritə] n interprèt mf.

interrogate [in'terəgeit] *vt* interroger, questionner.
interrogation [in,terə'geiʃən] *n* interrogation *f*; — **mark** point d'interrogation *m*.
interrogative [,intə'rɔgətiv] *a* interrogateur.
interrupt [,intə'rʌpt] *vti* interrompre.
interrupter [,intə'rʌptə] *n* interrupteur, -trice, coupe-circuit *m*.
interruption [,intə'rʌpʃən] *n* interruption *f*.
intersect [,intə'sekt] *vt* entrecouper,
entrecroiser.
intersection [,intə'sekʃən] *n* intersection *f*, croisement *m*.
interstice [in'tə:stis] *n* interstice *m*,
alvéole *m*.
interval ['intəvəl] *n* intervalle *m*,
entr'acte *m*, mi-temps *f*, récréation *f*.
intervene [,intə'vi:n] *vi* intervenir,
séparer, s'interposer.
intervening [,intə'vi:niŋ] *a* qui
sépare, qui intervient.
intervention [,intə'venʃən] *n* intervention *f*.
interview ['intəvju:] *n* interview *f*,
entrevue *f*; *vt* interviewer, avoir une
entrevue avec.
intestinal [in'testinl] *a* intestinal.
intestine [in'testin] *an* intestin *m*.
intimacy ['intiməsi] *n* intimité *f*.
intimate ['intimit] *an* intime *mf*;
['intimeit] *vt* intimer, indiquer,
notifier.
intimation [,inti'meiʃən] *n* intimation *f*, avis *m*.
intimidate [in'timideit] *vt* intimider.
intimidation [in,timi'deiʃən] *n* intimidation *f*.
into ['intu] *prep* dans, en, entre.
intolerable [in'tɔlərəbl] *a* insupportable, intolérable.
intolerance [in'tɔlərəns] *n* intolérance *f*.
intolerant [in'tɔlərənt] *a* intolérant.
intonation [,intou'neiʃən] *n* intonation *f*.
intone [in'toun] *vt* psalmodier, entonner.
intoxicate [in'tɔksikeit] *vt* enivrer,
tourner la tête à.
intoxication [in,tɔksi'keiʃən] *n*
ivresse *f*, intoxication *f*, enivrement
m.
intractable [in'træktəbl] *a* intraitable, opiniâtre.
intrepid [in'trepid] *a* intrépide.
intrepidity [,intri'piditi] *n* intrépidité *f*.
intricacy ['intrikəsi] *n* complication
f, complexité *f*.
intricate ['intrikit] *a* compliqué,
embrouillé.
intrigue [in'tri:g] *n* intrigue *f*, cabale
f; *vi* intriguer.
intrinsic [in'trinsik] *a* intrinsèque.
introduce [,intrə'dju:s] *vt* introduire,
présenter, initier.

introduction [,intrə'dʌkʃən] *n* introduction *f*, présentation *f*, avant-
propos *m*.
introspection [,introu'spekʃən] *n*
introspection *f*.
introverted [,introu'və:tid] *a* recueilli, introverti.
intrude [in'tru:d] *vi* faire intrusion,
être importun, empiéter (sur upon).
intruder [in'tru:də] *n* intrus(e) *mf*,
resquilleur, -euse.
intrusion [in'tru:ʒən] *n* intrusion *f*.
intuition [,intju'iʃən] *n* intuition *f*.
inundate ['inʌndeit] *vt* inonder,
déborder.
inundation [,inʌn'deiʃən] *n* inondation *f*.
inure [in'juə] *vt* habituer, endurcir.
invade [in'veid] *vt* envahir, violer.
invader [in'veidə] *n* envahisseur *m*.
invalid [in'vælid] *a* invalide.
invalid ['invælid] *an* malade *mf*,
infirme *mf*; *vt* réformer.
invalidate [in'vælideit] *vt* invalider,
casser.
invalidation [in,væli'deiʃən] *n* invalidation *f*.
invalidity [,invə'liditi] *n* invalidité *f*.
invaluable [in'væljuəbl] *a* inestimable.
invariable [in'vɛəriəbl] *a* invariable.
invasion [in'veiʒən] *n* invasion *f*,
envahissement *m*.
invective [in'vektiv] *n* invective *f*.
inveigh [in'vei] *vi* se déchaîner,
invectiver.
inveigle [in'vi:gl] *vt* séduire, attirer,
entraîner.
inveiglement [in'vi:glmənt] *n* séduction *f*, leurre *m*.
invent [in'vent] *vt* inventer.
invention [in'venʃən] *n* invention *f*.
inventiveness [in'ventivnis] *n* imagination *f*.
inventor [in'ventə] *n* inventeur *m*.
inverse [in'və:s] *an* inverse *m*;
contraire *m*.
inversion [in'və:ʃən] *n* renversement
m, inversion *f*.
invert [in'və:t] *vt* retourner, renverser.
invest [in'vest] *vt* (re)vêtir, investir,
placer.
investigate [in'vestigeit] *vt* examiner,
faire une enquête sur, informer sur.
investigation [in,vesti'geiʃən] *n* investigation *f*, enquête *f*.
investment [in'vestmənt] *n* placement *m*, investissement *m*.
investor [in'vestə] *n* actionnaire *m*,
capitaliste *m*.
inveterate [in'vetərit] *a* invétéré,
acharné.
invidious [in'vidiəs] *a* odieux, qui
fait envie.
invigilate [in'vidʒileit] *vt* surveiller.
invigilation [in,vidʒi'leiʃən] *n* surveillance *f*.
invigilator [in'vidʒileitə] *n* surveil-
lant(e) *mf*.

invigorating [in'vigəreitiŋ] *a* fortifiant, tonifiant.
invincibility [in.vinsi'biliti] *n* invincibilité *f*.
invincible [in'vinsəbl] *a* invincible.
inviolability [in.vaiələ'biliti] *n* inviolabilité *f*.
inviolable [in'vaiələbl] *a* inviolable.
invisibility [in.vizə'biliti] *n* invisibilité *f*.
invisible [in'vizəbl] *a* invisible, (ink) sympathique.
invitation [.invi'teiʃən] *n* invitation *f*.
invite [in'vait] *vt* inviter, demander.
invitingly [in'vaitiŋli] *ad* de manière engageante, tentante.
invocation [.invou'keiʃən] *n* invocation *f*.
invoice ['invɔis] *n* facture *f*.
invoke [in'vouk] *vt* invoquer, évoquer.
involuntary [in'vɔləntəri] *a* involontaire.
involve [in'vɔlv] *vt* envelopper, impliquer, engager, entraîner, nécessiter.
inward ['inwəd] *a* intérieur, interne.
iodine ['aiədiːn] *n* (teinture *f* d')iode *m*.
irascibility [i.ræsi'biliti] *n* irascibilité *m*.
irascible [i'ræsibl] *a* irascible, colérique.
irate [ai'reit] *a* en colère, courroucé.
Ireland ['aiələnd] *n* Irlande *f*.
iris ['aiəris] *n* iris *m*.
Irish ['aiəriʃ] *an* irlandais *m*.
Irishman ['aiəriʃmən] *n* Irelandais *m*.
irksome ['əːksəm] *a* ennuyeux, fatigant, ingrat.
iron ['aiən] *n* fer *m*; *a* de fer; *vt* repasser; to — out aplatir, effacer au fer chaud.
iron age ['aiəneidʒ] *n* âge *m* de fer.
ironclad ['aiənklæd] *an* cuirassé *m*.
iron-foundry ['aiən.faundri] *n* fonderie *f*.
iron-gray ['aiəngrei] *a* gris-fer.
ironical [ai'rɔnikəl] *a* ironique.
ironing ['aiəniŋ] *n* repassage *m*.
ironmonger ['aiən.mʌŋgə] *n* quincailler *m*.
ironmonger's ['aiən.mʌŋgəz] *n* quincaillerie *f*.
iron-ore ['aiən.ɔː] *n* minéral *m* de fer.
iron rations ['aiən'ræʃənz] *n pl* vivres de réserve *m pl*.
ironwork ['aiənwəːk] *n* serrurerie *f*, charpenterie *f* en fer.
irony ['aiərəni] *n* ironie *f*.
irradiate [i'reidieit] *vi* rayonner, iradier.
irradiation [i.reidi'eiʃən] *n* irradiation *f*, rayonnement *m*.
irrational [i'ræʃənl] *a* absurde, déraisonnable, irrationnel.
irrecognizable [i'rekəgnaizəbl] *a* méconnaissable.
irreconcilable [i.rekən'sailəbl] *a*

irreconcilable, inconciliable, implacable.
irrecoverable [.iri'kʌvərəbl] *a* irrécouvrable.
irredeemable [.iri'diːməbl] *a* non remboursable, irréparable, incorrigible.
irreducible [.iri'djuːsəbl] *a* irréductible.
irrefutable [.iri'fjuːtəbl] *a* irréfutable, irrécusable.
irregular [i'regjulə] *a* irrégulier, inégal.
irrelevant [i'reləvənt] *a* à côté de la question, hors de propos.
irreligious [.iri'lidʒəs] *a* irréligieux.
irremediable [.iri'miːdiəbl] *a* irrémédiable, sans remède.
irremovable [.iri'muːvəbl] *a* inamovible.
irreparable [i'repərəbl] *a* irréparable.
irreplaceable [.iri'pleisəbl] *a* irremplaçable.
irreproachable [.iri'proutʃəbl] *a* irréprochable.
irresistible [.iri'zistəbl] *a* irrésistible.
irresolute [i'rezəluːt] *a* irrésolu, hésitant, indécis.
irresoluteness [i'rezəluːtnis] *n* irrésolution *f*, indécision *f*.
irrespective [.iri'spektiv] *a* sans égard (à of), indépendamment (de of), indépendant.
irresponsible [.iris'pɔnsəbl] *a* irréfléchi, étourdi.
irresponsive [.iris'pɔnsiv] *a* figé, froid.
irretentive [.iri'tentiv] *a* peu fidèle, peu sûr.
irretrievable [.iri'triːvəbl] *a* irréparable.
irreverence [i'revərəns] *n* irrévérence *f*.
irreverent [i'revərənt] *a* irrévérencieux, irrévérent.
irrevocable [i'revəkəbl] *a* irrévocable.
irrigate ['irigeit] *vt* irriguer, arroser.
irrigation [.iri'geiʃən] *n* irrigation *f*.
irritability [.irita'biliti] *n* irritabilité *f*.
irritable ['iritəbl] *a* irritable.
irritate ['iriteit] *vt* irriter.
irritating ['iriteitiŋ] *a* irritant, agaçant.
irritation [.iri'teiʃən] *n* irritation *f*.
irruption [i'rʌpʃən] *n* irruption *f*.
Isabel ['izəbel] Isabelle *f*.
island ['ailənd] *n* île *f*, (street) refuge *m*.
islander ['ailəndə] *n* insulaire *mf*.
isle [ail] *n* îlot *m*.
islet ['ailit] *n* îlot *m*.
isolate ['aisouleit] *vt* isoler.
isolation [.aisə'leiʃən] *n* isolement *m*, solitude *f*.
issue ['isjuː] *n* issue *f*, progéniture *f*, question *f*, émission *f*, discussion *f*, débouché *m*, terme *m*, tirage *m*,

numéro m; *vti* sortir, résulter; *vt* émettre, publier, lancer.

isthmus ['isθməs] n isthme m.

Italian [i'tæliən] n Italien, -ienne; *an* italien m.

italics [i'tæliks] n italiques *f pl.*

it [it] *pn* il, le; ce, c', cela, ça.

Italy ['itəli] n Italie *f.*

itch [itʃ] n démangeaison *f*, prurit m, gale *f*; *vi* démanger.

itchy ['itʃi] *a* galeux, qui démange.

item ['aitəm] n item m de plus, article m, détail m, rubrique *f.*

itinerant [i'tinərənt] *a* ambulant, forain.

itinerary [ai'tinərəri] n itinéraire m.

its [its] *a* son, sa, ses.

itself [it'self] *pn* soi, lui-, elle-même, se.

ivory ['aivəri] n ivoire m.

ivy ['aivi] n lierre m.

jabber ['dʒæbə] n bafouillage m; *vi* bredouiller, baragouiner.

jack [dʒæk] n valet m, cric m, tourne-broche m, cochonnet m, pavillon m, brochet m; to — up hisser, soulever avec un cric; — of all trades n bricoleur m; — o' lantern n feu follet m.

jackal ['dʒækɔːl] n chacal m.

jackdaw ['dʒækdɔː] n choucas m.

jacket ['dʒækit] n veston m, veste *f*, (women) jaquette *f*, (books) chemise *f.*

jade [dʒeid] n jade m, rosse *f*, effrontée *f.*

jaded ['dʒeidid] *a* éreinté, fourbu, excédé.

jaguar ['dʒægjuə] n jaguar m.

jail [dʒeil] n prison *f*, geôle *f*; *vt* écrouer.

jailbird ['dʒeil.bəːd] n gibier de potence m.

jailer ['dʒeilə] n gardien de prison m, geôlier m.

jam [dʒæm] n confiture *f*, embarras m, embouteillage m, encombrement m; *vt* presser, bloquer, coincer, caler, enfoncer, fourrer, brouiller; *vi* se bloquer, se coincer, se caler.

Jane [dʒein] Jeanne *f.*

jangle ['dʒæŋgl] *vi* crier, grincer, cliqueter, s'entrechoquer.

January ['dʒænjuəri] n janvier m.

Japan [dʒə'pæn] n Japon m.

japan [dʒə'pæn] n laque m; *vt* laquer.

Japanese [.dʒæpə'niːz] n Japonais(e) *mf*; *an* japonais m.

jar [dʒaː] n jarre *f*, cruche *f*, bocal m, pot m, choc m, secousse *f*, grincement m; *vt* secouer, ébranler, agacer; *vi* jurer, détonner.

jargon ['dʒaːgən] n jargon m, baragouin m.

jasmine ['dʒæzmin] n jasmin m.

jasper ['dʒæspə] n jaspe m.

jaundice ['dʒɔːndis] n jaunisse *f.*

jaundiced ['dʒɔːndist] *a* envieux, bilieux.

jaunt [dʒɔːnt] n excursion *f*, sortie *f*, balade *f.*

jaunty ['dʒɔːnti] *a* enjoué, désinvolte, vaniteux.

jaw [dʒɔː] n mâchoire *f*, mords m, bec m, bouche *f*; *vi* bavarder, jaser; *vt* semoncer.

jay [dʒei] n geai m.

jazz [dʒæz] n jazz m; — band jazz m; *vi* danser le jazz.

jealous ['dʒeləs] *a* jaloux.

jealousy ['dʒeləsi] n jalousie *f.*

jeep [dʒiːp] n jeep *f.*

jeer [dʒiə] n sarcasme m, huée *f*; *vi* ricaner; to — at se moquer de, huer.

jelly ['dʒeli] n gelée *f.*

jellyfish ['dʒelifiʃ] n méduse *f.*

jemmy ['dʒemi] n pince-monseigneur *f.*

jeopardize ['dʒepədaiz] *vt* mettre en danger.

jeopardy ['dʒepədi] n danger m.

jerk [dʒəːk] n saccade *f*, à-coup m, secousse *f*, contraction *f*, convulsion *f*; *vt* secouer, tirer d'un coup sec, tirer par saccades.

jerkily ['dʒəːkili] *ad* par saccades.

jerky ['dʒəːki] *a* saccadé.

jersey ['dʒəːzi] n jersey m, tricot m, maillot m, vareuse *f.*

jest [dʒest] n plaisanterie *f*; *vi* plaisanter.

jester ['dʒestə] n bouffon m, fou m.

jet [dʒet] n jais m, jet m, gicleur m, bec m; — propulsion autopropulsion *f*; —propelled plane avion à réaction m.

jetsam ['dʒetsəm] n choses *fpl* jetées par-dessus bord, épaves *f pl.*

jettison ['dʒetizn] *vt* jeter par-dessus bord, se délester de.

jetty ['dʒeti] n jetée *f*, digue *f.*

Jew [dʒuː] n Juif m.

jewel ['dʒuːəl] n bijou m, joyau m.

jeweler ['dʒuːələ] n bijoutier m, joaillier m.

jewelry ['dʒuːəlri] n bijouterie *f*, joaillerie *f.*

Jew ['dʒuː] n Juif m, Juive *f.*

Jewish ['dʒuːiʃ] *a* juif.

Jewry ['dʒuəri] n monde juif m, juiverie *f.*

jib [dʒib] n foc m; *vi* se refuser, renâcler, regimber.

jiffy ['dʒifi] n clin d'œil m; in a — en un clin d'œil.

jig [dʒig] n gigue *f*, calibre m; *vi* danser la gigue, gigoter.

jigsaw puzzle ['dʒigsɔː'pʌzl] n puzzle m, jeu m de patience.

jilt [dʒilt] n coquette *f*; *vt* planter là, plaquer.

jingle ['dʒiŋgl] n tintement m, cliquetis m; *vi* cliqueter, tinter; *vt* faire sonner.

jingoism ['dʒiŋgouizəm] n chauvinisme m.

jitters ['dʒitəz] n frousse f, trouille f.

Joan [dʒoun] Jeanne f.

job [dʒɔb] n besogne f, affaire f, travail m, place f; vi bricoler.

jobber ['dʒɔbə] n tâcheron m, bricoleur m, tripoteur m.

jobbery ['dʒɔbəri] n tripotage m.

jockey ['dʒɔki] n jockey m; vt duper; vi manœuvrer.

jocose [dʒə'kous] a goguenard, facétieux.

jocular ['dʒɔkjulə] a rieur, badin.

jocund ['dʒɔkʌnd] a enjoué, jovial.

jog [dʒɔg] n cahot m, coup de coude m, petit trot m; vt secouer; vi to — along aller son (petit) train.

John [dʒɔn] Jean m.

join [dʒɔin] n point m, (ligne f de) jonction f, jointure f; vt se joindre à, (re)joindre, (ré)unir, s'inscrire à, relier; vi se (re)joindre; to — up s'engager.

joiner ['dʒɔinə] n menuisier m.

joint [dʒɔint] n joint m, jointure f, articulation f, gond m, pièce f (de viande), rôti m; boîte f (malfamée); gambling — tripot m; juice — cabaret m borgne; a (con)joint, (ré)uni, en commun; out of — déboîté, démis, déréglé.

jointed ['dʒɔintid] a articulé.

joint-heir ['dʒɔintsəə] n cohéritier m.

jointly ['dʒɔintli] ad conjointement.

joint-stock company ['dʒɔintstɔk'kʌmpæni] n société anonyme f.

joist [dʒɔist] n solive f, poutre f.

joke [dʒouk] n farce f, bon mot m, plaisanterie f, blague f; vi plaisanter; practical — farce f.

joker ['dʒoukə] n plaisant m, farceur, -euse; practical — mauvais plaisant m.

jollity ['dʒɔliti] n fête f, réjouissance f.

jolly ['dʒɔli] a gai, joyeux, éméché; ad (fam) drôlement, rudement.

jolt [dʒoult] n cahot m, secousse f; vt secouer; vi cahoter.

jonquil ['dʒɔŋkwil] n jonquille f.

Jordan ['dʒɔːdn] n Jordanie f.

jostle ['dʒɔsl] vt pousser, bousculer; vi jouer des coudes.

jot [dʒɔt] n fétu m, brin m; vt to — down noter, griffonner.

journal ['dʒəːnl] n journal m.

journalism ['dʒəːnəlizəm] n journalisme m.

journalist ['dʒəːnəlist] n journaliste mf.

journey ['dʒəːni] n voyage m, trajet m; vi voyager.

journeyman ['dʒəːnimən] n journalier m, compagnon m.

jovial ['dʒouviəl] a jovial.

joviality [dʒouvi'æliti] n jovialité f.

jowl [dʒaul] n mâchoire f, (ba)joue f.

joy [dʒɔi] n joie f.

joyful ['dʒɔiful] a joyeux.

jubilant ['dʒuːbilənt] a joyeux, réjoui; to be — jubiler, exulter.

jubilation [ˌdʒuːbi'leiʃən] n jubilation f.

jubilee ['dʒuːbiliː] n jubilé m.

Judas ['dʒuːdəs] n judas m.

judge [dʒʌdʒ] n juge m, arbitre m, connaisseur, -euse; vt juger, estimer.

judgment ['dʒʌdʒmənt] n jugement m, avis m, arrêt m, discernement m.

judicature ['dʒuːdikətʃə] n Justice f, Cour f.

judicial [dʒuː'diʃəl] a juridique, judiciaire, légal, impartial.

judicious [dʒuː'diʃəs] a judicieux.

jug [dʒʌg] n broc m, cruche f, (fam) violon m.

jugged [dʒʌgd] a cuit à l'étuvée, en civet; emprisonné, coffré.

juggle ['dʒʌgl] vi jongler, faire des tours de passe-passe; to — away escamoter.

juggler ['dʒʌglə] n jongleur m, bateleur m.

juggling ['dʒʌgliŋ] n jonglerie f, tours de passe-passe m pl.

juice [dʒuːs] n jus m.

juicy ['dʒuːsi] a juteux.

Julian ['dʒuːliən] Julien m.

July [dʒuː'lai] n juillet m.

jumble ['dʒʌmbl] n fouillis m; vt mêler, brouiller.

jump [dʒʌmp] n saut m, bond m, haut-le-corps m; vi bondir, tressaillir; vt sauter, franchir.

jumper ['dʒʌmpə] n sauteur, -euse, tricot m, vareuse f.

jumpiness ['dʒʌmpinis] n nervosité f.

jump rope ['dʒʌmproup] n corde f à sauter.

junction ['dʒʌŋkʃən] n jonction f, bifurcation f, gare d'embranchement f.

juncture ['dʒʌŋktʃə] n jointure f, conjoncture f.

June [dʒuːn] n juin m.

jungle ['dʒʌŋgl] n jungle f.

junior ['dʒuːniə] an cadet, -ette; a jeune; n subalterne m.

juniper ['dʒuːnipə] n genièvre m.

junk [dʒʌŋk] n vieilleries f pl, jonque f; piece of — rossignol m; drogue f.

junket ['dʒʌŋkit] n lait caillé m, bombance f.

jurisdiction [ˌdʒuəris'dikʃən] n juridiction f, ressort m.

jurist ['dʒuərist] n juriste m.

jury ['dʒuəri] n jury m.

just [dʒʌst] a juste, équitable; ad (tout) juste, au juste, justement, précisément, seulement, simplement, à l'instant, rien que; I have — seen him je viens de le voir; he — laughed il ne fit que rire; — as tout comme.

justice ['dʒʌstis] n justice f, juge m.

justifiable [ˌdʒʌsti'faiəbl] a justifiable, légitime.

justification [ˌdʒʌstifi'keiʃən] n justification f.

justify ['dʒʌstifai] vt justifier.
justness ['dʒʌstnis] n justice f, justesse f.
jut [dʒʌt] vi — out faire saillie, avancer.
jute [dʒuːt] n jute m.
juvenile ['dʒuːvənail] a juvenile, jeune.
juxtapose ['dʒʌkstəpouz] vt juxtaposer.

K

kangaroo [ˌkæŋgə'ruː] n kangourou m.
keel [kiːl] n quille f.
keen [kiːn] a (objet) aiguisé, affilé; vif, acerbe; fin, perçant; (pers) zélé, passionné (de on), enragé (de); I am not — on it je n'y tiens pas.
keenness ['kiːnnis] n (obj) acuité f; (pers) empressement m, ardeur f, enthousiasme m.
keep [kiːp] n donjon m, subsistance f; vt garder, tenir, observer, célébrer; — s.o. waiting faire attendre qn; vi se tenir rester, se conserver, continuer (de); — from s'empêcher de; — in entretenir; kept in en retenue; — on continuer de, à; — to tenir, garder.
keeper ['kiːpə] n gardien, -ienne, conservateur m, garde mf.
keeping ['kiːpiŋ] n garde f, harmonie f, observation f, célébration f.
keg [keg] n barillet m, caque f.
ken [ken] n portée f, connaissances f pl.
kennel ['kenl] n chenil m, niche f.
kept [kept] pp pt of **keep**.
kerchief ['kaːtʃif] n fichu m, mouchoir de tête m.
kernel ['kaːnl] n amande f, chair f, grain m, noyau m, essentiel m.
kettle ['ketl] n bouilloire f.
kettledrum ['ketldrʌm] n timbale f.
key [kiː] n clé f, clef f, touche f, mot m, corrigé m; a essentiel, clé; vt accorder; to — up stimuler.
keyboard ['kiːbɔːd] n clavier m.
keyhole ['kiːhoul] n trou de la serrure m.
keynote ['kiːnout] n clé f, tonique f, note dominante f.
key-ring ['kiːriŋ] n porte-clefs m inv.
keystone ['kiːstoun] n clé de voûte f.
kick [kik] n coup de pied m, ruade f, recul m, ressort m; plaintes f pl, critiques f pl; vi donner un coup de pied, ruer, reculer; vt pousser du pied, donner un coup de pied à, botter.
kick-off ['kikɔf] n coup d'envoi m.
kid [kid] n chevreau m, (fam) gosse mf.
kidnap ['kidnæp] vt enlever.
kidnapper ['kidnæpə] n ravisseur, -euse.

kidney ['kidni] n rein m, rognon m, acabit m, trempe f.
kill [kil] n mise à mort f; vt tuer, abattre.
killing ['kiliŋ] n tuerie f, massacre m; a meurtrier, tuant, mortel, tordant.
killjoy ['kildʒɔi] n rabat-joie m.
kiln [kiln] n four m.
kin [kin] n race f, souche f, parenté f, parents m pl; a allié, apparenté; next of — le plus proche parent, famille f.
kind [kaind] n espèce f, sorte f, genre m; in — en nature; a bon, aimable.
kindergarten ['kindəgaːtn] n école f maternelle, jardin m d'enfants.
kindle ['kindl] vt allumer, enflammer; vi s'allumer, prendre feu, flamber.
kindly ['kaindli] ad avec bonté, ayez l'obligeance de; a bon, bienveillant.
kindness ['kaindnis] n bonté f, amabilité f.
kindred ['kindrid] n parenté f; a analogue.
king [kiŋ] n roi m, (draughts) dame f.
kingdom ['kiŋdəm] n royaume m, règne m.
kingfisher ['kiŋfiʃə] n martin-pêcheur m.
kingly ['kiŋli] a royal.
kingship ['kiŋʃip] n art de régner m, royauté f.
kink [kiŋk] n nœud m, lubie f.
kinsfolk ['kinzfouk] n parenté f, famille f.
kipper ['kipə] n hareng fumé m; vt saler, fumer.
kirk [kaːk] n (Scot) église f.
kiss [kis] n baiser m; vt embrasser, baiser.
kissing ['kisiŋ] n embrassade.
kit [kit] n fourniment m, effets m pl, fourbi m, baluchon m, trousse f.
kit-bag ['kitbæg] n sac m.
kitchen ['kitʃin] n cuisine f.
kitchen-garden ['kitʃin'gaːdn] n jardin potager m.
kitchen-maid ['kitʃinmeid] n fille de cuisine f.
kitchen-range ['kitʃin'reindʒ] n fourneau m, cuisinière f.
kite [kait] n milan m, ballon d'essai m, cerf-volant m.
kitten ['kitn] n chaton m.
knack [næk] n tour m de main, adresse f, coup m, truc m.
knacker ['nækə] n équarrisseur m.
knapsack ['næpsæk] n sac m, havre-sac m.
knave [neiv] n gredin m, (cards) valet m.
knead [niːd] vt pétrir, masser.
kneading-trough ['niːdiŋ.trɔf] n pétrin m.
knee [niː] n genou m.
knee-breeches ['niː.briːtʃiz] n culotte f.
knee-cap ['niːkæp] n rotule f; genouillère f.

kneel [niːl] *vi* s'agenouiller.

knell [nel] *n* glas *m*.

knew [njuː] *pt of* **know**.

knickerbockers ['nikəbəkəz] *n* culotte *f*.

knickers ['nikəz] *n* pantalon *m* (de femme), culotte *f*.

knife [naif] *n* couteau *m*; *vt* donner un coup de couteau à, suriner.

knife-board ['naifbɔːd] *n* planche à couteaux *f*.

knife-grinder ['naif,graində] *n* rémouleur *m*.

knight [nait] *n* chevalier *m*; *vt* créer (armer) chevalier.

knighthood ['naithud] *n* rang de chevalier *m*.

knit [nit] *vt* tricoter; to — one's brows froncer les sourcils; well-—serré.

knitting ['nitiŋ] *n* tricotage *m*, tricot *m*; — needle aiguille à tricoter *f*.

knob [nɔb] *n* bosse *f*, bouton *m*, morceau *m*, pomme *f*.

knock [nɔk] *n* coup *m*; *vti* frapper, cogner; to — about bousculer, malmener; *vi* rouler sa bosse; to — down renverser, abattre, adjuger; to — off quitter le travail; to — out mettre hors de combat, mettre knock-out.

knocker ['nɔkə] *n* marteau *m*.

knock-kneed ['nɔk'niːd] *a* cagneux.

knoll [noul] *n* monticule *m*, tertre *m*.

knot [nɔt] *n* nœud *m*, groupe *m*; *vt* nouer, embrouiller.

knotty ['nɔti] *a* noueux, compliqué.

know [nou] *vt* connaître, reconnaître, savoir; to be in the — être dans le secret.

knowing ['nouiŋ] *a* averti, éveillé, fin, rusé, entendu.

knowingly ['nouiŋli] *ad* sciemment, finement, à bon escient.

knowledge ['nɔlidʒ] *n* connaissance *f*, savoir *m*, science *f*; not to my — pas que je sache; without my — à mon insu; to have a thorough — of connaître à fond.

knuckle ['nʌkl] *n* phalange *f*, articulation *f*, jointure *f*; — of veal jarret de veau *m*.

knuckle-bone ['nʌkl'boun] *n* osselet *m*.

knuckleduster ['nʌkl,dʌstə] *n* coup-de-poing américain *m*.

kola ['koulə] *n* — nut noix *f* de kola; — tree kolatier *m*.

Koran [kɔː'ræn] *n* Coran *m*.

L

label ['leibl] *n* étiquette *f*; *vt* étiqueter, classer.

labor ['leibə] *n* travail *m*, classe ouvrière *f*, main-d'œuvre *f*; — exchange bureau de placement *m*, bourse du Travail *f*; — party parti

travailliste *m*; *vt* élaborer, travailler; *vi* travailler, peiner.

laboratory [lə'bɔrətəri] *n* laboratoire *m*.

labored ['leibəd] *a* cherché, travaillé, pénible.

laborer ['leibərə] *n* manœuvre *m*.

laborious [lə'bɔːriəs] *a* laborieux, ardu, pénible.

laboriousness [lə'bɔːriəsnis] *n* application *f*.

laburnum [lə'bəːnəm] *n* cytise *m*.

labyrinth ['læbərinθ] *n* labyrinthe *m*, dédale *m*.

lace [leis] *n* lacet *m*, galon *m*, dentelle *f*, point *m*; *vt* lacer, galonner, garnir de dentelle, nuancer, corser.

lace-maker ['leis'meikə] *n* fabricant de dentelles *m*, dentellière *f*.

lacerate ['læsəreit] *vt* lacérer.

lachrymal ['lækriməl] *a* lacrymal.

lachrymatory ['lækrimətəri] *a* lacrymogène.

lachrymose ['lækrimous] *a* larmoyant.

lack [læk] *n* manque *m*, défaut *m*, besoin *m*; for — of faute de; *vt* manquer de.

lackadaisical [,lækə'deizikəl] *a* maniéré, affecté, langoureux.

lackey ['læki] *n* laquais *m*.

lacking ['lækiŋ] *a* qui manque, en défaut; *prep* à défaut de, faute de.

lacquer ['lækə] *n* laque *m*, vernis-laque *m*; *vt* laquer.

lad [læd] *n* (jeune) garçon *m*, gars *m*, gaillard *m*.

ladder ['lædə] *n* échelle *f*, maille *f* filée.

lade [leid] *vt* charger; *n* bief *m*.

lading ['leidiŋ] *n* chargement *m*.

ladle ['leidl] *n* louche *f*.

lady ['leidi] *n* dame *f*, Lady; *pl* mesdames, mesdemoiselles; —in-waiting dame d'honneur *f*; L— Day Annonciation *f*.

ladybird ['leidibəːd] *n* bête à bon Dieu *f*, coccinelle *f*.

ladylike ['leidilaik] *a* de dame, comme il faut.

lag [læg] *n* retard *m*, décalage *m*, cheval de retour *m*, repris de justice *m*; *vi* traîner, rester en arrière.

laggard ['lægəd] *n* traînard *m*, lambin(e) *mf*; *a* lent.

lagging ['lægiŋ] *n* revêtement calorifuge *m*.

lagoon [lə'guːn] *n* lagune *f*.

laic ['leiik] *n* laïque *m*.

laicize ['leiisaiz] *vt* laïciser.

laid [leid] *pt pp of* **lay**; — up mis en réserve, remisé, alité.

lain [lein] *pp of* **lie**.

lair [lɛə] *n* tanière *f*, repaire *m*.

laity ['leiiti] *n* laïques *m pl*, amateurs *m pl*.

lake [leik] *n* lac *m*; *a* lacustre.

lamb [læm] *n* agneau *m*.

lambkin ['læmkin] *n* agnelet *m*.

lame [leim] *a* boiteux, faible; *vt* rendre boiteux, estropier.

lameness ['leimnis] *n* boiterie *f*, claudication *f*, faiblesse *f*.

lament [lə'ment] *n* lamentation *f*; *vt* déplorer, pleurer; *vi* se lamenter.

lamentable ['læməntəbl] *a* lamentable, déplorable.

lamented [lə'mentid] *a* regretté.

lamp [læmp] *n* lampe *f*, lanterne *f*; **standard** — lampadaire *m*, lampe *f* de parquet.

lamplighter ['læmp'laitə] *n* allumeur de réverbères *m*.

lampoon [læm'pu:n] *n* libelle *m*; *vt* déchirer, chansonner.

lampoonist [læm'pu:nist] *n* libelliste *m*.

lamp-post ['læmppoust] *n* réverbère *m*.

lampshade ['læmpʃeid] *n* abat-jour *m*.

lance [lɑ:ns] *n* lance *f*.

lancer ['lɑ:nsə] *n* lancier *m*.

lancet ['lɑ:nsit] *n* lancette *f*.

land [lænd] *n* terre *f*, sol *m*, pays *m*; *vti* débarquer; *vi* atterrir, descendre; *vt* asséner.

landed ['lændid] *a* foncier.

land-holder ['lænd,houldə] *n* propriétaire *mf*, foncier, -ière.

landing ['lændiŋ] *n* débarquement *m*, atterrissage *m*, palier *m*; **forced** — atterrissage forcé *m*.

landing-place ['lændiŋpleis] *n* débarcadère *m*, terrain d'atterrissage *m*.

landing-net ['lændiŋnet] *n* épuisette *f*.

landlady ['læn,leidi] *n* propriétaire *f*.

landlord ['lænlɔ:d] *n* propriétaire *m*, patron *m*.

landowner ['lænd,ounə] *n* propriétaire *mf*, foncier, -ière.

landscape ['lænskeip] *n* paysage *m*.

landslide ['lændslaid] *n* éboulement *m*.

land-tax ['lændtæks] *n* impôt foncier *m*.

lane [lein] *n* sentier *m*, ruelle *f*.

language ['læŋgwidʒ] *n* langage *m*, langue *f*.

languid ['læŋgwid] *a* languissant, mou.

languidly ['læŋgwidli] *ad* languissamment, mollement.

languish ['læŋgwiʃ] *vi* languir.

languishing ['læŋgwiʃiŋ] *a* langoureux.

languor ['læŋgə] *n* langueur *f*.

languorous ['læŋgərəs] *a* langoureux.

lank [læŋk] *a* efflanqué, plat.

lantern ['læntən] *n* lanterne *f*, fanal *m*, falot *m*.

lap [læp] *n* giron *m*, sein *m*, pan *m*, lobe *m*, creux *m*, tour *m* (de piste), lapement *m*, lampée *f*, clapotis *m*; *vt* laper, lamper, (*sea*) lécher, faire le tour de; *vi* clapoter.

lapdog ['læpdɔg] *n* bichon *m*.

lapel [lə'pel] *n* revers *m*.

lapidary ['læpidəri] *n* lapidaire *m*.

Lapland ['læplænd] *n* Laponie *f*.

lapse [læps] *n* faux-pas *m*, lapsus *m*, laps de temps *m*, déchéance *f*; *vi* s'écouler, déchoir, manquer (à from).

lapsed [læpst] *a* déchu, périmé, caduc.

larboard ['lɑ:bəd] *n* bâbord *m*.

larceny ['lɑ:sni] *n* larcin *m*.

larch [lɑ:tʃ] *n* mélèze *m*.

lard [lɑ:d] *n* saindoux *m*.

larder ['lɑ:də] *n* garde-manger *m*.

large [lɑ:dʒ] *a* large, gros, grand, vaste; **at** — au large, en liberté.

largeness ['lɑ:dʒnis] *n* (*width*) largeur *f*, grandeur *f*, grosseur *f*.

lark [lɑ:k] *n* alouette *f*, farce *f*.

larkspur ['lɑ:kspə] *n* pied-d'alouette *m*.

laser ['leizə] *n* laser *m*.

lash [læʃ] *n* coup de fouet *m*, lanière *f*; *vti* fouailler, cingler; *vt* attacher, amarrer; **to** — **out** éclater, se ruer.

lass [læs] *n* fille *f*, bonne amie *f*.

lassitude ['læsitju:d] *n* lassitude *f*.

last [lɑ:st] *n* forme *f*, fin *f*; *a* dernier; — **but one** avant-dernier; — **night** cette nuit, la nuit dernière, hier soir; *vi* durer, tenir, faire.

lastly ['lɑ:stli] *ad* enfin.

latch [lætʃ] *n* loquet *m*; — **key** passe-partout *m*; *vt* fermer au loquet.

late [leit] *a* tard, tardif, en retard, dernier, feu; —**comer** retardataire; **to be** — **for** être en retard pour; **the train is** — le train a du retard; **it is getting** — il se fait tard.

lately ['leitli] *ad* récemment.

lateness ['leitnis] *n* heure tardive *f*, retard *m*.

latent ['leitənt] *a* latent.

lateral ['lætərəl] *a* latéral, transversal.

laterite ['lætərait] *n* terre de barre *f*, latérite *f*.

lath [lɑ:θ] *n* latte *f*.

lathe [leið] *n* tour *m*.

lather ['lɑ:ðə] *n* mousse *f*, écume *f*; *vt* savonner, rosser; *vi* mousser, écumer.

latitude ['lætitju:d] *n* largeur *f*, latitude *f*, liberté *f*.

latter ['lætə] *a* dernier, second, celui-ci, celle-ci, ceux-ci, celles-ci.

lattice ['lætis] *n* treillis *m*, treillage *m*.

laudable ['lɔ:dəbl] *a* louable.

laudatory ['lɔ:dətəri] *a* élogieux.

laugh [lɑ:f] *n* rire *m*; *vi* rire.

laughable ['lɑ:fəbl] *a* risible, ridicule.

laughing ['lɑ:fiŋ] *n* rire *m*; *a* à rire; — **gas** gaz hilarant *m*; — **stock** risée *f*.

laughter ['lɑ:ftə] *n* rire *m*; **to roar with** — rire aux éclats, rire à gorge déployée.

launch [lɔ:ntʃ] *n* lancement *m*, chaloupe *f*; *vt* lancer, déclencher; *vi* se lancer.

launderette [lɔːndəˈret] n laverie f, blanchisserie f automatique.

laundress [ˈlɔːndris] n blanchisseuse f.

laundry [ˈlɔːndri] n blanchissage m, blanchisserie f, linge n.

laureate [ˈlɔːriit] n lauréat m.

laurel [ˈlɔrəl] n laurier m.

lava [ˈlɑːvə] n lave f.

lavatory [ˈlævətəri] n lavabo m, cabinets m pl, toilette f.

lavender [ˈlævində] n lavande f.

lavish [ˈlæviʃ] a prodigue, somptueux; vt prodiguer, gaspiller.

lavishness [ˈlæviʃnis] n prodigalité f.

law [lɔː] n loi f, droit m; —abiding a respectueux de la loi; L— Courts Palais de Justice m.

lawful [ˈlɔːful] a légal, légitime.

lawfulness [ˈlɔːfulnis] n respect de la loi m, légalité f.

lawless [ˈlɔːlis] a sans foi ni loi, effréné, déréglé, anarchique.

lawlessness [ˈlɔːlisnis] n mépris de la loi m, anarchie f.

lawn [lɔːn] n pelouse f, gazon m.

lawn-mower [ˈlɔːnˌmouə] n tondeuse f.

lawsuit [ˈlɔːsjuːt] n procès m.

lawyer [ˈlɔːjə] n homme de loi m, jurisconsulte m.

lax [læks] a lâche, relâché, vague, mou, inexact.

laxity [ˈlæksiti] n laxité f, relâchement m, mollesse f.

lay [lei] pt of **lie** (être couché); n lai m, spécialité m; a lai, laïque, profane, amateur; vt coucher, étendre, abattre, placer, mettre, déposer, parier, pondre; to — the table mettre le couvert; to — aside se défaire de, mettre de côté; to — down déposer, quitter; to — off congédier; to — out étaler, aménager, assomer, tracer.

layer [ˈleiə] n couche f, marcotte f, banc m, pondeuse f.

lay-figure [ˈleiˌfigə] n mannequin m.

laying [ˈleiiŋ] n pose f, ponte f.

lay-off [ˈleiɔf] n (workers) mortesaison f.

layout [ˈleiaut] n tracé m, dessin m, disposition f typographique.

lazily [ˈleizili] ad nonchalamment, paresseusement.

laziness [ˈleizinis] n paresse f.

lazy [ˈleizi] a paresseux.

lead [liːd] n exemple m, tête f, (dogs) laisse f, (cards) main f, câble m, premier rôle m; vti mener, conduire; vt diriger, porter; vi (cards) avoir la main.

lead [led] n plomb m.

leaden [ˈledn] a de plomb, plombé, lourd.

leader [ˈliːdə] n chef m, directeur m, meneur m, guide m, éditorial m.

leadership [ˈliːdəʃip] n direction f, commandement m.

leading [ˈliːdiŋ] a principal, de tête; — case précédent n; — question question qui postule la réponse; — strings lisières f pl.

leaf, pl leaves [liːf, liːvz] n feuille f, rallonge f.

leafless [ˈliːflis] a sans feuilles, effeuillé, dépouillé.

leaflet [ˈliːflit] n feuillet m, prospectus m, papillon m.

leafy [ˈliːfi] a feuillu, touffu.

league [liːg] n lieue f, ligne f; L— of Nations Société des Nations f; vi se liguer.

leak [liːk] n fuite f, voie d'eau f; vi fuir, avoir une fuite, faire eau; to — out transpirer.

leakage [ˈliːkidʒ] n fuite f.

lean [liːn] a maigre; n inclinaison f; vt pencher, appuyer; vi s'appuyer, se pencher, incliner.

leaned [liːnd] pt pp of lean.

leaning [ˈliːniŋ] n penchant m, penchement m, tendance f.

leanness [ˈliːnnis] n maigreur f.

leap [liːp] n saut m; —frog sautemouton m; — year année bissextile f; vti sauter.

leapt [lept] pt pp of leap.

learn [ləːn] vt apprendre.

learned [ˈləːnid] a savant.

learning [ˈləːniŋ] n savoir m, érudition f.

lease [liːs] n bail m; on — à bail; vt louer, affermer.

leaseholder [ˈliːsˌhouldə] n locataire mf.

leash [liːʃ] n laisse f; vt tenir en laisse.

least [liːst] n le moins; a le, la moindre; at — au (de moins); not in the — pas le moins du monde; ad (le) moins.

leather [ˈleðə] n cuir m; patent — cuir verni m.

leave [liːv] n permission f, congé m; on — en permission, en congé; —taking départ m, adieu m; vt laisser, quitter; vi partir.

leaven [ˈlevn] n levain m; vt faire lever, tempérer.

Lebanon [ˈlebənən] n Liban m.

lecherous [ˈletʃərəs] a lascif, lubrique.

lechery [ˈletʃəri] n lasciveté f, luxure f.

lectern [ˈlektə(ː)n] n lutrin m.

lecture [ˈlektʃə] n conférence f, semonce f; vi faire des conférences; vt faire la leçon à; to — on faire un cours de.

lecturer [ˈlektʃərə] n conférencier m, maître de conférences m, chargé de cours m.

lectureship [ˈlektʃəʃip] n maîtrise de conférences f.

led [led] pt pp of lead.

ledge [ledʒ] n rebord m, corniche f, banc de rochers m.

ledger [ˈledʒə] n grand-livre m.

lee [liː] n abri m; a abrité.

leech [liːtʃ] n sangsue f.

leek [liːk] n poireau m.

leer [liə] n regard de côté m, œillade f; vi regarder de côté, faire de l'œil (à at).

lees [liːz] n lie f.

leeward ['liːwəd] a ad sous le vent.

leeway ['liːwei] n dérive f, retard m.

left [left] pt pp of **leave**; n gauche f; a gauche; on the — à gauche; ——handed gaucher, morganatique, de la main gauche; ——wing de gauche; — over laissé de côté; ——overs restes m pl.

leg [leg] n jambe f, cuisse f, gigot m, pied m.

legacy ['legəsi] n legs m.

legal ['liːgəl] a légal, judiciaire, licite.

legality [li(ː)'gæliti] n légalité f.

legalize ['liːgəlaiz] vt légaliser, autoriser.

legate ['legit] n légat m.

legatee [.legə'tiː] n légataire mf.

legation [li'geiʃən] n légation f.

legator ['legitə] n testateur m.

legend ['ledʒənd] n légende f.

leggings ['leginz] n jambières f pl, guêtres f pl.

leggy ['legi] a haut sur pattes, dégingandé.

legibility [.ledʒi'biliti] n lisibilité f.

legible ['ledʒəbl] a lisible.

legion ['liːdʒən] n légion f.

legionary ['liːdʒənəri] n légionnaire m.

legislate ['ledʒisleit] vi légiférer.

legislation [.ledʒis'leiʃən] n législation f.

legislative ['ledʒislətiv] a législatif.

legislator ['ledʒisleitə] n législateur m.

legislature ['ledʒisleitʃə] n législature f.

legitimacy [li'dʒitiməsi] n légitimité f.

legitimate [li'dʒitimit] a légitime.

legitimation [li.dʒiti'meiʃən] n légitimation f.

legitimize [li'dʒitimaiz] vt légitimer, reconnaître.

leisure ['leʒə] n loisir m.

leisurely ['leʒəli] a qui n'est jamais pressé, tranquille; ad à loisir, à tête reposée.

lemon ['lemən] n citron m.

lemonade [.lemə'neid] n limonade f.

lend [lend] vt prêter; — lease prêt-bail m.

lender ['lendə] n prêteur, -euse.

length [leŋθ] n longueur f; full — en pied; at — longuement, enfin.

lengthwise ['leŋθwaiz] a ad dans le sens de la longueur.

lengthy ['leŋθi] a long.

leniency ['liːniənsi] n douceur f, indulgence f.

lenient ['liːniənt] a indulgent, doux.

leniently ['liːniəntli] ad avec douceur (indulgence).

lenity ['leniti] n clémence f.

lens [lenz] n lentille f, loupe f.

lent [lent] pt pp of **lend**.

Lent [lent] n carême m.

lentil ['lentil] n lentille f.

leopard ['lepəd] n léopard m.

leper ['lepə] n lépreux, -euse.

leprosy ['leprəsi] n lèpre f.

lesbian ['lezbiən] an lesbien, -enne, saphiste.

lesion ['liːʒən] n lésion f.

less [les] n (le) moins; a moindre, moins de; prep ad moins, (in many compounds) sans.

lessee [le'siː] n locataire mf, tenancier, -ière, preneur m.

lessen ['lesn] vti diminuer; vi décroître.

lesser ['lesə] a moindre.

lesson ['lesn] n leçon f.

lessor [le'sɔː] n bailleur, -eresse.

lest [lest] cj de peur que.

let [let] vt laisser, louer; — us go partons; — him do it qu'il le fasse; — alone sans parler de; to — alone laisser tranquille; to — down baisser, descendre, laisser tomber; to — in faire, laisser entrer; to — on cafarder; to — off décharger; to — out laisser échapper, (re)lâcher; to — through laisser passer; to — up (rain) diminuer; se relâcher.

lethal ['liːθəl] a mortel, meurtrier.

lethargic [le'θɑːdʒik] a léthargique.

lethargy ['leθədʒi] n léthargie f.

letter ['letə] n lettre f; — bound a esclave de la lettre; ——box boîte aux lettres f; ——card carte-lettre f; — pad bloc-notes m.

lettuce ['letis] n laitue f.

leukemia [ljuˈkiːmiə] n leucémie f.

levee ['levi] n lever m.

level [levl] n niveau m; a uni, régulier, en palier; — with au même niveau que, au ras de; ——crossing passage m à niveau; ——headed pondéré; vt niveler, viser.

leveler ['levələ] n niveleur m.

leveling ['leviŋ] n nivellement m.

lever ['liːvə] n levier m, manette f.

leveret ['levərit] n levraut m.

levity ['leviti] n légèreté f.

levy ['levi] n levée f; vt lever, imposer, percevoir.

lewd [ljuːd] a luxurieux.

lewdness ['ljuːdnis] n luxure f, lasciveté f.

Lewis ['lu(ː)is] Louis m.

lexicon ['leksikən] n lexique m.

liability [.laiə'biliti] n responsabilité f; pl engagements m pl, passif m.

liable ['laiəbl] a passible (de for), responsable, sujet (à to).

liar ['laiə] n menteur, -euse.

libel ['laibəl] n diffamation f, libelle m; vt diffamer.

libeler ['laibələ] n diffamateur, -trice.

libelous ['laibələs] a diffamatoire, calomnieux.

liberal ['libərəl] n libéral m; a large, libéral, prodigue.

liberalism ['libərəlizəm] n libéralisme m.

liberality [,libə'ræliti] n libéralité f, générosité f.

liberate ['libəreit] vt libérer.

liberation [,libə'reiʃən] n libération f.

liberator ['libəreitə] n libérateur, -trice.

libertine ['libə(:)tiːn] an libertin m; n débauché m.

liberty ['libəti] n liberté f.

librarian [lai'brɛəriən] n bibliothécaire m.

library ['laibrəri] n bibliothèque f; lending — b. de prêt; free — b. publique; circulating — b. circulante.

lice [lais] n pl poux m pl.

license [laisəns] n permission f, autorisation f, permis m, licence f, patente f.

license ['laisəns] vt autoriser, patenter, accorder un permis à.

licentious [lai'senʃəs] a libre, licencieux.

licentiousness [lai'senʃəsnis] n licence f.

lichen ['laikən] n lichen m.

licit ['lisit] a licite.

lick [lik] n coup m de langue; vt lécher, rosser, battre à plate couture, (sur)passer; to — up laper; to — into shape dégrossir.

licking ['likiŋ] n râclée f.

lid [lid] n couvercle m.

lie [lai] n mensonge m, démenti m; disposition f, tracé m, gîte m; vi mentir, être couché, étendu, être resté, se trouver, (bank) déposer; it lies with cela dépend de; to — down se coucher, filer doux; to — up garder la chambre, désarmer; — in n (fam) grasse matinée f.

lieutenant [lef'tenənt] n lieutenant m; second — sous-lieutenant m.

life [laif] n vie f; —boat canot m de sauvetage; —buoy bouée m de sauvetage; — estate propriété f en viager; — saving sauvetage m; — savings économies f pl.

lifeless ['laiflis] a inanimé.

lifelike ['laiflaik] a d'après nature, vivant.

life-size ['laif'saiz] a en pied.

lifetime ['laiftaim] n vie f, vivant m.

lift [lift] n ascenseur m, montecharge m, montée f, (in a car) place f, coup d'épaule m; vt lever, soulever, pendre, voler; vi s'élever, se dissiper.

light [lait] n lumière f, clarté f, jour m, phare m, feu m; vt allumer, éclairer; vi s'allumer, s'éclairer, s'abattre, tomber; a léger, clair; —handedness légèreté de main f; —headed étourdi; —hearted gai, allègre; — minded frivole.

lighten ['laitn] vt alléger, soulager, éclairer, éclaircir; vi s'éclairer, faire des éclairs.

lighter ['laitə] n briquet m, chaland m.

lighthouse ['laithaus] n phare m.

lighting ['laitiŋ] n allumage m, éclairage m.

lightness ['laitnis] n légèreté f.

lightning ['laitniŋ] n éclair m, foudre f; a prompt comme l'éclair, foudroyant; — conductor paratonerre m.

light-ship ['laitʃip] n bateau-feu m, bouée lumineuse f.

lightweight ['laitweit] a léger, poids léger.

likable ['laikəbl] a sympathique.

like [laik] an semblable mf, pareil, -eille mf; a ressemblant; prep comme; vt aimer, vouloir, désirer.

likelihood ['laiklihud] n vraisemblance f, probabilité f.

likely ['laikli] a probable, propre, susceptible, plein de promesse; ad probablement.

liken ['laikən] vt comparer.

likeness ['laiknis] n ressemblance f, portrait m.

likewise ['laikwaiz] ad de même, aussi.

liking ['laikiŋ] n goût m, penchant m, sympathie f, gré m.

lilac ['lailək] n lilas m.

lily ['lili] n lis m; a de lis; — of the valley muguet m.

limb [lim] n membre m, bras m, branche maîtresse f.

limber ['limbə] n avant-train m; vt atteler; a souple.

limbo ['limbou] n limbes m pl.

lime [laim] n glu f, chaux f, tilleul m, limon m.

lime-juice ['laimdʒuːs] n limonade f, jus de limon m.

lime-kiln ['laimkiln] n four à chaux m.

limelight ['laimlait] n rampe f, feu de la publicité m, vedette f.

limestone ['laimstoun] n pierre à chaux f.

limit ['limit] n limite f, borne f; comble m; vt limiter, borner, restreindre.

limitation [,limi'teiʃən] n limitation f.

limited ['limitid] a à responsabilité limitée, restreint.

limp [limp] n claudication f; vi boiter; a souple, mou.

limpid ['limpid] a limpide.

limpidity [lim'piditi] n limpidité f.

limy ['laimi] a gluant, calcaire.

linden ['lindən] n tilleul m.

line [lain] n ligne f, file f, voie f, trait m, corde f, câble m, fil m, vers m; vt tracer, régler, sillonner, rider, aligner, border, doubler, remplir, garnir; vi s'aligner; to become lined se rider.

lineage ['liniidʒ] n lignage m, lignée f.

lineament ['liniəmənt] n lineament m.

linear ['liniə] *a* linéaire.

linen ['linin] *n* toile *f* (de lin), linge *m*.

liner ['lainə] *n* paquebot *m*.

linger ['liŋgə] *vi* tarder, traîner, subsister, s'attarder.

lingerer ['liŋgərə] *n* lambin(e) *mf*, retardataire *mf*.

lining ['lainiŋ] *n* doublure *f*, coiffe *f*, garniture *f*.

link [liŋk] *n* chaînon *m*, anneau *m*, lien *m*, maille *f*; *vt* (re)lier, enchaîner, unir, serrer; *vi* s'attacher (à to); to — arms se donner le bras.

links [liŋks] *n* (terrain *m* de) golf.

linnet ['linit] *n* linotte *f*.

linseed ['linsi:d] *n* graine de lin *f*.

lint [lint] *n* charpie *f*.

lintel ['lintl] *n* linteau *m*.

lion ['laiən] *n* lion *m*; — **cub** lionceau *m*.

lioness ['laiənis] *n* lionne *f*.

lip [lip] *n* lèvre *f*, babine *f*, bord *m*; *vt* toucher des lèvres.

lipstick ['lipstik] *n* rouge à lèvres *m*, bâton de rouge *m*

liquefaction [,likwi'fækʃən] *n* liquéfaction *f*.

liquefy ['likwifai] *vt* liquéfier.

liqueur [li'kjuə] *n* liqueur *f*; — **stand** cabaret *m*, cave à liqueurs *f*.

liquid ['likwid] *an* liquide *m*.

liquidate ['likwideit] *vt* liquider.

liquidation [,likwi'deiʃən] *n* liquidation *f*.

liquidator ['likwideitə] *n* liquidateur *m*.

liquidizer ['likwidaizə] *n*, mixe(u)r *m*.

liquor ['likə] *n* boisson alcoolique *f*.

liquorice ['likəris] *n* réglisse *f*.

lisp [lisp] *n* zézaiement *m*, bruissement *m*; *vi* zézayer.

lissom ['lisəm] *a* souple.

list [list] *n* liste *f*, tableau *m*, lisière *f*, bourrelet *m*, gîte *f*, (pl) lice *f*; **wine** — carte *f* des vins; **honors** — palmarès *m*; *vt* cataloguer; *vi* donner de la bande.

listen ['lisn] *vti* écouter.

listener ['lisnə] *n* écouteur, -euse, auditeur, -trice.

listless ['listlis] *a* apathique.

listlessness ['listlisnis] *n* apathie *f*.

lit [lit] *pt pp* of **light**.

litany ['litəni] *n* litanie *f*.

literal ['litərəl] *a* littéral.

literary ['litərəri] *a* littéraire; — **man** littérateur *m*, homme de lettres *m*.

literature ['litəritʃə] *n* littérature *f*.

lithe [laið] *a* souple.

litheness ['laiðnis] *n* souplesse *f*.

litigant ['litigənt] *n* plaideur, -euse, partie *f*.

litigate ['litigeit] *vi* plaider, être en procès.

litigation [,liti'geiʃən] *n* litige *m*.

litigious [li'tidʒəs] *a* litigieux, processif.

litter ['litə] *n* litière *f*, détritus *m*,

fouillis *m*, portée *f*; —**bin** poubelle *f*; *vt* encombrer.

little ['litl] *n* peu *m* (de chose); *ad* peu; *a* petit; **a** — un peu.

live [laiv] *a* vivant, vrai, vital, ardent, chargé.

live [liv] *vi* vivre, demeurer, habiter, durer; to — **down** user, faire oublier; to — up to se hausser à, faire honneur à; long — I vive!

livelihood ['laivlihud] *n* gagne-pain *m*, vie *f*.

liveliness ['laivlinis] *n* vivacité *f*, entrain *m*.

lively ['laivli] *a* vivant, vif, animé, plein de vie.

liven ['laivn] *vt* animer; to — **up** *vi* s'animer.

liver ['livə] *n* foie *m*.

liverish ['livəriʃ] *a* bilieux, amer.

livery ['livəri] *n* livrée *f*, compagnie *f*.

livestock ['laivstɔk] *n* bétail *m*, bestiaux *m pl*.

livid ['livid] *a* livide.

living ['liviŋ] *n* vie *f*, gagne-pain *m*, poste *m*, cure *f*; —**room** salle *f* de séjour, living-room *m*.

lizard ['lizəd] *n* lézard *m*.

load [loud] *n* charge *f*, chargement *m*, poids *m*, tas *m*; *vt* charger, accabler, combler; *vi* prendre charge.

loaded ['loudid] *a* chargé; — **cane** canne plombée *f*; — **dice** dés pipés *m pl*.

loadstone ['loudstoun] *n* aimant *m*.

loaf [louf] *n* pain *m*; *vi* fainéanter.

loafer ['loufə] *n* fainéant *m*, voyou *m*.

loam [loum] *n* glaise *f*, torchis *m*.

loan [loun] *n* prêt *m*, emprunt *m*.

loath [louθ] *a* qui répugne à.

loathe [louð] *vt* détester, abhorrer.

loathsome ['louðsəm] *a* répugnant, écœurant.

lobby ['lɔbi] *n* salle *f*, vestibule *m*, couloirs *m pl*; *vi* intriguer.

lobster ['lɔbstə] *n* homard *m*; — **pot** casier à homard *m*, langouste *f*.

local ['loukəl] *a* local, du lieu, du pays, en ville; — **road** route vicinale *f*; *n pl* examens locaux *m pl*.

locality [lou'kæliti] *n* localité *f*, emplacement *m*, parages *m pl*, région *f*, endroit *m*.

localize ['loukəlaiz] *vt* localiser.

locate [lou'keit] *vt* situer, repérer; *vi* s'établir, trouver.

location [lou'keiʃən] *n* position *f*, repérage *m*.

loch [lɔx] *n* (Scot) lac *m*, bras de mer *m*.

lock [lɔk] *n* flocon *m*, mèche *f*, serrure *f*, écluse *f*, embouteillage *m*, enrayure *f*; *vt* fermer à clef, mettre sous clef, caler, serrer, écluser; *vi* se bloquer, s'empoigner.

locker ['lɔkə] *n* casier *m*, caisson *m*, armoire *f*.

locket ['lɔkit] *n* médaillon *m*.

lockjaw ['lɔkdʒɔ:] *n* tétanos *m*.

lock-out ['lɔkaut] n lockout m.

locksmith ['lɔksmiθ] n serrurier m.

lock-up ['lɔkʌp] n fermeture f, (jail) violon m, garage m, box m.

locomotive ['loukə,moutiv] n locomotive f.

locum ['loukəm] n remplaçant(e) mf.

locust ['loukəst] n sauterelle f, locuste f.

lode [loud] n filon m; —stone aimant m.

lodge [lɔdʒ] n loge f, atelier m, pavillon m; vt loger, (con)tenir, déposer; to — a complaint porter plainte; vi (se) loger.

lodger ['lɔdʒə] n locataire mf, pensionnaire mf.

lodging ['lɔdʒiŋ] n logement m, chambres f pl meublées, garni m; — house hôtel meublé m, hôtel à la nuit m.

loft [lɔft] n grenier m, soupente f, galerie f, pigeonnier m.

loftiness ['lɔftinis] n hauteur f, sublimité f, élévation f.

lofty ['lɔfti] a haut, hautain, élevé, sublime.

log [lɔg] n bûche f; vt débiter en bûches, enregistrer; — book livre de bord m, carnet de route m.

loggerhead ['lɔgəhed] n bûche f; at —s à couteaux tirés.

logic ['lɔdʒik] n logique f.

logical ['lɔdʒikəl] a logique.

loin [lɔin] n rein m, (meat) longe f; —chop côtelette de filet f; —cloth pagne m.

loiter ['lɔitə] vi traîner (en route), s'attarder.

loiterer ['lɔitərə] n flâneur, -euse, rôdeur m.

loll [lɔl] vi pendre, se prélasser; to — back se renverser, s'appuyer; to — about flâner, fainéanter; to — out its tongue tirer la langue.

lollipop ['lɔlipɔp] n sucette f, sucre d'orge m.

London ['lʌndən] n Londres m.

lone [loun] a solitaire.

loneliness ['lounlinis] n solitude f, isolement m.

lonely ['lounli] ad esseulé, seul, solitaire.

loner ['lounə] n solitaire m.

long [lɔŋ] a long; ad (depuis, pendant, pour) longtemps; vi aspirer (à to, for), avoir bien envie (de to, for), attendre avec impatience; —sightedness presbytie f, prévoyance f; —suffering a patient.

longevity [lɔn'dʒeviti] n longévité f.

longhand ['lɔŋhænd] n écriture f ordinaire, courante.

longing ['lɔŋiŋ] n aspiration f, nostalgie f, grande envie f.

longitude ['lɔŋgitjuːd] n longitude f.

long-standing [lɔŋ'stændiŋ] a de longue terme, durée, connaissance, date f.

longways ['lɔŋweiz] ad dans le sens de la longueur.

look [luk] n regard m, air m, mine f; vi regarder, avoir l'air (de); to — after prendre soin de; to — at regarder; to — for attendre, chercher, guetter; to — in entrer dans, entrer en passant; to — out regarder au dehors, prendre garde; to — out on donner sur; to — through parcourir, repasser.

looker-on ['lukər'ɔn] n spectateur, -trice, badaud(e) mf.

look-out ['luk'aut] n qui-vive m, guet m, poste d'observation m, vigie f, guetteur m, perspective f.

looking-glass ['lukiŋglɑːs] n miroir m, glace f.

loom [luːm] n métier m; vi se montrer à l'horizon, surgir; to — ahead large paraître imminent, menacer.

loony ['luːni] a (fam) cinglé.

loop [luːp] n boucle f, anse f, huit m; vt boucler.

loophole ['luːphoul] n meurtrière f, trou m, échappatoire f.

loose [luːs] a libre, lâche, décousu, dissolu, desserré, détaché; vt délier, dénouer, défaire, détacher.

loosen ['luːsn] vt relâcher, desserrer, dénouer; vi se défaire, se relâcher, se desserrer.

loot [luːt] n butin m; vt piller, saccager.

lop [lɔp] n branchette f; vt élaguer, couper; vi pendre.

lopsided ['lɔp'saidid] a bancal, déjeté, de guingois.

lord [lɔːd] n Seigneur m, Lord m, maître m; vi to — it faire son grand seigneur.

lordly ['lɔːdli] a seigneurial, hautain.

lore [lɔː] n savoir m, science f.

lorry ['lɔri] n camion m.

lose [luːz] vt perdre.

loser ['luːzə] n perdant(e) mf.

loss [lɔs] n perte f; at a — à perte, désorienté; at a — to en peine de.

lost [lɔst] pt pp of lose; — and found bureau des objets trouvés m.

lot [lɔt] n (tirage m au) sort m, partage m, lot m tas m; ad beaucoup de, nombre de, quantité f.

lotion ['louʃən] n lotion f.

lottery ['lɔtəri] n loterie f.

loud [laud] a haut, fort, bruyant, criard, tapageur.

loudly ['laudli] ad à voix haute, bruyamment.

loudness ['laudnis] n hauteur f, force f, fracas m.

loudspeaker ['laud'spiːkə] n haut-parleur m.

lounge [laundʒ] n flânerie f, divan m, hall m, salon m (d'attente); vi flâner, tuer le temps, se prélasser.

lounger ['laundʒə] n flâneur, -euse.

lour ['lauə] vi se renfrogner, se couvrir, menacer.

louse [laus] n pou m; pl poux m pl.

lousy ['lauzi] a pouilleux; — **trick** sale coup m, cochonnerie f.

lout [laut] n butor m, rustre m, lourdaud m.

love [lʌv] n amour m, amitiés f pl; vt aimer; —**letter** billet-doux m, lettre d'amour f; —**making** cour f; —**match** mariage d'amour m.

loveliness ['lʌvlinis] n charme m, beauté f, fraîcheur f.

lovely ['lʌvli] a ravissant, charmant, adorable.

lover ['lʌvə] n amant m, amoureux m, fiancé m.

loving ['lʌviŋ] a affectueux, tendre.

lovingly ['lʌviŋli] ad tendrement, affectueusement.

low [lou] n beuglement m; vi beugler, meugler, mugir; a bas, décolleté, commun; —**down** n to give s.o. the —down renseigner qn; —**grade** de qualité inférieure; ad bas; **at** — **level** à rase-mottes, bas, en contre-bas.

lower ['louə] a (plus) bas; vt baisser, abaisser, affaiblir.

lowliness ['loulinis] n humilité f.

lowly ['louli] a humble.

loyal ['lɔiəl] a loyal, fidèle.

loyalty ['lɔiəlti] n loyauté f, fidélité f.

lozenge ['lɔzindʒ] n losange m, tablette f.

lubber ['lʌbə] n pataud m, empoté m; **land**— terrien m, marin d'eau douce m.

lubricate ['lu:brikeit] vt lubrifier, graisser.

lucerne [lu:'sə:n] n luzerne f.

lucid ['lu:sid] a lucide.

lucidity [lu:'siditi] n lucidité f, transparence f.

luck [lʌk] n chance f, veine f; **bad** — malchance f, déveine f, guignon m.

luckily ['lʌkili] ad heureusement, par bonheur.

lucky ['lʌki] a heureux; — **dog** veinard(e) mf; — **penny** porte-bonheur m.

lucrative ['lu:krətiv] a lucratif.

lucre ['lu:kə] n lucre m.

Lucy ['lu:si] Lucie f, Luce f.

ludicrous ['lu:dikrəs] a absurde, grotesque.

lug [lʌg] vt traîner, trimbaler.

luggage ['lʌgidʒ] n bagages m pl; — **rack** filet m; — **room** salle des bagages f; — **ticket** bulletin m; — **van** fourgon m.

lugubrious [lu:'gu:briəs] a lugubre.

lukewarm ['lu:kwɔ:m] a tiède.

lull [lʌl] n accalmie f, trêve f; vt bercer, endormir; vi se calmer, s'apaiser.

lullaby ['lʌləbai] n berceuse f.

lumbago [lʌm'beigou] n lumbago m.

lumber ['lʌmbə] n vieilleries f pl, fatras m, gros bois m; vt encombrer, entasser, embarrasser; vi marcher gauchement; — **mill** scierie f;

—**room** chambre de débarras f, capharnaüm m.

lumberjack ['lʌmbədʒæk] n bûcheron m.

luminosity [ˌlu:mi'nɔsiti] n luminosité f.

luminous ['lu:minəs] a lumineux.

lump [lʌmp] n morceau m, bosse f, (in the throat) boule f, tas m, enflure f, contusion f; **in the** — en bloc; — **sum** somme globale f; vt mettre dans le même sac, en tas.

lunacy ['lu:nəsi] n folie f.

lunar ['lu:nə] a lunaire.

lunatic ['lu:nətik] n fou, folle, aliéné(e) mf; a lunatique.

lunch [lʌntʃ] n déjeuner m, petit repas m.

lung [lʌŋ] n poumon m.

lunge [lʌndʒ] n longe f, (fencing) botte f, ruée f; vi se fendre, se ruer, lancer un coup (à at).

lurch [lə:tʃ] n embardée f, embarras m; **in the** — en plan; vi embarder, tituber.

lure [ljuə] n leurre m, appât m, fascination f; vt entraîner, leurrer, séduire.

lurid ['ljuərid] a sinistre.

lurk [lə:k] vi se tapir.

lurking ['lə:kiŋ] a furtif, vague; —**place** cachette f.

luscious ['lʌʃəs] a doux, savoureux, écœurant, fleuri.

lush [lʌʃ] a succulent.

lust [lʌst] n concupiscence f, désir m, soif f; vt **to** — **for** désirer violemment, avoir soif de, convoiter.

luster ['lʌstə] n lustre m, lustrine f, éclat m.

lustily ['lʌstili] ad de toutes ses forces, à pleins poumons.

lustrous ['lʌstrəs] a lustré, glacé, éclatant.

lusty ['lʌsti] a robuste.

lute [lu:t] n luth m.

luxuriance [lʌg'zjuəriəns] n luxuriance f.

luxuriant [lʌg'zjuəriənt] a luxuriant, abondant.

luxurious [lʌg'zjuəriəs] a somptueux, luxueux.

luxury ['lʌkʃəri] n luxe m, amour du luxe m, objet de luxe m.

lying ['laiiŋ] a menteur, étendu, couché; — **in** en couches.

lymph [limf] n lymphe f.

lymphatic [lim'fætik] a lymphatique.

lynch [lintʃ] vt lyncher.

lynx [liŋks] n lynx m.

lyre ['laiə] n lyre f.

lyrical ['lirikəl] a lyrique.

lyricism ['lirisizəm] n lyrisme m.

M

macaroni [ˌmækə'rouni] n macaroni m.

macaroon [ˌmækə'ruːn] n macaron m.

mace [meis] n masse f, (spice) macis m.

macebearer ['meisbeərə] n massier m.

macerate ['mæsəreit] vt macérer.

maceration [ˌmæsə'reiʃən] n macération f.

machine [mə'ʃiːn] n machine f, automate m, appareil m; vt usiner, façonner.

machine-gun [mə'ʃiːngʌn] n mitrailleuse f.

machinery [mə'ʃiːnəri] n machinerie f, machines f pl, mécanisme m, rouages m pl.

machinist [mə'ʃiːnist] n mécanicien m, machiniste m.

mackerel ['mækrəl] n maquereau m.

mac(kintosh) ['mæk(intɔʃ)] n imper (méable) m.

mad [mæd] a fou, fol, insensé, enragé, effréné.

madam ['mædəm] n Madame f.

madcap ['mædkæp] an étourdi(e) mf, écervelé(e) mf.

madden ['mædn] vt rendre fou, exaspérer.

maddeningly ['mædniŋli] ad à en devenir fou.

made [meid] pt pp of **make**.

madhouse ['mædhaus] n asile d'aliénés m.

madman ['mædmən] n fou m, aliéné m, forcéné.

madness ['mædnis] n folie f.

madonna [mə'dɔnə] n madone f.

magazine [mæɡə'ziːn] n magasin m, dépôt m, magazine m, revue f; — gun fusil m à répétition.

Magdelene ['mæɡdəlin] Madeleine f.

maggot ['mæɡət] n larve f, ver m, asticot m.

magic ['mædʒik] n magie f; a magique, enchanté.

magician [mə'dʒiʃən] n magicien, -ienne.

magisterial [ˌmædʒis'tiəriəl] a magistral, de magistrat.

magistracy ['mædʒistrəsi] n magistrature f.

magistrate ['mædʒistreit] n magistrat m, juge m.

magnanimity [ˌmæɡnə'nimiti] n magnanimité f.

magnanimous [ˌmæɡ'næniməs] a magnanime.

magnate ['mæɡneit] n magnat m, gros bonnet m.

magnesia [mæɡ'niːʃə] n magnésie f.

magnet ['mæɡnit] n aimant m.

magnetic [mæɡ'netik] a magnétique, hypnotique.

magnetism ['mæɡnitizəm] n magnétisme m.

magnetize ['mæɡnitaiz] vt magnétiser, aimanter.

magneto [mæɡ'niːtou] n magnéto f.

magnificence [mæɡ'nifisns] n magnificence f.

magnificent [mæɡ'nifisnt] a magnifique, somptueux.

magnify ['mæɡnifai] vt (a)grandir, grossir, exalter.

magnifying glass ['mæɡnifaiiŋ.glɑːs] n loupe f.

magniloquent [mæɡ'niləkwənt] a grandiloquent.

magnitude ['mæɡnitjuːd] n grandeur f, ampleur f.

magpie ['mæɡpai] n pie f.

mahogany [mə'hɔɡəni] n acajou m.

maid [meid] n fille f, pucelle f, bonne f; — of all work bonne à tout faire f; — of honor demoiselle d'honneur f.

maiden ['meidn] n jeune fille f, vierge f; a de jeune fille, non mariée; — voyage voyage de baptême m; — speech début à la tribune m.

maidenhood ['meidnhud] n célibat m.

maidenly ['meidnli] a chaste, modeste.

mail [meil] n (cotte de) mailles f pl, courrier m, poste f; vt expédier; — coach wagon postal m; — train train poste m.

maim [meim] vt mutiler.

main [mein] n force f, conduite principale f, océan m; in the — en gros; a principal, premier, essentiel.

mainland ['meinlənd] n continent m, terre ferme f.

mainly ['meinli] ad surtout, en grande partie, pour la plupart.

mainstay ['meinstei] n armature f, soutien m.

maintain [men'tein] vt soutenir, maintenir, entretenir, garder, conserver.

maintenance ['meintinəns] n moyens d'existence m pl, soutien m, maintien m, entretien m, pension f.

maize [meiz] n maïs m.

majestic [mə'dʒestik] a majestueux, auguste.

majesty ['mædʒisti] n majesté f.

major ['meidʒə] n commandant m, chef d'escadron m, majeure f; school) sujet m special; a majeur, principal, plus grand, aîné; vti passer les examens universitaires.

major-general ['meidʒə'dʒenərəl] n général de brigade m.

majority [mə'dʒɔriti] n majorité f, la plus grande partie.

make [meik] n fabrication f, marque f, taille f, façon f; vt faire, façonner, fabriquer, confectionner, rendre, gagner, arriver à; to — away with se débarrasser de; to — off décamper, se sauver; to — out comprendre, distinguer, dresser, établir; to — over transférer, céder; to — up compléter, compenser, combler, rattraper, arranger, préparer, dresser, inventer; **to — up to** faire des avances à.

make-believe ['meikbi,li:v] n trompe-l'œil m, feinte f.

maker ['meikə] n faiseur,- -euse, fabricant m, Créateur m.

makeshift ['meikʃift] n pis-aller m, expédient m; a de fortune.

make-up ['meikʌp] n maquillage m; composition f; vi se maquiller, se grimer.

making ['meikiŋ] n fabrication f, façon f, construction f, création f, main d'œuvre f; pl étoffe f, gains m pl.

maladjusted ['mælə'dʒʌstid] a inadapté.

malaria [mə'lɛəriə] n malaria f, paludisme m.

male [meil] an mâle m.

malefactor ['mælifæktə] n malfaiteur, -trice.

maleficent [mə'lefisnt] a malfaisant, criminel.

malevolence [mə'levələns] n malveillance f.

malevolent [mə'levələnt] a malveillant.

malice ['mælis] n méchanceté f, malice f.

malicious [mə'liʃəs] a méchant, malveillant.

malign [mə'lain] vt calomnier, diffamer.

malignancy [mə'lignənsi] n méchanceté f, malignité f.

malignant [mə'lignənt] a malin, -gne, méchant.

malinger [mə'liŋgə] vi tirer au flanc.

malingerer [mə'liŋgərə] n tireur au flanc m.

mail [mɔːl] n mail m.

mallard ['mæləd] n canard sauvage m.

mallet ['mælit] n maillet m.

mallow ['mælou] n mauve f.

malnutrition ['mælnju'triʃən] n sous-alimentation f, malnutrition f.

malodorous [mæ'loudərəs] a malodorant.

malpractice ['mæl'præktis] n négligence f, incurie f, malversation f.

malt [mɔːlt] n malt m.

maltreat [mæl'tri:t] vt maltraiter.

maltreatment [mæl'tri:tmənt] n mauvais traitement m.

man [mæn] n homme m, domestique m, pion m, pièce f; **— in the street** homme moyen; **— of war** vaisseau m de guerre; vt servir, occuper, garnir (d'hommes), armer, équiper.

manacle(s) ['mænəkl(z)] n menotte(s) f pl; vt passer les menottes à.

manage ['mænidʒ] vt manier, diriger, mener arranger, manœuvrer, maîtriser, réussir à, venir à bout de; vi s'arranger, en venir à bout, se débrouiller.

managed ['mænidʒd] pp of **manage** réussi, gouverné.

management ['mænidʒmənt] n direction f, conduite f, gestion f.

manager ['mænidʒə] n directeur m, régisseur m, gérant m, imprésario m.

manageress ['mænidʒəres] n directrice f, gérante f.

mandate ['mændeit] n mandat m.

mandate ['mændeit] vt mandater.

mandatory ['mændətəri] an mandataire mf, obligatoire.

mandible ['mændibl] n mandibule f.

mandrake ['mændreik] n mandragore f.

mane [mein] n crinière f.

man-eater ['mæn,i:tə] n cannibale m, mangeur d'hommes m.

maneuver [mə'nu:və] vti manœuvrer.

manful ['mænful] a viril, courageux.

mange [meindʒ] n gale f.

manger ['meindʒə] n mangeoire f, crèche f.

mangle ['mæŋgl] n calandreuse f; vt déchiqueter, estropier, défigurer, calandrer.

mango ['mæŋgou] n mangue f.

mangy ['meindʒi] a galeux.

manhandle ['mænhændl] vt faire à bras d'hommes, manutentionner, malmener.

manhood ['mænhud] n âge viril m, virilité f, humanité.

mania ['meiniə] n manie f.

maniac ['meiniæk] n fou furieux, maniaque mf, enragé(e) mf.

maniacal [mə'naiəkəl] a maniaque, de fou.

manicure ['mænikjuə] vt se faire faire les mains; n manucure f.

manicurist ['mænikjuərist] n manucure mf.

manifest ['mænifest] a manifeste; vti (se) manifester.

manifestation [,mænifes'teiʃən] n manifestation f.

manifesto [,mæni'festou] n manifeste m.

manifold ['mænifould] a divers, multiple; vt polycopier.

manikin ['mænikin] n mannequin m, gringalet m.

manipulate [mə'nipjuleit] vt manipuler, actionner, manœuvrer.

mankind [mæn'kaind] n humanité f, genre humain m.

manliness ['mænlinis] n virilité f.

manly ['mænli] a viril, mâle, d'homme.

manner ['mænə] n manière f, sorte f; pl manières f pl, mœurs f pl, savoir-vivre m.

mannered ['mænəd] a élevé, maniéré.

mannerism ['mænərizəm] n maniérisme m, particularité f, tic m.

mannerly ['mænəli] a poli, bien, courtois.

mannish ['mæniʃ] a masculin, hommassé, d'homme.

manor-house ['mænəhaus] n manoir m.

manpower ['mæn'pauə] n main d'œuvre f.

manse [mæns] n cure f, presbytère m.

mansion ['mænʃən] n résidence f, château m; hôtel m.

manslaughter ['mæn,slɔːtə] n homicide involontaire m.

mantelpiece ['mæntlpiːs] n manteau de cheminée m.

mantis ['mæntis] n mante f; **praying —** mante religieuse.

mantle ['mæntl] n mante f, manteau m, (gas) manchon m; vt couvrir, dissimuler.

manual ['mænjuəl] an manuel m; n clavier m.

manufacture [,mænju'fæktʃə] n fabrication f; vt fabriquer, confectionner.

manufacturer [,mænju'fæktʃərə] n manufacturier m, fabricant m, industriel m.

manure [mə'njuə] n fumier m, engrais m; vt fumer, engraisser.

manuscript ['mænjuskript] an manuscrit m.

many ['meni] n foule f, masse f; a beacoup de, bien des, nombre de, nombreux; as — autant de, que; how —? combien?; too — trop (de), de trop.

many-sided ['meni'saidid] a complexe, multilatère.

many-sidedness ['meni'saididnis] n complexité f.

map [mæp] n carte f, (world) mappemonde f, plan m.

maple ['meipl] n érable m; — **sugar** sucre d'érable m.

mar [maː] vt ruiner, troubler, gâter.

maraud [mə'rɔːd] vti marauder.

marauder [mə'rɔːdə] n maraudeur m.

marble ['maːbl] n marbre m, bille f; — **quarry** carrière de marbre f.

March [maːtʃ] n mars m.

march [maːtʃ] vi marcher, défiler; vt faire marcher; n marche f, pas m, frontière f; **forced —** marche forcée f; **quick —** pas accéléré m; — **past** défilé m

marchioness ['maːʃənis] n marquise f.

mare [mɛə] n jument f.

Margaret ['maːgərit] Marguerite f.

margarine [,maːdʒə'riːn] n margarine f.

margin ['maːdʒin] n bordure f, lisière f, marge f.

marginal ['maːdʒinl] a marginal.

marigold ['mærigould] n souci m.

marine [mə'riːn] n marine f, fusilier marin m; a marin, maritime.

mariner ['mærinə] n marin m.

mark [maːk] n but m, point m, note f, marque f, empreinte f, signe m, repère m; up to the — à la hauteur; of — d'importance; vt marquer,

repérer, montrer; — **you** remarquez bien.

markedly ['maːkidli] ad nettement.

marker ['maːkə] n marqueur m, signet m, jeton m, carnet-bloc m.

market ['maːkit] n marché m, débouché m; vt trouver un débouché pour; vi faire son marché.

marketable ['maːkitəbl] a qui a un marché, d'un débit facile.

market-gardener ['maːkit'gaːdnə] n maraicher, -ère.

market research ['maːkitri'səːtʃ] n étude f des marchés

marksman ['maːksmən] n bon tireur m.

marl [maːl] n marne f.

marmalade ['maːməleid] n marmelade f.

marmoset ['maːməzet] n ouistiti m.

marmot ['maːmət] n marmotte f.

maroon [mə'ruːn] an marron pourpré m; n pétard m, nègre marron m; to be —**ed** être coupé, isolé.

marquee [maː'kiː] n (tente-)marquise f.

marquess, marquis ['maːkwis] n marquis m.

marriage ['mæridʒ] n mariage m; — **lines** extrait de mariage m.

marriageable ['mæridʒəbl] a nubile, mariable, à marier.

married ['mærid] a en ménage.

marrow ['mærou] n moelle f, courge f.

marry ['mæri] vt épouser, (of parent, priest) marier; vi se marier.

marsh [maːʃ] n marais m.

marshal ['maːʃəl] n maréchal m, maître des cérémonies m; vt ranger, rassembler, introduire, trier.

marshmallow [maːʃ'mælou] n guimauve f.

marshy ['maːʃi] a marécageux.

marten ['maːtin] n mattre f; **stone- — fouine** f; **pine —** martre m des pins.

martial ['maːʃəl] a martial, guerrier.

martin ['maːtin] n martinet m

martinet [,maːti'net] n to be a — être à cheval sur la discipline.

martyr ['maːtə] n martyr(e) mf.

martyrdom ['maːtədəm] n martyre m.

marvel ['maːvəl] n merveille f, prodige m; vi s'étonner, s'émerveiller (de at).

marvelous ['maːviləs] a merveilleux, prodigieux.

Mary ['mɛəri] Marie f.

masculine ['mæskjulin] an masculin m.

mash [mæʃ] n moût m, mixture f, pâtée f; vt brasser, écraser, mettre en purée, broyer.

mask [maːsk] n masque m; vt masquer, déguiser, voiler.

mason ['meisn] n maçon m.

masquerade [,mæskə'reid] n bal

masqué m, déguisement m, mascarade f; vi se déguiser, poser (pour as).
mass [mæs] n messe f; high — grand'messe; low — messe basse; foule f, masse f; — meeting meeting m; vt masser; vi se masser, s'amonceler.
massacre ['mæsəkə] n massacre m; vt massacrer.
massage ['mæsɑːʒ] n massage m; vt masser, malaxer.
massive ['mæsiv] a massif.
mass-production [,mæsprə'dʌkʃən] m fabrication f en série.
mast [mɑːst] n mât m, faîne f.
master ['mɑːstə] n maître m; vt maîtriser, surmonter, dompter, posséder à fond
masterful ['mɑːstəful] a impérieux, autoritaire.
master-key ['mɑːstəkiː] n passe-partout m.
masterly ['mɑːstəli] ad de maître.
masterpiece ['mɑːstəpiːs] n chef d'œuvre m.
masterstroke ['mɑːstəstrouk] n coup de maître m.
mastery ['mɑːstəri] n maîtrise f, connaissance parfaite f.
mastic ['mæstik] n mastic m.
masticate ['mæstikeit] vt mâcher.
mastication [,mæsti'keiʃən] n mastication f.
mastiff ['mæstif] n mâtin m, dogue m.
mat [mæt] n natte f, paillasson m, dessous de plat m; vt emmêler, tresser; vi s'emmêler.
match [mætʃ] n allumette f, match m, partie f; assortiment m, parti m, égal(e) mf, pareil, -eille (à with), opposer (à), assortir, apparier, rivaliser avec, égaler; vi s'assortir; well——ed bien assorti.
matchet ['mætʃet] n coupe-coupe.
matchless ['mætʃlis] a sans égal, incomparable.
match-maker ['mætʃ,meikə] n marieuse f.
mate [meit] n camarade mf, copain m, compagnon m, compagne f, second m, aide m, époux m, épouse f; vi se marier, s'accoupler; vt accoupler.
material [mə'tiəriəl] n matériaux m pl, matière(s) f pl, matériel m, fournitures f pl; raw — matières premières f pl; a matériel, important, sensible.
materialism [mə'tiəriəlizəm] n matérialisme m.
materialist [mə'tiəriəlist] n matérialiste mf.
materialize [mə'tiəriəlaiz] vi se matérialiser, prendre corps, se réaliser.
maternal [mə'təːnl] a maternel.
maternity [mə'təːniti] n maternité f.
mathematician [,mæθimə'tiʃən] n mathématicien, -ienne.

mathematics [,mæθi'mætiks] n mathématiques f pl.
matriculate [mə'trikjuleit] vt immatriculer; vi s'inscrire (à l'université).
matriculation [mə,trikju'leiʃən] n (university) inscription f.
matrimonial [,mætri'mouniəl] a matrimonial, conjugal.
matrimony ['mætriməni] n mariage m.
matron ['meitrən] n mère f, matrone f, infirmière en chef f.
matter ['mætə] n matière f, pus m, affaire f, question f; vi importer, suppurer; — of course a tout naturel, positif, prosaïque; no — n'importe; what is the — qu'est ce qu'il y a; for that — quant à cela; —of-fact pratique.
Matthew ['mæθjuː] Mathieu m.
mattock ['mætək] n hoyau m.
mattress ['mætris] n matelas m, spring — sommier m.
mature [mə'tjuə] a mûr; vti mûrir; vi échoir.
maturity [mə'tjuəriti] n maturité f, échéance f.
Maud [mɔːd] Mathilde f.
maudlin ['mɔːdlin] a larmoyant, pompette.
maul [mɔːl] n maillet m; vt battre, abîmer, malmener.
mausoleum [,mɔːsə'liəm] n mausolée m.
maw [mɔː] n panse f, gueule f.
mawkish ['mɔːkiʃ] a fade.
mawkishness ['mɔːkiʃnis] n fadeur f, sensiblerie f.
maxim ['mæksim] n maxime f.
maximum ['mæksiməm] n maximum m.
May [mei] n mai m.
may [mei] n aubépine f; v aux pouvoir; maybe peut-être.
mayor [mɛə] n maire m.
mayoress ['mɛəris] n mairesse f.
maze [meiz] n labyrinthe m, dédale m.
me [miː] pn me, moi.
meadow ['medou] n pré m, prairie f.
meager ['miːgə] a maigre, rare, chiche.
meagerness ['miːgənis] n maigreur f, rareté f.
meal [miːl] n repas m, farine f.
mealy ['miːli] a farineux, en bouillie, doucereux.
mean [miːn] n milieu m, moyenterme m, moyenne f; pl moyens m pl, ressources f pl; a moyen, intermédiaire, minable, médiocre; — job besogne ennuyeuse; to feel — se sentir mal en train, mesquin, vilain, ladre; vt signifier, vouloir dire, avoir l'intention (de to), destiner, adresser.
meander [mi'ændə] n méandre m; vi serpenter.
meaning ['miːniŋ] n sens f.
meanness ['miːnnis] n mesquinerie f.

ladrerie f, médiocrité f, bassesse f.

means [mi:nz] n moyens m pl.

means-test ['mi:nztest] n relevé m des revenus.

meantime, -while ['mi:ntaim, -wail] ad en attendant, cependant.

measles ['mi:zlz] n rougeole f.

measure ['meʒə] n mesure f, démarche f; vt mesurer; vi — up égaler qn, être l'égal de.

measurement ['meʒəmənt] n mesurage m, dimension f, tour m, mesure f.

meat [mi:t] n viande f.

Mecca ['mekə] n La Mecque.

mechanic [mi'kænik] n méchanicien m; pl mécanique f.

mechanical [mi'kænikəl] a mécanique, machinal, automatique.

mechanism ['mekənizəm] n mécanisme m, appareil m.

medal ['medl] n médaille f.

medallion [mi'dæljən] n médaillon m.

meddle ['medl] vi se mêler (de with), s'immiscer (dans in), toucher (à with).

meddlesome ['medlsəm] a indiscret, fouinard, officieux.

mediate ['mi:dieit] vi s'entremettre, s'interposer.

mediator ['mi:dieitə] n médiateur, -trice.

medical ['medikəl] a médical, de (en) médecine.

medicine ['medsin] n médecine f, médicament m, purgatif m, sorcellerie f.

medicinal [me'disnl] a médicinal.

medieval [.medi'i:vəl] a médiéval, moyenâgeux.

mediocre [.mi:di'oukə] a médiocre, quelconque.

meditate ['mediteit] vti méditer; vi se recueillir.

meditation [.medi'teiʃən] n méditation f, recueillement m.

meditative ['meditətiv] a méditatif, pensif, recueilli.

Mediterranean [.meditə'reiniən] a méditerranéen; — Sea n Méditerranée f.

medium ['mi:djəm] n milieu m, moyen m, médium m, intermédiaire m; a moyen.

medlar ['medlə] n nèfle f.

medley ['medli] n mélange m, bigarrure f, pot pourri m.

meek [mi:k] a doux, résigné.

meekness ['mi:knis] n douceur f, humilité.

meet [mi:t] n rendez-vous m de chasse; vt faire la connaissance de, se retrouver, aller à la rencontre, joindre, se croiser, payer; to — with trouver, subir; vi se recontrer, se retrouver, se rejoindre.

meeting ['mi:tiŋ] n rencontre f, réunion f, meeting m; a convenable, séant.

megalomania ['megəlou'meiniə] n mégalomanie f.

megaton ['megətʌn] n mégatonne f.

melancholy ['melənkəli] n mélancolie f; a mélancolique, triste.

mellow ['melou] a succulent, moëlleux, adouci, mûr, cordial; vti mûrir; vt adoucir; vi s'adoucir.

melodious [mi'loudiəs] a mélodieux, harmonieux.

melodrama ['melə.drɑ:mə] n mélodrame m.

melodramatic [.meloudrə'mætik] a mélodramatique.

melody ['melədi] n mélodie f, air m.

melon ['melən] n melon m.

melt [melt] vti fondre; vt attendrir; vi se fondre, s'attendrir.

melting ['meltiŋ] n fonte f.

melting-pot ['meltiŋpɔt] n creuset m.

member ['membə] n membre m.

membership ['membəʃip] n nombre des membres m, qualité de membre f.

memento [mi'mentou] n mémento m, souvenir m.

memoir ['memwa:] n mémoire m.

memorable ['memərəbl] a mémorable.

memorandum [.memə'rændəm] n mémorandum m.

memorial [mi'mɔ:riəl] n monument m, pétition f; a commémoratif.

memorize ['meməraiz] vt apprendre par cœur.

memory ['meməri] n mémoire f.

menace ['menəs] n menace f; vt menacer.

mend [mend] n réparation f; vt raccommoder, réparer, (fig) améliorer, arranger; vi se rétablir, se corriger.

mendacious [men'deiʃəs] a menteur, mensonger.

mendacity [men'dæsiti] n penchant au mensonge m, fausseté f.

mendicant ['mendikənt] an mendiant(e) mf.

mendicity [men'disiti] n mendicité f.

menial ['mi:niəl] n domestique mf; a servile.

meningitis [.menin'dʒaitis] n méningite f.

menses ['mensi:z] n pl menstrues f, règles f.

mental ['mentl] a mental, de tête.

mentality [men'tæliti] n mentalité f.

mention ['menʃən] n mention f; vt mentionner, citer, prononcer, faire mention de.

mercantile ['mə:kəntail] a marchand, mercantile, commerçant.

mercenary ['mə:sinəri] an mercenaire m.

mercer ['mə:sə] n mercier, -ière.

merchandise ['mə:tʃəndaiz] n marchandise f.

merchant ['mə:tʃənt] n négociant(e) commerçant(e); a marchand.

merciful ['mə:siful] *a* clément.
mercifulness ['mə:sifulnis] *n* clémence *f*.
merciless ['mə:silis] *a* inexorable, impitoyable.
mercilessness ['mə:silisnis] *n* implacabilité *f*.
mercurial [mə:'kjuəriəl] *a* vif, inconstant, (*med*) mercuriel.
mercury ['mə:kjuri] *n* mercure *m*, vif-argent *m*.
mercy ['mə:si] *n* pitié *f*, merci *f*, grâce *f*.
mere ['miə] *a* pur, simple, seul; *n* lac *m*.
merely ['miəli] *ad* tout simplement.
merge [mə:dʒ] *vt* fondre, fusionner, amalgamer; *vi* se (con)fondre, s'amalgamer.
merger ['mə:dʒə] *n* fusion *f*, combine *f*.
meridian [mə'ridiən] *n* méridian *m*.
merino [mə'ri:nou] *n* mérinos *m*.
merit ['merit] *n* mérite *m*, valeur *f*; *vt* mériter.
meritorious [,meri'tɔ:riəs] *a* méritoire, méritant.
mermaid ['mə:meid] *n* sirène *f*.
merriment ['merimənt] *n* gaieté *f*, réjouissance *f*.
merry ['meri] *a* joyeux, gai.
merry-go-round ['merigou,raund] *n* chevaux de bois *m pl*, carrousel *m*.
mesh [meʃ] *n* maille *f*, filets *m pl*; *vt* prendre, engrener; *vi* s'engrener.
mesmerize ['mezməraiz] *vt* hypnotiser.
ness [mes] *n* (*food*) plat *m*, pâtée *f*; saleté *f*, désordre *m*, pétrin *m*; (*army*) mess *m*; *vt* salir, gâcher; *vi* manger au mess, faire table.
message ['mesidʒ] *n* message *m*, course *f*, commission *f*.
messenger ['mesindʒə] *n* messager, -ère, chasseur *m*.
Messiah [mi'saiə] *n* Messie *m*.
metal ['metl] *n* métal *m*; — **fatigue** fatigue *f* des métaux.
metallic [mi'tælik] *a* métallique.
metallurgy [me'tælədʒi] *n* métallurgie *f*.
metamorphosis [,metə'mɔ:fəsis] *n* métamorphose *f*.
metaphor ['metəfə] *n* métaphore *f*, image *f*.
meteor ['mi:tiə] *n* météore *m*.
meteorology [,mi:tjə'rɔlədʒi] *n* météorologie *f*.
meter ['mi:tə] *n* compteur *m*, mètre *m*, mesure *f*.
method ['meθəd] *n* méthode *f*, ordre *m*, façon *f*, procédé *m*, manière *f*.
methodical [mi'θɔdikəl] *a* méthodique, réglé, qui a de l'ordre.
methylated spirits ['meθileitid spiritz] *n* alcool à brûler *m*.
meticulous [mi'tikjuləs] *a* méticuleux, exact.
metric ['metrik] *a* métrique.

metropolis [mi'trɔpəlis] *n* métropole *f*.
metropolitan [,metrə'pɔlitən] *an* métropolitain *m*.
mettle ['metl] *n* fougue *f*, ardeur *f*, courage *m*.
mettlesome ['metlsəm] *a* fougueux, ardent.
mew [mju:] *n* mue *f*, mouette *f*, miaulement *m*, piaillement *m*; *vt* enfermer; *vi* miauler, piailler.
mew *see* **miaow**.
Mexican ['meksikən] *a* mexicain.
miaow [mi'au] *vi* miauler, piailler; *n* miaulement, piaillement.
miasma [mi'æzmə] *n* miasme *m*.
mice [mais] *n pl* souris *f pl*.
Michael ['maikl] Michel *m*.
microbe ['maikroub] *n* microbe *m*.
microphone ['maikrəfoun] *n* micro *m*.
microscope ['maikrəskoup] *n* microscope *m*.
microscopic [,maikrəs'kɔpik] *a* microscopique.
midday ['middei] *n* midi *m*.
middle ['midl] *n* milieu *m*; *a* du milieu, moyen.
middle-aged ['midl'eidʒd] *a* d'âge mûr.
middle class ['midl'kla:s] *n* (haute) bourgeoisie *f*.
middleman ['midlmæn] *n* intermédiaire *mf*.
middling ['midliŋ] *a* passable.
midge [midʒ] *n* moucheron *m*, cousin *m*.
midget ['midʒit] *n* nain(e) *mf*, nabot(e) *mf*.
midlands ['midləndz] *n* comtés *m pl* du centre (de l'Angleterre).
midnight ['midnait] *n* minuit *m*.
midshipman ['midʃipmən] *n* aspirant *m*, midship *m*.
midsummer ['mid,sʌmə] *n* mi-été *f*, la Saint-Jean.
midwife ['midwaif] *n* sage-femme *f*.
mien [mi:n] *n* mine *f*, air *m*.
might [mait] *pt of* **may**; *n* puissance *f*, force *f*.
mighty ['maiti] *a* puissant; *ad* très.
migrate [mai'greit] *vi* émigrer.
migratory ['maigrətəri] *a* — **bird(s)**, oiseau(x) migrateur(s).
milch-cow ['miltʃkau] *n* vache à lait *f*.
mild [maild] *a* doux, faible, mou.
mildness ['maildnis] *n* douceur *f*, clémence *f*.
mile [mail] *n* mille *m*.
mileage ['mailidʒ] *n* indemnité *f* de déplacement; carnets de billets de chemin de fer.
milestone ['mailstoun] *n* borne milliaire *f*, étape *f*, événement *m*.
militant ['militənt] *a* militant, activiste.
militarist ['militərist] *n* militariste *m*.

military ['militəri] *a* militaire; *n* armée *f*.
militate ['militeit] *vi* militer.
militia [mi'liʃə] *n* milice *f*.
milk [milk] *n* lait *m*; *vt* traire; *a* de lait, lacté.
milkman, -maid ['milkmən, -meid] *n* laitier, -ière.
milksop ['milksɔp] *n* poule mouillée *f*.
milky ['milki] *a* laiteux, lacté; the M— Way la Voie Lactée.
mill [mil] *n* moulin *m*, usine *f*; moteur *m* d'avion; *vti* moudre; *vt* fouler, fraiser, battre; *vi* tourner en rond.
millennial [mi'leniəl] *an* millénaire *m*.
miller ['milə] *n* meunier *m*, minotier *m*.
millet ['milit] *n* mil *m*, millet *m*.
milliard ['miljɑ:d] *n* milliard *m*.
milliner ['milinə] *n* modiste *f*.
millinery ['milinəri] *n* modes *f pl*.
million ['miljən] *n* million *m*.
millionaire [,miljə'nɛə] *n* millionnaire *mf*, milliardaire *mf*.
millstone ['milstoun] *n* meule *f*; (fig) boulet *m*.
mimeograph ['mimiəgrɑ:f] *n* autocopiste *m* (au stencil).
mimic ['mimik] *n* imitateur -trice, mime *m*; *vt* contrefaire, singer, imiter.
mimicry ['mimikri] *n* mimique *f*, imitation *f*.
mince [mins] *n* hachis *m*; *vt* hacher; not to — one's words ne pas mâcher ses mots.
mincing ['minsiŋ] *a* affecté, minaudier.
mind [maind] *n* pensée *f*, esprit *m*, avis *m*, décision *f*, attention *f*, souvenir *m*, parti *m*; *vt* s'occuper de, garder, avoir soin de, faire attention à, regarder à, soigner, s'inquiéter de; I don't — cela m'est égal, je veux bien, ça ne me fait rien.
minded ['maindid] *a* disposé.
mindful ['maindful] *a* réfléchi, attentif, soucieux.
mine [main] *n* mine *f*; *vt* miner, creuser, mouiller des mines dans; *pn* le(s) mien(s), la mienne, les miennes, à moi.
minefield ['mainfi:ld] *n* région *f* minière, champ *m* de mines.
minelayer ['main,leiə] *n* mouilleur *m* de mines.
miner ['mainə] *n* mineur *m*.
mineralogy [,minə'rælədʒi] *n* minéralogie *f*.
minesweeper ['main,swi:pə] *n* dragueur *m* de mines.
mingle ['miŋgl] *vt* mêler, mélanger; *vi* se mêler, se mélanger.
miniature ['minətʃə] *n* miniature *f*; *a* en miniature, en petit.
miniaturist ['minətʃuərist] *n* miniaturiste *mf*.

minimize ['minimaiz] *vt* diminuer, minimiser.
minimum ['miniməm] *n* minimum *m*.
mining ['mainiŋ] *a* minier; *n* industrie *f* minière.
minion ['minjən] *n* favori, -ite.
minister ['ministə] *n* ministre *m*, pasteur *m*; to — to soigner, veiller, subvenir à.
ministerial [,minis'tiəriəl] *a* ministériel, exécutif.
ministration [,minis'treiʃən] *n* bons soins *m pl*, bons offices *m pl*.
ministry ['ministri] *n* ministère *m*.
mink [miŋk] *n* vision *m*.
minor ['mainə] *an* mineur(e) *mf*; *a* moindre, jeune.
minority [mai'nɔriti] *n* minorité *f*.
minster ['minstə] *n* cathédrale *f*.
minstrel ['minstrəl] *n* ménestrel *m*, chanteur *m*.
mint [mint] *n* Monnaie *f*, trésor *m*, menthe *f*; *vt* frapper, forger.
minuet [,minju'et] *n* menuet *m*.
minus ['mainəs] *prep* moins, en moins; *a* négatif.
minute ['minit] *n* minute *f*; *pl* procès-verbal *m*.
minute [mai'nju:t] *a* menu, tout petit, minutieux.
minuteness [mai'nju:tnis] *n* minutie *f*, petitesse *f*.
minx [miŋks] *n* luronne *f*, friponne *f*.
miracle ['mirəkl] *n* miracle *m*, prodige *m*.
miraculous [mi'rækjuləs] *n* miraculeux, extraordinaire.
mirage ['mirɑ:ʒ] *n* mirage *m*.
mire ['maiə] *n* bourbier *m*, fange *f*, bourbe *f*, boue *f*.
mirror ['mirə] *n* miroir *m*, glace *f*, *vt* refléter.
mirth [mə:θ] *n* gaieté *f*.
misadventure ['misəd'ventʃə] *n* mésaventure *f*.
misalliance ['misə'laiəns] *n* mésalliance *f*.
misanthrope ['mizənθroup] *n* misanthrope *m*.
misapprehend ['mis,æpri'hend] *vt* comprendre de travers, se méprendre sur.
misapprehension ['mis,æpri'henʃən] *n* malentendu *m*, méprise *f*.
misappropriate ['misə'prouprieit] *vt* détourner.
misbegotten ['misbi'gɔtn] *a* illégitime.
misbehave ['misbi'heiv] *vi* se conduire mal.
miscalculate ['mis'kælkjuleit] *vt* mal calculer; *vi* se tromper.
miscarriage [mis'kæridʒ] *n* fausse couche *f*, égarement *m*, déni de justice *m*.
miscarry [mis'kæri] *vi* échouer, faire une fausse couche.
miscellaneous [,misi'leiniəs] *a* varié, divers.

miscellany [mi'seləni] n mélange m, recueil m.

mischance [mis'tʃɑːns] n malchance f, malheur m.

mischief ['mistʃif] n malice f, méchant tour m, tort m, mal m.

mischievous ['mistʃivəs] a malicieux, malfaisant, méchant.

misconduct [mis'kɔndəkt] n inconduite f, mauvaise gestion f.

misconduct ['miskən'dʌkt] vt mal gérer.

misconstrue ['miskən'struː] vt interpréter de travers.

miscount [mis'kaunt] n malcompte m, erreur d'addition f; vi mal compter.

miscreant ['miskriənt] n mécréant m, gredin m.

misdeal [mis'diːl] n mal donne f; vt mal donner.

misdeed [mis'diːd] n méfait m, crime m.

misdemeanor [ˌmisdi'miːnə] n délit m, méfait m.

misdirect ['misdi'rekt] vt mal diriger, mal adresser.

miser ['maizə] n avare mf.

miserable ['mizərəbl] a malheureux, misérable.

miserliness ['maizəlinis] n avarice f.

miserly ['maizəli] a avare, sordide.

misery ['mizəri] n misère f.

misfire ['mis'faiə] vi rater, faire long feu, manquer son effet.

misfit ['misfit] n malfaçon f, laissé-pour-compte m, misfit m.

misfortune [mis'fɔːtʃən] n malchance f, malheur m.

misgiving [mis'giviŋ] n défiance f, soupçon m, inquiétude f.

misguided ['mis'gaidid] a mal dirigé.

mishap ['mishæp] n accident m, mésaventure f.

misinformed ['misin'fɔːmd] a mal informé.

misjudge ['mis'dʒʌdʒ] vt maljuger.

mislay, -lead [mis'lei, -'liːd] vt égarer.

mismanage ['mis'mænidʒ] vt mal diriger, gâcher.

mismanagement ['mis'mænidʒmənt] n gestion inhabile f.

misplace ['mis'pleis] vt mal placer, déplacer, égarer.

misprint ['misprint] n coquille f, faute d'impression f.

misrepresent ['mis,repri'zent] vt fausser, dénaturer, travestir.

miss [mis] n Mademoiselle f; ratage m, raté m, coup manqué m; vt manquer, rater.

missal ['misəl] n missel m.

missile ['misail] n projectile m, missile m.

missing ['misiŋ] a manquant, qui manque.

mission ['miʃən] n mission f.

missionary ['miʃnəri] m missionnaire mf.

miss out [mis'aut] vt oublier, omettre; n omission f.

misspell ['mis'spel] vt mal orthographier.

misspent ['mis'spent] a dissipé, dépensé à tort et à travers, mal employé.

mist [mist] n brume f, brouillard m.

mistake [mis'teik] n erreur f, méprise f, faute f; vt mal comprendre, se méprendre sur, se tromper de, confondre.

mistaken [mis'teikn] a dans l'erreur, faux, erroné.

mistakenly [mis'teiknli] ad par erreur.

mister ['mistə] n Monsieur m.

mistletoe ['misltou] n gui m.

mistress ['mistris] n maîtresse f.

mistrust ['mistrʌst] n méfiance f; vt se méfier de.

misty ['misti] a brumeux, confus, vague, estompé.

misunderstand ['misʌndə'stænd] vt mal comprendre, se méprendre sur.

misunderstanding ['misʌndə'stændiŋ] n malentendu m, mésintelligence f.

misuse ['mis'juːs] n mauvais usage m, abus m.

misuse ['mis'juːz] vt mésuser de, maltraiter.

mite [mait] n obole f, brin m, un rien m, (fam) môme mf.

miter ['maitə] n mitre f.

mitigate ['mitigeit] vt apaiser, soulager, mitiger, atténuer.

mitigation [ˌmiti'geiʃən] n adoucissement m, atténuation f.

mitten ['mitn] n mitaine f.

mix [miks] vt mêler, mélanger, brasser, confondre; vi se mêler, se mélanger, frayer.

mixture ['mikstʃə] n mélange m, mixture f, panaché m.

mix-up ['miks'ʌp] n mélange f; vi confondre.

moan [moun] n gémissement m, plainte f; vt gémir.

moat [mout] n fossé m, douves f pl.

mob [mɔb] n foule f, racaille f, ramassis m; vt faire foule autour de, malmener.

mobile ['moubail] a mobile.

mobilization [ˌmoubilai'zeiʃən] n mobilisation f.

mock [mɔk] a d'imitation, simili, faux; vt se moquer de, narguer, en imposer à, contrefaire.

mockery ['mɔkəri] n raillerie f, parodie f, farce f.

mode [moud] n (fashion) mode f, mode m, manière f.

model ['mɔdl] n modèle m, (fashion) mannequin; vt modeler, copier.

modeling ['mɔdliŋ] n modelage m.

moderate ['mɔdərit] a modéré, médiocre, moyen, sobre.

moderate ['mɔdəreit] vt modérer, tempérer; vi se modérer.

moderation [‚mɔdə'reiʃən] n modération f, sobriété f, mesure f.

modern ['mɔdən] a moderne.

modernize ['mɔdənaiz] vt moderniser, renover.

modest ['mɔdist] a modeste, chaste, modéré.

modesty ['mɔdisti] n modestie f, modération f.

modification [‚mɔdifi'keiʃən] n modification f.

modify ['mɔdifai] vt modifier, atténuer.

modish ['moudiʃ] a à la mode, faraud.

modulate ['mɔdjuleit] vt moduler, ajuster.

modulation [‚mɔdju'leiʃən] n modulation f.

mohair ['mouheə] n mohair m.

moist [mɔist] a humide, moite, mouillé.

moisten ['mɔisn] vt humecter, mouiller.

moisture ['mɔistʃə] n humidité f, buée f, moiteur f.

molar ['moulə] an molaire f.

molasses [mə'læsiz] n pl mélasse f.

mold (mould) n terreau m, moule m, moisissure f; vt mouler, façonner, pétrir, former.

molder ['mouldə] vi tomber en poussière, pourrir; n mouleur m.

molding ['mouldiŋ] n moulage m, moulure f, formation f.

moldy ['mouldi] a moisi.

mole [moul] n jetée f, môle m, taupe f, grain de beauté m.

molecular [mou'lekjulə] a moléculaire.

molecule ['mɔlikju:l] n molécule m.

molehill ['moulhil] n taupinière f.

molest [mou'lest] vt molester.

mollify ['mɔlifai] vt apaiser, adoucir.

mollusk ['mɔləsk] n mollusque m.

molt [moult] n mue f; vi muer.

molten ['moultən] a fondu.

moment ['moumənt] n moment m, instant m, importance f; of — d'importance.

momentarily ['moumentərili] ad momentanément, pour l'instant.

momentary ['moumentəri] a momentané, passager.

momentous [mou'mentəs] a important, de conséquence.

monarch ['mɔnək] n monarque m.

monarchy ['mɔnəki] n monarchie f.

monastery ['mɔnəstəri] n monastère m.

monastic [mə'næstik] a monastique, monacal.

Monday ['mʌndi] n lundi m.

money ['mʌni] n argent m; monnaie f; —box n tire-lire f, caisse f; —changer n changeur m; —grubber n grippe-sous m; —lender n usurier m, bailleur de fonds m; —market n marché financier m; —order n mandat m; ready —

argent comptant; public — trésor m public.

moneyed ['mʌnid] a riche.

monger ['mʌŋgə] n marchand (de . . .).

mongrel ['mʌŋgrəl] n métis, -isse, bâtard(e) mf.

monk [mʌŋk] n moine m.

monkey ['mʌŋki] n singe m (f guenon); vti singer; vi jouer des tours; — business filouterie f; — wrench clé anglaise f.

monkish ['mʌŋkiʃ] a monastique, monacal.

monogamy [mɔ'nɔgəmi] n monogamie f.

monogram ['mɔnəgræm] n monogramme m.

monologue ['mɔnəlɔg] n monologue m.

monomania ['mɔnou'meiniə] n monomanie f.

monopolist [mə'nɔpəlist] n accapareur, -euse.

monopoly [mə'nɔpəli] n monopole m.

monosyllabic ['mɔnəsi'læbik] a monosyllabique.

monosyllable ['mɔnə‚siləbl] n monosyllabe m.

monotonous [mə'nɔtənəs] a monotone.

monotony [mə'nɔtəni] n monotonie f.

monsoon [mɔn'su:n] n mousson f.

monster ['mɔnstə] n monstre m.

monstrance ['mɔnstrəns] n ostensoir m.

monstrosity [mɔns'trɔsiti] n monstruosité f, énormité f.

monstrous ['mɔnstrəs] a monstrueux, énorme.

month [mʌnθ] n mois m.

monthly ['mʌnθli] a mensuel; ad mensuellement.

monument ['mɔnjumənt] n monument m.

monumental [‚mɔnju'mentl] a monumental.

mood [mu:d] n humeur f, mode m, disposition f.

moody ['mu:di] a morose, qui a des lubies, mal luné.

moon [mu:n] n lune f; vi rêvasser; to — about musarder.

moonlight ['mu:nlait] n clair de lune m.

moonshine ['mu:nʃain] n clair de lune m, blague f.

moonstruck ['mu:nstrʌk] a lunatique, toqué.

moor [muə] n lande f, bruyère f; vt amarrer; vi s'amarrer.

Moor [muə] n Maure m, Mauresque f.

moorhen ['muəhen] n poule f d'eau.

mooring ['muəriŋ] n amarrage m, mouillage m; pl amarres f pl.

mooring rope ['muəriŋroup] n amarre f.

Moorish ['muəriʃ] a maure, mauresque.

moot [mu:t] *a* discutable.

mop [mɔp] *n* balai *m* à laver, lavette *f*, (*hair*) tignasse, (*naut*) faubert; *vt* éponger, s'essuyer, fauberder.

mope [moup] *n* ennuyé(e) *mf*, *pl* le cafard; *vi* s'ennuyer, avoir le spleen.

moral [ˈmɔrəl] *a* moral; *n* moralité *f*; *pl* mœurs *f pl*.

morale [mɔˈrɑːl] *n* moral *m*.

moralist [ˈmɔrəlist] *n* moraliste *mf*.

moralize [ˈmɔrəlaiz] *vi* moraliser.

morass [məˈræs] *n* marais *m*, fondrière *f*.

morbid [ˈmɔːbid] *a* morbide, maladif.

more [mɔː] *a ad* plus (de); *prep* davantage; — and — de plus en plus; the — ... the — ... plus ... plus ...

moreover [mɔːˈrouvə] *ad* en outre, d'ailleurs.

morning [ˈmɔːniŋ] *n* matin *m*, matinée *f*; *a* du matin, matinal.

Moroccan [məˈrɔkən] *an* marocain *m*; *n* Marocain(e) *mf*.

Morocco [məˈrɔkou] *n* Maroc *m*, (*leather*) maroquin *m*.

morose [məˈrous] *a* morose.

moroseness [məˈrousnis] *n* maussaderie *f*, morosité *f*.

morphia [ˈmɔːfiə] *n* morphine *f*.

morrow [ˈmɔrou] *n* lendemain *m*.

morsel [ˈmɔːsəl] *n* morceau *m*, bouchée *f*.

mortal [ˈmɔːtl] *a* mortel, funeste; — fear peur jaune *f*.

mortality [mɔːˈtæliti] *n* mortalité *f*.

mortar [ˈmɔːtə] *n* mortier *m*; *vt* cimenter.

mortgage [ˈmɔːgidʒ] *n* hypothèque *f*; *vt* hypothéquer.

mortification [ˌmɔːtifiˈkeiʃən] *n* mortification *f*, (*med*) gangrène *f*.

mortify [ˈmɔːtifai] *vti* mortifier, (*med*) se gangrener.

mortise [ˈmɔːtis] *n* mortaise *f*.

mortuary [ˈmɔːtjuəri] *n* morgue *f*; *a* mortuaire.

mosaic [məˈzeiik] *a n* mosaïque *f*.

Moscow [ˈmɔskou] *n* Moscou *m*.

Moslem [ˈmɔzlem] *an* musulman(ne).

mosque [mɔsk] *n* mosquée *f*.

mosquito [məsˈkiːtou] *n* moustique *m*; — net moustiquaire *f*.

moss [mɔs] *n* mousse *f*.

mossy [ˈmɔsi] *a* moussu.

most [moust] *a* le plus, la plupart de; *ad* le (au) plus, très; presque.

mostly [ˈmoustli] *ad* surtout, pour la plupart.

motel [mouˈtel] *n* motel *m*.

moth [mɔθ] *n* phalène *f*, mite *f*.

moth-ball [ˈmɔθbɔːl] *n* boule de naphtaline *f*.

moth-eaten [ˈmɔθˌiːtn] *a* mangé aux mites, des vers.

mother [ˈmʌðə] *n* mère *f*; *vt* choyer, servir de mère à; — country mère-patrie *f*; —-in-law belle-mère *f*; —-of-pearl nacre *f*; — tongue

langue maternelle *f*.

motherhood [ˈmʌðəhud] *n* maternité *f*.

motion [ˈmouʃən] *n* mouvement *m*, geste *m*, signe *m*; motion *f*, proposition *f*; — picture cinéma *m*; *vt* diriger d'un geste, faire signe à.

motionless [ˈmouʃənlis] *a* immobile.

motivate [ˈmoutiveit] *vt* motiver.

motivating [ˈmoutiveitiŋ] *a* moteur.

motive [ˈmoutiv] *n* motif *m*, mobile *m*.

motley [ˈmɔtli] *n* bariolage *m*; *a* bariolé, mêlé.

motor [ˈmoutə] *a* moteur, automobile; *n* moteur *m*, automobile *f*; *vt* conduire en automobile; *vi* voyager, aller, en automobile; — car *n* auto(mobile) *f*; —-cycle *n* motocyclette *f*.

motoring [ˈmoutriŋ] *n* automobilisme *m*.

motorist [ˈmoutərist] *n* automobiliste *mf*.

motorway [ˈmoutəwei] *n* autoroute *f*.

mottle [ˈmɔtl] *n* marbrure *f*, veine *f*; *vt* marbrer, veiner.

motto [ˈmɔtou] *n* devise *f*.

mound [maund] *n* tertre *m*.

mount [maunt] *n* mont *m*, monture *f*, cadre *m*; *vti* monter; *vt* monter sur.

mountain [ˈmauntin] *n* montagne *f*.

mountaineer [ˌmauntiˈniə] *n* alpiniste *mf*, montagnard(e) *m(f)*.

mountaineering [ˌmauntiˈniəriŋ] *n* alpinisme *m*.

mountainous [ˈmauntinəs] *a* de montagne, montagneux.

mountebank [ˈmauntibæŋk] *n* saltimbanque *m*, charlatan *m*.

mourn [mɔːn] *vti* pleurer; *vi* se lamenter, être en deuil.

mourners [ˈmɔːnəz] *n pl* le cortège *m* funèbre.

mournful [ˈmɔːnful] *a* triste, lugubre, endeuillé.

mournfulness [ˈmɔːnfulnis] *n* tristesse *f*.

mourning [ˈmɔːniŋ] *n* deuil *m*.

mouse [maus] *n* souris *f*; *vi* chasser les souris, fureter.

mousetrap [ˈmaustræp] *n* souricière *f*.

mouth [mauθ] *n* bouche *f*, embouchure *f*, orifice *m*, grimace *f*, gueule *f*; *vti* déclamer; *vi* grimacer, discourir.

mouthful [ˈmauθful] *n* bouchée *f*.

mouthpiece [ˈmauθpiːs] *n* embouchure *f*, porte-parole *m*.

movable [ˈmuːvəbl] *a* mobile, mobilier; *n pl* biens meubles *m pl*, effets mobiliers *m pl*.

move [muːv] *n* mouvement *m*, coup *m*, démarche *f*; *vt* (é)mouvoir, exciter, pousser, proposer, déplacer; *vi* bouger, déménager; to — on (faire) circuler; to — back *vt* faire reculer; *vi* (se) reculer; to — forward *vti* avancer; to — in emménager; to — on s'avancer, circuler; to — out déménager.

movement ['mu:vmənt] n mouvement m, déplacement m.

movies ['mu:viz] n ciné(ma) m.

moving ['mu:viŋ] a émouvant, mobile, en marche.

mow [mou] vt faucher.

mower ['mouə] n faucheur, -euse, (machine) tondeuse f.

mown [moun] pp of **mow**.

Mr ['mistə] Monsieur m.

Mrs ['misiz] n Madame f.

much [mʌtʃ] a beaucoup de; pn beaucoup, ad de beaucoup, très; too — pn trop; a trop de.

mucilage ['mju:silidʒ] n colle f (de bureau).

muck [mʌk] n fumier m, ordure f; vt salir, gâcher.

mud [mʌd] n boue f, banco m; mud walls murs en banco.

muddle ['mʌdl] n confusion f, désordre m, pagaille f, gâchis m; vt (em)brouiller, emmêler; to — through se débrouiller, finir par s'en tirer.

muddleheaded ['mʌdl,hedid] a brouillon.

muddy ['mʌdi] a boueux, terne, épais, trouble, limoneux.

mudguard ['mʌdgɑ:d] n pareboue m.

muff [mʌf] n manchon m, pataud(e) mf, empoté(e) mf; vt rater.

muffle ['mʌfl] n mufle m, moufle m; vt emmitoufler, assourdir, étouffer.

muffled ['mʌfld] a étouffé, feutré, voilé.

muffler ['mʌflə] n cache-nez m inv.

mug [mʌg] n gobelet m, chope f, poire f, nigaud(e) mf.

muggy ['mʌgi] a étouffant, lourd et humide.

mulatto [mju:'lætou] n mulâtre, -esse.

mulberry ['mʌlbəri] n mûre f.

mulberry-tree ['mʌlbəritri:] n mûrier m.

mulct [mʌlkt] n amende f; vt mettre à l'amende.

mule [mju:l] n mule f, mulet m.

multifarious [,mʌlti'fɛəriəs] a multiple, divers, varié.

multiple ['mʌltipl] an multiple m.

multiplication [,mʌltipli'keiʃən] n multiplication f.

multiplicity [,mʌlti'plisiti] n multiplicité f.

multiply ['mʌltiplai] vt multiplier; vi se multiplier.

multitude ['mʌltitju:d] n multitude f, foule f.

mum [mʌm] a silencieux; n maman f; excl silence! motus!

mumble ['mʌmbl] n marmottage m; vti marmonner, marmotter.

mummify ['mʌmifai] vt momifier.

mummy ['mʌmi] n maman f; momie f.

mumps [mʌmps] n pl oreillons m pl.

munch [mʌntʃ] vti mastiquer; vt mâcher.

mundane ['mʌndein] a mondain, terrestre.

municipal [mju:'nisipəl] a municipal.

municipality [mju:,nisi'pæliti] n municipalité f.

munificent [mju:'nifisnt] a généreux, munificent.

munitions [mju:'niʃəns] n pl munitions f pl.

mural ['mjuərəl] a mural.

murder ['mə:də] n meurtre m, assassinat m; vt assassiner, (fig) massacrer.

murderer ['mə:dərə] n meurtrier m, assassin m.

murderous ['mə:dərəs] a meurtrier, homicide.

murky ['mə:ki] a sombre, épais, ténébreux.

murmur ['mə:mə] n murmure m; vti murmurer.

muscle ['mʌsl] n muscle m; vi s'immiscer (dans in), usurper.

muscular ['mʌskjulə] a musclé musculaire.

muse [mju:z] n muse f; vi méditer rêver.

museum [mju:'ziəm] n musée m.

mushroom ['mʌʃrum] n champignon m; vi champignonner.

music ['mju:zik] n musique f; stand pupitre m; — stool tabouret m.

musical ['mju:zikəl] a musical mélodieux, musicien; n opérette f.

musician [mju:'ziʃən] n musicien -ienne.

musing ['mju:ziŋ] n rêverie f méditation f.

musk [mʌsk] n musc m.

musket ['mʌskit] n mousquet m.

musketeer [,mʌski'tiə] n mousquetaire m.

muslin ['mʌzlin] n mousseline f.

musquash ['mʌskwɒʃ] n rat musqué m, castor m.

mussel ['mʌsl] n moule f.

mussy ['mʌsi] a dérangé, sale.

must [mʌst] n moût m, moisissure f; v aux devoir; falloir; they — go il leur faut partir, ils doivent partir.

mustard ['mʌstəd] n moutarde f; — plaster sinapisme m.

muster ['mʌstə] n appel m, rassemblement m; vt rassembler, faire l'appel de, compter; vi se rassembler.

musty ['mʌsti] a moisi, désuet.

mutable ['mju:təbl] a sujet à déplacement, changeant.

mutation [mju:'teiʃən] n mutation f.

mute [mju:t] a muet, sourd; assourdir, mettre la sourdine à.

mutilate ['mju:tileit] vt mutiler.

mutilation [,mju:ti'leiʃən] n mutilation f.

mutineer [,mju:ti'niə] n révolté m, mutiné m.

mutinous ['mju:tinəs] *a* mutin, rebelle.
mutiny ['mju:tini] *n* mutinerie *f*, révolte *f*.
mutter ['mʌtə] *n* murmure *m*; *vti* murmurer, marmotter.
mutton ['mʌtn] *n* mouton *m*; — chop côtelette *f*.
mutual ['mju:tjuəl] *a* mutuel, réciproque, respectif, commun.
mutuality [ˌmju:tju'æliti] *n* mutualité *f*.
muzzle ['mʌzl] *n* museau *m*, (gun) gueule *f*, muselière *f*; *vt* museler, bâillonner.
my [mai] *a* mon, ma, mes.
myrtle ['mə:tl] *n* myrte *m*.
myself [mai'self] *pn* moi-même.
mysterious [mis'tiəriəs] *a* mystérieux.
mystery ['mistəri] *n* mystère *m*.
mystic ['mistik] *an* mystique *mf*.
mysticism ['mistisizəm] *n* mysticisme *m*.
mystification [ˌmistifi'keiʃən] *n* mystification *f*, fumisterie *f*.
myth [miθ] *n* mythe *m*.
mythical ['miθikəl] *a* mythique.
mythology [mi'θɔlədʒi] *n* mythologie *f*.
myxomatosis [ˌmiksəmə'tousis] *n* myxomatose *f*.

N

nab [næb] *vt* pincer.
nabob ['neibɔb] *n* nabab *m*.
nag [næg] *n* bidet *m*; *vt* chamailler; *vi* grogner sur tout.
nagging ['nægiŋ] *a* hargneux; — **woman** chipie *f*.
nail [neil] *n* clou *m*, ongle *m*; *vt* clouer, fixer, empoigner.
naïve [nɑ:'i:v] *a* naïf, ingénu.
naked ['neikid] *a* nu, à poil.
nakedness ['neikidnis] *n* nudité *f*.
name [neim] *n* nom *m*, renom *m*, mot *m*; *vt* nommer, dire, fixer; **Christian** — prénom *m*; **assumed** — nom d'emprunt, pseudonyme *m*.
nameless ['neimlis] *a* sans nom, innommable, anonyme.
namely ['neimli] *ad* à savoir.
namesake ['neimseik] *n* homonyme *m*.
nap [næp] *n* somme *m*, poil *m*; *vi* sommeiller.
napalm ['neipɑ:m] *n* napalm *m*.
nape [neip] *n* nuque *f*.
napkin ['næpkin] *n* serviette *f*.
napping ['næpiŋ] *a* endormi, hors de garde, au dépourvu.
narcissus [nɑ:'sisəs] *n* narcisse *m*.
narcotic [nɑ:'kɔtik] *n* narcotique *m*; *an* stupéfiant *m*.

narrate [næ'reit] *vt* conter.
narration [næ'reiʃən] *n* narration *f*, récit *m*.
narrative ['nærətiv] *n* récit *m*, narration *f*.
narrator [næ'reitə] *n* narrateur, -trice.
narrow ['nærou] *a* étroit, étranglé; *vt* rétrécir, resserrer, restreindre; *vi* se resserrer, se rétrécir, s'étrangler.
narrowness ['nærounis] *n* étroitesse *f*, exiguïté *f*.
narrows ['nærouz] *n* détroit *m*, défilé *m*, étranglement *m*.
nasal ['neizəl] *n* nasale *f*; *a* nasal, de nez.
nastily ['nɑ:stili] *ad* méchamment.
nastiness ['nɑ:stinis] *n* méchanceté *f*, saleté *f*.
nasty ['nɑ:sti] *a* méchant, vilain, sale.
natal ['neitl] *a* natal.
nation ['neiʃən] *n* nation *f*.
national ['næʃənl] *a* national.
nationalism ['næʃnəlizəm] *n* nationalisme *m*.
nationality [ˌnæʃə'næliti] *n* nationalité *f*.
nationalize ['næʃnəlaiz] *vt* nationaliser.
native ['neitiv] *n* originaire *mf*, indigène *mf*; *a* naturel, de naissance, natif du pays.
nativity [nə'tiviti] *n* nativité *f*.
natty ['næti] *a* soigné, adroit.
natural ['nætʃrəl] *a* naturel, inné, foncier.
naturalism ['nætʃrəlizəm] *n* naturalisme *m*.
naturalist ['nætʃrəlist] *n* naturaliste *m*.
naturalization [ˌnætʃrəlai'zeiʃən] *n* naturalisation *f*.
naturalize ['nætʃrəlaiz] *vt* naturaliser.
naturally ['nætʃrəli] *ad* naturellement, bien sûr.
naturalness ['nætʃrəlnis] *n* naturel *m*, simplicité *f*.
nature ['neitʃə] *n* nature *f*, sorte *f*, tempérament *m*.
naught [nɔ:t] *n* rien *m*, zéro *m*; **to come to** — échouer.
naughtiness ['nɔ:tinis] *n* méchanceté *f*.
naughty ['nɔ:ti] *a* vilain, méchant, polisson.
nausea ['nɔ:siə] *n* nausée *f*.
nauseating ['nɔ:sieitiŋ] *a* écœurant, nauséabond.
nauseous ['nɔ:siəs] *a* nauséabond, dégoûtant.
naval ['neivəl] *a* naval, maritime, de marine; — **base** port de guerre *m*.
nave [neiv] *n* nef *f*, moyeu *m*.
navel ['neivəl] *n* nombril *m*.
navigate ['nævigeit] *vi* naviguer; *vt* diriger, gouverner, piloter.
navigation [ˌnævi'geiʃən] *n* navigation *f*, manœuvre *f*, conduite *f*.

navigator ['nævigeitə] n navigateur m, pilote m.

navvy ['nævi] n terrassier m.

navy ['neivi] n marine f.

nay [nei] ad non, ou plutôt, voire.

near [niə] a proche, prochain, (r)approché; prep près de; ad (de) près, à peu de chose près.

nearly ['niəli] ad de près, presque.

nearness ['niənis] n proximité f, ladrerie f, fidélité f.

neat [ni:t] a net, élégant, bien tenu, en ordre, adroit, nature, (drink) pur.

neatness ['ni:tnis] n netteté f, (bon) ordre m, finesse f.

nebulous ['nebjuləs] n nébuleux.

necessary ['nesisəri] n nécessaire, indispensable.

necessitate [ni'sesiteit] vt nécessiter.

necessitous [ni'sesitəs] a nécessiteux, besogneux.

necessity [ni'sesiti] n nécessité f, besoin m, contrainte f.

neck [nek] n cou m, col m, collet m, encolure f, goulot m.

neckerchief ['nekətʃif] n fichu m, foulard m.

necklace ['neklis] n collier m.

necktie ['nektai] n cravate f.

need [ni:d] n besoin m, nécessité f; vt avoir besoin de, exiger, réclamer, falloir; he needs money il lui faut une livre.

needful ['ni:dful] an nécessaire m.

needle ['ni:dl] n aiguille f; —woman n lingère f, couturière f.

needless ['ni:dlis] a inutile.

needs [ni:dz] ad nécessairement; he must — refuse force lui est de refuser.

needy ['ni:di] a nécessiteux, besogneux.

nefarious [ni'fɛəriəs] a inique, abominable.

negative ['negətiv] a négatif; n négative f négatif m, cliché m; vt rejeter, nier, neutraliser.

neglect [ni'glekt] n négligence f, incurie f; vt négliger.

neglectful [ni'glektful] a négligent, insoucieux.

negligently ['neglidʒəntli] ad négligemment.

negligible ['neglidʒəbl] a négligeable.

negotiable [ni'gouʃiəbl] a négociable.

negotiate [ni'gouʃieit] vti négocier; vt conclure, surmonter, franchir.

negotiation [ni,gouʃi'eiʃən] n négociation f.

negotiator [ni'gouʃieitə] n négociateur, -trice.

Negress ['ni:gris] n négresse f.

Negro ['ni:grou] n nègre m.

neigh [nei] n hennissement; vi hennir.

neighbor ['neibə] n voisin(e) mf.

neighborhood ['neibəhud] n voisinage m, région f.

neighboring ['neibəriŋ] a voisin, avoisinant.

neither ['naiðə] pn ni l'un ni l'autre; ad ni, non plus.

neo-colonialism [,ni:oukə'louniəlizm] n néo-colonialisme m.

nephew ['nevju] n neveu m.

nephritis [ne'fraitis] n néphrite f.

nepotism ['nepətizəm] n népotisme m.

nerve ['nə:v] n nerf m, sang-froid m, toupet m; vt fortifier; to — oneself se raidir, s'armer de courage.

nerveless ['nə:vlis] a mou, inerte.

nervous ['nə:vəs] a nerveux, excitable.

nervousness ['nə:vəsnis] n timidité f, nervosité f, peur f.

nest [nest] n nid m, nichée f; vi faire son nid, (se) nicher.

nestle ['nesl] vi se blottir, se nicher.

nestling ['nesliŋ] n oisillon m.

net [net] n filet m, réseau n, résille f, tulle m; vt rapporter net, prendre au filet, tendre des filets sur, dans; vi faire du filet; vt prendre au filet, couvrir de filets, tendre des filets dans; a net.

nether ['neðə] a inférieur, infernal.

Netherlands ['neðələndz] n Pays-Bas m pl.

netting ['netiŋ] n filet m, treillis m, pose de filets f.

nettle ['netl] n ortie f; vt piquer, irriter; —rash n urticaire f.

network ['netwə:k] n réseau m, ligne f.

neuralgia [njuə'rældʒə] n neuralgie f.

neurasthenia [,njuərəs'θi:niə] n neurasthénie f.

neurasthenic ['njuərəs'θenik] a neurasthénique.

neuritis [njuə'raitis] n névrite f.

neurology [njuə'rɔlədʒi] n neurologie f.

neuropath [njuərə'pɑ:θ] n névropathe m.

neurosis [njuə'rousis] n névrose f.

neurotic [njuə'rɔtik] a névrosé.

neuter ['nju:tə] an neutre m.

neutral ['nju:trəl] a neutre.

neutrality [nju'træliti] n neutralité f.

neutralize ['nju:trəlaiz] vt neutraliser.

neutron ['nju:trɔn] n neutron m.

never ['nevə] ad jamais, ne . . . jamais.

nevertheless [,nevəðə'les] ad cependant, néanmoins.

new [nju:] a neuf, nouveau, jeune, frais; —born nouveau-né; New Year le Nouvel An; New Year's Day le jour de l'an.

newly ['nju:li] ad nouvellement, fraîchement.

newness ['nju:nis] n nouveauté f, fraîcheur f.

news [nju:z] n nouvelle(s) f pl, (radio) informations f pl; a piece of — une nouvelle; —agent, —dealer marchand m de journaux; —boy n vendeur de journaux m.

newspaper ['nju:s,peipə] *n* journal *m*.

news-reel ['nju:zri:l] *n* informations *f pl*, actualités *f pl*.

news-stand ['nju:zstænd] *n* kiosque à journaux *m*.

newt [nju:t] *n* salamandre *f*.

next [nekst] *a* le plus proche, prochain, suivant; *prep* près de, sur, à même; *ad* ensuite, après, près.

nib [nib] *n* bec *m*, pointe *f*.

nibble ['nibl] *vt* grignoter, mordiller, égratigner.

nice [nais] *a* délicat, gentil, joli, doux, fin, subtil.

nicely ['naisli] *ad* gentiment, précisément, bien.

nicety ['naisiti] *n* subtilité *f*; **to a —** exactement, à point.

niche [nitʃ] *n* niche *f*.

nick [nik] *n* entaille *f*, encoche *f*; *vt* entailler, deviner, attraper, pincer, couper au court; **in the — of time** juste à temps.

nickname ['nikneim] *n* surnom *m*, sobriquet *m*; *vt* baptiser, surnommer.

niece [ni:s] *n* nièce *f*.

niggard ['nigəd] *n* ladre *m*, pingre *m*.

niggardliness ['nigədlinis] *n* ladrerie *f*, pingrerie *f*.

niggardly ['nigədli] *a* ladre, pingre, mesquin.

nigh [nai] *a* proche; *ad* presque.

night [nait] *n* nuit *f*, soir *m*; *a* du soir, nocturne; **last night** hier soir; **tonight** ce soir.

night-club ['naitklʌb] *n* boîte de nuit *f*.

nightdress ['naitdres] *n* chemise de nuit *f*.

nightfall ['naitfɔ:l] *n* tombée de la nuit *f*.

nightingale ['naitiŋgeil] *n* rossignol *m*.

nightlight ['naitlait] *n* veilleuse *f*.

nightly ['naitli] *a* nocturne, de nuit.

nightmare ['naitmɛə] *n* cauchemar *m*.

night-watchman ['nait'wɔtʃmən] *n* veilleur de nuit *m*.

nil [nil] *n* rien *m*, zéro *m*; *a* nul.

nimble ['nimbl] *a* agile, délié, ingambe.

nincompoop ['ninkəmpu:p] *n* gros bêta *m*, nigaud *m*.

nine [nain] *an* neuf *m*, équipe *f* de baseball.

ninepins ['nain'pinz] *n* quilles *f pl*.

nineteen ['nain'ti:n] *an* dix-neuf *m*.

nineteenth ['nain'ti:nθ] *an* dix-neuvième *mf*.

ninetieth ['naintiiθ] *an* quatre-vingt-dixième *mf*.

ninety ['nainti] *an* quatre-vingt-dix *m*.

ninny ['nini] *n* benêt *m*, niais(e) *mf*.

ninth [nainθ] *a* neuvième.

nip [nip] *n* pincement *m*, pinçon *m*, morsure *f*, sarcasme *m*, goutte *f*;

vt pincer, mordre, piquer, flétrir.

nipper ['nipə] *n* gosse *m*; *pl* pince *f*, tenailles *f pl*.

nipple ['nipl] *n* tétin *m*, mamelon *m*.

no [nou] *nm ad* non; *a* aucun, nul; **— longer** ne . . . plus.

nobility [nou'biliti] *n* noblesse *f*.

noble ['noubl] *an* noble *mf*; *a* grandiose, majestueux.

nobody ['noubədi] *pn* personne; *n* nullité *m*, pauvre type *m*.

nocturnal [nɔk'tə:nl] *a* nocturne.

nod [nɔd] *n* signe de tête *m*; *vi* faire un signe de tête, dodeliner, somnoler.

nodding ['nɔdiŋ] *a* à la tête dodelinante.

node [noud] *n* nœud *m*.

noise [nɔiz] *n* bruit *m*, vacarme *m*; *vt* répandre, ébruiter.

noiseless ['nɔizlis] *a* sans bruit, silencieux.

noisily ['nɔizili] *ad* bruyamment.

noisome ['nɔisəm] *a* nuisible, offensant, malodorant, désagréable.

noisy ['nɔizi] *a* bruyant.

no-man's-land ['noumænzlænd] *n* zone neutre *m*, terrains *mpl* vagues, zone *m*.

nominal ['nɔminl] *a* nominal.

nominally ['nɔminəli] *ad* de nom, soi-disant.

nominate ['nɔmineit] *vt* proposer, désigner, nommer.

nomination [,nɔmi'neiʃən] *n* nomination *f*.

non-aligned countries *npl* le tiers monde *m*.

non-alignement ['nɔnə'lainmənt] *n* neutralisme *m*.

non-appearance ['nɔnə'piərəns] *n* absence *f*; (*law*) défaut *m*.

non-committal ['nɔnkə'mitl] *a* évasif, (de) normand.

nondescript ['nɔndiskript] *a* vague, hétéroclite.

none [nʌn] *a pn* aucun, nul; *pn* pas une personne; *ad* en rien, pas.

nonentity [nɔ'nentiti] *n* nullité *f*, zéro *m*.

non-intervention ['nɔn,intə'venʃən] *n* non-intervention *f*.

non-payment ['nɔn'peimənt] *n* défaut de payement *m*.

nonplus ['nɔn'plʌs] *vt* interloquer, interdire.

nonsense ['nɔnsəns] *n* nonsens *m*, galimatias *m*, absurdité *f*, bêtise *f*.

nonsensical [nɔn'sensikəl] *a* absurde.

non-stop ['nɔn'stɔp] *a* sans arrêt, direct.

noodle ['nu:dl] *n* nigaud(e) *mf*, benêt *m*; *pl* nouilles *f pl*.

nook [nuk] *n* (re)coin *m*.

noon [nu:n] *n* midi *m*.

noose [nu:s] *n* nœud coulant *m*.

nor [nɔ:] *ad* ni, et ne pas.

normal ['nɔ:məl] *a* normal, moyen, ordinaire.

Norman ['nɔ:mən] *n* Normand(e) *mf*; *a* normand.

Normandy ['nɔ:məndi] n Normandie f.

north [nɔ:θ] an nord m; a du nord, septentrional.

northward ['nɔ:θwəd] a vers le nord. au nord.

Norway ['nɔ:wei] n Norvège f.

nose [nouz] n nez m, flair m; vt sentir, flairer; to — about fureter; to — out éventer, flairer; —bag musette f; —dive descente en piqué f; vi piquer du nez.

nosegay ['nouzgei] n bouquet m.

nostril ['nɔstril] n narine f, naseau m.

nostrum ['nɔstrəm] n orviétan m, panacée f.

not [nɔt] ad ne . . . pas, pas, non.

notable ['noutəbl] a notable, éminent, insigne.

notch [nɔtʃ] n (en)coche f, défilé m, gorge f; vt encocher, faire une coche à.

note [nout] n note f, ton m, signe m, mot m, marque f, réputation f; vt noter.

notebook ['noutbuk] n carnet m, bloc-notes m.

noted ['noutid] a connu, remarquable, célèbre (par for).

notepaper ['nout.peipə] n papier à lettres m.

noteworthy ['nout.wə:ði] a remarquable.

nothing ['nʌθiŋ] n pn rien m; n zéro m, néant m; ad en rien, nullement.

nothingness ['nʌθiŋnis] n néant m.

notice ['noutis] n avis m, informé m, avertissement m, affiche f, annonce f, compte m, connaissance f, congé m, notice f; vt remarquer, prendre garde à, s'apercevoir de. apercevoir.

noticeable ['noutisəbl] a sensible, perceptible, digne de remarque.

noticeboard ['noutisbɔ:d] n panneau m, écriteau m.

notifiable ['noutifaiəbl] a à déclarer.

notification [.noutifi'keiʃən] n avis m, déclaration f, notification f.

notify ['noutifai] vt avertir, notifier, déclarer.

notion ['nouʃən] n notion f, idée f.

notoriety [.noutə'raiəti] n notoriété f.

notorious [nou'tɔ:riəs] a notoire, malfamé.

notwithstanding [.nɔtwið'stændiŋ] prep malgré; ad néanmoins; cj bien que.

nought [nɔ:t] n rien m, zéro m.

noun [naun] n nom m.

nourish ['nʌriʃ] vt nourrir, sustenter, alimenter.

nourishment ['nʌriʃmənt] n nourriture f.

Nova Scotia ['nouvə'skouʃjə] la Nouvelle-Écosse.

novel ['nɔvəl] a original, étrange, nouveau; n roman m.

novelist ['nɔvəlist] n romancier m.

novelty ['nɔvəlti] n nouveauté f, innovation f.

November [nou'vembə] n novembre m.

novice ['nɔvis] a apprenti(e) mf, débutant(e) mf, novice mf.

now [nau] ad à présent, maintenant, tout de suite, dès lors, alors, tantôt, or; cj maintenant que.

nowadays ['nauədeiz] ad de nos jours, aujourd'hui.

nowhere ['nouwɛə] ad nulle part.

noxious ['nɔkʃəs] a nuisible, nocif.

nozzle ['nɔzl] n bec m, lance f, tuyau m, buse f.

nuclear ['nju:kliə] a nucléaire, atomique.

nucleus ['nju:kliəs] n noyau m.

nude [nju:d] an nu m.

nudge [nʌdʒ] n coup de coude m; vt pousser du coude.

nudity ['nju:diti] n nudité f.

nugget ['nagit] n pépite f.

nuisance ['nju:sns] n délit m, ennui m; to be a — être gênant, assommant.

null [nʌl] a nul, nulle.

nullify ['nʌlifai] vt annuler, infirmer.

numb [nʌm] a engourdi; vt engourdir.

number ['nʌmbə] n nombre m, numero m, chiffre m; vt compter, numéroter.

numberless ['nʌmbəlis] a innombrable.

numbness ['nʌmnis] n engourdissement m.

numerator ['nju:məreitə] n numérateur m.

numerical [nju(:)'merikəl] a numérique.

numerous ['nju:mərəs] a nombreux.

nun [nʌn] n nonne f, religieuse f.

nunnery ['nʌnəri] n couvent m.

nuptial ['nʌpʃəl] a nuptial; pl noces f pl.

nurse [nə:s] n infirmière f, nurse f, nourrice f, bonne f; vt nourrir, élever, soigner, bercer, ménager, entretenir.

nursery ['nə:sri] n (plants) pépinière f, garderie f, nursery f.

nurseryman ['nə:srimən] n pépiniériste m.

nursing-home ['nə:siŋhoum] n clinique f, maison f de santé.

nursling ['nə:sliŋ] n nourrisson m, poupon. -onne.

nurture ['nə:tʃə] n éducation f, soin m, nourriture f, soin m, nourriture f; vt nourrir, élever, soigner.

nut [nʌt] n noix f, écrou m, (fam) tête f, caboche f; cinglé m; —crackers n casse-noix m.

nutmeg ['nʌtmeg] n muscade f.

nutrition [nju(:)'triʃən] n nutrition f.

nutritious [nju(:)'triʃəs] a nourrissant.

nutritive ['nju:tritiv] a nutritif.

nutshell ['nʌtʃel] n coquille de noix f; in a — en deux mots.

nut-tree ['nʌttri:] n noyer m.

nutty ['nʌti] *a* à goût de noisette, toqué.
nuzzle ['nʌzl] *vt* flairer, fouiller, fourrer son nez dans, (contre); *vi* se blottir.
nymph [nimf] *n* nymphe *f*.

O

oak [ouk] *n* chêne *m*.
oakum ['oukəm] *n* étoupe *f*.
oar [ɔː] *n* rame *f*, aviron *m*; *vi* ramer.
oarsman ['ɔːzmən] *n* rameur *m*, nageur *m*.
oasis [ou'eisis] *n* oasis *f*.
oat(s) [outs] *n* avoine *f*; to sow one's wild — jeter sa gourme.
oath [ouθ] *n* serment *m*, juron *m*.
oatmeal ['outmiːl] *n* gruau *m*.
obduracy ['ɔbdjurəsi] *n* endurcissement *m*, obstination *f*.
obdurate ['ɔbdjurit] *a* endurci, obstiné.
obedience [ə'biːdjəns] *n* obéissance *f*, obédience *f*.
obedient [ə'biːdjənt] *a* obéissant, docile.
obeisance [ou'beisəns] *n* révérence *f*, hommage *m*.
obelisk ['ɔbilisk] *n* obélisque *m*.
obese [ou'biːs] *a* obèse.
obesity [ou'biːsiti] *n* obésité *f*.
obey [ə'bei] *vi* obéir; *vt* obéir à.
obituary [ə'bitjuəri] *n* notice nécrologique *f*.
object ['ɔbdʒikt] *n* objet *m*, but *m*, complément *m*.
object [əb'dʒekt] *vt* objecter; *vi* to — to trouver à redire à, s'opposer à, désapprouver.
objection [əb'dʒekʃən] *n* objection *f*, inconvénient *m*.
objectionable [əb'dʒekʃnəbl] *a* choquant, répugnant, désagréable.
objective [ɔb'dʒektiv] *an* objectif *m*; *n* but *m*.
objectivity [,ɔbdʒek'tiviti] *n* objectivité *f*.
obligation [,ɔbli'geiʃən] *n* obligation *f*, engagement *m*.
obligatory [ɔ'bligətəri] *a* obligatoire, de rigueur.
oblige [ə'blaidʒ] *vt* obliger, rendre service à.
obliging [ə'blaidʒiŋ] *a* obligeant, serviable.
oblique [ə'bliːk] *a* oblique.
obliterate [ə'blitəreit] *vt* effacer, oblitérer.
oblivion [ə'bliviən] *n* oubli *m*.
oblivious [ə'bliviəs] *a* oublieux.
oblong ['ɔblɔŋ] *a* oblong.
obloquy ['ɔbləkwi] *n* blâme *m*, opprobre *m*.
obnoxious [əb'nɔkʃəs] *a* offensa t déplaisant, odieux.
oboe ['oubou] *n* hautbois *m*.
obscene [ɔb'siːn] *a* impur, immonde, obscène.

obscenity [ɔb'seniti] *n* obscénité *f*, impiété *f*.
obscure [əb'skjuə] *a* obscur; *vt* obscurcir, éclipser, cacher.
obscurity [əb'skjuəriti] *n* obscurité *f*.
obsequies ['ɔbsikwiz] *n* obsèques *f pl*.
obsequious [əb'siːkwiəs] *a* obséquieux.
obsequiousness [əb'siːkwiəsnis] *n* obséquiosité *f*.
observable [əb'zəːvəbl] *a* observable.
observance [əb'zəːvəns] *n* observation *f*, observance *f*.
observant [əb'zəːvənt] *a* observateur.
observation [,ɔbzə'veiʃən] *n* observation *f*.
observatory [əb'zəːvətri] *n* observatoire *m*.
observe [əb'zəːv] *vt* observer, faire remarquer.
obsess [əb'ses] *vt* obséder.
obsession [əb'seʃən] *n* obsession *f*, hantise *f*.
obsolete ['ɔbsəliːt] *a* désuet, hors d'usage.
obstacle ['ɔbstəkl] *n* obstacle *m*.
obstinacy ['ɔbstənəsi] *n* obstination *f*.
obstinate ['ɔbstinit] *a* obstiné, têtu, acharné.
obstinately ['ɔbstinitli] *ad* obstinément.
obstreperous [əb'strepərəs] *a* bruyant, turbulent.
obstreperousness [əb'strepərisnis] *n* rouspétance *f*.
obstruct [əb'strʌkt] *vt* obstruer, boucher, entraver, encombrer.
obstruction [əb'strʌkʃən] *a* obstruction *f*, encombrement *m*, obstacle *m*.
obtain [əb'tein] *vt* se procurer, obtenir; *vi* prévaloir, régner.
obtainable [əb'teinəbl] *a* qui peut s'obtenir, procurable.
obtrude [əb'truːd] *vti* (s')imposer, (se) mettre en avant.
obtrusion [əb'truːʒən] *n* ingérence *f*, intrusion *f*.
obtrusive [əb'truːsiv] *a* importun, indiscret.
obtuse [əb'tjuːs] *a* émoussé, obtus.
obtuseness [əb'tjuːsnis] *n* stupidité *f*.
obviate ['ɔbvieit] *vt* parer à, prévenir.
obvious ['ɔbviəs] *a* évident, manifeste, indiqué.
occasion [ə'keiʒən] *n* cause *f*, occasion *f*, sujet *m*, affaires *f pl*; *vi* occasionner.
occasional [ə'keiʒənl] *a* de circonstance, occasionnel; — hand extra *m*; épars.
occasionally [ə'keiʒənəli] *ad* à l'occasion, de temps en temps.
occident ['ɔksidənt] *n* occident *m*.
occult [ɔ'kʌlt] *a* occulte.
occultism ['ɔkəltizəm] *n* occultisme *m*.

occupant ['ɔkjupant] n occupant(e) mf, habitant(e) mf, locataire mf.

occupation [ˌɔkju'peiʃən] n métier m, occupation f.

occupy ['ɔkjupai] vt occuper, habiter, tenir.

occur [ə'kə:] vi arriver, se produire, venir à l'esprit.

occurrence [ə'kʌrəns] n occurrence f, événement m.

ocean ['ouʃən] n océan m.

October [ɔk'toubə] n octobre m.

octopus ['ɔktəpəs] n pieuvre f.

ocular ['ɔkjulə] a oculaire.

oculist ['ɔkjulist] n oculiste mf.

odd [ɔd] a impair, de plus, de reste, dépareillé, curieux, bizarre.

oddity ['ɔditi] n bizarrerie f, curiosité f, excentricité f.

oddments ['ɔdmənts] n pl fins de série f pl, articles soldés m pl, fonds de boutique m pl.

odds [ɔdz] n inégalité f, avantage m, chances f pl; — and ends pièces et morceaux.

odious ['oudiəs] a odieux.

odor ['oudə] n odeur f.

odorless ['oudəlis] a inodore, sans odeur.

odorous ['oudərəs] a odorant.

of [ɔv] prep de, d'entre, depuis, par, à, en.

off [ɔf] prep de, sur, sans, de dessus, au large de, à la hauteur de; a éloigné, extérieur, de liberté; ad coupé, fermé, libre, parti, éloigné; I'm — je m'en vais; day — jour de congé.

offal ['ɔfəl] n abats m pl, rebut m.

offend [ə'fend] vt offenser, enfreindre, blesser.

offender [ə'fendə] n délinquant(e) mf, coupable mf.

offense [ə'fens] n contravention f, délit m, offense f.

offensive [ə'fensiv] n offensive f; a offensant, répugnant, offensif.

offer ['ɔfə] n offre f; vt offrir; vi s'offrir, se présenter.

offering ['ɔfəriŋ] n offrande f.

offertory ['ɔfətəri] n quête f.

offhand ['ɔf'hænd] a improvisé, désinvolte.

offhandedly ['ɔf'hændidli] ad de haut, avec désinvolture.

office ['ɔfis] n poste m, bureau m, office m; good —s bons offices m pl.

officer ['ɔfisə] n officier m.

official [ə'fiʃəl] a officiel, réglementaire; n employé m, fonctionnaire m.

officialdom [ə'fiʃəldəm] n monde officiel m, bureaucratie f.

officiate [ə'fiʃieit] vi officier, remplir les fonctions (de as).

officious [ə'fiʃəs] a trop zélé, officieux.

officiousness [ə'fiʃəsnis] n excès de zèle m.

offing ['ɔfiŋ] n (sea) large m, perspective f.

off-peak ['ɔfpi:k] a — hours heures creuses f pl; — tariff tarif de nuit m.

off-season ['ɔf'si:zn] n morte saison f.

offset ['ɔfset] n œilleton m, rejeton m, éperon m, compensation f, repoussoir m.

offshoot ['ɔfʃu:t] n rejeton m.

offshore ['ɔfʃɔ:] ad a de terre, éloigné de la côte.

offside ['ɔf'said] a hors jeu.

offspring ['ɔfspriŋ] n rejeton m, résultat m.

often ['ɔfn] ad souvent; — and — à mainte reprise.

ogle ['ougl] n œillade f; vt lorgner, faire de l'œil à.

oil [ɔil] n huile f, pétrole m; crude — mazout m; vt huiler, graisser; vi faire son plein de mazout; —can n burette f; —painting n peinture à l'huile; coconut — huile f de copra.

oilcake ['ɔilkeik] n tourteau m.

oilcloth ['ɔilklɔθ] n toile cirée f.

oiliness ['ɔilinis] n onctuosité f, état graisseux m.

oilskin ['ɔilskin] n ciré m.

oil-tanker ['ɔiltæŋkə] n pétrolier m.

oil-well ['ɔilwel] n puits pétrolifère m.

oily ['ɔili] a huileux, onctueux.

ointment ['ɔintmənt] n onguent m, pommade f.

old [ould] a vieux, vieil, vieille, ancien, âgé; to grow — vieillir; — age vieillesse f; —timer n vieillard m.

old-fashioned ['ould'fæʃənd] a démodé, suranné.

oldish ['ouldiʃ] a vieillot.

olive ['ɔliv] n olive f; a d'olive; — tree olivier m.

omen ['oumen] n présage m, augure m.

ominous ['ɔminəs] a menaçant, de mauvais augure.

omission [ou'miʃən] n omission f, oubli m.

omit [ou'mit] vt omettre, oublier.

omnifarious [ˌɔmni'fɛəriəs] a de toute espèce.

omnipotence [ɔm'nipətəns] n toute-puissance f.

omnivorous [ɔm'nivərəs] a omnivore.

on [ɔn] prep sur, à, lors de, en, sous, par, contre; ad en cours, en avant, mis, passé, allumé, ouvert.

once [wʌns] ad une fois; at — immédiatement, à la fois; —over n un coup d'œil scrutateur.

one [wʌn] a un, un seul; pn on.

one-eyed ['wʌn'aid] a borgne.

one's [wʌnz] a son, sa, ses.

oneself [wʌn'self] pn soi-même.

one-sided ['wʌn'saidid] a unilatéral, borné.

one-way ['wʌn'wei] n sens unique m; a à sens unique.

onerous ['ounərəs] a onéreux.

onion ['ʌnjən] n oignon m.

only ['ounli] a unique, seul; ad seulement; cj sauf que, mais.

onset ['ɔnset] n attaque f, assaut m, départ m, début m.

onslaught ['ɔnslɔːt] see onset.

onus ['ounəs] n poids m, charge f, responsabilité f.

onward ['ɔnwəd] a progressif, avancé, avançant; ad en avant, dorénavant.

ooze [uːz] n boue f, limon m, suintement m; vi suinter, dégoutter.

opal ['oupəl] n opale f; a opalin.

opaque [ou'peik] a opaque.

opaqueness [ou'peiknis] n opacité f.

open ['oupən] a ouvert, public, exposé, franc, débouché, libre; in the — (air) en plein air, au grand air; vt ouvrir, entamer, déboucher, percer, engager; vi s'ouvrir, débuter, commencer, s'épanouir.

opening ['oupəniŋ] n ouverture f, début m, débouché m, inauguration f.

opera ['ɔpərə] n opéra m.

operate ['ɔpəreit] vti opérer; vt accomplir, actionner, faire marcher; vi fonctionner, agir; gérer, exploiter.

operation [,ɔpə'reiʃən] n opération f, action f, fonctionnement m.

operative ['ɔpərətiv] n ouvrier, -ière; a efficace, actif, opératif, en vigueur.

opinion [ə'pinjən] n opinion f, avis m.

opinionated [ə'pinjəneitəd] a obstiné, entier.

opium ['oupjəm] n opium m.

opponent [ə'pounənt] n adversaire m, antagoniste mf.

opportune ['ɔpətjuːn] a opportun.

opportunely ['ɔpətjuːnli] ad à propos, en temps opportun.

opportunism ['ɔpətju:nizəm] n opportunisme m.

opportunity [,ɔpə'tjuːniti] n occasion f, chance f.

oppose [ə'pouz] vt s'opposer à, opposer.

opposite ['ɔpəzit] a opposé, correspondant; prep face à, en face de; ad en face, en regard; n contraire m, contre-pied m.

opposition [,ɔpə'ziʃən] n opposition f, concurrence f.

oppress [ə'pres] vt opprimer.

oppression [ə'preʃən] a oppression f.

oppressive [ə'presiv] a oppressif, lourd.

oppressor [ə'presə] n oppresseur m.

opprobrious [ə'proubriəs] a déshonorant, injurieux.

opprobrium [ə'proubriəm] n opprobre m.

opt [ɔpt] vi opter; — out s'esquiver.

optic ['ɔptik] a optique.

optician [ɔp'tiʃən] n opticien m.

optics ['ɔptiks] n optique f.

optimism ['ɔptimizəm] n optimisme m.

optimistic [,ɔpti'mistik] a optimiste.

option ['ɔpʃən] n option f, choix m.

optional ['ɔpʃənl] a facultatif.

opulence ['ɔpjuləns] n opulence f.

opulent ['ɔpjulənt] a opulent.

or [ɔː] cj ou, sinon.

oracle ['ɔrəkl] n oracle m.

oracular [ɔ'rækjulə] a oraculaire, obscur.

oral ['ɔːrəl] a oral.

orange ['ɔrindʒ] n orange f.

oration [ɔː'reiʃən] n discours m, harangue f.

orator ['ɔrətə] n orateur m.

oratorical [,ɔrə'tɔrikəl] a oratoire, ampoulé, disert.

orb [ɔːb] n orbe m, globe m, sphère f.

orbit ['ɔːbit] n orbite f.

orchard ['ɔːtʃəd] n verger m.

orchestra ['ɔːkistrə] n orchestre m.

orchestrate ['ɔːkistreit] vt orchestrer.

orchid ['ɔːkid] n orchidée f.

ordain [ɔː'dein] vt ordonner, conférer les ordres à.

ordeal [ɔː'diːl] n épreuve f.

order ['ɔːdə] n ordre m; to — sur commande; out of — détraqué, déplacé, irrégulier; in — to afin de; vt commander, ordonner.

orderliness ['ɔːdəlinis] n (esprit m d') ordre m.

orderly ['ɔːdəli] n infirmier militaire m, planton m; a en ordre, rangé, discipliné.

ordinary ['ɔːdnri] a ordinaire, typique, normal.

ordnance ['ɔːdnəns] n artillerie f, intendance f.

ore [ɔː] n minéral m.

organ ['ɔːgən] n organe m, orgue m.

organic [ɔː'gænik] a organique.

organism ['ɔːgənizəm] n organisme m.

organist ['ɔːgənist] n organiste mf.

organization [,ɔːgənai'zeiʃən] n organisation f, organisme m.

organize ['ɔːgənaiz] vt organiser, arranger.

organizer ['ɔːgənaizə] n organisateur, -trice.

orient ['ɔːriənt] n orient m.

oriental [,ɔːri'entl] a oriental, d'orient.

orientation [,ɔːrien'teiʃən] n orientation f.

orifice ['ɔrifis] n orifice m, ouverture f.

origin ['ɔridʒin] n origine f.

original [ə'ridʒənl] an original m; a originel.

originality [ə,ridʒi'næliti] n originalité f.

originate [ə'ridʒineit] vt donner naissance à; vt descendre, provenir, naître.

originator [ə'ridʒineitə] n auteur m, source f.

ornament ['ɔːnəmənt] n ornement m.

ornament [ɔːnə'ment] vt orner, agrémenter.

ornamental [ɔːnə'mentl] a ornemental, décoratif.
ornamentation [ɔːnəmen'teiʃən] n
ornementation f, décoration f.
orphan ['ɔːfən] n orphelin(e) mf.
orphanage ['ɔːfənidʒ] n orphelinat
m.
orthodox ['ɔːθədɔks] a orthodoxe.
orthodoxy ['ɔːθədɔksi] n orthodoxie
f.
orthography [ɔː'θɔgrəfi] n orthographe f.
oscillate ['ɔsileit] vi osciller.
osier ['ouʒə] n osier m.
ostensible [ɔs'tensəbl] a soi-disant,
prétendu.
ostentation [ɔsten'teiʃən] n ostentation f, faste m.
ostentatious [ɔsten'teiʃəs] a
fastueux.
ostler ['ɔslə] n garçon d'écurie m.
ostracize ['ɔstrəsaiz] vt ostraciser,
mettre au ban.
ostrich ['ɔstritʃ] n autruche f.
other ['ʌðə] an pn autre; pl d'autres,
les autres.
otherwise ['ʌðəwaiz] ad autrement,
sans quoi.
otter ['ɔtə] n loutre f.
ought [ɔːt] v aux devoir.
ounce [auns] n once f.
our ['auə] a notre, nos; ——**self**,
(**selves**) pn nous-même(s), nous.
ours ['auəz] pn le, la, les nôtre(s),
à nous, nôtre.
oust [aust] vt jeter dehors, évincer,
supplanter.
out [aut] ad dehors, au dehors, au
large, sur pied, en grève; a épuisé,
à bout, sorti, éteint, éclos; — **of**
prep hors de, à l'abri de, dans, à,
par, d'entre, parmi.
outbid [aut'bid] vt (r)enchérir sur.
outboard ['autbɔːd] an hors bord m.
outbreak ['autbreik] n explosion f,
éruption f, émeute f, accès m.
outbuilding ['autbildiŋ] n dépendance f, annexe f.
outburst ['autbəːst] n explosion f,
éclat m, élan m.
outcast ['autkɑːst] n paria m,
proscrit(e) mf, exilé(e) mf.
outclass [aut'klɑːs] vt surclasser,
surpasser.
outcome ['autkʌm] n résultat m,
issue f.
outcrop ['autkrɔp] n affleurement m.
outcry ['autkrai] n clameur f, tollé
m.
outdo [aut'duː] vt surpasser.
outer ['autə] a plus éloigné, extérieur,
externe.
outfall ['autfɔːl] n embouchure f.
outfit ['autfit] n équipement m,
trousseau m, trousse f, attirail m,
équipe f d'ouvriers.
outflank ['aut'flæŋk] vt déborder,
circonvenir.
outflow ['autflou] n écoulement m,
décharge f; vi provenir.

outgrow [aut'grou] vt dépasser,
devenir trop grand pour, faire
craquer.
outhouse ['authaus] n dépendance f.
outing ['autiŋ] n sortie f, excursion f.
outlandish [aut'lændiʃ] a étranger,
étrange, barbare, écarté, reculé.
outlaw ['autlɔː] n hors-la-loi m,
proscrit(e) mf; vt proscrire.
outlay ['autlei] n dépenses f pl, frais
m pl.
outlet ['autlet] n issue f, débouché m,
départ m.
outline ['autlain] n contour m,
esquisse f, silhouette f; vt esquisser,
silhouetter.
outlive [aut'liv] vt survivre à.
outlook ['autluk] n (point m de) vue
f, perspective f, philosophie f,
aguets m pl.
outlying ['aut.laiiŋ] a éloigné, excentrique.
outmatch [autmætʃ] vt surpasser
en finesse.
outpost ['autpoust] n avant poste m.
outpouring ['aut.pɔːriŋ] effusion f,
débordement m.
output ['autput] n production f,
rendement m.
outrage ['autreidʒ] n outrage m; vt
outrager, violenter.
outrageous [aut'reidʒəs] a outra-
geux, outrageant, excessif, indigne.
outrageously [aut'reidʒəsli] ad outre
mesure, immodérément.
outright ['autrait] a net, direct; ad
du (sur le) coup, complètement; a
franc.
outset ['autset] n début m.
outshine [aut'ʃain] vt éclipser, dépasser.
outside ['aut'said] n dehors m,
impériale f, extérieur m, maximum
m; a extérieur, du dehors; ad (en)
dehors, à l'extérieur; prep hors de,
en (au) dehors de.
outsider ['aut'saidə] n étranger, -ère,
intrus(e) mf, outsider m.
outskirts ['autskəːts] n lisière f,
banlieue f, faubourgs m pl.
outspoken [aut'spoukən] a franc,
brutal, rond, entier.
outstanding [aut'stændiŋ] a éminent, marquant, en suspens, à
recouvrer.
outstretch [aut'stretʃ] vt (é)tendre
déployer.
outstrip [aut'strip] vt dé-,sur-
passer, distancer.
outward ['autwəd] a extérieur, de
dehors, externe; ad pour l'étranger
vers le dehors.
outwards ['autwədz] ad see outward
outwit [aut'wit] vt déjouer, rouler
dépister.
outworn [aut'wɔːn] a usé jusqu'à la
corde, désuet.
oval ['ouvəl] an ovale m.
ovary ['ouvəri] n ovaire m.
ovation [ou'veiʃən] n ovation f.

oven ['ʌvn] n four m.

over ['ouvə] prep sur, contre, par dessus, au dessus de, plus de; ad au dessus, et plus, au delà, de trop, à l'excès.

overall ['ouvərɔ:l] n salopette f, combinaison f, bleu m de travail, blouse f; a général.

overawe [,ouvər'ɔ:] vt en imposer à, intimider.

overbalance [,ouvə'bæləns] vi perdre l'équilibre; vt renverser.

overbearing [,ouvə'bɛəriŋ] a arrogant, autoritaire.

overboard ['ouvəbɔ:d] ad par dessus bord, à la mer.

overcast ['ouvəkɑ:st] a couvert, assombri.

overcharge ['ouvə'tʃɑ:dʒ] n majoration f, prix excessif m, surcharge f; vt surfaire, faire payer trop cher à, surcharger.

overcoat ['ouvəkout] n pardessus m.

overcome [,ouvə'kʌm] vt surmonter, dominer, venir à bout de, triompher de, vaincre, accabler.

overdo [,ouvə'du:] vt exagérer, outrer, trop cuire.

overdose ['ouvədous] n dose excessive f.

overdraft ['ouvədrɑ:ft] n dépassement de crédit m, découvert m.

overdraw ['ouvə'drɔ:] vt tirer à découvert, charger.

overdrive ['ouvə'draiv] n vitesse surmultipliée f.

overdue ['ouvə'dju:] a en retard, périmé, échu.

overestimate ['ouvər'estimeit] vt surestimer.

overflow ['ouvəflou] n trop plein m, déversoir m; [ouvə'flou] vi déborder; vt inonder.

overflowing [,ouvə'flouiŋ] n débordement m, inondation f; a débordant.

overgrow ['ouvə'grou] vt envahir; vi trop grandir.

overhang ['ouvə'hæŋ] vt surplomber.

overhaul ['ouvəhɔ:l] vt réviser, remettre en état, rattraper; n remise en état f, révision f, examen détaillé m.

overhead ['ouvəhed] a ad aérien; n pl frais généraux m pl.

overhear [,ouvə'hiə] vt surprendre.

overheat ['ouvə'hi:t] vt surchauffer.

overjoyed [,ouvə'dʒɔid] a transporté de joie, enchanté.

overland ['ouvəlænd] a ad par voie de terre.

overlap ['ouvəlæp] vt chevaucher; vi se chevaucher.

overleaf ['ouvə'li:f] ad au revers, au verso.

overlook [,ouvə'luk] vt avoir vue sur, dominer, oublier, laisser passer, négliger, surveiller.

overmuch ['ouvə'mʌtʃ] ad par trop, excessif.

overpass ['ouvəpɑ:s] n enjambement m.

overpopulated ['ouvə'pɔpjuleitid] a surpeuplé.

overpower [ouvə'pauə] vt terrasser, subjuger, maîtriser, accabler.

overpowering [,ouvə'pauəriŋ] a irrésistible, accablant.

overproduction ['ouvəprə'dʌkʃən] n surproduction f.

overrate ['ouvə'reit] vt surfaire, surtaxer, présumer de.

overreach [,ouvə'ri:tʃ] vt duper, dépasser; to — oneself se surmener, se donner un effort.

overripe ['ouvə'raip] a trop mûr, trop fait, blet.

overrule [,ouvə'ru:l] vt annuler par autorité supérieure, casser, passer outre à.

overrun [,ouvə'rʌn] vt envahir, infester, excéder, dépasser, surmener.

oversea(s) ['ouvə'si:(z)] a d'outremer; ad outre-mer.

oversee ['ouvə'si:] vt surveiller.

overseer ['ouvəsiə] n surveillant(e) mf, contremaître, -tresse.

overshadow [,ouvə'ʃædou] vt ombrager, éclipser.

overshoes ['ouvəʃu:z] n pl caoutchoucs m pl.

overshoot ['ouvə'ʃu:t] vi tirer trop loin; vt dépasser.

oversight ['ouvəsait] n inadvertance f, oubli m.

overspill ['ouvəspil] n déversement m de population.

overstate ['ouvə'steit] vt exagérer.

overstatement ['ouvə'steitmənt] n exagération f.

overstep ['ouvə'step] vt outrepasser, dépasser.

overstrain ['ouvəstrein] vt tendre à l'excès, surmener.

overstrung ['ouvə'strʌŋ] a hypertendu.

overt ['ouvə:t] a public, évident.

overtake [,ouvə'teik] vt dépasser, doubler, rattraper, surprendre.

overthrow [,ouvə'θrou] vt renverser, mettre à bas.

overtime ['ouvətaim] n heures supplémentaires f pl; ad au delà du temps normal.

overtly ['ouvə:tli] ad au grand jour.

overture ['ouvətjuə] n ouverture f.

overturn ['ouvətə:n] vt tourner sens dessus dessous, renverser; vi verser, chavirer, se renverser, capoter.

overvaluation ['ouvə,vælju'eiʃən] n surestimation f.

overvalue ['ouvə'vælju:] vt surestimer.

overweening [,ouvə'wi:niŋ] a présomptueux.

overweight ['ouvə'weit] n excédent m, prépondérance f.

overwhelm [,ouvə'welm] vt accabler, écraser, combler.

overwork ['ouvǝ'wǝ:k] n surmenage m.

overwork ['ouvǝ'wǝ:k] vt surmener; vi se surmener.

overwrought ['ouvǝ'rɔ:t] a surmené, surexcité.

owe [ou] vt devoir.

owing ['ouiŋ] a dû; — to grâce à.

owl [aul] n hibou m, chouette f.

owlish ['auliʃ] a solennel, prétentieux, de hibou.

own [oun] a propre, à moi etc; vt posséder, admettre, reconnaître, avouer.

ownership ['ounǝʃip] n propriété f, possession f.

ox [ɔks] (pl **oxen**) n bœuf m.

oxide ['ɔksaid] n oxyde m.

oxidize ['ɔksidaiz] vt oxyder; vi s'oxyder.

oxygen ['ɔksidʒǝn] n oxygène m.

oxygenate [ɔk'sidʒineit] vt oxygéner.

oyster ['ɔistǝ] n huître f; — bed banc d'huîtres m.

P

pace [peis] n pas m, allure f, vitesse f; vt arpenter, mesurer au pas, entraîner; vi marcher (à pas mesurés).

pacific [pǝ'sifik] a pacifique, paisible; n Pacifique m.

pacification [.pæsifi'keiʃǝn] n pacification f.

pacifier ['pæsifaiǝ] n pacificateur, -trice.

pacifism ['pæsifizǝm] n pacifisme m.

pacifist ['pæsifist] n pacifiste mf.

pacify ['pæsifai] vt pacifier, apaiser.

pack [pæk] n paquet m, ballot m, jeu m (de cartes), bande f, meute f; —ice banquise f; vt empaqueter, emballer, envelopper, entasser, bourrer; vi se presser, s'attrouper, se tasser, faire ses malles.

package ['pækidʒ] n empaquetage m, paquet m; — tour voyage organisé m.

packer ['pækǝ] n emballeur m.

packet ['pækit] n paquet m, colis m, paquebot m.

packing ['pækiŋ] n emballage m, tassement m.

pact [pækt] n pacte m.

pad [pæd] n bourrelet m, tampon m, coussin m, sous-main m, (paper) bloc m, (fam) pieu m; vt rembourrer, capitonner, garnir.

padding ['pædiŋ] n rembourrage m, capitonnage m, remplissage m.

paddle ['pædl] n pagaie f, palette f, aube f; vti pagayer; vi patauger, barboter, faire trempette.

paddock ['pædǝk] n pré m, paddock m, pesage m.

padlock ['pædlɔk] n cadenas m; vt cadenasser.

pagan ['peigǝn] an païen, -ienne.

paganism ['peigǝnizǝm] n paganisme m.

page [peidʒ] n page f, (boy) page m, chasseur m, groom m; vt paginer.

pageant ['pædʒǝnt] n cortège m, cavalcade f, fête f, spectacle m.

pail(ful) ['peil(ful)] n seau m.

pain [pein] n peine f, douleur f; vt faire mal à, faire de la peine à.

painful ['peinful] a douloureux, pénible.

pain-killer ['peinkilǝ] n calmant m, anodin m.

painless ['peinlis] a indolore, sans douleur.

painstaking ['peinz.teikiŋ] a laborieux, assidu, soigné.

paint [peint] n peinture f; vti peindre; vi faire de la peinture.

painter ['peintǝ] n peintre m, peintre décorateur m.

pair [pɛǝ] n paire f, couple mf; vt accoupler, apparier, assortir.

pajamas [pǝ'dʒɑːmǝz] n pyjama(s) m (pl).

pal [pæl] n copain m, copine f.

palace ['pælis] n palais m.

palatable ['pælǝtǝbl] a délectable, agréable.

palate ['pælit] n palais m.

palaver [pǝ'lɑːvǝ] n palabre f; vi palabrer.

pale [peil] n pieu m, pal m; a pâle; vi pâlir.

palette ['pælit] n palette f.

paling ['peiliŋ] n palissade f, clôture f.

palish ['peiliʃ] a pâlot.

pall [pɔːl] n drap mortuaire m, voile m; vi s'affadir, se blaser.

pallbearer ['pɔːl.bɛǝrǝ] n qui tient un cordon du poêle.

pallet ['pælit] n paillasse f.

palliate ['pælieit] vt pallier, atténuer.

palliative ['pæliǝtiv] an palliatif m.

pallid ['pælid] a blême, pâle.

palm [pɑːm] n paume f, palmier m, palme f, rameau m; P— Sunday dimanche des Rameaux; —nut noix f de palme; — wine vin n de palme; vt escamoter; to — off repasser, refiler.

palmist ['pɑːmist] n chiromancien, -ienne.

palmistry ['pɑːmistri] n chiromancie f.

palmy ['pɑːmi] a triomphant, beau, heureux.

palpable ['pælpǝbl] a palpable, évident.

palpitate ['pælpiteit] vi palpiter.

palsy ['pɔːlzi] n paralysie f.

paltry ['pɔːltri] a mesquin, pauvre, malheureux.

pamper ['pæmpǝ] vt dorloter, gâter.

pamphlet ['pæmflit] n brochure f, opuscule m.

pamphleteer [.pæmfli'tiǝ] n publiciste m, auteur m de brochures.

pan [pæn] n casserole f, sauteuse f,

poêle *f*, bac *m*; to — out se passer, s'arranger.

panacea [ˌpænəˈsiə] *n* panacée *f*.

pancake [ˈpænkeik] *n* crêpe *f*.

pandemonium [ˌpændiˈmouniəm] *n* charivari *m*, tapage infernal *m*.

pander [ˈpændə] to — to se prêter à, encourager.

pane [pein] *n* carreau *m*, vitre *f*.

panel [ˈpænl] *n* tableau *m*, panneau *m*, lambris *m*, jury *m*; *vt* lambrisser, plaquer.

paneling [ˈpænliŋ] *n* lambrissage *m*.

pang [pæŋ] *n* serrement de cœur *m*, douleur *f*; —s of death affres de la mort *f pl*.

panic [ˈpænik] *an* panique *f*; *vi* s'affoler; —monger *n* fauteur *m* de panique, paniquard *m*.

panicky [ˈpæniki] *a* alarmiste, qui s'affole pour rien.

panoply [ˈpænəpli] *n* panoplie *f*.

pansy [ˈpænzi] *n* pensée *f*.

pant [pænt] *vi* haleter, panteler, aspirer (à after).

panties [ˈpæntiz] *n pl* slip *m*, culotte *f*.

pantheism [ˈpænθiizəm] *n* panthéisme *m*.

panther [ˈpænθə] *n* panthère *f*.

pantry [ˈpæntri] *n* office *m*, garde-manger *m*.

pants [pænts] *n* caleçon *m*, pantalon *m*.

pap [pæp] *n* tétin *m*, mamelon *m*, bouillie *f*.

papacy [ˈpeipəsi] *n* papauté *f*.

paper [ˈpeipə] *n* papier *m*, journal *m*, article *m*, essai *m*, épreuve *f*, copie *f*; *vt* tapisser; —hanger *n* colleur de papier *m*; —knife *n* coupe-papier *m*; —weight *n* presse-papier *m*; —clip *n* trombone *m*, pince *f*.

papermill [ˈpeipəmil] *n* papeterie *f*.

papist [ˈpeipist] *n* papiste *mf*.

par [pɑ:] *n* égalité *f*, pair *m*, moyenne *f*.

parable [ˈpærəbl] *n* parabole *f*.

parachute [ˈpærəʃu:t] *n* parachute *m*.

parachutist [ˈpærəʃu:tist] *n* parachutiste *mf*.

parade [pəˈreid] *n* parade *f*, revue *f*, défilé *m*; *vt* faire étalage de, faire défiler, passer en revue; *vi* défiler, parader.

paradise [ˈpærədais] *n* paradis *m*.

paradox [ˈpærədɔks] *n* paradoxe *m*.

paradoxical [ˌpærəˈdɔksikəl] *a* paradoxal.

paraffin [ˈpærəfin] *n* paraffine *f*, pétrole *m*.

paragon [ˈpærəgən] *n* parangon *m*.

paragraph [ˈpærəgrɑ:f] *n* paragraphe *m*, alinéa *m*, entrefilet *m*.

parakeet [ˈpærəki:t] *n* perruche *f*.

parallel [ˈpærəlel] *a* parallèle, pareil; *n* parallèle *mf*; *vt* mettre en parallèle, comparer.

paralysis [pəˈrælisis] *n* paralysie *f*.

paralyze [ˈpærəlaiz] *vt* paralyser.

paramount [ˈpærəmaunt] *a* suprême.

parapet [ˈpærəpit] *n* parapet *m*, garde-fou *m*.

paraphernalia [ˌpærəfəˈneiljə] *n* attirail *m*, boutique *f*, bataclan *m*, affaires *f pl*.

paraphrase [ˈpærəfreiz] *n* paraphrase *f*; *vt* paraphraser.

parasite [ˈpærəsait] *n* parasite *m*, pique-assiette *m*.

paratrooper [ˈpærətru:pə] *n* parachutiste *m*.

parasol [ˈpærəsɔl] *n* parasol *m*, ombrelle *f*.

parcel [ˈpɑ:sl] *n* paquet *m*, colis *m*, parcelle *f*, bande *f*; *vt* morceler, emballer.

parch [pɑ:tʃ] *vt* rôtir, (des)sécher, griller.

parchment [ˈpɑ:tʃmənt] *n* parchemin *m*.

pardon [ˈpɑ:dn] *n* pardon *m*; *vt* pardonner.

pardonable [ˈpɑ:dnəbl] *a* pardonnable, excusable.

pare [peə] *vt* peler, rogner, tailler.

parent [ˈpeərənt] *n* père *m*, mère *f*; *pl* parents *m pl*.

parentage [ˈpeərəntidʒ] *n* extraction *f*, naissance *f*.

parenthesis [pəˈrenθisis] *n* parenthèse *f*.

pariah [ˈpæriə] *n* paria *m*.

parish [ˈpæriʃ] *n* paroisse *f*.

parishioner [pəˈriʃənə] *n* paroissien, -ienne.

Parisian [pəˈriziən] *an* parisien.

park [pɑ:k] *n* parc *m*, jardin public *m*; *vt* parquer; *vi* stationner.

parking [ˈpɑ:kiŋ] *n* stationnement *m*, parcage *m*; — meter *n* parcomètre *m*, compteur *m*.

parley [ˈpɑ:li] *n* pourparlers *m pl*; *vi* parlementer, entrer en pourparlers.

parliament [ˈpɑ:ləmənt] *n* parlement *m*.

parliamentary [ˌpɑ:ləˈmentəri] *a* parlementaire.

parlor [ˈpɑ:lə] *n* salle *f*, petit salon *m*, parloir *m*; **beauty** — salon de coiffure *m*.

parochial [pəˈroukiəl] *a* paroissial, étroit.

parochialism [pəˈroukiəlizem] *n* esprit de clocher *m*.

parody [ˈpærədi] *n* parodie *f*, pastiche *m*; *vt* parodier, pasticher.

parole [pəˈroul] *n* parole *f*.

paroxysm [ˈpærəksizəm] *n* paroxysme *m*, crise *f*.

parricide [ˈpærisaid] *n* parricide (crime) *m*, (person) *mf*.

parrot [ˈpærət] *n* perroquet *m*.

parry [ˈpæri] *n* parade *f*; *vt* parer, détourner.

parse [pɑ:z] *vt* analyser.

parsimonious [.pa:si'mouniəs] *a* parcimonieux, ladre.

parsimony ['pa:siməni] *n* parcimonie *f*, ladrerie *f*.

parsley ['pa:sli] *n* persil *m*.

parsnip ['pa:snip] *n* panais *m*.

parson ['pa:sn] *n* prêtre *m*, pasteur *m*.

parsonage ['pa:snidʒ] *n* cure *f*, presbytère *m*.

part [pa:t] *n* partie *f*, parti *m*, région *f*, (*theatre*) rôle *m*, côté *m*; *vt* diviser, séparer; *vi* se séparer, se rompre; to — with céder, se séparer de.

partake [pa:'teik] to — of participer à, prendre part à, partager, tenir de, sentir.

partial ['pa:ʃəl] *a* partial, qui a un faible (pour).

partiality [.pa:ʃi'æliti] *n* partialité *f*, penchant *m*.

participate [pa:'tisipeit] *vi* participer (à, de, in).

participation [pa:,tisi'peiʃən] *n* participation *f*.

participle ['pa:tsipl] *n* participe *m*.

particle ['pa:tikl] *n* particule *f*, parcelle *f*, brin *m*, semblant *m*.

particular [pə'tikjulə] *a* spécial, minutieux, difficile; *n pl* détails *m pl*, renseignements *m pl*.

particularity [pə.tikju'læriti] *n* particularité *f*, minutie *f*.

particularize [pə'tikjuləraiz] *vt* spécifier; *vi* préciser.

parting ['pa:tiŋ] *n* séparation *f*, rupture *f*, (*hair*) raie *f*, (*ways*) croisée *f*; *a* de départ, d'adieu.

partisan [.pa:ti'zæn] *n* partisan *m*.

partition [pa:'tiʃən] *n* partage *m* démembrement *m*, morcellement *m*, cloison *f*; *vt* démembrer, morceler, partager, cloisonner.

partner ['pa:tnə] *n* partenaire *mf*, associé(e) *mf*, cavalier *m*, danseuse *f*; *vt* associer, être associé à, mener, être le partenaire de.

partnership ['pa:tnəʃip] *n* association *f*, société *f*.

partridge ['pa:tridʒ] *n* perdrix *f*.

part-time ['pa:t'taim] *a* à mi-temps.

party ['pa:ti] *n* parti *m*, réception *f*, partie *f*, bande *f*, détachement *m*.

pass [pa:s] *n* défilé *m*, col *m*, permission *f*, passe *f*, (*school*) moyenne *f*; *vt* (faire) passer, passer près de, disparaître, dépasser, franchir, doubler, voter, approuver, réussir à (un examen), recevoir; *vi* passer, s'écouler, se passer, être reçu.

passable ['pa:səbl] *a* passable, praticable, traversable.

passage ['pæsidʒ] *n* passage *m*, corridor *m*, échange *m*, passe d'armes *f*, traversée *f*.

pass-book ['pa:sbuk] *n* carnet de comptes *m*.

passenger ['pæsindʒə] *n* passager, -ère, voyageur, -euse.

passer-by ['pa:sə'bai] *n* passant(e) *mf*.

passing ['pa:siŋ] *n* passage *m*, mort *f*, écoulement *m*; *a* passager, fugitif.

passion ['pæʃən] *n* passion *f*, colère *f*.

passionate ['pæʃənit] *a* ardent, passionné, irascible.

passionately ['pæʃənitli] *ad* passionnément.

passive ['pæsiv] *a* passif.

passiveness ['pæsivnis] *n* passivité *f*, inertie *f*.

pass-key ['pa:ski:] *n* passe-partout *m*.

passport ['pa:spɔ:t] *n* passeport *m*.

password ['pa:swə:d] *n* mot de passe *m*.

past [pa:st] *an* passé *m*; *a* ancien, ex—; *prep* après, au delà de, plus loin que.

paste [peist] *n* pâte *f*, colle *f*; *vt* coller, (*fam*) rosser.

pasteboard ['peistbɔ:d] *n* carton *m*.

pastel ['pæstəl] *n* pastel *m*.

pasteurize ['pæstəraiz] *vt* pasteuriser.

pastime ['pa:staim] *n* passetemps *m*, distraction *f*.

pastor ['pa:stə] *n* pasteur *m*.

pastoral ['pa:stərəl] *a* pastoral.

pastry ['peistri] *n* pâtisserie *f*, pâte *f*; —cook *n* pâtissier, -ière; —shop *n* pâtisserie *f*.

pasture ['pa:stʃə] *n* pâture *f*, pâturage *m*, pacage *m*; *vt* faire paître.

pasty ['peisti] *n* pâté *m*; *a* pâteux, terreux.

pat [pæt] *n* tape *f*, coquille *f*, motte *f*, rondelle *f*; *vt* tapoter, caresser; *ad* à point, du tac au tac, tout prêt.

patch [pætʃ] *n* pièce *f*, emplâtre *m*, mouche *f*, tache *f*, (*peas*) planche *f*, carré *m*; *vt* rapiécer; to — up replâtrer, rafistoler.

patchwork ['pætʃwə:k] *n* rapiéçage *m*, mosaïque *f*.

patchy ['pætʃi] *a* fait de pièces et de morceaux, inégal, irrégulier.

paten ['pætən] *n* patène *f*.

patent ['peitənt] *n* brevet *m*, lettres patentes *f pl*; *a* breveté, patenté, manifeste; *vt* faire breveter.

paternal [pə'tə:nl] *a* paternel.

paternity [pə'tə:niti] *n* paternité *f*.

path [pa:θ] *n* sentier *m*, course *f*, chemin *m*.

pathetic [pə'θetik] *a* pathétique, triste, attendrissant.

pathfinder ['pa:θ.faində] *n* éclaireur *m*, pionnier *m*.

patience ['peiʃəns] *n* patience *f*, (*cards*) réussite *f*.

patient ['peiʃənt] *n* malade *mf*, patient(e) *mf*; *a* patient.

patiently ['peiʃəntli] *ad* patiemment, avec patience.

patriarch ['peitria:k] *n* patriarch *m*.

patriarchal [ˌpeitriˈɑːkəl] a patriarcal.

Patrick [ˈpætrik] Patrice m.

patrimony [ˈpætriməni] n patrimoine m.

patriot [ˈpeitriət] n patriote mf.

patriotic [ˌpætriˈɔtik] a patriotique, (person) patriote.

patriotism [ˈpætriətizəm] n patriotisme m.

patrol [pəˈtroul] n patrouille f, ronde f; vti patrouiller.

patron, **-ess** [ˈpeitrən, is] n patron, -onne, protecteur, -trice, client(e) mf, habitué(e) mf.

patronage [ˈpætrənidʒ] n patronage m, protection f, clientèle f, airs protecteurs m pl.

patronize [ˈpætrənaiz] vt patronner, protéger, traiter de haut, accorder sa clientèle à, se fournir chez.

patter [ˈpætə] n crépitement m, trottinement m, piétinement m, fouettement m, bagout m, boniment m; vi crépiter, trottiner, jaser.

pattern [ˈpætən] n modèle m, échantillon m, dessin m.

patty [ˈpæti] n petit pâté m.

paucity [ˈpɔːsiti] n rareté f, disette f, manque m.

Paul [pɔːl] Paul m.

paunch [ˈpɔːntʃ] n panse f, bedaine f.

pauper [ˈpɔːpə] n indigent(e) mf, mendiant(e) mf.

pause [pɔːz] n pause f, arrêt m, silence m, point d'orgue m; vi s'arrêter, faire la pause, hésiter.

pave [peiv] vt paver, carreler, frayer (la voie).

pavement [ˈpeivmənt] n pavé m, pavage m, trottoir m; chaussée f.

pavilion [pəˈviljən] n tente f, pavillon m.

paw [pɔː] n patte f; vt frapper du pied, tripoter; vi piaffer.

pawn [pɔːn] n pion m, gage m; vt mettre en gage.

pawnbroker [ˈpɔːnˌbroukə] n prêteur m sur gages.

pawnshop [ˈpɔːnʃɔp] n mont-de-piété m; (fam) tante f.

pawpaw [ˈpɔːpɔː] n papaye f.

pay [pei] n paie f, gages m pl, salaire m, solde f; vt payer, rétribuer, acquitter, faire; ⌐ in verser, encaisser; — a visit rendre visite (à to).

payer [ˈpeiə] n payeur, -euse, payant(e) mf.

paying-guest [ˈpeiiŋˌgest] n hôte payant m.

paymaster [ˈpeiˌmɑːstə] n trésorier m, payeur m.

payment [ˈpeimənt] n paiement m, rémunération f, règlement m, versement m.

pea [piː] n pois m; green —s petits pois; sweet — pois de senteur.

peace [piːs] n paix f; justice of the

— juge de paix m; vi to hold one's — se taire.

peaceful [ˈpiːsful] a paisible, pacifique.

peacefulness [ˈpiːsfulnis] n paix f, humeur paisible f.

peacemaker [ˈpiːsˌmeikə] n pacificateur, -trice.

peach [piːtʃ] n pêche f.

peach-tree [ˈpiːtʃtriː] n pêcher m.

peacock [ˈpiːkɔk] n paon m.

peahen [ˈpiːhen] n paonne f.

peak [piːk] n pic m, cime f, pointe f, visière f, apogée f, plus fort m; a maximum, de pointe.

peaked [ˈpiːkt] a à (en) pointe, pointu, hâve.

peal [piːl] n carillon m, volée de cloches f, coup m, grondement m; vti sonner; vi carillonner, gronder, retentir.

peanut [ˈpiːnʌt] n cacahuète f.

pear [pɛə] n poire f.

pearl [pəːl] n perle f.

pearly [ˈpəːli] a nacré, perlé.

pear-tree [ˈpɛətriː] n poirier m.

peasant [ˈpezənt] n paysan, -anne.

peasantry [ˈpezəntri] n paysans m pl.

peat [piːt] n tourbe f; — bog tourbière f.

pebble [ˈpebl] n galet m, caillou m.

peck [pek] n coup de bec m, bécot m; vt picoter, donner un coup de bec à, bécoter; vti manger du bout des lèvres; vi picorer.

peculiar [piˈkjuːliə] a particulier, excentrique, singulier.

peculiarity [piˌkjuːliˈæriti] n singularité f, particularité f.

pecuniary [piˈkjuːniəri] a pécuniaire, d'argent.

pedal [ˈpedl] n pédale f; vi pédaler.

pedant [ˈpedənt] n pédant(e) mf.

pedantic [piˈdæntik] a pédantesque, pédant.

pedantry [ˈpedəntri] n pédantisme m.

peddle [ˈpedl] vt colporter; vi faire le colportage.

peddler [ˈpedlə] n colporteur m, porteballe m; itinerant — dioula m.

pedestrian [piˈdestriən] n piéton m; a à pied, terre à terre, banal; — crossing passage clouté m.

pedigree [ˈpedigriː] n généalogie f, pedigree m.

pediment [ˈpedimənt] n fronton m.

peel [piːl] n peau f, écorce f, pelure f; vti peler; vt éplucher; vi s'écailler.

peep [piːp] n coup d'œil m, point du jour m, pépiement m, piaulement m; vi pépier, risquer un coup d'œil, se montrer; —hole n judas m.

peer [piə] n pair m, pareil, -eille, égal(e) mf; vi risquer un coup d'œil; to — at scruter.

peerage [ˈpiəridʒ] n pairie f.

peerless [ˈpiəlis] a incomparable, sans pareil.

peevish ['pi:viʃ] a bougon, revêche, irritable, maussade.

peevishness ['pi:viʃnis] n humeur bourrue f.

peg [peg] n cheville f, patère f, piquet m; **to come down a —** en rabattre; vt cheviller, marquer, accrocher; **— away** bûcher.

pellet ['pelit] n boulette f, pilule f, grain de plomb m.

pelt [pelt] n peau f; **at full —** à toutes jambes; vt bombarder; vi (rain) tomber à verse.

pen [pen] n parc m, plume f, stylo m; vt enfermer, parquer, écrire.

penal ['pi:nl] a pénal, punissable; **— servitude** n travaux forcés m pl.

penalty ['penlti] n amende f, peine f, sanction f, pénalité f; (football) penalty m; inconvénient m, rançon f.

penance ['penəns] n pénitence f.

pencil ['pensl] n crayon m, faisceau m; vt crayonner, marquer au crayon.

pendant ['pendənt] n pendant(if) m, pendeloque f, (flag) flamme f.

pending ['pendiŋ] prep pendant, en attendant.

pendulum ['pendjuləm] n pendule m, balancier m.

penetrate ['penitreit] vti pénétrer.

penetrating ['penitreitiŋ] a pénétrant, perçant.

penguin ['peŋgwin] n pingouin m.

penholder ['pen,houldə] n porteplume m.

penicillin [,peni'silin] n pénicilline f.

peninsula [pi'ninsjulə] n péninsule f.

penitence ['penitəns] n pénitence f.

penitent ['penitənt] an pénitent(e) mf; a contrit.

penitentiary [,peni'tenʃəri] n pénitencier m, prison f.

penknife ['pennaif] n canif m.

pen-name ['penneim] n pseudonyme m.

pennant ['penənt] n flamme f, banderole f.

penniless ['penilis] a sans le sou.

penny ['peni] n sou m, deux sous m pl; **—worth** pour deux sous; **—wise** a lésineur.

pension ['penʃən] n pension f, retraite f; vt pensionner, **to — off** mettre à la retraite.

pensive ['pensiv] a pensif.

pensiveness ['pensivnis] n rêverie f, air rêveur m.

pent [pent] a **— in** renfermé, confiné; **— up** contenu, refoulé.

Pentecost ['pentikɔst] n Pentecôte f.

penthouse ['penthaus] n appentis m, auvent m.

penurious [pi'njuəriəs] a pauvre, avare.

penury ['penjuri] n pénurie f, misère f.

peony ['piəni] n pivoine f.

people ['pi:pl] n peuple m, habitants m pl, gens m pl, personnes f pl, monde m, famille f, on, vous; vt peupler.

pep [pep] n vigueur f, allant m; **to — up** remonter.

pepper ['pepə] n poivre m; vt poivrer, cribler.

pepper-box, -pot ['pepəbɔks, -pɔt] n poivrière f.

peppermint ['pepəmint] n menthe poivrée f.

peppery ['pepəri] a poivré, emporté, colérique.

pep-pill ['pep'pil] n remontant m.

per [pə:] prep par, pour, à, par l'entremise de.

peradventure [pərəd'ventʃə] ad d'aventure, par hasard.

perambulate [pə'ræmbjuleit] vi déambuler, se promener.

perambulator ['præmbjuleitə] n voiture d'enfant f.

perceive [pə'si:v] vt percevoir, comprendre, s'apercevoir (de).

percentage [pə'sentidʒ] n pourcentage m, proportion f.

perceptible [pə'septəbl] a perceptible, sensible.

perception [pə'sepʃən] n perception f.

perch [pə:tʃ] n perche f, perchoir m; vi se percher, se jucher.

perchance [pə'tʃɑ:ns] ad par hasard.

percolate ['pə:kəleit] vt filtrer.

percolator ['pə:kəleitə] n percolateur m, filtre m.

percussion [pə:'kʌʃən] n percussion f, choc m.

perdition [pə:'diʃən] n ruine f, perte f.

peremptory [pə'remptəri] a péremptoire, catégorique, absolu.

perennial [pə'reniəl] a perpétuel, vivace.

perfect ['pə:fikt] a parfait.

perfect [pə'fekt] vt perfectionner, parfaire, achever.

perfection [pə'fekʃən] n perfection f.

perfidious [pə:'fidiəs] a perfide, traître.

perfidy ['pə:fidi] n perfidie f.

perforate ['pə:fəreit] vt perforer, percer.

perforation [,pə:fə'reiʃən] n perforation f, percement m.

perforce [pə'fɔ:s] ad de (par) force.

perform [pə'fɔ:m] vt remplir, exécuter; vti jouer.

performance [pə'fɔ:məns] n exécution f, (theatre) représentation f, (cine) séance f, exploit m, fonctionnement m, performance f.

performer [pə'fɔ:mə] n exécutant(e) mf, artiste mf.

perfume ['pə:fju:m] n parfum m.

perfume [pə'fju:m] vt parfumer.

perfumery [pə'fju:məri] n parfumerie f.

perfunctory [pə'fʌŋktəri] a de pure forme, superficiel, négligent.

perhaps [pə'hæps] *ad* peut-être.
peril ['peril] *n* péril *m*, danger *m*; **at your —** à vos risques et périls.
perilous ['periləs] *a* périlleux, dangereux.
period ['piəriəd] *n* période *f*, délai *m*, époque *f*, point *m*, phase *f*, style *m*; *pl* (med) règles *f pl*.
perish ['periʃ] *vi* périr, mourir, se détériorer.
perishable ['periʃəbl] *a* périssable, éphémère.
perished ['periʃt] *a* mort, détérioré.
peritonitis [.peritə'naitis] *n* péritonite *f*.
periwinkle ['peri.wiŋkl] *n* pervenche *f*, bigorneau *m*.
perjure ['pəːdʒə] *vt* **to — oneself** se parjurer.
perjurer ['pəːdʒərə] *n* parjure *mf*.
perjury ['pəːdʒəri] *n* parjure *m*, faux témoignage *m*.
perk [pəːk] *vt* **to — up** ravigoter, remettre le moral à; *vi* se ranimer, se retaper.
perky ['pəːki] *a* impertinent, coquet, dégagé, guilleret.
permanent ['pəːmənənt] *a* permanent, fixe.
permanent wave ['pəːmənənt'weiv] *n* ondulation *f* permanente.
permanently ['pəːmənəntli] *ad* de façon permanente, à titre définitif.
permeable ['pəːmiəbl] *a* perméable.
permeate ['pəːmieit] *vt* pénétrer; *vi* s'insinuer, filtrer.
permission [pə'miʃən] *n* permission *f*, autorisation *f*.
permit ['pəːmit] *n* permis *m*, autorisation *f*.
permit [pə'mit] *vt* permettre (à), autoriser.
pernicious [pəː'niʃəs] *a* pernicieux, fatal.
perpendicular [.pəːpən'dikjulə] *an* perpendiculaire *f*.
perpetrate ['pəːpitreit] *vt* commettre, perpétrer.
perpetration [.pəːpi'treiʃən] *n* perpétration *f*.
perpetrator ['pəːpitreitə] *n* auteur *m*.
perpetual [pə'petjuəl] *a* éternel, perpétuel.
perpetuate [pə'petjueit] *vt* perpétuer.
perpetuity [.pəːpi'tjuˈ(ː)iti] *n* perpétuité *f*.
perplex [pə'pleks] *vt* embarrasser.
perplexed [pə'plekst] *a* perplexe, embarrassé.
perplexity [pə'pleksiti] *n* perplexité *f*.
perquisite ['pəːkwizit] *n* profit *m*, pourboire *m*, casuel *m*, gratte *f*.
persecute ['pəːsikjuːt] *vt* persécuter.
persecution [.pəːsi'kjuːʃən] *n* persécution *f*.
perseverance [.pəːsi'viərəns] *n* persévérance *f*.

persevere [.pəːsi'viə] *vi* persévérer, s'obstiner.
persevering [.pəːsi'viəriŋ] *a* persévérant, assidu.
Persia ['pəːʃə] *n* Perse *f*.
Persian ['pəːʃən] *n* Persan(e) *mf*; *an* persan *m*.
persist [pə'sist] *vi* persister, s'obstiner, s'entêter.
persistency [pə'sistənsi] *n* persistance *f*, obstination *f*.
person ['pəːsn] *n* personne *f*.
personage ['pəːsnidʒ] *n* personnage *m*.
personal ['pəːsnl] *a* personnel, individuel.
personality [.pəːsə'næliti] *n* personnalité *f*, personnage *m*.
personification [pəː.sɔnifi'keiʃən] *n* personnification *f*.
personify [pəː'sɔnifai] *vt* personnifier.
personnel [.pəːsə'nel] *n* personnel *m*.
perspective [pə'spektiv] *n* perspective *f*.
perspicacious [.pəːspi'keiʃəs] *a* perspicace.
perspicacity [.pəːspi'kæsiti] *n* perspicacité *f*.
perspicuity [.pəːspi'kjuˈ(ː)iti] *n* clarté *f*, netteté *f*.
perspicuous [pə'spikjuəs] *a* clair, évident.
perspiration [.pəːspə'reiʃən] *n* transpiration *f*.
perspire [pəs'paiə] *vi* transpirer.
persuade [pə'sweid] *vt* persuader, décider.
persuasion [pə'sweiʒən] *n* persuasion *f*, conviction *f*, confession *f*.
persuasive [pə'sweisiv] *a* persuasif.
pert [pəːt] *a* effronté, impertinent.
pertinacious [.pəːti'neiʃəs] *a* opiniâtre, entêté, obstiné.
pertinacity [.pəːti'næsiti] *n* opiniâtreté *f*.
pertinence ['pəːtinəns] *n* pertinence *f*, à-propos *m*.
pertinent ['pəːtinənt] *a* pertinent, juste.
pertinently ['pəːtinəntli] *ad* pertinemment, à-propos.
perturb [pə'təːb] *vt* bouleverser, troubler, inquiéter.
perturbation [.pəːtəː'beiʃən] *n* bouleversement *m*, inquiétude *f*, trouble *m*.
perusal [pə'ruːzəl] *n* examen *m*, lecture *f*.
peruse [pə'ruːz] *vt* étudier, prendre connaissance de.
pervade [pəː'veid] *vt* pénétrer, animer, régner dans.
perverse [pə'vəːs] *a* pervers, contrariant.
perversion [pə'vəːʃən] *n* perversion *f*, travestissement *m*.
perversity [pə'vəːsiti] *n* perversité *f*, esprit de contradiction *m*.
pervert ['pəːvəːt] *n* perverti(e) *mf*, apostat *m*.

pervert [pə'vəːt] *vt* pervertir, fausser.

pervious ['pəːviəs] *a* perméable, accessible.

pessimism ['pesimizəm] *n* pessimisme *m*.

pessimistic [.pesi'mistik] *a* pessimiste.

pest [pest] *n* peste *f*, fléau *m*.

pester ['pestə] *vt* tracasser, importuner, infester.

pestilence ['pestiləns] *n* pestilence *f*.

pestilential [.pesti'lenʃəl] *a* pestilentiel, pernicieux.

pestle ['pesl] *n* pilon *m*; *vt* piler, broyer.

pet [pet] *a* animal *m* familier, favori *m*, chouchou *m*; to take the — prendre la mouche; *vt* caresser, choyer.

petal ['petl] *n* pétale *m*.

Peter ['piːtə] Pierre *m*.

peter out ['piːtə'aut] *vi* faire long feu, s'épuiser, s'arrêter.

petition [pə'tiʃən] *n* pétition *f*, prière *f*, demande *f*; *vt* adresser une pétition à.

petitioner [pə'tiʃənə] *n* pétitionaire *mf*, requérant(e) *mf*.

petrel ['petrəl] *n* pétrel *m*.

petrify ['petrifai] *vt* pétrifier.

petrol ['petrəl] *n* essence *f*.

petroleum [pi'trouliəm] *n* pétrole *m*.

petticoat ['petikout] *n* jupon *m*, jupe *f*.

pettifoggery ['petifɔgəri] *n* chicane *f*.

pettiness ['petinis] *n* mesquinerie *f*.

pettish ['petiʃ] *a* grincheux.

petty ['peti] *a* petit, mesquin; — **cash** menue monnaie *f*.

petty-officer ['peti'ɔfisə] *n* contre-maître *m*; *pl* maistrance *f*.

petulance ['petjuləns] *n* pétulance *f*, vivacité *f*.

petulant ['petjulənt] *a* pétulant, vif.

pew [pjuː] *n* banc *m*.

pewit ['piːwit] *n* vanneau *m*.

pewter ['pjuːtə] *n* étain *m*.

phantom ['fæntəm] *n* fantôme *m*; *a* illusoire.

Pharisee ['færisiː] *n* pharisien *m*.

pharyngitis [.færin'dʒaitis] *n* pharingite *f*.

pharynx ['færiŋks] *n* pharynx *m*.

phase [feiz] *n* phase *f*.

pheasant ['feznt] *n* faisan *m*, faisane *f*.

phenomenal [fi'nɔminl] *a* phénoménal.

phenomenon [fi'nɔminən] *n* phénomène *m*.

phial [faiəl] *n* fiole *f*.

philander [fi'lændə] *vi* papillonner, conter fleurette (à).

philanderer [fi'lændərə] *n* flirteur *m*.

philologist [fi'blədʒist] *n* philologue *m*.

philology [fi'blədʒi] *n* philologie *f*.

philosopher [fi'bsəfə] *n* philosophe *m*.

philosophy [fi'bsəfi] *n* philosophie

f; **moral** — morale *f*; **natural** — physique *f*.

philter ['filtə] *n* philtre *m*.

phlebitis [fli'baitis] *n* phlébite *f*.

phlegm [flem] *n* flegme *m*.

phlegmatic [fleg'mætik] *a* flegmatique.

phonetician [.fɔni'tiʃən] *n* phonéticien *m*.

phonetics [fə'netiks] *n* phonétique *f*.

phony ['founi] *a* drôle, faux.

phosphate ['fɔsfeit] *n* phosphate *m*.

phosphorous ['fɔsfərəs] *a* phosphoreux.

phosphorus ['fɔsfərəs] *n* phosphore *m*.

photograph ['foutəgraːf] *n* photographie *f*; *vt* photographier.

photographer [fə'tɔgrəfə] *n* photographe *m*.

photographic [.foutə'græfik] *a* photographique.

phrase [freiz] *n* phrase *f*, locution *f*, expression *f*; *vt* exprimer, rédiger.

phraseology [.freizi'ɔlədʒi] *n* phraséologie *f*.

phthisis ['θaisis] *n* phtisie *f*.

physic ['fizik] *n* (*fam*) médecine *f*, médicaments *m pl*.

physical ['fizikəl] *a* physique.

physician [fi'ziʃən] *n* médecin *m*.

physicist ['fizisist] *n* physicien, -ienne.

physics ['fiziks] *n* physique *f*.

physiognomy [.fizi'ɔnəmi] *n* physionomie *f*.

pianist ['piənist] *n* pianiste *mf*.

piano ['piænou] *n* piano *m*; *ad* piano; **grand** — piano à queue; **upright** — piano droit.

pick [pik] *n* pic *m*, pioche *f*, élite *f*, dessus du panier *m*; *vt* piocher, picorer, cueillir, choisir, trier, (lock) crocheter; to — out repérer, choisir, faire le tri de; to — up vt ramasser, prendre, relever, racoler, draguer; *vi* reprendre des forces.

pickaback ['pikabæk] *ad* sur le dos.

pickax ['pikæks] *n* pioche *f*.

picket ['pikit] *n* piquet *m*, pieu *m*.

picking ['pikiŋ] *n* cueillette *f*, épluchage *m*, crochetage *m*; *pl* bribes *f pl*, glanures *f pl*, gratte *f*.

pickle ['pikl] *n* saumure *f*, marinade *f*; *pl* condiments *m pl*, conserves au vinaigre *f pl*; *vt* conserver, mariner.

pickpocket ['pik.pɔkit] *n* pickpocket *m*, voleur à la tire *m*.

picnic ['piknik] *n* piquenique *m*; *vi* faire un piquenique.

pictorial [pik'tɔːriəl] *a* illustré, pittoresque.

picture ['piktʃə] *n* tableau *m*, image *f*; *pl* cinéma *m*; *vt* représenter, se figurer.

picturesque [.piktʃə'resk] *a* pittoresque.

picturesqueness [.piktʃə'resknis] *n* pittoresque *m*.

pie [pai] n pâté m, tourte f, tarte f.

piece [pi:s] n morceau m, pièce f; vt assembler, rapiécer.

piecemeal ['pi:smi:l] ad pièce à pièce, un à un.

piecework ['pi:swə:k] n travail à la pièce m.

pier [piə] n jetée f, pile f, pilier m.

pierce [piəs] vt percer, pénétrer.

piety ['paiəti] n piété f.

pig [pig] n porc m, pourceau m, cochon m.

pigeon ['pidʒin] n pigeon m; —hole n casier m; to —hole vt classer.

pigheaded ['pig'hedid] a buté, têtu.

pigsty ['pigstai] n porcherie f, étable f, bauge f.

pigtail ['pigteil] n natte f.

pike [paik] n pique f, brochet m, tourniquet m.

pikestaff ['paiksta:f] n hampe f.

pile [pail] n pieu m, pilotis m, pile f, (fam) fortune f, poil m; pl hémorroïdes f pl; vt empiler, entasser, (fam) charrier.

pilfer ['pilfə] vt chaparder.

pilferer ['pilfərə] n chapardeur, -euse.

pilfering ['pilfəriŋ] n chapardage m.

pilgrim ['pilgrim] n pèlerin(e) mf.

pilgrimage ['pilgrimidʒ] n pèlerinage m.

pill [pil] n pilule f.

pillage ['pilidʒ] n pillage m; vt piller, saccager.

pillar ['pilə] n pilier m, colonne f.

pillar-box ['piləbɔks] n boîte aux lettres f.

pill-box ['pilbɔks] n blockhaus m, boîte f à pilules.

pillow ['pilou] n oreiller m.

pillow-case ['piloukeis] n taie f.

pilot ['pailət] n pilote m; vt piloter.

pimple ['pimpl] n bouton m, pustule f.

pimply ['pimpli] a boutonneux.

pin [pin] n épingle f, cheville f, (fam) quille f; vt épingler, clouer, lier, accrocher, goupiller; —s and needles fourmis f pl.

pinafore ['pinəfɔ:] n tablier m.

pincers ['pinsəz] n pince f, tenailles f pl.

pinch [pintʃ] n pincée f, prise f, pincement m; vt pincer, blesser, gêner, chiper.

pincushion ['pin,kuʃin] n pelote à épingles f.

pine [pain] n pin m; vi languir, dépérir; to — for soupirer après, aspirer à.

pineapple ['pain,æpl] n ananas m.

pinion ['pinjən] n aileron m, aile f, (tec) pignon m; vt couper les ailes à, lier.

pink [piŋk] n œillet m; an rose m; vt percer; vi (motor) cliqueter.

pin-money ['pin,mʌni] n argent de poche m.

pinnacle ['pinəkl] n clocheton m, cime f, apogée f.

pinprick ['pinprik] n piqûre d'épingle f.

pint [paint] n pinte f.

pioneer [,paiə'niə] n pionnier m.

pious ['paiəs] a pieux.

pip [pip] n pépie f, pépin m, point m, cafard m.

pipe [paip] n tuyau m, pipe f, pipée f, sifflet m, chalumeau m; pl cornemuse f; vi jouer de la cornemuse, siffler, crier; vt jouer sur la cornemuse.

piper ['paipə] n joueur de cornemuse m.

pippin ['pipin] n reinette f.

piquancy ['pi:kənsi] n piquant m, sel m.

pique [pi:k] n pique f, dépit m; vt piquer, dépiter.

pirate ['paiərit] n pirate m.

pistol ['pistl] n pistolet m.

piston ['pistən] n piston m.

pit [pit] n trou m, puits m, fosse f, creux m, marque f, arène f, aisselle f; vt enfouir, mettre face à face, marquer, opposer.

pitch [pitʃ] n poix m, degré m, hauteur f, diapason m, comble m, terrain m, tangage m; a noir; vt dresser, poisser, régler le ton de, lancer, jeter; vi tanguer, tomber.

pitched [pitʃt] a rangé, en règle.

pitcher ['pitʃə] n cruche f, broc m.

pitchfork ['pitʃfɔ:k] n fourche f.

piteous ['pitiəs] a lamentable, piteux.

pitfall ['pitfɔ:l] n trappe f, traquenard m, piège m.

pith [piθ] n moelle f, essence f, vigueur f, sève f.

pitiable ['pitiəbl] a pitoyable.

pitiful ['pitiful] a compatissant, lamentable, qui fait pitié.

pitiless ['pitilis] a impitoyable, cruel.

pittance ['pitəns] n pitance f.

pitted ['pitid] a troué, marqué.

pity ['piti] n pitié f; it is a — c'est dommage; vt plaindre.

pivot ['pivət] n pivot m; vt monter sur pivot, faire pivoter; vi pivoter.

placard ['plæka:d] n affiche f; vt placarder, afficher, couvrir d'affiches.

placate [plə'keit] vt calmer, apaiser.

place [pleis] n place f, endroit m, lieu m, résidence f; vt placer, mettre, situer, poser, classer.

placebo [plə'si:bou] n remède factice m.

plagiarism ['pleidʒiərizəm] n plagiat m.

plagiarist ['pleidʒiərist] n plagiaire m.

plagiarize ['pleidʒiəraiz] vt plagier, contrefaire.

plague [pleig] n peste f, fléau m; vt tracasser.

plaice [pleis] n plie f, carrelet m.

plain [plein] n plaine f; a plan, plat,

clair, uni, franc, simple, commun, ordinaire; in — clothes en civil; she is — elle n'est pas belle; —**dealing** n loyauté f; —**spoken** a franc, rond, carré.

plainly ['pleinli] ad clairement, simplement, sans détours.

plainness ['pleinnis] n air m, commun, clarté f, netteté f, franchise f, simplicité f.

plaint [pleint] n plainte f.

plaintiff ['pleintif] n plaignant(e) mf, demandeur, -eresse.

plaintive ['pleintiv] a plaintif.

plait [plæt] n pli m, tresse f, natte f; vt plisser, natter.

plan [plæn] n plan m, projet m; vt relever, projeter, arrêter le plan de, combiner.

plane [plein] n platane m, rabot m, plan m, niveau m, avion m; a plan, uni; vt raboter, aplanir; vi voler, planer.

planet ['plænit] n planète f.

plank [plæŋk] n planche f, programme m.

plant [plɑːnt] n plante f, outillage m, machinerie f; vt planter (là), établir, fonder; to — out dépoter, déplanter.

plantation [plæn'teiʃən] n plantation f, bosquet m.

planter ['plɑːntə] n planteur m.

plash [plæʃ] n flac m, clapotis m, éclaboussure f; vi faire flac, clapoter, éclabousser.

plaster ['plɑːstə] n (em)plâtre m; vt plâtrer, enduire, couvrir.

plasterer ['plɑːstərə] n plâtrier m.

plastic ['plæstik] an plastique f.

plate [pleit] n plaque f, planche f, assiette f, vaisselle f, dentier m; vt plaquer; —ful n assiettée f; —**rack** n égouttoir m.

platform ['plætfɔːm] n plate-forme f, estrade f, quai m, trottoir m.

platinum ['plætinəm] n platine m.

platitude ['plætitjuːd] n platitude f, lieu commun m.

platoon [plə'tuːn] n peloton m, section f.

plausible ['plɔːzəbl] a plausible, vraisemblable.

plausibility [ˌplɔːzə'biliti] n plausibilité f.

play [plei] n jeu m, pièce f (de théâtre), carrière f; fair — franc jeu m; vti jouer; vⁱ folâtrer, gambader.

player ['pleiə] n joueur, -euse, acteur, -trice, exécutant(e) mf.

playful ['pleiful] a enjoué.

playground ['pleigraund] n terrain de jeu m, cour f.

playmate ['pleimeit] n camarade mf de jeu, ami(e) d'enfance.

playpen ['pleipen] n parc m (d'enfant).

playtime ['pleitaim] n récréation f.

plaything ['pleiθiŋ] n jouet m.

playwright ['pleirait] n auteur dramatique m.

plea [pliː] n argument m, plaidoyer m, excuse f.

plead [pliːd] vti plaider; vt prétexter, invoquer; vi s'avouer.

pleader ['pliːdə] n défenseur m, plaideur m.

pleasant ['pleznt] a agréable, aimable.

pleasantly ['plezntli] ad agréablement.

pleasantness ['plezntnis] n agrément m, affabilité m, charme m.

please [pliːz] vt plaire à; vi plaire; s'il vous plaît.

pleased [pliːzd] a très heureux, content.

pleasure ['pleʒə] n plaisir m, gré m, plaisance f.

pleat [pliːt] n pli m: vt plisser.

plebiscite ['plebisit] n plébiscite m.

pledge [pledʒ] n gage m, promesse f, toast m; vt mettre en gage, engager, porter un toast à.

plenipotentiary [ˌplenipə'tenʃəri] an plénipotentiaire m.

plentiful ['plentiful] a abondant, copieux.

plenty ['plenti] n abondance f.

pleurisy ['pluərisi] n pleurésie f.

pliability [ˌplaiə'biliti] n souplesse f, flexibilité f.

pliant ['plaiənt] a souple, flexible, complaisant.

pliers ['plaiəz] n pince f.

plight [plait] n (triste) état m; vt engager.

plighted ['plaitid] a engagé, lié.

plod [plod] n lourde tâche f; vi avancer (cheminer) péniblement, travailler laborieusement, bûcher.

plot [plot] n lopin m, complot m, intrigue f; vt tracer, relever; vti comploter; vi conspirer.

plotter ['plotə] n intrigant(e) mf, conspirateur, -trice.

plover ['plʌvə] n pluvier m.

plow [plau] n charrue f; vt labourer, rider, sillonner, (exam) refuser, recaler.

plowman ['plaumən] n laboureur m.

plowshare ['plauʃeə] n soc m.

pluck [plʌk] n courage m cran m; vt cueillir, arracher, plumer, tirer; to — up courage prendre courage.

plug [plʌg] n cheville f, bouchon m, tampon m, prise de courant f; vt boucher, tamponner.

plum [plʌm] n prune f, meilleur morceau m, poste etc.

plumage ['pluːmidʒ] n plumage m.

plumb [plʌm] n plomb m; a d'aplomb, vertical, tout pur; vt sonder; ad d'aplomb, juste, en plein.

plumber ['plʌmə] n plombier m.

plumb-line ['plʌmlain] n fil à plomb m.

plume [pluːm] n plume f, plumet m, panache m; to — oneself on se piquer de, se flatter de.

plummet ['plʌmit] n plomb m, sonde f.

plump [plʌmp] a rondelet, dodu, bien en chair; n chute f, bruit sourd m, plouf m; ad tout net; vt laisser tomber, flanquer; vi tomber, se laisser tomber lourdement.

plum-tree ['plʌmtri:] n prunier m.

plunder ['plʌndə] n pillage m, butin m; vt piller.

plunderer ['plʌndərə] n pillard m.

plunge [plʌndʒ] n plongeon m; vtl plonger; vi se jeter, s'enfoncer, piquer du nez, tanguer.

plural ['pluərəl] an pluriel m; a plural.

plus [plʌs] prep plus; a positif, actif.

plush [plʌʃ] n peluche f.

plutocracy [plu:'tɔkrəsi] n ploutocratie f.

ply [plai] n pli m, épaisseur f; vt manier, exercer, travailler, gorger, assaillir; vi faire la navette, faire le service.

plywood ['plaiwud] n contre-plaqué m.

pneumatic [nju(:)'mætik] an pneumatique m.

pneumonia [nju(:)'mouniə] n pneumonie f.

poach [poutʃ] vt pocher; vi braconner; vt braconner (dans); vi to — upon empiéter sur.

poacher ['poutʃə] n braconnier m.

poaching ['poutʃiŋ] n braconnage m.

pocket ['pɔkit] n poche f, sac m; —book calepin m, portefeuille m; vt empocher, mettre dans sa poche.

pock-marked ['pɔk,mɑːkt] a grêlé.

pod [pɔd] n cosse f, (coco) cabosse f; vt écosser, écaler.

poem ['pouim] n poème m.

poet ['pouit] n poète m.

poetry ['pouətri] n poésie f.

poignant ['pɔinənt] a âpre, piquant, poignant.

point [pɔint] n point m, pointe f, extrémité f, sujet m; (rl) aiguille f; —blank à bout portant; on — duty de faction; vt tailler, aiguiser, pointer, diriger, braquer; to — out indiquer, représenter, montrer du doigt, faire observer; to — at montrer du doigt; to — to annoncer, laisser supposer.

pointed ['pɔintid] a pointu, aigu, en pointe, mordant, direct.

pointer ['pɔintə] n aiguille f, baguette f, chien d'arrêt m, tuyau m, indication f.

pointless ['pɔintlis] a émoussé, qui manque d'à-propos, fade.

pointsman ['pɔintsmən] n aiguilleur m.

poise [pɔiz] n équilibre m, port m, dignité f, attente f; vt équilibrer, soupeser, balancer.

poison ['pɔizn] n poison m; vt empoisonner, intoxiquer.

poisoning ['pɔizniŋ] n empoisonnement m, intoxication f.

poisonous ['pɔiznəs] a empoisonné, toxique, (plant) vénéneux, (animal) venimeux.

poke [pouk] n coup m (de coude etc), poussée f; vt piquer, pousser du coude, tisonner, fourrer, passer; to — about fureter, fouiller; to — fun at se moquer de.

poker ['poukə] n tisonnier m, (game) poker m.

Poland ['poulənd] n Pologne f.

polar ['poulə] a polaire; — bear ours m blanc.

pole [poul] n perche f, échalas m, mât m, poteau m, montant m, timon m, pôle m; —jump saut m à la perche.

Pole [poul] n Polonais(e) mf.

police [pə'li:s] n police f; vt maintenir l'ordre dans, policer.

policeman [pə'li:smən] n agent m.

police station [pə'li:s'steiʃən] n commissariat m de police, poste m.

policy ['pɔlisi] n politique f, police d'assurance f.

polish ['pɔliʃ] n poli m, éclat m, cirage m, encaustique f, vernis m, blanc d'Espagne m, raffinement m; vt cirer, astiquer, fourbir, polir; to — off finir, régler son compte à, expédier.

Polish ['pouliʃ] an polonais m.

polite [pə'lait] a poli, cultivé, élégant.

politely [pə'laitli] ad poliment.

politeness [pə'laitnis] n politesse f, courtoisie.

political [pə'litikəl] a politique.

politician [,pɔli'tiʃən] n homme politique m, politicien m.

politics ['pɔlitiks] n politique f.

poll [poul] n scrutin m, vote m; vt obtenir les voix, étêter, écorner; vi voter.

pollute [pə'lu:t] vt polluer, profaner.

poltroon [pɔl'tru:n] n poltron m.

polygamist [pɔ'ligəmist] n polygame m.

polygamy [pɔ'ligəmi] n polygamie f.

polyglot ['pɔliglɔt] an polyglotte mf.

polygon ['pɔligən] n polygone m.

pomegranate ['pɔmi,grænit] n grenade f.

pomp [pɔmp] n pompe f, faste m, apparat m.

pomposity [pɔm'pɔsiti] n solennité f, pompe f, suffisance f, emphase f.

pompous ['pɔmpəs] a pompeux, suffisant, ampoulé.

pond [pɔnd] n bassin m, étang m, vivier m.

ponder ['pɔndə] vt peser, réfléchir sur, considérer; vi ruminer, réfléchir.

ponderous ['pɔndərəs] a pesant, lourd.

pontiff ['pɔntif] n pontife m, prélat m.

pontificate [pɔn'tifikeit] n pontificat m; vi pontifier.
pontoon [pɔn'tu:n] n ponton m.
pontoon bridge [pɔn'tu:nbridʒ] n pont de bateaux m.
pony ['pouni] n poney m.
poodle ['pu:dl] n caniche mf.
pooh-pooh [pu:'pu:] vt tourner en dérision; excl bah!
pool [pu:l] n mare f, flaque f, (swimming-) piscine f, (games) poule f, fonds commun m, cartel m; vt mettre en commun, répartir.
poop [pu:p] n poupe f, dunette f.
poor [puə] a pauvre, malheureux, médiocre, maigre, piètre, faible; the — les pauvres.
poorly ['puəli] ad tout doucement, pas fort, médiocrement; a souffrant.
poorness ['puənis] n pauvreté f, manque m, infériorité f.
pop [pɔp] n bruit sec m; excl pan! vi sauter, péter, éclater; vt faire sauter, fourrer, mettre au clou.
pope [poup] n pape m, pope m.
popery ['poupəri] n papisme m.
poplar ['pɔplə] n peuplier m.
poplin ['pɔplin] n popeline f.
poppy ['pɔpi] n coquelicot m, pavot m.
pop-song ['pɔpsɔŋ] n chanson f (à la mode).
populace ['pɔpjuləs] n peuple m, populace f.
popular ['pɔpjulə] a populaire, aimé, couru, à la mode.
popularity [‚pɔpju'læriti] n popularité f.
popularize ['pɔpjuləraiz] vt populariser, vulgariser.
populate ['pɔpjuleit] vt peupler.
population [‚pɔpju'leiʃən] n population f.
populous ['pɔpjuləs] a populeux.
porch [pɔːtʃ] n porche m, marquise f.
porcupine ['pɔːkjupain] n porc-épic m.
pore [pɔː] n pore m; vi to — over s'absorber dans.
pork [pɔːk] n porc m; —-butcher n charcutier m.
porous ['pɔːrəs] a poreux, perméable.
porpoise ['pɔːpəs] n marsouin m.
porridge ['pɔridʒ] n bouillie d'avoine f.
porringer ['pɔrindʒə] n écuelle f.
port [pɔːt] n port m; home — port d'attache; sabord m, bâbord m, allure f; (wine) porto m; vt mettre à bâbord, présenter; vi venir sur bâbord.
portable ['pɔːtəbl] a portatif, transportable.
portal ['pɔːtl] n portail m.
portcullis [pɔːt'kʌlis] n herse f.
portend [pɔː'tend] vt présager, faire pressentir, annoncer.
portent ['pɔːtent] n présage m.
portentous [pɔː'tentəs] a formidable, menaçant, de mauvais augure.

porter ['pɔːtə] n portier m, concierge m, porteur m, chasseur m.
porterage ['pɔːtəridʒ] n factage m, transport m.
portfolio [pɔːt'fouliou] n portefeuille m, chemise f, serviette f, carton m.
porthole ['pɔːthoul] n hublot m, sabord m.
portico ['pɔːtikou] n portique m.
portion ['pɔːʃən] n portion f, part f, partie f, dot f; vt partager, doter.
portly ['pɔːtli] a corpulent, imposant.
portmanteau [pɔːt'mæntou] n valise f.
portrait ['pɔːtrit] n portrait m.
portray [pɔː'trei] vt faire le portrait de, (dé)peindre.
Portugal ['pɔːtjugəl] n Portugal m.
Portuguese [‚pɔːtju'giːz] an Portugais(e).
pose [pouz] n pose f, affectation f; vti poser, (fam) coller; to — as s'ériger en, se faire passer pour.
poser ['pouzə] n question embarrassante f, colle f.
position [pə'ziʃən] n position f, condition f, place f, état m.
positive ['pɔzətiv] a positif, catégorique, formel, authentique.
possess [pə'zes] vt posséder, tenir, s'approprier, avoir.
possession [pə'zeʃən] n possession f.
possessive [pə'zesiv] a possessif.
possibility [‚pɔsə'biliti] n possibilité f, éventualité f.
possible ['pɔsəbl] an possible m; a éventuel.
possibly ['pɔsəbli] ad peut-être.
post [poust] n poste f, courrier m, levée f, mât m, poteau m, place f, emploi m; vt mettre à la poste, poster, affecter; first — appel m; last — sonnerie aux morts f, retraite f; — no bills défense d'afficher.
postage ['poustidʒ] n affranchissement m; — stamp timbre (-poste) m.
postcard ['poustkaːd] n carte postale f.
post-date ['poust'deit] vt postdater.
poster ['poustə] n affiche f, afficheur m.
posterior [pɔs'tiəriə] an postérieur m.
posterity [pɔs'teriti] n postérité f.
postern ['poustəːn] n poterne f, porte de derrière f.
post-free ['poust'friː] a franco, en franchise.
posthumous ['pɔstjuməs] a posthume.
postman ['poustmən] n facteur m.
postmark ['poustmaːk] n timbre d'oblitération m; vt timbrer.
postmaster ['poust‚maːstə] n receveur m, directeur des postes m.
post-mortem ['poust'mɔːtəm] n autopsie f.
post office ['poust ɔfis] n (bureau m de) poste f.

post-paid ['poust'peid] *a* port payé.

postpone [poust'poun] *vt* ajourner, remettre, reculer.

postscript ['pousskript] *n* postscriptum *m*.

postulate ['postjulit] *n* postulat *m*; ['postjuleit] *vt* postuler, demander, stipuler.

posture ['postʃə] *n* posture *f*, état *m*, attitude *f*.

posy ['pouzi] *n* petit bouquet *m*.

pot [pot] *n* pot *m*, marmite *f*.

potash ['potæʃ] *n* potasse *f*.

potato [pə'teitou] *n* pomme de terre *f*.

pot-bellied ['pot,belid] *a* ventru, bedonnant.

pot-boiler ['pot,boilə] *n* besogne *f* alimentaire.

potent ['poutənt] *a* puissant, fort, violent.

potential [pə'tenʃəl] *an* potentiel *m*, possible *m*; *a* en puissance, latent.

potentiality [pə,tenʃi'æliti] *n* virtualité *f*, potentialité *f*, potentiel *m*.

pother ['poðə] *n* nuage *m*, tapage *m*, embarras *m* *pl*.

potion ['pouʃən] *n* potion *f*, sirop *m*, philtre *m*.

pot-luck ['pot'lʌk] *n* fortune du pot *f*.

potter ['potə] *n* potier *m*; *vi* baguenauder, bricoler.

pottery ['potəri] *n* poterie *f*.

pouch [pautʃ] *n* blague *f*, cartouchière *f*, sac *m*, poche *f*, bourse *f*.

poulterer ['poultərə] *n* marchand de volailles *m*.

poultice ['poultis] *n* cataplasme *m*.

poultry ['poultri] *n* volaille *f*; —-yard *n* basse-cour *f*.

pounce [pauns] *n* serre *f*, attaque *f*; *vt* poncer; **to — on** fondre sur, sauter sur.

pound [paund] *n* livre *f*, fourrière *f*, enclos *m*; *vt* piler, broyer, (*mil*) pilonner.

pour [po:] *n* pluie torrentielle *f*; *vt* verser; *vi* se jeter, pleuvoir à verse.

pout [paut] *n* moue *f*, bouderie *f*; *vi* faire la moue, bouder.

poverty ['povəti] *n* pauvreté *f*, rareté *f*, misère *f*.

powder ['paudə] *n* poudre *f*; *vt* (sau)poudrer, pulvériser.

powdered ['paudəd] *a* en poudre.

powder-magazine ['paudəmægə,zi:-n] *n* poudrière *f*.

powder-puff ['paudəpʌf] *n* houppe *f*.

powdery ['paudəri] *a* poudreux, friable.

power ['pauə] *n* pouvoir *m*, puissance *f*, faculté *f*, vigueur *f*, (*el*) force *f*; *vt* actionner.

powerful ['pauəful] *a* puissant, énergique, vigoureux.

powerlessness ['pauəlisnis] *n* impuissance *f*, inefficacité *f*.

practicable ['præktikəbl] *a* praticable, faisable, pratique.

practical ['præktikəl] *a* pratique.

practice ['præktis] *n* pratique *f*, étude *f*, clientèle *f*, usage *m*, habitude *f*, exercice *m*, entraînement *m*.

practice ['præktis] *vt* pratiquer, exercer, s'exercer à, étudier; *vi* s'entraîner, faire des exercices.

practitioner [præk'tiʃnə] *n* praticien *m*; **general —** omnipraticien *m*.

prairie ['prɛəri] *n* prairie *f*, savane *f*.

praise [preiz] *n* éloge *m*, louange *f*; *vt* louer, glorifier.

praiseworthy ['preiz,wə:ði] *a* louable.

prance [pra:ns] *vi* se cabrer, piaffer, se pavaner.

prank [præŋk] *n* farce *f*, niche *f*, fredaine *f*, les cents coups *m* *pl*; *vt* orner, pavoiser.

prate [preit] *n* bavardage *m*; *vi* bavarder.

prattle ['prætl] *n* babil *m*; *vi* babiller, jaser.

prattling ['prætliŋ] *a* jaseur.

prawn [pro:n] *n* crevette rose *f*.

pray [prei] *vti* prier.

prayer [prɛə] *n* prière *f*.

prayer book ['prɛəbuk] *n* rituel *m*, livre de messe *m*, paroissien *m*.

preach [pri:tʃ] *vti* prêcher.

preamble [pri:'æmbl] *n* préambule *m*.

precarious [pri'kɛəriəs] *a* précaire, incertain.

precariousness [pri'kɛəriəsnis] *n* précarité *f*.

precaution [pri'ko:ʃən] *n* précaution *f*.

precede [pri(:)'si:d] *vt* précéder, préfacer.

precedence ['presidəns] *n* préséance *f*, pas *m*.

precedent ['presidənt] *n* précédent *m*.

precept ['pri:sept] *n* précepte *m*.

preceptor [pri'septə] *n* précepteur *m*.

precincts ['pri:siŋkts] *n* *pl* enceinte *f*, limites *f* *pl*, circonscription *f* électorale.

precious ['preʃəs] *a* précieux, de grand prix.

preciousness ['preʃəsnis] *n* haute valeur *f*, préciosité *f*.

precipice ['presipis] *n* précipice *m*.

precipitate [pri'sipitit] *n* précipité *m*; [pri'sipiteit] *vt* précipiter, brusquer.

precipitation [pri,sipi'teiʃən] *n* précipitation *f*.

precipitous [pri'sipitəs] *a* à pic, escarpé.

precise [pri'sais] *a* précis, exact, pointilleux.

precisely [pri'saisli] *ad* précisément, avec précision.

precision [pri'siʒən] *n* précision *f*.

preclude [pri'klu:d] *vt* exclure, prévenir, priver.

precocious [pri'kouʃəs] *a* précoce.

precociousness [pri'kouʃəsnis] *n* précocité *f*.

precursor [pri(:)'kə:sə] n précurseur m, avant-coureur m, devancier m.
predate [pri'deit] vt antidater.
predatory ['predətəri] a rapace, de proie, de brigand.
predecessor [pri:disesə] n prédécesseur m.
predicament [pri'dikəmənt] n difficulté f, situation fâcheuse f.
predict [pri'dikt] vt prédire.
predilection [.pri:di'lekʃən] n predilection f.
predispose ['pri:dis'pouz] vt prédisposer.
predisposition ['pri:.dispə'ziʃən] n prédisposition f.
predominate [pri'dɔmineit] vi prédominer.
pre-eminence [pri(:)'eminəns] n prééminence f.
preen [pri:n] to — oneself se bichonner, se faire beau, faire des grâces, se piquer (de on).
preface ['prefis] n préface f; vt préfacer, préluder à.
prefect ['pri:fekt] n préfet m.
prefer [pri'fə:] vt préférer, aimer mieux, avancer.
preferably ['prefərəbli] ad de préférence.
preference ['prefərəns] n préférence f.
preferential [.prefə'renʃəl] a préférentiel, de faveur.
preferment [pri'fə:mənt] n avancement m.
pregnancy ['pregnənsi] n grossesse f.
pregnant ['pregnənt] a enceinte, grosse, fertile, plein.
prejudice ['predʒudis] n préjudice m, tort m, préjugé m; vt faire tort à, prévenir.
prejudicial [.predʒu'diʃəl] a préjudiciable, nuisible.
prelate ['prelit] n prélat m.
preliminary [pri'liminəri] an préliminaire m; a préalable; n prélude m; pl préliminaires m pl.
prelude ['prelju:d] n prélude m; vi préluder (à); vt annoncer.
premature [.premə'tjuə] a prématuré.
prematurely [.premə'tjuəli] ad prématurément.
premeditate [pri(:)'mediteit] vt préméditer.
premeditation [pri(:).medi'teiʃən] n préméditation f.
premier ['premjə] a premier; n premier ministre m, président du conseil m.
premise ['premis] n prémisse f; pl maison f, lieux m pl, local m.
premium ['pri:mjəm] n prime f, boni m; to be at a — faire prime.
preoccupation [pri(:).ɔkju'peiʃən] n préoccupation f.
preoccupied [pri(:)'ɔkjupaid] a préoccupé.
preparation [.prepə'reiʃən] n pré-

paration f; pl préparatifs m pl.
preparatory [pri'pærətəri] a préparatoire, préalable.
prepare [pri'pɛə] vt préparer, apprêter; vi se préparer, se disposer (à).
prepay ['pri:'pei] vt payer d'avance.
preponderance [pri'pɔndərəns] n prépondérance f.
preponderate [pri'pɔndəreit] vi l'emporter (sur over).
preposition [.prepə'ziʃən] n préposition f.
prepossessing [.pri:pə'zesiŋ] a captivant, prévenant.
preposterous [pri'pɔstərəs] a absurde, saugrenu.
prerequisite ['pri:'rekwizit] n condition préalable f; a nécessaire.
prerogative [pri'rɔgətiv] n prérogative f, apanage m.
presage ['presidʒ] n présage m, pressentiment m, vt présager, annoncer, augurer.
prescribe [pris'kraib] vt prescrire, ordonner.
prescription [pris'kripʃən] n ordonnance f, prescription f, ordre m.
presence ['prezns] n présence f, distinction f, maintien m, prestance f.
present ['preznt] n cadeau m, présent m; a présent.
present [pri'zent] vt présenter, offrir, faire cadeau de, soumettre.
presentation [.prezen'teiʃən] n présentation f, don m, remise f, cadeau-souvenir m.
presentiment [pri'zentimənt] n pressentiment m.
presently ['prezntli] ad avant (sous) peu, tout à l'heure, bientôt.
preservation [.prezə(:)'veiʃən] n préservation f, conservation f.
preservative [pri'zə:vətiv] an préservatif m.
preserve [pri'zə:v] n chasse (pêche) gardée f; pl conserves f pl, confiture f; vt préserver, conserver, confire, maintenir, garder, observer, garantir (de from).
preside [pri'zaid] vi présider.
presidency ['prezidənsi] n présidence f.
president ['prezidənt] n président(e) mf.
press [pres] n presse f, pressoir m, pression f, foule f, hâte f, placard m, imprimerie f; vt appuyer sur, presser, serrer, pressurer, donner un coup de fer à; vi appuyer, se serrer, peser.
press-button ['pres'bʌtn] n bouton pression m.
pressing ['presiŋ] a pressant, urgent; n pressage m, pression f.
pressure ['preʃə] n pression f, poussée f, urgence f.
pressure-cooker ['preʃə.kukə] n cocotte minute f.
prestige [pres'ti:ʒ] n prestige, embarras m, tension f.

prestressed ['pri'strest] *a* précontraint.

presume [pri'zju:m] *vt* présumer, supposer, se permettre de croire, aimer à croire; **to — on** se prévaloir de, abuser de.

presumption [pri'zʌmpʃən] *n* présomption *f*.

presumptive [pri'zʌmptiv] *a* présomptif.

presumptuous [pri'zʌmptjuəs] *a* présomptueux.

pretend [pri'tend] *vt* feindre, faire semblant de, simuler, prétendre.

pretender [pri'tendə] *n* prétendant *m*, soupirant *m*.

pretense [pri'tens] *n* prétence *f*, prétexte *m*, (faux) semblant *m*.

pretension [pri'tenʃən] *n* prétention *f*.

pretentious [pri'tenʃəs] *a* prétentieux.

pretext ['pri:tekst] *n* prétexte *m*.

prettiness ['pritinis] *n* joliesse *f*, mignardise *f*.

pretty ['priti] *a* joli, beau, mignon, gentil; *ad* à peu près, assez.

prevail [pri'veil] *vi* l'emporter (sur over), prévaloir (contre, sur over), régner; **to — upon s.o. to** amener qn à, décider qn à, persuader à qn de.

prevailing [pri'veiliŋ] *a* courant, régnant, général.

prevalent ['prevələnt] *a* prédominant, répandu.

prevaricate [pri'værikeit] *vi* tergiverser, ergoter, mentir.

prevarication [pri,væri'keiʃən] *n* chicane *f*, tergiversation *f*, mensonge *m*.

prevent [pri'vent] *vt* empêcher, prévenir.

prevention [pri'venʃən] *n* empêchement *m*, protection *f*.

preventive [pri'ventiv] *an* préventif *m*.

preview ['pri:vju:] *n* exhibition préalable *f*, avant-première *f*.

previous ['pri:viəs] *a* précédent, préalable, antérieur.

previously ['pri:viəsli] *ad* précédemment, auparavant, au préalable.

prey [prei] *n* proie *f*; **to — upon** vivre sur, dévorer.

price [prais] *n* prix *m*; *vt* mettre un prix à, estimer.

priceless ['praislis] *a* sans prix, impayable.

prick [prik] *n* piqûre *f*, remords *m*; *vt* piquer, tendre, dresser.

pricker ['prikə] *n* poinçon *m*.

prickle ['prikl] *n* épine *f*, piquant *m*, picotement *m*; *vti* piquer, picoter.

pride [praid] *n* orgueil *m*, fierté *f*; **to — oneself on** s'enorgueillir de, se piquer de.

priest [pri:st] *n* prêtre *m*, prêtresse *f*.

priesthood ['pri:sthud] *n* prêtrise *f*.

prig [prig] *n* poseur *m*.

priggish ['prigiʃ] *a* pédantesque, poseur, bégueule, suffisant.

priggishness ['prigiʃnis] *n* bégueulerie *f*, suffisance *f*.

prim [prim] *a* affecté, collet monté, compassé.

primary ['praiməri] *a* primaire, premier, primitif, brut.

primate ['praimit] *n* primat *m*.

prime [praim] *n* fleur *f* (de l'âge), force *f*, commencement *m*; *a* premier, primordial, de première qualité; *vt* préparer, (engine) amorcer.

primer ['praimə] *n* abécédaire *m*, éléments *m pl*.

primeval [prai'mi:vəl] *a* primordial, primitif, vierge.

primitive ['primitiv] *a* primitif (-ve), primaire.

primness ['primnis] *n* affectation *f*, air pincé *m*, air collet monté *m*.

primrose ['primrouz] *n* primevère *f*.

prince [prins] *n* prince *m*.

princely ['prinsli] *a* princier, royal.

princess ['prinses] *n* princesse *f*.

principal ['prinsəpəl] *an* principal *m*; *n* directeur *m*, chef *m*.

principality [,prinsi'pæliti] *n* principauté *f*.

principle ['prinsəpl] *n* principe *m*.

print [print] *n* empreinte *f*, imprimé *m*, gravure *f*, estampe *f*, impression *f*, épreuve *f*, (tissu *m*) imprimé (*m*).

printer ['printə] *n* imprimeur *m*, typographe *m*.

printing ['printiŋ] *n* impression *f*, imprimerie *f*, tirage *m*, typographie *f*; **— office** *n* imprimerie *f*.

prior ['praiə] *n* prieur *m*; *a* antérieur, préalable; *ad* antérieurement (à to).

prism ['prizəm] *n* prisme *m*.

prison ['prizn] *n* prison *f*.

prisoner ['priznə] *n* prisonnier, -ière.

privacy ['praivəsi] *n* intimité *f*, solitude *f*, secret *m*.

private ['praivit] *n* soldat *m* sans grade, particulier, -ière; *a* privé, personnel, intime, confidentiel, retiré, particulier.

privately ['praivitli] *ad* en particulier, dans l'intimité, en confidence.

privation [prai'veiʃən] *n* privation *f*, manque *m*.

privet ['privit] *n* troène *m*.

privilege ['privilidʒ] *n* privilège *m*, bonne fortune *f*.

privileged ['privilidʒd] *a* privilégié.

privy ['privi] *n* privé *m*, cabinets *m pl*.

prize [praiz] *n* prix *m*, (at sea) prise *f*; *vt* apprécier, évaluer, faire grand cas de.

pro [prou] *prep* pour; *an* professionel, -elle.

probability [,probə'biliti] *n* probabilité *f*, vraisemblance *f*.

probable ['probəbl] *a* probable, vraisemblable.

probation [prə'beiʃən] *n* noviciat *m*,

épreuve *f*, surveillance *f*, stage *m*.

probe [proub] *n* sonde *f*; enquête *f*, sondage *m*; *vt* sonder, examiner, approfondir.

probity ['proubiti] *n* probité *f*.

problem ['problem] *n* problème *m*.

problematic [.probli'mætik] *a* problématique, incertain.

procedure [prə'si:dʒə] *n* procédure *f*, façon d'agir *f*.

proceed [prə'si:d] *vi* continuer, poursuivre, passer, se rendre, venir, procéder, se prendre.

proceeding [prə'si:diŋ] *n* procédé *m*, façon d'agir *f*; *pl* poursuites *f pl*, débats *m pl*, réunion *f*, cérémonie *f*.

proceeds ['prousi:dz] *n pl* produit *m*, recette *f*.

process ['prouses] *n* cours *m*, marche *f*, procédé *m*, processus *m*; *vt* apprêter.

procession [prə'seʃən] *n* procession *f*, défilé *m*, cortège *m*.

proclaim [prə'kleim] *vt* proclamer, déclarer, trahir.

proclamation [.proklə'meiʃən] *n* proclamation *f*.

procrastinate [prou'kræstineit] *vi* temporiser.

procrastination [prou.kræsti'neiʃən] *n* temporisation *f*.

procuration [.prokjuə'reiʃən] *n* procuration *f*, commission *f*, obtention *f*.

procure [prə'kjuə] *vt* obtenir, (se) procurer.

procurement [prə'kjuəmənt] *n* approvisionnement *m* (d'un service).

procurer [prə'kjuərə] *n* proxénète *m*.

prod [prod] *vt* bourrer les côtes à, pousser.

prodigal ['prodigəl] *an* prodigue *mf*.

prodigality [.prodi'gæliti] *n* prodigalité *f*.

prodigious [prə'didʒəs] *a* prodigieux, mirobolant.

prodigy ['prodidʒi] *n* prodige *m*, merveille *f*.

produce ['prodju:s] *n* produit *m*, rendement *m*, fruits *m pl*, denrées *f pl*.

produce [prə'dju:s] *vt* produire, présenter, provoquer, *(theatre)* monter, mettre en scène.

producer [prə'dju:sə] *n* producteur, -trice, metteur en scène *m*.

product ['prodəkt] *n* produit *m*, résultat *m*.

production [prə'dʌkʃən] *n* production *f*, produit *m*, œuvre *f*, (re)présentation *f*, mise en scène *f*, fabrication *f*.

productive [prə'dʌktiv] *a* productif, qui rapporte, fécond.

profane [prə'fein] *a* profane, impie; *vi* profaner, violer.

profanity [prə'fæniti] *n* impiété *f*, blasphème *m*.

profess [prə'fes] *vt* professer, faire profession de, exercer, prétendre; **to —** to be se faire passer pour.

professed [prə'fest] *a* déclaré, avoué, soi-disant.

profession [prə'feʃən] *n* profession *f*, carrière *f*, métier *m*, déclaration *f*, affirmation *f*.

professional [prə'feʃənl] *an* professionel, -elle; *a* de carrière, de métier.

professor [prə'fesə] *n* professeur *m* (d'université).

proffer ['profə] *vt* offrir, présenter.

proficiency [prə'fiʃənsi] *n* aptitude *f*, compétence *f*.

proficient [prə'fiʃənt] *a* bon, fort, compétent, capable.

profile ['proufail] *n* profil *m*.

profit ['profit] *n* profit *m*, gain *m*, bénéfice(s) *m* (*pl*); *vti* profiter (à, de by).

profitable ['profitəbl] *a* profitable, lucratif, avantageux.

profiteer [.profi'tiə] *n* mercanti *m*, exploitation *f*, mercantilisme *m*.

profligacy ['profligəsi] *n* débauche *f*.

profligate ['profligit] *an* débauché(e) *mf*, libertin(e) *mf*.

profound [prə'faund] *a* profond, approfondi.

profoundly [prə'faundli] *ad* profondément.

profuse [prə'fju:s] *a* prodigue, copieux, excessif.

profusely [prə'fu:sli] abondamment.

profusion [prə'fju:ʒən] *n* profusion *f*, abondance *f*.

progeny ['prodʒini] *n* rejeton *m*, progéniture *f*.

prognostic [prəg'nostik] *n* prognostic *m*.

prognosticate [prəg'nostikeit] *vt* prognostiquer, prédire.

program ['prougræm] *n* programme *m*.

progress ['prougres] *n* progrès *m*, cours *m*.

progress [prə'gres] *vi* (s')avancer, progresser.

progression [prə'greʃən] *n* progression *f*.

progressive [prə'gresiv] *a* progressif, de progrès, progressiste, d'avant-garde.

prohibit [prə'hibit] *vt* défendre, interdire (de).

prohibition [.proui'biʃən] *n* prohibition *f*, défense *f*, interdiction *f*.

prohibitive [prə'hibitiv] *a* prohibitif, inabordable.

project ['prodʒekt] *n* projet *m*.

project [prə'dʒekt] *vt* projeter; *vi* s'avancer, faire saillie.

projectile [prə'dʒektail] *n* projectile *m*.

projection [prə'dʒekʃən] *n* projection *f*, saillie *f*.

projector [prə'dʒektə] *n* lanceur *m*, projecteur *m*.

proletarian [.proule'tɛəriən] *an* prolétaire *mf*.

proletariat [.proule'tɛəriət] *n* prolétariat *m*.

prolific [prə'lifik] *a* prolifique, fécond.

prolix ['prouliks] *a* prolixe.

prolong [prə'lɒŋ] *vt* allonger, prolonger.

prolongation [.proulɒŋ'geiʃən] *n* prolongation *f*, prolongement *m*.

promenade [.prɔmi'nɑːd] *n* promenade *f*, esplanade *f*, promenoir *m*; *vi* se promener.

prominence ['prɔminəns] *n* (pro) éminence *f*, importance *f*.

prominent ['prɔminənt] *a* saillant, éminent, en vue, proéminent.

promiscuity [.promis'kju(:)iti] *n* promiscuité *f*.

promiscuous [prə'miskjuəs] *a* confus, mêlé, en commun.

promise ['prɔmis] *n* promesse *f*; *vt* promettre.

promising ['prɔmisiŋ] *a* qui promet, prometteur.

promontory ['prɔməntri] *n* promontoire *m*.

promote [prə'mout] *vt* promouvoir, nommer, avancer, encourager, soutenir.

promoter [prə'moutə] *n* promoteur *m*, lanceur *m*, auteur *m*.

promotion [prə'mouʃən] *n* avancement *m*, promotion *f*.

prompt [prɔmpt] *a* actif, prompt; *vt* pousser, inspirer, souffler.

prompter ['prɔmptə] *n* souffleur *m*; —'s box trou du souffleur m.

promptitude ['prɔmptitjuːd] *n* promptitude *f*, empressement *m*.

prone [proun] *a* couché sur le ventre, porté (à to).

prong [prɔŋ] *n* branche *f*, dent *f*, fourchon *m*.

pronoun ['prounaun] *n* pronom *m*.

pronounce [prə'nauns] *vt* prononcer, déclarer.

pronouncement [prə'naunsmənt] *n* déclaration *f*.

pronunciation [prə.nʌnsi'eiʃən] *n* prononciation *f*.

proof [pruːf] *n* preuve *f*, épreuve *f*; *a* à l'épreuve de, à l'abri (de **against**), imperméable, étanche, insensible; *vt* imperméabiliser.

prop [prɔp] *n* étai *m*, tuteur *m*, soutien *m*; *vt* étayer, soutenir, appuyer.

propaganda [.prɔpə'gændə] *n* propagande *f*.

propagate ['prɔpəgeit] *vt* propager, répandre.

propagation [.prɔpə'geiʃən] *n* propagation *f*, dissémination *f*.

propel [prə'pel] *vt* lancer, propulser.

propeller [prə'pelə] *n* hélice *f*.

propensity [prə'pensiti] *n* penchant *m*, inclination *f*, tendance *f* (à, vers **to, toward**).

proper ['prɔpə] *a* propre, approprié, décent, vrai, correct, convenable, bon, opportun.

properly ['prɔpəli] *ad* bien, comme il faut, convenablement, correctement, complètement.

property ['prɔpəti] *n* propriété *f*, biens *m pl*, immeuble *m*; *pl* accessoires *m pl*; —**man** *n* machiniste *m*.

prophecy ['prɔfisi] *n* prophétie *f*.

prophesy ['prɔfisai] *vti* prophétiser; *vt* prédire.

prophet ['prɔfit] *n* prophète *m*.

propinquity [prə'piŋkwiti] *n* voisinage *m*, proche parenté *f*, ressemblance *f*.

propitiate [prə'piʃieit] *vt* apaiser, se concilier.

propitious [prə'piʃəs] *a* propice, favorable.

proportion [prə'pɔːʃən] *n* proportion *f*, rapport *m*, part *f*; *vt* proportionner.

proportional [prə'pɔːʃənl] *a* proportionnel, proportionné.

proposal [prə'pouzəl] *n* offre *f*, proposition *f*, projet *m*, demande en mariage *f*.

propose [prə'pouz] *vt* (se) proposer; *vi* demander en mariage.

proposition [.prɔpə'ziʃən] *n* proposition *f*, affaire *f*, entreprise *f*.

propound [prə'paund] *vt* proposer, produire, exposer, émettre.

proprietary [prə'praiətəri] *a* possédant, de propriétaire, de propriété.

proprietor [prə'praiətə] *n* propriétaire *mf*.

propriety [prə'praiəti] *n* convenances *f pl*, bienséance *f*, propriété *f*, correction *f*.

proscribe [prəs'kraib] *vt* proscrire, interdire.

proscription [prəs'kripʃən] *n* proscription *f*, interdiction *f*.

prose [prouz] *n* prose *f*, thème *m*.

prosecute ['prɔsikjuːt] *vt* poursuivre, mener.

prosecution [.prɔsi'kjuːʃən] *n* poursuite(s) *f* (*pl*), accusation *f*, le ministère public *m*, plaignants *m pl*, exercice m (d'un métier).

prosecutor ['prɔsikjuːtə] *n* demandeur *m*, le ministère public *m*, (UK) procureur du roi *m*.

prose-writer ['prouz'raitə] *n* prosateur *m*.

prospect ['prɔspekt] *n* vue *f*, perspective *f*, chance *f*; *pl* espérances *f pl*.

prospect [prəs'pekt] *vti* prospecter.

prospective [prəs'pektiv] *a* futur, à venir, éventuel.

prospector [prəs'pektə] *n* prospecteur *m*.

prosper ['prɔspə] *vi* prospérer, réussir.

prosperity [prɔs'periti] *n* prospérité *f*.

prosperous ['prɔspərəs] *a* prospère.

prostitute ['prɔstitjuːt] *n* prostituée *f*; *vt* (se) prostituer, se vendre.

prostrate ['prɔstreit] *a* prosterné, prostré, abattu.

prostrate [prɔs'treit] vt abattre, accabler; to — oneself se prosterner.

prostration [prɔs'treiʃən] n prostration f, prosternement m, abattement m.

prosy ['prouzi] a prosaïque, fastidieux.

protect [prə'tekt] vt protéger, défendre, sauvegarder.

protection [prə'tekʃən] n protection f, défense f, sauvegarde f.

protective [prə'tektiv] a protecteur.

protein ['proutiːn] n protéine f.

protest ['proutest] n protestation f, protêt m.

protest [prə'test] vti protester; vt protester de.

protestant ['prɔtistənt] n protestant (e) mf.

protocol ['proutəkɔl] n protocole m.

prototype ['proutətaip] n prototype m, archétype m.

protract [prə'trækt] vt prolonger.

protraction [prə'trækʃən] n prolongation f.

protrude [prə'truːd] vi faire saillie, s'avancer.

proud [praud] a fier, orgueilleux.

prove [pruːv] vt prouver, démontrer; vi se montrer, s'avérer.

provender ['prɔvində] n fourrage m.

proverb ['prɔvəb] n proverbe m.

provide [prə'vaid] vt fournir, pourvoir, munir, stipuler; vi to — against se prémunir contre.

provided [prə'vaidid] cj pourvu que.

providence ['prɔvidəns] n prévoyance f, économie f, Providence f.

provident ['prɔvidənt] a prévoyant, économe.

providential [,prɔvi'denʃəl] a providentiel.

province ['prɔvins] n province f.

provincial [prə'vinʃəl] an provincial (e) mf.

provision [prə'viʒən] n provision f, approvisionnement m, stipulation f.

proviso [prə'vaizou] n condition f, clause f.

provocation [,prɔvə'keiʃən] n provocation f.

provocative [prə'vɔkətiv] a provoquant, provocateur.

provoke [prə'vouk] vt provoquer, exciter, exaspérer.

provost ['prɔvəst] n prévôt m, maire m.

prow [prau] n proue f.

prowess ['prauis] n courage m, prouesse f.

prowl [praul] vi rôder.

proximate ['prɔksimit] a prochain, proche.

proximity [prɔk'simiti] n proximité f.

proxy ['prɔksi] n procuration f, mandataire mf, fondé m de pouvoir(s).

prudence ['pruːdəns] n prudence f, sagesse f.

prudent ['pruːdənt] a prudent, sage.

prudery ['pruːdəri] n pruderie f, pudibonderie f.

prudish ['pruːdiʃ] a prude, bégueule, pudibond.

prune [pruːn] n pruneau m; vt émonder, tailler, élaguer (de off).

pruning ['pruːniŋ] n élagage m, émondage m, taille f; —shears n sécateur m.

pry [prai] vi fureter, fourrer le nez (dans into).

psalm [sɑːm] n psaume m.

psalmody ['sælmədi] n psalmodie f.

pseudonym ['psjuːdənim] n pseudonyme m.

psychiatrist [sai'kaiətrist] n psychiatre m.

psychoanalysis [,saikouə'nælisis] n psychanalyse f.

psychologist [sai'kɔlədʒist] n psychologue m.

psychology [sai'kɔlədʒi] n psychologie f.

pub [pʌb] n bistro m, bar m.

puberty ['pjuːbəti] n puberté f.

public ['pʌblik] an public m.

publication [,pʌbli'keiʃən] n publication f.

publicist ['pʌblisist] n publiciste m.

publicity [pʌb'lisiti] n publicité f, réclame f.

publish ['pʌbliʃ] vt publier, faire paraître.

publisher ['pʌbliʃə] n éditeur m.

publishing ['pʌbliʃiŋ] n publication f; — house maison f d'édition.

puck [pʌk] n lutin m, palet m.

pucker ['pʌkə] n ride f, pli m, fronce f; vt plisser, rider, froncer; vi se froncer.

pudding ['pudiŋ] n pudding m; black — boudin m.

puddle ['pʌdl] n flaque f, gâchis m; vi barboter; vt brasser, corroyer.

puff [pʌf] n souffle m, bouffée f, houppe f, bouffant m, feuilleté m, réclame f; vi haleter, souffler, lancer des bouffées; vt vanter, gonfler, essouffler.

puffed ['pʌft] a essoufflé, bouffant.

puffy ['pʌfi] a gonflé, bouffi.

pug(-nose) ['pʌgnouz] n nez m épaté.

pugnacious [pʌg'neiʃəs] a batailleur.

pull [pul] n tirage m, influence f, avantage m, piston m, lampée f, effort m; vt traîner; vti tirer; to — down démolir, baisser, renverser; to — off enlever, gagner; to — out vt tirer, arracher; vi démarrer, sortir; to — through vt tirer d'affaire; vi se tirer d'affaire; to — up vt arracher, relever, arrêter; vi s'arrêter; to — oneself together se ressaisir.

pullet ['pulit] n poulette f.

pulley ['puli] n poulie f.

pullover ['pul,ouvə] n pull-over m, tricot m.

pulp [pʌlp] n pulpe f, pâte f, chair f.

pulpit ['pulpit] n chaire f.

pulsate [pʌl'seit] vi battre, palpiter, vibrer.

pulse [pʌls] n pouls m, pulsation f, battement m; vi battre, palpiter.

pulverize ['pʌlvəraiz] vt pulvériser, broyer.

pumice(-stone) ['pʌmis(stoun)] n pierre ponce f.

pump [pʌmp] n pompe f; vt pomper, tirer les vers du nez à.

pumpkin ['pʌmpkin] n citrouille f.

pun [pʌn] n jeu de mots m, calembour m.

punch [pʌntʃ] n poinçon m, Polichinelle m, coup de poing m; vt poinçonner, trouer, étamper, donner un coup de poing à.

punctilious [pʌnk'tiliəs] a pointilleux, chatouilleux.

punctual ['pʌnktjuəl] a exact, ponctuel.

punctuality [,pʌnktju'æliti] n ponctualité f, exactitude f.

punctuate ['pʌnktjueit] vt ponctuer.

punctuation [,pʌnktju'eiʃən] n ponctuation f.

puncture ['pʌnktʃə] n piqûre f, crevaison f; vti crever.

pundit [pʌndit] n pontife m.

pungency ['pʌndʒənsi] n âcreté f, mordant m, saveur f.

pungent ['pʌndʒənt] a aigu, -uë, mordant, piquant, âcre.

punish ['pʌniʃ] vt punir, corriger.

punishable ['pʌniʃəbl] a punissable, délictueux.

punishment ['pʌniʃmənt] n punition f.

punt [pʌnt] n bachot m, coup de volée m.

puny ['pju:ni] a chétif, mesquin.

pup(py) ['pʌp(i)] n chiot m, petit chien m.

pupil ['pju:pl] n élève mf, (eye) pupille f.

puppet ['pʌpit] n marionnette f, pantin m.

purblind ['pə:blaind] a myope, obtus.

purchase ['pə:tʃəs] n achat m, acquisition f, prise f, point d'appui m; vt acheter.

purchaser ['pə:tʃəsə] n acheteur, -euse, acquéreur, -euse.

pure [pjuə] a pur.

purgation [pə:'geiʃən] n purification f, purgation f, purge f.

purgative ['pə:gətiv] an purgatif m.

purgatory ['pə:gətəri] n purgatoire m.

purge [pə:dʒ] n purge f, épuration f; vt purger, épurer.

purify ['pjuərifai] vt purifier.

Puritan ['pjuəritən] an puritain(e) mf.

purity ['pjuəriti] n pureté f.

purl [pə:l] n murmure m; vi murmurer.

purlieu ['pə:lju:] n lisière f, alentours m pl, bornes f pl.

purloin ['pə:lɔin] vt voler, soustraire.

purple ['pə:pl] an violet m, cramoisi m, pourpre m; n pourpre f.

purport ['pə:pət] n sens m, teneur f.

purport [pə:'pɔ:t] vt signifier, impliquer.

purpose ['pə:pəs] n dessein m, intention f, objet m; vt se proposer (de).

purposeful ['pə:pəsful] a calculé, réfléchi, énergique, avisé.

purposeless ['pə:pəslis] a sans objet, inutile.

purposely ['pə:pəsli] ad à dessein.

purr [pə:] n ronronnement m: vi ronronner.

purse [pə:s] n porte-monnaie m, bourse f; vt plisser, serrer, froncer.

purser ['pə:sə] n commissaire m.

pursuance [pə'sju(:)əns] n exécution f, conséquence f; in — of conformément à.

pursue [pə'sju:] vti poursuivre.

pursuit [pə'sju:t] n poursuite f, occupation f, recherche f.

purvey [pə:'vei] vt fournir.

purveyor [pə:'veiə] n fournisseur, -euse.

purview ['pə:vju:] n teneur f, portée f.

pus [pʌs] n pus m.

push [puʃ] n poussée f, coup m (d'épaule), effort m, pression f, crise f, entregent m; vti pousser; vt presser, appuyer.

pushing ['puʃiŋ] a intrigant, entreprenant, débrouillard, ambitieux.

puss [pus] n minet, -ette, minou m.

put [put] vt mettre, remettre, placer, estimer, lancer, verser; to — back retarder, remettre à sa place; to — by mettre de côté; to — down (dé)poser, réprimer, supprimer, noter, attribuer, rabattre; to — in vt installer, introduire, glisser, passer; vi to — in at faire escale à; to — off vt ajourner, remettre, ôter, dérouter; vi démarrer; to — on mettre, passer, revêtir, feindre; to — out éteindre, tendre, déconcerter, mettre à la porte, sortir, démettre, publier; to — through exécuter, mettre en communication; to — up vt (faire) dresser, construire, monter, hausser, lever, apposer, présenter, loger, héberger, proposer; vi descendre, loger; to — up with s'accommoder de, supporter.

putrefy ['pju:trifai] vi pourrir, se putréfier.

putrid ['pju:trid] a putride, infect.

putty ['pʌti] n mastic m.

puzzle ['pʌzl] n énigme f, devinette f, embarras m; jigsaw — puzzle m; vt intriguer, embarrasser; vi se creuser la tête.

puzzling ['pʌzliŋ] a embarrassant, intrigant.

pygmy ['pigmi] n pygmée m.

pylon ['pailən] n pylône m.

pyramid ['pirəmid] n pyramide f.
pyre ['paiə] n bûcher m.
pyx [piks] n ciboire m.

Q

quack [kwæk] n charlatan m, couin-couin m.
quackery ['kwækəri] n charlatanisme m.
quadrangle ['kwɔ,dræŋgl] n quadrilatère m, cour f.
quadruple ['kwɔdrupl] an quadruple m.
quaff [kwɑːf] vt lamper, vider d'un seul trait.
quagmire ['kwægmaiə] n fondrière f.
quail [kweil] n caille f; vi flancher, défaillir.
quaint [kweint] a désuet, délicat, étrange, archaïque, fantasque, vieux jeu.
quake [kweik] vi trembler.
qualification [,kwɔlifi'keiʃən] n réserve f, atténuation f, condition f, nom m; pl titres m.
qualify ['kwɔlifai] vt qualifier, traiter (de), atténuer, modifier, modérer; vi acquérir les titres, se qualifier.
quality ['kwɔliti] n qualité f.
qualm [kwɔːm] n scrupule m, remords m.
quandary ['kwɔndəri] n embarras m, impasse f.
quantity ['kwɔntiti] n quantité f.
quarantine ['kwɔrəntiːn] n quarantaine f.
quarrel ['kwɔrəl] n querelle f, dispute f; vi se quereller, se disputer.
quarrelsome ['kwɔrəlsəm] a querelleur.
quarry ['kwɔri] n proie f, carrière f; vt extraire.
quarter ['kwɔːtə] n quart m, trimestre m, région f, fogement m, quartier m, pièce d'½ dollar; vt couper en quatre, loger, équarrir, écarteler; — of an hour quart d'heure m; a — to moins le quart; a — past et quart; —deck n gaillard d'arrière m; —master-sergeant n maréchal des logis m.
quarterly ['kwɔːtəli] a trimestriel.
quartet [kwɔː'tet] n quatuor m.
quarto ['kwɔːtou] n inquarto m.
quash [kwɔʃ] vt casser, annuler.
quaver ['kweivə] n chevrotement m, trille m, croche f; vi faire des trilles, trembloter, chevroter.
quay [kiː] n quai m.
queasy ['kwiːzi] a barbouillé, scrupuleux.
queen ['kwiːn] n reine f, (cards) dame f.
queer ['kwiə] a étrange, bizarre, louche.
quell [kwel] vt réprimer, écraser, apaiser.

quench [kwentʃ] vt éteindre, étancher.
querulous ['kweruləs] a plaintif, grognon.
query ['kwiəri] n question f, (point m d')interrogation f; vt demander, mettre en question.
quest [kwest] n quête f, recherche f.
question ['kwestʃən] n question f, hésitation f, doute m; excl c'est à savoir! vt interroger, questionner, mettre en doute, contester; — mark n point d'interrogation m.
questionable ['kwestʃənəbl] a douteux, contestable.
queue [kjuː] n queue f; vi faire la queue.
quibble ['kwibl] n jeu m de mots, faux-fuyant m, équivoque f; vi ergoter.
quibbler ['kwiblə] n ergoteur, -euse.
quick [kwik] n vif m, fond m, moelle f; a vif, éveillé, rapide, fin; ad rapidement, vite; —tempered emporté; —witted vif.
quicken ['kwikən] vt hâter, exciter, animer; vi s'animer, s'accélérer.
quicklime ['kwiklaim] n chaux vive f.
quickly ['kwikli] ad vite.
quickness ['kwiknis] n vivacité f, promptitude f, rapidité f, acuité f.
quicksand ['kwiksænd] n sable mouvant m.
quicksilver ['kwik,silvə] n mercure m, vif-argent m.
quiet ['kwaiət] n calme m; paix f; a tranquille, en paix; vt apaiser, calmer.
quietly ['kwaiətli] ad doucement, silencieusement.
quietness ['kwaiətnis] n tranquillité f, repos m, quiétude f, sagesse f.
quill [kwil] n plume f (d'oie), curedent m, bobine f; vt gaufrer, enrouler, rucher.
quilt [kwilt] n couverture piquée f, édredon m; vt piquer, ouater.
quince [kwins] n coing m.
quinine [kwi'niːn] n quinine f.
quinsy ['kwinzi] n angine f.
quip [kwip] n sarcasme m, mot fin m, pointe f.
quire ['kwaiə] n main f (de papier).
quirk [kwəːk] n argutie f, méchant tour m, fioriture f.
quit [kwit] a libre, quitte, débarrassé; vt quitter; vi démissionner, abandonner la partie.
quite ['kwait] ad tout (à fait), bien.
quits [kwits] n ad quitte(s).
quiver ['kwivə] n carquois m, tremblement m; vi trembler, frémir.
quiz [kwiz] n jeu m, colle f, mystification f, original m; vt dévisager, lorgner, railler.
quizzical ['kwizikəl] a ironique, railleur.
quoit [kɔit] n anneau m, palet m.
quota ['kwoutə] n quotepart f.

quotation ['kwou'teiʃən] n citation f, cote f, cours m; — **marks** n pl guillemets m pl.

quote [kwout] vt citer, coter; n citation f.

quotient ['kwouʃənt] n quotient m.

R

rabbi ['ræbai] n rabbin m.

rabbit ['ræbit] n lapin m.

rabble ['ræbl] n canaille f.

rabid ['ræbid] a enragé, acharné, fanatique.

rabies ['reibiz] n rage f.

race [reis] n race f, course f, courant m, cours m; vi faire une course, lutter de vitesse, courir; vt faire courir, (engine) emballer; —**course** n champ de course m; —**horse** n cheval de course m.

raciness ['reisinis] n verve f, saveur f, goût de terroir m.

rack [ræk] n râtelier m, filet m, égouttoir m, étagère f, chevalet m; vt torturer, pressurer; to — one's **brains** se creuser la cervelle; —**ed by hunger** tenaillé par la faim.

racket ['rækit] n raquette f, vacarme m, vie joyeuse, f, affaire véreuse f, **combine** f.

racketeer [,ræki'tiə] n gangster m, combinard m.

racy ['reisi] a de terroir, savoureux, piquant, salé.

radiance ['reidiəns] n rayonnement m, éclat m.

radiant ['reidiənt] a rayonnant, radieux, resplendissant.

radiate ['reidieit] vi rayonner, irradier; vt dégager, émettre.

radiator ['reidieitə] n radiateur m.

radical ['rædikəl] a radical, foncier.

radicalism ['rædikəlizəm] n radicalisme m.

radio ['reidiou] n radio f; vt émettre par la radio; — **control** téléguidage m; vt téléguider.

radioactive ['reidiou'æktiv] a radioactif; — **material** matière f rayonnante.

radiograph ['reidiougrɑːf] vt radiographier; n radio(graphie) f.

radiography [reidi'ɔgrəfi] n radiographie f.

radish ['rædiʃ] n radis m.

radius ['reidiəs] n rayon m.

raffle ['ræfl] n loterie f, tombola f; vt mettre en loterie, en tombola.

raft [rɑːft] n radeau m, train de bois m.

rafter ['rɑːftə] n chevron m.

rag [ræg] n chiffon m, haillon m, chahut m, monôme m, brimade f; vt chahuter, brimer.

ragamuffin ['rægə,mʌfin] n loqueteux, -euse, va-nu-pieds m.

rage [reidʒ] n rage f, fureur f; vi rager, faire rage; **to be all the —** faire fureur.

rugged ['rægid] a en loques, déchiqueté, désordonné.

raging ['reidʒiŋ] a furieux, démonté, fou, brûlant.

ragman ['rægmæn] n chiffonnier m.

raid [reid] n raid m, rafle f; vt razzier, faire une rafle dans, bombarder.

rail [reil] n rail m, rampe f, balustrade f, barrière f, parapet m, garde-fou m; pl bastingages m pl; vi se déchaîner (contre at).

railhead ['reilhed] n tête f de ligne.

railing(s) ['reiliŋ(z)] n grille f, clôture f.

railroad ['reilroud] n chemin m de fer; vt faire voter en vitesse un projet de loi.

railway ['reilwei] n chemin de fer m; — **line** n voie ferrée f; — **station** n gare f, station f.

rain [rein] n pluie f; vi pleuvoir.

rainbow ['reinbou] n arc-en-ciel m.

raincoat ['reinkout] n imperméable m.

rainfall ['reinfɔːl] n précipitation f.

rain-pipe ['rein,paip] n (tuyau m de) descente f.

rainy ['reini] a pluvieux.

raise [reiz] vt (é-, sou-, re-)lever, faire pousser, cultiver, (res)susciter, provoquer, dresser, hausser, augmenter; n augmentation f (de salaire).

raisin ['reizn] n raisin sec m.

rake [reik] n râteau m, roué m; vt ratisser, râcler, balayer; — **off** gratte f; to — **up** vt attiser, raviver.

rakish ['reikiʃ] a coquin, dissolu, désinvolte, bravache.

rally ['ræli] n ralliement m, réunion f, rallye m, rétablissement m, dernier effort m; vt rallier, rétablir; vi se rallier, se reformer, retrouver des forces, se reprendre.

Ralph [rælf] Raoul m.

ram [ræm] n bélier m, éperon m, marteau-pilon m; vt éperonner, pilonner, tasser, bourrer, enfoncer, tamponner.

ramble ['ræmbl] n flânerie f, promenade f, divagation f; vi errer, flâner, divaguer.

rambler ['ræmblə] n flâneur, -euse, plante grimpante f.

rambling ['ræmbliŋ] a errant, vagabond, décousu; n pl promenades f pl, divagations f pl.

ramp [ræmp] n rampe f, pente f, scandale m, affaire véreuse f, supercherie f, coup monté m.

rampant ['ræmpənt] a forcené, répandu, envahissant, rampant.

rampart ['ræmpɑːt] n rempart m.

ramshackle ['ræm,ʃækl] a branlant, délabré.

ran [ræn] pt of run.

ranch [rɑːntʃ] n ranch m, prairie f

d'élevage; vi faire de l'élevage.

rancid ['rænsid] a rance.

rancidness ['rænsidnis] n rancidité f.

rancor ['ræŋkə] n rancœur f, rancune f.

rancorous ['ræŋkərəs] a rancunier.

random ['rændəm] n at — à l'aventure, au hasard.

rang [ræŋ] pt of ring.

range [reindʒ] n rangée f, étendue f, gamme f, rang m, direction f, portée f, fourneau m de cuisine, champ de tir m, grand pâturage m; vt ranger, (gun) porter, braquer; vi s'étendre, errer.

rank [ræŋk] n rang m, classe f, grade m; vt ranger; vi se ranger, compter; a luxuriant, rance, fort, absolu, flagrant, criant, pur.

rankle ['ræŋkl] vi s'envenimer, laisser une rancœur.

ransack ['rænsæk] vt fouiller, piller.

ransom ['rænsəm] n rançon f; vt rançonner, racheter.

rant [rænt] n tirade enflammée f, rodomontades f pl; vi pérorer.

rap [ræp] n tape f, coup sec m, (fig) pomme f; vt donner sur les doigts à; vti frapper.

rapacious [rə'peiʃəs] a rapace.

rape [reip] n viol m, (bot) colza m; vt violer.

rapid ['ræpid] a rapide.

rapt [ræpt] a ravi, recueilli.

rapture ['ræptʃə] n ravissement m, ivresse f.

rapturous ['ræptʃərəs] a ravissant, frénétique, extasié.

rare [rɛə] a rare.

rarefaction [,rɛəri'fækʃən] n raréfaction f.

rarefy ['rɛərifai] vt raréfier.

rarity ['rɛəriti] n rareté f.

rascal ['raːskəl] n gredin m, fripon m, coquin m.

rash [ræʃ] n éruption f; a impulsif, casse-cou, irréfléchi.

rasher ['ræʃə] n tranche de lard f.

rashness ['ræʃnis] n impulsivité f, témérité f.

rasp [raːsp] n râpe f; vt râper, racler; vi grincer.

raspberry ['raːzbəri] n framboise f.

rat [ræt] n rat m, faux frère m, mouchard n; to smell a — soupçonner anguille sous roche; vi tourner casaque.

ratchet ['rætʃit] n cliquet m, rochet m.

rate [reit] n taux m, prix m, raison f, vitesse f, impôt municipal m, cas m; at any — en tout cas; vt estimer, compter, considérer, classer, imposer; vi passer, être classé.

ratepayer ['reit,peiə] n contribuable mf.

rather ['raːðə] ad plutôt, assez.

ratification [,rætifi'keiʃən] n ratification f.

ratify ['rætifai] vt ratifier, approuver.

ratio ['reiʃiou] n proportion f, raison f.

ration ['ræʃən] n ration f; vt rationner.

rational ['ræʃənl] a raisonnable, raisonné, rationnel.

rationalist ['ræʃnəlist] an rationaliste mf.

rationing ['ræʃniŋ] n rationnement m.

rat-race ['rætreis] n course f aux sous.

rattle ['rætl] n (bruit de) crécelle f, hochet m, râle m, cliquetis m, tintamarre m, fracas m, crépitement m; vt faire cliqueter, faire sonner, bouleverser; vi ferrailler, cliqueter, crépiter, trembler; —snake m serpent m à sonnettes.

raucous ['rɔːkəs] a rauque.

ravage ['rævidʒ] n ravage m; vt ravager, dévaster.

rave [reiv] vi hurler, délirer, radoter, s'extasier (sur about), raffoler (de about).

ravel ['rævəl] vt embrouiller; to — out débrouiller, effilocher.

raven ['reivn] n corbeau m.

ravenous ['rævinəs] a dévorant, vorace, affamé.

ravine [rə'viːn] n ravin m.

raving ['reiviŋ] n hurlement m, délire m, a délirant; — mad fou à lier.

ravish ['ræviʃ] vt ravir, violer.

raw [rɔː] n vif m; a cru, (oil) brut, âpre, mal dégrossi, inexpérimenté — materials matières premières f pl.

rawness ['rɔːnis] n crudité f, âpreté f, inexpérience f.

ray [rei] n rayon m, (fish) raie f.

rayon ['reiɔn] n soie artificielle f, rayonne f.

raze [reiz] vt raser.

razor ['reizə] n rasoir m.

reach [riːtʃ] n portée f, (sport) allonge f, brief m; vt atteindre, arriver à, parvenir à, (é)tendre; vi s'étendre.

react [ri:'ækt] vi réagir.

reaction [ri:'ækʃən] n réaction f, contre-coup m.

reactor [ri:'æktə] n réacteur m, atomique; breeder — pile couvreuse

read [riːd] pp red vt lire, étudier, to — through parcourir.

readable ['riːdəbl] a lisible, d'un lecture facile.

reader ['riːdə] n lecteur, -trice, liseur, -euse, professeur adjoint m, livre de lecture m.

readily ['redili] ad volontiers, facilement.

readiness ['redinis] n empressement m, alacrité f, facilité f.

reading ['riːdiŋ] n lecture f, interprétation f.

readjust ['riːə'dʒʌst] vt rajuster, rectifier.

ready ['redi] *a* prêt, facile, prompt ;
— made *a* prêt à porter, tout fait ;
— reckoner *n* barême *m*.

real [riəl] *n* réel *m*; *a* vrai, naturel,
réel, foncier.

reality [ri'æliti] *n* réalité *f*.

realization [.riəlai'zeiʃən] *n* réalisation *f*.

realize ['riəlaiz] *vt* comprendre, se
rendre compte de, réaliser.

really ['riəli] *ad* vraiment, en effet.

realm [relm] *n* royaume *m*, domaine
m.

realtor ['ri:əltə] *n* agent *m* immobilier.

ream [ri:m] *n* rame *f*.

reap [ri:p] *vt* moissonner, récolter.

reaper ['ri:pə] *n* moissonneur, -euse,
(machine *f*) moissonneuse *f*.

reaping-hook ['ri:piŋhuk] *n* faucille
f.

reappear ['ri:ə'piə] *vi* réapparaître.

rear [riə] *n* arrière(s) *m* (pl), derrière
m, queue *f*, dernier rang *m*; *a* (d')
arrière, de queue; *vt* élever, dresser, ériger; *vi* se cabrer, s'élever, se
dresser; —guard *n* arrière-garde *f*.

reason ['ri:zn] *n* raison *f*, motif *m*;
vi raisonner.

reasonable ['ri:znəbl] *a* raisonnable.

reassemble ['ri:ə'sembl] *vt* rassembler, remonter.

rebate ['ri:beit] *n* rabais *m*, ristourne
f, escompte *m*.

rebel [rebl] *n* rebelle *mf*; *a* insurgé.

rebel [ri'bel] *vi* se révolter.

rebellion [ri'beljən] *n* rébellion *f*,
révolte *f*.

rebellious [ri'beljəs] *a* rebelle.

rebound [ri'baund] *n* recul *m*,
ricochet *m*, réaction *f*; *vi* rebondir,
ricocher.

rebuff [ri'bʌf] *n* rebuffade *f*, échec
m; *vt* rabrouer, repousser.

rebuke [ri'bju:k] *n* semonce *f*,
réprimande *f*; *vt* rembarrer, réprimander.

rebut [ri'bʌt] *vt* repousser, réfuter.

recall [ri'kɔ:l] *n* rappel *m*, annulation
f; *vt* (se) rappeler, révoquer, reprendre.

recant [ri'kænt] *vt* retirer, rétracter ;
vi se rétracter.

recapitulate [.ri:kə'pitjuleit] *vt* récapituler.

recede [ri'si:d] *vi* reculer, se retirer,
baisser, s'enfuir, fuir.

receipt [ri'si:t] *n* réception *f*,
recette *f*, reçu *m*, récépissé *m*,
quittance *f*; *vt* acquitter.

receive [ri'si:v] *vt* recevoir, admettre,
accueillir.

receiver [ri'si:və] *n* receleur, -euse,
recepteur *m*, destinataire *mf*; official
— syndic.

recent ['ri:snt] *a* récent.

recently ['ri:sntli] *ad* récemment,
dernièrement.

receptacle [ri'septəkl] *n* réceptacle
m, récipient *m*.

reception [ri'sepʃən] *n* réception *f*,
accueil *m*.

recess [ri'ses] *n* vacances parlemen-
taires *f pl*, repli *m*, recoin *m*, alcôve *f*.

recipe ['resipi] *n* recette *f*, ordonnance *f*, formule *f*.

reciprocal [ri'siprəkəl] *a* réciproque.

reciprocate [ri'siprəkeit] *vt* (se)
rendre, payer de retour; *vi* rendre la
pareille.

recital [ri'saitl] *n* exposé *m*, recitation *f*, récital *m*.

recite [ri'sait] *vt* réciter, énumérer.

reckless ['reklis] *a* imprudent,
forcené, casse-cou.

recklessness ['reklisnis] *n* imprudence *f*, témérité *f*.

reckon ['rekən] *vt* calculer, compter;
vi estimer.

reckoning ['rekniŋ] *n* règlement de
comptes *m*, calcul *m*, compte *m*.

reclaim [ri'kleim] *vt* reprendre,
réformer, récupérer.

recline [ri'klain] *vt* pencher, étendre,
reposer; *vi* (se) reposer, être appuyé.

recluse [ri'klu:s] *an* reclus(e) *mf*; *n*
anachorète *m*.

recognition [.rekəg'niʃən] *n* reconnaissance *f*.

recognizable [.rekəg'naizəbl] *a* re-
connaissable.

recognizance [ri'kɔgnizəns] *n* engagement *m*, caution *f*.

recognize ['rekəgnaiz] *vt* reconnaître,
avouer.

recoil [ri'kɔil] *n* recul *m*, rebondisse-
ment *m*; *vi* reculer, retomber,
rejaillir, se détendre.

recollect [.rekə'lekt] *vt* se rappeler,
se souvenir de.

recollection [.rekə'lekʃən] *n* mémoire *f*, souvenir *m*.

recommend [.rekə'mend] *vt* confier,
recommander, conseiller.

recompense ['rekəmpens] *n* récompense *f*, compensation *f*; *vt* récompenser, dédommager.

reconcilable ['rekənsailəbl] *a* con-
ciliable.

reconcile ['rekənsail] *vt* (ré)concilier
(à, avec).

reconciliation [.rekənsili'eiʃən] *n*
(ré)conciliation *f*.

recondite [ri'kɔndait] *a* abstrus,
obscur.

recondition [.ri:kən'diʃən] *vt* remettre en état, à neuf.

reconnoiter [.rekə'nɔitə] *vt* reconnaître; *vi* faire une reconnaissance.

record ['rekɔ:d] *n* document *m*,
dossier *m*, casier *m*, record *m*,
disque *m*, enregistrement *m*, passé
m; — player tourne-disques *m inv*.

record [ri'kɔ:d] *vt* rapporter, enregistrer, prendre acte de.

recorder [ri'kɔ:də] *n* archiviste *m*,
greffier, appareil enregistreur *m*,
flûte à bec *f*.

recount [ri'kaunt] *vt* raconter.

recoup [ri'ku:p] *vt* défalquer, dédommager; **to — one's losses** se rattraper de ses pertes.

recourse [ri'kɔ:s] n recours m.

recover [ri'kʌvə] vt recouvrer, récupérer, reprendre, rattraper; vi se rétablir, se remettre, se ressaisir.

recovery [ri'kʌvəri] n recouvrement m, récupération f, rétablissement m, relèvement m.

recreation [ˌrekri'eiʃən] n délassement m, divertissement m.

recriminate [ri'krimineit] vi récriminer.

recruit [ri'kru:t] n recrue f; vt recruter, racoler.

recruiting [ri'kru:tiŋ] n recrutement m.

rectangle ['rek.tæŋgl] an rectangle m.

rectification [ˌrektifi'keiʃən] n rectification f, redressement m.

rectify ['rektifai] vt rectifier, réparer, redresser.

rector ['rektə] n recteur m.

recumbent [ri'kʌmbənt] a couché.

recuperate [ri'kju:pəreit] vt récupérer; vi se rétablir.

recur [ri'kə:] vi revenir, se reproduire.

red [red] a rouge, roux; **—handed** a pris sur le fait; **— herring** n hareng saur m, diversion f; **—hot** chauffé au rouge; **—letter** a heureux, mémorable; **— tape** n paperasserie f, bureaucratie f.

redbreast ['redbrest] n rouge-gorge m.

Red Cross ['red'krɔs] n Croix-Rouge f.

redden ['redn] vti rougir.

reddish ['rediʃ] a rougeâtre.

redeem [ri'di:m] vt racheter, sauver.

redeemer [ri'di:mə] n sauveur m, rédempteur m.

redemption [ri'dempʃən] n rédemption f, salut m, rachat m.

redness ['rednis] n rougeur f, rousseur f.

redolent ['redələnt] a qui sent, parfumé.

redouble [ri'dʌbl] vti redoubler; vt plier en quatre, (bridge) surcontrer.

redoubt [ri'daut] n redoute f.

redoubtable [ri'dautəbl] a redoutable.

redress [ri:'dres] n réparation f; vt redresser, réparer.

reduce [ri'dju:s] vt réduire, diminuer, ravaler, ramener; vi maigrir.

reduced [ri'dju:st] a diminué, appauvri.

reducible [ri'dju:səbl] a réductible.

reduction [ri'dʌkʃən] n réduction f, baisse f, rabais m.

redundant [ri'dʌndənt] a redondant, superflu.

reed [ri:d] n roseau m, pipeau m, anche f.

reef [ri:f] n récif m, écueil m, filon m, ris m.

reek [ri:k] n fumée f, vapeur f,

relent m; vi fumer; **to — of** empester.

reel ['ri:l] n bobine f, dévidoir m, moulinet m; vt enrouler, dévider; vi tituber, tourner, être ébranlé.

re-elect ['ri:i'lekt] vt réélire.

re-embark ['ri:im'ba:k] vti rembarquer.

re-embarkation ['ri:.emba:'keiʃən] n rembarquement m.

re-enter ['ri:'entə] vi rentrer, se présenter de nouveau.

re-establish ['ri:is'tæbliʃ] vt rétablir.

re-establishment ['ri:is'tæbliʃmənt] n rétablissement m.

refection [ri'fekʃən] n réfection f, collation f.

refectory [ri'fektəri] n réfectoire m.

refer [ri'fə:] vt rapporter, référer, renvoyer, attribuer; vi se reporter, se rapporter, se référer, avoir trait (à to), faire allusion (à to).

referee [ˌrefə'ri:] n arbitre m, répondant m; vti arbitrer.

reference ['refrəns] n référence f, renvoi m, rapport m, allusion f, mention f.

refine [ri'fain] vt purifier, (r)affiner.

refinement [ri'fainmənt] n (r)affinage m, finesse f, raffinement m.

refinery [ri'fainəri] n raffinerie f.

refit ['ri:'fit] vt radouber, rééquiper, réarmer, rajuster, remonter.

reflect [ri'flekt] vti réfléchir; vt refléter, renvoyer; vi méditer, rejaillir, faire du tort (à upon).

reflection [ri'flekʃən] n réflexion f, reflet m, image f, critique f, atteinte f.

reflector [ri'flektə] n réflecteur m, cabochon m.

reflex [ri:fleks] n réflexe m, reflet m.

reflexive [ri'fleksiv] a réfléchi.

reform [ri'fɔ:m] n réforme f; vt réformer; vi se reformer.

reformation [ˌrefə'meiʃən] n réforme f, réformation f.

reformer [ri'fɔ:mə] n réformateur, -trice.

refract [ri'frækt] vt réfracter.

refraction [ri'frækʃən] n réfraction f.

refractory [ri'fræktəri] a réfractaire, insoumis.

refrain [ri'frein] n refrain m; vi s'abstenir, s'empêcher.

refresh [ri'freʃ] vt rafraîchir, ranimer.

refreshment [ri'freʃmənt] n rafraîchissement m; **— room** n buffet m, buvette f.

refrigerator [ri'fridʒəreitə] n réfrigérateur m, glacière f.

refuel [ri'fjuəl] vt ravitailler en combustible; vi se ravitailler en combustible, faire le plein (d'essence).

refuge ['refju:dʒ] n refuge m, abri m.

refugee [ˌrefju:'dʒi:] n réfugié(e) mf.

refund ['ri:fʌnd] n remboursement m; ['ri:fʌnd] vt rembourser.

refusal [ri'fju:zəl] n refus m.
refuse [re'fju:z] n rebut m, ordures f pl, déchets m pl, détritus m.
refuse [ri'fju:z] vt refuser, repousser.
refutation [.refju:'teiʃən] n réfutation f.
refute [ri'fju:t] vt réfuter.
regain [ri'gein] vt regagner, reprendre, recouvrer.
regal ['ri:gəl] a royal.
regale [ri'geil] vt régaler.
regalia [ri'geiliə] n joyaux m pl, insignes m pl.
regard [ri'gɑ:d] vt regarder, considérer, concerner, tenir compte de; n égard m, attention f, estime f; pl compliments m pl; with — to quant à, en égard à.
regardless [ri'gɑ:dlis] a inattentif; — of sans égard à, sans regarder à.
regency ['ri:dʒənsi] n régence f.
regenerate [ri'dʒenəreit] vt régénérer.
regent ['ri:dʒənt] n régent(e) mf.
regiment [.redʒimənt] n régiment m; vt enrégimenter.
regimentals [.redʒi'mentlz] n uniforme m.
region ['ri:dʒən] n région f.
register ['redʒistə] n registre m; vt enregistrer, inscrire, (post) recommander, immatriculer.
registrar [.redʒis'trɑ:] n secrétaire m, greffier m, officier de l'état civil m.
registry ['redʒistri] n mairie f, bureau de l'état civil m, bureau de placement m.
regret [ri'gret] n regret m; vt regretter.
regretful [ri'gretful] a désolé.
regretfully [ri'gretfuli] ad à (avec) regret.
regular ['regjulə] a régulier, habituel, réglé, rangé, normal, réglementaire, permanent.
regularity [.regju'læriti] n régularité f.
regularize ['regjuləraiz] vt régulariser.
regulate ['regjuleit] vt régler, ajuster, réglementer.
regulation [.regju'leiʃən] n règlement m, réglementation f, réglage m; a réglementaire, d'ordonnance.
rehearsal [ri'hə:səl] n répétition f, dress — répétition générale.
rehearse [ri'hə:s] vt répéter, énumérer.
reign [rein] n règne m; vi régner.
rein [rein] n rêne f, guide f.
reindeer ['reindiə] n renne m.
reinforce [.ri:in'fɔ:s] vt renforcer, appuyer.
reinforced [.ri:in'fɔ:st] a renforcé, armé.
reinforcement [.ri:in'fɔ:smənt] n renforcement m.
reinstate ['ri:in'steit] vt rétablir, réintégrer.
reinstatement ['ri:in'steitmənt] n rétablissement m, réintégration f.

reinvest ['ri:in'vest] vt replacer.
reiterate [ri:'itəreit] vt réitérer.
reiteration [.ri:itə'reiʃən] n réitération f.
reject [ri'dʒekt] vt rejeter, refuser, repousser; ['ri:dʒekt] n rebut m, article de rebut m.
rejection [ri'dʒekʃən] n rejet m, refus m, rebut m.
rejoice [ri'dʒɔis] vt réjouir; vi se réjouir.
rejoicing [ri'dʒɔisiŋ] n réjouissance f, allégresse f.
rejoin ['ri:'dʒɔin] vt riposter, répliquer.
rejoin ['ri:'dʒɔin] vt rejoindre, rallier; vi se rejoindre, se réunir.
rejoinder [ri'dʒɔində] n riposte f, réplique f.
relapse [ri'læps] n rechute f; vi retomber, avoir une rechute.
relate [ri'leit] vt (ra)conter, relater, rapporter, rattacher; vi avoir rapport (à to), se rapporter (à to).
related [ri'leitid] a apparenté, connexe, parent.
relation [ri'leiʃən] n relation f, rapport m, récit m, parent(e) m(f).
relationship [ri'leiʃənʃip] n parenté f, connexion f, rapport m.
relative ['relətiv] n parent(e) m(f); a relatif.
relax [ri'læks] vt détendre, relâcher, délasser, adoucir; vi se détendre, se relâcher, s'adoucir.
relaxation [.ri:læk'seiʃən] n distraction f, détente f, adoucissement m.
relaxing [ri:'læksiŋ] a apaisant, reposant, énervant.
relay [ri'lei] vt relayer; n relais m, relève f.
release [ri'li:s] n délivrance f, élargissement m, décharge f, déclenchement m, lancement m, reçu m, transfert m; vt remettre, déclencher, lâcher, dégager, desserrer, faire jouer.
relegate ['religeit] vt reléguer, confier.
relent [ri'lent] vi se radoucir.
relentless [ri'lentlis] a inexorable, implacable, acharné.
relentlessness [ri'lentlisnis] n inflexibilité f, acharnement m.
relevant ['relivənt] a pertinent, qui a rapport (à to).
reliability [ri.laiə'biliti] n sûreté f, régularité f.
reliable [ri'laiəbl] a sûr, de confiance, sérieux, solide, digne de foi.
reliance [ri'laiəns] n confiance f.
relic ['relik] n relique f; pl restes m pl, souvenirs m pl.
relief [ri'li:f] n soulagement m, secours m, délivrance f, relève f, relief m.
relieve [ri'li:v] vt soulager, secourir, délivrer, relever, mettre en relief.
religion [ri'lidʒən] n religion f, culte m.

religious [ri'lidʒəs] *a* religieux, pieux, dévot.

relinquish [ri'liŋkwiʃ] *vt* abandonner, renoncer à.

relinquishment [ri'liŋkwiʃmənt] *n* abandon *m*, renonciation *f*.

relish ['reliʃ] *n* saveur *f*, goût *m*, assaisonnement *m*; *vt* relever, aimer, goûter.

reluctance [ri'lʌktəns] *n* répugnance *f*.

reluctantly [ri'lʌktəntli] *ad* à contre-cœur, à regret.

rely [ri'lai] *vi* s'appuyer (sur on), compter (sur on).

remain [ri'mein] *vi* rester, demeurer.

remainder [ri'meində] *n* reste *m*, restant *m*.

remains [ri'meinz] *n* restes *m pl*, dépouille mortelle *f*.

remand [ri'ma:nd] *n* renvoi *m*; *vt* renvoyer en prison.

remark [ri'ma:k] *n* attention *f*, remarque *f*, observation *f*; *vt* remarquer, (faire) observer.

remarkable [ri'ma:kəbl] *a* remarquable, frappant.

remedy ['remidi] *n* remède *m*; *vt* remédier à.

remember [ri'membə] *vt* se souvenir de, se rappeler, penser à.

remembrance [ri'membrəns] *n* mémoire *f*, souvenir *m*.

remind [ri'maind] *vt* rappeler, faire penser.

reminder [ri'maində] *n* agenda *m*, rappel *m*.

remiss [ri'mis] *a* négligent, lent, apathique.

remission [ri'miʃən] *n* rémission *f*, remise *f*, relâchement *m*, pardon *m*.

remit [ri'mit] *vt* remettre, relâcher, (r)envoyer.

remittance [ri'mitəns] *n* envoi de fonds *m*.

remnant ['remnənt] *n* reste *m*, (*cloth*) coupon *m*.

remonstrance [ri'mɔnstrəns] *n* remontrance *f*.

remonstrate [ri'mɔnstreit] to — with faire des représentations à.

remorse [ri'mɔ:s] *n* remords *m*.

remorseful [ri'mɔ:sful] *a* plein de remords.

remorseless [ri'mɔ:slis] *a* sans remords, implacable.

remote [ri'mout] *a* lointain, reculé, écarté, vague, peu probable, distant.

remoteness [ri'moutnis] *n* éloignement *m*.

removable [ri'mu:vəbl] *a* amovible, détachable.

removal [ri'mu:vəl] *n* déménagement *m*, enlèvement *m*, suppression *f*.

remove [ri'mu:v] *vt* enlever, supprimer, déplacer, effacer, révoquer, retirer, écarter, déménager.

remunerate [ri'mju:nəreit] *vt* rémunérer.

remuneration [ri,mju:nə'reiʃən] *n* rémunération *f*.

remunerative [ri'mju:nərətiv] *a* rémunérateur.

rend [rend] *vt* déchirer, arracher, fendre.

render ['rendə] *vt* rendre, remettre, fondre.

renegade ['renəgeid] *n* renégat *m*.

renew [ri'nju:] *vt* renouveler, rafraîchir.

renewal [ri'nju:əl] *n* renouvellement *m*, reprise *f*.

renounce [ri'nauns] *vt* renoncer à, dénoncer, répudier, renier.

renouncement [ri'naunsmənt] *n* renoncement *m*.

renovate ['renəveit] *vt* rénover, remettre à neuf.

renovation [,renə'veiʃən] *n* rénovation *f*, remise à neuf *f*.

renown [ri'naun] *n* renom *m*, renommée *f*.

renowned [ri'naund] *a* célèbre, illustre.

rent [rent] *n* déchirure *f*, accroc *m*, loyer *m*; *vt* louer, affermer.

renunciation [ri,nʌnsi'eiʃən] *n* renoncement *m*, renonciation *f*, reniement *m*.

reopen ['ri:'oupən] *vti* rouvrir; *vi* se rouvrir, rentrer.

reopening ['ri:'oupniŋ] *n* rentrée *f*, réouverture *f*.

repair [ri'pɛə] *n* (état de) réparation *f*, radoub *m*; *vt* réparer, raccommoder; *vi* se rendre.

repartee [,repa:'ti:] *n* repartie *f*.

repast [ri'pa:st] *n* repas *m*.

repatriate [ri:'pætrieit] *vt* rapatrier.

repatriation ['ri:pætri'eiʃən] *n* rapatriement *m*.

repay [ri:'pei] *vt* rembourser, rendre, s'acquitter envers.

repayment [ri:'peimənt] *n* remboursement *m*, récompense *f*.

repeal [ri'pi:l] *n* abrogation *f*; *vt* abroger, révoquer.

repeat [ri'pi:t] *vt* répéter, rapporter, renouveler.

repeatedly [ri'pi:tidli] *ad* à maint... reprise.

repeating [ri'pi:tiŋ] *a* à répétition.

repel [ri'pel] *vt* repousser, répugner à.

repellent [ri'pelənt] *a* répugnant, repoussant.

repent [ri'pent] *vt* regretter, s... repentir de; *vi* se repentir.

repentance [ri'pentəns] *n* repentir *m*.

repertory ['repətəri] *n* répertoire *m*.

repetition [,repi'tiʃən] *n* répétition *f*, reprise *f*, récitation *f*.

replace [ri'pleis] *vt* remplacer, re... placer, remettre en place.

replaceable [ri'pleisəbl] *a* rempla... çable.

replacement [ri'pleismənt] *n* rem... placement *m*, pièce de rechange *f*.

replenish [ri'pleniʃ] *vt* remplir d... nouveau, regarnir, remonter.

replete [ri'pli:t] *a* plein, bondé, rassasié.

reply [ri'plai] *n* réponse *f*; *vi* répondre.

report [ri'pɔ:t] *n* bruit *m*, nouvelle *f*, compte-rendu *m*, bulletin *m*, rapport *m*, réputation *f*, détonation *f*; *vt* faire un rapport sur, rendre compte de, signaler, faire le reportage de; *vi* se présenter, dénoncer.

reporter [ri'pɔ:tə] *n* reporter *m*, journaliste *mf*, rapporteur *m*.

repose [ri'pouz] *n* repos *m*; *vi* (se) reposer.

reposeful [ri'pouzful] *a* reposant.

reprehend [,repri'hend] *vt* blâmer, reprendre.

reprehensible [repri'hensəbl] *a* répréhensible.

represent [,repri'zent] *vt* représenter.

representative [,repri'zentətiv] *n* représentant(e) *mf*; *a* représentatif.

repress [ri'pres] *vt* réprimer, refouler, étouffer.

repression [ri'preʃən] *n* répression *f*.

reprieve [ri'pri:v] *n* sursis *m*, grâce *f*, répit *m*; *vt* surseoir à, gracier.

reprimand ['reprimɑ:nd] *n* réprimande *f*; *vt* réprimander.

reprint ['ri:'print] *n* réimpression *f*; *vt* réimprimer.

reprisal [ri'praizəl] *n* représaille(s) *f* (pl).

reproach [ri'proutʃ] *n* honte *f*, reproche *m*; *vt* reprocher, faire des reproches à.

reproachfully [ri'proutʃfuli] *ad* sur un ton de reproche.

reprobate ['reproubeit] *n* réprouvé(e) *mf*, scélérat *m*.

reproduce [,ri:prə'dju:s] *vt* reproduire.

reproduction [,ri:prə'dʌkʃən] *n* reproduction *f*.

reproof [ri'pru:f] *n* blâme *m*, reproche *m*, rebuffade *f*.

reprove [ri'pru:v] *vt* blâmer, réprouver, réprimander, reprendre, condamner.

reptile ['reptail] *n* reptile *m*.

republic [ri'pʌblik] *n* république *f*.

republican [ri'pʌblikən] *an* républicain(e) *mf*.

repudiate [ri'pju:dieit] *vt* répudier, désavouer, renier.

repudiation [ri,pju:di'eiʃən] *n* répudiation *f*, reniement *m*.

repugnance [ri'pʌgnəns] *n* répugnance *f*, antipathie *f*.

repugnant [ri'pʌgnənt] *a* répugnant, incompatible.

repulse [ri'pʌls] *n* échec *m*, rebuffade *f*; *vt* repousser.

repulsion [ri'pʌlʃən] *n* répulsion *f*, aversion *f*.

repulsive [ri'pʌlsiv] *a* répulsif, repoussant.

reputable ['repjutəbl] *a* honorable, estimable.

reputation [,repju'teiʃən] *n* réputation *f*, renom *m*.

repute [ri'pju:t] *n* réputation *f*, renommée *f*, renom *m*.

reputed [ri'pju:təd] *a* réputé, censé, putatif.

request [ri'kwest] *n* requête *f*, prière *f*; *vt* demander, prier.

require [ri'kwaiə] *vt* requérir, exiger, réclamer, avoir besoin de, falloir.

requirement [ri'kwaiəmənt] *n* exigence *f*, besoin *m*, demande *f*.

requisite ['rekwizit] *n* condition *f*; *pl* articles *m* *pl*, accessoires *m* *pl*; *a* requis, voulu, indispensable.

requisition [,rekwi'ziʃən] *n* requête *f*, réquisition(s) *f* (*pl*), commande *f*; *vt* réquisitionner.

requital [ri'kwaitl] *n* revanche *f*, monnaie de sa pièce *f*, retour *m*.

requite [ri'kwait] *vt* recompenser, rendre, payer de retour.

rescind [ri'sind] *vt* annuler.

rescission [ri'siʒən] *n* annulation *f*, abrogation *f*.

rescue ['reskju:] *n* délivrance *f*, sauvetage *m*; *vt* délivrer, sauver.

rescuer ['reskjuə] *n* sauveteur *m*, libérateur, -trice.

research [ri'sə:tʃ] *n* recherche(s) *f* (*pl*).

resemblance [ri'zembləns] *n* ressemblance *f*, image *f*.

resemble [ri'zembl] *vt* ressembler à.

resent [ri'zent] *vt* ressentir, s'offenser de.

resentful [ri'zentful] *a* plein de ressentiment, rancunier.

resentment [ri'zentmənt] *n* ressentiment *m*, dépit *m*.

reservation [,rezə'veiʃən] *n* réservation *f*, réserve *f*, place retenue *f*.

reserve [ri'zə:v] *n* réserve *f*; *vt* réserver, retenir, louer.

reservoir ['rezəvwɑ:] *n* réservoir *m*.

reshuffle ['ri:'ʃʌfl] *n* refonte *f*, remaniement *m*; *vt* refondre, remanier, rebattre.

reside [ri'zaid] *vi* résider.

residence ['rezidəns] *n* résidence *f*, séjour *m*.

resident ['rezidənt] *a* résident; *n* habitant(e) *mf*.

residue ['rezidju:] *n* reste *m*, reliquat *m*, résidu *m*.

resign [ri'zain] *vt* résigner; *vi* démissionner.

resignation [,rezig'neiʃən] *n* résignation *f*, démission *f*, abandon *m*.

resilience [ri'ziliəns] *n* élasticité *f*, ressort *m*.

resilient [ri'ziliənt] *a* élastique, rebondissant, qui a du ressort.

resin ['rezin] *n* résine *f*.

resist [ri'zist] *vt* résister à; *vi* résister.

resistance [ri'zistəns] *n* résistance *f*.

resolute ['rezəlu:t] *a* résolu.

resolutely ['rezəlu:tli] *ad* résolument, avec fermeté.

resolution [rezə'lu:ʃən] n résolution f.

resolve [ri'zɔlv] vt résoudre; vi se résoudre.

resort [ri'zɔ:t] n recours m, ressort m, séjour m, station (balnéaire) f; vi recourir (à to), se rendre (à to).

resound [ri'zaund] vi retentir, résonner.

resource [ri'sɔ:s] n ressource f.

resourceful [ri'sɔ:sful] a débrouillard, ingénieux.

resourcefulness [ri'sɔ:sfulnis] n ingéniosité f.

respect [ris'pekt] n respect m, égard m, rapport m; vt respecter.

respectability [ris,pektə'biliti] n respectabilité f.

respectable [ris'pektəbl] a respectable.

respectful [ris'pektful] a respectueux.

respecting [ris'pektiŋ] prep relativement à, quant à.

respective [ris'pektiv] a respectif.

respiration [,respə'reiʃən] n respiration f.

respiratory [ris'paiərətəri] a respiratoire.

respite ['respait] n répit m, sursis m; soulager, différer.

resplendent [ris'plendənt] a resplendissant.

respond [ris'pɔnd] vi répondre, obéir réagir.

response [ris'pɔns] n réponse f, réaction f.

responsibility [ris,pɔnsə'biliti] n responsabilité f.

responsible [ris'pɔnsəbl] a responsable (devant to); to be — for répondre de.

responsive [ris'pɔnsiv] a sympathique, sensible, souple.

rest [rest] n repos m, appui f, reste, m, réserves f pl; vt (faire) reposer, appuyer; vi se reposer, s'appuyer.

restaurant ['restərɔ̃:ŋ] n restaurant m.

restful ['restful] a reposant, paisible.

restitution [,resti'tju:ʃən] n restitution f.

restive ['restiv] a rétif, nerveux, impatient.

restless ['restlis] a agité.

restlessness ['restlisnis] n agitation f, impatience f.

restoration [,restə'reiʃən] n restitution f, restauration f, rétablissement m.

restorative [ris'tɔrətiv] an fortifiant m.

restore [ris'tɔː] vt restituer, restaurer, rétablir.

restrain [ris'trein] vt réprimer, retenir, contenir, empêcher.

restraint [ris'treint] n discrétion f, contrôle m, sobriété f, contrainte f.

restrict [ris'trikt] vt réduire, limiter, restreindre.

restriction [ris'trikʃən] n restriction f, réduction f.

result [ri'zʌlt] n résultat m; vi résulter, aboutir (à in).

resume [ri'zju:m] vt reprendre, résumer.

resumption [ri'zʌmpʃən] n reprise f.

resurrection [,rezə'rekʃən] n résurrection f.

resuscitate [ri'sʌsiteit] vt ressusciter.

retail ['ri:teil] n vente au détail f.

retail [ri:'teil] vt vendre au détail.

retailer [ri:'teilə] n détaillant m.

retain [ri'tein] vt (con-, sou-, re-) tenir, conserver.

retainer [ri'teinə] n provision f, honoraires m pl, suivant m; pl suite f.

retaliate [ri'tælieit] vi rendre la pareille (à on), riposter.

retaliation [ri,tæli'eiʃən] n représailles f pl, revanche f.

retard [ri'tɑ:d] vt retarder.

retch ['ri:tʃ] n haut-le-cœur m; vi avoir des haut-le-cœur.

retentive [ri'tentiv] a fidèle.

retina ['retinə] n rétine f.

retinue [ri'tinju:] n suite f.

retire [ri'taiə] vt mettre à la retraite, retirer; vi se retirer, reculer, battre en retraite, prendre sa retraite.

retirement [ri'taiəmənt] n retraite f, retrait m.

retort [ri'tɔ:t] n riposte f, cornue f; vi riposter, rétorquer.

retrace [ri'treis] vt reconstituer, revenir sur.

retract [ri'trækt] vt rétracter, rentrer, escamoter; vi se rétracter.

retreat [ri'tri:t] n retraite f, abri m; vi battre en retraite.

retrench [ri:'trentʃ] vt retrancher; vi faire des économies; —ment n retranchement m.

retribution [,retri'bju:ʃən] n juste récompense f.

retrieve [ri'tri:v] vt rapporter, retrouver, réparer, rétablir.

retrograde ['retrougreid] vi rétrograder; a rétrograde.

retrospect ['retrouspekt] n regard m en arrière.

retrospective [,retrou'spektiv] a rétrospectif.

return [ri'tə:n] n retour m, restitution f, rendement m, échange m, revanche f, rapport m; pl recettes f pl, profit m; — ticket (billet m d') aller et retour m; vi retourner, revenir, rentrer; vt rendre, renvoyer, répliquer, élire.

reunion ['ri:'ju:njən] n réunion f.

reunite ['ri:ju:'nait] vt réunir; vi se réunir.

reveal [ri'vi:l] vt révéler, découvrir, faire voir.

reveille [ri'væli] n réveil m, diane f.

revel ['revl] n fête f, orgie f; pl réjouissances f pl; vi faire la fête, se délecter (à in).

revelation [ˌreviˈleiʃən] n révélation f.

reveler [ˈrevlə] n noceur, -euse, fêtard(e) mf.

revenge [riˈvendʒ] n revanche f, vengeance f; vt venger; to — oneself se venger.

revengeful [riˈvendʒful] a vindicatif, vengeur, -eresse.

revenue [ˈrevinjuː] n revenu m.

reverberate [riˈvəːbəreit] vt réfléchir, renvoyer; vti réverbérer; vi se réfléchir.

reverberation [riˌvəːbəˈreiʃən] n réverbération f, répercussion f.

revere [riˈviə] vt révérer.

reverence [ˈrevərəns] n révérence f.

reverend [ˈrevərənd] a révérend, vénérable.

reverent [ˈrevərənt] a respectueux.

reverse [riˈvəːs] n revers m, envers m, marche arrière f, contraire m; a contraire, opposé; vt renverser, faire reculer, annuler; vi faire machine arrière.

review [riˈvjuː] n revue f, révision f, compte-rendu m; vt revoir, passer en revue, admettre à révision, faire le compte-rendu de.

reviewer [riˈvjuːə] n critique m.

revile [riˈvail] vt vilipender, injurier.

revise [riˈvaiz] vt réviser, revoir, corriger.

revision [riˈviʒən] n révision f.

revival [riˈvaivəl] n renaissance f, renouveau m, reprise f.

revive [riˈvaiv] vt ranimer, renouveler, remonter; vi revivre, renaître, reprendre connaissance, se ranimer.

revocation [ˌrevəˈkeiʃən] n révocation f, annulation f.

revoke [riˈvouk] vt annuler, révoquer.

revolt [riˈvoult] n révolte f; vt révolter; vi se révolter.

revolution [ˌrevəˈluːʃən] n révolution f.

revolutionary [ˌrevəˈluːʃnəri] an révolutionnaire mf.

revolutionize [ˌrevəˈluːʃnaiz] vt révolutionner.

revolve [riˈvolv] vt faire tourner, retourner; vi rouler, tourner.

reward [riˈwɔːd] n récompense f; vt récompenser, payer (de retour).

rhetoric [ˈretərik] n éloquence f, rhétorique f.

rheumatic [ruːˈmætik] an rhumatisant(e) mf.

rheumatism [ˈruːmətizəm] n rhumatisme m.

rhubarb [ˈruːbɑːb] n rhubarbe f.

rhyme [raim] n rime f; vi rimer; vt faire rimer.

rhythm [ˈriðəm] n rythme m.

rib [rib] n côte f, nervure f, baleine f.

ribald [ˈribəld] a paillard, graveleux.

ribaldry [ˈribəldri] n obscénité f, paillardises f pl.

ribbon [ˈribən] n ruban m, cordon m.

rice [rais] n riz m.

rich [ritʃ] a riche, somptueux, magnifique.

riches [ˈritʃiz] n pl richesses f pl.

rick [rik] n meule f.

rickets [ˈrikits] n rachitisme m.

rickety [ˈrikiti] a rachitique, branlant.

rid [rid] inf pt pp of rid; vt débarrasser; to get — of se débarrasser de.

riddance [ˈridəns] n débarras m.

ridden [ˈridn] pp of ride.

riddle [ˈridl] n crible m, énigme f, devinette f; vt cribler.

ride [raid] n promenade à cheval f, en auto, tour m; vi monter (aller) à cheval (à bicyclette), chevaucher, flotter, voguer, être mouillé; vt monter.

rider [ˈraidə] n cavalier, -ière, amazone f, écuyer, -ère, jockey m, annexe f, recommandation f.

ridge [ridʒ] n arête f, crête f, faite f, ride f.

ridicule [ˈridikjuːl] n ridicule m, raillerie f; vt ridiculiser, se moquer de.

ridiculous [riˈdikjuləs] a ridicule, absurde.

riding-school [ˈraidiŋskuːl] n manège m, école f d'équitation.

rife [raif] a commun, courant, fourmillant; to be — sévir.

rifle [ˈraifl] n carabine f; vt dévaliser, vider, fouiller, rayer.

rift [rift] n fente f, fêlure f.

rig [rig] n gréement m, accoutrement m, tenue f; vt gréer, accoutrer, truquer; to — up installer, monter.

rigging [ˈrigiŋ] n agrès m pl, équipement m.

right [rait] n droite f, droit m, dû m; a juste, exact, droit; to be — avoir raison; ad droit, juste, très bien; vt redresser, réparer, corriger.

righteous [ˈraitʃəs] a pur, juste, sans faute, vertueux.

righteousness [ˈraitʃəsnis] n impeccabilité f, rectitude f, vertu f.

rightful [ˈraitful] a légitime, équitable.

right-handed [ˈraitˈhændid] a droitier.

rightness [ˈraitnis] n justesse f.

rigid [ˈridʒid] a rigide, raide, strict, inflexible.

rigidity [riˈdʒiditi] n rigidité f, sévérité f.

rigmarole [ˈrigməroul] n calembredaine f.

rigor [ˈrigə] n rigueur f, sévérité f.

rigorous [ˈrigərəs] a rigoureux.

rim [rim] n bord m, cercle m, jante f.

rime [raim] n rime f, givre m; vi rimer.

rimmed [rimd] a cerclé, bordé, cerné, à bord.

rind [raind] n peau f, croûte f, écorce f, couenne f.

ring [riŋ] n anneau m, bague f, cercle m, cerne f, bande f, piste f,

sonnerie *f*, coup *m* de sonnette; *vti*
sonner; to — off couper; — **finger**
n annulaire *m*.
ringleader ['riŋ,li:də] *n* meneur *m*.
ringworm ['riŋ wə:m] *n* pelade *f*,
teigne *f*.
rink [riŋk] *n* patinoire *f*.
rinse [rins] *vt* rincer; *n* rinçage *m*.
riot ['raiət] *n* émeute *f*, orgie *f*; *vi*
s'ameuter.
rioter ['raiətə] *n* émeutier *m*.
riotous ['raiətəs] *a* turbulent, tapageur.
rip [rip] *n* déchirure *f*; *vt* déchirer,
fendre; *vi* se déchirer, se fendre.
ripe [raip] *a* mûr.
ripen ['raipən] *vti* mûrir.
ripping ['ripiŋ] *a* épatant.
ripple ['ripl] *n* ride *f*, murmure *m*;
vi se rider, onduler, perler; *vt* rider.
rise [raiz] *n* montée *f*, éminence *f*,
avancement *m*, augmentation *f*,
hausse *f*, source *f*, naissance *f*, essor
m; *vi* se lever, s'élever, se soulever,
monter, naître.
risen ['rizn] *pp of* **rise**.
rising ['raiziŋ] *n* lever *m*, crue *f*,
soulèvement *m*, résurrection *f*,
hausse *f*.
risk [risk] *n* risque *m*, péril *m*; *vt*
risquer.
risky ['riski] *a* risqué, hasardeux.
rite [rait] *n* rite *m*.
ritual ['ritjuəl] *an* rituel *m*.
rival ['raivəl] *an* rival(e) *mf*; *n*
émule *mf*; *vt* rivaliser avec.
rivalry ['raivəlri] *n* rivalité *f*.
rive [raiv] *vt* fendre.
riven ['rivən] *pp of* **rive**.
river ['rivə] *n* rivière *f*, fleuve *m*.
rivet ['rivit] *n* rivet *m*; *vt* river.
rivulet ['rivjulit] *n* ruisselet *m*.
roach [routʃ] *n* gardon *m*.
road [roud] *n* route *f*, rue *f*, rade *f*.
roadside ['roud,said] *n* bas-côté *m*;
— **repairs** dépannage *m*.
roadway ['roudwei] *n* chaussée *f*.
roam [roum] *vi* rôder, errer.
roar [rɔ:] *n* mugissement *m*, rugissement *m*, grondement *m*, vrombissement *m*, gros éclat de rire *m*; *vi*
rugir, mugir, vrombir, hurler, s'esclaffer.
roast [roust] *n* rôti *m*, rosbif *m*; *vt*
rôtir, griller.
rob [rɔb] *vt* dérober, voler, piller,
détrousser.
robber ['rɔbə] *n* voleur, -euse.
robbery ['rɔbəri] *n* vol *m*, brigandage
m.
robe [roub] *n* robe *f*.
Robert ['rɔbət] Robert *m*.
robin ['rɔbin] *n* rouge-gorge *m*.
robot ['roubɔt] *n* automate *m*; *a*
automatique.
robust [rə'bʌst] *a* robuste, vigoureux.
rock [rɔk] *n* roc *m*, rocher *m*, roche,
f; *vt* bercer, balancer, (é)branler,
basculer; *vi* osciller, (se) balancer.

rocket ['rɔkit] *n* fusée *f*; *a* à fusée.
rocking ['rɔkiŋ] *a* à bascule.
rocky ['rɔki] *a* rocheux, rocailleux,
instable.
rod [rɔd] *n* baguette *f*, tringle *f*,
perche *f*, gaule *f*, canne à pêche *f*,
verge(s) *f* (*pl*), piston *m*.
rode [roud] *pt of* **ride**.
rodent ['roudənt] *an* rongeur *m*.
roe [rou] *n* **hard** — œufs *m pl*; **soft** —
laitance *f*.
roe(buck) ['rou(bʌk)] *n* chevreuil *m*.
rogue [roug] *n* coquin(e) *mf*, fripon,
-onne, gredin *m*.
roguish ['rougiʃ] *a* fripon, coquin,
espiègle, malin, -igne.
roll [roul] *n* rouleau *m*, boudin *m*,
petit pain *m*, tableau *m*, roulis *m*,
roulement *m*; *vt* rouler, enrouler,
laminer; *vi* (se) rouler, s'enrouler.
roller ['roulə] *n* rouleau *m*, bande *f*,
laminoir *m*, grosse lame *f*; — **skates**
patins à roulettes *m pl*.
Roman ['roumən] *a* romain; *n*
Romain(e) *mf*.
romance [rə'mæns] *an* roman *m*; *n*
idylle *f*, romanesque *m*; *vi* romancer,
faire du roman, exagérer.
romantic [rə'mæntik] *a* romanesque,
romantique.
romanticism [rə'mæntisizəm] *n* romantisme *m*.
Romany ['rɔməni] *n* bohémien,
-ienne.
romp [rɔmp] *n* petit(e) diable(sse),
jeu de vilain *m*, gambades *f pl*; *vi*
jouer, s'ébattre, gambader.
rood [ru:d] *n* crucifix *n*, quart
d'arpent *m*.
roof [ru:f] *n* toit *m*, toiture *f*, (*mouth*)
palais *m*.
rook [ruk] *n* corneille *f*, bonneteur
m, escroc *m*.
room [rum] *n* chambre *f*, pièce *f*,
salle *f*, place *f*, lieu *m*.
roomy ['rumi] *a* spacieux, ample.
roost [ru:st] *n* perchoir *m*; *vi* se
percher, se jucher.
root [ru:t] *n* racine *f*, source *f*; *vt*
planter, enraciner, clouer; *vi* s'enraciner.
rope [roup] *n* corde *f*, cordage *m*,
câble *m*, glane *f*, collier *m*; *vt* corder,
lier, hâler.
rosary ['rouzəri] *n* rosaire *m*,
chapelet *m*.
rose [rouz] *n* rose *f*, rosace *f*, rosette
f, pomme d'arrosoir *f*; —**bud** *n*
bouton *m* de rose; —**bush** *n* rosier *m*.
rosemary ['rouzməri] *n* romarin *m*.
rosin ['rɔzin] *n* colophane *f*.
roster ['rɔstə] *n* tableau *m*, liste *f*,
roulement *m*.
rosy ['rouzi] *a* rose, rosé, attrayant.
rot [rɔt] *n* pourriture *f*, carie *f*,
démoralisation *f*, bêtises *f pl*; *vti*
pourrir; *vi* se carier, se décomposer.
rota ['routə] *n* liste *f*, roulement *m*.
rotate [rou'teit] *vt* faire tourner,
alterner; *vi* tourner, pivoter.

rote [rout] n routine f; by — machinalement.

rotten ['rɔtn] a pourri, carié, fichu, moche, patraque.

rottèr ['rɔtə] n propre à rien m, sale type m, salaud m.

rotund [rou'tʌnd] a arrondi, sonore.

rouge [ru:ʒ] n rouge m, fard m; vt farder.

rough [rʌf] a rugueux, grossier, brutal, rude, brut, approximatif; to — it vivre à la dure.

roughcast ['rʌfkɑ:st] vt ébaucher, crépir; n crépi m.

rough copy ['rʌf'kɔpi] n brouillon m.

roughen ['rʌfn] vt rendre grossier, rude; vi grossir.

roughly ['rʌfli] ad en gros, brutalement, à peu près.

roughness ['rʌfnis] n rugosité f, rudesse f, grossièreté f.

roughshod ['rʌfʃɔd] a ferré à glace; to ride — over s.o. fouler qn aux pieds.

round [raund] n rond m, ronde f, tournée f, tour m, échelon m, (sport) circuit m, reprise f, série f, cartouche f, salve f; a rond; prep autour de; ad en rond, à la ronde; vt arrondir, contourner, doubler; to — up rassembler, rafler.

roundabout ['raundəbaut] n manège m (de chevaux de bois), rondpoint m.

roundly ['raundli] ad rondement, net.

roundworm ['raund,wə:m] n chique f.

rouse [rauz] vt réveiller, exciter, remuer.

rousing ['rauziŋ] a retentissant, vibrant.

rout [raut] n bande f. déroute f; vt. mettre en déroute.

route [ru:t] n itinéraire m, parcours m, route f.

routine [ru:'ti:n] n routine f.

rove [rouv] vi rôder; vt parcourir.

rover ['rouvə] n vagabond m, coureur m, pirate m.

row [rou] n rang m, rangée f, file f, partie de canotage f; vi ramer, faire du canotage; vt conduire à l'aviron.

row [rau] n dispute f, bagarre f, semonce f; vt attraper; vi se chamailler.

rowdy ['raudi] n voyou m; a violent, turbulent.

rowdyism ['raudiizəm] n désordre m, chahutage m.

rower ['rouə] n rameur m, -euse, canotier m.

rowlock ['rɔlək] n tolet m

royal ['rɔiəl] a royal.

royalist ['rɔiəlist] n royaliste mf.

royalty ['rɔiəlti] n royauté f; pl droits d'auteur m pl.

rub [rʌb] n frottement m, friction f, hauts et bas m pl, hic m; vti frotter; vt frictionner, calquer, polir, masser; to — out effacer.

rubber ['rʌbə] n gomme f, caoutchouc m, frotteur, -euse; — tree n hévia m.

rubbish ['rʌbiʃ] n ordures f pl, détritus m, décombres m pl, niaiseries f pl; — chute vide-ordures m.

rubble ['rʌbl] n gravats m pl.

rubric ['ru:brik] n rubrique f.

ruby ['ru:bi] n rubis m.

rudder ['rʌdə] n gouvernail m.

ruddy ['rʌdi] a coloré, rougeaud, rougeoyant.

rude [ru:d] a grossier, mal élevé, violent, brusque, brut.

rudeness ['ru:dnis] n rudesse f, grossièreté f.

rudiment ['ru:dimənt] n rudiment m.

rudimentary [,ru:di'mentəri] a rudimentaire.

rue [ru:] vt regretter, se repentir de.

rueful ['ru:ful] a triste.

ruefulness ['ru:fulnis] n tristesse f, regret m.

ruffian ['rʌfiən] n bandit m, brute f, polisson m.

ruffle ['rʌfl] n ride f, manchette f, jabot m; vt hérisser, rider, ébouriffer, émouvoir.

rug [rʌg] n couverture f, tapis m.

rugged ['rʌgid] a rugueux, inégal, sauvage, rude.

ruin ['ruin] n ruine f; vt ruiner.

ruinous ['ruinəs] a ruineux.

rule [ru:l] n règle f, règlement m, autorité f; vt régir, gouverner, régler, décider; to — out écarter.

ruler ['ru:lə] n souverain(e) mf, dirigeant(e) mf, règle f.

ruling ['ru:liŋ] n décision f.

rum [rʌm] n rhum m; a bizarre, louche.

rumble ['rʌmbl] n grondement m, roulement m; vi rouler, gronder.

ruminate ['ru:mineit] vti ruminer.

rummage ['rʌmidʒ] vti fouiller; vi fureter.

rumor ['ru:mə] n rumeur f, bruit m; vt it is —ed le bruit court.

rump [rʌmp] n croupe f, croupion m, culotte f.

rumple ['rʌmpl] vt froisser, friper.

run [rʌn] n course f, marche f, promenade f, direction f, série f, demande f, ruée f, moyenne f, enclos m, libre usage m; vti courir; vi marcher, fonctionner, couler, s'étendre, passer, déteindre, tenir l'affiche; vt diriger, exploiter, tenir, entretenir, promener.

runaway ['rʌnəwei] a fugitif, emballé.

rung [rʌŋ] pp of ring; n barreau m, échelon m.

runner ['rʌnə] n coureur, -euse, messager m, glissoir m, patin m.

running ['rʌniŋ] n course f, marche f, direction f; a courant, coulant, continu, de suite.

running-board ['rʌniŋ bɔ:d] s marche-pied m.

runway ['rʌnwei] n piste f.
rupee [ru:'pi:] roupie f.
rupture ['rʌptʃə] n rupture f, hernie f; vt rompre; vi se rompre.
rural ['ruərəl] a rural, agreste, des champs.
rush [rʌʃ] n jonc m, ruée f, hâte f, presse f, montée f; a de pointe, urgent; vt précipiter, brusquer, expédier, bousculer, envahir; vi s'élancer, se précipiter, se jeter, faire irruption.
rusk [rʌsk] n biscotte f.
russet ['rʌsit] n reinette grise f; a brun-roux.
Russia ['rʌʃə] n Russie f.
Russian ['rʌʃən] an russe m; n Russe mf.
rust [rʌst] n rouille f; vt rouiller; vi se rouiller.
rustic ['rʌstik] n paysan, -anne, campagnard(e) mf, rustre m; a rustique, paysan.
rustle ['rʌsl] n frou-frou m, bruissement m; vi bruire, faire frou-frou; vt froisser.
rustless ['rʌstlis] a inoxydable.
rusty ['rʌsti] a rouillé.
rut [rʌt] n ornière f, rut m.
ruthless ['ru:θlis] a implacable, impitoyable.
ruthlessness ['ru:θlisnis] n férocité f, implacabilité f.
rye [rai] n seigle m.

S

Sabbath ['sæbəθ] n sabbat m, dimanche f.
saber ['seibə] n sabre m.
sable ['seibl] n zibeline f; a noir.
sabotage ['sæbəta:ʒ] n sabotage m; vt saboter.
saccharine ['sækərin] n saccharine f.
sack [sæk] n sac m, pillage; vt saccager, renvoyer, mettre en sac.
sacrament ['sækrəmənt] n sacrement m.
sacred ['seikrid] a sacré, saint, religieux, consacré.
sacrifice ['sækrifais] n sacrifice m, victime f; vt sacrifier, immoler.
sacrilege ['sækrilidʒ] n sacrilège m.
sad [sæd] a triste, cruel, lourd, déplorable.
sadden ['sædn] vt attrister.
saddle ['sædl] n selle f; vt seller, mettre sur le dos de.
saddler ['sædlə] n sellier m, bourrelier m.
sadness ['sædnis] n tristesse f.
safe [seif] n garde-manger m, coffre-fort m; a sauf, sûr, prudent, à l'abri, en sûreté.
safe-conduct ['seif'kɔndəkt] n sauf-conduit m.
safeguard ['seifga:d] n sauvegarde f, garantie f.
safely ['seifli] ad sain et sauf, bien.

safety ['seifti] n sûreté f, sécurité f; a de sûreté.
sag [sæg] vi céder, fléchir, se détendre, gondoler, baisser; n fléchissement m, ventre m.
sagacious [sə'geiʃəs] a sagace, perspicace, intelligent.
sagacity [sə'gæsiti] n sagacité f, intelligence f.
sage [seidʒ] n (bot) sauge f; an sage m.
sago ['seigou] n tapioca m.
said [sed] pt pp of say.
sail [seil] n voile f, voiture f, aile f, traversée f, promenade en bateau f; vi naviguer, mettre à la voile, planer, voguer; vt conduire, naviguer; —ing n mise à la voile f, départ m, navigation f; to go sailing faire du bateau.
sailor ['seilə] n matelot m, marin m; to be a good — avoir le pied marin.
saint [seint] an saint(e) mf.
sake [seik] for the — of par égard pour, pour l'amour de, pour les beaux yeux de, dans l'intérêt de.
salable ['seiləbl] a vendable, de vente courante.
salad ['sæləd] n salade f.
salaried ['sælərid] a rétribué, salarié.
salary ['sæləri] n traitement m, appointements m pl.
sale [seil] n vente f, solde(s) f.
salesman ['seilzmən] n vendeur m, courtier m, commis m.
salient ['seiliənt] an saillant m.
saliva [sə'laivə] n salive f.
sallow ['sælou] a blafard, jaunâtre, olivâtre.
sally ['sæli] n sortie f, saillie f; vi faire une sortie, sortir.
salmon ['sæmən] n saumon m; —trout n truite saumonée f.
saloon [sə'lu:n] n salon m, salle f, cabaret m; — car n (voiture f à) conduite intérieure f.
salt [sɔ:lt] n sel m, loup m de mer; a salé; vt saler; —cellar n salière f.
saltpeter ['sɔ:lt,pi:tə] n salpêtre m.
salubrious [sə'lu:briəs] a salubre, sain.
salubrity [sə'lu:briti] n salubrité f.
salutary ['sæljutəri] a salutaire.
salute [sə'lu:t] n salut m, salve f; vt saluer.
salvage ['sælvidʒ] n sauvetage m, matériel récupéré m; vt récupérer.
salvation [sæl'veiʃən] n salut m.
salve [sælv] vt calmer, apaiser; n pommade f, baume m.
salver ['sælvə] n plateau m.
salvo ['sælvou] n salve f.
same [seim] a même, monotone; to do the — faire de même.
sameness ['seimnis] n ressemblance f, monotonie f, uniformité f.
sample ['sa:mpl] n échantillon m; vt éprouver, tâter de, échantillonner, déguster.
sanctify ['sæŋktifai] vt sanctifier, consacrer.

sanctimonious [ˌsæŋktiˈmouniəs] a papelard, hypocrite.

sanction [ˈsæŋkʃən] n sanction f, approbation f; vt sanctionner, approuver.

sanctity [ˈsæŋktiti] n sainteté f, inviolabilité f.

sanctuary [ˈsæŋktjuəri] n sanctuaire m, asile m, refuge m.

sand [sænd] n sable m; pl plage f; — dune dune f; —paper papier de verre m; —shoes souliers mpl bains de mer, espadrilles f pl.

sandal [ˈsændl] n sandale f, samara m.

sandalwood [ˈsændlwud] n santal m.

sandbag [ˈsændbæg] n sac de terre m, assommoir m; vt protéger avec des sacs de terre, assommer.

sandy [ˈsændi] a sablonneux, blond-roux.

sandwich [ˈsænwidʒ] n sandwich m.

sane [sein] a sain, sensé.

sang [sæŋ] pt of sing.

sanguinary [ˈsæŋgwinəri] a sanglant, sanguinaire.

sanguine [ˈsæŋgwin] a sanguin, convaincu, optimiste.

sanitary [ˈsænitəri] a sanitaire, hygiénique.

sanity [ˈsæniti] n raison f, santé f mentale.

sank [sæŋk] pt of sink.

sap [sæp] n sève f, sape f; vt épuiser, saper, miner.

sapling [ˈsæpliŋ] n plant m, baliveau m, adolescent(e).

sapper [ˈsæpə] n sapeur m.

sapphire [ˈsæfaiə] n saphir m.

sarcasm [ˈsɑːkæzəm] n sarcasme m, ironie f.

sarcastic [sɑːˈkæstik] a sarcastique; —ally ad d'un ton sarcastique.

sardine [sɑːˈdiːn] n sardine f.

Sardinia [sɑːˈdiniə] n Sardaigne f.

sash [sæʃ] n châssis m, ceinture f, écharpe f; — window n fenêtre à guillotine f.

sat [sæt] pt pp of sit.

satchel [ˈsætʃəl] n sacoche f, cartable m.

sate [seit] vt assouvir, rassasier.

sated [ˈseitid] a repu.

sateen [sæˈtiːn] n satinette f.

satiate [ˈseiʃieit] vt apaiser, rassasier.

satiety [səˈtaiəti] n satiété f.

satin [ˈsætin] n satin m.

satire [ˈsætaiə] n satire f.

satirical [səˈtirikl] a satirique.

satirist [ˈsætərist] n satirique m.

satisfaction [ˌsætisˈfækʃən] n paiement m, rachat m, satisfaction f.

satisfactory [ˌsætisˈfæktəri] a satisfaisant.

satisfy [ˈsætisfai] vt satisfaire, convaincre, remplir.

saturate [ˈsætʃəreit] vt tremper, imprégner, saturer.

Saturday [ˈsætədi] n samedi m.

satyr [ˈsætə] n satyre m.

sauce [sɔːs] n sauce f, assaisonnement m, insolence f; —boat n saucière f; —pan n casserole f.

saucer [ˈsɔːsə] n soucoupe f.

sauciness [ˈsɔːsinis] n impertinence f.

saucy [ˈsɔːsi] a impertinent, effronté, fripon.

saunter [ˈsɔːntə] n flânerie f; vt flâner.

sausage [ˈsɔsidʒ] n saucisse f, saucisson m.

sausage-meat [ˈsɔsidʒmiːt] n chair à saucisse f.

savage [ˈsævidʒ] n sauvage mf; a féroce, brutal, barbare.

savagery [ˈsævidʒəri] n sauvagerie f, férocité f, barberie f.

savanna(h) [səˈvænə] n savane f.

save [seiv] vt sauver, préserver, économiser, épargner, ménager; prep sauf, excepté.

saving [ˈseiviŋ] n salut m, économie f; a économe, qui rachète.

savior [ˈseivjə] n sauveur m.

savor [ˈseivə] n saveur f, goût m, pointe f; vi to — of sentir, tenir de.

savory [ˈseivəri] a relevé, savoureux, succulent.

Savoy [səˈvɔi] Savoie f.

savvy [ˈsævi] n jugeotte f; vti piger.

saw [sɔː] n scie f; adage m; maxime f, proverbe m; vt scier.

sawdust [ˈsɔːdʌst] n sciure f.

sawmill [ˈsɔːmil] n scierie f.

sawyer [ˈsɔːjə] n scieur m.

sawn [sɔːn] pp of saw.

say [sei] n mot m, voix f; vti dire.

saying [ˈseiiŋ] n dicton m, récitation f.

scab [skæb] n croûte, gourme f, gale f, jaune m, faux-frère m; vi se cicatriser.

scabbard [ˈskæbəd] n fourreau m, gaine f.

scabby [ˈskæbi] a galeux, croûteux, mesquin.

scabies [ˈskeibiiz] n gale f.

scabrous [ˈskeibrəs] a scabreux, raboteux.

scaffold [ˈskæfəld] n échafaud m.

scaffolding [ˈskæfəldiŋ] n échafaudage m.

scald [skɔːld] n brûlure f; vt ébouillanter, échauder.

scale [skeil] n plateau m, balance f, bascule f, échelle f, gamme f, écaille f, dépôt m, tartre m; vt écailler, peler, écosser, râcler, décrasser, escalader, graduer; vi s'écailler, s'incruster.

scallop [ˈskɔləp] n coquille Saint-Jacques f, feston m.

scalp [skælp] n cuir chevelu m, scalpe m; vt scalper.

scalpel [ˈskælpəl] n scalpel m.

scamp [skæmp] n vaurien m; vt bâcler.

scamper [ˈskæmpə] vi détaler.

scan [skæn] vt scander, scruter, embrasser du regard, parcourir.

scandal ['skændl] n scandale m, honte f, cancans m pl.

scandalize ['skændəlaiz] vt scandaliser.

scandalous ['skændələs] a scandaleux, honteux.

scansion ['skænʃən] n scansion f.

scanty ['skænti] a mince, rare, insuffisant, étroit, peu de, juste, sommaire.

scapegoat ['skeipgout] n bouc émissaire m, souffre-douleur m.

scapegrace ['skeipgreis] n étourneau m, mauvais sujet m.

scar [ska:] n cicatrice f; vt balafrer; vi se cicatriser.

scarab ['skærəb] n scarabée m.

scarce [skeəs] a rare.

scarcely ['skeəsli] ad à peine, ne ... guère.

scarcity ['skeəsiti] n rareté f, pénurie f.

scare [skeə] n panique f, alarme f; vt terrifier, effrayer; —crow n épouvantail m; —monger n alarmiste mf.

scarf [ska:f] n écharpe f, foulard m, cache-col m.

scarlet ['ska:lit] an écarlate f; — fever n (fièvre) scarlatine f.

scathing ['skeiðiŋ] a mordant, cinglant.

scatter ['skætə] vt disperser, éparpiller, semer; vi se disperser, s'égailler, se dissiper; —brain n écervelé(e).

scattered ['skætəd] a épars, éparpillé, semé.

scattering ['skætəriŋ] n dispersion f, éparpillement m, poignée f.

scavenger ['skævindʒə] n balayeur m, boueux m.

scene [si:n] n scène f, spectacle m, lieu m, théâtre m.

scenery ['si:nəri] n décor(s) m (pl), paysage m.

scenic ['si:nik] a scénique, théâtral.

scent [sent] n odeur f, parfum m, piste f, flair m; vt flairer, parfumer, embaumer.

scepter ['septə] n sceptre m.

schedule ['skedjul] n horaire m, plan m, annexe f.

scheme [ski:m] n plan m, projet m, intrigue f, combinaison f; vi comploter, intriguer; vt combiner, projeter.

schemer ['ski:mə] n homme m à projets, intrigant(e) mf.

schism ['sizəm] n schisme m.

scholar ['skolə] n érudit m, savant(e) mf, boursier, -ière, écolier, -ière.

scholarship ['skoləʃip] n science f, érudition f, bourse f.

school [sku:l] n école f, faculté f; vt instruire, dresser, formerent, raîner; —summer—cours de vacances; night — école, classe, cours du soir; to go to —aller en classe.

schoolmaster ['sku:l,ma:stə] n instituteur m, professeur m, directeur m.

schoolmate ['sku:lmeit] n camarade de classe mf.

schoolroom ['sku:lrum] n (salle de) classe f.

schooner ['sku:nə] n goélette f.

science ['saiəns] n science f.

scientist ['saiəntist] n savant(e) mf, homme de science m, scientifique m.

scion ['saiən] n rejeton m, bouture f.

scissors ['sizəz] n ciseaux m pl.

scoff [skof] n raillerie f; vt railler; vi se moquer (de at).

scold [skould] n mégère f; vti gronder; vt attraper.

scolding ['skouldiŋ] n semonce f, savon m.

sconce [skons] n applique f, bobèche.

scoop [sku:p] n pelle f, louche f, écope f, cuiller f, reportage m en exclusivité; vt creuser, vider, écoper, rafler.

scope [skoup] n portée f, envergure f, champ m, carrière f, compétence f.

scorch [sko:tʃ] vt brûler, roussir, rôtir; vi filer à toute vitesse, brûler le pavé.

score [sko:] n marque f, score m, point m, compte m, partition f, coche f, éraflure f, vingt; vt marquer, remporter, (en)cocher, érafler, orchestrer; vi marquer les points, avoir l'avantage; réprimander, censurer.

scorn [sko:n] n mépris m; vt mépriser.

scornful ['sko:nful] a méprisant.

Scotch ['skotʃ] n Écossais(e) mf; an écossais m; n whisky m.

scotfree ['skot'fri:] a indemne, sans rien payer.

Scotland ['skotlənd] n Écosse f.

Scot(sman, -swoman) [skot(smən, wumən)] n Écossais, Écossaise.

Scots, Scottish [skots, 'skotiʃ] a écossais, d'Écosse.

scoundrel ['skaundrəl] n canaille f, gredin m, coquin m.

scour ['skauə] vt frotter, récurer, purger, battre, balayer, (par)courir.

scourge [skə:dʒ] n fléau m; vt châtier, flageller.

scout [skaut] n éclaireur m, scout m; vt reconnaître, rejeter; vi partir en reconnaissance.

scowl [skaul] n air renfrogné m; vi faire la tête, se renfrogner.

scrag [skræg] n squelette m, cou m, collet m.

scraggy ['skrægi] a décharné.

scramble ['skræmbl] n mêlée f, lutte f; vt (eggs) brouiller; vi se battre, se bousculer.

scrap [skræp] n morceau m, chiffon m, coupure f, bribe f, bagarre f, déchets m pl, restes m pl; vt mettre au rebut, réformer; vi se battre, se bagarrer.

scrape [skreip] n grincement m,

grattage m, embarras m; vti gratter, frotter; vt râcler, décrotter.

scraper ['skreipə] n grattoir m, décrottoir m.

scratch [skrætʃ] n égratignure f, trait (grincement m) de plume mf, coup de griffe m; — pad n bloc-notes m; vti égratigner, gratter, griffonner.

scrawl [skrɔːl] n gribouillage m; vt gribouiller.

scream [skriːm] n cri (perçant m); vi pousser un cri, crier, se tordre (de rire).

screaming ['skriːmiŋ] a désopilant, criard.

screen [skriːn] n écran m, paravent m, rideau m, crible m, jubé m; vt couvrir, cacher, protéger, projeter, cribler, mettre à l'écran.

screw [skruː] n vis f, hélice f, écrou m, pingre m; vt visser, (res)serrer, pressurer; to — up one's courage prendre son courage à deux mains.

screwdriver ['skruːˌdraivə] n tournevis m.

scribble ['skribl] see **scrawl**.

scrimmage ['skrimidʒ] n bagarre f, mêlée f.

scrimp [skrimp] vti lésiner (sur), saboter.

scripture ['skriptʃə] n Écriture f.

scroll [skroul] n rouleau m, volute f, fioriture f.

scrounge [skraundʒ] vt chiper, écornifler.

scrounger ['skraundʒə] n chipeur m, pique-assiette m.

scrub [skrʌb] n broussailles f pl, coup de brosse m, frottée f; vt frotter, récurer.

scrubbing ['skrʌbiŋ] n frottage m, récurage m.

scrubby ['skrʌbi] a rabougri, chétif.

scruple ['skruːpl] n scrupule m; vi se faire scrupule (de about).

scrupulous ['skruːpjuləs] a scrupuleux, méticuleux.

scrutinize ['skruːtinaiz] vt scruter, examiner de près.

scrutiny ['skruːtini] n examen serré m, second compte m.

scuffle ['skʌfl] n bousculade f; vi bousculer.

scull [skʌl] n godille f; vi godiller, ramer.

sculptor ['skʌlptə] n sculpteur m.

sculpture ['skʌlptʃə] n sculpture f; vt sculpter.

scum [skʌm] n écume f, rebut m; vti écumer.

scurf [skəːf] n pellicule f.

scurrilous ['skʌriləs] a grossier, ordurier, obscène.

scurvy ['skəːvi] n scorbut m; a bas, méprisable.

scuttle ['skʌtl] n seau m, hublot m, fuite f; vt saborder; vi décamper.

scythe [saið] n faux f; vt faucher.

sea [siː] n mer f; a marin, maritime, de mer; —coast n littoral m;

—gull n mouette f; —horse n mouton m; —level n niveau de la mer m; —plane n hydravion m; —port n port (maritime) m; —sickness n mal de mer m; —wall n digue f.

seal [siːl] n (zool) phoque m; cachet m, sceau m; vt sceller, cacheter.

sealing-wax ['siːliŋwæks] n cire à cacheter f.

seam [siːm] n couture f, suture f, cicatrice f, veine f, filon m.

seaman ['siːmən] n marin m, matelot m.

seamstress ['semstris] n couturière f.

seamy side ['siːmisaid] n envers m, les dessous m pl.

sear [siə] a séché, flétri; vt brûler au fer rouge, flétrir.

search [səːtʃ] n quête f, visite f, perquisition f, recherche(s) f (pl); vt fouiller, inspecter, scruter, sonder, examiner; vti chercher.

searching ['səːtʃiŋ] a pénétrant, minutieux.

searchlight ['səːtʃlait] n projecteur m, phare m.

season ['siːzn] n saison f, période f, bon moment m; vt endurcir, aguerrir, mûrir, assaisonner, tempérer.

seasonable ['siːznəbl] a de saison, saisonnier, opportun.

seasoning ['siːzniŋ] n assaisonnement m.

season-ticket ['siːznˈtikit] n abonnement m.

seat [siːt] n siège m, selle f, centre m, foyer m, propriété f, fond m (de culotte); vt contenir, faire asseoir, installer.

seaweed ['siːwiːd] n goémon m, algue f, varech m.

secede [siˈsiːd] vi se séparer.

secession [siˈseʃən] n sécession f.

seclude [siˈkluːd] vt écarter.

seclusion [siˈkluːʒən] n retraite f, solitude f.

second ['sekənd] n seconde f, second m; a second, deuxième; — to none sans égal; vt seconder, appuyer, (mil) détacher; —hand a d'occasion; —rate a médiocre, inférieur.

secrecy ['siːkrisi] n secret m, réserve f, dissimulation f.

secret ['siːkrit] a secret, réservé, retiré; n secret m, confidence f.

secretariat [ˌsekrəˈtɛəriət] n secrétariat m.

secretary ['sekrətri] n secrétaire mf.

secrete [siˈkriːt] vt cacher, sécréter.

secretion [siˈkriːʃən] n sécrétion f.

secretive [siˈkriːtiv] a secret, réservé, cachottier, renfermé.

sect [sekt] n secte f.

sectarian [sekˈtɛəriən] n sectaire m.

section ['sekʃən] n section f, coupe f, tranche f, profil m.

sector ['sektə] n secteur m.

secular ['sekjulə] a séculier, profane, séculaire.

secure [si'kjuə] *a* sûr, assuré, en sûreté, assujetti; *vt* mettre en lieu sûr, fixer, s'assurer, obtenir, assujettir.
security [si'kjuəriti] *n* sécurité *f*, sûreté(s) *f* (pl), sauvegarde *f*, garantie *f*, solidité *f*.
sedate [si'deit] *a* posé.
sedentary ['sedntəri] *a* sédentaire.
sedge [sedʒ] *n* jonc *m*, laîche *f*.
sediment ['sedimənt] *n* sédiment *m*, lie *f*, dépôt *m*.
sedition [si'diʃən] *n* sédition *f*.
seditious [si'diʃəs] *a* séditieux.
seduce [si'djuːs] *vt* séduire.
seducer [si'djuːsə] *n* séducteur *m*.
seduction [si'dʌkʃən] *n* séduction *f*.
seductive [si'dʌktiv] *a* séduisant.
seductiveness [si'dʌktivnis] *n* attrait *m*, séduction *f*.
sedulous ['sedjuləs] *a* assidu, empressé.
see [siː] *n* évêché *m*, siège *m*; *vti* voir, saisir, comprendre; — here! toi, écoute!
seed [siːd] *n* semence *f*, graine *f*, pépin *m*; *vi* monter en graine; *vt* ensemencer, semer.
seedling ['siːdliŋ] *n* plant *m*, sauvageon *m*.
seedy ['siːdi] *a* monté en graine, râpé, souffreteux, minable.
seek [siːk] *vt* (re)chercher.
seem [siːm] *vi* sembler, paraître.
seeming ['siːmiŋ] *a* apparent, soidisant.
seemingly ['siːmiŋli] *ad* apparemment.
seemly ['siːmli] *a* séant.
seemliness ['siːmlinis] *n* bienséance *f*.
seesaw ['siːsɔː] *n* bascule *f*, balançoire *f*.
seethe [siːð] *vi* bouillonner, grouiller, être en effervescence.
seize [siːz] *vt* saisir, s'emparer de; *vi* se caler, gripper.
seizure ['siːʒə] *n* saisie *f*, attaque *f*.
seldom ['seldəm] *ad* rarement.
select [si'lekt] *a* choisi, de choix, d'élite; *vt* choisir, trier, sélectionner.
selection [si'lekʃən] *n* choix *m*, sélection *f*.
self [self] *n* personnalité *f*, moi *m*, égoïsme *m*; *a* même, monotone, uniforme, auto-; —conscious emprunté, gêné, conscient; —contained (ren)fermé, indépendant; —control maîtrise *f* de soi, sangfroid *m*; —defence légitime défense *f*; —denial sacrifice *m*, abnégation *f*; —educated autodidacte; —government autonomie *f*; —indulgence *n* complaisance *f* (pour soi-même), faiblesse; —interest égoïsme, intérêt personnel *m*; —respect amour-propre *m*; —same *a* identique.
self-determination ['selfdi təmi'neiʃən] *n* autodétermination *f*.
selfish ['selfiʃ] *a* égoïste.

selfishness ['selfiʃnis] *n* égoïsme *m*.
selfless ['selflis] *a* désintéressé.
selflessness ['selflisnis] *n* abnégation *f*.
self-possessed ['selfpə'zest] *a* maître de soi, qui à de l'aplomb *m*.
self-starter ['self'stɑːtə] *n* démarreur *m*.
self-willed ['self'wild] *a* obstiné, volontaire.
sell [sel] *vt* vendre; *v* —se vendre, se placer, populariser.
seller ['selə] *n* vendeur, -euse, marchand(e) *mf*.
semblance ['sembləns] *n* air *m*, apparence *f*, semblant *m*.
semi-colon ['semi'koulən] *n* pointvirgule *m*.
seminary ['seminəri] *n* séminaire *m*, pépinière *f*.
semi-official ['semiə'fiʃəl] *a* officieux.
semolina [ˌsemə'liːnə] *n* semoule *f*.
senate ['senit] *n* sénat *m*.
send [send] *vt* envoyer, expédier; to — down renvoyer; to — for faire venir; to — off reconduire, expédier.
sender ['sendə] *n* envoyeur, -euse, expéditeur, -trice.
sending ['sendiŋ] *n* envoi *m*, expédition *f*.
senior ['siːnjə] *an* ancien, -ienne, aîné(e) *mf*.
seniority [ˌsiːni'ɔriti] *n* ancienneté *f*, aînesse *f*.
sensation [sen'seiʃən] *n* sentiment *m*, sensation *f*, impression *f*.
sensational [sen'seiʃənl] *a* sensationnel, à sensation.
sense [sens] *n* (bon) sens *m*, sentiment *m*; *vt* sentir, pressentir.
senseless ['senslis] *a* déraisonnable, sans connaissance.
sensibility [ˌsensi'biliti] *n* sensibilité *f*.
sensible ['sensəbl] *a* raisonnable, sensé, perceptible, sensible.
sensitive ['sensitiv] *a* sensible, impressionnable.
sensual ['sensjuəl] *a* sensuel.
sensuality [ˌsensju'æliti] *n* sensualité *f*.
sent [sent] *pt pp* of **send**.
sentence ['sentəns] *n* phrase *f*, sentence *f*; *vt* condamner.
sententious [sen'tenʃəs] *a* sentencieux.
sentiment ['sentimənt] *n* sentiment *m*, opinion *f*.
sentimentality [ˌsentimen'tæliti] *n* sentimentalité *f*.
sentry ['sentri] *n* sentinelle *f*, factionnaire *m*.
sentry-box ['sentriboks] *n* guérite *f*.
separate ['seprit] *a* distinct, détaché, séparé.
separate ['sepəreit] *vt* séparer, détacher, dégager; *vi* se séparer, se détacher.
sepoy ['siːpɔi] *n* cipaye *m*.

September [səp'tembə] n septembre m.

septic ['septik] a septique.

sepulcher ['sepəlkə] n sépulcre m.

sequel ['si:kwəl] n suite f.

sequence ['si:kwəns] n série f, suite f, séquence f.

sequester [si'kwestə] vt séquestrer, enfermer.

seraglio [sə'rɑːliou] n sérail m.

serene [si'ri:n] a serein, calme.

serenity [si'reniti] n sérénité f, calme m.

serf [sə:f] n serf m.

serfdom ['sə:fdəm] n servage m.

serge [sə:dʒ] n serge f.

sergeant ['sɑːdʒənt] n sergent m, maréchal des logis m, (police) brigadier m.

serial ['siəriəl] n feuilleton m; a en série.

seriatim [,siəri'eitim] ad point par point.

series ['siəri:z] n série f, suite f.

serious ['siəriəs] a sérieux, grave.

seriousness ['siəriəsnis] n sérieux m, gravité f.

sermon ['sə:mən] n sermon m.

sermonize ['sə:mənaiz] vt sermonner.

serpent ['sə:pənt] n serpent m.

serpentine ['sə:pəntain] a serpentin, sinueux.

servant ['sə:vənt] n domestique mf, serviteur m, servante f.

serve [sə:v] vt servir, être utile à, subir, remettre, desservir, purger.

service ['sə:vis] n service m, emploi m, entretien m, office m, culte m; a d'ordonnance, de service.

serviceable ['sə:visəbl] a serviable, de bon usage, pratique, utilisable.

servile ['sə:vail] a servile.

servility [sə:'viliti] n servilité f.

servitude ['sə:vitju:d] n servitude f, esclavage m.

session ['seʃən] n session f, séance f, classe f, cours m pl.

set [set] n (tools etc) jeu m, collection f, (people) groupe m, cercle f, (tea etc) service m, (TV etc) poste m, appareil m, (theatre) décor(s) m (pl), (pearls) rangée f, (linen) parure f, (hair) mise-en-plis f, (idea) direction f; a fixe, pris, stéréotype; vt régler, mettre (à in), fixer, (print) composer, (jewels) sertir, (trap) tendre, (blade) aiguiser; vi se mettre (à), prendre, durcir, se fixer, (sun) se coucher; to — going commencer; to — aside mettre de côté, écarter; to — forth exposer, faire valoir; to — in vi avancer; — off vi partir, vt déclencher; to — out vi partir, vt arranger; to — up vi monter, s'établir, préparer; to — upon attaquer.

set-back ['setbæk] n recul m, échec m.

set-off ['set'ɔf] n contraste m, repoussoir m.

set-to ['set'tu:] n pugilat m, échauffourré m.

settee [se'ti:] n divan m.

setter ['setə] n chien d'arrêt m.

setting ['setiŋ] n monture f, pose f, cadre m, mise f (en scène, en marche etc), coucher m.

settle ['setl] vt établir, installer, fixer, ranger, poser, régler, placer; vi s'établir, s'installer, se poser, déposer, s'arranger; n banc m, canapé m.

settlement ['setlmənt] n établissement m, colonie f, contrat m, règlement m.

settler ['setlə] n colon m, immigrant m.

seven ['sevn] an sept m.

sevenfold ['sevnfould] a septuple; ad sept fois autant.

seventeen ['sevn'ti:n] an dix-sept m.

seventeenth ['sevn'ti:nθ] an dix-septième mf.

seventh ['sevnθ] an septième mf.

seventy ['sevnti] an soixante-dix m.

sever ['sevə] vt séparer, trancher, couper.

several ['sevrəl] a respectif, personnel; a pn plusieurs.

severe [si'viə] a sévère, rigoureux, vif.

severity [si'veriti] n sévérité f, rigueur f, violence f.

sew [sou] vt coudre, suturer.

sewage ['sjuidʒ] n vidanges f pl, eaux f pl d'égout.

sewer ['souə] n couturière, brocheuse f.

sewer ['sjuə] n égout m.

sewing-machine ['souiŋmə,ʃi:n] n machine à coudre f.

sewn [soun] pp of sew.

sex [seks] n sexe m; — appeal n sex-appeal m.

sexton ['sekstən] n sacristain m, fossoyeur m.

sexual ['seksjuəl] a sexuel.

sexy ['seksi] a (fam) capiteuse, excitante; to be — avoir du sex-appeal.

shabby ['ʃæbi] a pingre, râpé, minable, délabré, mesquin, défraîchi.

shackle ['ʃækl] n chaîne f, maillon m; pl fers m pl, entraves f pl; vt enchaîner, entraver.

shade [ʃeid] n ombre f, retraite f, nuance f, store m; pl lunettes de soleil f pl; vt abriter, ombrager, masquer, assombrir, ombrer; vi dégrader.

shadow ['ʃædou] n ombre f; vt filer.

shadowy ['ʃædoui] a ombrageux, vaseux.

shady ['ʃeidi] a ombragé, ombreux, furtif, louche.

shaft [ʃɑːft] n hampe f, trait m, tige f, fût m, manche m, brancard m, arbre m, puits m.

shaggy ['ʃægi] a hirsute, touffu, en broussailles.

shake [ʃeik] n secousse f, hochement m, tremblement m; vt secouer, agiter, hocher, ébranler, serrer; vi trembler, branler.

shaky ['ʃeiki] a branlant, tremblant, chancelant.

shallot [ʃə'lɔt] n échalote f.

shallow ['ʃælou] n bas-fond m, haut-fond m; a peu profond, creux, superficiel.

sham [ʃæm] n feinte f, trompe-l'œil m, faux semblant m; a faux, simulé, postiche, en toc; vt feindre, simuler, faire semblant de.

shamble ['ʃæmbl] vi traîner les pieds.

shambles ['ʃæmblz] n abattoir m, tuerie f.

shame [ʃeim] n honte f, pudeur f; vt faire honte à, couvrir de honte.

shameful ['ʃeimful] a honteux, scandaleux.

shameless ['ʃeimlis] a éhonté, effronté.

shampoo [ʃæm'pu:] n shampooing m; vt donner un shampooing à.

shamrock ['ʃæmrɔk] n trèfle m.

shandy ['ʃændi] n bière panachée f.

shank [ʃæŋk] n jambe f, tige f, fût m, manche m, tibia m.

shape [ʃeip] n forme f, tournure f, moule m; vt former, façonner; vi prendre forme, prendre tournure.

shapeless ['ʃeiplis] a informe.

shapely ['ʃeipli] a gracieux, bien fait.

share [ʃɛə] n part f, action f, contribution f, soc m; vti partager; vt prendre part à.

shareholder ['ʃɛə,houldə] n actionnaire mf.

shark [ʃɑ:k] n requin m, n fort (en maths).

sharp [ʃɑ:p] a pointu, aigu, tranchant, aigre, vif, fin, malhonnête, expert; ad juste, brusquement; tapant.

sharpen ['ʃɑ:pən] vt aiguiser, affiler, tailler.

sharper ['ʃɑ:pə] n tricheur m, escroc m.

sharply ['ʃɑ:pli] ad vertement, d'un ton tranchant.

sharpness ['ʃɑ:pnis] n acuité f, netteté f, finesse f.

sharpshooter ['ʃɑ:p,ʃu:tə] n bon tireur m, tirailleur m.

shatter ['ʃætə] vt mettre en pièces, fracasser.

shave [ʃeiv] vt raser, frôler; vi se raser; to have a — se (faire) raser; to have a close — l'échapper belle.

shaving ['ʃeiviŋ] n copeau m; —brush n blaireau m.

shawl [ʃɔ:l] n châle m.

she [ʃi:] pn elle, (ship) il; n femelle f.

sheaf [ʃi:f] n gerbe f, liasse f.

shear [ʃiə] vt tondre.

shearing ['ʃiəriŋ] n tonte f.

shears [ʃiəz] n cisailles f pl.

sheath [ʃi:θ] n fourreau m, gaine f, étui m.

sheathe [ʃi:ð] vt (r)engainer, encaisser, doubler.

shed [ʃed] n hangar m, remise f, étable f, appentis m; vt perdre, mettre au rencart, se dépouiller de, verser.

sheep [ʃi:p] n mouton m.

sheepdog ['ʃi:pdɔg] n chien de berger m.

sheepish ['ʃi:piʃ] a gauche, timide, penaud, honteux.

sheer [ʃiə] a pur, à pic, transparent.

sheet [ʃi:t] n drap m, feuille f, nappe f, tôle f.

shelf [ʃelf] n rayon m, corniche f.

shell [ʃel] n coquille f, coque f, cosse f, écaille f, carapace f, douille f, obus m; vt écosser, décortiquer, bombarder.

shellfish ['ʃelfiʃ] n coquillage m.

shelter ['ʃeltə] n abri m, couvert m, asile m; vt abriter, couvrir, recueillir; vi s'abriter, se mettre à l'abri.

shelve [ʃelv] vt mettre à l'écart, (en disponibilité, au panier), ajourner.

shepherd ['ʃepəd] n berger m; vt rassembler, garder, conduire.

sherry ['ʃeri] n Xérès m.

shield [ʃi:ld] n bouclier m, défense f; vt protéger, couvrir.

shift [ʃift] n changement m, équipe f, expédient m, faux-fuyant m; to work in —a se relayer; vti changer; vt déplacer; vi se déplacer; to — for oneself se débrouiller.

shifty ['ʃifti] a fuyant, retors, sournois.

shin(-bone) ['ʃin(boun)] n tibia m; vi grimper.

shine [ʃain] n brillant m, éclat m, beau-temps m; vi briller, reluire, rayonner.

shingle ['ʃiŋgl] n galets m pl; vt couper court.

shingles ['ʃiŋglz] n pl zona m.

ship [ʃip] n vaisseau m, navire m, bâtiment m; vt embarquer, charger, expédier; —broker courtier m maritime; —load chargement m, cargaison f; —building construction f navale.

shipping ['ʃipiŋ] n marine f, tonnage m, expédition f, navires m pl.

shipwreck ['ʃiprek] n naufrage m; vi faire échouer, faire naufrager; to be —ed faire naufrage.

shipwright ['ʃiprait] n charpentier de navires m.

shipyard ['ʃipjɑːd] n chantier maritime m.

shirk [ʃə:k] vt esquiver, renâcler à, se dérober à.

shirker ['ʃə:kə] n tire-au-flanc m, renâcleur m.

shirt [ʃə:t] n chemise f.

shirt-front ['ʃə:tfrʌnt] n plastron m.

shiver ['ʃivə] n frisson m; vi frissonner, grelotter.

shoal [ʃoul] n banc m, masse f, haut-fond m.

shock [ʃɔk] n secousse f, heurt m, choc m, coup m; vt choquer, frapper, scandaliser.

shoddy ['ʃɔdi] n camelote f; a de pacotille.

shoe [ʃuː] n soulier m, chaussure f, fer à cheval m; vt chausser, ferrer, armer; —black cireur m; —horn chausse-pied m; —lace lacet m, cordon m; —maker cordonnier m.

shone [ʃɔn] pt pp of shine.

shoot [ʃuːt] n pousse f, sarment m, gourmand m, rapide m, partie de chasse f, chasse f; vi pousser, jaillir, tirer, filer; vt tirer, abattre, fusiller, lancer, décocher, darder.

shooting ['ʃuːtiŋ] n tir m, fusillade f, chasse (gardée) f; —box pavillon de chasse m; —party partie de chasse f; —range m champ de tir m; —star n étoile filante f.

shop [ʃɔp] n magasin m, boutique f, atelier m; vi faire ses achats; —assistant vendeur m, vendeuse f; —boy (-girl) garçon (demoiselle f) de magasin m; —keeper boutiquier m, marchand m; —lifter voleur m à l'étalage; — window vitrine f.

shore [ʃɔː] n côte f, rivage m, étai m; vt étayer.

shorn [ʃɔːn] pp of shear.

short [ʃɔːt] n brève f, court-métrage m, (drinks) alcool m; a bref, court(aud), concis, à court de, cassant; in — bref; —ly ad brièvement, de court, sous peu.

shortage ['ʃɔːtidʒ] n manque m, crise f, pénurie f.

shortbread ['ʃɔːtbred] n sablé m.

short-circuit ['ʃɔːt'səːkit] n court-circuit m.

shortcoming [ʃɔːt'kʌmiŋ] n défaut m, insuffisance f, imperfection f.

shorten ['ʃɔːtn] vti raccourcir, abréger.

shorthand ['ʃɔːthænd] n sténographie f.

shortness ['ʃɔːtnis] n brièveté f, manque m.

shorts [ʃɔːts] n culotte f, short m.

short-sighted ['ʃɔːt'saitid] a myope, imprévoyant, de myopie.

short-sightedness ['ʃɔːt'saitidnis] n myopie f, imprévoyance f.

short-tempered ['ʃɔːt'tempəd] a irritable.

short-winded ['ʃɔːtwindid] a court d'haleine, poussif.

shot [ʃɔt] pt pp of shoot; n balle f, boulet m; plombs m pl, coup m (de feu), tireur m, tentative f, portée f, prise de vue f; —gun fusil m.

shoulder ['ʃouldə] n épaule f; vt mettre, charger, porter, sur l'épaule; —blade omoplate f; —strap bretelle f, patte d'épaule f; — bag sac m en bandoulière.

shout [ʃaut] n cri m; vti crier; to —

down huer.

shove [ʃʌv] n coup d'épaule m; vti pousser; vt fourrer.

shovel ['ʃʌvl] n pelle f.

shovelful ['ʃʌvlful] n pelletée f.

show [ʃou] n spectacle m, exposition f, montre f, étalage m, apparence f, simulacre m, affaire f, ostentation f; motor — salon m de l'automobile; vt montrer, exposer, exhiber, accuser, indiquer, faire preuve de; vi se montrer, paraître; to — in faire entrer, introduire; to — out reconduire; to — off vt faire étalage de, mettre en valeur; vi faire de l'épate, se faire valoir; to — up démasquer.

show-case ['ʃoukeis] n vitrine f.

shower ['ʃauə] n ondée f, averse f, pluie f, douche f, volée f; vt faire pleuvoir, arroser, accabler.

showiness ['ʃouinis] n ostentation f, épate f.

showman ['ʃoumən] n forain m, imprésario m.

shown [ʃoun] pp of show.

showroom ['ʃourum] n salon d'exposition m.

show-window ['ʃou'windou] n étalage m.

showy ['ʃoui] a voyant, criard, prétentieux.

shrank [ʃræŋk] pt of shrink.

shred [ʃred] n pièce f, lambeau m, brin m; vt mettre en pièces, effilocher.

shrew [ʃruː] n mégère f; (mouse) musaraigne f.

shrewd [ʃruːd] a perspicace, entendu, judicieux.

shrewdness ['ʃruːdnis] n sagacité f, perspicacité f, finesse f.

shriek [ʃriːk] n cri aigu m; vi crier, déchirer l'air, pousser un cri.

shrill [ʃril] a aigu, -uë, perçant.

shrimp [ʃrimp] n crevette (grise) f, gringalet m.

shrine [ʃrain] n châsse f, tombeau m, sanctuaire m.

shrink [ʃriŋk] vt rétrécir; vi se rétrécir, reculer.

shrinkage ['ʃriŋkidʒ] n rétrécissement m.

shrivel ['ʃrivl] vi se ratatiner, se recroqueviller; vt ratatiner, brûler.

shroud [ʃraud] n linceul m, suaire m, hauban m, voile m; vt envelopper, cacher, voiler.

Shrove Tuesday ['ʃrouv'tjuːzdi] n mardi gras m.

shrub [ʃrʌb] n arbrisseau m.

shrubbery ['ʃrʌbəri] n taillis m, bosquet m.

shrug [ʃrʌg] n haussement d'épaules m; vi to — one's shoulders hausser les épaules.

shudder ['ʃʌdə] n frisson m; vi frissonner.

shuffle ['ʃʌfl] vt brouiller, (cards) battre, mêler, traîner; vi traîner la jambe, louvoyer, tergiverser.

shun [ʃʌn] vt éviter, fuir.

shunt [ʃʌnt] *vt* garer, manœuvrer, écarter.

shunting ['ʃʌntiŋ] *n* garage *m*, manœuvre *f*.

shut [ʃʌt] *vti* fermer, serrer; *vi* (se) fermer; to — down arrêter, fermer; to — in enfermer, confiner; to — off couper; to — up *vt* enfermer; *vi* fermer çà.

shut-out ['ʃʌtaut] *n* lock-out *m*.

shutter ['ʃʌtə] *n* volet *m*, obturateur *m*.

shuttle ['ʃʌtl] *n* navette *f*.

shuttlecock ['ʃʌtlkɔk] *n* volant *m*.

shy [ʃai] *n* sursaut *m*, écart *m*, essai *m*; *a* timide, ombrageux; to be — of être à court de; to — sursauter, faire un écart; *vt* lancer.

sick [sik] *a* malade, écœuré, dégoûté, —room *n* chambre *f* de malade.

sicken ['sikn] *vi* tomber malade; *vt* écœurer.

sickle ['sikl] *n* faucille *f*.

sickly ['sikli] *a* maladif, malsain, fade, pâle.

sickness ['siknis] *n* maladie *f*, mal de cœur *m*.

side [said] *n* côté *m*, flanc *m*, côte *f*, parti *m*, équipe *f*, chichi *m*; *a* de coté, latéral.

sideboard ['saidbɔd] *n* dressoir *m*, buffet *m*.

sidecar ['saidkɑ:] *n* sidecar *m*.

sidelong ['saidlɔŋ] *a* oblique, de côté, en coulisse.

siding ['saidiŋ] *n* voie de garage *f*.

sidewalk ['saidwɔ:k] *n* trottoir *m*.

sideways ['saidweiz] *ad* de côté.

siege [si:dʒ] *n* siège *m*.

sieve [siv] *n* tamis *m*, crible *m*, écumoire *f*.

sift [sift] *vt* cribler, tamiser.

sigh [sai] *n* soupir *m*; *vi* soupirer.

sight [sait] *n* vue *f*, hausse *f*, guidon *m*, spectacle *m*; *vt* apercevoir, aviser; (gun) pointer.

sightless ['saitlis] *a* aveugle.

sightly ['saitli] *a* bon à voir, avenant.

sightseeing ['sait,si:iŋ] *n* tourisme *m*, visite *f*.

sign [sain] *n* signe *m*, marque *f*, indication *f*, enseigne *f*; *vt* signer; *vi* faire signe; —board enseigne *f*; —post poteau indicateur *m*.

signal ['signl] *n* signal *m*, indicatif *m*; *vti* signaler.

signatory ['signətəri] *n* signataire *mf*.

signature ['signitʃə] *n* signature *f*; — tune indicatif musical *m*.

significance [sig'nifikəns] *n* sens *m*, importance *f*.

significant [sig'nifikənt] *a* significatif, important.

signification [,signifi'keiʃən] *n* signification *f*.

signify ['signifai] *vt* annoncer, signifier; *vi* importer.

silence ['sailəns] *n* silence *m*; *excl* motus! chut!; *vt* réduire au silence, faire taire, étouffer.

silencer ['sailənsə] *n* silencieux *m*.

silent ['sailənt] *a* silencieux, muet, taciturne.

silk [silk] *n* soie *f*; *a* de, en, soie; —worm ver à soie *m*.

silken ['silkən] *a* soyeux, suave, doucereux.

sill [sil] *n* seuil *m*, rebord *m*.

silliness ['silinis] *n* sottise.

silly ['sili] *a* sot, sotte, bête.

silt [silt] *n* vase *f*; *vt* ensabler, envaser; *vi* s'ensabler.

silver ['silvə] *n* argent *m*, argenterie *f*; *a* d'argent, argenté; *vt* argenter, étamer; — gilt vermeil *m*;— paper papier d'étain *m*; —side gîte à la noix *m*; —smith orfèvre *m*.

silvery ['silvəri] *a* argenté, argentin.

similar ['similə] *a* semblable; —ly *ad* de même.

similarity [simi'læriti] *n* similarité *f*, ressemblance *f*.

simile ['simili] *n* comparaison *f*.

similitude [si'militju:d] *n* ressemblance *f*, apparence *f*, similitude *f*.

simmer ['simə] *vti* mijoter; *vi* frémir, fermenter.

simper ['simpə] *n* sourire *m* apprêté; *vi* minauder.

simple ['simpl] *a* simple.

simpleton ['simpltən] *n* niais(e) *mf*.

simplicity [sim'plisiti] *n* simplicité *f*, candeur *f*.

simplify ['simplifai] *vt* simplifier.

simplification [,simplifi'keiʃən] *n* simplification *f*.

simulate ['simjuleit] *vt* simuler, feindre, imiter.

simulation [,simju'leiʃən] *n* simulation *f*.

simulator ['simjuleitə] *n* simulateur, -trice.

simultaneous [,siməl'teiniəs] *a* simultané.

simultaneousness [,siməl'teiniəsnis] *n* simultanéité *f*.

sin [sin] *n* péché *m*; *vi* pécher.

since [sins] *prep* depuis; *ad* depuis; *cj* depuis que, puisque.

sincere [sin'siə] *a* sincère.

sincerely [sin'siəli] *ad* yours — recevez l'expression de mes sentiments distingués.

sincerity [sin'seriti] *n* sincérité *f*, bonne foi *f*.

sinecure ['sainikjuə] *n* sinécure *f*.

sinew ['sinju:] *n* tendon *m*, muscle *m*, force *f*; *pl* nerf(s) *m* (*pl*).

sinewy ['sinju:i] *a* musclé, musculeux, nerveux.

sinful ['sinful] *a* coupable.

sing [siŋ] *vti* chanter.

singe [sindʒ] *vt* roussir, flamber.

singer ['siŋə] *n* chanteur, -euse, chantre *m*; praise — griot *m*.

single ['siŋgl] *a* seul, singulier, pour une personne, célibataire, droit, sincère; *n* (ticket) aller *m*, (tennis) simple *m*; *vt* to — out distinguer, désigner; —**handed** sans aide, d'une seule main.

singleness ['singlnis] n unité f, droiture f.

singular ['singjulə] a singulier.

singularity [,singju'læriti] n singularité f.

sinister ['sinistə] a sinistre, mauvais.

sink [sink] n évier m, cloaque m, trappe f; vi baisser, tomber, s'abaisser, défaillir, sombrer, couler au fond, s'enfoncer; vt placer à fonds perdus, couler, baisser, forer, abandonner, sacrifier.

sinking ['sinkin] n coulage m, défaillance f, enfoncement m, abaissement m; —**fund** fonds d'amortissement m.

sinner ['sinə] n pécheur, pécheresse.

sinuous ['sinjuəs] a sinueux, souple.

sip [sip] n gorgée f goutte f; vt siroter, déguster.

siphon ['saifən] n siphon m.

sir [sə:] n monsieur m.

sire [saiə] n sire m, père m.

siren ['saiərin] n sirène f.

sirloin ['sə:lɔin] n aloyau m, fauxfilet m.

sister ['sistə] n sœur f; —**in-law** belle sœur f.

sisterhood ['sistəhud] n état de sœur m, communauté f.

sisterly ['sistəli] a de sœur.

sit [sit] vi être assis, rester assis, se tenir, (s')asseoir, siéger, couver, poser; to — in occuper; vt asseoir.

site [sait] n terrain m, emplacement m.

sitter ['sitə] n couveuse f, modèle m.

sitting ['sitin] n séance f, couvaison f, siège m; a assis.

sitting room ['sitinrum] n petit salon m, salle f de séjour.

situated ['sitjueitid] a situé.

situation [,sitju'eifən] n situation f, place f.

six [siks] an six m.

sixteen ['siks'ti:n] an seize m.

sixteenth ['siks'ti:nθ] an seizième m.

sixth [siksθ] an sixième mf.

sixty ['siksti] an soixante m.

size [saiz] n taille f, dimension f, grandeur f, pointure f, format m, calibre m; to — up mesurer, juger.

skate [skeit] n patin m, (fish) raie f; vi patiner.

skating-rink ['skeitinrink] n patinoire f.

skein [skein] n écheveau m.

skeleton ['skelitn] n squelette m, charpente f, canevas m; — **in the cupboard** secret m, tare f; —**key** passe-partout m, rossignol m.

skeptical ['skeptikəl] a sceptique.

skepticism ['skeptisizəm] n scepticisme m.

sketch [sketf] n croquis m, sketch m; vt esquisser.

skew [skju:] a oblique, de biais.

skewer ['skjuə] n brochette f.

skid [skid] n dérapage m, sabot m, patin m; vi déraper, patiner.

skill [skil] n habileté f, adresse f, tact m.

skilled [skild] a qualifié, expert, habile, versé.

skim [skim] vti écumer, écrémer, effleurer; to — **through** parcourir, feuilleter.

skimmer ['skimə] n écumoire f.

skimp [skimp] vt lésiner sur, mesurer.

skin ['skin] n peau f, outre f, robe f, pelure f; — **deep** à fleur de peau; vt écorcher, peler, éplucher, se cicatriser.

skinner ['skinə] n fourreur m.

skinny ['skini] a décharné.

skip [skip] n saut m; vi sauter, gambader.

skipper ['skipə] n patron m.

skirmish ['skə:mif] n escarmouche f.

skirt [skə:t] n jupe f, basque f, pan m, lisière f; vt longer, contourner.

skit [skit] n pièce satirique f, charge f.

skittle ['skitl] n quille f; pl jeu de quilles m.

skulk [skʌlk] vi se terrer, tirer au flanc, rôder.

skull [skʌl] n crâne m, tête de mort f.

skull-cap ['skʌlkæp] n calotte f.

skunk [skʌnk] n sconse m, mouffette f, salaud m.

sky [skai] n ciel m; —**lark** alouette f; —**light** lucarne f; —**line** horizon m; —**scraper** gratte-ciel m.

slab [slæb] n dalle f, plaque f, tablette f, pavé m.

slack [slæk] n poussier m, mou m, jeu m; a mou, flasque, veule, desserré, creux; vi (fam) flemmarder, se relâcher.

slacken ['slækən] vt ralentir, (re)lâcher, détendre, desserrer; vi ralentir, se relâcher.

slacker ['slækə] n flemmard(e) mf.

slackness ['slæknis] n veulerie f, laisser-aller m, relâchement m, marasme m, mollesse f, mou m.

slag [slæg] n scorie f, mâchefer m, crasses f pl.

slain [slein] pp of slay.

slake [sleik] vt étancher, assouvir.

slam [slæm] n claquement m, schlem m; vt claquer.

slander ['slɑ:ndə] n calomnie f, diffamation f; vt calomnier, diffamer.

slanderer ['slɑ:ndərə] n diffamateur, -trice, calomniateur, -trice.

slanderous ['slɑ:ndərəs] a diffamatoire, calomnieux.

slang [slæn] n argot m.

slant [slɑ:nt] n obliquité f, pente f, biais m, point m de vue; vi diverger, obliquer, s'incliner, être en pente; vt incliner, déverser.

slap [slæp] n gifle f, soufflet m, tape f; vt gifler; ad en plein.

slash [slæf] n estafilade f, balafre f, taillade f; vt balafrer, taillader, fouailler, éreinter, (*price*) réduire.

slashing ['slæʃiŋ] *a* cinglant, mordant.

slate [sleit] *n* ardoise *f*; *vt* ardoiser, tancer, éreinter.

slaughter ['slɔːtə] *n* abattage *m*, massacre *m*, boucherie *f*; *vt* massacrer, égorger, abattre; —**house** abattoir *m*.

slave [sleiv] *n* esclave *mf*; *vi* travailler comme un nègre, s'échiner.

slaver ['sleivə] *n* bave *f*, lèche *f*; *vi* baver, flagorner.

slave-trade ['sleivtreid] *n* traite des nègres *f*.

slavery ['sleivəri] *n* esclavage *m*, asservissement *m*.

slavish ['sleiviʃ] *n* servile.

slay [slei] *vt* égorger, tuer.

sledge [sledʒ] *n* traineau *m*.

sledge(-hammer) ['sledʒ(ˌhæmə)] *n* masse *f*; (*fig*) massue *f*.

sleek [sliːk] *a* lisse, lustré, onctueux.

sleep [sliːp] *n* sommeil *m*; *vi* dormir, coucher; to go to — s'endormir, s'engourdir.

sleeper ['sliːpə] *n* dormeur, traverse *f*, wagon-lit *m*.

sleeping-car ['sliːpiŋkɑː] *n* wagon-lit *m*.

sleeping-pill ['sliːpiŋpil] *n* somnifère *m*.

sleeping-sickness ['sliːpiŋˈsiknis] *n* maladie du sommeil *f*.

sleeplessness ['sliːplisnis] *n* insomnie *f*.

sleepy ['sliːpi] *a* ensommeillé, endormi.

sleet [sliːt] *n* neige fondue *f*, grésil *m*, giboulée *f*; *vi* grésiller.

sleeve [sliːv] *n* manche *f*.

sleigh [slei] *n* traineau *m*.

sleight [slait] *n* — of hand adresse *f*, tour de main *m*, prestidigitation *f*.

slender ['slendə] *a* mince, élancé, svelte, faible, maigre.

slenderness ['slendənis] *n* sveltesse *f*, exiguité *f*.

slept [slept] *pt pp of* **sleep**.

slew [sluː] *pt of* **slay**.

slice [slais] *n* tranche *f*, rond *m*, rondelle *f*, (*fish*) truelle *f*; *vt* couper (en tranches), trancher.

slid [slid] *pt pp of* **slide**.

slide [slaid] *vti* glisser; *vi* faire des glissades; *n* glissement *m*, glissement *m*, glissade *f*, glissoire *f*, coulisse *f*.

sliding ['slaidiŋ] *a* à coulisse, à glissières, gradué, mobile.

slight [slait] *n* affront *m*; *vt* manquer d'égards envers; *a* léger, frêle, peu de.

slightest ['slaitist] *a* le, la (les) moindre(s).

slim [slim] *a* mince, svelte, délié, rusé.

slime [slaim] *n* vase *f*, limon *m*, bave *f*.

slimy ['slaimi] *a* gluant, visqueux.

sling [sliŋ] *n* fronde *f*, bretelle *f*,

slink [sliŋk] *vi* marcher furtivement, raser les murs.

slip [slip] *n* faux-pas *m*, lapsus *m*, peccadille *f*, erreur *f*, bouture *f*, bande *f*, coulisse *f*, laisse *f*, enveloppe *f*, slip *m*; *vt* glisser, filer, échapper à; *vi* (se) glisser, se tromper; to — away se sauver, fuir; to — off enlever; to — on enfiler, passer.

slipper ['slipə] *n* pantoufle *f*, patin *m*.

slippery ['slipəri] *a* glissant, fuyant, souple, rusé.

slipshod ['slipʃɔd] *a* négligé, bâclé.

slit [slit] *n* incision *f*, fente *f*, entre-bâillement *m*; *vt* déchirer, couper, fendre; *vi* se fendre, se déchirer.

slogan ['slougən] *n* slogan *m*, mot d'ordre *m*.

slogger ['slɔgə] *n* cogneur *m*, bûcheur *m*.

slope [sloup] *n* pente *f*, rampe *f*, talus *m*; *vi* incliner, pencher, être en pente.

slop [slɔp] *vt* répandre; *vt* to — over *vt* s'attendrir sur.

slop-pail ['slɔppeil] *n* seau *m* de toilette.

slops [slɔps] *n* eaux sales *f pl*, bouillie *f*.

sloppy ['slɔpi] *a* détrempé, inondé, sale, pleurard, larmoyant, bâclé.

slot [slɔt] *n* rainure *f*, fente *f*.

slot-machine ['slɔtməˌʃiːn] *n* distributeur automatique *m*.

sloth ['slouθ] *n* paresse *f*.

slothful ['slouθful] *a* paresseux, indolent.

slouch [slautʃ] *n* démarche penchée *f*; *a* au bord rabattu; *vi* pencher, se tenir mal, trainer le pas; *vt* rabattre le bord de (son chapeau).

slough [slau] *n* fondrière *f*.

slough [slʌf] *n* dépouille *f*, tissu mort *m*; *vi* faire peau neuve, muer; *vt* jeter.

Slovak ['slouvæk] *n* Slovaque *mf*; *a* slovaque.

sloven ['slʌvn] *n* souillon *f*.

slovenly ['slʌvnli] *a* négligé, sale, désordonné.

slow [slou] *a* lent, en retard.

slowly ['slouli] *ad* lentement, au ralenti.

slowness ['slounis] *n* lenteur *f*.

slug [slʌg] *n* limace *f*, limaçon *m*, lampée *f* (d'alcool); (*tec*) lingot *m*; *vt* terrasser.

sluggard ['slʌgəd] *n* paresseux *m*, flemmard *m*.

sluggish ['slʌgiʃ] *a* paresseux, inerte, endormi, lourd.

sluggishly ['slʌgiʃli] *ad* indolemment, lentement.

sluggishness ['slʌgiʃnis] *n* inertie *f*, paresse *f*.

sluice [sluːs] *n* écluse *f*; *vt* vanner, laver à grande eau; —**gate** vanne

slum [slʌm] n taudis m.
slumber ['slʌmbə] n somme m, sommeil m; vt somnoler, sommeiller.
slump [slʌmp] n crise f, dégringolade f; vi baisser, dégringoler, se laisser tomber.
slung [slʌŋ] pt pp of **sling**.
slunk [slʌŋk] pt pp of **slink**.
slur [slə:] n blâme m, tache f, bredouillement m, liaison f, macule f, griffonnage m; vt bredouiller, griffonner, couler, passer (sur over).
sly [slai] a retors, malin, madré, en dessous.
smack [smæk] n arrière-goût m, teinture f, bateau de pêche, claquement m, gifle f, essai m, gros baiser m; vt gifler, faire claquer, taper; ad tout droit, en plein, paf; to — of sentir.
small [smɔ:l] a petit, faible, mesquin, modeste, peu important, peu de.
smallness ['smɔ:lnis] n petitesse f, mesquinerie f.
smallpox ['smɔ:lpɔks] n variole f, petite vérole f.
smart [smɑ:t] n douleur cuisante f; vi faire mal, picoter, en cuire à; a vif, débrouillard, fin, malin, chic.
smartness ['smɑ:tnis] n vivacité f, finesse f, élégance f.
smash [smæʃ] n collision f, coup de poing m, faillite f, sinistre m, effondrement m; vt mettre en pièces, écraser, heurter; vi faire faillite, se fracasser.
smattering ['smætəriŋ] n teinture f, notions f pl.
smear [smiə] n tache f, souillure f; vt graisser, barbouiller, enduire.
smell [smel] n odorat m, flair m, odeur f; vt flairer; vti sentir.
smelled [smeld] pt pp of **smell**; n éperlan m; vt fondre.
smile [smail] nm vi sourire.
smirch [smə:tʃ] vt salir, souiller.
smirk [smə:k] n sourire m affecté; vi minauder.
smite [smait] vt punir, frapper.
smitten ['smitn] pp atteint, épris.
smith [smiθ] n forgeron m.
smithereens ['smiðə'ri:nz] n miettes f pl, morceaux m pl.
smithy ['smiθi] n forge f.
smock [smɔk] n blouse f, sarrau m.
smoke [smouk] n fumée f; vti fumer; vi sentir la fumée; vt enfumer.
smoker ['smoukə] n fumeur m.
smokeless ['smouklis] a sans fumée.
smoking-car ['smoukiŋ,kɑ:] n compartiment pour fumeurs m.
smoking-room ['smoukiŋ,rum] n fumoir m.
smoky ['smouki] a fumeux, enfumé, noirci par la fumée.
smolder ['smouldə] vi couver, brûler et fumer.
smooth [smu:ð] a lisse, uni, calme, doux, aisé, flatteur, apaisant, souple;
smoothly doucement; vt aplanir, adoucir, lisser, apaiser, pallier.
smoothness ['smu:ðnis] n égalité f, calme m, douceur f, souplesse f.
smote [smout] pt of **smite**.
smother ['smʌðə] vt étouffer, couvrir, suffoquer.
smudge [smʌdʒ] n barbouillage m; vt barbouiller, salir.
smug [smʌg] a bête et solennel, content de soi, béat.
smuggle ['smʌgl] vt passer en fraude.
smuggler ['smʌglə] n contrebandier m.
smuggling ['smʌgliŋ] n contrebande f, fraude f.
smut [smʌt] n (grain m de) suie f, nielle f, obscénités f pl.
snack [snæk] n casse-croûte m.
snail [sneil] n escargot m, limace f.
snake [sneik] n serpent m.
snap [snæp] n claquement m, bruit sec m, déclic m, bouton-pression m, fermoir m, coup m (de froid), instantané m; a immédiat, vt happer, dire aigrement, casser, (faire) claquer, prendre un instantané de; vi claquer, se casser.
snappish ['snæpiʃ] n hargneux, irritable.
snapshot ['snæpʃɔt] n instantané m.
snare [snɛə] n piège m; vt prendre au piège.
snarl [snɑ:l] n grognement m; vi grogner, gronder.
snatch [snætʃ] n geste pour saisir m, fragment m, à-coup m, bribe f; vt saisir, arracher, enlever.
sneak [sni:k] n louche individu m, mouchard m; vi se glisser, cafarder, moucharder.
sneaking ['sni:kiŋ] a furtif, inavoué, servile.
sneer [sniə] n ricanement m; vi ricaner; to — at bafouer, dénigrer.
sneeze [sni:z] n éternuement m; vi éternuer.
sniff [snif] n reniflement m; vt humer; vti renifler.
snipe [snaip] n bécassine f; to — at canarder.
sniper ['snaipə] n tireur embusqué m, canardeur m.
snob [snɔb] n snob m, prétentieux m.
snobbery ['snɔbəri] n snobisme m, prétention f.
snooze [snu:z] n somme m; vi faire un somme.
snore [snɔ:] n ronflement m; vi ronfler.
snort [snɔ:t] vi renâcler, s'ébrouer, ronfler, dédaigner.
snout [snaut] n museau m, mufle m, groin m, boutoir m.
snow [snou] n neige f; vi neiger; to — under accabler; —drop perce-neige m or f; —flake flocon m; —plow chasse-neige m; —shoes raquettes f pl; —storm tempête f, rafale f de neige; —field champ m de neige; —ball boule f de neige.

snub [snʌb] *n* rebuffade *f*; *vt* rabrouer; *a* camus, retroussé.

snuff [snʌf] *n* tabac à priser *m*, prise *f*; *vi* priser; *vt* moucher, éteindre; ——box tabatière *f*.

snuffle ['snʌfl] *vi* renifler, nasiller.

snug [snʌg] *a* abrité, douillet, gentil, petit, bien.

so [sou] *ad* si, tellement, ainsi, comme ça, de même, à peu près, le; *cj* donc, si bien que; ——called soi-disant; — far jusqu'ici (là); — long à bientôt; — much tant, autant de; — much for assez; — on ainsi de suite; — and — un(e) tel(le), machin; in — far as en tant que, dans la mesure où; — that de manière à (que), si bien que; — as to de façon à, afin de; so so comme ci, comme ça.

soak [souk] *vt* tremper, imbiber, pénétrer, abattre, donner un coup de bambou; *vi* s'imbiber, s'infiltrer, baigner.

soaking ['soukiŋ] *n* trempage *m*, douche *f*.

soap [soup] *n* savon *m*; *vt* savonner.

soapy ['soupi] *a* savonneux, onctueux.

soar [sɔː] *vi* prendre l'essor, monter, planer.

sob [sɔb] *n* sanglot *m*; *vi* sangloter.

sober ['soubə] *a* sobre, sérieux, impartial, non ivre.

soberness ['soubənis] *n* sobriété *f*, modération *f*.

sociable ['souʃəbl] *a* sociable.

sociability [.souʃə'biliti] *n* sociabilité *f*.

social ['souʃəl] *n* réunion *f*; *a* social; — events mondanités *f pl*.

socialism ['souʃəlizəm] *n* socialisme *m*.

socialist ['souʃəlist] *n* socialiste *mf*.

socialize ['souʃəlaiz] *vt* socialiser.

society [sə'saiəti] *n* société *f*, monde *m*.

sock [sɔk] *n* chaussette *f*.

socket ['sɔkit] *n* trou *m*, orbite *m*, godet *m*, douille *f*, alvéole *m*.

sod [sɔd] *n* motte de gazon *f*.

soda ['soudə] *n* soude *f*, cristaux *m pl*; ——water eau de Seltz *f*.

sodden ['sɔdn] *a* (dé)trempé, pâteux, hébété, abruti.

sofa ['soufə] *n* canapé *m*, sofa *m*.

soft [sɔft] *a* mou, tendre, doux, facile, ramolli.

soften ['sɔfn] *vt* amollir, adoucir, attendrir.

softness ['sɔftnis] *n* douceur *f*, mollesse *f*, tendresse *f*.

soil [sɔil] *n* terre *f*, sol *m*; *vt* salir, souiller; *vi* se salir.

sojourn ['sɔdʒəːn] *n* séjour *m*; *vi* séjourner.

solace ['sɔləs] *n* consolation *f*; *vt* consoler.

sold [sould] *pt pp* of **sell**.

solder ['sɔldə] *n* soudure *f*; *vt* souder; ——ing iron lampe *f* à souder.

soldier ['souldʒə] *n* soldat *m*.

soldiery ['souldʒəri] *n* troupe *f*, (pej) soldatesque *f*.

sole [soul] *n* plante du pied *f*, semelle *f*, sole *f*; *vt* ressemeler; *a* seul, unique.

solemn ['sɔləm] *a* solennel.

solemnity [sə'lemniti] *n* solennité *f*.

solemnize ['sɔləmnaiz] *vt* célébrer, solenniser.

solicit [sə'lisit] *vt* solliciter.

solicitation [sə.lisi'teiʃən] *n* sollicitation *f*.

solicitor [sə'lisitə] *n* avoué *m*.

solicitous [sə'lisitəs] *a* zélé, anxieux, préoccupé.

solicitude [sə'lisitjud] *n* sollicitude *f*, anxiété *f*.

solid ['sɔlid] *an* solide *m*; *a* massif.

solidify [sə'lidifai] *vt* solidifier; *vi* se solidifier, se fixer.

solidity [sə'liditi] *n* solidité *f*.

soliloquy [sə'liləkwi] *n* soliloque *m*, monologue *m*.

solitary ['sɔlitəri] *a* solitaire.

solitude ['sɔlitjuːd] *n* solitude *f*, isolement *m*.

soluble ['sɔljubl] *an* soluble *m*.

solution [sə'luːʃən] *n* solution *f*.

solvability [.sɔlvə'biliti] *n* solvabilité *f*.

solve [sɔlv] *vt* résoudre.

solvency ['sɔlvənsi] *n* solvabilité *f*.

solvent ['sɔlvənt] *an* dissolvant *m*; *a* solvable.

some [sʌm] *a* du, de la, des, un peu de, quelques, certains; *pn* quelques-un(e)s, certains, en; *ad* quelque, environ.

somebody ['sʌmbədi] *pn* quelqu'un(e).

somehow ['sʌmhau] *ad* de manière ou d'autre; — or other je ne sais comment.

someone ['sʌmwʌn] *pn* quelqu'un.

somersault ['sʌməsɔːlt] *n* saut périlleux *m*, culbute *f*; *vi* faire la culbute, culbuter, capoter.

something ['sʌmθiŋ] *pn* quelque chose.

sometime ['sʌmtaim] *ad* un de ces jours, autrefois.

sometimes ['sʌmtaimz] *ad* quelquefois.

somewhat ['sʌmwɔt] *ad* quelque peu.

somewhere ['sʌmwɛə] *ad* quelque part.

son [sʌn] *n* fils *m*; ——in-law gendre *m*, beau-fils *m*.

song [sɔŋ] *n* chant *m*, chanson *f*.

songster ['sɔŋstə] *n* chanteur *m*.

sonority [sə'nɔriti] *n* sonorité *f*.

sonorous ['sɔnərəs] *a* sonore.

soon [suːn] *ad* (bien)tôt; as — as aussitôt que, dès que.

sooner ['suːnə] *ad* plus tôt, plutôt.

soot [sut] *n* suie *f*.

soothe [suːð] *vt* calmer, apaiser, flatter.

sooty ['suti] *a* noir de (comme) suie, fuligineux.

sop [sɔp] *n* trempette *f*, gâteau *m*; *vt* tremper; *vi* être trempé.

sophisticated [sə'fistikeitid] *a* artificiel, blasé, sophistiqué, frelaté.

soporific [.sɔpə'rifik] *an* soporifique *m*.

sorcerer ['sɔːsərə] *n* sorcier *m*.

sorcery ['sɔːsəri] *n* sorcellerie *f*.

sordid ['sɔːdid] *a* sordide.

sordidness ['sɔːdidnis] *n* sordidité *f*.

sore [sɔː] *n* mal *m*, plaie *f*, blessure *f*; *a* douloureux, envenimé, sévère, malade.

sorely ['sɔːli] *ad* fâcheusement, cruellement, gravement.

sorrel ['sɔrəl] *n* oseille *f*.

sorrow ['sɔrou] *n* chagrin *m*; *vi* s'affliger.

sorrowful ['sɔrəful] *a* affligé, pénible.

sorry ['sɔri] *a* désolé, fâché, pauvre, pitoyable, triste, méchant; —I pardon! excusez-moi.

sort [sɔːt] *n* sorte *f*, espèce *f*; — of pour ainsi dire; out of —s hors de son assiette; *vt* trier, assortir, classifier.

sorting ['sɔːtiŋ] *n* triage *m*, assortiment *m*.

sot [sɔt] *n* ivrogne *m*.

sottish ['sɔtiʃ] *a* abruti par la boisson.

sough [sau] *vi* gémir, siffler, soupirer, susurrer.

sought [sɔːt] *pt pp of* seek; — after *a* demandé, recherché.

soul [soul] *n* âme *f*; not a — pas âme qui vive, pas un chat.

soulful ['soulful] *a* pensif, sentimental, expressif.

sound [saund] *n* son *m*, sonde *f*, détroit *m*, chenal *m*; *vt* sonner, prononcer, sonder, ausculter; *vi* (ré)sonner, retentir; *a* sain, solide.

sounding ['saundiŋ] *n* sondage *m*, auscultation *f*.

soundless ['saundlis] *a* silencieux.

soup [suːp] *n* potage *m*, soupe *f*.

sour [sauə] *a* aigre, vert; *vti* aigrir; *vi* s'aigrir.

source [sɔːs] *n* source *f*, origine *f*, foyer *m*.

sourish ['sauriʃ] *a* aigrelet.

south [sauθ] *n* sud *m*, midi *m*; *a* du sud.

southern ['sʌðən] *a* méridional, du midi, du sud.

southward ['sauθwəd] *ad* vers le sud, au sud.

sovereign ['sɔvrin] *an* souverain(e) *mf*.

sovereignty ['sɔvrənti] *n* souveraineté *f*.

sow [sau] *n* truie *f*.

sow [sou] *vt* semer, ensemencer.

sower ['souə] *n* semeur, -euse.

sowing ['souiŋ] *n* semailles *f pl*, semis *m*.

sown [soun] *pp of* sow.

spa [spaː] *n* station thermale *f*.

space [speis] *n* espace *m*, place *f*, durée *f*, intervalle *m*, étendue *f*; *vt* espacer.

spacious ['speiʃəs] *a* spacieux, vaste, ample.

spade [speid] *n* bêche *f*, (*cards*) pique *m*.

Spain [spein] *n* Espagne *f*.

span [spæn] *pt of* spin; *n* durée *f*, longueur *f*, arche *f*, envergure *f*, écartement *m*; *vt* enjamber, embrasser, mesurer.

spangle ['spæŋgl] *n* paillette *f*.

Spaniard ['spænjəd] *n* Espagnol(e).

spaniel ['spænjəl] *n* épagneul *m*.

Spanish ['spæniʃ] *a* espagnol.

spank [spæŋk] *vt* fesser; to — along aller grand trot, filer.

spanking ['spæŋkiŋ] *n* fessée *f*; *a* épatant.

spanner ['spænə] *n* clef *f*; screw — clef anglaise *f*.

spar [spaː] *n* épar *m*, mât *m*, perche *f*; *vi* boxer, se harceler, s'escrimer.

spare [spɛə] *a* frugal, frêle, libre, de reste, de réserve, de rechange, à perdre; *vt* ménager, se passer de, épargner, accorder.

sparing ['spɛəriŋ] *a* économe, avare, chiche.

spark [spaːk] *n* étincelle *f*; *vi* étinceler, pétiller, mousser; — plug *n* bougie *f* (d'allumage).

sparkle ['spaːkl] *vi* étinceler, pétiller, chatoyer.

sparkling ['spaːkliŋ] *a* mousseux, brillant.

sparrow ['spærou] *n* moineau *m*.

sparse [spaːs] *a* clairsemé.

spasm ['spæzəm] *n* spasme *m*, accès *m*, quinte *f*, crampe *f*, à-coup *m*.

spat [spæt] *pt pp of* spit.

spat [spæt] *n* guêtre *f*, querelle *f*.

spate [speit] *n* crue *f*, flot *m*.

spatter ['spætə] *n* éclaboussure *f*; *vt* éclabousser.

spawn [spɔːn] *n* frai *m*; *vi* frayer.

speak [spiːk] *vti* parler, dire.

speaker ['spiːkə] *n* parleur, -euse, orateur *m*, président des communes *m*; loud — haut-parleur *m*.

spear [spiə] *n* lance *f*, javelot *m*, épieu *m*, harpon *m*, sagaie *f*; —head *n* extrême pointe *f*.

special ['speʃəl] *a* spécial, particulier; — delivery express *m*, pneumatique *m*.

specialist ['speʃəlist] *n* spécialiste *mf*.

speciality [.speʃi'æliti] *n* spécialité *f*, particularité *f*.

specialize ['speʃəlaiz] *vt* spécialiser; *vi* se spécialiser.

species ['spiːʃiːz] *n* espèce *f*.

specific [spi'sifik] *a* spécifique, explicite, précis.

specify ['spesifai] *vt* spécifier, déterminer.

specimen ['spesimin] n spécimen m, échantillon m.

specious ['spi:ʃəs] a spécieux, captieux.

speck [spek] n grain m, point m, tache f.

speckled ['spekld] a taché, tacheté, grivelé.

spectacle ['spektəkl] n spectacle m; pl lunettes f pl.

spectacular [spek'tækjulə] a spectaculaire, à grand spectacle.

spectator [spek'teitə] n spectateur, -trice, assistant(e) mf.

specter ['spektə] n spectre m.

spectral ['spektrəl] a spectral.

speculate ['spekjuleit] vi spéculer.

speculation [,spekju'leiʃən] n spéculation f.

speculative ['spekjulətiv] a spéculatif.

speculator ['spekjuleitə] n spéculateur m.

speech [spi:tʃ] n parole f, discours m.

speechless ['spi:tʃlis] a interdit, interloqué.

sped [sped] pt pp of **speed**.

speed [spi:d] n vitesse f; vt activer, hâter, régler; vi se presser, se hâter, faire de la vitesse, filer.

speediness ['spi:dinis] n promptitude f, rapidité f.

speedometer [spi'dɔmitə] n indicateur de vitesse m.

speedy ['spi:di] a rapide, prompt.

spell [spel] n charme m, sort m, maléfice m, tour m, moment m, période f; vt épeler, écrire, signifier.

spellbound ['spelbaund] a fasciné, sous le charme.

spelled [speld] pt pp of **spell**.

spelling ['speliŋ] n orthographe f.

spend [spend] vt dépenser, passer, épuiser.

spendthrift ['spendθrift] n dépensier, -ière, panier percé m.

spent [spent] pt pp of **spend**; a fini, à bout, éteint, mort.

spew [spju:] vti vomir; vt cracher.

sphere [sfiə] n sphère mf, domaine m, zone f, ressort.

spherical ['sferikəl] a sphérique.

spice [spais] n épice f, pointe f; vt épicer, relever.

spick and span [,spikən'spæn] a flambant neuf, tiré à quatre épingles, propret.

spicy ['spaisi] a épicé, poivré, relevé, pimenté, criard.

spider ['spaidə] n araignée f.

spike [spaik] n épi m, clou m, crampon m, pointe f; vt (en)clouer.

spill [spil] n chute f, bûche f, allume-feu m; vt (ren)verser, jeter bas; vi se répandre.

spilt [spilt] pt pp of **spill**.

spin [spin] n tour m, effet m, vrille f; ----drier n essoreuse f; vt filer; vi tourner, rouler, patiner.

spinach ['spinidʒ] n épinards m pl.

spindle ['spindl] n fuseau m, broche f, essieu m.

spindly ['spindli] a fluet, de fuseau.

spine [spain] n épine dorsale f.

spineless ['spainlis] a mou.

spinner ['spinə] n métier m, tisse-rand(e) mf, filateur m.

spinney ['spini] n petit bois m.

spinning-mill ['spiniŋmil] n filature f.

spinning-wheel ['spiniŋwi:l] n rouet m.

spinster ['spinstə] n vieille fille f, célibataire f.

spiny ['spaini] a épineux.

spiral ['spaiərəl] n spirale f; a en spirale, en colimaçon, spiral.

spire ['spaiə] n flèche f, aiguille f, pointe f.

spirit ['spirit] n esprit m, âme f, humeur f, cran m, ardeur f, feu m, alcool m; to ---- away escamoter.

spirited ['spiritid] a animé, fougueux, vif, hardi.

spiritless ['spiritlis] a déprimé, mou, terne.

spiritual ['spiritjuəl] a spirituel.

spiritualism ['spiritjuəlizəm] n spiritisme m, spiritualisme m.

spiritualist ['spiritjuəlist] n spirite mf.

spirituous ['spiritjuəs] a spiritueux, alcoolique.

spit [spit] n broche f, langue f (de terre), crachement m, crachat m; vt embrocher, mettre à la broche, cracher; vi cracher, bruiner, crachiner.

spite [spait] n dépit m, rancune f; vt mortifier, vexer; in ---- of malgré, en dépit de.

spiteful ['spaitful] a rancunier, méchant.

spitfire ['spitfaiə] n boute-feu m, soupe-au-lait mf, rageur m, rageuse f.

spittle ['spitl] n crachat m.

spittoon [spi'tu:n] n crachoir m.

splash [splæʃ] n éclaboussement m, éclaboussure f, tache f, clapotis m, sensation f; vt éclabousser, asperger; vi piquer un plat ventre, clapoter, barboter; to **make a** ---- faire de l'épate.

splay [splei] n ébrasure f; a plat, large, évasé; vt ébraser.

spleen [spli:n] n rate f, spleen m, bile f.

splendid ['splendid] a splendide, magnifique.

splendor ['splendə] n splendeur f, éclat m.

splint [splint] n attelle f, éclisse f.

splinter ['splintə] n éclat m, esquille f, écharde f; vt faire voler en éclats; vi voler en éclats.

split [split] n fente f, fissure f, scission f; pl grand écart m; vt fendre, couper, diviser, partager; vi se fendre, se diviser, se briser.

spoil(s) [spɔil(z)] n butin m; pl dépouilles f pl, profits m pl.

spoil [spɔil] vt dépouiller, gâter, abîmer, avarier, déparer; vi s'abîmer, se gâter.

spoilsport ['spɔilspɔːt] n trouble-fête m, rabat-joie m.

spoke [spouk] n rayon m, échelon m, bâton m (dans les roues).

spoke, -ken [spouk, spoukǝn] pt pp of **speak**.

spokesman ['spouksmǝn] n porte-parole m.

spoliation [ˌspouli'eiʃǝn] n spoliation f, pillage m.

sponge [spʌndʒ] n éponge f; vt passer l'éponge sur, éponger, effacer; **to — on** someone vivre sur qn, vivre aux crochets de qn.

sponge-cake ['spʌndʒ'keik] n gâteau de Savoie m.

sponger ['spʌndʒǝ] n parasite m, pique-assiette m.

spongy ['spʌndʒi] a spongieux.

sponsor ['spɔnsǝ] n parrain m, marraine f, garant m.

spontaneity [ˌspɔntǝ'niːiti] n spontanéité f.

spontaneous [spɔn'teiniǝs] a spontané.

spontaneously [spɔn'teiniǝsli] ad spontanément.

spool [spuːl] n bobine f, tambour m, rouleau m.

spoon [spuːn] n cuiller f.

spoonful ['spuːnful] n cuillerée f.

sport ['spɔːt] n jeu m, jouet m, sport m, chic type m; vi s'amuser, se divertir; vt arborer.

sporting ['spɔːtiŋ] a loyal, de chasse, sport, sportif.

sportive ['spɔːtiv] a enjoué, folâtre.

sportsman ['spɔːtsmǝn] n sportif m, beau joueur m, chasseur m.

sportsmanship ['spɔːtsmǝnʃip] n franc jeu m, l'esprit sportif m.

spot [spɔt] n endroit m, tache f, bouton m, pois m, marque f, goutte f; vt tacher, marquer, dépister, repérer.

spotted ['spɔtid] a tacheté, marqueté, à pois.

spotless ['spɔtlis] a sans tache, immaculé.

spouse [spauz] n époux m, épouse f.

spout [spaut] n bec m, jet m, gouttière f, colonne f; vt lancer, déclamer; vi jaillir, pérorer.

sprain [sprein] n entorse f, foulure f; vt se fouler.

sprang [spræŋ] pt of **spring**.

sprawl [sprɔːl] vi s'étendre, se vautrer, tomber les quatre pattes en l'air, rouler.

spray [sprei] n branche f, embrun m, vaporisateur m, bouquet m; vt asperger, vaporiser.

spread [spred] n envergure f, largeur f, diffusion f, propagation f; vtir répandre, (é)tendre, déployer;

vi se répandre, s'étendre, se disperser.

sprig [sprig] n branchette f, brin m, rejeton m.

sprightliness ['spraitlinis] n gaîté f, vivacité f.

sprightly ['spraitli] a vif, sémillant, allègre.

spring [spriŋ] n printemps m, source f, saut m, bond m, ressort m, élasticité f; vi bondir, s'élever, poindre, sortir, (wood) jouer, se fendre; vt lancer, (trap) tendre, suspendre.

spring-board ['spriŋbɔːd] n tremplin m.

springy ['spriŋi] a élastique, flexible.

sprinkle ['spriŋkl] n pincée f; vt asperger, éparpiller, saupoudrer.

sprinkler ['spriŋklǝ] n aspersoir m, goupillon m.

sprinkling ['spriŋkliŋ] n aspersion f, saupoudrage m.

sprite [sprait] n lutin m.

sprout [spraut] n pousse f; **Brussels — ** chou de Bruxelles m; vti pousser.

spruce [spruːs] n sapin m; a net, pimpant, soigné.

sprung [sprʌŋ] pp of **spring**.

spun [spʌn] pp of **spin**.

spur [spǝː] n éperon m, ergot m, coup de fouet m; vt éperonner, exciter, stimuler.

spurious ['spjuǝriǝs] a faux, controuvé, contrefait.

spurn [spǝːn] vt rejeter, dédaigner, traiter avec dédain.

sputter ['spʌtǝ] vti bredouiller; vi grésiller, cracher.

spy [spai] n espion m; vt espionner, épier; **—glass** longue-vue f; **—hole** judas m.

squabble ['skwɔbl] n bisbille f; vi se chamailler.

squad [skwɔd] n escouade f, peloton m, équipe f.

squadron ['skwɔdrǝn] n escadron m, escadre f.

squalid ['skwɔlid] a sordide.

squall [skwɔːl] n rafale f, grain m, cri m; pl grabuge m; vi piailler.

squander ['skwɔndǝ] vt gaspiller, dissiper, manger.

squanderer ['skwɔndǝrǝ] n prodigue m, gaspilleur, -euse.

square [skwɛǝ] n carré m, équerre f, square m, place f; a carré, régulier, loyal, tout net, quitté; vt accorder, régler, payer, carrer, équarrir; vi s'accorder, cadrer.

squash [skwɔʃ] n foule f, presse f, (drink) jus de fruit m; bouillie f, bruit mou m; vt écraser, rembarrer; vi se serrer, s'écraser.

squat [skwɔt] vi s'accroupir; a trapu, ramassé.

squeak [skwiːk] n cri aigu m, grincement m, couic m; vi grincer, crier.

squeal [skwiːl] n cri aigu m; vi crier,

criailler, protester; **to —** on dénoncer, moucharder, vendre.

squeamish ['skwiːmiʃ] *a* dégoûté, scrupuleux, prude.

squeamishness ['skwiːmiʃnis] *n* bégueulerie *f*, délicatesse *f*.

squeeze [skwiːz] *n* pression *f*, presse *f*, écrasement *m*, (*pol*) l'austérité *f*; *vt* presser, serrer, écraser, faire pression sur, extorquer, faire entrer sur, extorquer, faire entrer de force; *vi* **to — up** se serrer.

squint [skwint] *n* strabisme *m*, coup d'œil oblique *m*; *vi* loucher.

squirrel ['skwirəl] *n* écureuil *m*, petit gris *m*.

squirt [skwəːt] *n* seringue *f*, jet *m*; *vt* lancer, injecter; *vi* jaillir, gicler.

stab [stæb] *n* coup *m* de couteau; *vt* poignarder, porter un coup de couteau à.

stability [stə'biliti] *n* stabilité *f*, constance *f*.

stabilize ['steibilaiz] *vt* stabiliser.

stable ['steibl] *n* écurie *f*; *a* stable, consistant, solide.

stack [stæk] *n* meule *f*, pile *f*, cheminée *f*, (*mil*) faisceau *m*; *vt* entasser, empiler.

staff [staːf] *n* bâton *m*, mât *m*, hampe *f*, crosse *f*, état-major *m*, personnel *m*.

stag [stæg] *n* cerf *m*.

stage [steidʒ] *n* scène *f*, estrade *f*, échafaudage *m*, étape *f*, phase *f*, relais *m*, débarcadère *m*; *vt* monter, mettre en scène.

stage-coach ['steidʒkoutʃ] *n* diligence *f*.

stage-fright ['steidʒfrait] *n* trac *m*.

stage-hand ['steidʒhænd] *n* machiniste *m*.

stagger ['stægə] *vt* faire chanceler, ébranler, renverser, échelonner; *vi* chanceler, tituber.

stagnant ['stægnənt] *a* stagnant.

stagnate ['stægneit] *vi* croupir, être stagnant, s'encroûter.

stagnation [stæg'neiʃən] *n* stagnation *f*, marasme *m*.

staid [steid] *a* posé, rangé.

stain [stein] *n* tache *f*, colorant *m*; *vti* tacher, colorer.

stainless ['steinlis] *n* inoxydable, immaculé.

stair [stɛə] *n* marche *f*; *pl* escalier *m*.

staircase ['stɛəkeis] *n* escalier *m*.

stake [steik] *n* poteau *m*, bûcher *m*, pieu *m*, (en)jeu *m*, risque *m*, pari *m*; *vt* parier, risquer, jouer, miser.

stale [steil] *a* rassis, éventé, vicié, rebattu.

stalemate ['steil'meit] *n* point mort *m*, pat *m*.

stalk [stɔːk] *n* tige *f*, pied *m*, trognon *m*, queue *f*.

stall [stɔːl] *n* stalle *f*, banc *m*, baraque *f*, étal *m*, étalage *m*; *vt* bloquer; *vi* se bloquer.

stallion ['stæljən] *n* étalon *m*.

stalwart ['stɔːlwət] *a* solide, résolu, robuste.

stamen ['steimən] *n* étamine *f*.

stamina ['stæminə] *n* vigueur *f*, fond *m*.

stammer ['stæmə] *n* bégaiement *m*; *vti* bégayer.

stammerer ['stæmərə] *n* bègue *mf*.

stamp [stæmp] *n* timbre *m*, cachet *m*, poinçon *m*, coin *m*, estampille *f*, marque *f*, trempe *f*; *vt* timbrer, imprimer, marquer, affranchir; *vi* frapper du pied.

stampede [stæm'piːd] *n* débandade *f*, panique *f*; *vi* se débander, se ruer.

stanch [staːntʃ] *vt* étancher.

stand [stænd] *n* halte *f*, position *f*, station *f*, socle *m*, guéridon *m*, étalage *m*, stand *m*, barre *f*; *vi* se tenir (debout), se dresser, s'arrêter, rester, durer, tenir; *vt* supporter, offrir, payer; **to — for** représenter; **to — out** ressortir.

standard ['stændəd] *n* étendard *m*, étalon *m*, moyenne *f*, niveau *m*, qualité *f*; *a* classique, définitif, standard, courant.

standardize ['stændədaiz] *vt* standardiser, unifier.

standing ['stændiŋ] *n* réputation *f*, situation *f*, ancienneté *f*; *a* établi, permanent.

stand-offish ['stænd'ɔfiʃ] *a* distant.

stand-offishness ['stænd'ɔfiʃnis] *n* réserve *f*, hauteur *f*.

standpoint ['stændpoint] *n* point de vue *m*.

stank [stæŋk] *pt of* **stink**.

stanza ['stænzə] *n* stance *f*, strophe *f*.

staple ['steipl] *n* gâche *f*, crampon *m*, agrafe *f*; *a* principal.

stapler ['steiplə] *n* agrafeuse *f*.

star [staː] *n* étoile *f*, astre *m*, astérisque *m*; *vi* tenir le premier rôle, être en vedette.

starboard ['staːbəd] *n* tribord *m*.

starch [staːtʃ] *n* amidon *m*, raideur *f*; *vt* empeser.

starched [staːtʃt] *a* empesé, gourmé, collet monté.

stare [stɛə] *n* regard fixe *m*; *vi* regarder fixement, s'écarquiller; **to — at** regarder fixement, fixer, dévisager; **it is staring you in the face** cela vous saute aux yeux.

staring ['stɛəriŋ] *a* éclatant, fixe.

stark [staːk] *a* raide, tout pur; *ad* complètement.

start [staːt] *n* sursaut *m*, départ *m*, début *m*, avance *f*; *vi* commencer; *vt* lancer, entamer, mettre en marche, provoquer.

starter ['staːtə] *n* démarreur *m*, starter *m*, partant *m*, auteur *m*.

startle ['staːtl] *vt* faire tressaillir, effarer, effrayer.

startling ['staːtliŋ] *a* saisissant, sensationnel.

starvation [staː'veiʃən] *n* faim *f*, inanition *f*, famine *f*.

starve [stɑːv] vi mourir de faim, être transi; vt affamer, priver, faire mourir de faim.

state [steit] n état m, rang m, situation f, pompe f; a d'état, d'apparat; vt déclarer, prétendre, énoncer, fixer.

stately ['steitli] a noble, imposant, princier, majestueux.

statement ['steitmənt] n déclaration f, énoncé m, rapport m, expression f, relevé m.

statesman ['steitsmən] n homme d'état m.

station ['steiʃən] n poste m, gare f, station f, rang m; vt poster, placer; — house poste m de police.

stationary ['steiʃnəri] a station-naire, immobile.

stationer ['steiʃnə] n papetier m.

stationery ['steiʃnəri] n papeterie f.

stationmaster ['steiʃən,mɑːstə] n chef de gare m.

statistics [stə'tistiks] n statistique f.

statue ['stætjuː] n statue f.

stature ['stætʃə] n stature f, taille f.

status ['steitəs] n rang m, titre m, position f, statu quo m.

statute ['stætjuːt] n statut m, ordonnance f.

statutory ['stætjutəri] a statutaire, réglementaire.

staunch [stɔːntʃ] a ferme, loyal, étanche; vt étancher.

stave [steiv] n douve f, barreau m, stance f, portée f; vt — in défoncer, enfoncer; to — off détourner, conjurer, écarter.

stay [stei] n séjour m, sursis m, frein m, soutien m; vi rester, séjourner, tenir; vt arrêter, ajourner, soutenir.

stay-at-home ['steiəthoum] an casa-nier, -ière.

stays [steiz] n corset m.

stead [sted] n lieu m, place f; to stand s.o. in good — être d'un grand secours à qn.

steadfast ['stedfəst] a ferme, con-stant.

steadfastness ['stedfəstnis] n con-stance f, fixité f.

steadiness ['stedinis] n fermeté f, régularité f, stabilité f.

steady ['stedi] a ferme, régulier, constant, tranquille, rangé, continu, persistant; n petit(e) ami(e); vt assurer, (r)affermir, caler.

steak [steik] n tranche f, bifteck m, entrecôte f.

steal [stiːl] vti voler; vt dérober; to — in entrer à pas de loup.

stealth [stelθ] n secret m.

stealthily ['stelθili] ad secrètement, à la dérobée.

stealthy ['stelθi] a furtif.

steam [stiːm] n vapeur f, buée f; vt cuire à l'étuvée, vaporiser; vi fumer, marcher à la vapeur.

steamboat, -ship ['stiːmbout, -ʃip] n vapeur m.

steamer ['stiːmə] n steamer m; mar-mite à vapeur f.

steaming ['stiːmiŋ] a fumant, sous vapeur, tout chaud.

steed [stiːd] n étalon m.

steel [stiːl] n acier m, baleine f; vt tremper, aciérer; to — oneself se raidir, s'armer de courage.

steep [stiːp] a raide, escarpé, fort.

steeple ['stiːpl] n clocher m, flèche f.

steeplechase ['stiːpl'tʃeis] n steeple m, course d'obstacles f.

steer [stiə] vt diriger, gouverner, piloter.

steering-wheel ['stiəriŋwiːl] n volant m.

steersman ['stiəzmən] n barreur m, timonier m.

stem [stem] n tige f, queue f, souche f, étrave f, branche f, pied m, tuyau m; vt arrêter, endiguer, remonter.

stench [stentʃ] n puanteur f.

stencil ['stensl] n pochoir m, poncif m; vt imprimer au pochoir, poly-copier.

step [step] n pas m, marche f, marche-pied m, échelon m, promo-tion f, démarche f; pl échelle f, escalier m, mesures f pl; — ladder escabeau m; vi échelonner.

stepbrother ['step,brʌðə] n demi-frère m; —daughter belle-fille f; —father beau-père m; —mother belle-mère f; —sister demi-sœur f; —son beau-fils m.

Stephen ['stiːvn] Étienne m.

stepping-stone ['stepiŋstoun] n marche-pied m, tremplin m.

sterile ['sterail] a stérile.

sterility [ste'riliti] n stérilité f.

sterilize ['sterilaiz] vt stériliser.

sterling ['stəːliŋ] a pur, d'or, de bon aloi, massif.

stern [stəːn] n arrière m, poupe f; a sévère, austère.

sternness ['stəːnnis] n austérité f, sévérité f.

stevedore ['stiːvidɔː] n débardeur m.

stew [stjuː] n ragoût m, civet m; in a — sur les charbons ardents; vt cuire à la casserole, (faire) mijoter; vi mijoter, faire une compote.

steward ['stjuəd] n intendant m, gérant m, économe m, garçon m, commissaire m.

stewardess ['stjuədis] n femme de chambre f, hôtesse f de l'air.

stick [stik] n bâton m, canne f, baguette f, manche m, crosse f; pl du petit bois, brindilles f pl; vt enfoncer, fourrer, piquer, percer, afficher, coller, supporter, tenir; vi s'enfoncer, se ficher, se piquer, s'attacher, (s'en) tenir, coller, happer, rester (en panne), persister; to — it tenir le coup, tenir bon; to — at repugner à, reculer devant, s'obstiner à; to — out vt passer, bomber, tirer; vi faire saillie, saillir; to — to s'en tenir à, persister à, adhérer à, rester fidèle à.

sticky ['stiki] *a* collant, visqueux, difficile.

stiff [stif] *a* raide, ardu, (*price*) salé, courbaturé, engourdi, gourmé.

stiffen ['stifn] *vt* raidir; *vi* se raidir.

stiff-necked ['stif'nekt] *a* têtu, intraitable.

stiffness ['stifnis] *n* raideur *f*, contrainte *f*, difficulté *f*, fermeté *f*, courbatures *f pl*.

stifle ['staifl] *vt* étouffer, asphyxier, suffoquer.

stigma ['stigmə] *n* marque *f*, stigmate *m*.

stigmatize ['stigmataiz] *vt* stigmatiser, flétrir.

stile [stail] *n* échalier *m*.

still [stil] *n* alambic *m*; *a* immobile, tranquille, silencieux; *vt* apaiser, calmer; *ad* encore, toujours, cependant.

still-born ['stilbɔ:n] *a* mort-né.

still-life ['stil'laif] *n* nature morte *f*.

stillness ['stilnis] *n* calme *m*, paix *f*.

stilt [stilt] *n* échasse *f*.

stilted ['stiltid] *a* guindé.

stimulate ['stimjuleit] *vt* stimuler, aiguillonner.

stimulant ['stimjulant] *an* stimulant *m*.

stimulation [,stimju'leiʃən] *n* stimulation *f*.

stimulus ['stimjuləs] *n* stimulant *m*, coup de fouet *m*, aiguillon *m*.

sting [stiŋ] *n* dard *m*, aiguillon *m*, crochet *m*, piqûre *f*, pointe *f*; *vti* piquer, mordre.

stinginess ['stindʒinis] *n* ladrerie *f*, lésine *f*.

stingy ['stindʒi] *a* ladre, chiche, pingre, radin.

stink [stiŋk] *n* puanteur *f*; *vti* puer; *vt* empester.

stint [stint] *n* limite *f*, relâche *f*, tâche *f*; *vt* limiter, regarder à, mesurer.

stipend ['staipend] *n* traitement *m*, appointements *m pl*.

stipulate ['stipjuleit] *vt* stipuler.

stipulation [,stipju'leiʃən] *n* stipulation(s) *f* (*pl*).

stir [stə:] *n* remue-ménage *m*, sensation *f*, émoi *m*; *vt* remuer, secouer, agiter, émouvoir; *vi* remuer, bouger.

stirring ['stə:riŋ] *a* excitant, vibrant, mouvementé, empoignant.

stirrup ['stirəp] *n* étrier *m*.

stitch [stitʃ] *n* point *m*, maille *f*, suture *f*; *vt* coudre, raccommoder, brocher, suturer.

stoat [stout] *n* ermine *f* d'été.

stock [stɔk] *n* tronc *m*, souche *f*, provision *f*, stock *m*, fonds *m pl*, girofiée *f*, bouillon; — cube concentré *m*; *pl* rentes *f pl*; *vt* approvisionner, tenir, meubler, garnir, stocker; —**account** inventaire *m*; —**broker** agent de change *m*;

— **exchange** bourse *f*; — **jobber** agioteur *m*.

stocking ['stɔkiŋ] *n* bas *m*.

stock-phrase ['stɔk'freiz] *n* cliché *m*.

stocky ['stɔki] *a* épais, trapu.

stodgy ['stɔdʒi] *a* lourd, indigeste, bourré.

stoker ['stoukə] *n* chauffeur *m*.

stole [stoul] *pt of* **steal**; *n* étole *f*, écharpe *f*.

stolen ['stoulən] *pp of* **steal**.

stolid ['stɔlid] *a* stupide, obstiné, flegmatique.

stolidity [stɔ'liditi] *n* stupidité *f*, fiegme *m*.

stomach ['stʌmək] *n* estomac *m*, ventre *m*, bedaine *f*, appétit *m*, courage *m*, patience *f*; *vt* manger, avaler, supporter.

stone [stoun] *n* pierre *f*, caillou *m*, noyau *m*, pépin *m*, calcul *m*, 14 livres; *vt* lapider, empierrer, énoyauter.

stony ['stouni] *a* pierreux, dur, glacial, glacé.

stool [stu:l] *n* tabouret *m*, escabeau *m*, selle *f*.

stoop [stu:p] *vi* se pencher, être voûté, daigner, s'abaisser.

stop [stɔp] *n* arrêt *m*, halte *f*, fin *f*; **full** — point *m*; *vt* arrêter, boucher, (*tooth*) plomber, barrer, mettre fin à, ponctuer, empêcher, bloquer, couper; *vi* s'arrêter, cesser.

stoppage ['stɔpidʒ] *n* arrêt *m*, encombrement *m*, occlusion *f*, obstruction *f*.

stopper ['stɔpə] *n* bouchon *m*.

storage ['stɔ:ridʒ] *n* emmagasinage *m*, entrepôts *m pl*.

store [stɔ:] *n* dépôt *m*, entrepôt *m*, magasin *m*, provision *f*, réserve *f*; *vt* garnir, rentrer, entreposer, tenir, emmagasiner, meubler, mettre en réserve.

stork [stɔ:k] *n* cigogne *f*.

storm [stɔ:m] *n* orage *m*, tempête *f*, assaut *m*; *vt* emporter d'assaut; *vi* faire rage, tempêter.

stormy ['stɔ:mi] *a* orageux, houleux.

story ['stɔ:ri] *n* histoire *f*, version *f*, conte *m*, récit *m*, étage *m*; —**teller** raconteur *m*, narrateur *m*, griot *m*.

stout [staut] *a* brave, résolu, fort, gros, vigoureux.

stoutness ['stautnis] *n* courage *m*, grosseur *f*, embonpoint *m*, corpulence *f*.

stove [stouv] *pt pp of* **stave**; *n* poêle *m*.

stow [stou] *vt* bien empaqueter, arrimer.

stowaway ['stouəwei] *n* voyageur *d* fond de cale *m*.

straddle ['strædl] *vt* enfourcher, enjamber, s'installer sur, (*artillery*) encadrer.

strafe [stra:f] *vt* (*fam*) punir.

straggle ['strægl] *vi* trainer *e* arrière, s'écarter.

straggler ['stræglə] n retardataire mf, attardé m, traînard m.

straight [streit] n ligne droite f; ad droit, juste, directement; a droit, rectiligne, loyal, juste.

straighten ['streitn] vt redresser, arranger, défausser.

straightforward [streit'fɔːwəd] a loyal, droit.

straightforwardness [streit'fɔːwədnis] n droiture f, franchise f.

strain [strein] n tension f, effort m, ton m, veine f, entorse f; pl accents m pl; vt (é)tendre, tirer (sur), forcer, filtrer, fatiguer, faire violence à, (se) fouler.

strainer ['streinə] n passoire f, filtre m.

strait [streit] n détroit m.

straits [streits] n détroit m, gêne f.

strait-jacket ['streit'dʒækit] n camisole de force f.

strand [strænd] n rive f; vt échouer.

stranded ['strændid] a perdu, en panne, sans ressources.

strange [streindʒ] a étrange, singulier, étranger, dépaysé.

strangeness ['streindʒnis] n étrangeté f, nouveauté f.

stranger ['streindʒə] n étranger, inconnu.

strangle ['stræŋgl] vt étrangler, étouffer.

strangulation [‚stræŋgju'leiʃən] n strangulation f, étranglement m.

strap [stræp] n courroie f, sangle f, bande f, étrivière f; vt sangler, attacher, aiguiser, bander, frapper.

strapping ['stræpiŋ] a robuste, solide.

stratagem ['strætidʒəm] n stratagème m, ruse f.

strategist ['strætidʒist] n stratège m.

strategy ['strætidʒi] n stratégie f.

straw [strɔː] n paille f, fétu m; it is the last — il ne manquait plus que cela.

strawberry ['strɔːbəri] n fraise f, fraisier m.

stray [strei] n bête perdue f; a égaré, espacé, épars, perdu; vi se perdre, s'égarer.

streak [striːk] n raie f, bande f, veine f; vt rayer, strier; to — past passer en trombe.

streaked ['striːkt] a rayé, zébré.

stream [striːm] n cours d'eau m, courant m, ruisseau m, flot m, (Africa) marigot m; down—, up— en aval, en amont; vi couler, ruisseler, flotter.

street [striːt] n rue f.

street-arab ['striːt‚ærəb] n gavroche m, voyou m.

strength [streŋθ] n force(s) f (pl), solidité f, complet m, effectifs m pl.

strengthen ['streŋθən] vt renforcer, fortifier, (r)affermir.

strenuous ['strenjuəs] a énergique, appliqué, ardu.

strenuousness ['strenjuəsnis] n vigueur f, ardeur f.

stress [stres] n accent m, force f, pression f, tension f; vt accentuer, insister sur, souligner, fatiguer.

stretch [stretʃ] n étendue f, extension f, envergure f, élasticité f; vt (é)tendre, étirer, exagérer, élargir, bander; vi s'étendre, s'étirer, s'élargir.

stretcher ['stretʃə] n civière f, brancard m.

strew [struː] vt semer, joncher.

strict [strikt] a strict, sévère, rigoureux, formel.

strictures ['striktʃəz] n critiques f pl.

stride [straid] n enjambée f; vi marcher à grands pas.

strife [straif] n conflict m.

strike [straik] n grève f; vt frapper, heurter contre, sonner, trouver, frotter, conclure, (flag) amener; vi faire grève, porter coup.

striker ['straikə] n gréviste mf, marteau m.

striking ['straikiŋ] a frappant, saisissant.

string [striŋ] n ficelle f, corde f, chapelet m, enfilade f, cordon m, fil m, lacet m, file f, (journal) série f; pl instruments à cordes m; vt ficeler, enfiler.

stringent ['strindʒənt] a strict, rigoureux, étroit, serré.

strip [strip] n bande f, langue f; vt dépouiller, dégarnir, vider, écorcer; vi se déshabiller, se dévêtir.

stripe [straip] n bande f, barre f, raie f, (mil) galon m, chevron m; vt barrer, rayer.

strive [straiv] vi s'efforcer, lutter, rivaliser.

strode [stroud] pt of stride.

stroke [strouk] n coup m, attaque f, trait m, brassée f, caresse f; vt caresser, flatter.

stroll [stroul] vi flâner, faire un tour; n tour m, balade f.

strolling ['strouliŋ] a ambulant, forain, vagabond.

strong [strɔŋ] a fort, robuste, vigoureux, ferme, accusé, puissant, énergique.

strong-box ['strɔŋbɔks] n coffre fort m.

stronghold ['strɔŋhould] n forteresse f.

strong-minded ['strɔŋ'maindid] a volontaire, décidé.

strop [strɔp] n cuir m; vt affiler, repasser.

structure ['strʌktʃə] n structure f, construction f, édifice m, bâtiment m.

struck [strʌk] pt pp of strike.

struggle ['strʌgl] n lutte f; vi lutter, se démener.

strung [strʌŋ] pt pp of string.

strut [strʌt] n étai m, traverse f; vi

se pavaner; *vt* étayer, entretoiser.
stub [stʌb] *n* bout *m*, mégot *m*,
chicot *m*, tronçon *m*, souche *f*,
talon *m* de chèque; *vt* déraciner,
heurter; — out éteindre.
stubble ['stʌbl] *n* chaume *m*.
stubbly ['stʌbli] *a* hérissé, couvert de
chaume.
stubborn ['stʌbən] *a* têtu, obstiné.
stubbornness ['stʌbənnis] *n* entêtement *m*, ténacité *f*.
stuck [stʌk] *pt pp of* stick.
stud [stʌd] *n* bouton *m*, clou *m*, rivet
m, écurie *f*, haras *m*.
studded ['stʌdid] *a* semé, orné,
clouté.
student ['stjuːdənt] *n* étudiant(e)
mf, homme *m* qui étudie.
studied ['stʌdid] *a* étudié, délibéré,
recherché.
studio ['stjuːdiou] *n* atelier *m*, studio
m.
studious ['stjuːdiəs] *a* studieux,
étudié.
study ['stʌdi] *n* étude *f*, cabinet de
travail *m*; *vti* étudier; *vi* faire ses
études, apprendre (à).
stuff [stʌf] *n* étoffe *f*, marchandise *f*,
camelote *f*, substance *f*, sottise *f*;
vt bourrer, empiler, empailler, farcir,
fourrer, boucher.
stuffy ['stʌfi] *a* étouffant, mal aéré,
guindé.
stultify ['stʌltifai] *vt* rendre ridicule,
infirmer, ruiner.
stumble ['stʌmbl] *n* faux-pas *m*; *vi*
trébucher, se fourvoyer.
stumbling-block ['stʌmblɪŋblɔk] *n*
pierre d'achoppement *f*.
stump [stʌmp] *n* souche *f*, tronçon
m, chicot *m*, moignon *m*, bout *m*,
(*cricket*) piquet *m*; *vt* estomper,
coller; to — in entrer clopin-
clopant.
stumpy ['stʌmpi] *a* trapu, ramassé.
stung [stʌŋ] *pt pp of* sting.
stun [stʌn] *vt* étourdir, assommer,
assourdir, renverser.
stunk [stʌŋk] *pp of* stink.
stupefaction [ˌstjuːpiˈfækʃən] *n* stupéfaction *f*.
stupefy ['stjuːpifai] *vt* hébéter, stupéfier, engourdir.
stupefying ['stjuːpifaiɪŋ] *a* stupéfiant.
stupendous [stjuːˈpendəs] *a* prodigieux, formidable.
stupid ['stjuːpid] *a* stupide, bête.
stupidity [stjuːˈpiditi] *n* stupidité *f*,
bêtise *f*.
sturdy ['stəːdi] *a* robuste, vigoureux.
sturgeon ['stəːdʒən] *n* esturgeon *m*.
stutter ['stʌtə] *vti* bredouiller, bégayer.
sty [stai] *n* porcherie *f*, bouge *m*,
orgelet *m*.
style [stail] *n* style *m*, genre *m*, titre
m, espèce *f*; *vt* appeler.
stylish ['stailiʃ] *a* qui a du style, chic,
élégant.

subaltern ['sʌbltən] *an* subalterne *m*.
subdue [səbˈdjuː] *vt* soumettre,
maîtriser, dompter, adoucir, tamiser.
subdued [səbˈdjuːd] *a* vaincu, tamisé,
étouffé.
subject ['sʌbdʒikt] *n* sujet *m*;
matière *f*, objet *m*; *an* sujet, -ette;
a soumis, assujetti, passible; *ad* sous
réserve (de to).
subject [səbˈdʒekt] *vt* soumettre,
subjuguer, exposer.
subjection [səbˈdʒekʃən] *n* sujétion
f, assujettissement *m*, soumission *f*.
subjugation [ˌsʌbdʒuˈgeiʃən] *n* soumission *f*, assujettissement *m*.
subjugate ['sʌbdʒugeit] *vt* subjuguer.
sublime [səˈblaim] *a* sublime, suprême.
sublimity [səˈblimiti] *n* sublimité *f*.
submarine ['sʌbməriːn] *an* sous-
marin *m*.
submerge [səbˈməːdʒ] *vt* submerger;
vi plonger.
submersion [səbˈməːʃən] *n* submersion *f*.
submission [səbˈmiʃən] *n* soumission
f.
submit [səbˈmit] *vt* soumettre; *vi* se
soumettre.
subordinate [səˈbɔːdənit] *an* infé-
rieur(e) *mf*, subordonné(e) *mf*; *vt*
subordonner.
subordination [səˌbɔːdiˈneiʃən] *n*
subordination *f*.
suborn [sʌˈbɔːn] *vt* suborner.
subpoena [səbˈpiːnə] *n* assignation *f*;
vt citer.
subscribe [səbˈskraib] *vt* souscrire
(pour); to — to s'abonner à, être
abonné à.
subscriber [səbˈskraibə] *n* souscrip-
teur *m*, abonné(e) *mf*.
subscription [səbˈskripʃən] *n* sou-
scription *f*.
subsequent ['sʌbsikwənt] *a* subséquent, ultérieur.
subsequently ['sʌbsikwəntli] *ad* sub-
séquemment, dans la suite.
subservience [səbˈsəːvjəns] *n* soumission *f*, obséquiosité *f*.
subservient [səbˈsəːvjənt] *a* utile,
obséquieux.
subside [səbˈsaid] *vi* s'affaisser,
déposer, s'apaiser.
subsidence [səbˈsaidəns] *n* affaissement *m*, baisse *f*.
subsidize ['sʌbsidaiz] *vt* subventionner, primer.
subsidy ['sʌbsidi] *n* subvention *f*,
prime *f*.
subsist [səbˈsist] *vi* subsister, persister, vivre.
substance ['sʌbstəns] *n* substance *f*,
matière *f*, fond *m*, fortune *f*.
substantial [səbˈstænʃəl] *a* matériel,
substantiel, solide, riche, important,
copieux.
substantiate [səbˈstænʃieit] *vt* fonder,
justifier.
substitute ['sʌbstitjuːt] *n* substitut

m, équivalent m, doublure f, suppléant(e) mf, remplaçant(e) mf; vt substituer; to — for remplacer.

substitution [ˌsʌbstiˈtjuːʃən] n substitution f, remplacement m.

subterfuge [ˈsʌbtəfjuːdʒ] n subterfuge m, faux-fuyant m.

subtle [ˈsʌtl] a subtil, fin, astucieux.

subtlety [ˈsʌtlti] n subtilité f, finesse f.

subtract [səbˈtrækt] vt retrancher, soustraire.

subtraction [səbˈtrækʃən] n soustraction f.

suburb [ˈsʌbəːb] n faubourg m, banlieue f; a suburbain, de banlieue.

subvention [səbˈvenʃən] n subvention f.

subversion [səbˈvəːʃən] n subversion f.

subversive [səbˈvəːsiv] a subversif.

subvert [sʌbˈvəːt] vt renverser.

subway [ˈsʌbwei] n passage souterrain m; métro m.

succeed [səkˈsiːd] vti succéder (à), réussir.

success [səkˈses] n succès m, réussite f, suite f.

successful [səkˈsesful] a heureux, réussi, reçu, qui a du succès.

succession [səkˈseʃən] n succession f, suite f, série f.

successive [səkˈsesiv] a successif, consécutif, de suite.

successor [səkˈsesə] n successeur m.

succinct [səkˈsiŋkt] n succinct, concis.

succor [ˈsʌkə] n secours m; vt secourir.

succumb [səˈkʌm] vi succomber.

such [sʌtʃ] a tel, pareil, le même; pn tel, celui (qui), en qualité de; —as tel que, comme.

suchlike [ˈsʌtʃlaik] a analogue, de la sorte.

suck [sʌk] n tétée f, succion f, sucée f; vti sucer; vt téter.

sucking [ˈsʌkiŋ] a à la mamelle, de lait, en herbe.

suckle [ˈsʌkl] vt allaiter.

suckling [ˈsʌkliŋ] n nourrisson m, allaitement m.

sudden [ˈsʌdn] a soudain, brusque, subit; —ly adv tout à coup.

suddenness [ˈsʌdnnis] n soudaineté f, brusquerie f.

sue [suː] vt poursuivre, demander.

suet [suit] n graisse de rognon f.

suffer [ˈsʌfə] vti souffrir; vt subir, éprouver, supporter.

sufferance [ˈsʌfərəns] n tolérance f.

sufferer [ˈsʌfərə] n patient(e) mf, victime f.

suffering [ˈsʌfəriŋ] n souffrance f.

suffice [səˈfais] vi suffire.

sufficiency [səˈfiʃənsi] n fortune suffisante f, suffisance f, aisance f, assez de.

sufficient [səˈfiʃənt] a suffisant, assez de.

sufficiently [səˈfiʃəntli] ad suffisamment, assez.

suffocate [ˈsʌfəkeit] vti étouffer, suffoquer.

suffocation [ˌsʌfəˈkeiʃən] n suffocation f, asphyxie f.

suffrage [ˈsʌfridʒ] n suffrage m, droit de vote m.

suffuse [səˈfjuːz] vt colorer, humecter, se répandre sur.

sugar [ˈʃugə] n sucre m; castor — sucre en poudre; loaf — sucre en pain; vt sucrer; —bowl sucrier m; —beet betterave à sucre f; —cane canne à sucre f; —tongs pince f.

sugary [ˈʃugəri] a sucré, mielleux, doucereux, mièvre.

suggest [səˈdʒest] vt suggérer, inspirer, proposer.

suggestion [səˈdʒestʃən] n suggestion f, nuance f.

suggestive [səˈdʒestiv] a suggestif, équivoque.

suicide [ˈsjuisaid] n suicide m, suicidé(e) mf.

suit [sjuːt] n requête f, demande f, procès m, (cards) couleur f, complet m, tailleur m; vt adapter, accommoder, arranger, convenir à, aller à.

suitable [ˈsjuːtəbl] a approprié, convenable, assorti, qui convient.

suite [swiːt] n suite f, appartement m, mobilier m.

suitor [ˈsjuːtə] n plaignant m, solliciteur m, prétendant m, soupirant m.

sulk [sʌlk] vi bouder; —s n pl bouderie f; —y a bouderur.

sullen [ˈsʌlən] a rancunier, maussade, renfrogné.

sullenness [ˈsʌlənnis] n maussaderie f, air renfrogné m.

sully [ˈsʌli] vt salir, souiller.

sulphur [ˈsʌlfə] n soufre m.

sultan [ˈsʌltən] n sultan m.

sultana [səlˈtɑːnə] n raisin de Smyrne m; sultane f.

sultriness [ˈsʌltrinis] n lourdeur f.

sultry [ˈsʌltri] a étouffant, lourd.

sum [sʌm] n somme f, calcul m; to — up calculer, récapituler, resumer.

summary [ˈsʌməri] n sommaire m, résumé m; a sommaire, récapitulatif.

summer [ˈsʌmə] n été m; a estival, d'été.

summing-up [ˈsʌmiŋˈʌp] n résumé m.

summit [ˈsʌmit] n sommet m, cime f, comble m.

summon [ˈsʌmən] vt citer, convoquer.

summons [ˈsʌmənz] n citation f, convocation f, procès-verbal m.

sumptuous [ˈsʌmptjuəs] a somptueux, fastueux.

sumptuousness [ˈsʌmptjuəsnis] n somptuosité f.

sun [sʌn] n soleil m; vt exposer (chauffer) au soleil; —burn hâle m; —burnt a hâlé, basané, bronzé; —glasses lunettes f pl de soleil.

Sunday [ˈsʌndi] n dimanche m.

sundial ['sʌndaiəl] n cadran solaire m.

sunder ['sʌndə] vt séparer.

sundry ['sʌndri] a chacun à part, divers, différent; n pl faux frais m pl.

sung [sʌŋ] pp of sing.

sunk [sʌŋk] pp of sink.

sunny ['sʌni] a ensoleillé, de soleil.

sunrise ['sʌnraiz] n lever du soleil m.

sunset ['sʌnset] n coucher du soleil m.

sunshade ['sʌnʃeid] n ombrelle f, parasol m.

sunshine ['sʌnʃain] n (lumière f du) soleil, grand jour m.

sunstroke ['sʌnstrouk] n coup de soleil m, insclation f.

sup [sʌp] n gorgée f; vt boire à petites gorgées; vi souper.

superabundance [,sju:pərə'bʌndəns] n surabondance f.

superabundant [,sju:pərə'bʌndənt] a surabondant.

superannuated [,sju:pə'rænjueitid] a en (à la) retraite, suranné.

superb [sju:'pə:b] a superbe, magnifique, sensationel.

supercilious [,sju:pə'siliəs] a dédaigneux, pincé.

superficial [,sju:pə'fiʃəl] a superficiel.

superficiality [,sju:pə,fiʃi'æliti] n superficialité f.

superfluous [sju:'pə:fluəs] a superflu, de trop.

superfluity [,sju:pə'flu:iti] n superfluité f, embarras m, excédent m.

superhuman [,sju:pə'hju:mən] a surhumain.

superintend [,sju:prin'tend] vt contrôler, surveiller.

superintendence [,sju:prin'tendəns] n surintendance f, surveillance f.

superintendent [,sju:prin'tendənt] n surintendant m, surveillant(e) mf.

superior [sju:'piəriə] an supérieur(e) mf.

superiority [sju:,piəri'ɔriti] n supériorité f.

superlative [sju:'pə:lətiv] an superlatif m; a suprême.

superman ['sju:pəmæn] n surhomme m.

supernatural [,sju:pə'nætʃrəl] an surnaturel m.

superpose [,sju:pə'pouz] vt superposer.

supersede [,sju:pə'si:d] vt supplanter, écarter, remplacer.

superstition [,sju:pə'stiʃən] n superstition f.

superstitious [,sju:pə'stiʃəs] a superstitieux.

superstructure ['sju:pə,strʌktʃə] n superstructure f, tablier m.

supertax ['sju:pətæks] n surtaxe f.

supervise ['sju:pəvaiz] vt surveiller, contrôler.

supervision [,sju:pə'viʒən] n surveillance f, contrôle m.

supervisor ['sju:pəvaizə] n surveillant(e) mf.

supine ['sju:pain] a couché sur le dos, indolent.

supper ['sʌpə] n souper m.

supplant [sə'plɑ:nt] vt supplanter, évincer.

supple ['sʌpl] a souple, flexible.

supplement ['sʌplimənt] n supplément m.

supplement ['sʌpliment] vt ajouter à, augmenter.

suppleness ['sʌplnis] n souplesse f.

supplicate ['sʌplikeit] vti supplier.

supplication [,sʌpli'keiʃən] n supplication f.

supplier [sə'plaiə] n fournisseur, -euse.

supply [sə'plai] n offre f, fourniture f, provision f; pl vivres m pl; fournitures f pl, intendance f; vt fournir, munir.

support [sə'pɔ:t] n support m, soutien m, appui m; vt supporter, appuyer, soutenir.

supporter [sə'pɔ:tə] n soutien m, partisan m, supporter m.

suppose [sə'pouz] vt supposer, s'imaginer.

supposing [sə'pouziŋ] cj à supposer que.

supposition [,sʌpə'ziʃən] n supposition f.

suppress [sə'pres] vt supprimer, réprimer, étouffer, refouler.

suppression [sə'preʃən] n suppression f, répression f.

suppurate ['sʌpjuəreit] vi suppurer.

supremacy [sju:'preməsi] n suprématie f.

supreme [sju:'pri:m] a suprême.

sura, surat ['suərə, su'ræt] n sourate f.

surcharge ['sə:tʃɑ:dʒ] n surcharge f, surtaxe f; vt surcharger, surtaxer.

sure [ʃuə] a sûr, assuré, certain; to be — ad sûrement.

surety ['ʃuəti] n garant(e) mf, caution f.

surf [sə:f] n ressac m, surf m, barre f.

surface ['sə:fis] n surface f, apparence f.

surfboard ['sə:fbɔ:d] n aquaplane m.

surfboat ['sə:fbout] n pirogue f.

surfing ['sə:fiŋ] n planking m.

surfeit ['sə:fit] n excès m, satiété f, indigestion f, écœurement m; vt gaver, rassasier.

surge [sə:dʒ] n lame f, houle f, soulèvement m; vi se soulever, onduler, se répandre en flots.

surgeon ['sə:dʒən] n chirurgien m.

surgery ['sə:dʒəri] n chirurgie f, clinique f.

surgical ['sə:dʒikəl] a chirurgical.

surliness ['sə:linis] n morosité f, air bourru m.

surly ['sə:li] a revêche, bourru, morose.

surmise ['sə:maiz] n soupçon m

conjecture *f*; [sə'maiz] *vt* soupçonner, conjecturer.
surmount [sə:'maunt] *vt* surmonter,
triompher de.
surname ['sə:neim] *n* nom *m* de
famille; *vt* nommer.
surpass [sə:'pa:s] *vt* surpasser, dépasser, excéder.
surplice ['sə:pləs] *n* surplis *m*.
surplus ['sə:pləs] *n* surplus *m*,
excédent *m*, boni *m*, rabiot *m*.
surprise [sə'praiz] *n* surprise *f*; *vt*
surprendre; by — à l'improviste.
surprising [sə'praiziŋ] *a* surprenant,
étonnant.
surrealism [sə'ri:alizm] *n* sur-
réalisme *m*.
surrender [sə'rendə] *n* reddition *f*,
capitulation *f*; *vt* rendre, renoncer à,
livrer; *vi* se rendre, se livrer.
surreptitious [ˌsʌrəp'tiʃəs] *a* subreptice, clandestin.
surround [sə'raund] *vt* entourer,
cerner.
surrounding [sə'raundiŋ] *a* environ-
nant.
surroundings [sə'raundiŋs] *n* pl
environs *m* pl, ambiance *f*, alentours
m pl.
surtax ['sə:tæks] *n* surtaxe *f*.
survey ['sə:vei] *n* coup d'œil *m*,
examen *m*, arpentage *m*, cadastre
m, aperçu *m*, expertise *f*, plan *m*.
survey [sə:'vei] *vt* examiner, relever,
arpenter, embrasser du regard,
contempler.
surveyor [sə:'veiə] *n* arpenteur *m*,
inspecteur *m*, ingénieur *m* du service
vicinal.
survival [sə'vaivəl] *n* survivance *f*.
survive [sə'vaiv] *vi* survivre; *vt*
survivre à.
Susan ['su:zn] Suzanne *f*.
susceptibility [sə,septə'biliti] *n* susceptibilité *f*, sensibilité *f*.
susceptible [sə'septəbl] *a* susceptible,
sensible, impressionnable.
suspect [səs'pekt] *vt* soupçonner,
suspecter, se douter de.
suspect ['sʌspekt] *a* suspect.
suspend [səs'pend] *vt* (sus)pendre,
mettre à pied, surseoir à.
suspenders [səs'pendəz] *n* jarretelles
f pl, fixe-chaussettes *n* pl,
bretelles *f* pl.
suspense [səs'pens] *n* attente *f*,
inquiétude *f*, suspens *m*.
suspension [səs'penʃən] *n* suspension
f, mise à pied *f*, retrait *m*.
suspicion [səs'piʃən] *n* suspicion *f*,
soupçon *m*.
suspicious [səs'piʃəs] *a* soupçonneux,
suspect, méfiant, louche.
sustain [səs'tein] *vt* soutenir, sustenter, souffrir, subir.
sustenance ['sʌstinəns] *n* moyens de
se soutenir *m* pl, nourriture *f*.
swab [swɔb] *n* faubert *m*, tampon *m*;
vt balayer, nettoyer, laver à grande
eau.

swaddle ['swɔdl] *vt* emmailloter.
swaddling-clothes ['swɔdliŋklouðz]
n langes *m* pl.
swagger ['swægə] *n* suffisance *f*,
rodomontades *f* pl; *vi* se gober, se
pavaner, crâner.
swain [swein] *n* berger *m*, amoureux
m, tourtereau *m*.
swallow ['swɔlou] *n* hirondelle *f*,
gosier *m*, gorgée *f*; *vt* avaler, engloutir.
swam [swæm] *pt of* **swim**.
swamp ['swɔmp] *n* marais *m*; *vt*
inonder, déborder.
swan [swɔn] *n* cygne *m*.
swank [swæŋk] *vi* faire de l'épate,
se donner des airs.
swap [swɔp] *vt* troquer, échanger.
sward [swɔ:d] *n* gazon *m*.
swarm [swɔ:m] *n* essaim *m*, nuée *f*;
vi essaimer, fourmiller, grimper.
swarthy ['swɔ:ði] *a* hâlé, boucané.
swash [swɔʃ] *n* clapotis *m*; *vi*
clapoter.
swastika ['swɔstikə] *n* croix gammée
f.
swath [swɔ:θ] *n* andain *m*.
swathe [sweið] *vt* emmailloter, emmitoufler.
sway [swei] *n* balancement *m*,
pouvoir *m*, gouvernement *m*; *vi* se
balancer, vaciller, incliner; *vt* balancer, courber, porter, faire pencher,
gouverner.
swear [sweə] *n* — word juron *m*; *vti*
jurer; *vt* assermenter.
sweat [swet] *n* sueur *f*, transpiration
f; *vti* suer; *vi* transpirer, peiner; *vt*
exploiter.
sweater ['swetə] *n* sweater *m*, pull-
over *m*, chandail *m*, exploiteur *m*.
sweating ['swetiŋ] *n* suée *f*, transpiration *f*.
swede [swi:d] *n* rutabaga *m*.
Swede [swi:d] *n* Suédois(e) *mf*.
Sweden ['swi:dn] *n* Suède *f*.
Swedish ['swi:diʃ] *an* suédois *m*.
sweep [swi:p] *n* mouvement *m*,
large courbe *f*, allée *f*, portée *f*, coup
de balai *m*, godille *f*, ramoneur *m*;
vt balayer, emporter, ramoner,
draguer; *vi* s'élancer, fondre,
s'étendre; to — aside écarter; to —
down *vt* charrier, emporter; *vi*
dévaler.
sweeper ['swi:pə] *n* balayeur *m*,
balai *m* mécanique, balayeuse *f*;
mine— dragueur *m* de mines.
sweeping ['swi:piŋ] *n* balayage *m*,
dragage *m*, ramonage *m*; *a* excessif,
radical, impétueux, large.
swept [swept] *pt pp of* **sweep**.
sweet [swi:t] *a* doux, sucré, gentil; *n*
bonbon *m*; pl sucreries *f* pl, bonbons
m pl, douceurs *f* pl.
sweetbread ['swi:tbred] *n* ris de
veau *m*.
sweeten ['swi:tn] *vt* sucrer, adoucir.
sweetheart ['swi:tha:t] *n* ami(e) *mf*,
fiancé(e) *mf*, chéri(e) *mf*.

sweetish ['swiːtiʃ] *a* douceâtre.

sweetmeat ['swiːtmiːt] *n* bonbon *m*; *pl* sucreries *f pl*.

sweetness ['swiːtnis] *n* douceur *f*, charme *m*.

sweet-pea ['swiːt'piː] *n* pois de senteur *m*.

swell [swel] *n* enflure *f*, houle *f*; *pl* (*fam*) élégants *m pl*, gens de la haute *m pl*; *a* (*fam*) chic, épatant; *vt* enfler, gonfler; *vi* se gonfler, (s')enfler, se soulever.

swelter ['sweltə] *n* fournaise *f*; *vi* étouffer de chaleur, être en nage.

swerve [swəːv] *vi* faire un écart, une embardée, donner un coup de volant.

swift [swift] *n* martinet *m*; *a* rapide, prompt.

swiftness ['swiftnis] *n* rapidité *f*, vitesse *f*, promptitude *f*.

swill [swil] *n* rinçage *m*, lavasse *f*, pâtée *f*; *vt* rincer, boire goulûment, lamper.

swim [swim] *vi* nager, flotter, tourner; *vt* traverser à la nage.

swimmer ['swimə] *n* nageur, -euse.

swimming ['swimiŋ] *n* natation *f*, nage *f*.

swindle ['swindl] *n* escroquerie *f*; *vt* escroquer.

swindler ['swindlə] *n* escroc *m*.

swine [swain] *n* cochon *m*, porc *m*, pourceau *m*, salaud *m*.

swing [swiŋ] *n* oscillation *f*, balancement *m*, balançoire *f*, cours *m*, courant *m*, entrain *m*, revirement *m*; *vi* se balancer, tourner, ballotter, danser; *vt* balancer, faire osciller, tourner.

swirl [swəːl] *n* tourbillon *m*, remous *m*; *vi* tourbillonner.

swish [swiʃ] *n* banco *m*; latérite *f*; *vi* bruire.

Swiss [swis] *a* suisse; *n* Suisse, -esse.

switch [switʃ] *n* baguette *f*, badine *f*, (*rails*) aiguille *f*, commutateur *m*, bouton *m*; *vt* cingler, remuer, aiguiller; to — on (off) donner (couper) le courant.

switchboard ['switʃbɔːd] *n* tableau *m*.

Switzerland ['switsələnd] la Suisse *f*.

swivel ['swivl] *n* pivot *m*; *vi* pivoter, tourner.

swoon [swuːn] *n* syncope *f*, défaillance *f*; *vi* s'évanouir.

swoop [swuːp] *n* descente *f*, attaque foudroyante *f*, rafle *f*; *vi* fondre, s'abattre.

sword [sɔːd] *n* sabre *m*, épée *f*, glaive *m*.

swore [swɔː] *pt of* swear.

sworn [swɔːn] *pp of* swear; *a* assermenté, intime, juré.

swung [swʌŋ] *pt pp of* swing.

syllable ['siləbl] *n* syllabe *f*, mot *m*.

syllabus ['siləbəs] *n* programme *m*, ordre du jour *m*.

symbol ['simbəl] *n* symbole *m*, emblème *m*.

symbolic(al) [sim'bɔlik(əl)] *a* symbolique.

symbolism ['simbəlizəm] *n* symbolisme *f*.

symbolize ['simbəlaiz] *vt* symboliser.

symmetrical [si'metrikəl] *a* symétrique.

symmetry ['simitri] *n* symétrie *f*.

sympathetic [,simpə'θetik] *a* compatissant, de sympathie, sympathique.

sympathize ['simpəθaiz] *vi* compatir, partager la douleur (de), comprendre.

sympathy ['simpəθi] *n* compassion *f*, sympathie *f*.

symphony ['simfəni] *n* symphonie *f*.

symptom ['simptəm] *n* symptôme *m*.

synagogue ['sinəgɔg] *n* synagogue *f*.

syndicate ['sindikit] *n* syndicat *m*; ['sindikeit] *vt* syndiquer.

synod ['sinəd] *n* synode *m*.

synonym ['sinənim] *n* synonyme *m*.

synonymous [si'nɔniməs] *a* synonyme.

synopsis [si'nɔpsis] *n* vue d'ensemble *f*, résumé *m*, mémento *m*.

synoptic(al) [si'nɔptik(əl)] *a* synoptique.

syntax ['sintæks] *n* syntaxe *f*.

synthesis ['sinθisis] *n* synthèse *f*.

synthetic(al) [sin'θetik(əl)] *a* synthétique.

Syria ['siriə] *n* Syrie *f*.

Syrian ['siriən] *a* syrien; *n* Syrien, -ienne.

syringe ['sirindʒ] *n* seringue *f*.

syrup ['sirəp] *n* sirop *m*.

syrupy ['sirəpi] *a* sirupeux.

system ['sistim] *n* système *m*.

systematic [,sisti'mætik] *a* systématique.

systematize ['sistimətaiz] *vt* systématiser.

T

tab [tæb] *n* étiquette *f*, oreille *f*, patte *f*, ferret *m*, touche *f*.

table ['teibl] *n* table *f*, tablier *m*, plaque *f*, tablée *f*.

tablecloth ['teiblklɔθ] *n* nappe *f*.

tableland ['teiblænd] *n* plateau *m*.

table-leaf ['teibliːf] *n* rallonge *f*.

tablespoon ['teiblspuːn] *n* cuiller à bouche *f*.

tablet ['tæblit] *n* tablette *f*, cachet *m*, comprimé *m*, plaque *f*, commémorative *f*.

tabloid ['tæblɔid] *n* journal *m* à sensation.

taboo [tə'buː] *n* tabou *m*; *vt* interdire.

tabulate ['tæbjuleit] *vt* cataloguer, classifier.

tacit ['tæsit] *a* tacite.

taciturn ['tæsitəːn] *a* taciturne.

taciturnity [,tæsi'tə:niti] n taciturnité f.

tack [tæk] n faufil m, (nail) semence f, bordée f, voie f; vt clouer, faufiler; vi louvoyer, tirer des bordées, virer.

tackle ['tækl] n poulie f, attirail m, palan m, engins m pl; vt empoigner, aborder, s'attaquer à, plaquer.

tact [tækt] n tact m, savoir-faire m, doigté m.

tactful ['tæktful] a de tact, délicat.

tactician [tæk'tiʃən] n tacticien m.

tactics ['tæktiks] n tactique f.

tactless ['tæktlis] a sans tact, indiscret.

tactlessness ['tæktlisnis] n manque de tact m.

tadpole ['tædpoul] n têtard m.

tag [tæg] n aiguillette f, bout m, appendice m, cliché m, refrain m; fiche f.

tail [teil] n queue f, basque f, pan m, (tossing) pile m; to — off s'éteindre; vt suivre, pister.

tail-light ['teil'lait] n feu arrière m.

tailor ['teilə] n tailleur m; — made a tailleur, fait sur mesure.

taint [teint] n grain m, touche f, trace f, corruption f, tare f; vt corrompre, vicier, gâter.

take [teik] vti prendre; vt gagner, captiver, tenir (pour), falloir, mettre, demander, vouloir; to — off décoller; to — out (faire) sortir, tirer, emmener; to — to prendre goût à, se prendre d'amitié pour; to — up monter, relever, ramasser, occuper.

take in ['teik'in] vt tromper.

take-off ['teikɔf] n départ m, décollage m.

taking ['teikiŋ] a attrayant; n prise f.

takings ['teikiŋz] n pl recette f.

taken ['teikən] pp of **take.**

tale [teil] n conte m, racontar m.

tale-teller ['teil,telə] n conteur m, cancanier m, rapporteur, -euse, cafard(e) mf.

talent ['tælənt] n talent m.

talented ['tæləntid] a de talent, doué.

talk [tɔ:k] n conversation f, parole f, causerie f, fable f; vi causer; vti parler.

talkative ['tɔ:kətiv] a bavard, loquace.

talking of [tɔ:kiŋəv] prep à propos de.

tall [tɔ:l] a très grand, haut, raide, fort, extravagant.

tallow ['tælou] n suif m; — candle chandelle f.

tally ['tæli] n taille f, coche f, étiquette f; vt compter, concorder; vi s'accorder, cadrer.

talon ['tælən] n serre f.

tame [teim] a apprivoisé, domestique, banal, plat; vt apprivoiser, aplatir.

tameness ['teimnis] n soumission f, banalité f, fadeur f.

tamper ['tæmpə] vi se mêler; to —

with se mêler de, toucher à, falsifier, altérer.

tan [tæn] n tan m, hâle m; vt tanner, hâler, bronzer; vi brunir, se basaner.

tandem ['tændəm] n tandem m.

tang [tæŋ] n saveur f, piquant m, goût m.

tangent ['tændʒənt] n tangente f; a tangent.

tangerine [,tændʒə'ri:n] n mandarine f.

tangible ['tændʒəbl] a tangible, sensible, réel, palpable.

tangle ['tæŋgl] n confusion f, enchevêtrement m, fouillis m; vt embrouiller; vi s'embrouiller, s'emmêler.

tank [tæŋk] n réservoir m, citerne f, cuve f, tank m, char d'assaut m.

tankard ['tæŋkəd] n pot m, chope f.

tanner ['tænə] n tanneur m, pièce de sixpence f.

tannery ['tænəri] n tannerie f.

tantalize ['tæntəlaiz] vt tantaliser, tourmenter.

tantalizing ['tæntəlaiziŋ] a provoquant, décevant.

tantamount ['tæntəmaunt] a équivalent, qui revient à.

tantrum ['tæntrəm] n accès de colère m.

tap [tæp] n robinet m, tape f; vt mettre en perce, inciser, ponctionner, intercepter, taper, tapoter.

tape [teip] n ruban m, ganse f, bande f; vt attacher, border, brocher.

tape-measure ['teip,meʒə] n mètre ruban m.

taper ['teipə] n cierge m, bougie f, rat de cave m; vt effiler; vi amincir, s'effiler.

tape-recorder ['teipri,kɔːdə] n magnétophone m.

tapestry ['tæpistri] n tapisserie f.

tapeworm ['teipwə:m] n ver solitaire m, ténia m.

tapioca [,tæpi'oukə] n tapioca m.

tar [tɑ:] n goudron m, (fam) loup m de mer; vt goudronner.

tardiness ['tɑ:dinis] n lenteur f, tardivité f, retard m.

tardy ['tɑːdi] a lent, tardif.

tare [tɛə] n tare f, ivraie f.

target ['tɑːgit] n cible f, disque m, objectif m.

tariff ['tærif] n tarif m.

tarmac ['tɑːmæk] n macadam m, piste de décollage f.

tarnish ['tɑːniʃ] n ternissure f; vt ternir; vi se ternir.

tarpaulin [tɑː'pɔːlin] n bâche (goudronnée) f.

tarragon ['tærəgən] n estragon m.

tarry ['tæri] vi rester, attendre, s'attarder.

tart [tɑːt] n tarte f, fourte f; (fam) putain f; a acide, âpre, piquant, aigre.

tartness ['tɑːtnis] n aigreur f, verdeur f, acidité f.

task [tɑːsk] n tâche f,, devoir m, besogne f; to take to — prendre à partie.

tassel ['tæsəl] n gland m, signet m.

taste [teist] n goût m, saveur f; vt goûter (à), sentir, toucher à, déguster.

tasteful ['teistful] a qui a du goût, de bon goût.

tasteless ['teistlis] a insipide, fade, sans goût.

taster ['teistə] n dégustateur m.

tasty ['teisti] a savoureux.

tatter ['tætə] n chiffon m; pl loques f pl, guenilles f pl.

tattle ['tætl] n bavardage m, commérages m pl; vi bavarder.

tattler ['tætlə] n bavard(e) mf, cancanier, -ière.

tattoo [tə'tuː] n (mil) retraite f, tatouage m; vi tambouriner; vt tatouer.

taught [tɔːt] pt pp of **teach**.

taunt [tɔːnt] n reproche m, quolibet m; vt reprocher (à), accabler de quolibets, se moquer de, se gausser de.

taut [tɔːt] a tendu, raide.

tavern ['tævən] n taverne f, cabaret m.

tawdriness ['tɔːdrinis] n clinquant m, faux luxe m.

tawdry ['tɔːdri] a criard.

tawny ['tɔːni] a fauve, basané.

tax [tæks] n impôt m, taxe f, contribution f; vt taxer, imposer, frapper d'un impôt.

taxation [tæk'seifən] n imposition f, taxation f.

tax-collector ['tækskə,lektə] n percepteur m.

taxi ['tæksi] n taxi m.

tarpayer ['tæks,peiə] n contribuable mf.

tea [tiː] n thé m; —caddy boîte f à thé; —cloth napperon m; —pot théière f; —spoon cuiller f à thé; — chest caisse f à thé.

teach [tiːtʃ] vt enseigner, apprendre (à), instruire.

teacher ['tiːtʃə] n professeur m, (primary) instituteur m, institutrice f, maître m, maîtresse f.

teaching ['tiːtʃiŋ] n enseignement m, doctrine f, leçons f pl.

teak [tiːk] n tek m.

team [tiːm] n équipe f, attelage m; vt atteler.

tear [tiə] n larme f, goutte f, bulle f.

tear [teə] n déchirure f, accroc m; vt déchirer, arracher.

tearful ['tiəful] a larmoyant, en larmes, éploré.

tease [tiːz] vt taquiner, effilocher, démêler; n taquin(e) mf.

teasel ['tiːzl] n chardon m, carde f.

teaser ['tiːzə] n problème m, colle f.

teasing ['tiːziŋ] n taquinerie f, effilochage m; a taquin.

teat [tiːt] n tétin m, tétine f, tette f.

technical ['teknikəl] a technique.

technicality [,tekni'kæliti] n technicité f, détail m d'ordre technique.

technique [tek'niːk] n technique f.

tedious ['tiːdjəs] a ennuyeux, fastidieux.

teem [tiːm] vi pulluler, abonder, fourmiller, grouiller.

teeth [tiːθ] n pl of **tooth**.

teethe [tiːð] vi faire ses dents.

teething ['tiːðiŋ] n dentition f.

teetotal [tiː'toutl] a de tempérance, antialcoolique.

teetotaler [tiː'toutlə] n abstinent(e) mf.

telegram ['teligræm] n télégramme m, dépêche f.

telegraph ['teligrɑːf] n télégraphe m; vt télégraphier.

telegraphic [,teli'græfik] a télégraphique.

telegraphist [ti'legrəfist] n télégraphiste mf.

telepathy [ti'lepəθi] n télépathie f.

telephone ['telifoun] n téléphone m; vt téléphoner.

telescope ['teliskoup] n télescope f, longue-vue f; vt télescoper; vi se télescoper.

television ['teli,viʒən] n télévision f.

tell [tel] vt dire, conter, parler de, distinguer; vi porter, compter, militer; all told tout compris.

teller ['telə] n caissier m, conteur, -euse, recenseur m.

telltale ['telteil] n rapporteur, cafard (e) mf; a révélateur.

temerity [ti'meriti] n témérité f.

temper ['tempə] n humeur f, colère f, sang-froid m, mélange m, trempe f; vt mêler, tremper, tempérer.

temperament ['tempərəmənt] n tempérament m.

temperamental [,tempərə'mentl] a inégal, capricieux, nerveux, quinteux.

temperance ['tempərəns] n tempérance f, sobriété f, retenue f.

temperate ['tempərit] a tempéré, modéré, tempérant, sobre.

temperature ['tempritʃə] n température f, fièvre f.

tempest ['tempist] n tempête f.

tempestuous [tem'pestjuəs] a tempétueux, orageux, violent.

temple ['templ] n temple m, tempe f.

tempo ['tempou] n rythme m.

temporal ['tempərəl] a temporel.

temporary ['tempərəri] a temporaire, provisoire.

temporize ['tempəraiz] vi temporiser.

temporizer ['tempəraizə] n temporisateur m.

tempt [tempt] vt tenter.

temptation [temp'teifən] n tentation f.

tempter ['temptə] n tentateur m, séducteur m.

ten [ten] ad dix.

tenable ['tenəbl] *a* (sou)tenable, défendable.

tenacious [ti'neiʃəs] *a* tenace.

tenacity [ti'næsiti] *n* ténacité *f*.

tenancy ['tenənsi] *n* location *f*.

tenant ['tenənt] *n* locataire *mf*.

tench [tenʃ] *n* tanche *f*.

tend [tend] *vi* tendre (à), se diriger (vers); *vt* soigner, veiller sur, servir.

tendency ['tendənsi] *n* tendance *f*, disposition *f*.

tendentious [ten'denʃəs] *a* tendancieux.

tender ['tendə] *n* devis *m*, offre *f*, monnaie *f*, tender *m*; *vt* offrir; *vi* soumissionner; *a* tendre, délicat, sensible, fragile.

tenderness ['tendənis] *n* tendresse *f*, sensibilité *f*.

tendril ['tendril] *n* vrille *f*.

tenement ['tenimənt] *n* propriété *f*, appartement *m*, maison de rapport *f*.

tenet ['tenit] *n* doctrine *f*, opinion *f*, article de foi *m*.

tenfold ['tenfould] *a* décuple; *ad* dix fois.

tennis ['tenis] *n* tennis *m*; —**court** tennis *m*, court *m*.

tenor ['tenə] *n* teneur *f*, cours *m*, ténor *m*.

tense [tens] *n* temps *m*; *a* tendu, raide.

tension ['tenʃən] *n* tension *f*.

tent [tent] *n* tente *f*.

tentacle ['tentəkl] *n* tentacule *m*.

tentative ['tentətiv] *a* d'essai, expérimental.

tentatively ['tentətivli] *ad* à titre d'essai.

tenth [tenθ] *an* dixième *mf*, dix *m*.

tenuity [te'nju:iti] *n* rareté *f*, ténuité *f*.

tenuous ['tenjuəs] *a* délié, ténu, mince.

tenure ['tenjuə] *n* exercice de fonctions *m*, occupation *f*, tenure *f*.

tepid ['tepid] *a* tiède.

term [tə:m] *n* durée *f*, fin *f*, trimestre *m*, terme *m*; *pl* conditions *f pl*; *vt* nommer, désigner.

terminate ['tə:mineit] *vt* terminer; *vi* se terminer.

termination [.tə:mi'neiʃən] *n* terminaison *f*, conclusion *f*, fin *f*.

terminus ['tə:minəs] *n* terminus *m*, tête de ligne *f*.

terrace ['terəs] *n* terrasse *f*.

terrestrial [ti'restriəl] *a* terrestre.

terrible ['terəbl] *a* terrible, atroce, affreux.

terrific [tə'rifik] *a* terrifiant, terrible, formidable.

terrify ['terifai] *vt* terrifier, effrayer.

territorial [.teri'tɔ:riəl] *a* territorial, terrien.

territory ['teritəri] *n* territoire *m*.

terror ['terə] *n* terreur *f*.

terrorism ['terərizəm] *n* terrorisme *m*.

terrorize ['terəraiz] *vt* terroriser.

terse [tə:s] *a* net, délié, sobre, concis.

terseness ['tə:snis] *n* netteté *f*, concision *f*.

test [test] *n* pierre de touche *f*, épreuve *f*, test *m*, réactif *m*; *vt* éprouver, essayer, mettre à l'épreuve, vérifier.

testament ['testəmənt] *n* testament *m*.

testamentary [.testə'mentəri] *a* testamentaire.

testify ['testifai] *vt* attester, témoigner; *vi* déposer.

testily ['testili] *ad* en bougonnant, avec humeur.

testimonial [.testi'mouniəl] *n* recommandation *f*, certificat *m*.

testimony ['testiməni] *n* déposition *f*, témoignage *m*.

testiness ['testinis] *n* irascibilité *f*, susceptibilité *f*.

testy ['testi] *a* chatouilleux, irascible.

tetanus ['tetənəs] *n* tétanos *m*.

tether ['teðə] *n* longe *f*, attache *f*, moyens *m pl*, rouleau *m*; *vt* attacher.

text [tekst] *n* texte *m*.

text-book ['tekstbuk] *n* manuel *m*.

textile ['tekstail] *an* textile *m*; *a* tissu *m*.

textual ['tekstjuəl] *a* textuel, de texte.

texture ['tekstʃə] *n* (con)texture *f*, structure *f*, grain *m*, trace *f*.

Thames [temz] *n* la Tamise *f*.

than [ðən] *cj* que, de.

thank [θæŋk] *vt* remercier, rendre grâce(s) à.

thanks [θæŋks] *n pl* remerciements *m pl*, grâces *f pl*; — to grâce à.

thankful ['θæŋkful] *a* reconnaissant.

thankfulness ['θæŋkfulnis] *n* reconnaissance *f*.

thankless ['θæŋklis] *a* ingrat.

thanklessness ['θæŋklisnis] *n* ingratitude *f*.

thanksgiving ['θæŋks'giviŋ] *n* action de grâces *f*; fête *f* d'action de grâces.

that [ðæt] *a* ce, cet, cette; *pn* celui, celle (-là), cela, ça, qui, que, tant de; *cj* que, pour que, si seulement, plaise à Dieu que, dire que.

thatch [θætʃ] *n* chaume *m*; *vt* couvrir de chaume.

thatched [θætʃt] *a* (couvert) de chaume.

thaw [θɔ:] *n* dégel *m*; *vi* dégeler.

the [ðə] *def art* le, la, l', les, ce, cet, cette, ces, quel(s), quelle(s); *ad* d'autant; — more plus.

theater ['θiətə] *n* théâtre *m*.

theatrical [θi'ætrikəl] *a* théâtral, scénique.

thee [ði:] *pn* te, toi.

theft [θeft] *n* vol *m*.

their [ðeə] *a* leur(s).

theirs [ðeəz] *pn* le (la) leur, les leurs, à eux (elles).

them [ðem] *pn* les, eux, elles, leur.

theme [θi:m] *n* thème *m*, motif *m*.

themselves [ðəm'selvz] *pn* se, eux-(elles)-mêmes.

then [ðen] *ad* alors, puis, ensuite, donc.

thence [ðens] *ad* de là, par conséquent.

thenceforth ['ðens'fɔːθ] *ad* dès (depuis) lors, désormais.

theologian [θiə'loudʒjən] *n* théologien m.

theological [θiə'lɔdʒikəl] *a* théologique.

theology [θi'ɔlədʒi] *n* théologie f.

theorem ['θiərəm] *n* théorème m.

theoretic(al) [θiə'retikəl] *a* théorique.

theory ['θiəri] *n* théorie f.

there [ðɛə] *ad* là, y, il; *excl* voilà.

thereabout(s) ['ðɛərəbauts] *ad* par là, environ.

thereby ['ðɛə'bai] *ad* de ce fait, par là, par ce moyen.

therefore [ðɛə'fɔː] *ad* donc.

thereupon ['ðɛərə'pɔn] *ad* sur quoi, en conséquence, là-dessus.

thermometer [θə'mɔmitə] *n* thermomètre m.

these [ðiːz] *a* ces; *pn* ceux, celles(-ci).

thesis ['θiːsis] *n* thèse f.

they [ðei] *pn* ils, elles, on, eux, elles, ceux, celles.

thick [θik] *a* épais, touffu, dur, gros, fort, obtus; *ad* dur; *n* plus fort m.

thicken ['θikən] *vt* épaissir, lier; *vi* s'épaissir, se lier.

thicket ['θikit] *n* fourré m, bosquet m.

thickness ['θiknis] *n* épaisseur f.

thief [θiːf] *n* voleur, -euse.

thieve [θiːv] *vti* voler.

thigh [θai] *n* cuisse f; **—bone** fémur m.

thimble ['θimbl] *n* dé m.

thimbleful ['θimblful] *n* dé m, doigt m.

thin [θin] *a* mince, faible, fin, léger, grêle, clair(semé); *vt* éclaircir, amincir; *vi* s'éclaircir, maigrir, s'amincir.

thine [ðain] *pn* à toi, le (les) tien(s), la (les) tienne(s).

thing [θiŋ] *n* chose f, objet m, machin m, être m; *pl* affaires f *pl*, effets m *pl*.

thingummy ['θiŋəmi] *n* chose m, machin m, truc m.

think [θiŋk] *vti* penser, réfléchir; *vt* trouver, juger, s'imaginer; to **— about** penser à, songer à; to **— of** penser de, (à), avoir égard à.

thinker ['θiŋkə] *n* penseur mf.

thinness ['θinnis] *n* minceur f, maigreur f, fluidité f.

third [θəːd] *n* tiers m, tierce f; *a* troisième, tiers.

thirdly ['θəːdli] *ad* tertio, en troisième lieu, troisièmement.

thirst [θəːst] *n* soif f; *vi* avoir soif (de for).

thirsty ['θəːsti] *a* altéré, assoiffé.

thirteen ['θəː'tiːn] *an* treize m.

thirteenth ['θəː'tiːnθ] *an* treizième mf, treize m.

thirtieth ['θəːtiiθ] *an* trentième mf, trente m.

thirty ['θəːti] *an* trente m.

this [ðis] *a* ce, cet(te); *pn* ceci, ce, celui-ci, ceux-ci, celle(s)-ci.

thistle ['θisl] *n* chardon m.

thither ['ðiðə] *ad* y, là.

thong [θɔŋ] *n* courroie f, lanière f.

thorn [θɔːn] *n* épine f.

thorny ['θɔːni] *a* épineux.

thorough ['θʌrə] *a* soigné, minutieux, complet, achevé.

thoroughbred ['θʌrəbred] *an* pursang m.

thoroughfare ['θʌrəfɛə] *n* rue f, voie f, passage m; **no — entrée interdite**.

thoroughly ['θʌrəli] *ad* à fond, complètement, parfaitement.

thou [ðau] *pn* tu, toi.

though [ðou] *cj* bien que, quoique, même si; *ad* cependant, mais.

thought [θɔːt] *pt pp of* **think**; *n* pensée f, considération f, idée f, réflexion f.

thoughtful ['θɔːtful] *a* réfléchi, pensif, rêveur, attentionné, plein de prévenance.

thoughtfulness ['θɔːtfulnis] *n* réflexion f, méditation f, égards m *pl*, prévenance f.

thoughtless ['θɔːtlis] *a* étourdi, mal avisé.

thoughtlessness ['θɔːtlisnis] *n* étourderie f, manque d'égards m, imprévoyance f.

thousand ['θauzənd] *an* mille m.

thralldom ['θrɔːldəm] *n* esclavage m, servitude f.

thrash [θræʃ] *vt* battre, rosser.

thrashing ['θræʃiŋ] *n* battage m, correction f, raclée f.

thread [θred] *n* fil m, filet m, filon m; *vt* enfiler; to **— one's way** se faufiler.

threadbare ['θredbɛə] *a* usé jusqu'à la corde, râpé.

threat [θret] *n* menace f.

threaten ['θretn] *vti* menacer.

threefold ['θriːfould] *a* triple; *ad* trois fois autant.

thresh [θreʃ] *vt* battre.

threshing ['θreʃiŋ] *n* battage m.

threshing-machine ['θreʃiŋmə,ʃin] *n* batteuse f.

threshold ['θreʃhould] *n* seuil m.

threw [θruː] *pt of* **throw**.

thrice [θrais] *ad* trois fois.

thrift [θrift] *n* frugalité f, économie f.

thriftless ['θriftlis] *a* dépensier, prodigue.

thriftlessness ['θriftlisnis] *n* prodigalité f.

thrifty ['θrifti] *a* frugal, économe ménager.

thrill [θril] *n* frisson m, émotion *vt* émouvoir, électriser, faire frémir *vi* frémir, frissonner; tressaillir (de).

thriller ['θrilə] n roman à sensation m; roman série noire.

thrilling ['θriliŋ] a émouvant, empoignant, palpitant, sensationnel.

thrive [θraiv] vi prospérer, pousser dru, bien marcher.

thriving ['θraiviŋ] a prospère, vigoureux.

throat [θrout] n gorge f.

throaty ['θrouti] a guttural, rauque.

throb [θrɔb] n battement m, pulsation f, palpitation f, vrombissement m; vi battre, vibrer, vrombir.

throes [θrouz] n pl douleurs f pl, affres f pl, agonie f.

throne [θroun] n trône m.

throng [θrɔŋ] n foule f, cohue f; vt encombrer, remplir; vi affluer, se presser.

throttle ['θrɔtl] n régulateur m, obturateur m; vt étrangler.

through [θru:] a direct; prep à travers, par, au travers de, pendant, dans, à cause de, faute de; ad à travers, en communication, jusqu'au bout, à bonne fin, hors d'affaire; **I am — with you** j'en ai fini avec toi.

throughout [θru:'aut] ad de fond en comble, d'un bout à l'autre; prep d'un bout à l'autre de, partout dans.

throw [θrou] n lancement m, jet m, distance f, portée f; vt (re)jeter (bas, dehors etc), lancer, projeter, désarçonner; piquer; **to — away** (re)jeter, gaspiller; **to — back** renvoyer, réverbérer; **to — off** secouer, abandonner, quitter, dégager; **to — out** chasser, mettre à la porte, rejeter, lancer; **to — over** abandonner, plaquer; **to — up** abandonner, rendre, jeter en l'air.

thrown [θroun] pp of **throw**.

thrush [θrʌʃ] n grive f.

thrust [θrʌst] n coup de pointe m, coup d'estoc m, attaque f, trait m, poussée f, botte f; vt pousser, imposer, enfoncer.

thug [θʌg] n assassin m, bandit m, voyou m.

thumb [θʌm] n pouce m, influence f; **—tack** punaise f; vt feuilleter, manier; (fam) **to — a lift** faire de l'autostop.

thump [θʌmp] n coup de poing m, bruit sourd m; vt frapper à bras raccourcis, cogner sur.

thunder ['θʌndə] n tonnerre m; vti tonner, fulminer; **—bolt** foudre f; **—clap** coup de tonnerre m; **—storm** orage m; **—struck** foudroyé, renversé, sidéré.

Thursday ['θə:zdi] n jeudi m.

thus [ðʌs] ad ainsi, de cette façon, donc.

thwart [θwɔ:t] vt déjouer, contrecarrer.

thy [ðai] a ton, ta, tes.

thyme [taim] n thym m; **wild —** serpolet m.

thyself [ðai'self] pn te, toi-même.

tiara [ti'ɑ:rə] n tiare f.

tick [tik] n déclic m, tic-tac m, marque f, coche f, toile f, tique f, crédit m, instant m; vi faire tic-tac; **to — off** pointer, (fam) rembarrer.

ticket ['tikit] n billet m, ticket m, bulletin m, étiquette f, programme m; vt étiqueter; **—collector** contrôleur m; **—punch** poinçon m.

tickle ['tikl] n chatouillement m; vt chatouiller, amuser.

ticklish ['tikliʃ] a chatouilleux, délicat.

tidal wave ['taidl'weiv] n ras de marée m.

tide [taid] n marée f, courant m.

tidings ['taidiŋz] n nouvelles f pl.

tidy ['taidi] a bien rangé, ordonné, bien tenu, qui a de l'ordre, coquet; vt ranger, arranger, mettre de l'ordre dans.

tie [tai] n cravate f, lien m, match nul m; vt attacher, lier, nouer; vi faire match nul, être premier ex aequo.

tier [tiə] n gradin m, étage m.

tiff [tif] n pique f, petite querelle f bisbille f.

tiger ['taigə] n tigre m.

tight [tait] a compact, étroit, serré, tendu, étanche, ivre.

tighten ['taitn] vt (re)serrer, rétrécir, renforcer.

tight-fisted ['tait'fistid] a avare, pingre, radin.

tight-fitting ['tait'fitiŋ] a collant, bien ajusté.

tightly ['taitli] ad ferme, dur, bien, hermétiquement.

tightness ['taitnis] n compacité f, étanchéité f, étroitesse f, tension f.

tights [taits] n (maillot) collant m.

tigress ['taigris] n tigresse f.

tile [tail] n tuile f, carreau m; vt couvrir de tuiles, carreler.

till [til] n caisse f; vt labourer; prep jusqu'à; cj jusqu'à ce que.

tillage ['tilidʒ] n culture f, labourage m.

tiller ['tilə] n cultivateur m, laboureur m.

tiller ['tilə] n barre f.

tilt [tilt] n bâche f, pente f, joute f; vt bâcher, incliner, faire basculer, (faire) pencher; vi jouter, pencher, s'incliner, basculer.

timber ['timbə] n bois de charpente m, poutre f, calibre m, envergure f.

timbrel ['timbrəl] n tambourin m.

time [taim] n temps m, fois f, époque f, moment m, cadence f, mesure f; vt choisir le temps de, fixer l'heure de, noter la durée de, chronométrer, régler, juger, mesurer; **—server** opportuniste mf; **—table** horaire m, emploi du temps m.

timeless ['taimlis] a éternel, sans fin.

timely ['taimli] a opportun.

timid ['timid] a timide.

timorous ['timərəs] *a* peureux, timoré.

Timothy ['timəθi] Timothé *m*.

tin [tin] *n* étain *m*, fer-blanc *m*, *vt* étamer; — **can** bidon en fer-blanc.

tinfoil ['tinfɔil] *n* papier d'étain *m*, tain *m*.

tinned [tind] *a* en boîte, de conserve.

tin-hat ['tin'hæt] *n* casque *m*.

tin-opener ['tinoupənə] *n* ouvre-boîte *m*.

tinplate ['tinpleit] *vt* étamer; *n* ferblanterie *f*.

tinware ['tinwɛə] *n* vaisselle d'étain *f*.

tincture ['tiŋktʃə] *n* teinture *f*, saveur *f*, teinte *f*; *vt* colorer, relever, teinter.

tinder ['tində] *n* amadou *m*.

tinge [tindʒ] *n* teinte *f*, nuance *f*, saveur *f*, point *f*; *vt* colorer, teinter, nuancer.

tingle ['tiŋgl] *n* fourmillement *m*, picotement *m*, tintement *m*; fourmiller, cuire, picoter, tinter.

tinker ['tiŋkə] *n* rétameur *m*; *vt* rétamer, retaper; *vi* toucher, bricoler, tripoter.

tinkle ['tiŋkl] *n* tintement *m*, drelin *m*; *vi* tinter; *vt* faire tinter.

tinsel ['tinsəl] *n* paillette *f*, clinquant *m*; *vt* pailleter.

tint [tint] *n* teinte *f*, nuance *f*; *vt* teinter, colorer.

tiny ['taini] *a* tout petit, minuscule.

tip [tip] *n* bout *m*, pointe *f*, pourboire *m*, tuyau *m*; *vt* donner un pourboire à, graisser la patte à, donner un tuyau à, faire basculer, faire pencher, renverser, effleurer.

tippet ['tipit] *n* pèlerine *f*.

tipple ['tipl] *vt* boire sec.

tipsy ['tipsi] *a* ivre, gris.

tiptoe ['tiptou] *n* pointe des pieds *f*.

tiptop ['tip'tɔp] *n* le nec plus ultra; *a* de premier ordre.

tirade [tai'reid] *n* tirade *f*, diatribe *f*.

tire ['taiə] *vt* fatiguer; *vi* se fatiguer, se lasser; *vt* pneu *m*.

tired ['taiəd] *a* fatigué, las, dégoûté, contrarié.

tireless ['taiəlis] *a* infatigable.

tiresome ['taiəsəm] *a* fatigant, ennuyeux.

tissue ['tisju:] *n* tissu *m*, étoffe *f*.

tissue-paper ['tisju:'peipə] *n* papier de soie *m*.

tit [tit] *n* mésange *f*.

titbit ['titbit] *n* morceau de choix *m*, friandise *f*.

tithe [taið] *n* dîme *f*.

titillate ['titileit] *vt* chatouiller, émoustiller, titiller.

titillation [ˌtiti'leiʃən] *n* titillation *f*, chatouillement *m*, émoustillement *m*.

title ['taitl] *n* titre *m*, droit *m*.

titled ['taitld] *a* titré.

titter ['titə] *n* rire étouffé *m*; *vi* rire sous cape.

tittle ['titl] *n* fétu *m*.

tittle-tattle ['titl,tætl] *n* cancans *m pl*, potins *m pl*; *vi* cancaner.

titular ['titjulə] *a* titulaire.

to [tu:] *prep* à, de, pour, jusqu'à, (en)vers, contre, à côté de, à l'égard de.

toad [toud] *n* crapaud *m*.

toady ['toudi] *n* parasite *m*, flagorneur *m*; **to —** to faire du plat à, flagorner.

toast [toust] *n* rôtie *f*, pain grillé *m*, toast *m*, canapé *m*; *vti* griller, rôtir; *vt* boire à la santé de, porter un toast à.

tobacco [tə'bækou] *n* tabac *m*; **— pouch** blague à tabac *f*.

tobacconist [tə'bækənist] *n* marchand de tabac *m*.

tobacconist's [tə'bækənists] *n* bureau (débit *m*) de tabac *m*.

today [tə'dei] *n* ad aujourd'hui *m*; **— week** d'aujourd'hui en huit.

toddle ['tɔdl] *vt* trottiner, flâner.

to-do [tə'du:] *n* grabuge *m*, scène *f*.

toe [tou] *n* doigt de pied *m*, orteil *m*.

toffee ['tɔfi] *n* caramel *m*.

tog [tɔg] to **— oneself up** se faire beau.

together [tə'geðə] *ad* ensemble, à la fois.

toil [tɔil] *n* peine *f*, tâche *f*; *vi* peiner.

toilet ['tɔilit] *n* toilette *f*.

toilsome ['tɔilsəm] *a* pénible, fatigant.

token ['toukən] *n* signe *m*, gage *m*, jeton *m*, bon *m*.

told [tould] *pt pp of* **tell**.

tolerable ['tɔlərəbl] *a* tolérable, passable.

tolerance ['tɔlərəns] *n* tolérance *f*.

tolerant ['tɔlərənt] *a* tolérant.

tolerate ['tɔləreit] *vt* tolérer.

toll [toul] *n* droit *m*, péage *m*, octroi *m*; *vi* tinter, sonner le glas.

tolling ['toulin] *n* tintement *m*, glas *m*.

tomato [tə'mɑːtou] *n* tomate *f*.

tomb [tu:m] *n* tombe *f*, tombeau *m*, fosse *f*.

tombstone ['tu:mstoun] *n* pierre tombale *f*.

tomboy ['tɔmbɔi] *n* garçon manqué *m*, luronne *f*.

tomcat ['tɔm'kæt] *n* matou *m*.

tome [toum] *n* tome *m*.

tomfool ['tɔm'fu:l] *n* nigaud *m*.

tomfoolery ['tɔm'fu:ləri] *n* pasquinade *f*, niaiseries *f pl*.

tomtit ['tɔm'tit] *n* mésange *f*.

tomorrow [tə'mɔrou] *n* demain *m* **— week** demain en huit.

ton [tʌn] *n* tonne *f*, (ship) tonneau *m*.

tone [toun] *n* son *m*, bruit *m*, ton *m*, accent *m*; *vt* aviver, accorder; **to — down** dégrader, adoucir; **to — up** tonifier, ravigoter, remonter.

tongs [tɔŋz] *n* pincettes *f pl*, tenailles *f pl*.

tongue [tʌŋ] *n* langue *f*, languette *f*

tonic ['tɔnik] *an* tonique m; n fortifiant m.

tonight [tə'nait] *ad* ce soir m, cette nuit f.

tonnage ['tʌnidʒ] n tonnage m.

tonsil ['tɔnsl] n amygdale f.

tonsilitis [.tɔnsi'laitis] n amygdalite f, angine f.

tonsure ['tɔnʃə] n tonsure f; vt tonsurer.

too [tu:] *ad* trop (de), aussi, et de plus.

took [tuk] *pt of* **take.**

tool [tu:l] n outil m, instrument m.

tooth [tu:θ] n dent f; **milk —** dent de lait; **molar —** molaire f; **wisdom —** dent de sagesse; **false —** fausse dent; **—ache** mal de dents m; **—brush** brosse à dents f; **—paste** pâte dentifrice f; **—pick** cure-dents m.

toothless ['tu:θlis] *a* édenté, sans dents.

toothsome ['tu:θsəm] *a* succulent, friand.

top [tɔp] n haut m, sommet m, premier m, tête f, toupie f, impériale f, dessus m, haut bout m, prise directe f, hune f; *a* supérieur, plus haut, dernier, du (de) dessus, du haut, premier; *vt* couvrir, étêter, atteindre, dominer, couronner, dé(sur)passer, surmonter, être à la tête de.

top coat ['tɔp'kout] n pardessus m.

top hat ['tɔp'hæt] n chapeau haut de forme m.

top-heavy ['tɔp'hevi] *a* trop lourd par le haut.

topaz ['toupæz] n topaze f.

toper ['toupə] n ivrogne m.

topic ['tɔpik] n sujet m, thème m, question f.

topical ['tɔpikəl] *a* d'actualité, local, topique.

topmost ['tɔpmoust] *a* le plus haut.

topple ['tɔpl] *vi* culbuter, s'écrouler, trébucher; to — over *vt* faire tomber, *vi* tomber.

topsy-turvy ['tɔpsi'tə:vi] *a* sens dessus dessous, en désordre.

torch [tɔ:tʃ] n torche f, flambeau m, lampe électrique f.

tore [tɔ:] *pt of* **tear.**

torment ['tɔ:mənt] n souffrance atroce f, supplice m, tourment m.

torment [tɔ:'ment] *vt* tourmenter, torturer.

torn [tɔ:n] *pp of* **tear.**

tornado [tɔ:'neidou] n tornade f, ouragan m.

torpedo [tɔ:'pi:dou] n torpille f; **—boat** torpilleur m; **—tube** lance-torpilles m.

torpid ['tɔ:pid] *a* engourdi, paresseux, inerte.

torrent ['tɔrənt] n torrent m.

torrential [tə'renʃəl] *a* torrentiel.

torrid ['tɔrid] *a* torride.

torridity [tə'riditi] n chaleur torride f.

tortoise ['tɔ:təs] n tortue f; **—shell** écaille f.

tortuous ['tɔ:tjuəs] *a* tortueux, sinueux, enchevêtré.

torture ['tɔ:tʃə] n torture f, supplice m; *vt* torturer, mettre au supplice.

toss [tɔs] *vt* lancer (en l'air), jeter, ballotter, secouer; *vi* s'agiter, être ballotté, se tourner et se retourner, jouer à pile ou face.

tossing ['tɔsiŋ] n ballottement m.

total ['toutl] *an* total m; n montant m; *vt* totaliser, additionner; *vi* se monter à.

totalizator ['toutəlai.zeitə] n totalisateur m, pari-mutuel m.

totter ['tɔtə] *vi* chanceler, tituber.

touch [tʌtʃ] n toucher m, touche f, attouchement m, brin m, soupçon m, contact m, communication f, courant m; *vt* toucher, effleurer, égaler; *vi* se toucher.

touchiness ['tʌtʃinis] n susceptibilité f, irascibilité f.

touchstone ['tʌtʃstoun] n pierre de touche f.

touchy ['tʌtʃi] *a* chatouilleux, susceptible.

tough [tʌf] *a* dur, coriace, tenace, ardu, solide; n apache m; **— guy** dur à cuire m.

toughness ['tʌfnis] n dureté f, ténacité f, coriacité f.

tour [tuə] n tour m, tournée f, voyage m, excursion f; *vt* faire le tour de, parcourir; *vi* être en voyage, être en tournée.

touring ['tuəriŋ] n tourisme f.

tourist ['tuərist] n touriste mf.

tournament ['tuənəmənt] n tournoi m, concours m.

tousle ['tauzl] *vt* tirer, emmêler, ébouriffer.

tout [taut] n démarcheur m, racoleur m, pisteur m, espion m; to — for relancer (-ère) municipal(e) m; *vt* relancer (les clients), pister, solliciter.

tow [tou] n filasse f, étoupe f, remorque f; *vt* haler, remorquer, prendre à la remorque; **—path** chemin m de halage.

toward(s) [tə'wɔ:d(z)] *prep* vers, envers, en vue de, pour, à l'égard de.

towel ['tauəl] n essuie-mains m, serviette (de toilette) f; *vt* essuyer avec une serviette; **—rail** porte-serviettes m inv.

tower ['tauə] n tour f; *vi* planer, dominer; **church —** clocher m; **water —** château m d'eau.

towing ['touiŋ] n halage m, remorquage m, remorque f.

town [taun] n ville f.

town council ['taun'kaunsl] n conseil municipal m.

town councillor ['taun'kaunsilə] n conseiller (-ère) municipal(e) m.

town hall ['taun'hɔ:l] n hôtel de ville m, mairie f.

town-planning ['taun'plæniŋ] n urbanisme m.

townsman ['taunzmən] n citadin m, concitoyen m.

toy [tɔi] n jouet m, joujou m, jeu m; vi jouer, s'amuser.

trace [treis] n trace f, vestige m, trait m; vt tracer, calquer, suivre, trouver trace de, suivre la piste de; to — back to faire remonter à.

tracer ['treisə] n obus traceur m, balle traceuse f.

track [træk] n trace f; piste f, sillage m, sens m, sentier m, (rails) voie f, chenille f; vt suivre à la piste, traquer.

trackage ['trækidʒ] n (rails) réseau m.

tracing paper ['treisiŋ peipə] n papier-calque m.

tract [trækt] n étendue f, tract m.

tractable ['træktəbl] a traitable, maniable, arrangeant.

traction ['trækʃən] n traction f; a moteur.

tractor ['træktə] n tracteur m.

trade [treid] n commerce m, métier m, échange m, affaires f pl; vi être dans le commerce, faire le commerce (de in); to — on abuser de, exploiter.

trader ['treidə] n négociant(e) mf, commerçant(e) mf, navire marchand m.

trade-mark ['treidmɑ:k] n marque de fabrique f.

tradesman ['treidzmən] n commerçant m.

trade-union [,treid'ju:njən] n syndicat m (ouvrier).

trade-unionism [,treid'ju:njənizəm] n syndicalisme m.

trade-unionist [,treid'ju:njənist] n syndicaliste mf.

trade wind ['treidwind] n (vent) alizé m.

trading ['treidiŋ] n commerce m; — in reprise f (en compte); — station n factorerie f.

tradition [trə'diʃən] n tradition f.

traditional [trə'diʃənl] a traditionnel.

traditionalist [trə'diʃnəlist] n traditionaliste mf.

traduce [trə'dju:s] vt calomnier, diffamer.

traducer [trə'dju:sə] n calomniateur, -trice.

traffic ['træfik] n trafic m, circulation f, traite f.

traffic indicator ['træfik'indikeitə] n indicateur m (de direction), flèche f.

traffic jam ['træfikdʒæm] n embouteillage m.

trafficker ['træfikə] n trafiquant m, trafiqueur m.

traffic-light ['træfiklait] n feu m, signal m.

tragedian [trə'dʒi:djən] n poète mf, (acteur, -trice) tragique.

tragedy ['trædʒidi] n tragédie f, drame m.

tragic ['trædʒik] a tragique.

trail [treil] n trainée f, trace f, piste f, sillon m; vti trainer; vt remorquer, traquer, filer; to — off s'éteindre, se perdre.

trailer ['treilə] n baladeuse f, remorque f.

train [trein] n traine f, suite f, file f, série f, convoi m, train m; express — rapide m; slow — omnibus m; through — train direct m; corridor — train à couloirs m; vt former, dresser, entrainer, élever, exercer, préparer, braquer; vi s'entrainer.

trainer ['treinə] n entraineur m, dresseur m.

training ['treiniŋ] n éducation f, instruction f, formation f, entrainement m; — college école normale f; — ship vaisseau école m.

traitor ['treitə] n traitre m.

trajectory ['trædʒiktəri] n trajectoire f.

tramcar ['træmkɑ:] n tramway m, tram m.

trammel ['træməl] n entrave f, crémaillère f.

tramp [træmp] n bruit de pas m, marche f, chemineau m; vi marcher (lourdement), trimarder; vt parcourir à pied, faire à pied.

trample ['træmpl] vt fouler aux pieds, piétiner.

trampoline ['træmpouli:n] n matelas m élastique.

trance [trɑ:ns] n transe f, hypnose f, catalepsie f, extase f.

tranquil ['træŋkwil] a tranquille.

tranquilizer ['træŋkwilaizə] n tranquillisant, calmant.

tranquillity [træŋ'kwiliti] n tranquillité f, calme m.

transact [træn'zækt] vt passer, traiter.

transaction [træn'zækʃən] n conduite f; pl transactions f pl, rapports m pl.

transcend [træn'send] vt dépasser, exceller, surpasser.

transcribe [træns'kraib] vt transcrire.

transcription [træns'kripʃən] n transcription f.

transept ['trænsept] n transept m.

transfer [træns'fə:] vt transférer, déplacer, calquer.

transfer ['trænsfə] n transfert m, déplacement m, transport m.

transfigure [træns'figə] vt transfigurer.

transfix [træns'fiks] vt transpercer, (fig) pétrifier.

transform [træns'fɔ:m] vt transformer, convertir.

transformer [træns'fɔ:mə] n transformateur m.

transfuse [træns'fju:z] vt transfuser.

transfusion [træns'fju:ʒən] n transfusion f.

transgress [træns'gres] vt transgresser, violer.

transgressor [træns'gresə] n transgresseur m, pécheur m.

tranship [træn'ʃip] vt transborder; vi changer de vaisseau.

transient ['trænziənt] a passager, éphémère.

transistor [træn'sistə] n transistor m.

transit ['trænsit] n traversée f, passage m, transit m.

transition [træn'siʒən] n transition f, passage m.

transitory ['trænsitəri] a transitoire, fugitif.

translatable [træns'leitəbl] a traduisible.

translate [træns'leit] vt traduire, interpréter, transférer.

translation [træns'leiʃən] n traduction f.

translator [træns'leitə] n traducteur m.

transmission [trænz'miʃən] n transmission f.

transmit [træns'mit] vt transmettre; —ter n émmetteur m, transmetteur.

transmute [trænz'mjuːt] vt transmuer.

transparency [træns'peərənsi] n transparence f.

transparent [træns'peərənt] a transparent.

transpire [træns'paiə] vi transpirer.

transplant [træns'plɑːnt] vt transplanter, repiquer, greffer.

transport ['trænspɔːt] n transport m.

transport [træns'pɔːt] vt transporter.

transposable [træns'pouzəbl] a transposable.

transpose [træns'pouz] vt transposer.

trap [træp] n trappe f, piège m, traquenard m, cabriolet m; vt attraper, tendre un piège à, prendre; vi trapper.

trapdoor ['træp‚dɔː] n trappe f.

trapper ['træpə] n trappeur m.

trappings ['træpiŋz] n harnachement m, falbalas m, atours m pl, apparat m.

trash [træʃ] n camelote f, fatras m, niaiserie f, racaille f.

trashy ['træʃi] a de camelote, sans valeur.

trauma ['trɔːmə] n traumatisme m.

travel ['trævl] n voyage(s) m pl; vi voyager, être en voyage, marcher, aller; vt parcourir.

travel agency ('trævl'eidʒinsi] n agence f de voyages.

traveler ['trævlə] n voyageur, -euse; commercial — commis voyageur m.

traveling ['trævliŋ] a de voyage, ambulant; n voyages m pl.

traverse ['trævəs] n traverse f, bordée f, plaque tournante f; vt traverser.

travesty ['trævisti] n travestissement m; vt travestir, parodier.

trawl [trɔːl] n chalut m; vi pêcher au chalut.

trawler ['trɔːlə] n chalutier m.

tray ['trei] n plateau m, (trunk) compartiment m, éventaire m.

treacherous ['tretʃərəs] a traître, infidèle.

treachery ['tretʃəri] n traîtrise f, perfidie f.

treacle ['triːkl] n mélasse f.

tread [tred] n pas m, allure f, (of tire) chape f; vi marcher; vt fouler, écraser.

treadle ['tredl] n pédale f.

treason ['triːzn] n trahison f; high — lèse-majesté f.

treasure ['treʒə] n trésor m; vt garder précieusement, priser.

treasurer ['treʒərə] n trésorier, -ière, économe mf.

treasury ['treʒəri] n trésor m, trésorerie f.

treat [triːt] n plaisir m, fête f, régal m; vti traiter; vt régaler, payer.

treatise ['triːtiz] n traité m.

treatment ['triːtmənt] n traitement m, cure f.

treaty ['triːti] n traité m, accord m.

treble ['trebl] n triple m, soprano m; a triple, trois fois.

tree [triː] n arbre m.

trefoil ['trefɔil] n trèfle m.

trellis ['trelis] n treillis m, treillage m.

tremble ['trembl] n tremblement m; vi trembler.

tremendous [tri'mendəs] a énorme, formidable.

tremor ['tremə] n tremblement m, frisson m, secousse f.

tremulous ['tremjuləs] a tremblant, craintif, tremblotant.

trench [trentʃ] n tranchée f, fossé m; vt creuser.

trencher ['trentʃə] n trenchoir m.

trend [trend] n direction f, tendance f; vi se diriger, tendre.

trepan [tri'pæn] n trépan m; vt trépaner.

trepanning [tri'pæniŋ] n trépanation f.

trepidation [‚trepi'deiʃən] n tremblement m, trépidation f.

trespass ['trespəs] n délit m, péché m, intrusion f, offense f; vi entrer sans permission; to — upon empiéter sur, abuser de, offenser.

trespasser ['trespəsə] n délinquant m, intrus m, transgresseur m.

tress [tres] n tresse f, natte f; vt natter, tresser.

trestle ['tresl] n tréteau m, chevalet m.

trial ['traiəl] n épreuve f, essai m, procès m, jugement m, ennui m.

triangle ['traiæŋgl] n triangle m.

triangular [trai'æŋgjulə] a triangulaire.

tribal ['traibəl] a de la tribu, tribal.

tribe [traib] n tribu f.

tribulation [‚tribju'leiʃən] n tribulation f, affliction f.

tribunal [trai'bjuːnl] n tribunal m, cour f.

tribune ['tribju:n] n tribun m, tribune f.

tributary ['tribjutəri] an tributaire m; n affluent m.

tribute ['tribju:t] n tribut m, hommage m.

trick [trik] n tour m, farce f, ruse f, truc m, levée f; vt tromper, (dé)jouer.

trickery ['trikəri] n tromperie f, fourberie f.

trickle ['trikl] vi couler goutte à goutte, dégouliner; n filet m.

trickster ['trikstə] n escroc m, fourbe m.

tricky ['triki] a rusé, épineux.

tricycle ['traisikl] n tricycle m.

trifle ['traifl] n bagatelle f, (cook) diplomate m; vi badiner, jouer.

trifling ['traifliŋ] a insignifiant, futile, minime.

trigger ['trigə] n détente f, gâchette f, manette f.

trill [tril] n trille m, chant perlé m; vi vibrer, trembler; vt rouler, triller.

trim [trim] n ordre m, état m; a net, soigné, propret, en ordre; vt arranger, tailler, rafraîchir, soigner, orner, arrimer.

trimming ['trimiŋ] n mise en état f, arrangement m, taille f; pl fournitures f pl, garniture f, passementerie f, rognures f pl.

trinity ['triniti] n trinité f.

trinket ['triŋkit] n babiole f, bibelot m.

trip [trip] n excursion f, faux-pas m, croc-en-jambe m; vi marcher légèrement, trébucher, déraper, se tromper; vt pincer, faire trébucher, faucher les jambes à.

tripe [traip] n tripes f pl, bêtises f pl.

triple ['tripl] a triple; vti tripler.

triplet ['triplit] n trio m, tercet m, l'un de trois jumeaux.

triplicate ['triplikit] a triple, triplé; in — en trois exemplaires; vt tripler.

tripod ['traipəd] n trépied m.

trite [trait] a banal, usé, rebattu.

triteness ['traitnis] n banalité f.

triumph ['traiəmf] n triomphe m, miracle m; vi triompher, exulter.

triumphal [trai'ʌmfəl] a triomphal, de triomphe.

triumphant [trai'ʌmfənt] a triomphant, de triomphe.

trivial ['triviəl] a trivial, banal, futile.

triviality [.trivi'æliti] n trivialité f, futilité f, insignifiance f.

trod, trodden [trɔd, 'trɔdn] pp of tread.

trolley ['trɔli] n tramway m, chariot m, diable m, serveuse f, trolley m.

trombone [trɔm'boun] n trombone m.

troop [tru:p] n troupe(s) f (pl), bande f; vi s'attrouper, marcher en troupe.

trooper ['tru:pə] n cavalier m.

troop-ship ['tru:pʃip] n transport m.

trophy ['troufi] n trophée m.

tropic ['trɔpik] an tropique m; a tropical.

tropical ['trɔpikəl] a tropical.

trot [trɔt] n trot m; vi trotter; vt faire trotter.

trotter ['trɔtə] n (bon) trotteur m.

trouble ['trʌbl] n difficulté f, trouble m, ennui m, peine f, affection f, panne f, conflits m pl, discorde f; vt inquiéter, affliger, soucier, déranger, embarrasser, troubler, prier; vi s'inquiéter, se déranger, se donner la peine (de to).

troublemaker ['trʌbl,meikə] n trublion m.

troublesome ['trʌblsəm] a ennuyeux, gênant, fatigant, énervant.

trough [trɔf] n auge f, cuve f, pétrin m, creux m.

trounce [trauns] vt rouer de coups, rosser, battre à plates coutures, écraser.

trousers ['trauzəz] n pantalon m.

trout [traut] n truite f.

trowel ['trauəl] n truelle f, déplantoir m.

truant ['truənt] a fainéant m, vagabond(e) mf; to play — faire l'école buissonnière.

truce [tru:s] n trève f.

truck [trʌk] n camion m, chariot m, troc m, camelote f.

trudge [trʌdʒ] vi traîner la jambe, clopiner.

true [tru:] a vrai, loyal, sincère.

truffle ['trʌfl] n truffe f.

truly ['tru:li] ad à vrai dire, sincèrement.

trump [trʌmp] n atout m, trompette f; vt couper; to — up inventer.

trumpet ['trʌmpit] n trompette f, cornet acoustique m; vi trompeter, barir; vt proclamer.

trumpeter ['trʌmpitə] n trompette m, trompettiste m.

truncate ['trʌŋkeit] vt tronquer.

truncheon ['trʌntʃən] n matraque f, bâton m.

trundle ['trʌndl] n roulette f; vti rouler; vt pousser, trimbaler.

trunk [trʌŋk] n tronc m, malle f, trompe f; — call appel interurbain m; — line grande ligne f; — road grand-route f, artère f.

truss [trʌs] n trousse f, botte f, cintre m, bandage m; vt botteler, renforcer, soutenir, trousser, ligoter.

trust [trʌst] n confiance f, espoir m, parole f, dépôt m, charge f, trust m; vt confier, en croire, se fier à, faire crédit à; vi espérer, mettre son espoir (en in).

trustee [trʌs'ti:] n administrateur m, curateur, -trice.

trusteeship [trʌs'ti:ʃip] n administration f, curatelle f.

trustful ['trʌstful] a confiant.

trustworthiness ['trʌst,wə:ðinis] n loyauté f, exactitude f.

trustworthy ['trʌst,wəːðl] *a* sûr, fidèle, digne de foi.

trusty ['trʌstl] *a* sûr, loyal.

truth [truːθ] *n* vérité *f*; the — is, to tell the — à vrai dire.

truthful ['truːθful] *a* véridique, fidèle.

truthfulness ['truːθfulnis] *n* véracité *f*, fidélité *f*.

try [traɪ] *vt* essayer, mettre à l'épreuve, juger; *n* tentative *f*, essai *m*, coup *m*.

trying ['traɪiŋ] *a* fatigant, pénible.

try-on ['traɪɔn] *n* bluff *m*.

tsetse fly ['tsetsiflaɪ] *n* tsé-tsé *f*.

tub [tʌb] *n* cuve *f*, baquet *m*, caisse *f*, tub *m*, bain *m*.

tube [tjuːb] *n* tube *m*, tuyau *m*, métro *m*, chambre à air *f*.

tubercle ['tjuːbəːkl] *n* tubercule *m*.

tuberculosis [tjuː,bəːkjuːˈlousis] *n* tuberculose *f*.

tuck [tʌk] *n* pli *m*, rempli *m*, pâtisserie *f*; *vt* (re)plier, remplier, plisser, border; to — in *vi* bouffer; *vt* border, retrousser.

Tuesday ['tjuːzdɪ] *n* mardi *m*.

tuft [tʌft] *n* touffe *f*, houpe *f*, huppe *f*, flocon *m*, mèche *f*.

tug [tʌg] *n* effort *m*, secousse *f*, remorqueur *m*; *vti* tirer fort; *vt* remorquer, tirer; to — at tirer sur.

tuition [tjuːˈiʃən] *n* leçons *f pl*, instruction *f*.

tulip ['tjuːlip] *n* tulipe *f*.

tumble ['tʌmbl] *n* chute *f*, culbute *f*, désordre *m*; *vi* dégringoler, tomber, faire des culbutes; *vt* déranger, bouleverser, ébouriffer.

tumbledown ['tʌmbldaun] *a* délabré, croulant.

tumbler ['tʌmblə] *n* acrobate *mf*, gobelet *m*.

tumbrel ['tʌmbrəl] *n* caisson *m*, tombereau *m*.

tumor ['tjuːmə] *n* tumeur *f*.

tumult [tjuːmʌlt] *n* tumulte *m*, agitation *f*, émoi *m*.

tun [tʌn] *n* tonneau *m*.

tune [tjuːn] *n* air *m*, ton *m*, note *f*, accord *m*; *vt* accorder, adapter; to — in régler.

tuneful ['tjuːnful] *a* harmonieux.

tuneless ['tjuːnlis] *a* discordant.

tuner ['tjuːnə] *n* accordeur *m*.

tuning-fork ['tjuːniŋfɔːk] *n* diapason *m*.

tunic ['tjuːnik] *n* tunique *f*.

tunnel ['tʌnl] *n* tunnel *m*.

tunny ['tʌnɪ] *n* thon *m*.

turbid ['təːbid] *a* trouble.

turbine ['təːbin] *n* turbine *f*.

turbot ['təːbət] *n* turbot *m*.

turbulent ['təːbjulənt] *a* turbulent.

tureen [təˈriːn] *n* soupière *f*.

turf [təːf] *n* gazon *m*, motte *f*, turf *m*.

turgid ['təːdʒid] *a* boursouflé, enflé, ampoulé.

Turk [təːk] *n* Turc, Turque.

Turkey ['təːkɪ] *n* Turquie *f*.

turkey ['təːkɪ] *n* dinde *f*; —cock dindon *m*.

Turkish ['təːkiʃ] *an* turc *m*.

turmoil ['təːmɔil] *n* effervescence *f*, remous *m*.

turn [təːn] *n* tour *m*, tournant *m*, virage *m*, tournure *f*, numéro *m*, crise *f*, service *m*; in — à tour de rôle; to a — à point; *vti* tourner; *vt* retourner, changer, faire tourner, diriger; *vi* prendre, se tourner, se transformer, recourir (à to); to — down baisser, refuser, rabattre; to — off fermer, couper, renvoyer; to — on *vt* ouvrir, donner; *vi* dépendre de; to — out *vt* mettre dehors, à la porte, faire sortir, éteindre, retourner, produire; *vi* tourner, arriver, s'arranger; to — up *vt* relever, retrousser, déterrer, retourner, remonter; *vi* se présenter, se retrousser.

turncoat ['təːnkout] *n* renégat *m*, girouette *f*.

turner ['təːnə] *n* tourneur *m*.

turning ['təːniŋ] *n* tournant *m*.

turning-lathe ['təːniŋleið] *n* tour *m*.

turning point ['təːniŋpɔint] *n* tournant *m*.

turnip ['təːnip] *n* navet *m*.

turn-out ['təːn,aut] *n* assistance *f*, grève *f*, équipage *m*, tenue *f*, production *f*.

turnover ['təːn,ouvə] *n* chiffre d'affaires *m*, (cook) chausson *m*.

turnpike ['təːnpaik] *n* barrière *f*.

turnspit ['təːnspit] *n* tournebroche *m*.

turnstile ['təːnstail] *n* tourniquet *m*.

turntable ['təːn,teibl] *n* plaque tournante *f*.

turpentine ['təːpəntain] *n* térébenthine *f*.

turret ['tʌrit] *n* tourelle *f*.

turtle ['təːtl] *n* tortue *f*.

turtle-dove ['təːtldʌv] *n* tourterelle *f*.

tusk [tʌsk] *n* défense *f*.

tussle ['tʌsl] *n* lutte *f*; *vi* se battre, s'escrimer.

tutelage ['tjuːtilidʒ] *n* tutelle *f*.

tutor ['tjuːtə] *n* précepteur *m*, directeur d'études *m*, méthode *f*.

twaddle ['twɔdl] *n* verbiage *m*, balivernes *f pl*; *vi* bavasser, radoter.

twain [twein] *an* (old) deux.

twang [twæŋ] *n* grincement *m*, nasillement *m*; *vi* grincer, nasiller, vibrer; *vt* pincer.

tweed [twiːd] *n* tweed *m*.

tweezers ['twiːzəz] *n* pince *f*.

twelfth [twelfθ] *an* douzième *mf*; *a* douze.

twelve [twelv] *an* douze *m*.

twentieth ['twentiiθ] *an* vingtième *mf*; *a* vingt.

twenty ['twentɪ] *an* vingt *m*.

twice [twais] *ad* deux fois.

twig [twig] *n* branchette *f*, brindille *f*.

twilight ['twailait] *n* crépuscule *m*, petit jour *m*.

twin [twin] *n* jumeau *m*, jumelle *f*; *a* accouplé, jumeau, jumelé.

twine [twain] *n* ficelle *f*; *vt* tordre, entrelacer, enrouler.

twinge [twind3] *n* élancement *m*, lancinement *m*.

twinkle ['twiŋkl] *n* clignement *m*, scintillement *m*, lueur *f*; *vi* cligner, scintiller.

twinkling ['twiŋkliŋ] *n* clin d'œil *m*, scintillement *m*.

twirl [twə:l] *n* tournoiement *m*, fioriture *f*, pirouette *f*; *vi* tournoyer, tourbillonner, pirouetter; *vt* (*moustache*) tortiller.

twist [twist] *n* cordonnet *m*, torsion *f*, papillote *f*, rouleau *m*, torsade *f*, tour *m*; *vt* tortiller, tordre, entrelacer, se fouler, fausser; *vi* se tordre, tourner, vriller.

twit [twit] *vt* reprocher, railler.

twitch [twitʃ] *n* secousse *f*, tic *m*, contraction *f*, crispation *f*; *vt* crisper, tirer, contracter; *vi* se crisper, se contracter.

twitter ['twitə] *n* gazouillement *m*; *vi* gazouiller.

two [tu:] *an* deux.

two-edged ['tu:'ed3d] *a* à double tranchant.

twofold ['tu:fould] *a* double; *ad* deux fois.

tympan ['timpæn] *n* tympan *m*.

type [taip] *n* type *m*, modèle *m*, caractère d'imprimerie *m*; *vt* taper à la machine, dactylographier.

typescript ['taipskript] *n* texte *m* dactylographié.

typewriter ['taip,raitə] *n* machine à écrire *f*.

typhoid ['taifoid] *n* typhoïde *f*.

typhus ['taifəs] *n* typhus *m*.

typhoon [tai'fu:n] *n* typhon *m*.

typical ['tipikəl] *a* caractéristique, typique.

typify ['tipifai] *vt* incarner, représenter, être caractérisque de.

typist ['taipist] *n* dactylo(graphe) *mf*.

typographer [tai'pɔgrəfə] *n* typographe *m*.

typography [tai'pɔgrəfi] *n* typographie *f*.

tyrannical [ti'rænikəl] *a* tyrannique.

tyrannize ['tirənaiz] *vt* tyranniser.

tyranny ['tirəni] *n* tyrannie *f*.

tyrant ['taiərənt] *n* tyran *m*.

U

U-boat ['ju:bout] *n* sous-marin *m* allemand.

udder ['ʌdə] *n* pis *m*, mamelle *f*, tétine *f*.

ugliness ['ʌglinis] *n* laideur *f*.

ugly ['ʌgli] *a* laid.

ulcer ['ʌlsə] *n* ulcère *m*.

ulcerate ['ʌlsəreit] *vt* ulcérer; *vi* s'ulcérer.

ulterior [ʌl'tiəriə] *a* ultérieur, caché.

ultimate ['ʌltimit] *a* dernier, définitif, fondamental.

ultimately ['ʌltimitli] *ad* en fin de compte.

ultimatum [,ʌlti'meitəm] *n* ultimatum *m*.

ultimo ['ʌltimou] *a* du mois dernier.

umbrage ['ʌmbrid3] *n* ombrage *m*.

umbrella [ʌm'brelə] *n* parapluie *m*.

umbrella-stand [ʌm'breləstænd] *n* porte-parapluies *m inv*.

umpire ['ʌmpaiə] *n* arbitre *m*; *vt* arbitrer.

umpiring ['ʌmpaiəriŋ] *n* arbitrage *m*.

unabated ['ʌnə'beitid] *a* dans toute sa force, non diminué.

unable ['ʌn'eibl] *a* incapable, hors d'état (de to).

unabridged ['ʌnə'brid3d] *a* intégral, non abrégé.

unaccomplished ['ʌnə'kʌmpliʃd] *a* inachevé, inaccompli.

unaccountable ['ʌnə'kauntəbl] *a* inexplicable.

unaccustomed ['ʌnə'kʌstəmd] *a* inaccoutumé.

unacknowledged ['ʌnək'nɔlid3d] *a* sans réponse, non reconnu.

unacquainted ['ʌnə'kweintid] *a* to be — with ne pas connaître.

unadorned ['ʌnə'dɔ:nd] *a* simple, nu, pur.

unadulterated [,ʌnə'dʌltəreitid] *a* non frelaté, pur.

unadvisable ['ʌnəd'vaizəbl] *a* malavisé, imprudent.

unaffected ['ʌnə'fektid] *a* naturel, sincère, insensible.

unaffectedly [,ʌnə'fektidli] *ad* sans affectation.

unalleviated [,ʌnə'li:vieitid] *a* sans soulagement.

unalloyed ['ʌnə'lɔid] *a* pur, sans alliage (mélange).

unambiguous ['ʌnæm'bigjuəs] *a* catégorique, clair.

unambitious [,ʌnæm'biʃəs] *a* sans ambition.

unanimous [ju'næniməs] *n* unanime.

unanimity [,ju:nə'nimiti] *n* unanimité *f*.

unanswerable [ʌn'ɑ:nsərəbl] *a* sans réplique.

unanswered ['ʌn'ɑ:nsəd] *a* sans réponse, irréfuté.

unarmed ['ʌn'ɑ:md] *a* sans arme.

unassailable [,ʌnə'seiləbl] *a* inattaquable, indiscutable.

unassisted ['ʌnə'sistid] *a* sans aide, tout seul.

unassuming ['ʌnə'sju:miŋ] *a* sans prétention(s), modeste.

unattainable ['ʌnə'teinəbl] *a* hors d'atteinte, inaccessible.

unattractive [,ʌnə'træktiv] *a* peu attrayant.

unavailable [,ʌnə'veiləbl] *a* inaccessible, impossible à obtenir, indisponible.

unavailing ['ʌnə'veiliŋ] *a* inutile, vain.

unavoidable [ˌʌnə'vɔidəbl] *a* inévitable.

unaware ['ʌnə'wɛə] *a* to be — of ignorer, ne pas avoir conscience de.

unawares ['ʌnə'wɛəz] *ad* à l'improviste, au dépourvu.

unbalanced ['ʌn'bælənst] *a* déséquilibré, instable.

unbearable [ʌn'bɛərəbl] *a* intolérable.

unbecoming [ˌʌnbi'kʌmiŋ] *a* malséant.

unbeknown ['ʌnbi'noun] *ad* — to à l'insu de.

unbelief ['ʌnbi'liːf] *n* incrédulité *f*.

unbelievable [ˌʌnbi'liːvəbl] *a* incroyable.

unbeliever ['ʌnbi'liːvə] *n* incrédule *mf*, incroyant(e) *mf*.

unbend ['ʌn'bend] *vt* détendre; *vi* se dérider, se détendre.

unbending ['ʌn'bendiŋ] *a* raide, inflexible.

unbiased ['ʌn'baiəst] *a* impartial, objectif, sans parti pris.

unbind ['ʌn'baind] *vt* délier, dénouer.

unbleached ['ʌn'bliːtʃt] *a* non blanchi, écru.

unblemished [ʌn'blemiʃt] *a* sans tache, immaculé.

unblended [ʌn'blendid] *a* pur.

unblushing [ʌn'blʌʃiŋ] *a* effronté, éhonté.

unbolt ['ʌn'boult] *vt* déverrouiller.

unborn ['ʌn'bɔːn] *a* encore à naître, futur.

unbosom [ʌn'buzəm] *vt* révéler; to — oneself ouvrir son cœur.

unbound ['ʌn'baund] *a* délié, broché.

unbounded [ʌn'baundid] *a* illimité, sans bornes.

unbreakable [ʌn'breikəbl] *n* incassable.

unbreathable ['ʌn'briːðəbl] *a* irrespirable.

unbroken ['ʌn'broukən] *a* intact, ininterrompu, continu.

unburden [ʌn'bɔːdn] *vt* décharger, alléger, épancher.

unburied ['ʌn'berid] *a* sans sépulture.

unbusinesslike [ʌn'biznislaik] *a* peu pratique, sans méthode.

unbutton ['ʌn'bʌtn] *vt* déboutonner.

uncalled-for [ʌn'kɔːldfɔː] *a* non désiré, indiscret, déplacé, immérité.

uncanny [ʌn'kæni] *a* fantastique, inquiétant, mystérieux.

uncared-for ['ʌn'kɛədfɔː] *a* négligé.

uncaring [ʌn'kɛəriŋ] *a* insouciant.

unceasing [ʌn'siːsiŋ] *a* incessant, soutenu.

unceasingly [ʌn'siːsiŋli] *ad* sans cesse.

unceremoniously ['ʌn,seri'mouni-

liʃ] *ad* sans cérémonie, sans gêne, sans façons.

uncertain [ʌn'sɔːtn] *a* incertain, inégal, douteux.

unchallenged ['ʌn'tʃælindʒd] *a* sans provocation, indisputé.

unchangeable [ʌn'tʃeindʒəbl] *a* immuable.

uncharitable [ʌn'tʃæritəbl] *a* peu charitable.

unchaste ['ʌn'tʃeist] *a* impudique.

unchecked ['ʌn'tʃekt] *a* sans opposition, non maîtrisé.

uncivil ['ʌn'sivil] *a* impoli.

unclasp ['ʌn'klɑːsp] *vt* dégrafer, desserrer.

uncle ['ʌnkl] *n* oncle *m*; (*pawnbroker*) tante *f*.

unclean ['ʌn'kliːn] *a* malpropre, impur.

unclothe ['ʌn'klouð] *vt* dévêtir.

unclouded ['ʌn'klaudid] *a* sans nuage, limpide, pur.

uncomfortable [ʌn'kʌmfətəbl] *a* mal à l'aise, incommode, peu confortable.

uncommon [ʌn'kɔmən] *a* peu commun, rare, singulier.

uncommonly [ʌn'kɔmənli] *ad* singulièrement.

uncomplimentary ['ʌn,kɔmpli'mentəri] *a* peu flatteur.

uncompromising [ʌn'kɔmprəmaiziŋ] *a* intransigeant, intraitable.

unconcern ['ʌnkən'sɔːn] *n* indifférence *f*, détachement *m*.

unconcerned ['ʌnkən'sɔːnd] *a* comme étranger, indifférent, dégagé.

unconcernedly ['ʌnkən'sɔːnidli] *ad* d'un air détaché.

unconditional ['ʌnkən'diʃnəl] *a* sans conditions, absolu.

uncongenial ['ʌnkən'dʒiːnjəl] *a* antipathique, ingrat.

unconquerable [ʌn'kɔnkərəbl] *a* invincible.

unconquered ['ʌn'kɔnkəd] *a* invaincu.

unconscionable [ʌn'kɔnʃnəbl] *a* inconcevable, sans conscience.

unconscious [ʌn'kɔnʃəs] *a* inconscient, sans connaissance.

unconsciousness [ʌn'kɔnʃəsnis] *n* inconscience *f*, évanouissement *m*.

unconstitutional ['ʌn,kɔnsti'tjuːʃənl] *n* inconstitutionnel.

uncontrollable [ˌʌnkən'trouləbl] *a* incontrôlable, irrésistible, ingouvernable.

unconventional ['ʌnkən'venʃənl] *a* original.

unconvinced ['ʌnkən'vinst] *a* sceptique.

uncooked ['ʌn'kukt] *a* mal cuit, cru.

uncork ['ʌn'kɔːk] *vt* déboucher.

uncouth [ʌn'kuːθ] *a* rude, grossier, gauche, négligé.

uncover [ʌn'kʌvə] *vt* découvrir, dévoiler.

uncrossed ['ʌn'krɔst] *a* non barré.

unction ['ʌŋkʃən] n onction f.

unctuous ['ʌŋktjuəs] a onctueux, huileux.

undaunted [ʌn'dɔːntid] a indompté, intrépide.

undeceive ['ʌndi'siːv] vt détromper.

undecided ['ʌndi'saidid] a indécis, irrésolu, mal défini.

undecipherable ['ʌndi'saifərəbl] a indéchiffrable.

undefiled ['ʌndi'faild] a sans tache, pur.

undeniable [.ʌndi'naiəbl] a indéniable, incontestable.

under ['ʌndə] prep sous, au-dessous de; a de dessous, inférieur, subalterne.

underclothes ['ʌndəklouðz] n pl sous-vêtements m pl, linge de corps m.

underdeveloped ['ʌndədi'veləpt] a sous-développé.

underdog ['ʌndədɔg] n (fam) lampiste m, faible m.

underdone ['ʌndə'dʌn] a saignant.

underfed ['ʌndə'fed] a sous-alimenté.

undergo [.ʌndə'gou] vt souffrir, subir.

undergraduate [.ʌndə'grædjuit] n étudiant(e) mf.

underground ['ʌndəgraund] n métro m; a souterrain, clandestin; ad sous terre.

undergrowth ['ʌndəgrouθ] n taillis m, fourré m.

underhand ['ʌndəhænd] a souterrain, sournois, clandestin; ad par dessous main, en dessous.

underline ['ʌndəlain] vt souligner.

underling ['ʌndəliŋ] n sous-ordre m, barbin m, subordonné(e) mf.

undermine [.ʌndə'main] vt miner, saper.

underneath [.ʌndə'niːθ] prep au-dessous de, sous; ad dessous, par-dessous, au-dessous; a de dessous.

underrate [.ʌndə'reit] vt sous-estimer.

under-secretary ['ʌndə'sekrətəri] n sous-secrétaire mf.

undersell ['ʌndə'sel] vt vendre moins cher que.

undershirt ['ʌndəʃəːt] n tricot m, gilet m (de corps).

undersigned [.ʌndə'saind] a soussigné.

understand [.ʌndə'stænd] vt comprendre, s'entendre à, sous-entendre.

understandable [.ʌndə'stændəbl] a intelligible, compréhensible.

understanding [.ʌndə'stændiŋ] n entendement m, intelligence f, compréhension f.

understatement ['ʌndə'steitmənt] n atténuation f, amoindrissement m.

understood [.ʌndə'stud] pp of understand compris.

understudy ['ʌndə'stʌdi] n doublure f; vt doubler.

undertake [.ʌndə'teik] vt entreprendre, s'engager à, se charger de.

undertaker ['ʌndə.teikə] n entrepreneur de pompes funèbres m.

undertaking [.ʌndə'teikiŋ] n entreprise f, engagement m.

undertook [.ʌndə'tuk] pp of undertake.

undertow ['ʌndətou] n ressac m, barre f.

underwear ['ʌndəwεə] n sous-vêtements m pl, dessous m pl, lingerie f.

underwood ['ʌndəwud] n sous-bois m.

underworld ['ʌndəwəːld] n pègre f, bas fonds m pl, enfers m pl.

underwrite ['ʌndərait] vt souscrire, assurer.

underwriter ['ʌndə.raitə] n assureur maritime m.

undeserved ['ʌndi'zəːvd] a immérité.

undeserving ['ʌndi'zəːviŋ] a indigne.

undesignedly ['ʌndi'zainidli] ad sans intention, innocemment.

undesirable ['ʌndi'zaiərəbl] a indésirable.

undigested ['ʌndi'dʒestid] a mal digéré, indigeste.

undignified [ʌn'dignifaid] a sans dignité.

undiluted ['ʌndai'ljuːtid] a pur, non dilué.

undimmed [ʌn'dimd] a non voilé, brillant.

undiscernible ['ʌndi'səːnəbl] a indiscernable, imperceptible.

undiscerning ['ʌndi'səːniŋ] a sans discernement.

undischarged ['ʌndis'tʃɑːdʒd] a non libéré, inacquitté, inaccompli.

undisguised ['ʌndis'gaizd] a sans déguisement, évident, franc.

undismayed ['ʌndis'meid] a imperturbable.

undisputed ['ʌndis'pjuːtid] a incontesté.

undistinguished ['ʌndis'tiŋgwiʃt] a commun, médiocre, banal.

undisturbed ['ʌndis'təːbd] a non dérangé, non troublé, paisible.

undivided ['ʌndi'vaidid] a entier, indivisé, unanime.

undo ['ʌn'duː] vt défaire, dénouer, dégrafer, ruiner, annuler.

undoing ['ʌn'duiŋ] n perte f, ruine f.

undone ['ʌn'dʌn] a défait, inachevé, perdu.

undoubted [ʌn'dautid] a certain, incontestable.

undoubtedly [ʌn'dautidli] ad sans aucun doute.

undreamt [ʌn'dremt] a dont on n'osait rêver, merveilleux.

undress ['ʌn'dres] n petite tenue f, négligé m; vt déshabiller; vi se déshabiller.

undrinkable ['ʌn'driŋkəbl] a imbuvable, non potable.

undue ['ʌn'djuː] a excessif, indu.

undulate ['ʌndjuleit] vti onduler.

undulating ['ʌndjuleitiŋ] a vallonné, ondoyant, onduleux.

unduly ['ʌn'dju:li] ad indûment, à l'excès.

undying [ʌn'daiiŋ] a immortel, impérissable.

unearned ['ʌn'ə:nd] a — income plus-value f.

unearth ['ʌn'ə:θ] vt déterrer, exhumer.

unearthly [ʌn'ə:θli] a qui n'est pas de ce monde, surnaturel.

uneasiness [ʌn'i:zinis] a inquiétude f, gêne f.

uneasy [ʌn'i:zi] a mal à l'aise, inquiet, gêné.

uneatable ['ʌn'i:təbl] a immangeable.

uneducated ['ʌn'edjukeitid] a inculte, sans éducation.

unemployable [ʌnim'plɔiəbl] a bon à rien.

unemployed ['ʌnim'plɔid] a désœuvré, sans travail; the — les chômeurs m pl.

unemployment [ʌnim'plɔimənt] n chômage m.

unending [ʌn'endiŋ] a interminable, sans fin.

unequal ['ʌn'i:kwəl] a inégal; to be — to ne pas être à la hauteur de, ne pas être de force à.

unequaled ['ʌn'i:kwəld] a sans égal, inégalé.

unessential ['ʌni'senʃəl] a secondaire.

uneven ['ʌn'i:vən] a inégal, irrégulier, rugueux.

uneventful ['ʌni'ventful] a sans incident, terne, monotone.

unexceptionable [,ʌnik'sepʃnəbl] a irréprochable.

unexpected ['ʌniks'pektid] a inattendu, inespéré, imprévu.

unexpectedly ['ʌniks'pektidli] ad à l'improviste.

unexpectedness ['ʌniks'pektidnis] n soudaineté f, caractère imprévu m.

unexplored ['ʌniks'plɔ:d] a inexploré.

unfailing [ʌn'feiliŋ] a immanquable, impeccable, inaltérable.

unfair ['ʌn'feə] a injuste, déloyal.

unfairness ['ʌn'feənis] n injustice f, déloyauté f, mauvaise foi f.

unfaithful ['ʌn'feiθful] a infidèle; — ness n infidélité.

unfamiliar ['ʌnfə'miliə] a peu familier, étranger.

unfashionable ['ʌn'fæʃnəbl] a pas à la mode, démodé.

unfasten ['ʌn'fɑ:sn] vt détacher, dégrafer, déverrouiller.

unfathomable [ʌn'fæðəməbl] a insondable, impénétrable.

unfavorable ['ʌn'feivərəbl] a défavorable, impropice, desavantageux.

unfeasible ['ʌn'fi:zəbl] a infaisable, irréalisable.

unfeeling [ʌn'fi:liŋ] a insensible, froid, sec.

unfettered ['ʌn'fetəd] a sans entraves, libre.

unfinished ['ʌn'finiʃt] a inachevé.

unfit ['ʌn'fit] a inapte, en mauvaise santé.

unflagging [ʌn'flægiŋ] a sans défaillance, soutenu.

unfledged ['ʌn'fledʒd] a sans plumes, novice.

unflinchingly [ʌn'flintʃiŋli] ad sans fléchir, de pied ferme.

unfold ['ʌn'fould] vt déplier, dérouler, révéler; vi se dérouler, se déployer.

unforeseeable ['ʌnfɔ:'siəbl] a imprévisible.

unforeseen ['ʌnfɔ:'si:n] a imprévu.

unforgettable ['ʌnfə'getəbl] a inoubliable.

unforgivable ['ʌnfə'givəbl] a impardonnable.

unforgiving ['ʌnfə'giviŋ] a implacable.

unforgotten ['ʌnfə'gɔtn] a inoublié.

unfortunate [ʌn'fɔ:tʃnit] a malheureux.

unfortunately [ʌn'fɔ:tʃnitli] ad malheureusement.

unfounded ['ʌn'faundid] a sans fondement.

unfrequented ['ʌnfri'kwentid] a solitaire, écarté.

unfriendly ['ʌn'frendli] a inamical, hostile.

unfruitful ['ʌn'fru:tful] a infructueux, stérile.

unfulfilled ['ʌnful'fild] a irréalisé, inexaucé, inachevé.

unfurl [ʌn'fə:l] vt dérouler, déployer, déferler.

unfurnished ['ʌn'fə:niʃt] a non meublé.

ungainly [ʌn'geinli] a gauche, (fam) mastoc, dégingandé.

ungentlemanly [ʌn'dʒentlmənli] a indigne d'un galant homme, impoli.

ungovernable [ʌn'gʌvənəbl] a ingouvernable, irrésistible.

ungracious ['ʌn'greiʃəs] a sans grâce, désagréable.

ungrateful [ʌn'greitful] a ingrat.

ungratefulness [ʌn'greitfulnis] n ingratitude f.

ungrudgingly [ʌn'grʌdʒiŋli] ad sans grogner, de bon cœur, sans compter.

unguarded ['ʌn'gɑ:did] a sans défense, non gardé, inconsidéré.

unhallowed [ʌn'hæloud] a profane, impie.

unhandy [ʌn'hændi] a difficile à manier, incommode, gauche.

unhappiness [ʌn'hæpinis] n malheur m.

unhappy [ʌn'hæpi] a malheureux, infortuné.

unharmed ['ʌn'hɑ:md] a indemne, sain et sauf.

unharness ['ʌn'hɑ:nis] vt dételer.

unhealthiness [ʌn'helθinis] n état malsain m, insalubrité f.

unhealthy [ʌn'helθi] a malsain, insalubre, maladif.

unheard of [ʌn'hə:dɔv] a inouï, inconnu.

unheeded ['ʌn'hi:did] a inaperçu, négligé.

unhelpful ['ʌn'helpful] a peu serviable, de pauvre secours, inutile.

unhesitatingly [ʌn'heziteitiŋli] ad sans hésitation.

unhinge [ʌn'hindʒ] vt faire sortir des gonds, déranger.

unholy [ʌn'houli] a impie, impur, (fam) du diable, affreux.

unhonored [ʌn'ɔnəd] a sans honneur, dédaigné.

unhook ['ʌn'huk] vt décrocher, dégrafer.

unhoped for [ʌn'houptfɔ:] n inespéré.

unhurt ['ʌn'hə:t] a sans mal, indemne.

unicorn ['ju:nikɔ:n] n licorne f.

unification [,ju:nifi'keiʃən] n unification f.

uniform ['ju:nifɔ:m] an uniforme m.

uniformly ['ju:nifɔ:mli] ad uniformément.

unify ['ju:nifai] vt unifier.

unilateral ['ju:ni'lætərəl] a unilatéral.

unimaginable [,ʌni'mædʒinəbl] a inimaginable.

unimaginative ['ʌni'mædʒinətiv] a sans imagination.

unimpaired ['ʌnim'pɛəd] a dans toute sa force, intact.

unimpeachable [,ʌnim'pi:tʃəbl] a irréprochable, irrécusable.

unimportant ['ʌnim'pɔ:tənt] a sans importance.

unimpressed ['ʌnim'prest] a non impressionné, froid.

unimpressive [ʌn'impresiv] a peu impressionnant.

uninhabitable ['ʌnin'hæbitəbl] a inhabitable.

uninhabited ['ʌnin'hæbitid] a inhabité.

unintelligent ['ʌnin'telidʒənt] a inintelligent.

unintentional ['ʌnin'tenʃənl] a sans (mauvaise) intention, involontaire.

uninteresting ['ʌn'intristiŋ] a sans intérêt.

uninterrupted ['ʌn,intə'rʌptid] a ininterrompu.

union ['ju:njən] n union f, accord m, syndicat ouvrier m.

unionist ['ju:njənist] n syndiqué(e) mf, syndicaliste mf, unioniste mf.

Union Jack ['ju:njən'dʒæk] n pavillon britannique m.

unique [ju:'ni:k] a unique.

unison ['ju:nizn] n unisson m.

unit ['ju:nit] n unité f.

unite [ju:'nait] vt unir, unifier; vi s'unir.

unity ['ju:niti] n unité f, union f.

universal [,ju:ni'və:səl] a universel.

universe ['ju:nivə:s] n univers m.

university [,ju:ni'və:siti] n université f.

unjust ['ʌn'dʒʌst] a injuste.

unjustifiable [ʌn'dʒʌstifaiəbl] a injustifiable.

unkempt ['ʌn'kempt] a mal peigné, dépeigné, mal tenu.

unkind [ʌn'kaind] a peu aimable, désobligeant, dur.

unkindness [ʌn'kaindnis] n méchanceté f, désobligeance f.

unknowingly ['ʌn'nouiŋli] ad sans le savoir (vouloir).

unknown to ['ʌn'nountu:] ad à l'insu de.

unlamented [ʌnlə'mentid] a non pleuré.

unlatch ['ʌnlætʃ] vt ouvrir.

unlawful ['ʌn'bɔ:ful] a illégal, illicite.

unlawfulness ['ʌn'bɔ:fulnis] n illégalité f.

unlearn ['ʌn'lə:n] vt désapprendre, oublier.

unleash [ʌn'li:ʃ] vt détacher, déchaîner, lâcher.

unleavened ['ʌn'levnd] a sans levain, azyme.

unless [ən'les] cj à moins que (de), si . . . ne pas.

unlike ['ʌn'laik] a différent; ad à la différence de.

unlikely [ʌn'laikli] a improbable.

unlimited [ʌn'limitid] a illimité.

unload ['ʌn'loud] vt décharger.

unlock ['ʌn'lɔk] vt ouvrir.

unlooked for [ʌn'luktfɔ:] a inattendu, inespéré.

unlucky [ʌn'lʌki] a malchanceux, malheureux, maléfique.

unmanageable [ʌn'mænidʒəbl] a intraitable, impossible, difficile à manœuvrer.

unmanly ['ʌn'mænli] a peu viril, efféminé.

unmanneriness [ʌn'mænəlinis] n manque d'éducation m, impolitesse f.

unmannerly [ʌn'mænəli] a mal élevé, malappris.

unmarketable [ʌn'mɑ:kitəbl] a sans marché (demande), invendable.

unmarried ['ʌn'mærid] a célibataire, non marié.

unmask ['ʌn'mɑ:sk] vt démasquer, dévoiler.

unmentionable [ʌn'menʃnəbl] a innommable, dont on ne peut parler.

unmerciful [ʌn'mə:siful] a sans pitié, impitoyable.

unmerited ['ʌn'meritid] a immérité.

unmindful [ʌn'maindful] a oublieux, insouciant.

unmistakable ['ʌnmis'teikəbl] a impossible à méconnaître.

unmistakably ['ʌnmis'teikəbli] ad à n'en pas douter, à ne pas s'y méprendre.

unmitigated [ʌn'mitigeited] *a* pur, complet, fieffé, parfait.

unmoor ['ʌn'muə] *vt* démarrer.

unmoved ['ʌn'mu:vd] *a* indifférent, impassible.

unnamed ['ʌn'neimd] *a* sans nom, innomé, anonyme.

unnatural [ʌn'nætʃrəl] *a* pas naturel, dénaturé, anormal.

unnecessary [ʌn'nesisəri] *a* pas nécessaire, inutile, gratuit.

unneighborly ['ʌn'neibəli] *a* de mauvais voisin.

unnerve ['ʌn'nə:v] *vt* énerver, faire perdre son sang-froid à.

unnoticed ['ʌn'noutist] *a* inaperçu.

unnumbered ['ʌn'nʌmbəd] *a* innombrable, non-numéroté.

unobjectionable [ʌnəb'dʒekʃnəbl] *a* qui défie toute objection.

unobliging ['ʌnə'blaidʒiŋ] *a* désobligeant, peu obligeant.

unobservant [ʌnəb'zə:vənt] *a* peu observateur.

unobtainable ['ʌnəb'teinəbl] *a* introuvable.

unobtrusive ['ʌnəb'tru:siv] *a* effacé, discret, pas gênant.

unoccupied ['ʌn'ɔkjupaid] *a* inoccupé.

unoffending ['ʌnə'fendiŋ] *a* qui n'a rien de blessant, innocent.

unofficial ['ʌnə'fiʃəl] *a* officieux, inofficiel.

unostentatious ['ʌn,ɔsten'teiʃəs] *a* sans ostentation, simple.

unpack ['ʌn'pæk] *vt* dépaqueter, déballer, défaire; *vi* défaire sa malle.

unpalatable [ʌn'pælətəbl] *a* dur à avaler, amer, désagréable.

unparalleled [ʌn'pærəleld] *a* incomparable, sans précédent.

unpardonable [ʌn'pɑ:dnəbl] *a* impardonnable.

unperceived ['ʌnpə'si:vd] *a* inaperçu.

unperturbed ['ʌnpə'tə:bd] *a* imperturbable, peu ému, impassible.

unpleasant [ʌn'pleznt] *a* déplaisant, désagréable.

unpleasantness [ʌn'plezntnis] *n* désagrément *m*, ennui *m*.

unpolished ['ʌn'pɔliʃt] *a* terne, brut, mat, fruste, grossier.

unpopular ['ʌn'pɔpjulə] *a* impopulaire.

unpopularity ['ʌn,pɔpju'læriti] *n* impopularité *f*.

unpractical ['ʌn'præktikəl] *a* peu pratique, chimérique.

npracticed [ʌn'præktist] *a* mal entraîné, novice, inexpérimenté.

unprecedented [ʌn'presidəntid] *a* sans précédent.

unpredictable ['ʌnpri'diktəbl] *a* imprévisible.

unprejudiced [ʌn'predʒudist] *a* impartial.

unpremeditated ['ʌnpri'mediteitid] *a* sans préméditation, inopiné.

unprepared ['ʌnpri'pɛəd] *a* pas préparé, inapprêté, improvisé.

unprepossessing ['ʌn,pri:pə'zesiŋ] *a* peu engageant, de mauvaise mine.

unprincipled [ʌn'prinsəpld] *a* sans principes.

unproductive ['ʌnprə'dʌktiv] *a* improductif, stérile.

unprofitable [ʌn'prɔfitəbl] *a* sans profit, ingrat, peu lucratif.

unprogressive ['ʌnprə'gresiv] *a* stagnant, rétrograde.

unprompted [ʌn'prɔmptid] *a* spontané.

unpropitious ['ʌnprə'piʃəs] *a* de mauvais augure, impropice.

unprotected ['ʌnprə'tektid] *a* sans protection, exposé, inabrité.

unprovided ['ʌnprə'vaidid] *a* sans ressources, démuni.

unpublished ['ʌn'pʌbliʃt] *a* inédit, non publié.

unqualified ['ʌn'kwɔlifaid] *a* incompétent, sans titres, sans réserve, absolu, catégorique.

unquestionable [ʌn'kwestʃənəbl] *a* indiscutable.

unravel [ʌn'rævəl] *vt* démêler, affiler.

unreasonable [ʌn'ri:znəbl] *a* déraisonnable, exorbitant, extravagant.

unreasonableness [ʌn'ri:znəblnis] *n* déraison *f*, extravagance *f*.

unreciprocated ['ʌnri'siprəkeitid] *a* non payé de retour.

unrecognizable ['ʌn'rekəgnaizəbl] *a* méconnaissable.

unreconcilable ['ʌn'rekənsailəbl] *a* irréconciliable.

unredeemed ['ʌnri'di:md] *a* non racheté, inaccompli, sans compensation.

unrelated ['ʌnri'leitid] *a* étranger, sans rapport.

unrelenting ['ʌnri'lentiŋ] *a* inexorable, acharné.

unreliable ['ʌnri'laiəbl] *a* peu sûr, incertain.

unremitting [,ʌnri'mitiŋ] *a* incessant, acharné; — **efforts** efforts soutenus.

unrepentant ['ʌnri'pentənt] *a* impénitent.

unreservedly [,ʌnri'zə:vidli] *ad* sans réserve.

unresponsive ['ʌnris'ponsiv] *a* renfermé, réservé, froid.

unrest ['ʌn'rest] *n* inquiétude *f*, agitation *f*, malaise *m*.

unrestrained ['ʌnris'treind] *a* déréglé, déchaîné, immodéré.

unrestricted ['ʌnris'triktid] *a* sans restriction, absolu.

unripe ['ʌn'raip] *a* pas mûr, vert.

unrivaled [ʌn'raivəld] *a* inégalé, sans rival.

unroll ['ʌn'roul] *vt* dérouler; *vi* se dérouler.

unruffled ['ʌn'rʌfld] *a* imperturbable, serein, calme.

unruly [ʌn'ruːlɪ] a indiscipliné, turbulent, déréglé.

unsafe ['ʌn'seɪf] a dangereux, hasardeux.

unsalable ['ʌn'seɪləbl] a invendable.

unsavory ['ʌn'seɪvərɪ] a fade, nauséabond, repugnant, vilain.

unsay ['ʌn'seɪ] vt retirer, rétractér, se dédire de.

unscathed ['ʌn'skeɪðd] a sans une égratignure, indemne.

unscrew ['ʌn'skruː] vt dévisser.

unscripted ['ʌn'skrɪptəd] a en direct.

unscrupulous [ʌn'skruːpjuləs] a sans scrupules, indélicat.

unseal ['ʌn'siːl] vt décacheter, désceller.

unseasonable [ʌn'siːznəbl] a hors de saison, inopportun, déplacé.

unseat ['ʌn'siːt] vt démonter, désarçonner, invalider, faire perdre son siège à.

unseemly [ʌn'siːmlɪ] ad inconvenant.

unseen ['ʌn'siːn] a inaperçu, invisible.

unselfish ['ʌn'selfɪʃ] a désintéressé, généreux.

unserviceable ['ʌn'sɜːvɪsəbl] a hors de service, usé, inutilisable.

unsettled ['ʌn'setld] a indécis, variable, impayé.

unshaken ['ʌn'ʃeɪkən] a inébranlable.

unsheathe ['ʌn'ʃiːð] vt dégainer.

unship ['ʌn'ʃɪp] vt décharger, débarquer.

unshrinkable ['ʌn'ʃrɪnkəbl] a irrétrécissable.

unsightly [ʌn'saɪtlɪ] a laid, vilain.

unskilled ['ʌn'skɪld] a inexpert.

unsociable ['ʌn'səʊʃəbl] a insociable, farouche.

unsoiled [ʌn'sɔɪld] a sans tache.

unsold ['ʌn'səʊld] a invendu.

unsolicited ['ʌnsə'lɪsɪtɪd] a spontané.

unsophisticated ['ʌnsə'fɪstɪkeɪtɪd] a naturel, nature, ingénu.

unsound ['ʌn'saʊnd] a malsain, dérangé, erroné.

unsparing [ʌn'speərɪŋ] a prodigue, infatigable.

unspeakable [ʌn'spiːkəbl] a indicible, innommable.

unspoiled ['ʌn'spɔɪld] a non gâté vierge, bien élevé.

unstable ['ʌn'steɪbl] a instable.

unstamped ['ʌn'stæmpt] a non affranchi, non estampillé.

unsteadiness ['ʌn'stedɪnɪs] n instabilité f, indécision f, variabilité f, irrégularité f.

unsteady ['ʌn'stedɪ] a instable, mal assuré, irrésolu, irrégulier, chancelant, variable.

unstuck ['ʌn'stʌk] a to come — se décoller, se dégommer, (fig) s'effondrer.

unsuccessful [ʌnsək'sesful] a malheureux, manqué, raté, vain.

unsuccessfully ['ʌnsək'sesfulɪ] ad sans succès.

unsuitable ['ʌn'sjuːtəbl] a inapproprié, impropre, inapte, inopportun.

unsuited ['ʌn'sjuːtɪd] a impropre (à for), mal fait (pour for).

unsullied ['ʌn'sʌlɪd] a sans tache.

unsurpassable ['ʌnsə'pɑːsəbl] a impossible à surpasser.

unsurpassed ['ʌnsə'pɑːst] a sans égal.

unsuspected ['ʌnsəs'pektɪd] a insoupçonné.

unsuspicious ['ʌnsəs'pɪʃəs] a confiant, qui ne se doute de rien.

untamable ['ʌn'teɪməbl] a indomptable.

untaught ['ʌn'tɔːt] a ignorant, illettré.

untenanted ['ʌn'tenəntɪd] a vacant, inoccupé.

unthankful ['ʌn'θæŋkful] a ingrat.

unthankfulness ['ʌn'θæŋkfulnɪs] n ingratitude f.

unthinkable [ʌn'θɪŋkəbl] a inconcevable.

unthoughtful ['ʌn'θɔːtful] a irréfléchi.

untidy [ʌn'taɪdɪ] a négligé, débraillé, en désordre, mal tenu, mal peigné.

untie ['ʌn'taɪ] vt délier, détacher, défaire.

until [ən'tɪl] prep jusqu'à, avant, ne . . . que; cj jusqu'à ce que, avant que, ne . . . que quand.

untimely [ʌn'taɪmlɪ] a prématuré, intempestif, mal à propos.

untiring [ʌn'taɪərɪŋ] a infatigable.

untold ['ʌn'təʊld] a tu, passé sous silence, inouï, incalculable.

untoward [ʌn'təʊəd] a fâcheux, malencontreux.

untrammeled [ʌn'træməld] a sans entraves, libre.

untranslatable ['ʌntræns'leɪtəbl] a intraduisible.

untried ['ʌn'traɪd] a neuf, qui n'a pas été mis à l'épreuve.

untrodden ['ʌn'trɒdn] a vierge, inexploré.

untrue ['ʌn'truː] a faux, infidèle, déloyal.

untrustworthy ['ʌn'trʌst wɜːðɪ] a indigne de confiance.

untruth ['ʌn'truːθ] n mensonge m.

untruthful ['ʌn'truːθful] a menteur, mensonger, faux.

unusual [ʌn'juːʒuəl] a insolite, rare.

unutterable [ʌn'ʌtərəbl] a inexprimable, parfait.

unveil [ʌn'veɪl] vt dévoiler, inaugurer.

unveiling [ʌn'veɪlɪŋ] n inauguration f.

unwarranted ['ʌn'wɒrəntɪd] a injustifié, déplacé, gratuit.

unwary [ʌn'weərɪ] a imprudent.

unwavering [ʌn'weɪvərɪŋ] a constant, inaltérable, résolu.

unwaveringly [ʌn'weɪvərɪŋlɪ] ad de pied ferme, résolument.

unwearying [ʌn'wɪərɪɪŋ] a infatigable.

unwelcome [ʌn'welkəm] a mal venu, importun, désagréable.

unwell ['ʌn'wel] a indisposé, mal en train, souffrant.

unwholesome ['ʌn'houlsəm] a malsain, insalubre.

unwieldy [ʌn'wi:ldi] a difficile à manier, encombrant.

unwilling ['ʌn'wiliŋ] a malgré soi, de mauvaise volonté.

unwillingly [ʌn'wiliŋli] ad à contre cœur.

unwind ['ʌn'waind] vt dérouler, dévider, débobiner.

unwise ['ʌn'waiz] a malavisé, imprudent.

unwittingly [ʌn'witiŋli] ad sans y penser, étourdiment, sans le savoir.

unwonted [ʌn'wountid] a rare, inaccoutumé.

unworkable ['ʌn'wə:kəbl] a impraticable, inexploitable.

unworthiness [ʌn'wə:ðinis] a indignité f, peu de mérite m.

unworthy [ʌn'wə:ði] a indigne.

unwrap ['ʌn'ræp] vt déballer, défaire.

unwritten ['ʌn'ritn] a tacite, oral, non écrit.

unyielding [ʌn'ji:ldiŋ] a inflexible, intransigeant.

up [ʌp] a debout, levé, droit, fini, expiré; ad en dessus, plus fort, en montant, en l'air, en avance; — to jusque, jusqu'à; **it is all — with him** il est fichu, perdu; — **there** là-haut; **to be — to sth.** mijoter qch, être à la hauteur de qch; **the —s and downs** les vicissitudes f pl, accidents m pl; **to walk — and down** marcher de long en large.

upbraid [ʌp'breid] vt morigéner, faire des reproches à.

upbraiding [ʌp'breidiŋ] n réprimande f.

upbringing ['ʌp.briŋiŋ] n éducation f.

upheaval [ʌp'hi:vəl] n soulèvement m, convulsion f.

uphill ['ʌp'hil] a ardu, montant; ad en montant.

uphold [ʌp'hould] vt soutenir.

upholder [ʌp'houldə] n partisan m, soutien m.

upholster [ʌp'houlstə] vt tapisser.

upholsterer [ʌp'houlstərə] n tapissier m.

upholstery [ʌp'houlstəri] n tapisserie f, garniture f, capitonnage m.

upkeep ['ʌpki:p] n entretien m.

uplift ['ʌplift] n inspiration f, prêchi-prêcha m; [ʌp'lift] vt élever, exalter.

upon [ə'pɔn] prep sur; see **on**.

upper ['ʌpə] n empeigne f; a supérieur, de dessus, haut.

uppermost ['ʌpəmoust] a le plus haut, premier, du premier rang; ad en dessus.

uppish ['ʌpiʃ] a hautain, présomptueux.

upright ['ʌprait] a vertical, droit, debout, juste, honnête.

uprightness ['ʌp.raitnis] n droiture f.

uprising [ʌp'raiziŋ] n soulèvement m, lever m.

uproar ['ʌp.rɔ:] n tumulte m, brouhaha m.

uproarious [ʌp'rɔ:riəs] a bruyant, tapageur.

uproot [ʌp'ru:t] vt déraciner, extirper, arracher.

upset [ʌp'set] n bouleversement m, renversement m, dérangement m; vt bouleverser, renverser, déranger, indisposer.

upshot ['ʌpʃɔt] n conclusion f, issue f, fin mot m.

upside-down ['ʌpsaid'daun] ad sens dessus dessous, à l'envers, la tête en bas.

upstairs ['ʌp'stɛəz] ad en haut.

upstart ['ʌpstɑ:t] n parvenu(e) mf.

up-to-date ['ʌptu'deit] a à la page, au courant.

upturn [ʌp'tə:n] vt retourner, (re)lever.

upward ['ʌpwəd] a montant, ascendant; ad en montant, en-(au-)dessus; ad en haut, au-dessus, plus de.

urban ['ə:bən] a urbain.

urbane [ə:'bein] a affable, suave, courtois.

urbanity [ə:'bæniti] n urbanité f.

urchin ['ə:tʃin] n oursin m, gosse mf, gamin(e) mf.

urge [ə:dʒ] n impulsion f, besoin m; vt presser, talonner, alléguer, pousser, recommander.

urgency ['ə:dʒənsi] n urgence f.

urgent ['ə:dʒənt] a urgent, pressant, instant.

urgently ['ə:dʒəntli] ad instamment, avec urgence.

urn [ə:n] n urne f.

us [ʌs] pn nous.

usable ['ju:zəbl] a utilisable.

usage ['ju:zidʒ] n traitement m, usage m, emploi m.

use [ju:s] n usage m, emploi m; **it is no —** il ne sert à rien; **what is the —?** à quoi bon?

use [ju:z] vt employer, se servir de, traiter, avoir l'habitude de; **to — up** consommer, épuiser; **to get — to** s'habituer, s'accoutumer à.

useful ['ju:sful] a utile, pratique.

usefulness ['ju:sfulnis] n utilité f.

useless ['ju:slis] a inutile.

user ['ju:zə] n usager, -ère.

usher ['ʌʃə] n huissier m, répétiteur m, pion m; ouvreuse f; **to — in** inaugurer, annoncer, introduire, faire entrer; **to — out** reconduire.

usual ['ju:ʒuəl] a usuel, courant, d'usage.

usually ['ju:ʒuəli] ad d'habitude, d'ordinaire.

usufruct ['ju:sjufrʌkt] n usufruit m.

usurer ['ju:ʒərə] n usurier m.

usurp [juːˈzəːp] vt usurper, empiéter sur.

usurpation [ˌjuːzəːˈpeiʃən] n usurpation f.

usury [ˈjuːʒuri] n usure f.

utensil [juˈtensl] n ustensile m, attirail m, outil m.

utilitarian [ˌjuːtiliˈtɛəriən] a utilitaire.

utilitarianism [ˌjuːtiliˈtɛəriənizəm] n utilitarisme m.

utility [juˈtiliti] n utilité f.

utilization [ˌjuːtilaiˈzeiʃən] n utilisation f.

utilize [ˈjuːtilaiz] vt utiliser, tirer parti de.

utmost [ˈʌtmoust] n tout le possible; a extrême, dernier, le plus grand.

utopia [juːˈtoupiə] n utopie f.

utopian [juːˈtoupiən] a utopique.

utter [ˈʌtə] a extrême, absolu, achevé; vt émettre, exprimer, dire, pousser.

utterance [ˈʌtərəns] n voix f, parole f, expression f, articulation f.

utterly [ˈʌtəli] ad absolument.

V

vacancy [ˈveikənsi] n vacance f, vide m.

vacant [ˈveikənt] a vacant, vide, absent, hébété.

vacate [vəˈkeit] vt vider, évacuer, quitter, annuler.

vacation [vəˈkeiʃən] n vacances f pl.

vaccinate [ˈvæksineit] vt vacciner.

vaccination [ˌvæksiˈneiʃən] n vaccination f.

vaccine [ˈvæksiːn] n vaccin m.

vacillate [ˈvæsileit] vi vaciller, hésiter.

vacuous [ˈvækjuəs] a vide, hébété, niais.

vacuum [ˈvækjuəm] n vide m.

vagabond [ˈvægəbɔnd] n vagabond(e) mf, chemineau m.

vagabondage [ˈvægəbɔndidʒ] n vagabondage m.

vagary [ˈveigəri] n lubie f, chimère f, fantaisie f.

vagrancy [ˈveigrənsi] n vagabondage m.

vagrant [ˈveigrənt] n vagabond(e) mf, chemineau m; a errant, vagabond.

vague [veig] a vague, estompé, indécis.

vagueness [ˈveignis] n vague m, imprécision f.

vain [vein] a vain, inutile, vaniteux.

vainglorious [veinˈglɔːriəs] a fier, glorieux.

vainglory [veinˈglɔːri] n gloriole f.

vainly [ˈveinli] ad en vain, avec vanité.

vale [veil] n val m.

valiant [ˈvæljənt] a vaillant.

valiantly [ˈvæljəntli] ad vaillamment.

valid [ˈvælid] a valide, valable, solide.

validate [ˈvælideit] vt rendre valide, ratifier.

validity [vəˈliditi] n validité f.

valley [ˈvæli] n vallée f.

valor [ˈvælə] n valeur f.

valorous [ˈvælərəs] a valeureux.

valuable [ˈvæljuəbl] a de grande valeur, de prix, précieux; n objet de prix m.

valuation [ˌvæljuˈeiʃən] n évaluation f, prix m, expertise f.

value [ˈvælju:] n valeur f, prix m; vt évaluer, apprécier, estimer.

valve [vælv] n soupape f, valve f, valvule f, lampe f.

vamp [væmp] n femme fatale f, vamp f, empeigne f; vt flirter avec, rapiécer, (fam) retaper, improviser.

vampire [ˈvæmpaiə] n vampire m.

van [væn] n camion m, fourgon m, avant-garde f.

vane [vein] n girouette f, aile f, pale(tte) f.

vanilla [vəˈnilə] n vanille f.

vanish [ˈvæniʃ] vi disparaître, s'évanouir.

vanity [ˈvæniti] n vanité f.

vanquish [ˈvæŋkwiʃ] vt vaincre, venir à bout de.

vantage [ˈvɑːntidʒ] n avantage m.

vapid [ˈvæpid] a fade, plat.

vapor [ˈveipə] n vapeur f, buée f.

vaporization [ˌveipəraiˈzeiʃən] n vaporisation f.

vaporize [ˈveipəraiz] vt vaporiser; vi se vaporiser.

vaporizer [ˈveipəraizə] n vaporisateur m, atomiseur m.

variable [ˈvɛəriəbl] a variable, inconstant.

variance [ˈvɛəriəns] n désaccord m, discorde f.

variant [ˈvɛəriənt] n variante f.

variation [ˌvɛəriˈeiʃən] n variation f, écart m.

varicose [ˈværikous] a variqueux; — vein vein varice f.

varied [ˈvɛərid] a varié.

variegated [ˈvɛərigeitid] a bigarré, panaché, diapré.

variety [vəˈraiəti] n variété f, diversité f.

various [ˈvɛəriəs] a varié, divers, plusieurs.

variously [ˈvɛəriəsli] ad diversement.

varnish [ˈvɑːniʃ] n vernis m; vt vernir.

varnishing [ˈvɑːniʃiŋ] n vernissage m.

vary [ˈvɛəri] vti varier; vi différer, ne pas être d'accord.

vase [vɑːz] n vase m.

vast [vɑːst] a vaste, énorme.

vat [væt] n cuve f.

vault [vɔːlt] n voûte f, cave f,

caveau m, saut m; vt voûter; vti sauter.

vaunt [vɔːnt] n vantardise f; vt se vanter de.

veal [viːl] n veau m.

veer [viə] vi tourner, virer, sauter.

vegetable ['vedʒitəbl] n légume m; a végétal.

vegetarian [,vedʒi'teəriən] an végétarien, -ienne.

vegetate ['vedʒiteit] vi végéter.

vegetation [,vedʒi'teiʃən] n végétation f.

vehemence ['viːiməns] n véhémence f.

vehement ['viːimənt] a véhément.

vehicle ['viːikl] n véhicule m, voiture f.

veil [veil] n voile m, voilette f; vt voiler, masquer.

vein [vein] n veine f, humeur f.

veined [veind] a veiné.

vellum ['veləm] n vélin m.

velocity [vi'lɔsiti] n vélocité f, rapidité f.

velvet ['velvit] n velours m; a de velours, velouté.

velveteen ['velvi'tiːn] n velours de coton m.

venal ['viːnl] a vénal.

venality [viː'næliti] n vénalité f.

vendor ['vendɔː] n vendeur, -euse, marchand(e) mf.

veneer [və'niə] n placage m, glacis m, vernis m, mince couche f; vt plaquer.

venerable ['venərəbl] a vénérable.

venerate ['venəreit] vt vénérer.

veneration [,venə'reiʃən] n vénération f.

venereal [vi'niəriəl] a vénérien.

venetian blind [vi'niːʃən'blaind] n jalousie f.

vengeance ['vendʒəns] n vengeance f.

vengeful ['vendʒful] a vindicatif.

venial ['viːniəl] a véniel.

venison ['venzn] n venaison f.

venom ['venəm] n venin m.

venomous ['venəməs] a venimeux, méchant.

vent [vent] n trou m, passage m, cours m, carrière f, fente f; vt décharger.

ventilate ['ventileit] vt aérer, produire en public.

ventilation [,venti'leiʃən] n ventilation f, aération f.

ventilator ['ventileitə] n ventilateur m, soupirail m.

ventriloquist [ven'triləkwist] n ventriloque mf.

venture ['ventʃə] n risque m, entreprise f; vt s'aventurer à, oser, hasarder.

venturesome ['ventʃəsəm] a aventureux, risqué.

veracious [və'reiʃəs] a véridique.

veracity [və'ræsiti] n véracité f.

verb [vəːb] n verbe m.

verbal ['vəːbəl] a verbal, oral.

verbally ['vəːbəli] ad de vive voix.

verbatim [vəː'beitim] ad mot pour mot.

verbena [vəː(ː)'biːnə] n verveine f.

verbose [vəː'bous] a verbeux.

verbosity [vəː'bɔsiti] n verbosité f.

verdant ['vəːdənt] a verdoyant.

verdict ['vəːdikt] n verdict m, jugement m.

verge [vəːdʒ] n bord m, bordure f, point m, verge f, lisière f; to — on longer, côtoyer, friser.

verger ['vəːdʒə] n bedeau m, huissier m.

verifiable ['verifaiəbl] a vérifiable.

verification [,verifi'keiʃən] n vérification f, contrôle m.

verify ['verifai] vt vérifier, confirmer, justifier.

verisimilitude [,verisi'militjuːd] n vraisemblance f.

veritable ['veritəbl] a véritable.

vermicelli [,vəːmi'seli] n vermicelle m.

vermin ['vəːmin] n vermine f.

versatile ['vəːsətail] a aux talents variés, universel, souple, étendu.

versatility [,vəːsə'tiliti] n diversité f, universalité f, souplesse f.

verse [vəːs] n vers m, strophe f, verset m, poésie f.

versed [vəːst] a instruit (de in), rompu (à in), fort (en in), versé (en in).

versification [,vəːsifi'keiʃən] n versification f.

versify ['vəːsifai] vti versifier, écrire en vers.

version ['vəːʃən] n version f, interprétation f.

vertebra ['vəːtibrə] n vertèbre f.

vertical ['vəːtikəl] a vertical.

very ['veri] a vrai, même, seul, propre; ad très, fort, bien, tout.

vespers ['vespəz] n vêpres f pl.

vessel ['vesl] n vaisseau m, vase m, récipient m.

vest [vest] n gilet m, maillot m (de corps); vt investir (de with), conférer (à with).

vested ['vestid] a acquis.

vestibule ['vestibjuːl] n vestibule m.

vestige ['vestidʒ] n vestige m, trace f, ombre f.

vestment ['vestmənt] n vêtement m.

vestry ['vestri] n sacristie f, conseil de fabrique m.

veteran ['vetərən] n vétéran m.

veterinary ['vetərinəri] an vétérinaire m.

veto ['viːtou] n veto; vt mettre son veto (à, sur).

vex [veks] vt irriter, vexer.

vexation [vek'seiʃən] n dépit m, colère f, ennui m.

vexatious [vek'seiʃəs] a vexant, fâcheux, vexatoire.

vexed [vekst] a très discuté, vexé.

via ['vaiə] prep par, via.

viaduct ['vaiədʌkt] n viaduc m.

vial ['vaiəl] n fiole f.

viands ['vaiəndz] n pl victuailles f pl.
viaticum [vai'ætikəm] n viatique m.
vibrate [vai'breit] vi osciller, vibrer.
vibration [vai'breiʃən] n vibration f.
vicar ['vikə] n curé m, vicaire m.
vice [vais] n vice m, étau m; prep à la place de; prefix vice-.
vicinity [vi'siniti] n voisinage m, alentours m pl.
vicious ['viʃəs] a vicieux, pervers, méchant.
viciousness ['viʃəsnis] n perversité f, méchanceté f.
vicissitude [vi'sisitju:d] n vicissitude f, péripétie f.
victim ['viktim] n victime f.
victimize ['viktimaiz] vt persécuter, tromper.
victor ['viktə] n vainqueur m.
victorious [vik'tɔ:riəs] a victorieux.
victory ['viktəri] n victoire f.
victuals ['vitlz] n pl comestibles m pl, vivres m pl.
vie [vai] vi rivaliser, le disputer (à with).
view [vju:] n (point m de) vue f, perspective f, panorama m, regard m, opinion f; vt voir, regarder; with a — to dans l'intention de; bird's eye — vue f à vol d'oiseau.
viewer ['vju:ə] n téléspectateur, -trice, visionneuse f, viseur m, inspecteur, -trice.
view-finder ['vju:.faində] n viseur m.
vigil ['vidʒil] n veille f, vigile f.
vigilance ['vidʒiləns] n vigilance f.
vigilant ['vidʒilənt] a vigilant, alerte.
vigor ['vigə] n vigueur m, énergie f.
vigorous ['vigərəs] a vigoureux, solide.
vile [vail] a vil, infâme, abominable.
vileness ['vailnis] n bassesse f.
vilify ['vilifai] vt vilipender.
village ['vilidʒ] n village m.
villager ['vilidʒə] n villageois(e) mf.
villain ['vilən] n scélérat m, coquin(e) mf.
villainous ['vilənəs] a vil, infâme.
villainy ['viləni] n scélératesse f, infamie f.
vindicate ['vindikeit] vt défendre, justifier.
vindication [.vindi'keiʃən] n défense f, justification f.
vindicator ['vindikeitə] n vengeur m, défenseur m.
vindictive [vin'diktiv] a vindicatif.
vindictiveness [vin'diktivnis] n esprit vindicatif m.
vine [vain] n vigne f.
vinegar ['vinigə] n vinaigre m.
vineyard ['vinjəd] n vignoble m.
vintage ['vintidʒ] n vendange f, cru m, année f.
vintner ['vintnə] n marchand de vins m.
viol ['vaiəl] n viole f.
violate ['vaiəleit] vt violer.
violation [.vaiə'leiʃən] n viol m, violation f, infraction f.

violator ['vaiəleitə] n violateur, -trice, ravisseur m.
violence ['vaiələns] n violence f.
violent ['vaiələnt] a violent.
violently ['vaiələntli] ad violemment.
violet ['vaiələt] n violette f; a violet.
violin [.vaiə'lin] n violon m.
violinist ['vaiəlinist] n violoniste mf.
violoncello [.vaiələn'tʃelou] n violoncelle m.
viper ['vaipə] n vipère f.
virago [vi'rɑ:gou] n mégère f.
virgin ['və:dʒin] n vierge f.
virginal ['və:dʒinl] a virginal.
virginity [və:'dʒiniti] n virginité f.
virile ['virail] a viril, mâle.
virility [vi'riliti] n virilité f.
virtual ['və:tjuəl] a virtuel, de fait, vrai.
virtue ['və:tju:] n vertu f, qualité f.
virtuoso [.və:tju'ouzou] n virtuose mf.
virtuous ['və:tjuəs] a vertueux.
virulence ['virjuləns] n virulence f.
virulent ['virjulənt] a virulent.
virus ['vaiərəs] n virus m.
visa ['vi:zə] n visa m.
viscount ['vaikaunt] n vicomte m.
viscountess ['vaikauntis] n vicomtesse f.
viscous ['viskəs] a visqueux.
visibility [vizi'biliti] n visibilité f.
visible ['vizəbl] a visible.
vision ['viʒən] n vision f, vue f.
visionary ['viʒnəri] an visionnaire mf; a chimérique.
visit ['vizit] n visite f; vt rendre visite à, visiter.
visitation [.vizi'teiʃən] n tournée d'inspection f, épreuve f, calamité f, (fam) visite fâcheuse f, (eccl) visitation.
visiting ['vizitiŋ] a en (termes de) visite; — card carte de visite f.
visitor ['vizitə] n visiteur, -euse, visite f, voyageur, -euse, estivant, -ante.
visor ['vaizə] n visière f.
vista ['vistə] n perspective f, percée f, échappée f.
visual ['vizjuəl] a visuel.
visualize ['vizjuəlaiz] vt se représenter, envisager.
vital ['vaitl] a vital, mortel, capital, essentiel; — statistics statistiques démographiques f pl, (fam) mensurations f pl.
vitality [vai'tæliti] n vitalité f, vigueur f.
vitamin ['vitəmin] n vitamine f.
vitiate ['viʃieit] vt vicier, corrompre.
vituperate [vi'tju:pəreit] vt injurier, vilipender.
vituperation [vi.tju:pə'reiʃən] n injures f pl.
vivacious [vi'veiʃəs] a vif, vivace.
vivacity [vi'væsiti] n vivacité f, animation f.
viva voce ['vaivə'vousi] an oral m; ad de vive voix.

Vivian ['viviən] Vivianne, Vivienne f.
vivid ['vivid] a vif, éclatant.
vividness ['vividnis] n éclat m.
vivify ['vivifai] vt vivifier, animer.
vivisect [,vivi'sekt] vt disséquer à vif.
vivisection [,vivi'sekʃən] n vivisection f.
vixen ['viksn] n renarde f, mégère f.
viz [viz] ad c'est à dire.
vocable ['voukəbl] n vocable m.
vocabulary [və'kæbjuləri] n vocabulaire m.
vocal ['voukəl] a vocal.
vocation [vou'keiʃən] n vocation f, carrière f.
vocational [vou'keiʃənl] a professionnel.
vociferate [vou'sifəreit] vti vociférer.
vociferation [vou,sifə'reiʃən] n vociferation f, clameurs f pl.
vogue [voug] n vogue f.
voice [vɔis] n voix f; vt exprimer, énoncer.
voiceless ['vɔislis] a aphone, muet.
void [vɔid] n vide m; a vide, vacant, dénué, non avenu.
volatile ['vɔlətail] a volatil, vif, gai, volage.
volcanic [vɔl'kænik] a volcanique.
volcano [vɔl'keinou] n volcan m.
volley ['vɔli] n volée f, décharge f, salve f; vi tirer à toute volée; vt reprendre de volée, lâcher.
volt [voult] n volte f, volt m.
volubility [,vɔlju'biliti] n volubilité f.
voluble ['vɔljubl] a volubile, facile, coulant.
volume ['vɔljum] n volume m, tome m, livre m.
voluminous [və'ljuːminəs] a volumineux, ample.
voluntary ['vɔləntəri] an volontaire mf; a spontané.
volunteer [,vɔlən'tiə] n volontaire m, homme de bonne volonté m; vt offrir spontanément; vi s'offrir, s'engager comme volontaire.
voluptuous [və'lʌptjuəs] a voluptueux.
voluptuousness [və'lʌptjuəsnis] n volupté f, sensualité f.
vomit ['vɔmit] vti vomir, rendre.
vomiting ['vɔmitiŋ] n vomissement m.
voracious [və'reiʃəs] a vorace.
voracity [və'ræsiti] n voracité f.
vortex ['vɔːteks] n tourbillon m.
vote [vout] n vote m, voix f; vti voter; vt proposer.
voter ['voutə] n votant m, électeur, -trice.
voting ['voutiŋ] n scrutin m; — paper bulletin de vote m.
vouch [vautʃ] vt attester, garantir; to — for répondre de.
voucher ['vautʃə] n garantie f, attestation f, reçu m, bon m.
vouchsafe [vautʃ'seif] vt daigner, accorder.

vow [vau] n serment m, vœu m; vt vouer, jurer.
vowel ['vauəl] n voyelle f.
voyage [vɔiidʒ] n voyage m (par eau).
vulgar ['vʌlgə] a vulgaire.
vulgarity [vʌl'gæriti] n vulgarité f.
vulgarization [,vʌlgərai'zeiʃən] n vulgarisation f.
vulgarize ['vʌlgəraiz] vt vulgariser.
vulnerability [,vʌlnərə'biliti] n vulnérabilité f.
vulnerable ['vʌlnərəbl] a vulnérable.
vulture ['vʌltʃə] n vautour m, charognard m.

W

wad [wɔd] n bourre f, liasse f, tampon m; vt (rem)bourrer, ouater.
waddle ['wɔdl] n dandinement m; vi marcher comme un canard, se dandiner.
wade [weid] vi patauger; vti passer à gué.
wadi ['wɔdi] n oued m.
wafer ['weifə] n oublie f, gaufrette f, hostie f, pain à cacheter m.
waffle ['wɔfl] n gaufre f, (fam) radotages m pl; vi parloter, radoter.
waft [wɑːft] n bouffée f, souffle m, coup d'aile m; vt glisser, porter; vi flotter.
wag [wæg] n hochement m, branlement m, mouvement m, farceur m; vt remuer, hocher, lever; vi se remuer, aller.
wage(s) ['weidʒ(iz)] n salaire m, gages m pl; — freeze n blocage m des salaires.
wager ['weidʒə] n pari m, gageure f; vt parier.
waggish ['wægiʃ] a facétieux, blagueur, fumiste.
waggishness ['wægiʃnis] n espièglerie f.
waggle ['wægl] vti remuer.
wagon ['wægən] n camion m, chariot m, fourgon m, wagon m, voiture f.
wagoner ['wægənə] n camionneur m, charretier m, roulier m.
wagtail ['wægteil] n bergeronnette f, hochequeue m.
waif [weif] n enfant abandonné m, épave f.
wail [weil] n lamentation f, plainte f; vi se lamenter, vagir.
wainscot ['weinskət] n boiserie f, lambris m; vt lambrisser.
waist [weist] n taille f, ceinture f.
waistband ['weistbænd] n ceinture f, ceinturon m.
waistcoat ['weiskout] n gilet m.
wait [weit] n attente f, embuscade f, battement m; pl chanteurs de Noël m pl; vti attendre; vi servir à table.
waiter ['weitə] n garçon m.
waiting-room ['weitiŋrum] n salle d'attente f.

waitress ['weitris] n serveuse f.
waitress l mademoiselle l

waive [weiv] vt écarter, renoncer à, lever.

wake [weik] n veillée f, sillage m; vi s'éveiller; vt réveiller.

wakeful ['weikful] a éveillé, vigilant.

wakefulness ['weikfulnis] n insomnie f, vigilance f.

waken ['weikən] vi s'éveiller, se réveiller; vt (r)éveiller.

Wales [weilz] n pays de Galles m.

walk [wɔːk] n (dé)marche f, promenade f, allée f, promenoir m; vi se promener, marcher, aller à pied; vt promener, faire à pied, faire marcher; to — in entrer; to — off vi s'en aller; vt emmener.

walker ['wɔːkə] n marcheur, -euse, piéton m, promeneur, -euse.

walking ['wɔːkiŋ] a ambulant; in marche f; — stick canne f.

walk-out ['wɔːkaut] n grève f (spontanée).

walk-over ['wɔːk'ouvə] n victoire f par forfait, jeu d'enfant m.

wall [wɔːl] n mur m, muraille f, paroi f.

wallet ['wɔlit] n porte-feuille m, besace f, sacoche f.

wallflower ['wɔːlflauə] n giroflée f; to be a — faire tapisserie.

wallop ['wɔləp] n coup vigoureux m; vt rosser, fesser.

walloping ['wɔləpiŋ] n rossée f, fessée f, raclée f.

wallow ['wɔlou] vi rouler, se vautrer, se baigner.

wallpaper ['wɔːlpeipə] n papier peint m, tenture f.

walnut ['wɔːlnʌt] n noix f; — tree noyer m.

walrus ['wɔːlrəs] n morse m.

waltz [wɔːls] n valse f; vi valser.

wan [wɔn] a blafard, pâle.

wand [wɔnd] n baguette f, bâton m.

wander ['wɔndə] vi errer, se perdre, divaguer; vt (par)courir.

wanderer ['wɔndərə] n voyageur, -euse, promeneur, -euse.

wandering ['wɔndəriŋ] a errant, vagabond, distrait, égaré; n vagabondage m; pl divagations f pl.

wane [wein] n déclin m; vi décliner, décroître.

wanness ['wɔnnis] n pâleur f, lividité f.

want [wɔnt] n manque m, défaut m, gêne f, besoin m; for — of faute de; vt manquer de, avoir besoin de, demander, réclamer.

wanted ['wɔntid] a on demande, recherché (par la police).

wanton ['wɔntən] n gourgandine f, femme impudique f; a joueur, capricieux, impudique, débauché, gratuit.

war [wɔː] n guerre f.

warble ['wɔːbl] n gazouillement m; vt gazouiller.

warbler ['wɔːblə] n fauvette f.

ward [wɔːd] n garde f, tutelle f, pupille mf, arrondissement m, division f, cellule f, salle f (d'hôpital); vt garder; to — off écarter, parer.

warden ['wɔːdn] n directeur m (d'une institution, d'une prison) f recteur m; gardien m, conservateur m; game — garde-chasse m.

warder ['wɔːdə] n gardien m.

wardrobe ['wɔːdroub] n armoire f, garde-robe f.

wardroom ['wɔːdrum] n carré des officiers m.

ware [wɛə] n vaisselle f; pl marchandises f pl.

warehouse ['wɛəhaus] n entrepôt m, magasin m; vt entreposer, emmagasiner.

warfare ['wɔːfɛə] n guerre f.

wariness ['wɛərinis] n prudence méfiance f.

warlike ['wɔːlaik] a belliqueux.

warm [wɔːm] a chaud, chaleureux, pimenté, vif, échauffé, au chaud; vt (ré)chauffer; vi se (ré)chauffer, s'animer, s'échauffer.

warming ['wɔːmiŋ] n chauffage m.

warming-pan ['wɔːmiŋpæn] n bassinoire f.

warmth [wɔːmθ] n chaleur f, ardeur f.

warn [wɔːn] vt avertir, mettre en garde, prévenir.

warning ['wɔːniŋ] n avertissement m, congé m.

warp [wɔːp] n chaîne f, corde f, (wood) jeu m, gauchissement m, dépôt m; vt ourdir, remorquer, jouer, gauchir, fausser; vi gauchir, se voiler, se déformer.

warrant ['wɔrənt] n autorité f, garantie f, bon m, brevet m, mandat m (d'amener), pouvoir m; vt autoriser, garantir, justifier.

warrantable ['wɔrəntəbl] a justifiable.

warrantor ['wɔrəntɔː] n garant m, répondant m.

warren ['wɔrin] n garenne f.

warrior ['wɔriə] n guerrier m, soldat m; a martial, guerrier.

wart [wɔːt] n verrue f.

wart-hog ['wɔːthɔg] n phacochère m.

wary ['wɛəri] a prudent, méfiant, avisé.

wash [wɔʃ] n lavage m, lessive f, lavasse f, lotion f, remous m, sillage m, couche f, lavis m; vt laver, blanchir, badigeonner; vi se laver; to — away emporter; to — down arroser, laver à grande eau; to — out rincer, passer l'éponge sur, supprimer; to — up faire la vaisselle.

washable ['wɔʃəbl] a lavable.

wash-basin ['wɔʃ͵beisn] n cuvette f.

washed-out ['wɔʃt'aut] a (fam) lessivé; délavé, (fam) flapi.

washer ['wɔʃə] n laveur, -euse, rondelle f; —-up plongeur m.

washerwoman ['wɔʃə,wumən] n blanchisseuse f, lavandière f.

wash-house ['wɔʃhaus] n buanderie f, lavoir m.

washing ['wɔʃiŋ] n lavage m, linge m, vaisselle f, lessive f, blanchissage m.

wash-out ['wɔʃaut] n fiasco m, four m, débâcle f, raté(e).

washstand ['wɔʃstænd] n lavabo m.

washy ['wɔʃi] a insipide, fade.

wasp [wɔsp] n guêpe f; —'s nest guêpier m; **mason** — guêpe maçonne f.

waspish ['wɔspiʃ] a venimeux, méchant, de guêpe.

waste [weist] n désert m, usure f, déchets m pl, gaspillage m, perte f; a inculte, désert, de rebut; v. gaspiller, épuiser, perdre, rater, gâcher; vi s'user, se perdre, s'épuiser.

wasteful ['weistful] a ruineux, prodigue, gaspilleur.

waste-paper basket [weist'peipə-,baːskit] n corbeille à papier f.

waster ['weistə] n vaurien m, gaspilleur, -euse.

watch [wɔtʃ] n garde f, guet m, quart m, montre f; vt (sur)veiller, observer, regarder, guetter; vi prendre garde, veiller, faire attention.

watchdog ['wɔtʃdɔg] n chien m de garde; — **committee** comité f de surveillance.

watchful ['wɔtʃful] a attentif, vigilant.

watchfulness ['wɔtʃfulnis] n vigilance f.

watchmaker ['wɔtʃ,meikə] n horloger m.

watchman ['wɔtʃmən] n veilleur de nuit m, guetteur m.

watchword ['wɔtʃwəːd] n mot d'ordre m.

water ['wɔːtə] n eau f; vt arroser, abreuver; vi faire de l'eau, (eyes) se mouiller; to — **down** affaiblir, diluer, atténuer, frelater.

water bottle ['wɔːtə,bɔtl] n bidon m, gourde f; **hot**— bouillotte f.

water-closet ['wɔːtə,klɔzit] n cabinets m pl.

water-color ['wɔːtə,kʌlə] n aquarelle f.

watercress ['wɔːtəkres] n cresson m.

waterfall ['wɔːtəfɔːl] n cascade f.

watering ['wɔːtəriŋ] n arrosage m, dilution f.

watering-can ['wɔːtəriŋkæn] n arrosoir m.

watering-place ['wɔːtəriŋpleis] n abreuvoir m, ville d'eau f, plage f.

water-lily ['wɔːtə,lili] n nénuphar m.

waterline ['wɔːtəlain] n ligne de flottaison f.

waterlogged ['wɔːtəlɔgd] a plein d'eau, détrempé.

watermark ['wɔːtəmaːk] n filigrane m.

water-melon ['wɔːtə'melən] n pastèque f.

water-pipe ['wɔːtəpaip] n conduite f d'eau.

water-power ['wɔːtə,pauə] n force hydraulique f.

waterproof ['wɔːtəpruːf] an imperméable m.

watershed ['wɔːtəʃed] n ligne de partage des eaux f.

waterskiing ['wɔːtə'skiːiŋ] n ski nautique m.

waterspout ['wɔːtəspaut] n trombe f.

watertight ['wɔːtətait] a étanche.

waterway ['wɔːtəwei] n voie navigable f.

waterworks ['wɔːtəwəːks] n pl canalisations f pl, usine hydraulique f.

watery ['wɔːtəri] a aqueux, humide, dilué, déteint, chargé de pluie, insipide.

wattle ['wɔtl] n claie f, fanon m, barbe f.

wave [weiv] n vague f, ondulation f, (radio) onde f, signe m; vt brandir, agiter; vti onduler, ondoyer; vi s'agiter, flotter, faire signe (de la main).

wavelength ['weivleŋθ] n longueur f d'onde.

waver ['weivə] vi hésiter, défaillir, fléchir, vaciller, trembler.

wavy ['weivi] a ondulé, onduleux, tremblé.

wax [wæks] n cire f, (cobbler's) poix f; vt cirer, encaustiquer; vi croître, devenir.

waxwork ['wækswəːk] n figure de cire f, modelage en cire m; pl musée des figures de cire m.

waxy ['wæksi] a de cire, cireux, plastique.

way [wei] n chemin m, voie f, distance f, côté m, sens m, habitude f, manière f, point de vue m, état m; by the — à propos; by — of par manière de, en guise de; this — par ici; under — en train; out of the — insolite, écarté.

wayfarer ['wei,fɛərə] n voyageur, -euse.

waylay [wei'lei] vt dresser un guet-apens à.

way-out ['wei'aut] n sortie f, échappatoire f.

wayside ['weisaid] n bord m de route, bas côté m; a du bord de la route.

way train ['wei,trein] n train m omnibus.

wayward ['weiwəd] a entêté, capricieux.

waywardness ['weiwədnis] n humeur fantasque f.

we [wiː] pn nous.

weak [wiːk] a faible, chétif, léger, doux.

weaken ['wiːkən] vt affaiblir; vi s'affaiblir, fléchir.

weakish ['wiːkiʃ] a faiblard.

weakness ['wi:knis] n faiblesse f, faible m.
weal [wi:l] n bien m, zébrure f.
wealth [welθ] n richesse(s) f (pl), profusion f.
wealthy ['welθi] a riche.
wean [wi:n] vt sevrer, guérir.
weaning ['wi:niŋ] n sevrage m.
weapon ['wepən] n arme f.
wear [wɛə] n usage m, usure f; vt porter, mettre, user; vi s'user, tirer.
weariness ['wiərinis] n fatigue f, lassitude f.
wearisome ['wiərisəm] a ennuyeux, fastidieux.
weary ['wiəri] a fatigué, assommant; vt ennuyer, fatiguer; vi s'ennuyer, languir.
weasel ['wi:zl] n belette f.
weather ['weðə] n temps m; vt exposer aux intempéries, échapper à, survivre à, (cape) doubler.
weather-beaten ['weðə,bi:tn] a battu par la tempête, hâlé.
weather-bound ['weðəbaund] a retenu par le mauvais temps.
weathercock ['weðəkɔk] n girouette f.
weathered ['weðəd] a décoloré, rongé, patiné.
weather forecast ['weðə'fɔ:ka:st] n bulletin météorologique m.
weather station ['weðə'steiʃən] n station météorologique f.
weave [wi:v] vt tisser, tramer.
weaver ['wi:və] n tisserand m.
weaving ['wi:viŋ] n tissage m.
web [web] n tissu m, toile f.
webbing ['webiŋ] n sangles f pl, ceinture f.
web-footed ['web,futid] a palmé.
wed [wed] vt marier, se marier avec, épouser.
wedded ['wedid] a conjugal, marié.
wedding ['wediŋ] n mariage m, noce(s) f (pl).
wedding breakfast ['wediŋ'brekfəst] n repas de noces m.
wedge [wedʒ] n coin m, cale f, part f; vt coincer, presser, caler.
wedlock ['wedlɔk] n (état m de) mariage m, vie conjugale f.
Wednesday ['wenzdi] n mercredi m.
wee [wi:] a tout petit; vi faire pipi.
weed [wi:d] n mauvaise herbe f, tabac m; vt sarcler; to — out trier, éliminer.
weeds [wi:dz] n pl deuil de veuve m.
week [wi:k] n semaine f; today — d'aujourd'hui en huit.
weekday ['wi:kdei] n jour m de semaine.
weekend ['wi:k'end] n weekend m.
weekly ['wi:kli] a hebdomadaire; ad tous les huit jours.
weep [wi:p] vi pleurer, suinter.
weeping willow ['wi:piŋ'wilou] n saule pleureur m.
weft [weft] n trame f.
weigh [wei] vt peser; vi (anchor)

lever, calculer; to — down courber, accabler.
weight [weit] n poids m, pesanteur f, gravité f.
weighty ['weiti] a pesant, de poids, puissant.
weir [wiə] n barrage m.
weird [wiəd] a fantastique, bizarre, mystérieux.
welcome ['welkəm] n bienvenue f, accueil m; a bienvenu, acceptable; vt (bien) accueillir, souhaiter la bienvenue à.
weld [weld] vt souder, unir.
welding ['weldiŋ] n soudure f, soudage m.
welfare ['welfɛə] n bien-être m, bonheur m.
well [wel] n puits m, source f, fontaine f, cage d'escalier f, godet m; vi jaillir, sourdre; a bien portant; ad bien; — enough pas mal; all very — bel et bien; excl eh bien!
wellbeing ['wel'bi:iŋ] n bien-être m.
well-bred ['wel'bred] a bien élevé, (horse) racé.
well-built ['wel'bilt] a bien bâti.
well-done ['wel'dʌn] a bien fait, (cook) bien cuit; excl bravo!
well-meaning ['wel'mi:niŋ] a bien intentionné.
well-off ['wel'ɔf] a cossu, à l'aise.
Welsh [welʃ] an gallois m.
Welshman ['welʃmən] n Gallois(e) mf.
welter ['weltə] n confusion f, fatras m; vi baigner, se vautrer.
wen [wen] n loupe f, goitre m.
wench [wentʃ] n fille f, gaillarde f.
went [went] pt of go.
wept [wept] pt pp of weep.
west [west] n ouest m, occident m; a à (de, vers) l'ouest, ouest, occidental.
western ['westən] a see west.
westward ['westwəd] ad vers l'ouest.
wet [wet] n humidité f, pluie f; a humide, mouillé, trempé; — blanket rabat-joie m; vt mouiller, humecter.
wet-nurse ['wetnə:s] n nourrice f.
wetting ['wetiŋ] n douche f; to get a — se faire tremper.
whack [wæk] n coup de bâton m, essai m, part f; vt bâtonner, rosser écraser; excl vlan!
whacking ['wækiŋ] n rossée f, raclée f.
whale [weil] n baleine f.
whaleboat ['weilbout] n baleinière f.
whalebone ['weilboun] n fanon m, baleine f.
wharf [wɔ:f] n quai m.
what [wɔt] rel pn ce qui, ce que, ce dont; inter pn qu'est-ce qui? qu'est ce que?, que?, quoi? combien?; a inter quel quel(s)? quelle(s); excl quoi! comment!
what(so)ever [,wɔt(sou)'evə] pn tout ce qui, tout ce que, quoi qui, quoi

que, n'importe quoi; *a* quel que, quelque ... qui (que), quelconque.

wheat [wi:t] *n* blé m, froment m.

wheatear ['wi:tiər] *n* traquet m.

wheedle ['wi:dl] *vt* cajoler, engager; to — out of soutirer par cajolerie.

wheedler ['wi:dlə] *n* enjôleur, -euse.

wheel [wi:l] *n* roue f, tour m, cercle m, vélo m; *vt* rouler, tourner; *vi* tournoyer; to — around se retourner, faire volte-face, demi-tour.

wheelbarrow ['wi:l,bærou] *n* brouette f.

wheelwright ['wi:lrait] *n* charron m.

wheeze [wi:z] *n* respiration asthmatique f; *vi* respirer péniblement.

wheezing ['wi:ziŋ] *n* sifflement m, râle m.

wheezy ['wi:zi] *a* asthmatique, poussif.

whelp [welp] *n* jeune chien etc, petit m, drôle m; *vi* mettre bas.

when [wen] *cj* quand, lorsque, où, que; *inter ad* quand?

whence [wens] *ad* d'où.

whenever [wen'evə] *cj* toutes les fois que.

where [wɛə] *ad* où, là où, (à) l'endroit où.

whereabouts ['wɛərəbauts] *ad* où (donc); *n* lieu m où on est; his — où il est.

whereas [wɛər'æz] *cj* vu que, tandis que, alors que.

whereby [wɛə'bai] *ad* par quoi? par lequel.

wherefore ['wɛəfɔ:] *ad* en raison de quoi, donc, pourquoi.

wherein [wɛər'in] *ad* en quoi, où.

whereupon [,wɛərə'pɔn] *ad* sur quoi.

wherever [wɛər'evə] *ad* partout où, où que.

wherewithal ['wɛəwi'ðɔ:l] *n* moyen(s) de quoi m (pl).

whet [wet] *vt* aiguiser, repasser, affiler, exciter.

whether ['weðə] *cj* si; — ... or soit (que) ... soit (que).

whetstone ['wetstoun] *n* pierre à aiguiser f.

whey [wei] *n* petit lait m.

which [witʃ] *a* quel(s), quelle(s); *rel pn* qui, que, lequel, laquelle, lesquels, lesquelles, ce qui, ce que, ce dont; *inter pn* lequel etc.

whichever [witʃ'evə] *rel pn* celui qui, celui que, n'importe lequel; *a* que que, quelque ... que, n'importe quel.

whiff [wif] *n* bouffée f.

while [wail] *n* temps m, instant m; *cj* pendant que, tandis que, tout en; once in a — à l'occasion; to — away passer, tuer, tromper.

whim [wim] *n* caprice m, toquade f, fantaisie f.

whimper ['wimpə] *n* geignement m, pleurnichement m; *vi* geindre, pleurnicher.

whimsical ['wimzikəl] *a* fantasque, bizarre.

whimsicality [,wimzi'kæliti] *n* bizarrerie f, humeur f fantasque.

whine [wain] *n* gémissement m, jérémiade f; *vi* gémir, pleurnicher, se plaindre.

whinny ['wini] *n* hennissement m; *vi* hennir.

whip [wip] *n* fouet m, cravache f, cocher m, piqueur m, chef de file m, convocation urgente f; *vti* fouetter; *vt* battre; to — off enlever vivement; to — around se retourner brusquement, faire un tête à queue; to — up fouetter, activer.

whipcord ['wipkɔ:d] *n* corde f.

whiphand ['wip'hænd] *n* haute main f, avantage m.

whiplash ['wip'læʃ] *n* mèche de fouet f.

whipping ['wipiŋ] *n* fouettée f; to give a — to donner le fouet à.

whir(r) [wə:] *n* bourdonnement m, battement d'ailes m, ronronnement m, ronflement m; *vi* bourdonner, ronfler, ronronner.

whirl [wə:l] *n* tourbillon m, tournoiement m; to be in a — avoir la tête à l'envers; *vi* tournoyer, tourbillonner, pirouetter, tourner, virevolter.

whirlpool ['wə:lpu:l] *n* tourbillon m, remous m.

whirlwind ['wə:lwind] *n* trombe f, tourbillon m.

whisk [wisk] *n* fouet m (à crème), frétillement m; plumeau m, épousette f; *vt* fouetter, battre, remuer; to — away enlever vivement, escamoter, chasser.

whisker(s) ['wiskə(z)] *n* (of cat) moustache(s) f (pl), favoris m pl.

whisper ['wispə] *n* murmure m, chuchotement m, bruissement m; *vti* murmurer, chuchoter.

whistle ['wisl] *n* sifflet m, sifflement m; *vt* siffler; to — for siffler.

whistler ['wislə] *n* siffleur, -euse.

white [wait] *a* blanc, à blanc; *n* blanc m; — heat incandescence f; — caps moutons m pl; — hot chauffé à blanc; — lead céruse f; — paper rapport ministériel m; — slavery traite des blanches f.

whiten ['waitn] *vt* blanchir; *vi* pâlir.

whiteness ['waitnis] *n* blancheur f, pâleur f.

whitening ['waitniŋ] *n* blanchiment m, blanchissement m.

whitewash ['waitwɔʃ] *n* lait de chaux m, badigeon m, poudre aux yeux f; *vt* blanchir, badigeonner en blanc.

whither ['wiðə] *ad* où, là où.

whiting ['waitiŋ] *n* merlan m.

whitish ['waitiʃ] *a* blanchâtre.

whitlow ['witlou] *n* panaris m, mal blanc m.

Whitsun ['witsn] *n* Pentecôte f.

whistle ['witl] *vt* (dé)couper, amenuiser, amincir, diminuer, rògner.

whizz [wiz] *n* sifflement *m*; *vi* siffler; to — along filer à toute vitesse.

who [hu:] *rel pn* qui, lequel *etc*; *inter pn* qui? qui est-ce qui? quel?

who(so)ever [,hu:(sou)'evə] *pn* quiconque, toute personne qui.

whole [houl] *n* tout *m*, ensemble *m*, totalité *f*; on the — en somme, à tout prendre, dans l'ensemble; *a* tout, entier, complet, intégral, intact.

wholeheartedly ['houl'ha:tidli] *ad* de grand (tout) cœur.

wholeheartedness ['houl'ha:tidnis] *n* cordialité *f*, ardeur *f*, ferveur *f*.

wholesale ['houlseil] *n* vente en gros *f*; *a* général, en masse; *ad* en gros.

wholesome ['houlsəm] *a* salubre, sain, salutaire.

wholesomeness ['houlsəmnis] *n* santé *f*, salubrité *f*.

wholly ['houlli] *ad* sans réserve, intégralement, entièrement, tout à fait.

whom [hu:m] *rel pn* que, lequel *etc*; *inter pn* qui? qui est-ce que?

whoop [hu:p] *vi* huer.

whooping-cough ['hu:piŋkɔf] *n* coqueluche *f*.

whore [hɔ:] *n* prostituée *f*.

whose [hu:z] *rel pn* dont, de qui, duquel *etc*; *poss pn* à qui? de qui?

why [wai] *nm ad* pourquoi; *excl* allons! mais! tiens! voyons!

wick [wik] *n* mèche *f*.

wicked ['wikid] *a* méchant, vicieux, pervers, inique.

wickedly ['wikidli] *ad* méchamment.

wickedness ['wikidnis] *n* méchanceté *f*.

wicker ['wikə] *n* osier *m*.

wicket ['wikit] *n* guichet *m*, tourniquet *m*, barrière *f*, portillon *m*.

wide [waid] *a* large, vaste, (tout) grand; — of *prep* loin de, au large de.

wide awake ['waidə'weik] *a* bien éveillé, (*fam*) déluré.

widely ['waidli] *ad* grandement, très, largement.

widen ['waidn] *vt* élargir, étendre; *vi* s'élargir.

widening ['waidniŋ] *n* élargissement *m*, extension *f*.

widespread ['waidspred] *a* très répandu.

widow ['widou] *n* veuve *f*.

widowed ['widoud] *a* (devenu(e)) veuf, veuve.

widower ['widouə] *n* veuf *m*.

width [widθ] *n* largeur *f*.

wield [wi:ld] *vt* (de)manier, tenir, exercer.

wife [waif] *n* femme *f*, épouse *f*.

wig [wig] *n* perruque *f*.

wild [waild] *a* sauvage, fou, égaré, violent, farouche, déréglé.

wilderness ['wildənis] *n* déser. *m*, pays inculte *m*.

wildfire ['waild,faiə] *n* feu grégeois *m*, (*fig*) poudre *f*; like — comme une traînée de poudre.

wildly ['waildli] *ad* sauvagement, à l'aveugle, d'une façon extravagante.

wilds [waildz] *n pl* désert *m*, solitude *f*, brousse *f*, bled *m*, pays sauvage *m*.

wile [wail] *n* astuce *f*, ruse *f*.

will [wil] *n* volonté *f*, vouloir *m*, (*free*) arbitre *m*, testament *m*; *vt* vouloir, ordonner, léguer.

willful ['wilful] *a* volontaire, obstiné, prémédité.

willfulness ['wilfulnis] *n* opiniâtreté *f*, obstination *f*.

William ['wiljam] Guillaume *m*.

willing ['wiliŋ] *a* tout disposé, de bonne volonté.

willingly ['wiliŋli] *ad* volontiers.

willingness ['wiliŋnis] *n* empressement *m*, bonne volonté *f*.

will-o'-the-wisp ['wiləðə'wisp] *n* feu follet *m*, chimère *f*.

willow ['wilou] *n* saule *m*.

willy-nilly ['wili'nili] *ad* bon gré mal gré.

wilt [wilt] *vi* dépérir, se flétrir, se dégonfler.

wily ['waili] *a* retors, rusé.

win [win] *vt* gagner, remporter, vaincre; to — over gagner.

wince [wins] *n* haut-le-corps *m*, tressaillement *m*; *vi* tressaillir, broncher.

winch [wintʃ] *n* treuil *m*, manivelle *f*.

wind [wind] *n* vent *m*, instruments à vent *m pl*, souffle *m*, haleine *f*; to have the — up avoir la trouille; *vt* essouffler.

wind [waind] *vt* enrouler, remonter, sonner; *vi* serpenter, tourner, s'enrouler; to — up remonter, liquider, régler.

windbag ['windbæg] *n* moulin à paroles *m*.

winded ['windid] *a* essoufflé, hors d'haleine.

windfall ['windfɔ:l] *n* aubaine *f*, fruit tombé *m*.

winding ['waindiŋ] *a* sinueux, tortueux, tournant; *n* enroulement *m*, cours sinueux *m*; *pl* méandres *m pl*, sinuosités *f pl*, lacets *m pl*.

winding-sheet ['waindiŋʃi:t] *n* linceul *m*.

winding-up ['waindiŋ'ʌp] *n* conclusion *f*, liquidation *f*, remontage *m*.

windlass ['windləs] *n* cabestan *m*, treuil *m*.

windmill ['winmil] *n* moulin à vent *m*.

window ['windou] *n* fenêtre *f*, croisée *f*, (*shop*) vitrine *f*; stained-glass — verrière *f*.

window-dressing ['windou,dresiŋ] *n* art de l'étalage *m*, trompe-l'œil *m*.

window fastening ['windou'fa:sniŋ] *n* espagnolette *f*.

window frame ['windou'freim] *n* châssis *m* de fenêtre.

window pane ['windoupein] n carreau m, vitre f, glace f.

window-shopping ['windou'ʃɔpiŋ] n lèche-vitrine m.

windscreen ['windskri:n] n paravent m, pare-brise m.

windshield ['windʃi:ld] n pare-brise m; — **wiper** n essuie-glace m.

windswept ['windswept] a (hair style) en coup de vent, (place) venteux.

windy ['windi] a venteux, balayé par le vent, agité, creux, verbeux, vide, qui a la frousse.

wine [wain] n vin m.

wine-merchant ['wain'mə:tʃənt] n négociant en vins m.

wine-press ['wainpres] n pressoir m.

wing [wiŋ] n aile f, essor m, vol m; vt donner des ailes à, empenner, blesser à l'aile.

winged [wiŋd] a ailé.

winger ['wiŋə] n ailier m.

wink [wiŋk] n clin d'œil m; vi cligner, clignoter, faire de l'œil (à at); to — at fermer les yeux sur.

winker ['wiŋkə] n (aut) clignotant m.

winner ['winə] n gagnant(e) mf, vainqueur m, grand succès m.

winning ['winiŋ] a gagnant, engageant, décisif; —**post** n poteau d'arrivée m.

winnow ['winou] vt vanner, trier.

winnower ['winouə] n vanneur, -euse, (machine) vanneuse f.

winsome ['winsəm] a charmant, séduisant.

winter ['wintə] n hiver m; vi passer l'hiver, hiverner.

wintry ['wintri] a d'hiver, hivernal, glacial.

wipe [waip] n coup de balai m, de torchon, d'éponge; vt balayer, essuyer; to — out effacer, liquider, anéantir.

wire ['waiə] n fil de fer m, dépêche f, télégramme m; vt grill(ag)er, rattacher avec du fil de fer; vti télégraphier.

wire-cutter ['waiə.kʌtə] n cisailles f pl.

wire-haired ['waiəhɛəd] a à poil rêche.

wireless ['waiəlis] n radio f, télégraphie sans fil f; vt envoyer par la radio; vi envoyer un sans-fil; a sans-fil.

wire-netting ['waiə'netiŋ] n treillis (métallique) m.

wire-puller ['waiə.pulə] n combinard m, intrigant(e) mf.

wire-pulling ['waiə.puliŋ] n manipulation f, intrigues f pl, manigances f pl.

wiry ['waiəri] a tout nerfs, sec, nerveux, en fil de fer.

wisdom ['wizdəm] n sagesse f, prudence f.

wise [waiz] n manière f; a sage,

savant, prudent, informé, averti.

wiseacre ['waiz.eikə] n gros bêta m, faux sage m.

wisecrack ['waizkræk] n bon mot m; vi faire de l'esprit.

wish [wiʃ] n souhait m, désir m, vœu m; vt souhaiter, désirer, vouloir.

wishful ['wiʃful] a désireux, d'envie; — **thinking** optimisme béat m.

wisp [wisp] n bouchon m (de paille), petit bout m, mèche folle f, trainée f (de fumée).

wistful ['wistful] a pensif, plein de regret, insatisfait, d'envie.

wistfully ['wistfuli] ad d'un air pensif, avec envie.

wit [wit] n esprit m, homme d'esprit m (de ressource); to — à savoir.

witch [witʃ] n sorcière f, ensorceleuse f; vt ensorceler.

witchcraft ['witʃkra:ft] n sorcellerie f, magie noire f.

witch-doctor ['witʃ.dɔktə] n sorcier m.

with [wið] prep avec, à, au, à la, aux, chez, auprès de, envers, pour ce qui est de; to be — it être dans le vent.

withal [wi'ðɔ:l] ad avec cela, d'ailleurs, en même temps.

withdraw [wið'drɔ:] vt (re)tirer, reprendre, annuler, soustraire; vi se retirer, se replier, se rétracter.

withdrawal [wið'drɔ:əl] n retrait m, retraite f, rétraction f, repliement m, rappel m.

wither ['wiðə] vt dessécher, flétrir; vi se flétrir, se faner, dépérir.

withhold [wið'hould] vt retenir, refuser, cacher.

within [wi'ðin] prep dans, en dedans de, à l'intérieur de, en, entre, en moins de, à . . . près; ad au (en) dedans, à l'intérieur.

without [wi'ðaut] prep sans, hors de, en (au) dehors de; ad en (au) dehors, à l'extérieur.

withstand [wið'stænd] vt résister à, soutenir.

witness ['witnis] n témoin m, témoignage m; vi témoigner; vt attester, certifier, assister à, être témoin de.

witness-box ['witnis.bɔks] n banc m, barre des témoins f.

witticism ['witisizəm] n mot (trait m) d'esprit m, bon mot m.

wittingly ['witiŋli] ad à dessein, sciemment.

witty ['witi] a spirituel.

wizard ['wizəd] n magicien m, sorcier m, escamoteur m.

wizened ['wiznd] a ratatiné, desséché.

wobble ['wɔbl] n vacillation f, dandinement m; vi aller de travers, vaciller, trembler, branler, tituber, zigzaguer.

woe [wou] n malheur m.

woebegone ['woubi.gɔn] a lamentable, désolé.

woeful ['wouful] *a* triste, 'atroce, déplorable, affligé.

wold [would] *n* lande *f.*

wolf [wulf] *n* loup *m;* — **whistle** (*fam*) sifflement admiratif *m.*

wolf-cub ['wulfkʌb] *n* louveteau *m.*

woman ['wumən] *n* femme *f.*

womanhood ['wumənhud] *n* âge de femme *m,* fémininité *f.*

womanish ['wuməniʃ] *a* efféminé.

womanly ['wumənli] *a* féminin, de femme.

womb [wu:m] *n* matrice *f,* sein *m.*

won [wʌn] *pt pp of* **win.**

wonder ['wʌndə] *n* merveille *f,* prodige *m,* émerveillement *m;* no — rien d'étonnant, (*fam*) bien entendu; *vi* s'étonner; *vt* se demander; **to** — **at** admirer, s'étonner de.

wonderful ['wʌndəful] *a* étonnant, merveilleux.

wonderingly ['wʌndəriŋli] *ad* d'un air étonné.

wonderment ['wʌndəmənt] *n* étonnement *m,* émerveillement *m.*

wont [wount] *n* habitude *f;* **to be** — **to** avoid l'habitude de.

wonted ['wountid] *a* habituel, coutumier.

woo [wu:] *vt* courtiser, faire la cour à.

wood [wud] *n* bois *m,* forêt *f.*

woodcock ['wudkɔk] *n* bécasse *f.*

woodcut ['wudkʌt] *m* gravure sur bois *f.*

woodcutter ['wudkʌtə] *n* bûcheron *m,* graveur sur bois *m.*

wooden ['wudn] *a* de (en) bois.

woodland ['wudlənd] *n* pays boisé *m.*

woodman ['wudmən] *n* garde forestier *m,* bûcheron *m.*

woodpecker ['wud,pekə] *n* pic *m,* pivert *m.*

woodwork ['wudwə:k] *n* boisage *m,* boiserie *f,* menuiserie *f,* charpenterie *f.*

wool [wul] *n* laine *f.*

woolen ['wulin] *n* lainage *m; a* de laine, laineux.

woolly ['wuli] *a* de laine, laineux, ouaté, flou, cotonneux, (*fig*) confus, vaseux; *n* vêtement de laine *m,* pull-over *m.*

word [wə:d] *n* mot *m,* parole *f; vt* exprimer, rédiger, formuler, énoncer.

wordiness ['wə:dinis] *n* verbosité *f.*

wording ['wə:diŋ] *n* expression *f,* rédaction *f,* énoncé *m,* libellé *m.*

wordy ['wə:di] *a* verbeux, diffus, prolixe.

wore [wɔ:] *pt of* **wear.**

work [wə:k] *n* travail *m* (*pl* travaux), ouvrage *m,* œuvre *f; pl* usine *f,* atelier *m,* chantier *m,* mécanisme *m; vti* travailler; *vi* marcher, fonctionner, agir; *vt* faire travailler, faire marcher, actionner, exploiter, diriger, opérer, façonner; **to** — **out** *vt* élaborer, calculer; *vi* se monter (à **at**); **to** — **up** *vt* perfectionner, développer, préparer, exciter; *vi* se

développer, se préparer, remonter.

workable ['wə:kəbl] *a* faisable, réalisable, exploitable.

work-basket ['wə:k,bɑ:skit] *n* corbeille à ouvrage *f.*

workday ['wə:kdei] *n* jour ouvrable *m.*

worker ['wə:kə] *n* ouvrier, -ière.

workhouse ['wə:khaus] *n* asile *m,* hospice *m.*

working ['wə:kiŋ] *n* travail *m,* (*wine*) fermentation *f,* fonctionnement *m; a* — **class** classe ouvrière *f,* prolétariat *m;* — **majority** majorité suffisante *f.*

workmanlike ['wə:kmənlaik] *a* bien fait, pratique, en bon ouvrier.

workmanship ['wə:kmənʃip] *n* habileté manuelle *f,* fin travail *m,* façon *f.*

workshop ['wə:kʃɔp] *n* atelier *m,* usine *f.*

work-table ['wə:k,teibl] *n* table à ouvrage *f.*

world [wə:ld] *n* monde *m.*

worldliness ['wə:ldlinis] *n* mondanité *f.*

worldly ['wə:ldli] *a* de ce monde, matériel, du siècle.

worldwide ['wə:ldwaid] *a* mondial, universel.

worm [wə:m] *n* ver *m; vi* ramper, se glisser; **to** — **it out of s.o.** tirer les vers du nez à qn; **to** — **one's way into** se faufiler dans, s'insinuer dans.

worm-eaten ['wə:m,i:tn] *a* mangé des vers, vermoulu.

wormwood ['wə:mwud] *n* absinthe *f.*

worn [wɔ:n] *pp of* **wear.**

worn-out ['wɔ:n'aut] *a* épuisé, usé.

worried ['wʌrid] *a* soucieux.

worry ['wʌri] *n* souci *m,* tracas *m,* ennui *m; vt* tourmenter, inquiéter; *vi* se tourmenter, s'inquiéter.

worse [wə:s] *n* pis; *an* pire *m; ad* pis, moins bien, plus mal.

worsen ['wə:sn] *vti* empirer; *vt* aggraver; (*fam*) avoir le dessus sur; *vi* s'aggraver.

worship ['wə:ʃip] *n* culte *m,* adoration *f,* Honneur *m; vt* adorer, rendre un culte à.

worshipper ['wə:ʃipə] *n* fidèle *mf,* adorateur, -trice.

worst [wə:st] *n* le pis *m,* le pire *m,* le dessous *m,* désavantage *m; a* le pire; *ad* au pis, le pis, le plus mal; *vt* battre.

worsted ['wustid] *n* laine *f,* peigné *m.*

worth [wə:θ] *n* valeur *f,* mérite *m; a* qui vaut (la peine de), de la valeur de; **to be** — **valoir.**

worthiness ['wə:ðinis] *n* mérite *m,* justice *f.*

worthless ['wə:θlis] *a* sans valeur, bon à rien.

worthwhile ['wə:θ'wail] *a* de valeur, qui en vaut la peine.

worthy ['wə:ði] *a* digne, respectable; *n* personnage (notable) *m.*

would [wud] *part. of* **will.**

would-be ['wudbiː] *a* soi-disant, prétendu.

wound [waund] *pt pp of* **wind.**

wound [wuːnd] *n* blessure *f*, plaie *f*; *vt* blesser, atteindre.

wove, woven [wouv, 'wouvən] *pt pp of* **weave.**

wrack [ræk] *n* varech *m*.

wraith [reiθ] *n* fantôme *m*, apparition *f*.

wrangle ['ræŋgl] *n* dispute *f*; *vi* se disputer.

wrap [ræp] *vt* envelopper.

wrapped [ræpt] *a* enveloppé, absorbé.

wrapper ['ræpə] *n* bande *f*, couverture *f*, écharpe *f*.

wrath [rɔθ] *n* courroux *m*.

wreak [riːk] *vt* assouvir, décharger.

wreath [riːθ] *n* couronne *f*, volute *f*.

wreathe [riːð] *vt* couronner de fleurs, tresser, entourer, enrouler.

wreathed [riːðd] *a* enveloppé, baigné; — in smiles épanoui, rayonnant.

wreck [rek] *n* ruine *f*, naufrage *m*, épave(s) *f* (*pl*); *vt* perdre, ruiner, saboter, démolir, faire dérailler.

wreckage ['rekidʒ] *n* débris *m pl*; piece of — épave *f*.

wrecked [rekt] *a* jeté à la côte, naufragé, ruiné; to be — faire naufrage.

wrecker ['rekə] *n* naufrageur *m*, pilleur d'épaves *m*, dérailleur *m*, dépanneur *m* (*aut*), récupérateur *m* (d'épaves).

wrecking ['rekiŋ] *n* sauvetage *m*, renflouage *m* (de navire); — **train** carvée *f* de secours; — **lorry** dépanneuse *f*.

wren [ren] *n* roitelet *m*.

wrench [rentʃ] *n* torsion *f*, tour *m*, secousse *f*, coup *m*, clé *f*, entorse *f*; *vt* tordre, arracher; to — **open** ouvrir violemment, forcer.

wrest [rest] *vt* tourner, forcer, arracher.

wrestle ['resl] *n* lutte *f*; *vi* lutter; — **with** lutter contre, s'attaquer à.

wrestler ['reslə] *n* lutteur *m*.

wrestling ['resliŋ] *n* lutte *f*, catch *m*.

wretch [retʃ] *n* malheureux, -euse, scélérat *m*, pauvre diable *m*, triste sire *m*, fripon(ne).

wretched ['retʃid] *a* misérable, lamentable, minable.

wretchedness ['retʃidnis] *n* état *m* misérable, malheur *m*, misère *f*.

wriggle ['rigl] *n* tortillement *m*; *vt* tortiller, agiter; *vi* se tortiller, s'insinuer, se faufiler, frétiller.

wring [riŋ] *n* torsion *f*, pression *f*; *vt* presser, tordre, détourner, extorquer.

wrinkle ['riŋkl] *n* ride *f*, tuyau *m*; *vt* rider, froncer; *vi* se rider, se plisser.

wrist [rist] *n* poignet *m*.

wrist-watch ['ristwɔtʃ] *n* montre-bracelet *f*.

writ [rit] *n* écriture *f*, assignation *f*, mandat d'arrêt *m*.

write [rait] *vti* écrire; to — **down** noter, coucher par écrit, estimer, décrier; to — **off** réduire, défalquer, déduire, annuler; to — **up** rédiger, faire un éloge exagéré de, faire de la réclame pour, décrire, mettre à jour.

writer ['raitə] *n* écrivain *m*, auteur *m*, commis aux écritures *m*.

writhe [raið] *vi* se tordre, se crisper.

writing ['raitiŋ] *n* écriture *f*, œuvre *f*, écrit *m*, métier d'écrivain *m*.

writing-case ['raitiŋkeis] *n* nécessaire à écrire *m*.

writing-desk ['raitiŋdesk] *n* bureau *m*.

writing-pad ['raitiŋpæd] *n* sous-main *m*, bloc *m* de papier à lettres.

writing-paper ['raitiŋ.peipə] *n* papier à lettres *m*.

written ['ritn] *pp of* **write.**

wrong [rɔŋ] *n* tort *m*, mal *m*, injustice *f*, préjudice *m*; *a* dérangé, mauvais, faux, inexact; *ad* mal, à tort, de travers; *vt* léser, faire tort à; to be — se tromper, avoir tort.

wrongdoer ['rɔŋ'duːə] *n* malfaiteur, -trice, coupable *mf*.

wrongdoing ['rɔŋ'du(ː)iŋ] *n* méfaits *m pl*, mauvaises actions *f pl*.

wrongful ['rɔŋful] *a* injuste, faux.

wrongfully ['rɔŋfuli] *ad* à tort, de travers.

wrote [rout] *pt of* **write.**

wroth [rouθ] *a* en colère.

wrung [rʌŋ] *pt pp of* **wring.**

wrought [rɔːt] *pt pp of* **work;** *a* travaillé, forgé, excité.

wry [rai] *a* tors, tordu, de travers.

X

X-ray ['eks'rei] *n pl* rayons X *m pl*; *vt* radiographier, passer aux rayons X; — **treatment** radiothérapie.

Y

yacht [jɔt] *n* yacht *m*.

yam [jæm] *n* igname *f*.

yank [jæŋk] *vt* tirer brusquement; *n* coup sec *m*.

yap [jæp] *n* jappement *m*; *vi* japper.

yard [jɑːd] *n* mètre *m*, cour *f*, chantier *m*, vergue *f*; —**stick** mètre *m*, aune *f*.

yarn [jɑːn] *n* fil *m*, conte *m*, histoire *f*.

yaw [jɔː] *n* embardée *f*; *vi* embarder.

yawl [jɔːl] *n* yole *f*.

yawn [jɔːn] *n* bâillement *m*; *vi* bâiller, béer.

ye [jiː] *pn* vous.

yea [jei] *ad* oui, voire.

year [jəː] *n* an *m*, année *f*.

year-book ['jə:buk] n annuaire m.
yearling ['jə:liŋ] a d'un an.
yearly ['jə:li] a annuel; ad annuellement.
yearn [jə:n] vi aspirer (à after), soupirer (après after).
yearning ['jə:niŋ] n aspiration f, désir passionné m; a ardent.
yeast [ji:st] n levure f, levain m.
yell [jel] n hurlement m; vti hurler.
yellow ['jelou] an jaune m; a lâche.
yellowish ['jelouiʃ] a jaunâtre.
yellowness ['jelounis] n couleur jaune f.
yelp [jelp] n jappement m, glapissement m; vi japper, gémir, glapir.
yes [jes] n oui m; ad oui, si.
yes-man ['jesmæn] n qui dit amen à tout, béni-oui-oui m.
yesterday ['jestədi] n aa hier m; **the day before** — avant-hier.
yet [jet] ad encore, de plus, jusqu'ici, déjà; cj pourtant, tout de même.
yew [ju:] n if m.
yield [ji:ld] n produit m, rendement m, rapport m, revenu m, production f; vt rendre, rapporter, donner; vi céder; vi se rendre, succomber, plier, fléchir.
yielding ['ji:ldiŋ] a arrangeant, faible, mou.
yoke [jouk] n joug m, paire (de bœufs) f; vt atteler, lier, unir.
yolk [jouk] n jaune d'œuf m, suint m.
yonder ['jondə] ad là-bas.
yore [jo:] n of — d'antan, du temps jadis.
you [ju:] pn vous.
young [jʌŋ] n petit, jeune; a jeune.
younger ['jʌŋgə] a jeune, cadet, puîné.

youngish ['jʌŋiʃ] a jeunet.
youngster ['jʌŋstə] n enfant mf, gosse mf.
your [jo:] a votre, vos, ton, ta, tes.
yours [jo:z] pn vôtre(s), à vous; le, la, (les) vôtre(s); tien(s), tienne(s), à toi; le(s) tien(s), la tienne, les tiennes.
yourself, -selves [jo:'self, selvz] pn vous-même(s).
youth [ju:θ] n jeunesse f, jeune homme m.
youthful ['ju:θful] a jeune, juvénile.

Z

zeal [zi:l] n zèle m, empressement m.
zealous ['zeləs] a zélé, empressé.
zealously ['zeləsli] ad avec empressement.
zebra ['zi:brə] n zèbre m.
zebu ['zi:bu] n zébu m.
zenith ['zeniθ] n zénith m.
zero ['ziərou] n zéro m.
zest [zest] n piquant m, enthousiasme m, entrain m.
zigzag ['zigzæg] n zigzag m; vi zigzaguer.
zinc [ziŋk] n zinc m.
zip [zip] n sifflement m: — **fastener** fermeture éclair f.
zither ['ziðə] n cithare f.
zone [zoun] n zone f, ceinture f.
zoo [zu:] n jardin d'acclimatation m, jardin zoologique m.
zoological [.zouə'lɔdʒikəl] a zoologique.
zoologist [zou'ɔlədʒist] n zoologiste m.
zoology [zou'ɔlədʒi] n zoologie f.

Mesures et monnaies françaises
French measures, weights and money

MESURES DE LONGUEUR—LENGTH

1 millimètre = ·001 mètre   = ·0394 inch.
1 centimètre = ·01 mètre   = ·394 inch.
1 mètre   = 39·4 inches = *1 yard.
1 kilomètre = 1000 mètres = *1094 yards or ⅝ mile.
8 kilomètres = 5 miles.

MESURES DE SURFACE—AREA

1 are   = *120 square yards.
1 hectare = 100 ares = *2½ acres.

MESURES DE CAPACITÉ—CAPACITY (FLUIDS AND GRAIN)

1 centilitre = ·01 litre   = ·0176 pint.
1 litre   = *1¾ pints = ·2201 gallon.
1 hectolitre = 100 litres = *22 gallons = 2¾ bushels.
1 kilolitre = 1000 litres = *220 gallons = 27½ bushels.

MESURES DE POIDS—WEIGHTS

1 milligramme = ·001 gramme   = ·0154 grain.
1 centigramme = ·01 gramme   = ·1543 grain.
1 gramme   = 15·43 grains.
1 hectogramme = 100 grammes = *3½ oz.
1 livre   = 500 grammes = 1 lb. 1½ oz.
1 kilogramme = 1000 grammes = *2 lbs. 3 oz.
1 quintal   = 100 kilogrammes = *2 cwts.
1 tonne   = 1000 kilogrammes = *1 ton.

MESURES THERMOMÉTRIQUES—THE THERMOMETER

Point de congélation⎫ —Centigrade 0°
Freezing point   ⎬ —Fahrenheit 32°
Point d'ébullition   ⎫ —Centigrade 100°
Boiling point   ⎭ —Fahrenheit 212°

To convert Centigrade to Fahrenheit degrees, divide by 5, multiply by 9 and add 32.

MONNAIES—MONEY

100 centimes   = 1 franc.
* roughly.

Notes on French Grammar

A. THE ARTICLE

(i) The *definite article* is **le** (*m*), **la** (*f*), and **les** (*mf pl*). **Le** and **la** are shortened to **l'** before a vowel or H-mute.

(ii) The *indefinite article* is **un** (*m*), **une** (*f*).

(iii) When the prepositions **à** or **de** are used before the definite article they combine with **le** to form **au** and **du** respectively. They combine with **les** to form **aux** and **des**. They make no change before **la** or **l'**.

(iv) The partitive article, **du** (*m*), **de la** (*f*), **des** (*mf pl*), corresponds to the English *some* or *any* when the latter denotes an indefinite quantity. e.g. Have you any milk? **Avez-vous du lait?**

B. THE NOUN

(i) The plural is usually formed in **s**. Nouns ending in **s**, **x**, **z** have the same form in the plural. Those ending in **au**, and **eu** (except **bleu**) and some in **ou** (**bijou, caillou, hibou, genou, chou, pou, joujou**) form their plural in **x**. Those ending in **al** and **ail** form their plural in **aux**. **Aïeul, ciel, œil** become **aïeux, cieux** and **yeux**.

(ii) All French nouns are either masculine or feminine in gender. Most nouns ending in mute **e** are feminine, except those in **isme, age** (**image, rage, nage** are *f*) and **iste** (often either *m* or *f*). Most nouns ending in a consonant or a vowel other than mute **e** are masculine, but nouns ending in **tion** and **té** (**été, pâté** are *m*) are feminine.

(iii) The feminine is usually formed by adding **e** to the masculine. Nouns ending in **er** have a femine in **ère**, and those ending in **en, on** have a feminine in **enne, onne**. Nouns ending in **eur** have a feminine in **euse**, except those ending in **ateur** which give **atrice**. A few words ending in **e** have a feminine in **esse**.

C. THE ADJECTIVE

i) The plural is usually formed by adding an **s**. Adjectives ending in **s**, **x** are the same in the plural. Those ending in **al** have a plural in **aux**, but the following take an **s**: **bancal, fatal, final, glacial, natal, naval**.

ii) The feminine is usually formed by adding **e** to the masculine form. Adjectives ending in **f** change **f** into **ve**, and those ending in **x** change **x** into **se**. Adjectives ending in **er** have **ère** in the feminine form. To form the feminine of adjectives ending in **el, eil, en, et, on**, the final consonant must be doubled before adding an **e**.

(iii) Comparison of adjectives. The Comparative is formed regularly by adding **plus** to the ordinary form, and the Superlative by adding **le, la,** or **les,** as required, to the Comparative form. **Moins** (= less) is employed in the same way as **plus,** giving, for example, **moins long**—less long, **les moins récentes**—the least recent. Irregular forms are: **bon, meilleur, le meilleur; mauvais, pire** or **plus mauvais, le pire** or **le plus mauvais; petit, moindre** or **plus petit, le moindre** or **le plus petit.** 'Than' is always rendered by **que.** Other expressions of comparison are: **aussi ... que,** as ... as; **pas si ... que,** not so (as) ... as; **autant (de) ... que,** as much (or many) ... as; **pas tant (de) ... que,** not so much (or many) ... as.

(iv) The demonstrative adjectives 'this' and 'that' and their plural 'these' or 'those' are in French **ce, cet** (m), **cette** (f) and **ces** (pl). **Ce** is used with all masculine words except before those beginning with a vowel or an H-mute, in which case **cet** is used. The opposition between 'this' and 'that' may be emphasized by adding the suffix **-ci** or **-là** to the noun concerned. 'That of' is in French **celui** (f **celle,** pl **ceux, celles**) **de.** Expressions such as 'he who', 'the one which', 'those or they who' should be translated by **celui** (**celle, ceux, celles**) **qui.**

(v) Possessive adjectives.

my	**mon** (m)	**ma** (f)	**mes** (pl)
your	**ton**	**ta**	**tes**
his	**son**	**sa**	**ses**
our	**notre**	**notre**	**nos**
your	**votre**	**votre**	**vos**
their	**leur**	**leur**	**leurs**

All of these agree in gender with the following noun.

D. THE PRONOUN

I. (i) Unstressed forms.

	Nom.	Acc.	Dat.	Gen.
1st sing.	je	me	me	
2nd sing.	tu	te	te	
3rd sing.	il, elle	le, la (se)	lui, y	en
	Nom.	Acc.	Dat.	Gen.
1st plur.	nous	nous	nous	
2nd plur.	vous	vous	vous	
3rd plur.	ils, elles	les (se)	leur, y (se)	en

(i) **Tu** and **te** are normally used when speaking to one person who is a close relative or an intimate friend. They

481

are also used to any child or an animal. Otherwise the 2nd plural **vous** is normally used to address single persons. In this use it retains a plural verb, but its other agreements (with adjectives, participles etc.) are singular, provided it refers to a single person.

(ii) The forms **me, te, se, nous, vous,** se may be used in reflexive verbs, and also to denote mutual participation in an action. E.g. they looked at each other, **ils se regardaient.**

II. Stressed forms.

	Singular	*Plural*
1st Person	**moi**	**nous**
2nd Person	**toi**	**vous**
3rd Person m	**lui**	**eux**
f	**elle**	**elles**
Reflexive	**soi**	

(i) This form is used when the pronoun is governed by a preposition.

(ii) It is used where people are singled out or contrasted, i.e. for emphasis.

(iii) It is also used when a pronoun stands as the sole word in a sentence, stands as the antecedent of a relative, forms part of a double subject or object of a verb, is the complement of **être** or when it stands after **que** in comparative sentences.

III. When used together, personal pronouns are positioned according to the following scheme.

me	le	lui	y	en
te	la	leur		
nous	les			
vous				
se				

IV. Possessive pronouns.

	Singular	*Plural*
1st sing. m	**le mien**	**les miens**
f	**la mienne**	**les miennes**
2nd sing. m	**le tien**	**les tiens**
f	**la tienne**	**les tiennes**
3rd sing. m	**le sien**	**les siens**
f	**la sienne**	**les siennes**
1st plur.	**le (la) nôtre**	**les nôtres**
2nd plur.	**le (la) vôtre**	**les vôtres**
3rd plur.	**le (la) leur**	**les leurs**

E.g. I have lost my pen; lend me yours = **j'ai perdue ma plume, prêtez-moi la vôtre.**

V. Relative pronouns. 'Who' is translated by **qui**; 'whom' by **que** (or by **qui** after a preposition); 'whose' by **dont**; 'which' by **qui** (subject) or **que** (object). After a preposition 'which' is translated by **lequel** (*m*), **laquelle** (*f*), **lesquels** (*m pl*) and **lesquelles** (*f pl*). With the prepositions **à** and **de** the following contractions take place: **auquel** (but **à laquelle**), **auxquels, auxquelles; duquel** (but **de laquelle), desquels, desquelles.**

VI. Interrogative pronouns. 'Who' and 'whom' are both **qui**. 'What', when object, is **que** and when subject is **qu'est-ce qui**. When 'what' is used adjectivally it should be translated by **quel, quelle, quels, quelles.**

E. ADVERBS

Most French adverbs are formed by adding **ment** to the feminine form of the corresponding adjective. Adjectives ending in **ant** and **ent** have adverbial endings in **amment** and **emment** respectively.

Negative forms. 'Not' is **ne . . . pas,** 'nobody' **ne . . . personne,** 'nothing' **ne . . . rien** and 'never' is **ne . . . jamais.**

Examples. I do not know, **je ne sais pas.** I know nothing, **je ne sais rien.**

'Nobody and 'nothing' when subject are rendered by **personne ne . . ., rien ne . . .**

F. VERBS

I. Regular verbs.

There are three principal types of regular conjugation of French verbs, corresponding to the three infinitive endings: **-er, -ir, -re.** They provide patterns for conjugating large numbers of verbs which have one or other of these infinitive endings. As a convenient simplification, each part of a verb may be stated to consist of a basic stem and a characteristic ending. From the stem and ending of the present infinitive and of the present participle, all parts of a regular verb may be built up.

Examples. **parler, finir, vendre.**

Present infinitive	**parl/er**	**fin/ir**	**vend/re**
Present participle	**parl/ant**	**finiss/ant**	**vend/ant**
Past participle	stem+-é	stem+-i	stem+-u

483

Present indicative	stem+-e, stem+-is, stem+-s,
	-es, -e, -is, -it, -s, -,
	-ons, -ez, -issons, -ons, -ez,
	-ent -issez, -ent
	-issent

Imperative: 2nd singular, 1st plural and 2nd plural of present indicative, without subject pronouns. First conjugation drops final **s** of 2nd singular, except before **y, en.**

Imperfect: stem of present participle+-**ais**, -ais, -ait, -ions, -iez, -aient.

Past historic: stem+-**ai**, -**as**, stem+-**is**, -**is**, -a, -âmes, -âtes, -it, -îmes, -îtes, -èrent -irent

Future: infinitive+-**ai**, -**as**, -**a**, -**ons**, -**ez**, -**ont**. Third conjugation drops final e of infinitive.

Conditional: infinitive+-**ais**, -**ais**, -**ait**, -**ions**, -**iez**, -**aient**. Third conjugation drops final e of infinitive.

Present subjunctive: stem of present participle+ -**e**, -**es**, -**e**, -**ions**, -**iez**, -**ent**.

Imperfect subjunctive: remove final e from 2nd singular of past historic and add -**sse**, -**sses**, **ît**, -**ssions**, -**ssiez**, -**ssent**.

Compound tenses are formed with the auxiliary **avoir** and the past participle, except reflexive verbs and some common intransitive verbs (like **aller, arriver, devenir, partir, rester, retourner, sortir, tomber, venir** etc.) which are conjugated with **être**. The following scheme is applicable to all three conjugations.

Perfect: present indicative of **avoir** (or **être**)+past participle.

Pluperfect: imperfect of **avoir** (or **être**)+ past participle.

Future perfect: future of **avoir** (or **être**)+past participle.

Conditional perfect: conditional of **avoir** (or **être**)+ past participle.

Perfect infinitive: infinitive of **avoir** (or **être**)+ past participle.

Note on agreement. The French past participle always agrees with the noun to which it is either an attribute or an adjective. It agrees with the object of a verb conjugated with **avoir** only when the object comes before it. E.g. I loved that woman, **j'ai aimé cette femme**; the women I have loved, **les femmes que j'ai aimées.**

For the conjugation of the auxiliaries **avoir** and **être** consult the list of irregular verbs.

G. MISCELLANEOUS NOTES

(i) Verbs having a mute **e** or closed **é** in the last syllable but one of the present infinitive, change the mute **e** or closed **é** to open **è** before a mute syllable (except in the future and conditional tenses). E.g. **espérer, j'espère, il espérera, il espérerait.**

(ii) Verbs with infinitive endings in **-cer** have **ç** before endings in **a, o.** E.g. **commencer, je commençais, nous commençons.**

(iii) Verbs with infinitive endings in **-ger** have an additional **e** before endings in **a, o.** E.g. **manger, je mangeais, nous mangeons.**

(iv) Verbs ending in **-eler, -eter** double the **l** or **t** before a mute **e.** E.g. **appeler, j'appelle; jeter, je jette.** The following words do not obey this rule and take only **è: acheter, agneler, bégueter, celer, ciseler, congeler, corseter, crocheter, déceler, dégeler, démanteler, écarteler, fureter, geler, harceler, marteler, modeler, peler, racheter, receler, regeler.**

(v) Verbs with infinitive endings in **-yer** change **y** into **i** before a mute **e.** They require a **y** and an **i** in the first two persons plural of the imperfect indicative and of the present subjunctive. Verbs with infinitive endings in **-ayer** may keep the **y** or change it to **i** before a mute **e.** Verbs with infinitive endings in **-eyer** keep the **y** throughout the conjugation.

IRREGULAR VERBS

Order of principal tenses and essential parts of the French irregular verbs in most frequent use. (1) Present Participle; (2) Past Participle; (3) Present. Indicative; (4) Imperfect Indicative; (5) Preterite; (6) Future; (7) Present Subjunctive.

Prefixed verbs not included in this list follow the root verb, e.g., sourire—rire: abattre—battre.

acquérir (1) acquérant; (2) acquis; (3) acquiers, acquiers, acquiert, acquérons, acquérez, acquièrent; (4) acquérais; (5) acquis; (6) acquerrai; (7) acquière.

aller (1) allant; (2) allé; (3) vais, vas, va, allons, allez, vont; (4) allais; (5) allai; (6) irai; (7) aille.

asseoir (1) asseyant; (2) assis; (3) assieds, assieds, assied, asseyons, asseyez, asseyent; (4) asseyais; (5) assis; (6) assiérai or asseyerai; (7) asseye.

atteindre (1) atteignant; (2) atteint; (3) atteins, atteins, atteint, atteignons, atteignez, atteignent; (4) atteignais; (5) atteignis; (6) atteindrai; (7) atteigne.

avoir (1) ayant; (2) eu; (3) ai, as, a, avons, avez, ont; (4) avais; (5) eus; (6) aurai; (7) aie. *N.B.*—Imperative aie, ayons, ayez.

battre (1) battant; (2) battu; (3) bats, bats, bat, battons, battez, battent; (4) battais; (5) battis; (6) battrai; (7) batte.

boire (1) buvant; (2) bu; (3) bois, bois, boit, buvons, buvez, boivent; (4) buvais; (5) bus; (6) boirai; (7) boive.

bouillir (1) bouillant; (2) bouilli; (3) bous, bous, bout, bouillons, bouillez, bouillent; (4) bouillais; (5) bouillis; (6) bouillirai; (7) bouille.

conclure (1) concluant; (2) conclu; (3) conclus, conclus, conclut, concluons, concluez, concluent; (4) concluais; (5) conclus; (6) conclurai; (7) conclue.

conduire (1) conduisant; (2) conduit; (3) conduis, conduis, conduit, conduisons, conduisez, conduisent; (4) conduisais; (5) conduisis; (6) conduirai; (7) conduise.

connaître (1) connaissant; (2) connu; (3) connais, connais, connaît, connaissons, connaissez, connaissent; (4) connaissais; (5) connus; (6) connaîtrai; (7) connaisse.

coudre (1) cousant; (2) cousu; (3) couds, couds, coud, cousons, cousez, cousent; (4) cousais; (5) cousis; (6) coudrai; (7) couse.

courir (1) courant; (2) couru; (3) cours, cours, court, courons, courez, courent; (4) courais; (5) courus; (6) courrai; (7) coure.

couvrir (1) couvrant; (2) couvert; (3) couvre, couvres, couvre, couvrons, couvrez, couvrent; (4) couvrais; (5) couvris; (6) couvrirai; (7) couvre.

craindre (1) craignant; (2) craint; (3) crains, crains, craint, craignons, craignez, craignent; (4) craignais; (5) craignis; (6) craindrai; (7) craigne.

croire (1) croyant; (2) cru; (3) crois, crois, croit, croyons, croyez, croient; (4) croyais; (5) crus; (6) croirai; (7) croie.

croître (1) croissant; (2) crû, crue (*pl* crus, crues); (3) croîs, croîs, croît, croissons, croissez, croissent; (4) croissais; (5) crûs; (6) croîtrai; (7) croisse.

cueillir (1) cueillant; (2) cueilli; (3) cueille, cueilles, cueille, cueillons, cueillez, cueillent; (4) cueillais; (5) cueillis; (6) cueillerai; (7) cueille.

devoir (1) devant; (2) dû, due (*pl* dus, dues); (3) dois, dois,

doit, devons, devez, doivent; (4) devais; (5) dus; (6) devrai; (7) doive.

dire (1) disant; (2) dit; (3) dis, dis, dit, disons, dites, disent; (4) disais; (5) dis; (6) dirai; (7) dise.

dormir (1) dormant; (2) dormi; (3) dors, dors, dort, dormons, dormez, dorment; (4) dormais; (5) dormis; (6) dormirai; (7) dorme.

écrire (1) écrivant; (2) écrit; (3) écris, écris, écrit, écrivons, écrivez, écrivent; (4) écrivais; (5) écrivis; (6) écrirai; (7) écrive.

être (1) étant; (2) été; (3) suis, es, est, sommes, êtes, sont; (4) étais; (5) fus; (6) serai; (7) sois. *N.B.*—Imperative sois, soyons, soyez.

faire (1) faisant; (2) fait; (3) fais, fais, fait, faisons, faites, font; (4) faisais; (5) fis; (6) ferai; (7) fasse.

falloir (2) fallu; (3) faut; (4) fallait; (5) fallut; (6) faudra; (7) faille.

fuir (1) fuyant; (2) fui; (3) fuis, fuis, fuit, fuyons, fuyez, fuient; (4) fuyais; (5) fuis; (6) fuirai; (7) fuie.

joindre (1) joignant; (2) joint; (3) joins, joins, joint, joignons, joignez, joignent; (4) joignais; (5) joignis; (6) joindrai; (7) joigne.

lire (1) lisant; (2) lu; (3) lis, lis, lit, lisons, lisez, lisent; (4) lisais; (5) lus; (6) lirai; (7) lise.

luire (1) luisant; (2) lui; (3) luis, luis, luit, luisons, luisez, luisent; (4) luisais; (5) luisis; (6) luirai; (7) luise.

maudire (1) maudissant; (2) maudit; (3) maudis, maudis, maudit, maudissons, maudissez, maudissent; (4) maudissait; (5) maudis; (6) maudirai; (7) maudisse.

mentir (1) mentant; (2) menti; (3) mens, mens, ment, mentons, mentez, mentent; (4) mentais; (5) mentis; (6) mentirai; (7) mente.

mettre (1) mettant; (2) mis; (3) mets, mets, met, mettons, mettez, mettent; (4) mettais; (5) mis; (6) mettrai; (7) mette.

mourir (1) mourant; (2) mort; (3) meurs, meurs, meurt, mourons, mourez, meurent; (4) mourais; (5) mourus; (6) mourrai; (7) meure.

naître (1) naissant; (2) né; (3) nais, nais, naît, naissons, naissez, naissent; (4) naissais; (5) naquis; (6) naîtrai; (7) naisse.

offrir (1) offrant; (2) offert; (3) offre, offres, offre, offrons, offrez, offrent; (4) offrais; (5) offris; (6) offrirai; (7) offre.

partir (1) partant; (2) parti; (3) pars, pars, part, partons, partez, partent; (4) partais; (5) partis; (6) partirai; (7) parte.

plaire (1) plaisant; (2) plu; (3) plais, plais, plaît, plaisons, plaisez, plaisent; (4) plaisais; (5) plus; (6) plairai; (7) plaise.

pleuvoir (1) pleuvant; (2) plu; (3) pleut, pleuvent; (4) pleuvait; (5) plut; (6) pleuvra; (7) pleuve.

pourvoir (1) pourvoyant; (2) pourvu; (3) pourvois, pourvois, pourvoit, pourvoyons, pourvoyez, pourvoient; (4) pourvoyais; (5) pourvus; (6) pourvoirai; (7) pourvoie.

pouvoir (1) pouvant; (2) pu; (3) puis or peux, peux, peut, pouvons, pouvez, peuvent; (4) pouvais; (5) pus; (6) pourrai; (7) puisse.

prendre (1) prenant; (2) pris; (3) prends, prends, prend, prenons, prenez, prennent; (4) prenais; (5) pris; (6) prendrai; (7) prenne.

prévoir like voir. *N.B.*—(7) prévoirai.

recevoir (1) recevant; (2) reçu; (3) reçois, reçois, reçoit, recevons, recevez, reçoivent; (4) recevais; (5) reçus; (6) recevrai; (7) reçoive.

résoudre (1) résolvant; (2) résolu; (3) résous, résous, résout, résolvons, résolvez, résolvent; (4) résolvais; (5) résolus; (6) résoudrai; (7) résolve.

rire (1) riant; (2) ri; (3) ris, ris, rit, rions, riez, rient; (4) riais; (5) ris; (6) rirai; (7) rie.

savoir (1) sachant; (2) su; (3) sais, sais, sait, savons, savez, savent; (4) savais; (5) sus; (6) saurai; (7) sache. *N.B.*— Imperative sache, sachons, sachez.

servir (1) servant; (2) servi; (3) sers, sers, sert, servons, servez, servent; (4) servais; (5) servis; (6) servirai; (7) serve.

sortir (1) sortant; (2) sorti; (3) sors, sors, sort, sortons, sortez, sortent; (4) sortais; (5) sortis; (6) sortirai; (7) sorte.

souffrir (1) souffrant; (2) souffert; (3) souffre, souffres, souffre, souffrons, souffrez, souffrent; (4) souffrais; (5) souffris; (6) souffrirai; (7) souffre.

suffire (1) suffisant; (2) suffi; (3) suffis, suffis, suffit, suffisons, suffisez, suffisent; (4) suffisais; (5) suffis; (6) suffirai; (7) suffise.

suivre (1) suivant; (2) suivi; (3) suis, suis, suit, suivons, suivez, suivent; (4) suivais; (5) suivis; (6) suivrai; (7) suive.

taire (1) taisant; (2) tu; (3) tais, tais, tait, taisons, taisez, taisent; (4) taisais; (5) tus; (6) tairai; (7) taise.

tenir (1) tenant; (2) tenu; (3) tiens, tiens, tient, tenons, tenez, tiennent; (4) tenais; (5) tins; (6) tiendrai; (7) tienne.

vaincre (1) vainquant; (2) vaincu; (3) vaincs, vaincs, vainc, vainquons, vainquez, vainquent; (4) vainquais; (5) vainquis; (6) vaincrai; (7) vainque.

valoir (1) valant; (2) valu; (3) vaux, vaux, vaut, valons, valez, valent; (4) valais; (5) valus; (6) vaudrai; (7) vaille.

venir (1) venant; (2) venu; (3) viens, viens, vient, venons,

venez, viennent; (4) venais; (5) vins; (6) viendrai; (7) vienne.
vivre (1) vivant; (2) vécu; (3) vis, vis, vit, vivons, vivez,
vivent; (4) vivais; (5) vécus; (6) vivrai; (7) vive.
voir (1) voyant; (2) vu; (3) vois, vois, voit, voyons, voyez,
voient; (4) voyais; (5) vis; (6) verrai; (7) voie.
vouloir (1) voulant; (2) voulu; (3) veux, veux, veut,
voulons, voulez, veulent; (4) voulais; (5) voulus; (6)
voudrai; (7) veuille. *N.B.*—Imperative veuille, veuillons,
veuillez.

U.S. *and* U.K. *measures, weights and money*
Mesures et monnaies anglaises

LENGTH—MESURES DE LONGUEUR
Inch (in.) = 25 millimètres.
Foot (ft.) (12 in.) = 304 mm.
Yard (yd.) (3 ft.) = 914 mm. (approximativement 1 mètre).
Fathom (fthm.) (2 yds.) = 1 mètre 828 mm.
Mile (8 furlongs, 1760 yds.) = 1609 mètres
   (approximativement 1 kilomètre et demi).
Nautical mile, knot = 1853 mètres.
5 miles = 8 kilomètres.

AREA—MESURES DE SURFACE
Square inch = 6 centimètres carrés.
Square foot = 929 centimètres carrés.
Square yard = 0·8360 mètre carré.
Acre   = 4047 mètres carrés.

CAPACITY (FLUIDS AND GRAIN)—MESURES DE CAPACITÉ
Pint = 0·567 litre (approximativement ½ litre).
Quart (2 pints) = 1·135 litre.
Gallon (4 quarts) = 4·543   litres.
Peck (2 gallons) = 9·086 litres.
Bushel (8 gallons) = 36·348 litres.
Quarter (8 bushels) = 290·781 litres.

WEIGHTS (AVOIRDUPOIS)—MESURES DE POIDS
Ounce (oz.) = 28·35 grammes.
Pound (lb.—16 oz.) = 453·59 grammes.
Stone (st.—14 lb.) = 6 kilos 350 grammes.
Quarter (qr.—28 lb.) = 12·7 kilos.
Hundredweight (cwt.—112 lb.) = 50·8 kilos.
Ton (T.—20 cwts.) = 1016 kilos.

Freezing point ⎱ — Fahrenheit 32°
Point de congélation ⎰ — Centigrade 0°
Boiling point ⎱ — Fahrenheit 212°
Point d'ébullition ⎰ — Centigrade 100°

Pour convertir les mesures Fahrenheit en mesures Centigrade soustraire 32, multiplier par 5 et diviser par 9

MONEY—MONNAIES

USA

100 cents = 1 dollar

UK

A partir de 1971:
100 pence = 1 pound

Verbes forts et irréguliers anglais

PRÉSENT	PRÉTÉRIT	PARTICIPE PASSÉ
abide	abode	abode
arise	arose	arisen
awake	awoke, awaked	awaked, awoke
be	was	been
bear	bore	born(e)
beat	beat	beaten
become	became	become
befall	befell	befallen
begin	began	begun
behold	beheld	beheld
bend	bent	bent
bereave	bereft	bereft
beseech	besought	besought
bespeak	bespoke	bespoke(n)
bet	bet	bet
bid	bade, bid	bidden
bid	bid	bid
bind	bound	bound
bite	bit	bitten
bleed	bled	bled
blow	blew	blown
break	broke	broken
breed	bred	bred
bring	brought	brought
build	built	built
burn	burnt, burned	burnt, burned
burst	burst	burst
buy	bought	bought
cast	cast	cast
catch	caught	caught
chide	chid	chid(den)
choose	chose	chosen
cling	clung	clung
come	came	come

cost	cost	cost
creep	crept	crept
cut	cut	cut
deal	dealt	dealt
dig	dug	dug
do	did	done
draw	drew	drawn
dream	dreamt, dreamed	dreamt, dreamed
drink	drank	drunk
drive	drove	driven
dwell	dwelt	dwelt
eat	ate	eaten
fall	fell	fallen
feed	fed	fed
feel	felt	felt
fight	fought	fought
find	found	found
flee, fly	fled	fled
fling	flung	flung
fly	flew	flown
forbid	forbade	forbidden
forget	forgot	forgotten
forgive	forgave	forgiven
forsake	forsook	forsaken
freeze	froze	frozen
get	got	got
give	gave	given
go	went	gone
grind	ground	ground
grow	grew	grown
hang	hung	hung
have	had	had
hear	heard	heard
hew	hewed	hewn
hide	hid	hid(den)
hit	hit	hit
hold	held	held
hurt	hurt	hurt
keep	kept	kept
kneel	knelt	knelt
know	knew	known
lay	laid	laid
lead	led	led
lean	leaned, leant	leaned, leant
leap	leapt, leaped	leapt, leaped
learn	learned, learnt	learned, learnt
leave	left	left
lend	lent	lent
let	let	let
lie	lay	lain
light	lit	lit
lose	lost	lost
make	made	made
mean	meant	meant
meet	met	met
mow	mowed	mown
pay	paid	paid
put	put	put
quit	quit	quit

PRÉSENT	PRÉTÉRIT	PARTICIPE PASSÉ
read	read	read
rend	rent	rent
rid	rid	rid
ride	rode	ridden
ring	rang	rung
rise	rose	risen
run	ran	run
saw	sawed	sawn
say	said	said
see	saw	seen
seek	sought	sought
sell	sold	sold
send	sent	sent
set	set	set
sew	sewed	sewn
shake	shook	shaken
shed	shed	shed
shine	shone	shone
shoe	shod	shod
shoot	shot	shot
show	showed	shown
shrink	shrank	shrunk
shrive	shrove	shriven
shut	shut	shut
sing	sang, sung	sung
sink	sank, sunk	sunk
sit	sat	sat
slay	slew	slain
sleep	slept	slept
slide	slid	slid
sling	slung	slung
slink	slunk	slunk
slit	slit	slit
smell	smelled, smelt	smelled, smelt
smite	smote, smit	smitten, smit
sow	sowed	sown
speak	spoke	spoken
speed	sped	sped
spend	spent	spent
spill	spilt	spilt
spin	spun, span	spun
spit	spat, spit	spat, spit
split	split	split
spoil	spoiled, spoilt	spoiled, spoilt
spread	spread	spread
spring	sprang	sprung
stand	stood	stood
steal	stole	stolen
stick	stuck	stuck
sting	stung	stung
stink	stank, stunk	stunk
strew	strewed	strewn, strewed
stride	strode	stridden, strid
strike	struck	struck
string	strung	strung
strive	strove	striven
swear	swore	sworn

sweep	swept	swept
swell	swelled	swollen
swim	swam	swum
swing	swung	swung
take	took	taken
teach	taught	taught
tear	tore	torn
tell	told	told
think	thought	thought
thrive	throve	thriven
throw	threw	thrown
thrust	thrust	thrust
tread	trod	trodden
wake	woke	woken
wear	wore	worn
weave	wove	woven, wove
weep	wept	wept
wet	wet	wet
win	won	won
wind	wound	wound
wring	wrung	wrung
write	wrote	written

English Abbreviations

ABRÉVIATIONS ANGLAISES

A adults (*adultes*)

AAA American Automobile Association (*association américaine d'automobilistes*)

AA Alcoholics Anonymous (*société antialcoolique*)

a/c account (current) (*compte courant*)

AC alternating current (*current alternatif*)

AF of L American Federation of Labor (*fédération américaine du travail*)

am before noon (L. *ante meridiem*) (*avant midi*)

AMA American Medical Association (*conseil de l'ordre de médecins américains*)

approx approximately (*approximativement*)

assn association (*association*)

asst assistant (*auxiliaire ou aide*)

av average (*moyen*)

b born (*né*)

BA Bachelor of Arts (*Licencié ès Lettres*)

BC Before Christ (*avant Christ*); British Columbia (*Colombie Britannique*)

BD Bachelor of Divinity (*diplôme d'études théologiques*)

Bd Board (*conseil d'administration*)

BDS Bachelor of Dental Surgery (*diplôme sanctionnant les études dentaires*)

B/E Bill of exchange (*lettre de change, bon*)

BEA British European Airways (*compagnie aérienne qui dessert l'Europe*)

B. Litt. Bachelor of Letters (*diplôme d'études littéraires, diplôme d'études supérieures*)

B. Mus. Bachelor of Music (*diplôme des études musicales*)

BOAC British Overseas Airways Corporation (*compagnie aérienne qui dessert le monde entier*)

Brit	Britain (*Bretagne*); British (*Britannique*)
Bros	Brothers (*Frères*)
B/S	Bill of Sale (*acte de vente, reçu*)
BSc	Bachelor of Science (*diplôme de sciences*)
C	Cape (*cap*); centigrade (*centigrade*); central (*central*)
c	cent (*cent*); centime (*centime*); century (*siècle*); chapter (*chapitre*); about (*L. circa*) (*vers*)
CIA	Central Intelligence Agency (*agence américaine de contre-espionnage*)
CID	Criminal Investigation Department (*section de la police anglaise qui s'occupe de l'investigation des actes criminels*)
cif	Cost, Insurance and Freight (*coût, assurance et fret*)
CO	Commanding Officer (*commandant*); conscientious objector (*objecteur de conscience*)
Co	Company (*Cie, compagnie*)
c/o	care of (*aux bons soins de, chez*)
COD	cash on delivery (*payable à la livraison, livraison contre remboursement*)
CP	Communist Party (*parti communiste*)
cwt	hundredweight (*quintal*)
d	died (*mort*); date (*date*); daughter (*fille*); penny
DA	district attorney (*procureur de l'état*)
DC	District of Columbia (*district fédéral de Columbia*); direct current (*courant continu*)
DD	Doctor of Divinity (*docteur en théologie*)
doz	dozen (*douzaine*)
EEC	European Economic Community—Common Market (*Communauté économique européenne—Marché commun*)
EFTA	European Free Trade Association (*Association européenne pour le libre échange*)
eg	for example ((*L. exampli gratia*) *par exemple*)
esp	especially (*spécialement*)
est	established (*établi*)
FBI	Federal Bureau of Investigation (*police fédérale américaine*)
fob	free on board (*franco à bord*)
ft	foot (*pied*); feet (*pieds*); fort (*fort*)
gal	gallon(s) (*gallon(s)—5 litres = 1.1 gallons*)
GB	Great Britain (*Grande Bretagne*)
GI	Government issue (American private soldier) (*nom donné au simple soldat américain*)
GMT	Greenwich mean time (*l'heure de Greenwich*)
GOP	Republican Party (*parti républicain*)
Govt	government (*gouvernement*)
GP	General practitioner (*médecin de médecine générale, omnipraticien*)
GPO	General Post Office (*= P et T*)
h & c	hot and cold (*chaud et froid*)
HM(S)	Her Majesty('s Service, Her Majesty's Ship) (*Le Service de Sa Majesté, Le Bateau de Sa Majesté*)
Hon.	Honorary (*Honoraire*); Honourable (*Honorable*)
hp	Horse-power (*cheval-vapeur*)
HQ	Headquarters (*quartier général*)
HRH	His (Her) Royal Highness (*Son Altesse Royale*)
I, Is	islands (*îles*)
ICBM	Inter-Continental Ballistic Missile (*missile intercontinental*)
i.e.	that is; namely (*L. id est*) (*c'est-à-dire*)

ILO	International Labour Organization (*Bureau international du travail*)
IMF	International Monetary Fund (*Fond monétaire international*)
in	inch(es) (*pouce(s)*)
Inc, Incorp	Incorporated (*incorporé*)
incl	included; including; inclusive (*ci-joint, ci-inclus*)
IOU	I owe you (*traite*)
IQ	Intelligence Quotient (*quotient intellectuel, coefficient de l'âge mental*)
JP	Justice of the Peace (*juge de paix*)
jr	junior (*cadet, subalterne*)
L	Latin (*latin*); law (*le Droit*)
l	lake (*lac*); left (*gauche*); lira (*lire*)
lb	pound (*livre (poids)*)
LLB	Bachelor of Law (*licencié en droit*)
LP	Long-Playing (record) (*longue durée*); Labour Party (*le parti travailliste*)
LSD	lysergic acid diethylamide (*stupéfiant*); (also £sd) pounds, shillings and pence (*monnaie anglaise*)
Ltd	Limited (*Limité*)
m	male (*mâle*); married (*marié*); meter (*mètre*); mile (*mille*) minute (*minute*); month (*mois*)
MA	Master of Arts (*Licencié ès Lettres*)
MB, ChB	Bachelor of Medicine (*docteur en médecine*); Bachelor of Surgery (*docteur en chirurgie*)
MC	Master of Ceremonies (*maître de cérémonies*); Member of Congress (*député*); Military Cross (*croix militaire*)
MD	Doctor of Medicine (*docteur en médecine, médecin*)
Messrs	the plural of Mr. (*le pluriel de M. (MM), employé avec le nom d'une maison commerciale ou en tête d'une liste de plusieurs noms*)
MI	Military Intelligence (*service du contre-espionnage*)
MP	Member of Parliament (*membre de la chambre des communes, député*); Military Police (*police militaire*); Metropolitan Police (*police métropolitain*)
mph	miles per hour (*milles à l'heure*)
Mr.	Mister (*monsieur*)
Mrs.	Mistress (*madame*)
Mt	mount (*mont*); mountain (*montagne*)
n	name (*nom*); noun (*nom*); neuter (*neutre*); noon (*midi*); nephew (*neveu*); born (*L. natus*) (*né*)
NAM	National Association of Manufacturers (*association nationale de fabricants*)
Nat	National (*national*); Nationalist (*nationaliste*)
NATO	North Atlantic Treaty Organization (*l'Organisation du traité de l'Atlantique Nord*)
NCO	Non-commissioned officer (*sous-officier*)
NHS	National Health Service (*service de santé nationale—sécurité sociale*)
no(s)	number(s) (*L. numero*) (*numéro(s)*)
NW	nord-west (*nord-ouest*)
NY	New York
NZ	New Zealand (*Nouvelle Zélande*)
OAS	Organization of American States (*Organisation d'etats américains*); (*Organisation de l'armée secrète*)
OK	all correct (*correct*); all right (*d'accord*)

OM	Order of Merit (*décoration civile accordée à certaines personnes en récompense de leur mérite particulier*)
PhD	Doctor of Philosophy (*docteur en philosophie*)
PM	Prime Minister (*premier ministre*); Past Master (*ancien maître*)
pm	afternoon (*L. post meridiem*) (*après-midi*); after death (*L. post mortem*) (*après décès*)
PO	Post office (*bureau de poste*)
POB	Post Office Box (*boîte postale*)
POW	Prisoner of War (*prisonnier de guerre*)
pp	on behalf of (*pour le compte de*); pages (*pages*)
Pres	President (*président*)
PRO	Public Relations Officer (*un agent de Public Relations*)
PTO	Please Turn Over (*tournez s'il vous plaît*)
QED	quod erat demonstrandum (*C.Q.F.D.*)
qt	quart (*quart de gallon*)
qv	which see (*L. quod vide*)
RA	Royal Academy (*académie royale*)
RAF	Royal Air Force (*forces aériennes royales*); Royal Air Factory (*camp de RAF*)
RC	Roman Catholic (*catholique romain*); Red Cross (*Croix-Rouge*)
regd	registered (*recommandé, enregistré, inscrit*)
Rep	Representative (*reps*); Republic (*république*); Republican (*républicain*); Repertory (*répertoire, compagnie en tournée ou compagnie provinciale*); Reporter (*journaliste, correspondant*)
Rev	Reverend (*révérend*); Revelations (*Apocalypse*)
RN	Registered nurse (*infirmière diplômée*)
Rt. Hon.	Right Honorable (*très honorable—titre accordé à un ministre ou ancien ministre du gouvernement britannique*)
s	second (*deuxième*); shilling (*shilling*); son (*fils*); singular (*singulier*); substantive (*substantif*); solubility (*solubilité*)
Sch	School (*école*)
Sec, Secy	Secretary (*secrétaire*)
SHAPE	Supreme Headquarters Allied Powers Europe (*Quartier général des alliés en Europe*)
St	Saint (*saint*); Strait (*détroit*); street (*rue*)
SW	South-west (*sud-ouest*))
TB	Tuberculosis (*tuberculose*)
TNT	trinitrotoluene (explosive) (*explosif*)
TT	total abstainer (teetotal) (*abstinent, antialcoolique*)
TV	Television (*télévision, téléviseur*)
TWA	Trans World Airlines (*compagnie aérienne américaine*)
UK	United Kingdom (*royaume uni*)
UN(O)	United Nations (Organization) (*Organisation des Nations Unies*)
UNESCO	United Nations Educational, Scientific and Cultural Organization (*Organisation des Nations Unies pour l'Education, la Science et la Culture*) *qui s'occupe de l'éducation et de la vie scientifique et culturelle des pays sous-développés*)
UNICEF	UN International Children's Emergency Fund (*fonds spécial pour l'assistance des enfants réfugiés*)
US(A)	United States (of America) (*États-Unis*)
USAF	United States Air Force (*forces aériennes des États-Unis*)
USN	United States Navy (*la marine américaine*)
USSR	Union of Socialist Soviet Republics (*URSS*)

VD	Veneral Disease (*maladie venérienne*)
VHF	very high frequency (*très haute fréquence*)
VIP	(*fam*) very important person (*fam—personnage très important*)
viz	namely (*L. videlicet*) (*nommément*)
W	West (*ouest*); Western (*de l'ouest*)
wc	water closet (*W.C., toilet*)
WHO	World Health Organization (*Organisation mondiale de la santé*)
wk	week (*semaine*)
wp	weather permitting (*si le temps le permet*)
yd	yard(s) (*yard = approx. 1 mètre*)
YHA	Youth Hostels Association (*les Auberges de jeunesse*)
YMCA	Young Men's Christian Association (*association de jeunes chrétiens*)
yr	year (*an*); younger (*cadet*); your (*ton, votre*)
YWCA	Young Women's Christian Association (*association de jeunes chrétiennes*)

Abréviations Françaises

FRENCH ABBREVIATIONS

a.b.s.	aux bon soins de (*c/o*)
AC	Avant Christ (*before Christ*)
a.c.	argent comptant (*ready money*)
ACF	Automobile Club de France (*French automobile club*)
AEF	Afrique Equatoriale Française (*French Equatorial Africa*)
AF	Air France (*French airline company*)
AFP	Agence France Presse (*French Press Agency*)
AM	Assurance mutuelle (*mutual assurance*)
Amal	Amiral (*Admiral*)
anme	Anonyme (*limited liability company*)
AOF	Afrique Occidentale Française (*French West Africa*)
AP	Assistance publique (*public assistance*)
AR	Arrière (*rear*)
arr.	arrondissement (*district*)
AS	Assurance sociale (*social security*)
ASLV	Assurance sur la vie (*life assurance*)
asse	Assurance (*insurance*)
AT	Ancien Testament (*Old Testament*)
à t.p.	à tout prix (*at any cost*)
auj.	aujourd'hui (*today*)
av.	avenue (*avenue*)
AV	avant (*front*)
Bac	Baccalauréat (*certificate of secondary education*)
b à p	billet à payer (*bill payable*)
b à r	billet à recevoir (*bill receivable*)
bd	boulevard (*boulevard*)
BF	Banque de France (*Bank of France*)
Bib	Bible (*Bible*), Bibliothèque (*library*)
BIT	Bureau international du travail (*International Labor Office*)
BN	Bibliothèque Nationale (*national library*)
BO	Bulletin officiel (*official bulletin*)
BNP	Banque Nationale de Paris (*large banking house*)
BP	Boîte postale (*Post Office Box*)

BSGDC	Breveté sans garantie du gouvernement (*patent without government guarantee of quality*)
bté	breveté (*patented*)
ca	courant alternatif (*alternating current*)
c-à-d	c'est-à-dire (*that is*)
CAF	Coût, assurance, fret (*cost, insurance, freight*)
CAP	Certificat d'aptitude professionelle (*certificate of general proficiency in industry*)
	Certificat d'aptitude pédagogique (*teaching certificate*)
Cap.	capitaine (*captain*)
CAPES	Certificat d'aptitude au professorat de l'enseignement secondaire (*certificate for teaching in secondary schools*)
cc	courant continu (*direct current*)
c/c	compte courant (*current account*)
CCP	Compte chèques postaux (*Post Office Account*)
CD	Corps diplomatique (*Diplomatic Corps*)
CEE	Communauté économique européenne—Marché commun (*European Economic Community—Common Market*)
CEG	Collège d'enseignement général (*Secondary Modern School*).
CEI	Commission Electro-technique international (*International electro-technical commission*)
CEP	Certificat d'études primaires (*certificate for primary studies*)
CES	College d'enseignement secondaire (*Secondary School*)
CFDT	Confédération française démocratique de travail (*Catholic trade union—branch of CFTC*)
CFTC	Confédération française de travailleurs chrétiens (*union of Catholic workers*)
cg	centigramme (*centigram*)
CGC	Confédération générale des cadres (*communist white collar union*)
CGE	Compagnie générale d'électricité (*large electronics company*)
CGT	Confédération générale du travail (*communist trade union*)
ch-l	chef-lieu (*=county seat*)
CICR	Commission internationale de la Croix-Rouge (*International Commission of the Red Cross Organization*)
CM	Croix Militaire (*Military Cross*)
CNI	Centre National d'Information (*official government information department*)
CNRS	Centre national de la recherche scientifique (*national research board*)
CQFD	ce qu'il fallait démontré (*QED*)
CR	Croix-Rouge (*Red Cross*)
CRS	Compagnie républicaine de sécurité (*State Security Police*)
CT	Cabine téléphonique (*telephone booth*)
c.v.	cheval-vapeur (*horse-power*)
cv	chevaux (*horses*); curriculum vitae
d	diamètre (*diameter*)
DCA	Défense contre avions (*anti-aircraft defense*)
déb	débit (*debit*)
déc	décédé (*deceased*); décembre (*December*)
dép	département (*administrative department*)
DM	Docteur Médecin (*Doctor of Medicine*)
DP	défense passive (*civil defense*)

EC	École centrale (*Central School of Engineering at Paris*)
éd(it)	édition (*edition*)
ÉLO	École des langues orientales (*School of Oriental Languages*)
É-M	État-major (*headquarters*).
ÉNA	École nationale d'administration (*national administrative school*)
env	environ (*about*)
et Cie	et Compagnie (*and Company, & Co.*)
Éts	Établissements (*establishments*)
EV	en ville (*Post. local*)
ex	exemple (*example*)
exempl.	exemplaire (*copy*)
F	Franc : NF Nouveau France (*new franc*) AF Ancien Franc (*old franc*)
fàb	franco à bord (*free on board, fob*)
fab	fabrication (*make*)
FEN	Fédération de l'éducation nationale (*University teachers' union*); Fédération des étudiants nationalistes (*extreme right union of student*)
FFI	Forces françaises de l'intérieur (*internal security forces*)
FFLT	Fédération française de Lawn-Tennis (*French Lawn Tennis Federation*)
FGDS	Fédération de la gauche démocratique et socialiste (*left-wing political grouping*)
FIFA	Fédération Internationale de Football Association (*body governing international football*)
FLN	Front de libération nationale (*nationalist movement in Algerian War*)
FMI	Fond monétaire international (*International Monetary Fund*)
FO	Fédération ouvrière (*left-wing trade union*)
fo(l)	folio (*folio*)
FS	faire suivre (*please forward*)
g	gramme (*gram*)
GC	Grand-Croix (*Grand cross of Legion of Honour*)
GQG	Grand quartier général (*General Headquarters*)
h	heure (*hour*)
HC	hors concours (*not competing*); hors cadre (*not on the strength*)
HÉC	Hautes études commerciales (*business school*)
HLM	Habitations à loyer modéré (*accommodation at reasonable rents*)
hp	haute pression (*high pressure*)
HS	hors de service (*unfit for service*)
inéd	inédit (*unpublished*)
inf	infanterie (*infantry*); faites infuser (*infuse*)
in-f(o), infol	in-folio (*folio*)
IDHÉC	Institut des hautes études cinématographiques (*school for cinema-arts*)
in-pl	in plano (*broadsheet*)
JÉC	Jeunesse étudiante catholique (*catholic student association*)
JOC	Jeunesse ouvrière catholique (*young catholic workers*)
kil(o)	kilogramme (*kilogram*)
km/h	kilomètres par heure (*kilometers per hour*)
labo	laboratoire (*laboratory*)
l.c. or loc. cit.	L. loco citato (*at the place cited*)

liv(r)	livraison (*delivery*)
liv. st.	livre sterling (*pound sterling*)
M	Monsieur (*Mister, Mr.*)
MA	Moyen Age (*Middle Ages*)
Me	Maître (*Master—title given to some lawyers*)
Mgr	Monseigneur (*monsignor*)
Mlle	Mademoiselle (*miss*)
MM	Messieurs (*Messrs.*)
Mme	Madame (*Mistress, Mrs.*)
Mon	Maison (*Firm*)
M-P	Mandat-poste (*post-office order*)
MRP	Mouvement républicain populaire (*Catholic center party*)
n/c	notre compte (*our account*)
NDÉ	note de l'éditeur (*editor's note*)
négt	négotiant (*wholesaler*)
N du T	note du traducteur (*translator's note*)
NRF	Nouvelle Revue Française (*editions of Gallimard publishing house*)
O	à l'ordre de (*to the order of*)
OAS	Organisation de l'armée secrète (*extreme right army group during Algerian War*)
OCDE	Organisation de coopération et de développement économique (*Organization for Economic Co-operation and Development*)
OER	Officiers élèves de la réserve (*officer cadets*)
ONU	Organisation des Nations Unies (*United Nations Organization*)
ORTF	Office de radiodiffusion et télévision françaises (*national broadcasting body*)
OTAN	Organisation du traité de l'Atlantique Nord (*North Atlantic Treaty Organization*)
p	page (*page*); par (*per*); pour (*per*); poids (*weight*)
pass	passim (*in various places*)
P-B	Pays-Bas (*Netherlands*)
p/c	pour compte (*on account*)
PC	Parti communiste (*Communist Party*); poste de commandement (*command post*)
PCC	pour copie conforme (*true copy*)
PG	prisonnier de guerre (*prisoner of war*)
p.ex.	par exemple (*for example*)
p.g.	pour garder (*to be called for, poste restante*)
PJ	Police judiciaire
PMU	Pari mutuel urbain (*licensed betting shop*)
PN	passage à niveau (*level crossing*)
pp	port payé (*carriage paid*)
PSU	Parti socialiste unifié (*left-wing party formed in* 1960)
PSV	Pilotage sans visibilité (*automatic pilot*)
P et T	Postes et Télécommunications (*=GPO*)
PV	procès-verbal (*parking ticket, etc*)
QG	Quartier général (*headquarters*)
QM	Quotient mental (*intelligence quotient*)
qq	quelques (*some*); quelqu'un (*someone*)
qqf	quelquefois (*sometimes*)
r	rue (*road, street*); recommandé (*registered*)
RATP	Régie autonome des transports parisiens (*body which runs Paris transport*)
RAU	République Arabe Unie (*United Arab Republic*)
RDF	Rassemblement démocratique français (*political grouping of center parties*)

rd-vs	rendez-vous (*meeting place*)
rel	relié (*bound*)
Rép	République (*republic*)
RF	République française (*French Republic*)
le RP	le Révérend père (*the Reverend Father*)
RSVP	Répondez s'il vous plaît (*please reply*);
SA	Son Altesse (*His (Her) Highness*);
	Société anonyme (*limited company*)
SAR	Son Altesse Royale (*His (Her) Royal Highness*)
SARL	Société anonyme à responsabilité limitée (*limited liability company*)
s/c	son compte (*his account*);
	sous le couvert (*under (plain) cover*)
SE	Son Excellence (*His (Her) Excellency*);
	Son Eminence (*His Eminence*)
sept	Septentrional (*northern*)
SFIO	Section française de l'Internationale ouvrière (*French Socialist party*)
SI	Syndicat d'initiative (*tourist information bureau*)
slnd	sans lieu ni date (*of no place and no date*)
SM	Sa Majesté (*His (Her) Majesty*)
SMAG	Salaire minimum agricole garanti (*minimum agricultural wage*)
SMIG	Salaire minimum interprofessionnel garanti (*guaranteed minimum wage*)
SNCF	Société nationale des chemins de fer français (*French government railways*)
SNES	Syndicat national de l'enseignement secondaire (*teachers' union*)
SS	Sécurité sociale (*social security*);
	Sa Sainteté (*His Holiness*)
Sté	Société (*society*)
suiv.	suivant (*following*)
svp	s'il vous plaît (*please*)
tàv	tout à vous (*ever yours*)
TEP	Théâtre de l'Est Parisien (*Parisian theater*)
TNP	Théâtre national populaire (*Parisian theater company*)
t-p	timbre-poste (*stamp*)
tpm	tours par minute (*revolutions per minute*)
TSF	télégraphie sans fil (*wireless telegraphy*)
TSVP	tournez s'il vous plaît (*please turn over*)
TVA	taxe à la valeur ajoutée (*sales tax*)
UD	Union démocratique (*political grouping*)
UFF	Union familiale française (*Family association*)
UNAF	Union nationale des associations familiales (*Family association*)
UNEF	Union nationale des etudiants de France (*left-wing union of students*)
UNR	Union pour la Nouvelle République (*Gaullist political party*)
UP	Union postale (*Postal Union*)
URSS	Union de Républiques Socialistes Soviétiques (*USSR*)
UTA	Union de transports aériens (*united transport airline*)
v/c	votre compte (*your account*)
V-C	Vice-Consul (*Vice Consul*)
vo	verso (*back of page*)
Vte	Vicomte (*Viscount*)
WL	Wagons-lits (*sleeping cars*)
WR	Wagons-restaurants (*dining cars*)
XP	Exprès payé (*express paid*)